COUNTER-TERRORISM
LAW AND PRACTICE
An International Handbook

COUNTER-TERRORISM LAW AND PRACTICE

An International Handbook

ARVINDER SAMBEI
ANTON DU PLESSIS
MARTIN POLAINE

OXFORD

UNIVERSITY PRESS

OXFORD

UNIVERSITY PRESS

Great Clarendon Street, Oxford ox2 6DP

Oxford University Press is a department of the University of Oxford.
It furthers the University's objective of excellence in research, scholarship,
and education by publishing worldwide in

Oxford New York

Auckland Cape Town Dar es Salaam Hong Kong Karachi
Kuala Lumpur Madrid Melbourne Mexico City Nairobi
New Delhi Shanghai Taipei Toronto

With offices in

Argentina Austria Brazil Chile Czech Republic France Greece
Guatemala Hungary Italy Japan Poland Portugal Singapore
South Korea Switzerland Thailand Turkey Ukraine Vietnam

Oxford is a registered trade mark of Oxford University Press
in the UK and in certain other countries

Published in the United States
by Oxford University Press Inc., New York

British Library Cataloguing in Publication Data

Data available

Library of Congress Cataloging in Publication Data

Sambei, Arvinder.
 Counter-terrorism law and practice : an international handbook / Arvinder Sambei,
Anton du Plessis, Martin Polaine.
  p. cm.
 Includes index.
 ISBN 978-0-19-955380-8
 1. Terrorism—Prevention—International cooperation. 2. Terrorism. I. du Plessis,
Anton. II. Polaine, Martin. III. Title.
 K5256.S26 2009
 345′.02—dc22   2009006272

Typeset by Cepha Imaging Private Ltd, Bangalore, India
Printed in Great Britain
on acid-free paper by
CPI Antony Rowe, Chippenham, Wilts

ISBN 978–0–19–955380–8

1 3 5 7 9 10 8 6 4 2

FOREWORD

This is a significant and useful work, covering a broad and complex area in an accessible and referable form. The authors use their wide experience to approach their task from a practical standpoint and give a clear and thoroughly researched overview of a subject where understanding is all important and where so often the theory gives little guide to either the legislator or the practitioner.

The spectre of international terrorism this century has changed life as we know it. What were once regarded as internal problems now occur with little regard to national borders. Traditional views of sovereignty have had to be reviewed and globalization in its many forms, good and bad, is here to stay. Any hopes of international jurists that the world community could rise to the challenge and provide a fair and humane legal and judicial framework for a criminal justice response have failed to materialize. Despite the apparent uniformity of response and the rapid adoption after 9/11 of UNSCR 1373, the real result has been a rash of counter-terrorism measures and obligations which rarely sit comfortably together. Despite the development of international human rights law, the subsequent US-led 'Global War on Terror' has done little to win uncommitted support.

This book traces not only the historical backdrop of counter-terrorism law; it also deals lucidly with the many difficulties that the changed landscape has thrown up. It highlights the likely problems for the practitioner and provides a coherent guide to modern practice. It reviews the attempts by the League of Nations and the United Nations to produce resolutions, conventions, or protocols that could be both effective and supportable, and the difficulty of producing any sort of common strategic approach that would have universal appeal. It examines the barrier presented by expanding treaty law's being dependant on individual ratification, the problems of differing definitions, perceptions and interpretations, and the problems of applying appropriate sentences. What surfaces is that States have reacted on a case-by-case basis, and rather than set their star by some unworkable universal definition, many have seen the advantage of regarding a terrorist act as a crime against the national criminal law alone.

This view was encouraged by the design of the international conventions and protocols which imposed obligations on States to address the crimes committed by terrorists under their own law. A strength of this book is its analysis of the growing criminalization of terrorist acts and of the attempts to deal with the broad spectrum of problems by incorporation into, and use of, domestic law.

In the United Kingdom in recent years, the diversion of resources and expertise into the monitoring of activities and the investigation and presentation of terrorist cases has led to a considerable increase in the use of high-level judicial and court time for such purposes. A commensurate growth in appropriate practice and procedure has been an inevitable consequence, and this book helpfully addresses issues and pitfalls in this area. Developments in such thorny areas as covert investigations and disclosure also receive appropriate attention.

Another area of expansion and real concern which is explored in this book is the vital role played by money laundering and cross-border financing. A particularly significant trend is the exploitation of alternative remittance systems (such as *hawala*). The advantages of this system to the user are easy to recognize but far harder to police; the authors examine the attempts by the international community and national governments to counter such support for terrorist activities.

This work is a welcome addition to a growth area. It provides a picture not only of the worthy attempts to deal at the highest levels with the peace-defying problems of terrorism, but also of a contemporary working template for international cooperation and for the investigation and presentation of cases within the domestic, criminal system.

HH Judge Brian Barker QC
The Common Serjeant of London
Central Criminal Court
October, 2008

PREFACE

The domestic horrors of *la Terreur* in 18th century France have been replaced by a new form of transnational terrorism that threatens global peace, security, and stability. Since the attacks on the United States on the 11th of September 2001, countering this threat has been cast as a global priority. In this context, legal practitioners, law enforcement agents, and government officials are faced with the challenge of complying with a plethora of international and regional obligations, and implementing new or revised national counter-terrorism laws. This book is aimed primarily at that audience. By bringing together wide-ranging materials on counter-terrorism and related aspects, and providing detailed and practical analysis, we hope to assist colleagues in many jurisdictions, in their practice of a complex, but always fascinating, area of law.

Any consideration of modern counter-terrorism throws into sharp relief the US-led 'Global War on Terror': on the one hand, with its emphasis on an extrajudicial response, and, on the other, the normative and preventive approach of the UN's Global Counter-Terrorism Strategy. This book focuses on the latter, with a specific emphasis on the legal aspects of the law enforcement and criminal justice response to terrorism.

The authors are honoured that His Honour Judge Brian Barker QC, the Common Serjeant of London, took time away from his busy schedule at the Central Criminal Court, London to write the Foreword.

We are indebted to the following for their time, advice, and assistance: David Perry QC of 6 King's Bench Walk, Temple; Ranganath Manthripragada of the Department of Justice, Washington DC; Anneli Botha of the Institute for Security Studies, South Africa; Melissa Khemani, graduate law student at Georgetown University Law Center, Washington DC; Professor Max du Plessis of the University of KwaZulu-Natal; Anton Katz of the Cape Town Bar; and Alistair Millar, Eric Rosand, and Jason Ipe of the Center on Global Counterterrorism Cooperation, Washington DC.

Particular thanks must go to Graham Waller for his skill and good humour in the face of endless research requests, and to Karen Smith for her unsurpassed typing ability mixed with patience and understanding!

Thanks are also due to the team at Oxford University Press, Jane Kavanagh, Faye Judges, Lucy Ford, and Katie Heath, for keeping the authors to the deadlines they set themselves, and for their assistance and advice in the production of this book.

This book would not have been written without the understanding and support of colleagues and the encouragement and forbearance of families: our heartfelt thanks to them all.

As always, the fault for any errors or omissions lies entirely with the authors.

The law is stated as at 31 August 2008, but, where possible within the context of the final editing process, reference has been made to later events.

Arvinder Sambei
Anton du Plessis
Martin Polaine

ACKNOWLEDGEMENTS

The following pieces appear in this book by kind permission. Every effort has been made to contact the Copyright holders of the items reproduced here. However, the Publisher will be delighted to rectify any omission upon reprinting of this book.

1. Appendix 17: OAU Convention on the Prevention and Combating of Terrorism, 1999 – *The Commission of the African Union*
2. Appendix 19: FATF Special Recommendations on Terrorist Financing – *Financial Action Task Force*
3. Appendix 20: Commonwealth Secretariat Model Legislative Provisions on Measures to Combat Terrorism – *Commonwealth Secretariat*

SUMMARY CONTENTS

Foreword	v
Preface	vii
Acknowledgements	ix
Table of Cases	xxi
Tables of Legislation, Treaties, and Conventions	xxvii

1. Introduction	1
2. The United Nations Counter-Terrorism Instruments	17
3. Criminalization and Jurisdiction	85
4. Investigations and Prosecutions	147
5. Pre-Trial and Trial Issues	219
6. General Overview of International Efforts to Combat the Financing of Terrorism	275
7. Alternative Remittance Systems	319
8. Human Rights in the Context of Counter-Terrorism	337
9. International Cooperation	375

Appendices	447
Index	759

CONTENTS

Foreword   v
Preface   vii
Acknowledgements   ix
Table of Cases   xxi
Tables of Legislation, Treaties, and Conventions   xxvii

1. **Introduction**

   A. Introduction   1.01

   B. What is Terrorism?   1.06

   C. International Legal Responses to Terrorism   1.14
      The definition of terrorism in international law   1.18
      Terrorism as an international treaty crime   1.28
      Terrorism as a crime under customary international law   1.38
      Terrorism in armed conflict   1.39
      Domestic measures   1.40

   D. Overview of This Book   1.48

2. **The United Nations Counter-Terrorism Instruments**

   A. Introduction: Development of a Global Legal
      Regime against Terrorism   2.01
      The role of the UN Security Council   2.09
      Other UN Security Council resolutions pertaining to terrorism   2.15
      The United Nations Global Counter-Terrorism Strategy   2.21

   B. Overview of the UN Counter-Terrorism Instruments   2.23
      Common elements of the UN counter-terrorism instruments   2.29
      Criminalizing terrorist acts   2.32
      Forms of participation in an offence   2.38
      Jurisdiction provisions   2.42
      International cooperation mechanisms and the principle of
         aut dedere aut judicare   2.44

C. Relevant Extracts from the UN
Counter-Terrorism Instruments 2.47
   Agreements developed by the International
     Civil Aviation Organization (ICAO) 2.47
   Agreements developed by the International Maritime
     Organization (IMO) 2.75
   Instruments developed by the International
     Atomic Energy Agency (IAEA) 2.93
   Agreements developed at the initiative of the UN
     General Assembly aimed at protecting civilians 2.103

3. **Criminalization and Jurisdiction**

A. Criminalization 3.01
   The Hague Convention 3.02
   The Montreal Convention 3.28
   The Montreal Protocol 3.40
   The Diplomats Convention 3.46
   The Hostages Convention 3.51
   The Nuclear Convention 3.58
   The Rome Convention 3.61
   The Rome Protocol 3.72
   The 2005 Protocol to the Rome Convention 3.76
   The 2005 Protocol to the Rome Protocol 3.82
   The Bombings Convention 3.83
   The Financing Convention 3.92
   The Nuclear Terrorism Convention 3.103

B. Criminalization of Terrorism Offences in National Laws 3.108

C. United Nations Security Council Resolution 1373 3.123

D. Principal Terrorist Offences in the UK Reflecting Domestic
Implementation of the UN Counter-Terrorism Instruments 3.125

E. Jurisdiction 3.126
   Introduction 3.126
   Principles of criminal jurisdiction 3.127
   Jurisdiction based upon the territory where the offence
     was committed 3.132
   Jurisdiction based upon registration of aircraft or maritime vessels 3.134
   Extra-territorial jurisdiction 3.137
   The approach adopted by the UN instruments 3.155
   Jurisdiction based upon the presence of a person in the
     national territory 3.188
   Extension of jurisdiction for UK terrorism offences 3.192

4. **Investigations and Prosecutions**

  A. Reactive Investigations 4.02
    Evidence from an accomplice 4.03
    Resident sources/cooperating defendants 4.08
    Witness protection 4.20
    Anonymous witnesses 4.30

  B. Stop and Search 4.57

  C. Arrest 4.65

  D. Detention 4.67

  E. Admissions and Confessions 4.85
    Oppression and unfairness 4.93
    Silence as an admission 4.101
    Admissions occasioned by tricks 4.103
    At what stage should an admission/confession be challenged? 4.107

  F. Bomb/Explosion Scene Management 4.112

  G. Proactive Investigations 4.124

  H. Covert Methodologies 4.130
    Interception of communications 4.130
    Covert investigative techniques and human rights law 4.161
    Covert human sources 4.177
    Surveillance 4.213
    Entrapment 4.248

  I. Membership of a Proscribed Organization 4.266

5. **Pre-Trial and Trial Issues**

  A. Burden of Proof 5.01
    Burden of proof under the UK's counter-terrorism legislation 5.42

  B. Case Management 5.50

  C. Disclosure 5.52
    Disclosure of material by the prosecution 5.55
    Disclosure of third party material 5.79
    Mechanism for handling sensitive material 5.82
    Material held by authorities in a foreign state 5.84
    Ongoing duty of disclosure at trial and thereafter 5.85

  D. The Media and Adverse Comment 5.86

  E. Hearings in Camera 5.108

  F. The Accused's Right of Silence and Access to Legal Advice 5.110

6. **General Overview of International Efforts to**
   Combat the Financing of Terrorism

   A. Introduction   6.01

   B. International Efforts to Combat the Financing of Terrorism   6.07
       International Convention for the Suppression of the Financing of
          Terrorism (1999) ('Financing Convention')   6.09
       The International Convention against Transnational Organized
          Crime (2000) ('Palermo Convention')   6.23

   C. Key Extracts of Relevant UN Security Council Resolutions   6.24
       UN Security Council Resolution 1267 (1999)   6.24
       UN Security Council Resolution 1390 (2002)   6.29
       UN Security Council Resolution 1452 (2002)   6.30
       UN Security Council Resolution 1730 (2006)   6.31
       UN Security Council Resolution 1735 (2006)   6.32
       UN Security Council Resolution 1373 (2001)   6.33
       Summary of the criminalization, freezing, and forfeiture obligations
          under the Financing Convention (1999) and Security
          Council Resolutions 1267 (1999) and 1373 (2001)   6.42
       Legal and human rights issues relevant to the implementation
          of UN Security Council asset-freezing obligations   6.43

   D. The Financial Action Task Force   6.51
       FATF Nine Special Recommendations on terrorist financing   6.55

   E. Other International Initiatives   6.56
       The International Monetary Fund (IMF)   6.56
       The Egmont Group of Financial Intelligence Units   6.58
       Wolfsberg Group of Banks   6.62

7. **Alternative Remittance Systems**

   A. Introduction   7.01

   B. What is an Alternative Remittance System?   7.07
       Advantages of alternative remittance systems   7.12

   C. FATF Recommendations for Alternative Remittance Systems   7.15
       Special Recommendation VI: Interpretative Note   7.20

   D. Abu Dhabi Conferences   7.22

   E. Other Payment Methods   7.28

   F. Conclusion   7.33

8. **Human Rights in the Context of Counter-Terrorism**

   A. International Human Rights Law and International
       Humanitarian Law   8.02

   B. The Sources of IHRL   8.07

   C. Extra-Territorial Reach of Human Rights Instruments   8.15

   D. The Nature of the Rights Engaged   8.30
       What amounts to an absolute right   8.32
       Who comprises 'the State'?   8.42

   E. The Rights Likely to be Engaged During the
       Course of an Investigation   8.46
       Right to life   8.46
       Prohibition on torture   8.52
       Arbitrary, prolonged, and indefinite detention   8.94
       Right to a fair trial   8.107

   F. Privacy, Confidentiality, and Personal Information Issues   8.113

9. **International Cooperation**

   A. Introduction   9.01

   B. Mutual Legal Assistance: General Principles   9.03
       Mutual legal assistance and informal requests   9.03
       The UN instruments   9.05
       The legal bases for assistance   9.17
       Grounds for refusal   9.20
       Execution of requests in accordance with the laws of the requested state   9.28

   C. Mutual Legal Assistance or Mutual Assistance?   9.60
       Formal requests (mutual legal assistance)   9.70
       The form of the letter of request   9.75
       Particular problems experienced in mutual legal assistance
          sought in counter-terrorism cases   9.99
       Sensitive information contained within the letter of request   9.100
       Adducing evidence obtained from abroad   9.101
       Challenging a refusal to execute a letter of request   9.102

   D. Extradition   9.113
       What is 'extradition'?   9.113
       Comity: disguised/irregular extradition   9.119
       European Arrest Warrant   9.138
       The UN counter-terrorism instruments   9.148

Extradition crime and dual criminality   9.152
'Extradite or prosecute' (*aut dedere aut judicare*)   9.162
Political offence exception   9.168
Other protections   9.209
Human rights considerations   9.219

Appendices

Appendix 1. UNSCR 1267, 1456, 1540, 1566, 1617, 1624, 1735   449

Appendix 2. UNSCR 1373   479

Appendix 3. Tokyo Convention   483

Appendix 4. Hague Convention   491

Appendix 5. Montreal Convention and Protocol   497

Appendix 6. Diplomats Convention   509

Appendix 7. Hostages Convention   515

Appendix 8. Nuclear Materials Convention   521

Appendix 9. Rome Convention and Protocols   531

Appendix 10. Plastic Explosives Convention   561

Appendix 11. Bombings Convention   567

Appendix 12. International Convention for the
               Suppression of the Financing of Terrorism   575

Appendix 13. International Convention for the
               Suppression of Acts of Nuclear Terrorism   587

Appendix 14. The United Nations Global
               Counter-Terrorism Strategy   597

Appendix 15. European Convention on the
               Suppression of Terrorism   605

Appendix 16. American States Convention No. 24381   617

Appendix 17. OAU Convention on the Prevention
               and Combating of Terrorism, 1999   621

Appendix 18. The Arab Convention for the
               Suppression of Terrorism   631

Appendix 19. Financial Action Task Force on Money
               Laundering Special Recommendations on Terrorist Financing   643

Appendix 20. Commonwealth Secretariat Model Legislative
               Provisions on Measures to Combat Terrorism   645

Appendix 21. Criminal Evidence (Witness Anonymity) Act 2008   689

Appendix 22. Police & Criminal Evidence
    Act 1984 (PACE), Code H   697

Appendix 23. Ratification Status and Depository
    Information on the UN Counter-Terrorism Legal Instruments   739

Appendix 24. UNSC Resolution 1822   743

Appendix 25. The USA PATRIOT Act   751

Index   759

TABLE OF CASES

A v Secretary of State for the Home Department [2004] UKHL 56 . . . . 4.67
A v Secretary of State for the Home Department (No 2) [2005] UKHL 71 . . . . 4.86
A v Secretary of State for the Home Department: D v Secretary of State for the Home
    Department: C v Secretary of State for the Home Department [2005] UKHL 71 . . . . . 8.58
A v Secretary of State for the Home Department: X v Secretary of State for the
    Home Department [2004] UKHL 56 . . . . 8.36, 8.53
A, K, M, Q and G v Her Majesty's Treasury [2008] EWCA Civ 1187 . . . . 6.49
Ahmad and Another v Government of the United States of America [2006]
    All ER (D) 418 (Nov) 9.224
Ahmad v Wigen, 726 F Supp 389, 402 (EDNY 1989); 910 F 2d 1063,
    1066 (2d Cir 1990) 9.201
Ajodha v Trinidad and Tobago [1982] AC 204 . . . . 4.107
(Akamu and Others) v Nigeria (2000) AHRLR 8.112
Al-Fawwaz and Others *See* R (Al-Fawwaz) v Governor of Brixton Prison
Al-Fawwaz, Re [2001] UKHL 69, [2002] 1 AC 556 . . . . 9.146, 9.157
Al-Hamdi, 356 F 3d 9.201
Al-Skeini & Others v Secretary of State for Defence [2007] UKHL 26 . . . . 8.20
American Civil Liberties et al v National Security Agency et al US Court of Appeals,
    6th Circuit, 6 July 2007 . . . . 4.139
Arrest Warrant Case (Democratic Republic of the Congo v Belgium),
Arrest Warrant of 11 April 2000, ICJ Report 2002, 3 . . . . 3.175, 3.185
Arton, Re (No 2) [1896] 1 QB 509 . . . . 9.146
Asan and others v Turkey (App No 56003/00) 10 July 2007 . . . . 8.56, 8.95
Attorney General's Reference (3 of 2000) [2002] Cr App R 29 . . . . 4.250, 4.252, 4.260
Attorney General's Reference (No.4 of 2002), Re: Sheldrake v DPP
    [2004] UKHL 43 . . . . 5.27, 5.34, 5.42
Attorney-General of Hong Kong v Lee Kwong-Kut [1993] AC 951 . . . . 5.11
Averill v UK (2001) 31 EHRR 839 . . . . 5.115, 5.136
Bámaca-Velásquez v Guatemala Series C No 70, Judgment of 25 November 2000,
    Inter-Am CHR 8.14
Banković and Others v Belgium and 16 other Contracting States 11 BHRC 435;
    (2007) 44 EHRR SE5 . . . . 8.16, 8.18, 8.26
Barapind v Enomoto 1069 (9th Cir) 2004 . . . . 9.195
Bloggs v Secretary of State for the Home Department [2003] EWCA Civ 686 . . . . 4.13
Boumediene et al v Bush, President of the United States et al 12 June 2008 . . . . 8.101
Brady v Maryland 373 US 83 (1963) 5.68, 5.69
Brennan v UK (2002) 34 EHRR 18 . . . . 5.137
Brogan v United Kingdom ((1989) 11 EHRR 117 . . . . 8.95
Brussels v Cando Armas and Another [2004] EWHC 2019 (Admin) 9.146
Castioni, Re [1891] 1 Q.B. 149 . . . . 9.181, 9.184, 9.201
Chahal v UK (1996) 23 EHRR 413 . . . . 8.59, 8.84, 8.88
Chan Wai-Keung v The Queen [1995] 1 WLR 251 . . . . 4.07
Coard et al v the United States (Case 10.951) Report No 109/99, September 29, 1999,
    Inter-Am CHR 8.26
Cohen v The State of Israel 29(1) PD 340 . . . . 8.57

Condron v UK (2001) 31 EHRR 1 . . . . 5.114
Cooper Indus v British Aerospace, 102 FRD 918, 920 (SDNY 1984) 9.59
DPP v Ping Lin [1976] AC 574 . . . . 4.93
Doorson v Netherlands (1996) 22 EHRR 330 . . . . 4.26, 4.27, 4.35, 4.52
Eain 641 F 2d 504, 521(7th Cir 1981) 9.195
Ergin v Turkey (App no 47533/99) (2008) 47 EHRR 36. . . . . 8.112
Esbester v United Kingdom (18601/91) (1994) 18 EHRR CD72 . . . . 4.170
Escobedo v United States, 623 F 2d 1098, 1104 (5th Cir 1980) 9.201
Evans v Bartlam [1937] AC 473 . . . . 5.97
Ex parte Kebilene *See* R v DPP ex parte Kebilene 5.44
Faraj Hassan Faraj v Government of Italy [2004] EWHC 2950 (Admin) 9.233
Foucher v France [1997] 25 EHRR 234 . . . . 5.78
Gboko v The State (2007) 17 NWLR Pt 1063 . . . . 5.57
Ghaidan v Godin-Mendoza [2004] 3 WLR 113 . . . . 5.37
Gil v Canada (Minister of Employment and Immigration) [1995] 1 FC 508 . . . . . . .9.175, 9.204
Hadž Boudellaa, Boumediene Lakhdar, Mohamed Nechle; Saber Lahmar v Bosnia and
    Herzegovina and the Federation of Bosnia and Herzegovina Case Nos
    CH/02/8679, CH/02/8689, CH/02/8690 and CH/02/8691 (11 October 2002) 9.128
Halford v United Kingdom (20605/92) [1997] IRLR 471; (1997) 24 EHRR 523 . . . . 4.219
Hall (Dennis) v Queen, The (1971) 55 Cr App R 108, PC 4.101
Imbler v Pachtman 424 US 409 (1976). 5.85
Imbrioscia v Switzerland (1993) judgment of 24 November 2003 . . . . 5.133
Ireland v United Kingdom (A/25) (1979-80) 2 EHRR 25. . . . . 4.92
Issa & Others v Turkey (App no 31821/96) (2005) 41 EHRR 27 . . . . 8.17
Juma & Others v AG [13.2.2003]. 5.57
Kadi v Council and Commission (T-315/01) [2005] ECR II-3649 ('Kadi'). 6.45
Khouzam v Ashcroft: Khouzam v Hogan 361 F 3d 161, 171 (2d Cir 2004). 8.93
Kindler v Canada (Minister of Justice) [1991] 2 SCR 779 . . . . 9.228
Kirkwood v United (1984) 6 EHRR CD373 . . . . 4.33
Klass v Germany (A/28) (1979-80) 2 EHRR 214 . . . . .4.170, 5.114
Kopp v Switzerland (1999) 27 EHRR 91 . . . . 4.169
Kyles v Whitley 514 US 419 (1995) 5.69
Lam Chi-Ming v Queen, The [1991] 2 AC 212 . . . . 8.53
Liangsiriprasert v United States [1991] 1 AC 225 . . . . 3.138
Lotus Case PCIJ, Ser A, No 10, 1927 . . . . 3.129
Magee v UK (2001) 31 EHRR 35. . . . . 5.135
Malone v UK [1984] 7 EHRR 14 . . . . .4.170, 8.118
Marc Rich & Co v United States, 736 F 2d 864, 866 (2d Cir 1984). 9.59
Mariadas v The State SLR 96, Vol 1 of 1995 [1993] LKCA 14; (1995) 1 Sri LR 96 . . . . 4.96
McCann v United Kingdom (App no 18984/91) (1996) 21 EHRR 97 . . . . 8.47
Mete v Turkey (App No 77649/01). 8.96
Meunier, Re [1894] 2 QB 415 . . . . 9.186
Meziane and Benmerzouga, unreported, 25 June 2004 . . . . 5.106
Mironescu v Costner (4th Circuit 2007) 9.211
Moevao v The Department of Labour [1980] 1 NZLR 464. . . . . 9.135
Mohamed Salah Ben Hamadi Khemiri, Habib Ignaoua, Ali Ben Zidane Chehidi v
    The Court of Milan Italy [2008] EWHC 1988 (Admin) 9.237
Mohammed Fakhar Al Zaman Lodhi v The Governor of HMP Brixton and the
    Government of the United Arab Emirates [2001] EWHC Admin 178. . . . . 9.151
Montgomery v HM Advocate and Another [2203] 1 AC 641 . . . . 5.107
Morgans v DPP [2001] 1 AC 315. . . . . 4.130
Murray v UK (1996) EHRR 29 . . . . .5.118, 5.139
Ng Extradition, Re [1991] 2 SCR 858 . . . . 9.228
Niemietz v Germany (A/251-B) (1993) 16 EHRR 97 . . . . 4.219

Nimmo v Alexander Cowan & Sons Ltd [1968] AC 107 . . . . 5.34
Öcalan v Turkey [2003] ECHR 125 . . . . 8.108
Office of King's Prosecutor, Brussels v Cando Armas and Another [2004]
 EWHC 2019 (Admin) 9.146
Ouko v Kenya (2000) AHRLR 135 . . . . 8.97
Ozkan v Turkey App (No 21689/93) [2004] ECHR 133 . . . . 8.50
PG v United Kingdom: JH v United Kingdom (2008) 46 EHRR 51; [2002]
 Crim. L.R. 308 . . . . 4.219
Pakkan v Turkey (App No 13017/02) 8.96
Pinochet (No 3) [2000] 1 AC 147 . . . . 9.152, 9.159
Piracy Jure Gentium [1934] AC 586 . . . . 3.128
Prosecutor v Galic (Case No IT-98-29-T), Judgement 5 December 2003 . . . . 1.39
Quinn v Robinson 783 F 2d 776; 54 USLW 2449(9th Cir) 9.182, 9.195
R v A (No2) [2002] 1 AC 45 . . . . 5.36
R v Abdul-Hussain [1998] EWCA Crim 3528; [1999] Crim LR 570, CA 3.15, 3.26
R v Abdullah Ibrahim El-Faisal No: 03/1860/C2, [2004] EWCA Crim 343 . . . . 8.02, 8.03
R v Abu Hamza [2006] EWCA Crim 2918 . . . . 5.106, 8.02, 8.03
R v Alibhai [2004] EWCA Crim 681 . . . . 5.81
R v Bailey, Brewin and Gungai, unreported, 15 March 2001 . . . . 4.175
R v Bailey (Jason Gregory): R v Smith (Steven Simon) [1993] 3 All ER 513;
 (1993) 97 Cr App R 365 . . . . 4.106
R v Birtles (Frank Alexander) [1969] 1 WLR 1047 . . . . 4.182, 4.196
R v Boodhoo, Allen and Bunting [2001] EWCA Crim 1025 . . . . 4.154
R v Central Criminal Court, ex parte The Telegraph Plc (1994) 98 Cr App R 91 . . . . 5.106
R v Davis (Iain): R v Simms (Rodrigo Fernando); R v Ellis (Marcus Junior);
 R v Gregory (Michael); R v Martin (Nathan), *The Times* 1 June 2006, CA;
 [2008] UKHL 36, HL 4.35, 4.538.111,
R v DJX: R v SCY; R v GCZ (1990) 91 Cr App R 36 . . . . 4.48
R v DPP ex parte Kebilene [2000] 2 AC 326 . . . . 5.44
R v Drury [2001] EWCA Crim 1753 . . . . 4.13, 4.16
R v E [2004] EWCA Crim 1243 . . . . 4.158
R v F [2007] 2 Cr App R 3 . . . . 3.111
R v Ford (Royston) (1989) Cr App R 278; [1989] 3 WLR 762 . . . . 5.89
R v Fulling (Ruth Susan) [1987] Q.B. 426; (1987) 85 Cr App R 136 . . . . 4.94
R v Governor of Ashford Remand Centre, Ex p Postlethwaite [1988] AC 924 . . . . 9.146
R v Governor of Brixton Prison ex p Schtraks [1964] AC 556 . . . . 9.187
R v GS [2005] EWCA Crim 887 . . . . 4.222
R v Guney [1998] 2 Cr App R 242 . . . . 5.77
R v H and C [2004] UKHL 3 . . . . 5.82
R v Hardy (Brian): R v Hardy (Danny) [2002] EWCA Crim 3012 . . . . 4.158
R v Horseferry Road Magistrates' Court ex p Bennett [1994] 1 AC 42 . . . . 9.129, 9.131
R v Horseferry Road Magistrates' Court ex p Bennett (No 3) [1995] 1 Cr App R 147 . . . . . 9.131
R v Hudson and Taylor [1971] 55 Cr App R 1 . . . . 3.25
R v Hughes [1986] 2 NZLR 129 . . . . 4.44
R v Hunt (Richard) [1987] AC 352 . . . . 5.34
R v Hurst (Marnie Michelle) [1995] 1 Cr App R 82 . . . . 3.25
R v Jelen (Lawrence); R v Katz (Anthony) (1990) 90 Cr App R 456, CA (Crim Div) 4.105
R v Johnstone [2003] UKHL 28; [2003] 1 WLR 1736 . . . . 5.04, 5.38
R v Keane [1994] 1 WLR 746 . . . . 5.62
R v Khan [1997] AC 558 . . . . 4.240
R v Lambert [2001] UKHL 37 . . . . 5.13, 5.21, 5.38
R v Latif [1996] 1 WLR 104 . . . . 4.255
R v Liverpool City Magistrates Court ex parte DPP (1997) 161 JP 43 . . . . 4.49

R v Looseley (Grant Spencer) (No.1) Transcript: 200000730 Y5,
CA (Crim Div)..................................4.103, 4.250. 4.251, 4.257
R v Lucas (1981) 73 Cr App R 159..5.141
R v Makin [2004] EWCA Crim 1607..5.66
R v Mann (Brian Peter) (1972) 56 Cr App R 750 ....4.102
R v Martin (Colin) (1989) 88 Cr App R 343, CA 3.25, 3.26
R v Mason (Carl) (1988) 86 Cr App R 349....................................4.104
R v McCann: R v Cullen:R v Shanahan [1991] 92 Cr App R 239 ....5.87, 5.104
R v Melvin, unreported, 20 Dec 1993..5.62
R v Membar [1983] Crim LR 618, CA...3.13
R v Murphy [1990] NI 306, CA (NI)...4.47
R v Mushtaq (Ashfaq Ahmed) [2005] UKHL 25....................................8.53
R v P (Telephone Intercepts: Admissibility of Evidence) [2002] 1 AC 146;
[2001] 2 WLR 463..4.159
R v Payne (Robert Anthony) [1950] 1 All ER 102..............................4.06
R v Pommell (Fitzroy Derek) [1995] 2 Cr App R 607, CA........................3.25
R v Raviraj (Thaneran) (1987) 85 Cr App R 93................................4.102
R v Roger and Rose, unreported, 9 July 1997 ....3.25
R v Rowe (Andrew) [2007] EWCA Crim 635; [2007] 3 All ER 36 ....4.62
R v Sang [1980] AC 402..4.254
R v Secretary of State for the Home Department ex parte:R v Secretary of
State for the Home Department ex parte Ogun [1999] Q.B. 611;
[1998] 2 WLR 618..9.156
R v Shannon [2002] Crim LR 1001 ....4.257
R v Smurthwait: R v Gill [1994]1 AER 898 ....4.259
R v Taillefer and Duguay [2003] 3 SCR 307 ....5.65
R v Taylor (Michelle Ann) (1994) 98 Cr App R 361 ....5.104
R v Taylor (G) *The Times*, 17 August 1994, CA..............................4.34
R v Taylor and Crabb, unreported, 22 July 1994, CA..........................4.50
R v the Bow Street Magistrates ex parte Sir Rupert Henry Mackeson
(1982) 75 Cr App R 24..9.130
R v Thomas [2006] VSCA 165; [2008] Crim LR, 121 ....9.81, 9.98
R v Ward [1993] 1 WLR 619 ....5.61
R v Watford Magistrates Court ex parte Lenman [1993] Crim. L.R. 388..............4.48
R v Weekes (Alan John) (1982) 74 Cr App R 161 ....4.07
R v Whitehead (Job) [1929] 1 K.B. 99; (1930) 21 Cr App R 23, CCA................4.101
R v Whyte (1988) 51 DLR (4th) 481 ....5.11
R v Winston Brown [1998] AC 367, HL...5.75
R v Z [2005] 2 AC 467; [2005] UKHL 35, HL...........................3.27, 4.267
R (Al-Fawwaz) v Governor of Brixton Prison [2001] UKHL 69;
[2002] 1 AC 556 ....3.146, 3.147, 4.30,
4.35, 4.50
R (Islamic Human Rights Commission) v Civil Aviation Authority [2006]
EWHC 2465 (Admin); [2007] ACD 5...3.110
R (on the application of Gillan) v Commissioner of Police of the Metropolis
[2006] UKHL 12; 4.57
R (Amin) v Sec of State for the Home Department [2003] UKHL 51 ....8.51
R (on the application of Al-Skeini and others) v Secretary of State for Defence
[2004] EWHC 2911 (Admin) 8.49
R (on the application of Middleton) v West Somerset Coroner [2004] 2 All ER 465 ....8.48
Raissi v Commissioner of Police of the [2007] EWHC 2842; [2008]
EWCA Civ 1237, CA 4.65
Republic of Namibia v Kakaena Likunga Alfred & Others Court of Appeal,
Botswana 64/03, July 2004..9.177

Republic v Kamlesh Mansuklal Damji Pattni (2005) Eklr. Criminal
    case 229 of 2003 . . . . 5.57
Rochin v California, US Supreme Court (1952) 8.107
Saadi v Italy (37201/06) 24 BHRC 123; [2008] Imm. A.R. 519;
    [2008] Crim. L.R. 898; 8.84, 9.237
Salabiaku v France (1988) 13 EHRR 379 . . . . 5.11, 5.20, 5.35, 5.41
Saunders v UK (1996) 23 EHRR 313 . . . . 5.114
Schenk v Switzerland (A/140) (1991) 13 EHRR 242 . . . . 4.176
Scott v Scott [1913] AC 417 . . . . 5.108
Sealed Case, Re 825 F 2d 494, 497 (DC Cir 1987) 9.53, 9.59
Seckin & Others v Turkey (App no 56016/00) 8.112
Senthilnayagam and Others v Seneviratne and Another [1981] LKCA 44;
    (1981) 2 Sri LR 187 . . . . 4.74
Silver v United Kingdom (A/161) (1983) 5 EHRR 347 . . . . 4.169
Smith v United Kingdom: Grady v United Kingdom [1999] IRLR 734;
    (2000) 29 EHRR 493 . . . . 8.38
Soering v United Kingdom (1989) 11 EHRR 439 . . . . 9.232
South Africa v Leepile 1986 (4) SA 187 . . . . 4.45
Southwark LBC v Williams [1971] Ch 734, CA 3.25
St John v Governor of Brixton Prison; St John, Re; St John v United States
    [2001] EWHC Admin 543 . . . . 9.221
Sumitomo Shoji Am, Inc v Avagliano, 457 US 176, 184–85 (1982) 9.201
Tzu-Tsai Cheng v Governor of Pentonville Prison [1973] AC 931, HL 9.189
Ulusoy v Turkey (App no 52709/99) 8.112
United States v Pitawanakwat 120 F Supp 2d 921 . . . . 9.182
United States v Toscanino, 500 F 2d 267 . . . . 9.135
US v Alvarez-Machain, (15 June 1992) 504 US 655 (1992) 9.129
Vayic v Turkey (App No 18078/02) 8.96
Vo v Benov, 447 F 3d 1235, 1241 (9th Cir 2006) 9.201
Wijeratne Banda v State SLR 86, Vol 3 of 1998 [1998] LKCA 24;
    (1998) 3 Sri LR 86 . . . . 4.108
Wilmer Yarleque Ordinola v John Hackman US Court of Appeals for the
    Fourth Circuit No 06-6126 [22 December 2007] 9.195
Woolmington v Director of Public Prosecutions [1935] AC 462 . . . . 5.34
X v United Kingdom (1993) 15 EHRR CD113 . . . . 4.24
Yusuf and Al Barakaat International Foundation v Council and Commission
    (T-306/01) [2005] ECR-II 3533 . . . . 6.45

TABLE OF LEGISLATION, TREATIES, AND CONVENTIONS

Paragraph references in **bold** indicate that the text is reproduced in full

CONVENTIONS AND TREATIES

African Charter on Human and Peoples'
    Rights 1981/1986 . . . . 8.11
    Art 5. . . . . .9.231
    Art 7. . . . . .5.52, 8.94, 8.107, 8.112
    Art 27. . . . . .8.31
American Convention on Human Rights
    1969. . . . . 8.11, **App 16**
    Art 5. . . . . .9.231
    Art 8. . . . . .5.52
Arab Convention on the Suppression of
    Terrorism 1998. . . . .1.32, 2.08, **App 18**
Bombings Convention 1997
    (Suppression of Terrorist
    Bombings) 1.29, 2.23, 2.47, 3.83,
             3.136, 3.154, 6.19, **App 11**
    Art 1. . . . .**2.48**
    Art 1(1) 3.88
    Art 1(3) 3.91
    Art 2 . . . .**2.49, 2.127**, 3.83
    Art 2.1 . . . . .2.34
    Art 2.3 . . . . .2.40
    Art 3 . . . . **2.50, 2.128**
    Art 4 . . . .**2.51**
    Art 5 . . . .**2.130**
    Art 6 . . . . **2.131**, 3.171, 3.190
    Art 7 . . . .**2.132**
    Art 8 . . . .**2.134**, 3.190, 9.165
    Art 9 . . . .**2.135**
    Art 10. . . . . **2.46, 2.136**, 9.10, 9.13
    Arts 10-15 .2.46
    Art 10(1) **9.13**
    Art 11. . . . . **2.137**, 9.172
    Art 12. . . . . **2.138**, 9.208
    Art 13. . . . . **2.46, 2.139**
    Art 14. . . . .**2.133**
    Art 15. . . . . **2.46, 2.140**
    Art 19. . . . . .3.84
Civil Aviation Convention 1963. . . . . .3.135
Civil Aviation Convention 1970. . . . . .3.135
Civil Aviation Convention 1971. . . . . .3.135

Diplomats Convention 1973
    (Prevention and Punishment of
    Crimes against Internationally
    Protected Persons) 1.29, 2.46, 9.09,
                 9.110, **App 6**
    Art 1 . . . .**2.104**
    Art 1(1) 3.47
    Art 2 . . . . **2.105**, 3.46, 3.48, 3.50
    Art 2(1) **3.46**, 3.49
    Art 3 . . . . **2.106**, 3.166
    Art 4 . . . .**2.108**
    Art 5 . . . .**2.109**
    Art 6 . . . .**2.107**
    Art 7 . . . . **2.110**, 9.163
    Art 8 . . . .**2.111**
    Art 9 . . . .**2.112**
    Art 10. . . . .**2.113**
European Convention on
    Extradition 1957 . . . . .9.116
    Art 2 . . . . .9.154
    Art 6(2) 9.163
European Convention on Human
    Rights and Fundamental Freedoms
    1950 (ECHR) 4.33, 8.11, 8.20,
                      9.208
    Art 1 . . . . .4.265
    Art 3 . . . . 8.82, 8.88, 9.231
    Art 5 . . . . 4.33, 8.31, 8.94
    Art 5(1) 4.58
    Art 6 . . . . 4.33, 4.172, 4.253, 5.15,
             5.52, 5.128, 5.134, 8.88,
                 8.107, 8.112
    Art 6(1) 5.135
    Art 6(2) 5.03, 5.21, 5.27, 5.29, 5.46
    Art 6(3)(c) 5.135
    Art 7 . . . . .5.25
    Art 8 . . . . 4.165, 4.166, 4.171
    Art 8(1) 4.171, 4.172, 4.187
    Art 8(2) 4.58, 4.172, 4.187
    Art 10. . . . . 5.29, 8.121
    Art 15. . . . . .4.87

European Convention on the Suppression
    of Terrorism 1997. . .1.32, 2.08, **App 15**
Financing Convention 1999
    (Suppression of Financing of
    Terrorism) 1.29, 2.23, 2.33, 2.41,
                3.136, 6.08, 6.10, **App 12**
  Art 1 . . . . .6.15
  Art 1(1) 3.95
  Art 2 . . . . . .**2.142, 3.92**, 3.93, 6.17, 6.22
  Art 2(1) 1.39, 6.11, 6.12
  Art 2(3) 6.13
  Art 2(4) 6.14
  Art 2(5) 6.16
  Art 3 . . . .**2.143, 3.157**, 6.22
  Art 4 . . . .**2.144**, 6.14, 6.22
  Art 5 . . . .**2.145**, 6.17, 6.22
  Art 6 . . . . **2.146**, 6.22
  Art 7 . . . . **2.147, 3.157**, 3.172, 6.22
  Art 7(2) 6.18
  Art 8 . . . .**2.148**, 6.22, 9.14
  Art 8(1) 6.21
  Art 8(4) 6.22
  Art 9 . . . . **2.149**, 6.22
  Art 10. . . . . **2.151**, 6.22
  Art 11. . . . . **2.152**, 6.22
  Art 12. . . . .**2.153**, 6.22, 9.14
  Art 12(2) 9.25
  Art 13. . . . .**2.154**, 6.22, 9.24
  Art 14. . . . .**2.155**, 6.22, 9.173
  Art 15. . . . . **2.156**, 6.19, 6.22, 9.208
  Art 16. . . . .**2.157**
  Art 17. . . . .**2.150**
  Art 18. . . . . .6.22
Geneva Conventions 1949 . . . . . . 3.55, 8.06
  Art 1 . . . . .8.16
Geneva Convention IV (Protection of
    Civilian Persons in Time of War). . . 1.26
Additional Protocol I 1977 (Protection of
    Victims of International Armed
    Conflicts). 3.55, 8.06
  Art 51(2) 1.26
Additional Protocol II (Protection of Victims
    of Non-International Armed Conflicts).
    3.55, 8.06
  Art 13(2) 1.26
Hague Convention 1970 (Suppression
    of Unlawful Seizure of Aircraft) . . 2.23,
                2.39, 2.52, 3.02, 3.28,
                3.39, 3.133, **App 4**
  Art 1 . . . .**2.53**, 3.03, **3.05**, 3.09, 3.11
  Art 1(1)(a) 3.33, 3.38
  Art 1(1)(b) 3.34, 3.38
  Art 1(1)(c) 3.34, 3.38
  Art 1(1)(d) 3.35, 3.36

  Art 1(1)(e) .3.36
  Art 1(4) **3.03**
  Art 2 . . . . **2.54**, 3.32
  Art 3 . . . .**2.55**
  Art 3(1) 3.10
  Art 3(2) 3.03, 3.29
  Art 3(3) 3.10
  Art 4 . . . . .2.45, **2.56**, 3.161
  Art 4(5) **3.35**
  Art 5 . . . . .3.162
  Art 6 . . . .**2.57**
  Art 7 . . . .**2.58**
  Art 8 . . . . **2.59**, 9.150
  Art 9 . . . .**2.60**
  Art 10. . . . . **2.61**, 9.05
  Art 10.1 . . . . 2.45, 9.05
Hostages Convention 1979 (Against the
    Taking of Hostages) . . .1.29, 2.23, 2.46,
                3.145, **App 7**
  Art 1 . . . . **2.115, 3.51**
  Art 2 . . . .**2.116**
  Art 4 . . . . **2.121**, 3.57
  Art 5 . . . . **2.119**, 3.167
  Art 6 . . . .**2.120**
  Art 8 . . . . **2.122**, 9.165
  Art 9 . . . . **2.123**, 9.208
  Art 10. . . . .**2.124**
  Art 11. . . . . **2.125, 9.09**
  Art 12. . . . .**2.117**, 3.55, 3.56
  Art 13. . . . . **2.118**, 3.53
Inter-American Convention on Extradition
    1981. . . . . .9.208
Montreal Convention 1971 (Suppression
    of Unlawful Acts against the
    Safety of Civil
    Aviation) 1.29, 2.23, 2.39,
                2.46, 3.28, 3.39,
                9.11, **App 5**
  Art 1 . . . . **2.63**, 3.41
  Art 1(1) **3.30**, 3.43
  Art 1(2) 3.44
  Art 2 . . . .**2.64**
  Art 3 . . . . **2.65**, 3.165
  Art 4 . . . .**2.66**
  Art 4(1) 3.29
  Art 5 . . . .**2.67**, 3.164, 9.08
  Art 6 . . . .**2.68**
  Art 7 . . . .**2.69**
  Art 8 . . . .**2.70**
  Art 11. . . . . **2.71**, 9.06
  Art 12. . . . . **2.72**, 9.06
Montreal Protocol 1989 . . . . .3.40
  Art II 3.41
  Art II(2) 3.44

Mutual Assistance in Criminal
    Matters 1986 . . . . .9.111
    Art 1 . . . . .9.112
    Art 2 . . . . .9.112
    Art 3 . . . . .9.112
    Art 17 . . . . .9.112
Nuclear Materials Convention 1979
    (Physical Protection of
    Nuclear Material) 1.29, 2.23, 2.24,
               3.136, 9.148, **App 8**
    Art 7 . . . .**2.94, 3.58**, 3.59
    Art 8 . . . .**2.95**
    Art 9 . . . .**2.97**
    Art 10. . . . .**2.98**
    Art 11. . . . .**2.99**
    Art 11A **2.100**, 9.173
    Art 11B **2.101**, 9.208
    Art 12. . . . . **2.96**, 9.10
    Art 13. . . . .**2.102**
Nuclear Terrorism Convention 2005
    (Suppression of Acts of Nuclear
    Terrorism) 1.29, 2.23, 2.25,
            2.158, 3.136, 3.154,
                   9.148, **App 13**
    Art 1(1) .3.107
    Art 2 . . . .**2.159, 3.103**
    Art 2(1)(a) 3.104
    Art 2(1)(b) 3.105
    Art 2(2) .3.106
    Art 2(3) .3.107
    Art 2(4) .3.107
    Art 3 . . . .**2.160**
    Art 4 . . . .**2.161**
    Art 5 . . . .**2.162**
    Art 6 . . . .**2.163**
    Art 7 . . . .**2.168**
    Art 8 . . . . **2.169**, 3.168
    Art 9 . . . .**2.165**
    Art 10. . . . .**2.166**
    Art 11. . . . .**2.164**
    Art 12. . . . .**2.167**
    Art 13. . . . .**2.170**
    Art 14. . . . .**2.171**
    Art 15. . . . . **2.172**, 9.173
    Art 16. . . . . **2.173**, 9.208
    Art 17. . . . .**2.174**
OAS Convention to Prevent
    and Punish Acts of
    Terrorism 1971. . . . . 1.32, 2.08
OAU Convention on the Prevention
    and Combating of Terrorism
    1999. . . . . .1.32, 2.08, **App 17**
UN Convention against Corruption
    Art 43(2) .9.22

Organisation of the Islamic Conference on
    Combating International Terrorism
    1999. . . . . 1.32, 2.08
Plastic Explosives Convention 1991
    (Marking of Plastic Explosives
    for the Purpose of
    Identification) 1.29, 2.23,
                     9.150, **App 10**
Palermo Convention *See* United
    Nations Convention against
    Transnational Organised
    Crime 2000
Prevention and Punishment of Terrorism
    Convention 1937 (1937 Draft
    Convention). 1.19, 1.24, 2.01
    Art 2 . . . . .1.25
    Art 18. . . . . .1.25
Refugee Convention 1951 . . . . 9.208, 9.231
    Art 33(1) .9.209
    Art 33(2) .9.209
Rome Convention 1988 . . . . 3.61, **App 9**
    Art 1 . . . . 3.63, 3.65
    Art 2 . . . . .3.65
    Art 2(2) .3.67
    Art 3 . . . . 3.62, 3.68
    Art 3(1) **3.62**, 3.73
    Art 3 *ter* .3.79
    Art 3 *qater* 3.80
    Art 6 . . . . .3.169
Rome Protocol 1998. . . . . 3.73, 3.82
Rome Protocol 2005. . . . . 3.77, 3.82
SAARC Regional Convention
    on Suppression of
    Terrorism 1987. . . . . .1.32
Safety of Maritime Navigation 1988
    (Suppression of Unlawful Acts
    against the Safety of
    Maritime Navigation
    Convention). 1.29, 2.36, 3.134,
                     3.154, 9.148
    Art 1 . . . .**2.76**
    Art 2 . . . .**2.77**
    Art 3 . . . .**2.78**
    Art 6 . . . .**2.79**
    Art 7 . . . .**2.80**
    Art 8 . . . .**2.81**
    Art 9 . . . .**2.82**
    Art 10. . . . .**2.83**
    Art 11. . . . .**2.84**
    Art 12. . . . .**2.85**
    Art 13. . . . . **2.86**, 9.10
    Art 14. . . . .**2.87**
Terrorist Bombing Convention *See* Bombings
    Convention

Tokyo Convention 1963 (Offences and
    Certain Other Acts Committed on
    Board Aircraft) 1.29, 2.23, 2.30,
                            3.02, 9.150, 9.162,
                            9.170, **App 3**
    Art 1(4) 3.29
    Art 3 . . . . **3.157**, 3.160
    Art 4 . . . . **3.157**, 3.160
Torture Convention (against Torture and
    other Cruel, Inhuman, or
    Degrading Treatment)
    (CAT) 1984 . . . . 8.53, 9.208, 9.231
    Art 2 . . . . .8.54
    Art 12. . . . . .8.54
    Art 15. . . . . .8.66
Treaty of Cooperation among States
    Members of the Commonwealth of
    Independent States in Combating
    Terrorism 1999. . . . . .1.32
Treaty of Rome. 1.40
United Nations Convention on the Law
    of the Sea 1982 (UNCLOS) 3.66
    Art 29. . . . . .3.66
    Art 76. . . . . .3.74
United Nations Convention against Illicit
    Traffic in Narcotic Drugs and
    Psychotropic Substances (1988) (Vienna
    Convention). 6.05, 6.55,
                            9.151
United Nations Convention against
    Transnational Organised
    Crime 2000 (Palermo
    Convention). 6.05, 6.23
    Art 24. . . . . .4.28
Vienna Convention on Diplomatic Relations
    1961. . . . . .2.103
Vienna Convention on the Law of
    Treaties 1969
    Art 31. . . . . .9.112

NATIONAL LEGISLATION BY COUNTRY

Australia
Crimes Act 1914. . . . . .9.96

Barbados
Anti Terrorism Act 2002. . . . . .3.113

Belgium
Penal Code. . . . . Art 7 3.177, 3.185

Canada
Mutual Legal Assistance in Criminal Matters
    Act 1985
    s 18 . . . . .9.31
    s 18(1) 9.32
    s 20 . . . . 9.31, 9.32

Nigeria
Constitution
    s 36(6)(c) 5.57

Sri Lanka
Prevention of Terrorism
    (Temporary Provisions)
    Act No 48 1979 . . . . 4.97, 4.108, 4.110
    s 6 . . . . .4.82
    s 7 . . . . .4.82
    s 9 . . . . .4.82
    s 16 . . . . .4.99
    s 31 . . . . .4.83
Public Security Act No 28 1988 . . . . . .4.110

Switzerland
Criminal Code
    Art 25. . . . . .9.37
    Art 148. . . . . .9.37
Geneva Code of Criminal Procedure. . . .9.52
    Art 134. . . . . .9.52
    Art 138. . . . . .9.52
    Art 143. . . . . .9.52
    Art 234-8 .9.45
    Art 330-3 .9.45

Uganda
Anti Terrorism Act 2002. . . . . .3.113

South Africa
Aliens Control Act 96 1991 . . . . .9.124
Constitution. .9.124

UK Statutes
Anti Terrorism Crime and Security
    Act 2001 . . . . .3.108
    s 23 . . . . 4.67, 8.36, 8.37
    s 25 . . . . .4.88
    s 47 . . . . 3.125, 3.142
    s 50 . . . . 3.125, 3.142
    s 56 . . . . .3.142
Aviation and Maritime Security
    Act 1990 . . . . .3.45
    s 1 . . . . 3.45, 3.125
    ss 9-13 . . . . .3.125

Aviation Security Act 1982 . . . . 3.12
  s 1 . . . . **3.12**, 3.125
  s 1(1) 3.15
  s 2 . . . . 3.39, 3.125
  s 2(6) 3.39
  s 3 . . . . 3.39, 3.125
Biological Weapons Act 1974
  s 1 . . . . 3.125, 3.192, 5.51
Chemical Weapons Act 1996
  s 2 . . . . 3.125, 3.192, 5.51
Contempt of Court Act 1981
  s 5 . . . . .5.96
Crime and Disorder Act 1998
  s 51 . . . . .5.51
Crime (International Cooperation)
    Act 2003 . . . . .3.108
Criminal Appeal (Northern Ireland) Act 1980
  s 15(1) .4.269
Criminal Damage Act 1971
  s 1(2) 5.51
Criminal Evidence (Northern Ireland) Order
    1988 (SI 1988/1987) 5.119
  art 3 . . . . .5.113
  art 4 . . . . .5.113
  art 6 . . . . .5.113
Criminal Evidence (Witness Anonymity)
    Act 2008 . . . . 4.53, **App 21**
Criminal Jurisdiction Act 1975
  s 7 . . . . .3.192
  s 13 . . . . .3.192
Criminal Justice Act 1987
  s 4 . . . . .5.51
  s 9(3) .3.192
Criminal Justice and Public Order
    Act 1994 . . . . .5.112
  s 34 . . . .**5.112**
  s 35 . . . .**5.112**
  s 37 . . . .**5.112**
Criminal Justice (Terrorism and Conspiracy)
    Act 1998
  s 5 . . . . .3.192
Criminal Law Act 1997
  s 1A 3.192
Criminal Procedure and Investigations
    Act 1996 . . . . 5.59, 5.67
  s 31(3) 3.192
Explosive Substances Act 1883 . . . .
  s 2 . . . . 3.38, 3.125,
                            3.192, 5.51
  s 3 . . . . .3.192, 3.192, 5.49, 5.51
  s 3(1) .3.125
  s 4 . . . . .3.125
  s 5 . . . . 3.125, 3.192, 5.51
Extradition Act 2003 . . . . 9.115, 9.138

Firearms Act 1968
  s 16 . . . . .3.192
  s 17 . . . . .3.192
Human Rights Act 1998 . . . 5.15, 5.114, 8.20
  s 2 . . . . .5.23
  s 3 . . . . 5.19, 5.36
  s 3(1) .5.12
  s 6 . . . . 5.24, 8.21, 8.23
  s 7 . . . . 5.24, 8.21
  s 22 . . . . .5.24
Intelligence Services Act 1994
  s 5 . . . . .4.215
Interception of Communications
    Act 1985 . . . . .4.151
International Criminal Court
    Act 2001 . . . . .3.141
Internationally Protected Persons Act 1978
  s 1 . . . . .3.48
  s 1(4) 3.48
Jury's Act 1974
  s 5(1) 5.89
Misuse of Drugs Act 1971 . . . . .5.14
  s 5 . . . . .5.16
  s 28(2) .5.20
  s 28(3)(b)(i) 5.14
Nuclear Material Offences Act 1983
  s 1 . . . . .3.125
Offences against the Person Act 1861
  s 18 . . . . 3.38, 5.51
  ss 20-24 . . . . 3.38, 5.51
  s 28 . . . . 3.38, 3.192, 5.51
  s 29 . . . . 3.38, 3.192, 5.51
  s 30 . . . . .3.192
Official Secrets Act 1920
  s 8(4) .5.109
Police Act 1997 . . . . 4.170, 4.215
  Pt III .4.234
Police and Criminal Evidence
    Act 1984 (PACE)
  s 76 . . . . .4.93
  s 78 . . . . 4.253, 4.256, 8.67
  s 92 . . . . .4.241
  s 93 . . . .**4.243**
  s 94(4) .4.345
  s 95(1)-(3) 4.346
  Code H . . . . 5.140, **App 22**
Prevention of Terrorism Act 1984
  s 12 . . . . .5.135
Prevention of Terrorism (Temporary
    Provisions) Act 1989
  s 16A 5.44-5.46
Refugees Convention (United Nations 1951
    Convention on the Status of Refugees)
  Art 33 . . . . .8.82

Regulation of Investigatory Powers Act 2000
    (RIPA) 4.151, 4.166
  s 1(1) 4.152
  s 1(2) 4.153
  s 3   . . . . .4.155
  s 4   . . . . .4.155
  s 5   . . . . .4.156
  s 17 . . . . .4.157
  s 18 . . . . .4.157
  s 26(2) 4.218
  s 26(3) 4.225
  s 26(4) 4.227
  s 26(5) 4.228
  s 26(7) 4.184
  s 26(8) 4.183
  s 26(9) 4.186
  s 26(11) 4.227
  s 27(1) 4.221, 4.230
  s 27(2) 4.221
  s 27(3) 4.192
  s 28(2) 4.222
  s 28(3) 4.222
  s 29(3) 4.189
  s 29(5) 4.190
  s 32(1) 4.229
  s 32(2) 4.230, 4.237
  s 32(3) 4.230
  s 32(6) 4.229
  s 33(1) 4.191
  s 33(5) 4.234
  s 35(1) 4.235
  s 35(3) 4.235
  s 35(9) 4.236
  s 36(2) 4.236
  s 36(3) 4.236
  s 37(2)-(4) .4.237
  s 38(2) 4.239
  s 38(3) 4.239
  s 43(1) 4.233
  s 48(1) 4.227
  s 48(2) 4.214
  s 48(3) 4.216
  s 81(3) 4.232, 4.244
Regulation of Investigatory Powers
    (Prescription of Offices, Ranks
    and Positions) Order
    (SI 2000/2417). 4.191, 4.223
Road Traffic Act 1988. . . . . .5.27
  s 5   . . . .**5.27**
  s 5(2) 5.33
Serious Organised Crime and Police
    Act 2005 . . . . .3.108

Special Immigration Appeals
    Act 1997 .8.59
Suppression of Terrorism Act 1978
  s 4(1) 3.192
Taking of Hostages Act 1982
  s 1   . . . . .3.125
Terrorism Act 2000. . . . . .4.60
  s 1   . . . . 2.34, **3.108**, 3.112, 5.51
  s 1(1) **2.34**
  s 2   . . . .**3.38**
  s 3   . . . .**3.38**
  s 3(1) 4.267, 4.269
  s 11 . . . .**5.27**
  s 11(1) 3.192, 4.267
  s 11(2) 5.29, 5.40, 5.43
  s 12(2) 5.49
  ss 15-18 . . . . .5.43
  ss 15-19 . . . . .3.192
  s 18(2) 5.43
  ss 19-21 . . . . .5.43
  s 19(3) 5.43
  s 19(4) 5.43
  s 21(5) 5.43
  s 36(3) 5.43
  s 39(3) 5.49
  s 39(4) 5.49
  s 41 . . . . .5.140
  s 41(1) 4.65
  s 44 . . . . 4.57, 4.61
  s 44(3) 4.58
  s 54 . . . . 3.192, 5.49
  s 56 . . . . 3.125, 5.51
  s 57 . . . . 4.62, 5.01, 5.49
  s 58 . . . . 4.63, 5.49
  s 58(1)(b) .3.112
  s 59 . . . . 3.125, 5.51
  s 62 . . . . 3.192, 5.51
  s 63 . . . . .3.192
  s 77(1) 5.49
  s 118 . . . . 5.44, **5.48**
  s 183(1) 5.49
  Sch 8 . . . . 5.116, 5.140
Terrorism Act 2006. . . . . .3.108
  s 1   . . . . .3.192
  s 5   . . . . .5.51
  s 6   . . . . .3.192
  ss 8-11 . . . . .3.192
  s 17 . . . . .3.192
  s 17(5) 3.125
Theft Act 1968. . . . . .9.130
Trade Marks Act 1994 . . . . .5.04
  ss 10-12 . . . . .5.08

s 92 . . . . **5.04**
s 92(5) 5.05, 5.11, 5.12
United Nations Personnel Act 1997
   s 1 . . . . .3.125
   s 2 . . . . .3.125
   s 3 . . . . .3.125
Youth Justice and Criminal Evidence
   Act 1999
   s 58 . . . . .5.139

USA
Foreign Corrupt Practices Act
   1977 (FCPA) 3.150
Foreign Surveillance Act
   1978 (FISA) 4.146, 4.148
Military Commissions Act 2006 . . . . . .8.105

1

INTRODUCTION

A. Introduction	1.01	Terrorism as a crime under	
B. What is Terrorism?	1.06	customary international law	1.38
C. International Legal Responses		Terrorism in armed conflict	1.39
to Terrorism	1.14	Domestic measures	1.40
The definition of terrorism in		D. Overview of This Book	1.48
international law	1.18		
Terrorism as an international			
treaty crime	1.28		

A. Introduction

Although not a new phenomenon, terrorism has become an increasingly serious **1.01** threat to international peace, security, and stability. Traditionally considered a domestic security problem, terrorism has evolved over time to become a sophisticated form of transnational crime that poses a threat to all nations. The attacks on the United States (US) on 11 September 2001 (9/11) were the most stark acts of terrorism in recent history.[1] Together with a number of other serious incidents in several parts of the world in the 1990s,[2] they demonstrated that terrorists had developed the capacity and global infrastructure to launch attacks capable of causing massive destruction of life and property.

Modern-day forms of large-scale international terrorism, in the context of highly **1.02** complex and increasingly transnational networks, constitute a growing challenge to global, regional, and domestic security, including States' existing concepts of jurisdiction, law enforcement, and prosecution of offences. This brand of international terrorism is partly a phenomenon of globalization, where terrorists

---

[1] In total, 2,974 people were killed in the 9/11 attacks. The National Commission on Terrorist Attacks, *The 9/11 Commission Report: Final Report of the National Commission on Terrorist Attacks Upon the United States* (Authorized edn WW Norton, New York 2004).
[2] Including the simultaneous attacks on the US Embassies in Kenya and Tanzania in 1998, and the attack on the World Trade Centre in New York in 1993.

exploit the availability of a worldwide information and communication infrastructure for logistical purposes and political mobilization, and access to international travel to broaden the scope of their activities. Further, the prospect of terrorists gaining access to weapons of mass destruction adds a new dimension to the nature and extent of the threat posed by them.

1.03 The events of 9/11 catapulted terrorism up the list of international priorities. In the wake of those attacks, the world witnessed a proliferation of new legal obligations and measures, including United Nations (UN) Security Council resolutions, and international and regional conventions that imposed wide-reaching obligations on all Member States to prevent and combat terrorism. The most notable development came out of the UN Security Council when it adopted United Nations Security Resolution (UNSCR) 1373 (2001)[3] which targeted the diverse and widely dispersed transnational networks of Al-Qaida and other related non-State actors. UNSCR 1373 mandated all UN Member States to deny finances, travel, or assistance of any kind to terrorists and those who support them.[4]

1.04 Terrorist acts are serious crimes that must be addressed using the full range of available legal mechanisms, including international human rights law, international humanitarian law (IHL), international criminal law, and the domestic criminal justice system. By its very nature, terrorism cannot exclusively be dealt with within the framework of an international order defined by the nation-State; rather, it requires a multilateral effort that, inter alia, relies on enhanced international cooperation in criminal matters and improved criminal justice responses, both of which should uphold human rights and the rule of law.

1.05 Whilst some of these challenges continue to test the limits of the current international law paradigm, there is no need for an entirely new legal approach to address the problem of terrorism, even though it is true that not all relevant branches of international law possess an equal level of sophistication and that some are, in fact, in need of further development.

B. What is Terrorism?

1.06 Terrorism has blighted societies since earliest times. Leaders have been assassinated; acts of extreme violence have been committed against civilians in the name of religion, political belief, and other ideologies. Terrorism usually connotes evil, indiscriminate violence and brutality. It is commonly perceived that terrorists

---

[3] UNSCR 1373 (2001), 28 September 2001, UN Doc S/RES/1373 (2001).
[4] See Chapter 2 at 2.13 for further discussion on UNSCR 1373.

attack governments, and even international organizations, in order to undermine or destroy a political system, or a way of life. Such attacks, however, are often directed against innocent civilians.

These basic descriptions may seem banal, but political scientists, scholars, and **1.07** politicians have to this day not been able to agree on a clear definition of terrorism. This lack of agreement is easy to understand, especially when one considers the very nature of international relations and politics, and the associated differing views on what constitutes a legitimate government or accepted way of life.

It is, therefore, not surprising that there have been a multitude of proposed defini- **1.08** tions for terrorism; some exceedingly complicated, others too simplified. For the purposes of this discussion, the following definition captures the most important elements of terrorism as we know it today:

> Terrorism involves political aims and motives. It is violent or threatens violence. It is designed to generate fear in a targeted audience that extends beyond the immediate victims of the violence. The violence is conducted by an identifiable organisation. The violence involves a non-state actor or actors as either the perpetrator, the victim of violence, or both. Finally, the acts of violence are designed to create power in situations in which power previously had been lacking (ie, the violence attempts to enhance the power base of the organisation undertaking the actions).[5]

Whilst it is not within the scope of this book to provide a comprehensive overview **1.09** of the phenomenon of terrorism and how it has developed over time, it is, however, important to point out that terrorism is not a new phenomenon that surfaced on 9/11. It is also important to summarize briefly how terrorism has changed over the years from a predominantly domestic threat, into the global and transnational one that we face today.

Some theorists trace the origin of terrorism back to the eighteenth century when **1.10** it was frequently employed as a tactic during the French Revolution. According to the 1798 supplement of the *Dictionnaire* of the *Académie Française*, the words 'terrorism' and 'terrorist' stem from the *'régime de la terreur'*, which is a period of French history that followed the storming of the Bastille and the 1789 uprisings.[6] Terrorism was used to consolidate and entrench a newly established revolutionary State by intimidating counter-revolutionaries and other dissidents regarded as enemies of the people. Revolutionary leader Maximilien Robespierre held the view that revolution and terrorism had to work together to ensure the success

---

[5] J M Lutz and B J Lutz, *Global Terrorism* (Routledge, New York and London 2004) 10.
[6] A Hubschle, 'The T-word: Conceptualising Terrorism' (2006) 15 African Security Review, Institute for Security Studies 3, 2.

of democracy.[7] The very purpose of terrorism was to deal swiftly with international anarchy and external invasion by other European monarchs.

1.11 The Revolution, and its associated reign of terror, ended in 1794 when Robespierre and his closest allies were executed. Thereafter the terminology of terrorism become synonymous with abuse of office and power, and terrorists were viewed as people who tried to further their views or aims by a system of coercive intimidation. Although, initially, terrorism was understood to apply only to the actions by States, the notion was later expanded to describe a variety of acts of violence by non-State actors. There are a number of examples of this expanded notion of terrorism, including the ritualistic killings of African Americans by the Ku Klux Klan in the US, several political assassinations of Japanese prime ministers during the 1920s and 1930s, and frequent political murders in India in the decade before the First World War.

1.12 Throughout history, terrorism has been deeply woven into the fabric of social and political conflict.[8] Although that element of terrorism has not changed, modern terrorism has evolved into a more complex and dangerous threat. Terrorists are able to exploit new technologies, global communication networks, and loose cell-based terror networks, with limited command and control structures to plan and perpetrate sophisticated attacks around the world. Terrorist groups have been skilful in their use of information technology and the Internet to create unprecedented opportunities for violent extremists and their group members to broadcast their messages across the globe. Besides using the Internet for propaganda and recruitment purposes, terrorists are also able to share information and technical advice in relation to explosives, operational tactics, and terror training.

1.13 Many more present-day acts of terrorism have demonstrated little or no remorse over the killing of large number of civilians in the name of the cause. The underlying motivations for these terror campaigns encompass a broad range of political and religious beliefs and ideologies. The most well-known of these groups is Al-Qaida which has been responsible for a number of terrorist attacks in addition to 9/11, including: the attacks on the US Embassies in Kenya and Tanzania in 1998; the attack on the US destroyer, the *USS Cole*, in Aden in 2003; the attack on a commuter train in Madrid in 2004; and the attacks on UK public transport in London on 7 July 2005.

---

[7] B Hoffman, 'Defining Terrorism' in R Howard and R Sawyer (eds), *Terrorism and Counter-Terrorism* (McGraw-Hill/Dushkin, Connecticut 2002) 4.
[8] G Martin, *Understanding Terrorism: Challenges, Perspective and Issues* (Second Edition, Sage Publications, London 2006) 9.

C. International Legal Responses to Terrorism

The post-9/11 responses to terrorism have proved controversial. The US-led **1.14** 'Global War on Terror', in particular, has highlighted the dangers of a predomi- nantly military-focused and extrajudicial approach to countering terrorism. The first phase of post-9/11 efforts included robust and targeted US-led military action against the Taliban and Al-Qaida. Whilst these efforts were possibly justifi- able at the time, the ongoing US focus on a military-driven counter-terrorism campaign has failed to track down diverse terrorist funding sources and bring perpetrators of terrorist crimes to justice. It has also failed to adhere to interna- tionally accepted standards of human rights, due process, and the rule of law; and, in flouting these principles, has failed to win the long-term support of the inter- national community.

Attempts have been made to justify this approach partly on the premise that ter- **1.15** rorism lies somewhere between crime and war, and partly on the premise that terrorists are not ordinary criminals. They are particularly dangerous criminals, the argument goes, who are also our enemies. This has resulted in sympathy, in some quarters, for using techniques of preventive detention against these battle- field criminals. The US base at Guantanamo Bay has become synonymous with this approach.

Many of these practices have not survived the scrutiny of international law, and **1.16** there is now widespread recognition that all efforts to counter-terrorism must be taken in full conformity with the law, in accordance with human rights and due process.[9] In light of this, there is a need to enhance legitimate criminal justice responses to terrorism that provide a legal and judicial framework, and remedies, with built-in human rights protections. This response must consist of a number of elements, including:

- clear and accessible laws;
- law enforcement personnel and criminal justice practitioners who are able to apply these laws properly in practice;
- the operational capacity of those officials to engage in international cooperation, including mutual legal assistance and extradition;
- an independent judiciary capable of dispensing free, fair, and transparent justice that complies with international standards and norms, including human rights and due process.

---

[9] UN Global Counter-Terrorism Strategy, UNSCR 1456. To be found at Appendix 14 and Appendix 1 respectively.

1.17 A criminal justice-based response to terrorism must be guided by the framework provided by international and regional counter-terrorism standards and norms, and embedded in respect for the rule of law and human rights. This requires strengthening the capacity of national criminal justice systems to bring perpetrators to justice, or to extradite them to another State for trial, in full compliance with these legal standards. In addition to bringing perpetrators of terrorism crimes to justice, a criminal justice response to terrorism also provides effective preventive mechanisms (for instance, the criminalization of support conduct, financing of terrorism, incitement, and conspiracy to commit crime), with human rights safeguards. It deals with terrorists as criminals and not as soldiers or warriors based upon a clear non-political legal foundation.

The definition of terrorism in international law

1.18 While historians and political scientists have been able to describe and define terrorism in relatively clear terms, the same cannot be said for legal scholars and practitioners. Despite widespread condemnation of terrorism, there is still no all- embracing legal definition of it. Various diplomatic attempts (some of which are still ongoing) to draft a global counter-terrorism convention have failed due to the lack of consensus on a single definition. The crux of the problem is summed up in the aphorism 'one man's terrorist is another man's freedom fighter'. States have not been able to agree on the scope of application of the definition of international terrorism and whether it should apply to the actions of both national liberation movements and States.

1.19 In the aftermath of the Second World War there was a significant measure of agreement among States on the main elements of what could amount to terrorism. The most widely accepted definition was contained in the Convention for the Prevention and Punishment of Terrorism of 16 November 1937 (known as the 1937 Draft Convention) adopted by the League of Nations.[10] Article 1 defines 'terroristic acts' as 'criminal acts directed against the State and intended to create a state of terror in the minds of particular persons, or a group of persons or the general public'.

1.20 This progress towards consensus on a definition of terrorism was hampered by the political developments of the Cold War and the number of movements towards decolonization. During the 1960s, 70s, and 80s, a number of 'freedom fighters' resorted to acts of violence to express their resistance against oppressive and/or colonial regimes. Although these acts fit squarely within the normal definition of

---

[10] The Convention was ratified only by India and never came into force. For a discussion of the Convention see B Saul, 'The Legal Response of the League of Nations to Terrorism' (2006) 4 Journal of International Criminal Justice 18.

terrorism, many of these freedom fighters or national liberation movements had the political support of certain world powers that were fighting proxy wars against their Cold War adversaries. This led to a political gridlock between negotiating States that made it almost impossible to reach agreement on the definition of terrorism.

In 1972 the UN stepped in and mandated an Ad Hoc Committee of the General **1.21** Assembly to consider a Draft Comprehensive Convention and to produce a definition of terrorism. The Committee's report was rejected by Member States and served merely to highlight the challenges associated with efforts to reach consensus on a definition.

As described in Chapter 2, this political deadlock in reaching agreement on the **1.22** definition of terrorism caused the international community to adopt a reactive, case-by-case approach to terrorism. Instead of focusing on an all-inclusive definition of terrorism, Member States agreed on a piecemeal approach that provided for the criminalization of specific acts of terrorism, expansion of traditional jurisdictional limitations, and increased mechanisms and obligations to promote international cooperation in terrorism cases.

Efforts to reach agreement on a generally acceptable definition resumed after the **1.23** collapse of the Cold War and *apartheid*, the achievement of independence from colonialism by a number of African countries, and several positive developments in the Middle East. In a 1994 General Assembly Resolution,[11] the UN reaffirmed its unequivocal condemnation of all acts, methods, and practices of terrorism; declaring that acts of terrorism were unjustifiable whatever the considerations, be they political, religious, ethnic, or ideological. Interestingly, this Resolution dropped the reference to peoples' legitimate struggle for freedom and independence. Then in 1996, a new Ad Hoc Committee was created to lead the process towards the elaboration of a comprehensive convention on terrorism.[12] This spirit of unqualified condemnation of terrorism was carried forward in a number of subsequent General Assembly resolutions and UNSCRs on terrorism.[13]

The negotiations on the Draft Comprehensive Convention against International **1.24** Terrorism are still ongoing in the Sixth Committee of the United Nations.[14] This Draft Convention (which is based on the original instrument proposed by India in 1937) has the political support of the current UN Secretary General and his

---

[11] GA Resolution 49/60 of 9 December 1994.
[12] See GA Resolution No 51/210 of 17 December 1996, UN Doc A/RES/51/210.
[13] See Chapter 2 for more details on these resolutions.
[14] Draft Comprehensive Convention against International Terrorism, UN Doc A/59/894 App II.

immediate predecessor, as well as many Member States. Its most recent draft definition of terrorism, contained in Article (2) defines terrorism as:

> . . . unlawfully and internationally causing (a) death or serious bodily injury to any person; (b) serious damage to public and private property, including a State or government facility; or (c) other damage that is likely to result in economic loss. In terms of the definition, the purpose of the conduct described above must by its nature and context be performed to intimidate a population, or compel a government or an international organisation to do or abstain from doing any act.[15]

1.25 Despite ongoing diplomatic efforts at the UN and the appointment of a new Coordinator of the Working Group, the text of the Convention has still not gained the support of all Member States. Two main points of contention remain. First is the age-old issue of scope of application and whether the Convention applies to the legitimate struggle of people for independence and freedom, specifically whether it applies to National Liberation Movements (NLMs). To deal with this point of contention, Article 18 of the Draft Comprehensive Convention excludes from the scope of the Article 2 definition acts carried out during armed conflicts. It does this on the basis that another body of international law, namely IHL, expressly governs situations of armed conflict, including wars of national liberation.[16] Interestingly though, the current draft only excludes 'armed forces' from its scope, and in so doing, exempts only State forces and not other actors whose conduct may be covered by IHL, including NLMs in the context of wars. This inclusion of NLMs and other non-combatants continues to encounter firm resistance from a number of Member States, especially from the Organization of the Islamic Conference (OIC) block. A counter-proposal attempts to exclude both 'parties to a conflict', and to ensure that NLMs are considered within the scope of this exclusion. Negotiations in this issue are still continuing.

1.26 The second contentious issue relates to the relationship between 'individual' terrorism as a criminal offence and terrorism carried out by State agents as proscribed in the Fourth Geneva Convention and the Additional Protocols.[17] In respect of whether State conduct can constitute a terrorist act, it is worth highlighting the following key points. First, it should be recognized that the use of violence to instill terror among civilians is not the exclusive preserve of non-State actors. A number of States have engaged and continue to engage in violence against populations in a manner designed to create fear among them,

---

[15] Informal text of Article 2, Report of the Working Group on Measures to Eliminate International Terrorism, UN Doc a/s.6/56/L.9, Annex I B.

[16] These wars may be treated as international armed conflicts under Article 1(4) of Additional Protocol I of the Geneva Conventions.

[17] Article 51(2) Additional Protocol I and Art 13(2) Additional Protocol II: 'Acts or threats of violence the primary purpose of which is to spread terror among the civilian population are prohibited.'

especially in internal conflicts. Although State violence is popularly referred to as 'State terrorism', this term is not recognized in international law. The majority of international terrorism instruments do not address State terrorism as such.[18] This approach is, in theory, justified by the fact that States are, or should be, accountable through other branches of law, including human rights, IHL, and the law on the use of force. Specifically, violence perpetrated by a State against its citizens may constitute a threat to international peace and security which could lead the UN Security Council to invoke its Chapter VII powers.[19]

The question of State terrorism should be distinguished from State responsibility **1.27** carried out by private actors, and State sponsorship and support of terrorism. These concepts are explicitly covered in a number of counter-terrorism instruments. Finally, for the most part, 'State terrorism' would entail acts of terror committed against people of that State (thus not meeting the threshold for international terrorism) and most acts of 'State terrorism' would take place during a situation of armed conflict (falling explicitly outside the scope of most counter-terrorism instruments as these situations are covered by IHL).

Terrorism as an international treaty crime

The failure of the international community to reach agreement on a draft compre- **1.28** hensive convention against terrorism, including a broad definition of terrorism itself, did not completely thwart international counter-terrorism efforts. Faced with the daily reality of a growing threat of international terrorism, Member States adopted a reactive case-by-case approach to specific incidents of international terrorism. These included civilian aircraft and ship hijackings, hostage taking, terrorist bombings, and threats of nuclear terrorism from non-State actors.

Since 1963 the international community, supported by several regional initia- **1.29** tives, has developed a number of specific conventions and protocols addressing particular forms of terrorist activities and providing for enhanced international cooperation mechanisms and jurisdictional grounds.[20] Another key aim of these

---

[18] *International Bar Association's Task Force on International Terrorism, International Terrorism: Legal Challenges and Responses* (Transnational Publishers, USA 2003) 3.

[19] In terms of Article 39 of the UN Charter, the Security Council can determine the existence of a threat to international peace and security and utilize its Chapter VII powers, which include economic sanctions against the State under Article 41 and military action under Article 42.

[20] Convention on Offences and Certain Other Acts Committed on Board Aircraft (1963); Convention for the Suppression of Unlawful Seizure of Aircraft (1970); Convention for the Suppression of Unlawful Acts against the Safety of Civil Aviation (1971); Convention on the Prevention and Punishment of Crimes against Internationally Protected Persons, Including Diplomatic Agents (1973); International Convention against the Taking of Hostages (1979); Convention on the Physical Protection of Nuclear Material (1979); Protocol for the Suppression of Unlawful Acts of Violence at Airports Serving International Civil Aviation (1988), Supplementary to the

instruments is to provide a seamless international criminal law regime that reduces the existence of safe havens for those who commit and/or attempt to commit terrorist acts as defined in the conventions and protocols. This aim finds expression in the *aut dedere aut judicare* (States must either extradite or prosecute those accused of committing terrorist acts) obligation, which forms the cornerstone of virtually all of the instruments.

1.30 These treaties have the effect of criminalizing certain conduct by imposing obligations on acceding and ratifying States to implement the criminalization provisions in domestic law. The UN Security Council has also passed a number of counter-terrorism resolutions under Chapter VII that support those instruments.[21]

1.31 Whilst the piecemeal approach provided by this treaty regime provides a useful alternative to the lack of an international convention or definition of terrorism, it does have some limitations. First, these instruments are for the most part applicable to terrorist acts committed during peacetime and against civilian targets. Most of the conventions and protocols apply only to completed or attempted terrorist acts and cannot be used to prosecute inchoate crimes such as conspiracy or incitement. Moreover, being part of treaty law, these counter-terrorism instruments are only binding on State parties, and the prosecution of the specific terrorist crimes contained in the treaties is only possible if States have incorporated the treaties into domestic law.

1.32 In addition to these international counter-terrorism instruments, several regional organizations have also assumed responsibility for addressing terrorism. This has led to the adoption of a number of regional counter-terrorism conventions.[22]

Convention for the Suppression of Unlawful Acts against the Safety of Civil Aviation; Convention for the Suppression of Unlawful Acts against the Safety of Maritime Navigation (1988); Protocol for the Suppression of Unlawful Acts against the Safety of Fixed Platforms Located on the Continental Shelf (1988); Convention on the Marking of Plastic Explosives for the Purpose of Identification (1991); International Convention for the Suppression of Terrorist Bombings (1997); International Convention for the Suppression of the Financing of Terrorism (1999); International Convention for the Suppression of Acts of Nuclear Terrorism (2005); Amendment to the Convention on the Physical Protection of Nuclear Material (2005); Protocol of 2005 to the Convention for the Suppression of Unlawful Acts against the Safety of Maritime Navigation; Protocol of 2005 to the Protocol for the Suppression of Unlawful Acts against the Safety of Fixed Platforms Located on the Continental Shelf (1988).

[21] This international counter-terrorism legal regime is discussed in more detail in Chapters 2 and 3.

[22] Arab Convention on the Suppression of Terrorism, 22 April 1998; Convention of the Organization of the Islamic Conference on Combating International Terrorism, 1 July 1999; European Convention on the Suppression of Terrorism, 27 January 1997; OAS Convention to Prevent and Punish Acts of Terrorism Taking the Form of Crimes against Persons and Related Extortion that are of International Significance, Washington DC, 2 February 1971, OAU Convention on the Prevention and Combating of Terrorism, 1999; SAARC Regional Convention on Suppression of Terrorism, 4 November 1987; Treaty of Cooperation among States Members of the Commonwealth of Independent States in Combating Terrorism, 4 June 1999.

Many of these conventions contain their own definitions of terrorism and terrorist acts as well as detailed provisions on international cooperation in terrorist cases. State parties to these conventions are obligated to implement these provisions in their domestic law.

It may be worth setting out the mechanism through which a State implements its **1.33** treaty obligations. There are two major approaches as to how international treaties enter into force domestically. This process depends on whether a State subscribes to a monist or dualist system governing the relationship between international and national law. Monist systems reflect a unitary nature between international and domestic law, whereby both sources of law are considered to belong to the same legal family. Under this approach, when a State ratifies a treaty, the treaty is given the domestic force of law without the need to enact subsequent, implementing legislation. Democratic processes leading to the domestic approval of a treaty is attained during the treaty-making process. Under monist systems, domestic courts and other public bodies refer to the language of the treaty provisions itself as a source of law. Monist legal systems may exhibit variations in approach. These include:

1. Systems where only certain treaties are considered to be directly applicable in domestic law and where the treaty provisions share the same level of hierarchy as federal laws, in line with the principle that the latest in time prevails;
2. Systems where the provisions of certain treaties are superior to later legislation, but which remain lower in status to Constitutional provisions;
3. Systems where the Constitution provides for the direct applicability of certain treaties and where treaty provisions are considered superior to all laws.

Examples of States with monist legal systems, or variations thereof, include **1.34** Germany, the Netherlands, and the United States. However, even in a monist legal system, the effect of the constitution may be that domestic legislation will be needed to address sanctions before any criminal proceedings can be instituted.

Dualist systems stress that international law and domestic law exist separately, and **1.35** mostly operate independently of each other. Unlike monist systems, when a dualist State expresses its consent to be bound to an international treaty, the treaty does not directly assume the domestic force of law. Rather, the enactment of domestic legislation is first required in order for the treaty to have domestic legal effect.

The process by which an international treaty is given the force of law domestically **1.36** is referred to as the 'act of transformation'; the treaty is expressly transformed into domestic law by the use of relevant constitutional mechanisms (ie, an Act of Parliament). Therefore, in dualist systems, a State can express its consent to be bound by a treaty through ratification, placing the State under international legal obligations, but the same treaty provisions would have no domestic legal effect until the act of transformation. Furthermore, before the act of transformation, domestic courts are not strictly bound by the provisions of the treaty, although in practice, such sources of law are considered highly persuasive.

1.37 Following the British practice, most common law or Commonwealth States have dualist legal systems. Some have made it their practice to pass a single Act of Parliament simply incorporating their international obligations (even if under more than one instrument) into domestic law, whilst others have chosen to give effect to the treaty by passing comprehensive domestic legislation based on the requirements of the treaty, that establishes the necessary infrastructure or systems, and creates the necessary offences.

Terrorism as a crime under customary international law

1.38 In certain circumstances, an act which would otherwise amount to a terrorist offence, may amount to a crime under 'international criminal law', including customary international law. The limited circumstances envisaged are those in which such an act is carried out during an armed conflict and against a civilian population with the requisite intent to make out one or other of the crimes against 'international criminal law'. It is acknowledged that a terrorist act is not a crime under 'international criminal law'. However it should be stressed that, ordinarily, a terrorist act will be a crime under the general criminal law alone.

Terrorism in armed conflict

1.39 IHL also provides a definition of terrorism that may occur during an armed conflict. It prohibits acts or threats of violence which aim to spread terror among the civilian population in international and non-international armed conflict.[23] Serious violations of these and other IHL violations may also amount to a war crime for which an individual may be held to account. This principle was upheld by the International Criminal Tribunal for the Former Yugoslavia (ICTY) in the *Prosecutor v Galic* case in 2003.[24] As terrorist acts in armed conflict are covered by IHL, most of the specific counter-terrorism instruments referred to above do not apply in time of armed conflict. The Financing Convention of 1999[25] is one exception in this regard in that it includes situations of armed conflict within its scope. Article 2(1) of the Convention refers to:

> [a]ny other act intended to cause death or serious bodily injury to a civilian or to any other person not taking an active part in hostilities in a situation of armed conflict, when

---

[23] Article 52 of Additional Protocol I and Article 13 of Additional Protocol II. See also Article 33(1) of the Fourth Geneva Convention which provides clearly that 'terrorism is prohibited'.

[24] Case No IT-98-29-T, Judgment 5 December 2003.

[25] International Convention for the Suppression of the Financing of Terrorism (1999).

the purpose of such act, by its nature or context, is to intimidate a population, or compel a government or an international organisation to do or to abstain from doing any act.

Domestic measures

Despite being regarded as a threat to international peace and security by the UN **1.40** Security Council, for the most part, acts of international terrorism do not fall into the category of 'core international' crimes such as genocide, war crimes, and crimes against humanity. There are therefore no international criminal courts or tribunals with jurisdiction over these crimes.[26] Terrorist crimes (as defined in the international and regional counter-terrorism instruments) fall in the category of national criminal law of international concern. The duty to bring terrorist perpetrators to justice therefore rests solely on national criminal justice systems. Without adequate domestic capacity to discharge this duty, international counter-terrorism efforts will almost certainly fail.

The criminal justice response to terrorism is, therefore, essentially framed by **1.41** national law, which itself must comply with various aspects of international law. Ensuring that criminal justice practices are in compliance with national law and applicable international law is the responsibility of all law enforcement practitioners and prosecutors. Successful prosecution of terrorist crimes depends almost entirely on the capacity and expertise of national law enforcement and criminal justice officials that have to work within the framework of domestic counter-terrorism and related criminal laws. The duty to prevent the crimes being committed in the first place rests on, inter alia, national intelligence services.

Many States had counter-terrorism laws in place before 9/11 and the subsequent **1.42** passing of UNSCR 1373. Many of those laws were passed in response to specific domestic terrorist threats, and in an effort to implement relevant international and regional treaties that had been signed and ratified by the particular State. They often included a general definition of terrorism and terrorist act, which in most situations reflected the particular historical or political national context.

The post 9/11 proliferation of counter-terrorism measures and legal obligations **1.43** stemming from several international and regional conventions, protocols, and action plans, as well as the far-reaching obligations imposed by UNSCR 1373, resulted in the expeditious passing of a number of new national counter-terrorism

---

[26] The International Criminal Court, created in 1998 by the Treaty of Rome, is granted jurisdiction over the crime of genocide, crimes against humanity, war crimes, and the crime of aggression. Jurisdiction over acts of terrorism was rejected during the negotiations that resulted in the Court's creation.

laws and policies.[27] Specifically relevant in this regard is the legally binding obligation under UNSCR 1373 that obliges States to ensure that 'terrorist acts' are criminalized in domestic law, and to afford one another 'the greatest measure of assistance' in the investigation of terrorist acts.[28]

1.44   However, although UNSCR 1373 obliges States to criminalize terrorist acts in domestic law, it does not offer a definition of terrorism to guide lawmakers in this process. Rather, it makes reference to the terrorist acts as contained in the UN counter-terrorism conventions and protocols. This lack of clarity has the potential to allow certain States to abuse counter-terrorism laws to stigmatize political or other opponents under the guise of the fight against terrorism. This concern has been underscored by the Special Rapporteur on the Promotion and Protection of Human Rights and Fundamental Freedoms while Countering Terrorism who in his report drew attention to the risk of abusing the national laws on terrorism, especially on the part of oppressive regimes.[29]

1.45   Some progress towards providing more clarity on the definition of terrorism was made by UNSCR 1566 (2004). In that Resolution, the UN Security Council identified the *actus reus* and the *mens rea* that States should include in their definitions of terrorist acts.[30] Specifically, the Resolution refers to:

> criminal acts, including against civilians, committed with the intent to cause death or serious bodily injury, or taking of hostages . . . which constitute offences within the scope of and as defined in the international conventions and protocols relating to terrorism . . . with the purpose to provoke a state of terror in the general public or in a group of persons or particular persons, intimidate a population or compel a government or an international organisation to do or to abstain from doing any act.

1.46   The UN Security Council established a Working Group to consider practical measures to advance the implementation of UNSCR 1566, including measures imposed on individuals, groups, and entities involved in, or associated with, terrorist activities, other than those on the Al-Qaida and Taliban Consolidated List, and to look into possibilities of creating an international fund for victims of terrorism. Unfortunately, differences among members of the UN Security Council

---

[27] Within two months of the 9/11 attacks, the US and UK had passed new and amended counter-terrorism laws that afforded wide-ranging powers to domestic law enforcement and intelligence agencies. Both the USA PATRIOT Act, and the UK Anti-Terrorism, Crime and Security Act of 2001 have been criticized for restricting human rights and due process protections. Several other countries drafted and passed new counter-terrorism laws as an immediate response to these attacks, including Uganda and Tanzania.

[28] UNSCR 1373 (n 3) para 2(f).

[29] Report of the Special Rapporteur on the Promotion and Protection of Human Rights and Fundamental Freedoms while Countering Terrorism, UN Doc E/CN.4/2006/98 27.

[30] UNSCR 1566 (2004) Art 3.

have undermined the efforts of the Working Group, which has been unable to reach consensus on any meaningful recommendations.

In light of the above, it is not surprising that national definitions of terrorism **1.47** post-9/11 differ markedly. Another consequence of this lack of normative guidance from the UN Security Council relates to the lack of human rights and due process protections in these new counter-terrorism laws and policies. It is therefore important to observe the development of counter-terrorism policy and practice at domestic levels to ensure that it complies with the principle of legality and international legal standards.

D. Overview of This Book

This book aims to provide a comprehensive overview of the most relevant legal **1.48** principles applicable to law enforcement and criminal justice responses to terrorism. It intends to set out the international framework created by the UN counter-terrorism instruments and UNSCRs, along with regional initiatives, and to highlight the key measures which impact upon criminalization, the assuming of jurisdiction, and international cooperation. At the same time, the book considers national laws with an emphasis on the criminal justice response by the UK and other common law jurisdictions without, it is to be hoped, neglecting the civil law tradition.

2

THE UNITED NATIONS
COUNTER-TERRORISM INSTRUMENTS

A. Introduction: Development of a
   Global Legal Regime
   against Terrorism   2.01
   The role of the UN Security Council 2.09
   Other UN Security Council
      resolutions pertaining to terrorism 2.15
   The United Nations Global
      Counter-Terrorism Strategy   2.21
B. Overview of the UN
   Counter-Terrorism Instruments   2.23
   Common elements of the UN
      counter-terrorism instruments   2.29
   Criminalizing terrorist acts   2.32
   Forms of participation in an offence 2.38
   Jurisdiction provisions   2.42
   International cooperation
      mechanisms and the principle
      of *aut dedere aut judicare*   2.44

C. Relevant Extracts from the UN
   Counter-Terrorism
   Instruments   2.47
   Agreements developed by the
      International Civil Aviation
      Organization (ICAO)   2.47
   Agreements developed by the
      International Maritime
      Organization (IMO)   2.75
   Instruments developed by the
      International Atomic Energy
      Agency (IAEA)   2.93
   Agreements developed at the initiative
      of the UN General Assembly
      aimed at protecting civilians   2.103

A. Introduction: Development of a Global Legal
Regime against Terrorism

As described in the opening chapter, international efforts to combat terrorism **2.01** have been evolving for several decades, originating with the drafting of the Convention for the Prevention and Suppression of Terrorism by the League of Nations in 1937[1] and culminating most recently in the adoption of the United Nations Global Counter-Terrorism Strategy[2] by the United Nations General

---

[1] Convention for the Prevention and Punishment of Terrorism (Geneva, 1937, never entered into force), League of Nations Doc C.546M.383 1937 V.

[2] A/RES/60/288.

Assembly on 6 September 2006. Terrorism remained an item on the agenda of the international community throughout these years, but in the 1970s it became a much more pressing priority following a number of serious terrorist incidents, including the hijackings of several transnational airliners and the assault on the Olympic Games in Munich, Germany in 1972. The kidnapping of Ministers of the Organization of the Petroleum Exporting Countries (OPEC) in Vienna, Austria in 1975, and the increasing prevalence and severity of terrorist attacks in the following decades, further strengthened international resolve to respond to the growing threat.

2.02   The United Nations and its numerous specialized agencies have played a pivotal role in this global effort. Initially, the General Assembly was at the forefront of the UN's counter-terrorism programme until the 1990s when the issue was taken up on the agenda of the UN Security Council after the Council declared terrorism a threat to international security.[3] Like all UN counter-terrorism efforts, the progress in the General Assembly was dramatically shaped by the political realities of the day. Political divisions on essential points (such as the question of State terrorism), coupled with the existence of several recognized wars of national liberation fought against former colonial powers in the 1970s and 1980s, fuelled disagreements on the scope of application of any possible definition of terrorism and therefore attempts to reach consensus were abandoned.[4] Instead, it was considered more effective to develop a string of international treaties to suppress specific acts of terrorism on which some consensus could be reached, mostly after tragic events.

2.03   The General Assembly has addressed international terrorism in two ways: first, by contributing to the development of a normative framework that defines acts of terrorism as a common problem, and second, by encouraging concerted government action to develop more effective international and local rules for dealing with terrorists. In doing so, it has contributed significantly to the development of the global response to terrorism including the elaboration of UN counter-terrorism legal instruments.[5]

2.04   The 1990s saw a major shift in global politics with the end of the Cold War and *apartheid*, and achievement of independence from colonialism for several African countries. By its Resolution 49/60 of 9 December 1994, the General Assembly adopted a milestone Declaration on Measures to Eliminate International Terrorism.

---

[3] A Bianchi, 'Security Council's Anti-terror Resolutions and their implementation by Member States' (2006) 4 JICJ,1044–73.

[4] S Makinda, 'Terrorism, counter-terrorism and norms in Africa' (2006) 15 African Security Review, Institute for Security Studies 3, 19.

[5] The term universal is used to describe those agreements open to membership to all States of the United Nations or its affiliated specialized agencies, such as the International Civil Aviation Organization, as opposed to agreements open only to members of a regional or other restricted grouping, such as the Council of Europe.

The Declaration reaffirmed Member States' unequivocal condemnation of all acts, methods, and practices of terrorism as criminal and unjustifiable, wherever and by whomever committed. Moreover, it determined that criminal acts intended to provoke a state of terror in the general public, a group of persons, or particular persons for political purposes were in any circumstances unjustifiable, whatever the considerations of a political, philosophical, ideological, racial, ethnic, religious, or any other nature that might be invoked to justify them. It also urged States to become parties to the universal counter-terrorism instruments.

Two years later, in 1996, the General Assembly adopted another Declaration **2.05** (Resolution 51/210) to supplement the 1994 Declaration. It reaffirmed the fundamental principles of the previous Declaration and proclaimed that knowingly financing, planning, and inciting terrorist acts is contrary to the principles of the United Nations. It also contained new provisions relating to the granting of refugee status to suspected terrorist suspects, specifically that States should take appropriate measures in accordance with relevant provisions of national and international law before granting refugee status to persons seeking asylum. While recognizing the sovereign right of States in extradition matters, States were encouraged not to regard offences connected with terrorism as political offences. They were also encouraged to enhance sharing of information and international cooperation in terrorism matters.

In December 1996, the Secretary-General submitted a report to the General **2.06** Assembly on the implementation of the 1994 Declaration (A/51/336). The report contained a detailed review of the existing universal counter-terrorism instruments in force at the time and concluded that the United Nations was uniquely placed to take the lead in promoting global counter-terrorism activities and international cooperation. In order to enhance this role for the organization, the report suggested that there was a need for new universal counter-terrorism instruments in the areas not covered by the existing instruments, including terrorist bombings, terrorist financing, trafficking in arms, money laundering, use of weapons of mass destruction by terrorists, and the use of modern information technology for terrorist purposes. As a result of this report, the General Assembly established an Ad Hoc Committee tasked to elaborate an international convention for the suppression of terrorist bombings and an international convention for the suppression of acts of nuclear terrorism to supplement the existing counter-terrorism legal instruments. Both these conventions, as well as the International Convention for the Suppression of Terrorist Financing, were elaborated and have come into force.

In 1999, the General Assembly entrusted the Ad Hoc Committee with the notori- **2.07** ously tough task of resuming efforts towards the elaboration of a comprehensive convention on international terrorism. Negotiations within the Ad Hoc Committee on this convention started in 2000 and despite important progress being made, the Working Group encountered serious difficulties in finding solutions to three seemingly intractable points of contention among Member States: the definition of terrorism, including its scope of application; the relationship between the comprehensive convention and existing and future counter-terrorism legal instruments; and the issue of differentiating between acts of terrorism and the right of peoples to pursue self-determination and to combat foreign occupation.

2.08   However, despite the lack of consensus on a comprehensive convention against terrorism (or a definition of terrorism), a wide variety of act-specific UN counter-terrorism instruments, General Assembly and Security Council resolutions, and a universally accepted Global Counter-Terrorism Strategy have evolved over time to provide a global framework that, to a large extent, fills the normative and legal gaps created by lack of a comprehensive convention or agreement on the definition of terrorism. In addition, several regional counter-terrorism instruments have also been adopted to supplement the universal legal regime.[6]

The role of the UN Security Council

2.09   Although international terrorism had been a concern of the UN Member States for decades, it finally got onto the agenda of the UN Security Council in the early 1990s. This was largely as a result of the end of the Cold War, which created considerable new space for the constructive multilateral engagement on issues of international peace and security. This is illustrated by the drastic increase in the number of UNSCRs dealing with these issues and the decrease in the use of the veto by P5[7] countries.

2.10   On 31 January 1992, the UN Security Council held its first-ever meeting of Heads of State and government. At this meeting the members of the UN Security Council expressed their 'deep concern over acts of international terrorism and emphasized the need for the international community to deal effectively with such acts'. Initially the UN Security Council's response was mostly reactive, responding in particular to three cases: the downing of Pan AM and UTA flights in 1988, the attempted assassination of Egypt's president in 1991, and the bombing of the United States embassies in Tanzania and Kenya in 1998. Those events led to sanctions against Libya and Sudan for refusing to extradite the suspects and against the

---

[6] Some examples of these regional instruments are: Arab Convention on the Suppression of Terrorism (1998), Convention of the Organization of the Islamic Conference on Combating International Terrorism (1999), European Convention on the Suppression of Terrorism (1977), OAS Convention to Prevent and Punish Acts of Terrorism (1971), OAU Convention on the Prevention and Combating of Terrorism (1999), SAARC Regional Convention on the Suppression of Terrorism (1987).

[7] The five permanent member countries on the UN Security Council (known as P5 countries) are: the United States of America, Britain, France, Russia, and China.

Taliban in Afghanistan for supporting terrorist groups and refusing to extradite the Al-Qaida leader, Osama Bin Laden.[8] Several commentators have characterized the 1998 bombings of the US embassies in Dar es Salaam, Tanzania, and Nairobi, Kenya, as the forerunners to the attacks on the US on 11 September 2001.[9] Following these attacks, US President Bill Clinton in a speech to the General Assembly in 1998 placed the fight against terrorism 'at the top of the US agenda'.[10] In 1999, the UN Security Council recognized international terrorism as a threat to international peace and security and strongly condemned all such acts in UNSCR 1269.[11]

Then came the attacks on New York City and Washington DC on 11 September **2.11** 2001. The world witnessed a new scale of terrorist attack that resulted in significant loss of life and destruction of property. This event sparked immediate, unprecedented, and unified international action and political cohesion against terrorism, epitomized by the rapid adoption of UNSCR 1373 (2001)[12] just two weeks after the 9/11 attack. And although this attack did not mark the beginning of the international response to terrorism, it certainly galvanized global counter-terrorism action and commitment.

Adopted on 28 September 2001, UNSCR 1373 heralded a new (and relatively **2.12** controversial) quasi-legislative role for the UN Security Council; it imposed legally binding obligations on all States to undertake wide-ranging legal reforms and introduced several new counter-terrorism measures, focusing heavily on prevention through the targeting of persons and entities that support and finance terrorism. UNSCR 1373 also recognized in its preamble the 'inherent right of individual or collective self defense' as a legitimate response to terrorism.

UNSCR 1373 required every country to freeze the financial assets of terrorists and **2.13** their supporters, deny them travel or safe haven, prevent terrorist recruitment and weapons supply, and cooperate with other countries in information sharing and criminal prosecution. Member States are also called upon to sign and ratify the international UN Conventions and Protocols against terrorism. In addition, they are to afford one another 'the greatest measure of assistance' in investigating terrorist acts. And unlike previous UNSCRs on terrorism, UNSCR 1373 is not

---

[8] Sanctions against the Taliban were imposed under the well-known UNSCR 1267 (1999). This Resolution (together with its related successor resolutions) imposed sanctions in the form of travel bans, asset freezing, and arms embargoes against individual and entities listed by the UN Security Council pursuant to these resolutions.

[9] J Cilliers, 'Africa, root causes, and the "war on terror"' (2006) 15 African Security Review, Institute for Security Studies 3, 58.

[10] C de Jonge Oudraat, 'The Role of the Security Council' in J Boulden and T Weiss (eds), *Terrorism and the UN: Before and After September 11* (Indiana University Press 2004) 151.

[11] Boulden (n 10).

[12] United Nations Security Council, Security Council Resolution 1373 (2001), S/RES/1373, New York, 28 September 2001.

temporal or limited in application to a specific group or territory. It is an open-ended and far-reaching Resolution that imposes extensive counter-terrorism legal obligations on all UN Member States.[13]

2.14 UNSCR 1373 also created the Counter-Terrorism Committee (CTC),[14] which is fashioned as a committee of the whole, consisting of all fifteen members of the Security Council. It received priority attention within the UN and was described by then UN Secretary-General Kofi Annan as the 'centre of global efforts to fight terrorism'.[15] The primary function of the CTC has been to strengthen the counter-terrorism capacity of UN Member States. Its mission, wrote one observer, is to 'raise the average level of government performance against terrorism across the globe'.[16] The committee serves as a 'switchboard' helping to facilitate the provision of technical assistance to countries needing assistance in implementing counter-terrorism mandates. It has also attempted to coordinate the counter-terrorism efforts of a wide range of international, regional, and sub-regional organizations inside and outside the UN system. To reinforce the Committee's efforts towards more effective collaboration and State capacity building, the Committee established the Counter-Terrorism Committee Executive Directorate (CTC/CTED), which became fully operational late in 2005. The Executive Directorate also enhances the Committee's capacity to identify and prioritize the technical assistance needs of Member States.

Other UN Security Council resolutions pertaining to terrorism

2.15 UNSCR 1373 proceeded, and was followed up by, several other Chapter VII UNSCRs, including 1267, 1456, 1540, and 1566. The most important element of these resolutions are summarized below:

2.16 UNSCR 1267 was passed on 15 October 1999 for the purpose of overseeing the implementation of sanctions (including freezing of assets, arms embargo,

---

[13] UNSCR 1373 was passed under Chapter VII of the UN Charter, which permits the Security Council to take legally binding decisions under Article 25, directing Member States to impose economic sanctions or to use force to maintain international peace. Because of the serious consequences of such action, the permanent members of the Council have not hesitated to use their veto power to obstruct action of this kind where their interests have been involved.

[14] The CTC website is available at <http://www.un.org/Docs/sc/committees/1373/> (accessed 14 November 2007).

[15] United Nations Secretary-General Kofi Annan, 'Statement at Ministerial Level Meeting of the UN Security Council'. See United Nations Security Council, *High-level Meeting of the Security Council: Combating Terrorism*, S/PV.4688, New York, 20 January 2003.

[16] E Rosand, 'Security Council Resolution 1373 and the Counter-Terrorism Committee: the Cornerstone of the United Nations Contribution to the Fight Against Terrorism' in Cyrille Fijnaut, Jan Wouters, and Frederik Naert (eds) *Legal Instruments in the Fight Against International Terrorism* (Brill Academic Publishers 2004) 603, 606.

and travel ban) on Taliban-controlled Afghanistan for its support of Osama bin Laden following the 1998 simultaneous bombings of US embassies in Nairobi, Kenya and Dar es Salaam, Tanzania, that killed 257 people and wounded over 4,000. The 1267 sanctions regime received added impetus, however, after the 9/11 attacks on the USA due to the involvement of Al-Qaida and the Taliban in the planning and execution of the attacks. Since then, it has been modified and strengthened by UNSCRs 1390 (2002), 1455 (2003), 1526 (2004), 1617 (2005), 1730 (2006), 1735 (2006), and 1822 (2008).

UNSCR 1456 was passed on 20 January 2003. Its operative paragraph six declares **2.17** that 'States must ensure that any measure taken to combat terrorism comply with all their obligations under international law, and should adopt such measures in *accordance with international law, in particular international human rights, refugee, and humanitarian law*.'[17] UNSCR 1456, often regarded by many human rights NGOs as a flagship resolution for safeguarding human rights in the fight against terrorism, reminds States that 'terrorism can only be defeated, in accordance with the Charter of the United Nations and international law, by a sustained comprehensive approach involving the active participation and collaboration of all States, international and regional organizations, and by redoubled efforts at the national level'.

UNSCR 1540 was passed on 28 April 2004 in the immediate aftermath of **2.18** Dr. Abdul Qadeer Khan's confession to sharing nuclear technology with Iran, Libya, and North Korea. The UN Security Council adopted the non-proliferation Resolution in which it decided that all States shall refrain from supporting by any means non-State actors that attempt to acquire, use, or transfer nuclear, chemical, or biological weapons and their delivery systems. Unanimously adopting the Resolution under Chapter VII of the UN Charter, the UN Security Council also decided that all States would establish domestic controls to prevent the proliferation of such weapons and means of delivery, in particular for terrorist purposes, including by establishing appropriate controls over related materials, and adopt legislative measures in that respect. The Resolution also established a Committee to monitor State implementation of its provisions relating to domestic controls to prevent the proliferation of nuclear, chemical, or biological weapons and their means of delivery.

UNSCR 1566 was passed in October 2004, following the school massacre at **2.19** Beslan in North Ossetia. This Russian-drafted resolution urged greater cooperation in the fight against terrorism and established a working group to consider additional counter-terrorism measures. These new resolutions demonstrated the Council's resolve in countering terrorism, but they also created potential overlap with the

---

[17] Emphasis added.

mission of the CTC and generated uncertainty about how the new bodies would work together. Unfortunately, implementation of this Resolution has been lax. The working group established by the Resolution has not met regularly, and little progress is foreseen in the near future.[18]

2.20 Like the UN counter-terrorism instruments discussed below, most of these UNSCRs deal with, and respond to, specific types of terrorist threats. However, the difference between these resolutions and the universal instruments is that the instruments, in the form of Conventions or Protocols, are international treaties, and as such are only binding on State Parties that have signed and ratified (or acceded to) them. Most UNSCRs relating to terrorism have been passed under Chapter VII of the UN Charter and are therefore legally binding on all Member States. In this regard, it is important to note that UNSCRs, while developing and adding to international law through the executive arm of the United Nations, intensify an already existing legal framework against terrorism agreed upon by its main deliberative body, the General Assembly, which represents all UN Member States.

The United Nations Global Counter-Terrorism Strategy

2.21 Another important counter-terrorism development in recent years was the eventual elaboration of the United Nations Global Counter-Terrorism Strategy that was adopted by the General Assembly on 8 September 2006.[19] The Strategy—in the form of a Resolution and an annexed Plan of Action—is a unique instrument that aims to enhance national, regional, and international efforts to counter terrorism. For the first time, all Member States agreed on a common strategic approach to fight terrorism, not only sending a clear message that terrorism is unacceptable in all its forms and manifestations, but also expressing their resolve to take practical steps individually and collectively to prevent and combat terrorism. Those practical steps include a wide array of measures ranging from strengthening State capacity to counter terrorist threats, to improving coordination of counter-terrorism activities within the United Nations.

2.22 An additional positive aspect of the Strategy is its focus on broader terrorism prevention aspects, including addressing the underlying contributing and motivating factors that lead to terrorism. The fact that the Strategy was negotiated under the auspices of the General Assembly is also of positive significance, as the General Assembly generally carries more legitimacy than the Security Council

---

[18] V Comras, 'The United Nations and the Fight Against Terrorism and Nonproliferation' (Statement, Committee on International Relations, US House of Representatives, Washington, DC, 17 March 2005) 4.

[19] Cf (n 2).

due to its broader representational base. The adoption of the Strategy fulfils the commitment made by world leaders at the 2005 September Summit and builds on many of the elements proposed by the Secretary-General in his 2 May 2006 report, entitled 'Uniting against Terrorism: Recommendations for a Global Counter-Terrorism Strategy'.[20]

B. Overview of the UN Counter-Terrorism Instruments

The UN's counter-terrorism efforts span more than three decades, involving the General Assembly, the Security Council, the Economic and Social Council (ECOSOC), as well as specialized United Nations agencies such as the International Atomic Energy Agency (IAEA), the International Civil Aviation Organization (ICAO), and the International Maritime Organization (IMO). Together, they have long been active in the development of a wide range of universal legal instruments aimed at suppressing various acts of international terrorism[21] and promoting global cooperation in criminal matters aimed at bringing perpetrators to justice. This common legal framework consists of sixteen Conventions (meaning multilateral treaties) and Protocols (meaning agreements supplementary to Conventions) that cover almost every conceivable kind of international terrorist act.[22] The terrorist acts covered by these instruments are summarized in Table 1 below.

2.23

Table 1 UN Counter-Terrorism Instruments

UN Counter-Terrorism Instrument	Summary
1963 Convention on Offences and Certain Other Acts Committed on Board Aircraft ('The Tokyo Convention')[23]	Any acts on board an aircraft flying over the high seas that may or does endanger the safety of the aircraft or good order and discipline on board.
	Authorizes the aircraft commander to impose reasonable measures, including restraint, on any person he or she has reason to believe has committed or is about to commit such an act, where necessary to protect the safety of the aircraft.

[20] <http://www.un.org/terrorism/strategy-counter-terrorism.shtml> (Last accessed 10 November 2008).

[21] All the universal counter-terrorism instruments form part of international law. The instruments also explicitly confine their application to terrorist acts of an international nature. Roughly speaking, there is internationality if an act has international consequences, in the sense that it affects the duties or rights of more than one State or foreign interest.

[22] Two of the counter-terrorism instruments do not contain offence-creating provisions. These are the 1963 Convention on Offences and Certain Other Acts Committed on Board Aircraft and the 1991 Convention on the Marking of Plastic Explosives.

[23] Signed at Tokyo on 14 September 1963. In force on 4 December 1969. United Nations, Treaty Series, vol 704, No 10106. Depositary: International Civil Aviation Organization.

Table 1 *Cont.*

UN Counter-Terrorism Instrument	Summary
1970 Convention for the Suppression of Unlawful Seizure of Aircraft ('The Hague Convention')[24]	Unlawful acts of aircraft hijacking, including forcing the pilot to divert to a different destination.
1971 Convention for the Suppression of Unlawful Acts against the Safety of Civil Aviation ('The Montreal Convention')[25]	Unlawful acts of aviation sabotage, including interfering with the aircraft navigation systems, damaging an aircraft on the ground that makes it incapable of or endangers its flight, placement of explosives on board, communications of false information that endangers the safety of an aircraft in flight.
1979 Convention on the Physical Protection of Nuclear Material ('Nuclear Material Convention')[26]	Unlawful acts of taking and possession of nuclear material, including unlawful receipt, possession, or disposal of those isotopes of uranium and plutonium most useful for making weapons.
1979 International Convention against the Taking of Hostages ('Hostages Convention')[27]	Unlawful acts of hostage taking, including holding any person with the intention to compel a government or international organization to do or abstain from doing any act.
1988 Protocol for the Suppression of Unlawful Acts of Violence at Airports Serving International Civil Aviation.[28] (Supplementary to the Convention for the Suppression of Unlawful Acts against the Safety of Civil Aviation)	Unlawful acts of violence at airports, including violence against person, facilities, or aircraft in airports serving civil aviation that cause death or serious bodily injury and destruction or damage to property that disrupts operations at such airport.
1988 Convention for the Suppression of Unlawful Acts against the Safety of Maritime Navigation ('1988 Safety of Maritime Navigation Convention')[29]	Unlawful acts against the safety of maritime navigation, applying aviation-type rules to maritime safety, including prohibiting hijacking of ships on the high seas.

---

[24] Signed at The Hague on 16 December 1970. In force on 14 October 1971. United Nations, Treaty Series, vol 860, No 12325. Depositary: Russian Federation, United Kingdom of Great Britain and Northern Ireland, and the United States of America.

[25] Concluded at Montreal on 23 September 1971. In force on 26 January 1973. United Nations, Treaty Series, vol 974, No 14118. Depositary: Russian Federation, United Kingdom of Great Britain an Northern Ireland, and the United States of America.

[26] Adopted at Vienna on 26 October 1979. In force on 8 February 1987. United Nations, Treaty Series, vol 1456, No 24631. Depositary: Director General of the International Atomic Energy Agency.

[27] Adopted by the General Assembly of the United Nations on 17 December 1979. In force on 3 June 1983. United Nations, Treaty Series, vol 1316, No 21931. Depositary: Secretary-General of the United Nations.

[28] Done at Montreal on 24 February 1988. In force on 6 August 1989. ICAO Doc 9518. Depositary: Russian Federation, United Kingdom of Great Britain and Northern Ireland, the United States of America, and the International Civil Aviation Organization.

[29] Done at Rome on 10 March 1988. In force on 1 March 1992. IMO Doc SUA/CONF/15/Rev 1. Depositary: Secretary-General of the International Maritime Organization.

Table 1 *Cont.*

UN Counter-Terrorism Instrument	Summary
1988 Protocol for the Suppression of Unlawful Acts against the Safety of Fixed Platforms Located on the Continental Shelf [30]	Unlawful acts against the safety of fixed platforms located on the continental shelf. Extends Maritime Navigation Convention provisions to fixed platforms.
1991 Convention on the Marking of Plastic Explosives for the Purpose of Detection ('Plastic Explosives Convention')[31]	Designed to control and limit the use of unmarked and undetectable plastic explosives.
1997 International Convention for the Suppression of Terrorist Bombings ('Terrorist Bombing Convention')[32]	Unlawful acts of terrorist bombings, including intentionally delivering, placing, discharging, or detonating an explosive or other lethal device in, into, or against a place of public use, a State or government facility, a public transportation system, or an infrastructure facility with the intent to cause death or serious bodily injury or extensive destruction to property.
1999 International Convention for the Suppression of the Financing of Terrorism ('Financing Convention')[33]	Unlawful acts of support and funding of terrorist organizations. Requires State Parties to take steps to prevent and counteract the financing of terrorists. Provides for the identification, freezing, and seizure of funds allocated for terrorist activities.
2005 Protocols to the Convention for the Suppression of Unlawful Acts against the Safety of Maritime Navigation and to the Protocol for the Suppression of Unlawful Acts against the Safety of Fixed Platforms Located on the Continental Shelf[34]	Unlawful using against or discharging from a ship explosive, radioactive, biological, chemical, or nuclear materials or weapons in a manner likely to cause death, serious injury, or damage; discharging other hazardous or noxious substances likely to cause death or serious injury or damage; or using a ship in a manner that causes death or serious injury or damage; or threatening to do so. Transportation on board a ship of certain materials with intent to intimidate a population or to coerce a government or international organization.

[30] Done at Rome 10 March 1988. In force on 1 March 1992. IMO Doc SUA/CONF/16/Rev 2. Depositary: Secretary-General of the International Maritime Organization.

[31] Adopted by the International Civil Aviation Organisation (ICAO) on 1 March 1991. Entry into force 21 June 1998. Depository: Secretary-General of ICAO.

[32] Adopted by the General Assembly of the United Nations on 15 December 1997. Entry into force in accordance with Article 22. UN Doc A/RES/52/164, Annex. Depositary: Secretary-General of the United Nations.

[33] Adopted by the General Assembly of the United Nations on 9 December 1999. Entry into force in accordance with Article 26. UN Doc A/RES/54/109, Annex. Depositary: Secretary-General of the United Nations.

[34] Protocols to both the 1988 Maritime Convention and its Fixed Platform Protocol were negotiated in 2005. These instruments provide that upon coming into force with the requisite number of adoptions they shall be combined with the earlier instruments, and designated portions will be called the Convention for the Suppression of Unlawful Acts against the Safety of Maritime Navigation, 2005 and the Protocol for the Suppression of Unlawful Acts against the Safety of Fixed Platforms Located on the Continental Shelf, 2005.

Table 1 *Cont.*

UN Counter-Terrorism Instrument	Summary
	Unlawfully transporting a person knowing that the person has committed an offence defined in the 2005 Protocol.
2005 Amendment to the Convention on the Physical Protection of Nuclear Material	Unlawful acts directed against or interfering with a nuclear facility likely to cause serious injury or damage, as well as unauthorized movement of such material into or out of a State without lawful authority.
	Unlawful demand for nuclear material by threat or use of force; a threat to use such materials to cause death or serious injury or damage to property or to the environment or to commit an offence in order to coerce a person, international organization, or State.[35]
2005 International Convention for the Suppression of Acts of Nuclear Terrorism ('Nuclear Terrorism Convention')[36]	Acts of nuclear terrorism by non-State actors, including the possession or use of radioactive material or a nuclear explosive or radiation dispersal device with the intent to cause death or serious bodily injury or substantial damage to property or the environment; the use of radioactive material or a device, or the use of or damage to a nuclear facility which risks the release of radioactive material with the intent to cause death or serious injury or substantial damage to property or to the environment, or with the intent to compel a natural or legal person, an international organization, or a State to do or refrain from doing any act.

2.24   The original ten of the sixteen UN instruments were elaborated incrementally under the leadership of the following organizations and entities: four conventions and one protocol elaborated by the International Civil Aviation Organization (ICAO);[37] two conventions developed under the leadership of the General Assembly;[38] one convention elaborated by the International Atomic Energy

---

[35] 2005 Amendment to the Convention on the Physical Protection of Nuclear Material, creating a new agreement to be called the Convention on the Physical Protection of Nuclear Material and Nuclear Facilities.

[36] Adopted by the United Nations General Assembly on 13 April 2005. Entry into force 7 July 2007. Depository: Secretary-General of the United Nations.

[37] Convention on Offences and Certain Other Acts Committed on Board Aircraft, 1963; Convention for the Suppression of Unlawful Seizure of Aircraft, 1970; Convention for the Suppression of Unlawful Acts against the Safety of Civil Aircraft, 1971; Convention on the Marking of Plastic Explosives for the Purpose of Detection, 1991.

[38] Convention on the Prevention and Punishment of Crimes against Internationally Protected Persons, including Diplomatic Agents, 1973; International Convention against the Taking of Hostages, 1979.

Agency (IAEA);[39] and one convention and a protocol developed by the International Maritime Organization (IMO).[40]

As noted above, the Ad Hoc Committee established by the 1996 General Assembly **2.25** Resolution 51/210 was tasked to draw up an international convention for the suppression of terrorist bombings and an international convention for the suppression of acts of nuclear terrorism, to supplement related existing international instruments. Within a year, that Committee had finalized the 1997 International Convention for the Suppression of Terrorist Bombings. It was then given an additional mandate by the General Assembly to develop an agreement on terrorist financing, resulting in the International Convention for the Suppression of the Financing of Terrorism of 1999. The International Convention for the Suppression of Acts of Nuclear Terrorism was adopted in 2005 and came into force in July 2007. The instruments developed by the specialized agencies were also updated. The IMO developed two protocols in 2005 to update its 1988 Convention for the Suppression of Unlawful Acts against the Safety of Maritime Navigation and the 1988 Protocol for the Suppression of Acts against the Safety of Fixed Platforms on the Continental Shelf. The IAEA adopted Amendments in 2005 to its 1980 Convention on the Physical Protection of Nuclear Material.[41]

---

[39] Physical Protection of Nuclear Material Convention, 1979.

[40] Convention for the Suppression of Unlawful Acts against the Safety of Maritime Navigation, 1988; Protocol for the Suppression of Unlawful Acts against the Safety of Fixed Platforms Located on the Continental Shelf, 1988.

[41] The organization sponsoring negotiations for a convention typically becomes the treaty depository. All of the terrorism-related treaties developed by a General Assembly committee name the UN Secretary-General in New York as their depository. The specialized agency agreements vary. The 1963 Convention on Offences and Certain Other Acts Committed on Board Aircraft names the ICAO as its depository. The 1970 Convention for the Suppression of Unlawful Seizure of Aircraft and the 1971 Convention for the Suppression of Unlawful Acts against the Safety of Civil Aircraft identify the Governments of the Union of Soviet Socialist Republics, the United Kingdom, and the United States of America as the depositaries for instruments of ratification, accession, and denunciation. The 1988 Protocol for the Suppression of Unlawful Acts of Violence at Airports Serving International Civil Aviation identifies the same three depositary governments and adds the International Civil Aviation Organization in Montreal, which became the sole depositary for the 1991 Convention on the Marking of Plastic Explosives for the Purpose of Detection. The 1979 Physical Protection of Nuclear Material Convention and its 2005 Amendment both provide for signature either at the IAEA in Vienna or at UN Headquarters in New York, and identify the Director General of the IAEA as the depositary for the original convention text. This reference to the IAEA Director General appears to be treated as an implied designation of the IAEA as the depositary for subsequent treaty purposes, although no explicit reference is made in either instrument to the place of deposit of instruments of ratification, accession, or denunciation. The IMO instruments all designate the Secretary General of that organization, headquartered in London, as their depositary. The practical significance of these varying designations is that a ratification or accession document sent to the wrong depositary may never take effect, and one cannot assume that the UN Secretary General in New York is the depositary for all sixteen of the universal terrorism-related instruments. Moreover, advisory services on technical aspects of certain specialized instruments may be within

2.26   None of the Conventions or Protocols defines terrorism. Rather they offer the legal infrastructure to address *serious crimes* committed by terrorists by focusing instead on defining specific international terrorist acts by non-State actors. The instruments themselves do not purport to criminalize conduct, but impose obligations on State Parties to do so in domestic law. They are based on the premise that perpetrators of terrorist crimes should be brought to trial by their national governments, or should be extradited to a country willing to bring them to trial. The well-known principle of *aut dedere aut judicare* (extradite or prosecute) is meant to make the world inhospitable to terrorists, and those who finance and support them, by denying them safe havens.

2.27   The instruments form part of the broader international law response to terrorism. As discussed in Chapter 1, acts also commonly referred to as 'terrorist' may amount to crimes under international criminal law, including customary international law. Notably, they can amount to war crimes (if carried out in armed conflict) and crimes against humanity (whether or not there is an armed conflict), provided the necessary element of those crimes are met, including that they be committed against the civilian population.

2.28   As treaty law, the instruments are only binding on State Parties to them. Their effectiveness, therefore, depends upon their widespread ratification by States and, importantly, the extent to which States implement their provisions and build relevant criminal justice capacity to apply the new laws and procedural mechanisms. It is essential to emphasize that the duty and legal authority to enforce these measures against terrorism falls exclusively within the responsibility of sovereign States. No international tribunal exists with competence to prosecute terrorist offences contained in these instruments (for example, aircraft or ship hijacking, bombings of civilian targets, or financing of terrorism).[42] The legal instruments developed over decades to deal with those offences can only be implemented under national legislation which criminalizes the defined offences, creates appropriate jurisdiction in domestic courts, and authorizes the cooperation mechanisms provided in the international instruments and essential to their effectiveness.

---

the particular competence of the organization that developed the agreement, such as information from the IAEA in Vienna on the levels of protection required under the 2005 Amendment to the IAEA Physical Protection of Nuclear Material Convention, or from the IMO in London on ship boarding procedures under the 2005 Protocol to the Maritime Safety Convention.

[42]   The International Criminal Court (ICC), created in 1998 by the Treaty of Rome, was granted jurisdiction over certain 'core' international crimes such as crimes against humanity, genocide, and war crimes. Terrorism does not currently fall under the jurisdiction of the ICC.

Common elements of the UN counter-terrorism instruments

The instruments were adopted with the primary aim of suppressing terrorist **2.29**
acts by ensuring the criminalization of specific acts, promoting international
cooperation between State Parties, and denying safe haven to terrorist offenders
through the obligation on State Parties to either prosecute offenders found on
their territory (regardless of other links to the offence) or to extradite them to
a country that is willing to prosecute them.[43]

Two of the sixteen instruments do not create any offences. The 1963 Convention **2.30**
on Offences and Certain Other Acts Committed on Board Aircraft establishes
procedures for return of the aircraft and treatment of passengers and crew after
an unlawful diversion. It also requires a State Party to establish its jurisdiction to
punish offences committed on board aircraft registered in that State, but does not
establish any offences that State Parties are obligated to punish. The 1991
Convention on the Marking of Plastic Explosives for the Purpose of Detection
requires a State Party to take measures to control explosives that do not contain
volatile chemicals subject to detection by scanning equipment, but those measures
need not be penal in nature.

The remaining nine conventions, four protocols, and one amendment, all have **2.31**
the following common elements:

1) *Criminalization* of the conduct defined in a particular agreement as a punishable
   offence.
2) Establishment of specified grounds of *jurisdiction* over that offence.
3) Establishment of the *aut dedere aut judicare* principle, ie, the obligation
   on State Parties to refer a case against a suspected or accused offender to domestic authorities for prosecution if extradition is not granted pursuant to the
   applicable agreement.
4) An obligation to furnish related forms of *international cooperation,* especially
   mutual legal assistance and extradition where appropriate.

The rest of the chapter provides an overview of these common elements of the
UN counter-terrorism instruments and highlights their incremental development
between the elaboration of the first instrument in 1963 and the most recent one
in 2005.

---

[43] Most of the instruments apply to acts against civilians occurring during peacetime. There are,
however, a few exceptions such as the 1999 Financing Convention that in Article 1(b) covers the collection of funds for acts intended to cause death or serious bodily injury to a civilian, *or to any other person
not taking an active part in the hostilities in a situation of armed conflict* (emphasis added).

Criminalizing terrorist acts

2.32 All the offence-creating instruments contain clear articles that require the crimi-nalization of a number of terrorist acts in the areas they regulate.[44] None of the instruments use the word 'terrorism' or 'terrorist' in their offence definitions. The definitions employ traditional criminal law terminology: a description of a wrongful act, such as bombing, hostage-taking, or use of a ship to distribute dangerous materials, and a general or specific unlawful intent, without any requirement that terrorism be mentioned or defined, and without specifying any particular motive for the commission of the offence. Each of these instruments presents a complete description of the physical deed (*actus reus*) and subjective element (*mens rea*) required for the commission of the relevant offence. They also require attempted crimes and complicity to be criminalized.

2.33 Three of the instruments require specific intent: the 1999 Convention on the Suppression of the Financing of Terrorism which refers to providing funds *knowing or intending* that the funds will be used to commit a terrorist act; 1979 Hostage Taking Convention which refers to taking a person hostage with the *intent to compel* a State, international organization etc to do, or refrain from doing some-thing; and the 1997 Convention for the Suppression of Terrorist Bombings which refers to detonating explosives in a public place with the *intention to cause* death or serious bodily injury, or to cause extensive damage to property etc.[45]

2.34 Although not required by the universal instruments, certain State Parties have elected to include a terrorist motive as an element of the offence, meaning that the act must be committed with a *political, ideological, or religious motive*.[46] This is a separate and additional requirement of motivation, in addition to a general criminal intent to kill or injure, or to the specific criminal intent described above. For example, Section 1 of the Terrorism Act 2000 of the United Kingdom provides as follows:

> (1) In this Act 'terrorism' means the use or threat of action where—
>> (a) the action falls within subsection (2),
>> (b) the use or threat is designed to influence the government or to intimidate the public or a section of the public, and

---

[44] The two counter-terrorism instruments that do not include definitions of offences are the 1963 Convention on Offences and Certain Other Acts Committed on Board Aircraft and the 1991 Convention on the Marking of Plastic Explosives.

[45] This element of specific intention should not be confused with motive to commit the crime. The offender's motive, ie, reason for committing the offence, is not regarded as an element of the crime.

[46] The offence created by Article 2.1 of the 1999 Terrorist Bombing Convention is an example of a general criminal intent crime, defined as the doing of certain acts involving specified weapons or devices: '(a) With the intent to cause death or serious bodily injury; or (b) With the intent to cause extensive destruction . . . where such destruction results or is likely to result in major economic loss'.

(c) the use or threat is made for the purpose of advancing a political, religious or ideological cause.

However, due to the evidentiary difficulties associated with the inclusion of a specific motive as *an element of the offence*, States should carefully consider the implications of this route when domesticating the instruments.

International lawyers and legal drafters would agree that no single formula for the **2.35** domestic criminalization of international treaty crimes is applicable to all countries. The approach to criminalization will depend upon the national dynamics, security threats facing a country, its history and political circumstances, and the legal tradition and jurisprudence that dictate how laws will be interpreted. However, it is desirable to repeat the terminology used in the universal instruments in domestic implementing legislation.[47] This is because differences in offence definitions between countries can create problems with the double criminality requirement of international cooperation. Moreover, none of the instruments provide for a proscribed punishment for any of the offences. They do, however, require State Parties to ensure that the offences are punishable by appropriate penalties which take into account the grave nature of the offences. The exact nature of this punishment is left to the discretion of the State Party.

Indeed, when ratifying and implementing the UN counter-terrorism instru- **2.36** ments, politicians and lawmakers will understandably first want to assess whether a particular Convention or Protocol is relevant to the specific political and geographic circumstances applicable in their country. Officials of a land-locked State may for instance question how their country could experience a violation of the Convention for the Suppression of Unlawful Acts against the Safety of Maritime Navigation if the country has no seacoast and no registered ships or offshore platforms.

However, these decisions should be taken with due consideration to the nature **2.37** and scope of terrorism as a form of international crime that requires global cooperation to counter it effectively. One of the country's nationals might commit such a crime; its citizens could be among the passengers threatened or killed; the unlawful seizure and threats to kill or destroy could be directed to force that country to release a particular prisoner or refrain from taking a certain action; or the offender could be found on its territory. These are all grounds of jurisdiction found in the 1988 Maritime Convention, and there are many reasons why a country might wish to have the option to extradite or to prosecute in its own courts, or to be able to ask for extradition of an offender from another country.

---

[47] UN Office on Drugs and Crime, *Guide to the Legislative Implementation of the Universal Instruments Against Terrorism* (UNODC 2006).

Forms of participation in an offence

2.38 The type of criminal participation required for the offences created by the UN counter-terrorism instruments has evolved over time. The eight conventions and protocols negotiated between 1970 and 1988 create reactive criminal offences. They require that criminal liability be imposed, assuming the existence of the necessary guilty state of mind, in the following three circumstances:

(a) The *physical commission* of the conduct established in a particular convention as an offence, usually called responsibility as a principal. A principal would be the person who personally seizes an aircraft or maritime vessel, or takes hostages, attacks diplomats or passengers at an international airport, steals or unlawfully uses nuclear material, or makes threats prohibited by certain of the universal instruments;

(b) An *attempt to commit* a prohibited offence, that fails for reasons beyond the offender's control, such as an armed attack on passengers at an airport that was foiled by security guards outside the airport;

(c) *Intentional participation* as an abettor or accomplice in the commission or attempted commission of an offence. Examples would include an airport employee who shares airport architecture information to assist the attackers with their attack plan and escape route, or someone who provides false identity documents to aid the flight of members of a group that has placed and detonated a bomb in a marketplace.

2.39 These forms of participation developed incrementally. The 1970 Hijacking Convention applied only to an accomplice on board an aircraft in flight. The 1971 Convention for the Suppression of Unlawful Acts against the Safety of Civil Aviation was expanded to cover any attempt, or to any accomplice, wherever located. In subsequent instruments other forms of criminal responsibility were introduced, including an act constituting participation in the principal offence (the 1979 Physical Protection of Nuclear Materials Convention) or abetting its commission (the 1988 Convention for the Suppression of Unlawful Acts against the Safety of Maritime Navigation).

2.40 Prior to 1997 it was clear that the instruments required the punishment only of completed or attempted acts. In 1997 Article 2.3 of the Terrorist Bombing Convention established two new forms of criminal liability for a person who:

- organizes or directs others to commit an offence as set forth in paragraph 1 or 2 (meaning either accomplishment of the principal offence or its attempted commission); or

- in any other way contributes to the commission of one or more offences as set forth in paragraph 1 or 2 by a group of persons acting with a common purpose.

The 1999 International Convention for the Suppression of the Financing of **2.41** Terrorism repeats the same forms of participation listed in the 1997 Terrorist Bombing Convention that is as a principal, attempter, accomplice, organizer or director, or contributor to group action. However, the conduct criminalized is no longer a violent terrorist act. Instead, what is prohibited for the first time by a counter-terrorism instrument is the non-violent financial preparation that precedes nearly every significant terrorist act. Moreover, that preparation or contribution is explicitly made independently punishable by Article 2–3 of the Convention, regardless of whether the intended terrorist act is actually accomplished or attempted.

Jurisdiction provisions

The traditional approach of States was that 'all crime is local' and therefore the **2.42** courts could only try cases that occurred within the territory of the State. The main reason behind this reasoning is founded in the concept of State sovereignty: it was for each State to try offenders within its own geographical territory or its own nationals. However the concept of territorial jurisdiction has been subject to revision over time, with States slowly recognizing and accepting extra-territorial jurisdiction in relation to certain serious crimes.[48] Extra-territorial jurisdiction can be asserted on the following grounds: active personality (nationality of the offender), passive personality (nationality of the victim), and national security.[49]

These recognized grounds on which States can assert jurisdiction have been built **2.43** into the UN counter-terrorism instruments, with most providing both mandatory (where appropriate) and discretionary measures to extend extra-territorial criminal jurisdiction. The rationale is to give effect to the principle of 'extradite or prosecute' (*aut dedere aut judicare*).[50]

International cooperation mechanisms and the principle of aut dedere aut judicare

The main objective of the UN counter-terrorism instruments is to ensure the **2.44** apprehension, prosecution, or extradition of persons suspected of committing acts of terrorism. As there are no international tribunals with competence for acts of terrorism as defined in the counter-terrorism instruments, the duty to bring the

---

[48] See discussion on jurisdiction in Chapter 3, below.
[49] Ibid.
[50] See Chapters 5 and 9 for detailed discussion.

perpetrators of terrorist acts to justice therefore rests solely on domestic courts. The international community has come to recognize the challenges facing domestic law enforcement and criminal justice authorities when dealing with international crimes that are committed across national borders by criminals determined to exploit the potential legal gaps in the domestic prosecution of these complex crimes. The counter-terrorism instruments provide essential international cooperation tools, including extradition and mutual legal assistance, so that national authorities can effectively conduct cross-border investigations and ensure that there are no safe havens from prosecution and extradition. This objective underpins the *aut dedere aut judicare* principle that is found in all the instruments that define criminal offences and is reinforced by UNSCR 1373, which obliges all Member States to deny safe haven to terrorists.[51]

2.45   The requirement that Parties afford assistance in criminal proceedings appeared first in Article 10.1 of the 1970 Convention for the Suppression of Unlawful Seizure of Aircraft which provides that:

> Contracting States shall afford one another the greatest measure of assistance in connection with criminal proceedings brought in respect of the offence and other acts mentioned in Article 4. The law of the State requested shall apply in all cases.

2.46   This practice was then adopted in all subsequent Conventions that create criminal offences. In the 1979 Hostages Convention and subsequent instruments, that assistance is specified as including the obtaining of evidence at a State Party's disposal. Beginning with the 1971 Convention for the Suppression of Unlawful Acts against the Safety of Civil Aviation, the Conventions obligate parties to take measures to prevent offences against other parties. This obligation was broadened in the 1973 Convention on Internationally Protected Persons, including Diplomatic Agents, to a duty to exchange information and coordinate administrative and other preventive measures. A good example of expanded mutual legal assistance provisions is found in Articles 10–15 of the 1997 Terrorist Bombings Convention:[52]

Article 10

1. States Parties shall afford one another the greatest measure of assistance in connection with investigations or criminal or extradition proceedings brought in respect of the offences set forth in article 2, including assistance in obtaining evidence at their disposal necessary for the proceedings.

2. States Parties shall carry out their obligations under paragraph 1 of the present article in conformity with any treaties or other arrangements on mutual legal assistance that may exist between them. In the absence of such treaties or arrangements, States Parties shall afford one another assistance in accordance with their domestic law.

---

[51]   Section 2 (c) of UNSCR 1373.
[52]   A fuller discussion on international cooperation is set out in Chapter 9.

Article 13

1. A person who is being detained or is serving a sentence in the territory of one State Party whose presence in another State Party is requested for purposes of testimony, identification or otherwise providing assistance in obtaining evidence for the investigation or prosecution of offences under this Convention may be transferred if the following conditions are met:

    a. The person freely gives his or her informed consent; and

    b. The competent authorities of both States agree, subject to such conditions as those States may deem appropriate.

2. For the purposes of the present article:

    a. The State to which the person is transferred shall have the authority and obligation to keep the person transferred in custody, unless otherwise requested or authorized by the State from which the person was transferred;

    b. The State to which the person is transferred shall without delay implement its obligation to return the person to the custody of the State from which the person was transferred as agreed beforehand, or as otherwise agreed, by the competent authorities of both States;

    c. The State to which the person is transferred shall not require the State from which the person was transferred to initiate extradition proceedings for the return of the person;

    d. The person transferred shall receive credit for service of the sentence being served in the State from which he was transferred for time spent in the custody of the State to which he was transferred.

3. Unless the State Party from which a person is to be transferred in accordance with the present article so agrees, that person, whatever his or her nationality, shall not be prosecuted or detained or subjected to any other restriction of his or her personal liberty in the territory of the State to which that person is transferred in respect of acts or convictions anterior to his or her departure from the territory of the State from which such person was transferred.

Article 15

States Parties shall cooperate in the prevention of the offences set forth in article 2, particularly:

    a. By taking all practicable measures, including, if necessary, adapting their domestic legislation, to prevent and counter preparations in their respective territories for the commission of those offences within or outside their territories, including measures to prohibit in their territories illegal activities of persons, groups and organizations that encourage, instigate, organize, knowingly finance or engage in the perpetration of offences as set forth in article 2;

    b. By exchanging accurate and verified information in accordance with their national law, and coordinating administrative and other measures taken as appropriate to prevent the commission of offences as set forth in article 2;

    c. Where appropriate, through research and development regarding methods of detection of explosives and other harmful substances that can cause death or bodily injury, consultations on the development of standards for marking explosives in order to identify their origin in post-blast investigations, exchange of information on preventive measures, cooperation and transfer of technology, equipment and related materials.

C. Relevant Extracts from the UN Counter-Terrorism Instruments

*Agreements developed by the International
Civil Aviation Organization (ICAO)*

1963 Convention on Offences and Certain Other Acts Committed on Board Aircraft ('The Tokyo Convention')

2.47 The 1963 Tokyo Convention deals with acts committed on board a commercial aircraft which are prejudicial to good order and safety of the aircraft while it is in flight in the territory outside that of the State Party (including on the surface of the high seas). It was followed by additional civil aviation conventions in 1970 and 1971 as well as a supplementary Protocol in 1988. These instruments were elaborated in response to a spate of well-publicized aircraft hijackings in the 1960s and 70s. As noted above, the 1963 Tokyo Convention does not contain any criminalization provisions. It is a regulatory Convention that requires State Parties to take 'such measures as may be necessary to establish its jurisdiction as the State of registration over offences committed on board aircraft registered in such State'.[53] There is no requirement to define any particular conduct endangering the safety of an aircraft or of persons on board as an offence. Moreover, the requirement to establish jurisdiction only applies to acts committed on board an aircraft in flight, defined as from the moment when power is applied for the purpose of take-off until the moment when the landing run ends.

Key provisions

Article 1

2.48 1. This Convention shall apply in respect of:
   a. offences against penal law;
   b. acts which, whether or not they are offences, may or do jeopardize the safety of the aircraft or of persons or property therein or which jeopardize good order and discipline on board.

2. Except as provided in Chapter III, this Convention shall apply in respect of offences committed or acts done by a person on board any aircraft registered in a Contracting State, while that aircraft is in flight or on the surface of the high seas or of any other area outside the territory of any State.

3. For the purposes of this Convention, an aircraft is considered to be in flight from the moment when power is applied for the purpose of take- off until the moment when the landing run ends.

4. This Convention shall not apply to aircraft used in military, customs or police services.

---

[53] 1963 Tokyo Convention (Art 3.2).

Article 2

Without prejudice to the provisions of Article 4 and except when the safety of the aircraft or of persons or property on board so requires, no provision of this Convention shall be interpreted as authorizing or requiring any action in respect of offences against penal laws of a political nature or those based on racial or religious discrimination.

2.49

Jurisdiction provisions

Article 3

1. The State of registration of the aircraft is competent to exercise jurisdiction over offences and acts committed on board.

2.50

2. Each Contracting State shall take such measures as may be necessary to establish its jurisdiction as the State of registration over offences committed on board aircraft registered in such State.

3. This Convention does not exclude any criminal jurisdiction exercised in accordance with national law.

Article 4

A Contracting State which is not the State of registration may not interfere with an aircraft in flight in order to exercise its criminal jurisdiction over an offence committed on board except in the following cases:

2.51

    a. the offence has effect on the territory of such State;
    b. the offence has been committed by or against a national or permanent resident of such State;
    c. the offence is against the security of such State;
    d. the offence consists of a breach of any rules or regulations relating to the flight or manoeuvre of aircraft in force in such State.

1970 Convention for the Suppression of Unlawful Seizure of Aircraft ('The Hague Convention')

The spate of aircraft hijackings in the 1970s introduced a new dimension to the threat posed by international terrorism. These incidents resulted in a concerted global effort to address the growing phenomenon, including the elaboration of additional and more forceful UN counter-terrorism instruments finalized in 1970, 1971, and supplemented by an Additional Protocol in 1988. These instruments were the first to include detailed criminalization, jurisdiction, and international cooperation provisions, specifically aimed at addressing acts of terrorism affecting civil aviation.

2.52

Criminalization provisions

Article 1

Any person who on board an aircraft in flight:

2.53

    a. unlawfully, by force or threat thereof, or by any other form of intimidation, seizes, or exercises control of, that aircraft, or attempts to perform any such act, or

b. is an accomplice of a person who performs or attempts to perform any such act

commits an offence (hereinafter referred to as 'the offence').

Article 2

2.54 Each Contracting State undertakes to make the offence punishable by severe penalties.

Article 3

2.55 1. For the purposes of this Convention, an aircraft is considered to be in flight at any time from the moment when all its external doors are closed following embarkation until the moment when any such door is opened for disembarkation. In the case of a forced landing, the flight shall be deemed to continue until the competent authorities take over the responsibility for the aircraft and for persons and property on board.

2. This Convention shall not apply to aircraft used in military, customs or police services.

3. This Convention shall apply only if the place of take-off or the place of actual landing of the aircraft on board which the offence is committed is situated outside the territory of the State of registration of that aircraft; it shall be immaterial whether the aircraft is engaged in an international or domestic flight.

4. In the cases mentioned in Article 5, this Convention shall not apply if the place of take-off and the place of actual landing of the aircraft on board which the offence is committed are situated within the territory of the same State where that State is one of those referred to in that Article.

5. Notwithstanding paragraphs 3 and 4 of this Article, Articles 6, 7, 8, and 10 shall apply whatever the place of take-off or the place of actual landing of the aircraft, if the offender or the alleged offender is found in the territory of a State other than the State of registration of that aircraft.

Jurisdiction provisions

Article 4

2.56 1. Each Contracting State shall take such measures as may be necessary to establish its jurisdiction over the offence and any other act of violence against passengers or crew committed by the alleged offender in connection with the offence, in the following cases:

a. when the offence is committed on board an aircraft registered in that State;
b. when the aircraft on board which the offence is committed lands in its territory with the alleged offender still on board;
c. when the offence is committed on board an aircraft leased without crew to a lessee who has his principal place of business or, if the lessee has no such place of business, his permanent residence, in that State.

2. Each Contracting State shall likewise take such measures as may be necessary to establish its jurisdiction over the offence in the case where the alleged offender is present in its territory and it does not extradite him pursuant to Article 8 to any of the States mentioned in paragraph 1 of this Article.

3. This Convention does not exclude any criminal jurisdiction exercised in accordance with national law.

Procedural and due process provisions

Article 6

1. Upon being satisfied that the circumstances so warrant, any Contracting State in the territory of which the offender or the alleged offender is present, shall take him into custody or take other measures to ensure his presence. The custody and other measures shall be as provided in the law of that State but may only be continued for such time as is necessary to enable any criminal or extradition proceedings to be instituted.

2. Such State shall immediately make a preliminary enquiry into the facts.

3. Any person in custody pursuant to paragraph 1 of this Article shall be assisted in communicating immediately with the nearest appropriate representative of the State of which he is a national.

4. When a State, pursuant to this Article, has taken a person into custody, it shall immediately notify the State of registration of the aircraft, the State mentioned in Article 4, paragraph 1(c), the State of nationality of the detained person and, if it considers it advisable, any other interested States of the fact that such person is in custody and of the circumstances which warrant his detention. The State which makes the preliminary enquiry contemplated in paragraph 2 of this Article shall promptly report its findings to the said States and shall indicate whether it intends to exercise jurisdiction.

2.57

International cooperation mechanisms and the aut dedere aut judicare *principle*

Article 7

The Contracting State in the territory of which the alleged offender is found shall, if it does not extradite him, be obliged, without exception whatsoever and whether or not the offence was committed in its territory, to submit the case to its competent authorities for the purpose of prosecution. Those authorities shall take their decision in the same manner as in the case of any ordinary offence of a serious nature under the law of that State.

2.58

Article 8

1. The offence shall be deemed to be included as an extraditable offence in any extradition treaty existing between Contracting States. Contracting States undertake to include the offence as an extraditable offence in every extradition treaty to be concluded between them.

2. If a Contracting State which makes extradition conditional on the existence of a treaty receives a request for extradition from another Contracting State with which it has no extradition treaty, it may at its option consider this Convention as the legal basis for extradition in respect of the offence. Extradition shall be subject to the other conditions provided by the law of the requested State.

3. Contracting States which do not make extradition conditional on the existence of a treaty shall recognize the offence as an extraditable offence between themselves subject to the conditions provided by the law of the requested State.

4. The offence shall be treated, for the purpose of extradition between Contracting States, as if it had been committed not only in the place in which it occurred but also

2.59

in the territories of the States required to establish their jurisdiction in accordance with Article 4, paragraph 1.

Article 9

2.60   1. When any of the acts mentioned in Article 1(a) has occurred or is about to occur, Contracting States shall take all appropriate measures to restore control of the aircraft to its lawful commander or to preserve his control of the aircraft.

2. In the cases contemplated by the preceding paragraph, any Contracting State in which the aircraft or its passengers or crew are present shall facilitate the continuation of the journey of the passengers and crew as soon as practicable, and shall without delay return the aircraft and its cargo to the persons lawfully entitled to possession.

Article 10

2.61   1. Contracting States shall afford one another the greatest measure of assistance in connection with criminal proceedings brought in respect of the offence and other acts mentioned in Article 4. The law of the State requested shall apply in all cases.

2. The provisions of paragraph 1 of this Article shall not affect obligations under any other treaty, bilateral or multilateral, which governs or will govern, in whole or in part, mutual assistance in criminal matters.

1971 Convention for the Suppression of Unlawful Acts against the Safety of Civil Aviation ('The Montreal Convention')

2.62   This agreement was adopted after the destruction of four civilian aircraft on the ground in the Middle East in September 1970.[54] It requires criminalization of attacks on aircraft 'in service' as 'from the beginning of the pre-flight preparation of the aircraft by ground personnel or by the crew for a specific flight until twenty-four hours after any landing'. It also requires the criminalization of any act of violence against a person on board an aircraft in flight and any damage to or interference with air navigation facilities likely to endanger the safety of an aircraft.

Criminalization provisions

Article 1

2.63   1. Any person commits an offence if he/she unlawfully and intentionally:

    a. performs an act of violence against a person on board an aircraft in flight if that act is likely to endanger the safety of that aircraft; or

    b. destroys an aircraft in service or causes damage to such an aircraft which renders it incapable of flight or which is likely to endanger its safety in flight; or

    c. places or causes to be placed on an aircraft in service, by any means whatsoever, a device or substance which is likely to destroy that aircraft, or to cause damage

---

[54] The Popular Front for the Liberation of Palestine (PFLP) hijacked four planes between the 7 and 9 September 1970. The hijackings were an attempt to publicize Palestinian issues, and after releasing the hostages the planes were blown up.

    to it which renders it incapable of flight, or to cause damage to it which is likely to endanger its safety in flight; or

    d. destroys or damages air navigation facilities or interferes with their operation, if any such act is likely to endanger the safety of aircraft in flight; or

    e. communicates information which he knows to be false, thereby endangering the safety of an aircraft in flight.

2. Any person also commits an offence if he:

    a. attempts to commit any of the offences mentioned in paragraph 1 of this Article; or

    b. is an accomplice of a person who commits or attempts to commit any such offence.

Article 2

For the purposes of this Convention:

    a. an aircraft is considered to be in flight at any time from the moment when all its external doors are closed following embarkation until the moment when any such door is opened for disembarkation; in the case of a forced landing, the flight shall be deemed to continue until the competent authorities take over the responsibility for the aircraft and for persons and property on board;

    b. an aircraft is considered to be in service from the beginning of the preflight preparation of the aircraft by ground personnel or by the crew for a specific flight until twenty-four hours after any landing; the period of service shall, in any event, extend for the entire period during which the aircraft is in flight as defined in paragraph (a) of this Article.

2.64

Article 3

Each Contracting State undertakes to make the offences mentioned in Article 1 punishable by severe penalties.

2.65

Article 4

1. This Convention shall not apply to aircraft used in military, customs or police services.

2.66

2. In the cases contemplated in subparagraphs (a), (b), (c) and (e) of paragraph 1 of Article 1, this Convention shall apply, irrespective of whether the aircraft is engaged in an international or domestic flight, only if:

    a. the place of take-off or landing, actual or intended, of the aircraft is situated outside the territory of the State of registration of that aircraft; or

    b. the offence is committed in the territory of a State other than the State of registration of the aircraft.

3. Notwithstanding paragraph 2 of this Article, in the cases contemplated in subparagraphs (a), (b), (c) and (e) of paragraph 1 of Article 1, this Convention shall also apply if the offender or the alleged offender is found in the territory of a State other than the State of registration of the aircraft.

4. With respect to the States mentioned in Article 9 and in the cases mentioned in subparagraphs (a), (b), (c) and (e) of paragraph 1 of Article 1, this Convention shall not apply if the places referred to in subparagraph (a) of paragraph 2 of this Article are situated within the territory of the same State where that State is one of those referred to in

Article 9, unless the offence is committed or the offender or alleged offender is found in the territory of a State other than that State.

5. In the cases contemplated in subparagraph (d) of paragraph 1 of Article 1, this Convention shall apply only if the air navigation facilities are used in international air navigation.

6. The provisions of paragraphs 2, 3, 4 and 5 of this Article shall also apply in the cases contemplated in paragraph 2 of Article 1.

Jurisdiction provisions

Article 5

2.67 1. Each Contracting State shall take such measures as may be necessary to establish its jurisdiction over the offences in the following cases:

    a. when the offence is committed in the territory of that State;

    b. when the offence is committed against or on board an aircraft registered in that State;

    c. when the aircraft on board which the offence is committed lands in its territory with the alleged offender still on board;

    d. when the offence is committed against or on board an aircraft leased without crew to a lessee who has his principal place of business or, if the lessee has no such place of business, his permanent residence, in that State.

2. Each Contracting State shall likewise take such measures as may be necessary to establish its jurisdiction over the offences mentioned in Article 1, paragraph 1 (a), (b) and (c), and in Article 1, paragraph 2, in so far as that paragraph relates to those offences, in the case where the alleged offender is present in its territory and it does not extradite him pursuant to Article 8 to any of the States mentioned in paragraph 1 of this Article.

3. This Convention does not exclude any criminal jurisdiction exercised in accordance with national law.

Procedural and due process provisions

Article 6

2.68 1. Upon being satisfied that the circumstances so warrant, any Contracting State in the territory of which the offender or the alleged offender is present, shall take him into custody or take other measures to ensure his presence. The custody and other measures shall be as provided in the law of that State but may only be continued for such time as is necessary to enable any criminal or extradition proceedings to be instituted.

2. Such State shall immediately make a preliminary enquiry into the facts.

3. Any person in custody pursuant to paragraph 1 of this Article shall be assisted in communicating immediately with the nearest appropriate representative of the State of which he is a national.

4. When a State, pursuant to this Article, has taken a person into custody, it shall immediately notify the States mentioned in Article 5, paragraph 1, the State of nationality of the detained person and, if it considers it advisable, any other interested State of the fact that such person is in custody and of the circumstances which warrant his detention. The State which makes the preliminary enquiry contemplated in paragraph 2 of this Article shall promptly report its findings to the said States and shall indicate whether it intends to exercise jurisdiction.

International cooperation mechanisms and the
aut dedere aut judicare *principle*

Article 7

The Contracting State in the territory of which the alleged offender is found shall, if it does not extradite him, be obliged, without exception whatsoever and whether or not the offence was committed in its territory, to submit the case to its competent authorities for the purpose of prosecution. Those authorities shall take their decision in the same manner as in the case of any ordinary offence of a serious nature under the law of that State.

2.69

Article 8

1. The offences shall be deemed to be included as extraditable offences in any extradition treaty existing between Contracting States. Contracting States undertake to include the offences as extraditable offences in every extradition treaty to be concluded between them.

2.70

2. If a Contracting State which makes extradition conditional on the existence of a treaty receives a request for extradition from another Contracting State with which it has no extradition treaty, it may at its option consider this Convention as the legal basis for extradition in respect of the offences. Extradition shall be subject to the other conditions provided by the law of the requested State.

3. Contracting States which do not make extradition conditional on the existence of a treaty shall recognize the offences as extraditable offences between themselves subject to the conditions provided by the law of the requested State.

4. Each of the offences shall be treated, for the purpose of extradition between Contracting States, as if it had been committed not only in the place in which it occurred but also in the territories of the States required to establish their jurisdiction in accordance with Article 5, paragraph 1 (b), (c) and (d).

Article 11

1. Contracting States shall afford one another the greatest measure of assistance in connection with criminal proceedings brought in respect of the offences. The law of the State requested shall apply in all cases.

2.71

2. The provisions of paragraph 1 of this Article shall not affect obligations under any other treaty, bilateral or multilateral, which governs or will govern, in whole or in part, mutual assistance in criminal matters.

Article 12

Any Contracting State having reason to believe that one of the offences mentioned in Article 1 will be committed shall, in accordance with its national law, furnish any relevant information in its possession to those States which it believes would be the States mentioned in Article 5, paragraph 1.

2.72

1988 Protocol for the Suppression of Unlawful Acts of Violence at Airports Serving International Civil Aviation

Only States that are parties to the 1971 Montreal Convention may join this Protocol. Its negotiation followed attacks on travellers in airports in Vienna, Rome, and elsewhere in the 1980s. It requires criminalization of acts of violence

2.73

at airports serving international civil aviation likely to cause death or serious injury, as well as destroying or seriously damaging aircraft or facilities if such acts endanger or are likely to endanger safety at that airport. After negotiation of the 1971 Convention, a number of countries approved legislation implementing the 1963, 1970, and 1971 Conventions in a single law.[55] Some consolidated laws enacted after negotiation of the 1988 Airport Protocol incorporate not only the offences defined therein, but also the unauthorized introduction of weapons and other dangerous articles into airports and on board aircraft.[56]

Criminalization provisions

Article 2

2.74   1. In Article 1 of the Convention, the following shall be added as new paragraph 1 bis: '1 bis. Any person commits an offence if he unlawfully and intentionally, using any device, substance or weapon:

> a. performs an act of violence against a person at an airport serving international civil aviation which causes or is likely to cause serious injury or death; or
> b. destroys or seriously damages the facilities of an airport serving international civil aviation or aircraft not in service located thereon or disrupts the services of the airport, if such an act endangers or is likely to endanger safety at that airport.'

Agreements developed by the International Maritime Organization (IMO)

1988 Convention for the Suppression of Unlawful Acts against the Safety of Maritime Navigation ('1988 Safety of Maritime Navigation Convention') and its Fixed Platform Protocol

2.75   This Convention applies many of the provisions developed in the preceding decades to deal with attacks upon aircraft to maritime vessels. It was elaborated following the 1985 hijacking of the cruise ship *Achille Lauro* in the Mediterranean and the murder of a passenger. The agreement requires the criminalization of

---

[55] Among these were the New Zealand Aviation Crimes Act 1972, the Malawi Hijacking Act of 1972, the Malaysian Aviation Offences Act 1984, and the Mauritius Civil Aviation (Hijacking and Other Offences) Act 1985. Some of the statutes were later amended by insertion of an article incorporating the 1988 Airport Protocol, as was done by Mauritius. Its 1985 Hijacking and Other Offences Act was amended in 1994 by the addition of Article 6A, which criminalized the conduct defined as an offence in the 1988 Airport Protocol to the 1971 Safety of Civil Aviation Convention, as well as any act at an airport using a device, substance, or weapon likely to cause serious damage to the environment.

[56] The Australia Crimes (Aviation) Act of 1991 and the Fiji Civil Aviation (Security) Act 1994 are comprehensive post-1988 rewritings of prior air travel safety legislation and incorporate airport security measures forbidding the introduction of weapons and other dangerous articles, and in the law of Fiji, provisions on airport access, security searches, and related topics.

a ship seizure, damage to a ship or its cargo that is likely to endanger its safe navigation, introduction of a device or substance likely to endanger the ship, endangering safe navigation by serious damage to navigation facilities, and injuring or killing any person in connection with the previously listed offences. Its contemporaneous Protocol for the Suppression of Unlawful Acts against the Safety of Fixed Platforms on the Continental Shelf[57] extended similar provisions to attacks upon those platforms.[58]

Criminalization provisions

Article 1

For the purposes of this Convention, 'ship' means a vessel of any type whatsoever not permanently attached to the sea-bed, including dynamically supported craft, submersibles, or any other floating craft.

2.76

Article 2

1. This Convention does not apply to:

   a. a warship; or
   b. a ship owned or operated by a State when being used as a naval auxiliary or for customs or police purposes; or
   c. a ship which has been withdrawn from navigation or laid up.

2. Nothing in this Convention affects the immunities of warships and other government ships operated for non-commercial purposes.

2.77

Article 3

1. Any person commits an offence if that person unlawfully and intentionally:

   a. seizes or exercises control over a ship by force or threat thereof or any other form of intimidation; or
   b. performs an act of violence against a person on board a ship if that act is likely to endanger the safe navigation of that ship; or
   c. destroys a ship or causes damage to a ship or to its cargo which is likely to endanger the safe navigation of that ship; or
   d. places or causes to be placed on a ship, by any means whatsoever, a device or substance which is likely to destroy that ship, or cause damage to that ship or

2.78

---

[57] A definition of the continental shelf is found in the UN Convention on the Law of the Sea. In very simplified terms it is the natural prolongation of a State's land territory to the point where the deep ocean floor begins. However, there are very technical limits and qualifications in the Convention on the Law of the Sea that need to be examined to determine whether a particular location constitutes part of the continental shelf.

[58] Article 1.1 of the Protocol stipulates that the provisions of Articles 5 and 7 and of Articles 10 to 16 of the Convention for the Suppression of unlawful Acts against the Safety of Maritime Navigation shall also apply *mutatis mutandis* to the offences set forth in Article 2 of this Protocol where such offences are committed on board or against fixed platforms located on the continental shelf.

its cargo which endangers or is likely to endanger the safe navigation of that ship; or

e. destroys or seriously damages maritime navigational facilities or seriously interferes with their operation, if any such act is likely to endanger the safe navigation of a ship; or

f. communicates information which he knows to be false, thereby endangering the safe navigation of a ship; or

g. injures or kills any person, in connection with the commission or the attempted commission of any of the offences set forth in subparagraphs (a) to (f).

2. Any person also commits an offence if that person:

a. attempts to commit any of the offences set forth in paragraph 1; or

b. abets the commission of any of the offences set forth in paragraph 1 perpetrated by any person or is otherwise an accomplice of a person who commits such an offence; or

c. threatens, with or without a condition, as is provided for under national law, aimed at compelling a physical or juridical person to do or refrain from doing any act, to commit any of the offences set forth in paragraph 1, subparagraphs (b), (c) and (e), if that threat is likely to endanger the safe navigation of the ship in question.

Jurisdiction provisions

Article 6

2.79   1. Each State Party shall take such measures as may be necessary to establish its jurisdiction over the offences set forth in article 3 when the offence is committed:

a. against or on board a ship flying the flag of the State at the time the offence is committed; or

b. in the territory of that State, including its territorial sea; or

c. by a national of that State.

2. A State Party may also establish its jurisdiction over any such offence when:

a. it is committed by a stateless person whose habitual residence is in that State; or

b. during its commission a national of that State is seized, threatened, injured or killed; or

c. it is committed in an attempt to compel that State to do or abstain from doing any act.

3. Any State Party which has established jurisdiction mentioned in paragraph 2 shall notify the Secretary-General of the International Maritime Organization (hereinafter referred to as 'the Secretary-General'). If such State Party subsequently rescinds that jurisdiction, it shall notify the Secretary-General.

4. Each State Party shall take such measures as may be necessary to establish its jurisdiction over the offences set forth in article 3 in cases where the alleged offender is present in its territory and it does not extradite him to any of the States Parties which have established their jurisdiction in accordance with paragraphs 1 and 2 of this article.

5. This Convention does not exclude any criminal jurisdiction exercised in accordance with national law.

Procedural and due process provisions

Article 7

1. Upon being satisfied that the circumstances so warrant, any State Party in the territory of which the offender or the alleged offender is present shall, in accordance with its law, take him into custody or take other measures to ensure his presence for such time as is necessary to enable any criminal or extradition proceedings to be instituted.

2.80

2. Such State shall immediately make a preliminary inquiry into the facts, in accordance with its own legislation.

3. Any person regarding whom the measures referred to in paragraph 1 are being taken shall be entitled to:

   a. communicate without delay with the nearest appropriate representative of the State of which he is a national or which is otherwise entitled to establish such communication or, if he is a stateless person, the State in the territory of which he has his habitual residence;
   b. be visited by a representative of that State.

4. The rights referred to in paragraph 3 shall be exercised in conformity with the laws and regulations of the State in the territory of which the offender or the alleged offender is present, subject to the proviso that the said laws and regulations must enable full effect to be given to the purposes for which the rights accorded under paragraph 3 are intended.

5. When a State Party, pursuant to this article, has taken a person into custody, it shall immediately notify the States which have established jurisdiction in accordance with article 6, paragraph 1 and, if it considers it advisable, any other interested States, of the fact that such person is in custody and of the circumstances which warrant his detention. The State which makes the preliminary inquiry contemplated in paragraph 2 of this article shall promptly report its findings to the said States and shall indicate whether it intends to exercise jurisdiction.

Article 8

1. The master of a ship of a State Party (the 'flag State') may deliver to the authorities of any other State Party (the 'receiving State') any person who he has reasonable grounds to believe has committed one of the offences set forth in article 3.

2.81

2. The flag State shall ensure that the master of its ship is obliged, whenever practicable, and if possible before entering the territorial sea of the receiving State carrying on board any person whom the master intends to deliver in accordance with paragraph 1, to give notification to the authorities of the receiving State of his intention to deliver such person and the reasons therefor.

3. The receiving State shall accept the delivery, except where it has grounds to consider that the Convention is not applicable to the acts giving rise to the delivery, and shall proceed in accordance with the provisions of article 1. Any refusal to accept a delivery shall be accompanied by a statement of the reasons for refusal.

4. The flag State shall ensure that the master of its ship is obliged to furnish the authorities of the receiving State with the evidence in the master's possession which pertains to the alleged offence.

5. A receiving State which has accepted the delivery of a person in accordance with paragraph 3 may, in turn, request the flag State to accept delivery of that person. The flag

State shall consider any such request, and if it accedes to the request it shall proceed in accordance with article 7. If the flag State declines a request, it shall furnish the receiving State with a statement of the reasons therefor.

Article 9

2.82   Nothing in this Convention shall affect in any way the rules of international law pertaining to the competence of States to exercise investigative or enforcement jurisdiction on board ships not flying their flag.

International cooperation mechanisms and the aut dedere aut judicare *principle*

Article 10

2.83   1. The State Party in the territory of which the offender or the alleged offender is found shall, in cases to which article 6 applies, if it does not extradite him, be obliged, without exception whatsoever and whether or not the offence was committed in its territory, to submit the case without delay to its competent authorities for the purpose of prosecution, through proceedings in accordance with the laws of that State. Those authorities shall take their decision in the same manner as in the case of any other offence of a grave nature under the law of that State.

2. Any person regarding whom proceedings are being carried out in connection with any of the offences set forth in article 3 shall be guaranteed fair treatment at all stages of the proceedings, including enjoyment of all the rights and guarantees provided for such proceedings by the law of the State in the territory of which he is present.

Article 11

2.84   1. The offences set forth in article 3 shall be deemed to be included as extraditable offences in any extradition treaty existing between any of the States Parties. States Parties undertake to include such offences as extraditable offences in every extradition treaty to be concluded between them.

2. If a State Party which makes extradition conditional on the existence of a treaty receives a request for extradition from another State Party with which it has no extradition treaty, the requested State Party may, at its option, consider this Convention as a legal basis for extradition in respect of the offences set forth in article 3. Extradition shall be subject to the other conditions provided by the law of the requested State Party.

3. States Parties which do not make extradition conditional on the existence of a treaty shall recognize the offences set forth in article 3 as extraditable offences between themselves, subject to the conditions provided by the law of the requested State.

4. If necessary, the offences set forth in article 3 shall be treated, for the purposes of extradition between States Parties, as if they had been committed not only in the place in which they occurred but also in a place within the jurisdiction of the State Party requesting extradition.

5. A State Party which receives more than one request for extradition from States which have established jurisdiction in accordance with article 7 and which decides not to prosecute shall, in selecting the State to which the offender or alleged offender is to be extradited, pay due regard to the interests and responsibilities of the State Party whose flag the ship was flying at the time of the commission of the offence.

6. In considering a request for the extradition of an alleged offender pursuant to this Convention, the requested State shall pay due regard to whether his rights as set forth in article 7, paragraph 3, can be effected in the requesting State.

7. With respect to the offences as defined in this Convention, the provisions of all extradition treaties and arrangements applicable between States Parties are modified as between States Parties to the extent that they are incompatible with this Convention.

Article 12

1. State Parties shall afford one another the greatest measure of assistance in connection with criminal proceedings brought in respect of the offences set forth in article 3, including assistance in obtaining evidence at their disposal necessary for the proceedings.

2.85

2. States Parties shall carry out their obligations under paragraph 1 in conformity with any treaties on mutual assistance that may exist between them. In the absence of such treaties, States Parties shall afford each other assistance in accordance with their national law.

Article 13

1. States Parties shall co-operate in the prevention of the offences set forth in article 3, particularly by:

2.86

   a. taking all practicable measures to prevent preparations in their respective territories for the commission of those offences within or outside their territories;
   b. exchanging information in accordance with their national law, and co-ordinating administrative and other measures taken as appropriate to prevent the commission of offences set forth in article 3.

2. When, due to the commission of an offence set forth in article 3, the passage of a ship has been delayed or interrupted, any State Party in whose territory the ship or passengers or crew are present shall be bound to exercise all possible efforts to avoid a ship, its passengers, crew or cargo being unduly detained or delayed.

Article 14

Any State Party having reason to believe that an offence set forth in article 3 will be committed shall, in accordance with its national law, furnish as promptly as possible any relevant information in its possession to those States which it believes would be the States having established jurisdiction in accordance with article 6.

2.87

Protocols to the Convention for the Suppression of Unlawful Acts against the Safety of Maritime Navigation and to the Protocol for the Suppression of Unlawful Acts against the Safety of Fixed Platforms located on the Continental Shelf (2005)

Protocols to both the Convention and Protocol of 1988 were negotiated in 2005. These instruments provide that upon coming into force with the requisite number of adoptions they shall be combined with the earlier instruments, and designated portions will be called the Convention for the Suppression of Unlawful Acts against the Safety of Maritime Navigation, 2005 and the Protocol for the Suppression of Unlawful Acts against the Safety of Fixed Platforms Located on

2.88

the Continental Shelf, 2005. The new agreements create additional offences, including: using against or discharging from a ship explosive, radioactive, biological, chemical, or nuclear materials or weapons in a manner likely to cause death, serious injury, or damage; discharging other hazardous or noxious substances likely to cause death or serious injury or damage; or using a ship in a manner that causes death or serious injury or damage; or threatening to do so.

2.89 Transportation on board a ship of certain materials must be criminalized if done with an intent to intimidate a population or to coerce a government or international organization, as well as any equipment, material, software, or technology that significantly contributes to the design of a biological, chemical, or nuclear weapon. Additional articles require the creation of offences for transporting a person knowing that the person has committed an offence defined in the 2005 Protocol or in the annexed list of terrorism-related treaties and for injuring a person in connection with the commission of the defined offences.

Criminalization provisions

2.90 The following text is added as Article 3bis of the Convention:

[Article 3bis]

1. Any person commits an offence within the meaning of this Convention if that person unlawfully and intentionally:

    (a) when the purpose of the act, by its nature or context, is to intimidate a population, or to compel a government or an international organization to do or to abstain from doing any act:

        (i) ses against or on a ship or discharges from a ship any explosive, radioactive material or BCN weapon in a manner that causes or is likely to cause death or serious injury or damage; or

        (ii) discharges, from a ship, oil, liquefied natural gas, or other hazardous or noxious substance, which is not covered by subparagraph (a)(i), in such quantity or concentration that causes or is likely to cause death or serious injury or damage; or

        (iii) uses a ship in a manner that causes death or serious injury or damage; or

        (iv) threatens, with or without a condition, as is provided for under national law, to commit an offence set forth in subparagraph (a)(i), (ii) or (iii); or

    (b) transports on board a ship:

        (i) any explosive or radioactive material, knowing that it is intended to be used to cause, or in a threat to cause, with or without a condition, as is provided for under national law, death or serious injury or damage for the purpose of intimidating a population, or compelling a government or an international organization to do or to abstain from doing any act; or

        (ii) any BCN weapon, knowing it to be a BCN weapon as defined in article 1; or

        (iii) any source material, special fissionable material, or equipment or material especially designed or prepared for the processing, use or production of special fissionable material, knowing that it is intended to be used in a nuclear explosive activity or in any other nuclear activity not under safe-guards pursuant to an IAEA comprehensive safeguards agreement; or

(iv) any equipment, materials or software or related technology that significantly contributes to the design, manufacture or delivery of a BCN weapon, with the intention that it will be used for such purpose.

2. It shall not be an offence within the meaning of this Convention to transport an item or material covered by paragraph 1(b)(iii) or, insofar as it relates to a nuclear weapon or other nuclear explosive device, paragraph 1(b)(iv), if such item or material is transported to or from the territory of, or is otherwise transported under the control of, a State Party to the Treaty on the Non-Proliferation of Nuclear Weapons where:

(a) the resulting transfer or receipt, including internal to a State, of the item or material is not contrary to such State Party's obligations under the Treaty on the Non-Proliferation of Nuclear Weapons and,

(b) if the item or material is intended for the delivery system of a nuclear weapon or other nuclear explosive device of a State Party to the Treaty on the Non-Proliferation of Nuclear Weapons, the holding of such weapon or device is not contrary to that State Party's obligations under that Treaty.

The following text is added as Article 3ter of the Convention: 2.91

[Article 3ter]

Any person commits an offence within the meaning of this Convention if that person unlawfully and intentionally transports another person on board a ship knowing that the person has committed an act that constitutes an offence set forth in article 3, 3bis or 3quater or an offence set forth in any treaty listed in the Annex, and intending to assist that person to evade criminal prosecution.

The following text is added as Article 3quater of the Convention: 2.92

[Article 3quater]

Any person also commits an offence within the meaning of this Convention if that person:

(a) unlawfully and intentionally injures or kills any person in connection with the commission of any of the offences set forth in article 3, paragraph 1, article 3bis, or article 3ter; or

(b) attempts to commit an offence set forth in article 3, paragraph 1, article 3bis, paragraph 1(a)(i), (ii) or (iii), or subparagraph (a) of this article; or

(c) participates as an accomplice in an offence set forth in article 3, article 3bis, article 3ter, or subparagraph (a) or (b) of this article; or

(d) organizes or directs others to commit an offence set forth in article 3, article 3bis, article 3ter, or subparagraph (a) or (b) of this article; or

(e) contributes to the commission of one or more offences set forth in article 3, article 3bis, article 3ter or subparagraph (a) or (b) of this article, by a group of persons acting with a common purpose, intentionally and either:

(i) with the aim of furthering the criminal activity or criminal purpose of the group, where such activity or purpose involves the commission of an offence set forth in article 3, 3bis or 3ter; or

(ii) the knowledge of the intention of the group to commit an offence set forth in article 3, 3bis or 3ter.

*Instruments developed by the International
Atomic Energy Agency (IAEA)*

1979 Convention on the Physical Protection of Nuclear Material ('Nuclear Material Convention') and its 2005 Amendment

2.93   In 1979 the IAEA developed the Convention on the Physical Protection of Nuclear Material, establishing obligations concerning the protection and transportation of defined materials. The Convention requires the States Parties to create offences of unlawful handling of nuclear materials or a threat thereof; a theft, robbery, or other unlawful acquisition of or demand for such material; or a threat of such unlawful acquisition in order to coerce a person, international organization, or State. In 2005 that instrument was amended to criminalize acts directed against or interfering with a nuclear facility likely to cause serious injury or damage, as well as: unauthorized movement of such material into, or out of a State without lawful authority; a demand for nuclear material by threat, or use of force; a threat to use such materials to cause death or serious injury, or damage to property, or to the environment, or to commit an offence in order to coerce a person, international organization, or State.[59] The application of this agreement should be considered in conjunction with an instrument developed by the General Assembly's Ad Hoc Committee in 2005, the International Convention for the Suppression of Acts of Nuclear Terrorism.

Criminalization provisions

Article 7

2.94   1. The intentional commission of:

    a. an act without lawful authority which constitutes the receipt, possession, use, transfer, alteration, disposal or dispersal of nuclear material and which causes or is likely to cause death or serious injury to any person or substantial damage to property;

    b. a theft or robbery of nuclear material;

    c. an embezzlement or fraudulent obtaining of nuclear material;

    d. an act constituting a demand for nuclear material by threat or use of force or by any other form of intimidation;

    e. a threat:

        i. to use nuclear material to cause death or serious injury to any person or substantial property damage, or

        ii. to commit an offence described in sub-paragraph (b) in order to compel a natural or legal person, international organization or State to do or to refrain from doing any act;

    f. an attempt to commit any offence described in paragraphs (a), (b) or (c); and

---

[59] 2005 Amendment to the Convention on the Physical Protection of Nuclear Material, creating a new agreement to be called the Convention on the Physical Protection of Nuclear Material and Nuclear Facilities.

g. an act which constitutes participation in any offence described in paragraphs (a) to (f) shall be made a punishable offence by each State Party under its national law.

Changes introduced by Article 9 of the 2005 Amendment: Paragraph 1 of Article 7 of the Convention is replaced by the following text: **2.95**

1. The intentional commission of:

   (a) an act without lawful authority which constitutes the receipt, possession, use, transfer, alteration, disposal or dispersal of nuclear material and which causes or is likely to cause death or serious injury to any person or substantial damage to property or to the environment;

   (b) a theft or robbery of nuclear material;

   (c) an embezzlement or fraudulent obtaining of nuclear material;

   (d) an act which constitutes the carrying, sending, or moving of nuclear material into or out of a State without lawful authority;

   (e) an act directed against a nuclear facility, or an act interfering with the operation of a nuclear facility, where the offender intentionally causes, or where he knows that the act is likely to cause, death or serious injury to any person or substantial damage to property or to the environment by exposure to radiation or release of radioactive substances, unless the act is undertaken in conformity with the national law of the State Party in the territory of which the nuclear facility is situated;

   (f) an act constituting a demand for nuclear material by threat or use of force or by any other form of intimidation;

   (g) a threat: (i) to use nuclear material to cause death or serious injury to any person or substantial damage to property or to the environment or to commit the offence described in sub-paragraph (e), or (ii) to commit an offence described in sub-paragraphs (b) and (e) in order to compel a natural or legal person, international organization or State to do or to refrain from doing any act;

   (h) an attempt to commit any offence described in sub-paragraphs (a) to (e);

   (i) an act which constitutes participation in any offence described in sub-paragraphs (a) to (h);

   (j) an act of any person who organizes or directs others to commit an offence described in sub-paragraphs (a) to (h); and

   (k) an act which contributes to the commission of any offence described in sub-paragraphs (a) to (h) by a group of persons acting with a common purpose; such act shall be intentional and shall either: (i) be made with the aim of furthering the criminal activity or criminal purpose of the group, where such activity or purpose involves the commission of an offence described in sub-paragraphs (a) to (g), or (ii) be made in the knowledge of the intention of the group to commit an offence described in sub-paragraphs (a) to (g) shall be made a punishable offence by each State Party under its national law.

2. Each State Party shall make the offences described in this article punishable by appropriate penalties which take into account their grave nature.

Jurisdiction provisions

Article 8

2.96 1. Each State Party shall take such measures as may be necessary to establish its jurisdiction over the offences set forth in article 7 in the following cases:

   a. when the offence is committed in the territory of that State or on board a ship or aircraft registered in that State;

   b. when the alleged offender is a national of that State.

2. Each State Party shall likewise take such measures as may be necessary to establish its jurisdiction over these offences in cases where the alleged offender is present in its territory and it does not extradite him pursuant to article 11 to any of the States mentioned in paragraph 1.

3. This Convention does not exclude any criminal jurisdiction exercised in accordance with national law.

4. In addition to the States Parties mentioned in paragraphs I and 2, each State Party may, consistent with international law, establish its jurisdiction over the offences set forth in article 7 when it is involved in international nuclear transport as the exporting or importing State.

Procedural and due process provisions

Article 12

2.97 Any person regarding whom proceedings are being carried out in connection with any of the offences set forth in article 7 shall be guaranteed fair treatment at all stages of the proceedings.

International cooperation mechanisms and the
aut dedere aut judicare *principle*

Article 9

2.98 Upon being satisfied that the circumstances so warrant, the State Party in whose territory the alleged offender is present shall take appropriate measures, including detention, under its national law to ensure his presence for the purpose of prosecution or extradition. Measures taken according to this article shall be notified without delay to the States required to establish jurisdiction pursuant to article 8 and, where appropriate, all other States concerned.

Article 10

2.99 The State Party in whose territory the alleged offender is present shall, if it does not extradite him, submit, without exception whatsoever and without undue delay, the case to its competent authorities for the purpose of prosecution, through proceedings in accordance with the laws of that State.

Article 11

2.100 1. The offences in article 7 shall be deemed to be included as extraditable offences in any extradition treaty existing between States Parties. States Parties undertake to include those offences as extraditable offences in every future extradition treaty to be concluded between them.

2. If a State Party which makes extradition conditional on the existence of a treaty receives a request for extradition from another State Party with which it has no

extradition treaty, it may at its option consider this Convention as the legal basis for extradition in respect of those offences. Extradition shall be subject to the other conditions provided by the law of the requested State.

3. States Parties which do not make extradition conditional on the existence of a treaty shall recognize those offences as extraditable offences between themselves subject to the conditions provided by the law of the requested State.

4. Each of the offences shall be treated, for the purpose of extradition between States Parties, as if it had been committed not only in the place in which it occurred but also in the territories of the States Parties required to establish their jurisdiction in accordance with paragraph 1 of article 8.

Changes introduced by Article 10 of the 2005 Amendment. After Article 11 **2.101** of the Convention, two new articles, Article 11A and Article 11B, are added as follows:

Article 11A

None of the offences set forth in article 7 shall be regarded for the purposes of extradition or mutual legal assistance, as a political offence or as an offence connected with a political offence or as an offence inspired by political motives. Accordingly, a request for extradition or for mutual legal assistance based on such an offence may not be refused on the sole ground that it concerns a political offence or an offence connected with a political offence or an offence inspired by political motives.

Article 11B

Nothing in this Convention shall be interpreted as imposing an obligation to extradite or to afford mutual legal assistance, if the requested State Party has substantial grounds for believing that the request for extradition for offences set forth in article 7 or for mutual legal assistance with respect to such offences has been made for the purpose of prosecuting or punishing a person on account of that person's race, religion, nationality, ethnic origin or political opinion or that compliance with the request would cause prejudice to that person's position for any of these reasons.

Article 13

1. States Parties shall afford one another the greatest measure of assistance in connec- **2.102** tion with criminal proceedings brought in respect of the offences set forth in article 7, including the supply of evidence at their disposal necessary for the proceedings. The law of the State requested shall apply in all cases.

2. The provisions of paragraph 1 shall not affect obligations under any other treaty, bilateral or multilateral, which governs or will govern, in whole or in part, mutual assistance in criminal matters.

Agreements developed at the initiative of the
UN General Assembly aimed at protecting civilians

1973 Convention on the Prevention and Punishment of Crimes against Internationally Protected Persons ('Diplomats Convention')

The 1973 Convention on the Prevention and Punishment of Crimes against **2.103** Internationally Protected Persons, including Diplomatic Agents, requires States

Parties to criminalize violent attacks directed against heads of State and foreign ministers and their family members, as well as against diplomatic agents entitled to special protection under international law. The term 'diplomatic agents' and the circumstances under which such persons are entitled to special protections can be found in the Vienna Convention on Diplomatic Relations 1961.[60]

Criminalization provisions

Article 1

2.104   For the purposes of this Convention:

1. 'internationally protected person' means:

   a. a Head of State, including any member of a collegial body performing the functions of a Head of State under the constitution of the State concerned, a Head of Government or a Minister for Foreign Affairs, whenever any such person is in a foreign State, as well as members of his family who accompany him;

   b. any representative or official of a State or any official or other agent of an international organization of an intergovernmental character who, at the time when and in the place where a crime against him, his official premises, his private accommodation or his means of transport is committed, is entitled pursuant to international law to special protection from any attack on his person, freedom or dignity, as well as members of his family forming part of his household;

2. 'alleged offender' means a person as to whom there is sufficient evidence to determine prima facie that he has committed or participated in one or more of the crimes set forth in article 2.

Article 2

2.105   1. The intentional commission of:

   a. a murder, kidnapping or other attack upon the person or liberty of an internationally protected person;

   b. a violent attack upon the official premises, the private accommodation or the means of transport of an internationally protected person likely to endanger his person or liberty;

   c. a threat to commit any such attack;

   d. an attempt to commit any such attack; and

   e. an act constituting participation as an accomplice in any such attack shall be made by each State Party a crime under its internal law.

2. Each State Party shall make these crimes punishable by appropriate penalties which take into account their grave nature.

---

[60] Entered into force 24 April 1964, UN Treaty Series, vol 500, 95.

3. Paragraphs 1 and 2 of this article in no way derogate from the obligations of States Parties under international law to take all appropriate measures to prevent other attacks on the person, freedom or dignity of an internationally protected person.

Jurisdiction provisions

Article 3

1. Each State Party shall take such measures as may be necessary to establish its jurisdiction over the crimes set forth in article 2 in the following cases: **2.106**

   a. when the crime is committed in the territory of that State or on board a ship or aircraft registered in that State;
   b. when the alleged offender is a national of that State;
   c. when the crime is committed against an internationally protected person as defined in article 1 who enjoys his status as such by virtue of functions which he exercises on behalf of that State.

2. Each State Party shall likewise take such measures as may be necessary to establish its jurisdiction over these crimes in cases where the alleged offender is present in its territory and it does not extradite him pursuant to article 8 to any of the States mentioned in paragraph 1 of this article.

3. This Convention does not exclude any criminal jurisdiction exercised in accordance with internal law.

Procedural and due process provisions

Article 6

1. Upon being satisfied that the circumstances so warrant, the State Party in whose territory the alleged offender is present shall take the appropriate measures under its internal law so as to ensure his presence for the purpose of prosecution or extradition. Such measures shall be notified without delay directly or through the Secretary-General of the United Nations to: **2.107**

   a. the State where the crime was committed;
   b. the State or States of which the alleged offender is a national or, if he is a stateless person, in whose territory he permanently resides;
   c. the State or States of which the internationally protected person concerned is a national or on whose behalf he was exercising his functions;
   d. all other States concerned; and
   e. the international organization of which the internationally protected person concerned is an official or an agent.

2. Any person regarding whom the measures referred to in paragraph 1 of this article are being taken shall be entitled:

   a. to communicate without delay with the nearest appropriate representative of the State of which he is a national or which is otherwise entitled to protect his rights or, if he is a stateless person, which he requests and which is willing to protect his rights, and
   b. to be visited by a representative of that State.

International cooperation mechanisms and the
aut dedere aut judicare *principle*

Article 4

2.108   States Parties shall co-operate in the prevention of the crimes set forth in article 2, particularly by:

> a. taking all practicable measures to prevent preparations in their respective territories for the commission of those crimes within or outside their territories;
> b. exchanging information and co-ordinating the taking of administrative and other measures as appropriate to prevent the commission of those crimes.

Article 5

2.109   1. The State Party in which any of the crimes set forth in article 2 has been committed shall, if it has reason to believe that an alleged offender has fled from its territory, communicate to all other States concerned, directly or through the Secretary-General of the United Nations, all the pertinent facts regarding the crime committed and all available information regarding the identity of the alleged offender.

2. Whenever any of the crimes set forth in article 2 has been committed against an internationally protected person, any State Party which has information concerning the victim and the circumstances of the crime shall endeavour to transmit it, under the conditions provided for in its internal law, fully and promptly to the State Party on whose behalf he was exercising his functions.

Article 7

2.110   The State Party in whose territory the alleged offender is present shall, if it does not extradite him, submit, without exception whatsoever and without undue delay, the case to its competent authorities for the purpose of prosecution, through proceedings in accordance with the laws of that State.

Article 8

2.111   1. To the extent that the crimes set forth in article 2 are not listed as extraditable offences in any extradition treaty existing between States Parties, they shall be deemed to be included as such therein. States Parties undertake to include those crimes as extraditable offences in every future extradition treaty to be concluded between them.

2. If a State Party which makes extradition conditional on the existence of a treaty receives a request for extradition from another State Party with which it has no extradition treaty, it may, if it decides to extradite, consider this Convention as the legal basis for extradition in respect of those crimes. Extradition shall be subject to the procedural provisions and the other conditions of the law of the requested State.

3. States Parties which do not make extradition conditional on the existence of a treaty shall recognize those crimes as extraditable offences between themselves subject to the procedural provisions and the other conditions of the law of the requested State.

4. Each of the crimes shall be treated, for the purpose of extradition between States Parties, as if it had been committed not only in the place in which it occurred but also in the territories of the States required to establish their jurisdiction in accordance with paragraph 1 of article 3.

Article 9

Any person regarding whom proceedings are being carried out in connection with any of the crimes set forth in article 2 shall be guaranteed fair treatment at all stages of the proceedings.

2.112

Article 10

1. States Parties shall afford one another the greatest measure of assistance in connection with criminal proceedings brought in respect of the crimes set forth in article 2, including the supply of all evidence at their disposal necessary for the proceedings.

2.113

2. The provisions of paragraph 1 of this article shall not affect obligations concerning mutual judicial assistance embodied in any other treaty.

1979 International Convention against the Taking of Hostages ('Hostages Convention')

The 1979 Hostage Taking Convention was enacted in response to the Entebbe hostage crisis of 1976 in which a group of Palestinians hijacked and forced an Air France flight to land at Entebbe airport in Uganda, demanding the release of fifty-three accused terrorists detained in Israel in exchange for the life of the hostages. The Convention requires criminalization of any seizure or detention and threat to kill, injure, or continue to detain any hostage, not merely diplomatic agents, in order to compel any State, international organization, or person to do or abstain from doing any act. This Convention only addresses detentions and related threats, and not any resulting death or injury, and applies only when there is an international dimension to the event. Another interesting aspect of the Convention is that Article 12 grants priority to the 1949 Geneva Conventions and the 1977 Additional Protocols, whenever they can apply. In line with the other instruments, the scope of the Convention is restricted to acts occurring in peacetime.

2.114

Criminalization provisions

Article 1

1. Any person who seizes or detains and threatens to kill, to injure or to continue to detain another person (hereinafter referred to as the 'hostage') in order to compel a third party, namely, a State, an international intergovernmental organization, a natural or juridical person, or a group of persons, to do or abstain from doing any act as an explicit or implicit condition for the release of the hostage commits the offence of taking of hostages ('hostage-taking') within the meaning of this Convention.

2.115

2. Any person who:

    a. attempts to commit an act of hostage-taking, or

    b. participates as an accomplice of anyone who commits or attempts to commit an act of hostage-taking likewise commits an offence for the purposes of this Convention.

Article 2

Each State Party shall make the offences set forth in article 1 punishable by appropriate penalties which take into account the grave nature of those offences.

2.116

Article 12

2.117   In so far as the Geneva Conventions of 1949 for the protection of war victims or the Additional Protocols to those Conventions are applicable to a particular act of hostage-taking, and in so far as States Parties to this Convention are bound under those conventions to prosecute or hand over the hostage-taker, the present Convention shall not apply to an act of hostage-taking committed in the course of armed conflicts as defined in the Geneva Conventions of 1949 and the Protocols thereto, including armed conflicts mentioned in article 1, paragraph 4, of Additional Protocol I of 1977, in which peoples are fighting against colonial domination and alien occupation and against racist regimes in the exercise of their right of self-determination, as enshrined in the Charter of the United Nations and the Declaration on Principles of International Law concerning Friendly Relations and Co-operation among States in accordance with the Charter of the United Nations.

Article 13

2.118   This Convention shall not apply where the offence is committed within a single State, the hostage and the alleged offender are nationals of that State and the alleged offender is found in the territory of that State.

Jurisdiction provisions

Article 5

2.119   1. Each State Party shall take such measures as may be necessary to establish its juris-diction over any of the offences set forth in article 1 which are committed:

   a. in its territory or on board a ship or aircraft registered in that State;
   b. by any of its nationals or, if that State considers it appropriate, by those stateless persons who have their habitual residence in its territory;
   c. in order to compel that State to do or abstain from doing any act; or
   d. with respect to a hostage who is a national of that State, if that State considers it appropriate.

2. Each State Party shall likewise take such measures as may be necessary to establish its jurisdiction over the offences set forth in article 1 in cases where the alleged offender is present in its territory and it does not extradite him to any of the States mentioned in paragraph 1 of this article.

3. This Convention does not exclude any criminal jurisdiction exercised in accordance with internal law.

Procedural and due process provisions

Article 6

2.120   1. Upon being satisfied that the circumstances so warrant, any State Party in the territory of which the alleged offender is present shall, in accordance with its laws, take him into custody or take other measures to ensure his presence for such time as is necessary to enable any criminal or extradition proceedings to be instituted. That State Party shall immediately make a preliminary inquiry into the facts.

2. The custody or other measures referred to in paragraph 1 of this article shall be notified without delay directly or through the Secretary-General of the United Nations to:

   a. the State where the offence was committed;
   b. the State against which compulsion has been directed or attempted;

    c. the State of which the natural or juridical person against whom compulsion has been directed or attempted is a national;

    d. the State of which the hostage is a national or in the territory of which he has his habitual residence;

    e. the State of which the alleged offender is a national or, if he is a stateless person, in the territory of which he has his habitual residence;

    f. the international intergovernmental organization against which compulsion has been directed or attempted;

    g. all other States concerned.

3. Any person regarding whom the measures referred to in paragraph 1 of this article are being taken shall be entitled:

    a. to communicate without delay with the nearest appropriate representative of the State of which he is a national or which is otherwise entitled to establish such communication or, if he is a stateless person, the State in the territory of which he has his habitual residence;

    b. to be visited by a representative of that State.

4. The rights referred to in paragraph 3 of this article shall be exercised in conformity with the laws and regulations of the State in the territory of which the alleged offender is present subject to the proviso, however, that the said laws and regulations must enable full effect to be given to the purposes for which the rights accorded under paragraph 3 of this article are intended.

5. The provisions of paragraphs 3 and 4 of this article shall be without prejudice to the right of any State Party having a claim to jurisdiction in accordance with paragraph 1(b) of article 5 to invite the International Committee of the Red Cross to communicate with and visit the alleged offender.

6. The State which makes the preliminary inquiry contemplated in paragraph 1 of this article shall promptly report its findings to the States or organization referred to in paragraph 2 of this article and indicate whether it intends to exercise jurisdiction.

The **aut dedere aut judicare** *principle and international cooperation elements*
Article 4

States Parties shall co-operate in the prevention of the offences set forth in article 1, particularly by:　　　　　　　　　　　　　　　　　　　　　　　　　　　　　**2.121**

    a. taking all practicable measures to prevent preparations in their respective territories for the commission of those offences within or outside their territories, including measures to prohibit in their territories illegal activities of persons, groups and organizations that encourage, instigate, organize or engage in the perpetration of acts of taking of hostages;

    b. exchanging information and co-ordinating the taking of administrative and other measures as appropriate to prevent the commission of those offences.

Article 8

1. The State Party in the territory of which the alleged offender is found shall, if it does not extradite him, be obliged, without exception whatsoever and whether or not the offence was committed in its territory, to submit the case to its competent authorities for the purpose of prosecution, through proceedings in accordance with the laws of　　**2.122**

that State. Those authorities shall take their decision in the same manner as in the case of any ordinary offence of a grave nature under the law of that State.

2. Any person regarding whom proceedings are being carried out in connexion with any of the offences set forth in article 1 shall be guaranteed fair treatment at all stages of the proceedings, including enjoyment of all the rights and guarantees provided by the law of the State in the territory of which he is present.

Article 9

2.123   1. A request for the extradition of an alleged offender, pursuant to this Convention, shall not be granted if the requested State Party has substantial grounds for believing:

> a. that the request for extradition for an offence set forth in article 1 has been made for the purpose of prosecuting or punishing a person on account of his race, religion, nationality, ethnic origin or political opinion; or
> b. that the person's position may be prejudiced:
>> i. for any of the reasons mentioned in subparagraph (a) of this paragraph, or
>> ii. for the reason that communication with him by the appropriate authorities of the State entitled to exercise rights of protection cannot be effected.

2. With respect to the offences as defined in this Convention, the provisions of all extradition treaties and arrangements applicable between States Parties are modified as between States Parties to the extent that they are incompatible with this Convention.

Article 10

2.124   1. The offences set forth in article 1 shall be deemed to be included as extraditable offences in any extradition treaty existing between States Parties. States Parties undertake to include such offences as extraditable offences in every extradition treaty to be concluded between them.

2. If a State Party which makes extradition conditional on the existence of a treaty receives a request for extradition from another State Party with which it has no extradition treaty, the requested State may at its option consider this Convention as the legal basis for extradition in respect of the offences set forth in article 1. Extradition shall be subject to the other conditions provided by the law of the requested State.

3. States Parties which do not make extradition conditional on the existence of a treaty shall recognize the offences set forth in article 1 as extraditable offences between themselves subject to the conditions provided by the law of the requested State.

4. The offences set forth in article 1 shall be treated, for the purpose of extradition between States Parties, as if they had been committed not only in the place in which they occurred but also in the territories of the States required to establish their jurisdiction in accordance with paragraph 1 of article 5.

Article 11

2.125   1. States Parties shall afford one another the greatest measure of assistance in connexion with criminal proceedings brought in respect of the offences set forth in article 1, including the supply of all evidence at their disposal necessary for the proceedings.

2. The provisions of paragraph 1 of this article shall not affect obligations concerning mutual judicial assistance embodied in any other treaty.

1997 International Convention for the Suppression of Terrorist Bombings ('Terrorist Bombing Convention')

As mentioned previously, General Assembly 51/20 of 1996 established an Ad **2.126**
Hoc Committee open to all Member States of the UN and charged with negotiating instruments for the suppression of various manifestations of terrorism. The first result of the Committee's work was the International Convention for the Suppression of Terrorist Bombings (1997).

Criminalization provisions

Article 2

1. Any person commits an offence within the meaning of this Convention if that person **2.127**
unlawfully and intentionally delivers, places, discharges or detonates an explosive or other lethal device in, into or against a place of public use, a State or government facility, a public transportation system or an infrastructure facility:

    a. With the intent to cause death or serious bodily injury; or
    b. With the intent to cause extensive destruction of such a place, facility or system, where such destruction results in or is likely to result in major economic loss.

2. Any person also commits an offence if that person attempts to commit an offence as set forth in paragraph 1 of the present article.

3. Any person also commits an offence if that person:

    a. Participates as an accomplice in an offence as set forth in paragraph 1 or 2 of the present article; or
    b. Organizes or directs others to commit an offence as set forth in paragraph 1 or 2 of the present article; or
    c. In any other way contributes to the commission of one or more offences as set forth in paragraph 1 or 2 of the present article by a group of persons acting with a common purpose; such contribution shall be intentional and either be made with the aim of furthering the general criminal activity or purpose of the group or be made in the knowledge of the intention of the group to commit the offence or offences concerned.

Article 3

This Convention shall not apply where the offence is committed within a single State, **2.128**
the alleged offender and the victims are nationals of that State, the alleged offender is found in the territory of that State and no other State has a basis under article 6, paragraph 1 or paragraph 2, of this Convention to exercise jurisdiction, except that the provisions of articles 10 to 15 shall, as appropriate, apply in those cases.

Article 4

Each State Party shall adopt such measures as may be necessary: **2.129**

    a. To establish as criminal offences under its domestic law the offences set forth in article 2 of this Convention;
    b. To make those offences punishable by appropriate penalties which take into account the grave nature of those offences.

Article 5

2.130   Each State Party shall adopt such measures as may be necessary, including, where appropriate, domestic legislation, to ensure that criminal acts within the scope of this Convention, in particular where they are intended or calculated to provoke a state of terror in the general public or in a group of persons or particular persons, are under no circumstances justifiable by considerations of a political, philosophical, ideological, racial, ethnic, religious or other similar nature and are punished by penalties consistent with their grave nature.

Jurisdiction provisions

Article 6

2.131   1. Each State Party shall take such measures as may be necessary to establish its jurisdiction over the offences set forth in article 2 when:

   a. The offence is committed in the territory of that State; or
   b. The offence is committed on board a vessel flying the flag of that State or an aircraft which is registered under the laws of that State at the time the offence is committed; or
   c. The offence is committed by a national of that State.

2. A State Party may also establish its jurisdiction over any such offence when:

   a. The offence is committed against a national of that State; or
   b. The offence is committed against a State or government facility of that State abroad, including an embassy or other diplomatic or consular premises of that State; or
   c. The offence is committed by a stateless person who has his or her habitual residence in the territory of that State; or
   d. The offence is committed in an attempt to compel that State to do or abstain from doing any act; or
   e. The offence is committed on board an aircraft which is operated by the Government of that State.

3. Upon ratifying, accepting, approving or acceding to this Convention, each State Party shall notify the Secretary-General of the United Nations of the jurisdiction it has established under its domestic law in accordance with paragraph 2 of the present article. Should any change take place, the State Party concerned shall immediately notify the Secretary-General.

4. Each State Party shall likewise take such measures as may be necessary to establish its jurisdiction over the offences set forth in article 2 in cases where the alleged offender is present in its territory and it does not extradite that person to any of the States Parties which have established their jurisdiction in accordance with paragraph 1 or 2 of the present article.

5. This Convention does not exclude the exercise of any criminal jurisdiction established by a State Party in accordance with its domestic law.

Procedural and due process provisions

Article 7

2.132   1. Upon receiving information that a person who has committed or who is alleged to have committed an offence as set forth in article 2 may be present in its territory, the State Party concerned shall take such measures as may be necessary under its domestic law to investigate the facts contained in the information.

2. Upon being satisfied that the circumstances so warrant, the State Party in whose territory the offender or alleged offender is present shall take the appropriate measures under its domestic law so as to ensure that person's presence for the purpose of prosecution or extradition.

3. Any person regarding whom the measures referred to in paragraph 2 of the present article are being taken shall be entitled to:

    a. Communicate without delay with the nearest appropriate representative of the State of which that person is a national or which is otherwise entitled to protect that person's rights or, if that person is a stateless person, the State in the territory of which that person habitually resides;

    b. Be visited by a representative of that State;

    c. Be informed of that person's rights under subparagraphs (a) and (b).

4. The rights referred to in paragraph 3 of the present article shall be exercised in conformity with the laws and regulations of the State in the territory of which the offender or alleged offender is present, subject to the provision that the said laws and regulations must enable full effect to be given to the purposes for which the rights accorded under paragraph 3 are intended.

5. The provisions of paragraphs 3 and 4 of the present article shall be without prejudice to the right of any State Party having a claim to jurisdiction in accordance with article 6, subparagraph 1 (c) or 2 (c), to invite the International Committee of the Red Cross to communicate with and visit the alleged offender.

6. When a State Party, pursuant to the present article, has taken a person into custody, it shall immediately notify, directly or through the Secretary-General of the United Nations, the States Parties which have established jurisdiction in accordance with article 6, paragraphs 1 and 2, and, if it considers it advisable, any other interested States Parties, of the fact that that person is in custody and of the circumstances which warrant that person's detention. The State which makes the investigation contemplated in paragraph 1 of the present article shall promptly inform the said States Parties of its findings and shall indicate whether it intends to exercise jurisdiction.

Article 14

Any person who is taken into custody or regarding whom any other measures are taken   **2.133** or proceedings are carried out pursuant to this Convention shall be guaranteed fair treatment, including enjoyment of all rights and guarantees in conformity with the law of the State in the territory of which that person is present and applicable provisions of international law, including international law of human rights.

The *aut dedere aut judicare principle and international cooperation elements*

Article 8

1. The State Party in the territory of which the alleged offender is present shall, in cases   **2.134** to which article 6 applies, if it does not extradite that person, be obliged, without exception whatsoever and whether or not the offence was committed in its territory, to submit the case without undue delay to its competent authorities for the purpose of prosecution, through proceedings in accordance with the laws of that State. Those authorities shall take their decision in the same manner as in the case of any other offence of a grave nature under the law of that State.

2. Whenever a State Party is permitted under its domestic law to extradite or otherwise surrender one of its nationals only upon the condition that the person will be returned to

that State to serve the sentence imposed as a result of the trial or proceeding for which the extradition or surrender of the person was sought, and this State and the State seeking the extradition of the person agree with this option and other terms they may deem appropriate, such a conditional extradition or surrender shall be sufficient to discharge the obligation set forth in paragraph 1 of the present article.

Article 9

2.135 1. The offences set forth in article 2 shall be deemed to be included as extraditable offences in any extradition treaty existing between any of the States Parties before the entry into force of this Convention. States Parties undertake to include such offences as extraditable offences in every extradition treaty to be subsequently concluded between them.

2. When a State Party which makes extradition conditional on the existence of a treaty receives a request for extradition from another State Party with which it has no extradition treaty, the requested State Party may, at its option, consider this Convention as a legal basis for extradition in respect of the offences set forth in article 2. Extradition shall be subject to the other conditions provided by the law of the requested State.

3. States Parties which do not make extradition conditional on the existence of a treaty shall recognize the offences set forth in article 2 as extraditable offences between themselves, subject to the conditions provided by the law of the requested State.

4. If necessary, the offences set forth in article 2 shall be treated, for the purposes of extradition between States Parties, as if they had been committed not only in the place in which they occurred but also in the territory of the States that have established jurisdiction in accordance with article 6, paragraphs 1 and 2.

5. The provisions of all extradition treaties and arrangements between States Parties with regard to offences set forth in article 2 shall be deemed to be modified as between State Parties to the extent that they are incompatible with this Convention.

Article 10

2.136 1. States Parties shall afford one another the greatest measure of assistance in connection with investigations or criminal or extradition proceedings brought in respect of the offences set forth in article 2, including assistance in obtaining evidence at their disposal necessary for the proceedings.

2. States Parties shall carry out their obligations under paragraph 1 of the present article in conformity with any treaties or other arrangements on mutual legal assistance that may exist between them. In the absence of such treaties or arrangements, States Parties shall afford one another assistance in accordance with their domestic law.

Article 11

2.137 None of the offences set forth in article 2 shall be regarded, for the purposes of extradition or mutual legal assistance, as a political offence or as an offence connected with a political offence or as an offence inspired by political motives. Accordingly, a request for extradition or for mutual legal assistance based on such an offence may not be refused on the sole ground that it concerns a political offence or an offence connected with a political offence or an offence inspired by political motives.

Article 12

2.138 Nothing in this Convention shall be interpreted as imposing an obligation to extradite or to afford mutual legal assistance, if the requested State Party has substantial grounds for believing that the request for extradition for offences set forth in article 2 or for mutual legal assistance with respect to such offences has been made for the purpose of prosecuting or punishing a person on account of that person's race, religion, nationality, ethnic origin or political opinion or that compliance with the request would cause prejudice to that person's position for any of these reasons.

Article 13

1. A person who is being detained or is serving a sentence in the territory of one State Party whose presence in another State Party is requested for purposes of testimony, identification or otherwise providing assistance in obtaining evidence for the investigation or prosecution of offences under this Convention may be transferred if the following conditions are met:

    a. The person freely gives his or her informed consent; and
    b. The competent authorities of both States agree, subject to such conditions as those States may deem appropriate.

2. For the purposes of the present article:

    a. The State to which the person is transferred shall have the authority and obligation to keep the person transferred in custody, unless otherwise requested or authorized by the State from which the person was transferred;
    b. The State to which the person is transferred shall without delay implement its obligation to return the person to the custody of the State from which the person was transferred as agreed beforehand, or as otherwise agreed, by the competent authorities of both States;
    c. The State to which the person is transferred shall not require the State from which the person was transferred to initiate extradition proceedings for the return of the person;
    d. The person transferred shall receive credit for service of the sentence being served in the State from which he was transferred for time spent in the custody of the State to which he was transferred.

3. Unless the State Party from which a person is to be transferred in accordance with the present article so agrees, that person, whatever his or her nationality, shall not be prosecuted or detained or subjected to any other restriction of his or her personal liberty in the territory of the State to which that person is transferred in respect of acts or convictions anterior to his or her departure from the territory of the State from which such person was transferred.

2.139

Article 15

States Parties shall cooperate in the prevention of the offences set forth in article 2, particularly:

2.140

    a. By taking all practicable measures, including, if necessary, adapting their domestic legislation, to prevent and counter preparations in their respective territories for the commission of those offences within or outside their territories, including measures to prohibit in their territories illegal activities of persons, groups and organizations that encourage, instigate, organize, knowingly finance or engage in the perpetration of offences as set forth in article 2;
    b. By exchanging accurate and verified information in accordance with their national law, and coordinating administrative and other measures taken as appropriate to prevent the commission of offences as set forth in article 2;

c. Where appropriate, through research and development regarding methods of detection of explosives and other harmful substances that can cause death or bodily injury, consultations on the development of standards for marking explosives in order to identify their origin in post-blast investigations, exchange of information on preventive measures, cooperation and transfer of technology, equipment and related materials.

1999 International Convention for the Suppression of the Financing of Terrorism ('Financing Convention')

2.141   The second result of the Ad Hoc Committee's work was the 1999 International Convention for the Suppression of the Financing of Terrorism. Convention Article 2-3 is part of a highly important advance in the use of anti-terrorism measures to prevent rather than merely to react to terrorist violence. Although the Financing Convention parallels the Terrorist Bombing Convention in its structure and language, it achieves a strategic breakthrough against the planning and preparation that precedes almost every terrorist attack. It accomplishes this result by two innovations. Instead of prohibiting a particular form of violence associated with terrorism, the Financing Convention criminalizes the non-violent logistical preparation and support that make significant terrorist groups and terrorist operations possible. Moreover, Article 2-3 eliminates any ambiguity by expressly providing that the prohibited provision or collection of funds need not result in a violent act specified in paragraph 1 of the Convention to be punishable. Meeting all of the international standards applicable to the financing of terrorism can be fully achieved only by legislation establishing the Convention offence, and not by reliance upon theories of complicity, conspiracy, money laundering, or other offences not specific to the financing of terrorism.

Criminalization provisions

Article 2

2.142   1. Any person commits an offence within the meaning of this Convention if that person by any means, directly or indirectly, unlawfully and wilfully, provides or collects funds with the intention that they should be used or in the knowledge that they are to be used, in full or in part, in order to carry out:

(a) An act which constitutes an offence within the scope of and as defined in one of the treaties listed in the annex; or

(b) Any other act intended to cause death or serious bodily injury to a civilian, or to any other person not taking an active part in the hostilities in a situation of armed conflict, when the purpose of such act, by its nature or context, is to intimidate a population, or to compel a Government or an international organization to do or to abstain from doing any act.

2. (a) On depositing its instrument of ratification, acceptance, approval or accession, a State Party which is not a party to a treaty listed in the annex may declare that, in the application of this Convention to the State Party, the treaty shall be deemed not to be included in the annex referred to in paragraph 1, subparagraph (a). The declaration shall

cease to have effect as soon as the treaty enters into force for the State Party, which shall notify the depositary of this fact;

(b) When a State Party ceases to be a party to a treaty listed in the annex, it may make a declaration as provided for in this article, with respect to that treaty.

3. For an act to constitute an offence set forth in paragraph 1, it shall not be necessary that the funds were actually used to carry out an offence referred to in paragraph 1, subparagraph (a) or (b).

4. Any person also commits an offence if that person attempts to commit an offence as set forth in paragraph 1 of this article.

5. Any person also commits an offence if that person:

(a) Participates as an accomplice in an offence as set forth in paragraph 1 or 4 of this article;

(b) Organizes or directs others to commit an offence as set forth in paragraph 1 or 4 of this article;

(c) Contributes to the commission of one or more offences as set forth in paragraph 1 or 4 of this article by a group of persons acting with a common purpose. Such contribution shall be intentional and shall either:

(i) Be made with the aim of furthering the criminal activity or criminal purpose of the group, where such activity or purpose involves the commission of an offence as set forth in paragraph 1 of this article; or

(ii) Be made in the knowledge of the intention of the group to commit an offence as set forth in paragraph 1 of this article.

Article 3

This Convention shall not apply where the offence is committed within a single State, the alleged offender is a national of that State and is present in the territory of that State and no other State has a basis under article 7, paragraph 1 or 2, to exercise jurisdiction, except that the provisions of articles 12 to 18 shall, as appropriate, apply in those cases. **2.143**

Article 4

Each State Party shall adopt such measures as may be necessary: **2.144**

(a) To establish as criminal offences under its domestic law the offences as set forth in article 2;

(b) To make those offences punishable by appropriate penalties which take into account the grave nature of the offences.

Article 5

1. Each State Party, in accordance with its domestic legal principles, shall take the necessary measures to enable a legal entity located in its territory or organized under its laws to be held liable when a person responsible for the management or control of that legal entity has, in that capacity, committed an offence as set forth in article 2. Such liability may be criminal, civil or administrative. **2.145**

2. Such liability is incurred without prejudice to the criminal liability of individuals who have committed the offences.

3. Each State Party shall ensure, in particular, that legal entities liable in accordance with paragraph 1 above are subject to effective, proportionate and dissuasive criminal, civil or administrative sanctions. Such sanctions may include monetary sanctions.

Article 6

2.146   Each State Party shall adopt such measures as may be necessary, including, where appropriate, domestic legislation, to ensure that criminal acts within the scope of this Convention are under no circumstances justifiable by considerations of a political, philosophical, ideological, racial, ethnic, religious or other similar nature.

Jurisdiction provisions

Article 7

2.147   1. Each State Party shall take such measures as may be necessary to establish its jurisdiction over the offences set forth in article 2 when:

(a) The offence is committed in the territory of that State;

(b) The offence is committed on board a vessel flying the flag of that State or an aircraft registered under the laws of that State at the time the offence is committed;

(c) The offence is committed by a national of that State.

2. A State Party may also establish its jurisdiction over any such offence when:

(a) The offence was directed towards or resulted in the carrying out of an offence referred to in article 2, paragraph 1, subparagraph (a) or (b), in the territory of or against a national of that State;

(b) The offence was directed towards or resulted in the carrying out of an offence referred to in article 2, paragraph 1, subparagraph (a) or (b), against a State or government facility of that State abroad, including diplomatic or consular premises of that State;

(c) The offence was directed towards or resulted in an offence referred to in article 2, paragraph 1, subparagraph (a) or (b), committed in an attempt to compel that State to do or abstain from doing any act;

(d) The offence is committed by a stateless person who has his or her habitual residence in the territory of that State;

(e) The offence is committed on board an aircraft which is operated by the Government of that State.

3. Upon ratifying, accepting, approving or acceding to this Convention, each State Party shall notify the Secretary-General of the United Nations of the jurisdiction it has established in accordance with paragraph 2. Should any change take place, the State Party concerned shall immediately notify the Secretary-General.

4. Each State Party shall likewise take such measures as may be necessary to establish its jurisdiction over the offences set forth in article 2 in cases where the alleged offender is present in its territory and it does not extradite that person to any of the States Parties that have established their jurisdiction in accordance with paragraphs 1 or 2.

5. When more than one State Party claims jurisdiction over the offences set forth in article 2, the relevant States Parties shall strive to coordinate their actions appropriately, in particular concerning the conditions for prosecution and the modalities for mutual legal assistance.

6. Without prejudice to the norms of general international law, this Convention does not exclude the exercise of any criminal jurisdiction established by a State Party in accordance with its domestic law.

Procedural and due process provisions

Article 8

1. Each State Party shall take appropriate measures, in accordance with its domestic legal principles, for the identification, detection and freezing or seizure of any funds used or allocated for the purpose of committing the offences set forth in article 2 as well as the proceeds derived from such offences, for purposes of possible forfeiture.

2. Each State Party shall take appropriate measures, in accordance with its domestic legal principles, for the forfeiture of funds used or allocated for the purpose of committing the offences set forth in article 2 and the proceeds derived from such offences.

3. Each State Party concerned may give consideration to concluding agreements on the sharing with other States Parties, on a regular or case-by-case basis, of the funds derived from the forfeitures referred to in this article.

4. Each State Party shall consider establishing mechanisms whereby the funds derived from the forfeitures referred to in this article are utilized to compensate the victims of offences referred to in article 2, paragraph 1, subparagraph (a) or (b), or their families.

5. The provisions of this article shall be implemented without prejudice to the rights of third parties acting in good faith.

2.148

Article 9

1. Upon receiving information that a person who has committed or who is alleged to have committed an offence set forth in article 2 may be present in its territory, the State Party concerned shall take such measures as may be necessary under its domestic law to investigate the facts contained in the information.

2. Upon being satisfied that the circumstances so warrant, the State Party in whose territory the offender or alleged offender is present shall take the appropriate measures under its domestic law so as to ensure that person's presence for the purpose of prosecution or extradition.

3. Any person regarding whom the measures referred to in paragraph 2 are being taken shall be entitled:

    (a) To communicate without delay with the nearest appropriate representative of the State of which that person is a national or which is otherwise entitled to protect that person's rights or, if that person is a stateless person, the State in the territory of which that person habitually resides;

    (b) To be visited by a representative of that State;

    (c) To be informed of that person's rights under subparagraphs (a) and (b).

4. The rights referred to in paragraph 3 shall be exercised in conformity with the laws and regulations of the State in the territory of which the offender or alleged offender is present, subject to the provision that the said laws and regulations must enable full effect to be given to the purposes for which the rights accorded under paragraph 3 are intended.

5. The provisions of paragraphs 3 and 4 shall be without prejudice to the right of any State Party having a claim to jurisdiction in accordance with article 7, paragraph 1, subparagraph (b), or paragraph 2, subparagraph (b), to invite the International Committee of the Red Cross to communicate with and visit the alleged offender.

2.149

6. When a State Party, pursuant to the present article, has taken a person into custody, it shall immediately notify, directly or through the Secretary-General of the United Nations, the States Parties which have established jurisdiction in accordance with article 7, paragraph 1 or 2, and, if it considers it advisable, any other interested States Parties, of the fact that such person is in custody and of the circumstances which warrant that person's detention. The State which makes the investigation contemplated in paragraph 1 shall promptly inform the said States Parties of its findings and shall indicate whether it intends to exercise jurisdiction.

Article 17

2.150   Any person who is taken into custody or regarding whom any other measures are taken or proceedings are carried out pursuant to this Convention shall be guaranteed fair treatment, including enjoyment of all rights and guarantees in conformity with the law of the State in the territory of which that person is present and applicable provisions of international law, including international human rights law.

The aut dedere aut judicare *principle and international cooperation elements*

Article 10

2.151   1. The State Party in the territory of which the alleged offender is present shall, in cases to which article 7 applies, if it does not extradite that person, be obliged, without exception whatsoever and whether or not the offence was committed in its territory, to submit the case without undue delay to its competent authorities for the purpose of prosecution, through proceedings in accordance with the laws of that State. Those authorities shall take their decision in the same manner as in the case of any other offence of a grave nature under the law of that State.

2. Whenever a State Party is permitted under its domestic law to extradite or otherwise surrender one of its nationals only upon the condition that the person will be returned to that State to serve the sentence imposed as a result of the trial or proceeding for which the extradition or surrender of the person was sought, and this State and the State seeking the extradition of the person agree with this option and other terms they may deem appropriate, such a conditional extradition or surrender shall be sufficient to discharge the obligation set forth in paragraph 1.

Article 11

2.152   1. The offences set forth in article 2 shall be deemed to be included as extraditable offences in any extradition treaty existing between any of the States Parties before the entry into force of this Convention. States Parties undertake to include such offences as extraditable offences in every extradition treaty to be subsequently concluded between them.

2. When a State Party which makes extradition conditional on the existence of a treaty receives a request for extradition from another State Party with which it has no extradition treaty, the requested State Party may, at its option, consider this Convention as a legal basis for extradition in respect of the offences set forth in article 2. Extradition shall be subject to the other conditions provided by the law of the requested State.

3. States Parties which do not make extradition conditional on the existence of a treaty shall recognize the offences set forth in article 2 as extraditable offences between themselves, subject to the conditions provided by the law of the requested State.

4. If necessary, the offences set forth in article 2 shall be treated, for the purposes of extradition between States Parties, as if they had been committed not only in the place in which they occurred but also in the territory of the States that have established jurisdiction in accordance with article 7, paragraphs 1 and 2.

5. The provisions of all extradition treaties and arrangements between States Parties with regard to offences set forth in article 2 shall be deemed to be modified as between States Parties to the extent that they are incompatible with this Convention.

Article 12

1. States Parties shall afford one another the greatest measure of assistance in connection with criminal investigations or criminal or extradition proceedings in respect of the offences set forth in article 2, including assistance in obtaining evidence in their possession necessary for the proceedings.

2.153

2. States Parties may not refuse a request for mutual legal assistance on the ground of bank secrecy.

3. The requesting Party shall not transmit or use information or evidence furnished by the requested Party for investigations, prosecutions or proceedings other than those stated in the request without the prior consent of the requested Party.

4. Each State Party may give consideration to establishing mechanisms to share with other States Parties information or evidence needed to establish criminal, civil or administrative liability pursuant to article 5.

5. States Parties shall carry out their obligations under paragraphs 1 and 2 in conformity with any treaties or other arrangements on mutual legal assistance or information exchange that may exist between them. In the absence of such treaties or arrangements, States Parties shall afford one another assistance in accordance with their domestic law.

Article 13

None of the offences set forth in article 2 shall be regarded, for the purposes of extradition or mutual legal assistance, as a fiscal offence. Accordingly, States Parties may not refuse a request for extradition or for mutual legal assistance on the sole ground that it concerns a fiscal offence.

2.154

Article 14

None of the offences set forth in article 2 shall be regarded for the purposes of extradition or mutual legal assistance as a political offence or as an offence connected with a political offence or as an offence inspired by political motives. Accordingly, a request for extradition or for mutual legal assistance based on such an offence may not be refused on the sole ground that it concerns a political offence or an offence connected with a political offence or an offence inspired by political motives.

2.155

Article 15

Nothing in this Convention shall be interpreted as imposing an obligation to extradite or to afford mutual legal assistance, if the requested State Party has substantial grounds for believing that the request for extradition for offences set forth in article 2 or for mutual legal assistance with respect to such offences has been made for the purpose of prosecuting or punishing a person on account of that person's race, religion, nationality, ethnic origin or political opinion or that compliance with the request would cause prejudice to that person's position for any of these reasons.

2.156

Article 16

2.157   1. A person who is being detained or is serving a sentence in the territory of one State Party whose presence in another State Party is requested for purposes of identification, testimony or otherwise providing assistance in obtaining evidence for the investigation or prosecution of offences set forth in article 2 may be transferred if the following conditions are met:

(a) The person freely gives his or her informed consent;

(b) The competent authorities of both States agree, subject to such conditions as those States may deem appropriate.

2. For the purposes of the present article:

(a) The State to which the person is transferred shall have the authority and obligation to keep the person transferred in custody, unless otherwise requested or authorized by the State from which the person was transferred;

(b) The State to which the person is transferred shall without delay implement its obligation to return the person to the custody of the State from which the person was transferred as agreed beforehand, or as otherwise agreed, by the competent authorities of both States;

(c) The State to which the person is transferred shall not require the State from which the person was transferred to initiate extradition proceedings for the return of the person;

(d) The person transferred shall receive credit for service of the sentence being served in the State from which he or she was transferred for time spent in the custody of the State to which he or she was transferred.

3. Unless the State Party from which a person is to be transferred in accordance with the present article so agrees, that person, whatever his or her nationality, shall not be prosecuted or detained or subjected to any other restriction of his or her personal liberty in the territory of the State to which that person is transferred in respect of acts or convictions anterior to his or her departure from the territory of the State from which such person was transferred.

2005 International Convention for the Suppression of Acts of Nuclear Terrorism ('Nuclear Terrorism Convention')

2.158   The Nuclear Terrorism Convention was also a product of the work of the Ad Hoc Committee. It defines as offences: (a) the possession or use of radioactive material or a nuclear explosive or radiation dispersal device with the intent to cause death or serious bodily injury or substantial damage to property or the environment; (b) the use of radioactive material or a device, or the use of or damage to a nuclear facility which risks the release of radioactive material with the intent to cause death, or serious injury, or substantial damage to property or to the environment, or with the intent to compel a natural or legal person, an international organization, or a State to do, or refrain from doing any act. These offences focus more explicitly on nuclear devices specifically constructed to do harm than do those in the 1979 Convention on the Physical Protection of Nuclear Materials, but the IAEA agreements also contain prohibitions against harmful use, theft, robbery, embezzlement, or other illegal means of obtaining such materials, and to related threats. Both conventions define their terminology, and these definitions must be reviewed carefully by experts in the legislative drafting process. For example, a 'nuclear facility' is protected by both agreements, but the term is defined differently in the two instruments.

Criminalization provisions

Article 2

1. Any person commits an offence within the meaning of this Convention if that person unlawfully and intentionally: **2.159**

    (a) Possesses radioactive material or makes or possesses a device:

        (i) With the intent to cause death or serious bodily injury; or

        (ii) With the intent to cause substantial damage to property or to the environment;

    (b) Uses in any way radioactive material or a device, or uses or damages a nuclear facility in a manner which releases or risks the release of radioactive material:

        (i) With the intent to cause death or serious bodily injury; or

        (ii) With the intent to cause substantial damage to property or to the environment; or

        (iii) With the intent to compel a natural or legal person, an international organization or a State to do or refrain from doing an act.

2. Any person also commits an offence if that person:

    (a) Threatens, under circumstances which indicate the credibility of the threat, to commit an offence as set forth in paragraph 1(b) of the present article; or

    (b) Demands unlawfully and intentionally radioactive material, a device or a nuclear facility by threat, under circumstances which indicate the credibility of the threat, or by use of force.

3. Any person also commits an offence if that person attempts to commit an offence as set forth in paragraph 1 of the present article.

4. Any person also commits an offence if that person:

    (a) Participates as an accomplice in an offence as set forth in paragraph 1, 2 or 3 of the present article; or

    (b) Organizes or directs others to commit an offence as set forth in paragraph 1, 2 or 3 of the present article; or

    (c) In any other way contributes to the commission of one or more offences as set forth in paragraph 1, 2 or 3 of the present article by a group of persons acting with a common purpose; such contribution shall be intentional and either be made with the aim of furthering the general criminal activity or purpose of the group or be made in the knowledge of the intention of the group to commit the offence or offences concerned.

Article 3

This Convention shall not apply where the offence is committed within a single State, the alleged offender and the victims are nationals of that State, the alleged offender is found in the territory of that State and no other State has a basis under article 9, paragraph 1 or 2, to exercise jurisdiction, except that the provisions of articles 7, 12, 14, 15, 16 and 17 shall, as appropriate, apply in those cases.   **2.160**

Article 4

2.161   1. Nothing in this Convention shall affect other rights, obligations and responsibilities of States and individuals under international law, in particular the purposes and principles of the Charter of the United Nations and international humanitarian law.

2. The activities of armed forces during an armed conflict, as those terms are understood under international humanitarian law, which are governed by that law are not governed by this Convention, and the activities undertaken by military forces of a State in the exercise of their official duties, inasmuch as they are governed by other rules of international law, are not governed by this Convention.

3. The provisions of paragraph 2 of the present article shall not be interpreted as condoning or making lawful otherwise unlawful acts, or precluding prosecution under other laws.

4. This Convention does not address, nor can it be interpreted as addressing, in any way, the issue of the legality of the use or threat of use of nuclear weapons by States.

Article 5

2.162   Each State Party shall adopt such measures as may be necessary:

   (a) To establish as criminal offences under its national law the offences set forth in article 2;
   (b) To make those offences punishable by appropriate penalties which take into account the grave nature of these offences.

Article 6

2.163   Each State Party shall adopt such measures as may be necessary, including, where appropriate, domestic legislation, to ensure that criminal acts within the scope of this Convention, in particular where they are intended or calculated to provoke a state of terror in the general public or in a group of persons or particular persons, are under no circumstances justifiable by considerations of a political, philosophical, ideological, racial, ethnic, religious or other similar nature and are punished by penalties consistent with their grave nature.

Article 11

2.164   1. The State Party in the territory of which the alleged offender is present shall, in cases to which article 9 applies, if it does not extradite that person, be obliged, without exception whatsoever and whether or not the offence was committed in its territory, to submit the case without undue delay to its competent authorities for the purpose of prosecution, through proceedings in accordance with the laws of that State. Those authorities shall take their decision in the same manner as in the case of any other offence of a grave nature under the law of that State.

2. Whenever a State Party is permitted under its national law to extradite or otherwise surrender one of its nationals only upon the condition that the person will be returned to that State to serve the sentence imposed as a result of the trial or proceeding for which the extradition or surrender of the person was sought, and this State and the State seeking the extradition of the person agree with this option and other terms they may deem appropriate, such a conditional extradition or surrender shall be sufficient to discharge the obligation set forth in paragraph 1 of the present article.

Jurisdiction provisions

Article 9

1. Each State Party shall take such measures as may be necessary to establish its jurisdiction over the offences set forth in article 2 when: **2.165**

   (a) The offence is committed in the territory of that State; or

   (b) The offence is committed on board a vessel flying the flag of that State or an aircraft which is registered under the laws of that State at the time the offence is committed; or

   (c) The offence is committed by a national of that State.

2. A State Party may also establish its jurisdiction over any such offence when:

   (a) The offence is committed against a national of that State; or

   (b) The offence is committed against a State or government facility of that State abroad, including an embassy or other diplomatic or consular premises of that State; or

   (c) The offence is committed by a stateless person who has his or her habitual residence in the territory of that State; or

   (d) The offence is committed in an attempt to compel that State to do or abstain from doing any act; or

   (e) The offence is committed on board an aircraft which is operated by the Government of that State.

3. Upon ratifying, accepting, approving or acceding to this Convention, each State Party shall notify the Secretary-General of the United Nations of the jurisdiction it has established under its national law in accordance with paragraph 2 of the present article. Should any change take place, the State Party concerned shall immediately notify the Secretary-General.

4. Each State Party shall likewise take such measures as may be necessary to establish its jurisdiction over the offences set forth in article 2 in cases where the alleged offender is present in its territory and it does not extradite that person to any of the States Parties which have established their jurisdiction in accordance with paragraph 1 or 2 of the present article.

5. This Convention does not exclude the exercise of any criminal jurisdiction established by a State Party in accordance with its national law.

Procedural and due process provisions

Article 10

1. Upon receiving information that an offence set forth in article 2 has been committed   **2.166** or is being committed in the territory of a State Party or that a person who has committed or who is alleged to have committed such an offence may be present in its territory, the State Party concerned shall take such measures as may be necessary under its national law to investigate the facts contained in the information.

2. Upon being satisfied that the circumstances so warrant, the State Party in whose territory the offender or alleged offender is present shall take the appropriate measures under its national law so as to ensure that person's presence for the purpose of prosecution or extradition.

3. Any person regarding whom the measures referred to in paragraph 2 of the present article are being taken shall be entitled:

   (a) To communicate without delay with the nearest appropriate representative of the State of which that person is a national or which is otherwise entitled to protect that person's rights or, if that person is a stateless person, the State in the territory of which that person habitually resides;

   (b) To be visited by a representative of that State;

   (c) To be informed of that person's rights under subparagraphs (*a*) and (*b*).

4. The rights referred to in paragraph 3 of the present article shall be exercised in conformity with the laws and regulations of the State in the territory of which the offender or alleged offender is present, subject to the provision that the said laws and regulations must enable full effect to be given to the purposes for which the rights accorded under paragraph 3 are intended.

5. The provisions of paragraphs 3 and 4 of the present article shall be without prejudice to the right of any State Party having a claim to jurisdiction in accordance with article 9, paragraph 1 (c) or 2 (c), to invite the International Committee of the Red Cross to communicate with and visit the alleged offender.

6. When a State Party, pursuant to the present article, has taken a person into custody, it shall immediately notify, directly or through the Secretary-General of the United Nations, the States Parties which have established jurisdiction in accordance with article 9, paragraphs 1 and 2, and, if it considers it advisable, any other interested States Parties, of the fact that that person is in custody and of the circumstances which warrant that person's detention. The State which makes the investigation contemplated in paragraph 1 of the present article shall promptly inform the said States Parties of its findings and shall indicate whether it intends to exercise jurisdiction.

Article 12

2.167 Any person who is taken into custody or regarding whom any other measures are taken or proceedings are carried out pursuant to this Convention shall be guaranteed fair treatment, including enjoyment of all rights and guarantees in conformity with the law of the State in the territory of which that person is present and applicable provisions of international law, including international law of human rights.

The aut dedere aut judicare *principle and international cooperation elements*

Article 7

2.168 1. States Parties shall cooperate by:

   (a) Taking all practicable measures, including, if necessary, adapting their national law, to prevent and counter preparations in their respective territories for the commission within or outside their territories of the offences set forth in article 2, including measures to prohibit in their territories illegal activities of persons, groups and organizations that encourage, instigate, organize, knowingly finance or knowingly provide technical assistance or information or engage in the perpetration of those offences;

   (b) Exchanging accurate and verified information in accordance with their national law and in the manner and subject to the conditions specified herein, and coordinating administrative and other measures taken as appropriate to detect, prevent, suppress and investigate the offences set forth in article 2 and also in order to institute criminal proceedings against persons alleged to have committed those crimes. In particular, a State Party shall take appropriate measures in order to inform without delay the other States referred to in article 9 in respect of the commission of the offences set forth in article 2 as well as preparations to commit such offences about which it has learned, and also to inform, where appropriate, international organizations.

2. States Parties shall take appropriate measures consistent with their national law to protect the confidentiality of any information which they receive in confidence by virtue of the provisions of this Convention from another State Party or through participation in an activity carried out for the implementation of this Convention. If States Parties provide information to international organizations in confidence, steps shall be taken to ensure that the confidentiality of such information is protected.

3. States Parties shall not be required by this Convention to provide any information which they are not permitted to communicate pursuant to national law or which would jeopardize the security of the State concerned or the physical protection of nuclear material.

4. States Parties shall inform the Secretary-General of the United Nations of their competent authorities and liaison points responsible for sending and receiving the information referred to in the present article. The Secretary-General of the United Nations shall communicate such information regarding competent authorities and liaison points to all States Parties and the International Atomic Energy Agency. Such authorities and liaison points must be accessible on a continuous basis.

Article 8

For purposes of preventing offences under this Convention, States Parties shall make every effort to adopt appropriate measures to ensure the protection of radioactive material, taking into account relevant recommendations and functions of the International Atomic Energy Agency.   **2.169**

Article 13

1. The offences set forth in article 2 shall be deemed to be included as extraditable offences in any extradition treaty existing between any of the States Parties before the entry into force of this Convention. States Parties undertake to include such offences as extraditable offences in every extradition treaty to be subsequently concluded between them.   **2.170**

2. When a State Party which makes extradition conditional on the existence of a treaty receives a request for extradition from another State Party with which it has no extradition treaty, the requested State Party may, at its option, consider this Convention as a legal basis for extradition in respect of the offences set forth in article 2. Extradition shall be subject to the other conditions provided by the law of the requested State.

3. States Parties which do not make extradition conditional on the existence of a treaty shall recognize the offences set forth in article 2 as extraditable offences between themselves, subject to the conditions provided by the law of the requested State.

4. If necessary, the offences set forth in article 2 shall be treated, for the purposes of extradition between States Parties, as if they had been committed not only in the place in which they occurred but also in the territory of the States that have established jurisdiction in accordance with article 9, paragraphs 1 and 2.

5. The provisions of all extradition treaties and arrangements between States Parties with regard to offences set forth in article 2 shall be deemed to be modified as between States Parties to the extent that they are incompatible with this Convention.

Article 14

2.171 1. States Parties shall afford one another the greatest measure of assistance in connection with investigations or criminal or extradition proceedings brought in respect of the offences set forth in article 2, including assistance in obtaining evidence at their disposal necessary for the proceedings.

2. States Parties shall carry out their obligations under paragraph 1 of the present article in conformity with any treaties or other arrangements on mutual legal assistance that may exist between them. In the absence of such treaties or arrangements, States Parties shall afford one another assistance in accordance with their national law.

Article 15

2.172 None of the offences set forth in article 2 shall be regarded, for the purposes of extradition or mutual legal assistance, as a political offence or as an offence connected with a political offence or as an offence inspired by political motives. Accordingly, a request for extradition or for mutual legal assistance based on such an offence may not be refused on the sole ground that it concerns a political offence or an offence connected with a political offence or an offence inspired by political motives.

Article 16

2.173 Nothing in this Convention shall be interpreted as imposing an obligation to extradite or to afford mutual legal assistance if the requested State Party has substantial grounds for believing that the request for extradition for offences set forth in article 2 or for mutual legal assistance with respect to such offences has been made for the purpose of prosecuting or punishing a person on account of that person's race, religion, nationality, ethnic origin or political opinion or that compliance with the request would cause prejudice to that person's position for any of these reasons.

Article 17

2.174 1. A person who is being detained or is serving a sentence in the territory of one State Party whose presence in another State Party is requested for purposes of testimony, identification or otherwise providing assistance in obtaining evidence for the investigation or prosecution of offences under this Convention may be transferred if the following conditions are met:

(a) The person freely gives his or her informed consent; and
(b) The competent authorities of both States agree, subject to such conditions as those States may deem appropriate.

2. For the purposes of the present article:

(a) The State to which the person is transferred shall have the authority and obligation to keep the person transferred in custody, unless otherwise requested or authorized by the State from which the person was transferred;
(b) The State to which the person is transferred shall without delay implement its obligation to return the person to the custody of the State from which the person was transferred as agreed beforehand, or as otherwise agreed, by the competent authorities of both States;

(c) The State to which the person is transferred shall not require the State from which the person was transferred to initiate extradition proceedings for the return of the person;

(d) The person transferred shall receive credit for service of the sentence being served in the State from which he or she was transferred for time spent in the custody of the State to which he or she was transferred.

3. Unless the State Party from which a person is to be transferred in accordance with the present article so agrees, that person, whatever his or her nationality, shall not be prosecuted or detained or subjected to any other restriction of his or her personal liberty in the territory of the State to which that person is transferred in respect of acts or convictions anterior to his or her departure from the territory of the State from which such person was transferred.

3

CRIMINALIZATION AND JURISDICTION

A. **Criminalization**	3.01	D.	**Principal Terrorist Offences in**	
The Hague Convention	3.02		**the UK Reflecting Domestic**	
The Montreal Convention	3.28		**Implementation of the UN**	
The Montreal Protocol	3.40		**Counter-Terrorism Instruments**	3.125
The Diplomats Convention	3.46	E.	**Jurisdiction**	3.126
The Hostages Convention	3.51		Introduction	3.126
The Nuclear Convention	3.58		Principles of criminal jurisdiction	3.127
The Rome Convention	3.61		Jurisdiction based upon the territory	
The Rome Protocol	3.72		where the offence was committed	3.132
The 2005 Protocol to the Rome			Jurisdiction based upon registration	
Convention[1]	3.76		of aircraft or maritime vessels	3.134
The 2005 Protocol to the Rome			Extra-territorial jurisdiction	3.137
Protocol[2]	3.82		The approach adopted by the	
The Bombings Convention	3.83		UN instruments	3.155
The Financing Convention	3.92		Jurisdiction based upon the presence	
The Nuclear Terrorism Convention	3.103		of a person in the national territory	3.188
B. **Criminalization of Terrorism**			Extension of jurisdiction for	
Offences in National Laws	3.108		UK terrorism offences	3.192
C. **United Nations Security Council**				
Resolution 1373	3.123			

A. Criminalization

As seen in Chapter 2,[3] the international legal framework contained in the universal **3.01** instruments includes criminalization requirements which cover most types of terrorist act. This chapter will examine those provisions in some detail, and will also highlight the approaches States have used to incorporate them into national law. If criminalization is the tool for effective prosecutions, then jurisdictional provisions provide the means by which the tool can set to work; accordingly, the later focus of this chapter is jurisdiction.

---

[1] Not yet in force.
[2] Not yet in force.
[3] See 2.32 ff.

The Hague Convention

Convention Offences

3.02 It is the second of the universal instruments, The Hague Convention, which is the first to contain penal provisions; the Tokyo Convention addresses jurisdiction, but not criminalization.

3.03 The Hague Convention establishes the effects of hijacking (at Article 1). Its provisions only apply to civil aircraft, not to aircraft used in military, customs, or police service (Article 3(2)). As to the type of aircraft within its ambit, therefore, it mirrors the provisions of the Tokyo Convention (at Article 1(4)).

3.04 It should be noted that the Hague Convention applies only to circumstances where the location of take-off or the place of actual landing of the aircraft on board which the Convention offence is committed is situated outside the territory of the State where the aircraft is registered (Article 3(3)). The scheduled destination is, however, irrelevant. It may be an international or domestic flight; thus, an aircraft registered in State A may be undertaking a domestic flight in that State when, as a result of a hijacking, it actually lands in a different State. In such circumstances, the Convention will apply.

3.05 The Article 1 offence is set out as follows:

> Any person who, on board an aircraft in flight:
>
> (a) unlawfully, by force or threat of there of, or by any other form of intimidation, seizes, or exercises control of, that aircraft, or attempts to perform any such act, or;
>
> (b) is an accomplice of a person who intends to perform any such act; commits an offence.
>
> Thus the following elements make up the offence:
>
> (i) seizure or exercise of control of an aircraft, or an attempt to do the same;
>
> (ii) by force, or threat of force, or by any other form of intimidation;
>
> (iii) such seizure or exercise of control being an unlawful one;
>
> (iv) the seizure or exercise of control or the attempt to do the same taking place on board the aircraft whilst in flight.

3.06 Seizure and exercise of control are not defined and may well, in certain circumstances, overlap. However the provisions cover circumstances where a pilot is replaced as the pilot by a hijacker, where a pilot is ordered to follow instructions given by a hijacker, or where a third person is prompted or forced by the hijacker to take control of the aircraft.

3.07 The offence can only be committed by a person who is actually on board the aircraft and the threat or use of force must come from within the aircraft itself. Thus, an attempt by another aircraft to force an aircraft to land or to change course, even if by threat or application of force, would not amount to the Convention offence. Similarly, the provisions do not cover the situation where any individual leaves, for instance, an explosive device on board an aircraft and then, from outside the aircraft, seeks to exercise control through making the threat that the device will be detonated.

A use or threat of force may, however, be against the crew, the passengers, or the aircraft. It may also be that the threat is to use force against a person or persons or property not on board the aircraft. It should also be noted that the phrase 'or by any other form of intimidation' would include any threat which is not a threat of force; for instance, blackmail. **3.08**

The threat or use of force must be an unlawful one. Thus the conduct must be without legal excuse or justification. Clearly, therefore, a regaining of control of an aircraft by, for instance, an air marshal in circumstances where an aircraft had already been seized by a hijacker would not amount to an offence. It is a moot point under which law the unlawfulness of the conduct is to be judged. It is suggested that it should be unlawfulness as understood by law of the State in which the aircraft is registered, since, it is difficult to imagine an act which is lawful under that State's law amounting to an offence within Article 1. **3.09**

The criminalization requirement under the Hague Convention is confined to the offence which is committed on board an aircraft in flight. Article 3(1) provides that an aircraft is considered to be in flight at any time from the time when all its external doors are closed following boarding until the moment when any external door is opened for the purposes of disembarkation. The effect of Article 3(1) is also that, in the case of a forced landing, an aircraft is deemed to be in flight until the competent authorities assume responsibility for both the aircraft and for those persons and property on board. Thus, if an attempt to seize an aircraft takes place during the boarding procedure, and before all the external doors have been closed, such conduct will not amount to an offence under Article 1. Even when all doors are closed, however, and the aircraft is, for the purpose of the Convention, 'in flight', the effect of Article 3(3) is that the Convention only appears to apply if the closing of the doors is then followed by take-off of the aircraft. Although such a conclusion seems at odds with the Convention definition of 'in flight', Article 3(3) is clear in saying that the provisions only bite 'if the place of take-off or the place of actual landing of the aircraft on board which the offence is committed is situated outside the territory of the State of registration of that aircraft . . .'. Although such a position is arguable, no sensible reading of the text can result in a construction of Article 3(3) which is at odds with the Article 3(1) definition of 'in flight'. It is therefore suggested that the phrase 'the place of take-off' should be read as the place of take-off or intended take-off. Without that reading, one is left with the position, suggested by some[4] that, notwithstanding that the aircraft is **3.10**

---

[4] See, for instance, the commentary to the Commonwealth Secretariat Implementation Kits for the International Counter Terrorism Conventions, 49. Available at: <http://www.thecommonwealth.org/Internal/38061/documents/>.

in flight, a Convention offence is only committed if the closing of the doors is followed by take-off thereafter.

3.11 Article 1 explicitly provides for secondary parties, and requires that accomplices be held equally liable for the Convention offence (Article 1(b)). In circumstances, however, where an accomplice assists by, for instance, placing equipment on an aircraft before a flight in order that a hijacker may make use of such equipment, he will not commit the Article 1 offence. Of course, the expectation is that such actions will amount to a criminal offence under national law in the territory of the State where that action takes place. It should be noted, in addition, that such assistance would in any event require to be criminalized under the Montreal Convention (see below).

The UK's Provisions

3.12 The UK's criminalization of hijacking is to be found in section 1 of the Aviation Security Act 1982. The key provisions of that section for present purposes are as follows:

> *1. Hijacking*
> (1) A person on board an aircraft in flight who, unlawfully, by the use of force or by threats of any kind, seizes the aircraft or exercises control of it commits the offence of hijacking, whatever his nationality, whatever the State in which the aircraft is registered and whether the aircraft is in the United Kingdom or elsewhere, but subject to subsection (2) below.
> (2) If—
>> (a) the aircraft is used in military, customs or police service, or
>> (b) both the place of take-off and the place of landing are in the territory of the State in which the aircraft is registered,
>> subsection (1) above shall not apply unless—
>>> (i) the person seizing or exercising control of the aircraft is a United Kingdom national; or
>>> (ii) his act is committed in the United Kingdom; or
>>> (iii) the aircraft is registered in the United Kingdom or is used in the military or customs service of the United Kingdom or in the service of any police force in the United Kingdom.
> (3) A person who commits the offence of hijacking shall be liable, on conviction on indictment, to imprisonment for life.
> (4) If the Secretary of State by order made by statutory instrument declares—
>> (a) that any two or more States named in the order have established an organisation or agency which operates aircraft; and
>> (b) that one of those States has been designated as exercising, for aircraft so operated, the powers of the State of registration,
>> the State declared under paragraph (b) of this subsection shall be deemed for the purposes of this section to be the State in which any aircraft so operated is registered; but in relation to such an aircraft subsection (2)(b) above shall have effect as if it referred to the territory of any one of the States named in the order.
> (5) For the purposes of this section the territorial waters of any State shall be treated as part of its territory.

The learned editors of Archbold[5] note that even when the commander of an **3.13**
aircraft may have been collaborating with a defendant, that does not preclude
a conviction under section 1 provided that the defendant is proved to have
threatened or used force on other members of the air crew (*R v Membar*).[6]

It will be noted that the section 1 offence is broader than the Hague Convention **3.14**
requires in an important respect. If an aircraft is seized or control is taken of it by
a UK national, the person committing the act commits it in the UK, or the aircraft
is registered in the UK or is used in the military, customs, or police service of
the UK, then the offence will be made out both in respect of military, customs,
or police aircraft and in a situation where take-off and landing are both in the
territory of the State of registration. Each of those circumstances, however, it will
be noted is outside of the Article 1 requirement.

In addition to general defences, the defence of necessity or duress of circumstances **3.15**
is capable of being a defence to the section 1 hijacking charge: *R v Abdul-Hussain*.[7]
In that case, Abdul-Hussain and six other defendants were convicted at the Central
Criminal Court of hijacking, contrary to section 1(1) of the Aviation and Security
Act 1982. They appealed on the basis that the trial judge had misdirected himself
in not leaving the defence of necessity to the jury.

The appellants were all Shiite Muslims from southern Iraq. Six out of the seven of **3.16**
them had offended against the laws of the Saddam Hussein regime, of which they
became fugitives. In 1996 they were living in Sudan and feared being returned
to Iraq by the Sudanese authorities. One of them, H, had a valid permit to reside
in the UK and where he would have become entitled to a right of permanent
settlement. He had helped fellow Iraqis obtain false papers and also appears to
have been involved in the bribing of officials.

In April 1996, H went to Jordan in order to assist his fiancée's family. His fiancée's **3.17**
father and two brothers had earlier been executed in Iraq and all the women of the
family had been imprisoned and tortured. H took his fiancée and the remainder
of the family with him to Sudan, believing that it would be easier to escape from
Sudan in due course. H believed that he was at risk of detection and deportation
to Iraq because of the help he had given to other fugitives from the then Iraqi
regime. He believed that, if returned to Iraq, he would probably be executed.
Abdul-Hussain, meanwhile, had been sentenced to death in his absence in Iraq in
1991, following a confession which had been extracted by torture. That sentence
of death had been reconfirmed by the regime in 1996. The remaining defendants

---

[5] J Richardson (ed), *Archbold: Criminal Pleading, Evidence and Practice* (56th edn Sweet &
Maxwell, London 2008) ch 25-178, 2348.
[6] [1983] Crim LR 618, CA.
[7] [1998] EWCA Crim 3528 and [1999] Crim LR 570, CA.

had been, variously, involved in an unsuccessful uprising in southern Iraq after the Gulf War and had, in the case of one, avoided service in the Iraqi army.

3.18 Each of the men became known to each other though a series of interrelationships. As a group they made several attempts to leave Sudan using false passports. On each occasion these false passports were rejected at Khartoum Airport but returned to them. Three weeks before the hijacking, Sudanese security officers had visited the group and confiscated their passports. H had managed to get these returned in due course, but had been warned by the Sudanese that he needed to take steps to resolve the position of the group in Sudan. H also feared that one of the consequences of the then UN sanctions, which were in force, was that Khartoum Airport might be closed.

3.19 In August 1996 several members of the group watched a film about a hijack and this prompted the idea to hijack an aircraft. H was the accepted leader and formulated the plans. By the end of August each member of the group was an overstayer in Sudan. H was the only one who did not have forged documents. All feared deportation to Iraq and, thereafter, torture and probable death.

3.20 On 27 August 1996 at Khartoum Airport the appellants boarded a Sudanese Airbus bound for Jordan. They were equipped with plastic knives and plastic mustard bottles filled with salt. The plastic bottles, once on board, were wrapped in black tape and modified with plasticine to give them the appearance of hand grenades.

3.21 When the flight was in Egyptian airspace, one of the group seized an air hostess and threatened her with a plastic knife. He was overpowered by security officials but, at that stage, another member of the group produced one of the imitation grenades and threatened to blow up the plane. Thereupon the pilot surrendered the control of the aircraft to the group with one of the hijackers remaining on the flight deck with the pilot, holding a knife to his back. As circumstance would have it, and quite separately from the group, one of the passengers on board was a butcher who had with him his trade knives. The group took possession of these knives and one passenger who resisted the group was stabbed in the arm. One of the group declined to participate in the hijack itself and, he was instead tied up and gagged by the rest of the group.

3.22 The intention of the group was to divert the plane to London but there was insufficient fuel and therefore permission was given for the plane to land in Cyprus. There, women and children were released and the plane was refuelled. Thereafter, it arrived in the UK landing at Stansted Airport. After eight hours of negotiations, the passengers and crew were released and the appellants surrendered.

3.23 Following arrest, H made full admissions in interview. He described how he had been trying to get his fiancée and family out of, initially, Jordan and then the Sudan. His account was largely supported by other passengers and crew.

Each appellant on arrival in the UK sought political asylum. At trial it was accepted   **3.24**
by all save the member of the group who did not actively participate whilst on
board, that the aircraft had been hijacked. However, it was said that this was done
as a last resort to escape death, be that of themselves or their families. However,
at the close of all the evidence, the learned trial judge ruled that the defence of
necessity or duress of circumstances should not be left to the jury. He ruled in the
following terms:

> On this aspect of the matter a considerable body of, if I may say so, convincing
> evidence has been called on behalf of the defendants to demonstrate the cruel, unjust
> and tyrannical nature of the Saddam Hussein regime in Iraq. Evidence has been
> called of summary executions, either without any or no more than a semblance of
> a trial, of arbitrary imprisonment in conditions of extreme hardship, more often
> than not with torture of the most revolting and horrifying kind for no greater offence
> than that of opposition to the current regime in power.

> The evidence of the defendants themselves in this regard is supported not only by
> independent expert evidence but also by the country briefs of the Immigration and
> National Directorate of the Home Office which have been placed before the jury by
> agreement between counsel on all sides . . . In general terms all the six defendants and
> their companions were overstayers in Sudan and, in the case of all but Hoshan [H],
> on forged documents. They feared that at any time they might be arrested by the
> Sudanese authorities and instead of being merely fined for overstaying and given
> a limited period to leave the country, they would either be deported directly to Iraq
> or handed over to the Iraqi Embassy with the same result. If that occurred they all
> feared that they and their families would receive savage punishment including, in all
> probability, execution.

> Nevertheless, in my judgment there was at no time any sufficient connection between
> the danger feared by the defendants and their families on the one hand, and the
> criminal act of hijacking the aircraft on the other of such a close and immediate
> nature as is established by the authorities as being required to lay the basis for the
> defence of necessity. There was no immediate threat of death or serious personal
> harm or, indeed, even of arrest in the meaning of that word which, in my judgment,
> the authorities I have cited require.

Having heard argument and having been referred to more than seventy authori-   **3.25**
ties, the Vice President, Rose LJ, gave judgment and, in so doing, set out the
propositions which the court had gleaned from the authorities placed before it:

> 1. Unless and until Parliament provides otherwise, the defence of duress, whether
>   by threats or from circumstances, is generally available in relation to all substan-
>   tive crimes, except murder, attempted murder and some forms of treason.[8]
>   Accordingly, if raised by appropriate evidence, it is available in relation to hijack-
>   ing aircraft; although, in such cases, the terror induced in innocent passengers will
>   generally raise issues of proportionality for determination, initially as a matter of
>   law by the judge and, in appropriate cases, [as a matter of fact] by the jury.

---

[8] *R v Pommell* [1995] 2 Cr App R 607 at 615 C.

2. The Courts have developed the defence on a case by case basis, notably during the last 30 years. Its scope remains imprecise.[9]

3. Imminent peril of death or serious injury to the defendant, or those to whom he has responsibility, is an essential element of both types of duress.[10]

4. The peril must operate on the mind of the defendant at the time when he commits the otherwise criminal act, so as to overbear his will, and this is essentially a question for the jury.[11]

5. But the execution of the threat need not be immediately in prospect.[12]

6. The period of time which elapses between the inception of the peril and the defendant's act, and between that act and execution of the threat are relative but not determinative factors for a judge and jury in deciding whether duress operates.[13]

7. All the circumstances of the peril, including the number, identity and status of those creating it, and the opportunities (if any) which exist to avoid it are relevant, initially for the judge, and, in appropriate cases, for the jury, when assessing whether the defendant's mind was affected as in 4 above.

8. As to 6 and 7, above, if Anne Frank had stolen a car to escape from Amsterdam and been charged with theft, the tenets of English law would not, in our judgment, have denied her a defence of duress of circumstances, on the ground that she should have waited for the Gestapo's knock on the door.

9. We see no reason of principle or authority for distinguishing the two forms of duress in relation to the elements of the defence which we have identified.

10. The judgment of the court, presided over by Lord Lane CJ, when delivered by Simon Brown LJ in *R v Martin*[14] affords, as it seems to us, the clearest and most authoritative guide to the relevant principles and appropriate direction in relation to both forms of duress . . . it applies a predominantly, but not entirely, objective test, and this court has recently rejected an attempt to introduce a purely subjective element divorced from extraneous influence.[15]

Having set out those principles, Rose LJ stated that the court was satisfied that the learned trial judge had erred and was wrong to withdraw the defence from the jury. The convictions were therefore quashed.

3.26 In relation to the case of *Martin*, relied upon by the Court of Appeal in *Abdul-Hussain*, it is perhaps valuable to set out the précis of the law of duress as set out by Simon Brown LJ in giving the judgment of the court:

> The principles may be summarised thus. First, English law does, in extreme circumstances, recognise the defence of necessity. Most commonly this defence arises as duress, that is pressure upon the accused's will from the wrongful threats or violence of another. Equally, however, it can arise from other objective dangers threatening the accused or others. Arising thus, it is conveniently called 'duress of circumstances'.

---

[9] Hurst [1995] 1 Cr App R 83 at 93 D.

[10] See *Southwark LBC v Williams* [1971] 1 Ch 734, per Edmond-Davies LJ at 746 A.

[11] *R v Hudson and Taylor* [1971] 55 Cr App R 1.

[12] *R v Hudson and Taylor* (n 11) 425.

[13] *R v Pommell* (n 8) 616.

[14] [1989] 88 Cr App R 343.

[15] See *R v Roger and Rose*, unreported, 9 July 1997.

Secondly, the defence is available only if, from an objective standpoint, the accused can be said to be acting reasonably and proportionately in order to avoid a threat of death or serious injury. Thirdly, assuming the defence to be open to the accused on his account of the fact, the issue should be left to the jury, who should be directed to determine these two questions: First, was the accused, or may he have been, impelled to act as he did because, as a result of what he reasonably believed to be the situation, he had good cause to fear that otherwise death or serious physical injury would result? Secondly, if so, may a sober person of reasonable firmness, sharing the characteristics of the accused, have responded to that situation by acting as the accused acted? If the answer to both those questions was yes, then the jury acquit: the defence of necessity would have been established.[16]

One important caveat to the decision in *Abdul-Hussain* is in relation to the posi- **3.27** tion where there is no immediate threat. It was suggested in *Abdul-Hussain* that the defence should be left to the jury even though the threat was not in the immediacy; however, doubts have now been cast on that position by the decision of the House of Lords in *R v Z*.[17] In that case, Their Lordships said it should be made clear to juries that if the peril or retribution threatened is not such as the defendant reasonably expects to follow immediately or almost immediately on his failure to comply with the threat, there may be little doubt that in such circumstances the defendant could have taken evasive action to avoid committing the crime in respect of which he faces trial.

The Montreal Convention

Convention Offences

The offence established by the Hague Convention does not extend to the use of **3.28** threat of force when such force is applied from outside an aircraft and does not, of course, include acts of sabotage and destruction of aircraft. It has been said elsewhere[18] that the universal instruments are, in most part, a reactive response, and so it will come as no surprise that, following the destruction of twenty-two aircraft and the deaths of 400 persons as a result of the detonation of explosives on board aircraft in the twenty years leading up to 1970, a new instrument, the Montreal Convention, was adopted in 1971.

Article 4(1) of the Montreal Convention[19] makes it clear that its provisions apply **3.29** to civil aircraft alone, and not to those aircraft used in military, customs, or police service.

---

[16] [1989] 88 Cr App R 345.
[17] [2005] 2 AC 467.
[18] See Chapter 2 at 2.141.
[19] A provision identical to Article 1(4) of the Tokyo Convention and Article 3(2) of the Hague Convention.

3.30 Article 1(1) is the offence-creating provision and provides that:

> Any person shall be guilty of an offence if he unlawfully or intentionally:
> (a) performs an act of violence against a person on board an aircraft in flight if that act is likely to endanger the safety of that aircraft; or
> (b) destroys an aircraft in service or causes damage to such an aircraft which renders it incapable of flight or which is likely to endanger its safety in flight; or
> (c) places or causes to be placed on an aircraft in service, by any means whatsoever a device or substance which is likely to destroy that aircraft or to cause damage to it which renders it incapable of flight, or to cause damage to it which is likely to endanger its safety in flight; or
> (d) destroys or damages air navigation facilities or interferes with their operation, if any such act is likely to endanger the safety of aircraft in flight; or
> (e) communicates information which he knows to be false, thereby endangering the safety of an aircraft in flight.

3.31 It will be noted from the above that, to amount to an offence, the conduct must be unlawful. In addition there is a requirement of intention, although it should be noted that 'intention' is in relation to the acts being carried out, not an intention as to consequences. It will also be noted that (1) (a), (c), & (d) do not require any circumstances to actually come about in order for the offence to be made out. They are predicated on the basis that certain consequences are likely.

3.32 As with the Hague Convention, an aircraft is in flight from the moment all its external doors are closed after boarding until the opening of an external door for disembarkation (Article 2(a)). In addition, for the purposes of the Montreal Convention, an aircraft 'is considered to be in service from the beginning of the pre-flight preparation of the aircraft by ground personnel or by the crew for a specific flight until 24 hours after landing; the period of service shall, in any event, extend for the entire period during which the aircraft is in flight . . .' (Article 2(b)).

3.33 The first offence under Article 1 is that contained in Article 1(1)(a). There, the act of violence must be such as is likely to endanger the safety of the aircraft. It must be an act against a person on board an aircraft in flight, but the person carrying out the attack does not have to be on board the aircraft. Although, of course, he or she can be. Nor, from the wording of the Article, does the act of violence have to be against a particular person or persons. Therefore, if an act of violence was perpetrated from outside, either by the firing of a rocket or missile or by the use of a remote control bomb, such actions would be within the criminalization provisions of (1)(a).

The offence in (1)(b) addresses destruction of or damage to an aircraft. The **3.34** destruction or damage envisaged must take place when the aircraft is in service.[20] (1)(b) will criminalize the actions of a person whether or not on board the aircraft. It will also include an attack on an aircraft in flight when that attack comes from another aircraft. The mischief sought to be addressed by (1)(c) is principally that of the explosive device placed on board an aircraft. Such a device, whether put into the aircraft itself or fixed to the outside of the aircraft, will still come within the ambit of (1)(c); however, again, the aircraft in question must be in service. For this offence, though, if an explosive device is placed on an aircraft before that aircraft is in service, and the device remains in place when the aircraft comes into service, then the Convention offence will still be made out.

For the offence in (1)(d) to be made out the air navigation facilities in question **3.35** must be ones used for international navigation (Article 4(5)). However, those navigation facilities may be at the airport, at a remote site or, presumably, even on the aircraft itself. For this offence to be completed, it is not required that a particular aircraft in flight has its safety endangered, rather that the act committed creates a danger to aircraft generally in flight. The provisions include interference with the operation of air navigation facilities, therefore the use of electronic interference or modification, such as the blocking of radio signals from a navigation facility, would come within the ambit of the offence.

The final offence under Article 1 is at Article 1(1)(e), which criminalizes the **3.36** communicating of information in circumstances in which the person communicating knows that the information is false, thereby endangering the safety of an aircraft in flight. The mischief that this is aimed at is the sending of false signals to an aircraft in order to divert it from its original course. A subtle difference in wording can be noted as compared to (1)(d). In (1)(d) the danger envisaged is a general danger to aircraft, whilst here, in (1)(e), conduct will amount to an offence if the safety of a particular aircraft in flight is endangered. It will be noted that in (1)(e) the word 'an' has been inserted before the phrase aircraft in flight.

As to secondary parties, and inchoate offences, an accomplice to the princi- **3.37** pal offence or offender commits an offence under Article 1 (Article 1(2)(b)). Indeed, unlike The Hague Convention, the act or conduct of the accomplice may take place on or off board the aircraft. In addition, any person who attempts to commit any of the offences under Article 1 also commits an offence (Article 1(2)(a)).

---

[20] See below, the Montreal Protocol at Article 2, which addresses such an eventuality.

The UK's Provisions

3.38 For the UK, the offences set out in Article 1(1)(a)–(c) are reflected in section 2 of the Aviation and Security Act 1982, whilst the offences in Article 1(1)(d)–(e) are provided for in section 3 of the same Act. As an example of the implementation into domestic law of the Montreal provisions, those sections provide as follows:

> 2. *Destroying, damaging or endangering safety of aircraft*
>
> (1) It shall, subject to subsection (4) below, be an offence for any person unlawfully and intentionally—
>> (a) to destroy an aircraft in service or so to damage such an aircraft as to render it incapable of flight or as to be likely to endanger its safety in flight; or
>> (b) to commit on board an aircraft in flight any act of violence which is likely to endanger the safety of the aircraft.
>
> (2) It shall also, subject to subsection (4) below, be an offence for any person unlawfully and intentionally to place, or cause to be placed, on an aircraft in service any device or substance which is likely to destroy the aircraft, or is likely so to damage it as to render it incapable of flight or as to be likely to endanger its safety in flight; but nothing in this subsection shall be construed as limiting the circumstances in which the commission of any act—
>> (a) may constitute an offence under subsection (1) above, or
>> (b) may constitute attempting or conspiring to commit, or aiding, abetting, counselling or procuring, or being art and part in, the commission of such an offence.
>
> (3) Except as provided by subsection (4) below, subsections (1) and (2) above shall apply whether any such act as is therein mentioned is committed in the United Kingdom or elsewhere, whatever the nationality of the person committing the act and whatever the State in which the aircraft is registered.
>
> (4) Subsections (1) and (2) above shall not apply to any act committed in relation to an aircraft used in military, customs or police service unless—
>> (a) the act is committed in the United Kingdom, or
>> (b) where the act is committed outside the United Kingdom, the person committing it is a United Kingdom national.
>
> (5) A person who commits an offence under this section shall be liable, on conviction on indictment, to imprisonment for life.
>
> (6) In this section unlawfully—
>> (a) in relation to the commission of an act in the United Kingdom, means so as (apart from this Act) to constitute an offence under the law of the part of the United Kingdom in which the act is committed, and
>> (b) in relation to the commission of an act outside the United Kingdom, means so that the commission of the act would (apart from this Act) have been an offence under the law of England and Wales if it had been committed in England and Wales or of Scotland if it had been committed in Scotland.
>
> (7) In this section act of violence means—
>> (a) any act done in the United Kingdom which constitutes the offence of murder, attempted murder, manslaughter, culpable homicide or assault or an offence under section 18, 20, 21, 22, 23, 24, 28 or 29 of the Offences against the Person Act 1861 or under section 2 of the Explosive Substances Act 1883, and

(b) any act done outside the United Kingdom which, if done in the United Kingdom, would constitute such an offence as is mentioned in paragraph (a) above.

3. *Other acts endangering or likely to endanger safety of aircraft*

(1) It shall, subject to subsections (5) and (6) below, be an offence for any person unlawfully and intentionally to destroy or damage any property to which this subsection applies, or to interfere with the operation of any such property, where the destruction, damage or interference is likely to endanger the safety of aircraft in flight.

(2) Subsection (1) above applies to any property used for the provision of air navigation facilities, including any land, building or ship so used, and including any apparatus or equipment so used, whether it is on board an aircraft or elsewhere.

(3) It shall also, subject to subsections (4) and (5) below, be an offence for any person intentionally to communicate any information which is false, misleading or deceptive in a material particular, where the communication of the information endangers the safety of an aircraft in flight or is likely to endanger the safety of aircraft in flight.

(4) It shall be a defence for a person charged with an offence under subsection (3) above to prove—

(a) that he believed, and had reasonable grounds for believing, that the information was true; or

(b) that, when he communicated the information, he was lawfully employed to perform duties which consisted of or included the communication of information and that he communicated the information in good faith in the performance of those duties.

(5) Subsections (1) and (3) above shall not apply to the commission of any act unless either the act is committed in the United Kingdom, or, where it is committed outside the United Kingdom—

(a) the person committing it is a United Kingdom national; or

(b) the commission of the act endangers or is likely to endanger the safety in flight of a civil aircraft registered in the United Kingdom or chartered by demise to a lessee whose principal place of business, or (if he has no place of business) whose permanent residence, is in the United Kingdom; or

(c) the act is committed on board a civil aircraft which is so registered or so chartered; or

(d) the act is committed on board a civil aircraft which lands in the United Kingdom with the person who committed the act still on board.

(6) Subsection (1) above shall also not apply to any act committed outside the United Kingdom and so committed in relation to property which is situated outside the United Kingdom and is not used for the provision of air navigation facilities in connection with international air navigation, unless the person committing the act is a United Kingdom national.

(7) A person who commits an offence under this section shall be liable, on conviction on indictment, to imprisonment for life.

(8) In this section civil aircraft means any aircraft other than an aircraft used in military, customs or police service and unlawfully has the same meaning as in section 2 of this Act.

Moving back to the Convention and the issue of the test of unlawfulness, and the **3.39** uncertainty (common to both the Montreal and the Hague Conventions) as to which system of law would govern the test of what was unlawful, the UK has made the position clear for the purposes of its offence-creating provisions by providing in section 2(6) of the Aviation and Security Act 1982 (a provision that applies to both section 2 and section 3) that 'unlawfully' means:

(a) in relation to an act in the United Kingdom, means so as (apart from this Act) to constitute an offence under the law of the part of the United Kingdom in which the act is committed, and

(b) in relation to the commission of an act outside the United Kingdom, means so that the commission of the act would (apart from this Act) have been an offence under the law of England and Wales if it had been committed in England and Wales or of Scotland if it had been committed in Scotland.

The Montreal Protocol

3.40 The Montreal Protocol, which was adopted in 1998 and entered into force on 6 August 1989, was a response to a terrorist attack at Rome Airport in January 1986. The Protocol seeks to supplement the Montreal Convention by extending the criminalization provisions of the convention to include offences involving acts of violence occurring at international airports.[21]

3.41 Given that the Protocol and the Convention must be read and interpreted as a single instrument, Article II of the Protocol has the effect of adding paragraph 1 bis to the Convention's Article 1. The new paragraph provides that:

> Any person commits an offence if he unlawfully and intentionally, using any device, substance or weapon:
> (a) performs an act of violence towards a person at an airport serving international aviation which causes or is likely to cause serious injury or death; or
> (b) destroys or seriously damages the facilities of an airport serving international civil aviation or aircraft not in service located thereon, or disrupts the services of the airport,
> if such an act endangers or is likely to endanger safety at that airport.

Thus two new offences are created. In either case, the act alleged must be intentional and unlawful. This issue of unlawfulness is not likely to cause a difficulty in the case of a Protocol offence, since the acts which amount to the offence are acts at an airport and therefore the test of what is unlawful will be in accordance with the law in the State in whose territory the airport is situated.

---

[21] A Aust, *Implementation Kits for the International Counter-Terrorism Conventions* (Commonwealth Secretariat, London 2002). As highlighted by Professor Antony Aust in his commentary at page 102, as between parties to the Protocol, the Convention and the Protocol are to be read and interpreted as one single instrument (Article I). Therefore a State which is not a party to the Convention may ratify or accede to the Protocol only if at the same time it ratifies or accedes to the Convention (Article V(2) and Articles VII(2). Therefore, as between those parties to the Convention which are not parties to the Protocol, the Convention will continue to apply in its original and un-amended form. It will also apply in that original form as between a party to the Protocol and the Convention and a party to the Convention alone.

The paragraph 1 bis offences can only be committed by a person using a device, **3.42** substance or weapon. In the case of (1) bis (a) the act of violence must be against a person or persons and must cause or be likely to cause serious injury or death. However, the intention required is in relation to the act of violence, not in relation to the consequence of death or serious injury. Thus there is no requirement that the accused must have intent to kill or to cause serious injury. The act of violence must take place at an airport which serves international civil aviation, and it must be presumed that the word 'airport' will include not just the airport buildings themselves, but all other areas within the airport including aprons, hangers and runways. The offence at para (1) bis (b) requires an act that involves the use of a device, substance, or weapon to destroy or to seriously damage facilities of such an airport, or an aircraft not in service which is situated there, or the disruption of services of the airport by use of a device, substance, or weapon.

It will be recalled that, in relation to the Montreal Convention, it was highlighted **3.43** that the offences under Article 1(1)(a)(d)(e) were confined to aircrafts in flight and that offences created by Article 1(1)(b)(c) related to aircraft in service; however, the (1) bis (b) offence plugs the gap and applies to aircraft not in service. It only applies, of course, to such aircraft when they are located at an airport serving international aviation. Thus, the lacuna in the original Convention offences, whereby destruction or damage to an aircraft when not in service was not addressed has now been remedied.

As for the original Convention offences, both the person who attempts to com- **3.44** mit one of the Protocol offences or an accomplice of a person who commits or attempts to commit Protocol offences, must be criminalized by a State party to the Protocol (Article 1(2)(a) of the Convention, as amended by Article II(2) of the Protocol).

The UK's Provisions

For the UK, the criminalization provisions compliant with the Montreal Protocol **3.45** are found at section 1, Aviation and Maritime Security Act 1990.

The Diplomats Convention

The criminalization provisions are to be found in Article 2 which provides **3.46** (at Article 2(1)) that:

The intentional commission of:
(a) a murder, kidnapping or other attack upon the person or liberty of an internationally protected person;
(b) a violent attack upon the official premises, the private accommodation or the means of transport of an internationally protected person likely to endanger his personal liberty;
(c) a threat to commit any such attack;

(d) an attempt to commit any such attack; and

(e) an act constituting participation as an accomplice in any such attack;

shall be made by each State Party a crime under its internal law.

3.47 The definition of an 'internationally protected person' (IPP) is to be found at Article 1, which provides that:

'internationally protected person' means:

(a) a Head of State, including any member of a collegial body performing the functions of a Head of State under the constitution of the State concerned, a Head of Government or a minister for foreign affairs, whenever any such person is in a foreign State, as well as members of his family who accompany him;

(b) any representative or official of the State or an official or agent of an international organisation of an intergovernmental character who, at the time when and in the place where a crime against him, his official premises, his private accommodation or his means of transport is committed, is entitled, pursuant to international law to any protection from any attack on his person, freedom or dignity, as well as members of his family forming part of his household (Article 1(1)).

It should be noted that the definition and indeed the term IPP used in the Diplomats Convention was not taken from a pre-existing term of art. It will be noted that Article 1(1)(a) applies whenever a person within that definition is present in a foreign State, whereas Article 1(1)(b) is only applicable to a person within the (1)(b) definition who is entitled to 'special protection' 'at the time when and in the place where . . .' the offence against him is committed. This is a reflection that whilst a Head of State or Head of Government retains his or her status wherever he might be, as a general rule, diplomats and officials or agents of international organizations who have an entitlement to special protection only enjoy that protection when they are in the State to which they are formally accredited or when in the course of exercising their official function.

3.48 Those acts set out under Article 2 as constituting the Convention offence will, for most States, already be criminal offences under national law. In such circumstances, it should be borne in mind that there is not a requirement to create a new offence to reflect, for instance, the murder of an IPP, although, for reasons of policy, a State may choose to do exactly that. Given the wording of Article 2 and the requirement that for an offence to be a Convention offence it must be committed intentionally, the effect is that a person who commits an act as set out in Article 2 against an IPP, but who does not know at the time of that act that the victim is, in fact, an IPP, is not guilty of a Convention offence. However, some States have chosen to criminalize in a way that goes beyond the Convention in that regard. Indeed, the UK, in section 1 of the Internationally Protected Persons Act 1978 explicitly provides at section 1(4) that 'for the purposes of the preceding subsection [the criminalizing provisions] it is immaterial whether a person knows that another person is a protected person'.

3.49 Article 2(1)(a) speaks of 'murder, kidnapping or other attack'; it is suggested here that, in order to meet the intention of the Convention and adhere to the proportionality of (a), 'other attack' should be construed as confined to an attack of equivalent seriousness to murder or kidnapping. Thus, it does not seem to have been the intention of the Convention to require a State Party to criminalize minor assaults. That having been said, it has to be noted that the UK's Internationally Protected Persons Act 1978 provides (at section 1) an IPP offence which includes assault occasioning actual bodily harm. Again, that appears to go beyond Convention requirements. Given that Article 2(2) provides that 'each State Party shall make these crimes punishable by appropriate penalties which take into account their grave nature' it seems even more apparent that less serious forms of assault or attack were not intended to be included.

Before leaving the criminalization provisions of the Diplomats Convention, it **3.50** should be noted that Article 2 also contains a preventive and proactive measure by providing: 'Paragraphs 1 and 2 of this Article in no way derogate from the obligations of States Parties under international law to take all appropriate measures to take all appropriate measure to prevent other attacks on the person, freedom or dignity of an internationally protected person.'

The Hostages Convention

Article 1 provides: **3.51**

  1) Any person who seizes or detains and threatens to kill, to injure or to continue to detain another person (hereinafter referred to as the 'hostage') in order to compel a third party, namely a State, an intergovernmental organisation, a national or juridical person or a group or person, to do or abstain from doing any act as an explicit or implicit condition for the release of the hostage commits the offence of taking hostages ('hostage-taking') within the meaning of this Convention.
  2) Any person who:
     (a) attempts to commit an act of hostage taking, or
     (b) participates as an accomplice of anyone who commits or attempts to commit an act of hostage-taking;
     likewise commits an offence for the purposes of this Convention.

The *actus reus* of the offence is seizure or detention of a person, coupled with a **3.52** threat to kill, to injure, or to continue to detain that person unless a third party does or abstains from doing a particular act—that last element being an explicit or implicit condition for the release of the hostage. The third party who is subject to the compulsion or attempt at compulsion may be a State, an organization, a corporation, or a natural person. It should be noted that the criminalization provisions do not include a requirement that force is used in order for the offence to be made out. Unlike the Diplomats Convention, the Hostages Convention does not extend the offence to the making of a threat to take a hostage; although, as seen from the provisions as set out above, an attempt is to be criminalized by State Parties.

Given the element of the Article 1 offence is the compelling of a third party to do **3.53** or to abstain from doing an act as an explicit or implicit condition for the release of the hostage, any kidnapping with an international element to it would, in principle at least, come within the ambit of the Convention. The importance of the international nature of the offence is made clear by Article 13 which provides that:

> The Convention shall not apply where the offence is committed within a single State, the hostage and the alleged offender are nationals of that State and the alleged offender is found in the territory of that State.

3.54   Although a kidnapping for political purposes was the spur to the adoption of the Hostages Convention, it does then extend to both the political and the non-political purpose. It should be remembered that an offence under one of the other conventions, such as hijacking under the Hague Convention, will very often amount to the hostage-taking offence as well. The Convention does not extend, though, to taking of an object or an animal. Thus, seizing or detaining a valuable racehorse will not fall within the terms of Article 1.

3.55   Unlike all other UN counter-terrorism instruments, the Hostages Convention specifically addresses its relationship with hostage-taking during an armed conflict and the provisions of the Geneva Conventions of 1949 and the 1977 Additional Protocols to those Conventions. Article 12 provides that:

> . . . insofar as the Geneva Conventions 1949 for the protection of war victims or the Protocols additional to those Conventions are applicable to a particular act of hostage taking, and insofar as States parties to this convention are bound under those conventions to prosecute or to hand over the hostage-taker, the present Convention shall not apply to an act of hostage-taking committed in the course of armed conflicts . . . as defined in the Geneva Conventions of 1949 and the Protocols thereto, including armed conflicts mentioned in Article (i) of 1977, in which peoples are fighting against colonial domination and alien occupation and against racist regimes in the exercise of their right of self-determination, as enshrined in the charter of the United Nations and the declarations on principles of international law concerning friendly relations and cooperation amongst States in accordance with the charter of the United Nations.

3.56   The effect of Article 12 is to exclude from the scope of the Convention hostage-taking which amounts to a grave breach of the Geneva Conventions. States parties to the Geneva Conventions have an obligation under those conventions to prosecute or extradite in circumstances where hostage-taking amounts to a grave breach.

3.57   Just as the Diplomats Convention has preventive provisions,[22] so the Hostages Convention (at Article 4) states that:

> The State Party should cooperate in the prevention of the offences set forth in Article 1, particularly by: (a) taking all practical measure to prevent preparation in their respective territories for the commission of those offences within or outside their territories, including measures to prohibit in their territories illegal activities of persons, groups and organisation that encourage, instigate, organise or engage in the perpetration of

---

[22]   See Article 2(3) and Article 4.

acts of taking of hostages; (b) exchanging information and coordinating the taking of administrative and other measures as appropriate to prevent the commission of those offences.

The Nuclear Convention

The offence-creating provision is Article 7 which provides: **3.58**

> The intentional commission of:
> (a) an act without lawful authority which constitutes the receipt, possession, use, transfer, alternation, and disposal or dispersal of nuclear material and which causes or is likely to cause death or serious injury to any person or substantial damage to property;
> (b) a theft or robbery of nuclear material;
> (c) an embezzlement or fraudulent obtaining of nuclear material;
> (d) an act constituting a demand for nuclear material by threat or use of force, or by any other form of intimidation;
> (e) a threat:
>   i. To use nuclear material to cause death or serious injury to any person or substantial property damage, or
>   ii. To commit an offence described in sub-paragraph (b) in order to compel a natural or legal person, international organisation or State to do or to refrain from doing any act;
> (f) an attempt to commit any offence described in (a), (b) or (c); and
> (g) an act which constitutes participation in any offence described in paragraphs (a) to (f) shall be made a punishable offence by each State Party under its national law.

Article 7 creates, arguably, six separate offences, each of which requires specific **3.59** intent. In addition Article 7(1)(f) and (g) criminalize attempt and participation respectively. As we have seen in relation to both the Diplomats and Hostages Conventions, the criminalization drafting is wide in the sense that the crimes are not confined to acts committed with a terrorist purpose. To that extent, each of the offences created could be said to be an expression of a general criminal act. The one exception is arguably the offence contained in Article 7(2)(e) which incorporates the ulterior purpose of 'in order to compel a natural or legal person, international organisation or State to do or to refrain from doing any act'. The offence in (a) is the key possession and transportation of material offence. It is committed not just when death or serious injury are in fact caused but when one of those outcomes is likely to be caused. The likelihood will be an objective test; in other words, are there reasonable grounds for believing that the act in question is/was likely to cause death or serious injury.

The theft or robbery offences in (b) should be given an ordinary construction, **3.60** whilst 'an embezzlement or fraudulent obtaining' in (c) should be read to include all acts and enterprises which would ordinarily constitute embezzlement, fraud, or deception.

The Rome Convention

3.61 This, the first of the so-called 'maritime conventions' was the result of the seizing in 1985 of the Italian cruise ship, the *Achille Lauro*. It was seized in international waters by members of the Palestine Liberation Front. Its passengers were held hostage and one passenger, an American Jew, was killed.

3.62 The offence-creating provision is contained in Article 3, which provides at Article 3(1) that:

> Any person commits an offence if that person unlawfully and intentionally:
> a) seizes or exercises control over a ship by force or threat thereof or any other form of intimidation; or
> b) performs an act of violence against a person on board a ship it that act is likely to endanger the safe navigation of that ship; or
> c) destroys a ship or causes damage to a ship or its cargo which is likely to endanger the safer navigation of that ship; or
> d) places or causes to be placed on a ship, by any means whatsoever, a device or substance which is likely to destroy that ship, or cause damage to that ship or its cargo, which endangers or is likely to endanger the safe navigation of that ship; or
> e) destroys or seriously damages maritime navigation abilities or seriously interferes with their operation, if any such act is likely to endanger the safe navigation of a ship; or
> f) communicates information which he knows to be false, thereby endangering the safe navigation of a ship; or
> g) injures or kills any person, in connection with the commission or the attempted commission of any of the offences set forth in sub para-graphs (a–f).

3.63 The word 'ship' is defined in Article 1 as 'a vessel of any type whatsoever not permanently attached to the sea-bed, including dynamically supported craft, submersibles, or any other floating craft'.

3.64 Thus, a drilling platform permanently attached to the sea-bed will not be covered by the Convention; however, hovercrafts and hydrofoils are included, along with submarines. It should be noted that there is no requirement, in order to be within the scope of the Convention, for a ship to be a registered vessel with a State Party.

3.65 However, not all categories of vessel falling into the Article 1 definition have been brought within the Convention. Article 2 provides for express exclusions. A warship is not covered and neither is a ship owned or operated by a State when such a ship is being used as a naval auxiliary, or for customs or police purposes. Similarly, a ship which has been withdrawn from navigation or has been laid up (for instance, 'mothballed') is, similarly, not caught by the Convention (see Article 1(1)).

A warship is not defined by the Rome Convention. The definition is to be found **3.66** in the United Nations Convention on the Law of the Sea[23] which provides:

> A ship belonging to the armed forces of a State bearing the external marks distinguishing such ships of its nationality, under the command of an officer duly commissioned by the government of the State and whose name appears in the appropriate service list or its equivalent, and manned by a crew which is under regular armed forces discipline.

In addition to providing those exclusions, Article 2(2), also provides that: 'nothing **3.67** in this Convention affects the immunities of warships and other government ships operated for non-commercial purposes'. This is simply a confirmation of the well-understood position. With respect, it is hard to see what it adds in this context, and why it was thought necessary to insert this provision.

The offences set out in Article 3 must each be committed unlawfully and inten- **3.68** tionally. The reader is referred to earlier discussions, above, in relation to the use of those words. Similarly, the use of the term 'seizing or exercising control' has already been examined in the context of the Hague Convention and reference should be made to that discussion, above. It will be noted that the offences set out in (b), (c), and (e) require that the act is likely to endanger safe navigation, whereas the offence in (d) is put on the basis of 'endangers or is likely to endanger . . .' and the offence in (f) does not include likelihood but rather 'thereby endangering the safe navigation of the ship'.

Article 3(1)(e) extends, it should be noted, to the destruction etc of maritime **3.69** navigational facilities which are not actually on a ship itself.

Article 3(2)(a) criminalizes attempts, whilst Article 3(2)(b) criminalizes the **3.70** accomplice who aids or abets.

Article 3(2)(c) creates an offence which is, on its wording, slightly unusual. It **3.71** criminalizes a threat which is made with the aim of compelling a natural or a legal person to do or refrain from doing an act, with the requisite threat being a threat to commit one of the offences set out in Article 3(1)(b), (c), or (e) if such a threat is likely to endanger the safe navigation of the ship in question. The threat, though, may be one made with or without a condition being attached, depending upon what the national law of the State in question provides for. Thus, the threat could be aimed at obtaining money or obtaining the release of a prisoner with the threat itself being, for instance, that a ship or its cargo would be destroyed or damaged if the money was not handed over or the prisoner released.

---

[23] UNCLOS (1982), Article 29.

The Rome Protocol

3.72 As seen from the above, the dangers to maritime navigation recognized in the Rome Convention did not lead to criminalization provisions which extended to those structures permanently attached to the sea-bed, in other words, those fixed offshore platforms used principally by the oil and gas industries.

3.73 The equivalent to Article 3(1) of the Rome Convention is Article 2(1) of the Protocol which provides that:

> Any person commits an offence if that person unlawfully and intention-ally:
> (a) seizes or exercises control over a fixed platform by force or threat thereof or any other form of intimidation; or
> (b) performs an act of violence against a person on board a fixed platform if that act is likely to endanger its safety; or
> (c) destroys a fixed platform or causes damage to it which is likely to endanger its safety; or
> (d) places or causes to be placed on a fixed platform, by any means whatsoever, a device or substance which is likely to destroy that fixed platform or likely to endanger its safety; or
> (e) injures or kills any person in connection with the commission or the attempted commission of any of the offences set forth in subparagraphs (a) to (d).

As to the above provisions, the reader is referred to the discussion in relation to the Rome Convention, above at 3.62, in addition, in relation to the Protocol, it will be seen that a 'fixed platform' is defined in Article 1(3) as 'an artificial island, installation or structure permanently attached to the sea-bed for the purpose of exploration or exploitation of resources or for other economic purposes'.

3.74 The above definition complements the definition in Article 1 of the Rome Convention, which, it will be recalled, will cover a platform which is not permanently attached to the sea-bed. It should be noted, however, that the Protocol's definition is less than clear in one regard. It is apparent from the Preamble, and Articles 3 and 4 that the Protocol addresses platforms attached to the continental shelf. Indeed, the title of the Protocol speaks of '. . . fixed platforms located on the continental shelf'. It is the sea-bed of the continental shelf with which the Protocol is concerned.[24]

3.75 Article 2(2)(a) and (b) criminalize attempting, and aiding and abetting as an accomplice respectively. Interestingly, though, and in contrast to the other penal counter-terrorism instruments, neither the Rome Convention nor its Protocol require the criminalization of aiding and abetting an attempt. Article 2(2)(c),

---

[24] The definition of continental shelf (for a coastal State) may be found at Article 76 of the United Nations Convention on the Law of the Sea 1982.

following the criminalization provision of Article 2(c) of the Convention, creates the offence of threatening to commit an offence under Article 2(1)(b) or (c). It is couched in similar terms to the Convention and the reader is referred to that discussion above.

The 2005 Protocol to the Rome Convention[25]

Two new Protocols were adopted in 2005 in relation to the safety of maritime **3.76** navigation. Neither is presently in force. The first of these is a Protocol to the Rome Convention, with a full title of 'Protocol of 2005 to the Convention for the Suppression of Unlawful Acts against the Safety of Maritime Navigation'. The second is a Protocol to the Rome Protocol and has a full title of 'Protocol of 2005 to the Protocol for the Suppression of Unlawful Acts against the Safety of Fixed Platforms Located on the Continental Shelf'.

Turning first to the 2005 Protocol to the Rome Convention, it is an amending **3.77** Protocol, which has the effect of making substantive amendments to the text of the original Convention. Given that it is not yet in force it is being addressed distinctly within this present section on criminalization.

The effect of this Protocol on the offence-creating provisions is as follows: **3.78**

- The Article 3(1)(g) offence (injuring or killing any person, in connection with an Article 3 offence) is deleted;
- The existing provision in respect of attempts (Article 3(2)) is replaced by the following:

  Any person also commits an offence if that person threatens, with or without a condition, as is provided for under national law, aimed at compelling a physical or juridical person to do or refrain from doing any act to commit any of the offences set forth in paragraph 1(b),(c) and (e) if that threat is likely to endanger the safe navigation of the ship in question.

- A new Article, Article 3*bis* is added. This Article provides:

  1. Any person commits an offence within the meaning of the Convention if that person unlawfully and intentionally:
     (a) When the purpose of the act, by its nature or context, is to intimidate a population, or to compel a Government or an international organization to do or to abstain from any act:
         (i) uses against or on a ship or discharging from a ship any explosive, radioactive material or BCN (biological, chemical, nuclear) weapon in a manner that causes or is likely to cause death or serious injury or damage;

---

[25] Not yet in force.

(ii) discharges, from a ship, oil, liquefied natural gas, or other hazardous or noxious substance, which is not covered by sub paragraph (a)(1) in such quantity or concentration that causes or is likely to cause death or serious injury or damage;

(iii) uses a ship in a manner that causes death or serious injury or damage; or

(iv) threatens, with or without a condition as is provided for under national law, to commit an offence set forth in sub paragraph (a)(i)(ii) or (iii); or

(b) Transports on board a ship:

(i) any explosive or radioactive material, knowing that it is intended to be used to cause, or in a threat to cause, with or without a condition, as is provided for under national law, death or serious injury or damage for the purpose of intimidating a population, or compelling a government or an international organisation to do or abstain from doing any act; or

(ii) any BCN weapon, knowing it will be a weapon as defined in article 1; or

(iii) any source material, special fissionable material or equipment or material especially designed or prepared for the processing, use or production of special fissionable material, knowing that it is intended to be used in a nuclear explosive activity or in any other nuclear activity not under safeguards pursuant to an IAEA comprehensive safeguards agreement; or

(iv) any equipment, material or software or related technology that significantly contributes to the design, manufacture or delivery of a BCN weapon with the intention it will used for such purpose.

2. It shall not be an offence within the meaning of this Convention to transport an item or material covered by paragraph 1(b)(iii) or, insofar as it relates to a nuclear weapon or other nuclear explosive device, paragraph 1(b)(vi), if such an item or material is transported to or from a territory of, or is otherwise transported under the control of a State Party to the Treaty on the Non-Proliferation of Nuclear Weapons where:

(a) The resulting transfer or receipt, including internal to a State, of the item or material is not contrary to such State Party's obligations under the treaty or the non-proliferation of nuclear weapons and,

(b) If the item or material is intended for the delivery system of a nuclear weapon or other nuclear explosive device of a State Party of a treaty on the non-proliferation of nuclear weapons, the holding of such weapon or device is not contrary to that State Party's obligations under that treaty.

3.79 The Protocol also inserts an Article 3*ter*:

[Article 3ter]
Any person commits an offence within the meaning of this Convention if that person unlawfully and intentionally transports another person on board a ship knowing that the person has committed an act that constitutes an offence set forth in article 3, 3*bis* or 3*quater* or an offence set forth in any treaty listed in the Annex, and intending to assist that person to evade criminal prosecution.

[Article 3quater]   **3.80**
Any person also commits an offence within the meaning of this Convention if that
person:
(a) unlawfully and intentionally injures or kills any person in connection with the
    commission of any of the offences set forth in article 3, paragraph 1, article 3*bis*,
or article 3*ter*; or
(b) attempts to commit an offence set forth in article 3, paragraph 1, article 3*bis*, para-
    graph 1(a)(i), (ii) or (iii), or subparagraph (a) of this article; or
(c) participates as an accomplice in an offence set forth in article 3, article 3*bis*, article
    3*ter*, or subparagraph (a) or (b) of this article; or
(d) organizes or directs others to commit an offence set forth in article 3, article 3*bis*,
    article 3*ter*, or subparagraph (a) or (b) of this article; or
(e) contributes to the commission of one or more offences set forth in article 3, article
    3*bis*, article 3*ter* or subparagraph (a) or (b) of this article, by a group of persons
    acting with a common purpose, intentionally and either:
    (i) with the aim of furthering the criminal activity or criminal purpose of the
        group, where such activity or purpose involves the commission of an offence
        set forth in article 3, 3*bis* or 3*ter*; or
    (ii) in the knowledge of the intention of the group to commit an offence set forth
        in article 3, 3*bis* or 3*ter*.

Just as was seen in relation to the Financing Convention, there is an obligation to **3.81**
impose liability on the legal person. This is provided for in new Article, Article 5*bis*:

[Article 5bis]
1. Each State Party, in accordance with its domestic legal principles, shall take the
necessary measures to enable a legal entity located in its territory or organized under its
laws to be held liable when a person responsible for management or control of that legal
entity has, in that capacity, committed an offence set forth in this Convention. Such
liability may be criminal, civil or administrative.

2. Such liability is incurred without prejudice to the criminal liability of individuals
having committed the offences.

3. Each State Party shall ensure, in particular, that legal entities liable in accordance
with paragraph 1 are subject to effective, proportionate and dissuasive criminal, civil or
administrative sanctions. Such sanctions may include monetary sanctions.

The 2005 Protocol to the Rome Protocol[26]

Again, this Protocol is not presently in force. Once in force, it will have the effect **3.82**
of making the following amendments to the criminalization provisions of the
earlier Protocol:

• Article 3 of the 2005 Protocol at paragraph 2 deletes Article 2(1)(e) of the 1998
  Protocol;
• Article 3(3) replaces Article 2(2) of the 1998 Protocol by the following text:
  'any person also commits an offence if that person threatens, with or without a

[26] Not yet in force.

condition as is provided for under national law, aimed at compelling a physical or juridical person to do or refrain from doing the act, to commit any of the offences set forth in paragraphs 1(b) and (c), if that threat is likely to endanger the safety of the fixed platform'.

- A new Article, Article 2*bis* is inserted. That provides as follows:

[Article 2bis]

Any person commits an offence within the meaning of this Protocol if that person unlawfully and intentionally, when the purpose of the act, by its nature or context, is to intimidate a population, or to compel a government or an international organization to do or to abstain from doing any act:

(a) uses against or on a fixed platform or discharges from a fixed platform any explosive, radioactive material or BCN weapon in a manner that causes or is likely to cause death or serious injury or damage; or

(b) discharges, from a fixed platform, oil, liquefied natural gas, or other hazardous or noxious substance, which is not covered by subparagraph (a), in such quantity or concentration that causes or is likely to cause death or serious injury or damage; or

(c) threatens, with or without a condition, as is provided for under national law, to commit an offence set forth in subparagraph (a) or (b).

- A further new Article, Article 2*ter* is inserted. That provides as follows:

[Article 2ter]

Any person also commits an offence within the meaning of this Protocol if that person:

(a) unlawfully and intentionally injures or kills any person in connection with the commission of any of the offences set forth in article 2, paragraph 1, or article 2*bis*; or

(b) attempts to commit an offence set forth in article 2, paragraph 1, article 2*bis*, subparagraph (a) or (b), or subparagraph (a) of this article; or

(c) participates as an accomplice in an offence set forth in article 2, article 2*bis* or subparagraph (a) or (b) of this article; or

(d) organizes or directs others to commit an offence set forth in article 2, article 2*bis* or subparagraph (a) or (b) of this article; or

(e) contributes to the commission of one or more offences set forth in article 2, article 2*bis* or subparagraph (a) or (b) of this article, by a group of persons acting with a common purpose, intentionally and either:

   (i) with the aim of furthering the criminal activity or criminal purpose of the group, where such activity or purpose involves the commission of an offence set forth in article 2 or 2*bis*; or

   (ii) in the knowledge of the intention of the group to commit an offence set forth in article 2 or 2*bis*.

The Bombings Convention

3.83 The 1997 Bombings Convention was, essentially, an initiative of the United States, arising from the bombing of the Federal Building in Oklahoma City. Its offence-creating provision is contained in Article 2. Article 2(1) provides that:

Any person commits an offence within the meaning of this Convention if that person— unlawfully or intentionally delivers, places, discharges, or detonates an explosive or other lethal device in, into or against, a place of public use, a State or government facility, a public transportation system or an infrastructure facility:

(a) with the intent to cause death or serious bodily injury, or,

(b) with the intent to cause extensive destruction of such a place or facility or system, where such destruction results in or is likely to result in major economic loss.

It will be noted that, once again, this is a crime of specific intent, and relates to **3.84** acts which are committed 'unlawfully and intentionally'. During the course of negations, there was much discussion as to whether the Convention should cover the activities of members of armed forces. The result of those discussions is Article 19 which provides that:

1) Nothing in this Convention shall affect other rights, obligations and responsibilities of States and individuals under international law, in particular the purposes and principles of the Charter of the United Nations and international humanitarian law.

2) The activities of armed forces during an armed conflict, as those terms are understood under international humanitarian law, which are governed by that law, are not governed by this Convention, and the activities undertaken by military forces of a State in the exercise of their official duties, inasmuch as they are governed by other rules of international law, are not governed by this Convention.

The effect of Article 19(1) confirms that the Convention does not affect rights **3.85** and obligations under, in particular, the Charter of the United Nations and international humanitarian law. It acts as a prelude to Article 19(2), which, in turn, has two distinct effects: the first part of paragraph 2 makes the activities of armed forces during an armed conflict acts which are outside the ambit of the Convention. Such acts continue to be governed by the law of armed conflict. 'Armed forces' will cover not only armed forces of a State, but also armed forces in armed conflicts where a population is fighting against foreign occupation and where there is an internal armed conflict, as reflected in Additional Protocol I and Additional Protocol II to the Geneva Conventions which cover, in the case of the former, those who take arms to counter foreign occupation and, in the case of the latter, those who take up arms in an internal armed conflict.

However, the second half of Article 19(2) is limited to the armed forces of a State **3.86** when they are acting within the course of their duty, but not taking part in an armed conflict. Thus, the net effect of the second half of 19(2) is that a member of the armed forces carrying out an official duty in another State, not during an armed conflict, would not be caught by the Convention if he carried out an explosion which proved to be unlawful.

Article 1 contains a number of key definitions which inform the criminalization **3.87** provision. As to the location of the offence, a place of 'public use' is defined at Article 1(5) as meaning:

. . . those parts of any building, land, street, waterway or other location that are accessible or open to members of the public, whether continuously, periodically or occasionally, and encompasses any commercial, business, cultural, historical, educational, religious, governmental, entertainment, recreational or similar place that is so accessible or open to the public.

3.88   In addition to the public place, the other possible locations in which or on which an explosive or other lethal device may be put include:

- 'A State or government facility' which, by virtue of Article 1(1) 'includes any permanent or temporary facility or conveyance that is used or occupied by representatives of a State, members of Government, the legislature or the judiciary, or by officials or employees of a State or any other public authority or entity or by employees or officials of an intergovernmental organization in connection with their official duties'.
- 'Infrastructure facility', which at Article 1(2), means 'any publicly or privately owned facility providing or distributing services for the benefit of the public, such as water, sewage, energy, fuel or communications'.
- A 'public transportation system' which means by virtue of Article 1(6) 'all facilities, conveyances and instrumentalities, whether publicly or privately owned, that are used in or for publicly available services for the transportation of persons or cargo'.

3.89   As will be seen, the definitions above as to location are deliberately broad. A place of public use, importantly, includes any place that is accessible or open to the public periodically or occasionally; thus, a private house that is open to the public on certain days would, on such occasions, be covered. Similarly broad is the definition of 'public transportation system' which will include buildings and other structures, such as tunnels and railway tracks.

3.90   Similarly, 'State or government facilities' will include buildings and vehicles whether or not, it is suggested, they are actually being used by the official or representative covered at the time of the bombing. Likewise, an ambassador's or minister's residence will fall within the definition since it is used or occupied in connection with official duties.

3.91   The definition of 'explosive or other lethal device' is set out in Article 1(3) as:

(a) An explosive or incendiary weapon or device that is designed, or has the capability, to cause death, serious bodily injury or substantial material damage; or
(b) A weapon or device that is designed, or has the capability, to cause death, serious bodily injury or substantial material damage through the release, dissemination or impact of toxic chemicals, biological agents or toxins or similar substances or radiation or radioactive material.

Again, the definition is wide and includes, at both (a) and (b) the device which although not designed to cause death, serious bodily injury, or substantial material damage, nevertheless has the capacity to cause death, serious bodily injury, or substantial material damage.

The Financing Convention

The 1999 Financing Convention criminalizes a number of acts, which are set out **3.92** in Article 2, which provides that:

1. Any person commits an offence within the meaning of this Convention if that person by any means, directly or indirectly, unlawfully and wilfully, provides or collects funds with the intention that they should be used or in the knowledge that they are to be used, in full or in part, in order to carry out:
   (a) An act which constitutes an offence within the scope of and as defined in one of the treaties listed in the annex; or
   (b) Any other act intended to cause death or serious bodily injury to a civilian, or to any other person not taking an active part in the hostilities in a situation of armed conflict, when the purpose of such act, by its nature or context, is to intimidate a population, or to compel a government or an international organization to do or to abstain from doing any act.
2. . . . .
3. For an act to constitute an offence set forth in paragraph 1, it shall not be necessary that the funds were actually used to carry out an offence referred to in paragraph 1, subparagraphs (a) or (b).
4. Any person also commits an offence if that person attempts to commit an offence as set forth in paragraph 1 of this Article.
5. Any person also commits an offence if that person:
   (a) Participates as an accomplice in an offence as set forth in paragraph 1 or 4 of this Article;
   (b) Organizes or directs others to commit an offence as set forth in paragraph 1 or 4 of this Article;
   (c) Contributes to the commission of one or more offences as set forth in paragraphs 1 or 4 of this Article by a group of persons acting with a common purpose. Such contribution shall be intentional and shall either:
       (i) Be made with the aim of furthering the criminal activity or criminal purpose of the group, where such activity or purpose involves the commission of an offence as set forth in paragraph 1 of this Article; or
       (ii) Be made in the knowledge of the intention of the group to commit an offence as set forth in paragraph 1 of this Article.

The offences in Article 2 may be committed by either a natural or legal person. **3.93** Although the word 'person' for the purposes of the Convention means only the natural person and is in accordance with the earlier penal UN counter-terrorism instruments, the application of Article 2 is extended by virtue of Article 5 which provides that:

Each State Party, in accordance with its domestic legal principles, shall take the necessary measures to enable a legal entity located in its territory or organized under its laws to be held liable when a person responsible for the management or control of that legal entity has, in that capacity, committed an offence set forth in Article 2. Such liability may be criminal, civil or administrative.

3.94 Given the nature of those offences created under this Convention, it was important that banks and other financial institutions should have the potential for liability. Such an approach, it was hoped, would act as a real deterrent to such institutions. Article 5 recognizes that different States approach the question of liability of the legal person in different ways. Thus, in a State which has administrative rather than civil liability (Germany and Italy are two obvious examples), the requirement, as a minimum, is that administrative liability will be imposed. The rationale underlying the phrase 'in accordance with its domestic legal principles' is that of functional equivalence. It should also be noted that liability is only required to be imposed when a senior individual within the company or entity has, in his official capacity, committed an Article 2 offence. Thus, the actions of a junior employee would not be sufficient to require the legal person under this provision to be held liable. At the same time, as Article 5(2) makes clear, the liability of the legal person is without prejudice to any concurrent or subsequent criminal liability accruing to a natural person in relation to the same offence or offences.

3.95 To make the Article 2 provisions meaningful in the context of countering the funding of terrorism, it was vital that 'funds' was defined in a broad way. Accordingly, Article 1(1) states that:

> 'Funds' means assets of every kind, whether tangible or intangible, movable or immovable, however acquired, and legal documents or instruments in any form, including electronic or digital, evidencing title to, or interest in, such assets, including, but not limited to, bank credits, travellers cheques, bank cheques, money orders, shares, securities, bonds, drafts, letters of credit.

3.96 It will be seen from the above that the types of instruments and assets set out in paragraph 1 are examples forming part of an inclusive rather than an exhaustive definition. It was also important that the definition of funds in no sense confined itself to illicitly obtained or acquired assets. By its very nature, the financing of terrorism depends upon monies and assets lawfully in the hands of a donor or supporter as well as assets acquired through illicit activity.

3.97 The provision or collection of funds is criminalized whether it takes place directly or indirectly; a reflection that an intermediary or middle person may well have an involvement, but an Article 2 offence must be unlawful and wilful and carried out with the intention that the funds should be used or in the knowledge that they are to be used, whether in full or in part, to carry out one of the acts set out in Arti-cle 2. The Convention is striking at the deliberate and intentional, not the reckless or negligent. However, one cannot help wonder whether 'wilfully' or, indeed 'unlawfully' actually adds anything to the definition. It might, one supposes, be argued that 'unlawful' is needed simply to ensure that a covert operation by law enforcement or the intelligence services which involved the handing over of funds to terrorist targets is not, unwittingly, brought within the ambit of the offences. It will be apparent, though, that Article 2 does not make any mention of a reverse burden, whether legal or evidential.[27]

It is the financing of the acts set out in paragraph 1 which amounts to offences **3.98** under the Convention. Article 1(a) relates to any act which amounts to an offence under one of the UN counter-terrorism instruments. This subparagraph includes not only substantial offences, but also inchoate offences (ie, attempt) and offences of complicity or participation.

Article 1(b) was inserted to fill any gap in respect of terrorist acts not covered by **3.99** the counter-terrorism instruments. It has been the result of much comment and discussion since, in the absence of a comprehensive definition of terrorism and 'terrorist act', it provides a partial definition for the purposes of this Convention. It is wide enough to embrace within it some acts which will, in any event, be criminalized under the other instruments and includes the purposive element of '. . . to intimidate a population, or to compel a government . . . .'. That insertion will, of course, ensure that general criminal offences, such as homicide or assault, are not brought within the definition. In relation to that purposive element, it should be subject to an objective test ('by its nature or context').

As to potential victims, sub-paragraph (b) relates to 'a civilian, or to any other person **3.100** not taking an active part in the hostilities in a situation of armed conflict . . .', the activation of the criminalization provisions then, in that regard, are wide and will sit alongside international humanitarian law during an armed conflict. However, the legitimate actions of military forces of States are, given the sub-paragraph (b) formulation, excluded from its reach.

Article 2(2) was a necessary insertion as not all States that became parties to **3.101** the Financing Convention were, or indeed are, parties to each of the instruments annexed. Thus, it is open to a State Party to the Financing Convention to have such an instrument deemed not to be included, in its case, in the annex. Thereafter, when such a State Party ratifies that other instrument, it will be included within its annex. A similar provision is provided in Article 2(2)(b) in circumstances where a State ceases to be a party to one of the instruments listed in the annex.

---

[27] See the discussion on the reverse burdens of proof in Chapter 5, below.

3.102 Article 2(3) makes it clear that it is not necessary that the funds in relation to an Article 2 offence were actually used to carry out one of the offences out in Article 2(1). Whilst the criminalization provisions are completed by paragraphs 4 and 5 of Article 2 which have the effect of criminalizing an attempt to commit a paragraph 1 offence and participation or directing others or contributing to paragraph 1 or paragraph 4 offences respectively.

The Nuclear Terrorism Convention

3.103 The 2005 Convention has wide criminalization provisions in relation to radioactive material set out in Article 2:

1. Any person commits an offence within the meaning of this Convention if that person unlawfully and intentionally:
    (a) Possesses radioactive material or makes or possesses a device:
        (i) With the intent to cause death or serious bodily injury; or
        (ii) With the intent to cause substantial damage to property or the environment;
    (b) Uses in any way radioactive material or a device, or uses or damages a nuclear facility in a manner which releases or risks the release of radioactive material:
        (i) With the intent to cause death or serious bodily injury; or
        (ii) With the intent to cause substantial damage to property or the environment; or
        (iii) With the intent to compel a natural or legal person, an international organization or a State to do or refrain from doing an act.
2. Any person also commits an offence if that person:
    (a) Threatens, under circumstances which indicate the credibility of the threat, to commit an offence as set forth in subparagraph 1 (b) of the present Article; or
    (b) Demands unlawfully and intentionally radioactive material, a device or a nuclear facility by threat, under circumstances which indicate the credibility of the threat, or by use of force.
3. Any person also commits an offence if that person attempts to commit an offence as set forth in paragraph 1 of the present Article.
4. Any person also commits an offence if that person:
    (a) Participates as an accomplice in an offence as set forth in paragraph 1, 2 or 3 of the present Article; or
    (b) Organizes or directs others to commit an offence as set forth in paragraph 1, 2 or 3 of the present Article; or
    (c) In any other way contributes to the commission of one or more offences as set forth in paragraph 1, 2 or 3 of the present Article by a group of persons acting with a common purpose; such contribution shall be intentional and either be made with the aim of furthering the general criminal activity or purpose of the group or be made in the knowledge of the intention of the group to commit the offence or offences concerned.

3.104 Article 2(1)(a) then creates an offence that may be committed in, broadly, two different ways: unlawfully and intentionally possessing radioactive material or

116

making or possessing a device with the intention of causing death or serious bodily injury, or with the intent to cause substantial damage etc. For the sub-paragraph (a) offences and, indeed, for the rest of Article 2, any offence must be, of course, unlawful and committed intentionally. The definition of 'radioactive material' is to be found at Article 1(1), and 'nuclear material', at Article 1(2). A 'device' is defined in Article 1(4) as '(a) Any nuclear explosive device; or (b) Any radioactive material dispersal or radiation-emitting device which may, owing to its radiological properties, cause death, serious bodily injury or substantial damage to property or the environment.'

Article 2(1)(b) contains the second set of offence-creating provisions, each of **3.105** which may be committed with one of three different intents. It is an offence unlawfully and intentionally to use radioactive material for a device with one of those intents (see the text to Article 2 above), and, equally, it is an offence to use or damage a facility in a manner which releases or risks the radioactive material again, with one of the three requisite intents. For this purpose, a 'nuclear facility' is defined as:

(a) Any nuclear reactor, including reactors installed on vessels, vehicles, aircraft or space objects for use as an energy source in order to propel such vessels, vehicles, aircraft or space objects or for any other purpose;

(b) Any plant or conveyance being used for the production, storage, processing or transport of radioactive material.

Article 2(2) criminalizes the person who threatens to commit a paragraph 1(b) **3.106** offence in circumstances which indicate the credibility of the threat. It also contains a second offence at Article 2(2)(b), providing that it is an offence for a person to make an unlawful and intentional demand for radioactive material, a device, or a nuclear facility by using a threat and, again, in circumstances where, objectively, that threat has credibility. The offence at (b) may also be committed where the demand is accompanied not by a threat but by the use of force.

Article 2(3) criminalizes an attempt to commit any of the offences set out in **3.107** Article 1(1) whilst Article 2(4) criminalizes the accomplice (at (a)), the person who organizes or directs others to commit a Convention offence (at (b)) and the person who in any other way contributes to the commission of one of the Convention offences, where such contribution is intentional, where the offence is committed by a group of persons acting with a common purpose and where the contributor makes his or her contribution with the aim of furthering either general criminal activity or the purpose of that group of people or where the contributor makes his contribution in the knowledge of the group's intention to commit the Convention offence or offences.

B. Criminalization of Terrorism Offences in National Laws

3.108   The UK's principal counter-terrorism criminalization provisions are contained in
the Terrorism Act 2000[28] and the definition of terrorism is contained in section 1
of the Act, which provides as follows:

> 1. *Terrorism: interpretation*
> (1) In this Act 'terrorism' means the use or threat of action where—
>   (a) the action falls within subsection (2),
>   (b) the use or threat is designed to influence the government [or an international
>   governmental organization] or to intimidate the public or a section of the
>   public, and
>   (c) the use or threat is made for the purpose of advancing a political, religious or
>   ideological cause.
> (2) Action falls within this subsection if it—
>   (a) involves serious violence against a person,
>   (b) involves serious damage to property,
>   (c) endangers a person's life, other than that of the person committing the action,
>   (d) creates a serious risk to the health or safety of the public or a section of the
>   public, or
>   (e) is designed seriously to interfere with or seriously to disrupt an electronic
>   system.
> (3) The use or threat of action falling within subsection (2) which involves the use of
>   firearms or explosives is terrorism whether or not subsection (1) (b) is satisfied.
> (4) In this section—
>   (a) 'action' includes action outside the United Kingdom,
>   (b) a reference to any person or to property is a reference to any person, or to prop-
>   erty, wherever situated,
>   (c) a reference to the public includes a reference to the public of a country other
>   than the United Kingdom, and
>   (d) 'the government' means the government of the United Kingdom, of a Part
>   of the United Kingdom or of a country other than the United Kingdom.
> (5) In this Act a reference to action taken for the purposes of terrorism includes a
>   reference to action taken for the benefit of a proscribed organisation.

3.109   As has been noted earlier in this work[29] there is no all-embracing or comprehensive definition of terrorism. It will be noted the UK's definition does not make
explicit reference to UN Convention offences; rather it provides a definition
(of terrorist acts and activities) which involves a consequence or a threat of a
certain consequence (see subsection 2 above at 3.108), but which avoids the

---

[28] The Act itself has been amended by, variously: The Anti Terrorism, Crime and Security Act
2001; The Crime (International Cooperation) Act 2003; The Serious Organised Crime and Police
Act 2005; The Terrorism Act 2006.
[29] See Chapter 2, 2.26.

purposive element seen in some States' law to the effect that a particular act is for the purpose of advancing a political, ideological, or religious cause.

As to the breadth of the UK's law, arguably the effect of subsection 3 is that the definition is wide enough to cover a lawful act of war. Indeed, that point was specifically addressed in *R (Islamic Human Rights Commission) v Civil Aviation Authority*[30]; there, Ouseley J accepted that wider construction, but rejected a submission that it therefore covered actions by the States of Israel, Lebanon, and Palestine. Although he did not give reasons for reaching that conclusion, the learned editors of *Archbold* suggest that one might infer that the learned judge took the view that lawful acts of war were impliedly, if not explicitly, excluded.[31] **3.110**

Section 1(b) speaks of a use or threat that is 'designed to influence the government . . .' and, by virtue of subsection 4(d), 'government' here means the United Kingdom, a part of the United Kingdom, and a country other than the United Kingdom. The issue arose in *R v F*[32] of whether the reference to the government of a country other than the UK is limited to countries which are governed by democratic or representative principle. **3.111**

F was charged with two counts of possession of a document or record containing information of a kind likely to be useful to a person committing or preparing an act of terrorism.[33] The prosecution alleged that F, a Libyan refugee who had been granted asylum in the UK, was in possession of twenty-one files downloaded from a Jihadist website. Those files were entitled 'A Special Training Course on the Manufacture of Explosives for the Righteous Fighting Group until God's Will is Established'. A handwritten document was also recovered which described how a terrorist cell could be set up. It addressed the concept of jihad, the removal of President Gaddafi from power in Libya, and the establishment of the rule of Allah. It gave advice on acquiring firearms for use within urban areas and also recommended mastering the use of 'explosives and mining'. At a preparatory hearing the trial judge ruled that the words 'the government' in section 1 were not limited to States governed by democratic principles, but also extended to governments which amounted to a dictatorship. The argument that a narrower definition confined to democratic governments should be construed, taking into account international human rights instruments, was rejected. The court held that the meaning of 'a country other than the United Kingdom' was plain and reinforced the international dimension of the protection against terrorism provided in domestic legislation. Section 1 was, therefore, broad and the 2000 Act did not **3.112**

---

[30] [2007] ACD 5, QBD.
[31] See *Archbold: 2008* (n 5) ch 25-57, 2265.
[32] [2007] 2 Cr App R, 3 CA.
[33] An offence contrary to s 58(1)(b) Terrorism Act 2000, see below.

create a defence for terrorism in a just cause. Terrorism was terrorism, regardless of motive.

3.113 By way of contrast, to seize on the example of a small State, the Anti-Terrorism Act 2002 of Barbados defines an offence of terrorism as including any offence under nine (of the ten) penal conventions and protocols to which Barbados is party. The tenth, the Financing Convention, being addressed by the creation of the separate crime of financing of terrorism in the Barbados statute. Under the Act, in addition to offences defined by reference to the conventions, terrorism is defined as:

> (b) any other act:
>> 1 (i) that has the purpose by its nature or context, to intimidate the public or to compel a government or an international organization to do or to refrain from doing any act; and
>> (ii) that is intended to cause:
>>> (A) death or serious bodily harm to a civilian or in a situation of armed conflict, to any other person not taking an active part in the hostilities;
>>> (B) serious risk to the health or safety of the public or any segment of the public;
>>> (C) substantial property damage, whether to public or private property, where the damage involves a risk of the kind mentioned in sub-paragraph (B) or an interference or disruption of the kind mentioned in subparagraph (D); or
>>> (D) serious interference with or serious disruption of an essential service, facility or system, whether public or private, not being an interference or disruption resulting from lawful advocacy, or from protest, dissent or stoppage of work and not involving a risk of the kind mentioned in sub-paragraph (B).

What some have seen as being a very wide definition of 'terrorism' in both of the above jurisdictions has provoked much controversy. However, these examples do not stand alone, with many States adopting an even broader definition.[34]

3.114 The conflicting arguments in the UK are set out in detail in the Criminal Law Review Commentary on *R v F*[35]. Those favouring a broad approach will argue that counter-terrorism criminalization is meant to prevent and to disrupt as well as provide a penal route. Given that such pre-emptive action is, by its nature, usually at an anticipatory stage of terrorist activity, a wider definition will prove more workable.

3.115 However, those opposed to that approach argue that such rationale is appropriate in respect of counter-terrorism powers such as arrest and the deployment of covert means, but should not form a basis of criminalization. In particular, they argue,

---

[34] See for example Uganda's 2002 Anti-Terrorism Act.
[35] Criminal Law Review [2008] 162ff.

the approach—ever since the passing of legislation to address domestic terrorism in Northern Ireland—has been to criminalize terrorist activity within mainstream criminal law and that criminalization on the basis of a broad definition of terrorism or terrorist act is a marked departure from the traditional and tested stance.

A further concern on the part of opponents of the broad approach is the extension **3.116** to encompass foreign terrorism. Certainly the 2000 Act was expressly drafted to include actions directed against foreign governments; it also needs to be viewed alongside the extraterritoriality provided for in the UK and elsewhere. However, such an argument is, to some extent, misconceived. Such an expansive approach reflects the obligations of the UK and other Member States following the adoption of UNSCR 1373 and the obligations which are incumbent on the UK as a State Party to the UN counter-terrorism instruments. A lynchpin of those so-called 'universal instruments' is the obligation on States Parties in many circumstances to take a much more expansive jurisdiction and, of course, to ensure that there is no safe haven for terrorists.[36]

As to the need to define terrorism or terrorist act, it is not possible for a State **3.117** to criminalize membership, support, and fund provision/collection offences without arriving at such a definition. However, the efforts of States to arrive at such a definition should not be seen as an attempt to arrive at a single international definition. Inevitably, it will be the domestic context for many States which dictates how broad or narrow the interpretation of terrorism actually is. An examination of approaches from around the world shows a degree of consistency. This may well be, however, because of capacity-building and technical assistance work undertaken by UNODC, the US, and certain Western governments. In general, the starting-point for a definition is the universal instruments coupled with a list or series of categories of underlying acts, and a requirement that such an act or acts was threatened or committed to intimidate or threaten the population of the State or in order to compel a government or international organization to do, or to refrain from doing, an act. Usually the definition is predicated on the basis that an act amounts to a terrorist act either because it reflects an act which has been set out in a penal provision of one of the universal instruments or because it amounts to one of the underlying acts decided upon for the purposes of criminalization by the State which is criminalizing. As already mentioned, a third element, found in the laws of some States is the additional requirement, the so-called purposive requirement, that the act is motivated by a political, religious, or ideological cause.

This approach to arriving at a definition which will then form the basis of crimi- **3.118** nalization provisions was examined by a Commonwealth Expert Group set up to arrive at model legislative provisions for counter-terrorism on behalf of

---

[36] See the discussion in relation to the principle of 'extradite or prosecute' in Chapter 2, 2.43–2.44.

Commonwealth States.[37] As a result of the Expert Group's deliberations and conclusions, an implementation kit for counter-terrorism legislation was also produced.[38]

3.119 Most States of which the authors are aware have criminalization provisions which simply rely on the universal instruments' penal formulations. Certainly for most States, the universal instruments are a starting point, providing, as they do, a minimum set of acts that must constitute offences in domestic law. The international instrument minimum is, however, supplemented by States by the criminalization of other acts which are not specifically addressed in the instruments themselves. The key issue for a State is how to provide a sufficiently comprehensive criminalization framework which does not extend beyond what would ordinarily be regarded as a terrorist act. Some States have been notably unsuccessful at striking this balance, particularly when addressing the relationship of a terrorism definition to activities such as protests or strike actions.

3.120 Many would argue that the inclusion of a purposive element is important in that it provides a true characterization to an offence separating the terrorist act from other criminal activity. The requirement of purpose also provides parameters and serves to narrow the application of an offence in such a way as to reduce the risk of abuse at the hands of State authorities. It has to be said, however, that many argue that as a matter of policy an act and intent alone should constitute the elements of the offence and that purpose, as a motive, should be of no relevance.

3.121 The Commonwealth Expert Group decided upon two separate options as to what amounts to a 'terrorist act' to put before Member States. The first of these defines as a terrorist act an act or omission which constitutes an offence within the scope of one of the UN counter-terrorism instruments, or any act or threat of action which involves one or more underlying acts or intentions. The second option includes each of these but also adds a purposive element. In each option, the second limb, 'an act or threat of action . . .', is limited by the need for there to be an intention to intimidate the public or section of public or to compel the government or international organization to do, or refrain from doing, the act.

3.122 It is to be noted, however, that these definitions, as the Expert Group's guidance itself points out, are examples and that a Member State may choose to adopt a much narrower definition so long as, from the standpoint of international obligations, that narrower definition at least meets all of the criminalization requirements contained in the universal instrument to which it is a State Party.

---

[37] That Expert Group produced model legislative provisions in September 2002. Those provisions are available at <http://www.thecommonwealth.org>.
[38] Available at <http://www.thecommonwealth.org>.

C. United Nations Security Council Resolution 1373

In respect of criminalization, as highlighted elsewhere,[39] Article 1 of UNSCR **3.123**
1373 requires that all States shall criminalize the wilful provision or collection,
whether direct or indirect, of funds by their nationals or in their territories where
there is an intention on behalf of the person providing or collecting the funds the
funds should be used, or in the knowledge that they are to be used, in order to
carry out terrorist acts.

In addition, Article 2(e) 1373 provides that States must ensure any person who **3.124**
participates in the financing, planning, preparation, or perpetration of terrorist
acts or supporting terrorist acts is brought to justice and that, inter alia, such
terrorist acts are established serious criminal offences, with commensurate sanctions in domestic law. In relation to compliance with UNSCR 1373, the reader is
referred to the Commonwealth's Model Legislative Provisions or Measures to
Combat Terrorism set out in Appendix 20 below.

D. Principal Terrorist Offences in the UK Reflecting Domestic Implementation of the UN Counter-Terrorism Instruments

Section 2, Explosive Substances Act 1883.	Causing an explosion likely to endanger life or property.	**3.125**
Section 3(1)(a) Explosive Substances Act 1883.	Attempting or conspiring to cause an explosion.	
Section 3(1)(b) Explosive Substances Act 1883.	Making or keeping an explosive with intent to endanger life or property.	
Section 4 Explosive Substances Act 1883.	Making or possessing an explosive under suspicious circumstances.	
Section 5 Explosive Substances Act 1883.	Being an accessory to an explosion.	
Section 1 Biological Weapons Act 1974.	The use of a biological weapon.	
Section 1 Taking of Hostages Act 1982.	Hostage-taking.	
Section 1 Aviation Security Act 1982.	Hijacking.	
Section 2 Aviation Security Act 1982.	Destroying, damaging, or endangering the safety of aircraft.	
Section 3 Aviation Security Act 1982.	Doing an act, endangering, or likely to endanger the safety of aircraft.	
Section 1 Nuclear Material (Offences) 1983.	Preparatory acts and the issuing of threats in respect of nuclear material.	
Section 1 Aviation and Maritime Security Act 1990.	Endangering safety at an aerodrome.	
Section 9 Aviation and Maritime Security Act 1990.	Hijacking of ships.	
Section 10 Aviation and Maritime Security Act 1990.	Seizing or exercising control of a fixed platform.	

---

[39] See Chapters 2, 6.

Section 11 Aviation and Maritime Security Act 1990.	Destroying a ship, a fixed platform, or endangering its safety.
Section 12 Aviation and Maritime Security Act 1990.	Doing an act endangering safe navigation.
Section 13 Aviation and Maritime Security Act 1990.	Offences involving the issuing of threats.
Section 2 Chemical Weapons Act 1996.	Using a chemical weapon
Section 1 United Nations Personnel Act 1997.	Attacks on UN workers.
Section 2 United Nations Personnel Act 1997.	Attacks in connection with UN premises and vehicles.
Section 3 United Nations Personnel Act 1997.	Threats of attack on UN workers.
Section 56 Terrorism Act 2000.	Directing a terrorist organization.[39a]
Section 59 Terrorism Act 2000.	Inciting terrorism overseas.
Section 47 Anti-Terrorism Crime and Security Act 2001.	Offences in respect of nuclear weapons.
Section 50 Anti-Terrorism Crime and Security Act 2001.	Assisting or inducing weapons-related acts overseas.

E. Jurisdiction

Introduction

3.126 The jurisdictional provisions of the universal instruments have a central importance both to criminalization and to the wider issues of international cooperation, in particular, extradition. It is those provisions which contain the following:

i) Clarity on whether a particular offence should be justiciable before the courts of a State, although, or course, domestic law will provide the answer on whether they actually are;

ii) The extradite or prosecute principle. In other words, *aut dedere aut judicare*—an area of law where States often face real difficulties.

iii) A starting point for addressing the issue of concurrent jurisdiction, so-called 'jurisdiction shopping'—an issue that has come into much sharper focus in recent times as crime generally has become much more transnational in character.

Principles of criminal jurisdiction

3.127 A State may assert criminal jurisdiction in one or more of the following ways:

i. Territorial

ii. Active personality (nationality of offender)

[39a] On 18 December 2008 at Manchester Crown Court, Rangzieb Ahmed became the first defendant in the UK to be convicted of directing terrorism. He was also convicted of membership of al-Qaida and possession of an article for a purpose connected to terrorism. His co-defendant, Habib Ahmed, was also found guilty of membership of al-Qaeda and of possessing books and a document for a purpose connected with terrorism. Habib Ahmed's wife, Mehreen Haji was found not guilty of arranging funding for the purposes of terrorism (*The Times*, 19 December 2008).

iii. Passive personality (nationality of victim)
iv. Protective personality (national security)
v. Universal jurisdiction.

The first two bases of asserting jurisdiction have been the bedrock of common law **3.128**
systems, save for piracy which has long been an exception to the territorial rule for
criminal jurisdiction under English law. As Viscount Sankey LC noted:

> whereas according to international law the criminal jurisdiction of municipal law is
> ordinarily restricted to crimes committed on its terra firma or territorial waters or its
> own ships, and to crimes by its own national wherever committed, it is also recog-
> nized as extending to piracy committed on the high seas by any national on any ship,
> because a person guilty of such piracy has placed himself beyond the protection of
> any State. He is no longer a national, but 'hostis humani generis' and as such he is
> justiciable by any State anywhere . . . [40]

However, the idea of territorial jurisdiction has been subject to revision over **3.129**
the centuries and in 1927, the Permanent Court of Justice in '*The Lotus case*'[41]
observed that:

> Though it is true that in all systems of law the principle of the territorial character of
> criminal law is fundamental, it is equally true that all or nearly all these systems of law
> extend their action to offences committed outside the territory of the State which
> adopts them, and they do so in ways which vary from State to State. The territoriality
> of criminal law, therefore, is not an absolute principle of international law and by no
> means coincides with territorial sovereignty . . . [42]

The Lotus case itself followed a criminal trial which resulted from a collision **3.130**
between a French steamer (the *SS Lotus*) and a Turkish vessel (the *SS Boz-Kourt*)
which occurred in August 1926. As a result of the accident, eight Turkish nationals drowned. The case was presented before the Permanent Court of International
Justice, the then judicial branch of the League of Nations. The central issue was
whether Turkey had jurisdiction to try the French officer who had been on watch
duty at the time of the collision. The incident had occurred on the high seas and
France claimed that only the State whose flag the vessel flew had jurisdiction to
conduct the trial. The court, however, rejected that argument and found that
there was no rule in international law which prohibited the taking of an extended
jurisdiction and that a sovereign state, in that regard, was able to take jurisdiction
as it wished so long as, by so doing, it did not breach an express prohibition in, for
instance, a formal instrument.

The position under common law however remained largely territorial unless **3.131**
jurisdiction was expressly extended by Statute. This is in contrast to civil law

---

[40] Viscount Sankey LC in *Piracy Jure Gentium* [1934] AC 586 PC.
[41] PCIJ, Ser A, No 10, 1927.
[42] PCIJ, Ser A, No 10, 1927, 21.

jurisdictions where the concept of jurisdiction is not seen as a concept separate to and from the aspect of statehood or indeed international law.

Jurisdiction based upon the territory where the offence was committed

3.132   The territory on which the offence was committed has traditionally been one of the most well recognized bases upon which a State can assert jurisdiction to punish an offence. However determining what constitutes the territory of a particular State is often subject to several interpretations. While offences committed on the principal territory[43] of a State would more clearly fall within that State's criminal jurisdiction, the determination of jurisdiction can become more complicated when cases involve subsidiary and extended territorial jurisdiction.

3.133   Nevertheless, this ground of jurisdiction was not recognized in the 1970 Convention for the Suppression of Unlawful Seizure of Aircraft. That agreement dealt with in-flight hijackings, many of which involved situations in which the territorial jurisdiction was either uncertain, in dispute, or not applicable, such as seizures over the high seas. However, the 1971 Convention for the Suppression of Unlawful Acts against the Safety of Civil Aviation protected aircraft 'in service', meaning on the ground in the twenty-four hours before and after a flight, as well as air navigation facilities. It therefore listed territoriality as its first ground of jurisdiction in Article 5.1(a). All of the UN instruments developed since then have included the territoriality basis of jurisdiction.

Jurisdiction based upon registration of aircraft or maritime vessels

3.134   The 1963 Convention on Offences and Certain Other Acts Committed on Board Aircraft provides that the State of registration of an aircraft is competent and obligated to exercise jurisdiction over criminal offences committed on board aircraft registered to that State. In recognition of the prevalence of aircraft leasing, the subsequent air travel safety conventions of 1970 and 1971 added a requirement to establish jurisdiction when the offence is committed against or on board an aircraft leased without crew to a lessee whose principal place of business is in that State. Article 6.1 of the 1988 Convention for the Suppression of Unlawful Acts against the Safety of Maritime Navigation used the traditional maritime approach for this registration concept, that jurisdiction exists when an offence established by the Convention is committed 'against or on board a ship flying the flag of the State at the time the offence is committed'.

---

[43]   Principal territory of a State usually comprises not only land but also maritime and air space linked to it.

The 1963, 1970, and 1971 Civil Aviation Conventions were all focused upon the **3.135**
safety of international civil aviation and specifically excluded aircraft used in military, customs, or police service.

The 1997 Terrorist Bombings Convention permits an optional ground of juris- **3.136**
diction if an offence established by that instrument is committed on board an
aircraft operated by the Government of a State, regardless of its use. That ground
is carried forward in the 1999 Financing Convention and the 2005 Nuclear
Terrorism Convention. The International Convention on the Physical Protection
of Nuclear Material and its 2005 Amendment do not specifically exclude aircraft
used in military, customs, or police service, and simply require jurisdiction to be
established 'when the offence is committed in the territory of the State or on board
a ship or aircraft registered in that State.'

Extra-territorial jurisdiction

A number of inroads have developed through both common law and statute **3.137**
which allow courts to consider acts or omissions which are not committed within
the territory, thus extending the scope of criminal jurisdiction. In other words, the
taking by a State of 'extra –territorial jurisdiction'.

The common law recognized and developed the limits of territorial jurisdiction in **3.138**
the Privy Council decision in *Liangsiriprasert v Government of the United States of
America.*⁴⁴

The appellant in that case was a Thai national who was the target of an undercover **3.139**
anti drug trafficking operation. In Thailand in 1998, an undercover agent from
the US arranged for the appellant to supply him with heroin which was to be
imported into the US for sale by a criminal organization there. Meetings took
place at which not only the appellant, but his cousin, were also present. In due
course the appellant travelled to northern Thailand to collect the heroin which he
then delivered to the agent. Two days later a quantity of that heroin was taken to
New York in a diplomatic bag by another agent, accompanied by a Thai police
officer. Meanwhile, and as arranged, the appellant and his cousin went to Hong
Kong to collect the payment and were arrested. The US sought the extradition of
the appellant and his cousin. In due course, a magistrate in Hong Kong committed them for extradition to the US. The appellant made an application to the
High Court in Hong Kong for a Writ of Habeas Corpus. That was dismissed
both by the judge and, on appeal, by the Court of Appeal. The appellant appealed

---

⁴⁴ [1991] 1 AC 225.

to the Privy Council. Giving the judgment of their Lordships, Lord Griffiths stated:

> As a broad general statement it is true to say that English criminal law is local in its effect and that the common law does not concern itself with crimes committed abroad. The reason for this is obvious; the criminal law is developed to protect English society and not that of other nationals which must be left to make and enforce such laws as they see fit to protect their own societies. To put the matter bluntly, it is no direct concern of English society if a crime is committed in another country. It is for this reason that the law of extradition was introduced between civilised nations for the fugitive offenders might be returned for trial in the country against whose law they had offended.
>
> There have, however, from medieval times been a number of exceptions to this general principal such as treason, piracy and murder committed by a British subject abroad. In more recent times, the British Parliament has legislated to make certain crimes committed abroad triable in England particularly those crimes which have been the subject of international conventions . . . .
>
> Unfortunately in this century crime has ceased to be largely local in origin and effect. Crime is now established on an international scale and the common law must face this new reality. Their Lordships can find nothing in precedent, comity or good sense that should inhibit the common law from regarding as justiciable in England inchoate crimes committed abroad which are intended to result in the commission of criminal offences in England. Accordingly, a conspiracy entered into in Thailand with the intention of committing the criminal offence of trafficking of drugs in Hong Kong is justiciable in Hong Kong even if no Act pursuant to the conspiracy has yet occurred in Hong Kong.

3.140 Extra-territorial jurisdiction is not one single basis of jurisdiction but rather a reflection of jurisdiction that may be asserted on any one of the following grounds:

   i. Active personality (nationality of offender)
   ii. Passive personality (nationality of victim)
   iii. Protective personality (National security).

Active personality (nationality of offender)

3.141 In common law systems, the exceptions to the basic principle of territoriality are based on the principle of active personality and are usually provided by statute. For instance, in the UK, the offences of murder or manslaughter of either a British or foreign victim which took place outside the UK may be tried by a UK court if the suspect is a British national. Similarly, Part 5 of the International Criminal Court Act 2001 gives domestic courts in the UK jurisdiction to prosecute International Criminal Court (ICC) crimes committed by UK nationals, persons resident in the UK, and UK service personnel, even where the alleged offences themselves have taken place outside of the UK.

3.142 In relation to counter-terrorism measures in particular, the UK's Anti-Terrorism, Crime and Security Act 2001 explicitly provides that proceedings for an offence committed under either section 47 or section 50 of the Act outside the UK may be tried in the UK and that the offences may, for incidental purposes, be treated as having been committed in any part of the UK. Section 47 provides for the offence of the use etc of nuclear weapons, whilst section 50 criminalizes the assisting or the inducing of certain weapons-related acts overseas. In each case, it should be noted that the application of sections is to acts done outside the UK if they are committed by a UK person. A UK person, by virtue of section 56, means a UK national, a Scottish partnership, or a body incorporated under the law of a part of the UK.

Most civil law systems, in contrast, assert criminal jurisdiction on this basis of **3.143** active personality. That, of course, is in addition to territorial jurisdiction, which civil law States invariably also assert, the rationale being that the State exercises jurisdiction over its own nationals wherever they may commit an offence. Equally, civil law systems would recognize passive personality; but until recently, this was not the case in respect of common law systems.

The 1973 Convention on the Prevention and Punishment of Crimes against **3.144** Internationally Protected Persons introduced the requirement that a State Party must establish jurisdiction over an alleged offender who is a national of that State. All of the subsequent instruments require the establishment of jurisdiction over nationals, with the exception of the 1988 Airport Protocol. That instrument supplemented the 1971 International Convention for the Suppression of Unlawful Acts against the Safety of Civil Aviation, which did not contain the nationality provision.

Some flexibility was introduced in the 1979 Hostage Taking Convention, which **3.145** recognized that a State might wish to also establish jurisdiction over stateless persons who have their habitual residence in its territory. That ground is listed with other optional grounds in the 1988 Convention for the Suppression of Unlawful Acts against the Safety of Maritime Navigation and its Fixed Platform Protocol (and therefore applies to the 2005 Protocols), in the 1997 Terrorist Bombings Convention, the 1999 Financing of Terrorism Convention, and the 2005 Nuclear Terrorism Convention.

Passive personality and protective personality

These bases are developing as a means of asserting criminal jurisdiction within **3.146** common law systems, particularly in the light of the attacks on the nationals of States by terrorists groups when those nationals are outside of their own State. The case of *Al-Fawwaz and others*[45] provides a useful illustration of the arguments centred around the reliance of these interlinked bases.

---

[45] [2001] UKHL 69.

3.147 The facts of the *Al-Fawwaz* case are set out in more detail in Chapter 9 below.[46] It concerned an extradition request to the UK from the USA in the wake of the US Embassy bombings in East Africa. The appellant, Al-Fawwaz, was accused in the USA District Court in New York of conspiring with Osama Bin Laden and others between 1993–1998. It was alleged that they had agreed between them that US citizens would be murdered both in the USA and elsewhere and that American officials in the Middle East and Africa, US soldiers deployed in the UN peace-keeping forces, American diplomats, and other internationally protected persons would be killed, and bombs planted at US Embassies and other American installations.

3.148 It was further alleged that, in furtherance of the alleged conspiracy, members of Al-Qaida, founded and led by Osama Bin Laden and committed to violent opposition to the US, had bombed the US Embassies in Nairobi, Kenya and Dar es Salaam, Tanzania.

3.149 A large number of people, including US nationals, were killed in those bombings. However, the US put its assertion of jurisdiction on two bases: passive personality (the US victims) and national security/protective personality (US interests being threatened and attacked).

3.150 The application of the protective personality basis was demonstrated in a recent US anti-corruption case, the so-called *Statoil* case [2006].[47] On 13 October 2006 Statoil ASA agreed to a three-year deferred prosecution agreement with US authorities, having admitted it had violated US law (contained in the Foreign Corrupt Practices Act (FCPA) 1977) on the bribery of foreign officials. The enforcement settlements reached with the Department of Justice and the Securities and Exchange Commission resulted in Statoil agreeing to pay $21,000,000 in order to settle. It was alleged that Statoil made two payments in 2002 and 2003 totalling $5,200,000 to an off-shore intermediary company which had ties to an Iranian official who was the head of the Iranian Fuel Consumption Optimising Organisation and was known by Statoil to be an advisor to the Iranian Minister of Oil. Statoil sought to use the official to gain improper business advantages. It did not perform due diligence on the official, and knew that his family was the subject of corruption allegations in relation to other matters. The payments made by Statoil went through a New York bank account to an account in Switzerland. Both payments were recorded as relating to consulting services.

3.151 The Department of Justice charged Statoil with criminal violations of the Anti-Bribery and the Book and Records Provisions of the FCPA, whilst the Securities

---

[46] See Chapter 9, 'Extradition' at 9.140.

[47] US Department of Justice Press Release, 13 October 2006. Available at: <http://www.usdoj.gov/opa/pr/2006/October /06_crm_700.html>.

and Exchange Commission alleged that Statoil had violated anti-bribery and accounting provisions. No 'active' conduct had taken place in the US and Statoil itself was registered in Norway. Indeed, it had already tendered a guilty plea to trading in influence in relation to the same conduct in Norway and had received a $3,000,000 penalty from the Norwegian authorities. The US asserted jurisdiction on the basis that US instrumentalities were used to transfer the bribe payments and that Statoil was quoted on the New York Stock Exchange. The FCPA grants jurisdiction where the legal person is a US issuer and so, to that extent, there was active personality jurisdiction. In addition, however, the underlying rationale for taking such jurisdiction here is, arguably, a protective one.

The assassination of the Jordanian Prime Minister in 1971 in Cairo and the murder of three foreign diplomats in Khartoum in 1973 were the preludes to an international response on passive personality as a basis for jurisdiction in the fight against terrorism. The 1973 Diplomats Convention was the first of the counterterrorism instruments that established jurisdiction based upon the status or nationality of the victim. In this Convention the protected status was that of '. . . an internationally protected person as defined in Article 1 who enjoys his status as such by virtue of functions which he exercises on behalf of that State'. **3.152**

Jurisdiction based upon the nationality of the hostage was established in the 1979 International Convention against the Taking of Hostages as an optional basis of jurisdiction. That Convention also introduced the protection of national interests principle in Article 5.1 as a mandatory ground of jurisdiction, when hostage-taking was committed '. . . in order to compel that State to do or abstain from doing any act'. **3.153**

The 1988 Maritime Safety Convention and its Fixed Platform Protocol included jurisdiction based upon the nationality of the victim and upon an effort to compel a State to do or abstain from doing any act, but treated them as optional rather than mandatory grounds. The optional treatment of both those grounds was continued in the Terrorist Bombings Convention 1997, which also established the optional ground of an offence committed against a State facility abroad. Those three options were repeated in the 1999 Financing of Terrorism Convention and the 2005 Nuclear Terrorism Convention. **3.154**

The approach adopted by the UN instruments

As crime transcends national boundaries, the United Nations instruments have sought to reflect this trend through mandatory (where appropriate) and discretionary measures to extend extra-territorial criminal jurisdiction. The rationale is to give effect to the principle of 'extradite or prosecute' (*aut dedere aut judicare*). **3.155**

3.156 Therefore in implementing the UN instruments, Member States must extend their jurisdiction provisions so as to give effect to the intent of the international community and to provide a truly international response through the denial of safe havens.

3.157 For example, since 1963 the counter-terrorism instruments have, as we have seen, made express mention of jurisdiction, a practice that is found in other UN Conventions such as the UN Convention against Corruption (UNCAC) of 2003, and created both mandatory and discretionary measures, reflecting a move from a territorial basis to a wider jurisdictional basis as may be seen by contrasting the 1962 Tokyo Convention with the 1999 Financing Convention:

Convention on Offences and Certain Other Acts Committed on Board Aircraft—'The Tokyo Convention' [1963]:

Jurisdiction provisions

Article 3

1. The State of registration of the aircraft is competent to exercise jurisdiction over offences and acts committed on board.
2. Each Contracting State shall take such measures as may be necessary to establish its jurisdiction as the State of registration over offences committed on board aircraft registered in such State.
3. This Convention does not exclude any criminal jurisdiction exercised in accordance with national law.

Article 4

A Contracting State which is not the State of registration may not interfere with an aircraft in flight in order to exercise its criminal jurisdiction over an offence committed on board except in the following cases:

a. the offence has effect on the territory of such State;
b. the offence has been committed by or against a national or permanent resident of such State;
c. the offence is against the security of such State;
d. the offence consists of a breach of any rules or regulations relating to the flight or manoeuvre of aircraft in force in such State;
e. the exercise of jurisdiction is necessary to ensure the observance of any obligation of such State under a multilateral international agreement.

International Convention for the Suppression of the Financing of Terrorism—'Financing of Terrorism' [1999]

Jurisdiction provisions

Article 3

This Convention shall not apply where the offence is committed within a single State, the alleged offender is a national of that State and is present in the territory of that State and no other State has a basis under article 7, paragraph 1 or 2, to exercise jurisdiction, except that the provisions of articles 12 to 18 shall, as appropriate, apply in those cases.

Article 7

1. Each State Party shall take such measures as may be necessary to establish its jurisdiction over the offences set forth in article 2 when:

(a) The offence is committed in the territory of that State *(territorial)*;

(b) The offence is committed on board a vessel flying the flag of that State or an aircraft registered under the laws of that State at the time the offence is committed; *(deemed extended jurisdiction)*

(c) The offence is committed by a national of that State. *(active personality)*

2. A State Party may also establish its jurisdiction over any such offence when:

(a) The offence was directed towards or resulted in the carrying out of an offence referred to in article 2, paragraph 1, subparagraph (a) or (b), in the territory of or against a national of that State; *(passive personality)*

(b) The offence was directed towards or resulted in the carrying out of an offence referred to in article 2, paragraph 1, subparagraph (a) or (b), against a State or government facility of that State abroad, including diplomatic or consular premises of that State; *(protective/active personality)*

(c) The offence was directed towards or resulted in an offence referred to in article 2, paragraph 1, subparagraph (a) or (b), committed in an attempt to compel that State to do or abstain from doing any act;

(d) The offence is committed by a stateless person who has his or her habitual residence in the territory of that State; *(active personality)*

(e) The offence is committed on board an aircraft which is operated by the Government of that State *(deemed extended jurisdiction)*.

Most UN Conventions, whether in the context of counter-terrorism or the more recent anti-corruption convention, tend to remain within the more traditional bases for asserting jurisdiction namely territorial (including deemed extended jurisdiction) or active personality, when setting out the mandatory basis. However, even in the discretionary provisions they tend not to go further than passive personality basis. So, the idea that the counter-terrorism conventions create universal jurisdiction is wholly incorrect. It is important to note that universal jurisdiction is limited both in its scope and application. **3.158**

The principal jurisdictional provisions in the UN instruments may be summarized as follows: **3.159**

Tokyo Convention

The effect of Articles 3 and 4 is to require the State of registration of an aircraft to take jurisdiction over offences committed on board. However, there is also the recognition that another State or States may also claim jurisdiction in a given case. Thus, Article 3(1) provides that: 'the State of registration of the aircraft is competent to exercise jurisdiction over offences and acts committed onboard'. It is competent, but it does not have sole claim to jurisdiction. In that sense, the Tokyo Convention has set a trend in counter-terrorism instruments: in relation to an act committed on board an aircraft the jurisdiction of the State of **3.160** registration is treated as the primary, but not the only, jurisdiction. There is not a duty on a State to exercise its jurisdiction. As in late conventions, there is no test of priority in relation to jurisdiction and there is the possibility of a conflict of jurisdiction, or 'jurisdiction shopping', arising. As against that, however, the requirement on States to extend their jurisdiction to cover acts committed on board aircraft registered in the State means that, wherever an offence is committed on board an aircraft, there will always be one State, if not more, able to exercise jurisdiction.

Hague Convention

3.161 Article 4 of the Hague Convention is, for its time, broad in reach. A State must establish jurisdiction when an offence is committed on board an aircraft registered to it, when an aircraft on board which an offence is committed lands in its territory in circumstances where the alleged offender is still on board, and when the offence is committed on board an aircraft leased without crew to a lessee who has his principal place of business or permanent residence (if he has no such place of business) in that State. Further, as a prelude to the central principle of 'no safe havens' which has been at the forefront of every subsequent penal counter-terrorism instrument, Article 4(2) provides for 'extradite or prosecute'.

3.162 Article 5 contains particular provisions where an aircraft is subject to joint or international registration. It requires that States which establish joint air transport/international operating organizations or agencies, or which operate jointly or internationally registered aircraft shall designate for each aircraft which State among them shall exercise jurisdiction and be treated at if it were the State of registration. However, it should be noted that Article 3(4) provides for an exception: 'in the cases mentioned in Article 5, this Convention shall not apply if the place of take-off and the place of actual landing of the aircraft on board which the offence is committed are situated within the territory of the same State where that State is one of those referred to in that Article (ie, in Article 5)'.

3.163 Thus the Convention does not apply if both places of take-off and actual landing are situated within the territory of the same party if that party is also one of the States operating the aircraft.

Montreal Convention

3.164 The jurisdiction-taking provisions of this Convention, set out in Article 5, are similar to those seen above in the Hague Convention. Again, these are reflected in Article 5(2). However, it should be noted that Article 5(2) does not extend to the Article 1(1)(d) offence.

3.165 It should be noted that Article 3 of the Montreal Protocol adds a new provision to Article 5 of the Montreal Convention. That new provision is Article 5(2) *bis*.

It relates solely to Protocol offences. The effect of the new paragraph is that a State which is party to the Protocol must establish its jurisdiction over a Protocol offence when such an offence is committed in its jurisdiction and also, it would appear, when a Protocol offence is committed on or against an aircraft in one of the circumstances set out in Article 5(1)(b), (c), or (d) of the Convention. Article 5(2) does not apply to Protocol offences; rather, Article 5(2)*bis* for Protocol offences is the equivalent of Article 5(2) of the Convention.

Diplomats Convention

Article 3 of the Convention takes jurisdiction for terrorism offences much further **3.166** than the preceding instruments. In addition to the extended territorial jurisdiction, Article 3(1)(b) provides for active personality jurisdiction and requires a State to establish its jurisdiction where the alleged offender is one of its nationals and it provides for mandatory passive personality jurisdiction under Article 3(1)(c) in circumstances where the offence is committed against a person who is an internationally protected person by virtue of the functions which he exercises on behalf of the State in question. Thus, a State must take jurisdiction where the victim is one of its own IPPs. Meanwhile Article 3(2) requires a State Party to establish its jurisdiction where the alleged offender is present in its territory and it does not extradite. This, just like the similar provisions that appear in the Hague and Montreal Conventions beforehand, is the jurisdiction-taking requirement which is needed to give effect to Article 7 (the extradite or prosecute principle).

Hostages Convention

Article 5 addresses the establishment of jurisdiction. It requires a State Party to **3.167** establish its jurisdiction on the extended territorial principle (in relation to a ship or an aircraft), on the active personality principle and where an offence is committed in order to compel a State to do or abstain from doing any act. In addition, there is discretionary 'active personality' jurisdiction provided for in the case of a stateless person having his residence in the State's territory or where the hostage is a national of the State. Again, Article 5(2) requires the establishment of jurisdiction to support the 'extradite or prosecute' principle.

Nuclear Convention

Article 8 of the Convention requires extended territorial jurisdiction (in respect of **3.168** a ship or an aircraft registered to the State in question and active personality jurisdiction).

Rome Convention

Article 6 requires each State Party to establish territorial jurisdiction, extended **3.169** territorial jurisdiction in relation to offences committed against or onboard a ship flying its flag at the time of the offence, and active personality jurisdiction. Those three mandatory limbs are contained at Article 6(1)(a) to (c) respectively. In addition, Article 6(2) allows States (but does not require them) to establish jurisdiction over: active personality where the alleged offender is a stateless person whose habitual residence is in this territory; passive personality jurisdiction when one of its nationals is seized, threatened, injured, or killed; and passive/protective personality jurisdiction when an offence is committed in an offence to compel the State in question to do or to abstain from doing any act. In addition, and as one would expect, to complement the 'extradite or prosecute' provision in Article 10(1), Article 6(4) requires the State Party to establish jurisdiction where the offender is present in its territory and it does not extradite to another State Party.

3.170 Meanwhile, the Rome Protocol contains Article 3, which follows, in essence, Article 6 of the Convention.

Bombings Convention

3.171 Article 6 of the Bombings Convention closely follows the approach of the Rome Convention in relation to mandatory jurisdiction being established: a territorial basis, extended territorial basis in respect of a ship or an aircraft flying the flag/registered to the State in question, and the active personality basis. In addition, at Article 6(2) a series of discretionary bases for taking jurisdiction are set out. If one compares that provision with the jurisdiction-taking provisions of the hostage-taking provisions one will see obvious similarities. However, the Bombings Convention goes further and allows for jurisdiction to be taken in the following circumstances: passive personality (in respect of a national who is a victim); protective personality, where an attack has taken place on a State or government facility abroad, including diplomatic or consulate premises; active personality in respect of a stateless person; and once again, the protective principle, where the offence is an attempt to compel the State from doing an act. One further basis appears at Article 6(2)(e) where a State may, but is not required to, take jurisdiction in relation to an offence committed on board an aircraft operated by its government. Finally, Article 6(4) is the establishment of jurisdiction to give effect to the 'extradite or prosecute' principle.

Financing Convention

3.172 At Article 7(1)(a) to (c) the territorial, extended territorial, and active personality bases are set out as a requirement for States Parties. In addition, Article 7(2)(a) to (e) provide five discretionary bases. It will be seen from the above test that those owe a great deal to the increasingly evolving trend of allowing States to criminalize on the basis of passive/protected personality. In addition, and as one would expect, the provision giving effect to extradite or prosecute by requiring a

State Party to establish jurisdiction in a case where the alleged offender is present in its territory but does not extradite that person to another State Party is found in Article 7(4).

Universal Jurisdiction

States had recognized and accepted extended jurisdiction in relation to those **3.173** crimes that were regarded as so abhorrent to mankind that they deserved international condemnation and censure such that any State could assert criminal jurisdiction over individuals wherever they were found. Universal jurisdiction however only applies to a narrow range of offences such as piracy, grave breaches of the Geneva Conventions, torture, and slavery. The list is limited and restricted to offences of grave concern.

Universal jurisdiction means exactly that—the power of the State to try an offender **3.174** irrespective of the nationality of the offender or where the crime occurred; at first blush it would appear that no nexus is required between the offender and the State asserting jurisdiction. The International Court of Justice in the *Arrest Warrant* case[48] made it clear, however, that a nexus was required and that universal jurisdiction could not be asserted if the offender was not within its territory or there was no other nexus with the State. Hence there are practical limitations to what amounts to universal jurisdiction.

In the *Arrest Warrant* case, a Belgium investigating judge issued an international **3.175** arrest warrant on 11 April 2000 against the Minister for Foreign Affairs of the Democratic Republic of the Congo (DRC), Mr Abdulaye Yerodia. The warrant was to seek the provisional detention of Yerodia pending a request for extradition to Belgium for alleged crimes constituting grave violations of international humanitarian law. The allegation, specifically, was that of inciting genocide; and related to a speech given by Yerodia which, it was alleged, directly incited mass killings.

The arrest warrant was transmitted to the DRC on 7 June 2000, and received by **3.176** the authorities there on 12 July the same year.

Article 7 of the Belgium Penal Code provides that: 'the Belgium courts shall have **3.177** jurisdiction in respect of the offences provided for, in the present law [genocide], where so ever they may have been committed'. It was Belgium's case that the complaints that initiated the proceedings, as a result of which the arrest warrant was

---

[48] Arrest Warrant of 11 April 2000 (*Democratic Republic of the Congo v Belgium*), ICJ Report 2002, 3.

issued, emanated from twelve individuals, all of whom were resident in Belgium and five of whom were Belgium nationals.

3.178   The DRC brought the matter before the International Court of Justice, arguing that by issuing and internationally circulating the arrest warrant, Belgium had initiated a violation in relation to DRC of the rule of customary international law concerning the absolute inviolability and immunity from criminal process of incumbent foreign ministers. In doing so, it was further alleged on behalf of DRC that Belgium had violated the principle of sovereign equality amongst States. It was argued that such violations of international law underline the issue and circulation of the warrant precluded any State, including Belgium, from executing it. The DRC therefore sought that Belgium should be required to recall and cancel the warrant, and to inform the foreign authorities to whom it had been circulated that Belgium no longer sought its execution. Belgium, for its part, argued before the ICJ that the court lacked jurisdiction in the case and/or the application by the DRC was inadmissible. It further argued that, if the court did have jurisdiction, and that the application to the Court by the DRC was admissible, then the court should reject the submissions of DRC and refuse to interfere with the warrant presently in force.

3.179   In argument, Belgium conceded that the matters to which the arrest warrant related were committed outside Belgium territory, that Mr Yerodia was not a Belgian national at the time of those acts and that he was not, in any event, in Belgium territory at the time the arrest warrant was issued and circulated. It was also accepted that no Belgian nationals were victims of the violence that was alleged to have resulted from Mr Yerodia's alleged incitement.

3.180   In giving its judgment, the court found that it did have jurisdiction and that the application by the DRC was, therefore, admissible. It found that, contrary to the submission of Belgium, there was a legal dispute between Belgium and the DRC and that such a dispute fell within the court's competence, being a disagreement on a point of law or fact and a conflict of legal views or interests between two persons. The court also went on to reject the submission that, because by the time of the hearing Mr Yerodia was no longer the foreign minister, the change in the situation had put an end to the dispute between the parties. The court concluded that a dispute remained and that the DRC continued to seek the cancellation of the warrant.

3.181   Having addressed the central argument on the issue of immunity and concluded that it was unable to deduce that there exists under customary international law any form of exception to the rule according immunity from criminal jurisdiction and inviolability from any act or authority of another State to a Minister of Foreign Affairs, the Court found that his functions are such that, throughout the duration of his office, he, when abroad, enjoys full immunity from criminal jurisdiction and inviolability. In that respect, no distinction can be drawn between acts performed by a Minister for Foreign Affairs in an official capacity and those claimed to have been performed in a private capacity or, for that matter, between acts performed before the person concerned assumed office and acts performed during the period of office.

However, no such protection would extend to a former minister in respect of acts **3.182** committed after he had left office. The Court went on to make it clear that this was the position even in circumstances where the minister in question was suspected of having committed war crimes or crimes against humanity. In addition, the court emphasized that after a person ceases to hold the office of Minister for Foreign Affairs he will no longer enjoy all of the immunities accorded by international law in other States. Thus, provided it has jurisdiction under international law, a court of one State may try a former Minister of Foreign Affairs of another State in respect of acts committed prior or subsequent to his period of office, as well as acts committed during that period of office in a private capacity.

The issue of the exercise of universal jurisdiction was very much a secondary **3.183** consideration, even on the admission of DRC itself. It argued that the arrest warrant amounted to an attempt to exercise excessive universal jurisdiction and that, in effect, the issues of international law raised by universal jurisdiction were being undertaken not at the request of DRC, but rather because of the defence strategy adopted by Belgium, which sought to maintain that the exercise of such jurisdiction can 'represent a valid counterweight to the observance of immunities'.[49]

The Court did not address the issue of universal jurisdiction in the reasoning for **3.184** its decision. Although the issue was raised in DRC's original application instituting proceedings, the DRC did not elaborate on that line of argument during the oral proceedings and did not include it in its final submissions. Therefore, the Court was not able to rule on the point expressly in its judgment. As was indicated in passing in the judgment, it would have perhaps been logical to have dealt with the issue of jurisdiction first, before going on to decide the question of immunity. However, it was the immunity argument which held centre stage. Nevertheless, most members of the Court, in giving separate opinions, dealt with the issue and concluded that a State did not have a right in international law to establish such jurisdiction over an alleged offender *in absentia* when there was no other nexus between the alleged offender and the State that was claiming jurisdiction.

The Belgium Law of 16 June 1993 was introduced to address serious violations of **3.185** international humanitarian law. Its remit included crimes against humanity and Article 7 of the Law provided that 'the Belgium courts shall have jurisdiction in

---

[49] *Statoil* (n 47) 19.

respect of the offences provided for in the present law, where so ever they may have been committed'.[50]

3.186 It was pointed out by Judge Guillaume amongst others that traditionally, customary international law recognized one case of universal jurisdiction, that of piracy. Judge Guillaume pointed out that following the Hague Convention of 1970 and the express principle contained therein of 'extradite or prosecute', the concept of universal jurisdiction has gained wider currency in respect of a broader range of offences. However, that did not provide an unfettered right to a State to take jurisdiction. Rather, there must be some connection or nexus between such a State and the offence (for instance, by virtue of the nationality of the victim or victims, or between the State and the offender, by the person being present in the territory).

3.187 The matter has, however, been reopened before the International Court of Justice in *Certain Criminal Proceedings in France (Republic of the Congo v France)*[51] when the issue will be revisited.

Jurisdiction based upon the presence of a person in the national territory

3.188 As already highlighted, a lynchpin of the UN instruments is the principle of 'extradite or prosecute' *(aut dedere aut judicare)*. To give practical effect to that obligation, States must ensure that their domestic courts are competent to exercise jurisdiction over an act which took place elsewhere and has no connection with a country's citizens or interests other than the alleged offender's presence. All of the counter-terrorism instruments that create criminal offences impose the obligation to refer for prosecution. As a consequence, so-called 'monist' countries that automatically incorporate treaties in domestic law may be able to exercise jurisdiction over an alleged offender found in the territory based simply upon the international treaty. However, not all countries provide that a non-citizen found in the territory may be prosecuted for an extra-territorial act simply based upon that person's presence, or upon presence plus a decision not to extradite.

3.189 The jurisdictional provisions of the Hague Convention 1970 provide a good example of the more limited grounds of jurisdiction found in some of the earlier instruments:

Article 4

1. Each Contracting State shall take such measures as may be necessary to establish its jurisdiction over the offence and any other act of violence against passengers or crew

---

[50] Arrest Warrant of 11 April 2000 (*Democratic Republic of the Congo v Belgium*), ICJ Report 2002, 3, separate opinion by Judge Guillaume at 36.

[51] Pleadings were due to be filed by 11 August 2008. See <http://www.icj-cij.org/docket/index.php?pr=653&p1=3&p2=1&case=129&p3=6>.

committed by the alleged offender in connection with the offence, in the following cases:

    a. when the offence is committed on board an aircraft registered in that State;

    b. when the aircraft on board which the offence is committed lands in its territory with the alleged offender still on board;

    c. when the offence is committed on board an aircraft leased without crew to a lessee who has his principal place of business or, if the lessee has no such place of business, his permanent residence, in that State.

2. Each Contracting State shall likewise take such measures as may be necessary to establish its jurisdiction over the offence in the case where the alleged offender is present in its territory and it does not extradite him pursuant to Article 8 to any of the States mentioned in paragraph 1 of this Article.

3. This Convention does not exclude any criminal jurisdiction exercised in accordance with national law.

The jurisdictional provisions, Articles 6 and 8 of the 1998 International Convention **3.190** for the Suppression of Terrorist Bombings serve as a good example of a more comprehensive mandatory and optional grounds of jurisdiction found in some of the recent instruments.

Article 6 provides:

1. Each State Party shall take such measures as may be necessary to establish its jurisdiction over the offences set forth in article 2 when:

    a. The offence is committed in the territory of that State; or

    b. The offence is committed on board a vessel flying the flag of that State or an aircraft which is registered under the laws of that State at the time the offence is committed; or

    c. The offence is committed by a national of that State.

2. A State Party may also establish its jurisdiction over any such offence when:

    a. The offence is committed against a national of that State; or

    b. The offence is committed against a State or government facility of that State abroad, including an embassy or other diplomatic or consular premises of that State; or

    c. The offence is committed by a stateless person who has his or her habitual residence in the territory of that State; or

    d. The offence is committed in an attempt to compel that State to do or abstain from doing any act; or

    e. The offence is committed on board an aircraft which is operated by the Government of that State.

4. Each State Party shall likewise take such measures as may be necessary to establish its jurisdiction over the offences set forth in Article 2 in cases where the alleged offender is present in its territory and it does not extradite that person to any of the States Parties which have established their jurisdiction in accordance with paragraph 1 or 2 of the present article.

Article 8 provides: **3.191**

1. The State Party in the territory of which the alleged offender is present shall, in cases to which Article 6 applies, if it does not extradite that person, be obliged, without exception whatsoever and whether or not the offence was committed in its territory, to

submit the case without undue delay to its competent authorities for the purpose of prosecution, through proceedings in accordance with the laws of that State. Those authorities shall take their decision in the same manner as in the case of any other offence of a grave nature under the law of that State.

Extension of jurisdiction for UK terrorism offences

3.192 In addition to those offences set out above, there are a number of jurisdiction provisions which have been introduced to comply with the UK's UN and other international obligations. These may be summarized as follows:

- In respect of conspiracy offences,[52] the Criminal Justice (Terrorism and Conspiracy) Act 1998 makes it an offence to conspire to commit a crime outside the UK. Section 5 of the 1998 Act inserts section 1A into the Criminal Law Act 1997. The effect of that is that any agreement formed after 4 September 1998 to commit an offence (not confined to terrorism offences) outside the jurisdiction is a criminal offence triable in England and Wales. However, for the offence to be capable of prosecution, certain conditions must be met. These are set out under section 1A as follows:

  (1) Where each of the following conditions is satisfied in the case of an agreement, this Part of this Act has effect in relation to the agreement as it has effect in relation to an agreement falling within section 1(1) above.
  (2) The first condition is that the pursuit of the agreed course of conduct would at some stage involve—
      (a) an act by one or more of the parties, or
      (b) the happening of some other event,
          intended to take place in a country or territory outside the United Kingdom.
  (3) The second condition is that that act or other event constitutes an offence under the law in force in that country or territory.
  (4) The third condition is that the agreement would fall within section 1(1) above as an agreement relating to the commission of an offence but for the fact that the offence would not be an offence triable in England and Wales if committed in accordance with the parties' intentions.
  (5) The fourth condition is that—
      (a) a party to the agreement, or a party's agent, did anything in England and Wales in relation to the agreement before its formation, or
      (b) a party to the agreement became a party in England and Wales (by joining it either in person or through an agent), or
      (c) a party to the agreement, or a party's agent, did or omitted anything in England and Wales in pursuance of the agreement.

---

[52] It should be noted that in many terrorist trials, the indictment will allege a conspiracy to perform an act which is an offence under the general criminal law, such as murder. On other occasions it may be a conspiracy to commit a substantive but terrorism-specific offence. However, when a conspiracy to cause an explosion is alleged, the charge should be under section 3 of the Explosive Substances Act 1883, not a statutory conspiracy under the Criminal Law Act 1977.

(6) In the application of this Part of this Act to an agreement in the case of which each of the above conditions is satisfied, a reference to an offence is to be read as a reference to what would be the offence in question but for the fact that it is not an offence triable in England and Wales.

(7) Conduct punishable under the law in force in any country or territory is an offence under that law for the purposes of this section, however it is described in that law.

(8) Subject to subsection (9) below, the second condition is to be taken to be satisfied unless, not later than rules of court may provide, the defence serve on the prosecution a notice—

   (a) stating that, on the facts as alleged with respect to the agreed course of conduct, the condition is not in their opinion satisfied,

   (b) showing their grounds for that opinion, and

   (c) requiring the prosecution to show that it is satisfied.

(9) The court may permit the defence to require the prosecution to show that the second condition is satisfied without the prior service of a notice under subsection (8) above.

(10) In the Crown Court the question whether the second condition is satisfied shall be decided by the judge alone, and shall be treated as a question of law for the purposes of—

   (a) section 9(3) of the [1987 c. 38.] Criminal Justice Act 1987 (preparatory hearing in fraud cases), and

   (b) section 31(3) of the [1996 c. 25.] Criminal Procedure and Investigations Act 1996 (preparatory hearing in other cases).

(11) Any act done by means of a message (however communicated) is to be treated for the purposes of the fourth condition as done in England and Wales if the message is sent or received in England and Wales.

(12) In any proceedings in respect of an offence triable by virtue of this section, it is immaterial to guilt whether or not the accused was a British citizen at the time of any act or other event proof of which is required for conviction of the offence.

(13) References in any enactment, instrument or document (except those in this Part of this Act) to an offence of conspiracy to commit an offence include an offence triable in England and Wales as such a conspiracy by virtue of this section (without prejudice to subsection (6) above).

(14) Nothing in this section—

   (a) applies to an agreement entered into before the day on which the Criminal Justice (Terrorism and Conspiracy) Act 1998 was passed, or

   (b) imposes criminal liability on any person acting on behalf of, or holding office under, the Crown.

• Jurisdiction in respect of sections 2, 3, and 5 Explosive Substances Act 1883, section 1 Biological Weapons Act 1974, and section 2 Chemicals Weapons Act 1996 has been extended by virtue of section 62 of the Terrorism Act 2000 to give the UK jurisdiction in respect of any such acts carried out abroad. The effect of this is to comply with, inter alia, the Bombing Convention and to ensure that on the extradite or prosecute principle, there is no safe haven in the UK for a bomber and that, in addition, active personality jurisdiction is in any event taken when a UK national commits one of the prescribed offences abroad.

- Section 63 of Terrorism Act 2000 extends the UK's jurisdiction in a similar way in relation to the terrorist financing offences contained in sections 15–18 of the Terrorism Act 2000.

- The offences contrary to section 3(1)(a) and 3(1)(b) Explosive Substances Act 1883 are extended to give the UK jurisdiction for acts committed anywhere in the world (again with a mind to the extradite or prosecute provision) by virtue of section 17(5) of the Terrorism Act 2006.

- The Suppression of Terrorism Act 1978, which incorporates the UK's obligations under the European Convention on the Suppression of Terrorism into national law provides that the offence under sections 28–30 of the Offence Against the Persons Act 1861 (Gunpowder Offences) may be tried in the UK if committed by any person in a State which is party to the Convention.[53]

- An offence under section 3 of the Explosive Substances Act 1883 may be tried in the UK when it is committed by a person in a State which is party to the European Convention on the Suppression of Terrorism (again by section 4(1) of the Suppression of Terrorism Act 1978).

- Sections 16 and 17 of the Firearms Act 1968 have also had their jurisdiction extended to cover an offence committed by a person in a State Party to the European Convention by virtue of schedule 1 of the Suppression of Terrorism Act 1978.

- An act which takes place on board a ship registered in a State Party to the European Convention is triable in the UK if, had the ship been registered in UK, the acts committed would have constituted an offence within the UK as provided by section 4(7)(a) of the Suppression of Terrorism Act 1978.

- Jurisdiction has similarly been extended in relation to aircraft registered in a Convention State by section 4(7)(b) of the Suppression of Terrorism Act 1978.

- Section 17(1)–(4) the Terrorism Act 2006 extends the jurisdiction of the UK to a number of offences committed abroad. It provides by virtue of section 17(1) that if a person does anything outside the UK and his action, if done in a part of the UK, constitutes an offence falling with subsection (2), he shall be guilty in that part of the UK of that offence. Subsection (2) for its part, sets out a list of offences which includes the encouragement of terrorism, terrorist training, the making or possessing of a radioactive device or materials, using or damaging a nuclear facility, causing radioactive materials to be released, making terrorist threats in relation to nuclear or radioactive devices, material or facilities, membership of a

---

[53] Section 4(1) of the Suppression of Terrorism Act 1978. A similar extension is provided to the offence of Causing an Explosion Likely to Endanger Life (Section 2 Explosive Substances Act 1883) by virtue of section 7 and 13 of the Criminal Jurisdiction Act 1975.

proscribed organization, weapons training and conspiracy, incitement or attempting to commit any of those offences, or aiding or abetting their commission. The provisions of the relevant subsections of section 17 are as follows:

(1) If—
  (a) a person does anything outside the United Kingdom, and
  (b) his action, if done in a part of the United Kingdom, would constitute an offence falling within subsection (2),
  he shall be guilty in that part of the United Kingdom of the offence.
(2) The offences falling within this subsection are—
  (a) an offence under section 1 or 6 of this Act so far as it is committed in relation to any statement, instruction or training in relation to which that section has effect by reason of its relevance to the commission, preparation or instigation of one or more Convention offences;
  (b) an offence under any of sections 8 to 11 of this Act;
  (c) an offence under section 11(1) of the Terrorism Act 2000 (c. 11) (membership of proscribed organisations);
  (d) an offence under section 54 of that Act (weapons training);
  (e) conspiracy to commit an offence falling within this subsection;
  (f) inciting a person to commit such an offence;
  (g) attempting to commit such an offence;
  (h) aiding, abetting, counselling or procuring the commission of such an offence.
(3) Subsection (1) applies irrespective of whether the person is a British citizen or, in the case of a company, a company incorporated in a part of the United Kingdom.
(4) In the case of an offence falling within subsection (2) which is committed wholly or partly outside the United Kingdom—
  (a) proceedings for the offence may be taken at any place in the United Kingdom; and
  (b) the offence may for all incidental purposes be treated as having been committed at any such place.

- Section 1(1)(a) and (b) extend jurisdiction to comply with the UK's obligations under the Diplomats Convention. But, in addition, section 17 of the Terrorism Act 2006, as discussed above, by virtue of section 17(2)(a) as set out above, extends the UK's jurisdiction in compliance with its Convention obligations to 'an offence under section 1 or 6 of the 2006 Act insofar as such an offence is committed in relation to any statement, instruction or training in relation to which that section has effect by reason of its relevance to the commission, preparation or instigation of one or more Convention offences'.

4

INVESTIGATIONS AND PROSECUTIONS[1]

A. Reactive Investigations	4.02	F. Bomb/Explosion Scene
Evidence from an accomplice	4.03	Management 4.112
Resident sources/cooperating defendants	4.08	G. Proactive Investigations 4.124
Witness protection	4.20	H. Covert Methodologies 4.130
Anonymous witnesses	4.30	Interception of communications 4.130
B. Stop and Search	4.57	Covert investigative techniques
C. Arrest	4.65	and human rights law 4.161
D. Detention	4.67	Covert human sources 4.177
E. Admissions and Confessions	4.85	Surveillance 4.213
Oppression and unfairness	4.93	Entrapment 4.248
Silence as an admission	4.101	I. Membership of a Proscribed
Admissions occasioned by tricks	4.103	Organization 4.266
At what stage should an admission/		
confession be challenged?	4.107	

The nature of the terrorist threat has changed since the 1990s, with ensuing **4.01** practical impact upon the way that investigations are conducted. The threat now for many States is of a network, or networks, of loosely-affiliated terrorist groups stretching to many parts of the world and having the aim, intent, and capability to attack without warning and to inflict mass casualties upon the public at large. Investigations, as a result, have become increasingly transnational, complex, and more likely to rely upon covert, or so-called 'special investigative' techniques.

A. Reactive Investigations

Traditionally, counter-terrorism investigations have tended to be reactive, as opposed **4.02** to the increasingly important proactive investigations which are discussed in detail later in this chapter.[2]

---

[1] The purpose of this chapter is not to provide a comprehensive discussion of investigative and prosecutorial issues, but rather to highlight those topics, cases, and materials which are likely to exercise the mind of the counter-terrorism practitioner.

[2] See 4.124 ff, below.

Evidence from an accomplice

4.03 Reactive investigations will often rely on forensic and financial evidence, along with eyewitness accounts. However, one of the most compelling pieces of testimony in a terrorist case, but equally one of the most dangerous to all sides, is that from an individual who has been within the terrorist group or organization. The risk of using such a witness is obvious; is he or she credible and has his or her evidence been distorted, or even fabricated, in the hope of reward? Equally, is he or she simply providing evidence because of some form of inducement, such as the expectation of a reduced sentence? All of this has also to be set against a background of possible risk to life, manipulation of the process, and, very often, a history of past criminality and related 'baggage'.

4.04 In a terrorist case, such a criminal associate or accomplice, perhaps faced with overwhelming evidence, may turn *State's*, or *Queen's*, *Evidence* and elect to give evidence against others. No particular difficulties of procedure should arise here for either prosecution or defence. Depending on the jurisdiction, it will usually be that a draft witness statement or witness account (in front of a magistrate or judge in civil law jurisdictions) is provided by an accused who has decided to cooperate. As a matter of practice in some States where a signature is required, such a witness statement will not be signed until after a plea of guilty has been entered. Sentence, meanwhile, will usually, but not invariably, be passed after he has given evidence at the trial or trials of his associates.

4.05 Jurisdictions vary in their approach as to whether sentencing for such a witness should take place before or after evidence has been given.

4.06 In the UK, the approach of judges until the end of the 1970s was that a co-accused should be sentenced before giving evidence. Lord Goddard CJ, giving judgment in *Payne*,[3] stated that co-accused should generally be sentenced together but, 'what I have said does not apply to the exceptional case where a man who pleads guilty is going to be called as a witness, in those circumstances it is right that he be sentenced there and then so that there can be no suspicion that his evidence is coloured by the fact that he hopes to get a lighter sentence'.

4.07 However, Boreham J, giving the judgment in the Court of Appeal in *Weekes*,[4] stated that an accused who gives evidence against his former co-accused should not be sentenced until after the co-accused's trial. He stated that:

> Here are made manifest difficulties that arise when persons involved with others are sentenced before the full facts have been heard, particularly where a trial is to take place, as it was to take place here . . . There may be exceptions, but generally it is

---

[3] [1950] 1 All ER 102.
[4] [1980] 73 Cr App R 161.

clearly right, it is clearly fairer and it is better for both the public and all the defendants concerned, that all are sentenced at the same time and at the same court whenever that is possible.[5]

That the position remains as it was stated in *Weekes* was confirmed by the Court of Appeal in *Chan Wai-Keung*.[6]

Resident sources/cooperating defendants

The same principles as regards timing of sentence and the dangers of relying on accomplice evidence alone will also be applicable in the case of what is variously called a resident informant, resident source, 'supergrass', or cooperating defendant. **4.08**

For present purposes, a resident informant or cooperating defendant is an active participant in a serious crime (or a number of serious crimes) who, after arrest or conviction, elects to identify, give evidence against, and provide intelligence about criminal associates involved in those or other offences. A member of a terrorist organization who decides to cooperate with the authorities may well fall into this category. **4.09**

In the UK, the use of resident informants fell into abeyance, perhaps even disrepute, in the 1980s. Previously, resident informants had been used in trials of organized criminals and in Northern Ireland terrorist cases. However, almost insurmountable problems were encountered in relation to the preservation of credibility of the resident informant as a witness and minimizing the risk of it being said that an individual had been induced by thought of rewards or advantage to give evidence which was unreliable or untrue. **4.10**

However, resident informants have been used with real effect from the late 1990s onwards in corruption and organized crime trials, the methodology now employed being better able to withstand challenge before a court. **4.11**

The method and basis for the handling of resident informants varies from State to State. In the UK, guidelines are contained in Home Office Circular 9/1992. However, it should be noted immediately that the guidance contained therein, although useful in some respects, is generally regarded as being out of date and in need of rewriting. It is believed that a revised guidance document is under consideration. **4.12**

There are, however, other sources of information providing detail of handling and management which will be of useful application across jurisdictions. The Court of Appeal considered the method of interviewing and debriefing resident **4.13**

---

[5] [1980] 73 Cr App R 161, 166.
[6] [1995] 1 WLR 251; [1995] 2 Cr App R 469.

informants in *R v Drury & Others*,[7] and concluded that both the interview as a suspect and the debriefing as a witness should be tape-recorded. Meanwhile, the Court of Appeal Civil Division set out details of the prison regime for prisoners categorized by the Prison Service as 'protected witnesses' in *Bloggs v The Secretary of State for the Home Department*.[8]

4.14 In the UK, before any attempt is made to debrief or to take a draft witness state-ment from a potential resident informant, he or she should be 'cleansed' of his/her criminality; in other words, there should be an interview as a suspect during which all previous offending should be admitted. Those admissions will, in due course, be reflected in criminal charges sufficient to represent the level and extent of the admitted offending.

4.15 It is, however, important that the potential resident informant is not misled: it might, therefore, be thought that only two promises should be given. First, that any assistance will be brought to the attention of the sentencing judge (in a so-called 'text'; that is to say, a written note outlining and evaluating the assistance that has been given) and that any duty of care issues arising will be properly addressed.

4.16 It is only after admissions have been obtained that the second stage, that of debrief-ing as a potential witness, should be undertaken. As already indicated, the Court of Appeal stated in *R v Drury & Others* that the debrief process should be tape-recorded (Code E of PACE applying in the UK), even though it will usually consist of 'free recall', rather than questions and answers. Those conducting the debrief should, however, not be part of the investigative team.

4.17 Typically, the potential resident informant will have been remanded in custody by a court and will then be produced (by a production order) for the purposes of further interview and debrief. It should, therefore, be remembered that he or she will remain the prison governor's responsibility and that decisions regarding privileges and visits rest ultimately with the governor.

4.18 A resident informant who admits the full extent of his/her criminality and who remains credible to the extent that he/she gives evidence for the prosecution, can expect to receive a discount on sentence. In some jurisdictions, this may amount to as much as about two-thirds reduction.

4.19 Finally, given the twin difficulties of credibility and accusations of 'inducement', it will usually be the position that the prosecution does not seek to rely for its case on the evidence of an uncorroborated single resident informant.

---

[7] [2001] EWCA Crim 1753.
[8] [2003] EWCA Civ 686.

Witness protection

In some jurisdictions witness protection is organized nationally, whilst, in others, **4.20** programmes are organized regionally or by individual police forces or law enforcement agencies.

Principle

The interests of justice require that vulnerable witnesses, both child and adult, are **4.21** afforded as much protection as possible to enable them to give evidence in a way which maintains the quality of that evidence and minimizes the trauma suffered.

Equally, justice requires that measures to protect vulnerable witnesses do not **4.22** deprive the defendant of his right to a fair trial, and that any restriction on the principle of open justice must be fully justified.

Protective measures such as the provision of screens

Some States have already made provision for special measures to assist vulnerable **4.23** and intimidated witnesses; including, for instance, the use of screens. The interests of the victims/witnesses must be balanced against the right of the defendant to have a fair trial as understood by international human rights law.[9]

In *X v United Kingdom*,[10] the Commission heard a complaint from Northern **4.24** Ireland where, during a single judge court (known as a 'Diplock Court'), witnesses were shielded so that the accused, the press, and the public were unable to see them. The witnesses could, however, be seen by counsel and the judge.

The Commission was of the opinion that the complaint was manifestly ill-founded **4.25** because:

- the applicant was able, through his legal representative, to put all questions to the witnesses in question;
- the evidence in question was 'far from being the only item of evidence on which the court based its judgment'; and,
- although the public was not able to see the screened witnesses, the interference with the right to a public hearing was kept to a minimum by the fact that the public was not excluded from the proceedings, but could hear all the questions put to and answers given by the witnesses.

In any wider consideration of the issues, the European Court of Human Rights **4.26** case of *Doorson v Netherlands*[11] on witness anonymity is useful. The decision not

---

[9] See Chapter 8, below.
[10] (1993)15 EHRR CD 113.
[11] (1996) 22 EHRR 330.

to disclose the identity of two anonymous witnesses to the defence was inspired by the need to obtain evidence from them while at the same time protecting them against possible reprisals by the applicant (the Court had noted that while there was no evidence that any of the witnesses had been threatened by the applicant, there was evidence that drug dealers in general resorted to terror against those who testified against them). The Court held that 'it is a relevant reason to allow them anonymity but it remains to be seen whether it was sufficient'.[12]

4.27 The Court in the *Doorson* case concluded that there were sufficient safeguards in the case to counterbalance 'the handicaps under which the defence laboured':

- the anonymous witnesses had been questioned in the presence of Counsel by an investigating magistrate who knew of their identity;
- the Magistrate was able to note the circumstances on the basis of which he was able to draw conclusions as to the reliability of their evidence;
- Counsel was not only present but was able to ask any questions he wished other than those which might lead to the identification of the witness;
- a conviction 'should not be based solely or to a decisive extent on anonymous statements'[13] (but that was not the case in *Doorson*); and
- 'evidence obtained from witnesses under conditions in which the rights of the defence cannot be secured to the extent normally required by the Convention should be treated with extreme care'.[14]

4.28 For those States that have not addressed witness protection, what should be the approach? A change to evidentiary rules may well be required in order to protect witnesses and, to that end, States may wish to consider procedural reforms of the kind envisaged by Article 24 of the UN Convention against Transnational Organized Crime (UNTOC).[15] In summary, those include providing evidentiary rules to permit witness testimony to be given in a manner that best ensures the

---

[12] *Doorson* (n 11) at para 71.
[13] *Doorson* (n 11) at para 76.
[14] *Doorson* (n 11) at para 77.
[15] Article 24 provides that:

1. Each State Party shall take appropriate measures within its means to provide effective protection from potential retaliation or intimidation for witnesses in criminal proceedings who give testimony concerning offences covered by this Convention and, as appropriate, for their relatives and other persons close to them.
2. The measures envisaged in paragraph 1 of this Article may include, inter alia, without prejudice to the rights of the defendant, including the right to due process:
(*a*) Establishing procedures for the physical protection of such persons, such as, to the extent necessary and feasible, relocating them and permitting, where appropriate, non-disclosure or limitations on the disclosure of information concerning the identity and whereabouts of such persons; (*b*) Providing evidentiary rules to permit witness testimony to be given in a manner that ensures the safety of the witness, such as permitting testimony to be given through the use of communications technology such as video links or other adequate means.

safety of the witness, such as permitting testimony to be given through the use of communications technology such as video links.

However, another practical inroad is a reform in procedure which allows the **4.29** evidential recognition of witness statements or their equivalent which are taken pre-trial. In most European States, pre-trial statements given by witnesses and informants are recognized as valid evidence in court, provided that the parties have had the opportunity to participate in the examination of witnesses. A report by a Council of Europe Group of Experts suggests that, in a system where pre-trial statements of witnesses or testimonies of anonymous witnesses are generally regarded as valid evidence during proceedings, such procedures can provide effective protection of witnesses. The need for other measures to ensure the physical protection of witnesses is perhaps less called for in a system that makes such procedural provision.

Anonymous witnesses

Another, but controversial, measure to protect a witness is by grant of anonymity. **4.30** In the context of terrorism, the issue was raised in *Al-Fawwaz & Others*.[16] There, Al-Fawwaz, Abdel Bary, and Eidarous were accused of a conspiracy to murder US nationals, diplomats, and personnel as part of the conspiracy by members of Al-Qaida. The US sought their extradition in respect of the bombings of the US Embassies in Nairobi and Dar es Salaam in 1998.

Following the committal hearing the defence lodged an application for habeas **4.31** corpus and raised two issues: (i) in order to constitute an extradition crime the conduct must be committed in the territory of the US; and (ii) the reliance on the evidence of an anonymous witness.

The Administrative Court held that in order to amount to an extradition crime, **4.32** the conduct must be committed in the territory of the USA and went on to identify a number of acts during the course of the conspiracy which touched the USA.

The matter went on appeal to the House of Lords, where Their Lordships were asked to address two issues: one of jurisdiction,[17] the other of witness anonymity.

On that second matter, Their Lordships did not accept that the magistrate had **4.33** erred in law in admitting the evidence of an anonymous witness and neither did it violate the rights of the fugitives under Article 5 or 6 of ECHR:

---

3. States Parties shall consider entering into agreements or arrangements with other States for the relocation of persons referred to in paragraph 1 of this Article 28.
4. The provisions of this Article shall also apply to victims insofar as they are witnesses.

[16] *In re Al-Fawwaz; In re Abdel Bary; In re Eidarous* [2001] UKHL 69.
[17] Addressed in Chapter 3, at 3.144.

In my opinion the two Administrative Courts were right to reject this argument as it is clear from the decision of the European Commission of Human *Rights in Kirkwood v United Kingdom* (1984) 37 DR 158 that the provisions of article 6 do not apply to a committal hearing on an application for extradition . . . I consider that at the committal proceedings the appellants were able to challenge the lawfulness of their detention, and as they cannot rely on article 6 in respect of that hearing they cannot claim the rights given by article 6 by relying on article 5(4).[18]

4.34 As to the position at common law in respect of the substantive issue of whether a witness's anonymity can be preserved, the Court of Appeal in *R v Taylor (G)*[19] set out relevant factors for a trial judge to consider when deciding whether a witness may be permitted to conceal his identity entirely from the accused:

i) There must be real grounds for fear of the consequences if the identity of the witness was to be revealed. However, the fear need not be the witness's own, nor need he be fearful for himself alone.

ii) The evidence the witness is able to give must be sufficiently important for it to be unfair to force the prosecution to proceed without it.

iii) The prosecution must satisfy the court that the creditworthiness of the witness has been fully investigated and disclosed to the defence.

iv) The court must be satisfied that there would be no undue prejudice to the accused. To that end, measures such as a video screen to enable the accused to see the witness, or a screen to shield the witness from the direct sight of the dock might be considered.

v) The court should balance the need for protection on the one hand, with unfairness or the appearance of unfairness to the accused.

4.35 Anonymity was further considered in *R v Dennis (Iain); R v Ellis, Gregory, Simms and Martin.*[20] There the Court of Appeal held that:

i) The court possesses an inherent jurisdiction at common law to control its own proceedings, if necessary by adapting and developing existing processes.

ii) The disadvantages of witness anonymity can be lessened if the defendant has the benefit of counsel who can pursue a substantial degree of cross-examination of the witness before the jury, and if the prosecution properly discharges its disclosure obligations.

iii) In broad terms, the same considerations apply to witnesses called by or on behalf of the defence.

iv) The seminal decisions of the ECtHR are *Doorson v Netherlands* and *Van Mechelen v Netherlands*.

---

[18] [2001] UKHL 69, per Lord Hutton at para 87.
[19] *R v Taylor (G)*, The Times 17 August 1994 (CA).
[20] *R v Dennis (Iain); R v Ellis, Gregory, Simms and Martin*, The Times 1 June 2006 (CA).

v) The discretion of a trial judge to permit anonymity is beyond question, but the principles in *Al-Fawwaz*[21] are not to be treated as obiter dicta and do not conflict with ECtHR case law. The application must be examined by applying the Strasbourg jurisprudence.

Recent Developments

This issue of witness anonymity in common law jurisdictions will need to be revisited in the light of the decision of the House of Lords in *R v Davis*.[22] **4.36**

The appellant D was extradited from the US and stood trial at the Central Criminal Court in London on two counts of murder. Those related to a shot which was fired from a gun at a New Year's Eve party in 2002, which had the effect of killing two men. D was convicted on the strength of evidence from witnesses who had been granted anonymity. He appealed to the Court of Appeal Criminal Division and, that appeal having been dismissed, thence to the House of Lords. **4.37**

At trial, D admitted that he had been at the New Year's Eve party but claimed that he had left before the shooting had taken place. He denied he was the gunman. However, he had left the UK and gone to the US on a false passport shortly after the killings. On return to the UK, he refused to answer questions in interview. He gave details of his alibi only when giving evidence himself at trial, and he called no further witnesses to substantiate that alibi. **4.38**

Three witnesses on behalf of the prosecution were able to identify the appellant as the gunman. Each of these witnesses claimed to be in fear of their lives if it became known they had given evidence against the appellant. Their claims of fear were investigated and accepted as genuine by both the trial judge and the Court of Appeal. To preserve their safety, and to ensure their willingness to give evidence, the trial judge made an order in the following terms: **4.39**

 i) the witnesses were each to give evidence under a pseudonym;
 ii) the addresses and any personal details and any particulars which might identify the witnesses, were to be withheld from the appellant and his legal advisors;
 iii) the appellant's counsel was permitted to ask the witnesses no question which might enable any of them to be identified;
 iv) the witnesses were each to give evidence behind screens so they could be seen by the judge and the jury, but not by the appellant;

---

[21] [2001] UKHL 69.
[22] [2008] UKHL 36 which, arguably, has the effect of rendering the use of anonymous evidence impermissible at common law. Accordingly, common law States will need to consider whether explicit provisions to allow for anonymity are required and, if so, will need to pass legislation to that effect.

v) the witnesses' voices were to be heard by the judge and the jury but were to be heard by the appellant and his counsel subject to mechanical distortion so as to prevent recognition by the appellant.

4.40 The effect of the trial judge's order was not to deny defence counsel the opportunity of seeing the witnesses as they gave evidence. However, defence counsel took the view that it was incompatible with his relationship with his lay client to receive information which he could not communicate to the appellant in order to obtain instructions. Accordingly, he submitted to the same restriction as was imposed on the appellant. At trial the defence objected to the restrictions, arguing that they were contrary to the common law of England, inconsistent with Article 6(3)(d) of the ECHR and rendered the trial of the appellant unfair. These arguments were also advanced before the Court of Appeal, but were rejected. However, the Court of Appeal certified a point of law of general public importance in the following terms: 'is it permissible for a defendant to be convicted where a conviction is based solely or to a decisive extent on the testimony of one or more anonymous witnesses?'

4.41 It should be noted that the challenge of the appellant, both before the Court of Appeal and the House of Lords, was not in relation to anonymity alone, but was, rather, to the range of measures imposed by the judge and described by the House of Lords as 'protective measures'.

4.42 Giving the leading speech, Lord Bingham of Cornhill observed that it was a long-established principle of the English common law that, subject to certain exceptions, the defendant in a criminal trial should be confronted by his accusers in order that he may cross-examine them and challenge their evidence. That, he said, was a principle that originated in ancient Rome. He noted that, although there had been long-recognized exceptions to the right of confrontation such as, dying declarations and statements which are part of the *res gestae*, there had not, until recently, been a precedent for protective measures of the kind which were now being considered, even when witness intimidation was an extreme problem, as in terrorist trials in Northern Ireland.

4.43 He noted that the 1972 commission, chaired by Lord Diplock, set up to report on 'Legal Procedures to Deal with Terrorist Activities' concluded that the problem with witness intimidation could not be overcome by any changes in the trial, the rules of evidence, or the onus of proof which it would regard as appropriate to trial by judicial process in a court of law. It considered that the minimum requirements for criminal trial by a court of law called for the accused to be informed in detail of the nature of the accusation against him and to examine, or have examined, witnesses against him. Lord Diplock's commission, Lord Bingham stated, could see no way of keeping the identity of witnesses secret without gravely compromising the defence or exposing defence counsel to a conflict of duty between that owed to his lay client and that to the State, consistent with the role of being a defence lawyer in a judicial process.

Surveying other jurisdictions, Lord Bingham noted that the right to confront **4.44** a witness was adopted in the US as a constitutional right, being described there as 'an essential and fundamental requirement for the kind of fair trial which is this country's constitutional goal'.[23] In other States which have taken their procedure from the common law tradition, Lord Bingham also noted that although the right to confrontation has not achieved constitutional protection, it has been treated as an important right.[24]

In his consideration of earlier authorities, Lord Bingham also highlighted the **4.45** South African case of *S v Leepile*.[25] In that case, the prosecution in a criminal trial applied to the trial judge to withhold the name and identity of a witness from the defendant. In the last of a number of rulings to which that application gave rise, Ackermann J stated:

> The wide direction regarding secrecy sought by the State in the present application has far more drastic consequences for the accused than an *in camera* hearing with a restriction of the publication to the public of a witness's identity. The consequences to the accused of such a wide direction are, *inter alia*, the following:
>
> (a) No investigation could be conducted by the accused's legal representatives into the witness's background to ascertain if he has a general reputation for untruthfulness, whether he as made previous inconsistent statements nor to investigate other matters which might be relevant to his credibility in general.
> (b) It would make it more difficult to make enquiries to establish that the witness was not at places on the occasions mentioned by him.
> (c) It would further heighten the witness's sense of impregnability and increase the temptation to falsify and exaggerate.[26]

It is to be noted that Ackerman J also went on to distinguish the wide anonymity **4.46** being sought by the prosecution in argument before him from the position in which the identity of a witness is withheld from the general public alone. Indeed, he observed that the prosecution had been unable to refer him to any case law, either in South Africa or from the UK, in which the principle of anonymity had, at that stage, been taken as far as was then being sought.[27]

---

[23] *Pointer v Texas* 380 US 400 (1965).
[24] See, for example, the decision of the Court of Appeal of New Zealand in *R v Hughes* [1986] 2 NZLR 129.
[25] This case gave rise to a number of rulings which may be found as follows (1–3) 1986(2) SA333; (4) 1986(3) SA661.
[26] *S v Leepile* (5) 1986(4) SA187, 198.
[27] *Leepile* (n 26) 90.

4.47   In his speech, Lord Bingham turned his attention to the UK case law[28] and noted that the first judicial departure from the basic principle of confrontation in the UK occurred in *R v Murphy & Another*.[29] In that case, two defendants were convicted of the murder of two British army corporals. The killings had received much publicity and, indeed, prosecution evidence presented at trial included that of a number of televisions journalists who had been filming the scene of the killing. The trial judge had ruled that those journalistic witnesses should not be identified by name and that, in giving their evidence, they should be screened so that their faces would only be seen by the judge and the lawyers, but not by the defendants or the public. On appeal, the Court of Appeal in Northern Ireland upheld that decision. It should be noted, however, that at trial, the defence had not raised any objection to the withholding of the identities and, indeed, that the evidence of the witnesses themselves, although establishing a necessary link in the prosecution case, did not implicate the defendants in the commission of the offences. In addition, the credibility, as opposed to the reliability, of the journalistic witnesses was not in issue.

4.48   Continuing his analysis of the case law, Lord Bingham discussed the decision of the Divisional Court in *R v Watford Magistrates' Court, ex parte Lenman*.[30] That case arose from a challenge to a decision made at committal proceedings heard by the Watford Justices. In a committal for violent disorder, the court was asked to put in place safeguards for the benefit of prosecution witnesses. The case concerned an incident in which it was alleged that a group of youths had rampaged through the town centre at Watford and, in so doing, had attacked a number of victims. Several witnesses, fearing for their safety if identified, had made witness statements to the police using pseudonyms. At the committal hearing an application was made that those witnesses should give evidence using the pseudonyms, should give evidence from behind screens, and should have their voices distorted. The applications were opposed on behalf of the defendants, but the magistrates ruled that they should maintain their anonymity. However, it was also ruled that counsel and their accompanying legal representatives should be able to see the witnesses. Referring to that case, Lord Bingham observed:

> Giving judgment, Beldam LJ said it was 'well-established that there may be occasions upon which the interests of justice require that the identity of witnesses should be withheld'. The only authority cited in support of that proposition was *R v DJX, DCY and GCZ*.[31] That was a case in which screens had been erected so that child victims and the defendants accused of abusing them could not see each other, a procedure approved by the Court of Appeal. But it was a case in which the victims

---

28   2008 UKHL 8.
29   [1990] NI 306.
30   [1993] Crim LR 388; Transcript 7 May 1992.
31   [1989] 91 Cr App R 36.

and the defendants were all related to each other and the identities of the child witnesses was very well known to the defendants. The witnesses did not give evidence anonymously and their identities were not withheld. This authority did not support the magistrate's courts decision or that of the divisional court upholding it. But the challenge in the *Watford* case related to committal proceedings, not a trial, and Beldam LJ accepted that the ruling might have to be reconsidered if it appeared that real prejudice might be caused to any defendant. He also expressly left open the question whether, if the defendant's were committed to trial, the witnesses should then be committed to withhold their identities and give evidence and conditions which would preserve their anonymity.

It is, of course, not just members of the public who make claims to be in fear or **4.49** danger; police or intelligence officer witnesses may also express similar concerns. Indeed one of the authorities reviewed by Lord Bingham in his speech, *R v Liverpool Magistrates' Court, ex parte DPP*,[32] addressed the issue of undercover officers. The application for judicial review on behalf of the DPP arose from an order made by a stipendiary magistrate who was hearing committal proceedings in a drugs matter. The magistrate ruled that undercover officers, although permitted to give evidence shielding their faces from the public in court, should not be permitted to withhold their true names and identity. The DPP's application for judicial review was heard by the Divisional Court and granted. The leading judgment was given by Beldam LJ, who relied on his earlier decision in the *Watford Justices* case.

The question of anonymity will, of course, have relevance in relation to written, **4.50** as well as oral, evidence. One of the authorities referred to the House of Lords was the earlier decision of the House in *Al-Fawwaz*,[33] already referred to above, where the House of Lords decision was given in relation to an application for habeas corpus which arose from an application to extradite Al-Fawwaz and others to the US. At the extradition hearing, the stipendiary magistrate had placed reliance on affidavit evidence which was anonymous. However, the House rejected an argument against such anonymity and largely followed the reasoning in an earlier unreported case of *R v Taylor and Crabb*.[34]

---

[32] (1996) 161 JP 43.

[33] *R (Al-Fawwaz) v Governor of Brixton Prison* [2001] UKHL 69, [2002] 1AC 556. See also the discussion of the case at 4.30, above.

[34] *R v Taylor and Crabb* (unreported 22 July 1994, CA) arose out of a murder trial at the Central Criminal Court. At trial a witness was allowed to give evidence anonymously, referred to as only Miss A, and was not obliged to reveal her address. In addition, she gave evidence from behind a screen so arranged so that she, the judge, jury, and counsel could see each other directly, but she and each of the defendants could not. However there was a video camera in operation which enabled the defendants to see her on screen as she gave evidence. That latter precaution, as the Court of Appeal noted, ensured that the defendants were able to satisfy themselves that Miss A was not a person known to them or, in so far as they were aware, a person who had an improper motive for giving evidence against them. Accordingly, the Court of Appeal concluded that the possibility of prejudice had been eliminated by the safeguards in place. In addition, although Miss A was an important witness, it seems that she was a corroborative witness whose accuracy, not honesty, was in issue.

4.51 Lord Bingham in *Davis* noted that the decision in *Al-Fawwaz* and the endorsement of the reasoning in *Taylor and Crabb* might appear to assist the Crown. However, as he went on to say:

> . . . in my opinion the assistance is small: the applicants (ie, in *Al-Fawwaz*) did not challenge the correctness of *R v Taylor and Crabb*, on which indeed they founded their argument; there was accordingly no consideration of fundamental principle and little of authority; extradition proceedings are not a criminal trial and cannot culminate in a conviction; there is, in any event, no right of cross examination where duly authenticated evidence is presented in extradition proceedings; and the United States Government had indicated that the anonymity of the anonymous deponent would be disclosed in the United States.

4.52 Lord Bingham also took the opportunity of considering the authorities from Strasbourg. He concluded that the line of Strasbourg authorities, including *Doorson v Netherlands*,[35] is that the essential principle is that no conviction should be based solely or to a decisive extent on the statements or testimony of anonymous witnesses. The reason is that such a conviction results from a trial which cannot be regarded as fair. However, as Lord Bingham went on to note, such a view reflects the stance traditionally adopted at common law. To that extent, the ECHR case law has taken things little further.

4.53 The prosecution in *Davis* relied, inter alia, on the proposition that witness intimidation is a problem which is real and prevalent. In a number of cases, witnesses simply will not give evidence unless their identity is withheld from the defence. If such witnesses do not give evidence, then dangerous criminals in serious cases will walk free. The end result is that both society and the administration of justice itself will suffer. The riposte to this, given by Lord Bingham and by other members of the House of Lords in *Davis*, is that the reality reflected in that proposition is entirely accepted. However, such a problem is not a new, although it is a serious one. The remedy, if one exists, may well be for statutory provision to be made by Parliament.[36]

4.54 Following such an extensive review of the authorities, Lord Bingham concluded:

> At no point in its judgment [in the *Davis* appeal] does the Court of Appeal acknowledge that the right to be confronted by one's accusers is a right recognized by the common law for centuries, and it is not enough if counsel see the accusers if they are unknown to, and unseen by, the defendant.

4.55 Accordingly, Lord Bingham concluded, reflecting a decision echoed by all the other members of the House of Lords in the case: 'I feel bound to conclude that

---

[35] (1996) 22 EHHR 330; see 4.26, supra.
[36] As a result of the decision by the House of Lords in *Davis*, the UK Parliament passed the Witness Anonymity Act 2008. That Act is set out at Appendix 21, below.

the protective measures imposed by the court in this case hampered the conduct of the defence in a manner and to an extent which was unlawful and rendered the trial unfair. I would accordingly allow this appeal . . .'.

In another speech, Lord Rodger of Earlsferry, in reaching the same conclusion, articulated in some detail the reasons why anonymity was unacceptable in the present case. That view may well be instructive to those in any jurisdiction considering the drafting of statutory provisions on anonymity: **4.56**

> I feel compelled to the view, not without some hesitation, that I am unable to agree with the conclusion of the Court of Appeal. The testimony of the witnessed concerned was central to the prosecution case. The defence was an attack upon their probity and credibility, yet the defendants and their advisors did not have their names and were unable to see their faces or hear their natural voices. The effect as intended, was to make it impossible to identify them, which may have been necessary if their testimony was to be obtained, but was a significant potential detriment to the conduct of the defence. The anonymising measures went beyond any which had been adopted in the reported cases. Where such thorough going measures are to be taken, the court should be very sure the hampering effect will not make the trial unfair. I do not think that one could be sufficiently sure of that in the present case.[37]

B. Stop and Search

R (on the application of Gillan and another) v Metropolitan Police Commissioner and another[38]

The claimants had been stopped and searched under the provisions of section 44 of the Terrorism Act 2000 whilst participating in a protest against the arms trade, but nothing incriminating was found on them. Their application for judicial review was dismissed both by the Divisional Court and the Court of Appeal. **4.57**

They appealed to the House of Lords on the following grounds: **4.58**

(i) that the expression 'expedient' in s 44(3) of the 2000 Act should be interpreted as permitting an authorization to be made only if the decision-maker had reasonable grounds for considering that the powers were necessary and suitable, in all the circumstances, for the prevention of terrorism;

(ii) that the authorization contravened the right to liberty guaranteed by Art 5(1) of the European Convention on Human Rights;

(iii) that the stop and search power involved an interference with the right for respect of a person's private life and, therefore, had to be justified under Art 8(2); and

---

[37] [2008] UKHL 36, 34.
[38] [2006] All ER (D) 114 (Mar); [2006] UKHL 12.

(iv) that, the expressions 'prescribed by law' in Art 5(1) and 'in accordance with the law' in Art 8(2), meant not only the 2000 Act, but also the authorization and confirmation, and that those were not accessible so that a person could not know whether, if he went to a particular place, he would be liable to be stopped and searched.

4.59 The House of Lords, in dismissing the appeal, examined the provisions of section 44 which permits 'stop and search',[39] and held:

(1) The word 'expedient' had a meaning quite distinct from 'necessary'. The effect of s 44(3) of the 2000 Act was that an authorization might be given if, and only if, the person giving it considered it likely that the stop and search powers would be of significant practical value and utility in seeking to achieve the prevention of acts of terrorism.

Parliament had chosen the word 'expedient' not the word 'necessary' and there was no basis for concluding that Parliament meant something which it did not say. Moreover, the statute in dispensing with the condition of reasonable suspicion, departed from the normal rule applicable where a constable exercises a power to stop and search. The statutory context also showed that the authorization and exercise of the power were very closely regulated, leaving no room for inference that Parliament did not mean what it said. There was indeed every indication that Parliament appreciated the significance of the power that it was conferring, but thought it an appropriate measure to protect the public against the grave risks posed by terrorism, provided the power was subject to effective constraints, which were embodied in the legislation.

(2) A person stopped and searched in accordance with the procedure prescribed by the 2000 Act and Code A was not deprived of his liberty within the autonomous meaning of that expression contained in Art 5(1) of the ECHR.

The aim of Art 5(1) was to ensure that no one should be dispossessed of his liberty in an arbitrary fashion. In order to determine whether there had been a deprivation of liberty, account had to be taken of a whole range of factors arising such as type, duration, effects, and the manner of implementation of the measure in question. Where a person was stopped and searched under sections 44 and 45, the procedures would ordinarily be relatively brief. The person stopped would not be arrested, handcuffed, confined, or removed to any different place. He, accordingly, could not

---

[39] Section 44 of the Terrorism Act 2000 provides, so far as material: '(1) An authorisation under this subsection authorises any constable in uniform to stop a vehicle in an area or at a place specified in the authorisation and to search—(a) the vehicle; (b) the driver of the vehicle; (c) a passenger in the vehicle; (d) anything in or on the vehicle or carried by the driver or a passenger. (2) An authorisation under this subsection authorises any constable in uniform to stop a pedestrian in an area or at a place specified in the authorisation and to search—(a) the pedestrian; (b) anything carried by him. (3) An authorisation under subsection (1) or (2) may be given only if the person giving it considers it expedient for the prevention of acts of terrorism. (4) An authorisation may be given—... (b) where the specified area or place is the whole or part of the metropolitan police district, by a police officer for the district who is of at least the rank of commander of the metropolitan police . . .'.

be regarded as being detained in the sense of confined or kept in custody, but more properly of being detained in the sense of kept from proceeding or kept waiting.

(3) A stop and search power was justified under Art 8(2) in that it was necessary in a democratic society and proportionate.

It was impossible to regard a proper exercise of the power, in accordance with Code A, as other than proportionate when seeking to counter the great danger of terrorism.

(4) The test which any interference with, or derogation from, an ECHR right had to meet if a violation was to be avoided was whether the exercise of power by public officials, as it affected members of the public, was governed by clear and publicly-accessible rules of law. The public were not to be made vulnerable to interference by public officials acting on any personal whim, caprice, malice, predilection, or purpose other than that for which the power was conferred.

The stop and search regime did meet that test. The Terrorism Act 2000 informed **4.60** the public that those powers were, if duly authorized and confirmed, available. It defines and limits the powers with considerable precision. Code A, a public document, described the procedures in detail. The Act and the Code did not require the fact or the details of any authorization to be publicized in any way, even retrospectively, but it was doubtful if they were to be regarded as 'law' rather than as procedure for bringing the law into potential effect. The efficacy of the measure would be gravely weakened if potential offenders were alerted in advance. Anyone stopped and searched had to be told, by the constable, all he needed to know. Moreover, in exercising the power the constable was not free to act arbitrarily. Although the constable did not need to have any suspicion before stopping and searching a member of the public, that could not, realistically, be interpreted as a warrant to stop and search people who were obviously not terrorist suspects. It was to ensure that a constable was not deterred from stopping and searching a person whom he did suspect as a potential terrorist by the fear that he could not show reasonable grounds for his suspicion.

The section 44 power has been the subject of consternation in some quarters on **4.61** the basis that it gives a power to stop and search a person who happens to be in or at a location which has been authorized for the purposes of the section without the officer conducting the stop having a reasonable suspicion in respect of the person stopped. This decision, though, goes some way to addressing those concerns by importing a purposive requirement. A person who is obviously not a terrorist suspect should not be stopped and searched under this provision, although, of course, a person who might be a terrorist suspect, even in the absence of a reasonable suspicion, can lawfully be. However, it is submitted that, in exercising this power, an officer should confine himself to the person whom he suspects as a potential terrorist (even though he may not demonstrably have reasonable grounds for that suspicion).

R v Rowe[40]

4.62 The defendant was convicted of two offences contrary to section 57 of the Terrorism Act 2000,[41] in relation to the following material in his possession:

(i) notes made on how to assemble and use of mortar;

(ii) a substitution code with ingredients of explosives, vulnerable targets, and countries.

4.63 It was submitted on his behalf that the term 'articles' did not extend to cover these sort of items, since section 58[42] specifically covered them in a separate offence, namely the collecting or making a record of information of a kind likely to be useful and 'record' included a photographic or electronic record.

---

[40] [2007] 3 All ER 36.

[41] Section 57 provides: Possession for terrorist purposes

(1) A person commits an offence if he possesses an article in circumstances which give rise to a reasonable suspicion that his possession is for a purpose connected with the commission, preparation or instigation of an act of terrorism.

(2) It is a defence for a person charged with an offence under this section to prove that his possession of the article was not for a purpose connected with the commission, preparation or instigation of an act of terrorism.

(3) In proceedings for an offence under this section, if it is proved that an article—

    (a) was on any premises at the same time as the accused, or

    (b) was on premises of which the accused was the occupier or which he habitually used otherwise than as a member of the public, the court may assume that the accused possessed the article, unless he proves that he did not know of its presence on the premises or that he had no control over it.

(4) A person guilty of an offence under this section shall be liable—

    (a) on conviction on indictment, to imprisonment for a term not exceeding 10 years, to a fine or to both, or

    (b) on summary conviction, to imprisonment for a term not exceeding six months, to a fine not exceeding the statutory maximum or to both.

[42] Section 58: Collection of information

(1) A person commits an offence if—

    (a) he collects or makes a record of information of a kind likely to be useful to a person committing or preparing an act of terrorism, or

    (b) he possesses a document or record containing information of that kind.

(2) In this section 'record' includes a photographic or electronic record.

(3) It is a defence for a person charged with an offence under this section to prove that he had a reasonable excuse for his action or possession.

(4) A person guilty of an offence under this section shall be liable—

    (a) on conviction on indictment, to imprisonment for a term not exceeding 10 years, to a fine or to both, or

    (b) on summary conviction, to imprisonment for a term not exceeding six months, to a fine not exceeding the statutory maximum or to both.

(5) A court by or before which a person is convicted of an offence under this section may order the forfeiture of any document or record containing information of the kind mentioned in subsection (1)(a).

(6) Before making an order under subsection (5) a court must give an opportunity to be heard to any person, other than the convicted person, who claims to be the owner of or otherwise interested in anything which can be forfeited under that subsection.

(7) An order under subsection (5) shall not come into force until there is no further possibility of it being varied, or set aside, on appeal (disregarding any power of a court to grant leave to appeal out of time).

It was held that: 'Although there was an overlap between sections 57 and 58 of the **4.64** 2000 Act it was not correct to conclude that section 58 would be almost superfluous if documents and records constituted articles for the purpose of section 57. The sections dealt with different aspects of activities relating to terrorism. Section 57 dealt with possessing articles for the purpose of terrorist acts and section 58 dealt with collecting or holding information that was of a kind likely to be useful to those involved in acts of terrorism. Section 57 included a specific intention and section 58 did not.'

C. Arrest

Raissi and another v Commissioner of Police of the Metropolis[43]

An action was brought by Raissi for wrongful arrest and false imprisonment. The **4.65** court ruled that it was settled law that the threshold of suspicion required for an arrest under section 41(1) of the Terrorism Act 2000[44] was low.

---

[43] [2007] EWHC 2842. The case was subsequently appealed by the Commissioner to the Court of Appeal (Civil Division): *Commissioner of Police of the Metropolis v Mohammed Raissi* [2008] EWCA Civ 1237. M having successfully challenged the decision to arrest him and having had damages awarded, the Commissioner appealed against the order: The arresting officer (B) had made the decision to arrest on the basis that his senior officers may have additional information regarding M to which he was not privy. The Court of Appeal held that it 'was not reasonable for B to infer that his superiors must have had good grounds for suspicion of terrorism and whether B had reasonable grounds for suspicion depended on the information that he had . . .' In addition, the fact that L and M were close brothers, that they lived close to each other, and that each had access to the other's house, did not afford B reasonable grounds to suspect that M was a terrorist.

[44] S 41, Terrorism Act 2000 (arrest without warrant):
  (1) A constable may arrest without a warrant a person whom he reasonably suspects to be a terrorist.
  (2) Where a person is arrested under this section the provisions of Schedule 8 (detention: treatment, review and extension) shall apply.
  (3) Subject to subsections (4) to (7), a person detained under this section shall (unless detained under any other power) be released not later than the end of the period of 48 hours beginning—
    (a) with the time of his arrest under this section, or
    (b) if he was being detained under Schedule 7 when he was arrested under this section, with the time when his examination under that Schedule began.
  (4) If on a review of a person's detention under Part II of Schedule 8 the review officer does not authorise continued detention, the person shall (unless detained in accordance with subsection (5) or (6) or under any other power) be released.
  (5) Where a police officer intends to make an application for a warrant under paragraph 29 of Schedule 8 extending a person's detention, the person may be detained pending the making of the application.
  (6) Where an application has been made under paragraph 29 or 36 of Schedule 8 in respect of a person's detention, he may be detained pending the conclusion of proceedings on the application.
  (7) Where an application under paragraph 29 or 36 of Schedule 8 is granted in respect of a person's detention, he may be detained, subject to paragraph 37 of that Schedule, during the period specified in the warrant.
  (8) The refusal of an application in respect of a person's detention under paragraph 29 or 36 of Schedule 8 shall not prevent his continued detention in accordance with this section.

4.66 Raissi was arrested on a US warrant in relation to the events of 11 September 2001. His wife and brother were also arrested. They now each brought an action. The court found that there were sufficient grounds to arrest Raissi's wife as she:

> was not merely the wife of a prime suspect for the terrorist offences in question, but she had been with her husband in a foreign country at a time when he might well have been thought to have been engaged, at the same time and at the same location, in the very training which was being undergone by one of the known perpetrators of the atrocities.[45]

However in respect of the brother: he lived a short distance away from Raissi and was simply assumed to be connected. That was not sufficient. Furthermore, the officer conducting the arrest had:

> ... been influenced by an opinion, arising from the briefings, that family links played a part in terrorist activity, but having failed to give any reasons of substance himself for that opinion, the second claimant's arrest could not have been justified. Accordingly, the first claimant's case would be dismissed, and the second claimant's case would be allowed. Furthermore, given that result, damages would be assessed for the second claimant.[46]

D. Detention

R (on the application of Q) v Secretary of State for the Home Department and Another [47]

4.67 In this case, Q had been certified by the Secretary of State for the Home Department under section 23 of the Anti-terrorism Crime and Security Act 2001 as a suspected international terrorist and detained in January 2003. Following the ruling of the House of Lords in *A and Others v Secretary of State for the Home Department*[48] in March 2005, Q was granted bail under strict conditions pursuant to the 2001 Act and then made the subject of a control order under section 1 of the 2005 Act. In August 2005 he was served with a notice of intention to deport, and was arrested and detained for that purpose.

4.68 The difficulty arose as to Q's real identity. He had several aliases with documents supporting the aliases. It was clear that he had not disclosed his true identity to the

---

(9) A person who has the powers of a constable in one Part of the United Kingdom may exercise the power under subsection (1) in any Part of the United Kingdom.

[45] [2007] EWHC 2842, para 47.

[46] [2007] EWHC 2842, para 48.

[47] [2006] EWCA Civ 2690 (Admin), QBD.

[48] [2004] UKHL 56. A case heard in respect of the indefinite detention of the so-called detainees at Belarsh Prison, SE London, who were being held under section 23. A declaration of incompatibility under the Human Rights Act 1998 was issued in relation to section 23. The House of Lords having determined that section 23 was incompatible with Article 5 of ECHR; the provision was subsequently replaced.

UK authorities. Following the notice of intention to deport, he gave the UK authorities another name together with supporting documents. He stated that this was his true identity. The details provided stated that he was an Algerian national. He also provided them with his father's name in order to verify his identity. He applied for bail, which was refused. He subsequently also withdrew his notice of appeal against the deportation order and the order was served on him.

In the meantime, the UK authorities had submitted the information to the Algerian authorities for verification. Both the UK authorities and Q's solicitors urged the Algerian authorities to expedite their enquiries so that he could be returned to Algeria; but no information was forthcoming. **4.69**

In August 2006, Q applied for a writ of habeas corpus and/or judicial review, claiming that his continued detention was unlawful. **4.70**

The Court dismissed the application and determined that the question of whether detention under paragraph 2(3) of Schedule 3 to the Act was lawful must be determined by the circumstances of each case and by looking at the reasons for the detention—in this instance it was for the removal of Q. The court had to draw a balance between the interests of the individual and the wider national interest, particularly in the present case. In the present instance Q had used several identities making it extremely difficult for the authorities to determine his true identity. The UK had, once his true details had been provided, taken every measure to expedite the enquiries. **4.71**

Ward v Police Service of Northern Ireland[49]

This matter from Northern Ireland dealt with the exclusion of defence representatives from applications to a judge for extension of time in which to interview the suspect, and the failure of the judge to reveal these reasons to the defence. **4.72**

It was held[50] that the power in paragraph 33(3) (of Schedule 8)[51] is: 'available where the judicial authority wishes to be satisfied that further detention is necessary to obtain relevant evidence by questioning the person to whom the **4.73**

---

[49] [2007] UKHL 50.
[50] At paragraph 30, page 9 of the judgment.
[51] Paragraph 33 of Part III of Schedule 8 provides:
   (1) The person to whom an application relates shall—
      (a) be given an opportunity to make oral or written representations to the judicial authority about the application, and
      (b) subject to sub-paragraph (3), be entitled to be legally represented at the hearing.
   (2) A judicial authority shall adjourn the hearing of an application to enable the person to whom the application relates to obtain legal representation where—
      (a) he is not legally represented,
      (b) he is entitled to be legally represented, and
      (c) he wishes to be so represented.

application relates. It enables the judicial authority, in the detained person's absence, to examine the topics that are to be the subject of that exercise. But it must be read subject to paragraph 34. So where the power to order that specified information be withheld from that person under that paragraph is available, an order to withhold it must be sought under that paragraph'.

Senthilnayagam and Others v Seneviratne and Another[52]

4.74 On 13 April 1981, police and army officers entered and searched the home of the claimant, S Arunagirinathan. They had no warrant and neither did they explain to the complainant the reason for the search. Nothing incriminating was found. Six days later, the officers returned to A's home address, again without a warrant and searched his property. Nothing incriminating was found and no reason was provided for the search. It is alleged that the officers, prior to arresting A, assaulted his wife, their 11-year-old son and A. The officers then took him away. The family informed their local MP of the events.

4.75 A alleges that he was not informed of the reasons for his arrest and upon his arrival at the Army Camp in Elephant Pass he was interrogated several times during which he was tortured. He stated that his testicles were tied with a string and tugged, he was beaten on his knuckles, buttocks, and knees with a wooden rod and forced to sign a statement. He was detained at the Army Camp for two weeks.

4.76 He was subsequently moved to another Army Camp in Panagoda, where he was held from May–July 1981. He was informed on 9 July 1981 that the Minister had authorized his detention on 20 April on the grounds that the Minister had 'reason to suspect that S Arunagirinathan was connected with or concerned in terrorist activity'.

4.77 On 21 July he was blindfolded and taken before a magistrate and made a statement. He alleges that the officers had told him what to say, but he had omitted to say everything he had been ordered to say. On his return to the Army Camp he was tortured as an act of reprisal in the following manner:

- handcuffed by both wrists to high railings on a door and window and was forced to stand erect with arms outstretched. He was kept in this position for long periods except for short spells of four to five hours each night to enable him to sleep, to have his meals, and to attend to his ablutions.

---

(3) A judicial authority may exclude any of the following persons from any part of the hearing—
    (a) the person to whom the application relates;
    (b) anyone representing him.
[52] A Sri Lankan case reported at: [1981] LKCA 44; (1981) 2 Sri LR 187 (10 September 1981).

- forced to roll on the floor for a long time until his body ached, after which he was forced together with another prisoner to hold each other's ears and repeatedly squat and stand up for a long time until he could barely stand.
- he was taken handcuffed to meet his lawyer and after the interview he was manacled in a standing position until bedtime.

A denied that he was a member of an organization whose aim was to set up   **4.78**
a separate state by means of an armed struggle, violence, or terrorism. He denied any involvement in criminal activities.

The officers alleged that he was indeed a member of an organization whose   **4.79**
declared aim was the establishment of a separate state and that A had assisted in the concealment and subsequent disposal of 8.1 million rupees, the proceeds of a robbery. The officers, for their part, deny that A had been subjected to any form of torture or physical harm whilst in their custody.

A had been examined by a doctor on 28 May and A had informed the doctor of   **4.80**
the 'torture'. The doctor examined him and concluded that the swelling on the right side of his scrotum had been caused by a natural disease and was not due to any physical abuse. The doctor found that the injuries in the buttock region had been caused with a blunt weapon. Apart from that A was deemed to be in satisfactory health.

The court considered three other applications for habeas corpus. The facts and   **4.81**
allegations of torture were similar to those of A. The Minister had made a similar determination in respect of all claimants namely, he had 'reason to suspect that . . . was connected with or concerned in terrorist activity'. The Minister later issued fresh detention orders stating 'unlawful activity' and removing any mention of 'terrorist activity'.

Colin-Thome P gave the leading judgment and in examining the relevant   **4.82**
provisions of the Prevention of Terrorism (Temporary Provisions) Act No 48 of 1979 stated:

> Sections 6, 7 and 9 deal with any arrested person who is 'connected with or concerned in or reasonably suspected of being connected with or concerned in any unlawful activity'. After a person is arrested under section 6 there are two alternatives open to a police officer. Firstly, within a period of 72 hours he may produce a suspect before a Magistrate and have him remanded until the conclusion of his trial. A police officer will adopt this procedure only when there is prima facie evidence to support a charge under section 2 or 3 or 5. The other alternative is that when a police officer has a reasonable suspicion that a person is connected with or concerned in any unlawful activity and the 72 hours period is inadequate for concluding his investigations he may move for a detention order from the Minister under section 9.

The words 'has reason to believe or suspect' in section 9 also envisage two categories of suspects:

(a) Where the Minister has reason to believe that any person is connected with or concerned in any unlawful activity; and

(b) Where the Minister has reason to suspect that any person is connected with or concerned in any unlawful activity.

The primary purpose of detention under section 9 is to facilitate further investigation and interrogation of both categories of persons and their confederates in order to achieve the object of eradicating terrorism. Section 9 is not intended merely as a negative form of preventive detention nor is it intended to be a punishment. 'Unlawful activity', as defined in section 31, extends to persons not only on the periphery of criminal liability, but it also encompasses any person whose acts 'by any means whatsoever' are connected with 'the commission of any offence under this Act', and that, we hold, includes a person who has committed an offence under Act No. 48 of 1979.

The detention orders X1 stated that the grounds for detention were 'terrorist activity'. The words 'terrorist activity' are not only lacking in particularity they do not fall under the definition of 'unlawful activity' in section 31 of the Act. We hold, therefore, that the detention orders X1 were invalid ab initio.

As we have held that 'unlawful activity' includes an offence under the Act No. 48 of 1979, the specifying of an offence under the Act, as has been done in the detention orders X2, as the basis for detention, does not invalidate the detention order. Therefore, we hold that the four detention orders X2 are valid ex facie.

4.83 The Court also examined the validity of the second detention order issued by the Minister and whether it could remedy the defect contained in the first orders. The Court examined case law from India and UK and concluded that the second detention orders were capable of rectifying the earlier defective orders.

The Court, in dismissing the applications, held, inter alia:

(1) The words 'unlawful activity' as defined in section 31 of the Prevention of Terrorism (Temporary Provisions) Act, No. 48 of 1979, extend to persons not only on the periphery of criminal liability but they also encompass any person whose acts 'by any means whatsoever' are connected with 'the commission of any offence under this Act', and that includes a person who has committed an offence under the Act.

(2) The detention orders marked 'X1' stated that the grounds for detention were 'terrorist activity'. The words 'terrorist activity' are not only lacking in particularity but they also do not fall under the definition of 'unlawful activity' in section 31 of the Act.

(3) The detention orders marked 'X2' were valid ex facie inasmuch as the said orders specified an offence under the Act as the basis for detention.

(4) The objection that the detention orders 'X1' and 'X2' were defective as they did not name the custodian of the person detained on the face of the documents is purely technical. There is no requirement in section 9 of the Act that the custodian should be named in the order itself.

(5) The words 'where the Minister has reason to believe or suspect' in section 9(1) of the Act, mean that there must be objective grounds and a rational basis for belief or suspicion.

In relation to the allegations of torture, the Court found that it was not possible **4.84** to conclusively say whether or not the claimants had been the victims of ill treatment by the officers and directed that their lawyers should have access to their clients at the Army Camp and each of them should be examined once a week by the Judicial Medical Officer of Colombo or a Deputy Judicial Medical Officer at their offices.

E. Admissions and Confessions

Notwithstanding that the prohibition against torture is, in international human **4.85** rights law, absolute,[53] there has been much debate internationally as to the use, if any, to which admissions or intelligence obtained through torture can be put.

The case of *A and Others v Secretary of State for the Home Department (No 2)*,[54] gave **4.86** an opportunity for the approach of the common law to this question to be examined in detail by the House of Lords.

Following the events of 9/11, the UK Government concluded that there was a **4.87** public emergency threatening the life of the nation within the meaning of Article 15 of the European Convention for the Protection of Human Rights and Fundamental Freedoms (ECHR) and took measures derogating from its obligations. Accordingly, the derogation from the right to liberty under the Convention was one such measure.[55] This provided for the detention of suspected foreign international terrorists if the Secretary of State believed their presence in the UK was a risk to national security and he suspected that they were terrorists who could not be deported because of fears for their safety or other practical considerations.

The applicants who were certified under this provision appealed to the Special **4.88** Immigration Appeals Commission (SIAC) against their detention.[56] The SIAC is permitted to receive evidence that would not in the usual course of events be admissible in a court of law. The evidence tendered was reviewed in respect of each applicant and, in a number of open and closed judgments, the appeals were dismissed.

---

[53] See Chapter 8, below, at 8.32–8.34.
[54] [2005] UKHL 71; [2006] 2 AC 221.
[55] Set out in a schedule to the Human Rights Act 1988 and temporary emergency powers subject to renewal were set out in Part 4 of the Anti-Terrorism, Crime and Security Act 2001.
[56] Under section 25 of the 2001 Act.

4.89   One of the applicants contended that the Secretary of State had relied on evidence of a third party obtained through his torture in a foreign state. The Commission held that, if there was such material which had been obtained without the complicity of British authorities, they might examine it and determine the proper weight to be attached to it and that there would be no prohibition on its admission within the meaning of Article 15 of the United Nations Convention against Torture and other Cruel, Inhuman or Degrading Treatment or Punishment (Torture Convention). They concluded, however, that there was no such material. The Court of Appeal, by a majority, upheld the Commission's decision and dismissed the applicants' appeals.

4.90   The applicants petitioned the House of Lords. Following a detailed analysis on the prohibition of torture to obtain confessions, Their Lordships, in allowing the appeals, held:

> (1) That evidence of a suspect or witness which had been obtained by torture had long been regarded by the common law as inherently unreliable, unfair, offensive to ordinary standards of humanity and decency and incompatible with the principles on which courts should administer justice, and that, in consequence, such evidence might not lawfully be admitted against a party to proceedings in a United Kingdom court, irrespective of where, by whom or on whose authority the torture had been inflicted; that the Secretary of State did not act unlawfully in relying on such tainted material when certifying, arresting and detaining a person under the 2001 Act whom he suspected of international terrorism; but that the Commission was established to exercise judicial supervision of his exercise of those powers and was required to assess whether at the time of the hearing before it there were reasonable grounds for his suspicion; that, although it might admit a wide range of material which was inadmissible in judicial proceedings, express statutory words would be required to override the exclusionary rule barring evidence procured by torture; that the wording of rule 44(3) could not be interpreted as authorizing the displacement of that rule and that, accordingly, the commission could not admit such evidence.
>
> (2) That, since a detainee had only limited access to material advanced against him in proceedings before the commission, a conventional approach to the burden of proof was inappropriate in determining whether a statement should be excluded as procured by torture; that a detainee could not be expected to do more than raise a plausible reason that material might have been so obtained and, where he did so, it was for the commission to initiate relevant inquiries; that (Lord Bingham of Cornhill, Lord Nicholls of Birkenhead and Lord Hoffmann dissenting) the commission should adopt the test of admissibility laid down in article 15 of the Torture Convention and consider whether it was established by such inquiry as it was practicable to carry out and on a balance of probabilities that the information relied on by the Secretary of State was obtained by torture; that if satisfied that it was so established the commission should decline to admit the material, but that, if they were doubtful, they should admit it, bearing their doubt in mind in evaluating it.

The cases were remitted to the Commission for reconsideration.

4.91   The effect of the House of Lords' decision here is confirmation that the principles of the common law when standing alone, and also when applied in accordance with international law (eg, the Torture Convention) and regional human rights instruments (such as the ECHR), dictate that evidence obtained by torture may not be admitted against a party in a common law jurisdiction, irrespective of where, or by whom, or on whose authority the torture was carried out.

It is also worthy of note that both Lord Bingham and Lord Hoffmann, in each of   **4.92** their speeches, held that the conduct previously characterized as inhuman and degrading by the ECtHR in *Ireland v UK*[57] *would now be characterized as torture.*

Oppression and unfairness

At common law, the test which determined the admissibility of confessions was   **4.93** that of voluntariness. Thus an admission obtained by fear, or hope of favour held out by a person in authority was liable to be excluded.[58] Some jurisdictions have provided further safeguards by statute, such as the provisions contained in section 76 of the UK's Police and Criminal Evidence Act 1984 (PACE).

In *R v Fulling*[59] the Court of Appeal held that 'oppression' (a ground for exclusion   **4.94** under section 76(2)(a) of PACE was to be given its ordinary dictionary meaning: 'The Oxford English Dictionary as its third definition of the word runs as follows: "exercise of authority or power in a burdensome, harsh, or wrongful manner; unjust or cruel treatment of subjects, inferiors, etc., or the imposition of unreasonable or unjust burdens"'.[60]

There, the court found it hard to envisage any circumstances in which such   **4.95** oppression would not entail some impropriety on the part of the interrogator.

Mariadas v The State[61] (Sri Lankan Court of Appeal)

This matter was an appeal from conviction and sentence entered by the High   **4.96** Court of Colombo, Sri Lanka.

The applicant, Mariadas, together with others for an offence of conspiracy to   **4.97** commit murder of a member of Parliament under the Prevention of Terrorism (Temporary Provisions) Act, No 48 of 1979 as amended by Act No 10 of 1982. He was convicted and sentenced for seven years rigorous imprisonment.

Mariadas appealed against both conviction and sentence on the following grounds: **4.98**

1. At the trial the prosecution had adduced a confession made by Mariadas to the Senior Superintendent of Police. The defence had objected to the confession

---

[57] (1978) 2 EHRR 25.
[58] *DPP v Ping Lin* [1976] AC 574.
[59] [1987] QB 426; 85 Cr App R 136.
[60] (n 59) per Lord Lane CJ, 432, 142.
[61] SLR 96, Vol 1 of 1995 [1993] LKCA 14; (1995) 1 Sri LR 96 (19 November 1993).

being admitted in evidence on the basis that he had in fact made no confessions but had been made to sign a typed statement by the officer which contained admissions by Mariadas that he was an active member of the LTTE organization and supported its activities. Following an inquiry into the circumstances of the confession evidence the High Court had erred in allowing the confession evidence.

2. The confession should not have been admitted as:
   - The confession was in English and the appellant did not have sufficient knowledge of English;
   - The confession had been typed out, apparently based on a number of interviews with the appellant and none of the notes nor the confession was read out to him;
   - The prosecution had failed to call the typist who had compiled the confession statement.

3. The prosecution had failed to produce/disclose the note books in which, it was said, the contemporaneous interview notes had been made.

4. He further alleged that he had been subjected to assaults whilst in custody; he suffered ill health and was not properly fed.

4.99 The Court of Appeal quashed his conviction and sentence:

> To support this contention the learned President's Counsel referred to the failure of the prosecution to produce the note book in which SSP Ariyasena had taken down notes, when he questioned the accused-appellant for two weeks regarding his involvement. In other words what the learned President's Counsel was seeking to show was that the material obtained by questioning the accused-appellant for two weeks was typed in the form of a confession and thereafter the signature of the accused-appellant had been obtained. As submitted by the learned Deputy Solicitor-General certainly the material that is available in the confession could not have been put into the confession unless all this material came from the accused appellant in some form. . . . It was the position of SSP Ariyasena that the note book he used during interrogation did not contain material relating to the confession, but contained other matters connected with the investigation of the accused-appellant's involvement. If that was the position, we are of the view that the production of the note book and making it available to the defence, which disclosed that it contained only the material referred to by SSP Ariyasena, would have enhanced his credibility specially in regard to the recording of the confession.

> Another point raised in this appeal by the learned President's Counsel was the failure of the prosecution to call the typist who recorded the confession. His contention was that this failure affected the prosecution, whose burden was to prove the making of the confession by the accused-appellant beyond reasonable doubt. We observe that the typist SA Peiris who typed the confession of the accused-appellant was a witness for the prosecution and his name appears in the indictment. Under normal circumstances this witness would have certainly provided corroborative evidence in regard to the material that was placed before the Court through SSP Ariyasena. For some unexplained reason, his evidence was not led by the prosecution at the trial. The evidence of this witness would have been very material in view of the various

allegations made by the defence in regard to the confession that was permitted to be led in the case . . .

Further we observe that the evidence of the typist was very material for yet another reason. The declaration made by the typist SA Peiris at the end of the alleged confession reads as follows:

'I, S A Peiris declare that I have typed the above statement of V W Mariadas correctly as dictated by G P S Ariyasena from pages 1 to 27.' According to the plain meaning of this declaration it appears that the statement that has been recorded by the typist has been what was dictated to him by SSP Ariyasena and not what was spoken to by the accused-appellant. This declaration in the absence of an explanation or clarification from SA Peiris goes contrary to evidence given by SSP Ariyasena and tends to support in some way, the stand taken by the accused-appellant that he never made this confession . . .

It is to be noted that Section 16(1)[62] of the Prevention of Terrorism (Temporary Provisions) Act has permitted the admissibility of a statement made to a police officer above the rank of an Assistant Superintendent of Police unless such a statement is irrelevant under Section 24 of the Evidence Ordinance. Section 16(2) of the said Act states that the burden of proving that such a statement is irrelevant under Section 24 of the Evidence Ordinance shall be on the person asserting it to be irrelevant. Section 24 of the Evidence Ordinance reads as follows:

A confession made by an accused person is irrelevant in a criminal proceeding if the making of the confession appears to the court to have been caused by any inducement, threat, or promise having reference to the charge against the accused person, proceeding from a person in authority, or proceeding from another person in the presence of a person in authority and with his sanction, and which inducement, threat, or promise is sufficient in the opinion of the court to give the accused person grounds, which would appear to him reasonable; for supposing that by making it he

---

[62] Section 16 of the Prevention of Terrorism (Temporary Provisions) Act reads as follows:
(1) Notwithstanding the provisions of any other law, where any person is charged with any offence under this Act, any statement made by such person at any time, whether—
 (a) it amounts to a confession or not;
 (b) made orally or reduced to writing;
 (c) such person was or was not in custody or presence of a police officer;
 (d) made in the course of an investigation or not;
 (e) it was or was not wholly or partly in answer to any question,
may be proved as against such person if such statement is not irrelevant under Section 24 of the Evidence Ordinance;
Provided, however, that no such statement shall be proved as against such person if such statement was made to a police officer below the rank of an Assistant Superintendent.
(2) The burden of proving that any statement referred to in subsection (1) is irrelevant under Section 24 of the Evidence Ordinance shall be on the person asserting it to be irrelevant.
(3) Any statement admissible under subsection (1) may be proved as against any other person charged jointly with the person making the statement, if, and only if, such statement is corroborated in material particulars by evidence than the statements referred to in subsection (1).
The court examined this provision and concluded that as it had been widely drafted, it was capable of including **any** statement and not just confession evidence if the statement was made to an officer not below the rank of an Asst Superintendent.

would gain any advantage or avoid any evil of a temporal nature in reference to the proceedings against him.

In the case of *Vivekanandan v Selvaratnam*, Malcolm Perera, J in dealing with Section 24 of the Evidence Ordinance said 'At the outset, the Court must determine the meaning of the word "appears". I think what the Court has to decide is not whether it has been proved that there was threat, inducement or promise, but whether it appears to Court that such threat, inducement or promise was present. I am inclined to the view that the word "appears" indicates a lesser degree of probability than it would have been, if the word "proof" as defined in Section 3 of the Evidence Ordinance had appeared in Section 24.'

'I should rather think that the legislature has decidedly used the word "appears" to guarantee to accused persons in criminal proceedings, absolute fairness. Thus Section 24 does not require positive proof of improper inducement, threat or promise to justify the rejection of a confession. If the Court after proper examination and a careful analysis of the evidence and the circumstances of the given case, comes to the view that there appears to have been a threat, inducement or promise offered, though this is not strictly proved, then the Court must refuse to receive in evidence the confession. I should venture to think that a strong possibility that the confession was made under the stimulus of an inducement, threat, or promise, would be sufficient to attract exclusionary provision of Section 24 of the Evidence Ordinance.' Therefore it is clear that the accused-person has very much a lighter burden to discharge, to bring himself under Section 24 of the Evidence Ordinance.

Since we are of the view that there is a grave doubt as to whether the document P1 which was produced as the confession made by the accused-appellant was in fact made by him specially in view of the fact that the officer who is alleged to have typed the statement has not been called as a witness. On a plain reading of his certificate which is appended to P1, a doubt necessarily arises as to whether P1 contains a verbatim record of what was uttered by the accused-appellant or which was dictated by SSP Ariyasena.[63]

4.100 On the allegation of the assault and the failure of the prosecution to call the officers accused of assaulting the appellant prior to the confession statement, the Court criticized the decision and remarked that some of the officers should have been called even if it would have just been to rebut the appellant's claim.

Silence as an admission

4.101 Where a defendant is informed by a police officer, who does not caution him, of an allegation made by a third party, for instance, a co-defendant, his silence when told of the allegation cannot per se amount to an acknowledgment by him of the truth of the allegation. The caution merely acts as a reminder to the suspect of the right he already possesses at common law. If in a particular instance, a suspect

---

[63] SLR 96, Vol 1 of 1995 [1993] LKCA 14; (1995) 1 Sri LR 96 (19 November 1993), per Yapa J.

has not been reminded of the right, there is still no ground for inferring that his silence was not in exercise of his common law right.[64]

Where the defendant's reaction to some of the questions put to him by a police officer was either to remain silent, shake his head, or say 'no comment', the court held that it was proper for the whole 'dialogue' to go before the jury. If the defendant has failed to respond to any of the questions it may well be, on the basis of *Hall v R*, above, that the evidence of the questions should not be admitted.[65]

4.102

Admissions occasioned by tricks

In the event of admissions made in response to a trick carried out by police officers or agents of the State, the reader is referred to the discussion, below, in respect of *Looseley*.[66] In general, the court will differentiate between a trick which gives a defendant an opportunity to confess to the offence, and one which induces a confession which, without the trick, would not otherwise have been made.

4.103

In *R v Mason*,[67] the defendant's conviction for arson was overturned because police officers tricked him into confessing. They told both the defendant and his lawyer, untruthfully, that his fingerprint had been found on fragments of a bottle used in starting the fire.

4.104

In *R v Jelen and Katz*,[68] one of three defendants, D, had pleaded guilty to a charge of conspiracy to commit false accounting. He had been the first defendant to be arrested. He admitted his role in interview and incriminated the two others (J and K), who in due course became his co-defendants. At the time of D's arrest, the police investigators were of the view that there was insufficient evidence to justify arresting and charging J, but that if they interviewed him they would have to caution him. They therefore sought D's help. He agreed to meet with J whilst wearing a concealed personal recording device. The meeting duly took place and the recording was adduced in evidence. D also gave evidence for the prosecution. D lied to J in the course of their conversation. He told him that he had not said anything to the police. The Court of Appeal held that the case went beyond simply eavesdropping on the defendant's conversation. There was entrapment. However, it was not unfair. There was a further submission that the statutory and Code of Practice provisions designed to protect those being questioned by the police had been circumvented by the method used here. However, the court

4.105

---

[64] See *Hall v R* [1970] 55 Cr App R 108 (PC), approving *R v Whitehead* [1929] 1 KB 99, 21 Cr App R 23; *R v Keeling*, 28 Cr App R 121.

[65] *R v Mann*, 56 Cr App R 750; *R v Raviraj*, 85 Cr App R 93.

[66] See 4.249, below.

[67] 86 Cr App R 349.

[68] 90 Cr App R 456.

observed that J had not been arrested; the safeguards in question were to protect those who were vulnerable because they were in police custody.

4.106   In *R v Bailey and Smith*,[69] police officers had secretly tape-recorded the suspects' conversations with each other when they were in a police station cell. The suspects had been tricked into believing that putting them in the same cell was against the investigating officer's wishes and had been insisted upon by the officer in control of the custody area. It was held that it did not undermine the suspects' right to silence; nor did the suspects need to be protected from the opportunity to converse with each other in an inculpatory manner. However, the court said that such a method should only be used in 'grave cases'.

At what stage should an admission/confession be challenged?

4.107   In the appeal to the Privy Council of *Adjodha v The State*,[70] Lord Bridge observed that the usual procedure to be followed where admissibility of a confession is being challenged is as follows: The confession would not be opened (if there is a jury) and the trial judge will determine its admissibility on a *voire dire*. The defence may, however, decide that the court/jury should hear the evidence relating to the confession. At the end of the prosecution case, the defence may then apply to the judge, if the confession is ruled inadmissible, to tell the jury to disregard the confession; alternatively, the trial judge is able to take that course of action on his own motion if he doubted the confession was made voluntarily.

4.108   In *Wijeratne Banda v State*,[71] the appellant was convicted and sentenced to a term of ten years rigorous imprisonment for two offences under the Prevention of Terrorism (Temporary Provisions) Act No 48 of 1979, namely, robbery of government property and possession of a gun. He was further charged with attempted murder. This appeal arises from these convictions and sentences.

4.109   On 20 October 1992, the Principal of Lunuwatte Maha Vidyalaya School, accompanied by three teachers, went to the bank to collect the monthly salaries of the teachers of the school. The total amount collected was Rs. 1,60,583.50. Having collected the money from the bank, it was divided into three parcels as a safety measure and the teachers made their way back to the school on foot. Whilst the group was walking through a tea estate a stranger went past them followed shortly by a second person carrying a weapon like a pistol who emerged from the bushes and demanded money. A struggle ensued and the money was taken from

---

[69]   97 Cr App R 365.
[70]   [1982] AC 204.
[71]   SLR 86, Vol 3 of 1998 [1998] LKCA 24; (1998) 3 Sri LR 86 (29 October 1998).

the school teachers. The witnesses noticed a third person in the vicinity who was armed.

Police were alerted and upon arrival they apprehended one of the suspects who was identified by the witnesses as the third person at the scene. He was arrested and charged with attempted murder and two counts under the terrorism legislation.

The appellant contended that the facts did not warrant a charge under the **4.110** Prevention of Terrorism (Temporary Provisions) Act No 48 of 1979 and the Public Security Act read with the Emergency Regulations and further, the High Court Judge had failed to consider this despite defence objections at the preliminary hearing. The judge considered the defence application but rejected it as the case papers contained a confession by the accused which supported the charges under the Prevention of Terrorism (Temporary Provisions) Act No 48 of 1979 as amended and the Public Security Act No 28 of 1988 as amended read with the Emergency Regulations No 1 of 1989.

The point of time at which such an objection and impugnment should be decided **4.111** and determined was considered by Canekeratne, J in *Weerakutty v Pullenayagam*. He referred to the judgment in *Choughhani v King Emperor* where it was held that the relevant point of time at which such objection to a charge should be considered is that of accusation and not the eventual result.

F. Bomb/Explosion Scene Management

Recovery of forensic evidence will be a priority for investigators. However, from **4.112** the standpoint of the lawyer, prosecution, or defence, the following should be borne in mind in relation to bomb/explosion scene management:

Post-incident investigations

Post-incident strategy will seek to: **4.113**

- Provide intelligence that may lead to the prevention of future attacks or the disruption of terrorist networks;
- Provide evidence in support of prosecution;
- Provide evidence for an inquest;
- Assist families of the deceased by the dignified recovery and return of the bodies.

The role of the Senior Investigating Officer

The Senior Investigating Officer is responsible for the criminal investigation and **4.114** should set the various lines of enquiry relevant to the investigation to ensure it remains focused and concentrates on the principle issues. He or she will be responsible for developing the various strategies in support of the overall objectives of the investigation. These are likely to include:

- scene strategies
- forensic strategy
- search strategy
- victim and witness strategy
- intelligence strategy
- suspect strategy
- CCTV strategy
- community strategy
- media strategy.

4.115 A Bomb Scene Manager is likely to be appointed. The role is to coordinate the overall response at the scene after the rescue phase is complete. His duties will comprise:

- health and safety
- welfare of staff
- equipment
- inter-agency liaison
- management of access to inner cordon
- fast track of crucial information found within scene
- media access (Allowing the media controlled access to the scene is often beneficial. It reduces intrusion and speculation and can support an effective media strategy).

Cordons

4.116 All scenes of suspect devices and bomb scenes require extensive cordons that have to be managed. These will be all inner cordons from which the evidence recovery will take place and an outer cordon to protect the crime scene. The bomb scene manager should strictly regulate access to the inner cordon. Access through the outer cordon should also be restricted to those with a legitimate purpose and agreed access.

Scene examiner

4.117 The scene examiner is responsible for the implementation of the scene strategy within the inner cordon. This includes:

- body and body part recovery strategy
- the search plan
- the fast track of crucial exhibits
- maximizing forensic recovery including explosive traces and component parts
- the direction of specialist scientific support
- zoning.

Zoning

The dividing of the area within the inner cordon into zones is likely to be used to **4.118** ensure an effective evidential recovery from within the scene. The setting of zones together with detailed scene photography is intended to provide a basis to which all can work throughout the investigation and any subsequent trial or inquest. The argument in favour of zoning is that experience has shown that there is little to be gained by recording exactly where or when each item is found (except bodies). It is arguably more efficient to recover by zone. This gives sufficient detail for the explosive scientists to evaluate and give an expert analysis on the size and type of explosion.

The zoning system is also flexible enough to be used in confined scenes such as **4.119** train carriages or scenes covering a huge area such as an aircraft disaster.

Interviewing of witnesses

The interviewing of witnesses may follow one of the various models which exist **4.120** for the effective interview of witnesses. For example, there is the so-called PEACE model:

P— Planning and preparation
E— Engage and explain
A— Account clarification and challenge
C— Closure
E— Evaluation.

CCTV

The increasing use of CCTV by governments, local authorities, businesses, and **4.121** private individuals has considerably increased the opportunities for investigators. Timely recovery and effective viewing can be instrumental in the success of a counter-terrorist investigation, however this potential is only likely to be fulfilled where the systems in place are maintained, of sufficient quality, and allow for easy retrieval. This is far from being the norm and a concerted effort in educating the operators of both analogue and digital CCTV systems is required.

A CCTV strategy is likely to include the following: **4.122**

Recovery:

- Divide into areas or zones starting at the centre of the incident.
- Conduct detailed survey of the area concerned. Databases are a guide but new cameras are installed all the time.
- Secure continuity evidence at point of seizure.
- Prioritize recovery; some systems will only record for a set time before recording over product.

Viewing:

- Undertaken by specialist and trained officers.
- Subject to regular briefings—do they know what they are looking for?
- A system for identifying individuals/vehicles to enable movement to be tracked across systems

Media strategy

4.123   It is inevitable that counter-terrorism investigations will result in significant media interest. Following a terrorist attack or arrests related to a terrorist investigation, the investigator, in most jurisdictions, will, for operational reasons, retain the media lead.

The strategic aims of the media strategy will be to:

- provide timely accurate information to maintain public confidence
- support the aims and objectives of the investigation
- provide community reassurance
- dispel speculation and prevent prejudicial reporting
- provide advice to the media in relation to inappropriate speculation that may prejudice judicial proceedings
- prevent disclosure of sensitive information or tactics.

G. Proactive Investigations

4.124   The nature of the threat means that law enforcement agencies may have to intervene at a very early stage in a conspiracy in order to protect public safety. This of course can create immense difficulty for those responsible for building an evidential case; the action may have been based largely upon intelligence and leaves investigators with little or no tangible evidence to develop. To combat this, all agencies need to work closely from the outset to ensure no evidential opportunity is missed.

4.125   Covert counter-terrorist investigation is a vital tool in combating international terrorism. It is particularly relevant given the threat of no notice attacks, where the objective of the terrorist is to inflict mass casualties of civilians. Covert activity is therefore a key component in the prevention and disruption of such attacks.

Strategic coordination

4.126   Counter-terrorism investigations are complex, crossing national and international boundaries. Equally, they frequently involve many agencies. In order to manage such investigations successfully, effective strategic coordination is vital. Key stakeholders should be identified and the roles and responsibilities should be known and understood by all. Each operation must have a clear command and control structure and a mechanism put in place to ensure all available material is considered to enable the effective implementation of a strategy to protect public safety.

Those familiar with the 'Gold, Silver, Bronze' system will recognize this as being **4.127** at Gold level. This system identifies three command levels in which operational decisions are made, providing a framework through which an operation is controlled and executed. The Gold command level focuses on 'what needs to be done', by determining the overall strategy of the operation and maintaining accountability.

Tactical coordination

It is essential that there is an effective implementation of the overarching strategy. **4.128** A group of the relevant tactical commanders should be formed who answer to the various leaders at the strategic level. This can include the coordination of covert resources such as electronic and human surveillance, the deployment of undercover operations, covert human intelligence sources, and the pursuit of evidential and intelligence leads. It is important that the areas of responsibility and accountability within this group are clearly documented and agreed by all.

This level focuses on carrying out the tactical plan of the strategy set out by the **4.129** 'Gold' level of command.

H. Covert Methodologies

Interception of communications

Many jurisdictions rely heavily on the product of telephone and email intercep- **4.130** tion to detect and, thereafter, to prosecute the most serious of crimes, including terrorist offences. The UK is the exception, with the use of domestic intercept product from a public intercept, which can only be authorized by a warrant issued by the Home Secretary, being restricted to intelligence purposes and not being capable of being admitted in evidence.[72]

---

[72] Although foreign intercept product may be used in UK courts; see the discussion on 'MLA' later in the present chapter. As to unlawful public interception, the House of Lords made it clear in *Morgans v Director of Public Prosecutions* [2001] 1 AC 315 that the product of an unlawful, unwarranted interception is inadmissible in evidence.

4.131 For those States able to deploy an intercept capability, the value to a counter-terrorism investigation may be significant. Investigations to date have, for instance, been assisted by evidence of the contents of emails in which terrorist suspects have asked associates in other jurisdictions for advice concerning the composition of explosives and the most effective location at which to deploy a bomb.

4.132 In Australia, a warrant is required, but may be granted by either a Federal Court judge or a nominated member of the Administrative Appeals Tribunal. Once granted, any product is admissible in criminal proceedings.

4.133 Meanwhile, in Jamaica, authorization is via a judicial warrant, and the product may be adduced in evidence; although without questions being allowed as to the methodology employed or the identity of those carrying out the deployment.

4.134 Similarly, in Canada, the USA, South Africa, Kenya, and Malaysia, amongst others, the authorization must be given by a judge (or, in the case of South Africa and Kenya, by a magistrate). There are, however, restrictions as to who may make or authorize the application; in Canada, Kenya, and Malaysia, it is the Attorney General, whilst in the US it is a senior Department of Justice representative or a Principal Prosecutor from a constituent State.

4.135 In the event that there is a 'live' deployment of intercept capability during an investigation, there will usually be real-time monitoring of conversations. Very often those monitoring will keep their own notes or summaries of what has been said, thus assisting later processes when relevant calls are being identified.

4.136 In those jurisdictions where there is no 'secrecy' attaching to the process of deployment and monitoring, and where there are positive obligations on investigators and prosecutors to consider disclosure, careful regard will have to be had to the notes made and, in particular, to any assistance which they might give to the defence in its case. Similarly, as to the product itself and particularly those parts which do not form part of the prosecution case, the need to comply with disclosure requirements should be recognized.

4.137 Live monitoring performs a number of important functions. With human rights issues in mind, monitoring will help to minimize the amount of so-called 'collateral intrusion' (ie, incidental, and non-relevant for the purpose of the investigation, intrusion into the private or personal life of a third party) which takes place, since, depending on the State, those carrying out the interception will, for instance, switch off monitoring and 'dip sample', but continue recording, or, switch off the recording, for the duration of the third party's call.

4.138 Care will need to be taken in relation to any product which is subject to legal professional privilege (LPP) which, for most States, will not include things said and done within the lawyer-client relationship for the furtherance of crime.

Again, practices will differ (between States and, indeed, between agencies within States): some cease recording, others will continue recording, but will then seal the recording without it having been listened to or monitored, save for, perhaps, dip sampling; whilst others still will record, listen, and transcribe, but then seal the recording and mark the transcription 'LPP' (or similar) and, of course, not allow the prosecutor or investigator to have access to it.

American Civil Liberties et al v National Security Agency et al[73]

The case concerns a group action against the National Security Agency (NSA). **4.139** The group comprised of lawyers, academics, and journalists brought an action in the Eastern District of Michigan seeking a permanent injunction against NSA for actions taken by them under the US 'Terrorist Surveillance Program' (TSP) and a declaration that the warrantless wiretapping and data mining by the NSA violated:

- the First and Fourth Amendments,
- the Separation of Powers Doctrine,
- the Administrative Procedures Act,
- Title III of the Omnibus Crime Control and Safe Streets,
- the Foreign Intelligence Surveillance Act (FISA).

The action was based on their belief that their communications with those abroad **4.140** who may be suspected of being Al-Qaida terrorists, affiliates, or supporters was being monitored and tapped by NSA, without a warrant. This they alleged caused them irreparable damage as they were not able to maintain their contact with these individuals and therefore required them to travel in order to meet their contacts thereby incurring costs.

The NSA invoked the State Secrets Doctrine to bar the discovery of any material **4.141** on the grounds of national security. They claimed that in the absence of such material, the group had no *locus standi*.

The District Court rejected the claim for the data mining but granted the relief **4.142** sought for the warrantless wiretapping. NSA appealed.

Following the events of 11 September 2001, President Bush authorized NSA to **4.143** deploy a counter-terrorism operation which is referred to as 'Terrorist Surveillance Program' (TSP). The details of the operation have never been disclosed save to say that it is commonly known that NSA does intercept communications (telephone and email) without a warrant where one party to the communication is outside the US and the NSA has a 'reasonable basis to conclude that one of the parties to the

---

[73] US Court of Appeals, 6th Circuit [6 July 2007].

communication is a member of Al Qaeda, affiliated with Al Qaeda or a member of an organization affiliated with Al Qaeda or working in support of Al Qaeda'.

4.144 The Court of Appeal, in granting the appeal concluded that the group had no *locus standi*, vacated the order of the District court, and remanded the matter to the district court for dismissal.

4.145 Her Hon Circuit Judge Batchelder gave the leading judgment. In holding that the group had no *locus*, she examined each of the grounds set out for the claim:

> The conduct giving rise to the alleged injuries is undisputed: the NSA (1) eavesdrops, (2) without warrants, (3) on international telephone and email communications in which at least one of the parties is reasonably suspected of Al Qaeda ties. The plaintiffs' objection to this conduct is also undisputed, and they demand NSA discontinue it. The plaintiffs do not contend—nor could they—that the mere practice of wiretapping is by itself, unconstitutional, illegal or even improper . . . According to the plaintiffs, it is the absence of these warrants that renders the NSA's conduct illegal and unconstitutional. But the plaintiffs do not—because of the State Secret Doctrine cannot—produce any evidence that any of their communications have ever been intercepted by the NSA, under TSP, or without warrants.
>
> Instead, they assert a mere belief, which they contend is reasonable and which they label a 'well founded belief', that: their overseas contacts are the types of people targeted by the NSA; the plaintiffs are consequently subjected to the NSA's eavesdropping; the eavesdropping leads the NSA to discover (and possibly disclose) private or privileged information; and the mere possibility of such discovery (or disclosure) has injured them in three particular ways . . . first . . . is their inability to communicate with their overseas contacts by telephone or email due to their self-governing ethical obligations . . . second . . . fear that the NSA's discovery . . . will lead to some direct reprisal by the United States Government, their own government or others. This fear causes the overseas contacts to refuse to communicate . . . third . . . NSA's violation of their legitimate expectation of privacy in their overseas telephone and email communications . . . The plaintiffs assert that the Fourth Amendment, Title III and FISA limit the occasions and circumstances in which, and the manner by which, the government can lawfully intercept overseas electronic communications, giving rise to a legitimate expectation that their overseas communications will be intercepted only in accordance with these limits . . . in the present case, the plaintiffs concede that there is no single plaintiff that can show that he or she has actually been wiretapped. Moreover, due to the State Secrets Doctrine, the proof needed either to make or negate such a showing is privileged . . .
>
> This is the premise upon which the plaintiffs' entire theory is built. But even though the plaintiffs' beliefs . . . may be reasonable, the alternative possibility remains that the NSA might not be intercepting, and might never actually intercept any communication by any of the plaintiffs named . . .
>
> Therefore, the injury that would support a declaratory judgment . . . is too speculative . . . the problem with asserting only a breach-of-privacy claim is that, because the plaintiffs cannot show that they have been or will be subjected to surveillance personally, they clearly cannot establish standing under the Fourth Amendment or FISA . . .

A wiretap is always 'secret'—that is its very purpose—and because of this secrecy, neither the plaintiffs nor their overseas contacts would know, with or without a warrant, whether their communication was being tapped. Therefore, the NSA's secret possession of a warrant would have no more effect on the subjective willingness or unwillingness of these parties to 'freely engage in conversations and correspond via email' . . . the plaintiffs have argued that if the NSA were to conduct its surveillance in compliance with FISA, they would no longer feel compelled to cease their international telephone and email communications . . . the imposition of FISA requirements into this scenario would not change the likelihood that these overseas contacts are the types of people who the plaintiffs believe would be monitored. Nor would it change the plaintiffs 'well founded belief' that NSA is intercepting . . .

Discussion on FISA **4.146**

The Foreign Surveillance Act of 1978 (FISA) . . . governs the interception of electronic communications involving foreign intelligence information . . . FISA is fraught with detailed statutory definitions and is expressly limited, by its own terms to situations in which the President has authorized 'electronic surveillance' for the purpose of acquiring 'foreign intelligence information'.

First, the surveillance in question must acquire 'foreign intelligence information' which includes 'information that relates to . . . the ability of the United States to protect against . . . international terrorism' . . . the proclaimed purpose is to prevent future terrorist attacks.

Next, the interception must occur by 'electronic surveillance' . . .

There are at least three reasons why the plaintiffs cannot maintain their claims under FISA . . . First, the plaintiffs have not alleged that they are 'aggrieved persons'. FISA defines 'aggrieved person' as a 'person who is the target of an electronic surveillance or any other person whose communications or activities were subject to electronic surveillance . . . the plaintiffs have not shown that they were actually the target of, or subject to, the NSA's surveillance . . .

Giving her judgment, Her Hon Circuit Judge Gibbons, in agreement with **4.147** Batchelder CJ, concluded on the state secret doctrine as follows:

Under any understanding of constitutional standing, the plaintiffs are ultimately prevented from establishing standing because of the state secrets privilege. As Judge Batchelder notes, plaintiffs have not challenged the government's invocation of the privilege or its application . . . The state secrets privilege operates as a bar to the admission of evidence to which the privilege attaches, the plaintiff must proceed without the benefit of such evidence . . . Where the privilege prevents the plaintiff from producing sufficient evidence to establish his or her prima facie case, the court must dismiss the claim . . . In this way, the state secrets privilege has prevented the plaintiffs from conducting discovery that might allow them to establish that they are personally subject to the TSP, as I believe constitutional standing requires.

However, where the privilege deprives the government of a valid defense to the plaintiff's claim, the court must also dismiss the claim . . . whether that evidence is favorable to plaintiffs or defendants, its unavailability requires dismissal. That it may be unsatisfying that facts pertinent to the standing inquiry are unavailable can have no bearing on the disposition of this case. If the state secret privilege prevents the plaintiffs from presenting adequate evidence of their standing, we must dismiss their claims. If the state secret privilege prevents the government from presenting evidence that might refute the plaintiffs' allegations that they are likely to be surveilled and undercut the reasonableness of their asserted fear, we must also dismiss the plaintiffs' claim.

4.148 In dissenting from his colleagues, Gilman CJ observed:

. . . a fundamental disagreement exists between the two of them and myself on what is required to show standing and whether any of the plaintiffs have met the requirement. Because of that disagreement, I respectfully dissent. Moreover, I would affirm the judgment of the district court because I am persuaded that the TSP as originally implemented violated the Foreign Surveillance Act of 1978 (FISA) . . .

4.149 Gilman CJ was of the view that even if the journalists and academics did not have *locus*, the attorneys most certainly did and this would suffice for the purpose of determining the claim:

In short, the critical question in this case is not whether the attorney-plaintiffs have actually been surveilled—because, as the lead opinion aptly notes, a wiretap by its nature is meant to be unknown to its targets—but whether the 'reasonableness of the fear' of such surveillance is sufficient . . . I believe that the plaintiffs have established such an injury in fact . . .

The lead opinion asserts that the attorney-plaintiffs cannot establish that they have a right to sue because they are not 'aggrieved person' under FISA . . . The attorney-plaintiffs challenge, however, is precisely that the TSP has operated outside of FISA despite the fact that Congress has declared FISA to be the 'exclusive means' for the government to engage in electronic surveillance for foreign intelligence purposes in this country . . .

The language of both the FISA statute and its legislative history is explicit: FISA was specifically drafted 'to curb the practice by which the Executive Branch may conduct warrantless electronic surveillance on its own unilateral determination that national security justifies it' . . . When debating FISA, Congress made it clear that it intended to prevent the Executive Branch from engaging in electronic surveillance in the United States without judicial oversight, even during times of war . . .

More to the point, the government has publicly admitted that the TSP has operated outside of the FISA and Title III statutory framework and that the TSP engages in 'electronic surveillance' . . . In January 2007 in fact, the Bush Administration announced that it had reached a secret agreement with the Foreign Intelligence Surveillance Court (FISC) whereby TSP would comply with FISA, a further acknowledgement that the TSP had previously been operating without FISA approval . . .

Moreover, the government's contention lacks merit. The Attorney General has publicly acknowledged that FISA 'requires a court order before engaging in this kind of surveillance . . . unless otherwise authorized by Congress'

Both FISA and Title III expressly prohibit electronic surveillance outside of their statutory framework . . . The language is unequivocal. In enacting FISA, Congress directed that electronic surveillance conducted inside the United States for foreign intelligence purposes was to be undertaken only as authorized by specific federal statutory authority . . . Title III criminalizes the interception and disclosure of wire, oral and electronic communications except under specified exceptions . . . I nonetheless reiterate that the legislative history of FISA clearly reinforces the conclusion that FISA and Title III constitute the sole means by which electronic surveillance may lawfully be conducted . . . Congress has thus unequivocally declared that FISA and Title III are the exclusive means by which electronic surveillance is permitted.

No other authorization can comply with the law. Congress further emphasized this point by criminalizing the undertaking of electronic surveillance not authorized by statute in two separate places in the US Code . . . The government, however, contends that Congress authorized TSP in the aftermath of September 11, 2001 . . . . But FISA itself expressly and specifically restricts the President's authority even in times of war . . . To be sure, Congress in 1978 likely did not contemplate a situation such as the one that arose with the attacks of September 11, 2001. But in the aftermath of those attacks, Congress has shown itself both willing and able to consider appropriate amendments to FISA. Congress has in fact amended FISA multiple times since September 11, 2001, increasing the President's authority by permitting 'roving' wiretaps and expanding the permissible use of pen-register devices. But Congress has never suspended FISA's application nor altered the 15-day limit on warrantless electronic surveillance . . .

In arguing that the TSP did not violate FISA, the government contends that Congress authorized such warrantless electronic surveillance when it passed AUMF . . . Nothing in the AUMF suggests that Congress intends to 'expand or alter the authorization' set forth in FISA. Moreover, the text and the legislative history of FISA and Title III make it quite clear that the TSP or a similar program can be authorized only through those two statutes. The TSP plainly violated FISA and Title III and, unless there exists some authority for the President to supersede this statutory authority, was therefore unlawful. [emphasis added]

Gilman CJ then examined the inherent authority of the President with particular **4.150** reference during wartime and concluded: 'the Constitution divides the nation's powers between the Executive and the Legislative Branches . . . in contrast to the government's suggestion, the President does not have exclusive war powers . . .'.

The UK's approach to interception of telecommunications

Part I of the Regulation of Investigatory Powers Act 2000 (RIPA 2000) governs **4.151** both interception and the acquisition of communications data. It repeals the Interception of Communications Act 1985, but replaces it with a very similar regime which, in broad terms, prohibits the interception of telecommunications, public and private (including emails, and items sent through the post), subject to certain exceptions. Also, and importantly, it creates a framework which has the effect of prohibiting the evidential use of the product of lawful public interception where the interception has been authorized (by warrant) by the Secretary of State.

Section 1(1) of RIPA 2000 creates an offence for a person who intentionally **4.152** and without lawful authority intercepts, within the United Kingdom, any communication which is in the course of transmission by means of a public postal service or a public telecommunication system. The definition of telecommunication system is wide and is such as to include mobile telephones and email traffic.[74]

4.153 Section 1(2) creates a further offence, that of intentionally and without lawful authority intercepting, within the United Kingdom, any communication in the course of its transmission by means of a private telecommunication system (otherwise than in circumstances in which such conduct is conducted by or on behalf of a person who has a right to control the operational use of the system.[75]

4.154 A private telecommunication system is one which is attached directly or indirectly (and whether or not for the purposes of the communication in question) to a public telecommunication system[76] and where there is apparatus comprised in the system which is both located in the United Kingdom and used (with or without other apparatus) for making the attachment to the public communications system.[77]

4.155 An interception will not amount to an offence if it is done with 'lawful authority'.[78] Lawful authority may take one of a number of forms, which are set out in detail in sections 3 and 4 of RIPA 2000. Importantly, if an interception is one which is consented to by one party to the transmission (be it the sender or recipient), such an interception will be lawful, the product will be capable of being used evidentially, and will be specifically treated under the 2000 Act as amounting to directed surveillance.[79]

4.156 If an interception of a public telecommunication system is required and does not fall within the scope of lawful authority within sections 3 and 4, then a warrant will need to be sought from the Secretary of State. Such a warrant may only be sought in accordance with the criteria set out in section 5. The effect of section 5(2) and (3) is that the Secretary of State shall only issue an interception warrant if he believes that: (a) interception is necessary on one of four specified grounds (in the interests of national security, for the purpose of preventing or detecting serious crime, for the purpose of safeguarding the economic well-being of the UK, and for the purpose of giving effect to the provisions of any international mutual assistance agreement); and (ii) the conduct authorized by the warrant is proportionate to what is sought to be achieved by it.

---

[74] RIPA 2000, s 2(1).
[75] s 1(6).
[76] Whether a telephone line is part of a public or private telecommunications system is a question of fact: *R v Boodhoo, Allen and Bunting* [2001] EWCA Crim 1025.
[77] s 2(1).
[78] s 1(1).
[79] s 48(4).

In the case of a warranted public interception, the restrictions should not be **4.157** underestimated. In essence, no evidence may be adduced, questions asked, assertions or disclosures made in any legal proceedings which are likely to reveal the existence of, or absence of, an interception warrant.[80] Of such exceptions as there are,[81] the most important is that in relation to the power of a judge to order disclosure to himself, where he is satisfied that there are exceptional circumstances which make disclosure essential in the interests of justice.[82] Effectively, however, the restrictions contained within Part I of RIPA 2000 mean that it is the prosecutor's duty to secure fairness in a trial in respect of which there is, in the background, either extant interception product or where there has been an interception but the product, and the notes thereof have been destroyed.[83] Looking at the combination of sections 17 and 18, only in circumstances where a prosecutor cannot fulfil his duty of securing fairness, should recourse be had to the trial judge, and even then only within the limitations imposed by sections 17 and 18.

It should be noted, however, that recording telephone conversations by, for instance, **4.158** the wearing of a device by an undercover officer, will not amount to an interception. The latest authority, which clarifies the point is *R v E*:[83a] In the course of an investigation into suspected large-scale drug dealing, the police placed an authorized listening device in the target's vehicle. The device picked up conversations between individuals actually in the vehicle and also words spoken by persons in it when they were using their mobile (cell) phones. No speech was picked up, though, from the person at the other end of the line. The defence argued that what occurred amounted to 'interception' which should have been authorized by means of a warrant. If no warrant was in place, the interception was unlawful and the product inadmissible. The Court of Appeal rejected that argument. It held that the natural

---

[80] RIPA 2000, s 17(1) and (2). Section 17 excludes evidence, questioning, or assertions in legal proceedings which are likely to reveal the existence or absence of a warrant. It does this directly by stating that the contents of intercepted material and related communications data may not be disclosed, and by the indirect route of prohibiting the disclosure of material which would lead to certain inferences being drawn.

[81] s 18.

[82] s 18(7), (6), and (8).

[83] For disclosure to the prosecutor, see RIPA 2000, s 18(7)(a). Section 18(7)(a) permits the disclosure of intercepted material which has not been destroyed to 'a person conducting a criminal prosecution' to enable that person to determine what he needs to do to ensure the fairness of the prosecution. Section 18(7)(b) permits the disclosure of such material to a 'relevant judge' where the judge has ordered disclosure to him. The term 'relevant judge' includes a circuit judge (s 18(11)). Section 18(8) provides that a judge will not order disclosure to himself unless satisfied that the 'exceptional circumstances of the case make the disclosure essential in the interests of justice'. Section 18(9) provides for a relevant judge who has ordered disclosure under section 18(7)(b) to direct the prosecutor, in 'exceptional circumstances', to make such admission of fact as the judge thinks essential in the interests of justice. However, the judge may not make such a direction if to do so would itself amount to a breach of section 17(1) (s 18(10)).

[83a] [2004] EWCA Crim 1243.

meaning of 'interception' denoted some interference or abstraction of the signal, whether it was passing along wires or by wireless telegraphy, during the process of transmission. The recording of a person's voice, independently of the fact that at the time he was using a telephone, did not become interception simply because what he said not only went into the recorder but was also transmitted, by a separate process, by a telecommunications system. See also the earlier Court of Appeal case of *R v Hardy and Hardy* [2002] EWCA Crim 3012, which is to the same effect.

4.159 In respect of foreign 'public' intercept product, however, the House of Lords held in *R v P and Others*[84] that, where telephone conversations have been lawfully monitored in another State by the authorities of that State, recordings of those conversations are admissible in evidence in a trial in the UK assuming that they are relevant. In circumstances where such product is obtained, though, by a UK prosecutor or investigator, all of the material will fall to be considered in accordance with the prosecution's disclosure obligations.

4.160 It should also be noted that if the UK requests such product from a State Party to the EU MLA Convention (EUMLAC), then the request should be made in accordance with the provisions of EUMLAC (the UK itself being a Party). The reader is referred to EUMLAC for further detail; however, for present purposes, the product of a foreign interception may be requested where the product is pre-existing, but a request for interception will mean that any product obtained through that deployment will be inadmissible.

Covert investigative techniques and human rights law

4.161 The deployment of covert, intrusive techniques is not new. However, since the early 1990s there has, worldwide, been ever-increasing reliance on intelligence-led and proactive criminal investigations. The use of such techniques may well, indeed, be the only way to investigate terrorism in any given instance, whether it is suspected on the part of a law enforcement officer with connections to organized crime or whether it is bribery within the commercial sphere.

4.162 Traditionally those States that had some regulation of the use of covert means relied on codes of practice or guidelines (in common law jurisdictions) and often a disparate range of laws (in civil law States). However, an increase in human rights challenges and the passing of specific, human rights compliant legislation in many States, has led to a recognition that covert activity must have an explicit and workable framework in domestic law.

---

[84] [2001] 2 WLR 463.

In the UK, the only real exception to a 'code of practice' approach was the statu- **4.163**
tory regime for the restricted, intelligence-only use of public telecommunications
intercept product provided for by the Interception of Communications Act 1985
(IOCA). However, with the passing of the Human Rights Act 1998 requiring
UK law to be compatible with the provisions of the ECHR, a re-think took place.
The UK example is an instructive one, given that the statutory regime introduced
(RIPA 2000) has, on the whole, steered away from requiring judicial authority for
intrusion, whilst recognizing that different levels of intrusion require different
levels of authorization.

The intrusive nature of many forms of covert investigation have to be considered **4.164**
in the light of international human rights instruments and, in particular, with the
qualified, or restricted, right to a personal/private life which will invariably be
found therein. A full discussion of those instruments will be found in Chapter 8,
below.

For States who are parties to the ECHR, Article 8 of the ECHR addresses privacy, **4.165**
and provides that:

1) Everyone has the right to respect for his private and family life, his home and
   correspondence.
2) There shall be no interference by a public authority with the exercise of this right,
   except such as is in accordance with the law and is necessary in a democratic society in
   the interests of national security, public safety, or the economic well-being of the
   country, for the prevention of disorder or crime, for the protection of health or morals,
   or for the protection of the rights and freedoms of others.

Article 8, then, guarantees a right to private and family life, home and correspondence. However, it is a qualified, not an absolute right. Thus, interference with
a right under Article 8(1) will amount to a breach of Article 8 unless the interference or intrusion in question can be justified on the basis of Article 8(2). From the
provisions of Article 8(2), above, it can be seen that to be justified under 8(2) there
must be a basis in law for the interference, the intrusion must have been 'necessary
in a democratic society' and, in accordance with established ECHR jurisprudence,
the intrusion must be proportionate. That is to say, the intrusion must correspond
to pressing social need and be proportionate to that need.[85]

In order to provide a basis in law for covert investigations which may involve **4.166**
interference with a subject's Article 8 rights, and to provide an authorization
regime based on the key principles of necessity and proportionality, RIPA 2000
was passed.

---

[85] See, eg, *Ludi v Switzerland* [1992] 15 EHRR 173.

4.167 RIPA 2000 establishes a permissive regime for a number of covert activities and powers. It has also been supplemented by subordinate legislation and by Codes of Practice. RIPA 2000 provides criteria for authorization and levels of authorization which become more restrictive the greater the degree of intrusion required. RIPA 2000 is divided as follows:

> Part I, Chapter 1: The Interception of Communications;
>
> Part I, Chapter 2: The Acquisition of Communications Related Data (eg, telephone billing)
>
> Part II: The use and conduct of the 'covert human intelligence source' (ie, informants, participating sources and undercover agents); 'Directed' surveillance and 'intrusive' surveillance (ie, surveillance on or in residential premises and private motor vehicles);
>
> Part III: The power to seize electronic keys or passwords which will give access to encrypted information (ie, computer material) [Part III not yet in force];
>
> Part IV: A regime of scrutiny in relation to the use of covert powers (ie, The Office of the Surveillance Commissioners);
>
> Part V: Miscellaneous provisions.

4.168 With covert investigations into terrorist activity in mind, the following should be noted:

'In Accordance with the Law'

4.169 There must be a basis in domestic law or legislation which provides for the deployment of the covert technique. Such legislation must be accessible to those liable to be affected.[86] In addition, such legislation, including that which authorizes the activity liable to interfere with the Article 8(1) right, must have sufficient clarity so as to give a person an indication as to the circumstances and conditions in which convert methods by a public authority may be used.[87]

4.170 The European Court of Human Rights (ECtHR) expects that there should be a regime of independent supervision of the use of covert, intrusive powers.[88] As to the process of authorization, the more independent the authorizing or reviewing individual/body is, the more likely that the ECtHR will regard the authorizing and reviewing regime to be in compliance with the requirements of Article 8(2). Indeed, in *Klass v Germany*[89] the ECtHR noted that judicial control of the authorization procedure provided 'the best guarantees of independent, impartiality and a proper procedure'. The use by the UK of domestic commissioners and tribunals

---

[86] Eg, *Silver v UK* [1983] 5 EHRR 347.
[87] *Copp v Switzerland* [1983] 27 EHRR 91.
[88] *Malone v UK* [1984] 7 EHRR 14.
[89] [1978] 2 EHRR 214.

(first provided for under IOCA and now found in both the Police Act 1997[90] and in RIPA) is capable of satisfying the demands of Article 8.[91]

'Necessary in a Democratic Society'

The interference with an individual's Article 8(1) rights must fulfil a pressing   **4.171**
social need, be in pursuit of one of the aims set out in Article 8(2) and any deployment must be only that which is necessary to achieve what is sought to be achieved
(ie, the detection of the particular crime). In addition, safeguards must be in place
to prevent abuse by intrusive techniques and remedies must be available in the
event of such abuse.

'Proportionality'

The interference must be proportionate to what is sought to be achieved by it.   **4.172**
Thus, for example, the deployment with a listening device in a target's bedroom
may require much greater justification than a deployment in a living room.

In considering, in any jurisdiction, whether a covert technique or deployment is   **4.173**
indeed proportionate to the legitimate aim which is being pursued, consideration
should be given to the following:

• Have sufficient, relevant reasons been set out in support of the deployment?
• Could the same aim have been achieved by use of a less intrusive method?
• Did the authorizing/decision-making process as to the deployment take place
  in a way which was procedurally fair?
• Do adequate safeguards exist to prevent abuse?
• Does the interference in question destroy the very essence of the Article 8(1) right?

'The effect of a breach, during an investigation, of the right to a private life'

A defendant is likely to argue that: **4.174**

i) The use by the prosecution of evidence that was obtained in breach of an
    Article 8(1) right, in circumstances where the breach cannot be justified under
    Article 8(2), has the effect of denying the defendant his right to a fair trail
    (in the case of the ECHR, under Article 6). Therefore, the proceedings in
    question should be stayed.

Alternatively,

ii) Evidence obtained as a result of an unjustified Article 8(1) breach should be
    excluded under the court's discretionary power to exclude (depending on the
    jurisdiction, this may be common law or statutory).

---

[90] See 4.239–4.246, below.
[91] *Esbester v UK* [1994] 18 EHRR 72.

4.175 However, in relation to either or both of the above arguments, the test is the same: what is the effect of the admission of the evidence on the fairness of the proceedings on a whole?[92]

4.176 The above approach by the domestic courts has the effect of mirroring the underlying rationale of human rights instruments: that questions of admissibility are matters for national courts. In contrast, the ECtHR, for example, is concerned with whether the proceedings as a whole are fair.[93]

Covert human sources

4.177 Information from human sources, increasingly, provides the basis for counter-terrorism investigations. A source in this context is a person who establishes or maintains a personal or other relationship with a person for the covert purpose of facilitating the doing of anything that:

• Covertly uses such a relationship to obtain information or to provide access to any information to another person, or
• Covertly discloses information obtained by the use of such a relationship, or as a consequence of the existence of such a relationship.[94]

4.178 It should be noted immediately that in most States, undercover agents and so-called participating sources will fall within this definition.

4.179 With the right to a personal life in mind, and recognizing that interaction with a target will probably result in the source obtaining personal information, an authorization process should be in place. Typically this will allow for deployment:

• In the interests of national security;
• For the purpose of preventing or detecting crime or of preventing disorder;
• In the interests of the economic well-being of the State in question;
• In the interests of public safety;
• For the purpose of protecting public health.

4.180 In addition, the authorizing process must require the authorizer to believe that the authorized conduct or use is proportionate to what is sought to be achieved by it.

---

[92] See support for this by the Court of Appeal in *R v Bailey, Brewin and Gangai* (15 March 2001, unreported).

[93] See, for example, *Shenck v Switzerland* [1988] 13 EHRR 242.

[94] The UK law enforcement authorities have also recognized the status of 'tasked witness'. That is a witness who has or is about to make a witness statement and who is tasked to obtain further information or evidence. The further evidence will usually form part of the prosecution case and so will be the subject of an additional witness statement in due course. That the information or evidence was obtained pursuant to a specific request will also be revealed. Such a witness will not, therefore, ordinarily fall to be classified as a covert human intelligence source (CHIS).

There should also be provision for handling and controlling the source, and for the keeping of records and maintaining of confidentiality.

Given the increasingly transactional nature of counter-terrorist investigations, the authorization process in a State should provide that authorizations may be given for the conduct and use of a human source both within and outside that State. However, it should be noted that in addition to authorization in the requesting State, consideration will need to be given to authorizations and permissions in the requested State, since such activity will usually need to be requested via a formal letter of request and will be undertaken by investigators of the requested State under its laws.[95]   **4.181**

Mention has been made of 'participating sources'. A participating source may be defined as an individual who, with the approval of an authorizing officer, is given permission to participate in a crime which the principals have already intended to commit. There is common law authority for the use of a participator; in particular, *R v Birtles*,[96] however, explicit provisions in law will also be required if the activity is to be capable of being human rights compliant. It is suggested that, inter alia, such provisions should address the role to be undertaken by a participator and specify that it must be a minor one, that the offences under investigation must amount to serious crime, and that there must be authorization at a sufficiently senior level, whether judicial or law enforcement.   **4.182**

The Covert Human Intelligence Source ('CHIS') in the UK

Increasingly, information from sources provides the basis for investigations into terrorist activity. Regard must therefore be had to Part II of RIPA 2000 which provides a regulatory framework for the conduct and use of the covert human intelligence source (CHIS). A CHIS is defined in section 26(8) of RIPA 2000 as a person who: **4.183**

> establishes or maintains a personal or other relationship with a person for the covert purpose of facilitating the doing of anything . . . [in (b) or (c) below]
>
> (b) he covertly uses such a relationship to obtain information or to provide access to any information to another person, or
> (c) he covertly discloses information obtained by the use of such a relationship, or as a consequence of the existence of such a relationship.

It should be noted immediately that undercover agents, test purchasers, and participating sources will fall within this definition.

---

[95] See Chapter 9, below.
[96] [1969] 1 WLR 1074, which set out two guidelines or principles: the offence for which participation is authorized must be 'already laid on' and the participator must not be used to entrap unlawfully (in other words, must not be used as an agent provocateur).

4.184 Any conduct and use of a CHIS must be authorized in accordance with section 29 of RIPA 2000. The effect of section 26(7) is to define 'conduct' as:

> Any conduct of a covert human intelligence source which establishes or maintains a personal or other relationship with a person for the covert purpose of facilitating (or is incidental to) the doing of anything that:
>
> Covertly uses such a relationship to obtain information or to provide access to any information to another person, or
>
> Covertly discloses information obtained by the use of such a relationship, or as a consequence of the existence of such a relationship.

4.185 The definition of 'use' of a CHIS is, meanwhile, defined in section 26(7)(b) as: '. . . inducing, asking or assisting a person to engage in the conduct of such a source, or to obtain information by means of the conduct of such a source'.

4.186 A key element of the above definitions is, of course, the notion of 'covert'. Covert is defined in section 26(9). It is, in effect, given its usual dictionary meaning. Thus, for example, a relationship is used covertly, for the purposes of the deployment of a CHIS, if it is used in a manner calculated to ensure that one of the parties to the relationship is unaware of the use in question.[97]

4.187 When RIPA 2000 was introduced, there was much discussion and concern that a large number of individuals might fall within the definition of a 'CHIS' even though they would not previously have been thought of as 'informants'. It is clear, however, that a restrictive definition should be applied. The 2000 Act is, after all, intended to ensure ECHR compliance; in particular, that any breach of Article 8(1) of the ECHR is justified and that deployment is authorized. The mischief which Article 8(2) seeks to prevent is an interference with an individual's Article 8(1) right by a public authority unless the qualifications contained within Article 8(2) are met. Thus, it must be that RIPA 2000 intends that an individual is a CHIS only if he or she is induced, asked, or assisted to engage in certain conduct (ie, that referred to in section 26(7)(b)) and the relationship that is established or maintained is for a covert purpose. The 'good citizen' who simply reports a matter will not, therefore, fall within the definition. Although the provisions of the Act do not provide for it, it is, in fact, hard to envisage circumstances where an individual will be a CHIS if he or she had not been tasked by a public authority to obtain information, etc by establishing or maintaining a relationship for a covert purpose. That having been said, the view of the Chief Surveillance Commissioner[98] appears to be that tasking is not actually a requirement.

---

[97] See RIPA 2000, s 26(9)(c).
[98] See the Office of the Surveillance Commissioner's website <http://www.surveillance commissioners.gov.uk>.

An application for the use and conduct of a CHIS should, unless urgent (see below), **4.188**
be in writing and should set out:

(1) the reasons why the authorization is necessary;
(2) the reasons why the authorization is considered proportionate to what it seeks
to achieve;
(3) the purpose for which the source will be tasked or deployed;
(4) the nature of the specific operation or investigation being undertaken;
(5) the nature of what the source will be tasked to do;
(6) the level of authorization needed;
(7) details of the risks of collateral intrusion, how that has been minimized and
why such intrusion as there is can be justified;
(8) in the event that confidential information is likely to be obtained, details of
any such information likely to result from the authorization.[99]

Section 29(2) of RIPA 2000 sets out the criteria for authorization for the conduct **4.189**
or the use of a CHIS. A person shall not grant such an authorization unless he or
she believes that:

The authorization is necessary on one or more of the following grounds:

(a) In the interests of national security;
(b) For the purpose of preventing or detecting crime or of preventing disorder;
(c) In the interests of the economic well-being of the UK;
(d) In the interests of public safety;
(e) For the purpose of protecting public health;
(f) For the purpose of assessing or collecting any tax, duty, levy or other imposition,
contribution or charge payable to a government department;
(g) For any other purpose specified by order of the Secretary of State.[100]

In addition, the authorizing officer must believe that the authorized conduct or **4.190**
use is proportionate to what is sought to be achieved by it and arrangements must
exist in respect of the source which satisfy matters set out in section 29(5), namely
provision for handling and controlling the CHIS, and for the keeping of records
and maintaining confidentiality, etc.

The Regulation of Investigatory Powers Act (Prescription of Offices, Ranks and **4.191**
Positions) Order 2000 requires that authorization for the conduct and use of
a CHIS shall be granted by an officer of at least superintendent rank. However,
in an urgent case, in the absence of an authorizing officer, authorization may be
given by an officer of inspector rank. However, where the likely consequence of
the conduct of the CHIS would be for knowledge of confidential material to be

---

[99] CHIS Code of Practice, para 4.14.
[100] RIPA 2000, 29(3).

acquired, then authorization must be given by the chief constable.[101] In the case of a police force, an authorization for conduct and use of a CHIS can only be granted on application from within the police force wishing to deploy the source.[102]

4.192 Given the increasingly transnational nature of counter-terrorism investigations, and with foreign investigation in mind, it should be noted that section 27(3) of RIPA 2000, in addressing the authorization of both the CHIS and of surveillance, provides that 'the conduct that may be authorized under this Part (ie, Part II) includes conduct outside the United Kingdom'.

4.193 In the case of the CHIS, the Code of Practice at para 1.6, provides that authorization may be given for the conduct and use of a source both within and outside the United Kingdom. However, it should be noted that, in addition to a RIPA authorization, consideration will need to be given to authorizations and permissions in the country concerned. Such activity will usually need to be initiated via a formal letter of request.

4.194 Part II of RIPA 2000 provides detailed regulation in respect of the form, renewal, and duration of authorization, along with cancellation of the same. The detailed requirements are outside the scope of the present book, therefore reference should be made to the provisions of the Act itself.

4.195 Taking into account the nature of investigations into alleged terrorist activity, it may well be necessary for investigators to deploy a participating source or undercover officer. However, RIPA 2000 makes no explicit provisions for such deployment. A 'participating source' may be defined as an individual who, with the approval of an authorizing officer, is given permission to participate in a crime which the principals have already intended to commit.

4.196 Despite the lack of provision in RIPA 2000, two passages in the CHIS Code of Practice do provide some basis for such a deployment. Paragraph 2.10 provides: 'in a very limited range of circumstances an authorization under Part II may . . . render lawful, conduct which otherwise would be criminal, if it is incidental to conduct falling within section 26(8) of the 2000 Act which the source is authorized to undertake'. In addition, para 1.4 of the Code of Practice states that: 'neither Part II of the 2000 Act nor this Code of Practice is intended to affect the practices and procedures surrounding criminal participation of sources'. The Code of Practice, then, gives a basis, but it is not, of course, a basis in law as required by the ECHR jurisprudence. There is, however, common law authority for the use of a participator; in particular, *R v Birtles*.[103]

---

[101] See CHIS Code of Practice, para 3.2.
[102] RIPA 2000, s 33(1).
[103] [1969] 1 WLR 1074, which set out two guidelines or principles: the offence for which participation is authorized must be 'already laid on' and the participator must not be used to entrap unlawfully (in other words, must not be used as an *agent provocateur*).

The common law, it might be said, is not a satisfactory basis in law in itself, since **4.197** it is not readily accessible to persons likely to be affected and lacks the clarity which Strasbourg demands. A further difficulty is that, because RIPA 2000 makes no explicit provisions for the participator, it does not address the proportionality of the participation. It does not, for instance, confine participation to certain types of crime of particular gravamen. In addition, it does not provide for any higher level of authorization in the case of participation. Indeed, there is less provision following the introduction of RIPA 2000, than existed when participation simply purported to be regulated by guidelines. Home Office Circular 97/1969 gave more detailed guidance and required that the role played by the participator was only a peripheral one when compared to that of the principal. The Circular also provided for authorization to be granted at assistant chief constable level. Indeed, in a period just prior to the passing of the 2000 Act, the Association of Chief Police Officers and what was then HM Customs and Excise agreed a Code of Practice on the use of sources which, again, was more stringent as to participation than RIPA 2000. It, too, provided for authorization at Assistant Chief Constable level.[104]

Those involved in counter-terrorism investigations and prosecutions must, there- **4.198** fore, note that an Article 8 challenge may be mounted in relation to the deployment of a participating source. Indeed, the difficulties have been, in part, addressed within the Manual of Minimum Standards in the Use of Covert Human Intelligence Sources. That document, which does not give a 'basis in law' for ECHR purposes, provides that the role to be undertaken by a participator must be a minor one, that the offences under investigation must amount to serious crime (as defined in section 81(3) of RIPA 2000) and must be authorized by an officer of at least assistant chief constable rank.

Possible Human Source Handling Model

The approach set out below seeks to give general guidance and to highlight **4.199** possible areas of compromise and the ways in which those handling/controlling sources might be expected to have safeguards in place. It is drawn from 'best practices' from the UK, Europe, and the Commonwealth.

'Recruitment and assessment'

Identification. Human sources are identified using a number of processes, the **4.200** most obvious one being through arrest or coming to notice as a suspect.

---

[104] Present 'Guidance' to UK law enforcement confirms, inter alia, that authorization must be at Assistant Chief Constable level and that the role to be played must be 'minor', with the evidence or information being essential and not being capable of being obtained by less intrusive means.

4.201 However in a terrorist case the best source may be a person on the borders or within the terrorist organization. The person on the border has particular advantages: he/she may not actually be involved in direct terrorist activity, but may be aware of what is happening.

4.202 **Research.** This is perhaps the key area of recruitment. A full profile of the person to be approached will be conducted. An informed prediction will be made on how the person will react when an approach is made. The questions to be asked will be: Is the person of a disposition to be able to cope with the approach and then to continue to assist? Have steps been taken to ensure that the person is not involved in terrorist activity?

To achieve this, a so-called lifestyle surveillance operation will be undertaken.

4.203 **Assessment of the information.** The intention must be to corroborate the information that the source is providing. Accuracy must be questioned. Does it progress the investigation? Is it timely and up to date? Is it actionable; in other words, can it be used to progress the investigation?

4.204 **Assessment of character.** Dedicated source handlers should be in place, and should give their views on the character of the person. Can he/she cope with stress? Will they maintain objectivity and focus? Can he/she be trusted not to compromise the investigation.

'Documentation'

4.205 **Recruitment.** The decision-making process used to recruit the source and the methods used should be detailed. The rationale is that during any subsequent prosecution, allegations might be directed at the methods used to recruit.

4.206 **Terms and conditions.** This sets the parameters in which a source may operate. It should show a clear audit trial in respect of tasking and use. It should also include informing the source of the consequences if he/she commits crime and or breaches the parameters set.

'Reviews'

4.207 There should be regular reviews of the use of the source and the taskings undertaken, along with, the results achieved by using them.

4.208 The objective of the review is to ensure that the source is being used appropriately. A review should also consider welfare and prevent over-use.

'Authorization of meetings'

4.209 An independent officer should ensure that the handling process is being conducted effectively and ethically.

At the outset this officer should authorize the handlers to meet with the source **4.210** and agree the meeting place.

Recording details of the meeting and the product obtained. A detailed **4.211** record of where the meeting took place, timing, and what information was obtained.

'Registrar'

The purpose of the role is to set and to have the responsibility of ensuring **4.212** that the agency keeps a central record of all authorized sources and their deployments.

'Process of dissemination'

• Intelligence placed onto a database with a unique number.
• An intelligence cell controls this database.

Surveillance

Some, but not all, jurisdictions have a regime in place for the authorization of **4.213** surveillance. Such authorization is, variously, senior law enforcement, judicial, or executive. The first and the last of these are, of course, more susceptible to challenge on human rights grounds. Given the variety of approaches adopted, the present section will address the process set out in the UK in RIPA 2000.

Surveillance is defined in section 48(2) of RIPA 2000 as including: **4.214**

(a) monitoring, observing or listening to persons, their movements, their conversations or their other activities or communications;
(b) recording anything monitored, recorded or listened to in the course of surveillance; and
(c) surveillance by or with the assistance of a surveillance device.

Section 48(3), meanwhile, goes on to provide that surveillance *does not* include: **4.215**

(a) Any conduct of a CHIS for obtaining or recording (whether or not using a surveillance device) any information which is disclosed in the presence of the source;
(b) The use of a CHIS for so obtaining or recording information; or
(c) Any such entry on, or interference with, property or wireless telegraphy as would be unlawful unless authorized under (i) section 5 of the Intelligence Services Act 1994 or (ii) Part III of the Police Act 1997.

The effect of section 48(3)(c) is that a covert deployment by a law enforcement **4.216** agency involving an interference with real or personal property will require an authorization under Part III of the Police Act 1997 in the event that the person entitled to give permission in relation to the property has not consented to the interference. Similarly, in relation to activity by the security services, authorization of deployment in such circumstances will be under section 5 of the Intelligence Services Act 1994.

4.217   Part II of RIPA 2000 creates two types of surveillance: directed and intrusive. Each will be of relevance to those conducting proactive investigations into alleged terrorist activity:

Directed surveillance

4.218   Section 26(2) of RIPA 2000 defines directed surveillance as being covert surveillance that is not intrusive and is undertaken for the purposes of a specific investigation in such a manner as is likely to result in the obtaining of private information about a person, whether or not that person is specifically identified for the purposes of the investigation or operation in question. Intrusive surveillance is addressed, in detail, below; however, for present purposes, intrusive surveillance is covert surveillance carried out in relation to anything taking place on any residential premises or in any private vehicle.[105]

4.219   'Private information' for the purposes of directed surveillance is addressed in section 26(10), which provides that, in relation to a person, private information includes any information relating to his private or family life. In addition, para 4.3 of the Surveillance Code of Practice provides that the notion of private or family life should be interpreted broadly to include an individual's private or personal relationships with others. Such a broad definition is in line with ECtHR case law which has never favoured a restrictive interpretation.[106]

4.220   In the event of an immediate response to events or circumstances, surveillance will not amount to directed surveillance (and hence will not require an authorization) where it would not have been reasonably practicable for an authorization to have been sought.[107] It should also be noted that overt CCTV surveillance will not amount to directed surveillance unless, for example, CCTV cameras are being used in a covert manner; for instance, targeting a particular individual or group of individuals on the basis of intelligence or information received rather than by immediate response.

4.221   Conduct which amounts to directed surveillance will be lawful, for all purposes, provided that an authorization has been granted and that the surveillance activity

---

[105]   RIPA 2000, s 26(3).
[106]   See eg, *PG and JH v UK* [2002] Crim LR 308; *Neimitz v Germany* (1992) 16 EHRR 97; and *Halford v UK* (1997) 24 EHRR 523.
[107]   RIPA 2000, s 26(2)(c).

in question is in accordance with that authorization.[108] Authorization, as in the case of the CHIS, may be given for activities taking place in the United Kingdom or by and on behalf of UK investigators in foreign states.[109]

The criteria for authorization of directed surveillance mirrors in large part that for **4.222** the CHIS.[110] However, the usual authorization duration for directed surveillance (and indeed for surveillance activity generally) is three months, as opposed to twelve months for the CHIS. An authorizing officer or official shall not grant authorization for directed surveillance unless he or she believes that:[111]

(1) the authorization is necessary on one of the following grounds:
    (a) in the interests of national security;
    (b) for the purpose of preventing or detecting crime or of preventing disorder;
    (c) in the interests of the economic well-being of the United Kingdom;
    (d) in the interests of public safety;
    (e) for the purpose of protecting the public health;
    (f) for the purpose of assessing or collecting any tax, duty, levy, or other impo-sition, contribution, or charge payable to a government department;
    (g) for any other purpose specified by order of the Secretary of State; and

(2) the authorized surveillance is proportionate to what is sought to be achieved by carrying it out.[112]

As in the case of the CHIS, the subordinate legislation[113] requires that the autho- **4.223** rizing officer be of superintendent rank or equivalent. In urgent cases, again as with the CHIS, an authorization can be given by an inspector where no superin-tendent is available. However, where the likely consequence of the surveillance activity would be for any person to acquire knowledge of confidential material, authorization must be given by the chief constable.

Urgent authorizations may be given and will last for seventy-two hours. If the **4.224** authorizing officer is at superintendent level or above the authorization may be given orally. If at inspector rank, the authorization, even for an urgent case, must be given in writing.

---

[108] (n 107) s 27(1).
[109] (n 107) s 27(3).
[110] The issue of whether there was a valid authorization in place in a common law State is likely to be one that goes to legality, not admissibility (although, of course, absence of legality may lead to admissibility or abuse of process arguments *(R v GS & Others* [2005] EWCA Crim 887).
[111] (n 107) s 28(2) and (3).
[112] (n 107) s 28(2).
[113] The Regulation of Investigatory Powers (Prescription of Offices, Ranks and Positions) Order 2000.

Intrusive surveillance

4.225 Intrusive surveillance is covert surveillance carried out in relation to anything taking place on any residential premises or in any private motor vehicle, which involves the presence of an individual on the premises or in the vehicle, or is carried out by means of a surveillance device.[114]

4.226 'Residential premises' for the purposes of section 26(3) refers to a premises or any part of a premises that is occupied or used, even if temporarily, for residential purposes, including those parts of hotel and prison accommodation used for residence. Common areas, such as landings, staircases, and corridors, are not, however, included.[115] From this, it will be seen that if a device is to be deployed in a police or prison cell, it will require an intrusive surveillance authorization.

4.227 A private vehicle is one used primarily for private purposes;[116] it does not include a taxi which is plying for hire or has been hired.[117] The use of the word 'in' any private motor vehicle will include a device being located on, under or attached to the vehicle.[118] In relation to tracking devices, in the event that the device only provides information about the location of the vehicle, the surveillance is specifically deemed to be directed and not intrusive.[119]

4.228 Surveillance which is carried out by means of a surveillance device in relation to anything taking place on any residential premises or in any private vehicle without the device being present on the premises or vehicle will not be intrusive, unless the device is such that it consistently provides information of the same quality and detail that might be expected from a device actually present on the premises or in the vehicle.[120] To assist further, paragraph 5.3 of the Covert Surveillance Code of Practice indicates that an external observation post, providing only limited view and no audio, will not be considered by the Surveillance Commissioners to be intrusive.

4.229 In relation to the authorization regime, the greater intrusion of intrusive surveillance has dictated a much higher level of authorizing officer. The level of authorization for intrusive surveillance mirrors that for property interference under the Police Act 1997, discussed in more detail below. Section 32(1) of RIPA 2000 provides that an authorization for intrusive surveillance may only be granted by the Secretary of State or by a senior authorizing officer. 'Senior authorizing officer' is defined in

---

[114] RIPA 2000, s 26(3).
[115] See (n 114) s 48(1) and (7)(b).
[116] (n 114) s 48(1).
[117] (n 114) s 48(7)(a).
[118] (n 114) s 26(11).
[119] (n 114) s 26(4).
[120] (n 114) s 26(5).

section 32(6) as being, for a police force, a chief constable. However, in an urgent case, an authorization may be granted by an officer of assistant chief constable rank or above.

Section 27(1) provides that conduct amounting to intrusive surveillance shall be **4.230** lawful for all purposes if an authorization conferring an entitlement to engage in such conduct is conferred and that the conduct that takes place is in accordance with that authorization. The authorizing officer must believe, by virtue of section 32(2) and (3), that the authorization is necessary:

(1) in the interests of national security;
(2) for the purpose of preventing or detecting serious crime; or
(3) in the interests of the economic well-being of the United Kingdom.

Further, the authorized surveillance must be believed to be proportionate to what **4.231** is sought to be achieved by carrying it out. In considering whether authorization is necessary and proportionate, the authorizing officer must take into account, inter alia, the question of whether the information which it is thought necessary to obtain by the authorized conduct could reasonably be obtained by other means.[121]

A 'serious crime' (see point (2) of the above list), for the purposes of RIPA 2000, **4.232** is defined in section 81(3) as an offence for which a person aged 21 years or over, with no previous convictions, could reasonably be expected to receive a sentence of three years' imprisonment or more; or where the alleged conduct involves the use of violence, results in substantial financial gain, or is conducted by a large number of persons in pursuit of a common purpose.

An authorization for intrusive surveillance must be in writing, unless the case is **4.233** urgent.[122] An urgent authorization will last for up to seventy-two hours; otherwise an authorization will last for up to three months. Renewal is available thereafter. The senior authorizing officer may only grant authorization in respect of an application made by a member of his or her own force.[123] Where an application for intrusive surveillance relates to residential premises, the premises in question must be in the 'area of operation' of the force making the application.

A single authorization may, by virtue of section 33(5), combine an application for **4.234** intrusive or directed surveillance under Part II of RIPA 2000 and an application for property interference under Part III of the Police Act 1997. However, the provisions and criteria of each will apply and need to be considered separately.

---

[121] (n 114) s 32(4).
[122] (n 114) s 43(1).
[123] (n 114) s 33(3).

4.235 Given the more intrusive nature of intrusive surveillance, and having regard to the view of the ECtHR that there should be judicial oversight, prior approval of a Surveillance Commissioner is required for an intrusive surveillance authorization to take effect (save in the case of an urgent authorization, see below). The senior authorizing officer must give written notice to a Surveillance Commissioner when a police or Customs authorization has been granted, renewed, or cancelled.[124] The notice must state one of two things: either that the approval of a Surveillance Commissioner is required before the authorization is able to take effect, or that the case is an urgent one.[125] If the matter is an urgent one, the grounds for that belief must be set out to the Surveillance Commissioner. Having received the notice, the Surveillance Commissioner must, as soon as practicable, consider the authorization and approve it or reject it.

4.236 An authorization will not take effect until approval by a Surveillance Commissioner has been given and written notice of that approval has been provided to the authorizing officer.[126] The notice requirements under section 35 may, however, be transmitted electronically.[127] If the notice states that it is an urgent one, then the authorization will be effective from the time it was granted by the senior authorizing officer.[128]

4.237 If a Surveillance Commissioner is satisfied that, at the time that the authorization was granted or renewed, there were no reasonable grounds for believing that section 32(2) criteria were fulfilled, he may quash the authorization, a decision which will be effective from the time of the authorization or from the time of the renewal (whichever is applicable).[129] Similarly where a Surveillance Commissioner is satisfied that, at any time while an authorization is extant, there are no longer any reasonable grounds for believing that the section 32(2) criteria are fulfilled, he may cancel the authorization. Such cancellation will take effect from the time at which it appears to the Surveillance Commissioner that the criteria ceased to be satisfied.[130]

4.238 If an urgent application has resulted in either a grant or a renewal by a senior authorizing officer, the Surveillance Commissioner may quash the authorization if he is not satisfied that, at the time of the grant or renewal as the case may be, there were reasonable grounds for believing that the case was an urgent one.[131]

(n 114) s 35(1).
[125] (n 114) s 35(3).
[126] (n 114) s 36(2).
[127] (n 114) s 35(9).
[128] (n 114) s 36(3).
[129] (n 114) s 37(2).
[130] (n 114) s 37(3).
[131] (n 114) s 37(4).

In the event that a Surveillance Commissioner refuses to approve an intrusive **4.239** surveillance authorization, or quashes or cancels an authorization, a senior authorizing officer may appeal to the Chief Surveillance Commissioner.[132] An appeal must be made within seven days from the day on which the decision appealed against was reported to the senior authorizing officer.[133] In the event that the Chief Surveillance Commissioner is satisfied that there were reasonable grounds for believing that the criteria in section 32(2) were fulfilled and if he is not satisfied that the authorization is not one in which the urgent application provisions have been abused, then the appeal must be allowed. Similarly, if there is an appeal against a decision to quash or cancel, the Chief Surveillance Commissioner may either reverse the decision of the Surveillance Commissioner or modify that decision (in a case where, for instance, he believes the decision should have been cancelled, but from a different time from that at which it was cancelled by the Surveillance Commissioner).

Interference with Property (Part III, Police Act 1997)

In the event that, during the course of a counter-terrorism investigation, the **4.240** investigator seeks to deploy any surveillance device in such a way as will involve an interference with property (real or personal) he must obtain an authorization under Part III of the Police Act 1997. The provisions of Part III were brought in as a result of the judgment of the House of Lords in *R v Khan*.[134]

Section 92 of the Police Act 1997 provides that no entry on or interference with **4.241** property or with wireless telegraphy shall be lawful unless authorized under the Act. In addition, paragraph 6.4 of the Covert Surveillance Code of Practice provides that 'authorizations under the 1997 Act may not be necessary where the public authority is acting with the consent of a person able to give permission in respect of relevant property, although consideration should still be given to the need to obtain an authorization under Part II of the 2000 Act'.

As already indicated, interference with property as envisaged in Part III of the **4.242** Police Act 1997 relates to both real and personal property. A gloss has, however, been put on the legislation by guidance issued from the Office of the Surveillance Commissioners. This is obtainable from the Office's website.[135] That guidance indicates, inter alia, that a Part III authorization will not be required for entry into an area open to the public, such as in shops, public houses, restaurants, or hotel or apartment common areas and to other premises where, with an implied consent from the occupier, the public are allowed access. In essence, the mere fact that an

---

[132] (n 114) s 38(1).
[133] (n 114) s 38(3).
[134] [1997] AC 558.
[135] Available at the OSC website: <http://www.surveillancecommissioners.gov.uk/>.

entry into a restaurant or other establishment is for a covert purpose will not vitiate the implied consent.

4.243 The grounds for authorization for property interference are contained within section 93, which provides that:

> (1) Where subsection (2) applies, an authorizing officer may authorize—
>> (a) the taking of such action, in respect of such property in the relevant area, as he may specify, or
>> (b) the taking of such action in the relevant area as he may specify, in respect of wireless telegraphy.
> (2) This subsection applies where the authorizing officer believes—
>> (a) that it is necessary for the actions specified to be taken on the ground that it is likely to be of substantial value in the prevention or detection of serious crime, and
>> (b) that what the action seeks to achieve cannot reasonably be achieved by other means.

Thus, the criteria of both necessity and proportionality need to be satisfied.

4.244 The definition of 'serious crime' for the purposes of Part III of the Police Act 1997 is identical to that in section 81(3) of RIPA 2000. Thus, conduct which constitutes one or more offences should only be regarded as serious crime if:

(1) it involves the use of violence, or results in substantial financial gain, or it is conducted by a large number of persons in pursuit of a common purpose; or
(2) the offence, or one of the offences, is an offence for which a person who has attained the age of 21 years and has no previous convictions could reasonably be expected to be sentenced to imprisonment for a term of three years or more.

4.245 Just as for intrusive surveillance, the level of authorization within the police is at chief constable level. However, where it is not reasonably practicable to obtain the authorization from the authorizing officer, a designated deputy[136] may grant the authorization.

4.246 Just as for RIPA 2000 surveillance authorizations, an authorization under Part III of the Police Act 1997 must be in writing[137] and may last for up to three months.[138] Oral authorization may be given in urgent cases and will have effect for seventy-two hours.[139] In the event that an urgent authorization is granted by a designated deputy, that must be in writing, but will, again, last for only seventy-two hours.[140] At any time before an authorization ceases, the authorizing officer may renew it

---

[136] Police Act 1997, s 94(4).
[137] (n 136) s 95(1).
[138] (n 136) s 95(2)(b).
[139] (n 136) s 95(2)(a).
[140] (n 136) s 95(1) and (2)(a).

for a period of up to three months, beginning on the day on which the authorization would otherwise cease to have effect.[141]

A Part III authorization is only effective in the geographical area of the police force **4.247**
in question.[142] However, in the case of a force or authority with national responsibility, the geographical area will be construed accordingly. An authorizing officer is only able to authorize property interference on application from a member of his own force.[143] But an authorizing officer is able to authorize maintenance and retrieval of equipment outside his own force area. However, any entry on to private property outside the authorizing officer's force area will require authorization from the authorizing officer from the force in whose area the private property (ie real property) is situated.

Entrapment

Given the increasing recourse to undercover deployment and 'sting' operations in **4.248**
counter-terrorism investigations, the parameters to which law enforcement, and indeed intelligence, agencies must have regard now fall to be examined.

A proactive investigation might take the form of the deployment of an undercover **4.249**
agent to infiltrate a terrorist group or involve participating status being afforded to an informant from such a group. Either way, those responsible for such operations must ensure that investigators remain investigators, not creators, of crime.

In the UK, the position in domestic law has been made relatively clear following **4.250**
the conjoined appeal to the House of Lords in *R v Looseley* and *Attorney General's Reference (3 of 2000).*[144] Although a drugs test purchase, not a terrorism case, the test set out in *Looseley* is equally applicable to a counter-terrorism investigation and, indeed, to any other circumstance of covert deployment. The facts of the two cases which made up the appeal were, in themselves, unremarkable, but the House of Lords took the opportunity to examine in detail the law on entrapment and to formulate a test which, in approach and formulation, is practical, secures the balance of fairness for all interests, and has due regard for international human rights law. Moreover, the criteria for covert operations set out by Their Lordships provides a test which will be applicable across the range of covert investigations from a short term covert operation against an individual soliciting or recruiting on behalf of a terrorist organization to a long term infiltration into the organization itself.

---

[141] (n 136) s 95(3).
[142] (n 136) s 93(1).
[143] (n 136) s 93(3).
[144] [2002] Cr App R 29.

4.251 The defendant in *Looseley* engaged with an undercover police officer, facilitated three drug deals, and faced an indictment containing three counts of being concerned in the supply of a controlled drug of class A, namely heroin. Having been unsuccessful at trial in arguing that the proceedings should have been stayed as an abuse of process or, alternatively, that the evidence of the undercover officer should have been excluded under the UK's exclusionary provisions contained in section 78 of the Police and Criminal Evidence Act 1984 (PACE), the defendant pleaded guilty. An appeal against conviction on the basis of the trial judge's rulings on the legal argument was dismissed. The matter, in due course, went to the House of Lords.

4.252 The facts of the case which form the basis of the *Attorney General's Reference (3 of 2000)* also related to an investigation concerning relatively low-level drug dealing. In essence, the undercover officers in that case went too far in their conversations with the defendant. Accordingly, the trial judge acceded to a defence application to stay proceedings as an abuse of process. The stay was subsequently lifted in order that the prosecution could offer no evidence.

4.253 Following that acquittal, a Reference was taken by the Attorney General to the Court of Appeal as to whether the exclusionary discretion under section 78 of PACE or the inherent jurisdiction of the court to stay proceedings as abuse of process had been changed or modified by Article 6 of the ECHR and the incorporation into domestic law of the ECHR itself. The Court of Appeal answered that question in the negative and, again, the matter came before the House of Lords.

4.254 Their Lordships confirmed that *R v Sang*[145] is still good law and that entrapment is not a substantive defence in English law. The basis for such a view being that even a defendant who is entrapped to commit an offence still has the necessary mental element and/or of course, has committed the *actus reus* of the offence.

4.255 If agents of the state, such as police officers, behave in an unacceptable and improper manner by creating crime, then the defendant will be excused, not because he is less culpable (although he may be) but because the police have behaved improperly.[146] As Lord Steyn had previously noted in *R v Latif*,[147] to prosecute in such circumstances 'would be an affront to the public conscience'.

4.256 Thus, the House of Lords concluded, where a defendant has been entrapped, a stay is the appropriate remedy, not because the defendant is not guilty of the offence or because he could not receive a fair trial, but because it would be unfair to try him at all. Conversely, such an argument is not a section 78 admissibility

---

[145] [1980] AC 402.
[146] Per Lord Nicholls [2002] Cr App R 29, 367.
[147] [1996] 1 WLR 104, 112.

argument: it is not being said that the admission of certain evidence renders the trial unfair; what is really being said is that there should be no trial at all.

However, in the eyes of the House of Lords in *Looseley*, there will be occasions **4.257** when it is still appropriate for there to be a section 78 argument. However, such occasions will be limited to those set out by Potter LJ in *R v Shannon*[148] (which was quoted by Lords Hoffman and Hutton in *Looseley*):

> If there is good reason to question the credibility of evidence given by an agent provocateur, or which casts doubt on the reliability of other evidence procured or resulting from his actions, and that question is not capable of being properly or fairly resolved in the course of the proceedings from the available, admissible and 'untainted' evidence, then the judge may readily conclude that such evidence should be excluded.

What then amounts to 'entrapment'? The key question is as to whether the agent **4.258** of the state, such as the undercover operative, has provided an opportunity to the target to commit a crime or has instigated or incited the target to commit an offence that he would not have otherwise committed. The opportunity in question must, in the words of Lord Hoffman,[149] be an 'unexceptional opportunity' and no more. As to what amounts to an unexceptional opportunity; the question will be whether the undercover agent, in his conduct, has done no more then might have been expected from someone in the role he was assuming. Thus, there will be something of a sliding scale. An undercover agent playing the role of a major organized criminal in, for instance, an infiltration will most probably be able to use, in the words of the House of Lords[150] 'a degree of persistence' in his dealing with major high-level targets. Conversely, an undercover agent assuming the role of a potential recruit in relation to an investigation of the soliciting of funds or the recruitment of low-level members by targets who are themselves at a relatively low level will be expected to speak and react as a person who is, effectively, a member of the public, would in the circumstances.

Before the decision in *Looseley*, the principal considerations in any entrapment **4.259** argument were the criteria set out by the Court of Appeal in *R v Smurthwaite; R v Gill*.[151] Those criteria included the question as to whether the conduct of the undercover agent was active or passive. The active/passive distinction was disapproved by the House of Lords in *Looseley* as being unhelpful. Recognizing a sliding scale of what amounts to acceptable behaviour by an investigator working undercover, depending on the nature of the operation and the targets, Lord Hoffman stated that: '. . . a good deal of active behaviour in the course of an authorized operation

---

[148] [2002] CLR 100 1.
[149] [2002] Cr App R 29, 381.
[150] (n 149) 381.
[151] [1994] 1 AER 898.

may therefore be acceptable without crossing the boundary between causing the offence to be committed and providing an opportunity to commit it.'[152]

4.260   However, in assessing whether an acceptable opportunity, but nothing more, has been given, there are also other considerations to be had. The more difficult an offence is to detect by conventional reactive means, and many aspects of terrorist activity will fall into this category, the more likely that the use of a proactive covert methodology will be justified. Further, in assessing the nature of inducements given by the undercover agent, regard will have to be had to the circumstances of the defendant and, in particular, as to whether the defendant is vulnerable. Again, the stronger the position of the defendant, the more likely that the inducement made will be regarded as acceptable. Nevertheless, the predisposition of a target to offend will not be a proper basis for a covert operation and will not render acceptable that which would be unacceptable in the case of a person without previous convictions. As Lord Hoffman noted, 'since the English doctrine assumes the defendant's guilt and is concerned with the standards of behaviour for the law enforcement officers, predisposition is irrelevant to whether a stay should be granted or not'.[153]

4.261   Given that one of the rationales for the test formulated in *Looseley* is what has been described[154] as a preventive or protective one (in other words a jurisdiction to prevent the abuse of executive power), and that another is the integrity principle (that is to say, a prosecution based on entrapment should be halted in order to protect the integrity of the criminal justice system), the court must be satisfied that the investigation was undertaken in good faith. As Lord Hoffman noted[155] one way that good faith may be established is by the investigators having reasonable ground for suspicion before the covert operation is launched. Suspicion may be as to an individual or group of individuals, but it may also be as to a location. Suspicion as to location will suffice. It might be there is scope for future argument to the effect that in circumstances where there is suspicion as to location, but not as to individuals, then for an investigation to be proportionate there should be intermediate steps taken (eg, surveillance) to identify a target or group of targets before the more intrusive measure of introducing undercover agents is adopted. However, for the time being and on the basis of the speeches in *Looseley*, suspicion as to location is clearly enough. Nonetheless, the days of speculative, so-called 'random virtue' operations are now at an end.

---

[152] [2002] Cr App R 29, 381.
[153] [2002] Cr App R 29, 380.
[154] See A Ashworth, 'Re-Drawing the Boundaries of Entrapment' (2002) Crim LR 161–79.
[155] [2002] Cr App R 29, 369.

Not only must there be reasonable suspicion for covert activity, the deployment **4.262**
itself must be properly supervised with appropriate authorizations for the activities
involved, in compliance with relevant Codes of Practice and with proper tasking
and debriefing.

In the light of the above, what is the test that can be inferred to judge the accept- **4.263**
ability of a proactive operation? As encapsulated by Andrew Ashworth,[156] that test
should now been seen as follows:

> There is no entrapment if:
>
> i) The investigators have reasonable grounds to suspect the target or targets of
>   involvement in a certain kind of offence, or at least the investigators have
>   reasonable grounds to suspect people frequenting a particular location to be thus
>   involved; and
> ii) The investigators are duly authorized to carry out the operation in compliance
>   with appropriate Codes of Practice etc; and
> iii) The undercover agent (agents) does no more than provide the target or targets
>   with an unexceptional opportunity to commit the offence.

Conversely, if the investigators do not have reasonable grounds for suspicion, or, **4.264**
although having reasonable grounds, go further than simply providing an
exceptionally opportunity, the conduct is likely to be viewed as entrapment and
a stay of criminal proceedings will be likely.

Increasingly, private individuals and organizations undertake sting operations; an **4.265**
obvious example will be that of an investigative journalist carrying out an undercover assignment for a newspaper or TV channel. In such circumstances, after
product has been obtained, material may be passed on to the police or prosecuting
authorities who may wish to make evidential use of it in criminal proceedings. In
those jurisdictions where there is an authorization regime for intrusive methods
and special investigative means, such as the UK's framework under RIPA, such
authorization may usually only be granted by a designated person, such as a senior
police officer or judge, on an application by a prescribed public authority. However,
it is submitted that the test that the court should apply if an abuse of process or
exclusion of evidence argument arises in the case of material obtained by, for
instance, a journalistic 'sting' will be the same as for an operation carried out by
a law enforcement agency. A court is, after all, a public authority or State entity
and must, therefore, act compatibly with an individual's human rights, even in
circumstances where proceedings are taking place, ostensibly, between two private
parties. Moreover, for those States that are Parties to the ECHR, a public authority
has a positive obligation, derived from Article 1 of the ECHR, to ensure that
Convention rights are properly and effectively protected. That obligation will fall

---

[156] See Ashworth (n 154).

to a court whether or not the rights have been infringed by a private organization or public authority. In all the circumstances, therefore, it is difficult to see that a court would be justified in applying a different, or less demanding, test.

I. Membership of a Proscribed Organization

4.266 Investigators and prosecutors each have a role in the charging or bringing of proceedings process, although the nature of that role will, of course, vary from State to State.

4.267 Both for the purposes of investigative strategy and for the purposes of charge, the question of whether a particular group amounts to a proscribed organization may be an important one.

In that regard, the case of *R v Z*, House of Lords,[157] is instructive. Z and three others were each charged under section 11(1) of the Terrorism Act 2000 with belonging to a proscribed organization, which for the purposes of the Act, was defined as being, by section 3(1)(a), an organization listed in Schedule 2 to the Act or, by section 3(1)(b), one that operated 'under the same name as an organization listed in that Schedule'.

4.268 The particulars of the offence alleged in each case that the person 'belonged to a proscribed organization, namely the Real Irish Republican Army'. At the conclusion of the prosecution case the judge ruled that since Schedule 2 referred to the 'Irish Republican Army' but not the 'Real Irish Republican Army', which had been formed in 1997 by a group of dissident members of the former organization, the latter was not proscribed for the purposes of section 11(1).

4.269 On a reference by the Attorney General for Northern Ireland under section 15(1) of the Criminal Appeal (Northern Ireland) Act 1980, the Court of Appeal in Northern Ireland held that the Real Irish Republican Army fell within the term 'Irish Republican Army' in Schedule 2 and was therefore proscribed by virtue of section 3(1)(a) or, alternatively, was a proscribed organization within section 3(1)(b).[158]

4.270 On an appeal by Z, the House of Lords held, dismissing the appeal, that the interpretation of a statute required a controversial provision to be read in the context of the statute as a whole in the historical context of the situation which led to its enactment; that since 1922 statutes had been enacted by the Westminster and

---

[157] [2005] UKHL 35.
[158] Terrorism Act 2000, s 3(1): see post, para 2 s 11(1): 'A person commits an offence if he belongs or professes to belong to a proscribed organization'.

Stormont Parliaments with the object of suppressing terrorism by stifling organizations which were dedicated to violence for political ends and, following the emergence of more than one body claiming to be the true embodiment of the Irish Republican Army, had adopted the legislative technique of using a blanket description to embrace all emanations, manifestations, and representations of that organization, whatever their relationship to each other; that such technique had been employed in Schedule 2 to the 2000 Act; and that, accordingly, the Real Irish Republican Army fell within the ambit of the term 'Irish Republican Army' in Schedule 2 and, whether on the basis (per Lord Rodger of Earlsferry, Lord Carswell, and Lord Brown of Eaton-under-Heywood) of section 3(1)(a) alone or (per Lord Bingham of Cornhill and Lord Woolf CJ) section 3(1)(a)(b) read as a single composite test. Membership of that body was therefore an offence under section 11(1) 67–69).

5

PRE-TRIAL AND TRIAL ISSUES

A. **Burden of Proof**	5.01	Material held by authorities in a foreign state	5.84
Burden of proof under the UK's counter-terrorism legislation	5.42	Ongoing duty of disclosure at trial and thereafter	5.85
B. **Case Management**	5.50	D. **The Media and Adverse Comment**	5.86
C. **Disclosure**	5.52	E. **Hearings in Camera**	5.108
Disclosure of material by the prosecution	5.55	F. **The Accused's Right of Silence and Access to Legal Advice**	5.110
Disclosure of third party material	5.79		
Mechanism for handling sensitive material	5.82		

A. Burden of Proof

In balancing human rights considerations, some jurisdictions have introduced **5.01** offences which place an evidential burden on the defendant. For example, section 57 of the UK's Terrorism Act (2000) creates the offence of possession of an article for a terrorist purpose and provides that, if someone resides at or is in habitual use of the premises, the court may assume that he is in possession of articles there, unless he adduces evidence sufficient to raise an issue as to his lack of knowledge in relation to the presence of the articles on the premises or as to his lack of control over them.

The reversal of the evidential burden might be subject to legal argument on human **5.02** rights issues in some jurisdictions, but is likely to withstand such challenges before the courts. However, prosecutors must recognize that it still falls to the prosecution to negative the assertion or fact raised by the defendant who has satisfied the evidential burden.

The notion of reverse burden is one that has raised concern, particularly in **5.03** common law jurisdictions. It arises where the offence-creating provision, either expressly or by clear implication, requires the defence to bear the burden. The key questions that the courts have grappled with is whether such a requirement poses a legal (persuasive) or evidential burden on the accused and, in the case of the UK and other signatories to the European Convention on Human Rights,

219

whether it violates the fundamental presumption of innocence contained in Article 6(2).[1]

5.04 In *R v Johnstone*,[2] a case concerning the infringement of trademarks in 'bootlegging' cases under section 92 of the Trade Marks Act 1994,[3] the issue before the House

---

[1] Article 6(2) provides:
Right to a fair trial
2. Everyone charged with a criminal offence shall be presumed innocent until proved guilty according to law.

[2] [2003] UKHL 28; [2003] 1 WLR 1736.

[3] Section 92 provides:
Unauthorised use of trade mark, &c. in relation to goods
(1) A person commits an offence who with a view to gain for himself or another, or with intent to cause loss to another, and without the consent of the proprietor—
  (a) applies to goods or their packaging a sign identical to, or likely to be mistaken for, a registered trade mark, or
  (b) sells or lets for hire, offers or exposes for sale or hire or distributes goods which bear, or the packaging of which bears, such a sign, or
  (c) has in his possession, custody or control in the course of a business any such goods with a view to the doing of anything, by himself or another, which would be an offence under paragraph (b).
(2) A person commits an offence who with a view to gain for himself or another, or with intent to cause loss to another, and without the consent of the proprietor—
  (a) applies a sign identical to, or likely to be mistaken for, a registered trade mark to material intended to be used—
    (i) for labelling or packaging goods,
    (ii) as a business paper in relation to goods, or
    (iii) for advertising goods, or
  (b) uses in the course of a business material bearing such a sign for labelling or packaging goods, as a business paper in relation to goods, or for advertising goods, or
  (c) has in his possession, custody or control in the course of a business any such material with a view to the doing of anything, by himself or another, which would be an offence under paragraph (b).
3) A person commits an offence who with a view to gain for himself or another, or with intent to cause loss to another, and without the consent of the proprietor—
  (a) makes an article specifically designed or adapted for making copies of a sign identical to, or likely to be mistaken for, a registered trade mark, or
  (b) has such an article in his possession, custody or control in the course of a business, knowing or having reason to believe that it has been, or is to be, used to produce goods, or material for labelling or packaging goods, as a business paper in relation to goods, or for advertising goods.
(4) A person does not commit an offence under this section unless—
  (a) the goods are goods in respect of which the trade mark is registered, or
  (b) the trade mark has a reputation in the United Kingdom and the use of the sign takes or would take unfair advantage of, or is or would be detrimental to, the distinctive character or the repute of the trade mark.
(5) It is a defence for a person charged with an offence under this section to show that he believed on reasonable grounds that the use of the sign in the manner in which it was used, or was to be used, was not an infringement of the registered trade mark.
(6) A person guilty of an offence under this section is liable—
  (a) on summary conviction to imprisonment for a term not exceeding six months or a fine not exceeding the statutory maximum, or both;
  (b) on conviction on indictment to a fine or imprisonment for a term not exceeding ten years, or both. [emphasis added]

220

of Lords was whether the prosecution must prove civil infringement of a registered trademark in order to prove an offence under section 92(1)(c) of the Trade Marks Act 1994.

Their Lordships in determining this issue considered the entire section and in **5.05** particular sub-section 92(5) imposed a legal or evidential burden on the accused.

The facts of the case are relatively straightforward. Mr Johnstone was involved in **5.06** bootlegging, and his activities came to light when a Mrs Luddington was errone-ously sent a parcel by Mr Johnstone containing a large quantity of compact discs. She alerted Polygram Records. Following a search of Mr Johnstone's home, the officers recovered some 500 compact discs and audio cassettes; all of these were also found to be bootleg recordings. He was charged with offences under section 92 of the Trade Marks Act 1994. As set out above, he claimed that in order for the offence to be proved, prosecution must prove as a constituent element of the offence that there had been civil infringement of the trademark in question and as the CDs merely contained the name of the performer this was not an indication of trade origin but simply a statement of who the performer was.

The trial judge ruled that there was no requirement to prove civil infringement as **5.07** section 92 was an offence-creating provision and not concerned with any other part of the Act which dealt with trademarks and was therefore to that extent a 'stand alone' provision. On that basis Mr Johnstone pleaded and was sentenced.

Mr Johnstone appealed, and the Court of Appeal in allowing the appeal, stated **5.08** that the prosecution does not have to prove civil infringement unless a defence is raised under sections 10–12 of the Act. If that occurs, the prosecution must then disprove such a defence.

The certified question to the House of Lords was as follows: **5.09**

> whether it is a defence to a criminal charge under section 92 of the Act that the defendant's acts do not amount to a civil infringement of the trade mark.

Lord Nicholls of Birkenhead, delivered the lead judgment and concluded that it **5.10** was implicit in the provisions of section 92 that the:

> . . . offending use of the sign must be use of a trade mark . . . within the section there are two clear indications confirming this interpretation . . . Secondly, section 92(5) presupposes that the conduct of the person charged was an infringement of a registered trade mark. It would make no sense for reasonable belief in non-infringement to provide a defence if infringement was irrelevant so far as the criminal offences are concerned . . .

Their Lordships then examined section 92(5) of the Act which provides a defence **5.11** (see footnote above) and the burden of proof and observed:

> It concerns the burden of proof. On this there are conflicting decisions of the Court of Appeal . . . I shall, therefore, state my views as shortly as may be. First, I entertain no doubt that, unless this interpretation is incompatible with article 6(2) of the

Convention, section 92(5) should be interpreted as imposing on the accused person the burden of proving the relevant facts on the balance of probability. Unless he proves these facts he does not make good the defence provided by section 92(5). The contrary interpretation of section 92(5) involves substantial re-writing of the subsection. It would not be sufficient to read the subsection as meaning that it is a defence for a person charged to raise an issue on the facts in question. That would not be sufficient, because raising an issue does not provide the person charged with a defence. It provides him with a defence only if, he having raised an issue, the prosecution then fails to disprove the relevant facts beyond reasonable doubt. I do not believe section 92(5) can be so read. I do not believe that is what Parliament intended.

The question which next arises is whether this interpretation, namely, that section 92(5) imposes a 'legal' or 'persuasive' onus on the person charged, is compatible with the presumption of innocence contained in article 6(2) of the European Convention on Human Rights. Prima facie this interpretation derogates from that principle. That much is clear. On this interpretation section 92(5) sets out facts a defendant must establish if he is to avoid conviction. These facts are presumed against him unless he establishes the contrary.

That is not the end of the matter. The European Court of Human Rights has recognised that the Convention does not, in principle, prohibit presumptions of fact or law. What article 6(2) requires is that they must be confined within reasonable limits which take into account the importance of what is at stake and maintain the rights of the defence: *Salabiaku v France*.[4] Thus, as elsewhere in the Convention, a reasonable balance has to be held between the public interest and the interests of the individual. In each case it is for the state to show that the balance held in the legislation is reasonable. The derogation from the presumption of innocence requires justification . . .

. . . of this paradox all that can be said is that for a reverse burden of proof to be acceptable there must be a compelling reason why it is fair and reasonable to deny the accused person the protection normally guaranteed to everyone by the presumption of innocence . . . . . sound starting point is to remember that if an accused is required to prove a fact on the balance of probability to avoid conviction, this permits a conviction in spite of the fact-finding tribunal having a reasonable doubt as to the guilt of the accused: see Dickson CJ in *R v Whyte*.[5]

This consequence of a reverse burden of proof should colour one's approach when evaluating the reasons why it is said that, in the absence of a persuasive burden on the accused, the public interest will be prejudiced to an extent which justifies placing a persuasive burden on the accused. The more serious the punishment which may flow from conviction, the more compelling must be the reasons. The extent and nature of the factual matters required to be proved by the accused, and their importance relative to the matters required to be proved by the prosecution, have to be taken into account. So also does the extent to which the burden on the accused relates to facts which, if they exist, are readily provable by him as matters within his own knowledge or to which he has ready access.

In evaluating these factors the court's role is one of review. Parliament, not the court, is charged with the primary responsibility for deciding, as a matter of policy, what

---

[4] (1988) 13 EHRR 379, 388, at para 28.
[5] (1988) 51 DLR (4th) 481, 493.

should be the constituent elements of a criminal offence. I echo the words of Lord Woolf in *Attorney-General of Hong Kong v Lee Kwong-Kut*.[6]

> 'In order to maintain the balance between the individual and the society as a whole, rigid and inflexible standards should not be imposed on the legislature's attempts to resolve the difficult and intransigent problems with which society is faced when seeking to deal with serious crime.'

The court will reach a different conclusion from the legislature only when it is apparent the legislature has attached insufficient importance to the fundamental right of an individual to be presumed innocent until proved guilty.

5.12 The Court concluded that section 92(5) did indeed place a legal/persuasive burden on the accused given the menace of counterfeiting and neither did such a burden violate the presumption of innocence as the facts would be known to the trader and to require the prosecution to prove that a trader acted dishonestly would have a counter-effect of fewer investigations in such cases:

> ... overall it is fair and reasonable to require a trader, should the need arise, to prove on the balance of probability that he honestly and reasonably believed the goods were genuine. I consider the persuasive burden placed on an accused person by the section 92(5) defence is compatible with article 6(2). This being so, it becomes unnecessary to consider whether, if this interpretation of section 92(5) were incompatible with article 6(2), section 92(5) might be open to a different interpretation pursuant to section 3(1) of the Human Rights Act 1998. (per Lord Nicholls[7])

5.13 In *R v Lambert*[8] the House of Lords was asked to consider the applicability of the Human Rights Act 1998 retrospectively.

5.14 The defendant, Lambert, was convicted in 1999 of an offence under the Misuse of Drugs Act 1971 for possession with intent to supply cocaine. At his trial, relying on section 28(3)(b)(i) of the Act, he submitted that he did not believe or suspect of the contents of his bag to contain cocaine and therefore was not in possession of drugs. He was convicted and sentenced seven years imprisonment. He appealed against conviction and sentence on the ground that the defence under section 28 imposed a legal rather than an evidentiary burden.

5.15 The Court of Appeal dismissed the appeal and found that there was a justification for the reverse burden and further it was a proportionate response in the context and therefore it did not violate Article 6. Although the Human Rights Act 1998 was not in force at the time of his trial, the Court of Appeal proceeded on the basis that the Act should apply even though it was not available to Lambert during the trial and the subsequent appeal.

---

[6] [1993] AC 951, 975.
[7] [2003] UKHL 28, para 53.
[8] [2001] UKHL 37.

5.16 The Court of Appeal dismissed the appeal but certified the following questions for determination by the House of Lords:

- Whether for an offence under section 5 of the 1971 Act, it is an essential element of the offence that the accused must know that he had a controlled drug in his possession;
- Whether on a charge under section 5 of the Act, the trial judge was right to direct the jury that the onus of proving the defence under section 28(2) imposed a legal rather than an evidentiary burden;
- Whether the accused could rely on the Convention rights which were not in force at the time of his trial.

5.17 The House of Lords was of the view that the last question which essentially dealt with the jurisdictional point should be addressed first. The majority of the House (Lord Steyn dissenting) was of the opinion that no reliance could be placed on the 1998 Act where the trial had taken place prior to its coming into force; in short, the Human Rights Act 1998 did not apply retrospectively.

5.18 However, their Lordships were of the view that a ruling should be given on the remaining two questions even though the Act and by extension, the Convention, could have no application in the present instance.

Legal or evidential burden?

5.19 The court applied section 3 of the Human Rights Act[9] and concluded that the presumption of innocence could be interfered with, but that any interference must be justified and proportionate. In the present case, there was sufficient justification of the interference but the transfer of a legal burden was not proportionate and should accordingly be read down to evidential burden. Lord Hutton, however, dissented.

5.20 Giving the leading speech, Lord Slynn said:

> The second question in effect asks whether, if the prosecution has proved the three elements to which I have referred, it is contrary to Article 6(2) of the Convention Rights for a judge to direct a jury that 'the defendant is guilty as charged unless he

---

[9] Interpretation of legislation:
  (1) So far as it is possible to do so, primary legislation and subordinate legislation must be read and given effect in a way which is compatible with the Convention rights.
  (2) This section—
      (a) applies to primary legislation and subordinate legislation whenever enacted;
      (b) does not affect the validity, continuing operation or enforcement of any incompatible primary legislation; and
      (c) does not affect the validity, continuing operation or enforcement of any incompatible subordinate legislation if (disregarding any possibility of revocation) primary legislation prevents removal of the incompatibility.

discharges a legal, rather than an evidential, burden of proof to the effect that he neither believed nor suspected nor had reason to suspect that the substance in question was a controlled drug'. If read in isolation there is obviously much force in the contention that section 28(2) imposes the legal burden of proof on the accused, in which case serious arguments arise as to whether this is justified or so disproportionate that there is a violation of Article 6(2) of the Convention rights (see *Salabiaku v France*[10])

In balancing the interests of the individual in achieving justice against the needs of society to protect against abuse of drugs this seems to me a very difficult question but I incline to the view that this burden would not be justified under Article 6(2) of the Convention rights . . . the House must still go on to consider section 3(1) of the 1998 Act. That section provides that 'So far as it is possible to do so, primary legislation must be read and given effect in a way which is compatible with the Convention rights'. This obligation applies to primary legislation 'whenever enacted'. Even if the most obvious way to read section 28(2) is that it imposes a legal burden of proof I have no doubt that it is 'possible', without doing violence to the language or to the objective of that section, to read the words as imposing only the evidential burden of proof. Such a reading would in my view be compatible with Convention rights since, even if this may create evidential difficulties for the prosecution as I accept, it ensures that the defendant does not have the legal onus of proving the matters referred to in section 28(2) which whether they are regarded as part of the offence or as a riposte to the offence prima facie established are of crucial importance.[11]

Lord Steyn, in dissenting on the retrospective application of the Human Rights **5.21** Act 1998, agreed with the majority that the transfer of a legal burden was not compatible with Article 6(2) of ECHR and must be read down to mean evidential burden. He was of the opinion that whilst such an inroad into the presumption could be said to be justified, it must still be a proportionate measure:

Counsel for the appellant submitted that the defence put forward by the appellant under section 28 is an ingredient of the offence under section 5(3). His argument was that knowledge of the existence and control of the contents of the container is the gravamen of the offence for which the legislature prescribed a maximum sentence of life imprisonment . . . Taking into account that section 28 deals directly with the situation where the accused is denying moral blameworthiness and the fact that the maximum prescribed penalty is life imprisonment, I conclude that the appellant's interpretation is to be preferred. It follows that section 28 derogates from the presumption of innocence.

I would, however, also reach this conclusion on broader grounds. The distinction between constituent elements of the crime and defensive issues will sometimes be unprincipled and arbitrary. After all, it is sometimes simply a matter of which drafting technique is adopted: a true constituent element can be removed from the definition of the crime and cast as a defensive issue whereas any definition of an offence can be reformulated so as to include all possible defences within it. It is necessary to concentrate not on technicalities and niceties of language but rather on

---

[10] (1988) 13 EHRR 37, para 28.
[11] [2001] UKHL 37, para 17.

matters of substance . . . There are other cases where the defence is so closely linked with *mens rea* and moral blameworthiness that it would derogate from the presumption to transfer the legal burden to the accused . . . A transfer of a legal burden amounts to a far more drastic interference with the presumption of innocence than the creation of an evidential burden of the accused. The former requires the accused to establish his innocence.[12]

5.22 Lord Clyde examined the likelihood of section 28 imposing a legal/persuasive burden on the accused and in agreement with the majority, he concluded that:

Of course trafficking in controlled drugs is a notorious social evil, but if any error is to be made in the weighing of the scales of justice it should be to the effect that the guilty should go free rather than that an innocent person should be wrongly convicted. By imposing a persuasive burden on the accused it would be possible for an accused person to be convicted where the jury believed he might well be innocent but have not been persuaded that he probably did not know the nature of what he possessed. The jury may have a reasonable doubt as to his guilt in respect of his knowledge of the nature of what he possessed but still be required to convict. Looking to the potentially serious consequences of a conviction at least in respect of class A drugs it does not seem to me that such a burden is acceptable.[13]

5.23 Lord Hutton, in his dissenting speech, was of the opinion that section 28 imposed a legal/persuasive burden, but that this did not contravene Article 6(2) of the Convention:

It is also relevant to observe that subsections 28(2) and (3) expressly impose not merely an evidential burden on the defendant but a persuasive (or legal) burden. Therefore the appellant derives no assistance from *B v Director of Public Prosecutions* as it is clear that Parliament has expressly provided that the prosecution need not prove the mental element of knowledge. A persuasive burden is one where the matter in question must be taken as proved against the defendant unless he satisfies the jury on the balance of probabilities to the contrary. An evidential burden is one where the matter must be taken as proved against the defendant unless there is sufficient evidence to raise an issue on the matter but, if there is sufficient evidence, then the burden rests on the prosecution to satisfy the jury as to the matter beyond reasonable doubt . . . [14]

. . . In my opinion the reasoning of the Commission can be relied on by the Crown in this case. In the present case the statutory presumption is restrictively worded in that it requires the prosecution to prove that the defendant is in possession of the container containing the controlled drug and that the substance inside the container is, in fact, a controlled drug. Only when this is proved is it presumed that he knew that the substance was a controlled drug and he is then entitled to disprove the presumption. The presumption is neither irrebuttable nor unreasonable. To oblige

---

[12] [2001] UKHL 37, per Lord Steyn, paras 35–7.
[13] Ibid, per Lord Clyde, para 156.
[14] Ibid, per Lord Hutton, para 182.

the prosecution to prove that the defendant knew that the substance was a controlled drug in many cases would make it very difficult to obtain a conviction.[15]

Therefore in considering whether a rebuttable presumption of knowledge created by section 28(2) and (3) is compatible with Article 6(2) a number of factors (which to some extent overlap) have to be considered:

(1) Is the presumption created by subsections 28(2) and (3) directed towards a clear and proper public objective?

In my opinion it clearly is. The taking of controlled drugs is a great social evil which causes widespread suffering and the possession of controlled drugs with intent to supply is a grave and frequently committed offence which ensures the continuation of this social evil.

(2) Is the creation of the presumption a reasonable measure for Parliament to take and is there a reasonable relationship of proportionality between the means employed and the aim sought to be realised?[16]

. . . In considering this matter it is necessary, as Lord Hope of Craighead stated in *Brown v Stott*, to assess whether a fair balance has been struck between the general interest of the community and the personal rights of the individual. In my opinion the threat posed by drugs to the welfare of society is so grave and the difficulty in some cases of rebutting a defence that the defendant believed that he was carrying something other than drugs is so great that it was reasonable for Parliament to impose a persuasive burden as to lack of knowledge on a defendant. The question whether a fair balance has been struck depends in large measure on whether the creation of an evidential burden as opposed to a persuasive burden on a defendant would be adequate to remedy the problem with which subsections 28(2) and (3) were intended to deal . . . In such cases it will often be very difficult to prove guilt if the prosecution has to prove beyond a reasonable doubt that the defendant knew that the bag contained a controlled drug or that the tablets were a controlled drug.[17]

It is clear from the decisions of the European Commission in *X v United Kingdom* and *AG v Malta* that the difficulty of proving knowledge on the part of the defendant is one of the factors which can justify the creation of a presumption against a defendant, where the presumption is neither irrebuttable nor unreasonable. I am, with respect, unable to agree with the view that the problem of obtaining a conviction against a guilty person can be surmounted by imposing an evidential burden on the defendant. All that a defendant would have to do to discharge such a burden would be to adduce some evidence to raise the issue that he did not know that the article in the bag or the tablets on the table were a controlled drug, and the prosecution would then have to destroy that defence in such a manner as to leave in the jury's mind no reasonable doubt that the defendant knew that it was a controlled drug in the bag or on the table.[18]

---

[15] Ibid, per Lord Hutton, para 187.
[16] Ibid, per Lord Hutton, para 190.
[17] Ibid.
[18] Ibid, per Lord Hutton, paras 191–2.

At the heart of the present case is the concept of a fair trial which is enshrined in Article 6. However the concept of a fair trial has been an integral part of the law of the United Kingdom long before it was set out in the Convention. It is clear that thirty years ago members of this House considered that it was not unfair for Parliament to place a persuasive burden as to lack of knowledge on the defendant in a drugs case . . .[19]

My Lords, when judges of such eminence considered that transferring the burden of proof in relation to knowledge would not result in an unfair trial to the defendant, I consider that thirty years later when the problem has not changed there is no reason for this House to take a different view. Section 2 of the 1998 Act now requires the House in determining a question which has arisen in connection with a Convention right to take into account judgments of the European Court and decisions of the European Commission, but in my opinion the judgments and decisions to which I have referred provide no basis for the view that under the jurisprudence of the European Court the transfer of the onus of proof as to knowledge in drugs cases would constitute a violation of Article 6(2).[20]

Therefore my conclusion is that the difficulty in some cases of convicting those guilty of the crime of possession of a controlled drug with intent to supply, if the burden of proving knowledge beyond a reasonable doubt rests on the prosecution, is not resolved by placing an evidential burden on the defendant, and that it is necessary to impose a persuasive burden as subsections 28(2) and (3) do. I further consider that the transfer of the onus satisfies the test that it has a legitimate aim in the public interest and that there is a reasonable relationship of proportionality between the means employed and the aim sought to be realised. Accordingly I am of the opinion that subsections 28(2) and (3) do not violate Article 6(2) and I am in full agreement with the Court of Appeal on this issue.[21]

5.24 In *Lambert*, the defence invited the Court to apply the provisions of the Human Rights Act 1998 retrospectively. In so doing they relied on section 6, 7, and 22 of the Act. Given that retrospective application of the 1998 Act would have been procedural rather than substantive, it is somewhat surprising that reliance was not placed on the fact that human rights law prohibits the application of a law retrospectively where the law creates a criminal offence and the conduct occurred before the act is criminalized,[22] but the same does not hold true for procedural change that would indeed benefit an accused or where a penalty is reduced.

---

[19] Ibid, per Lord Hutton, para 195.
[20] Ibid, per Lord Hutton, para 197.
[21] Ibid, per Lord Hutton, para 198.
[22] Article 15 of the ICCPR states:
    1. No one shall be held guilty of any criminal offence on account of any act or omission which did not constitute a criminal offence, under national or international law, at the time when it was committed. Nor shall a heavier penalty be imposed than the one that was applicable at the time when the criminal offence was committed. If, subsequent to the commission of the offence, provision is made by law for the imposition of the lighter penalty, the offender shall benefit thereby.
    2. Nothing in this article shall prejudice the trial and punishment of any person for any act or omission which, at the time when it was committed, was criminal according to the general principles of law recognized by the community of nations.

Therefore, the rule against retrospectivity would not apply in this instance as the **5.25** Act is not an offence-creating statute and therefore not 'penal' in character, but seeks to protect rights of a person, and therefore would not offend the rule. It is somewhat surprising that reliance was not placed on this simple principle. Support for this proposition can also be found in Article 7 of the European Convention on Human Rights

Following *Lambert,* the House of Lords looked at the recasting of a statutory legal **5.26** burden as an evidential one.

Attorney General's Reference No 4 of 2002 (On Appeal from the Court of Appeal (Criminal Division)) Sheldrake (Respondent) v Director of Public Prosecutions (Appellant) (Criminal Appeal from Her Majesty's High Court of Justice) (Conjoined Appeals)[23]

Following a conviction for an offence under section 5 of the Road Traffic Act **5.27** 1988[24] and an acquittal in a matter under section 11 of the Terrorism Act 2000,[25]

---

[23] [2004] UKHL 43.

[24] Section 5 provides:
Driving or being in charge of a motor vehicle with alcohol concentration above prescribed limit
(1) If a person—
    (a) drives or attempts to drive a motor vehicle on a road or other public place, or
    (b) is in charge of a motor vehicle on a road or other public place,
        after consuming so much alcohol that the proportion of it in his breath, blood or urine exceeds the prescribed limit he is guilty of an offence.
(2) It is a defence for a person charged with an offence under subsection (1)(b) above to prove that at the time he is alleged to have committed the offence the circumstances were such that there was no likelihood of his driving the vehicle whilst the proportion of alcohol in his breath, blood or urine remained likely to exceed the prescribed limit.
(3) The court may, in determining whether there was such a likelihood as is mentioned in subsection (2) above, disregard any injury to him and any damage to the vehicle.

[25] Section 11 provides: Membership
(1) A person commits an offence if he belongs or professes to belong to a proscribed organisation.
(2) It is a defence for a person charged with an offence under subsection (1) to prove—
    (a) that the organisation was not proscribed on the last (or only) occasion on which he became a member or began to profess to be a member, and
    (b) that he has not taken part in the activities of the organisation at any time while it was proscribed.
(3) A person guilty of an offence under this section shall be liable—
    (a) on conviction on indictment, to imprisonment for a term not exceeding ten years, to a fine or to both, or
    (b) on summary conviction, to imprisonment for a term not exceeding six months, to a fine not exceeding the statutory maximum or to both.
(4) In subsection (2) 'proscribed' means proscribed for the purposes of any of the following—
    (a) this Act;
    (b) the [1996 c. 22.] Northern Ireland (Emergency Provisions) Act 1996;
    (c) the [1991 c. 24.] Northern Ireland (Emergency Provisions) Act 1991;

the issue of reverse burden fell to be considered again by the House of Lords in the conjoined appeal and whether such a reversal violates the presumption of innocence enshrined in Article 6(2) of the European Convention on Human Rights (see (n 1) above) particularly when they are read as posing a legal/persuasive burden on the accused rather than an evidential burden.

5.28 The brief facts that give rise to this appeal are as follows:

Mr Sheldrake was convicted of an offence under section 5 of the Road Traffic Act 1988. At his trial he argued that he had no intention of driving whilst under the influence of alcohol, but the magistrates were not convinced and Sheldrake was convicted. He argued that section 5(2) which provided a defence, required him to prove that he did not intend to drive, thereby imposing upon him a legal reverse burden which ran counter to the presumption of innocence.

5.29 In the connected appeal, A was acquitted at the Crown Court for an offence under section 11 of the Terrorism Act 2000, namely that he was a member of a proscribed organization, 'Hamas IDQ' and professed to be a member of Hamas IDQ. The evidence was largely based on his continued bragging to his acquaintances that he was a member. Following legal argument, the trial judge ruled there was no case to answer and verdicts of not guilty were entered. The Attorney General referred the matter to the Court of Appeal for an opinion on the following questions:

- What are the ingredients of an offence contrary to section 11(1) of the Terrorism Act?
- Does the defence contained in section 11(2) of the Terrorism Act 2000 impose a legal, rather than an evidential, burden of proof on an accused, and if so, is such a legal burden compatible with the European Convention and, in particular, articles 6(2) and 10 of the Convention?

5.30 The Court of Appeal concluded that the ingredients of the offence were contained in the provision itself; however in respect of the defence set out in section 11(20), it imposed a legal rather than an evidential burden and it was compatible with Article 6(2) of ECHR.

5.31 The matter was then referred to Their Lordships on the application of A. Their Lordships took the opportunity to analyse the position in both domestic law and under ECHR jurisprudence. They also considered cases from the Commonwealth, but found that the value of such authorities were limited as they arose in jurisdictions

---

(d) the [1989 c. 4.] Prevention of Terrorism (Temporary Provisions) Act 1989;
(e) the [1984 c. 8.] Prevention of Terrorism (Temporary Provisions) Act 1984;
(f) the [1978 c. 5.] Northern Ireland (Emergency Provisions) Act 1978;
(g) the [1976 c. 8.] Prevention of Terrorism (Temporary Provisions) Act 1976;
(h) the [1974 c. 56.] Prevention of Terrorism (Temporary Provisions) Act 1974;
(i) the [1973 c. 53.] Northern Ireland (Emergency Provisions) Act 1973.

which are not signatories to ECHR and that they, the House of Lords, felt bound by the Strasbourg decisions.

Their Lordships held that, as a general principle, courts should, where possible, read **5.32** down provisions as imposing an evidential burden. A declaration of incompatibility in relation to the legislation falling to be considered in such circumstances, should be regarded as an action last resort.

Specifically, the House of Lords held, allowing the appeal by the DPP in Sheldrake, **5.33** and answering the questions referred, that the burden of proof provision in section 5(2) of the Road Traffic Act 1988 imposes a legal burden on an accused.

Giving the leading speech, Lord Bingham of Cornhill stated: **5.34**

> Thus the first question for consideration in each case is whether the provision in question does, unjustifiably, infringe the presumption of innocence. If it does the further question arises whether the provision can and should be read down in accordance with the courts' interpretative obligation under section 3 of the Human Rights Act 1998 so as to impose an evidential and not a legal burden on the defendant. An evidential burden is not a burden of proof. It is a burden of raising, on the evidence in the case, an issue as to the matter in question fit for consideration by the tribunal of fact. If an issue is properly raised, it is for the prosecutor to prove, beyond reasonable doubt, that that ground of exoneration does not avail the defendant . . .
>
> The governing principle of English criminal law, memorably affirmed by Viscount Sankey LC in *Woolmington v Director of Public Prosecutions*[26] is that the onus lies upon the prosecution in a criminal trial to prove all the elements of the offence with which the accused is charged. This principle has been regarded as supremely important, but not as absolute.
>
> In practice, Parliament has been very ready to impose legal burdens on, or provide for presumptions rebuttable by, the defendant . . . But the language of the statute may not, in some cases, make it plain whether a ground of exoneration must be established by the defendant or negatived by the prosecutor. In *Nimmo v Alexander Cowan & Sons Ltd* [27] the House was divided on the question. In such a case, as Lord Griffiths said in *R v Hunt (Richard)* [1987] AC 352, 374:
>
>> 'the court should look to other considerations to determine the intention of Parliament such as the mischief at which the Act was aimed and practical considerations affecting the burden of proof and, in particular, the ease or difficulty that the respective parties would encounter in discharging the burden. I regard this last consideration as one of great importance for surely Parliament can never lightly be taken to have intended to impose an onerous duty on a defendant to prove his innocence in a criminal case, and a court should be very slow to draw any such inference from the language of a statute'.[28]

---

[26] [1935] AC 462, 481.
[27] [1968] AC 107.
[28] [2004] UKHL 43, paras 1–5.

Until the coming into force of the Human Rights Act 1998, the issue now before the House could scarcely have arisen. The two statutory provisions which it is necessary to consider are not obscure or ambiguous. They afford the defendant (Mr Sheldrake) and the acquitted person a ground of exoneration, but in each case the provision, interpreted in accordance with the canons of construction ordinarily applied in the courts, would (as already noted) be understood to impose on the defendant a legal burden to establish that ground of exoneration on the balance of probabilities. Until October 2000 the courts would have been bound to interpret the provisions conventionally. Even if minded to do so, they could not have struck down or amended the provisions as repugnant to any statutory or common law rule. Domestic law would have required effect to be given to them according to their accepted meaning. Thus the crucial question is whether the European Convention and the Strasbourg jurisprudence interpreting it have modified in any relevant respect our domestic regime and, if so, to what extent . . . [29]

5.35 Their Lordships then considered the relevant jurisprudence from Strasbourg and considered the leading authority, *Salabiaku v France*[30] in which the Strasbourg Court recognized that such presumption did indeed exist in every legal system and the Convention did not prohibit such presumptions, and concluded:

> From this body of authority certain principles may be derived. The overriding concern is that a trial should be fair, and the presumption of innocence is a fundamental right directed to that end. The Convention does not outlaw presumptions of fact or law but requires that these should be kept within reasonable limits and should not be arbitrary. It is open to states to define the constituent elements of a criminal offence, excluding the requirement of *mens rea*.

> But the substance and effect of any presumption adverse to a defendant must be examined, and must be reasonable. Relevant to any judgment on reasonableness or proportionality will be the opportunity given to the defendant to rebut the presumption, maintenance of the rights of the defence, flexibility in application of the presumption, retention by the court of a power to assess the evidence, the importance of what is at stake and the difficulty which a prosecutor may face in the absence of a presumption. Security concerns do not absolve member states from their duty to observe basic standards of fairness. The justifiability of any infringement of the presumption of innocence cannot be resolved by any rule of thumb, but on examination of all the facts and circumstances of the particular provision as applied in the particular case.[31]

5.36 The application of section 3 of the Human Rights Act 1988 was considered and based on the guidance set down in an earlier decision of the House in *R v A (No 2)*[32]:

> In accordance with the will of Parliament as reflected in section 3 it will sometimes be necessary to adopt an interpretation which linguistically may appear strained.

---

[29] [2004] UKHL 43, para 7.
[30] (1988) 13 EHRR 379.
[31] [2004] UKHL 43, para 21.
[32] [2002] 1 AC 45.

The techniques to be used will not only involve the reading down of express language in a statute but also the implication of provisions. A declaration of incompatibility is a measure of last resort. It must be avoided unless it is plainly impossible to do so. (per Lord Steyn[33])

Their Lordships went on to consider the interpretative obligations under section 3 **5.37** as set out in *Ghaidan v Godin-Mendoza*.[34]

The interpretative obligation of the courts under section 3 of the 1998 Act was the subject of illuminating discussion in *Ghaidan v Godin-Mendoza* . . . The majority opinions of Lord Nicholls, Lord Steyn and Lord Rodger in that case (with which Lady Hale agreed) do not lend themselves easily to a brief summary. But they leave no room for doubt on four important points. First, the interpretative obligation under section 3 is a very strong and far reaching one, and may require the court to depart from the legislative intention of Parliament. Secondly, a Convention-compliant interpretation under section 3 is the primary remedial measure and a declaration of incompatibility under section 4 an exceptional course. Thirdly, it is to be noted that during the passage of the Bill through Parliament the promoters of the Bill told both Houses that it was envisaged that the need for a declaration of incompatibility would rarely arise. Fourthly, there is a limit beyond which a Convention-compliant interpretation is not possible . . . [35]

Their Lordships then considered the perceived differences in the test adopted **5.38** in *R v Lambert* and *R v Johnstone* and ruled that both decisions are binding on lower courts and that nothing in *Johnstone* 'suggests an intention to depart from or modify the earlier decision, which should not be treated as superseded or implicitly overruled'.

Differences of emphasis (and Lord Steyn was not a lone voice in *R v Lambert*) are **5.39** explicable by the difference in the subject matter of the two cases. The task of the court is never to decide whether a reverse burden should be imposed on a defendant, but always to assess whether a burden enacted by Parliament unjustifiably infringes the presumption of innocence. It may nonetheless be questioned whether (as the Court of Appeal ruled in para 52D) '. . . the assumption should be that Parliament would not have made an exception without good reason. Such an approach may lead the court to give too much weight to the enactment under review and too little to the presumption of innocence and the obligation imposed on it by section 3 . . .'.

The Court then examined section 11(2) of the Terrorism Act 2000 and Lord **5.40** Bingham, together with Lord Steyn, and Lord Phillips, agreed that the reverse

---

[33] [2002] 1 AC 45, at para 44.
[34] [2004] 3 WLR 113.
[35] [2004] UKHL 43, para 28.

burden under section 11(2) should be read down to mean an evidential rather than legal burden:

> It was argued for the Attorney General that section 11(2) could not be read down under section 3 of the 1998 Act so as to impose an evidential rather than a legal burden if (contrary to his submissions) the subsection were held to infringe, impermissibly, the presumption of innocence. He submitted that if the presumption of innocence were found to be infringed, a declaration of incompatibility should be made. I cannot accept this submission . . . In my opinion, reading down section 11(2) so as to impose an evidential instead of a legal burden falls well within the interpretative principles discussed above. The subsection should be treated as if section 118(2) applied to it. Such was not the intention of Parliament when enacting the 2000 Act, but it was the intention of Parliament when enacting section 3 of the 1998 Act. I would answer the first part of the Attorney General's second question by ruling that section 11(2) of the Act should be read and given effect as imposing on the defendant an evidential burden only.[36] (per Lord Bingham, paragraph 53)

5.41   Lord Rodger and Lord Carswell however were of the view that section 11(2) imposed a legal rather than evidential burden:[37]

> By enacting section 11(2) Parliament has singled out for favourable treatment those defendants who became members or began to profess to belong to the organization before it was proscribed. As I pointed out in para 65, there could have been no question of an infringement of the defendant's article 6 rights if this defence had not been included in section 11. On that hypothesis, whatever the circumstances of his initial involvement in the organization, he could have had a fair trial in terms of article 6 and could have been convicted of an offence under section 11(1) if the Crown had proved that he was a member or professed to belong to the organization after it was proscribed. All that has happened is that, without changing the definitional elements of the offence, Parliament has given these particular defendants the additional benefit of a defence if they can prove the two elements in subsection (2).
>
> The introduction of the defence does not involve the introduction into the proceedings of any presumption in favour of the Crown: the magistrate or jury decides the matter by considering and weighing the evidence led, unconstrained by any presumption of any kind. Parliament requires, however, that, before a defendant who has otherwise been proved to be guilty of the offence under section 11(1) is excused, the magistrate or jury must actually be satisfied that he did indeed join, or begin to profess to belong to, the organisation before it was proscribed and that he did not thereafter take any part in its activities.
>
> Parliament can lay down these preconditions for the defendant's acquittal in such a case without infringing article 6(2) as interpreted by the European Court in *Salabiaku* and the other authorities. And, when Parliament does so, it must inevitably be for the defendant to satisfy the magistrate or jury that the preconditions have been met. Who else could do it? If the defendant fails to establish either of the preconditions, the defence is to fail and the defendant is to be duly convicted—because, *ex hypothesi*, the Crown will already have proved all that is necessary to secure a conviction under section 11(1) . . .

---

[36] [2004] UKHL 43, para 53, per Lord Bingham.
[37] [2004] UKHL 43, paras 69ff, per Lord Rodger.

The defence in section 11(2) can be seen as relaxing the rigour of the offence in section 11(1) for defendants in these particular circumstances. If section 11(1) itself contains nothing to infringe article 6(1) or (2), then nothing in section 11(2), which serves only to improve the defendant's situation, can precipitate a violation of article 6(1) or (2) . . . I would hold, first, that section 11(2) of the Terrorism Act 2000 imposes a legal, rather than an evidential, burden of proof on an accused and, secondly, that the legal burden is compatible with articles 6 and 10 of the Convention. I would answer the Attorney General's second question accordingly.

Burden of proof under the UK's counter-terrorism legislation

Following the decision of the House of Lords in *Attorney General's Reference No 4 of 2002*[38] it can be seen that a number of offences contained within the UK's Terrorism Act 2000 carry with them defences which place a legal burden on the defendant. In addition, however, the 2000 Act also provides for a number of offences where the defence is subject to an evidential, rather than legal, burden.   **5.42**

Turning first to the shift of the legal burden to the defence, the following offences are caught: **5.43**

Offence	Statutory Defence
Belonging or professing to belong to a proscribed organization (section 11(1)).	That the organization was not proscribed when the defendant became a member/began to profess to be a member and the defendant has not taken part in activities of the organization while it was proscribed (section 11(2)).
Entering into or becoming concerned in an arrangement facilitating the retention or control by another of terrorist property (section 18(1)).	The defendant did not know and had no reasonable cause to suspect that the arrangement related to terrorist property (section 18(2)).
Failing to disclose information (section 19(1) and (2)).	The defendant has a reasonable excuse for not disclosing the information, or the defendant made a disclosure of the information to his employer in accordance with an established procedure for disclosing such information (section 19(3) and (4).[39]
Failing to comply with an order, prohibition or restriction imposed by a constable in uniform (section 36(1) and (2)).	Having a reasonable excuse for failing to comply (section 36(3)).

---

[38] [2004] UK HL 43.

[39] In addition, a defendant has a statutory defence by virtue of section 21(5) where he can show that he intended to make a disclosure and there was a reasonable excuse for his failure to do so *and* he has been charged in relation to an offence under any of the provisions contained in sections 15–18 of the 2000 Act. That is to say, where he has been charged in relation to terrorist fundraising, possessing money or property for the purposes of terrorism; being involved in terrorist funding arrangements and the money/asset laundering offence.

Offence	Statutory Defence
Parking a vehicle in contravention of a prohibition or restriction (section 51(1) and (2)).	Having a reasonable excuse for the act or omission in question (section 51(3)).
Contravening a restraint order (schedule 4, para 37(1)).	Having a reasonable excuse for a contravention (section 4 para 37(2)).
Failing to comply with a notice issued under para 16(1) of the schedule 5 to provide an explanation in respect of material seized pursuant to (schedule 5(15)).	Having a reasonable excuse for failing to comply with the notice (para 16(4)).
Failing to comply with an order under schedule 6, para (1(1)) requiring a financial institution to provide customer information for the purposes of an investigation (schedule 6, para (1(1–3)).	A financial institution was not in possession of the information required, or it was not reasonably practicable for the financial institution to comply with the requirement (para 1(4)).

5.44 Section 118 of the Terrorism Act 2000 provides for an evidential, rather than legal, burden in relation to certain offences which are listed within the section. It was incorporated into the Act following the decision of the House of Lords in *ex parte Kibilene*.[40] In *ex parte Kibilene*, the appellant K, a Nigerian national, was charged with two others with offences under section 16A of the Prevention of Terrorism (Temporary Provisions) Act 1989. Section 16A provided that:

> A person is guilty of an offence if he has any article in his possession in circumstances giving rise to a reasonable suspicion that the article is in his possession for a purpose connected with the commission, preparation or instigation of acts of terrorism to which this section applies.

5.45 In addition to creating the offence, however, section 16A also provided, at subsection 3, for a statutory defence: 'It is a defence for a person charged under this section to prove that, at the time of the alleged offence, the article in question was not in his possession for such a purpose as is mentioned in subsection (1) above.'

5.46 At the close of the prosecution case at trial, it was argued on behalf of the defence that section 16A reversed the legal burden of proof and was therefore in breach of Article 6(2) of the ECHR. The trial judge ruled that section 16A was indeed in conflict with Article 6(2) and, as a result, those acting for the

---

[40] [2000] 2 AC 326.

three defendants wrote to the DPP to request him to reconsider his consent to proceedings. Having considered matters, the DPP remained of the view that section 16A was not, in fact, inconsistent. In advance of a new trial date being set, the three defendants applied for and were granted leave to move for judicial review. The Divisional Court in due course granted a declaration that the DPP's decision to proceed with the prosecution was unlawful. Lord Bingham of Cornhill, sitting in the Divisional Court observed that: 'Under section 16A a defendant could be convicted even if the jury entertained a reasonable doubt whether he knew that the items were in his premises, whether he had the items for a terrorist purpose'.

In giving his judgment, Bingham CJ when on to say that although it was not **5.47** for the DPP to disapply legislative provisions which Parliament had enacted, nevertheless it was appropriate for the Divisional Court to review the soundness of the legal advice on which the DPP had acted. The House of Lords was called on to examine a number of issues but held, inter alia, that in respect of the reversal of burden, the section 16A provisions created an onus on the defendant that was incompatible with Article 6(2).

In the light of the decision of the House of Lords, section 118 of the 2000 Act **5.48** provides that:

(i)   Subsection (2) applies where in accordance with a provision mentioned in subsection (5) it is a defence for a person charged with an offence to prove a particular matter.
(ii) If the person adduces evidence which is sufficient to raise an issue with respect to the matter the court or jury shall assume that the defence is not satisfied unless the prosecution proves beyond reasonable doubt it is not.
(iii) Subsection (4) applies where in accordance with a provision mentioned in subsection (5) a court:
    (a) may make an assumption in relation to a person charged with an offence unless a particular matter is proved, or
    (b) may accept a fact as sufficient evidence unless a particular matter is proved.
(iv) If evidence is adduced which is sufficient to raise an issue with respect to the matter mentioned in sub section (3)(a) or (b) the court shall treat it as proved unless the prosecution disproves it beyond reasonable doubt.
(v)   The provisions in respect of which sub sections (2) and (4) apply are:
    (a) sections 12(4), 39(5)(a), 54, 57, 58, 77 and 103 of this Act, and
    (b) sections 13, 32 and 33 of the Northern Ireland (Emergency Provisions) Act 1996 (Possession and Information Offences) as they have effect by virtue of Schedule 1 to this Act.

The offences to which the evidential burden apply are, essentially, offences where **5.49** it is a defence for the accused to prove a particular matter or where the court may make an assumption about the accused or accept a fact as sufficient evidence against him (ie, as set out in section 118(1) to (4)). The offences under the 2000 Act which are covered by section 118 are:

Offence	Statutory Defence
Arranging, managing, or assisting in arranging or managing a meeting which the defendant knows is to be addressed by a person who belongs or professes to belong to a proscribed organization (section 12(2)(c)).	That the defendant had no reasonable cause to believe the address mentioned in sub-section (2) (c) would support a proscribed organization or further its activities.
Where a person knows or has reasonable cause to suspect that a disclosure has been or will be made under any of section 19-21 of the 2000 Act, that person commits an offence if he discloses to another anything that is likely to prejudice an investigation resulting from the disclosure under that section, or interferes with material that is likely to be relevant to an investigation resulting from the disclosure under that section (section 39(3) and (4)).	That he did not know and had know reasonable cause to suspect that the disclosure or interference was likely to affect a terrorist investigation, or that he had a reasonable excuse for the disclosure or interference (section 39(5)(a) and (b).
Providing weapons instruction or training etc (section 54(1) to (4)).	The defendant's action or involvement was wholly for a purpose other than assisting, preparing for or participating in terrorism (section 54(5)).
Possessing an article in circumstances which give rise to a reasonable suspicion that possession is for a purpose connected with the commission, preparation, or instigation of an act of terrorism (section 57(1)).	That possession of the article was not for a purpose with the commission, preparation, or instigation of an act of terrorism (section 57(2)).
Collection or making a record of information of a kind likely to be useful to a person committing or preparing an act of terrorism; or possessing a document or record containing information of that kind (section 58(1)).	That the defendant had a reasonable excuse for his action or possession (section 58(3)).
Possessing an explosive with intent to endanger life (section 3, the Explosive Substances Act 1883) or possessing an explosive in suspicious circumstances (section 4, the Explosive Substances Act 1883). (As provided for by section 77(1) of the 2000 Act.)	The defendant did not know of the presence of the article on his premises, or had no control of the said article (section 77(2)).
Collecting, recording, publishing, communicating, or attempting to elicit information about a person of a kind likely to be useful to a person committing or preparing an act of terrorism, or possessing a document or record containing information of that kind (section 183(1)).	That the defendant did not know of the presence of the document or record on the premises, or had no control over it (section 183(4)).

B. Case Management

A terrorist trial will often be complex and lengthy. Many jurisdictions, in both   **5.50**
common law and civil law, have struggled with putting in place an appropriate
management system for such cases which, whilst serving the public interest in
having matters resolved as expeditiously as possible, also does justice to both the
prosecution and the defence. Effective case management will ensure that, on the
one hand, a case is heard at an appropriate venue and that witnesses on both sides
are not unduly inconvenienced and, on the other, that vital safeguards in the process such as timely disclosure of material to the defence to enable it to prepare its
case, fully and appropriately, are put in place.

In the UK, the President of the Queen's Bench Division of the High Court issued,   **5.51**
on 30 January 2007, a *'Protocol on the Management of Terrorism Cases'*. The terms
of the Protocol are set out in full below and, in addition to their relevance to UK
practitioners, they may also assist other jurisdictions in deciding what measures
should be put in place to ensure that the public and all other interests are served.

Management of Terrorism Cases (issued 30 01 07 by Judge LJ, President of the Queen's Bench Divisions)

MANAGEMENT OF TERRORISM CASES
A PROTOCOL ISSUED BY THE PRESIDENT OF THE QUEEN'S BENCH
DIVISION
<u>Terrorism Cases</u>
1. This protocol applies to 'terrorism cases'. For the purposes of this Protocol a case is a 'ter-
    rorism case' where:
    a. One of the offences charged against any of the defendants is indictable only and it is
        alleged by the prosecution that there is evidence that it took place during an act of
        terrorism or for the purposes of terrorism as defined in s 1 of the Terrorism Act 2000.
        This may include, but is not limited to:
           i murder
          ii manslaughter
         iii an offence under section 18 of the Offences against the Person Act 1861
              (wounding with intent)
          iv an offence under section 23 or 24 of that Act (administering poison etc)
           v an offence under section 28 or 29 of that Act (explosives)
          vi an offence under section 2, 3 or 5 of the Explosive Substances Act 1883
              (causing explosions)
         vii an offence under section 1 (2) of the Criminal Damage Act 1971 (endangering
              life by damaging property)
        viii an offence under section 1 of the Biological Weapons Act 1974 (biological
              weapons)
          ix an offence under section 2 of the Chemical Weapons Act 1996 (chemical
              weapons)

  x an offence under section 56 of the Terrorism Act 2000 (directing a terrorist organisation)

  xi an offence under section 59 of that Act (inciting terrorism overseas)

  xii offences under (v), (vii) and (viii) above given jurisdiction by virtue of section 62 of that Act (terrorist bombing overseas) xiii an offence under section 5 of the Terrorism Act 2006 (preparation of terrorism acts)

 b. One of the offences charged is indictable only and includes an allegation by the prosecution of serious fraud that took place during an act of terrorism or for the purposes of terrorism as defined in s1 of the Terrorist Act 2000 and meets the test to be transferred to the Crown Court under section 4 of the Criminal Justice Act 1987.

 c. One of the offences charged is indictable only includes an allegation that a defendant conspired, incited or attempted to commit an offence under sub paragraphs (1) a) or b) above.

 d. It is a case (which can be indictable only or triable either way) that a judge of the terrorism cases list (see paragraph 2a) below) considers should be a terrorism case. In deciding whether a case not covered by subparagraphs (1) a), b) or c) above should be a terrorism case, the judge may hear representations from the Crown Prosecution Service.

The Terrorism cases list

2.

 a. All terrorism cases, wherever they originate in England and Wales, will be managed in a list known as the 'terrorism cases list' by the Presiding Judges of the South Eastern Circuit and such other judges of the High Court as are nominated by the President of the Queen's Bench Division.

 b. Such cases will be tried, unless otherwise directed by the President of the Queen's Bench Division, by a judge of the High Court as nominated by the President of the Queen's Bench Division.

3. The judges managing the terrorism cases referred to in paragraph (2) will be supported by the London and South Eastern Regional Co-ordinator's Office (the 'Regional Co-ordinator's Office'). An official of that office or nominated by that office will act as the case progression officer for cases in that list for the purposes of part 3.4 of the Criminal Procedure Rules.

Procedure after charge

4. Immediately after a person has been charged in a terrorism case, anywhere in England and Wales, a representative of the Crown Prosecution Service will notify the person on the 24 hour rota for special jurisdiction matters at Westminster Magistrates' Court of the following information:

 a. The full name of each defendant and the name of his solicitor of other legal representative, if known

 b. The charges laid

 c. The name and contact details of the Crown Prosecutor with responsibility for the case, if known

 d. Confirmation that the case is a terrorism case.

5. The person on the 24-hour rota will then ensure that all terrorism cases wherever they are charged in England and Wales are listed before the Chief Magistrate or other District Judge designated under the Terrorism Act 2000. Unless the Chief Magistrate or other District

Judge designated under the Terrorism Act 2000 directs otherwise the first appearance of all defendants accused of terrorism offences will be listed at Westminster Magistrates' Court.

6. In order to comply with section 46 of the Police and Criminal Evidence Act 1984, if a defendant in a terrorism case is charged at a police station within the local justice area in which Westminster Magistrates' Court is situated the defendant must be brought before Westminster Magistrates' Court as soon as is practicable and in any event not later than the first sitting after he is charged with the offence. If a defendant in a terrorism case is charged in a police station outside the local justice area in which Westminster Magistrates' Court is situated, unless the Chief Magistrate or other designated judge directs otherwise, the defendant must be removed to that area as soon as is practicable. He must then be brought before Westminster Magistrates' Court as soon as is practicable after his arrival in the area and in any event not later than the first sitting of Westminster Magistrates' Court after his arrival in that area.

7. As soon as is practicable after charge a representative of the Crown Prosecution Service will also provide the Regional Listing Co-ordinator's Office with the information listed in paragraph 4 above.

8. The Regional Co-ordinator's Office will then ensure that the Chief Magistrate and the Legal Services Commission have the same information.

Cases to be sent to the Crown Court under section 51 of the Crime and Disorder Act 1998

9. A preliminary hearing should normally be ordered by the Magistrates' Court in a terrorism case. The court should ordinarily direct that the preliminary hearing should take place about 14 days after charge.

10. The sending Magistrates' Court should contact the Regional Listing Co-ordinator's Office who will be responsible for notifying the Magistrates' Court as to the relevant Crown Court to which to send the case.

11. In all terrorism cases, the Magistrates' Court case progression form for cases sent to the Crown Court under section 51 of the Crime and Disorder Act 1998 should not be used. Instead of the automatic directions set out in that form, the Magistrates' Court shall make the following directions to facilitate the preliminary hearing at the Crown Court:

    a. Three days prior to the preliminary hearing in the terrorism cases list, the prosecution must serve upon each defendant and the Regional Listing co-ordinator:
        i   A preliminary summary of the case
        ii   The names of those who are to represent the prosecution, if known.
        iii An estimate of the length of the trial
        iv   A suggested provisional timetable which should generally include:
             • The general nature of further enquiries being made by the prose-cution
             • The time needed for the completion of such enquiries
             • The time required by the prosecution to review the case
             • A timetable for the phased service of the evidence
             • The time for the provision by the Attorney General for his consent if necessary
             • The time for service of the detailed defence case statement
             • The date for the case management hearing
             • Estimated trial date.
        v   A preliminary statement of the possible disclosure issues setting out the nature and scale of the problem including the amount of unused material, the manner

        in which the prosecution seeks to deal with these matters and a suggested timetable for discharging their statutory duty.

      vi Any information relating to bail and custody time limits

    b. One day prior to the preliminary hearing in the terrorist cases list, each defendant must serve in writing on the Regional Listing Co-ordinator and the prosecution:

      i The proposed representation

      ii Observations on the timetable

      iii An indication of plea and the general nature of the defence.

Cases to be transferred to the Crown Court under section 4(1) of the Criminal Justice Act 1987

12. If a terrorism case is to be transferred to the Crown Court the Magistrates' Court should proceed as if it is being sent to the Crown Court, as in paragraphs 9–11 above.

13. When a terrorism case is so sent or transferred the case will go into the terrorism list and be managed by a judge as described in paragraph 2 above.

The preliminary hearing at the Crown Court

14. At the preliminary hearing, the judge will determine whether the case is one to remain in the terrorism list and if so give directions setting the provisional timetable.

15. The Legal Services Commission must attend the hearing by an authorised officer to assist the court.

Use of video links

17. Unless a judge otherwise directs, all Crown court hearings prior to the trial will be conducted by video link for all defendants in custody.

Security

18. The police service and the prison service will provide the Regional Listing Co-ordinator's Office with an initial joint assessment of the security risks associated with any court appearance by the defendants within 14 days of charge. Any subsequent changes in circumstances or the assessment of risk which have the potential to impact upon the choice of trial venue will be notified to the Regional Listing Co-ordinator's Office immediately.

30 January 2007

C. Disclosure

5.52 One of the fundamental tenets of the rule of law is the right to a fair trial. This is reflected in the various international and regional and human rights instruments which set out the basic requirements that satisfy the guarantee of the right to fair trial. These are addressed in detail in Chapter 8, below, and include:

- the International Covenant on Civil and Political Rights 1966 (Article 14)
- the European Convention of Fundamental Rights 1950 (Article 6)
- the American Convention on Human Rights 1969 (Article 8)
- the African Charter on Human and Peoples' Rights 1981/1986 (Article 7)

5.53 A number of States, in particular in Asia, are not parties to these conventions and instruments. Therefore one needs also to refer to the rights set out in their national constitutions which must be construed in accordance with international human rights law. In any event, the constitution of a State, where applicable, is the primary source of safeguard of fundamental rights.

The right to a fair trial in essence enshrines the need for the defence to be fully **5.54** informed of the case against him and permit him to mount a 'full and robust' defence. As part of the proceedings therefore, the defendant must be served with the evidence that the prosecution seek to adduce during the course of the trial, and also be provided with relevant material that has come into existence as part of the investigation but which the prosecution does not intend to place reliance upon. However, practice across jurisdictions differs markedly and the discussion below, will therefore focus on the following:

- the traditional common law approach;
- the approach in civil law states;
- the consequences of a failure to disclose unused material.

Disclosure of material by the prosecution

Material which forms part of the prosecution case

The starting point must be what is meant by disclosure of material. **5.55**

During the course of any investigation, a large amount of material is gathered by **5.56** the investigators (both in the State of the alleged offence and, increasingly, from abroad). In common law jurisdictions, such 'material' is then considered by the prosecution to decide what material they will rely upon as admissible evidence to prove its case. This then is part of the prosecution case and must be made available to the defence, either by inspection or service, depending on the nature and gravity of the offence alleged.

However, practice even across common law states varies in this regard. To give some **5.57** examples:

- In The Gambia where, although a summary of the evidence and a list of exhibits are formally filed, such work is largely undertaken by the investigators, and in practice, the defence must first ask for the evidence before it is provided.
- The courts in Nigeria have interpreted that the rights granted under the Constitution[41] prohibit trial by ambush and have ruled that any witness whose name and written statement are not included in the application for leave to prefer a charge and also disclosed to the defence before the commencement of trial cannot be called to testify for the prosecution. The application of what has effectively become a rule was brought to bear in the case of *Gboko v The State*,[42] where the written statement of the Investigating Police had not been included

---

[41] In particular, Section 36 (6)(c).
[42] (2007) 17 NWLR Pt 1063.

at the preliminary hearing by the prosecution; and, as a consequence the court ruled that the prosecution could not rely upon that witness at trial.

- In Kenya, the practice of serving witness statements and any exhibits only after a witness had given evidence was subject to criticism in a decision of the Kenyan High Court[43] in 2003 which ruled that it would be contrary to the principles of a fair trial, and that such a practice of *ex post facto* disclosure does not give effect to the Constitution. Accordingly the Court further ruled that the prosecution must provide the defence with all the relevant evidence prior to a hearing. However, whilst the practice set out in this judgment has been adopted in Kenya, it appears that it is considered *per incuriam* by the prosecuting authorities and might be the subject of appeal. It does, however, seem unlikely that a future court would seek to overturn such a ruling which sits happily with general notions of prosecutorial fairness. By adopting a narrow construction of the rights protected by the Constitution, a court would go against the fundamental tenets of human rights law and an interpretation which, subsequently, has since been followed in Kenya by the case of *Pattni*.[44]

- In the UK there is an obligation to disclose all evidence the prosecution will rely on to prove its case, and that position is also reflected in Caribbean states such as Barbados and Jamaica.

- Turning to Asia, the current position in Malaysia is provided for in the Criminal Procedure Code [Act 593] which provides that an accused must be given, before trial, a copy of the information laid relating to the commission of the offence with which the accused is charged and a written statement of any document which it is intended to tender as part of the case against him.

- In contrast, in India there is no statutory provision on the point, but the courts have long held that all statements and documents relied upon by the prosecution should be served on the defence in order to ensure a fair trial.

Material not relied on by the prosecution

5.58 Turning now to material in the possession of the prosecution, but which is not to be relied upon at trial; such material is usually referred to as 'unused material' and, in a terrorist case, may include items which contain sensitive information attracting a claim of confidentiality or public interest immunity. It is the disclosure of such material that has been the subject of judicial comment and in some jurisdictions, such as the United Kingdom and Australia, a statutory regime has been put in place to meet the prosecution's obligations in this regard.

---

[43] *Juma & Others v AG* [13.2.2003].
[44] *Republic v Kamlesh Mansuklal Damji Pattni* (2005) Eklr. Criminal case 229 of 2003.

It is in the treatment of such material that a wide divergence exists among com- **5.59** mon law States in particular, and perhaps needs to be addressed internationally as it is central to the fundamental tenet of the right to a fair trial. At present, some States place no obligation on their prosecutors to disclose unused material, whilst others require prosecutors to consider the material and to disclose it to the defence if it either assists the defence or undermines the prosecution case. It may assist to highlight the position in several of the Member States to demonstrate the discrepancy in approach.

- In the UK, the disclosure of unused material is dealt with on a statutory basis under the Criminal Procedure and Investigations Act (CPIA) 1996, with clearly defined processes having evolved to deal with both sensitive and non-sensitive material. The disclosure to the defence of unused material must satisfy the disclosure test (see below), or else it will not be provided. An exception to this is material that can be withheld on the basis of public interest immunity, which will be determined by a judge.

- In Cyprus the prosecution must serve all material on the defence, and the defence can further request any other material arising from the investigation. However, the defence must apply to the court for the disclosure of sensitive information, and to examine any original documentation.

- In The Gambia there is no obligation to disclose any material to the defence. If the defence applies to the court however, it is likely to order the disclosure. There is also no obligation on the prosecution to alert the defence to material it is unaware of, whether or not such material may assist the defence case.

- Nigerian prosecutors have an obligation to disclose all material to the defence, including material which could undermine the prosecution's case. At Federal High Court level, the Court can order such material to be provided, whereas at the State High Court, there is an obligation to do so. Material cannot be withheld irrespective of whether it is exculpatory or inculpatory.

- The present position in Kenya, meanwhile, is that all relevant evidence in the possession of the prosecutor must be disclosed so as to enable the court to reach a fair decision.

- The Canadian position is governed by The Supreme Court of Canada which has provided guidelines on disclosure; if the information has relevance, then it must be disclosed, but the prosecution retains discretion when it comes to deciding on relevance and whether the information is privileged. Unused material may be subject to disclosure, unless there is privileged information (eg, covert methods of investigation) or if it would compromise an ongoing investigation. The prosecution also has a responsibility to disclose information received from a foreign agency.

- Similarly, in the Caribbean, the position generally is governed within jurisdictions by case law and, on occasion, by guidelines issued by Attorney Generals or DPPs. Thus, in Barbados the prosecution is under the obligation to disclose all materials, including making available for inspection unused material in its possession, except for information the release of which would be detrimental to national security or would breach the attorney-client privilege. The breadth of this obligation is based on the test of relevance (see *Francis v Quimby*[45]). A similar position holds true in Jamaica, where the prosecution has to disclose all the material upon which it intends to rely to prove its case. The prosecution is also obliged to disclose to the defence material that assists the defence case, and any other material requested unless there is a good reason, such as public interest immunity, to withhold it. The disclosure regime is governed by case law and by Guidelines issued by the DPP on 14 June 1996.

• In Malaysia, a written statement of facts favourable to the defence of the accused signed under the hand of the Public Prosecutor or any person conducting the prosecution must, by statute, be provided to the defence. Whilst in India, statements and other material not relied on but in the possession of the prosecution must be provided to the defence (save for the police diary, which is regarded as sensitive).

The common law approach to 'unused material'

5.60 Jurisprudence from the UK has provided two of the leading cases which set out the common law approach.

5.61 In 1992 the Court of Appeal gave its judgment in the case of *Ward*,[46] a prosecution which resulted from a series of explosions which formed part of the IRA terrorist campaign for the withdrawal of British troops from Northern Ireland. The case rested heavily on scientific/forensic evidence which was later found to be of dubious quality and the matter was referred to the Court of Appeal. At the appeal hearing the defence submitted that there had been a material irregularity on the part of the prosecution in that it had failed to disclose relevant, but unused, evidence. The court emphasized the positive duty on the prosecution to make full and proper disclosure, failure of which amounted to an 'irregularity in the course of the trial', but recognized one of the exceptions, namely public interest immunity.

5.62 In *R v Keane*,[47] the Court of Appeal provided a framework for the prosecution in its approach to disclosure. First, the prosecutor has to identify which unused items or documents are 'material' or 'relevant'. As to the test that a prosecutor should

---

[45] CR Apps Nos 8 and 10 of 2005.
[46] [1993] 1 WLR 619.
[47] [1994] 1 WLR 746.

apply in reaching that decision, the Court of Appeal adopted a formulation from the earlier case of *Melvin*[48] where the court said:

> I would judge to be material in the realm of disclosure that which can be seen on a sensible appraisal by the prosecution: (1) to be relevant or possibly relevant to an issue in the case, (2) to raise or possibly raise a new issue whose existence is not apparent from the evidence the prosecution proposes to use, (3) to hold out a real, as opposed to fanciful, prospect of providing a lead on evidence which goes to (1) or (2).

The court in *Keane* then went on to note that: **5.63**

> . . . it is open to the defence to indicate to the prosecution a defence or an issue they propose to raise as to which material in the prosecution may be of assistance, and if that is done the prosecution may wish to reconsider what should be disclosed.

Having identified relevant material thus, disclosure will then take place, without   **5.64** more, of non-sensitive items. If, however, an item or document contains sensitive details such as an informant's true identity, then the prosecutor will go before the court to seek a ruling from the judge on whether the material in question may be withheld. However, the court emphasized that:

- it is for the prosecution to put before the court only those documents which it regards as material but wishes to withhold, and the test for determining what documents are 'material' is for the prosecution to decide;

- when the court is seized of the material (that is, sensitive material), the judge must perform a balancing exercise by having regard to non-disclosure in the public interest on the one hand, and importance of the documents to the issues of interest to the defence, present and potential, on the other. If the disputed material might go to a defendant's innocence or avoid a miscarriage of justice, then the balance comes down resoundingly in favour of disclosure.

In setting out the above, the court emphasized that it was the duty of the prosecution to make a determination on the material and not simply 'dump all its unused material into the court's lap'.

Similarly in Canada, the Supreme Court in *R v Taillefer and Duguay*,[49] in clarifying   **5.65** the prosecution's duty of disclosure, upheld an earlier decision, and confirmed that the duty was 'triggered whenever there is a reasonable possibility of information being used by the defence either in meeting the case for the Crown, advancing a defence or otherwise in making a decision which may affect the conduct of the defence'. It applies whether the information is exculpatory or inculpatory. New Zealand adopts a similar approach.

---

[48] 20 Dec 1993, unreported.
[49] [2003] 3 SCR 307.

5.66 In subsequent cases in the UK, the courts have stressed that the 'duty of disclosure continues as long as proceedings remain whether at first instance or on appeal'.[50]

5.67 Both these leading cases subsequently provided the framework for the test which was later set out in England and Wales in statute.[51] In that regard, the following should be noted as to the statutory regime:

- The test of what amounts to relevant material is provided for in a Code of Practice issued under the CPIA: relevant material is defined as anything that appears to an investigator, or the officer in charge of an investigation or the disclosure officer to have some bearing on any offence under investigation or any person being investigated or on the surrounding circumstances unless it is incapable of having any impact on the case.

- The disclosure test under the CPIA is: disclosure of any material which might reasonably be considered capable of undermining the case for the prosecution against the accused, or of assisting the case for the accused, and which has not previously been disclosed.

5.68 By way of comparison, the United States adopts a disclosure framework similar in principle to the traditional common law position. The landmark case is *Brady v Maryland*,[52] in which the Supreme Court declared that, regardless of the good faith or bad faith of the prosecution, the suppression of evidence favourable to the accused violates due process where the evidence is material to either guilt or punishment.

5.69 In the more than thirty years since the *Brady* decision, the scope of its application has been found to include both direct and indirect evidence which is favourable to the defendant. In addition, and just as the position at common law, the duty of disclosure is not limited to evidence in the actual possession of the prosecutor, but, rather, it extends to evidence in the possession of the entire prosecution team, which includes investigative and other government agencies (see *Kyles v Whitley*[53]).

The disclosure approach in civil law States

5.70 In contrast to the practice in common law jurisdictions, the traditional civil law approach is that any material that is gathered as part of the investigative file will be disclosed to the parties, without any distinction being drawn between used and unused material. Such disclosure in civil law jurisdictions

---

[50] *R v Makin* [2004] EWCA Crim 1607.
[51] Criminal Procedure and Investigations Act 1996.
[52] 373 US 83 (1963).
[53] 514 US 419 (1995).

will usually be subject to the editing or excision of sensitive material before serving it on the defence. This determination is usually made by the investigating magistrate/judge.

Consequences of non-disclosure

The obligations under human rights instruments, and the established common **5.71** law requirement that proceedings as a whole must be fair have already been high-lighted. However, there are other, practical reasons why it is important that States without an established disclosure process take steps to introduce one, and that those with such a process already in place ensure that all involved are fully trained and aware of their responsibilities. A failure by the prosecutor or investigator to comply with their respective obligations may have the following consequences:

- the accused may raise a successful abuse of process argument at the trial;
- the prosecutor may be unable to argue for an extension of a remand in custody;
- the accused may be released from the duty to make defence disclosure (in those states where such an obligation exists);
- costs may be awarded against the prosecution for any time wasted if prosecution disclosure is delayed;
- the court may decide to exclude evidence, and the accused may be acquitted as a result;
- the appellate courts may find that a conviction is unsafe;
- disciplinary proceedings may be instituted against the prosecutor or investigator.

Revelation by investigator to prosecutor

At this point it should be noted that, in a common law jurisdiction, a prerequisite **5.72** to the disclosure process is a credible system of what might be called 'revelation'. Revelation refers to the investigator bringing to the attention of the prosecutor the existence of relevant material that has been retained in the investigation. The better the lines of communication, and the more that investigators and prosecutors are encouraged to adopt a 'team working' relationship, the more likely that revelation will take place effectively and in a timely manner. Revelation to the prosecutor does not, of course, mean automatic disclosure to the defence.

In order for both revelation and any subsequent disclosure to be effective and to ensure **5.73** fairness, all investigators should be under a duty to record and retain relevant material obtained or generated by them during the course of the investigation. Recording and retention should be at the heart of any investigation.

The range of information to be considered for disclosure

The importance of considering the contents of phone calls and emails made/ **5.74** received by the investigators during the investigation itself should not be discounted.

In addition, material going to the credibility of witnesses must be properly addressed and may be problematic. In particular, this will include previous convictions against any witness, and, in the case of any investigator and other professional witnesses, any finding of fact that he/she was untruthful or unreliable.

5.75 The common law duty of disclosure has always reflected the great importance to a case of the creditworthiness or otherwise of a prosecution witness. Indeed, in *R v Winston Brown*[54] the House of Lords held that it would be contrary to the great principle of open justice identified in *Keane* to withhold material which might undermine the case against the defendant or which might assist his defence. Lord Hope, delivering the leading speech, said that:

> If a defendant is to have a fair trial he must have adequate notice of the case which is to be made against him. Fairness also requires that the rules of natural justice must be observed . . . It would be contrary to that principle for the prosecution to withhold from the defendant material which might undermine their case against him or which might assist his defence.

5.76 Should there be any doubt that the obligation to disclose such findings arises even in the absence of any inquiry on the point by the defence, one need only think of the consequences if any other course were to be adopted:

   (i) to do otherwise would result in the duty of disclosure being determined by what an individual prosecutor might think a judge would permit to be used by way of conviction or findings. Thus, a subjective view by the prosecutor, with no opportunity for the defence to argue the matter, would prevail;

   (ii) the defence would be required to set out its defence in ignorance of all or some of the convictions or findings of the witnesses;

   (iii) both the court and defence would be, potentially, in ignorance of the full picture of a particular witness's creditworthiness. Similarly, the trial judge would no longer be in control of the issue of evidence going to credibility.

5.77 That common law principle was reconfirmed by the Court of Appeal in *R v Guney*,[55] namely that an express adverse finding against a police officer whether by virtue of the verdict of a jury in a criminal case, the answers to specific questions by a jury in a civil case, a previous decision of a prosecutor or of the police, should always be revealed to the prosecution and will, in the normal course of events, fall to be disclosed assuming that the credibility of that officer is to be an issue in any subsequent case (as it is certainly likely to be, if that officer is to be called).

---

[54] [1998] AC 367.
[55] Judgment 27 February 1998.

The unrepresented accused

The decision of the European Court of Human Rights in *Foucher v France*[56] indicates   **5.78**
that, in principle, the unrepresented accused has an equal right of access to the
investigative file (in a civil law state, so equivalent to used and unused material in
a common law jurisdiction), although the arrangements for providing access may
be different. The general principles of a right to a fair trial apply whether the
accused is represented or not. The difficulty for some States in this scenario is to
find a way of ensuring that the rights of victims, witnesses, and other parties are
protected, but that the accused gets access to information relevant to his defence.
Possible safeguards might be a limitation on the type of case in which an accused
can represent himself, and the provision of disclosure by inspection of material
rather than providing copies of it. States might also wish to have provided to
them a model legislative provision which makes any misuse of disclosed material
a criminal offence.

Disclosure of third party material

In a counter-terrorist investigation, it might well be that two or more investigating   **5.79**
agencies have undertaken a joint investigation, but one is taking the case forward.
Material obtained as part of that joint investigation should be treated as prosecution material and dealt with accordingly. From the point of view of the prosecution, both investigators and prosecutors must be encouraged to have regard to
whether relevant material may exist in relation to other linked investigations or
prosecutions. Reasonable enquiries must be carried out to establish this. From the
stance of the defence, multi-agency involvement should be borne in mind.
Reasonable lines of enquiry may include enquiries as to the existence of relevant
material in the possession of a third party. Very often the existence of such material
will be known or can be concluded from the circumstances.

Where an investigator believes that a third party holds material that may be   **5.80**
relevant to the investigation, a moot point in many jurisdictions is as to the
obligation of the investigator. It is suggested that such third party must be told of
the investigation and told to preserve relevant material. Consideration should
then be given by the investigator and prosecutor as to whether it is appropriate to
seek access to the material. Access should be sought if the material or item is likely
to satisfy the disclosure test. States will also have to consider how to deal with
a refusal by the third party (eg, a court order) and the stage at which the defence
should be notified, if at all.

---

[56] [1997] 25 EHRR 234 para 20.

5.81 There seems to be little authority giving general guidance on this point, but in *R v Alibhai*,[57] the Court of Appeal held that, under the CPIA for England and Wales, the prosecutor is only under a duty to disclose a third party's material if that material had come into the prosecutor's possession and the prosecutor was of the opinion that such material satisfied the disclosure test. Before taking steps to obtain third party material, the Court emphasized that it must be shown that there was a suspicion that the third party not only had relevant material and that the material was not merely neutral or damaging to the accused but satisfied the disclosure test.

Mechanism for handling sensitive material

5.82 The balance between wider public interests on the one hand, and the public interest in a particular defendant getting a fair trial have already been highlighted. Guidance should aim to help the prosecutor in balancing those competing interests. The House of Lords case of *R v H and C*,[58] has set out a valuable framework which the guidance might wish to replicate, since in many Member States the trial judge will play a role. The issue of sensitive material should, Their Lordships held, be treated thus:

> When any issue of derogation from the 'golden rule' of full disclosure comes before it, the court must address a series of questions:
>
> (1) What is the material which the prosecution seek to withhold? This must be considered by the court in detail.
>
> (2) Is the material such as may weaken the prosecution case or strengthen that of the defence? If No, disclosure should not be ordered. If Yes, full disclosure should (subject to (3), (4) and (5) below be ordered.
>
> (3) Is there a real risk of serious prejudice to an important public interest (and, if so, what) if full disclosure of the material is ordered? If No, full disclosure should be ordered.
>
> (4) If the answer to (2) and (3) is Yes, can the defendant's interest be protected without disclosure or disclosure be ordered to an extent or in a way which will give adequate protection to the public interest in question and also afford adequate protection to the interests of the defence?
>
> This question requires the court to consider, with specific reference to the material which the prosecution seek to withhold and the facts of the case and the defence as disclosed, whether the prosecution should formally admit what the defence seek to establish or whether disclosure short of full disclosure may be ordered. This may be done in appropriate cases by the preparation of summaries or extracts of evidence, or the provision of documents in an edited or anonymised form, provided the documents supplied are in each instance approved by the judge. In appropriate cases the appointment of special counsel may be a necessary step to ensure that the contentions of the prosecution are tested and the interests of the defendant protected (see paragraph 22 above). In cases of

---

[57] [2004] EWCA Crim 681.
[58] [2004] UKHL 3.

exceptional difficulty the court may require the appointment of special counsel to ensure a correct answer to questions (2) and (3) as well as (4).

(5) Do the measures proposed in answer to (4) represent the minimum derogation necessary to protect the public interest in question? If No, the court should order such greater disclosure as will represent the minimum derogation from the golden rule of full disclosure.

(6) If limited disclosure is ordered pursuant to (4) or (5), may the effect be to render the trial process, viewed as a whole, unfair to the defendant? If Yes, then fuller disclosure should be ordered even if this leads or may lead the prosecution to discontinue the proceedings so as to avoid having to make disclosure.

(7) If the answer to (6) when first given is No, does that remain the correct answer as the trial unfolds, evidence is adduced and the defence advanced?

It is important that the answer to (6) should not be treated as a final, once-and-for-all, answer but as a provisional answer which the court must keep under review.

The effect of *H and C* should be that applications to the court for the withholding of **5.83** sensitive material are rare. The starting point for the prosecutor will be that fairness ordinarily requires that all material that weakens the prosecution case or strengthens that of the defence should be disclosed. There should only be derogation from that 'golden rule' (in the words of the House of Lords) in exceptional circumstances. Those exceptional circumstances will be where one of the following applies:

- the prosecutor has identified material that fulfils the disclosure test, disclosure of which would create a real risk of serious prejudice to an important public interest and the prosecutor believes that the public interest in withholding the material outweighs the public interest in disclosing it to the defence;

- the above conditions are not fulfilled, but the police, other agencies or investigators, after consultation at a senior level, do not accept the prosecutor's assessment on this,

- the prosecutor has pursued all relevant enquiries of the police and the accused and yet is still unable to determine whether sensitive material satisfies the disclosure test and seeks the guidance of the court.

In each of the above, it should be borne in mind that material should only be placed before the court if the court's assistance is required to assess its disclosability.

Material held by authorities in a foreign state

As terrorism becomes increasingly transnational and as requests for evidence and **5.84** even joint investigations between investigators in different jurisdictions become more frequent, so the chances that unused relevant material is in existence outside the jurisdiction where the trial is being held becomes all the greater. The following should, therefore, be had in mind:

- 'ownership' of the material; particularly in relation to sensitive information (where, it is suggested, ownership will always vest with the requested state);

- the third party status for disclosure purposes of foreign authorities, save in the case of a joint investigation, and hence the 'reasonable lines of enquiry' duty;
- the dangers for the prosecution of a case of the prosecutor not knowing what a foreign state holds in relation to the case;
- mechanisms for obtaining the material from a foreign state in order to carry out disclosure consideration;
- the likely arguments to be faced at any trial in the event that such material cannot be obtained or inspected.

Ongoing duty of disclosure at trial and thereafter

5.85 The duty of disclosure should, it is submitted, remain for as a long as proceedings are extant, whether at first instance or on appeal. The continuing nature of this duty will be particularly important to have in mind during the course of the trial or hearing itself. The point was highlighted in the US case of *Imbler v Pachtman*[59] where it was held that: 'After a conviction the prosecutor also is bound by the ethics of his office to inform the appropriate authority of after-acquired or other information that casts doubt upon the correctness of the conviction'.

D. The Media and Adverse Comment

5.86 One abuse of process argument which is regularly put before the court in terrorist trials is the risk of prejudice to the defendant receiving a fair trial because of adverse comment in the media. Incidents of terrorism always, of course, receive much publicity and, very often, comment in all forms of media, particularly the printed media. The media regularly 'leads' the search for suspects and, inevitably, arrests, charging, and preliminary court appearances are all widely publicized. Of course, in many jurisdictions there will be fetters upon the details which can be reported. For instances, in the UK, the interlocutory process is subject to, inter alia, the provisions of the Magistrates' Courts Act 1980 which curtails the reporting of the detail given in preliminary and interlocutory hearings, and even later in proceedings restrictions may be imposed by orders made by the court under the Contempt of Court Act 1981. Nevertheless, the reporting that does take place can give rise to the argument that the nature of the publicity leading up to and surrounding the trial has been so prejudicial to the defendant as to put him in a position where he is unable to receive a fair trial.

---

[59] 424 US 409 (1976).

The issue of adverse publicity fell to be considered by the Court of Appeal in the **5.87** case of *R v McCann*.[60]

The three appellants were found by police close to the home of the then-Secretary **5.88** of State for Northern Ireland, the Right Honourable Tom King MP. His home was a large country house set in the countryside. It had extensive grounds. Two of the appellants, Cullen and Shanahan, were found by police sitting on a stone wall near one of the locations giving access to the wood which, itself, contains an area which commands a view over the house and its grounds. As a result of questions answered by the two and following the seizure of a number of items, the two were arrested. McCann, the third appellant, was arrested at a campsite nearby and, again, had in his possession a number of items which were to become of significance in the later trial, including a list of names of politicians and senior army officers with connections to Northern Ireland. Following an extensive police investigation, the three were charged with conspiracy to murder the Secretary of State and conspiracy to murder persons unknown.

The trial took place in Winchester, Hampshire, an army town. A number of appli- **5.89** cations were made by counsel for the appellants, including an application to change the venue of the trial and its timing (which coincided with that year's Conservative Party Conference); these applications, however, were refused by the trial judge. It should be noted that, in relation to the application concerning location, although the trial judge declined to move the trial, he did direct that the panel of jurors from which the jury was to be chosen should not be drawn from the Winchester or Aldershot (another army town) areas. That direction was given before a later judgment of the Court of Appeal in which it was held that a trial judge has no discretion to interfere with the way in which a random selection of jurors should take place. Rather, the arrangements to be made for the preparation of jury panels were the responsibility of the Lord Chancellor.[61]

When the case was opened by the prosecution it was put on the basis that the three **5.90** defendants standing trial were engaged on an enterprise which was to further the Republican cause in Northern Ireland. The opening of the case attracted a large amount of publicity, including what the Court of Appeal later described as 'some rather flamboyant reporting'. The trial continued and the defendants elected not to give evidence. However, as defence counsel were making their closing speeches to the jury, the Home Secretary, in answer to a written question in the House of Commons, announced the intention of the government to change the law on the

---

[60] [1991] 92 Cr App R 239. The *McCann* appeal was a consolidated appeal with the case of *R v Cullen* and *R v Shanahan*.
[61] See the case of *Ford (Royston)* (1989) Cr App R 278; [1989] 3WLR 762. See also, in respect of responsibility for jury panels, section 5(1) of the Jury's Act 1974.

right of silence. That statement caused great media interest and was a leading item on radio and television broadcasts and in the press. In the course of the radio and television broadcasts, the Secretary of State for Northern Ireland, and the alleged target of the three appellants, made a number of observations which, it was later argued by defence counsel, were capable of the interpretation that those who relied on the right to silence, particularly terrorists, did so to conceal their guilt. In addition, broadcasts also contained an interview with Lord Denning (himself a long-standing resident of Hampshire) which contained similar observations.

5.91 As a result of those events, defence counsel at the trial argued that the timing of the comments, so late in the trial, meant that it would be impossible to cure the prejudice caused or to restore the appearance of fairness to the proceedings. However, the trial judge ruled against those arguments and directed that the trial should proceed. On the jury's return, he warned them to disregard anything they may have seen on television in respect of the right of silence and undertook to counsel that he would warn the jury again in similar terms in his summoning up. The appellant Cullen was granted an opportunity by the trial judge to consider with his counsel whether he should reconsider his election not to give evidence, but he stood by his election and it was submitted later on his behalf that it would have been impracticable to go back on that. The jury deliberated for a total of fifteen hours and by a majority of 10:2 found each of the three appellants guilty of both counts. Each appellant was sentenced to twenty-five years' imprisonment on each of the counts, the sentences to run concurrently.

5.92 On appeal it was submitted, inter alia, on behalf of all three appellants that the radio and television broadcasts and press articles and comments in respect of the right of silence at such a crucial part of the trial rendered it impossible to say that the jury had not been influenced by what they must have seen or heard. It was submitted that the trial judge ought to have discharged the jury and ordered a retrial. It was further contended that, by refusing the defence application, the trial judge failed to exercise his discretion or exercised his discretion on a wrong principle, and was in error in believing he could cure the risk of injustice by giving directions to the jury. It was further submitted that he failed to have regard to the overriding principal that justice must not only be done, but must also be seen to be done.

5.93 In its judgment, the Court of Appeal set out some of the details of the broadcasts. The UK's commercial television station, ITV, carried the right of silence issue as its main story, under the heading 'King say suspected terrorist will no longer have the right to silence'. Its piece continued: 'the government has announced moves to curb the right to silence of terrorist suspects in Ulster. Northern Ireland Secretary Tom King says that it is aimed at terrorist and racketeers who were trying to defeat justice. Similar changes are being studied for courts in England and Wales'.

In addition, the Secretary of State for Northern Ireland was interviewed for the same news programme and expressed the view, the Court of Appeal said 'forcefully', that the measures to be introduced were 'aimed at people whom, if they were innocent, might have been expected by any fair-minded person to have been able to explain their behaviour, but remained silent and the court was not allowed to draw an inference. It was not common-sense . . .'.

Meanwhile, that same evening, the BBC News also carried the item as its main story and included an interview with the Secretary of State for Northern Ireland, who said:

5.94

> What I have to deal with is a sustained and deliberate attack on the whole system of justice and the fact that people who, if they were innocent could easily make their case, simply look at the wall and refuse to answer any questions whatsoever. It is a very old saying by a very distinguished jurist who said that innocence pleads for a chance to make its case and it is silence that is offering an opportunity for the guilty.

Other news channels also featured the story in a similarly prominent position. One of those channels also included an interview with Lord Denning, the former Master of the Rolls. He stated that, in essence, too many guilty people were being acquitted because the rules of criminal procedure favour the guilty far too much. As the Court of Appeal noted, 'for some lawyers and for most laymen his [Lord Denning's] pronouncements represent the law'.

5.95

In giving the judgment of the Court of Appeal, Beldam LJ highlighted that given that justice is usually public justice and that the media reaches into most homes it is unavoidable that those doing jury service may from time to time hear public comment or debate on aspects of the administration of justice. However, he went on to say, it is usually unlikely that such a debate will impinge upon the issues of a trial which is ongoing. Nevertheless, the fact that there may in certain circumstances be a risk prejudice to the course of justice in particular legal proceedings arising from a more general discussion of public affairs appears to be recognized by section 5 of the Contempt of Court Act 1981.[62] Nevertheless, public discussion in such circumstances may be such that it will not be necessary to discharge a jury in order to avoid the risk of injustice.

5.96

In addition to that consideration, Beldam LJ highlighted that the trial judge was exercising his discretion and that the Court of Appeal must give great weight to a trial judge's discretion. It will not be enough he said, that the Court of Appeal would have exercised its discretion differently. Rather, 'we must be clearly satisfied

5.97

---

[62] Section 5 reads as follows: 'A publication made as or as part of a discussion in good faith of public affairs or other matters of general public interest of public is not to be treated as a contempt of court under the strict liability rule if the risk of impediment or prejudice to particular legal proceedings is merely incidental to the discussion'.

that the judge is wrong . . .' The Court of Appeal, therefore, must, if it thinks it's necessary, 'examine anew the relevant facts and circumstances to exercise a discretion by way of review if it thinks the judge's ruling may have resulted in injustice to the appellants'.[63]

5.98   The Court of Appeal pointed out that several of the quotes from the broadcasts referred to the trial judge by counsel. In addition, it was highlighted on behalf of the defence that the effect of the publicity was that the jury were being told that 'the wisdom of the government and a leading member of the judiciary that silence equalled terrorism and thus guilt'.

5.99   In answer to the defence admissions, the Court of Appeal noted that the trial judge stated that if he thought a fair trial of the accused had been endangered, then he would have to discharge the jury. However, his view was that any harm that had been done could be cured and, in any event, he doubted that there had been such harm because he had previously directed the jury they must try the case on the basis of the evidence they had heard and not in respect of anything they read in the newspapers or heard about in broadcasts. Thereafter, the trial judge directed the jury and, as summarized by the Court of Appeal, reminded them that:

> The accused had certainly so far not given evidence. That was an inalienable right which any accused person had under the law. No person was obliged to answer any questions put to him or to give evidence in a case. That was their absolute right and nothing could take that away from them. He reminded them they must try the case on the evidence which they heard and not on anything which they heard on the radio or television or read in the newspapers, and he told them to totally disregard anything they might have read in the newspapers or seen on television that might have had any effect on their minds.

5.100   Beldam LJ went on to say that the Court of Appeal had formed the view that 'the power and nature of the statements which had been made in the course of the broadcasts did constitute a real and not a fanciful risk that the jury might be influenced to the view, particularly in a terrorist case, that a refusal to give an explanation in answer to questions or in evidence was the refuge of the guilty and incompatible with innocence'.

5.101   In addition the Court of Appeal noted that, at the time of the trial, neither the trial judge nor the prosecution had had the opportunity to see or hear the recordings themselves. The Court of Appeal was satisfied that if the trial judge had in fact seen the broadcasts he would have been less willing to have discounted the risk of prejudice and would have been less confident that a risk could be eliminated by a direction to the jury. Seen in that light, it was appropriate for the Court of

---

[63] *Evans v Bartlam* [1937] AC 473.

Appeal to review the exercise by the trial judge of his discretion in the light of the recordings of the broadcast which the Court of Appeal had viewed and, indeed by a concession made on behalf of the prosecution that there was a real, as opposed to fanciful, risk of prejudice.

The Court of Appeal noted that the media interest would have subsided and its **5.102** impact lessened in 'a matter of a month or two' and it also noted that 'two or three days would have elapsed before the jury retired to consider their verdict and that before they did so they would have had the advantage of a very fair summing up which the learned judge delivered to them'. They also had due regard to the fact that the jury deliberated for about fifteen hours before delivering a majority 10:2 verdict.

However, having taken all that into account, Beldam LJ concluded: **5.103**

> In the final analysis we are left with a definite impression that the impact which the statements in the television interviews may well have had on the fairness of the trial could not be overcome by any direction to the jury, and that the only way which justice could be done and be obviously seen to be done was by discharging the jury and ordering a retrial. In our judgement that is what the learned judge should have done.[64]

It will be seen from the *McCann* case that media reporting will be unlikely to result **5.104** in the discharge of the jury in those jurisdictions where the retrials take place or in a successful appeal, unless the media reporting itself has been intense and blatantly prejudicial. In many instances, it will be felt by a trial judge and appeal court alike that directions to the jury will ensure that any risk of prejudice is sufficiently minimized. If a process argument is being advanced, it is clear that the trial judge should have the opportunity to see or hear the offending material. Very often, the context of what is said and how it is said, and indeed by whom it is said, will prove to be important. Appeal Courts, though, will generally be slow to conclude that media reporting, even when a direction is given to the tribunal of fact, has caused a real risk of prejudice. It will need to be reporting approaching the level of that of *Taylor*[65] where the Court of Appeal quashed the appellant's convictions in a case in which the publicity during the trial, was, according to the Court of Appeal, 'unlimiting, extensive, sensational, inaccurate and misleading'.[66]

A theme which seems to emerge across jurisdiction is that criminal courts are keen **5.105** to restrict abuse or other arguments based on adverse publicity. Rather, they set store by a tribunal of fact's capacity not to be influenced by newspaper or broadcast

---

[64] [1991] 92 Cr App R 239, 253.
[65] (1994) 98 Cr App R 361.
[66] (1994) 98 Cr App R 361, 368.

media reports. A number of judgments have emphasized the ability of the jury or other tribunal of fact to put adverse publicity out of its collective mind.

5.106 In *R v Central Criminal Court, ex parte The Telegraph Plc*[67] then Lord Chief Justice, Lord Taylor, stated that a jury should be credited with the ability to be able to abide by a direction given to them to decide the case on the evidence, as in the terrorist case of *Meziane and Benmerzouga*.[68] The Court of Appeal highlighted that there must be an assumption that the trial process will normally take away the risk of prejudice and that it will therefore only be in an exceptional case that adverse publicity will mean that a fair trial could not take place.[69] Reliance on a combination of directions given by the tribunal of law and the ability of the tribunal of fact was further emphasized by the Lord Chief Justice, Lord Phillips, in *R v Abu Hamza*[70] *where he concluded that:*

> The fact that adverse publicity may have risked prejudicing a fair trial is no reason not to proceed with the trial if the judge concludes that, with his assistance, it will be possible to have a fair trial.

5.107 The assumption that the process of trial will usually ensure that the risk of protest is avoided and that only exceptionally will those safeguards be inadequate was implicit in the Privy Council's judgment in *Montgomery v HM Advocate and Another*.[71] There, the Privy Council stated that the test of whether the risk of prejudice from publicity occurring before the trial could be successfully met by a direction was whether that risk was so grave that no direction could reasonably be expected to remove it. One has to look, the Privy Council said, on what will be the effect of the publicity on the mind of a notional juror at the time of the trial, rather than, of course, at the time of publication. Moreover, in making that judgment, one has to weigh in the balance the safeguards which will be available to the trial judge as tribunal of law to minimize the risk and reduce the impact (by, for instance, the giving of directions). In addition, of course, the courts will bear in mind the time that has elapsed between the publicity itself and the trial. The reality often is that in a high-profile case, the initial reporting by the media at the time of arrest or first appearance is such that a real risk of prejudice would occur were the trial to be taking place at that time. The expectation in most cases is that lapse of time itself will remove the risk.

---

[67] (1994) 98 Cr App R 91.

[68] (Unreported, 25 June 2004).

[69] The authors are grateful to Barnaby Jameson and his co-authors of *A Practitioner's Guide to Terrorist Trials* (2007) for highlighting this unreported case.

[70] [2006] EWCA Crim 2918.

[71] [2203] 1 AC 641.

E. Hearings in Camera

Given the nature of material to be led in evidence or to be cross-examined upon **5.108** (as a result, for instance, of disclosure), it is sometimes necessary for terrorist trials, or parts of a trial, to be heard *in camera*. Such a decision by a court is, of course, an exceptional one as the presumption is that justice is open. However, the case of *Scott v Scott*[72] is authority for the court's inherent jurisdiction to order that matters be heard in private. That case concerned issues surrounding a committal for contempt in respect of communications of material following a divorce case. Viscount Haldane, Lord Chancellor, giving the leading speech in the House of Lords, stated:

> While the broad principle is that the courts of this country must, as between parties, administer justice in public, this principle is subject to apparent exceptions . . . but the exceptions are themselves the outcome of a more fundamental principle that the chief object of the courts of justice must be to secure that justice is done.

In addition to the common law position, there is a statutory provision which is **5.109** often used in terrorist cases, contained in the Official Secrets Act (1920) at section 8(4), which provides that:

> In addition, and without prejudice to any powers which a court may possess to order the exclusion of the public to any proceeding if, in the course of proceedings before a court against any person for an offence . . . application is made by the prosecution, on the grounds that the publication of any evidence to be given or of any statement to be made in the course of proceedings would be prejudicial to the national security, that all or any portion of the public should be excluded during any part of the hearing, the court may make an order to that effect.

F. The Accused's Right of Silence and Access to Legal Advice

The above two topics, although on one level distinct, are interrelated and will, **5.110** therefore, be examined side by side.

The position at common law is that every person has the right to exercise the **5.111** privilege against self-incrimination, and that an accused has the absolute right to say nothing in response to an accusation. However, in a number of jurisdictions, that right of silence has been effectively curtailed by statutory provisions which, in some instances, require an answer to be given to questions and which, in such instances, provide for a penalty in the event of non-compliance and which, in other cases, provide for silence to be maintained, but allow a court or other

---

[72] [1913] AC 417 is authority that the power of a court to order proceedings or part of proceedings to be held *in camera* exists at common law.

tribunal to draw inferences from that silence. In relation to the former approach, jurisdictions vary as to whether obligatory answers may be used in evidence against the accused.

5.112   In the UK, the right to silence has been curtailed by sections 34, 35, and 37 of the Criminal Justice and Public Order Act 1994. Those provisions provide as follows:

[Inferences from accused's silence]
34. Effect of accused's failure to mention facts when questioned or charged
(1)   Where, in any proceedings against a person for an offence, evidence is given that the accused—
   (a)   at any time before he was charged with the offence, on being questioned under caution by a constable trying to discover whether or by whom the offence had been committed, failed to mention any fact relied on in his defence in those proceedings; or
   (b)   on being charged with the offence or officially informed that he might be prose-cuted for it, failed to mention any such fact,

being a fact which in the circumstances existing at the time the accused could reasonably have been expected to mention when so questioned, charged or informed, as the case may be, sub-section (2) below applies.
(2)   Where this subsection applies—
   (a)   a magistrates' court, in deciding whether to grant an application for dismissal made by the accused under section 6 of the [1980 c. 43.] Magistrates' Courts Act 1980 (application for dismissal of charge in course of proceedings with a view to transfer for trial);
   (b)   a judge, in deciding whether to grant an application made by the accused under—
      (i)   section 6 of the [1987 c. 38.] Criminal Justice Act 1987 (application for dis-missal of charge of serious fraud in respect of which notice of transfer has been given under section 4 of that Act); or
      (ii)   paragraph 5 of Schedule 6 to the [1991 c. 53.] Criminal Justice Act 1991 (application for dismissal of charge of violent or sexual offence involving child in respect of which notice of transfer has been given under section 53 of that Act);
   (c)   the court, in determining whether there is a case to answer;
   and
   (d)   the court or jury, in determining whether the accused is guilty of the offence charged, may draw such inferences from the failure as appear proper.
(3)   Subject to any directions by the court, evidence tending to establish the failure may be given before or after evidence tending to establish the fact which the accused is alleged to have failed to mention.
(4)   This section applies in relation to questioning by persons (other than constables) charged with the duty of investigating offences or charging offenders as it applies in relation to ques-tioning by constables; and in subsection (1) above 'officially informed' means informed by a constable or any such person.
(5)   This section does not—
   (a)   prejudice the admissibility in evidence of the silence or other reaction of the accused in the face of anything said in his presence relating to the conduct in respect of which he is charged, in so far as evidence thereof would be admissible apart from this section; or

(b)   preclude the drawing of any inference from any such silence or other reaction of the accused which could properly be drawn apart from this section.

(6)   This section does not apply in relation to a failure to mention a fact if the failure occurred before the commencement of this section.

(7)   In relation to any time before the commencement of section 44 of this Act, this section shall have effect as if the reference in subsection (2)(a) to the grant of an application for dismissal was a reference to the committal of the accused for trial.

35. *Effect of accused's silence at trial*

(1)   At the trial of any person who has attained the age of fourteen years for an offence, subsections (2) and (3) below apply unless—

(a)   the accused's guilt is not in issue; or

(b)   it appears to the court that the physical or mental condition of the accused makes it undesirable for him to give evidence;

but subsection (2) below does not apply if, at the conclusion of the evidence for the prosecution, his legal representative informs the court that the accused will give evidence or, where he is unrepresented, the court ascertains from him that he will give evidence.

(2)   Where this subsection applies, the court shall, at the conclusion of the evidence for the prosecution, satisfy itself (in the case of proceedings on indictment, in the presence of the jury) that the accused is aware that the stage has been reached at which evidence can be given for the defence and that he can, if he wishes, give evidence and that, if he chooses not to give evidence, or having been sworn, without good cause refuses to answer any question, it will be permissible for the court or jury to draw such inferences as appear proper from his failure to give evidence or his refusal, without good cause, to answer any question.

(3)   Where this subsection applies, the court or jury, in determining whether the accused is guilty of the offence charged, may draw such inferences as appear proper from the failure of the accused to give evidence or his refusal, without good cause, to answer any question.

(4)   This section does not render the accused compellable to give evidence on his own behalf, and he shall accordingly not be guilty of contempt of court by reason of a failure to do so.

(5)   For the purposes of this section a person who, having been sworn, refuses to answer any question shall be taken to do so without good cause unless—

(a)   he is entitled to refuse to answer the question by virtue of any enactment, whenever passed or made, or on the ground of privilege; or

(b)   the court in the exercise of its general discretion excuses him from answering it.

(6)   Where the age of any person is material for the purposes of subsection (1) above, his age shall for those purposes be taken to be that which appears to the court to be his age.

(7)   This section applies—

(a)   in relation to proceedings on indictment for an offence, only if the person charged with the offence is arraigned on or after the commencement of this section;

(b)   in relation to proceedings in a magistrates' court, only if the time when the court begins to receive evidence in the proceedings falls after the commencement of this section.

37. *Effect of accused's failure or refusal to account for presence at a particular place*

(1)   Where—

(a)   a person arrested by a constable was found by him at a place at or about the time the offence for which he was arrested is alleged to have been committed; and

(b) that or another constable investigating the offence reasonably believes that the presence of the person at that place and at that time may be attributable to his participation in the commission of the offence; and

(c) the constable informs the person that he so believes, and requests him to account for that presence; and

(d) the person fails or refuses to do so, then if, in any proceedings against the person for the offence, evidence of those matters is given, subsection (2) below applies.

(2) Where this subsection applies—

(a) a magistrates' court, in deciding whether to grant an application for dismissal made by the accused under section 6 of the [1980 c. 43.] Magistrates' Courts Act 1980 (application for dismissal of charge in course of proceedings with a view to transfer for trial);

(b) a judge, in deciding whether to grant an application made by the accused under—

(i) section 6 of the [1987 c. 38.] Criminal Justice Act 1987 (application for dismissal of charge of serious fraud in respect of which notice of transfer has been given under section 4 of that Act); or

(ii) paragraph 5 of Schedule 6 to the [1991 c. 53.] Criminal Justice Act 1991 (application for dismissal of charge of violent or sexual offence involving child in respect of which notice of transfer has been given under section 53 of that Act);

(c) the court, in determining whether there is a case to answer; and

(d) the court or jury, in determining whether the accused is guilty of the offence charged, may draw such inferences from the failure or refusal as appear proper.

(3) Subsections (1) and (2) do not apply unless the accused was told in ordinary language by the constable when making the request mentioned in subsection (1)(c) above what the effect of this section would be if he failed or refused to comply with the request.

(4) This section applies in relation to officers of customs and excise as it applies in relation to constables.

(5) This section does not preclude the drawing of any inference from a failure or refusal of the accused to account for his presence at a place which could properly be drawn apart from this section.

(6) This section does not apply in relation to a failure or refusal which occurred before the commencement of this section.

(7) In relation to any time before the commencement of section 44 of this Act, this section shall have effect as if the reference in subsection (2)(a) to the grant of an application for dismissal was a reference to the committal of the accused for trial.

5.113 The introduction of the 1994 Act followed similar provisions being introduced in Northern Ireland by virtue of the Criminal Evidence (Northern Ireland) Order 1988 (at articles 3, 4, and 6). The Northern Ireland legislation arose directly from concerns on the part of the authorities that, in terrorist cases, the right of silence in interview was being frequently exercised and that investigations were being frustrated and a low proportion of convictions in terrorist cases resulted. However, the Northern Ireland experience is typical, rather than unique. Thus, in jurisdictions such as England and Wales, any terrorist trial is likely to feature the issue of whether, and if so what, adverse inferences should be drawn from silence.

Any jurisdiction which is party to a human rights instrument will also have to take **5.114** into account the obligations imposed under that instrument and jurisdictions, in general, and will also have to have regard to the international instrument and case law corpus which makes up international human rights law. The UK, as a result of the Human Rights Act 1998, has incorporated the ECHR into domestic law. Strasbourg jurisprudence has addressed adverse inferences from silence on a number of occasions. Some of the case law is conflicting, but general principles that have emerged are that the Strasbourg Court will want to see that the adverse inference is discretionary rather than mandatory, that the suspect or accused has been given clear and adequate warnings at each stage in the proceedings, and that the burden of proof has not in any sense been reversed so that the prosecution still has an obligation to establish a prima facie case before any inferences can be drawn.[73] The other overriding principle emerging from Strasbourg is that a conviction should not be based solely or mainly on the fact of silence.

The European Court of Human Rights has also emphasized that there may be **5.115** compelling reasons in a particular case why an innocent person has not been willing to speak. It may be that the person is not prepared to say anything until he or she has spoken with a lawyer and, indeed, that even having consulted with a lawyer, the exercise of the right to silence is based on advice given in good faith by that lawyer.[74] In any event, what can be said is that what was once regarded as an absolute right is now a right subject to qualification. At the same time though, the adverse inferences which are actually drawn are liable to be considered very carefully at any appeal and, in particular, before a human rights court.

Turning to the issue of access to legal advice, it will be seen from the principal **5.116** case law on the subject that most arguments are centred on the denial of access to legal advice at interview. Thus, the crossover between the twin issues of adverse inferences and denial of access to a lawyer.

As a result of the Terrorism Act 2000, there are special provisions for terrorist suspects in England and Wales with regards to their access to legal advice. Under schedule 8 part I, para 8(4) of the 2000 Act, a suspect's access to legal advice may be delayed in the following circumstances:
  (a) interference with or harm to evidence of a serious arrestable offence,
  (b) interference with or physical injury to any person,
  (c) the alerting of persons who are suspected of having committed a serious arrestable offence but who have not been arrested for it,
  (d) the hindering of the recovery of property obtained as a result of a serious arrestable offence or in respect of which a forfeiture order could be made under section 23,

---

[73] Relevant cases from the European Court of Human Rights include *Klass v Germany* (1978) 2 EHRR 214; *Saunders v UK* (1996) 23 EHRR 313; *Condron v UK* (2001) 31 EHRR 1.
[74] See *Averill v UK* (2001) 31 EHRR 839.

    (e)   interference with the gathering of information about the commission, preparation or instigation of acts of terrorism,

    (f)   the alerting of a person and thereby making it more difficult to prevent an act of terrorism, and

    (g)   the alerting of a person and thereby making it more difficult to secure a person's apprehension, prosecution, or conviction in connection with the commission, preparation, or instigation of an act of terrorism.

5.117   It has to be said that, bearing in mind the Strasbourg case law, the provisions in the 2000 Act are likely to be regarded as Convention-compliant so long as the decision-maker in the particular case has turned his mind to the right issues and has exercised his discretion reasonably.

5.118   The leading case on access to legal advice, which is a case arising from a counter-terrorism investigation, is that of *Murray v UK*.[75] That case, necessarily, also raises the issue of adverse inferences from the exercise of the right of silence.

5.119   Murray was found guilty in May 1991 of aiding and abetting unlawful imprisonment and was sentenced to eight years in prison. He had been arrested in January 1990 under terrorism prevention legislation in Northern Ireland and, following arrest, he was given the words of the caution under the Criminal Evidence (Northern Ireland) Order 1988. The effect of that caution was that he was informed that adverse inferences could be drawn at his trial if he elected to remain silent and did not answer questions put to him by the police. In addition, he was denied legal advice for forty-eight hours.

5.120   The trial was not in front of a jury, but was in front of a single judge 'Diplock Court'. When finding Murray guilty, the trial judge informed him that he had drawn adverse inferences from his failure to answer police questions, and because he had not given evidence at his trial. Having exhausted the appeal process in Northern Ireland, Murray brought his case to Strasbourg, contending the denial of legal advice of forty-eight hours and the adverse inferences drawn against him meant that he had not received a fair trial under Article 6. In a subsidiary argument, he also submitted that he had been discriminated against contrary to Article 14, in that he had been treated differently in Northern Ireland than he would have been if he had been an English person in England.

5.121   Murray was interviewed a total of twelve times over two days. During the first ten interviews, at a time when he had not had access to a solicitor, he made no comment in interview. After the tenth, but before the eleventh interview, he was able to consult with a solicitor. In the eleventh and twelfth interviews, he made no comment, but informed those interviewing him that he had been advised by his

---

[75] (1996) EHRR 29.

solicitor not to answer any of their questions. His solicitor, meanwhile, had not been permitted to be present at any interviews.

His trial took place in May 1991 and was heard by the Lord Chief Justice of **5.122** Northern Ireland. Murray faced three charges: conspiracy to murder, unlawful imprisonment, and belonging to a proscribed organization. At the close of the prosecution case, the trial judge, in accordance with Article 4 of the Criminal Evidence (Northern Ireland) Order 1988, warned Murray and his seven co-defendants that:

> I'm also required by law to tell you that if you refuse to come into the witness box to be sworn or if, after having been sworn, you refuse, without good reason, to answer any question, the court, in deciding whether you are guilty or not guilty, may take into account against you to the extent that it considers proper your refusal to give evidence or to answer any questions.

On advice, Murray did not give evidence. Nor were any witnesses called on his **5.123** behalf. However, there was evidence from a co-accused that Murray's presence in the house where the alleged false imprisonment was meant to have taken place was innocent and that he had only just arrived there before the police.

He was found guilty of aiding and abetting the unlawful imprisonment, but **5.124** acquitted of the remaining two charges.

The case against Murray had been put by the prosecution on the basis that he **5.125** knew before he arrived at that particular house that the alleged victim was being held there. In that knowledge, moreover, he assisted in falsely imprisoning the victim by directing him from the bedroom where he had been held and by giving him the directions, on the arrival of police, to go downstairs and pretend to be watching television. In respect of the unlawful imprisonment, that was the basis of Murray being said to be an aider and abettor. When the victim had been asked to take off his hood, Murray was the one captor seen by the victim and subsequently identified by him.

On appeal to the Court of Appeal of Northern Ireland, the court held that **5.126** there was a formidable case against Murray and that the evidence against him, in particular the evidence and identification given by the victim, called for an answer. Murray's silence meant that no answer was forthcoming either to the police during interview or during the trial. In those circumstances, the Court of Appeal of Northern Ireland said, 'It was inevitable that the judge would draw "very strong inferences" against him'. Murray's appeal was therefore dismissed.

In its judgment, the European Court of Human Rights addressed, inter alia, the **5.127** right of silence and access to legal advice.

Turning first to the right of silence, a majority of the court concluded: **5.128**

> Although not specifically mentioned in Article 6 of the Convention, there can be no doubt that the right to remain silent under police questioning and the privilege

against self incrimination are generally recognised international standards which lie at the heart of the notion of a fair procedure under Article 6. By providing the accused with protection against improper compulsion by the authorities, these immunities contribute to avoiding miscarriages of justice and to securing the aim of Article 6 . . .[76]

What is at stake in the present case is whether these immunities are absolute in the sense that the exercise of an accused of the right of silence cannot under any circumstances be used against him in the trial, or, alternatively, that informing him in advance that, under certain conditions, his silence may be used, is always to be regarded as 'improper coercion'.

On the one hand, it is self-evident that it is incompatible with the immunities under consideration to base a conviction solely or mainly on the accused's silence or on a refusal to answer questions or to give evidence himself. On the other hand, the Court deems it equally obvious that these immunities cannot and should not prevent that the accused's silence, in situations that clearly call for an explanation from him, be taken into account in assessing the persuasiveness of the evidence accused by the prosecution.[77]

Wherever the line between these two extremes is to be drawn, it follows from this understanding of the right to silence that the question whether the right is absolute must be answered in the negative.

It cannot be said therefore an accused's decision to remain silent throughout the proceedings should necessarily have no implications when the trial court seeks to evaluate the evidence against him. In particular, as the Government has pointed out, established international standards in this area, while providing for the right to silence and the privilege against self incrimination, are silent on this point.

Whether the drawing of adverse inferences from an accused silence infringes Article 6 is a matter to be determined in the light of all the circumstances in the case, having particular regard to the situations where inferences may be drawn, the weight attached to them by the national courts in their assessment of the evidence, and the degree of compulsion inherent in the situation.

As regards the degree of compulsion in the present case, it is recalled the applicant was in fact able to remain silent. Notwithstanding the repeated warnings as to the possibility that inferences may be drawn from his silence, he did not make any statements to the police and did not give evidence during his trial. Moreover, under Article 4(5) of the Order he remained a non-compellable witness. Thus his insistence in maintaining a silence throughout the proceedings did not amount to a criminal offence or contempt of court. Further, as has been stressed in national court decisions, silence, in itself, cannot be regarded as an indication of guilt . . .

Admittedly a system which warns the accused, who is possibly without legal assistance (as in the applicants cases), that adverse inferences may be drawn from a refusal to provide an explanation to the police for his presence at the scene of a crime or to testify during his trial, when taken in conjunction with the weight of the evidence against him, involves a certain level of indirect compulsion. However,

---

[76] (1996) 22 EHRR 29, 60.
[77] Ibid.

since the applicant could not compelled to speak or to testify, as indicated above, this factor on its own cannot be decisive. The court must rather concentrate its attention on the role played by the inferences in the proceedings against the applicant and especially in his conviction.

In this context, it is recalled that these were proceedings without a jury, the tryer of fact being an experienced judge. Furthermore, the drawing of inferences under the Order is subject to an important series of safeguards designed to respect the right of the defence and to limit the extent to which reliance is placed on inferences.[78]

The court, in its judgment, then went on to highlight the safeguards, which **5.129** included the warnings which had to be given to the accused, the prosecutor needing to establish a prima facie case against him before inferences could be drawn, and the need for each of the elements of the offence to be proved beyond reasonable doubt.

The court then went on to say: **5.130**

The question in each particular case is whether the evidence adduced by the prosecu-tion is evidently strong to require an answer . . . it is only if the evidence against the accused calls for an explanation which the accused ought to be in possession to give but a failure to give an explanation may as a matter of commonsense allow the draw-ing of an inference that there is no explanation and the that the accused is guilty. Conversely if the case presented by the prosecution had so little evidential value that it called for no answer, a failing to provide one could not justify an inference of guilt. In some, it is only commonsense inferences which the judge considers proper, in the light of the evidence against the accused, that can be drawn under the order.[79]

The Court then went on to say that the trial judge in the present case had a discre- **5.131** tion whether an inference should be drawn, and that the evidence presented against Murray was considered by the Court of Appeal in Northern Ireland to be formidable. The court then went on to conclude:

In the Court's view, having regard to the weight of the evidence against the applic-ant . . . the drawing of inferences from his refusal, at arrest, during police questioning, and at trial, to provide an explanation for his presence in the house was a matter of common sense and cannot be regarded as unfair or unreasonable in the circum-stances. As pointed out by the Delegate of the Commission, the courts in a consider-able number of countries where evidence is freely assessed may have regard to all relevant circumstances, including the manner in which the accused has behaved or has conducted his defence, when evaluating the evidence in the case. It considers that, what distinguishes the drawing of inferences under the Order, is that, in addi-tion to the existence of the specific safeguards mentioned above, it constitutes, as described the Commission, 'a formalised system which aims at allowing common-sense implications to play an open role in the assessment of evidence'.

---

[78] (1996) 22 EHRR 29, 61.
[79] Ibid, 62.

Nor can it be said, against this background, that the drawing of reasonable inferences from the applicant's behaviour had the effect of shifting the burden of proof from the prosecution to the defence save so as to infringe the principle of the presumption of innocence.[80]

5.132 The court then went on to address the issue of access to a lawyer. Murray, in the submissions made on his behalf, maintained that it was unfair to drawn inferences from his silence at interview when he had not had the benefit of legal advice. He argued that the question of access to a lawyer was inextricably linked with that of the drawing of adverse inferences from pre-trial silence. He submitted that, once an accused has remained silent, a trap is set from which he cannot escape: if he chooses to give evidence or call witnesses he is, by reason of his prior silence, exposed to the risk of an inference sufficient to bring about a conviction being drawn; on the other hand, if he maintains his silence, then inferences may be drawn against him at trial following the judge's warning.[81]

5.133 Turning to the issue of access to a lawyer, the court stated that the concept of fairness reflected in Article 6 requires that an accused has the benefit of a lawyer from the initial stages of police interrogation. Thus, to deny access to a lawyer for the first forty-eight hours of police questioning, as occurred in Murray's situation, in circumstances where the rights of the defence may well be retrievably prejudiced from that early stage, is incompatible with Article 6 whatever the justification for such a denial. The court reiterated that Article 6 applies even at the stage of preliminary investigation by the police into an offence.[82] In conclusion, on that point, the court stated: 'There has therefore been a breach of Article 6(1) in conjunction with paragraph 3(c) of the Convention as regards the applicant's denial of access to a lawyer during the first forty-eight hours of his police detention'.

5.134 However, the court, in its judgment, made clear, as a matter of principle, there may be circumstances in which the right to legal advice could be restricted. It stated:

> National laws may attach consequences to the attitude of an accused at the initial stages of police interrogation which are decisive for the prospects of the defence in any subsequent criminal proceedings. In such circumstances Article 6 will normally require that the accused be allowed to benefit from the assistance of a lawyer already at the initial stages of police interrogation. However, this right, which is not explicitly set out in the Convention, may be subject to restrictions for good cause. The question, in each case, is whether the restriction, in the light of the entirety of the proceedings, has deprived the accused of a fair hearing . . . although it is an important element to be taken into account, even a lawfully exercised power

---

[80] Ibid, 63.
[81] (1996) EHRR 29, para 3 of the Court's judgment.
[82] See *Imbrioscia v Switzerland* (1993) judgment of 24 November 2003.

of restriction is capable of depriving an accused, in certain circumstances, of a fair procedure.[83]

Three later cases from Northern Ireland which came before the European Court of Human Rights should also be noted.

In *Magee v UK*,[84] the applicant had been arrested under section 12 of the Prevention **5.135** of Terrorism Act 1984 in relation to an attempted bomb attack on the military. He was denied access to a lawyer for the first forty-eight hours of his detention, and during the first twenty-four of those hours he was interviewed five times and made no comment. During the course of the second twenty-four hours he was interviewed three more times. In the first and second interviews of the second twenty-four hours (in other words, his sixth and seventh interviews), he made admissions and signed a detailed series of written admissions. He was then interviewed twice on a third day, by this time having been given access to a lawyer in between those two interviews (ie, his ninth and tenth interviews). The confession evidence formed the basis of the case against him. The applicant did not give evidence and was convicted by Northern Ireland's Special Court (in other words, a Diplock Court). In its judgment, the European Court of Human Rights, adopting similar language to that used in the *Murray* case, found that there are circumstances where access to legal advice may be delayed for a good cause, but that, in the case of Magee, he had been held under conditions which were 'psychologically coercive'. The nature of his confinement had been created to induce a confession. It was therefore found there had been a violation of Article 6(1) in respect of Article 6(3)(c).

The second of these latter cases is that of *Averill v UK*.[85] There, the applicant, hav- **5.136** ing been arrested under the Prevention of Terrorism provisions, was denied access to a lawyer for twenty-four hours. Thereafter, he was able to consult freely with his lawyer. He maintained his right of silence throughout and, at trial, he gave evidence and called alibi witnesses on his behalf. He was convicted; the court, again a Diplock Court, having drawn an adverse inference from his silence in the interviews which took place during the first twenty-four hours of his detention (when he did not have access to a lawyer). The European Court of Human Rights found that there had been a violation of Article 6 on the basis that the refusal during those twenty-four hours of police questioning 'must still be considered incompatible with the rights guaranteed to him under Article 6'.

---

[83] (1996) 22 EHRR 29, 66f.
[84] (2001) 31 EHRR 35.
[85] (2001) 31 EHRR 36.

5.137 In *Brennan v UK*,[86] having been arrested on suspicion of terrorism offences in Northern Ireland, the applicant Brennan was denied access to a lawyer for the initial twenty-four hours of his detention. However, although the prohibition on consulting with the lawyer was removed after twenty-four hours, the applicant did not consult with one until forty-eight hours after arrest. In his first twenty-four hours of detention, the applicant made no comment. When the first consultation with a lawyer took place, a police officer was also deployed in the consultation room. The applicant was told the consultation was purely for the purpose of legal advice and, therefore, no names could be discussed, nor information concerning the nature of the case conveyed. The Special Criminal Court (a Diplock Court) convicted the applicant; however, in convicting him, it did not draw any adverse inferences from his silence during the first twenty-four hours he was detained.

5.138 Although no breach of the applicant's Article 6 was found in respect of the first twenty-four hours of his detention, the court did find there had been a violation (Article 6(1) in connection with Article 6(3)(c)) in relation to the police officer's presence in the consultation room within the hearing of the applicant and his lawyer. It held that the right of access to a lawyer carries with it the right to communicate freely and privately with that lawyer. Indeed, in reaching its conclusion, the European Court of Human Rights noted the express provision in the American Convention on Human Rights[87] which expressly provides for free communication in such circumstances. The court also took note that the Standard Minimum Rules for the Treatment of Prisoners, issued by the Council of Europe, at Article 93, provides that, although interviews between a detainee and a lawyer may be within sight of a police or prison officer, it may not be within the officer's hearing.

5.139 For England and Wales, the Attorney General issued guidance to prosecutors following the *Murray v UK* case. The effect of that guidance was that the prosecution should not seek to rely on inferences from silence before access to legal advice has been granted. However, subsequently the matter has been addressed expressly by statute. Section 58 of the Youth Justice and Criminal Evidence Act 1999 provides that an adverse inference may not be drawn where there has been a delay in, or denial of, access to legal advice.

5.140 In an attempt to enable terrorist investigations to progress in circumstances where, for instance, efforts were being made to locate a suspected bomber or to locate explosives or munitions, a new Code, H, was introduced under PACE. It has effect from 25 July 2006 and gives the power to police to conduct a so-called 'safety interview' for the purpose of public protection. The effect of Code H is that

---

[86] (2002) 34 EHRR 18.
[87] At Article 8(2)(d). See further, Chapter 8.

a suspect arrested in relation to terrorist offences may be interviewed before access to a lawyer is granted. Prior to 25 July 2006, the procedures for the detention and interview of terror suspects, as with all suspects for criminal offences, was governed by Code C of PACE. Code H is reproduced in full at Appendix 22. It applies to suspects detained under section 41 and Schedule 8 of the Terrorism Act 2000. It will be noted, upon appraisal of Code H, that it contains a so-called 'old style caution' which is to be given before a safety interview. No adverse inference may be drawn from silence at a safety interview in the absence of access to a lawyer.[88]

As to the admissibility of lies, however, in a safety interview: to the extent that a lie **5.141** is, in one sense, a failure to mention in interview something relied on at trial, an adverse inference may not be drawn from it. However, as a matter of common law, anything said by a suspect, including any lies, is capable of forming part of the case against him, subject to fairness and, at trial, subject to a direction by a judge in accordance with the case of *R v Lucas*.[89] Ironically, therefore, a suspect who lies during a safety interview may find that the lie tells against him, unlike the suspect who remains silent. Given that the purpose of such an interview is to protect the public, authorities in any jurisdiction adopting such an approach may wish to consider whether the suspect should be given an assurance or undertaking that anything said during the course of an interview will not be used in evidence against him.

---

[88] In other words, as in accordance with an interview for a non-terrorist suspect under Code C.
[89] See the case of *Ibrahim and Others* in (2007) per Fulford J, Woolwich CC. Again, the authors are grateful to B Jameson et al (n 70) for highlighting that first instance decision. R v Lucas may be found at (1981) 73 Cr App R 159.

6

GENERAL OVERVIEW OF INTERNATIONAL EFFORTS TO COMBAT THE FINANCING OF TERRORISM

A. **Introduction**	6.01	UN Security Council Resolution 1373 (2001)	6.33
B. **International Efforts to Combat the Financing of Terrorism**	6.07	Summary of the criminalization, freezing, and forfeiture obligations under the Financing	
International Convention for the Suppression of the Financing of Terrorism (1999) ('Financing Convention')	6.09	Convention (1999) and Security Council Resolutions 1267 (1999) and 1373 (2001)	6.42
The International Convention against Transnational Organized Crime (2000) ('Palermo Convention')	6.23	Legal and human rights issues relevant to the implementation of UN Security Council asset-freezing obligations	6.43
C. **Key Extracts of Relevant UN Security Council Resolutions**	6.24	D. **The Financial Action Task Force**	6.51
UN Security Council Resolution 1267 (1999)	6.24	FATF Nine Special Recommendations on terrorist financing	6.55
UN Security Council Resolution 1390 (2002)	6.29	E. **Other International Initiatives**	6.56
UN Security Council Resolution 1452 (2002)	6.30	The International Monetary Fund (IMF)	6.56
UN Security Council Resolution 1730 (2006)	6.31	The Egmont Group of Financial Intelligence Units	6.58
UN Security Council Resolution 1735 (2006)	6.32	Wolfsberg Group of Banks	6.62

A. Introduction

Preventing terrorists and terrorist organizations from funding their activities **6.01** and planned attacks is an essential component of any successful global counterterrorism campaign. Targeting the finances of terrorists and terrorist organizations can provide vital intelligence information concerning their activities and insight on how to formulate policies that deny terrorists access to funds and restrict their ability to function. By using methods of financial investigation, it has

275

become possible to identify and profile suspects, link addresses, storage facilities, and methods of communication. Furthermore financial investigations can reveal travel and spending patterns, valuable information on recruitment methods and operational strategies, as well as areas of vulnerability in terrorist organizations.

6.02   It is estimated that the 9/11 attacks on the United States cost no more than $500,000 to plan and execute.[1] Yet despite the relatively small amount required to mount the attack (especially when one considers the impact of the attack), it still involved the transfer of significant, and easily traceable, amounts of money that could conceivably have been linked to the hijackers prior to the attack.

6.03   Before the 9/11 attacks, tracking terrorist financing was not viewed as a priority for the international community. It was also not high on the list of priorities of national authorities, including law enforcement agencies. Combating money laundering was seen as more important and most policymakers and criminal justice officials believed that anti-money laundering capacity and policies were sufficient to deal with the threat of terrorist financing as well. This was a mistaken, and consequently a very dangerous, assumption.

6.04   While money laundering is conceptually linked to contemporary terrorist financing, there are several key differences between the two. Money laundering is the process by which money derived from criminal origins is processed through multiple, layered transactions in the financial system to conceal its illicit origins. Financing of terrorism on the other hand, is the financial support, in any form, of terrorism or of those who encourage, plan, or engage in such support.

6.05   Most States subscribe to the definition of money laundering adopted by the United Nations Convention Against Illicit Traffic in Narcotic Drugs and Psychotropic Substances (1988) (Vienna Convention)[2] and the United Nations Convention Against Transnational Organized Crime (2000) (Palermo Convention).[3] The key elements of these definitions are:

- The conversion or transfer of property, knowing that such property is derived from any [drug trafficking] offence or offences or from an act of participation in such offence or offences, for the purpose of concealing or disguising the illicit origin of the property or of assisting any person who is involved in the

---

[1]   M Pieth, 'Criminalizing the Financing of Terrorism' (2006) 4 JICJ1076. The first report of the Analytical Support and Sanctions Monitoring Team appointed under UN Security Council Resolution 1526 (2004) details that the bombings of the US embassies in Kenya and Tanzania in 1998 cost less than $50,000; the 2000 attack on the *USS Cole* cost less than $10,000; the Bali bombings in 2002 cost less than $50,000; the Madrid bombings in 2004 cost less than $10,000; and the London bombings in 2005 cost about $2,000. See S/2004/670 (New York, United Nations, August 2004) 12.

[2]   Available at <http://www.incb.org/pdf/e/conv/1988_convention_en.pdf>.

[3]   Available at <http://www.uncjin.org/Documents/Conventions/dcatoc/final_documents_2/convention_eng.pdf>.

commission of such an offence or offences to evade the legal consequences of his/her actions;

- The concealment or disguise of the true nature, source, location, disposition, movement, rights with respect to, or ownership of property, knowing that such property is derived from an offence or offences or from an act of participation in such an offence or offences, and;

The acquisition, possession or use of property, knowing at the time of receipt that such property was derived from an offence or offences or from an act of participation in such offence . . . or offences.

Money laundering and terrorist financing often have similar core operational fea- **6.06**
tures, mostly having to do with the way in which funds are concealed. Money launderers send illicit funds through legal channels in order to conceal their criminal origins, while those who finance terrorism transfer funds that may *be legal or illicit in origin* in such a way as to conceal the source of the funds and their ultimate use—to support terrorism. Such legitimate sources may include donations or gifts of cash or other assets to organizations, such as foundations or charities. This key difference requires special laws to deal with terrorist financing. However, to the extent that funds for financing terrorism are derived from illegal sources, such funds may already be covered by a State's anti-money laundering framework, depending upon the scope of predicate offences for money laundering. States are therefore under an obligation under UNSCR 1373 and the Financing Convention to criminalize the financing of terrorism, terrorist acts, and terrorist organizations, and designate such offences as money laundering predicate offences.

B. International Efforts to Combat the Financing of Terrorism

International efforts to combat transnational financial crime and terrorist financ- **6.07**
ing have evolved considerably in recent years. During the 1990s, most of these efforts were spearheaded by a small number of intergovernmental organizations, most notably the Financial Action Task Force (FATF) and associated regional bodies (also known as FATF-style regional bodies) and the International Monetary Fund (IMF). However, efforts to counter the financing of terrorism were drastically expanded as a result of the 9/11 attacks on the US as the international community's focus turned onto undermining terrorist organizations' ability to plan and perpetrate large-scale attacks like the ones seen in September 2001.

This chapter focuses on the most relevant legal and criminal justice develop- **6.08**
ments in the international counter-terrorism financing regime. These include the adoption of the International Convention for the Suppression of the Financing

of Terrorism[4] in 1999, the adoption of UN Security Council Resolution 1267 (1999) and 1373 (2001), the development of the FATF Special Recommendations of Terrorist Financing in October 2001 as well as subsequent Guidance Notes, and the related efforts of other intergovernmental organizations like the International Monetary Fund (IMF), European Union (EU), Organization for Security and Cooperation in Europe (OSCE), and Interpol.

International Convention for the Suppression of the Financing of Terrorism (1999) ('Financing Convention')[5]

6.09   As described in Chapter 2, the international community, acting through the UN, has since 1963 developed sixteen counter-terrorism conventions and protocols that deal with specific acts of terrorism. These instruments, supported by a number of UN Security Council resolutions dealing with terrorism, provide what is known as the international legal regime against terrorism. The Financing Convention was adopted by the General Assembly in 1999 and came into force in 2002. As of July 2008, it had been ratified by 112 Member States.[6]

6.10   The Financing Convention is unique in a number of ways. It is the first counter-terrorism instrument that takes a proactive and preventive approach by criminalizing the financing of terrorism as a stand-alone preparatory offence and requiring States to freeze and forfeit funds used for or derived from the commission of terrorist acts. Unlike the rest of the UN counter-terrorism instruments, the Financing Convention does not deal just with specific acts of terrorism, but is intended to suppress the financing of terrorism from a broader, more preventive, point of view.

Criminalization provisions

6.11   Article 2(1) envisages two categories of offences. The first is committed when a person who by any means, directly or indirectly, unlawfully and wilfully, provides or collects funds[7] with the intention that they should be used or in the knowledge

---

[4]   UN Doc A/Res/54/109, 9 December 1999.

[5]   Adopted by the General Assembly of the United Nations on 9 December 1999. Entry into force in accordance with Article 26. UN Doc A/RES/54/109, Annex. Depositary: Secretary-General of the United Nations.

[6]   Available at <http://www.unodc.org/tldb> (free access, user registration required). Accessed on 31 July 2008.

[7]   Art 1(1) of the Convention for the Suppression of the Financing of Terrorism (1999) gives a very general definition of 'funds': '1. "Funds" means assets of every kind, whether tangible or intangible, movable or immovable, however acquired, and legal documents or instruments in any form, including electronic or digital, evidencing title to, or interest in, such assets, including, but not limited to, bank credits, travellers cheques, bank cheques, money orders, shares, securities, bonds, drafts, letters of credit'.

that they are to be used, in full or in part, in order to carry out the financing of acts defined in the previous counter-terrorism instruments (nine at the time of passing) listed in the annex to the Convention. The criminalization of the funding of these acts does not necessarily require the ratification of the relevant Conventions and Protocols, Contracting States may specifically exclude specified instruments from the application of the Convention.[8]

The second part of the criminalization provision goes beyond focusing on the tra-   **6.12** ditional definitions of terrorist crimes and introduces a so-called 'mini-definition' of terrorism that focuses on the protection of civilians. Article 2(1)(b) consists of the financing of '[a]ny other act intended to cause death or serious bodily injury to a civilian, or any person not taking an active part in the hostilities in a situation of armed conflict, when the purpose of such act, by its nature or context, is to intimidate a population, or to compel a government or an international organization to do or abstain from doing any act'.

These criminalization provisions represent an important advance in the use of   **6.13** anti-terrorism measures to prevent rather than merely to react to terrorist violence. Instead of only prohibiting a particular form of violence associated with terrorism, the Financing Convention criminalizes the non-violent logistical preparation and support that make terrorist groups and terrorist operations possible. Moreover, Article 2(3) eliminates any ambiguity by expressly providing that the prohibited provision or collection of funds need not result in a violent act specified in paragraph 1 of the Convention to be punishable. This is an important element of the offence; one often misunderstood by policymakers and criminal justice officials.

Meeting all of the international standards applicable to the financing of terrorism   **6.14** can be fully achieved only by legislation establishing the Convention offence, and not by reliance upon complicity, conspiracy, money laundering, or other offences not specific to the financing of terrorism. Article 2(4) and Article 4 of the Convention require attempts to be criminalized, even without achieving the envisaged goal of the attempt.

The Convention's criminalization provision contains an interesting addition to   **6.15** the traditional subjective component of *mens rea* which is normally limited to a specific intention to commit the offence. Article 1 of the Convention adds 'or in the knowledge that they are to be used . . .'. Knowledge in the context of this Convention should be interpreted as a form of direct intent.

Article 2(5) deals with the three forms of co-perpetration and participation in the   **6.16** crime and obliges State Parties to criminalize these forms of participation under

---

[8] See Article 2(2).

their national laws, including: actual accomplices, organizers and instigators, and those contributing to the commission through a group.

Liability of legal persons

6.17 The Convention also obliges States to hold legal persons liable under specific circumstances. Article 5 obliges each State Party to take the necessary measures to enable a legal entity located in its territory or organized under its laws to be held liable when a person responsible for the management or control of that legal entity has, in that capacity, committed an offence as set forth in article 2. Such liability may be criminal, civil, or administrative, although recent practice leans more towards establishing criminal corporate liability whenever possible.[9]

Jurisdictional provisions

6.18 The jurisdiction provisions of the Financing Convention are in line with the expanded jurisdictional provisions found in most of the more recent counter-terrorism instruments. It provides for jurisdiction to be taken on the basis of territoriality, extended territoriality, and nationality (both active and passive). Article 7(2) goes further and includes additional, non-mandatory jurisdictional principles (see relevant extracts below).

International cooperation provisions

6.19 The Convention's international cooperation provisions are mostly standard. However, like the 1997 Bombings Convention, the Financing Convention also removes the political and fiscal offence exceptions as a bar to international cooperation in criminal matters. To counterbalance the removal of such exceptions, Article 15 provides for refusal of a request where it is made for the 'purpose of prosecuting or punishing a person on account of that person's race, religion, nationality, ethnic origin or political opinion or that compliance with the request would cause prejudice to that person's position for any of these reasons'.

Freezing, seizure, and forfeiture provisions

6.20 As noted above, the Financing Convention contains important provisions of freezing, seizure, and confiscation of terrorist funds. These must, however, be interpreted and applied within the context of the wider international counter-terrorism financing regime, especially UNSCRs 1267 (1999) and 1373 (2001). The freezing, seizing, and confiscation provisions of the Financing Convention adopt the more traditional, and less controversial, approach to the confiscation of criminal assets, based on the instrumentality and proceeds of crime. The two

---

[9] FATF. *The 40 Recommendations*, 20 June 2003, R 2(b).

freezing regimes under UNSCRs 1267 and 1373, discussed below, impose wider-reaching freezing obligations based on membership of a particular group or the reasonable belief that a person or group has committed or attempted to commit a terrorist act.

Article 8(1) obliges each State Party to take appropriate measures for the identifi- **6.21** cation, detection, and freezing or seizure of any funds *used or allocated* for the purpose of committing the offences set forth in article 2 as well as *the proceeds derived from such offences*, for purposes of possible forfeiture.

Interestingly, Article 8(4) requires each State Party to consider establishing **6.22** mechanisms whereby the funds derived from the forfeitures referred to in this article are utilized to compensate the victims (or their families) of offences referred to in the Convention.

Extracts of key provisions

Article 2

1. Any person commits an offence within the meaning of this Convention if that person by any means, directly or indirectly, unlawfully and wilfully, provides or collects funds[10] with the intention that they should be used or in the knowledge that they are to be used, in full or in part, in order to carry out:

(a) An act which constitutes an offence within the scope of and as defined in one of the treaties listed in the annex;[11] or

(b) Any other act intended to cause death or serious bodily injury to a civilian, or to any other person not taking an active part in the hostilities in a situation of armed conflict, when the purpose of such act, by its nature or context, is to intimidate a population, or to compel a Government or an international organization to do or to abstain from doing any act.

2. (a) On depositing its instrument of ratification, acceptance, approval or accession, a State Party which is not a party to a treaty listed in the annex may declare that, in the application of this Convention to the State Party, the treaty shall be deemed not to be included in the annex referred to in paragraph 1, subparagraph (a). The declaration shall cease to have effect as soon as the treaty enters into force for the State Party, which shall notify the depositary of this fact;

(b) When a State Party ceases to be a party to a treaty listed in the annex, it may make a declaration as provided for in this article, with respect to that treaty.

---

[10] Article 1 of the Convention defines 'Funds' as assets of every kind, whether tangible or intangible, movable or immovable, however acquired, and legal documents or instruments in any form, including electronic or digital, evidencing title to, or interest in, such assets, including, but not limited to, bank credits, travellers cheques, bank cheques, money orders, shares, securities, bonds, drafts, and letters of credit.

[11] The Annex to the Convention contained a list of all the Conventions and Protocols that preceded it.

3. For an act to constitute an offence set forth in paragraph 1, it shall not be necessary that the funds were actually used to carry out an offence referred to in paragraph 1, subparagraph (a) or (b).

4. Any person also commits an offence if that person attempts to commit an offence as set forth in paragraph 1 of this article.

5. Any person also commits an offence if that person:

(a) Participates as an accomplice in an offence as set forth in paragraph 1 or 4 of this article;

(b) Organizes or directs others to commit an offence as set forth in paragraph 1 or 4 of this article;

(c) Contributes to the commission of one or more offences as set forth in paragraph 1 or 4 of this article by a group of persons acting with a common purpose. Such contribution shall be intentional and shall either:

  (i) Be made with the aim of furthering the criminal activity or criminal purpose of the group, where such activity or purpose involves the commission of an offence as set forth in paragraph 1 of this article; or

  (ii) Be made in the knowledge of the intention of the group to commit an offence as set forth in paragraph 1 of this article.

Article 3

This Convention shall not apply where the offence is committed within a single State, the alleged offender is a national of that State and is present in the territory of that State and no other State has a basis under article 7, paragraph 1 or 2, to exercise jurisdiction, except that the provisions of articles 12 to 18 shall, as appropriate, apply in those cases.

Article 4

Each State Party shall adopt such measures as may be necessary:

(a) To establish as criminal offences under its domestic law the offences as set forth in article 2;

(b) To make those offences punishable by appropriate penalties which take into account the grave nature of the offences.

Article 5

1. Each State Party, in accordance with its domestic legal principles, shall take the necessary measures to enable a legal entity located in its territory or organized under its laws to be held liable when a person responsible for the management or control of that legal entity has, in that capacity, committed an offence as set forth in article 2. Such liability may be criminal, civil or administrative.

2. Such liability is incurred without prejudice to the criminal liability of individuals who have committed the offences.

3. Each State Party shall ensure, in particular, that legal entities liable in accordance with paragraph 1 above are subject to effective, proportionate and dissuasive criminal, civil or administrative sanctions. Such sanctions may include monetary sanctions.

Article 6

Each State Party shall adopt such measures as may be necessary, including, where appropriate, domestic legislation, to ensure that criminal acts within the scope of this Convention are under no circumstances justifiable by considerations of a political, philosophical, ideological, racial, ethnic, religious or other similar nature.

Article 7

1. Each State Party shall take such measures as may be necessary to establish its jurisdiction over the offences set forth in article 2 when:

(a) The offence is committed in the territory of that State;
(b) The offence is committed on board a vessel flying the flag of that State or an aircraft registered under the laws of that State at the time the offence is committed;
(c) The offence is committed by a national of that State.

2. A State Party may also establish its jurisdiction over any such offence when:

(a) The offence was directed towards or resulted in the carrying out of an offence referred to in article 2, paragraph 1, subparagraph (a) or (b), in the territory of or against a national of that State;
(b) The offence was directed towards or resulted in the carrying out of an offence referred to in article 2, paragraph 1, subparagraph (a) or (b), against a State or government facility of that State abroad, including diplomatic or consular premises of that State;
(c) The offence was directed towards or resulted in an offence referred to in article 2, paragraph 1, subparagraph (a) or (b), committed in an attempt to compel that State to do or abstain from doing any act;
(d) The offence is committed by a stateless person who has his or her habitual residence in the territory of that State;
(e) The offence is committed on board an aircraft which is operated by the Government of that State.

3. Upon ratifying, accepting, approving or acceding to this Convention, each State Party shall notify the Secretary-General of the United Nations of the jurisdiction it has established in accordance with paragraph 2. Should any change take place, the State Party concerned shall immediately notify the Secretary-General.

4. Each State Party shall likewise take such measures as may be necessary to establish its jurisdiction over the offences set forth in article 2 in cases where the alleged offender is present in its territory and it does not extradite that person to any of the States Parties that have established their jurisdiction in accordance with paragraphs 1 or 2.

5. When more than one State Party claims jurisdiction over the offences set forth in article 2, the relevant States Parties shall strive to coordinate their actions appropriately, in particular concerning the conditions for prosecution and the modalities for mutual legal assistance.

6. Without prejudice to the norms of general international law, this Convention does not exclude the exercise of any criminal jurisdiction established by a State Party in accordance with its domestic law.

Article 8

1. Each State Party shall take appropriate measures, in accordance with its domestic legal principles, for the identification, detection and freezing or seizure of any funds used or allocated for the purpose of committing the offences set forth in article 2 as well as the proceeds derived from such offences, for purposes of possible forfeiture.

2. Each State Party shall take appropriate measures, in accordance with its domestic legal principles, for the forfeiture of funds used or allocated for the purpose of committing the offences set forth in article 2 and the proceeds derived from such offences.

3. Each State Party concerned may give consideration to concluding agreements on the sharing with other States Parties, on a regular or case-by-case basis, of the funds derived from the forfeitures referred to in this article.

4. Each State Party shall consider establishing mechanisms whereby the funds derived from the forfeitures referred to in this article are utilized to compensate the victims of offences referred to in article 2, paragraph 1, subparagraph (a) or (b), or their families.

5. The provisions of this article shall be implemented without prejudice to the rights of third parties acting in good faith.

Article 9

1. Upon receiving information that a person who has committed or who is alleged to have committed an offence set forth in article 2 may be present in its territory, the State Party concerned shall take such measures as may be necessary under its domestic law to investigate the facts contained in the information.

2. Upon being satisfied that the circumstances so warrant, the State Party in whose territory the offender or alleged offender is present shall take the appropriate measures under its domestic law so as to ensure that person's presence for the purpose of prosecution or extradition.

3. Any person regarding whom the measures referred to in paragraph 2 are being taken shall be entitled:

(a) To communicate without delay with the nearest appropriate representative of the State of which that person is a national or which is otherwise entitled to protect that person's rights or, if that person is a stateless person, the State in the territory of which that person habitually resides;

(b) To be visited by a representative of that State;

(c) To be informed of that person's rights under subparagraphs (a) and (b).

4. The rights referred to in paragraph 3 shall be exercised in conformity with the laws and regulations of the State in the territory of which the offender or alleged offender is present, subject to the provision that the said laws and regulations must enable full effect to be given to the purposes for which the rights accorded under paragraph 3 are intended.

5. The provisions of paragraphs 3 and 4 shall be without prejudice to the right of any State Party having a claim to jurisdiction in accordance with article 7, paragraph 1, subparagraph (b), or paragraph 2, subparagraph (b), to invite the International Committee of the Red Cross to communicate with and visit the alleged offender.

6. When a State Party, pursuant to the present article, has taken a person into custody, it shall immediately notify, directly or through the Secretary-General of the United Nations, the States Parties which have established jurisdiction in accordance with article 7, paragraph 1 or 2, and, if it considers it advisable, any other interested States Parties, of the fact that such person is in custody and of the circumstances which warrant that person's detention. The State which makes the investigation contemplated in paragraph 1 shall promptly inform the said States Parties of its findings and shall indicate whether it intends to exercise jurisdiction.

Article 10

1. The State Party in the territory of which the alleged offender is present shall, in cases to which article 7 applies, if it does not extradite that person, be obliged, without exception whatsoever and whether or not the offence was committed in its territory, to submit the case without undue delay to its competent authorities for the purpose of prosecution, through proceedings in accordance with the laws of that State. Those authorities shall

take their decision in the same manner as in the case of any other offence of a grave nature under the law of that State.

2. Whenever a State Party is permitted under its domestic law to extradite or otherwise surrender one of its nationals only upon the condition that the person will be returned to that State to serve the sentence imposed as a result of the trial or proceeding for which the extradition or surrender of the person was sought, and this State and the State seeking the extradition of the person agree with this option and other terms they may deem appropriate, such a conditional extradition or surrender shall be sufficient to discharge the obligation set forth in paragraph 1.

Article 11

1. The offences set forth in article 2 shall be deemed to be included as extraditable offences in any extradition treaty existing between any of the States Parties before the entry into force of this Convention. States Parties undertake to include such offences as extraditable offences in every extradition treaty to be subsequently concluded between them.

2. When a State Party which makes extradition conditional on the existence of a treaty receives a request for extradition from another State Party with which it has no extradition treaty, the requested State Party may, at its option, consider this Convention as a legal basis for extradition in respect of the offences set forth in article 2. Extradition shall be subject to the other conditions provided by the law of the requested State.

3. States Parties which do not make extradition conditional on the existence of a treaty shall recognize the offences set forth in article 2 as extraditable offences between themselves, subject to the conditions provided by the law of the requested State.

4. If necessary, the offences set forth in article 2 shall be treated, for the purposes of extradition between States Parties, as if they had been committed not only in the place in which they occurred but also in the territory of the States that have established jurisdiction in accordance with article 7, paragraphs 1 and 2.

5. The provisions of all extradition treaties and arrangements between States Parties with regard to offences set forth in article 2 shall be deemed to be modified as between States Parties to the extent that they are incompatible with this Convention.

Article 12

1. States Parties shall afford one another the greatest measure of assistance in connection with criminal investigations or criminal or extradition proceedings in respect of the offences set forth in article 2, including assistance in obtaining evidence in their possession necessary for the proceedings.

2. States Parties may not refuse a request for mutual legal assistance on the ground of bank secrecy.

3. The requesting Party shall not transmit or use information or evidence furnished by the requested Party for investigations, prosecutions or proceedings other than those stated in the request without the prior consent of the requested Party.

4. Each State Party may give consideration to establishing mechanisms to share with other States Parties information or evidence needed to establish criminal, civil or administrative liability pursuant to article 5.

5. States Parties shall carry out their obligations under paragraphs 1 and 2 in conformity with any treaties or other arrangements on mutual legal assistance or information exchange that may exist between them. In the absence of such treaties or arrangements, States Parties shall afford one another assistance in accordance with their domestic law.

Article 13

None of the offences set forth in article 2 shall be regarded, for the purposes of extradition or mutual legal assistance, as a fiscal offence. Accordingly, States Parties may not refuse a request for extradition or for mutual legal assistance on the sole ground that it concerns a fiscal offence.

Article 14

None of the offences set forth in article 2 shall be regarded for the purposes of extradition or mutual legal assistance as a political offence or as an offence connected with a political offence or as an offence inspired by political motives. Accordingly, a request for extradition or for mutual legal assistance based on such an offence may not be refused on the sole ground that it concerns a political offence or an offence connected with a political offence or an offence inspired by political motives.

Article 15

Nothing in this Convention shall be interpreted as imposing an obligation to extradite or to afford mutual legal assistance, if the requested State Party has substantial grounds for believing that the request for extradition for offences set forth in article 2 or for mutual legal assistance with respect to such offences has been made for the purpose of prosecuting or punishing a person on account of that person's race, religion, nationality, ethnic origin or political opinion or that compliance with the request would cause prejudice to that person's position for any of these reasons.

Article 18

1. States Parties shall cooperate in the prevention of the offences set forth in article 2 by taking all practicable measures, inter alia, by adapting their domestic legislation, if necessary, to prevent and counter preparations in their respective territories for the commission of those offences within or outside their territories, including:

(a) Measures to prohibit in their territories illegal activities of persons and organizations that knowingly encourage, instigate, organize or engage in the commission of offences set forth in article 2;

(b) Measures requiring financial institutions and other professions involved in financial transactions to utilize the most efficient measures available for the identification of their usual or occasional customers, as well as customers in whose interest accounts are opened, and to pay special attention to unusual or suspicious transactions and report transactions suspected of stemming from a criminal activity. For this purpose, States Parties shall consider:

   (i) Adopting regulations prohibiting the opening of accounts, the holders or beneficiaries of which are unidentified or unidentifiable, and measures to ensure that such institutions verify the identity of the real owners of such transactions;

   (ii) With respect to the identification of legal entities, requiring financial institutions, when necessary, to take measures to verify the legal existence and the structure of the customer by obtaining, either from a public register or from the customer or both, proof of incorporation, including information concerning the customer's name, legal form, address, directors and provisions regulating the power to bind the entity;

   (iii) Adopting regulations imposing on financial institutions the obligation to report promptly to the competent authorities all complex, unusual large transactions and unusual patterns of transactions, which have no apparent economic or obviously lawful purpose, without fear of assuming criminal or civil liability for breach of any restriction on disclosure of information if they report their suspicions in good faith;

(iv) Requiring financial institutions to maintain, for at least five years, all necessary records on transactions, both domestic and international.

2. States Parties shall further cooperate in the prevention of offences set forth in article 2 by considering:

(a) Measures for the supervision, including, for example, the licensing, of all money-transmission agencies;

(b) Feasible measures to detect or monitor the physical cross-border transportation of cash and bearer negotiable instruments, subject to strict safeguards to ensure proper use of information and without impeding in any way the freedom of capital movements.

3. States Parties shall further cooperate in the prevention of the offences set forth in article 2 by exchanging accurate and verified information in accordance with their domestic law and coordinating administrative and other measures taken, as appropriate, to prevent the commission of offences set forth in article 2, in particular by:

(a) Establishing and maintaining channels of communication between their competent agencies and services to facilitate the secure and rapid exchange of information concerning all aspects of offences set forth in article 2;

(b) Cooperating with one another in conducting inquiries, with respect to the offences set forth in article 2, concerning:

(i) The identity, whereabouts and activities of persons in respect of whom reasonable suspicion exists that they are involved in such offences;

(ii) The movement of funds relating to the commission of such offences.

4. States Parties may exchange information through the International Criminal Police Organization (Interpol).

The International Convention against Transnational Organized Crime (2000)[12] (Palermo Convention)

In order to expand the effort to fight international organized crime, in 2000, the **6.23** UN adopted the International Convention against Transnational Organized Crime (2000) (also known as the Palermo Convention). With respect to money laundering, the Palermo Convention specifically obliges State Parties to:

• Criminalize money laundering and include all serious crimes as predicate offences of money laundering, whether committed in or outside of the State, and permit the required criminal knowledge or intent to be inferred from objective facts;

• Establish regulatory regimes to deter and detect all forms of money laundering, including customer identification, record-keeping, and reporting of suspicious transactions;

---

[12] <http://www.uncjin.org/Documents/Conventions/dcatoc/final_documents_2/convention_eng.pdf>.

- Authorize the cooperation and exchange of information among administrative, regulatory, law enforcement, and other authorities, both domestically and internationally, and consider the establishment of a financial intelligence unit to collect, analyse, and disseminate information; and

- Promote international cooperation.

This Convention came into force on the 29th of September 2003, having been signed by 147 States and ratified by 82 States.

C. Key Extracts of Relevant UN Security Council Resolutions

UN Security Council Resolution 1267 (1999)[13]

6.24 UNSCR1267 (1999) was passed on 15 October 1999 for the purpose of overseeing the implementation of sanctions, including freezing of assets, arms embargo, and travel bans, against the Taliban for its support of Osama bin Laden following the 1998 simultaneous bombings of US embassies in Nairobi, Kenya and Dar es Salaam, Tanzania. While Resolution 1267 (1999) focused initially on the Taliban, its reach was gradually broadened by a series of related Chapter VII Security Council Resolutions that expanded the sanctions regime to also cover Al-Qaida, its affiliates, and Osama bin Laden (Resolution 1333 (2000)[14]) due to their links to the Taliban and involvement in the planning and perpetration of several terrorist attacks, including 9/11. Since 1999, UNSCR 1267 has been modified and strengthened by subsequent resolutions, namely: 1390 (2002), 1455 (2003), 1526 (2004), 1617 (2005), 1730 (2006), 1735 (2006), and 1822 (2008).[15]

---

[13] Available at <http://www.un.org/Docs/scres/1999/sc99.htm>.
[14] Available at <http://www.un.org/Docs/scres/2000/sc2000.htm>.
[15] Available at <http://www.un.org/Docs/scres/2002/sc2002.htm>.
UNSCR 1822 was passed on 30 June 2008. It extended the mandate of the Al-Qaida/Taliban Monitoring Team for 18 months, and attempts to respond to longstanding calls for greater transparency and fairness of Committee procedures by:
- making accessible the publicly releasable reasons for listing all current and future individuals or entities contained in the Consolidated List;
- requiring States to take all possible measures to notify the listed individual or entity and providing a copy of the publicly releasable information leading to the listing, and informing the concerned individual or entity when they are removed from the Consolidated List;
- directing consideration of an annual review of names of individuals reportedly deceased;
- directing a review of all names on the Consolidated List by 30 June 2010, and thereafter, to conduct an annual review of all names that have not been reviewed in three or more years;
- encouraging the Committee to continue to ensure fair and clear listing and delisting procedures exist; and
- directing the review of the Committee's guidelines.

This 1267 Al-Qaida and Taliban regime relies on the arms embargo, travel ban, **6.25** freezing of funds sanctions directed against individuals and entities (Osama bin Laden and members of, or people associated with, Al-Qaida and the Taliban) as enumerated in the Consolidated List.[16] Today there are more than 480 names on this list, the vast majority of which were submitted by the US in the aftermath of 9/11 attacks.[17] The implementation of the regime is monitored by the 1267 Al-Qaida and Taliban Sanctions Committee, which is responsible for managing and updating the Consolidated List. To assist the Committee with its work, the Council established an Analytical Support and Sanctions Monitoring Team.

Despite its relatively promising start, the 1267 Al-Qaida and Taliban regime has **6.26** been shrouded in controversy, mostly due to the lack of transparency in the listing and de-listing process and human rights considerations that arise due to the lack of judicial oversight of the Council's listing decisions. To allay these concerns, the Committee has adopted several additional resolutions to provide guidelines and standards for States to follow in proposing names, including minimum evidentiary standards for the identification of individuals, and a more transparent listing and de-listing process to ensure that due process, the rule of law, and human rights standards are respected.

The asset-freezing obligations of the 1267 Al-Qaida and Taliban regime are wide- **6.27** reaching, especially when one considers that they are obligations stemming from a Security Council listing process that is not subject to domestic judicial review or challenge.[18] The core asset-freezing provisions of the regime require all States to freeze funds and other financial resources, including funds derived or generated from property owned or controlled directly or indirectly by the Taliban and Al-Qaida, or by any undertaking owned or controlled by them, as designated by the Committee, and ensure that neither they nor any other funds or financial resources so designated are made available, by their nationals or by any persons within their territory, to or for the benefit of the Taliban and Al-Qaida, except as may be authorized by the Committee on a case-by-case basis on the grounds of humanitarian need.[19]

---

[16] Entries into the list are made at the recommendation of States and often relevant information is provided by intelligence sources. Any change in the list is promptly communicated to States.

[17] E Rosand and A Millar, 'Strengthening International Law and Global Implementation', in D Cortright and G Lopez (eds) *Uniting Against Terror: Cooperative non-military responses to the global terrorist threat* (MIT Press, London 2007) 57.

[18] Watson Institute for International Studies, *Strengthening Targeted Sanctions Through Fair and Clear Procedures* (Brown University 2006); *The European Convention on Human Rights, Due Process and United Nations Security Council Counter-Terrorism Sanctions* (Report to the Council of Europe 2006); Professor Bardo Fassbinder, *Targeted Sanctions and Due Process* (Study Commissioned by the United Nations Office of Legal Affairs 2006).

[19] SC Res 1452 (2002) and 1735 (2006).

6.28 The way in which the Consolidated List is incorporated into domestic law varies considerably from State to State. Some States incorporate the list directly into national law on the basis of the special status of UNSCRs,[20] whilst others rely on an ad hoc act of incorporation to make the list part of domestic law. The Council of the European Union adopted Common Positions 1999/727/CFSP and 2001/931/CFSP and subsequent common positions and implementing regulations to give effect to UNSCRs 1267 and 1373 and their respective successors. Some States and regional organizations create their own lists of foreign or domestic persons and entities that commit, attempt to commit, or support terrorist acts and whose funds must be frozen. The relevant part of the Resolution provides as follows:

> Acting under Chapter VII of the Charter of the United Nations,
>
> 4. Decides further that . . . all States shall:
>
> (a) Deny permission for any aircraft to take off from or land in their territory if it is owned, leased or operated by or on behalf of the Taliban as designated by the Committee established by paragraph 6 below, unless the particular flight has been approved in advance by the Committee on the grounds of humanitarian need, including religious obligation such as the performance of the Hajj;
>
> (b) Freeze funds and other financial resources, including funds derived or generated from property owned or controlled directly or indirectly by the Taliban, or by any undertaking owned or controlled by the Taliban, as designated by the Committee established by paragraph 6 below, and ensure that neither they nor any other funds or financial resources so designated are made available, by their nationals or by any persons within their territory, to or for the benefit of the Taliban or any undertaking owned or controlled, directly or indirectly, by the Taliban, except as may be authorized by the Committee on a case-by-case basis on the grounds of humanitarian need;

UN Security Council Resolution 1390 (2002)

6.29 Acting under Chapter VII of the Charter of the United Nations:

> 2. Decides that all States shall take the following measures with respect to Usama bin Laden, members of the Al-Qaida organization and the Taliban and other individuals, groups, undertakings and entities associated with them, as referred to in the list created pursuant to resolutions 1267 (1999) and 1333 (2000) to be updated regularly by the Committee established pursuant to resolution 1267 (1999) hereinafter referred to as 'the Committee';
>
> (a) Freeze without delay the funds and other financial assets or economic resources of these individuals, groups, undertakings and entities, including funds derived from property owned or controlled, directly or indirectly, by them or by persons acting on their behalf or at their direction, and ensure that neither these nor any other funds, financial assets or economic resources are made available, directly or indirectly, for such persons' benefit, by their nationals or by any persons within their territory.

---

[20] For example, Angola and Belarus.

UN Security Council Resolution 1452 (2002)

Acting under Chapter VII of the Charter of the United Nations: **6.30**

1. Decides that the provisions of paragraph 4(b) of resolution 1267 (1999), and paragraphs 1 and 2(a) of resolution 1390 (2002), do not apply to funds and other financial assets or economic resources that have been determined by the relevant State(s) to be:

(a) necessary for basic expenses, including payments for foodstuffs, rent or mortgage, medicines and medical treatment, taxes, insurance premiums, and public utility charges, or exclusively for payment of reasonable professional fees and reimbursement of incurred expenses associated with the provision of legal services, or fees or service charges for routine holding or maintenance of frozen funds or other financial assets or economic resources, after notification by the relevant State(s) to the Committee established pursuant to resolution 1267 (1999) (hereinafter referred to as 'the Committee') of the intention to authorize, where appropriate, access to such funds, assets or resources and in the absence of a negative decision by the Committee within 48 hours of such notification;

(b) necessary for extraordinary expenses, provided that such determination has been notified by the relevant State(s) to the Committee and has been approved by the Committee.

UN Security Council Resolution 1730 (2006)

The resolution provides: **6.31**

1. Adopts the de-listing procedure in the document annexed to this resolution and requests the Secretary-General to establish within the Secretariat (Security Council Subsidiary Organs Branch), a focal point to receive de-listing requests and to perform the tasks described in the attached annex;

De-listing procedure

The Security Council requests the Secretary-General to establish, within the Secretariat (Security Council Subsidiary Organs Branch), a focal point to receive de-listing requests. Petitioners seeking to submit a request for de-listing can do so either through the focal point process outlined below or through their state of residence or citizenship.

The focal point will perform the following tasks:

1. Receive de-listing requests from a petitioner (individual(s), groups, undertakings, and/or entities on the Sanctions Committee's lists).

2. Verify if the request is new or is a repeated request.

3. If it is a repeated request and if it does not contain any additional information, return it to the petitioner.

4. Acknowledge receipt of the request to the petitioner and inform the petitioner on the general procedure for processing that request.

5. Forward the request, for their information and possible comments to the designating government(s) and to the government(s) of citizenship and residence. Those governments are encouraged to consult with the designating government(s) before recommending de-listing. To this end, they may approach the focal point, which, if the designating state(s) so agree(s), will put them in contact with the designating state(s).

6. (a) If, after these consultations, any of these governments recommend de listing, that government will forward its recommendation, either through the focal point or directly to the Chairman of the Sanctions Committee, accompanied by that government's explanation. The Chairman will then place the de-listing request on the Committee's agenda.

(b) If any of the governments, which were consulted on the de-listing request under paragraph 5 above oppose the request, the focal point will so inform the Committee and provide copies of the de-listing request. Any member of the Committee, which possesses information in support of the de-listing request, is encouraged to share such information with the governments that reviewed the de listing request under paragraph 5 above.

(c) If, after a reasonable time (3 months), none of the governments which reviewed the de-listing request under paragraph 5 above comment, or indicate that they are working on the de-listing request to the Committee and require an additional definite period of time, the focal point will so notify all members of the Committee and provide copies of the de-listing request. Any member of the Committee may, after consultation with the designating government(s), recommend de-listing by forwarding the request to the Chairman of the Sanctions Committee, accompanied by an explanation. (Only one member of the Committee needs to recommend de-listing in order to place the issue on the Committee's agenda.) If after one month, no Committee member recommends de-listing, then it shall be deemed rejected and the Chairman of the Committee shall inform the focal point accordingly.

7. The focal point shall convey all communications, which it receives from Member States, to the Committee for its information.

8. Inform the petitioner:

(a) Of the decision of the Sanctions Committee to grant the de-listing petition; or

That the process of consideration of the de-listing request within the Committee has been completed and that the petitioner remains on the list of the Committee.

UN Security Council Resolution 1735 (2006)

6.32 Acting under Chapter VII of the Charter of the United Nations:

1. Decides that all States shall take the measures as previously imposed by paragraph 4(b) of resolution 1267 (1999), paragraph 8(c) of resolution 1333 (2000), paragraphs 1 and 2 of resolution 1390 (2002), with respect to Al-Qaida, Usama bin Laden, and the Taliban and other individuals, groups, undertakings and entities associated with them, as referred to in the list created pursuant to resolutions 1267 (1999) and 1333 (2000) (the 'Consolidated List'):

(a) Freeze without delay the funds and other financial assets or economic resources of these individuals, groups, undertakings and entities, including funds derived from property owned or controlled, directly or indirectly, by them or by persons acting on their behalf or at their direction, and ensure that neither these nor any other funds, financial assets or economic resources are made available, directly or indirectly, for such persons' benefit, or by their nationals or by persons within their territory;

2. Reminds States of their obligation to freeze without delay the funds and other financial assets or economic resources pursuant to paragraph 1(a) of this resolution;

3. Confirms that the requirements in paragraph 1(a) of this resolution apply to economic resources of every kind;

Listing

5. Decides that, when proposing names to the Committee for inclusion on the Consolidated List, States shall act in accordance with paragraph 17 of resolution 1526 (2004) and paragraph 4 of resolution 1617 (2005) and provide a statement of case; the statement of case should provide as much detail as possible on the basis(es) for the listing, including: (i) specific information supporting a determination that the individual or entity meets the criteria above; (ii) the nature of the information and (iii) supporting information or documents that can be provided; States should include details of any connection between the proposed designee and any currently listed individual or entity;

6. Requests designating States, at the time of submission, to identify those parts of the statement of case which may be publicly released for the purposes of notifying the listed individual or entity, and those parts which may be released upon request to interested States;

9. Directs the Committee to encourage States to submit additional identifying and other information on listed individuals and entities, including updates on assets frozen and the movement of listed individuals as such information becomes available;

10. Decides that the Secretariat shall, after publication but within two weeks after a name is added to the Consolidated List, notify the Permanent Mission of the State or States where the individual or entity is believed to be located and, in the case of individuals, the State of which the person is a national (to the extent this information is known), and include with this notification a copy of the publicly releasable portion of the statement of case, a description of the effects of designation, as set forth in the relevant resolutions, the Committee's procedures for considering delisting requests, and the provisions of resolution 1452 (2002);

11. Calls upon States receiving notification as in paragraph 10 to take reasonable steps according to their domestic laws and practices to notify or inform the listed individual or entity of the designation and to include with this notification a copy of the publicly releasable portion of the statement of case, a description of the effects of designation, as provided in the relevant resolutions, the Committee's procedures for considering delisting requests, the provisions of resolution 1452 (2002);

Delisting

13. Decides that the Committee shall continue to develop, adopt, and apply guidelines regarding the de-listing of individuals and entities on the Consolidated List;

14. Decides that the Committee, in determining whether to remove names from the Consolidated List, may consider, among other things, (i) whether the individual or entity was placed on the Consolidated List due to a mistake of identity, or (ii) whether the individual or entity no longer meets the criteria set out in relevant resolutions, in particular resolution 1617 (2005); in making the evaluation in (ii) above, the Committee may consider, among other things, whether the individual is deceased, or whether it has been affirmatively shown that the individual or entity has severed all association, as defined in resolution 1617 (2005), with Al-Qaida, Usama bin Laden, the Taliban, and their supporters, including all individuals and entities on the Consolidated List.

UN Security Council Resolution 1373 (2001)[21]

6.33 Resolution 1373 (2001) was passed on the 28th of September 2001 as a direct consequence of the 9/11 attacks on the United States just two weeks earlier. Resolution 1373 is arguably the Security Council's most groundbreaking counter-terrorism resolution. It imposes wide-ranging obligations on all Member States and established the Counter-Terrorism Committee (CTC), comprised of all fifteen members of the Security Council, to monitor States' implementation of their obligations.

6.34 UNSCR 1373 is extremely ambitious. It aims to raise the average level of government capacity to respond more effectively to terrorism across the globe. This requires States to improve their counter-terrorism laws, develop specialized intelligence capabilities, law enforcement, and criminal justice capacity, strengthen international cooperation mechanisms, border and port security, and increase levels of political commitment to prevent and combat the threat of terrorism. To assist in achieving these aims, the CTC was strengthened in 2004 by the establishment of the Counter-Terrorism Executive Directorate (CTED). CTED provides the CTC with additional capacity and expertise in all of the substantive areas covered by Resolution 1373.[22]

6.35 Combating the financing of terrorism is one of the foremost priorities of Resolution 1373. The 9/11 attacks highlighted the importance of tracking and eliminating the funding of terrorist organizations like Al-Qaida. The Resolution recognized the need for States to complement international cooperation by taking additional measures to prevent and suppress the financing and preparation of any acts of terrorism. The first operative line of the Resolution is unambiguous in placing an obligation on all States to prevent and suppress the financing of terrorist acts.[23] It goes on to require States to criminalize the wilful provision or collection, by any means, directly or indirectly, of funds by their nationals or in their territories with the intention that the funds should be used, or in the knowledge that they are to be used, in order to carry out terrorist acts.[24]

6.36 UNSCR 1373 also contains a wide-ranging and 'non-traditional' freezing regime in that it is not based on the more recognized grounds of instrumentality and proceeds of crime. Rather, its freezing obligation requires States to:

> . . . freeze without delay funds and other financial assets or economic resources of persons who commit, or attempt to commit, terrorist acts or participate in or

---

[21] SC Res 1373 (2001).
[22] See Chapter 2 for additional information on the CTC and CTED.
[23] SC Res 1373 (2001) 1(a).
[24] SC Res 1373 (2001) 1(b).

facilitate the commission of terrorist acts; of entities owned or controlled directly or indirectly by such persons; and of persons and entities acting on behalf of, or at the direction of such persons and entities, including funds derived or generated from property owned or controlled directly or indirectly by such persons and associated persons and entities.[25]

Furthermore, it obliges States to prohibit their nationals or any persons and entities within their territories from making any funds, financial assets, economic resources, or financial or other related services available, directly or indirectly, for the benefit of persons who commit or attempt to commit or facilitate or participate in the commission of terrorist acts, of entities owned or controlled, directly or indirectly, by such persons and of persons and entities acting on behalf of or at the direction of such persons.[26]   **6.37**

Unlike UNSCR 1267, Resolution 1373 does not establish a list of individuals **6.38** or entities whose funds must be frozen. It also does not define 'terrorist act'. At a minimum, that phrase would include crimes that a State denominated as terrorism or terrorist acts under domestic law. However, most States would consider that the offences in the international terrorism-related Conventions and Protocols adopted by that State would be considered terrorist acts. In view of the many references describing terrorism and terrorist acts as victimization of civilians in the resolutions of the Security Council[27] and the General Assembly[28], the mini-definition in Article 2.1(b) of the Financing of Terrorism Convention provides another practical guide for identification of acts for which the provision or collection of funds should be forbidden.

An important aspect of UNSCR 1373 is that its scope of freezing must apply to **6.39** *all property* owned or controlled by persons *who commit or attempt to commit terrorist acts*. However, most domestic laws only permit the freezing of property that is ultimately subject to forfeiture, which in most States means instrumentalities and proceeds of crime. Proper implementation of UNSCR 1373 therefore requires an expanded freezing regime.

In summary, Resolution 1373 obliges States to: **6.40**

- Deny all forms of support for terrorist groups;
- Suppress the provision of safe haven or support for terrorists, including freezing funds or assets of persons, organizations, or entities involved in terrorist acts;

---

[25] SC Res 1373 (2001) 1(c).
[26] SC Res 1373 (2001) 1(d).
[27] Security Council Resolutions 1456 (2003), 1540 and 1566 (2004), 1624 (2005), and 1735 (2006).
[28] General Assembly Resolutions 56/88 (2002), 57/27 (2003), 58/81 and 58/174 (2004), 60/288 and 61/40 (2006).

- Prohibit active or passive assistance to terrorists; and
- Cooperate with other States in criminal investigations and sharing information about planned terrorist acts.

6.41 The key provisions of UNSCR 1373 are as follows:

> Acting under Chapter VII of the Charter of the United Nations,
> 1. Decides that all States shall:
>   (a) Prevent and suppress the financing of terrorist acts;
>   (b) Criminalize the wilful provision or collection, by any means, directly or indirectly, of funds by their nationals or in their territories with the intention that the funds should be used, or in the knowledge that they are to be used, in order to carry out terrorist acts;
>   (c) Freeze without delay funds and other financial assets or economic resources of persons who commit, or attempt to commit, terrorist acts or participate in or facilitate the commission of terrorist acts; of entities owned or controlled directly or indirectly by such persons; and of persons and entities acting on behalf of, or at the direction of such persons and entities, including funds derived or generated from property owned or controlled directly or indirectly by such persons and associated persons and entities;
>   (d) Prohibit their nationals or any persons and entities within their territories from making any funds, financial assets or economic resources or financial or other related services available, directly or indirectly, for the benefit of persons who commit or attempt to commit or facilitate or participate in the commission of terrorist acts, of entities owned or controlled, directly or indirectly, by such persons and of persons and entities acting on behalf of or at the direction of such persons;
> 2. Decides also that all States shall:
>   (a) Refrain from providing any form of support, active or passive, to entities or persons involved in terrorist acts, including by suppressing recruitment of members of terrorist groups and eliminating the supply of weapons to terrorists;
>   (b) Take the necessary steps to prevent the commission of terrorist acts, including by provision of early warning to other States by exchange of information;
>   (c) Deny safe haven to those who finance, plan, support, or commit terrorist acts, or provide safe havens;
>   (d) Prevent those who finance, plan, facilitate or commit terrorist acts from using their respective territories for those purposes against other States or their citizens;
>   (e) Ensure that any person who participates in the financing, planning, preparation or perpetration of terrorist acts or in supporting terrorist acts is brought to justice and ensure that, in addition to any other measures against them, such terrorist acts are established as serious criminal offences in domestic laws and regulations and that the punishment duly reflects the seriousness of such terrorist acts;
>   (f) Afford one another the greatest measure of assistance in connection with criminal investigations or criminal proceedings relating to the financing or support of terrorist acts, including assistance in obtaining evidence in their possession necessary for the proceedings;
>   (g) Prevent the movement of terrorists or terrorist groups by effective border controls and controls on issuance of identity papers and travel documents, and through

measures for preventing counterfeiting, forgery or fraudulent use of identity papers and travel documents;

3. Calls upon all States to:
   (a) Find ways of intensifying and accelerating the exchange of operational information, especially regarding actions or movements of terrorist persons or networks; forged or falsified travel documents; traffic in arms, explosives or sensitive materials; use of communications technologies by terrorist groups; and the threat posed by the possession of weapons of mass destruction by terrorist groups;
   (b) Exchange information in accordance with international and domestic law and cooperate on administrative and judicial matters to prevent the commission of terrorist acts;
   (c) Cooperate, particularly through bilateral and multilateral arrangements and agreements, to prevent and suppress terrorist attacks and take action against perpetrators of such acts;
   (d) Become parties as soon as possible to the relevant international conventions and protocols relating to terrorism, including the International Convention for the Suppression of the Financing of Terrorism of 9 December 1999;
   (e) Increase cooperation and fully implement the relevant international conventions and protocols relating to terrorism and Security Council resolutions 1269 (1999) and 1368 (2001);
   (f) Take appropriate measures in conformity with the relevant provisions of national and international law, including international standards of human rights, before granting refugee status, for the purpose of ensuring that the asylum-seeker has not planned, facilitated or participated in the commission of terrorist acts;
   (g) Ensure, in conformity with international law, that refugee status is not abused by the perpetrators, organizers or facilitators of terrorist acts, and that claims of political motivation are not recognized as grounds for refusing requests for the extradition of alleged terrorists;

4. Notes with concern the close connection between international terrorism and transnational organized crime, illicit drugs, money-laundering, illegal arms-trafficking, and illegal movement of nuclear, chemical, biological and other potentially deadly materials, and in this regard emphasizes the need to enhance coordination of efforts on national, sub-regional, regional and international levels in order to strengthen a global response to this serious challenge and threat to international security;

5. Declares that acts, methods, and practices of terrorism are contrary to the purposes and principles of the United Nations and that knowingly financing, planning and inciting terrorist acts are also contrary to the purposes and principles of the United Nations;

6. Decides to establish, in accordance with rule 28 of its provisional rules of procedure, a Committee of the Security Council, consisting of all the members of the Council, to monitor implementation of this resolution, with the assistance of appropriate expertise, and calls upon all States to report to the Committee, no later than 90 days from the date of adoption of this resolution and thereafter according to a timetable to be proposed by the Committee, on the steps they have taken to implement this resolution;

7. Directs the Committee to delineate its tasks, submit a work programme within 30 days of the adoption of this resolution, and to consider the support it requires, in consultation with the Secretary-General;

Summary of the criminalization, freezing, and forfeiture obligations
under the Financing Convention (1999) and Security Council
Resolutions 1267 (1999) and 1373 (2001)[29]

6.42 Summary: financing of terrorism criminalization and freezing provisions

	1999 Financing Convention	Security Council Resolution 1373	Security Council Resolution 1267 and related resolutions
Criminalization provisions	Unlawfully and wilfully, provides or collects funds with the intention that they should be used or in the knowledge that they are to be used, in full or in part, in order to carry out . . . (certain defined acts, including Convention offences and specific civilian-centred definition provided in the Convention).	Criminalize the wilful provision or collection, by any means, directly or indirectly, of funds by their nationals or in their territories with the intention that the funds should be used, or in the knowledge that they are to be used, in order to carry out terrorist acts.	No criminalization provision, only freezing, travel, and arms sanctions.
Freezing obligation	Identification, detection, and freezing or seizure of any funds used or allocated for the purpose of committing the offences set forth in the Convention as well as the proceeds derived from such offences, for purposes of possible forfeiture.	Freeze the funds, and other financial assets or economic resources of persons who commit, or attempt to commit, terrorist acts; of entities owned or controlled directly or indirectly by such persons; and of persons and entities acting on behalf of, or at the direction of such persons and entities.	Freeze funds and other financial resources, including funds derived or generated from property owned or controlled directly or indirectly by Al-Qaida and the Taliban, or by any undertaking owned or controlled by Al-Qaida and the Taliban, as designated by the Committee.
Confiscation/ forfeiture obligation	Take appropriate measures, in accordance with its domestic legal principles, for the forfeiture of funds used or allocated for the purpose of committing the offences set forth in the Convention and the proceeds derived from such offences.	No confiscation or forfeiture requirement. Only preventative (non-criminal) freezing required.	No confiscation or forfeiture requirement. Only preventative (non-criminal) freezing required.

---

[29] This table draws on the UNODC 2008 Legislative Guide to the universal legal regime against terrorism. Available at <http://www.unodc.org/documents/terrorism/LegislativeGuide2008.pdf >.

	1999 Financing Convention	Security Council Resolution 1373	Security Council Resolution 1267 and related resolutions
Other	For an act to constitute an offence set forth in the Convention, it shall not be necessary that the funds were actually used to carry out a defined terrorist purpose. Criminalization, freezing, and forfeiture apply to funds of innocent origin once provided or collected with the intention or in the knowledge they will be used for one of the defined terrorist purposes.	In the absence of a definitive explanation in Resolution 1373 of what acts trigger its freezing obligation, States apply their own interpretations. Many States have definitions of terrorism or terrorist acts in criminal statutes. The Resolution requires freezing all property of those who commit or support acts of terrorism, including innocent property not intended for criminal use.	Consolidated list: 142 individuals belonging to or associated with the Taliban; one entity belonging to or associated with the Taliban; 223 individuals belonging to or associated with Al-Qaida

Legal and human rights issues relevant to the implementation of UN Security Council asset freezing obligations

Despite efforts to address the human rights and due process concerns associated with the UN Security Council's asset freezing obligations under Resolutions 1267 (1999) and 1373 (2001), there have been a number of challenges to the legality of these resolutions, especially Resolution 1267. At the core of these challenges is the right to be heard, the right to effective judicial review by an independent tribunal, and the right to property. **6.43**

On 21 September 2005 in the *Yusuf* and *Kadi* cases,[30] the Court of First Instance of the European Communities (CFI) refused to review the European Regulation 881/2002 that contains the list of individuals and entities whose assets must be frozen, due to suspected terrorist links. Regulation 881 had been adopted by the Council of the European Union to ensure regional implementation of UN Security Council asset freezing regulations, particularly in relation to assets of individuals and entities affiliated with the Taliban and Al-Qaida. Yusuf, together with the company Al Barakaat and other individuals, filed a petition to the Court of First Instance in 2001, seeking the annulment of the Regulation according to Article 230 of the **6.44**

---

[30] Court of First Instance (CFI), case T-306/01, *Ahmed Ali Yusuf, Al Barakaat Int'l Found'n v Council and Commission* (21 Sept 2005), [2005] ECR II-3533, app'd under case C-415/05, [2006] OJ C48, 11; case T-315/01, *Yassin Abdullah Kadi v Council and Commission* (21 Sept 2005), [2005] ECR II-3649, app'd under case C-402/05, [2006] OJ C36, 19. Philippe Weckel, 'Chronique de jurisprudence internationale' (2005) 109 Revue Gén Dr Int Public 957.

European Communities Treaty. They held that the insertion of their names in the list was inaccurate and that the mechanism of listing breached their fundamental rights. The Court held that Regulation 881 and the list may not be challenged as they derive from Security Council Resolutions that bind Member States according to the UN Charter. Therefore, they cannot be impugned even when translated into European norms, unless they violate *jus cogens*. In this case, however, the Court found no breach of *jus cogens*, since the right to judicial review can be derogated in certain prescribed circumstances. This judgment was criticized by the EU Advocate-General, Miguel Poiares Maduro, who in January 2008 issued an opinion that argues that there is no basis in Community law for according supra-constitutional status to measures adopted by the EU Commission that are necessary for the implementation of resolutions adopted by the Security Council.[31]

6.45 In joined cases, Kadi and Al Barakaat International Foundation lodged appeals to the European Court of Justice on the 17th and 21st of November 2005, respectively. By their appeals, Mr Kadi (C-402/05 P) and Al Barakaat International Foundation (C-415/05 P) sought to set aside the judgments of the Court of First Instance of the European Communities of 21 September 2005 in Case T-315/01 *Kadi v Council and Commission* [2005] ECR II-3649 ('Kadi') and Case T-306/01 *Yusuf and Al Barakaat International Foundation v Council and Commission* [2005] ECR-II 3533.

6.46 In a landmark judgment on the 3rd of September 2008, the ECJ set aside the judgments of the Court of First Instance of the European Communities of 21 September 2005 and annulled Council Regulation (EC) No 881/2002 of 27 May 2002 which imposed certain restrictive measures directed against certain persons and entities associated with Osama bin Laden, the Al-Qaida network, and the Taliban, and repealed Council Regulation (EC) No 467/2001 which prohibited the export of certain goods and services to Afghanistan, in so far as it concerns Mr Kadi and the Al Barakaat International Foundation. In order to give the EU policymakers sufficient time to remedy the *lacuna* that would be created by the lack of EU regulations, the Court ordered that effects of Regulation No 881/2002 should be maintained for a period not exceeding three months from the date of the judgment.

6.47 The Court concluded that the Community courts must ensure the review, in principle the full review, of the lawfulness of all Community acts in the light of the fundamental rights forming an integral part of the general principles of Community law, including review of Community measures which, like the contested regulation, are designed to give effect to resolutions adopted by the Security Council. This

---

[31] Opinion of Advocate-General Poiares Maduro delivered on 16 January 2008 (1) Case C-402/05 P *Yassin Abdullah Kadi v Council of the European Union and Commission of the European Communities*. See <http://curia.europa.eu/en/actu/communiques/cp08/aff/cp080002en.pdf>.

ruling, which was welcomed by human rights advocates, affirms the jurisdiction of the EU Courts to examine the implementation of UN Security Council Resolutions and ensure their compliance with human rights law.

This case represents one of several judicial and political challenges now question- **6.48**
ing the legal effect of designation and the equity and fairness of the procedures employed by the UN Al-Qaida and Taliban Sanctions Committee in making designations or considering petitions for de-listing. According to the UN Al-Qaida Committee's own Monitoring Team, there are more than fifteen major lawsuits underway, in at least seven countries, challenging UN designations.[32] This includes cases in the United States, Italy, Netherlands, Pakistan, Switzerland, and Turkey.

In April 2008, the United Kingdom High Court in the case of *A, K, M, Q and G v* **6.49**
Her Majesty's Treasury,[33] overturned as ultra vires a UK freezing order against five individuals designated by the UN Al-Qaida and Taliban Sanctions Committee. The UK terrorist asset-freezing measures are contained in the Terrorism (United Nations Measures) Order 2006 and the Al-Qaida and Taliban (United Nations Measures) Order 2006. These measures were introduced directly by the Government through Orders in Council to implement UN Security Council Resolutions in order to strengthen domestic controls on the financing of terrorism and to comply with the British Government's international obligations to enforce UN Resolutions requiring such controls. They were never properly scrutinized, debated, or approved by Parliament. In a judgment condemning as impermissible the Government's ousting of Parliament, Mr. Justice Collins said:

> Counsel for the applicants have submitted that the means used to apply the obligations imposed by the UN Resolutions is unlawful. Parliament has been bypassed by the use of Orders in Council. But in deciding the appropriate way in which the obligation should be applied and in particular in creating the criminal offences set out in the Orders it was necessary that Parliamentary approval should be obtained. Those submissions are in my judgment entirely persuasive.[34]

The court ruling highlighted the risks associated with the creation of unchecked executive counter-terrorism policies and practices.[34a] Political challenges are also

---

[32] See Annex I to UN Doc S/2008/324 at <http://documents-dds-ny.un.org/doc/UNDOC/GEN/N08/341/88/pdf/N0834188.pdf?OpenElement>.

[33] See Annex I (n 32).

[34] See Annex I (n 32).

[34a] The Treasury appealed the decision of the Administrative Court in *G v HM Treasury; A & others v Same*, Court of Appeal. On 12 November 2008, the Court of Appeal held that the Orders were valid provided that the words 'or may be' were excised from Article 4(2) with the result that the Treasury was required to show 'reasonable grounds for suspecting ...and not simply suspecting that he might be involved'. The Treasury may no longer simply rely on a suspicion that the person may be involved in the abovementioned acts or be a designated person. Furthermore, in relation to the Al-Qaida and Taliban Order, the designated person should be entitled to a merits-based review. The Court of Appeal found that, once revised, the Orders would be compliant with the European Convention on Human Rights and that they were not unlawful at common law.

being debated in the European Parliament, the Council of Europe, and national parliaments around the world.[35]

6.50 Another notable development is a recent opinion by the Court of Justice of the European Communities in a case involving an attempted transaction with a listed person. In Möllendorf,[36] the Court, on request for a preliminary ruling from a German court, considered whether sellers of real estate to a partnership including Aqeel Abdulaziz Aqeel al-Aqeel (QI A 171.04) were precluded by European sanctions regulations from registering the change of ownership in a land registry even though the sale contract for the property and agreement to transfer ownership had been concluded before Aqeel was listed. The court concluded that article 2(3) of regulation EC 881/2002, which provides that '[n]o economic resources shall be made available, directly or indirectly, to, or for the benefit of a listed person so as to enable that person, group or entity to obtain funds, goods or services', prohibited the registration.[37] The Court of Justice referred back to the German court the question of whether a requirement under national law that the sellers refund the purchase price for such an incomplete sale disproportionately infringed their right to disposal of property.[38]

D. The Financial Action Task Force

6.51 The Financial Action Task Force (FATF) was established at the G-7 Summit in 1989 in direct response to growing international threat posed by money laundering. FATF is an intergovernmental policymaking body that prescribes both domestic and international anti-money laundering policy standards. It also conducts evaluations of States' current anti-money laundering procedures, and examines the techniques of money launderers and terrorist organizations, and developing annual typologies reports. In 1990, FATF issued Forty (40) Recommendations designed to assist with the fight against money laundering. These Recommendations were updated and revised in 1996 and 2003 to reflect the development in global money laundering trends and methodologies.

6.52 Although primarily an anti-money laundering organization in response to the 9/11 attacks, FATF expanded its mission to encompass terrorist financing and proceeded in October 2001 to issue a list of Eight Special Recommendations on

---

[35] See Annex I (n 32).
[36] See Annex I (n 32).
[37] See Annex I (n 32).
[38] See Annex I (n 32).

Terrorist Financing[39] with the aim of assisting private authorities in detecting the movement of terrorist funds. These were later followed by a ninth Recommendation on cash couriers. Many of the FATF Recommendations are similar to the obligations imposed by UN Security Council Resolution 1373 (2001), including the call to Member States to ratify and implement the universal legal instruments against terrorism. Security Council Resolution 1617 reinforces the FATF Special Recommendations and obliges States to implement them.[40]

Since the development of these Special Recommendations, FATF has become **6.53** one of the lead international institutions supporting the development of policy and good practice relating to the combating of terrorist financing. It currently has thirty-three Member States, and where necessary it imposes counter-measures on non-compliant members and non-members. To clarify provisions and assist with implementation, FATF produces a series of Interpretive Notes and International Best Practice papers that contain specific guidance on several of the Special Recommendations for States, relevant organizations, and departments.[41]

FATF operates on the basis of three main processes: the first focuses on setting **6.54** standards (through the 40 plus 9 Recommendations), the second on assessing and ensuring compliance, mostly through self-reporting and mutual peer review, and the third on exporting the model though regional FATFs. The last process is particularly important as it allows FATF to respond effectively to the various manifestations of terrorism as they differ so markedly from region to region. This approach has also enabled FATF to expand its reach beyond the core membership,[42] through the establishment of FATF-style regional bodies (FSRBs) in regions of concern.[43] FSRBs are regional bodies with structures and processes based on the FATF model. There are currently over 130 States that are members of FSRBs. These regional bodies have greatly expanded the impact of FATF and have contributed to the global effort to counter the financing of terrorism.[44]

---

[39] FATF Special Recommendations on Terrorist Financing (Oct 31, 2001), available at <http://www.fatf-gafi.org/document/9/0,3343,en_32250379_32236920_34032073_1_1_1_1, 00.html>.

[40] S/RES/1617, New York, 29 July 2005.

[41] See <http://www.fatf-gafi.org/document/53/0,3343,en_32250379_32236947_34261877_ 1_1_1_1,00.html>.

[42] Members of the Organization for Economic Co-operation and Development (OECD).

[43] The thirty-one Member States and territories are: Argentina, Australia, Austria, Belgium, Brazil, Canada, Denmark, Finland, France, Germany, Greece, Hong Kong-China, Iceland, Ireland, Italy, Japan, Luxemburg, Mexico, Kingdom of the Netherlands, New Zealand, Norway, Portugal, Russia, Singapore, South Africa, Spain, Sweden, Switzerland, Turkey, United Kingdom, and United States. The two regional organizations are the European Commission and the Gulf Co-operation Council.

[44] These bodies are: Asia/Pacific Group on Money Laundering (APG); Caribbean Financial Action Task Force (CFATF); Council of Europe MONEYVAL (previously PC-R-EV) Committee;

FATF Nine Special Recommendations on terrorist financing

6.55 As stated above, FATF adopted Nine Special Recommendations addressing the financing of terrorism together with Interpretive Notes to assist States when giving effect to the Special Recommendations. Given the importance of these Recommendations, they are summarized below with the accompanying interpretative note where appropriate:

1. Ratification and implementation of UN legal instruments against terrorism

The first Special Recommendation consists of two parts. The first requires each State to take immediate steps to ratify and fully implement the 1999 United Nations International Convention for the Suppression of the Financing of Terrorism. The second requires States to also fully implement the United Nations resolutions relating to the prevention and suppression of the financing of terrorist acts, particularly Security Council resolution 1373 (2001).

Implementation of the above obligations means that States need to adopt appropriate laws and related measures to ensure that the provisions of the Financing Convention and the relevant Security Council Resolutions are effective in practice. This can be accomplished by a dedicated implementing law, regulation, decree or other appropriate legislative or executive action.

2. Criminalizing the financing of terrorism and associated money laundering

The second Special Recommendation also contains two elements. The first requires that each State should criminalize the financing of terrorism, terrorist acts, and terrorist organizations. Secondly, States should ensure that such offences are designated as money laundering predicate offences. FATF has issued an Interpretive Note describing how a State should implement this recommendation. Relevant extracts of this Interpretive Note are reproduced at the end of this section.

> *Special Recommendation II (SR II): Criminalizing the financing of terrorism and associated money laundering*
>
> **Objective**
>
> 1. Special Recommendation II (SR II) was developed with the objective of ensuring that States have the legal capacity to prosecute and apply criminal sanctions to persons that finance terrorism. Given the close connection between international terrorism and inter alia money laundering, another objective of SR II is to emphasize this link by obligating States to include terrorist financing offences as predicate offences for money laundering.

Eastern and Southern Africa Anti-Money Laundering Group (ESAAMLG); and Financial Action Task Force on Money Laundering in South America (GAFISUD).

The basis for criminalizing terrorist financing should be the United Nations International Convention for the Suppression of the Financing of Terrorism, 1999.

Definitions

2. For the purposes of SR II and this Interpretative Note, the following definitions apply:

a) The term funds refers to assets of every kind, whether tangible or intangible, movable or immovable, however acquired, and legal documents or instruments in any form, including electronic or digital, evidencing title to, or interest in, such assets, including, but not limited to, bank credits, travellers cheques, bank cheques, money orders, shares, securities, bonds, drafts, letters of credit.

b) The term terrorist refers to any natural person who: (i) commits, or attempts to commit, terrorist acts by any means, directly or indirectly, unlawfully and wilfully; (ii) participates as an accomplice in terrorist acts; (iii) organises or directs others to commit terrorist acts; or (iv) contributes to the commission of terrorist acts by a group of persons acting with a common purpose where the contribution is made intentionally and with the aim of furthering the terrorist act or with the knowledge of the intention of the group to commit a terrorist act.

c) The term terrorist act includes:

   i) An act which constitutes an offence within the scope of, and as defined in one of the following treaties: Convention for the Suppression of Unlawful Seizure of Aircraft (1970), Convention for the Suppression of Unlawful Acts against the Safety of Civil Aviation (1971), Convention on the Prevention and Punishment of Crimes against Internationally Protected Persons, including Diplomatic Agents (1973), International Convention against the Taking of Hostages (1979), Convention on the Physical Protection of Nuclear Material (1980), Protocol for the Suppression of Unlawful Acts of Violence at Airports Serving International Civil Aviation, supplementary to the Convention for the Suppression of Unlawful Acts against the Safety of Civil Aviation (1988), Convention for the Suppression of Unlawful Acts against the Safety of Maritime Navigation (1988), Protocol for the Suppression of Unlawful Acts against the Safety of Fixed Platforms located on the Continental Shelf (1988), and the International Convention for the Suppression of Terrorist Bombings (1997); and

   ii) Any other act intended to cause death or serious bodily injury to a civilian, or to any other person not taking an active part in the hostilities in a situation of armed conflict, when the purpose of such act, by its nature or context, is to intimidate a population, or to compel a Government or an international organization to do or to abstain from doing any act.

d) The term terrorist financing includes the financing of terrorist acts, and of terrorists and terrorist organizations.

e) The term terrorist organization refers to any group of terrorists that:

   (i) commits, or attempts to commit, terrorist acts by any means, directly or indirectly, unlawfully and wilfully; (ii) participates as an accomplice in terrorist acts; (iii) organises or directs others to commit terrorist acts; or (iv) contributes to the commission of terrorist acts by a group of persons acting with a common purpose where the contribution is made intentionally and with the aim of furthering the terrorist act or with the knowledge of the intention of the group to commit a terrorist act.

Characteristics of the terrorist financing offence

3. Terrorist financing offences should extend to any person who wilfully provides or collects funds by any means, directly or indirectly, with the unlawful intention that

they should be used or in the knowledge that they are to be used, in full or in part: (a) to carry out a terrorist act(s); (b) by a terrorist organization; or (c) by an individual terrorist.

4. Criminalizing terrorist financing solely on the basis of aiding and abetting, attempt, or conspiracy does not comply with this Recommendation.

5. Terrorist financing offences should extend to any funds whether from a legitimate or illegitimate source.

6. Terrorist financing offences should not require that the funds: (a) were actually used to carry out or attempt a terrorist act(s); or (b) be linked to a specific terrorist act(s).

7. It should also be an offence to attempt to commit the offence of terrorist financing.

8. It should also be an offence to engage in any of the following types of conduct:

a) Participating as an accomplice in an offence as set forth in paragraphs 3 or 7 of this Interpretative Note;
b) Organising or directing others to commit an offence as set forth in paragraphs 3 or 7 of this Interpretative Note;
c) Contributing to the commission of one or more offence(s) as set forth in paragraphs 3 or 7 of this Interpretative Note by a group of persons acting with a common purpose. Such contribution shall be intentional and shall either: (i) be made with the aim of furthering the criminal activity or criminal purpose of the group, where such activity or purpose involves the commission of a terrorist financing offence; or (ii) be made in the knowledge of the intention of the group to commit a terrorist financing offence.

9. Terrorist financing offences should be predicate offences for money laundering.

10. Terrorist financing offences should apply, regardless of whether the person alleged to have committed the offence(s) is in the same State or a different State from the one in which the terrorist(s)/terrorist organization(s) is located or the terrorist act(s) occurred/ will occur.

11. The law should permit the intentional element of the terrorist financing offence to be inferred from objective factual circumstances.

12. Criminal liability for terrorist financing should extend to legal persons. Where that is not possible (ie, due to fundamental principles of domestic law), civil or administrative liability should apply.

13. Making legal persons subject to criminal liability for terrorist financing should not preclude the possibility of parallel criminal, civil or administrative proceedings in States in which more than one form of liability is available.

14. Natural and legal persons should be subject to effective, proportionate and dissuasive criminal, civil or administrative sanctions for terrorist financing.

3. Freezing and confiscating terrorist assets

The third Special Recommendation requires each State to implement measures to freeze without delay funds or other assets of terrorists, those who finance terrorism and terrorist organizations in accordance with the United Nations resolutions relating to the prevention and suppression of the financing of terrorist acts. Each State should also adopt and implement measures, including legislative ones, that would enable the competent authorities to seize and confiscate property that is the proceeds of, or used in, or intended or allocated for use in, the financing of terrorism, terrorist acts or terrorist organizations. FATF has issued an Interpretive Note describing how a State should implement this recommendation. Relevant extracts of this Interpretive Note are reproduced at the end of this section.

Interpretative Note to Special Recommendation III: Freezing and Confiscating Terrorist Assets

Objectives

1. FATF Special Recommendation III consists of two obligations. The first requires jurisdictions to implement measures that will freeze or, if appropriate, seize terrorist-related funds or other assets without delay in accordance with relevant United Nations resolutions. The second obligation of Special Recommendation III is to have measures in place that permit a jurisdiction to seize or confiscate terrorist funds or other assets on the basis of an order or mechanism issued by a competent authority or a court.

2. The objective of the first requirement is to freeze terrorist-related funds or other assets based on reasonable grounds, or a reasonable basis, to suspect or believe that such funds or other assets could be used to finance terrorist activity. The objective of the second requirement is to deprive terrorists of these funds or other assets if and when links have been adequately established between the funds or other assets and terrorists or terrorist activity. The intent of the first objective is preventative, while the intent of the second objective is mainly preventative and punitive. Both requirements are necessary to deprive terrorists and terrorist networks of the means to conduct future terrorist activity and maintain their infrastructure and operations.

Scope

3. Special Recommendation III is intended, with regard to its first requirement, to complement the obligations in the context of the United Nations Security Council (UNSC) resolutions relating to the prevention and suppression of the financing of terrorist acts—S/RES/1267(1999) and its successor resolutions,[45] S/RES/1373(2001) and any prospective resolutions related to the freezing, or if appropriate seizure, of terrorist assets. It should be stressed that none of the obligations in Special Recommendation III is intended to replace other measures or obligations that may already be in place for dealing with funds or other assets in the context of a criminal, civil or administrative investigation or proceeding.[46] The focus of Special Recommendation III

---

[45] When issued, S/RES/1267(1999) had a time limit of one year. A series of resolutions have been issued by the United Nations Security Council (UNSC) to extend and further refine provisions of S/RES/1267(1999). By successor resolutions are meant those resolutions that extend and are directly related to the original resolution S/RES/1267(1999). At the time of issue of this Interpretative Note, these resolutions included S/RES/1333(2000), S/RES/1363(2001), S/RES/1390(2002), and S/RES/1455(2003). In this Interpretative Note, the term S/RES/1267(1999) refers to S/RES/1267(1999) and its successor resolutions.

[46] For instance, both the UN Convention against Illicit Traffic in Narcotic Drugs and Psychotropic Substances (1988) and UN Convention against Transnational Organized Crime (2000) contain obligations regarding freezing, seizure, and confiscation in the context of combating transnational crime. Those obligations exist separately and apart from obligations that are set forth in S/RES/1267 (1999), S/RES/1373(2001) and Special Recommendation III.

instead is on the preventative measures that are necessary and unique in the context of stopping the flow or use of funds or other assets to terrorist groups.

4. S/RES/1267(1999) and S/RES/1373(2001) differ in the persons and entities whose funds or other assets are to be frozen, the authorities responsible for making these designations, and the effect of these designations.

5. S/RES/1267(1999) and its successor resolutions obligate jurisdictions to freeze without delay the funds or other assets owned or controlled by Al-Qaida, the Taliban, Osama bin Laden, or persons and entities associated with them as designated by the United Nations Al-Qaida and Taliban Sanctions Committee established pursuant to United Nations Security Council Resolution 1267 (the Al-Qaida and Taliban Sanctions Committee), including funds derived from funds or other assets owned or controlled, directly or indirectly, by them or by persons acting on their behalf or at their direction, and ensure that neither these nor any other funds or other assets are made available, directly or indirectly, for such persons' benefit, by their nationals or by any person within their territory. The Al-Qaida and Taliban Sanctions Committee is the authority responsible for designating the persons and entities that should have their funds or other assets frozen under S/RES/1267(1999). All jurisdictions that are members of the United Nations are obligated by S/RES/1267(1999) to freeze the assets of persons and entities so designated by the Al-Qaida and Taliban Sanctions Committee.[47]

6. S/RES/1373(2001) obligates jurisdictions to freeze without delay the funds or other assets of persons who commit, or attempt to commit, terrorist acts or participate in or facilitate the commission of terrorist acts; of entities owned or controlled directly or indirectly by such persons; and of persons and entities acting on behalf of, or at the direction of such persons and entities, including funds or other assets derived or generated from property owned or controlled, directly or indirectly, by such persons and associated persons and entities. Each individual jurisdiction has the authority to designate the persons and entities that should have their funds or other assets frozen. Additionally, to ensure that effective co-operation is developed among jurisdictions, jurisdictions should examine and give effect to, if appropriate, the actions initiated under the freezing mechanisms of other jurisdictions. When (i) a specific notification or communication is sent and (ii) the jurisdiction receiving the request is satisfied, according to applicable legal principles, that a requested designation is supported by reasonable grounds, or a reasonable basis, to suspect or believe that the proposed designee is a terrorist, one who finances terrorism or a terrorist organization, the jurisdiction receiving the request must ensure that the funds or other assets of the designated person are frozen without delay.

Definitions

7. For the purposes of Special Recommendation III and this Interpretive Note, the following definitions apply:

a) The term freeze means to prohibit the transfer, conversion, disposition or movement of funds or other assets on the basis of, and for the duration of the validity of, an action initiated by a competent authority or a court under a freezing mechanism. The frozen funds or other assets remain the property of the person(s) or entity(ies) that held an interest in the specified funds or other assets at the time of

---

[47] When the UNSC acts under Chapter VII of the UN Charter, the resolutions it issues are mandatory for all UN members.

the freezing and may continue to be administered by the financial institution or other arrangements designated by such person(s) or entity(ies) prior to the initiation of an action under a freezing mechanism.

b) The term seize means to prohibit the transfer, conversion, disposition or movement of funds or other assets on the basis of an action initiated by a competent authority or a court under a freezing mechanism. However, unlike a freezing action, a seizure is effected by a mechanism that allows the competent authority or court to take control of specified funds or other assets. The seized funds or other assets remain the property of the person(s) or entity(ies) that held an interest in the specified funds or other assets at the time of the seizure, although the competent authority or court will often take over possession, administration or management of the seized funds or other assets.

c) The term confiscate, which includes forfeiture where applicable, means the permanent deprivation of funds or other assets by order of a competent authority or a court. Confiscation or forfeiture takes place through a judicial or administrative procedure that transfers the ownership of specified funds or other assets to be transferred to the State. In this case, the person(s) or entity(ies) that held an interest in the specified funds or other assets at the time of the confiscation or forfeiture loses all rights, in principle, to the confiscated or forfeited funds or other assets.48

d) The term funds or other assets means financial assets, property of every kind, whether tangible or intangible, movable or immovable, however acquired, and legal documents or instruments in any form, including electronic or digital, evidencing title to, or interest in, such funds or other assets, including, but not limited to, bank credits, travellers cheques, bank cheques, money orders, shares, securities, bonds, drafts, or letters of credit, and any interest, dividends or other income on or value accruing from or generated by such funds or other assets.

e) The term terrorist refers to any natural person who: (i) commits, or attempts to commit, terrorist acts[49] by any means, directly or indirectly, unlawfully and wilfully; (ii) participates as an accomplice in terrorist acts or terrorist financing; (iii) organises or directs others to commit terrorist acts or terrorist financing; or (iv) contributes to the commission of terrorist acts or terrorist financing by a group of persons acting with a common purpose where the contribution is made intentionally and with the aim of furthering the terrorist act or terrorist financing or with the knowledge of the intention of the group to commit a terrorist act or terrorist financing.

---

[48] Confiscation or forfeiture orders are usually linked to a criminal conviction or a court decision whereby the confiscated or forfeited property is determined to have been derived from or intended for use in a violation of the law.

[49] A terrorist act includes an act which constitutes an offence within the scope of, and as defined in one of the following treaties: Convention for the Suppression of Unlawful Seizure of Aircraft; Convention for the Suppression of Unlawful Acts against the Safety of Civil Aviation; Convention on the Prevention and Punishment of Crimes against Internationally Protected Persons, Including Diplomatic Agents; International Convention against the Taking of Hostages; Convention on the Physical Protection of Nuclear Material; Protocol for the Suppression of Unlawful Acts of Violence at Airports Serving International Civil Aviation, supplementary to the Convention for the Suppression of Unlawful Acts against the Safety of Civil Aviation; Convention for the Suppression of Unlawful Acts against the Safety of Maritime Navigation; Protocol for the Suppression of Unlawful Acts against the Safety of Fixed Platforms located on the Continental Shelf; International Convention for the Suppression of Terrorist Bombings; and the International Convention for the Suppression of the Financing of Terrorism (1999).

f) The phrase those who finance terrorism refers to any person, group, undertaking or other entity that provides or collects, by any means, directly or indirectly, funds or other assets that may be used, in full or in part, to facilitate the commission of terrorist acts, or to any persons or entities acting on behalf of, or at the direction of such persons, groups, undertakings or other entities. This includes those who provide or collect funds or other assets with the intention that they should be used or in the knowledge that they are to be used, in full or in part, in order to carry out terrorist acts.

g) The term terrorist organization refers to any legal person, group, undertaking or other entity owned or controlled directly or indirectly by a terrorist(s).

h) The term designated persons refers to those persons or entities designated by the Al-Qaida and Taliban Sanctions Committee pursuant to S/RES/1267(1999) or those persons or entities designated and accepted, as appropriate, by jurisdictions pursuant to S/RES/1373(2001).

  i) The phrase without delay, for the purposes of S/RES/1267(1999), means, ideally, within a matter of hours of a designation by the Al-Qaida and Taliban Sanctions Committee. For the purposes of S/RES/1373(2001), the phrase without delay means upon having reasonable grounds, or a reasonable basis, to suspect or believe that a person or entity is a terrorist, one who finances terrorism or a terrorist organization. The phrase without delay should be interpreted in the context of the need to prevent the flight or dissipation of terrorist-linked funds or other assets, and the need for global, concerted action to interdict and disrupt their flow swiftly.

Freezing without delay terrorist-related funds or other assets

8. In order to fulfil the preventive intent of Special Recommendation III, jurisdictions should establish the necessary authority and adopt the following standards and procedures to freeze the funds or other assets of terrorists, those who finance terrorism and terrorist organizations in accordance with both S/RES/1267(1999) and S/RES/1373(2001):

a) Authority to freeze, unfreeze and prohibit dealing in funds or other assets of designated persons. Jurisdictions should prohibit by enforceable means the transfer, conversion, disposition or movement of funds or other assets. Options for providing the authority to freeze and unfreeze terrorist funds or other assets include:

  i) empowering or designating a competent authority or a court to issue, administer and enforce freezing and unfreezing actions under relevant mechanisms, or

  ii) enacting legislation that places responsibility for freezing the funds or other assets of designated persons publicly identified by a competent authority or a court on the person or entity holding the funds or other assets and subjecting them to sanctions for non-compliance. The authority to freeze and unfreeze funds or other assets should also extend to funds or other assets derived or generated from funds or other assets owned or controlled directly or indirectly by such terrorists, those who finance terrorism, or terrorist organizations. Whatever option is chosen there should be clearly identifiable competent authorities responsible for enforcing the measures. The competent authorities shall ensure that their nationals or any persons and entities within their territories are prohibited from making any funds or other assets, economic resources or financial or other related services available, directly or indirectly, wholly or jointly, for the benefit of: designated persons, terrorists; those who finance terrorism; terrorist organizations; entities owned or controlled, directly or indirectly, by such persons or entities; and persons and entities acting on behalf of or at the direction of such persons or entities.

b) Freezing procedures. Jurisdictions should develop and implement procedures to freeze the funds or other assets specified in paragraph (c) below without delay and without giving prior notice to the persons or entities concerned. Persons or entities holding such funds or other assets should be required by law to freeze them and should furthermore be subject to sanctions for non-compliance with this requirement. Any delay between the official receipt of information provided in support of a designation and the actual freezing of the funds or other assets of designated persons undermines the effectiveness of designation by affording designated persons time to remove funds or other assets from identifiable accounts and places. Consequently, these procedures must ensure (i) the prompt determination whether reasonable grounds or a reasonable basis exists to initiate an action under a freezing mechanism and (ii) the subsequent freezing of funds or other assets without delay upon determination that such grounds or basis for freezing exist. Jurisdictions should develop efficient and effective systems for communicating actions taken under their freezing mechanisms to the financial sector immediately upon taking such action. As well, they should provide clear guidance, particularly financial institutions and other persons or entities that may be holding targeted funds or other assets on obligations in taking action under freezing mechanisms.

c) Funds or other assets to be frozen or, if appropriate, seized. Under Special Recommendation III, funds or other assets to be frozen include those subject to freezing under S/RES/1267(1999) and S/RES/1373(2001). Such funds or other assets would also include those wholly or jointly owned or controlled, directly or indirectly, by designated persons. In accordance with their obligations under the United Nations International Convention for the Suppression of the Financing of Terrorism (1999) (the Terrorist Financing Convention (1999)), jurisdictions should be able to freeze or, if appropriate, seize any funds or other assets that they identify, detect, and verify, in accordance with applicable legal principles, as being used by, allocated for, or being made available to terrorists, those who finance terrorists or terrorist organizations. Freezing or seizing under the Terrorist Financing Convention (1999) may be conducted by freezing or seizing in the context of a criminal investigation or proceeding. Freezing action taken under Special Recommendation III shall be without prejudice to the rights of third parties acting in good faith.

d) De-listing and unfreezing procedures. Jurisdictions should develop and implement publicly known procedures to consider de-listing requests upon satisfaction of certain criteria consistent with international obligations and applicable legal principles, and to unfreeze the funds or other assets of de-listed persons or entities in a timely manner. For persons and entities designated under S/RES/1267(1999), such procedures and criteria should be in accordance with procedures adopted by the Al-Qaida and Taliban Sanctions Committee under S/RES/1267(1999).

e) Unfreezing upon verification of identity. For persons or entities with the same or similar name as designated persons, who are inadvertently affected by a freezing mechanism, jurisdictions should develop and implement publicly known procedures to unfreeze the funds or other assets of such persons or entities in a timely manner upon verification that the person or entity involved is not a designated person.

f) Providing access to frozen funds or other assets in certain circumstances. Where jurisdictions have determined that funds or other assets, which are otherwise subject to freezing pursuant to the obligations under S/RES/1267(1999), are necessary for basic expenses; for the payment of certain types of fees, expenses and service charges, or for extraordinary expenses, jurisdictions should authorise access to such funds or other assets in accordance with the procedures set out in S/RES/1452(2002) and subject to approval of the Al-Qaida and Taliban Sanctions Committee. On the same grounds, jurisdictions may authorise access to funds or other assets, if freezing measures are applied pursuant to S/RES/1373(2001).

g) Remedies. Jurisdictions should provide for a mechanism through which a person or an entity that is the target of a freezing mechanism in the context of terrorist financing can challenge that measure with a view to having it reviewed by a competent authority or a court.

h) Sanctions. Jurisdictions should adopt appropriate measures to monitor effectively the compliance with relevant legislation, rules or regulations governing freezing mechanisms by financial institutions and other persons or entities that may be holding funds or other assets as indicated in paragraph 8(c) above. Failure to comply with such legislation, rules or regulations should be subject to civil, administrative or criminal sanctions.

Seizure and confiscation

9. Consistent with FATF Recommendation 3, jurisdictions should adopt measures similar to those set forth in Article V of the United Nations Convention against Illicit Traffic in Narcotic Drugs and Psychotropic Substances (1988), Articles 12 to 14 of the United Nations Convention on Transnational Organised Crime (2000), and Article 8 of the Terrorist Financing Convention.

4. Reporting suspicious transactions related to terrorism

The fourth Special Recommendation places a duty on certain financial institutions to report suspicious activities to competent authorities. If financial institutions, or other businesses or entities subject to anti-money laundering obligations, suspect or have reasonable grounds to suspect that funds are linked or related to, or are to be used for terrorism, terrorist acts or by terrorist organizations, they should be required to report promptly their suspicions to the competent authorities.

This requirement applies to both financial institutions, and to the non-financial businesses and professions, as defined in The Forty Recommendations.[50] This recommendation involves reporting under two alternative circumstances: when there is a 'suspicion' that funds are linked to terrorist financing; and when there are 'reasonable grounds to suspect' that funds are linked to terrorist financing.

5. International cooperation

The fifth of the Special Recommendations provides that each State should afford another State, on the basis of a treaty, arrangement or other mechanism for mutual legal assistance or information exchange, the greatest possible measure of assistance

---

[50] FATF, Guidance Notes, at Paragraph 19.

in connection with criminal, civil enforcement, and administrative investigations, inquiries and proceedings relating to the financing of terrorism, terrorist acts and terrorist organizations. States should also take all possible measures to ensure that they do not provide safe havens for individuals charged with the financing of terrorism, terrorist acts or terrorist organizations, and should have procedures in place to extradite, where possible, such individuals.

'Mutual legal assistance' means the authority to provide a full range of legal assistance, including the taking of evidence; the search and seizure of documents or items relevant to criminal proceedings or criminal investigations; and the ability to enforce a foreign restraint, seizure, confiscation or forfeiture order in a criminal matter.[51] Exchange of information by means 'other than through mutual legal assistance' means any other arrangement, including an exchange occurring through financial intelligence units (FIUs) or other governmental agencies that exchange information bilaterally pursuant to memoranda of understanding (MOUs), exchange of letter or otherwise.[52]

6. Alternative remittance

The sixth Special Recommendation requires each State to take measures to ensure that persons or legal entities, including agents, that provide a service for the transmission of money or value, including transmission through an informal money or value transfer system or network, should be licensed or registered and subject to all the FATF Recommendations that apply to banks and non-bank financial institutions. Each State should ensure that persons or legal entities that carry out this service illegally are subject to administrative, civil or criminal sanctions.

FATF has issued an Interpretive Note as well as a set of Best Practices on Special Recommendation VI, in order to provide formal guidance and general assistance, respectively, to States on how to implement this recommendation.[53] Formal money remittance or transfer services are often provided by a distinct category of non-bank financial institutions, through which funds are moved on behalf of individuals or legal entities through a dedicated network or through the regulated banking system. For purposes of determining compliance with The Forty Recommendations, these money transmitters, which are included within the definition of the term 'financial institutions' should be subject to a State's anti-money laundering and counter-terrorism financing laws, and should be licensed or registered.[54]

---

[51] FATF, Guidance Notes, at Paragraph 24.
[52] Ibid, at Paragraph 25.
[53] See < http://www.fatf-gafi.org/dataoecd/53/34/34262291.PDF>.
[54] See Chapter 7.

7. Wire Transfers

Under the seventh Special Recommendation States need to take measures to require financial institutions, including money remitters, to include accurate and meaningful originator information (name, address, and account number) on funds transfers and related messages that are sent, and the information should remain with the transfer or related message through the payment chain. States should take measures to ensure that financial institutions, including money remitters, conduct enhanced scrutiny of and monitor for suspicious activity funds transfers which do not contain complete originator information (name, address, and account number).

8. Non-profit organizations

The eighth Recommendation sets out measures to prevent non-profit organizations as well as other legal entities and arrangements, from being misused by terrorists. It requires that each State should review the adequacy of its laws and regulations that relate to entities that can be abused for the financing of terrorism. Non-profit organizations are particularly vulnerable, and States should ensure that they cannot be misused:

- by terrorist organizations posing as legitimate entities;
- to exploit legitimate entities as conduits for terrorist financing, including for the purpose of escaping asset freezing measures; and
- to conceal or obscure the clandestine diversion of funds intended for legitimate purposes to terrorist organizations.

To that end, it identifies three areas for action by States under the recommendation:

1. Ensure financial transparency so that relevant organizations should have transparent financial records and conduct their activities in a way that can be audited and funds accounted for. Accounts should be published and disbursements of funds should be done through accounts with established financial institutions.
2. Programmatic verification should enable the organizations to know who receives funds and how they are spent and should take active steps to monitor these things. This is especially important when the recipients are in another State.
3. Promote effective administration to ensure that good records are kept for the activities of the organization and there should be clear governance structures and internal accountability.

9. Cash couriers

The ninth and final Special Recommendation requires States to have measures in place to detect the physical cross-border transportation of currency and bearer negotiable instruments, including a declaration system or other disclosure obligations. States should ensure that their competent authorities have the legal authority to stop or restrain currency or bearer negotiable instruments that are suspected to be related to terrorist financing or money laundering, or that are falsely declared or disclosed.

States should ensure that effective, proportionate, and dissuasive sanctions are available to deal with persons who make false declaration(s) or disclosure(s). In cases where the currency of bearer negotiable instruments are related to terrorist financing or money laundering, States should also adopt measures, including legislative ones consistent with Recommendation 3 and Special Recommendation III, which would enable the confiscation of such currency or instruments.

In summary, the main aim of this Special Recommendation is to ensure that terrorists and other criminals cannot finance their activities or launder the proceeds of their crimes through the transportation of currency and monetary instruments from one State to another.[55] FATF adopted a formal Interpretative Note to accompany the ninth Special Recommendation. The Interpretative Note provides a thorough definition of the terms used in the recommendation as well as a description of how a State may implement the requirements of this recommendation. FATF also adopted an International Best Practices paper, entitled 'Detecting and Preventing the Cross-Border Transportation of Cash by Terrorists and Other Criminals', to accompany this recommendation.

E. Other International Initiatives

The International Monetary Fund (IMF)

6.56 The IMF was established at the following the end of the Second World War to help promote and develop the world's economies, initially involving forty-five Member States. Today, IMF membership comprises of 184 members. Its core functions are:

- promoting international monetary cooperation;
- facilitating the expansion and balanced growth of international trade;
- promoting exchange stability;
- assisting in the establishment of a multilateral system of payments;
- making its resources available, under adequate safeguards, to members experiencing balance of payment difficulties.

---

[55] Interpretative Note to Special Recommendation IX, at Paragraph 1.

6.57 In 2004, after a twelve-month review, the IMF and the World Bank agreed they would fund a more integrated approach in the fight against terrorist financing. Part of this approach involves the delivery of technical assistance to vulnerable States. The IMF continues to provide valuable assistance to other organizations such as FATF in combating the financing of terrorism and money laundering.

The Egmont Group of Financial Intelligence Units

6.58 As part of the global money laundering efforts, governments created specialized agencies to analyse information submitted by specified entities and persons pursuant to accepted money laundering reporting requirements. These agencies are known as financial intelligent units (FIUs). These units serve as the focal point for national AML programmes as they provide for the exchange of information between financial institutions and law enforcement agencies.

6.59 In 1995, a number of FIUs began working together and formed the Egmont Group of Financial Intelligence Units (Egmont Group).[56] The main aim of the group is to provide a forum for FIUs to strengthen collaboration and the sharing of information and good practice in relation to the AML. This includes expanding and systematizing the exchange of financial intelligence information, improving expertise and capabilities of personnel, and fostering better communication among FIUs through technology.[57] The mission of the Egmont Group was expanded in 2004 to include specifically financial intelligence on terrorist financing.

6.60 To be a member of the Egmont Group, a State's FIU must first meet the Egmont FIU definition, which is

> . . . a central, national agency responsible for receiving (and, as permitted, requesting), analyzing and disseminating to the competent authorities, disclosures of financial information: (i) concerning suspected proceeds of crime and potential financing of terrorism, or (ii) required by national regulation, in order to counter money laundering and terrorist financing.[58]

6.61 A member must also commit to act in accordance with the Egmont Group's Principles for Information Exchange Between Financial Intelligence Units for Money Laundering Cases. These principles include conditions for the exchange of information, limitation on permitted uses of information, and confidentiality.

---

[56] See <http://www.egmontgroup.org/>.
[57] See Statement of Purpose, Egmont Group, available at <http://www.egmontgroup.org/files/library_egmont_docs/statement_of_purpose.pdf>.
[58] See <http://www.egmontgroup.org/info_paper_final_092003.pdf>.

Wolfsberg Group of Banks

The Wolfsberg Group is an association of twelve global banks, representing   **6.62**
primarily international private banking concerns.[59] The group, which was named
after the Château Wolfsberg in north-eastern Switzerland where the group was
formed, has established four sets of principles for private banking which cover a
range of good practices in relation to AML and related prevention and detection
mechanisms. The Group also released a statement on the suppression of the
financing of terrorism that describes the role that financial institutions should play
in combating terrorist financing, with a view toward enhancing the contribution
financial institutions can make toward this international problem.[60]

The statement emphasizes that financial institutions need to assist competent   **6.63**
authorities in fighting terrorist financing through prevention, detection, and
information sharing. This statement provides that 'know your customer' (KYC)
policies and procedures should be enhanced with searches of lists of known or
suspected terrorists. In addition, banks should play an active role in helping
governments by applying extra due diligence whenever they see suspicious or
irregular activities. Extra due diligence is especially important when customers are
engaged in sectors or activities that have been identified by competent authorities
as being used for the financing of terrorism. The statement goes on to endorse
the need for enhanced global cooperation and adoption of the FATF Special
Recommendations.

---

[59] The Wolfsberg Group consists of the following international banks: ABN Amro NV; Santander
Central Hispano SA; Bank of Tokyo-Mitsubishi Ltd; Barclays Bank; Citigroup; Credit Suisse
Group; Deutsche Bank AG; Goldman Sachs; HSBC; JP Morgan Chase; Société Générale; and UBS
AG. See <http://www.wolfsberg-principles.com/index.html>.
[60] See <http://www.wolfsberg-principles.com/financing-terrorism.html>.

7

ALTERNATIVE REMITTANCE SYSTEMS

A. Introduction	7.01	Special Recommendation VI:	
B. What is an Alternative		Interpretative Note	7.20
Remittance System?	7.07	D. Abu Dhabi Conferences	7.22
Advantages of alternative remittance		E. Other Payment Methods	7.28
systems	7.12	F. Conclusion	7.33
C. FATF Recommendations for			
Alternative Remittance Systems	7.15		

A. Introduction

Chapter 6 examined the international framework dealing with the financing of **7.01** terrorism and money laundering, in particular the responses by the UN and other bodies such as the Financial Action Task Force (FATF) to counter such financing, and the obligation on States to ensure that they had in place the necessary legislative framework to investigate and prosecute such activities.

It must be said at the outset that, to date, there have been no prosecutions specifically **7.02** relating to financing of terrorism offences—they are generally part of a case and may, if at all, be the subject of specific charges. The US practice is to proceed with charges of material support to capture such conduct or proceed with charges under revenue laws.* Therefore, the extensive efforts of the international community have been largely focused on building the intelligence picture by studying and examining the methodology and typology of the financing aspect through Financial Intelligence Units (FIUs) in order that trends can be identified and responses developed—this is particularly the case with the alternative remittance systems.[1]

---

* *Holy Land Foundation and 5 others:* On 24 November 2008 the Holy Land Foundation for Relief and Development and five defendants were convicted of a number of charges, including providing material support to a foreign terrorist organization, being engaged in prohibited financial transactions with a Specially Designated Global Terrorist, money laundering, conspiracy, and filing false tax returns. The organization and its leaders were accused of channelling some 12 million dollars to Hamas, which had been declared a terrorist group in the US in 1995.
[1] It is sometimes also referred to as a money or value transfer service.

7.03 It is difficult to precisely define terrorist financing. Terrorism can be conducted without large-scale funding and terrorist financing does not always rely on the proceeds of crime or necessarily involve money laundering. Therefore, to understand terrorist financing, it is perhaps more useful to describe the ways funds are raised, moved, and used in terrorist activity, rather than attempt to arrive at a specific definition.

7.04 The financing of terrorism must therefore be understood in two ways—first, how do terrorists finance their activities, and second, how is the money then moved? It is the second aspect that this chapter will address. Before proceeding to look at the channels for the movement of the funds, it may be useful to examine the first limb of financing.

7.05 How are terrorist activities funded? Essentially, the 'traditional' terrorist groups were local or national and their cause was, so to speak, contained within national boundaries. However, the landscape of terrorism has shifted in recent times, making it an 'international' phenomenon rather than a group solely concerned with 'local' issues. Therefore, it is inevitable that the nature of terrorist organizations has changed to reflect this reality—they are more organized and have a transnational reach. At the same time, they rely to a large extent on gathering their finance through partnership with other criminal organizations or 'setting up' their own criminal networks. In 2001, FATF identified a number of criminal activities that supported the financing of terrorism and these included: drug trafficking, kidnapping, corruption, donations being improperly channelled to terrorist acts,[2] etc.

7.06 Once the funding has been secured, it then needs to be moved to the intended recipients within the organization and this is achieved through both the formal banking channels and the informal non-banking channels, of which alternative remittance systems is one such mechanism.

B. What is an Alternative Remittance System?

7.07 An alternative remittance system is a mechanism by which money is transferred, within a country or internationally, without any reliance on banks or other financial institutions. To gain a better understanding, it may be useful to trace the development of this system.

7.08 One of the most popular mechanisms of an alternative remittance system is what is popularly referred to as the *hawala* system—which is an honour-based system where money is transferred via a network of *hawala* brokers—variations of it

---

[2] For example, an investigation into the 7 July 2005 incidents in the UK has revealed that part of the funding came from the misuse of legitimate money to a community project in Leeds. The matter has now been referred for further enquiries.

appear in most developing countries. Hitherto, such systems were largely ignored as they were either little understood or there was the lack of awareness in the financial community owing to the fact that such systems are largely culturally-based and serve a particular community. The presence of such systems is to be found in countries where formal banking is either scarce or unavailable (for example, in large parts of Africa, Asia, and South America where no banks or other financial institutions are present in remote villages), or where the financial sector is not operational due to conflicts (as in the case of Afghanistan whilst under the Taliban). In the case of developed economies, it is found in the migrant communities who regularly send money home for the upkeep of the family and find formal banking an expensive and relatively slow option.

The development of such an alternative remittance system owes largely to the **7.09** movement of people from villages to towns or indeed abroad who may well be the main wage-earner to sustain the family left behind. Prior to the relaxation in exchange controls, the prohibitive cost of banking led to the movement of funds in a parallel system and today it is used by millions of families across the world—it is therefore only logical that the informal banking has grown exponentially. Whilst it is an effective way of transferring money, it has an impact on not just the economy of a country but on the its openness to abuse by criminals and terrorists.

Hawala and other similar systems are based solely on trust and a reliable network **7.10** of connections—there is usually no audit trail or indeed any documentary proof of the transfer, minimal or no costs and money is 'transferred' to the beneficiary rapidly. The following illustrates how a *hawala* system works in practice:

> A works in country X, where the currency is the British pound, and would like to send money to B in country Y, where the currency is, for example, Bangladeshi takas. A approaches C, who is able to send the money to B and after a small fee an exchange rate is negotiated which is invariably a more favourable rate to that available through the bank.
> A would then give C the amount in sterling.
> C then contacts D in country Y, and gives him the details.
> D arranges to have the equivalent in Bangladeshi taka delivered to B.

Throughout this transaction there has been no audit trail and it is based on **7.11** trust between the parties. There is no requirement on A or B to have a bank account as the money is handed over in person. Such a transaction can be completed within a matter of minutes as opposed to the formal mechanisms that usually require a number of days and would not have the advantage of delivery to the recipient in person with no additional costs. The advantages of such a system are immediately apparent. The *hawala* system is widely used in the United Arab Emirates where there is a large migrant population, in the UK, and in Asia generally.

An example of how a similar system works in southern and eastern Africa was examined by the Eastern and Southern Africa Anti-Money Laundering Group (ESAAMLG) under a study conducted by the International Monetary Fund (IMF). The study found that large numbers of workers from Malawi, Mozambique, and Zambia working in South Africa generally left members of their families behind and as the main bread-winners, it led to the emergence of the informal 'banking' whereby money would be handed to the bus driver who would then hand it over to the families in the respective countries. This practice again illustrates the advantages to the community of rapid and cheap remittance.

Advantages of alternative remittance systems

7.12 Thus, the advantages of the alternative remittance systems such as *hawala*, or its equivalent in other parts of the world, can be broadly summarized as follows:

- As mentioned above, it is cost effective as the usually high banking costs do not form part of it.

- The system is efficient, as such transactions usually take place within a matter of hours compared to the time taken through the formal channels. The IMF study found that the *hawala* system operating in Afghanistan (the only active financial market) was able to transfer money from Kabul to surrounding cities within 6–12 hours, and slightly longer for delivery of money to villages and the more remote regions. The Afghanistan experience illustrates the importance of the informal system where the country has no formal banking to speak of. The study revealed that the *hawala* system was widely adopted by NGOs, donors, and development agencies in the absence of a banking system.

- Integral to the proper functioning of the system is trust and reliability. The studies show that it is rare for a *hawala* transaction not to be honoured—whether that is through the bus driver in South Africa or the dealer in Kabul.

- Another advantage is the absence of scrutiny—herein lies its weakness, too, for the system works on anonymity in that the authorities may not even be aware of the person's presence in the country. For example, if an illegal migrant wanted to transfer money to his family, there is no requirement on him to have a bank account or indeed any official documentation. The alternative remittance system dispenses with such formality and all that is required is payment in cash to the dealer or the person who will subsequently deliver the money. It therefore follows that criminals or terrorists may remit money with ease, safe in the knowledge that it is unlikely to be easily detected.

- Also of benefit to the sender and the 'dealer'—there is no audit trail and apart from a 'rough' accounting mechanism, the dealers would hardly submit such 'book-keeping' to the authorities. This avoids any tax implications for the dealer. At the same time, the sender is secure in the knowledge that the exchange rate works to his benefit and the costs are minimal. It is this aspect of the alternative remittance system that has proved to be most challenging both to intelligence and investigation agencies.

The benefits to a community of such informal transfers is immediately recog- **7.13** nized, however as stated above, it has become a vehicle of abuse by those either wishing to launder the proceeds of their criminality, or move their funds to finance their criminal conduct, including terrorism. Such a system offers them an inexpensive, anonymous, and virtually non-traceable transaction—this was recognized by the international intelligence units leading to the adoption of the 9 FATF Special Recommendations on Terrorist Financing thereby supplementing the 40 FATF Recommendations adopted initially in 1990 and subsequently amended in 1996. Following the events of 11 September 2001, FATF extended its mandate to look at typologies relating to the financing of terrorism and issued 8 Special Recommendations on Terrorist Financing followed shortly by the ninth recommendation relating to cash couriers—taken together, these are now the 9 Special Recommendations recognized by the international community as the current best practice in dealing with the financing of terrorism. Of course as new typologies are identified the recommendations are amended to reflect the trend. The Special Recommendations recognize alternative remittance systems[3] as a means of moving funds and provide for measures which should be adopted by States to prevent the abuse of such systems.

The establishment and the role of FATF has been examined in detail in the previ- **7.14** ous chapter, but it is worth setting out the key recommendations relating to the financing of terrorism. As stated previously, FATF was initially concerned with thelaunderingofdrug-traffickingproceedsandsotheoriginal40Recommendations focus on that; however, those are now as much part of the framework dealing with the 'detection, prevention and suppression' of the financing of terrorism and must be read together with the 9 Special Recommendations.

C. FATF Recommendations for Alternative Remittance Systems

In addition to the Recommendations, FATF have produced interpretative notes **7.15** to the 9 Special Recommendations which are extremely useful in understanding the mischief they seek to address. For ease of reference, they are set out in full in relation to the alternative remittance systems.

---

[3] Special Recommendation VI.

7.16 The relevant Recommendations contained in the original 40 Recommendations[4] are Recommendations 4–16 and 21–25 which provide as follows:

> *Recommendation 4*: 'Countries should ensure that financial institution secrecy laws do not inhibit implementation of the FATF Recommendations.'
>
> *Recommendation 5* deals with customer due diligence and record-keeping and states:
>
> Financial institutions should not keep anonymous accounts or accounts in obviously fictitious names. Financial institutions should undertake customer due diligence measures, including identifying and verifying the identity of their customers, when:
>
> - establishing business relations;
> - carrying out occasional transactions: (i) above the applicable designated threshold; or (ii) that are wire transfers in the circumstances covered by the Interpretative Note to Special Recommendation VII;
> - there is a suspicion of money laundering or terrorist financing; or
> - the financial institution has doubts about the veracity or adequacy of previously obtained customer identification data.
>
> The customer due diligence (CDD) measures to be taken are as follows:
>
> (a) Identifying the customer and verifying that customer's identity using reliable, independent source documents, data or information.
> (b) Identifying the beneficial owner, and taking reasonable measures to verify the identity of the beneficial owner such that the financial institution is satisfied that it knows who the beneficial owner is. For legal persons and arrangements this should include financial institutions taking reasonable measures to understand the ownership and control structure of the customer.
> (c) Obtaining information on the purpose and intended nature of the business relationship.
> (d) Conducting ongoing due diligence on the business relationship and scrutiny of transactions undertaken throughout the course of that relationship to ensure that the transactions being conducted are consistent with the institution's knowledge of the customer, their business and risk profile, including, where necessary, the source of funds. Financial institutions should apply each of the CDD measures under (a) to (d) above, but may determine the extent of such measures on a risk sensitive basis depending on the type of customer, business relationship or transaction. The measures that are taken should be consistent with any guidelines issued by competent authorities. For higher risk categories, financial institutions should perform enhanced due diligence. In certain circumstances, where there are low risks, countries may decide that financial institutions can apply reduced or simplified measures.
>
> Financial institutions should verify the identity of the customer and beneficial owner before or during the course of establishing a business relationship or conducting transactions for occasional customers. Countries may permit financial institutions to complete the verification as soon as reasonably practicable following the establishment of the relationship, where the money laundering risks are effectively managed and where this is essential not to interrupt the normal conduct of business.

---

[4] The FATF Recommendations, interpretive notes and best practice can be readily accessed through the FATF website at <http://www.fatf-gafi.org>.

Where the financial institution is unable to comply with paragraphs (a) to (c) above, it should not open the account, commence business relations or perform the transaction; or should terminate the business relationship; and should consider making a suspicious transactions report in relation to the customer.

These requirements should apply to all new customers, though financial institutions should also apply this Recommendation to existing customers on the basis of materiality and risk, and should conduct due diligence on such existing relationships at appropriate times.

Recommendation 6:

Financial institutions should, in relation to politically exposed persons, in addition to performing normal due diligence measures:

(a) Have appropriate risk management systems to determine whether thecustomer is a politically exposed person.

(b) Obtain senior management approval for establishing business relationships with such customers.

(c) Take reasonable measures to establish the source of wealth and source of funds.

(d) Conduct enhanced ongoing monitoring of the business relationship.

Recommendation 7:

Financial institutions should, in relation to cross-border correspondent banking and other similar relationships, in addition to performing normal due diligence measures:

(a) Gather sufficient information about a respondent institution to understand fully the nature of the respondent's business and to determine from publicly available information the reputation of the institution and the quality of supervision, including whether it has been subject to a money laundering or terrorist financing investigation or regulatory action.

(b) Assess the respondent institution's anti-money laundering and terrorist financing controls.

(c) Obtain approval from senior management before establishing new correspondent relationships.

(d) Document the respective responsibilities of each institution.

(e) With respect to 'payable-through accounts', be satisfied that the respondent bank has verified the identity of and performed ongoing due diligence on the customers having direct access to accounts of the correspondent and that it is able to provide relevant customer identification data upon request to the correspondent bank.

Recommendation 8:

Financial institutions should pay special attention to any money laundering threats that may arise from new or developing technologies that might favour anonymity, and take measures, if needed, to prevent their use in money laundering schemes. In particular, financial institutions should have policies and procedures in place to address any specific risks associated with non face-to-face business relationships or transactions.

Recommendation 9:

Countries may permit financial institutions to rely on intermediaries or other third parties to perform elements (a)–(c) of the CDD process or to introduce business, provided that the criteria set out below are met. Where such reliance is permitted, the ultimate responsibility for customer identification and verification remains with the financial institution relying on the third party.

The criteria that should be met are as follows:

(a) A financial institution relying upon a third party should immediately obtain the necessary information concerning elements (a)–(c) of the CDD process. Financial institutions should take adequate steps to satisfy themselves that copies of identification data and other relevant documentation relating to the CDD requirements will be made available from the third party upon request without delay.

(b) The financial institution should satisfy itself that the third party is regulated and supervised for, and has measures in place to comply with CDD requirements in line with Recommendations 5 and 10.

It is left to each country to determine in which countries the third party that meets the conditions can be based, having regard to information available on countries that do not or do not adequately apply the FATF Recommendations.

Recommendation 10:
Financial institutions should maintain, for at least five years, all necessary records on transactions, both domestic or international, to enable them to comply swiftly with information requests from the competent authorities. Such records must be sufficient to permit reconstruction of individual transactions (including the amounts and types of currency involved if any) so as to provide, if necessary, evidence for prosecution of criminal activity.

Financial institutions should keep records on the identification data obtained through the customer due diligence process (eg copies or records of official identification documents like passports, identity cards, driving licenses or similar documents), account files and business correspondence for at least five years after the business relationship is ended.

The identification data and transaction records should be available to domestic competent authorities upon appropriate authority.

Recommendation 11:
Financial institutions should pay special attention to all complex, unusual large transactions, and all unusual patterns of transactions, which have no apparent economic or visible lawful purpose. The background and purpose of such transactions should, as far as possible, be examined, the findings established in writing, and be available to help competent authorities and auditors.

Recommendation 12:
The customer due diligence and record-keeping requirements set out in Recommendations 5, 6, and 8 to 11 apply to designated non-financial businesses and professions in the following situations:

(a) Casinos—when customers engage in financial transactions equal to or above the applicable designated threshold.

(b) Real estate agents—when they are involved in transactions for their client concerning the buying and selling of real estate.

(c) Dealers in precious metals and dealers in precious stones—when they engage in any cash transaction with a customer equal to or above the applicable designated threshold.

(d) Lawyers, notaries, other independent legal professionals and accountants when they prepare for or carry out transactions for their client concerning the following activities:

- buying and selling of real estate;
- managing of client money, securities or other assets;

- management of bank, savings or securities accounts;
- organisation of contributions for the creation, operation or management of companies;
- creation, operation or management of legal persons or arrangements, and buying and selling of business entities.

(e) Trust and company service providers when they prepare for or carry out transactions for a client concerning the activities listed in the definition in the Glossary.

Recommendation 13 addresses the reporting of suspicious transactions and compliance:

If a financial institution suspects or has reasonable grounds to suspect that funds are the proceeds of a criminal activity, or are related to terrorist financing, it should be required, directly by law or regulation, to report promptly its suspicions to the financial intelligence unit (FIU).

Recommendation 14:
Financial institutions, their directors, officers and employees should be:

(a) Protected by legal provisions from criminal and civil liability for breach of any restriction on disclosure of information imposed by contract or by any legislative, regulatory or administrative provision, if they report their suspicions in good faith to the FIU, even if they did not know precisely what the underlying criminal activity was, and regardless of whether illegal activity actually occurred.

(b) Prohibited by law from disclosing the fact that a suspicious transaction report (STR) or related information is being reported to the FIU.

Recommendation 15:
Financial institutions should develop programmes against money laundering and terrorist financing. These programmes should include:

(a) The development of internal policies, procedures and controls, including appropriate compliance management arrangements, and adequate screening procedures to ensure high standards when hiring employees.

(b) An ongoing employee training programme.

(c) An audit function to test the system.

Recommendation 16:
The requirements set out in Recommendations 13 to 15, and 21 apply to all designated non-financial businesses and professions, subject to the following qualifications:

(a) Lawyers, notaries, other independent legal professionals and accountants should be required to report suspicious transactions when, on behalf of or for a client, they engage in a financial transaction in relation to the activities described in Recommendation 12(d). Countries are strongly encouraged to extend the reporting requirement to the rest of the professional activities of accountants, including auditing.

(b) Dealers in precious metals and dealers in precious stones should be required to report suspicious transactions when they engage in any cash transaction with a customer equal to or above the applicable designated threshold.

(c) Trust and company service providers should be required to report suspicious transactions for a client when, on behalf of or for a client, they engage in a transaction in relation to the activities referred to Recommendation 12(e).

Lawyers, notaries, other independent legal professionals, and accountants acting as independent legal professionals, are not required to report their suspicions if the relevant information was obtained in circumstances where they are subject to professional secrecy or legal professional privilege.

Recommendation 21:

Financial institutions should give special attention to business relationships and transactions with persons, including companies and financial institutions, from countries which do not or insufficiently apply the FATF Recommendations. Whenever these transactions have no apparent economic or visible lawful purpose, their background and purpose should, as far as possible, be examined, the findings established in writing, and be available to help competent authorities. Where such a country continues not to apply or insufficiently applies the FATF Recommen-dations, countries should be able to apply appropriate countermeasures.

Recommendation 22:

Financial institutions should ensure that the principles applicable to financial institutions, which are mentioned above are also applied to branches and majority owned subsidiaries located abroad, especially in countries which do not or insufficiently apply the FATF Recommendations, to the extent that local applicable laws and regulations permit. When local applicable laws and regulations prohibit this implementation, competent authorities in the country of the parent institution should be informed by the financial institutions that they cannot apply the FATF Recommendations.

Recommendation 23:

Countries should ensure that financial institutions are subject to adequate regulation and supervision and are effectively implementing the FATF Recommendations. Competent authorities should take the necessary legal or regulatory measures to prevent criminals or their associates from holding or being the beneficial owner of a significant or controlling interest or holding a management function in a financial institution.

For financial institutions subject to the Core Principles, the regulatory and supervisory measures that apply for prudential purposes and which are also relevant to money laundering, should apply in a similar manner for anti-money laundering and terrorist financing purposes.

Other financial institutions should be licensed or registered and appropriately regulated, and subject to supervision or oversight for anti-money laundering purposes, having regard to the risk of money laundering or terrorist financing in that sector. At a minimum, businesses providing a service of money or value transfer, or of money or currency changing should be licensed or registered, and subject to effective systems for monitoring and ensuring compliance with national requirements to combat money laundering and terrorist financing.

Recommendation 24:

Designated non-financial businesses and professions should be subject to regulatory and supervisory measures as set out below.

(a) Casinos should be subject to a comprehensive regulatory and supervisory regime that ensures that they have effectively implemented the necessary anti-money laundering and terrorist-financing measures. At a minimum:

- casinos should be licensed;
- competent authorities should take the necessary legal or regulatory measures to prevent criminals or their associates from holding or being the beneficial owner of a significant or controlling interest, holding a management function in, or being an operator of a casino;

- competent authorities should ensure that casinos are effectively supervised for compliance with requirements to combat money laundering and terrorist financing.

(b) Countries should ensure that the other categories of designated non-financial businesses and professions are subject to effective systems for monitoring and ensuring their compliance with requirements to combat money laundering and terrorist financing. This should be performed on a risk-sensitive basis. This may be performed by a government authority or by an appropriate self-regulatory organisation, provided that such an organisation can ensure that its members comply with their obligations to combat money laundering and terrorist financing.

Recommendation 25:
The competent authorities should establish guidelines, and provide feedback which will assist financial institutions and designated non-financial businesses and professions in applying national measures to combat money laundering and terrorist financing, and in particular, in detecting and reporting suspicious transactions.

Turning now to the Special Recommendation, in particular Special Recommenda- **7.17** tion VI which addresses alternative remittance systems and provides as follows:

Each country should take measures to ensure that persons or legal entities, including agents, that provide a service for the transmission of money or value, including transmission through an informal money or value transfer system or network, should be licensed or registered and subject to all the FATF Recommendations that apply to banks and non-bank financial institutions. Each country should ensure that persons or legal entities that carry out this service illegally are subject to administrative, civil or criminal sanctions.

The Recommendation aims to treat *hawala* and other dealers in a manner similar **7.18** to that adopted for banks and non-banks by requiring the licensing or registration of such dealers so that their activities are transparent and can be subject to scrutiny. The difficulty, however, lies in the fact that it is not necessary for a person to go to a dealer to transfer money as demonstrated by the bus driver example in the case of southern Africa, or indeed in countries where reliance is placed on strong family and community ties. For example, a person wishing to remit money from the UAE, UK, or elsewhere where there is a close-knit migrant community would simply rely on the connections within the family or community to remit the money to their dependants, or indeed for the purposes of financing acts of terrorism (where this is easily achieved when one considers the current wave of terrorism linked to strong religious and ideological beliefs engendering an environment of 'community'). It may well be that in such circumstances the Special Recommendation IX on cash couriers is of relevance.

The challenges facing both the intelligence gathering and investigation of the **7.19** financing of terrorism cannot be underestimated. These practical challenges were the subject of the Abu Dhabi Conferences held in 2002 and 2004 (discussed below).

Special Recommendation VI: Interpretative Note

7.20 Turning to the accompanying interpretative note to the Special Recommendation VI, it sets out in detail the components of Special Recommendation VI and the measures it recommends States should adopt in order to deal effectively with the financing of terrorism through this means. The note is self-explanatory and provides as follows:

Interpretative Note to Special Recommendation VI: Alternative Remittance

General

1. Money or value transfer systems have shown themselves vulnerable to misuse for money laundering and terrorist financing purposes. The objective of Special Recommendation VI is to increase the transparency of payment flows by ensuring that jurisdictions impose consistent anti-money laundering and counter-terrorist financing measures on all forms of money/value transfer systems, particularly those traditionally operating outside the conventional financial sector and not currently subject to the FATF Recommendations. This Recommendation and Interpretative Note underscore the need to bring all money or value transfer services, whether formal or informal, within the ambit of certain minimum legal and regulatory requirements in accordance with the relevant FATF Recommendations.

2. Special Recommendation VI consists of three core elements:

a. Jurisdictions should require licensing or registration of persons (natural or legal) that provide money/value transfer services, including through informal systems;

b. Jurisdictions should ensure that money/value transmission services, including informal systems (as described in paragraph 5 below), are subject to applicable FATF Forty Recommendations (2003) (in particular, Recommendations 4–16 and 21–25) and the Eight Special Recommen-dations (in particular SR VII); and

c. Jurisdictions should be able to impose sanctions on money/value transfer services, including informal systems, that operate without a license or registration and that fail to comply with relevant FATF Recommen-dations.

Scope and application

3. For the purposes of this Recommendation, the following definitions are used.

4. Money or value transfer service refers to a financial service that accepts cash, cheques, other monetary instruments or other stores of value in one location and pays a corresponding sum in cash or other form to a beneficiary in another location by means of a communication, message, transfer or through a clearing network to which the money/value transfer service belongs. Transactions performed by such services can involve one or more intermediaries and a third party final payment.

5. A money or value transfer service may be provided by persons (natural or legal) formally through the regulated financial system or informally through non-bank financial institutions or other business entities or any other mechanism either through the regulated financial system (for example, use of bank accounts) or through a network or mechanism that operates outside the regulated system. In some jurisdictions, informal systems are frequently referred to as alternative remittance services or underground (or parallel)

banking systems. Often these systems have ties to particular geographic regions and are therefore described using a variety of specific terms. Some examples of these terms include *hawala, hundi, fei-chien,* and the *black market peso exchange.*

6. Licensing means a requirement to obtain permission from a designated competent authority in order to operate a money/value transfer service legally.

7. Registration in this Recommendation means a requirement to register with or declare to a designated competent authority the existence of a money/value transfer service in order for the business to operate legally.

8. The obligation of licensing or registration applies to agents. At a minimum, the principal business must maintain a current list of agents which must be made available to the designated competent authority. An *agent* is any person who provides money or value transfer service under the direction of or by contract with a legally registered or licensed remitter (for example, licensees, franchisees, concessionaires).

Applicability of Special Recommendation VI

9. Special Recommendation VI should apply to all persons (natural or legal), which conduct for or on behalf of another person (natural or legal) the types of activity described in paragraphs 4 and 5 above as a primary or substantial part of their business or when such activity is undertaken on a regular or recurring basis, including as an ancillary part of a separate business enterprise.

10. Jurisdictions need not impose a separate licensing / registration system or designate another competent authority in respect to persons (natural or legal) already licensed or registered as financial institutions (as defined by the FATF Forty Recommendations (2003)) within a particular jurisdiction, which under such license or registration are permitted to perform activities indicated in paragraphs 4 and 5 above and which are already subject to the full range of applicable obligations under the FATF Forty Recommendations (2003) (in particular, Recommendations 4–16 and 21–25) and the Eight Special Recommendations (in particular SR VII).

Licensing or Registration and Compliance

11. Jurisdictions should designate an authority to grant licences and/or carry out registration and ensure that the requirement is observed. There should be an authority responsible for ensuring compliance by money/value transfer services with the FATF Recommendations (including the Eight Special Recommendations). There should also be effective systems in place for monitoring and ensuring such compliance. This interpretation of Special Recommendation VI (ie, the need for designation of competent authorities) is consistent with FATF Recommendation 23.

Sanctions

12. Persons providing money/value transfer services without a license or registration should be subject to appropriate administrative, civil or criminal sanctions. Licensed or registered money/value transfer services which fail to comply fully with the relevant measures called for in the FATF Forty Recommendations (2003) or the Eight Special Recommendations should also be subject to appropriate sanctions.

As discussed above, the challenges faced by the law enforcement agencies in the **7.21** detection and investigation of such activity was the subject of a conference held in

Abu Dhabi[5] in 2002 and a second conference in 2004. Both conferences aimed to deal with the regulation of alternative remittance systems (in particular the *hawala* system and how best the Special Recommendation VI could be adopted in order to have a meaningful response), as well as develop a detailed understanding of such systems.

D. Abu Dhabi Conferences

7.22 The Declaration from the first conference of 2002 concluded as follows:

1. Recognizing the need to better understand *Hawala* and other informal remittance systems and to ensure that this system is not abused by money launderers and terrorist financiers, the Government of the United Arab Emirates brought together experts and representatives of international and regional bodies and regulatory and law enforcement agencies, as well as bankers and money changers, in Abu Dhabi on May 15–16, 2002.

2. The word '*Hawala*' comes originally from the Arabic language and means transfer or remittance, but in this context refers specifically to informal money or value transfer systems or networks outside the formal financial sector.

3. The conference participants agreed that *Hawala* and other informal remittance systems have many positive aspects and that most of the activities conducted by *Hawaladars* (*Hawala* Operators) relate to legitimate business. *Hawala* provides a fast and cost-effective method for worldwide remittance of money or value, particularly for persons who may be outside the reach of the financial sector.

4. However, the participants also raised concerns about *Hawala* and other informal remittance systems, noting that a lack of transparency and accountability, as well as the absence of governmental supervisions, presents the potential for abuse by criminal elements.

5. In light of these concerns, the participants agreed:

- Countries should adopt the 40 Recommendations of the Financial Action Task Force (FATF) on Money Laundering and the 8 Special Recommendations on Terrorist Financing in relation to remitters, including *Hawaladars* and other alternative remittance providers.
- Countries should designate competent supervisory authorities to monitor and enforce the application of these recommendations to *Hawaladars* and other alternative remittance providers.
- Regulations should be effective but not overly restrictive.
- The continued success in strengthening the international financial system and combating money laundering and terrorist financing requires the close support and unwavering commitment of the international community.
- The international community should remain seized with the issue and should continue to work individually and collectively to regulate the *Hawala* system for legitimate commerce and to prevent its exploitation or misuse by criminals and others.

---

[5] The conferences were hosted by the United Arab Emirates (Central Bank) in collaboration with the IMF.

6. The participants wish to express their deep appreciation to the Government of the United Arab Emirates and particularly the Central Bank for their leadership in hosting this groundbreaking conference.

The Conference recognized the need for regulatory action. However, it acknowledged the fact that as such systems can be administered without the need for dealers, there is a grave danger that in imposing such regulations, the entire informal system through *hawala* and other similar mechanisms would simply go further 'underground' and would be counter-productive.   **7.23**

The Second International Conference in 2004[6] developed the 2002 Declaration   **7.24** and again was unable to reach any key decisions on how such systems should be regulated. The Second Conference recognized the importance of such a system being available to migrant communities (in the UAE, in particular, which relies heavily on a migrant population) and further:

- The Conference acknowledged and reaffirmed the important achievements of the First International Conference on *Hawala* as set out in the Abu Dhabi Declaration on *Hawala* (May 2002).
- The Conference recognized the key role that *hawala* and other informal funds transfer (IFT) systems play in facilitating remittances, particularly those of migrant workers. It noted, as well, the significance of IFT systems as an integral part of the international financial system.
- A major outcome of the Conference was its contribution in increasing awareness of the role of IFT systems. Participants emphasized that IFT systems need to be understood against the diversity of socio-cultural, legal, and economic contexts. Nevertheless, IFT systems, like other parts of the financial system, can also be misused for illegal purposes, and participants therefore re-emphasized the need for transparency and traceability of financial transactions. Furthermore, acknowledging the work of the Financial Action Task Force (FATF) in development standards and best practices in this area, the Conference highlighted the range of experience, practices, and approaches that could apply.
- The Conference identified the following challenges in implementing IFT regulatory regimes:
  - Overcoming imperfect information on the functioning IFT systems;
  - Ensuring authorities have adequate resources in dealing with this issue;
  - Designing regulatory solutions that are proportionate to the risks and sensitive to possible unintended consequences.
  - Avoiding over-regulation that might drive IFT operations underground; and
  - Demonstrating to the participants in IFT systems that the benefits of regulation outweigh the costs.
- With the aim of addressing these challenges, the Conference concluded that there was a need to:
  - Gather and analyze information on IFT systems and their operations;
  - Engage in a dialogue with IFT providers and users to develop constructive solutions;

---

[6] Held in Abu Dhabi, 3–5 April 2004.

- Conduct outreach to raise the awareness of the regulated community and public to IFT issues; and
- Remove any impediments to cost-effective, reliable, and convenient transmission of funds in the regulated financial sector.
  - Where IFT systems are permitted, countries should as a first step register and/or license IFT operators. Further anti-money laundering and combating the financing of terrorism (AML/CFT) requirements should then be implemented in the IFT sector by countries according to their capacity.
  - Finally, the Conference encouraged the FATF and the international financial institutions to take note of the conclusions of this Conference and work to develop further guidance.
  - The Conference expressed its gratitude to the Government and Central Bank of the United Arab Emirates, and the International Monetary Fund for organizing the Conference.

7.25 There are at present no new guidelines on the *hawala* system following the 2004 Conference—this is understandable given the real challenges the system poses and States are now aiming to regulate such activity through legislative and administrative measures.

7.26 There has however been the adoption of Special Recommendation IX and the accompanying 'international best practices' dealing with cash couriers and aims to address the physical transfer of cash across borders through stricter border checks and immediate confiscation of cash. Such measures have been adopted through domestic legislation in a number of countries—including Nigeria, South Africa, the UK, and the US.

7.27 The alternative remittance systems discussed above illustrate the practical difficulties in the gathering of evidence for the purposes of prosecution and provides some explanation as to the lack of case law dealing with the financing of terrorism. It does however assist in developing the intelligence picture which in turn informs the response of the international community.

E. Other Payment Methods

7.28 The systems discussed above focused on a cash-based transfer of money—where it is handed to an individual for ultimate delivery to the recipient. As with all financial markets, there is a move towards electronic transactions and given that alternative remittance systems can generally work through most mediums—electronic transfers, precious metals, and gemstones—essentially anything of value can be transferred through this mechanism.

7.29 In respect of electronic transfers, Special Recommendation VII dealing with wire transfers provides:

> Countries should take measures to require financial institutions, including money remitters, to include accurate and meaningful originator information (name, address

and account number) on funds transfers and related messages that are sent, and the information should remain with the transfer or related message through the payment chain.

Countries should take measures to ensure that financial institutions, including money remitters, conduct enhanced scrutiny of and monitor for suspicious activity funds transfers which do not contain complete originator information (name, address and account number).

The recommendation places an onus on remitters to conduct enhanced scrutiny **7.30** and ensure there is sufficient originator information—this would therefore place an obligation on remitters such as Western Union but it is not clear to what extent it would capture transfer of small amounts of money being transferred (ie, in one day). For example, a person can quite feasibly attend ten or more remitters in a day and transfer small amounts that may not necessarily raise any suspicion as individual transactions, but taken together could lead to the transfer of a sizeable amount—this could permit the transfer of funds for terrorist acts through legitimate means.

In 2006, FATF issued a report dealing with what it describes as 'New Payment **7.31** Methods' (NPM)[7] as a means of financing of terrorism which include transfers through the internet. The report identified the following methods of payments:

- pre-paid payment cards
- electronic purses
- mobile payments—these comprise of payments reliant on a bank account as well as payments which do not require a bank account
- digital precious metals.

The Report[8] examined each of these methods in detail and highlights the practical challenges in the investigation of such payment methods.

In essence most of these mechanisms have little or no face-to-face contact and in **7.32** the case of electronic purses or pre-paid payment cards simply require the purchase of the card—in that sense they share the same features of anonymity as discussed above. The challenges are therefore similar to that faced in the systems discussed above with the added difficulty of the use of the Internet. Like all Internet traffic, more than one service provider may be involved in a single transmission and depending on the location and applicable law for the service provider, this may vary greatly. This in turn creates difficulties when investigating or prosecuting such cases as it could give rise to competing jurisdictions, or the lack of

---

[7] NPM includes payment methods that were available but have simply been extended, as well as new methods.

[8] The full report can be accessed on the FATF website at <http://www.fatf-gafi.org/dataoecd/30/47/37627240.pdf>.

regulatory controls in a jurisdiction, which may have the result of frustrating an investigation or prosecution.

F. Conclusion

7.33 Alternative remittance systems, in whatever guise, present a real challenge in detecting and prosecuting the financing of terrorism. As discussed, the financing element of an investigation may usually either have intelligence value or it may form part of the background to a case rather than specific charges. Nevertheless, its importance must not be underestimated, particularly when all acts of terrorism rely on financing of one sort or another.

8

HUMAN RIGHTS IN THE CONTEXT OF COUNTER-TERRORISM

A. International Human Rights Law and International Humanitarian Law	8.02	E. The Rights Likely to be Engaged During the Course of an Investigation	8.46
B. The Sources of IHRL	8.07	Right to life	8.46
C. Extra-Territorial Reach of Human Rights Instruments	8.15	Prohibition on torture	8.52
		Arbitrary, prolonged, and indefinite detention	8.94
D. The Nature of the Rights Engaged	8.30	Right to a fair trial	8.107
What amounts to an absolute right	8.32	F. Privacy, Confidentiality, and Personal Information Issues	8.113
Who comprises 'the State'?	8.42		

The aim of this chapter is to give an overview of the engagement of human rights **8.01** law within the law enforcement measures when dealing with acts of terrorism rather than the use of force or military response to such acts. The laws of war or international humanitarian law (IHL) govern the conduct of the latter response and the establishment of the controversial detention facility at Guantanamo Bay which is governed exclusively by the laws of war.[1]

A. International Human Rights Law and International Humanitarian Law

It is, however, important to say at the outset that there have been some attempts **8.02** to merge the two disciplines[2] within the context of counter-terrorism, in particular,

---

[1] For a detailed study on international human rights law (IHRL) and IHL, readers are referred to other texts dealing exclusively with those subjects.

[2] *R v Abdullah Ibrahim El-Faisal* No: 03/1860/C2, [2004] EWCA Crim 343; *R v Abu Hamza* [2006] EWCA Crim 2118.

on the arguments being raised by defence on the issue of self-defence. It may assist to be aware of the application of IHL for the following reasons:

1. Though acts of terrorism have traditionally fallen almost exclusively within the ambit of law enforcement, this is no longer the case;
2. The UN Security Council determined that the events of 9/11 posed a threat to 'international peace and security';
3. All subsequent UNSCRs have determined that acts of terrorism are a threat to 'international peace and security';
4. Acts of terrorism represent a unique class of offences as, in addition to general criminal law, they may engage the laws of armed conflict.

8.03 In both *El-Faisal* and *Abu Hamza*, the defendants were charged with offences, inter alia, of soliciting to murder. Each encouraged his audience to wage Jihad against the enemies of Islam. At their appeals and trials respectively, they submitted that these were no more than words calling to kill in the course of an armed conflict and, therefore, did not amount to solicitation. The Court of Appeal rejected the argument and agreed with the trial judge's ruling in the case of *Abu Hamza*:

> Ground 10 raised issues the judge's directions about the circumstances in which killing, following the breakdown of the ordinary principles of law and order, whether by way of civil war, or armed conflict, should be approached. The way in which Mr Fitzgerald put his submission was that this was the kind of case to be equated with a defence of killing on the battle field. If that was what the appellant was exhorting, then it was not unlawful killing. Therefore, he was not soliciting to murder, and therefore the offence did not arise. We have read four pages of the judge's direction to the jury on this issue and it was impeccable. The judge distinguished between lawful killing, that is to say killing in self-defence or in defence of another person, and contrasted it with retaliation or counterattack . . .

He went on:

> . . . it is not the law that armed people participating in that kind of conflict cannot commit murder. An aggressive killing, other than in self-defence, in the course of such conflict is murder. There is no exception for such a situation.

That in law was an accurate direction. [Judge LJ][3]

8.04 It may assist if one looks at the historical development of IHRL[4] and IHL to gain an understanding of how the two disciplines evolved and their inter-relationship. It is often the view that IHL is *lex specialis* and, consequently, the two disciplines are mutually exclusive. However, given that both are aimed at the protection of citizens/civilians, it would be somewhat short-sighted to treat them as such.

[3] Para 14 of the judgment.
[4] International Human Rights Law.

The development of IHRL and IHL are largely attributable to the events of the Second World War and the subsequent emergence of the United Nations.

IHRL governs the relationship between a State and its citizens and is applicable **8.05** both in peacetime and during an armed conflict. For example, the prohibition on torture, the prohibition on death in custody, the right to a fair trial have resulted mainly from the grave violations of the rights of citizens by some States, in particular, by denying their citizens the most fundamental of rights; the right to life. The Holocaust and, more recently, the genocide in Rwanda are particularly poignant examples of a State's ability to violate this basic right whilst at the same time granting itself immunity from any legal process within its national jurisdiction.

IHL, sometimes referred to as the law of armed conflict, on the other hand, seeks **8.06** to protect civilians[5] during an armed conflict and limit the effects of war through controlling the methods and means of warfare. Such protected persons are entitled to enjoy legal guarantees (right to habeas corpus etc) as well as prohibition on torture etc. To that extent, the corpus of IHL seeks to provide the protection that would normally be available under IHRL, albeit that it is limited to the absolute rights under IHRL. It would, therefore, come into play where terrorist/ counter-terrorism acts arise in the context of the use of force[6]. IHL is made up of a number of conventions[7] but the key instruments are four Geneva Conventions of 1948 and the two Additional Protocols of 1977 relating to the protection of victims of armed conflicts. A key distinction from IHRL is that IHL obligations apply to all parties to a conflict—State and non-State organs; by contrast IHRL is generally only applicable to a State and its organs.

B. The Sources of IHRL

The primary source of IHRL is the UN Charter, which specifically recognizes **8.07** human rights in the Preamble, a section of which states as follows:

> We the peoples of the United Nations determined to save succeeding generations from the scourge of war, which twice in our lifetime has brought untold sorrow to mankind, and to reaffirm faith in fundamental human rights, in the dignity and worth of the human person, in the equal rights of men and women and of nations large and small, and to establish conditions under which justice and respect for the obligations arising from treaties

---

[5] Including those no longer taking part in hostilities.

[6] The Inter-American Court has on numerous occasions examined the application of IHL within the context of counter-terrorism.

[7] For example, the Torture Convention, Genocide Convention, 1954 Convention for the Protection of Cultural Property in the Event of Armed Conflict and its protocols, etc.

and other sources of international law can be maintained, and to promote social progress and better standards of life in larger freedom.

8.08 Further, Article 1 of the Charter provides as follows:

> To achieve international co-operation in solving international problems of an economic, social, cultural or humanitarian character, and in promoting and encouraging respect for human rights and for fundamental freedom for all without distinction as to race, sex, language, or religion . . .

8.09 However, the Charter itself remains silent on what rights are recognized and how they are to be enforced. This was not addressed until the adoption of the Universal Declaration of Human Rights 1948 (UDHR), often referred to as the Bill of Rights. The UDHR provides for comprehensive protection for all rights—civil, political, social, cultural, and economic. A political divergence of views between States on what rights could be guaranteed and enforced led to the splitting of the UDHR into two Covenants:

1. International Covenant on Civil and Political Rights 1966 (ICCPR)—1st Generation rights
2. International Covenant on Economic, Social and Cultural Rights 1966 (ICESCR)—2nd Generation rights

8.10 The Covenants set out the internationally recognized rights, but provided no mechanism to oversee their enforcement. In respect of civil and political rights this was remedied by the establishment of the Human Rights Committee (HRC) under the Optional Protocol to the ICCPR. The HRC was set up to monitor the implementation of the ICCPR by member States, but its competence has been extended to consider, inter alia, individual petitions. The Committee also provides useful guidance on the interpretation and application of the ICCPR through General Comments.

8.11 These were subsequently adopted regionally with each region creating a judicial body to oversee the enforcement of rights and address any violations (except criminal violations which remain a matter for national enforcement). The Regional instruments are as follows:

- European Convention on the protection of Human Rights and Fundamental Freedoms (1950) (ECHR)
- Organisation of American States Charter (OAS Charter) and the American Convention on Human Rights (came into force in 1978) (ACHR)
- African (Banjul) Charter on Human and Peoples' Rights (1986) (African Charter)
- Arab League (emerging).

8.12 Depending on a particular country's legal system, regional conventions are given effect in domestic law, either by an enabling statute or by adopting the Convention into national law.

There are, therefore, three tiers for the protection and enforcement of IHRL: **8.13**

1. International
2. Regional
3. Municipal/Domestic.

It is also worthy of note that IHRL still applies where there is an internal armed   **8.14**
conflict;[8] or where the existing State apparatus is replaced or removed following
an international armed conflict. In the latter case, the Occupying Power assumes
the responsibilities of the State and must ensure the protection of human rights
not just for 'protected persons' as defined under the Geneva Conventions but for
all those who fall under their jurisdiction.

C. Extra-Territorial Reach of Human Rights Instruments

The question of the extent of the obligations of a Contracting State in respect of   **8.15**
those who are within its 'jurisdiction' has been subject of judicial decision at the
European Court of Human Rights and in the UK by the House of Lords as well
as the American Court of Human Rights. The regional Human Rights Courts
considered whether the obligations of a State extended to those who may not
necessarily be present within the territorial boundaries of the State but are deemed
to be within the 'jurisdiction' of the State, that is to say, the obligations contained
in the Convention have extra-territorial application.

Within the European context, the seminal case is *Bankovic' and Others v Belgium*   **8.16**
and 16 other Contracting States,[9] a case concerning bombing by NATO of the
Radio-Television Serbia (RTS) headquarters in Belgrade in April 1999 during
the Kosovo conflict. The relatives of the deceased, and one injured, alleged,
inter alia, violation of Article 2 (right to life). The Court examined the phrase
'jurisdiction' contained within Article 1 of the Convention[10] and in rejecting
any jurisdictional link between the applicants and the respondent Member States,
the Court observed:

> As to the 'ordinary meaning' of the term jurisdiction in Article 1 of the Convention,
> the Court was satisfied that, from the standpoint of public international law, the

---

[8] The Inter-American Court of Human Rights in the *Bámaca-Velásquez v Guatemala* case,
involved a guerrilla fighter captured by the Guatemalan military during a battle, who was tortured
and murdered by them. The Court concluded that during an internal armed conflict, the State is not
exonerated from its human rights obligations. Rather, the very fact of the existence of such an armed
conflict 'obliged it to act in accordance with such obligations'. Merits, Series C No 70, Judgment of
25 November 2000, Inter-Am CHR.

[9] Application no 52207/99; [11BHRC435].

[10] Article 1 states: 'The High Contracting Parties shall secure to everyone within their jurisdiction
the rights and freedoms defined in Section I of this Convention.'

jurisdictional competence of a State was primarily territorial. While international law did not exclude a State's exercise of jurisdiction extra-territorially, the suggested bases of such jurisdiction (including nationality, flag, diplomatic and consular relations, effect, protection, passive personality, and universality) were, as a general rule, defined and limited by the sovereign territorial rights of the other relevant States. The Court considered that Article 1 of the Convention must be considered to reflect this ordinary and essentially territorial notion of jurisdiction, other bases of jurisdiction being exceptional and requiring special justification in the particular circumstances of each case.

The Court found State practice in the application of the Convention since its ratification to be indicative of a lack of any apprehension on the part of the Contracting States of their extra-territorial responsibility in contexts similar to the present case. Although there had been a number of military missions involving Contracting States acting extra-territorially since their ratification of the Convention (among others, in the Gulf, in Bosnia and Herzegovina and in the FRY), no State had indicated a belief that its extra-territorial actions involved an exercise of jurisdiction within the meaning of Article 1 by making a derogation pursuant to Article 15 (derogation in time of emergency) of the Convention.

The Court also observed that it had recognised *only exceptionally extra-territorial acts as constituting an exercise of jurisdiction*, when the respondent State, through the effective control of the relevant territory and its inhabitants abroad as a consequence of military occupation or through the consent, invitation or acquiescence of the Government of that territory, exercised all or some of the public powers normally to be exercised by that Government.

Regarding the applicants' claim that the positive obligation under Article 1 extended to securing the Convention rights in a manner proportionate to the level of control exercised in any given extra-territorial situation, the Court considered that this was tantamount to arguing that anyone adversely affected by an act imputable to a Contracting State, wherever in the world that act may have been committed or its consequences felt, was thereby brought within the jurisdiction of that State for the purpose of Article 1.

Regarding the applicants' claim that the positive obligation under Article 1 extended to securing the Convention rights in a manner proportionate to the level of control exercised in any given extra-territorial situation, the Court considered that this was tantamount to arguing that anyone adversely affected by an act imputable to a Contracting State, wherever in the world that act may have been committed or its consequences felt, was thereby brought within the jurisdiction of that State for the purpose of Article 1.

The Court considered that Article 1 did not provide any support for the applicants' suggestion that the positive obligation in Article 1 to secure 'the rights and freedoms defined in Section I of this Convention' could be divided and tailored in accordance with the particular circumstances of the extra-territorial act in question. The applicants' approach did not explain the application of the words 'within their jurisdiction' in Article 1 and went so far as to render those words superfluous and devoid of any purpose. Had the drafters of the Convention wished to ensure jurisdiction as extensive as that advocated by the applicants, they could have adopted a text the same as or similar to the contemporaneous Articles 1 of the four Geneva Conventions of 1949.

Furthermore, the applicants' notion of jurisdiction equated the determination of whether an individual fell within the jurisdiction of a Contracting State with the question of whether that person could be considered to be a victim of a violation of rights guaranteed by the Convention. These were separate and distinct admissibility conditions, each of which had to be satisfied before an individual could invoke the Convention provisions against a Contracting State.

However, there has been some confusion on this issue as in 2005, the European **8.17** Court in *Issa & Others v Turkey*[11] delivered its judgment and seems to have shifted its position on the necessary jurisdictional link between a complainant and the State to considering whether the actions of a State could render it liable. In *Issa & others v Turkey*, an action brought by the complainants resident in Northern Iraq, it was alleged that, following Turkish military action in the area, their relatives had been deliberately targeted and killed by the Turkish soldiers and two of them had been detained by the soldiers. The Turkish Government conceded that whilst there had been military action at the relevant time, they disputed any engagement in the area where the complainants were located. Furthermore, there were no records of complaint lodged to show that the complainants had in fact made contact with the Turkish soldiers. The complainants adduced documents, including post-mortem reports illustrating the death of the victims.

The Court rejected the complaint and found that there was insufficient evidence **8.18** to show that the Turkish soldiers were responsible for the actions alleged, although at the relevant time they were conducting military operations in Northern Iraq, albeit not in the area where the complainants were located. At the hearing, representatives of the Turkish Government invited the Court to reconsider its approach in *Banković*. In confirming its position on *Banković*, the Court ruled as follows:[12]

> However, the concept of 'jurisdiction' within the meaning of Article 1 of the Convention is not necessarily restricted to the national territory of the High Contracting Parties . . . In exceptional circumstances the acts of Contracting States performed outside their territory or which produce effects there ('extra-territorial act') may amount to exercise by them of their jurisdiction within the meaning of Article 1 of the Convention.

> According to the relevant principles of international law, a State's responsibility may be engaged where, as a consequence of military action—whether lawful or unlawful— that State in practice exercises effective control of an area situated outside its national territory. The obligation to secure, in such an area, the rights and freedoms set out in the Convention derives from the fact of such control, whether it be exercised directly, through its armed forces, or through a subordinate local administration..

> It is not necessary to determine whether a Contracting Party actually exercises detailed control over the policies and actions of the authorities in the area situated outside its national territory, since even overall control of the area may engage the responsibility of the Contracting Party concerned . . .

> Moreover, a State may also be held accountable for violation of the Convention rights and freedoms of persons who are in the territory of another State but who are

---

[11] Application no 31821/96.
[12] Paras 68–74 of the judgment.

found to be under the former State's authority and control through its agents operating—whether lawfully or unlawfully—in the latter State . . . Accountability in such situations stems from the fact that Article 1 of the Convention cannot be interpreted so as to allow a State party to perpetrate violations of the Convention on the territory of another State, which it could not perpetrate on its own territory . . .

The Court does not exclude the possibility that, as a consequence of this military action, the respondent State could be considered to have exercised, temporarily, effective overall control of a particular portion of the territory of northern Iraq. Accordingly, if there is a sufficient factual basis for holding that, at the relevant time, the victims were within that specific area, it would follow logically that they were within the jurisdiction of Turkey (and not that of Iraq, which is not a Contracting State and clearly does not fall within the legal space (*espace juridique*) of the Contracting States (see the above-cited *Banković* decision, § 80) . . . .

8.19   Therefore, although it rejected the applicants' submission that they were within the 'jurisdiction' of Turkey (on sufficiency of evidence only), the Court has made some interesting observations on the circumstances in which a State could be held liable for actions taken outside its own borders, however temporary those may be provided 'effective control' was exercised by the State or its agents.

8.20   The House of Lords in the UK was confronted by a similar complaint following UK military operations in Basra, Iraq in *Al-Skeini & Others v Secretary of State for Defence*.[13] The proceedings were brought by the relatives of six Iraqi nationals who had been killed by UK soldiers. In respect of five of them, the victims had been killed as a direct result of military operations, however, in the case of the sixth victim, he had been arrested and detained by British soldiers at the UK detention facility in Southern Iraq where it was alleged he was the subject of maltreatment and eventually died as a result of that treatment. The Court considered whether the complainants, residing in Iraq, fell within the ambit of the European Convention on Human Rights and the Human Rights Act 1998 for the purposes of an independent enquiry into the death of their relatives.

8.21   Their Lordships found that the case of the Iraqi national, Baha Mousa, who was held at the detention facility at the time of his death, warranted an independent enquiry into the circumstances of his death and remitted the matter to the Divisional Court. In respect of the remaining five Iraqi nationals, the House of Lords concluded that the Convention did not have extra-territorial application in this instance based on the reasoning of the European Court in *Banković*. Their Lordships also considered the extra-territorial application of the Human Rights Act 1998 and the majority concluded that the Act had extra-territorial reach (Lord Bingham, dissenting) although the reasoning differed to some extent.

---

[13] [2007] UKHL 26.

The cases indicate, therefore, that British individuals or firms or companies or other organisations readily fall within the legislative grasp of statutes passed by Parliament. So far as they are concerned, the question is whether, on a fair interpretation, the statute in question is intended to apply to them only in the United Kingdom or also, to some extent at least, beyond the territorial limits of the United Kingdom. Here, there is no doubt that section 6 applies to public authorities such as the armed forces within the United Kingdom: the only question is whether, on a fair interpretation, it is confined to the United Kingdom.[14]

Nevertheless, where a public authority has power to operate outside of the United Kingdom and does so legitimately . . . it would only be sensible to treat the public authority, so far as possible, in the same way as when it operates at home. [para 53] There is therefore nothing in the wider context of international law which points to the need to confine sections 6 and 7 of the 1998 Act to the territory of the United Kingdom. [para 54]

For these reasons, section 6 should be interpreted as applying not only when a public authority acts within the United Kingdom but also when it acts within the jurisdiction of the United Kingdom for purposes of article 1 of the Convention, but outside the territory of the United Kingdom. [para 59, Lord Rodger]

Baroness Hale in concurring with Lord Rodger that the Human Rights Act 1998 **8.22** had extra-territorial effect where, in the present instance, the detention facility was a British facility and operated by the army which would be sufficient to found a remedy by his family in the UK:

I can find nothing in the Act which indicates that section 6 should not apply to Mr Mousa's case and several good reasons why it should. In particular, it has many times been said that the object of the Human Rights Act was to give people who would be entitled to a remedy against the United Kingdom in the European Court of Human Rights in Strasbourg a remedy against the relevant public authority in the courts of this country. The United Kingdom now accepts that it would be answerable in Strasbourg for the conduct of the British army while Mr Mousa was detained in a British detention unit in Basra. It would be consistent with the purpose of the Act to give his father a remedy against the army in the courts of this country. [para 88]

Lord Carswell, whilst agreeing with the majority view that section 6 of the Human **8.23** Rights Act 1998 must be interpreted as applying when a public body acts within the UK or its jurisdiction. However, he expressed caution on the extra-territorial application of the Act and concluded that it would, 'in my opinion require a high degree of control by the agents of the State of an area in another State before it could be said that that area was within the jurisdiction of the former. The test for establishing that is and should be stringent, and in my judgment the British presence in Iraq falls well short of that degree of control.' [at para 97]

Lord Brown in concluding that the Act had extra-territorial application provided **8.24** it fell within the 'narrow categories of exception established under the Strasbourg

---

[14] Para 47, 28.

case law (as in the sixth appellant's case)' as it presently stood. Although he expressed some reservation should Strasbourg widen the application of the Convention, he was of the opinion that the Act would still have to 'have the same extra-territorial effect as the Convention'.

8.25 In his dissenting speech, Lord Bingham rejected a wider application of the Act and rejected the use of section 3 of the Act as a 'tool . . . to determine the extent of the rights':

> There is, I think, force in this point, unless a clear inference of extra-territorial appli-cation can otherwise be drawn from the terms of the Act. It cannot be doubted that, if Parliament had intended the Act to have extraterritorial application, words could very readily have been found to express that intention. [para 13]

> This makes it the more unlikely, in my opinion, that Parliament could, without any express provision to that effect, have intended to rebut the presumption of territorial application so as to authorise the bringing of claims, under the Act, based on the conduct of British forces outside the UK and outside any other contracting state. Differing from the courts below, I regard the statutory presumption of territorial application as a strong one, which has not been rebutted. [para 24].

8.26 The Inter-American Commission on Human Rights[15] [IACHR] in 1999, some two years before the European Court's decision in *Bankovic'*, considered the application of the American Declaration in *Coard et al v the United States*,[16] a case arising out of US military operations in Grenada. The complainants alleged that they had been detained and had been subject to physical abuse by US military and were denied any legal representation in relation to their detention. The Commission considered the application of the American Declaration and concluded that:

> Given that individual rights inhere simply by virtue of a person's humanity, each American State is obliged to uphold the protected rights of any person subject to its jurisdiction. While this most commonly refers to persons within a State's territory, it may, under given circumstances, refer to conduct with an extraterritorial locus where the person concerned is present in the territory of one State, but subject to the control of another State—usually through the acts of the latter's agents abroad . . . In principle, the inquiry turns not on the presumed victim's nationality or presence within a particular geographic area, but on whether, under the specific circumstances, the State observed the rights of a person subject to its authority and control.

8.27 Interestingly, the US objected to the reliance placed by the Commission on international humanitarian law on the basis that it was governed by its mandate which did not permit the application of international humanitarian law.

---

[15] The IACHR is an organ of the OAS and is one of the two major human rights bodies in the Inter-American human rights system.

[16] Case 10.951, Report No 109/99, September 29, 1999, Inter-Am CHR.

The Commission, in rightly rejecting that approach, emphasized on the inter-relationship between the disciplines and observed that:

> First, while international humanitarian law pertains primarily in times of war and the international law of human rights applies most fully in times of peace, the potential application of one does not necessarily exclude or displace the other. There is an integral linkage between the law of human rights and humanitarian law because they share a 'common nucleus of non-derogable rights and a common purpose of protecting human life and dignity', and there may be a substantial overlap in the application of these bodies of law. Certain core guarantees apply in all circumstances, including situations of conflict, and this is reflected, *inter alia*, in the designation of certain protections pertaining to the person as peremptory norms (*jus cogens*) and obligations *erga omnes*, in a vast body of treaty law, in principles of customary international law, and in the doctrine and practice of international human rights bodies such as this Commission. Both normative systems may be thus be applicable to the situation under study.

This decision together with the UN resolutions,[17] and the decision of the European Commission in *Cyprus v Turkey*, all explicitly recognize the symbiotic relationship of these regimes. Therefore, although IHRL applies both during peacetime and during an armed conflict (both internal and international), it does not, however, govern issues such as the conduct of hostilities, or the treatment of prisoners of war; that remains the remit of the laws of war or IHL. However, other Conventions, such as the Torture Convention, which are applicable during an armed conflict, must be read alongside the four Geneva Conventions and the Additional Protocols. **8.28**

IHRL and IHL appear to have had parallel developments, but it is now increasingly being acknowledged that both human rights systems should not be mutually exclusive such that the applications of IHRL cease during an armed conflict. This broader view is borne out by the more recent Conventions such as the Convention on the Rights of Children and the Rome Statute. **8.29**

D. The Nature of the Rights Engaged

Turning now to human rights issues likely to emerge in terrorist investigations, it is important to first recognize the right of a State to derogate from human rights provisions contained in the ICCPR and any relevant regional convention. **8.30**

Article 4 of the ICCPR permits a State to derogate in 'time of public emergency which threatens the life of the nation and the existence of which is officially **8.31**

---

[17] UNSCR 2675 (XXV)(1970); UNSCR 237 (1967) and the more recent UNSCR 1456, 1624 etc and the recently adopted global counter-terrorism (CT) strategy. For all CT-related UN documents see <http://www.un.org/terrorism/>.

proclaimed . . .'. A similar provision can be found in the regional conventions (Article 5 of ECHR; Article 27 ACHR). The UK, for example, has, since the events of 11 September 2001, derogated from some of the provisions of the ECHR. The criteria and procedures for derogation are set out in the relevant regional conventions. However, there are limits on what a State may derogate from. The ICCPR and general IHRL jurisprudence draw a distinction between those rights which are:

- Absolute
- Restrictive.

This, in effect, means that, despite any declaration of derogation, the rights which are determined as absolute may never be derogated.

What amounts to an absolute right

8.32 Under IHRL (and IHL) some rights are considered to be so fundamental that a State cannot derogate from these rights under any circumstances.

8.33 The two most significant absolute rights which are common to all IHRL/IHL instruments and which give rise to individual criminal responsibility are:

1. Right to life—(which implicitly prohibits murder, crimes against humanity, and genocide); and
2. Prohibition on torture.

8.34 However, the ICCPR and regional conventions also set out other additional rights which are considered as absolute (non-derogable). For example, under the ICCPR the additional absolute right includes no punishment without due process of law.[18] The regional conventions, by contrast, determine which rights are absolute by reference to the prevailing conditions in the region. Thus, the ECHR identifies only one other right in addition to the right to life and prohibition on torture,[19] whilst the American Convention on Human Rights includes nine additional rights[20] reflecting the situation in the Americas, and the African Charter does not permit any derogation.

8.35 Restrictive/derogable rights are those rights which a State may be permitted to restrict or limit in accordance with the criterion laid down in the relevant convention.

---

[18] The other absolute rights are: imprisonment for contractual obligations; recognition before the law; and freedom of thought, conscience, and religion.

[19] No punishment without due process of law.

[20] Recognition before the law; freedom from ex post facto laws; freedom of conscience and religion; rights of the family; right to a name; rights of the child; right to nationality; right to participate in Government; and judicial guarantees for the protection of these rights.

Broadly speaking, the restriction is generally for public order/safety. However such limitations must be: lawful, necessary, and proportionate.

That is:

1. All measures taken by States must be lawful. That is, they must be, by reference to and within, prescribed laws duly passed in the constitutional manner.
2. Measures and actions should not be 'arbitrary' and based only on an official's discretion or whim. For the law enforcement official, this means acting only where certain that one's actions are 'covered' or authorized by a valid law.
3. Limitations should be necessary and proportionate to the aim that is sought to be achieved.

Any limitation or restriction must be non-discriminatory and maintain equality **8.36** in its application.[21] This was confirmed, in the UK in *A (FC) and others (FC) (Appellants) v Secretary of State for the Home Department (Respondent); X (FC) and another (FC) (Appellants) v Secretary of State for the Home Department (Respondent)*[22] when dealing with an appeal in relation to the detention of foreign nationals under section 23 of the Anti-terrorism, Crime and Security Act 2001. The appellants challenged the lawfulness of their detention, and that the UK was not entitled to derogate from its obligations under ECHR. They further contended that the offending provisions of the Anti-terrorism, Crime and Security Act 2001 were incompatible with the Convention.

The House of Lords unanimously agreed that section 23 of the Anti-terrorism, **8.37** Crime and Security Act 2001 was incompatible with the ECHR on the grounds that it was disproportionate and discriminatory (on grounds of nationality or immigration status).

Lord Bingham gave the leading speech and on the issue of derogation and the **8.38** impact of the legislation adopted as a consequence of it, in particular, on foreign nationals, he opined at para 68 as follows:

> Article 15 requires any derogating measures to go no further than is strictly required by the exigencies of the situation and the prohibition of discrimination on grounds of nationality or immigration status has not been the subject of derogation. Article 14 remains in full force. Any discriminatory measure inevitably affects a smaller rather than a larger group, but cannot be justified on the ground that more people would be adversely affected if the measure were applied generally. What has to be justified is not the measure in issue but the difference in treatment between one person or group and another. What cannot be justified here is the decision to detain one group

---

[21] It is a fundamental principle of international human rights law that all persons have a right to be recognized as a person before the law, are to be treated as equal before the law, and entitled without any discrimination to equal protection of the law (Article 7 UDHR, Article 16 ICCPR).
[22] [2004] UKHL 56.

of suspected international terrorists, defined by nationality or immigration status, and not another. To do so was a violation of article 14. It was also a violation of article 26 of the ICCPR and so inconsistent with the United Kingdom's other obligations under international law within the meaning of article 15 of the European Convention . . .

He concluded that both SIAC[23] and the Court of Appeal had erred in their approach and observed:

> Assuming, as one must, that there is a public emergency threatening the life of the nation, measures which derogate from article 5 are permissible only to the extent strictly required by the exigencies of the situation, and it is for the derogating state to prove that that is so. The reasons given by SIAC do not warrant its conclusion. The first reason does not explain why the measures are directed only to foreign nationals. The second reason no doubt has some validity, but is subject to the same weakness. The third reason does not explain why a terrorist, if a serious threat to the UK, ceases to be so on the French side of the English Channel or elsewhere. The fourth reason is intelligible if the foreign national is not really thought to be a serious threat to the UK, but hard to understand if he is. I do not consider SIAC's conclusion as one to which it could properly come. In dismissing the appellants' appeal, Lord Woolf CJ broadly considered that it was sensible and appropriate for the Secretary of State to use immigration legislation, that deference was owed to his decisions (para 40) and that SIAC's conclusions depended on the evidence before it (para 43). Brooke LJ reached a similar conclusion (para 91), regarding SIAC's findings as unappealable findings of fact. Chadwick LJ also regarded SIAC's finding as one of fact (para 150). I cannot accept this analysis as correct. The European Court does not approach questions of proportionality as questions of pure fact: see, for example, *Smith and Grady v United Kingdom*, above. Nor should domestic courts do so. The greater intensity of review now required in determining questions of proportionality, and the duty of the courts to protect Convention rights, would in my view be emasculated if a judgment at first instance on such a question were conclusively to preclude any further review. So would excessive deference, in a field involving indefinite detention without charge or trial, to ministerial decision. In my opinion, SIAC erred in law and the Court of Appeal erred in failing to correct its error.[24]

8.39 Lord Hope in his speech highlighted the unlawfulness and irrationality of the discriminatory consequences of section 23 of the Anti-terrorism, Crime and Security Act 2001:

> To tell a man that he is to be incarcerated for a fixed period is one thing. To tell him that he is to be incarcerated for a period that has no end in sight is quite another. And the longer the time the incarceration will last with no end in sight the worse it is. The gravity of this interference leads inevitably to the question posed by article 15(1) which is whether, if this is the nature of the emergency, the derogation is strictly required to deal with it. This raises the further question whether there is some other way of dealing with the emergency which will not be incompatible with the

---

[23] Special Immigration Appeals Commission.
[24] Para 44 of the judgment.

Convention rights. If there is some other way of dealing with it that will meet this test, the prolonged and indefinite detention without trial of those affected by the Derogation Order cannot be said to be what the exigencies of the situation strictly require[25] . . .

I would hold that the indefinite detention of foreign nationals without trial has not been shown to be strictly required, as the same threat from British nationals whom the government is unable or unwilling to prosecute is being met by other measures which do not require them to be detained indefinitely without trial. The distinction which the government seeks to draw between these two groups—British nationals and foreign nationals—raises an issue of discrimination. But, as the distinction is irrational, it goes to the heart of the issue about proportionality also. It proceeds on the misconception that it is a sufficient answer to the question whether the derogation is strictly required that the two groups have different rights in the immigration context. So they do. But the derogation is from the right to liberty. The right to liberty is the same for each group. If derogation is not strictly required in the case of one group, it cannot be strictly required in the case of the other group that presents the same threat.[26]

Such an approach is consistent with the jurisprudence of the European Court **8.40** which has repeatedly emphasized on the non-derogation of Article 14. A similar approach is to be found in the decisions of the African Commission where the remedy of habeas corpus had been denied to a particular group of detainees who were held in Nigeria for reasons of state security. Given that the African Charter does not permit derogation in any event, the actions of Nigeria were held to be non-compatible with Article 6 of the Charter. The Commission said that whilst it was sympathetic to a State's need to maintain public peace, 'it must note that too often extreme measures to curtail rights simply create greater unrest. It is dangerous for the protection of human rights for the executive branch of the government to operate without such checks as the judiciary can usefully perform'.[27]

The Inter-American Commission on Human Rights in its report[28] on 'Terrorism **8.41** and Human Rights' emphasized the importance of States not to deny judicial protection through discriminatory measures as the right to non-discrimination is a non-derogable right. Therefore, where a State does legitimately derogate it must ensure that there is no discriminatory element.

Who comprises 'the State'?

Having highlighted the duties and obligations of a State, we now turn to examine **8.42** the issue of who is an integral part of the State?

---

[25] Para 124.
[26] Para 132.
[27] Para 33 of the Commission's findings in the *Constitutional Rights Project and Another v Nigeria* (2000) AHRLR 235.
[28] The report can be accessed on <http://www.cidh.oas.org/Terrorism/Eng/part.b.htm>.

8.43 As mentioned above, the protection of human rights relate to the relationship between the State and those (citizens or others) within its jurisdiction or under its control. IHRL prescribes certain duties that the State has towards such persons, and recognizes their right to claim that the State respects or observes these duties.

8.44 The State has an overarching duty to protect citizens. More generally, however, the duty of the State is to refrain from directly and arbitrarily (ie, without legal process) depriving individuals of their rights. Given the complex structure of any State apparatus it is inevitable that those caught within the definition will include law enforcement officials and agencies, as agents of the State, and be synonymous with it. Therefore, their day-to-day and operational conduct is governed by the State's obligations derived from international commitments or local constitutional constraints on State power. Violation of basic rights by State officials has implications both for the individual law enforcement officers (criminal and civil sanctions) and for the State (civil sanctions as well as political and diplomatic consequences arising out of its non-compliance of international obligations and duties).

8.45 In the context of investigations, all the agencies of the State apparatus involved would be caught within this definition.

E. The Rights Likely to be Engaged During the Course of an Investigation

Right to life

8.46 All IHRL instruments recognize the inherent right to life and in the European context this right, as expounded by a series of decisions essentially imposes three basic obligations on States:

1. A negative obligation; not to take life;
2. A positive obligation; to take steps to preserve life;
3. A procedural obligation; which is implied in Article 2 to ensure an adequate and effective investigation into death alleged to have arisen at hands of agents of State or from State's negligent failure to protect lives. A State must act of its own motion when matters are drawn to their attention.

8.47 The Court has in all its decisions construed Article 2 in the strictest manner given its fundamental importance as stated in *McCann & others v the UK*,[29] a case involving the shooting of IRA suspects in Gibraltar in 1988 by UK soldiers.

---

[29] [1995] Appl no 18984/91.

The applicants brought proceedings against the UK alleging a breach of Article 2 and an inadequacy of an independent investigation:

> It must also be borne in mind that, as a provision (art 2) which not only safeguards the right to life but sets out the circumstances when the deprivation of life may be justified, Article 2 (art 2) ranks as one of the most fundamental provisions in the Convention—indeed one which, in peacetime, admits of no derogation under Article 15 (art 15). Together with Article 3 (art 15+3) of the Convention, it also enshrines one of the basic values of the democratic societies making up the Council of Europe [. . .]. As such, its provisions must be strictly construed.[30]

> On the submission of an inadequate independent investigation, the Court established that 'a general legal prohibition of arbitrary killing by the agents of the State would be ineffective, in practice, if there existed no procedure for reviewing the lawfulness of the use of lethal force by State authorities'. The obligation to protect the right to life under this provision (art 2), read in conjunction with the State's general duty under Article 1 (art 2+1) of the Convention to 'secure to everyone within their jurisdiction the rights and freedoms defined in [the] Convention', requires by implication that there should be some form of effective official investigation when individuals have been killed as a result of the use of force by, inter alios, agents of the State.[31]

8.48 This need for an independent investigation has been the subject of legal ruling in the UK in *R (on the application of Middleton) v West Somerset Coroner*[32] relating to the nature of coroner's inquests following the death of a prisoner, the House of Lords found that whilst the procedure was compliant, there was a need to reflect the factual conclusions.

8.49 By contrast, the Divisional Court in *R (on the application of Al-Skeini and others) v Secretary of State for Defence*,[33] examining the nature of investigations conducted by the SIB in Iraq, found that they did not meet the procedural requirements of Article 2 and 3 of ECHR and ruled 'they were not independent; they were one-sided; and the commanders concerned were not trying to do their best according to the dictates of article 2.'[34]

> The Divisional Court set out the conditions of an independent investigation: 'It follows that for an investigation into a death occurring allegedly at the hands of state agents to comply with the requirements of the procedural obligation, it must be official, ie, initiated by the state; timely, ie, in both initiation and completion; independent, ie both formally and practically, from those implicated in the events; open, ie, to a sufficient element of public scrutiny as well as to the involvement of the next-of-kin; and effective, ie, capable of achieving objective accountability of the state agents and thus of leading, as appropriate, to conclusions about all the circumstances, including

---

[30] Para 147 of the judgment.
[31] Para 161 of the judgment.
[32] [2004] 2 All ER 465.
[33] [2004] EWHC 2911 (Admin).
[34] Para 340 of the judgment.

the background issues, leading to the death, as well as about responsibility for it, and the identification and punishment of those responsible.

In addition, where the death occurs in state custody, the burden is on the State, and it is a particularly stringent one, to account for the death: for it is the duty of the State to protect those in its custody.[35]

8.50 The European Court itself has been critical of Member States where the procedural obligation has been disregarded. For example in *Ozkan v Turkey [ECtHR]*[36] where security forces looking for members of the PKK (proscribed as a terrorist organization under Turkish law) had attacked Ormaniçi, and as a result of which two children had died and others had been taken away from the village and detained where they were tortured and subjected to ill-treatment. The Court concluded that there had been a violation of the substantive and procedural requirements under Article 2 and 3 by the Turkish authorities and observed:

> On the procedural aspect, bearing in mind the vulnerable position in which detainees find themselves and the authorities' obligation to protect them and to conduct an effective investigation where a person dies in detention, the Court further found that, as a result of the failure of the two public prosecutors who conducted an investigation into . . . to examine whether there existed a causal link between his fatal illness and his treatment in custody—including the failure by the Diyarbakır public prosecutor to verify the information allegedly given by the police about İbrahim Ekinci's personal history—no effective investigation into İbrahim Ekinci's death had been conducted. Accordingly, there had also been a violation of Article 2 of the Convention in respect of the authorities' investigation into the death of İbrahim Ekinci.

> In addition, in view of the total inactivity of the judicial authorities in the present case to investigate the manner in which the apprehended Ormaniçi villagers had sustained their foot injuries, the Court concluded that there had also been a violation of Article 3 of the Convention in its procedural aspect.

8.51 On the positive obligation to protect, the House of Lords in *R (Amin) v Sec of State for the Home Department*[37] laid down the following guidance:

- Persons in custody are vulnerable, and authorities are under a duty to protect. The obligation to account for the treatment of a prisoner is particularly stringent when that person dies;
- A systemic failure, resulting in death, may well call for even more anxious consideration;
- Investigation must be effective (ie, capable of leading to a proper determination);
- Person(s) responsible for and carrying out the investigation must be independent (ie, a lack of hierarchical, institutional, and practical connection);
- There must be public scrutiny and involvement of family.

---

[35] Para 322 and 323.
[36] Application No 21689/93 [2004] ECHR 133.
[37] [2003] UKHL 51.

Prohibition on torture

The prohibition on torture takes a number of forms which include: **8.52**

- Use of torture during interrogation and use evidence obtained through torture;
- The handing over of individuals for interrogation to third States which deploy torture tactics;
- The deportation of persons, either following sentence, or where entry is refused/ rejection of application for political asylum.

Use of torture as interrogation technique/use of evidence obtained through torture

The Convention against Torture and other cruel, inhuman, or degrading treatment **8.53** (CAT) [1984] criminalizes and provides for universal jurisdiction for torture committed by a State official in order to obtain information/confession etc[38] and renders the evidence so obtained inadmissible.[39] Equally, admissions obtained under torture in a third State may still be excluded by a court in the receiving country.[40]

The Convention establishes the non-derogable in Article 2 and requires States **8.54** to ensure that 'its competent authorities proceed to a prompt and impartial investigation, wherever there is reasonable ground to believe that an act of torture has been committee in any territory under its jurisdiction'.[41] In this regard, the absolute prohibition of torture and its attendant procedural obligation to conduct an independent investigation is akin to that engaged in the right to life.

Regional human rights courts have emphasized the importance of a procedural **8.55** obligation to conduct an independent investigation in instances where allegations of torture have been made against state officials. As mentioned above, the use of

---

[38] Article 1 defines torture as 'any act by which severe pain or suffering, whether physical or mental, is intentionally inflicted on a person for such purposes as obtaining from him or a third person information or a confession, punishing him for an act he or a third person has committed or is suspected of having committed, or intimidating or coercing him or a third person, or for any reason based on discrimination of any kind, when such pain or suffering is inflicted by or at the instigation of or with the consent or acquiescence of a public official or other person acting in an official capacity'.

[39] Article 15 provides: 'Each State Party shall ensure that any statement which is established to have been made as a result of torture shall not be invoked as evidence in any proceedings, except against a person accused of torture as evidence that the statement was made'.

[40] The common law (as well as international law) and 'the importance a civilised society attaches to proper behaviour by the police' compel the exclusion of 'evidence' obtained by torture. It is excluded as inherently unreliable, unfair, offensive to ordinary standards of humanity and decency and incompatible with principles which should inform a tribunal seeking to administer justice: *A & Others v Secretary of State Home Affairs* (UK House of Lords, December 2005; *R v Mushtaq* (UK House of Lords, 2005); *Lam Chi-Ming v The Queen* (Privy Council, 1991). See also Article 69 *Rome Statute (International Criminal Court)* and the *Rules of Procedure* of the International Criminal Tribunals (Former Yugoslavia and Rwanda).

[41] Article 12 of the Convention.

torture brings with it individual criminal responsibility and must therefore be the subject of investigation.

8.56   In a recent case before the European Court, *Asan and others v Turkey*,[42] an allegation of ill-treatment amounting to torture was made against the officers conducting an investigation. The applicants had been arrested and detained for some nine days before being brought to Court. The applicants complained to the prosecutor and the judge of their ill-treatment whilst in detention which was borne out by medical examination but no action had been taken by the authorities. The Court found that:

> It was trite that where an individual had been taken into custody in good health, but was found to be injured by the time of release, it was incumbent on the government concerned to produce a plausible explanation of how those injuries were caused and to produce evidence casting doubt on the victim's allegations, particularly if those allegations had been corroborated by medical reports.

> Indeed, the burden of proof might be regarded as resting on the authorities to provide a satisfactory and convincing explanation. In the instant case, the findings of the medical examinations of five of the applicants after their detention were, at the very least, consistent with their allegations of having been beaten, and the later medical evidence did not contain any statement that there had been no finding of physical violence on their bodies.

> Where an individual had an arguable claim that he had been subjected to ill-treatment by agents of the State, the notion of an 'effective remedy' for the purposes of art 13 of the Convention entailed a thorough and effective investigation capable to leading to the identification and punishment of those responsible, effective access to the investigatory procedure for the complainant, and the payment of compensation where appropriate . . .

8.57   This international standard has been adopted by all the regional human rights instruments and enforced through the regional human rights courts. Other human rights oversight bodies such as The Human Rights Committee in its General Comment 21 emphasized the importance of the obligation by States 'towards persons who are particularly vulnerable because of their status as persons deprived of liberty . . .', a fact that has been echoed by the Israeli Supreme Court when considering the use of interrogation techniques. The Court highlighted the effect of detention that:

> . . . by its very nature, places the suspect in a difficult position. 'The criminal's interrogation', wrote Justice Vitkon over twenty years ago, 'is not a negotiation process between two open and fair vendors, conducting their business on the basis of maximum mutual trust' (Cr A 216/74 *Cohen v The State of Israel*) 29(1) PD 340 at 352). An interrogation is a 'competition of minds', in which the investigator attempts

---

[42]   10 July 2007 App No 56003/00; [2007] ECHR 56003/00.

to penetrate the suspect's thoughts and elicit from him the information the investigator seeks to obtain.[43]

In the UK the House of Lords in *A (FC) and Others (FC) (Appellants) v Secretary of* **8.58** *State for the Home Department (Respondent) (2004); A and Others (Appellants) (FC) and Others v Secretary of State for the Home Department (Respondent) (Conjoined Appeals)*[44] considered the question of admissibility of evidence obtained by torture by the SIAC.

Following the detention of A and others under Part 4 of the Anti-Terrorism Crime **8.59** and Security Act 2001,[45] the appellants argued that SIAC had relied on evidence obtained by torture by officials of a foreign state. SIAC was set up in the UK under the Special Immigration Appeals Act 1997, as a response to the earlier ECHR decision,[46] to decide on cases as an appellate body on issues such as deportation in sensitive cases. It was a body set up as a compromise between dealing with human rights obligations under, for example, the Refugee Convention on the one part, and issues of national security on the other.

In order to discharge its functions, the rules governing the material that SIAC **8.60** could examine and take into account naturally was, either sensitive in nature, or intelligence led. It has the ability to receive evidence in both open and closed sessions with the option of special counsel in respect of those detained where a situation so demanded. It was this aspect that became the subject of the challenge, namely: can SIAC receive evidence that was obtained by torture?

At the hearing the appellants challenged the admission of evidence obtained by **8.61** torture by foreign officials, albeit without the complicity of British officials. SIAC found that it could admit such evidence where it was obtained only by foreign officials, and the only issue was what weight could be attached to such evidence. The Court of Appeal came to the same conclusion and the matter was then referred to the House of Lords.

The central question for decision by the House of Lords was whether SIAC may **8.62** 'receive evidence which has or may have been procured by torture inflicted, in order to obtain evidence, by officials of a foreign state without the complicity of the British authorities'?

The House of Lords unanimously decided that no evidence could be admitted **8.63** in any proceedings obtained through torture with, or without, the complicity of

---

[43] Para 22 of the judgment—Israeli Supreme Court Judgment concerning the legality of the GSS Interrogation Methods (1999).
[44] [2005] UKHL 71.
[45] See case discussed at (n 44).
[46] *Chahal v UK* (1996) 23 EHRR 413, as a case dealing with the principle of non-refoulment.

British officials. Given the importance of this decision it is worth considering it in some detail.

8.64 Lord Bingham gave the leading speech and in rejecting the submission on behalf of the Secretary of State on the admission of such evidence he observed:

> In rejecting the use of torture, whether applied to potential defendants or potential witnesses, the common law was moved by the cruelty of the practice as applied to those not convicted of crime, by the inherent unreliability of confessions or evidence so procured and by the belief that it degraded all those who lent themselves to the practice.[para 11]

8.65 Lord Hope echoed the inadmissibility of such evidence and the need to protect judicial integrity:

> The use of such evidence is excluded not on grounds of its unreliability—if that was the only objection to it, it would go to its weight, not to its admissibility—but on grounds of its barbarism, its illegality and its inhumanity. The law will not lend its support to the use of torture for any purpose whatever. It has no place in the defence of freedom and democracy, whose very existence depends on the denial of the use of such methods to the executive. [para 112]

8.66 Their Lordships considered the obligations under the Torture Convention, in particular Article 15,[47] and found that, even in instances of terrorist-related activities, it:

> . . . makes plain the blanket nature of this exclusionary rule. It cannot possibly be read, as counsel for the Secretary of State submits, as intended to apply only in criminal proceedings. Nor can it be understood to differentiate between confessions and accusatory statements, or to apply only where the state in whose jurisdiction the proceedings are held has inflicted or been complicit in the torture. It would indeed be remarkable if national courts, exercising universal jurisdiction, could try a foreign torturer for acts of torture committed abroad, but could nonetheless receive evidence obtained by such torture. [para 35]

> The Secretary of State is right to submit that SIAC is a body designed to enable it to receive and assess a wide range of material, including material which would not be disclosed to a body lacking its special characteristics. And it would of course be within the power of a sovereign Parliament (in breach of international law) to confer power on SIAC to receive third party torture evidence. But the English common law has regarded torture and its fruits with abhorrence for over 500 years, and that abhorrence is now shared by over 140 countries which have acceded to the Torture Convention. I am startled, even a little dismayed, at the suggestion (and the acceptance by the Court of Appeal majority) that this deeply-rooted tradition and an international obligation solemnly and explicitly undertaken can be overridden by a statute and a procedural rule which make no mention of torture at all. [para 51, per Lord Bingham]

---

[47] Article 15, which is cited in full at (n 39), prohibits any reliance on statements [confessions] obtained through torture in any proceedings; unless the proceedings are against the official accused of torture.

On the question of inhuman or degrading treatment and whether the treatment **8.67** of evidence obtained through inhuman or degrading treatment follows that obtained through torture, Lord Bingham and Lord Hope concluded that based on existing European Court jurisprudence, there is a distinction between the two. Where evidence is obtained through torture it is inadmissible in judicial proceedings per se, whilst evidence that is said to have been obtained as a result of inhuman or degrading treatment, such evidence in English proceedings may be rendered inadmissible by virtue of section 78 of the Police and Criminal Evidence Act 1984.

The judgment also considers the issue of whether the executive may consider **8.68** material that could be a product of torture when making operational decisions ('ticking time bomb') and in the present instance, whether the Secretary of State can rely upon material that may be tainted when considering whether or not to issue a certificate in respect of the detention of an individual (Lord Nicholls expressed some reservation in respect of any reliance being placed by the Secretary of State on such tainted information).

Their Lordships unanimously found that the executive could rely on such infor- **8.69** mation and acknowledged the inevitable 'mismatch' that arises particularly in the context of counter-terrorism when conflicting interests must be balanced.

> In my opinion the 'mismatch' to which counsel for the Secretary of State refers is almost inevitable in any case of judicial supervision of executive action. It is not the function of the courts to place limits upon the information available to the Secretary of State, particularly when he is concerned with national security. Provided that he acts lawfully, he may read whatever he likes . . . But the 2001 Act makes the exercise by the Secretary of State of his extraordinary powers subject to judicial supervision. [per Lord Hoffman, para 93]

Lord Nicholls in his speech highlighted the tension in such an instance: **8.70**

> The intuitive response to these questions is that if use of such information might save lives it would be absurd to reject it. If the police were to learn of the whereabouts of a ticking bomb it would be ludicrous for them to disregard this information if it had been procured by torture. No one suggests the police should act in this way. Similarly, if tainted information points a finger of suspicion at a particular individual: depending on the circumstances, this information is a matter the police may properly take into account when considering, for example, whether to make an arrest.[para 68]

> The next step is to consider whether the position is the same regarding the use of this information in legal proceedings and, if not, why not. In my view the position is not the same. The executive and the judiciary have different functions and different responsibilities. It is one thing for tainted information to be used by the executive when making operational decisions or by the police when exercising their investigatory powers, including powers of arrest. These steps do not impinge upon the liberty of individuals or, when they do, they are of an essentially short-term interim character. Often there is an urgent need for action. It is an altogether different matter for the

judicial arm of the State to admit such information as evidence when adjudicating definitively upon the guilt or innocence of a person charged with a criminal offence. In the latter case repugnance to torture demands that proof of facts should be found in more acceptable sources than information extracted by torture. [para 70]

8.71 Therefore, the Court in recognizing the need for rapid operational decisions by the executive found that reliance could be placed on material in their possession as there would eventually be judicial supervision where the matter could be considered more calmly than the initial executive decision.

8.72 Their Lordships all agreed that the traditional approach to the burden of proof would be of little use in the case of appeals before SIAC, given its unique character and, therefore, clear guidance was needed. However, the House was divided on the test to be adopted by SIAC and two separate approaches were developed, which can loosely be described as the 'Bingham' approach and the 'Hope' approach. The 'Bingham' approach[48] in a nutshell is that SIAC was best placed to discharge this duty given its:

> . . . knowledge and expertise in this field knows or suspects that evidence may have come from such a country, it is for SIAC to initiate or direct such inquiry as is necessary to enable it to form a fair judgment whether the evidence has, or whether there is a real risk that it may have been, obtained by torture or not. All will depend on the facts and circumstances of a particular case. If SIAC is unable to conclude that there is not a real risk that the evidence has been obtained by torture, it should refuse to admit the evidence. Otherwise it should admit it. [per Lord Bingham, para 56]

8.73 The 'Hope' approach differs to the extent that it found the 'Bingham' test to place a heavy burden on SIAC to satisfy itself that the evidence was not obtained through torture and suggested that the correct test is that 'SIAC should not admit the evidence if it concludes on a balance of probabilities that it was obtained by torture. In other words, if SIAC is left in doubt as to whether the evidence was obtained in this way, it should admit it' [Lord Hope, para 118]

By a majority of 4:3 the 'Hope' test was adopted.

8.74 Likewise the Israeli Supreme Court Judgment concerning the *Legality of the GSS Interrogation Methods* (6 September 1999) rejected the use of interrogation techniques involving the use of physical force such as shaking, the 'shabach'[49] position. The Supreme Court was considering an application by a number of bodies,

---

48 Adopted by Lord Nicholls and Lord Hoffman.

49 The 'shabach' position involves tying the hands behind the suspect's back. 'He is seated on a small and low chair, whose seat is tilted forward, towards the ground. One hand is tied behind the suspect, and placed inside the gap between the chair's seat and back support. His second hand is tied behind the chair, against its back support. The suspect's head is covered by an opaque sack, falling down to his shoulders. Powerfully loud music is played in the room.' Judgment by the presiding judge [President A Barak] in Legality of the GSS Interrogation Methods (6 September 1999) para 10.

including the Public Committee against Torture and Citizen's Rights in Israel etc on the methods of interrogation adopted by the General Security Service (GSS) in relation to terrorist suspects. The Supreme Court was asked to give an advisory opinion on the legality of the methods of interrogation used by the GSS.

The Public Committee against Torture submitted that there was no legal basis for **8.75** the GSS to conduct such investigations and in any event the adoption of such techniques was unlawful both under domestic law and international law. The Supreme Court found that there was no legal basis on which the actions of the GSS could be founded and in any event the methods adopted were impermissible in the absence of any permitting legislation. The Court concluded:

> In other words, general directives governing the use of physical means during inter-rogations must be rooted in an authorization prescribed by law and not from defences to criminal liability. The principle of 'necessity' cannot serve as a basis of authority [. . .]. If the State wishes to enable GSS investigators to utilize physical means in interrogations, they must seek the enactment of legislation for this purpose.

> Our conclusion is therefore the following: According to the existing state of the law, neither the government nor the heads of security services possess the authority to establish directives and bestow authorization regarding the use of liberty infringing physical means during the interrogation of suspects suspected of hostile terrorist activities, beyond the general directives which can be inferred from the very concept of an interrogation. Similarly, the individual GSS investigator—like any police officer—does not possess the authority to employ physical means which infringe upon a suspect's liberty during the interrogation, unless these means are inherently accessory to the very essence of an interrogation and are both fair and reasonable.

During the course of the hearing the issue of the 'ticking time bomb' was raised by **8.76** the Court and in particular if the methods of interrogation would be justified in such circumstances. Following submissions, the Court found that in such instances, it would be open to the interrogator to apply such methods with the caveat that the officer could be subject to criminal proceedings with the defence of 'necessity' being available to him. The Court stated:

> Consequently we are prepared to presume, as was held by the Inquiry Commission's Report, that if a GSS investigator—who applied physical interrogation methods for the purpose of saving human life—is criminally indicted, the 'necessity' defence is likely to be open to him in the appropriate circumstances . . .

In handing down the judgment, the Court emphasized their awareness of the Israeli **8.77** security position but emphasized that the nature of interrogation was such that:

> We are aware that this decision does not ease dealing with that reality. This is the destiny of democracy, as not all means are acceptable to it, and not all practices employed by its enemies are open before it. Although a democracy must often fight with one hand tied behind its back, it nonetheless has the upper hand. Preserving the Rule of Law and recognition of an individual's liberty constitutes an important component in its understanding of security. At the end of the day, they strengthen its

spirit and its strength and allow it to overcome its difficulties. This having been said, there are those who argue that Israel's security problems are too numerous, thereby requiring the authorization to use physical means. If it will nonetheless be decided that it is appropriate for Israel, in light of its security difficulties to sanction physical means in interrogations (and the scope of these means which deviate from the ordinary investigation rules), this is an issue that must be decided by the legislative branch which represents the people. We do not take any stand on this matter at this time. It is there that various considerations must be weighed. The pointed debate must occur there. It is there that the required legislation may be passed, provided, of course, that a law infringing upon a suspect's liberty 'befitting the values of the State of Israel', is enacted for a proper purpose, and to an extent no greater than is required. (Article 8 to the Basic Law: Human Dignity and Liberty).[50]

8.78 We now turn to the handing over of individuals for interrogation to third States which deploy torture tactics. This has been an area of growing concern. Since the events of 11 September 2001, the US has engaged in renditions of individuals and handed them to 'friendly' authorities for the purposes of interrogation where it is known that the country in question uses torture as a tool of interrogation. The US's own policy on what amounts to torture has also come under criticism particularly on the more recent 'water boarding' technique.

8.79 Recently, the Kenyan Government came under criticism[51] for its part in the handing over of some 100 individuals (between 2–31 January 2007), without due process, to either neighbouring countries or to the US.

8.80 In Canada[52] an inquiry[53] was held in relation to the actions of the Canadian, Syrian, and US Authorities in the handing over of Maher Arar, a dual Canadian/Syrian national detained at the airport in New York. The US Authorities detained and questioned him for twelve days and then sent him firstly to Jordan and then to Syria. He was interrogated for twelve days during which he alleged he was tortured. The report, in condemning the actions of the officers, found that the Canadian intelligence officials were under pressure to find terrorists following the events of 11 September 2001 and had provided incorrect information regarding Arar and condemned the deportation on intelligence only in the absence of sufficient safeguards.

8.81 Turning to the third aspect, the deportation of persons either following sentence or where entry is refused/rejection of application for political asylum.

8.82 The deportation of a person from a State also raises obligations for the State based on Article 33 of the United Nations 1951 Convention on the Status of Refugees

---

[50] Para 39.
[51] Report by the Muslim Human Rights Forum [6 July 2007].
[52] See Chapter 9.
[53] The two-and-a-half-year inquiry was concluded in September 2006.

(Refugees Convention)[54] *(non-refoulement),* in that it places a bar on the return of a person if there are fears that if returned, the person's 'life or freedom would be threatened'. At a regional level, the various human rights Courts have read the obligation in the context of prohibition on torture, for example, the European Court in *Chahal v UK* found that C could not be deported to India as there was a fear if returned there was a risk that he may be subjected to treatment contrary to Article 3 of the European Convention on Human Rights. In this regard, therefore, regional courts read the obligations for a Contracting State on a much wider basis than that provided for by the non-refoulement provision of the Refugee Convention.

Like any absolute prohibition on torture, this too is an absolute right and no dero- **8.83**
gation is permitted to a Contracting State to the European Convention on Human Rights however reprehensible the actions of the individual concerned. A practical solution was then found in the obtaining of relevant diplomatic assurances (as in extradition cases) from the State where the person was to be deported, guarantees that the person would not on return be subjected to adverse treatment.

The European Court of Human Rights was recently invited in the *Case of Saadi v* **8.84**
Italy[55] to reconsider its ruling in *Chahal* on the basis that it was too rigid a requirement, particularly in the current context on international terrorism.

Saadi, a national of Tunisia, had entered Italy via France and lived in Milan. In 2002 **8.85**
he was arrested on a number of terrorist-related offences, including conspiracy to commit acts of violence in States other than Italy with the aim of spreading terror. The Milan Assize Court took the view that the offences did not amount to acts of international terrorism but criminal conspiracy. The court sentenced Saadi to four years and six months' imprisonment and ordered that he be deported to Tunisia after serving his sentence. Both the applicant and the prosecutor appealed against the finding of the Milan Assize Court. The Appeal Court referred the matter to the Constitutional Court on the interpretation of the applicable law. In the interim, S was convicted and sentenced in his absence by a military court in Tunisia in relation to terrorism-related offences.

---

[54] Article 33. Prohibition of expulsion or return ('refoulement'):
  1. No Contracting State shall expel or return ('refouler') a refugee in any manner whatsoever to the frontiers of territories where his life or freedom would be threatened on account of his race, religion, nationality, membership of a particular social group or political opinion.
  2. The benefit of the present provision may not, however, be claimed by a refugee whom there are reasonable grounds for regarding as a danger to the security of the country in which he is, or who, having been convicted by a final judgement of a particularly serious crime, constitutes a danger to the community of that country.

[55] [Application no 37201/06] 28 February 2008.

8.86 On 8 August 2006, the Minister ordered him to be deported to Tunisia. S then applied for political asylum on the grounds that he had been sentenced in his absence for political reasons, and if returned he would be subjected to torture and 'political and religious reprisals'. A number of NGOs made representations to the Italian Government urging them not to deport S as their findings illustrated a general abuse of human rights, including torture.

8.87 The Italian Government received diplomatic assurances from Tunisia in respect of his retrial and confirmed his deportation including assurances that if he were deported he would not be subjected to treatment contrary to Article 3 of the ECHR.

8.88 S applied to the European Court of Human Rights against the deportation order on the grounds it violated Article 3, 6 of the Convention. At the hearing the UK intervened on the grounds that the ruling in *Chahal* should be reconsidered in the light of the present prevalent security situation and the absolute prohibition set out in *Chahal* was far too rigid and imposed difficulties on Contracting States when considering expulsion etc. The decision in *Chahal* in effect prevented a Contracting State from putting into the balance issues such as the protection of national security.

8.89 The Court rejected these observations and observed that whilst States had the right to control the entry, residence, and removal of aliens:

> . . . expulsion may give rise to an issue under Article 3, and hence engage the responsibility of that State under the Convention, where substantial grounds have been shown for believing that the person concerned, if deported, faces a real risk of being subjected to treatment contrary to Article 3. In such a case Article 3 implies an obligation not to deport the person in question to that country . . . In so far as any liability under the Convention is incurred, it is liability incurred by the Contracting State, by reason of its having taken action which has a direct consequence the exposure of an individual to the risk of proscribed ill-treatment . . .

8.90 In emphasizing the absolute bar imposed by Article 3, the Grand Chamber rejected the observations submitted by the UK and confirmed that:

> Article 3, which prohibits in absolute terms torture and inhuman or degrading treatment or punishment, enshrines one of the fundamental values of the democratic societies . . . Article 3 makes no provision for exceptions and no derogation from it is permissible under Article 15, even in the event of a public emergency threatening the life of a nation . . . As the prohibition of torture and of inhuman or degrading treatment or punishment is absolute, irrespective of the victim's conduct, the nature of the offence allegedly committed by the applicant is therefore irrelevant for the purposes of Article 3.

8.91 The Court then examined the distinction between ill-treatment and torture and recognized the practical difficulties faced by States but reiterated that irrespective of the current position the absolute nature of Article 3 is sacrosanct. The Court reaffirmed the decision in *Chahal* and confirmed that it is:

> . . . not possible to weigh the risk of ill-treatment against the reasons put forward for the expulsion in order to determine whether the responsibility of a State is engaged under Article 3, even where such treatment is inflicted by another State. In that connection, the conduct of the person concerned, however undesirable or dangerous, cannot be taken into account, with the consequence that the protection afforded by Article 3 is broader than that provided for in Article 32 and 33 of the 1951 United Nations Convention relating to the Status of Refugees . . .

On the issue of diplomatic assurances, the Court expressed some reservations on the manner in which Tunisia had responded to the initial queries by Italy and concluded that even if such assurances had been received it would not absolve the Court from its 'obligation to examine whether such assurances provided . . . a sufficient guarantee that the applicant would be protected against the risk of treatment prohibited by the Convention. The weight to be given to assurances from the receiving State depends in each case, on the circumstances obtaining at the relevant time'. **8.92**

This doubt surrounding diplomatic assurances has been echoed in the US in *Khouzam v Hogan*[56] when the court refused to deport Sameh Khouzam to Egypt based on diplomatic assurances alone. The District Judge concluded that 'no showing has been made . . . that removal based upon diplomatic assurances by a country known to have engaged in torture is consistent with the Convention against torture . . .'. **8.93**

Arbitrary, prolonged, and indefinite detention

Detention by police (pre-trial detention) should only be for a reasonable period of time and as provided for by law, and a person arrested or detained must be allowed to challenge the lawfulness of the arrest and detention before a court, and should be brought without undue delay before a competent and independent tribunal.[57] This provision seeks to preserve the right to habeas corpus proceedings where a person is detained without charge. Any person detained pending trial is entitled to regular supervision of the lawfulness of the detention by a court. However, what amounts to 'reasonable time' before a person is brought before a court depends on all the circumstances. **8.94**

---

[56] *Khouzam v Ashcroft*, 361 F 3d 161, 171 (2d Cir 2004) (US).
[57] Article 9 ICCPR; Article 5 ECHR; Article 7 ACHR; and Article 6 Banjul Charter.

8.95 However, there are minimum standards clearly set by national laws and international/regional law.[58] The European Court of Human Rights has, since *Brogan*, emphasized that pre-trial detention, even in terrorist related cases, must be for a reasonable period. In *Asan and others v Turkey*[59] the Court found that police detention for up to nine days violated Article 5(3), and:

> Although the investigation of terrorist offences undoubtedly presented the authorities with special problems, that did not mean that the authorities had carte blanche under art 5 to arrest suspects and detain them in police custody, free from effective control by the domestic courts and, in the final instance, by the Convention's supervisory institutions, whenever they considered that there had been a terrorist offence. Police detention for four days and six hours had previously been held to violate art 5(3) of the Convention, even though its purpose had been to protect the community as a whole against terrorism. In those circumstances, even supposing that the activities of which the applicants stood accused were linked to a terrorist threat, it had not been necessary to detain them for more than four days and six hours . . .

8.96 In earlier cases in 2005[60] and 2006[61], again involving Turkey, *Pakkan v Turkey*[62] the Court, in finding that a period of thirteen years in detention, despite several hearings at court, was wholly unreasonable coupled with the use of bland assertions by the national court for the grounds for detention, 'having regard to the nature of the offence and the state of evidence' was insufficient. The conduct of the domestic courts was found to be less than satisfactory and the Court reminded Contracting States the test for reasonable delay:

> The reasonableness of the length of proceedings should be assessed in the light of the circumstances of the case, with reference to the criteria established by its case-law, particularly the complexity of the case, the conduct of the applicant and of the relevant authorities, and what was at stake for the applicant. Even though the case involved a certain degree of complexity, it could not be said that that in itself justified the total length of the proceedings. Recalling that art 6(1) of the Convention imposed on the contracting States the duty to organise their legal systems in such a way that their courts could meet each of the requirements of that provision, including the obligation to decide cases within a reasonable time, the domestic court should

---

[58] The European Court of Human Rights in *Brogan v United Kingdom* ((1989) 11 EHRR 117, a Northern Ireland terrorism detention case) held that: 'The assessment of 'promptness' has to be made in the light of the object and purpose of [Article 9(3) ICCPR], which enshrines a fundamental right, namely the protection of the individual against arbitrary interferences by the State with his right to liberty. Judicial control of such interferences is an essential feature of this guarantee, which is intended to minimise the risk of arbitrariness'. It will depend on the circumstances. In that case, there had been excessive delay.

[59] [2007] ECHR 56003/00, para 3.

[60] *Vayic v Turkey* App No 18078/02; [2006] ECHR 18078/02.

[61] *Mete v Turkey* App No 77649/01; [2006] ECHR 77649/01, where a pre-trial detention of five days was found to have violated Article 5(3).

[62] App No 13017/02; [2006] ECHR 13017/02.

have applied stricter measures to speed up the proceedings. It followed that the proceedings in the instant case had been unnecessarily prolonged as the national court had failed to act with the necessary diligence.

The African Commission in *Ouko v Kenya*[63] in considering a complaint of torture **8.97** from O and in the absence of a response from Kenya held that his treatment whilst in detention for ten months without trial amounted to a violation of his dignity and freedom from inhuman and degrading treatment. O had alleged that he had been detained and held at the Secret Service Department in Nairobi where he had been subjected to denial of bathroom facilities, and a 250-watt electric bulb had been left on in his cell throughout the ten months.

The recent attempt to extend pre-trial detention in the UK to forty-two days in **8.98** terrorist cases proved to be controversial and was defeated by the House of Lords. Whether such an extension would have withstood the scrutiny of the European Court is less than likely.

However, the special security imperatives in terrorism cases may permit persons **8.99** detained to be subject to more stringent conditions than in other cases (eg, more restricted access to information and exchange of information). However they should otherwise enjoy no lesser rights than other detainees generally.[64]

The provisions also provide for the ability to challenge detention by seeking a writ **8.100** of habeas corpus. Whilst States may have derogated from certain provisions of the regional or international human rights instruments, it is generally accepted that such a remedy cannot be withheld. In the US this lack of remedy came into sharp focus in respect of those detained at Guantanamo Bay following their capture in Afghanistan or elsewhere. As discussed above, whilst the establishment of the detention facility and those detained therein is subject to *lex specialis* of international humanitarian law, the issue of the challenge to their detention by means of a writ of habeas corpus is of significance.

The US Supreme Court in *Boumediene et al v Bush, President of the United States* **8.101** *et al*, has recently[65] examined the availability of the remedy of habeas corpus in respect of those detained in Guantanamo Bay, and by a majority of 5:4 held that such a remedy is and should be available to foreign detainees held at the base.

This judgment comes after a history of uncertainty and numerous challenges to **8.102** the right of those detained to seek a remedy in the US courts whilst being held

---

[63] (2000) AHRLR 135.
[64] The prohibition on cruel, inhuman, and degrading treatment, Article 7 ICCPR, and Article 10: all persons deprived of their liberty shall be treated with humanity and respect for the inherent dignity of the person.
[65] 12 June 2008.

outside the territory of the US. The US Courts had previously rejected all such applications on the basis that they lacked jurisdiction over a facility based outside the US. There then followed a series of legislative measures seeking to deny such applications before US federal courts.

8.103 The Supreme Court considered the narrow question of whether the remedy of habeas corpus was available to foreign detainees held at Guantanamo Bay and whether the existing legislative regime operating in respect of the detention facility and detainees provide an effective substitute to a writ of habeas corpus. The Court found that the existing regime did not provide an effective remedy and the denial of such a remedy was unconstitutional. It rejected the Government submission that as they did not exercise sovereignty over the base no such remedy could lie. The Court held, inter alia:

> Whilst it accepted that Cuba retained de jure sovereignty, that is not the only criteria for permitting an application for habeas 'Common-law habeas' history provides scant support for this proposition, and it is inconsistent with the Court's precedents and contrary to fundamental separation-of-powers principles.

8.104 The Court found that the *de jure* sovereignty was not the correct test to be adopted as it:

> . . . raises troubling separation-of-powers concerns, which are illustrated by Guantanamo's political history. Although the United States has maintained complete and uninterrupted control of Guantanamo for over 100 years, the Government's view is that the Constitution has no effect there, at least as to non-citizens, because the United States disclaimed formal sovereignty in its 1903 lease with Cuba. The Nation's basic charter cannot be contracted away like this. The Constitution grants Congress and the President the power to acquire, dispose of, and govern territory, not the power to decide when and where its terms apply. To hold that the political branches may switch the Constitution on or off at will would lead to a regime in which they, not this Court, say 'what the law is'.

8.105 The Court found that there were no 'credible arguments that the military mission at Guantanamo would be compromised if habeas courts had jurisdiction . . . and furthermore the remedies available for reviewing detainees' status are not an adequate and effective substitute for the habeas writ . . . and the procedures under Military Commissions Act 2006 operated as "an unconstitutional suspension of the writ"'.

8.106 The Court concluded its findings in the following terms:

> In considering both the procedural and substantive standards used to impose detention to prevent acts of terrorism, the courts must accord proper deference to the political branches. However, security subsists, too, in fidelity to freedom's first principles, chief among them being freedom from arbitrary and unlawful restraint and the personal liberty that is secured by adherence to the separation of powers.

Right to a fair trial

Everyone is equal before the courts, and is entitled to a fair and public hearing **8.107** (unless exceptional circumstances exist) before an independent court.[66] There had previously been some debate on whether the right to a fair trial enjoyed the status of a non-derogable or absolute right or if the exigencies of a situation so demanded, a State could derogate or restrict such a right. This debate has, it would appear now, been settled through jurisprudence and the General Comment No 29, by the Human Rights Committee, which states:

> While article 14[67] is not included in the list of non-derogable rights of article 4, paragraph 2 of the Covenant, States derogating from normal procedures required under article 14 in circumstances of a public emergency should ensure that such derogations do not exceed those strictly required by the exigencies of the actual situation. The guarantees of fair trial may never be made subject to measures of derogation that would circumvent the protection of non-derogable rights. Thus, for example, as article 6 of the Covenant is non-derogable in its entirety, any trial leading to the imposition of the death penalty during a state of emergency must conform to the provisions of the Covenant, including all the requirements of article 14.[68] Similarly, as article 7 is also non-derogable in its entirety, no statements or confessions or, in principle, other evidence obtained in violation of this provision may be invoked as evidence in any proceedings covered by article 14, including during a state of emergency,[69] except if a statement or confession obtained in violation of article 7 is used as evidence that torture or other treatment prohibited by this provision occurred.[70] Deviating from fundamental principles of fair trial, including the presumption of innocence, is prohibited at all times.[71]

As is the case for other criminal trials, the presumption of innocence (Article 14.2) **8.108** remains valid. Article 14.3 of the ICCPR provides in full the minimum standards of justice and fairness for a person facing trial on criminal charges.[72]

In *Öcalan v Turkey*, O was detained in February 1999, and prison authorities did not provide him with the case file until the first hearing on 2 June 1999. On 29 June 1999 he was found guilty of security offences and sentenced to death. The European Court[73] held unanimously that there had been a violation of

---

[66] Article 14 ICCPR; Article 6 ECHR; Article 8 ACHR; and Article 7 Banjul Charter.
[67] General Comment No 32.
[68] General Comment No 29 (2001) on Article 4: Derogations during a state of emergency, para 15.
[69] Ibid, paras 7 and 15.
[70] Cf Convention against Torture and Other Cruel, Inhuman or Degrading Treatment or Punishment, Article 15.
[71] General Comment No 29 (2001) on Article 4: Derogations during a state of emergency, para 11.
[72] 'States in their prosecutions respect certain decencies . . . [these rules] express the notions of justice . . . even toward those charged with the most heinous offences'. (*Rochin v California*, US Supreme Court 1952).
[73] [2003] ECHR 125.

the right to a fair trial, adequate time and facilities for preparation of defence, and to legal assistance. The Court found that other rights had been breached, namely the failure to bring him before a judge promptly after his arrest and the right to have lawfulness of detention in police custody decided speedily by a court.

8.109 Of course, some restrictions on normal fair trial rights are justifiable. The *OECD Guidelines* (2002) on human rights in counter-terrorism provide the following:

> . . . the imperatives of the fight against terrorism may . . . justify certain restrictions to the right of defence, in particular with regard to:
>
> - the arrangements for access to and contacts with counsel;
> - the arrangements for access to the case-file;
> - the use of anonymous testimony.

8.110 Such restrictions to the right of defence must be strictly proportionate to their purpose, and compensatory measures to protect the interests of the accused must be taken so as to maintain the fairness of the proceedings and to ensure that procedural rights are not drained of their substance.

8.111 On the issue of anonymous witnesses, the House of Lords[74] in the UK has recently ruled that[75] such measures cannot be adopted as they do not provide for a fair trial and are, therefore, unlawful.

8.112 The essential thrust, therefore, is that terrorism cases should be treated for the purposes of guaranteeing a fair trial on the same principles as any other criminal case. Thus, the ECHR found that the use of military judges in Turkey in such cases violated Article 6 of ECHR.[76] Similarly, the African Commission in the *Constitutional Rights Project (in respect of Akamu and Others) v Nigeria*[77] found that the tribunals created under the Robbery and Firearms (Special Provisions) Act violated Article 7(1)(d)[78] of the Charter as it was made up of a judge, an officer

---

[74] *R v Davis (Iain)* [2008] UKHL 36 (18 June 2008).

[75] Discussed in more detail in Chapter 4.

[76] *Ulusoy v Turkey* Appln 52709/99; *Ergin v Turkey* Appln 47533/99; *Seckin & Others v Turkey* Appln 56016/00; *Kaya v Turkey* Appln 2624/02.

[77] (2000) AHRLR.

[78] Article 7 provides:

'Every individual shall have the right to have his cause heard. This comprises: (a) the right to an appeal to competent national organs against acts of violating his fundamental rights as recognized and guaranteed by conventions, laws, regulations and customs in force; (b) the right to be presumed innocent until proved guilty by a competent court or tribunal; (c) the right to defence, including the right to be defended by counsel of his choice; (d) the right to be tried within a reasonable time by an impartial court or tribunal. 2. No one may be condemned for an act or omission which did not constitute a legally punishable offence at the time it was committed. No penalty may be inflicted for an offence for which no provision was made at the time it was committed. Punishment is personal and can be imposed only on the offender.'

of the military services, and a police officer, essentially members of the executive branch who had been instrumental in the passing of the Act, and had no legal expertise.

F. Privacy, Confidentiality, and Personal Information Issues

It should be remembered that counter-terrorism operations often intrude into the private lives of persons and their personal information. As with interference with liberty, clear legal justification must exist for interfering with the privacy of individuals, by whatever means, technological, or otherwise. **8.113**

Measures such as searches, bugging, telephone tapping, surveillance, and use of undercover officers, and all measures to collect and process what may be private personal information must be legally authorized, necessary, proportionate to the information being sought, and, preferably, subject to a form of independent review. It must also be possible to challenge the lawfulness of such measures in court. **8.114**

The deployment of covert, intrusive techniques is not new and is not unique to counter-terrorism investigations. However, in recent years there has been an increasing reliance on covert intelligence-gathering and intelligence-led and proactive criminal investigations. Indeed, the use of such techniques may well be the only way to obtain information or evidence needed in certain cases. **8.115**

The right to a personal or private life is a qualified or derogable right. However, what amounts to 'private' or 'personal' will be widely construed and may include a person's activities in a public place and in the place of work. **8.116**

There must be a basis in domestic law or legislation which provides for the deployment of the covert activity or technique. Such legislation must be accessible to those liable to be affected and must have sufficient clarity to give a person an indication as to the circumstances and conditions in which convert methods by a public authority may be used. **8.117**

The practical effect of the regional initiatives is an expectation that there should be a regime of independent supervision of the use of covert, intrusive powers.[79] Interference with an individual's right to a private life must fulfil a pressing social need, be in pursuit of an aim which can be justified in law (eg, to prevent or detect crime), and any covert deployment must be only that which is necessary to achieve what is sought to be achieved (ie, the detection of a particular crime). In addition, safeguards must be in place to prevent abuse by intrusive techniques, and remedies must be available in the event of such abuse. **8.118**

---

[79] See, for example, the ECHR case of *Malone v UK* [1984] 7 EHRR 14.

8.119 The interference must also be proportionate to what is sought to be achieved by it. Thus, for example, a deployment with a listening device in a target's bedroom may require much greater justification than a deployment in a living room.

8.120 In considering whether a covert technique, or deployment, is indeed proportionate to the legitimate aim which is being pursued, consideration should be given to the following:

- Have sufficient, relevant reasons been set out in support of the deployment?
- Could the same aim have been achieved by use of a less intrusive method?
- Did the authorizing/decision-making process as to the deployment take place in a way which was procedurally fair?
- Do adequate safeguards exist to prevent abuse?
- Does the interference in question destroy the very essence of the right to a private/personal life?

8.121 The freedom of expression under Article 10 of the ECHR has been the subject of a recent decision (2 October 2008) before the European Court of Human Rights. The Court handed a judgment[80] in relation to the publication of cartoons by a French cartoonist shortly after the events of 11 September. The cartoons illustrated the attack on the World Trade Center with the words 'We have all dreamt about it . . . Hamas did it'. The cartoonist, Denis Leroy and the magazine responsible for the publication were prosecuted in France for offences relating to 'apology of terrorism'.

8.122 Before the European Court, L argued that his prosecution amounted to violation of his rights under Article 10 as he was simply expressing his Anti-American feelings. The Court dismissed the application and found that there had been no violation of Article 10, that being a restrictive right as it serves a legitimate aim.

8.123 This judgment is of significant importance in the terrorism cases where it relates to the freedom of expression given the current debates surrounding 'apology of terrorism'.

8.124 This chapter has, then, sought to address some of the key issues relating to human rights in the context of counter-terrorism which straddle both international human rights law and international humanitarian law as the response by States has, since the events of 11 September, engaged both military and non-military responses. Therefore an overlap is inevitable given that terrorism goes to the heart of national security and the protection of its citizens and property. This difficult balance has been acknowledged by national and regional courts in the protection of human rights as highlighted by the cases above. The challenges faced by a State

---

[80] Currently only available in French; AFFAIRE LEROY C FRANCE *(Requête n° 36109/03).*

has been crystallized by the President of the Israel Supreme Court, Aharon Barak, in the following terms:

> Democratic nations should conduct the struggle against terrorism with a proper balance between two conflicting values and principles. On one hand, we must consider the values and principles relating to the security of the State and its citizens. Human rights are not a stage for national destruction; they cannot justify undermining national security in every case and in all circumstances. Similarly, a constitution is not a prescription for national suicide. But on the other hand, we must consider the values and principles relating to human dignity and freedom. National security cannot justify undermining human rights in every case and under all circumstances. National security does not grant an unlimited license to harm the individual.[81]

---

[81] A Barak, *Judgments of the Israel Supreme Court: Fighting Terrorism within the Law* (Israel Supreme Court, Jerusalem 2005) 14.

9

INTERNATIONAL COOPERATION

A. Introduction   9.01
B. **Mutual Legal Assistance:**
   General Principles   9.03
   Mutual legal assistance and
      informal requests   9.03
   The UN instruments   9.05
   The legal bases for assistance   9.17
   Grounds for refusal   9.20
   Execution of requests in accordance
      with the laws of the requested state   9.28
C. **Mutual Legal Assistance or**
   Mutual Assistance?   9.60
   Formal requests
      (mutual legal assistance)   9.70
   The form of the letter of request   9.75
   Particular problems experienced in
      mutual legal assistance sought in
      counter-terrorism cases   9.99
   Sensitive information contained
      within the letter of request   9.100

Adducing evidence obtained
   from abroad   9.101
Challenging a refusal to execute a
   letter of request   9.102
D. **Extradition**   9.113
   What is 'extradition'?   9.113
   Comity: disguised/irregular
      extradition   9.119
   European Arrest Warrant   9.138
   The UN counter-terrorism
      instruments   9.148
   Extradition crime and dual
      criminality   9.152
   'Extradite or prosecute'
      (*aut dedere aut judicare*)   9.162
   Political offence exception   9.168
   Other protections   9.209
   Human rights considerations   9.219

A. Introduction

The adoption of UNSCR 1373 on 28 September 2001 gave an impetus never **9.01** before seen to counter-terrorism measures generally and to international cooperation in particular. Adopted under Chapter VII of the UN Charter, UNSCR 1373 imposes a number of obligations on Member States. Importantly for the purposes of the discussion below, although it was adopted in response to the 11 September 2001 terrorist attacks in the United States, the measures it sets forth are expressed in a much broader way and, arguably, seek to set new international norms in relation to counter-terrorism cooperation between States. The framework created by the 16 UN counter-terrorism (CT) instruments must be read in conjunction with the text of UNSCR 1373, and mutual legal assistance and extradition must be understood in the light of the following provisions:

Calling on States to work together urgently to prevent and suppress terrorist acts, including through increased cooperation and full implementation of the relevant international conventions relating to terrorism

2. Decides . . . that all States shall . . .

(f) Afford one another the greatest measure of assistance in connection with criminal investigations or criminal proceedings relating to the financing or support of terrorist acts, including assistance in obtaining evidence in their possession necessary for the proceedings;

3. Calls upon all States to . . .

(c) Cooperate, particularly through the bilateral and multilateral arrangements and agreements, to prevent and suppress terrorist attacks and take action against perpetrators of such acts;

. . .

(e) Increase cooperation and fully implement the relevant international conventions and protocols relating to terrorism and Security Council Resolutions 1269 (1999) and 1368 (2001).

9.02 International cooperation includes but is not limited to:

- mutual legal assistance (MLA)
- extradition
- seizure and forfeiture of terrorist property[1]
- transfer of convicted and serving prisoners.

This chapter will, however, focus on the first two of these measures.

B. Mutual Legal Assistance: General Principles

Mutual legal assistance and informal requests

9.03 The framework and procedures within which both formal assistance from State to State via a letter of request (referred to as 'mutual legal assistance') and informal cooperation, typically from investigator to investigator or prosecutor to prosecutor (referred to as 'mutual assistance') are obtained are sometimes bewildering and very often depend on the attitude and opinions of those 'on the ground' to whom the request is made. Whether formal or informal, the importance of such cooperation cannot be overstated.

---

[1] Although some of the comments in relation to MLA will assist on this topic, it is covered extensively in Chapter 6 on the Financing of Terrorism.

Counter-terrorism operations, by their very nature, are usually transnational in **9.04** character and scope; and, as such, require investigators and prosecutors to gather evidence across borders. However, if for the purposes of criminalization and even extradition, ratification and implementation of the UN CT instruments can be said to be 'the foundation of a successful global counter-terrorism strategy . . .',[2] they have been slow to provide a detailed framework for investigative and evidentiary cooperation between States. Largely reactive they might be, but the instruments are, nevertheless, the only truly global foundation for international cooperation in terrorism cases. Any discussion of mutual legal assistance must, therefore, pay due regard to them, whilst at the same time recognize that it is the UN CT instruments, regional agreements, bilateral treaties, and States' domestic laws which, taken together, have provided the precondition for building a comprehensive network for cooperation.

The UN Instruments

Unsurprisingly, the non-penal Tokyo Convention makes no mention of mutual **9.05** legal assistance. The requirement that State Parties afford assistance in criminal proceedings appeared first in Article 10.1 of the Hague Convention which provides that:

Article 10

1. Contracting States shall afford one another the greatest measure of assistance in connection with criminal proceedings brought in respect of the offence and other acts mentioned in Article 4. The law of the State requested shall apply in all cases.
2. The provisions of paragraph 1 of this Article shall not affect obligations under any other treaty, bilateral or multilateral, which governs or will govern, in whole or in part, mutual assistance in criminal matters.

The statement that the law of the requested State shall apply is one that will be **9.06** familiar to all mutual legal assistance practitioners, but that aside, the provision is wide and ill-defined, making no attempt to address mutual legal assistance specifically, nor create a workable mechanism. Looked at in the context of criminal investigations at a time when transnational crime was not yet a norm, the approach is, however, understandable. Indeed that assistance provision was replicated the following year, 1971, in Article 11 of the Montreal Convention. That instrument goes further in one respect, though, with recognition in

---

[2] Terrorism Prevention Branch, UN Office on Drugs and Crime, 'Preventing Terrorist Acts: A Criminal Justice Strategy' (Technical Assistance Working Paper, 2006) 37.

Article 12 of the need for a State to cooperate informally on an intelligence or law enforcement basis, particularly in relation to information sharing.

9.07 Article 12 provides: 'Any Contracting State having reason to believe that one of the offences mentioned in Article 1 will be committed shall, in accordance with its national law, furnish any relevant information in its possession to those States which it believes would be the States mentioned in Article 5, paragraph 1.'

9.08 The reference to Article 5(1) being to the jurisdiction provisions, and hence to the obligation on parties to provide information relevant to a convention offence to any Party in whose territory the suspect is presently situated, to whom the aircraft is registered, in which an affected aircraft has landed with the suspect still on board, or in which the lessee of an un-crewed aircraft has as his place of business or residence.

9.09 The general 'obligation to assist' provision appears again in both The Diplomats Convention [1973], and The Hostages Convention [1979], although in the latter with a supplement:

> Article 11 of the Hostages Convention provides:
> 1. States Parties shall afford one another the greatest measure of assistance in connexion with criminal proceedings brought in respect of the offences set forth in article 1, including the supply of all evidence at their disposal necessary for the proceedings.
> 2. The provisions of paragraph 1 of this article shall not affect obligations concerning mutual judicial assistance embodied in any other treaty.

9.10 That is the first explicit recognition in the UN counter-terrorism instruments of the need to transmit evidence from State to State, although stopping short still at this stage of addressing evidence-gathering itself. The wording is used again in almost identical form in Article 12 of the Nuclear Materials Convention [1980], Article 13 of the Convention for the Suppression of Unlawful Acts Against the Safety of Maritime Navigation [1988], and Article 10 of The Bombings Convention [1997].

9.11 In tracing the growing recognition in the instruments of the importance of cooperation, it is also worthy of note that from the Montreal Convention [1971], the UN CT instruments oblige parties to take measures to prevent offences against other Parties. Such a pre-emptive obligation broadened in The Diplomats Convention to a duty to exchange information and coordinate administrative and other preventive measures.

9.12 As an aside, until The Bombings Convention, the Articles in the instruments which dealt with the obligation to assist each referred to 'assistance in connection with criminal proceedings'. The choice of the words 'criminal proceedings' appears to have had in mind the evidence-gathering process in civil law systems, where criminal inquiries are usually conducted under the authority of an investigating magistrate who opens a formal proceeding. However that form of words may cause difficulties to the traditional approach in common law jurisdictions where the evidence-gathering phase of an investigation will be opened and conducted by the police without necessarily having any involvement of a prosecutor or judge until a formal charge is instituted; although, increasingly, in common law jurisdictions, prosecutors are called to advise upon, but not direct, aspects of the investigation.

In order to remedy that ambiguity, Article 10 of The Bombings Convention **9.13** introduced the language 'investigations or criminal or extradition proceedings', a formulation employed in the subsequent instruments developed by the General Assembly's Ad Hoc Committee:

> Article 10(1) provides: 'States Parties shall afford one another the greatest measure of assistance in connection with investigations or criminal or extradition proceedings brought in respect of the offences set forth in article 2, including assistance in obtaining evidence at their disposal necessary for the proceedings.'

It is with the 1999 Financing of Terrorism Convention that a truly proactive **9.14** approach in MLA is seen for the first time in the UN CT instruments. Having obliged States, in Article 8, to take measures to identify, detect, and freeze funds used or allocated for the purpose of a convention offence, as well as proceeds derived from such offences, Article 12 provides that:

1. States Parties shall afford one another the greatest measure of assistance in connection with criminal investigations or criminal or extradition proceedings in respect of the offences set forth in article 2, including assistance in obtaining evidence in their possession necessary for the proceedings.
2. States Parties may not refuse a request for mutual legal assistance on the ground of bank secrecy.
3. The requesting Party shall not transmit or use information or evidence furnished by the requested Party for investigations, prosecutions or proceedings other than those stated in the request without the prior consent of the requested Party.
4. Each State Party may give consideration to establishing mechanisms to share with other States Parties information or evidence needed to establish criminal, civil or administrative liability pursuant to article 5.
5. States Parties shall carry out their obligations under paragraphs 1 and 2 in conformity with any treaties or other arrangements on mutual legal assistance or information exchange that may exist between them. In the absence of such treaties or arrangements, States Parties shall afford one another assistance in accordance with their domestic law.

In addition to the urging for as permissive an assistance regime as possible, the **9.15** above can be seen to contain the denial of bank secrecy as a ground of refusal, and a push, albeit a non-mandatory one, to States to establish information and evidence-sharing mechanisms for the purposes of taking proceedings against legal persons.

Building on the UN instruments

9.16 In the immediate aftermath of the terrorist attacks of 9/11, a number of States issued decrees instructing governmental bodies to increase their involvement in international cooperation. Since much non-judicial cooperation can be accomplished by the executive branch within its existing powers, these orders may be an expeditious and effective means of implementing basic mutual assistance requirements. More formal and binding arrangements can be secured by ratification and implementation of the UN CT instruments and by negotiations of bilateral or multilateral mutual assistance treaties (see the Model Treaty on Mutual Assistance in Criminal Matters (General Assembly Resolution 45/117, Annex)[3] and the Manual on the Model Treaty on Mutual Assistance in Criminal Matters.[4]

The legal bases for assistance

9.17 As a general principle, MLA is the mechanism for evidence-gathering and informal assistance is for the provision of intelligence or information. However, the caveat is that many States will provide evidence from, for instance, a voluntary witness informally, without the need for a formal letter of request. If, therefore, a request for evidence does not involve the requested State exercising a coercive power that State may well agree to render assistance on the basis of investigator (or prosecutor) to investigator (or prosecutor).

9.18 If, however, a formal request is needed then it must, generally have a legal basis. Such a basis might be:

- A multilateral convention (such as one of the UN CT instruments or a regional convention);
- A bilateral treaty;
- A voluntary arrangement between States, such as the Scheme Relating to Mutual Assistance in Criminal Matters within the Commonwealth ('The Harare Scheme') for Commonwealth States;
- Domestic law, which may, or may not, impose a reciprocity requirement.

---

[3] Reproduced in Appendix 3, below.
[4] The Manual can be found at <http://www.un.org/documents/ga/res/45/a45r117.htm>.

In respect of the above, it should be borne in mind that there is no all-encompass- **9.19**
ing or 'universal' MLA convention and that assistance may be requested and
received in the absence of any treaty agreement and, indeed, in the case of some
States, in the absence of any domestic MLA law.

Grounds for refusal

The grounds for refusal of an MLA request are broadly similar to those in relation **9.20**
to extradition, which are addressed below,[5] save (i) that there is a strong international trend in favour of encouraging MLA to be as permissive as possible, even if
that means striking down some of the grounds of refusal that have been relied
upon by States, and (ii) most States in relation to MLA requests will assert in
national law and/or international agreements that there is a general ground for
refusal when a State is of the view that its national interests, sovereignty, or security
would be threatened thereby. However, it has to be said that, in practice, that
general ground is rarely exercised and that, where in a specific instance, that
ground does arise, there should be consultation between requesting and requested
State in order that a balance may be struck between, on the one hand, the importance of international cooperation and, on the other, national interests or national
security.

Dual criminality

The principle of dual, or double, criminality is dealt with in detail below,[6] in rela- **9.21**
tion to extradition. Whilst it is seen as an essential safeguard in extradition law, its
applicability in MLA varies greatly. Some States do not insist on dual criminality
to provide assistance, whilst others enforce the principle strictly. A third category
requires dual criminality only where the request involves a coercive power such as
search and seizure. To complicate matters even more, some of those States that
have a dual criminality requirement regard its absence as a discretionary ground
for refusal, whilst for others it is an essential precondition.

However, even where the requirement still exists, proactive provisions and **9.22**
interpretations are reducing its effect as a bar to cooperation. Indeed, Article 43,
para 2 of the UN Convention Against Corruption illustrates what is perhaps the
prevailing mood, by emphasizing a broad approach to the 'conduct' test:

> In matters of international cooperation, whenever dual criminality is considered a
> requirement, it shall be deemed fulfilled irrespective of whether the laws of the
> requested State Party place the offence within the same category of offence or
> denominate the offence by the same terminology as the requesting State Party, if the

---

[5] See 9.219 ff.
[6] See 9.152 ff.

conduct underlying the offence for which assistance is sought is a criminal offence under the laws of both States Parties.

Political offence

9.23 Denial of assistance in MLA on the basis of the political offence exception has traditionally posed great challenges; however, as discussed in relation to extradition, below, its importance in relation to terrorism offences has diminished considerably.

Fiscal offence exception and bank secrecy

9.24 Both international treaties and the domestic law of some States allow refusal of an MLA request on the ground that the offence under investigation is a fiscal one. However, The Terrorism Financing Convention specifically provides at Article 13 that: 'none of the offences set forth in article 2 shall be regarded, for the purposes of extradition or mutual legal assistance, as a fiscal offence. Accordingly, States Parties may not refuse a request for extradition or for mutual legal assistance on the sole ground that it concerns a fiscal offence'.

9.25 Similarly, in relation to bank secrecy, Article 12(2) provides that: 'States Parties may not refuse a request for mutual legal assistance on the ground of bank secrecy'.

Death penalty

9.26 Many States will deny assistance if the offence under consideration may attract the death penalty in the event of conviction. The determining factor is not that a State retains the death penalty, but rather whether the offence is punishable by death. However, this ground is more difficult for a State to apply in MLA than in extradition, since the investigation may be at an early stage and it may be impossible to say with any certainty whether there is a risk of the death penalty. In the event, though, that this consideration becomes a 'live' issue in respect of a letter of request, consultations will need to take place between the requesting and requested State in order to ascertain whether appropriate assurances can be given by those making the request.

Dual jeopardy (*non bis in idem*)

9.27 MLA may be refused on the basis of dual jeopardy. However, international treaties, both multilateral and bilateral, vary greatly on how this principle is addressed. Some treaties look at whether the suspect has been convicted or punished for the crime in the requesting or requested State, whilst others extend to consider proceedings in a third State. Similarly, some texts formulate the test as to whether a person has been acquitted or convicted, whilst others ask whether a person has been 'punished'. Practitioners must, therefore, examine the language of any relevant treaty closely.

Execution of requests in accordance with the laws of the requested state

An MLA request will be executed in accordance with the laws of the requested **9.28** State. However, where not inconsistent with those laws, a requesting State may ask that investigative processes be carried out in accordance with procedures set out in its law.

In deciding whether an enquiry is relevant, a court in the requested State should **9.29** adopt a wide interpretation and should have in mind that admissibility will be a matter for the trial court in the requesting State as illustrated by *Mutual Legal Assistance in Criminal Matters, Re* (CA (Ont)) Court of Appeal (Ontario), 13 September 1999.[7]

The Russian Federation submitted a request for mutual legal assistance to Canada **9.30** in respect of an investigation of theft and corruption involving Russian citizens and government officials. In executing the request, the Canadian authorities obtained search warrants and seized a number of documents from the business premises of X. They also seized documents held in three banks.

X appealed against an order made under the Mutual Legal Assistance in Criminal **9.31** Matters Act 1985 section 18, which directed that copies of the documents be handed to a specified official and a further order under section 20 of the same Act for the documents to be sent to the Russian Federation.

The Court[8] dismissed the appeal and held: **9.32**

(1) the Act did not require that a foreign State's request for assistance should comply with section 18(1);
(2) the issue of 'relevance' had to be given a wide judicial interpretation at the investigative stage of criminal proceedings, especially where commercial matters were concerned, as in the instant case. The judge making an order under section 20 was not concerned with the ultimate admissibility of any of the documents in a Russian court, and
(3) 'relevance' therefore meant information that would assist the foreign authorities in discovering and proving the events underlying the allegations that formed the subject matter of the Russian investigation.

---

[7] [2001] I L Pr 11.
[8] McMurtry, CJ.

Evidence to be used in proceedings in relation to which the request was made/ admissibility and exclusionary issues arising out of such evidence to be adjudicated upon by the trial court in the requested State

In re Request from L Kasper-Ansermet, Examining Magistrate for the Republic and Canton of Geneva, etc.[9]

9.33   This case concerns a request for assistance by the Swiss Authorities to the US. The facts of the case can be briefly summarized as follows:

9.34   In 1975 Salvatore Giordano and Salvatore Giordano Jr ['the Giordanos'] were employed by the Fedders Corporation.[10] The company entered into negotiations and allegedly sold a large quantity of refrigeration equipment to two Iranian companies, namely General Industrial Corporation and Loristan Refrigeration Industries. The Giordanos submit that they were not directly involved in the negotiation of the transaction, but recollect that Fedders sold certain refrigeration machinery and equipment for approximately $9 million and was paid only $7 million and further that Fedders' investment in an Iranian company was expropriated without compensation by the Islamic Republic of Iran.

9.35   Consequently in 1982, Fedders Corporation commenced an action against the Iranian companies before the Iran-US Claims Tribunal. Loristan filed a counter-claim against Fedders before the Claims Tribunal alleging fraud in this transaction.

9.36   The Iran-US Claims Tribunal reached no decision and a retrial was scheduled for 5 June 1989.

9.37   In or around 1985, the Examining Magistrate in Geneva, L Kasper-Ansermet, conducted an investigation and 'pronounced indictment' on Enayat Behbehani, who was the president of General Industrial Company for fraud under Articles 25 and 148 of the Swiss Criminal Code. It was alleged that the refrigeration equip-ment sold as new to Loristan for $25,279,122, was actually known to Behbehani to be used and repainted and only worth about $9,000,000. Secondly, Behbehani had allegedly received $4.5 million personally and illegally from this transaction, from the sums paid out by Loristan. The indictment also named Mr Bruno Giordano.

9.38   The Examining Magistrate, relying on the US-Swiss Treaty for Mutual Assistance, submitted a request to the US. The US authorities issued subpoenas for both Giordanos requiring them to attend before an Asst US Attorney in order to answer

---

[9]   132 FRD 622 (1990), US Dist.
[10]   The name of the company was subsequently changed to Rotorex Corporation and the Giordanos are members of the Board.

questions submitted by the Swiss Authorities and to permit the Swiss Magistrate to 'pronounce indictment' on both of them. The Giordanos challenged the Swiss request for assistance on a number of grounds, as follows:

1. That the Swiss investigation and the subsequent request for assistance was not for criminal purposes, but a disguise to permit the effort by the Iranians to subvert the exclusive civil jurisdiction of the Iran-US Claims Tribunal.

The Court, in expressing its disapproval of the disclosure of the evidence gathered **9.39** by the Examining Magistrate to a litigant in other proceedings stated:

> I have held that the previous Swiss request for the Giordanos' addresses was made in connection with a criminal prosecution and not for the improper purpose of coercion or harassment by the Swiss authorities, and that this court is not the proper forum to adjudicate a claim of unethical or unlawful conduct of the Iranians with respect to their behavior before the Claims Tribunal.

> I continue to have the impression that the Swiss investigation is primarily for criminal purposes, although it is troubling to learn that the Swiss Magistrate has shared information developed in his criminal investigation with the Iranians for their use before the Iran-US Claims Tribunal, as demonstrated by the letters of October 12, 1988 and November 21, 1988, above . . . Again, the concerns of the Giordanos and Fedders Corporation as to the impropriety of the Iranians' conduct before the Claims Tribunal is best addressed to that forum, in which the Fedders Corporation is a litigant. It is indeed repugnant to any concept of fair play for the Iranians to make ex parte submissions to the Claims Tribunal without notice being given to their adversaries . . .

2. The propriety of the civil subpoenas in order to compel their presence before the appointed Commissioner. In order to comply with the request, the United States authorities issued civil subpoenas to compel the Giordanos' appearances before the Asst District Attorney to give a deposition/information. The court acknowledged that the terms of the Treaty[11] permitted such a course of action and that the law of the requested State applied.

The Giordanos submitted that the issuance of the civil subpoenas was wholly **9.40** inappropriate and incorrect as the procedures to obtain testimony evidence in the course of an investigation are set out in the Federal Rules of Criminal Procedure. Furthermore, the Treaty recognizes that the criminal procedures of the requested State must be followed, which was not the case in this instance. The correct procedure they say was to issue a grand jury subpoena.

---

[11] Art 10, § 1 provides: 'A person whose testimony or statement is requested under this Treaty shall be compelled to appear, testify and produce documents, records and articles of evidence in the same manner and to the same extent as in criminal investigations or proceedings in the requested State. Such person may not be so compelled if under the law in either State he has a right to refuse . . .'.

9.41 The Government, for their part accepted that a civil subpoena, in general, had no application in a federal criminal investigation, and that the procedure which would be used to compel a criminal suspect or target witness to appear for identification purposes and for questioning during the course of a criminal investigation would be a grand jury subpoena, and further that such a subpoena is authorized under the Treaty. There was therefore, insufficient or no explanation as to why the authorities had proceeded in the manner they had done namely by civil subpoena rather than by grand jury subpoena save to say that the Federal Rules with respect to compelling testimony in civil litigation are essentially identical to the language for grand jury subpoenas.

9.42 The issue therefore to be determined by the Court was whether the civil subpoenas used in such circumstances, namely a criminal investigation are inconsistent with the Treaty's requirement for the use of procedures 'which would ordinarily be used in comparable investigations or proceedings' under federal law for criminal investigation.

9.43 The Magistrate examined the Treaty provisions and relevant domestic law,[12] including grand jury subpoena, and concluded that the civil subpoena was the appropriate procedure and that 'A grand jury subpoena, after all, is not a procedural document issued by the court, but is instead issued by a grand jury at the direction of the United States Attorney. A civil subpoena, on the other hand, is most certainly a "procedural document" in accordance with its own procedural law to require the attendance and statement or testimony of persons'.[13]

9.44 He also found that the subpoena was not limited to civil cases but rather extended to criminal investigations or proceedings. To construe otherwise would have the effect of rendering the Treaty ineffective for the purposes of evidence-gathering and he observed:

> Thus, the court holds that a civil subpoena to compel attendance of a witness for self-identification and testimony is an appropriate procedure under the Treaty. Alternatively, even if a civil subpoena were not in accordance with applicable Treaty provisions, it is a procedural document, issued under authority of the court to compel attendance and testimony of a witness, which is functionally identical in scope to a grand jury subpoena for these purposes; to reject the civil subpoena and to compel the Government to obtain and serve a grand jury subpoena for these purposes instead would elevate form over function. The spirit of the Treaty is to 'provide . . . for broad assistance between the United States and Switzerland in criminal matters . . . includ[ing] assistance in . . . the obtaining of statements and testimony of witnesses . . .'.

---

[12] 28 USC § 1782.
[13] Simandle, Magistrate.

3. Swiss proceedings are fundamentally unfair and deny due process of law. This ground of objection was put in a number of ways, as follows:

(i) Swiss Law permits trials and convictions in absence. This runs contrary to the protections afforded to US nationals under the Constitution.

(ii) Passage of time—given the amount of time that had lapsed since the transaction (fourteen years), they could not reasonably be expected to secure evidence in their defence particularly as some of the key witnesses were now dead.

(iii) Statute of limitation.

(iv) The right to silence, protected under the US Constitution, if exercised in the current proceedings would permit a Swiss jury to draw an adverse inference. This would have the effect of violating their right to silence.

(v) The Pronouncement of Indictment by the Swiss Magistrate during a hearing connected with evidence gathering ran counter to such proceedings as it had the effect of arraigning a defendant which would most certainly fall foul of the Treaty.

The Court examined each of these objections in turn.

Trials in absence

The evidence submitted on their behalf setting out the position under Swiss Law **9.45** confirmed that Articles 234–8 and 330–3 of the Geneva Code of Criminal Procedure provides for a criminal trial to be held and a conviction made *in absentia*. This could necessitate their being present at the hearing even though a request for extradition had not been made and no reliance could properly be placed on the MLA Treaty. The court, relying on a judgment in an extradition case, concluded that following the directions from the Supreme Court 'a federal court shall not require the foreign tribunal in which a criminal proceeding is pending to provide a process equivalent to the American protections of individual rights'.

On that basis, the fact that Swiss law provided for trial and conviction *in absentia* **9.46** did not in itself preclude the granting of assistance in a criminal investigation. The court observed that:

> First, there has been no trial in absentia in this matter; this is not a situation where the Swiss are seeking to identify and locate individuals who have actually been convicted in absentia. As the future unfolds, there may be no trial, or the defendants may choose to attend, or there may be an acquittal, or charges may be dropped. No one can say for sure. Second, the Treaty obligates American judicial assistance in this matter, notwithstanding the knowledge of the Treaty's ratifiers that the Swiss system's protection of rights of the accused is not the equal of our own. If a duty of inquiry were triggered by the Swiss request for assistance in this criminal matter, then it would be triggered in all such matters and assistance would be precluded if the hypothetical future Swiss trial would not protect US constitutional rights. Under that

scenario, the Treaty obligations would be undermined by general inquiry into the nature of rights protected by Swiss law in a hypothetical prosecution and trial. Such a duty of inquiry, at this stage of the proceedings, would thus be highly inappropriate, unless this right is addressed in the Treaty . . .

Statute of limitation and passage of time

9.47 Given the delay in commencing these proceedings, it was submitted that in similar circumstances in the US, a prosecution would be time barred. The Court rejected this objection as the Swiss Magistrate had confirmed that the statue of limitation did not expire until 1991.

9.48 On the related matter of the passage of time and the likely prejudice they would face in mounting their defence due to the death of some of the key players in the initial transactions and the general inability to secure evidence after all this time, the US magistrate was of the view that it would not be possible for him to judge the impact of this delay as the current matter before him concerned the gathering of evidence and he had no further information on the role of the Giordanos' in the original transactions or indeed the evidence already in the possession of the Swiss authorities. It would therefore be a matter for the Swiss courts to determine what prejudice, if any the delay had caused.

Right to remain silent

9.49 The Giordanos confirmed to the court that in accordance with their constitutional right, it was their intention to exercise the right to remain silent. This they submit could then be used against them in Swiss proceedings as the jury would be directed that an adverse inference can be drawn.

9.50 Further the Treaty itself specifically permits a refusal to answer questions[14] and prohibits the Swiss from penalizing the Giordanos based on such refusal. However the consequence of an adverse inference would have a harsh consequence, namely

---

[14] Art 10, § 1, provides in part:

'A person whose testimony or statement is requested under this Treaty shall be compelled to appear, testify and produce documents, records and articles of evidence in the same manner and in the same extent as in criminal investigations or proceedings in the requested State. Such person may not be so compelled if under the law in either State he has a right to refuse. If any person claims that such a right is applicable in the requesting State, the requesting State shall, with respect thereto, rely on a certification of the Central Authority of the requesting State.'

Art. 14 provides that: 'the requesting state may not subject a witness to any legal sanction solely because he exercised rights permitted under the Treaty', stating:

'No citizen of the requested State who has refused to give non-compulsory testimony or information or against whom compulsory measures had to be applied in the requested State pursuant to this Treaty shall be subjected to any legal sanction in the requesting State solely because he has exercised such rights as permitted under this Treaty.'

a finding of guilt. Therefore the Swiss trial, in any event, could have the effect of violating the Treaty. The magistrate observed that a:

> finding of guilt based solely upon refusal to testify would clearly violate Art. 14, because the Swiss authorities have agreed that no American citizen will be subjected to any legal sanction in Switzerland solely because the American citizen has exercised his right to silence. This court cannot presume that the Swiss authorities would violate their Treaty obligations. The Treaty does not, however, absolutely prohibit any use at trial of the fact of refusal to testify; the Treaty precludes the Swiss only from using the Giordanos' silence as the sole evidence supporting a guilty verdict. Otherwise, nothing in the Treaty alters the Swiss law's use of a defendant's refusal to testify as a source for adverse inference.

The magistrate, in concluding that even though there was a difference in the application of the right to remain silent between the jurisdictions it was not a basis for a refusal to provide assistance in criminal matters. However, the Court expressed some unease with the situation in the following terms: **9.51**

> The sovereign states, in negotiating the Treaty, could have provided instead that no adverse use whatsoever would be made of the fact that a witness exercised his right to refuse to testify; they did not do so, and this court is not free to rewrite the Treaty to conform to the strictures of evidence before an American court. The drafters were presumably well aware that a Swiss court could use silence as evidence from which adverse inferences may be drawn, and they were aware of the Swiss system of 'freedom of evidence', which permits admission in criminal cases of 'all the evidence, direct and indirect [and] investigations' . . .

Pronouncement of indictment by Swiss Magistrate

The Court at the outset recognized that the 'pronouncement of indictment' did not have a direct equivalent in the US criminal justice system. It examined the nature of the 'pronouncement of indictment' based on the evidence of the Swiss Magistrate[15] and found that it was akin to a pre-trial hearing. The Treaty is **9.52**

---

[15] The court provided a useful summary of the evidence of the Swiss Magistrate, L Kasper-Ansermet: Under the Geneva Code of Criminal Proceedings ['GPPG'] the Examining Magistrate conducts the criminal investigation and decides whether the information is sufficient to bring charges. According to Article 134 of the GPPG, 'as soon as the enquiries bring to light sufficient charges, the Examining Magistrate indicts the person who is the object of his preliminary investigation'. The indictment must be pronounced in person by the Examining Magistrate, communicated to the defendant present in his chambers, and recorded in the official minutes.
The consequence of pronouncing indictment is that the Public Prosecutor will bring up the case for trial. From that moment, 'the proceedings of the investigation become adversary proceedings and the defendant has the right to be assisted by a lawyer' (GPPG, Article 138). The defendant and his lawyer are summoned to all legal proceedings (GPPG, Article 143), may ask any pertinent questions, may request certain investigation actions (presumably in the nature of pre-trial discovery). The pronouncement of indictment is thus a necessary stage of the pre-trial process whereby the defendant is personally advised of the charge against him, is provided with an opportunity to inspect the Prosecutor's files and to prepare for the trial, which is conducted by the Public Prosecutor. The pronouncement of indictment makes the defendant susceptible to being

concerned with 'investigations or court proceedings' but it would appear that the pronouncement of indictment was a judicial proceeding against an accused in the requested State, which is not included.

> That the Treaty fundamentally pertains to assistance in exchanging information, rather than the conduct of judicial proceedings against the accused in the requested state, is shown again by reference to Treaty Art 29, pertaining to the 'Content of Requests'. Art 29, § 1(b) mandates that each request under the Treaty specify 'the principal need for the evidence or information sought'. If pronouncement of indictment were within the Treaty's functions, some reference to this proceeding would be expected in this Treaty requirement. The authority pronouncing indictment, of course, seeks no evidence or information; the authority instead imparts information to the accused, who becomes the defendant. Again, Art 29 is inconsistent with the procedure of pronouncing indictment . . . For these reasons, the court finds that the pronouncement of indictment is not authorized by the Treaty, and this aspect of the Swiss request finds no support under the Treaty. The Swiss request to pronounce indictment likewise finds no support under 28 USC § 1782.

Treaty not exclusive mechanism for MLA in absence of express provision to that effect

In re-Sealed Case[16]

9.53 This case addresses the production of documents in the possession or custody of a witness who was deemed to be the 'custodian' of eight foreign companies with whom he was allegedly associated.

9.54 Following the Iran-Contra affair an independent counsel was appointed to investigate the violations, if any, of US law by any person involved in the sale of arms to Iran as well as the provision of assistance to the Contras of Nicaragua.

9.55 On application by the independent counsel for a *subpoena duces tecum* directing the witness to produce any documents in their custody, the judge took the additional step of holding non-compliance of the subpoena as contempt.

9.56 The witnesses appealed against this order on the grounds, inter alia, that:

1. The District Court had erred in issuing the subpoena in his representational capacity as it had no personal jurisdiction over the foreign companies;
2. The Treaty on Mutual Assistance in Criminal Matters between the US and Switzerland was the only mechanism to secure the production of the

---

summoned before the Swiss court to appear and defend himself. Pronouncement of indictment, in person and upon the official record, is a 'hearing', as the Swiss Magistrate's Additional Letters Rogatory make clear that the Swiss wish to conduct 'the hearing of Salvatore Giordano, Senior and Salvatore Giordano, Junior, for them to be charged and indicted . . .'

[16] 832 F 2d 1268, 266 US App DC 30, 56 USLW 2283, United States Court of Appeals, District of Columbia Circuit.

documents, but this was limited in effect as the international comity pre-cluded enforcement of a subpoena to obtain business records protected by the secrecy laws of other nations.

The US Court of Appeals held,[17] in agreeing with the witness on the first ground **9.57** (above), the District Court for the District of Columbia did not have personal jurisdiction over each of the foreign companies and it did not suffice to issue the subpoena against the witness in his representational capacity:

> The mere fact that the court has jurisdiction over an alleged representative of the companies is patently insufficient to establish jurisdiction over the companies or to entitle the Independent Counsel to view company documents. Just as service of a subpoena duces tecum on a corporate officer vacationing in the United States would not allow the Independent Counsel access to corporate records absent proof that a United States court had jurisdiction over the corporation itself, service of a subpoena on the Witness as 'custodian' for the companies cannot confer on the Independent Counsel a right to inspect their records unless it can show that the District Court possesses personal jurisdiction over them ... The fact that the Witness is an American citizen, not just sojourning here, is also irrelevant to establishing jurisdiction over foreign companies. The Independent Counsel's repeated claim that the Witness has a 'duty'to comply with the subpoena simply because he enjoys United States citizenship is utterly baseless as an assertion about our law.[18]

The Court examined previous authorities and emphasized the requirement for a **9.58** corporation or business to have certain 'minimum contacts' in order for a federal court to have personal jurisdiction over the corporation or business entity; and in the case of foreign companies, such jurisdiction can be asserted if the conduct abroad causes a harmful effect/injury in the US.

On the objection, set out in point 2 above, that the Treaty on Mutual Assistance **9.59** in Criminal Matters between the US and Switzerland was the only mechanism to secure the production of the documents as the documents may well have been created and preserved on the understanding that the Swiss secrecy laws would have the effect of protecting them from voluntary disclosures. The Court of Appeal, not surprisingly, found this objection unconvincing for a number of reasons and set out its objections in the following terms:

> First, some of the documents sought may not be located in Switzerland.
>
> Second, it is not clear from the Witness' brief that Swiss law forbids the companies or their custodians from complying with the subpoena even in regard to documents located in Switzerland. The Witness cites three statutory provisions, none of which, on its face, is plainly pertinent.
>
> Third, even if the Witness might face possible prosecution in Switzerland if he complied with the subpoena, he would only run that risk if he travelled to Switzerland

---

[17] His Hon Harry T Edwards, Circuit Judge, gave the leading speech.
[18] Per Harry T Edwards, Circuit Judge.

voluntarily. In re: Sealed Case, 825 F 2d 494, 497 (DC Cir 1987), this court upheld a contempt order for failure to testify before a grand jury on similar facts, ruling that the Fifth Amendment 'does not protect against dangers voluntarily assumed'. We see no reason to depart from that precedent here.

Fourth, and most important, the Witness has offered no evidence that the United States Government, in signing the Treaty, understood it to supply the exclusive vehicle for obtaining documents in Switzerland whose production falls within the Treaty's ambit. The Swiss government, as amicus curiae, has indeed argued that any attempt to secure documents located in Switzerland and protected by Swiss secrecy laws would trammel Swiss sovereignty and offend common notions of international comity. See Marc Rich & Co v United States, 736 F 2d 864, 866 (2d Cir 1984). But the Witness has not cited any American decision adopting the Swiss government's view, and in fact almost all courts that have ruled on this issue or similar matters, such as the exclusivity of the discovery mechanisms contained in the Hague Convention on evidence, have squarely rejected it. The Second Circuit decided to order production of the corporate documents in Marc Rich, notwithstanding the Swiss government's plea. And although courts recognize comity as an important objective, there is little doubt that '[a] United States Court has the power to order any party within its jurisdiction to testify or produce documents regardless of a foreign sovereign's views to the contrary' . . . Most courts, including this one, are reluctant to embrace doctrines that would allow those who break American laws to escape sanctions by setting up base abroad. As one court noted, 'If one defendant could so easily evade discovery, every United States company would have a foreign affiliate for storing sensitive documents.' Cooper Indus v British Aerospace, 102 FRD 918, 920 (SDNY 1984) . . . . The Witness' claim that the companies and their officers expected protection when they chose to incorporate or operate in Switzerland or other countries is devoid of force, for in light of the importance this country attaches to its discovery procedures and to the prosecution of those who are believed to have flouted its laws, those expectations were both unreasonable and, on balance, of trivial importance.

C. Mutual Legal Assistance or Mutual Assistance?

9.60 The availability of informal assistance, even where evidence is being sought, has already been mentioned. Prosecutors and investigators sometimes have recourse to mutual legal assistance without exploring whether informal mutual assistance would, in fact, meet their needs. It is often forgotten that the country receiving the request might welcome an informal approach that can be dealt with efficiently and expeditiously. Prosecutors should first, therefore, ask themselves whether they really need a formal letter of request to obtain a particular piece of evidence.

9.61 The extent to which States are willing to assist with a formal request does, of course, vary greatly. In many cases, it will depend on a particular country's own domestic laws, on the nature of the relationship between that State and the requesting State and, it has to be said, the attitude and helpfulness of those practitioners to whom the request is made. Consequently, the importance of excellent working relationships being built up and maintained transnationally cannot be too greatly stressed.

Although no definitive list can be drawn up of the type of enquiries that may be dealt with informally, some general observations may be made. Variations from State to State, must, however, always be borne in mind.   **9.62**

- If the enquiry is a routine one and does not require the State of whom the request is made to seek coercive powers, then it may well be possible for the request to be made and complied with without a formal letter of request.
- The obtaining of public records, such as land registry documents and papers relating to registration of companies, may usually be obtained informally.
- Potential witnesses may be contacted to see if they are willing to assist the authorities of the requesting country voluntarily.
- A witness statement may be taken from a voluntary witness, particularly in circumstances where that witness's evidence is likely to be non-contentious.
- The obtaining of lists of previous convictions and of basic subscriber details from communications and service providers that do not require a court order may also be dealt with in the same, informal, way.

Equally, it is possible to draw up a guidance list of the sorts of request where a formal letter will be required: **9.63**

- Obtaining testimony from a non-voluntary witness.
- Seeking to interview a suspect under caution.
- Obtaining account information and documentary evidence from banks and financial institutions (generally).
- Requests for search and seizure.
- Internet records and the contents of emails.
- The transfer of consenting persons into custody in order for testimony to be given.

Confusion is likely to be avoided if prosecutors and investigators have regard to the limits of the conventions and treaties that relate to mutual legal assistance and remember that the regime of mutual legal assistance is for the obtaining of evidence; thus, the obtaining of intelligence and the locating of suspects for interview should only be sought by way of informal assistance to which, of course, agreement may or may not be forthcoming. As for the return of a fugitive, that is a process entirely governed by the law and practice of extradition, not mutual legal assistance.   **9.64**

It is sometimes forgotten just how many types of evidence and other material may be obtained informally. For example, some States have directories of telephone   **9.65** account holders available on the internet (although consideration will need to be given as to whether it is in a form that may be used evidentially).

9.66 Sometimes a degree of lateral thinking is required. In a given case, it might be quicker, cheaper, and easier for the requesting State's investigators to arrange and pay for a voluntary witness to travel to the requesting State to make a witness statement, rather than for the investigators themselves to travel to take the statement. Similarly, if the consent of the State in which an embassy is situated is obtained, witness statements may be taken by investigators at the requesting State's embassy.

9.67 Taking matters one stage further, many States have no objection to an investigator of the requesting State telephoning the witness, obtaining relevant information, and sending an appropriately drafted statement by post thereafter for signature and return. Of course, such a method may only be used as long as the witness is willing to assist the requesting authority and in circumstances where no objections arise from the authorities in the foreign State concerned, from whom prior permission must be sought.

9.68 There are certain key considerations which a person making a request should consider when deciding whether evidence is to be sought by informal means from abroad:

- It must be evidence that may be lawfully gathered under the requesting State's law, and there should be no reason to believe that it would be excluded in evidence when sought to be introduced at trial within the requesting State.

- It should be evidence that may be lawfully gathered under the laws of the requested State.

- The requested State should have no objection.

- The potential difficultly in failing to heed these elements might be that in States with an exclusionary principle in relation to evidence, such evidence will be excluded.

- In addition, but of no less importance, inappropriate actions by way of informal request may well irritate the authorities of the requested State, who might therefore be less inclined to assist with any future request.

- Ensure that any informal request is made and executed lawfully.

9.69 Any consideration of informal assistance should not overlook the use to which such assistance can be put in order to pave the way for a later, formal request. It might, for instance, be possible to narrow down an enquiry in a formal letter of request by first seeking informal assistance. For example, if a statement is to be taken from an employee of a telephone company in a foreign State, informal measures should be taken to identify the company in question, its address, and any other details that will assist and expedite the formal process. It is sometimes overlooked that an expectation always exists among those working in the field of mutual legal assistance that as much preparation work as possible will be undertaken by informal means.

Formal requests (mutual legal assistance)

Given that there is no universal instrument or treaty which governs the gathering of evidence abroad in criminal matters, the building blocks for formal requests are the conventions, schemes, and treaties that States have signed and ratified, including, in counter-terrorism investigations, the sixteen international conventions and protocols on the prevention and suppression of terrorist activity. **9.70**

Prosecutors, investigators, or judges making a formal request should always assert the international obligation of a requested State to assist where such an obligation exists by way of international instrument. Equally, the authority upon which the letter of request is written should also be spelt out.[19] **9.71**

Similarly, the person making a request must take care to ensure that his or her own domestic law allows the request that is actually being made to be made. For instance, a piece of domestic legislation might, in fact, disallow some requests or type of requests that many conventions, treaties, or other international instruments would appear to allow. For some States, the domestic legislation will have primacy. To make a request otherwise than in accordance with domestic law in such circumstances will be to invite arguments for exclusion of evidence. **9.72**

Investigators and prosecutors should make early contact with a counterpart in the State to which the request is to be made. Notwithstanding the existence of a convention or treaty and its broad and permissive approach, the requested State may well have entered reservations that limit the assistance that can, in fact, be given. For instance, some States have reserved the right to refuse judicial assistance when the offence is already the subject of a judicial investigation in their own territory, that is to say, within the requested State. **9.73**

The key principle should be this: regard should always be given to the fact that a requested State will have to comply with its own domestic law, both as regards whether assistance can be given at all and, if so, how that assistance is, in fact, given. **9.74**

---

[19] To give a practical example, the UK made a statement of good practice in accordance with Article 1 of the Joint Action of 29 June 1998 adopted by the Council of Europe, in which it declared that the UK Home Office (Interior Ministry) will ensure that requests are in conformity with relevant treaties and other international obligations. Persons issuing a request must take heed of any such declarations of such intent made by their own State and take action accordingly.

The form of the letter of request

9.75 The requesting authority should submit a letter that is a stand-alone document. It should provide the requested State with all the information needed to decide whether assistance is to be given and to undertake the requested enquiries. Of course, depending upon the nature of those enquiries and the type of case, the requested State may be quite content for officers from the requesting State to attend within its territory and to be present during the investigation or enquiries.

9.76 A problem that occurs in all jurisdictions in respect of both incoming and outgoing requests is that of time. A request may take weeks, sometimes months and, occasionally and unfortunately, years to execute. As soon as grounds emerge to issue the request and the need for such a request is clear, then the letter should be issued. It is important that urgent requests be kept to a minimum and that everyone involved in the process appreciates that an urgent request is indeed truly urgent and unavoidably so. If a request is urgent, the letter should say so clearly and, in terms, set out the reasons why.

9.77 The material conditions to be satisfied within a letter of request may be summarized as follows:

- If the requested State requires an undertaking of reciprocity on the part of the requesting State, then this should be given. In this respect, common law countries are usually more restrictive than those with a civil code. Equally, even where no undertaking is required, the requesting State should set out in the letter if it is making a request in respect of which it could not reciprocate.

- A general prerequisite for many jurisdictions is the crime under investigation is a criminal offence in both the requesting and requested State, the dual-criminality rule. This should therefore be addressed within the letter.

- The assistance must relate to criminal proceedings whether at an investigative stage, or after court proceedings have begun, in the strict and accepted sense; that is to say, an investigation or proceedings against the perpetrators of a criminal offence under ordinary law. The charges and any future possible charges should be set out; whilst if evidence is to be used in, for instance, confiscation proceedings as well as at trial, that should also be clearly stated.

- In addition, the principle of 'speciality' will mean that, if a charge changes after a request has been made, a new request will need to be made, unless the new charge was anticipated in the original letter.

- Although it need not be specifically asserted within the letter, a prerequisite for formal assistance is the guarantee of a fair trial, and respect of the fundamental rights laid down in the International Covenant on Civil and Political Rights as implemented within the legal system of the requesting State.

- Some requested States may require an assertion that the request does not relate to fiscal, political, or military misdemeanours.
- The letter must contain a description of the facts which form the basis of the investigations/proceedings. Such a description must be as detailed as possible and should indicate in what way the evidence being sought is necessary.
- If the requesting and requested States are each a party to a multilateral or bilateral agreement, then the international instrument concerned should be referred to and prayed in aid.

Although a request is executed by the Competent Judicial Authority of the **9.78** requested State in accordance with its own laws and its own rules and procedures, very often it will be possible for the requesting authority to make an express request that the requested State apply the requesting State's rules of procedure.

If a request in such terms is available to the requesting authority, advantage should be **9.79** taken of it. The reason is obvious. A fundamental difficulty, often overlooked, is that different States have different ways of presenting evidence. The whole purpose of a request is to obtain useable, admissible evidence. That evidence must therefore be in a form appropriate for the courts of the requesting State, or as near as possible to that form as circumstances allow. It should be made clear by the requesting State, therefore, as to the form in which, for instance, the testimony of a witness should be taken. The requested State cannot be expected to be familiar with the rules of evidence-gathering and evidence-adducing in the jurisdiction from which the request comes.

Further to the above, some instruments may contain a provision to the effect that **9.80** the method of execution specified in the request shall be followed to the extent that it is compatible with the laws and practices of the requested State. If in doubt, the requesting authority should provide examples to the requested authority of what is required.

The importance of adhering, wherever possible, to the procedures of the request- **9.81** ing State was highlighted in the recent Australian case of *R v Thomas*.[20]

Thomas was a decision of the Victoria Supreme Court of Appeal that the appeal by **9.82** Joseph Thomas against his convictions in the Supreme Court be allowed. The Court quashed Thomas's convictions but, following a submission by the Commonwealth Director of Public Prosecutions, adjourned the question of whether the conviction should be quashed or there should be a retrial for further hearing.

Thomas, an Australian national, was apprehended by Pakistani immigration offi- **9.83** cials at Karachi Airport in January 2003. He was in possession of a false passport, an airline ticket to Australia, and US $3,800 in cash. It was suspected that he was

---

[20] [2006] VSCA 165.

linked to Al-Qaida. He was detained and remained in the custody of the Pakistani authorities until he was released and returned to Australia on6 June 2003.

9.84   Whilst in detention in Pakistan, Thomas was initially taken to a military base where he was questioned by investigators from Pakistan and the USA. He was then transferred to another location where he was held in solitary confinement and questioned for two weeks. Thereafter he was flown to Islamabad where, in late January, he received a consular visit.

9.85   At that stage, arrangements were made for Thomas to be questioned by intelligence agencies from the USA, Pakistan, and Australia. Over the course of five days, four separate interviews were conducted by Pakistani officials and a joint Australian investigation team made up of two Federal Police officers and two members of the Australian Security and Intelligence Organisation (ASIO). During those interviews, the Australian investigators showed Thomas a photograph of himself with his wife and child and a letter from his family. They told him that they might allow him to read the letter again at a later time.

9.86   Thomas was then taken to Lahore and again questioned by officials from the USA and Pakistan. He was finally taken back to Islamabad thereafter for an interview with the Australian Federal Police (AFP) representatives. That interview took place on 8 March. By the time of that interview, Thomas had already made admissions that he had the received the US $3,800 from an associate of Osama Bin Laden, and that he had trained at a training camp under Al-Qaida direction.

9.87   In advance of the 8 March interview, the AFP communicated with the Pakistan authorities and requested that their interview with Thomas should be conducted as a formally recorded interview in order to obtain admissions which could be used as part of a criminal prosecution in Australia. They advised that, to that end, Thomas must be advised of his rights, including access to a lawyer, the ability to communicate with a friend or relative, and the right to remain silent.

9.88   AFP received permission to conduct the interview, but under certain conditions, including a maximum duration of two hours, and no access to a lawyer. The interview proceeded on that basis and Thomas repeated his earlier admissions. The AFP, for its part, protested to the Pakistani Intelligence Service that admissibility had been compromised thereby.

9.89   In early June 2003, Thomas was released from custody and returned to Australia. He was, however, arrested eighteen months later and charged with a number of offences, including being in possession of a false passport and receiving funds from a terrorist organization.

9.90   Thomas was subsequently tried and found guilty in the Supreme Court on both matters. Crucial to his conviction was the admission of the confessions made by him in the course of the 8 March interview.

He appealed against his conviction on a number of grounds, one of which **9.91** concerned the admission of the record of interview which, counsel submitted, was not voluntarily made and was therefore inadmissible.

Counsel for Thomas argued that to describe him as having had a free choice to **9.92** speak or be silent, in the position in which he was known to be by those interviewing him, was quite unrealistic. The Court, in agreeing with this argument, stated that the applicant had been repeatedly told by his Pakistani interrogators, to whose control he was subject, that what would befall him was, to a very great extent, dependent upon the extent of his cooperation. The applicant was explicitly proffered by the Pakistani officials the possibility of returning to his family on the one hand and a very different fate on the other. The Australians present made no attempt to distance themselves from this position; indeed, impliedly endorsed it. Importantly, the inducements were held out in the presence of one Australian Federal Police officer who was involved in all of the six joint AFP/ASIO interviews, and who took part in the formal AFP interview.

The Court was of the opinion that it certainly did not require any 'feat of imagina- **9.93** tion' to appreciate the character of the prospects with which Thomas was faced, when contemplating their potential to overbear his will. The Court stated that there could be little doubt that, from the perspective of Thomas and from that of any reasonable person in similar circumstances, Thomas was aware that, if he was to change his current situation of detention in Pakistan and reduce the risk of indeterminate detention there or in some unidentified location, cooperation was far more important than reliance on his rights under the law. Indeed, it was apparent that he believed that insistence upon his rights may well have resulted in antagonizing those in control of his fate.

The Court also found that it was not to the point that Thomas made the admis- **9.94** sions in the knowledge of the existence of a right to silence under Australian law if he had no real opportunity to exercise that right. The Court stated that Thomas could have declined to answer questions and subjected himself to what he reasonably perceived as an increased risk of indeterminate detention, but that prospect would have been so daunting that few would have been likely to accept the risk. What was important was whether the applicant could, in any real sense, be said to have had a free choice to speak or remain silent.

In the Court's view, there could be little doubt that Thomas was subjected to **9.95** externally-imposed pressure of a kind calculated to overbear his will, thereby restricting his available choices and the manner of their exercise. The Court ruled that what necessarily followed was that the evidence of the interview of 8 March 2003 should not have been admitted and that the conviction be set aside.

Having decided that the admissions in the record of interview were not voluntary, **9.96** it was not necessary for the Court to consider the remaining grounds. However, the

Court did consider whether, assuming the admissions in the record of interview were voluntary, they should have been excluded by the trial judge on the basis of unfairness or because of public policy considerations. The Court took into account the safeguards mandated under the Crimes Act 1914, specifically the requirement under Australian law that a person being interviewed in relation to a criminal investigation must be given an opportunity to secure legal advice. Given the conditions of his detention by Pakistani authorities, who would not allow him access to a lawyer, Thomas had no such opportunity. In these circumstances, the Court concluded, it was contrary to public policy to admit the evidence obtained in the record of interview.

9.97　Given the international impetus towards States adopting extra-territorial jurisdiction, particularly on the basis of active personality, the difficulties experienced in this case are likely to be repeated. The practical, operational limitations of such cases have to be recognized. In particular, that it is vital that the requested State complies with the main safeguards and procedures in, for instance, the interviewing of suspects which exist in the requesting State.

9.98　Additionally, it is clear from *Thomas* that there may well not be any substantial differences from a court's perspective between intelligence-gathering interviews and interviewing a suspect for the purposes of a criminal investigation. If the former is to be unregulated and without safeguards, the consequences in the present case are likely to be repeated.[21]

Particular problems experienced in mutual legal assistance sought in counter-terrorism cases

9.99　1.　If a counter-terrorism investigation also involves an allegation of corruption implicating an influential or powerful figure in the requested State, the assistance sought may never be provided. The requested authority might even cite 'national interest' or immunities enjoyed by certain sections of the community, for example, ministers of the government or judges.

　　　2.　It should be noted in respect of terrorism-financing investigations that in some countries the person in respect of whom the request for mutual legal assistance is made is able to appeal against the sharing of evidence with the requesting State. When such an appeal is available it may well cause lengthy delay and, of course, alert the target. In those European jurisdictions which have traditionally enjoyed favourable tax and banking conditions, for instance Liechtenstein and Switzerland, an appeal avenue is available in relation to the disclosure of

---

[21]　See the analysis by Dr Chris Corns, 'Interrogating Nationals Abroad: Jurisdictional Lessons from *R v Thomas*' [2008] Crim LR, 121ff.

information about a person's financial position, although not, generally, at the interlocutory or investigative stage. In those States, in addition, institutions such as banks may have similar rights of appeal.

3. Search and/or seizure generally can be problematic. Essentially, the authority making the request should be careful to provide as much information as possible about the location of the premises. Although some States have introduced more far-reaching powers in this regard to assist in the investigation of terrorist offences and suspects, it must be remembered that different jurisdictions set different thresholds. Search and seizure is a powerful weapon for investigators. It must be assumed that the requested State will only be able to execute a request and search/seizure if it has been demonstrated by the request that reasonable grounds exist to suspect that an offence has been committed and that there is evidence on the premises or person concerned which goes to that offence. These 'reasonable grounds' should be specifically set out within the letter therefore.

4. Generally, it will not be enough simply to ask for search and seizure without explaining why it is believed the process might produce evidence. For requests within Europe, it is undeniably good practice to have written regard to the core principles of the ECHR, namely necessity, proportionality, and legality. Interference with property and privacy in European countries is now frequently justified only if there are pressing social reasons, such as the need to prosecute criminals for serious offences. Even if all these factors are addressed it may well be that the searching of the person and taking fingerprints, DNA, and other samples will have less chance of success in some jurisdictions.

5. Accordingly, it is suggested that any State making a request to any other State, whether in Europe or not, should address the issue of fundamental/human rights, the nature of any breaches which execution of the request might bring about, the legal basis for such a breach, and why, in the particular circumstances of the investigation which is in hand, the breach is justifiable.

Sensitive information contained within the letter of request

9.100 There are likely to be extremely sensitive aspects to many counter-terrorism investigations. It may also be that, in a given case, sensitive information needs to be included in a formal request for assistance in order to satisfy the requested authority. At the same time, the disclosure of prospective witnesses and other information that could be exploited by terrorist groups or their sympathizers needs to be weighed in the balance. In reality, the system for obtaining mutual legal assistance, globally, is inherently insecure. The risk of unwanted disclosure will be greater or lesser depending on the identity of the requested state. When considering the issue, those making the request must have regard to the duty of care issues which arise. Sometimes, difficulties can be avoided by the issuing of a generalized letter which leaves out the most sensitive information, but provides enough detail to allow the request to be executed. Exceptionally, consideration can be given to the issuing of a conditional request for mutual legal assistance; in other words, a request that is only to be executed by the requested authority if it can be executed without requiring sensitive information to be disclosed.

Adducing evidence obtained from abroad

9.101 As set out above, it is always advisable for the requesting State to ask the requested State's authorities to allow the evidence sought to be gathered in the form usually expected by the requesting State's courts. However, this may not always be possible. Some, but not all States, have enacted provisions allowing the admission into evidence of material not in a form which would be regarded as the prescribed form if the evidence had been gathered domestically, subject to any other exclusion arguments which might be mounted.

Challenging a refusal to execute a letter of request

9.102 International cooperation, whether by way of formal MLA or an informal request, depends in very large part on goodwill, a willingness to assist, and the recognition that today's requested State might be the requesting State tomorrow. What then can be done in the event of a refusal to execute a request?

9.103 If a letter of request is issued on the basis of comity, without the force of a treaty obligation, the requested State will be at liberty to refuse to execute if it is unwilling to cooperate. However, if the request is made in reliance upon a treaty, whether bilateral or multilateral, an unjustified refusal will put the requested State in breach of its treaty obligation. Such a course may well risk embarrassment and might prompt executive or diplomatic pressure to accede to the request.

9.104 However, if a State remains steadfast in its refusal there is, in practical terms, little that can be done. Depending on the instrument concerned, the matter may be put before the conference or assembly of the States Parties and might result in censure, or it might be referred to the organization or body with 'ownership' of the instrument in question. Either way, rebuke and little more will be the outcome.

9.105 A further avenue that a requesting State might go down is to bring an action before the International Court of Justice (ICJ)[22] in The Hague. Indeed, at the time of writing, the ICJ brought down a judgment on 4 June 2008 following an action brought by Djibouti against France.

---

[22] Principal judicial organ of the United Nations.

Certain Questions of Mutual Assistance in Criminal Matters (*Djibouti v France*), ICJ

On 9 January 2006 the Republic of Djibouti, Djibouti filed an application against **9.106** France before the on the basis of 'the refusal by the French governmental and judicial authorities to execute an international letter rogatory regarding the transmission to the judicial authorities in Djibouti of the record relating to the investigation in the Case against X for the murder of Bernard Borrel'.

This is the first time that a requesting State has commenced proceedings against **9.107** the requested State for failure to provide assistance on mutual assistance in criminal matters and is therefore of key significance.

In its application Djibouti claims that the refusal constitutes a violation of France's **9.108** international obligations both under the Treaty of Friendship and Co-operation signed by the two States on 27 June 1977 and the Convention on Mutual Assistance in Criminal Matters between France and Djibouti dated 27 September 1986.

The second claim by Djibouti is that in summoning of certain internationally **9.109** protected nationals of Djibouti, including the Head of State, as témoins assistés, legally represented witnesses, in connection with a criminal complaint for subornation of perjury against X in the Borrel case, France had violated its obligation to prevent attacks on the person, freedom or dignity of individuals enjoying such protection.

The application before the International Court of Justice (ICJ) by Djibouti **9.110** broadly raised the following issues:

- The jurisdiction of the court to hear such an application under Article 38, paragraph 5, of the Rules of Court.
- The witness summonses issued by the French judicial authorities in relation to the Djiboutian Head of State and senior Djiboutian officials, 'in breach of the provisions of the Treaty of Friendship and Co-operation (concluded between France and Djibouti, 27 June 1977), the principles and rules governing the diplomatic privileges and immunities laid down by the Vienna Convention on Diplomatic Relations of 18 April 1961 and the principles established under customary international law relating to international immunities as reflected, in particular, by the Convention on the Prevention and Punishment of Crimes against Internationally Protected Persons, including Diplomatic Agents, of 14 December 1973'.
- The two arrest warrants issued by France in relation to senior Djibouti officials.
- The refusal by the French governmental and judicial authorities to execute an international letter rogatory 'in violation of the Convention on Mutual

Assistance in Criminal Matters between the [Djiboutian] Government and the [French] Government, of 27 September 1986 . . .'.

9.111 The Court found that it had jurisdiction to hear the matter under Article 38, paragraph 5, of the Rules of Court. Turning only to the issues concerning the refusal to provide assistance[23] under the Convention on Mutual Assistance in Criminal Matters of 27 September 1986, Djibouti relied on two grounds, as follows:

- Obligation to provide assistance to Djibouti on the basis of reciprocity under Article 1 of the Treaty.
- Failure to provide reasons for refusal.

9.112 Djibouti submitted that based on the past assistance it had provided to the French authorities, it had a level of expectation that a request from Djibouti would be reciprocated. The Court, in rejecting the reliance on reciprocity emphasized the principle that it is the law of the requested State that applies observed as follows:

> The Court notes that in the present case, the concept of reciprocity has been invoked in support of the contention that the execution by one State of a request for mutual assistance requires as a consequence the other State to do the same. However, the Court considers that, so far as the 1986 Convention is concerned, each request for legal assistance is to be assessed on its own terms by each Party. Moreover, the way in which the concept of reciprocity is advanced by Djibouti would render without effect the exceptions listed in Article 2. The Court observes that the Convention nowhere provides that the granting of assistance by one State in respect of one matter imposes on the other State the obligation to do likewise when assistance is requested of it in turn.

> The Court accordingly considers that Djibouti cannot rely on the principle of reciprocity in seeking execution of the international letter rogatory it submitted to the French judicial authorities.[24]

> The Court observes that the obligation to execute international letters rogatory laid down in Article 3 of the 1986 Convention is to be realized in accordance with the procedural law of the requested State. Thus, the ultimate treatment of a request for mutual assistance in criminal matters clearly depends on the decision by the competent national authorities, following the procedure established in the law of the requested State. While it must of course ensure that the procedure is put in motion, the State does not thereby guarantee the outcome, in the sense of the transmission of the file requested in the letter rogatory. Interpreted in context, as called for by the rule of customary law reflected in Article 31, paragraph 1, of the 1969 Vienna Convention on the Law of Treaties, Article 3 of the 1986 Convention must be read in conjunction with Articles 1 and 2 of the Convention. While Article 1 does provide that there must be 'the widest measure' of mutual assistance, there are cases in which it will not

---

[23] Readers are referred to the judgment on the other issues concerning the issuance of arrest warrants.

[24] Para 119 of the judgment [p 39].

be possible. Article 2, for its part, describes situations in which '[a]ssistance may be refused'. It follows that those who are empowered to address these matters will do so by applying the provisions of Article 2 or of other Articles in the Convention that may lead to the rejection of the requesting State's démarche.[25]

However the Court found unanimously that France, by not giving Djibouti the reasons for its refusal to execute the letter rogatory of 3 November 2004, failed to comply with its international obligation under Article 17 of the Convention.

D. Extradition

What is 'extradition'?

Extradition is the process by which States seek the return of a person accused or **9.113** convicted of crimes to the State where those crimes were allegedly committed. The practice of extradition has its roots in the idea of territorial jurisdiction; that is, traditionally a State could not prosecute or punish a person who had committed a crime in the territory of another State, as the courts of the State where the fugitive was found did not necessarily have jurisdiction over his conduct and therefore had to be returned to the State from which the person had fled. It must be emphasized however that there is no obligation in international law for a State to extradite a person found in its territory. It is, and always remains, a matter for the requested State to decide if a person is to be surrendered to the requesting State. Extradition is therefore an act of State and does, in most jurisdictions, engage both the executive and judicial processes, leaving the executive to make the final decision on surrender (particularly in common law countries), albeit with judicial oversight. The involvement of the executive is largely dependant on domestic law and arrangements. Some countries, in particular civil law jurisdictions, have no executive involvement in the extradition process, which is regarded entirely as a request from and to the judiciary.

In essence, extradition is an amalgam of judicial, executive, and diplomatic issues **9.114** and has been aptly described by McLachlin J in the unreported case of *Kindler v Crosbie & AG of Canada* as:

> . . . while the extradition process is an important part of our system of criminal justice, it would be wrong to equate it to the criminal trial process. It differs from the criminal process in purpose and procedure and, most importantly, in the factors which render it fair. Extradition procedure, unlike the criminal procedure, is founded on the concepts of reciprocity, comity and respect for difference in other jurisdictions. This unique foundation means that the law of extradition must accommodate many factors foreign to our internal criminal law. While our conceptions of what

---

[25] Para 123 of the judgment [p 40].

constitutes a fair criminal law are important to the process of extradition, they are necessarily tempered by other considerations.

9.115 A request for extradition is usually only acted upon where a treaty or arrangement exists between the requesting and requested State. Even where countries have attempted to move away from the need of a treaty and placing reliance on their own domestic law, it is often the case that treaties will still be seen as the preferred way forward. For example, the UK Extradition Act 2003 does not necessarily place reliance on the existence of a treaty in order to comply with a request for extradition; however a treaty or arrangement, whether general, ad hoc, or Memorandum of Understanding (MOU),[26] is still, in practice, required.

9.116 Historically, States entered into bilateral treaties. This, of course, meant that only parties to the treaty were bound by its terms and such agreements were, therefore, limited in impact. However as crime became more international in nature and travel became easier, the international community, acting either through the United Nations General Assembly or regionally, adopted a number of multilateral treaties. Equally regions that share a common legal tradition, such as the Commonwealth[27] or space, as in Europe[28] soon adopted arrangements or conventions to facilitate extradition amongst the Member States. This does not however mean that States cannot still enter into bilateral arrangements as was the case between India and the UK[29] (both members of the Commonwealth and have adopted the London Scheme in their domestic law) in the wake of terrorist acts in the 1990s to expedite such requests.

9.117 The advantage of such multilateral treaties is that it permits a number of countries to become State Parties which obviates the need for bilateral treaties. Further, every State Party is fully aware of the obligations of each party as well as any reservations/declarations that a State Party may enter.

9.118 In essence therefore, the bases of extradition are contained in:

1. Bilateral treaties.
2. Regional multilateral treaties eg, European Convention on Extradition, South African Development Community (SADC) Protocol on Extradition.
3. Mutual recognition of decisions—for example, European Arrest Warrant (EAW) and the proposed Caribbean Community (CARICOM) Arrest Warrant.
4. UN Conventions (including the 16 UN CT Conventions[30] and Protocols).

---

[26] Recent UK-Rwanda MOU [14 Dec 2006 amended 22 Dec 2006].
[27] London Scheme for Extradition within the Commonwealth—last amended in 2002 (previously referred to as the Commonwealth Scheme for the Rendition of Fugitive Offenders).
[28] European Convention on Extradition 1957 [ECE].
[29] UK-India treaty [22 Sep 1992].
[30] It is important to note however that although the Conventions and Protocols may provide the legal basis for extradition, in the absence of a treaty between the parties, the request can only proceed

5. Ad hoc arrangements between States.
6. Willingness to surrender in the absence of a treaty (comity).

Comity: disguised/irregular extradition

The last of these legal bases namely, comity, has come into sharp focus in the **9.119** context of terrorism. Comity (literally, courteousness of nations) is the recognition by one State of the legal procedures and jurisprudence of another. Following the bombing of the US embassies in Kenya and Tanzania and in particular after the events of 11 September 2001, the US has come under stern criticism for relying on comity rather than a formal extradition request to a requested State. The key concern lies in the fact that a request for surrender based on comity alone has the effect of denying the fugitive any legal protection to challenge the request or to ensure that there are adequate safeguards in place, particularly where the offence may attract the death penalty. Such surrenders are regarded as disguised or irregular extradition and fall foul of human rights considerations and have been the subject of adverse judicial comment in various jurisdictions.

The Constitutional Court of South Africa in the recent case of *Khalfan Khamis* **9.120** *Mohamed, Abdrurahman Dalvie and President of the Republic of South Africa and six others* [2001][31] condemned the handing over by deportation of Khalfan Khamis Mohammed to the US Authorities.

Given the significance of this judgment, it is worth setting out the facts of this **9.121** case. Following the US Embassy bombing in Dar-es-Salaam, Tanzania on 7 August 1998, Khalfan Khamis Mohammed, a Tanzanian national, left Tanzania on 8 August 1998 having obtained a visa from the South African High Commission on 6 August 1998. He entered South Africa by road on 16 August 1998. Upon entry into South Africa he settled in Cape Town and in due course applied for asylum under an assumed name. He was granted temporary residence status.

In the interim, he was indicted in New York for the embassy bombing and a war- **9.122** rant was issued for his arrest on 17 December 1998 by the Federal District Court for the Southern District of New York. The information was then transmitted to Interpol to secure his arrest.

The South African Police Service and the Department of Home Affairs were aware **9.123** of the US investigation. In August 1999, an FBI agent identified Khalfan Khamis

---

for the convention offence. For example, Algeria submitted an extradition request to the UK for Ait-Haddad under the Montreal Convention and Protocol dealing with acts of terrorism at civilian airports. Ait-Haddad was accused of acts of general acts of terrorism in Algeria and not connected to the bombing at Algiers Airport. The request could therefore not go ahead. Thus a request that places reliance on a UN Convention is necessarily limited to the offences under the relevant convention.

[31] CCT 17/01.

Mohammed (hereinafter referred to as Mohammed) whilst trawling through the South African records for asylum seekers and brought it to the attention of Chief Immigration Officer.

9.124 Mohammed was arrested in Cape Town on 5 October 1999 by immigration officers. He was detained and interrogated by South African immigration officers and thereafter handed over to FBI agents for interrogation. He was subsequently removed to New York on 6 October 1999 to stand trial in relation to the Tanzania US Embassy bombing and indicted. If convicted, he faced the death penalty.

9.125 During this time he was held at the detention facility near the airport and denied access to a lawyer. Moreover, when his lodgings were searched, his flatmate/landlord was informed that Mohammed was being deported to Tanzania and that it would not assist him to be legally represented.

9.126 Following his removal, his legal representatives sought declaratory and mandatory relief against the government on the basis that Mohammed's removal from South Africa was a disguised extradition and therefore in breach of both the South African Constitution and the Aliens Control Act 96 of 1991. Furthermore, South Africa had not sought assurances on the death penalty from the US before handing him over which infringed his constitutional right to life and dignity.

9.127 The Constitutional Court observed:

> The Bill of Rights which we find to have been infringed, is binding on all organs of State and it is our constitutional duty to ensure that appropriate relief is afforded to those who have suffered infringement of their constitutional rights . . . Republic of South Africa had no authority in law to deport or purportedly to deport or otherwise to remove or cause the removal of Mohammed from the Republic to the US.[32]

It is worth noting that at the relevant time, the US and South Africa were engaged in negotiations of a new extradition treaty.

9.128 Similarly, the Human Rights Chamber[33] in considering an application in relation to the removal and the handing over of four Algerians[34] to the US in the absence of a request for extradition, found that:

> There is no evidence to suggest that the hand-over of the applicants can be interpreted to be an extradition. In particular, the diplomatic note of 17 January 2002 from the US Embassy cannot be understood to be a valid extradition request of the United States of America. In this note the US Embassy in Sarajevo advised the Government of Bosnia and Herzegovina that it was prepared to assume custody of

---

[32] P 52 of the judgment.
[33] A judicial body established under the Dayton Peace Agreement (Bosnia and Herzegovina).
[34] *Hadž Boudellaa, Boumediene Lakhdar, Mohamed Nechle, and Saber Lahmar v Bosnia and Herzegovina and The Federation of Bosnia and Herzegovina* Case Nos CH/02/8679, CH/02/8689, CH/02/8690 and CH/02/8691 (11 October 2002).

the six specified Algerian citizens and it offered to arrange to take physical custody of the individuals at a time and location mutually convenient. This note, however, does not fulfil the requirements for a formal extradition of persons who have been charged or convicted as provided for in Chapter XXXI of the Code of Criminal Procedure of the Federation of Bosnia and Herzegovina [. . .]. In particular, it includes neither the indicting proposal against the applicants nor an extract of the criminal law to be applied in the United States.

Clearly such a practice is fraught with difficulties and has been the subject of **9.129** adverse comment by the international community and judiciary in national courts,[35] however it should equally be borne in mind that certain states, the US being a notable example, do not look behind the mechanisms used to bring a person before their courts.[36]

By contrast, the UK takes a different approach and in *The Queen v the Bow Street* **9.130** *Magistrates ex parte Sir Rupert Henry Mackeson*,[37] the applicant was accused of offences of fraud committed in May 1979 in the UK. He was at the time residing in Zimbabwe (then Rhodesia), and was deported to the UK in April 1980. Upon his arrival to the UK, he was arrested and charged with offences under the Theft Act 1968. The matter was set down for a committal hearing for 15 January 1981. The applicant lodged judicial review proceedings and sought an order prohibiting any committal from taking place on the basis that the deportation ('veiled extradition') was unlawful. The authorities in Rhodesia, following a request by the Metropolitan Police, for his return in circumstances when there was no extradition arrangement between the two countries had surrendered the applicant. Furthermore, the UK authorities could have applied for his extradition after December 1979 as 'legality had returned to Rhodesia', but the UK authorities chose not to submit an extradition request.

> . . . it seems clear to me that the object of this exercise was simply to achieve extradition by the back door. It seems equally plain to me that the English police authorities were, to say the least concurring in that exercise . . .

> On 20 April 1979 direct rule started, and in those circumstances, technically at least, the 1881 Act started once again to apply in Zimbabwe-Rhodesia, and would have been available had anyone seen fit to use it in order properly to extradite this applicant to the UK, whereas . . . that was not done . . .[38]

The leading authority on the practice of 'handing over' is the House of Lords **9.131** case of *ex p Bennett*.[39] The court was asked to consider the consequences for

---

[35] *R v Horseferry Road Magistrates' Court ex p Bennett* [1994] 1 AC 42. Similar reasoning was adopted in the subsequent case of R v Mullen [1999] 2 Cr App R 143.

[36] *US v Alvarez-Machain*, (15 June 1992) 504 US 655 (1992).

[37] Divisional Court, 25 June 1981 [unreported].

[38] Per The Lord Chief Justice.

[39] *R v Horseferry Road Magistrates' Court ex p Bennett* [1994] 1 AC 42; *R v Horseferry Road Magistrates' Court ex p Bennett* (No 3) [1995] 1 Cr App R 147.

a prosecution where a person has been removed from a country to the UK in the absence of an extradition arrangement. The question for Their Lordships was whether in the exercise of its supervisory jurisdiction the court has the power to inquire into the circumstances by which a person has been brought within the jurisdiction and if so what remedy, if any, is available to prevent his trial where that person has been lawfully arrested within the jurisdiction for a crime committed within it.

9.132 Bennett was a New Zealand national wanted by the UK authorities for an offence of fraud. He was traced in South Africa but as there was no extradition arrangement between UK and South Africa, a request could not be made. Officers received legal advice to that effect, but decided to liaise with their counterparts in South Africa, and Bennett was subsequently sent to the UK by the South African police, apparently in defiance of a South African court order.

9.133 By a majority (Lord Oliver dissenting) Their Lordships answered the certified question in the affirmative and in so doing extended the ambit of abuse of process to include the circumstance where there has been a misuse of executive power even where such misuse cannot be shown to have resulted in prejudice to the accused.

9.134 Giving the leading speech, Lord Griffiths said:

> In my view your Lordships should now declare that where process of law is available to return an accused to this country through extradition procedures our courts will refuse to try him if he has been forcibly brought within our jurisdiction in disregard of those procedures by a process to which our own police, prosecuting or other executive authorities have been a knowing party.
>
> I would accordingly affirm the power of the magistrates, whether sitting as committing justices or exercising their summary jurisdiction, to exercise control over their proceedings through an abuse of process jurisdiction. However this power should be strictly confined to matters directly affecting the fairness of the trial such as delay or unfair manipulation of court procedures. The wider responsibility for upholding the rule of law must be that of the High Court and that if a serious question arises as to the deliberate abuse of extradition *procedures* a magistrate should allow an adjournment so that an application can be made to the Divisional Court. The High Court in the exercise of its supervisory jurisdiction has power to enquire into the circumstances by which a person has been brought within the jurisdiction and if satisfied that it was in disregard of extradition procedures it may stay the prosecution and order the release of the accused.

9.135 This disapproval was echoed by Lord Bridge in the following terms:

> There is, I think, no principle more basic to any proper system of law than the maintenance of the rule of law itself. When it is shown that the law enforcement agency responsible for bringing a prosecution has only been enabled to do so by participating in violations of international law and of the laws of another state in order to secure the presence of the accused within the territorial jurisdiction of the court, I think that respect for the rule of law demands that the court take cognisance of that circumstance. To hold that the court may turn a blind eye to executive lawlessness beyond the frontiers of its own jurisdiction is, to my mind, an insular and

unacceptable view. Having then taken cognisance of the lawlessness it would again appear to me to be a wholly inadequate response for the court to hold that the only remedy lies in civil proceedings at the suit of the defendant or in disciplinary or criminal proceedings against the individual officers of the law enforcement agency who were concerned in the illegal action taken. Since the prosecution could never have been brought if the defendant had not been illegally abducted, the whole proceeding is tainted. If a resident in another country is properly extradited here, the time when the prosecution commences is the time when the authorities here set the extradition process in motion. By parity of reasoning, if the authorities, instead of proceeding by way of extradition, have resorted to abduction, that is the effective commencement of the prosecution process and is the illegal foundation on which it rests. It is apt, in my view, to describe these circumstances, in the language used by Woodhouse J in *Moevao v The Department of Labour* [1980] 1 NZLR 464, 467, as an 'abuse of the criminal jurisdiction in general' or indeed, in the language of Mansfield J in United States v Toscanino, 500 F 2d 267, as a 'degradation' of the court's criminal process. To hold that in these circumstances the court may decline to exercise its jurisdiction on the ground that its process has been abused may be an extension of the doctrine of abuse of process but is, in my view, a wholly proper and necessary one.[40]

In Canada an inquiry[41] was held in relation to the actions of the Canadian, Syrian, **9.136** and US Authorities in the handing over of *Maher Arar*. Arar, a dual Canadian/Syrian national was detained at the airport in New York. The US Authorities detained and questioned him for twelve days and then sent him firstly to Jordan and then to Syria. He was interrogated for twelve days, during which he alleged he was tortured. The report in condemning the actions of the officers found that the Canadian intelligence officials were under pressure to find terrorists following the events of 9/11 and had provided incorrect information regarding Arar and went on to condemn this practice.

Another practice that has often been employed by States is the luring of a person **9.137** into the jurisdiction where it is deemed to be easier by the State to do so for the sake of expediency. Thus, in the case of *Hemant Lakhani*, the fugitive, a UK national, was lured into the US from the UK in 2002 as part of an undercover operation relating to missile deals. Upon entry into the US he was arrested and prosecuted. All this despite the fact that a treaty existed between the US and UK.

European Arrest Warrant

In an attempt to simplify and expedite a usually complex and lengthy process, **9.138** a recent innovation through the Council of the European Union has been the adoption of the European Arrest Warrant (EAW).[42] This was one of the conclusions of the Tampere European Council of 15 and 16 October 1999 and was adopted

---

[40] Per Lord Bridge at p 20 of the judgment.
[41] The two-and-a-half-year inquiry was concluded in September 2006.
[42] The EAW has been given effect in the UK by the Extradition Act 2003.

through the Council Framework Decision of 13 June 2002. It has had the effect of replacing extradition proceedings between Member States and is based on mutual recognition of criminal decisions between Member States, being designed to have a uniform effect throughout the European Union.

9.139 One of the main drivers in the adoption of the European Arrest Warrant[43] was the delay inherent in extradition proceedings brought about by unnecessary complexities of the process such as authentication and certification, particularly in common law systems where an extradition request is seen both as an exercise of the executive and judicial branch. The European Arrest Warrant, by contrast, relies on mutual recognition and surrender and is a judicial decision issued by a Member State and has gone some way to remove some of the cumbersome requirements (for example, authentication and certification). The main aim of the EAW therefore is to ensure a swift surrender and avoid the delay usually associated with extradition requests and remove the requirement of involving the executive in extradition matters.

9.140 The objectives of the EAW are set out in the Preamble to the Council Framework Decision and some of the key objectives are as follows:

> (1) According to the Conclusions of the Tampere European Council of 15 and 16 October 1999, and in particular point 35 thereof, the formal extradition procedure should be abolished among the Member States in respect of persons who are fleeing from justice after having been finally sentenced and extradition procedures should be speeded up in respect of persons suspected of having committed an offence.
>
> . . .
>
> (5) The objective set for the Union to become an area of freedom, security and justice leads to abolishing extradition between Member States and replacing it by a system of surrender between judicial authorities. Further, the introduction of a new simplified system of surrender of sentenced or suspected persons for the purposes of execution or prosecution of criminal sentences makes it possible to remove the complexity and potential for delay inherent in the present extradition procedures. Traditional cooperation relations which have prevailed up till now between Member States should be replaced by a system of free movement of judicial decisions in criminal matters, covering both pre-sentence and final decisions, within an area of freedom, security and justice.

9.141 In essence, a warrant may be issued by a national issuing judicial authority and transmitted to the executing judicial authority. Once it is certified in the executing State it can be executed directly without the need to obtain a domestic warrant, unlike the procedure under existing extradition arrangements.

---

[43] And the more recent proposed CARICOM Arrest Warrant.

It has also sought to simplify the process by identifying a list of serious offences **9.142** which Member States regard as serious offences and removing the need for the requirement for dual criminality in respect of these offences. Article 2.1 of the European Framework Decision provides as follows:

> 1. A European Arrest Warrant may be issued for acts punishable by the law of the issuing Member State by a custodial sentence or a detention order for a maximum period of at least 12 months or, where a sentence has been passed or a detention order has been made, for sentences of at least four months. The following offences, if they are punishable in the issuing Member State by a custodial sentence or a detention order for a maximum period of at least three years and as they are defined by the law of the issuing Member State, shall, under the terms of this Framework Decision and without verification of the dual criminality of the act, give rise to surrender pursuant to a European Arrest Warrant.

It then lists a number of offences, including terrorism, trafficking, and corrup- **9.143** tion, which do not require verification of dual criminality.

The EAW has two distinct categories of extradition offence: **9.144**

1. offences punishable with twelve months or more imprisonment;
2. offences contained in the Framework list punishable with imprisonment of three years or more and as 'defined by the law of the issuing Member State, shall under the terms of this Framework Decision and *without verification of the double criminality* of the act, give rise to surrender pursuant to a European Arrest Warrant'[44] [emphasis added].

The Council Framework Decision of 13 June 2002 identifies a list of generic **9.145** serious offences which Member States regard as serious offences and common to all Member States (eg, corruption, terrorism, laundering of proceeds of crime). Consequently the Framework Decision seeks to remove the need for the transposition of conduct in order to satisfy the dual criminality rule. This perceived removal of the dual criminality rule raised a huge concern amongst practitioners as it was thought that extradition would be granted for offences which are not offences under English law. The House of Lords in *Dabas*,[45] a request from Spain for offences of 'terrorism', observed:

> These provisions show that the result to be achieved was to remove the complexity and potential for delay that was inherent in the existing extradition procedures. They were to be replaced by a much simpler system of surrender between judicial authorities. This system was to be subject to sufficient controls to enable the judicial authorities of the requested state to decide whether or not surrender was in

---

[44] Official Journal of the European Communities, 13 June 2002.
[45] [2007] UKHL 6.

accordance with the terms and conditions which the Framework Decision lays down. But care had to be taken not to make them unnecessarily elaborate. Complexity and delay are inimical to its objectives.

The scope of the European Arrest Warrant is described in article 2. It may be issued for acts punishable by the law of the issuing Member State by a custodial sentence or a detention order for a maximum period of at least 12 months or, where a sentence has been passed or a detention order has been made, for sentences of at least four months: article 2.1. Verification of the dual criminality of the act is dispensed with in the case of a European Arrest Warrant which is issued for any one or more of the 32 offences listed in article 2.2, provided that the act is punishable in the issuing Member State by a custodial sentence or a detention order for a maximum period of at least three years. Acts which constitute offences other than those on the list may be subject to the condition that they constitute an offence under the law of the executing Member State— that is, subject to verification of their dual criminality: article 2.4.[46]

9.146   In an earlier case in the UK, *Office of King's Prosecutor, Brussels v Cando Armas and Another*[47] dealing with the issue of extradition offence and the construction and interpretation of the relevant part of the Extradition Act 2003, the Administrative Court observed:

> The object of the Framework Decision was to facilitate extradition between Member States of the European Union: we refer to the recitals and to Article 1.2. The list of framework offences includes offences of the most serious kind. Many of them are by their nature often committed by conduct occurring in the territory of more than one Member State: terrorism, trafficking in human beings, illicit trafficking in narcotic drugs and weapons, illicit trafficking in endangered species and in cultural goods are some examples. We are reminded of the speech of Lord Slynn in *Re Al-Fawwaz* [2001] UKHL 69, [2002] 1 AC 556 at [37], when giving reasons for not regarding the jurisdiction of a state seeking extradition as being limited to its territory:
>
> > . . . It should not because in present conditions it would make it impossible to extradite for some of the most serious crimes now committed globally or at any rate across frontiers. Drug smuggling, money laundering, the abduction of children, acts of terrorism, would to a considerable extent be excluded from the extradition process. It is essential that that process should be available to them. To ignore modern methods of communication and travel as aids to criminal activities is unreal.
>
> It is not coincidence that all of the offences to which Lord Slynn referred are now framework offences. We also refer to Lord Bridge of Harwich in *R v Governor of Ashford Remand Centre, Ex p Postlethwaite* [1988] AC 924, 947, cited by Lord Hutton in *Re Al-Fawwaz* at [64]:
>
> > I also take the judgment in that case [In Re Arton (No 2) [1896] 1 QB 509, 517] as good authority for the proposition that in the application of the principle the court should not, unless constrained by the language used, interpret any

---

[46] Per Lord Hope of Craighead, para 18 and 19 of the judgment.
[47] [2004] EWHC 2019 (Admin).

extradition treaty in a way which would 'hinder the working and narrow the operation of most salutary international arrangements.'—Mr Justice Stanley Burnton, Queen's Bench Division (Administrative Court) 20 August 2004.[48]

This model has also inspired the proposal for the CARICOM Arrest Warrant **9.147** Treaty[49] and was endorsed by the Annual Meeting of the Conference of Heads of Government of the Caribbean Community in their Communiqué issued at the conclusion of the Twenty-Eighth Meeting of the Conference of Heads of Government of The Caribbean Community (CARICOM), 1–4 July 2007:

> Other measures to be finalised by September 2007 include a CARICOM Maritime and Airspace Agreement and a CARICOM Arrest Warrant Treaty. The Maritime and Airspace Agreement for CARICOM Member States will allow Member States to make best use of available resources in order to provide surveillance of the maritime environment; while the Arrest Warrant will put in place a legal mechanism to effect surrender of suspected persons and fugitives across borders. In the first instance, the focus will be on providing coverage for the maritime environment shared by Trinidad and Tobago, Barbados, Grenada, St. Vincent and the Grenadines and Saint Lucia.

The UN counter-terrorism instruments

There are at present sixteen UN counter-terrorism (CT) instruments which were **9.148** negotiated between 1963 and 2005 dealing with the prevention and suppression of terrorism, culminating, in April 2005, with the General Assembly adopting the International Convention for the Suppression of Acts of Nuclear Terrorism. Thereafter, three further instruments were adopted during 2005: the Amendment to the Convention on the Physical Protection of Nuclear Material, the Protocol of 2005 to the Convention for the Suppression of Unlawful Acts Against the Safety of Maritime Navigation, and the Protocol of 2005 to the Protocol for the Suppression of Unlawful Acts against the Safety of Fixed Platforms Located on the Continental Shelf.

These Conventions provide an important framework for international coopera- **9.149** tion in dealing with cases relating to acts of terrorism. They do so by providing, for the purposes of extradition:

- The legal basis for extradition where no treaty is in place between the requesting and requested State;

- The convention offences are deemed to be extradition crimes thereby assisting in the satisfaction of an essential safeguard in extradition, namely dual criminality.

---

[48] Office of King's Prosecutor, *Brussels v Cando Armas and Another* [2004] EWHC 2019 (Admin).
[49] CARICOM arrest warrant has not been finalized at the time of writing.

- The obligation to extradite or prosecute (*aut dedere aut judicare*).
- The removal of the political offence exception.
- The protection of human rights through the refusal of extradition if there are substantial grounds to believe that the request has been made for the purpose of prosecuting a person on account of race religion, nationality, ethnic origin, or political opinion.

Legal basis for extradition

9.150 Nine of the sixteen UN CT instruments[50] provide for a legal basis for extradition in the following general terms:

1. The offence shall be deemed to be included as an extraditable offence in any extradition treaty existing between Contracting States. Contracting States undertake to include the offence as an extraditable offence in every extradition treaty to be concluded amongst them.

2. If a Contracting State which makes extradition conditional on the existence of a treaty receives a request for extradition from another Contracting State with which it has no extradition treaty, it may at its option consider this Convention as the legal basis for extradition in respect of the offence. Extradition shall be subject to the other conditions provided by the law of the requested State.

3. Contracting States which to not make extradition conditional on the existence of a treaty shall recognize the offence as an extraditable offence between themselves subject to the conditions provided by the law of the requested State.

4. The offence shall be treated, for the purposes of extradition between Contracting States, as if it had been committed not only in the place in which it occurred but also in the territories of the States required to establish their jurisdiction in accordance with Article 4, paragraph 1.[51]

9.151 Although the instruments provide a legal basis for extradition, it is usually a matter for the law of the requested State as to whether or not the Convention/Protocol basis is accepted or a bilateral treaty is still required. Most States do however recognize this is a basis in the absence of a treaty. For example, the UAE requested the extradition of *Lodhi*[52] from the UK invoking the UN Convention against Illicit

---

[50] The following are non-penal instruments: the Convention on Offences and Certain Other Acts Committed on Board Aircraft (1963); Protocol for the Suppression of Unlawful Acts against the Safety of Fixed Platforms Located on the Continental Shelf (1988); Protocol for the Suppression of Unlawful Acts of Violence at Airports Serving International Civil Aviation (1988); Convention on the Marking of Plastic Explosives for the Purpose of Identification (1991).

[51] Article 8 of the Convention for the Suppression of Unlawful Seizure of Aircraft (1970).

[52] *Mohammed Fakhar Al Zaman Lodhi v The Governor of HMP Brixton and the Government of the United Arab Emirates* [2001] EWHC (Admin) 178.

Traffic in Narcotic Drugs and Psychotropic Substances (1988) (the 'Vienna Convention'). At the hearing the defence challenged the validity of placing reliance on the Convention and the Administrative Court, dismissing the argument stated:

> In these circumstances we are quite unable to accept the submission of Mr Fitzgerald QC that the UAE must somehow or other be regarded as a second class state in extradition terms because it is not a party to a general bilateral extradition treaty with this country. As is the case with anti-terrorist treaties, this country has bound itself by treaty to co-operate on an international stage in the fight against illicit traffic in narcotic drugs. In this respect we accept Mr Greenwood QC's submission that there should be a fundamental assumption of good faith on the part of the requesting state (*R v Governor of Pentonville Prison ex p Lee* [1993] 1 WLR 1294, 1300), and that we ought to accord the treaty and the statute 'a broad and generous construction so far as the texts permit to facilitate extradition' (*Re Ismail* [1999] AC 320, per Lord Steyn at pp 326–7) . . . [53]

Extradition crime and dual criminality

At the heart of extradition lies what has always been regarded as an essential safeguard—the rule of dual criminality. This rule requires that, for an extradition request to succeed, the conduct complained of in the requesting State must also amount to a crime in the requested State; a failure to satisfy this requirement leads to the discharge of the fugitive at the first step: 'For the purposes of the present case, the most important requirement is that the conduct complained of must constitute a crime under the law both of Spain and of the United Kingdom. This is known as the double criminality rule'—Lord Browne-Wilkinson, *Pinochet* (No 3) [2000] 1 AC 147. **9.152**

What amounts to an extradition crime varies between instruments. Broadly speaking, there are two different approaches to determining what amounts to an extradition crime: **9.153**

• The conduct test;
• The 'list' test.

The conduct test

Most recent extradition treaties adopt this approach, as it avoids the complexities usually associated with trying to fit the conduct in a general list. The main criteria under this test is that the offence is punishable under the laws of both the requesting and requested State for twelve months or more;[54] in some cases, the sentence threshold is set at two years or more.[55] **9.154**

---

[53] Per LJ Brooke.
[54] Eg, Article 2 of the European Convention on Extradition 1957.
[55] The London Scheme for Extradition within the Commonwealth (Nov 2000).

9.155   Therefore, when determining an extradition crime under the conduct test, the requested State transposes the conduct from the requesting State as if it has occurred within the requested State. If the conduct amounts to a crime, then the next stage is to look at the sentence threshold to ensure it satisfies the requirement. If the conduct does not amount either to a crime or does not satisfy the sentence threshold, it fails the dual criminality rule. This approach has been found to be more flexible and one that encompasses both statutory and common law offences.

The list test

9.156   In contrast, the list test has proven to be more difficult, particularly in relation to common law offences. For example, in the UK, 'conspiracy to defraud' is an extradition crime for requests emanating from European and Commonwealth/Colony countries, but was not deemed to be an extradition crime where it concerned requests from the US under the old US-UK treaty.[56]

9.157   Apart from the transposition of conduct, consideration must also be given to the following matters, all of which must be satisfied for the purposes of the dual criminality:

(i)   Date of the offence: as the offence has to be a crime under the law of both the requesting and requested State and must not fall foul of the retrospectivity rule. It follows therefore that where the offence is criminalized at a date later than when it occurred in the requesting State. For example, the extradition request submitted by Spain in respect of Pinochet related to offences of committed between 1973 and 1990 while he was Head of State of Chile. The crimes included genocide, torture, taking of hostages, and murder of Spanish citizens. The proposed English charges included conspiracy to torture between:
   • January 1972 and September 1973;
   • August 1973 and January 1990;
   • January 1972 and January 1990; and
   • Torture in June 1989.

   One of the grounds for challenge was whether the rule of dual criminality was satisfied given that the conduct alleged had occurred prior to torture being an offence under UK law. As torture was criminalized by the Criminal Justice Act of 1988 and hostage-taking after 1982, the conduct did not amount to an extradition crime.

   The House of Lords determined that for an offence to amount to an extradition crime required the conduct to be an offence in the UK at the date it took place and not merely the date of the request for extradition. Therefore,

---

[56] *The Secretary of State for the Home Dept ex parte Gilmore & Ogun* Divisional Court [6 June 1997].

only those parts of the conspiracy to torture and torture relating to the period after 29 September 1988 were extradition crimes.

This decision, although *per incuriam*, in effect overruled the Divisional Court decision in *Gotthold*[57] when the Court considered a similar argument but concluded that if the conduct was an offence at the time when a request for extradition is submitted then it would amount to an extradition crime and not at the date of commission of the offence.

(ii) Are there any extra-territorial elements to the conduct? Where the conduct spreads over a number of countries the transposition exercise still remains the same in order to determine if there is an extradition crime. Generally speaking, treaties and domestic law refer to conduct which occurs within the 'territory' of the State Party. However, courts have always read 'territory' to mean 'jurisdiction' in order to capture conduct in both the requesting State and elsewhere; this is now of particular relevance given that crime is no longer local in commission or effect. For example, in the US extradition request of *Al-Fawwaz & Others*,[58] Al-Fawwaz, Abdel Bary, and Eidarous were accused of a conspiracy to murder US nationals, American diplomats, and American personnel as part of the conspiracy by members of Al-Qaida. The US sought their extradition in respect of the Embassy bombings in East Africa in 1998. Following the committal hearing the defence lodged an application for habeas corpus and submitted that in order to amount to an 'extradition crime' the conduct should have occurred within the territory of the US, but in the present case the conduct was largely extraterritorial, and so it could not be considered as it had not occurred in the territory of the US. On behalf of the US it was submitted that the word 'territory' in the treaty had to be given

---

[57] Divisional Court, 8 May 1998 CO/2497/97. Gotthold was accused of cheating the Swedish public revenue between 1 February 1994 and 1 March 1994 by submitting a false VAT return. He submitted that: (i) the conduct alleged in count 4 (submitting a false VAT return) was not an extradition crime—the relevant dates being prior to the enactment of the European Convention on Extradition (Fiscal Offences) Order 1993. It was argued by defence that this order only applied to offences committed after 6 June 1994 and that the order does not contain any words to the effect that it applies to offences committed prior to its enactment. The applicant therefore has an accrued right not to be extradited in respect of this offence and that the Order is a penal enactment in that it expands the range of offences for which extradition can be ordered.
Decision:
(i) rejected—the present case does not concern any accrued right. The applicant is accused of an act which was a crime at the time he allegedly committed it. 'All that has happened is that, whereas previously he was entitled, if he could escape from Sweden, to remain in this country without being extradited back, Parliament has now decided that those accused of such crimes can be extradited back. It has not, in my judgment, imposed an extra penalty upon him and this is not a case where one should regard the position as being one where he had an accrued right which this court's sense of fairness should lead it to protect. The present case is manifestly not one where it can be said that the act was not a criminal offence at the time when it was committed, nor is there any question of any heavier penalty. I do not regard liability to extradition as being part of the penalty'— LJ Schieman.
[58] [2001] UKHL 69.

a broader interpretation, in line with paragraph 15 of Schedule 1 of the 1989 Act and the case of *Minervini*, to mean 'jurisdiction'.

The House of Lords stated that there was no requirement for the conduct to have occurred in the US and reliance could be placed on extra-territorial conduct in order for the offences to be justiciable in the US, particularly as serious crimes were committed globally, and 'an ordinary meaning of the term "the jurisdiction of the State", is the power of that State to try an offence and includes extra-territorial jurisdiction'.

9.158 Thus, to amount to an 'extradition crime' conduct must satisfy the following criteria:

- Dual criminality;
- Sentence;
- Within the 'jurisdiction' of the requesting state, which includes both territorial and extraterritorial offences.

9.159 It does not mean however, that if part of the conduct does not satisfy the dual criminality rule, it would lead to a refusal of extradition on the entire conduct. As illustrated in *Pinochet* and other cases, the requested State can find that part of the conduct satisfies the test and return a fugitive for part of the conduct. Such a finding would be binding on the requesting State under the speciality rule.[58a]

9.160 Dual criminality, as mentioned above, has long been regarded as one of the key safeguards in extradition, in that, if conduct did not amount to an extradition crime then no extradition could lie; but the adoption by the European Union of the European Arrest Warrant (EAW) under the Council Framework Decision of 13 June 2002 has identified a number of serious offences common to all State Parties and removed the verification of dual criminality for those offences.[59]

9.161 However, there is a practical limitation to reliance being placed on any of the UN Conventions as illustrated by the request from Algeria to the UK.[60] Equally where the conduct has not been criminalized in the requested State it would raise a challenge under the principle of *nullem crimen sine lege*.

'Extradite or prosecute' (aut dedere aut judicare)

9.162 The main objective of the UN CT instruments is to ensure the apprehension, prosecution, or extradition of persons suspected of committing acts of terrorism.

[58a] The speciality rule prohibits the requesting State from proceeding with matters other than those for which a person is returned. However, where the requesting State does proceed with charges which were not the basis of the extradition request, the avenue of judicial oversight in the requested State is limited—see the recent decision in *Farid Hilali* [2008] EWHC 2892 (Admin).

[59] See discussion above at paras 9.142–9.146.

[60] See (n 30) above.

This objective is reflected in the *aut dedere aut judicare* ('extradite or prosecute') principle that is found in all the UN CT instruments that create offences[61] and is reinforced by UNSCR 1373 which obliges all Member States to deny safe haven to those 'who finance, plan, support, or commit terrorist acts, or provide safe havens'.[62]

The 'extradite or prosecute' principle is reflected in most treaties[63] but is often limited to refusal on the basis of nationality. The UN Conventions, by contrast, do not limit the principle where refusal is on the grounds of nationality. For example, Article 7 of the Convention on the Prevention and Punishment of Crimes against Internationally Protected Persons [1973] provides that: 'The State Party in whose territory the alleged offender is present shall, if it does not extradite him, submit, without exception whatsoever and without undue delay, the case to its competent authorities for the purpose of prosecution, through proceedings in accordance with the laws of that State.' **9.163**

The wording in the two earlier Conventions was then amended in the Hostages Convention to include the requirement for a fair trial[64] in the requested State or temporary surrender where the domestic law of a State Party does not permit the extradition of its nationals, leading to the adoption of the following text which is found in subsequent Conventions. **9.164**

Thus, Article 8 of the International Convention against the Taking of Hostages [1979] provides as follows: **9.165**

1. The State Party in the territory of which the alleged offender is found shall, if it does not extradite him, be obliged, without exception whatsoever and whether or not the offence was committed in its territory, to submit the case to its competent authorities for the purposes of prosecution, through proceedings in accordance with the laws of that State. Those authorities shall take their decision in the same manner as in the case of any ordinary offence of a grave nature under the law of that State.

Article 8 of the International Convention for the Suppression of Terrorist Bombings [1997] ('Terrorist Bombing Convention'):

1. The State Party in the territory of which the alleged offender is present shall, in cases to which Article 6[65] applies, if it does not extradite that person, be obliged,

---

[61] Save for the Convention on Offences and Certain Other Acts Committed on Board Aircraft (1963), and Convention on the Marking of Plastic Explosives for the Purpose of Identification [1991] which does not create any offences.
[62] Paragraph 2(c) of UNSCR 1373.
[63] For example, Article 6(2) of the European Convention on Extradition 1957 imposes such an obligation where the requested State does not extradite its own national.
[64] See Appendix 7: Hostages Convention, Article 8.2.
[65] Article 6 sets out the jurisdiction provisions (also covered in Chapter 3 on Jurisdiction).

without exception whatsoever and whether or not the offence was committed in its territory, to submit the case without undue delay to its competent authorities for the purpose of prosecution, through proceedings in accordance with the laws of that State. These authorities shall take their decision in the same manner as in the case of any offence of a grave nature under the law of that State.

2. Whenever a State Party is permitted under its domestic law to extradite or otherwise surrender one of its nationals only upon the condition that the person will be returned to that State to serve the sentence imposed as a result of the trial or proceeding for which the extradition or surrender of the person was sought, and this State and the State seeking the extradition of the person agree with this option and other terms they may deem appropriate, such a conditional extradition or surrender shall be sufficient to discharge the obligation set forth in paragraph 1 of the present article.

9.166   The effectiveness of the principle of 'extradite or prosecute' however is largely dependent on the jurisdiction[66] provisions of the laws of the requested State. The position under common law remains largely territorial unless jurisdiction is expressly extended by Statute. This is in contrast to civil law jurisdictions where the concept of jurisdiction is not seen as a concept separate to and from the aspect of statehood or indeed international law.

9.167   Therefore, if such provisions do not extend jurisdiction, then it may well prove to be difficult to prosecute such a case no matter how willing the State may be to conduct the prosecution. Common law countries, by and large, tend only to extend jurisdiction on grounds of nationality (active personality basis), for example, The UK Terrorism Act 2000, whilst South Africa legislation permits a wider jurisdiction. In practice, this would mean that where an offence has been committed against the nationals of a requesting State (passive personality) but extradition has been refused by the requested State, it is obliged to refer the case to its competent authorities for consideration. If for instance, extra-territorial jurisdiction based on passive personality is not recognized under the law of the requested State, then no prosecution can lie, and this can inadvertently create the perception of a safe haven. It is for this reason that the instruments have created the mandatory and discretionary basis for asserting jurisdiction.

Political offence exception

9.168   If acts of violence directed at ordinary citizens were deemed 'political crimes' for the purposes of this subsection, then the Attorney General would be required to

---

[66] See Chapter 3 on Jurisdiction.

withhold deportation of the perpetrators. As the Seventh Circuit observed, if such were the law:

> [N]othing would prevent an influx of terrorists seeking a safe haven in America. Those terrorists who flee to this country would avoid having to answer to anyone anywhere for their crimes. The law is not so utterly absurd. Terrorists who have committed barbarous acts elsewhere would be able to flee to the United States and live in our neighbourhoods and walk our streets forever free from any accountability for their acts. We do not need them in our society. We have enough of our own domestic criminal violence with which to contend without importing and harbouring with open arms the worst that other countries have to export. We recognize the validity and usefulness of the political offense exception, but it should be applied with care lest our country become a social jungle and an encouragement to terrorists everywhere.—Eain, 641 F 2d at 520.

Historically, the political offence exception had constituted a ground for refusal for **9.169** extradition in many States. That exception was based upon an understanding amongst States not to assist in punishing political activity directed against the government of another State, such as treason, sedition, or attempts to force a ruling group to change or adopt certain policies, otherwise referred to as 'pure' offences. This approach is fairly straightforward and clear, however the difficulty arises in respect of 'relative' offences, that is, conduct that alleges criminality but is also linked with political activity. It is this latter range of offences that national courts and international bodies have sought to grapple with and is discussed below.

The Convention on Offences and Certain Other Acts Committed on Board **9.170** Aircraft [1963] reflects an attempt to allow a limited exception of a political nature without negating the purpose of the agreement. Its Article 2 provides in relevant part as follows:

> . . . except when the safety of the aircraft or of persons or property on board so requires, no provision of this Convention shall be interpreted as authorizng or requiring any action in respect of offences against penal laws of a political nature or those based on racial or religious discrimination.

For thirty-four years after 1963, no express reference is found to any form of **9.171** political offence exception in any of the counter-terrorism conventions and protocols; although reference to the political offence exception is found in bilateral and regional extradition treaties.[67]

The Terrorist Bombing Convention [1997] is the first Convention in which the **9.172** political offence exception is mentioned and explicitly rejected. Article 11 provides:

> None of the offences set forth in article 2 shall be regarded, for the purposes of extradition or mutual legal assistance, as a political offence or as an offence connected

---

[67] US-UK treaty; European Convention on Extradition [1957]; European Convention on the Suppression of Terrorism [1977].

with a political offence or as an offence inspired by political motives. Accordingly, a request for extradition or for mutual legal assistance based on such an offence may not be refused on the sole ground that it concerns a political offence or an offence connected with a political offence or an offence inspired by political motives.

9.173 This has been echoed in the subsequent conventions, namely Article 14 of the International Convention for the Suppression of the Financing of Terrorism (1999); Article 15 of International Convention for the Suppression of Acts of Nuclear Terrorism (2005); and Article 11A of the Amendment to the Convention on the Physical Protection of Nuclear Material (2005).

What does political offence exception mean?

9.174 Despite its common usage both in extradition and refugee law, there is no definition or an agreed meaning of this phrase. Treaties, whether bilateral, regional, or international have all remained silent. It has been largely left to national courts to interpret the term, assisted to some extent from the general comments and interpretation guidance issued by human rights committees and commissions.

9.175 The essential difficulty surrounding this notion has been well captured by Hugessen JA in *Gil v Canada (Minister of Employment and Immigration)* (CA) (1994), [1995] 1 FC 508:

> Although the terminology of 'political offence' is widespread, a satisfactory definition remains to be formulated. The term embraces two concepts: first, the purely political offence, which is an act directed against the political organization or government of a state and contains no element of common crime; and secondly, what is described in the Act as an offence of a political character, one that is a common crime but is so closely integrated with political acts or events that it is regarded as political and the rationale for the rule is clear enough.

9.176 It must be remarked at the outset that, in practice, there have been cases, few and far between, where the requested State has refused to extradite the fugitive on the grounds of the political offence exception, but given the significance of this principle and to gain an understanding as to the meaning of the exception, particularly for the 'relative' offences, and its application by national courts, it is important to consider the facts and the analysis of some of the leading cases in which the political offence exception was raised and its modern day application.

9.177 Turning first to the 'pure' political offence, an illustration of the application of the exception is the recent case from Botswana of *The Republic of Namibia v Kakaena Likunga Alfred & Others.*[68]

9.178 The case relates to an extradition request from The Republic of Namibia in respect of thirteen individuals for offences committed by them in the Caprivi region.

---

[68] Court of Appeal, Botswana 64/03 [July 2004].

It was alleged that the thirteen were members of an organization known as the Caprivi Liberation Army (CLA) which was seeking secession from Namibia. The CLA had set up training camps in Namibia securing arms and ammunitions. It was alleged that two of the group had shot and killed a victim who was attempting to escape the training camp. It was further alleged that the group had planned an attack on Namibia and to that end, some of them had participated in an attack on government installations in Kadma Mullo, killing a number of people. The group then fled to neighbouring Botswana.

9.179 Namibia sought the extradition[69] of these thirteen accused in respect of two charges: namely, high treason and the unlawful possession of arms and ammunition. Additional charges of murder, attempted murder, unlawful possession of explosives, and robbery with aggravating circumstances were laid against some of them.

9.180 All the accused were arrested in August 2000 and were ruled extraditable by the magistrate the following year. The accused appealed to the High Court and were discharged on the grounds that the offences of high treason, arms and ammunition charges, and the explosives charges were caught by the exception. The Government of Namibia, acting through the Attorney General of Botswana, lodged an appeal to the Court of Appeal against the findings of the High Court.

9.181 The Court of Appeal[70] in applying the exception had no difficulty in ruling that high treason was an offence that was political in nature and therefore a refusal to extradite must follow. With regard to the 'relative' offences, the Court relied on the incidence tests as expounded by the decision in *Re Castioni*.[71]

9.182 Tebbutt JP, in giving the leading speech, stated as follows:

> The exemption of political offence from extradition has been expressed as an important principle of extradition law since the middle of the 19th century . . . The objective of the exemption has been said to be two-fold: it mixes inseparably the humanitarian concept for the fugitive on the one hand and on the other the politically motivated unwillingness of the requested State to get involved in the internal political affairs of the requesting State . . . In the United States in *United States v*

---

[69] Namibia sought the request under the London Scheme for Extradition within the Commonwealth. Article 12 of the Scheme sets out the Political Offence Exception which is identical in terms with other extradition treaties and international instruments. The full text of the London Scheme can be found at <http://www.thecommonwealth.org/Internal/38061/documents/>.
[70] The Court set out a very helpful and detailed summary of the political position of the Caprivi region.
[71] Queen's Bench Division, November 1890.

Pitawanakwat 120 F Supp 2d 921, Janice Stewart J, quoting from *Quinn v Robinson* 783 F 2d 776, 786 (9th Cir) said the following:

> This exception, which arose in the aftermath of the American and French Revolutions, was first incorporated into treaties in the early nineteenth century and is 'now almost universally accepted in extradition law'. It was consciously designed to protect the right of citizens to rebel against unjust or oppressive government and is premised on the following justifications.

> First, its historical development suggests that it is grounded in a belief that individuals have a 'right to resort to political activism to foster political change'. This justification is consistent with the modern consensus that political crimes have greater legitimacy than common crimes. Second, the exception reflects a concern that individuals—particularly unsuccessful rebels—should not be returned to countries where they may be subjected to unfair trials and punishments because of their political opinions. Third, the exception comports with the notion that governments—and certainly their non-political branches—should not intervene in the internal political struggles of other nations . . .

> In the cases of the ten respondents charged with high treason and unlawful possession of arms and ammunition, the extradition application in respect of them had to be refused on the high treason charges as these were offences of a political character. This finding is made (a) because treason is per se a political offence and (b) because of the actions of the respondents on 2 August 1999 were, in the light of the background to them committed in the course of a political struggle against the Government of Namibia in pursuance of the respondents' political aims to secure the secession of Caprivi. On the criteria set out above they were therefore offences of a political character . . . The evidence that they were committed in pursuance of a political ideal is overwhelming. The possession by the respondents of arms and ammunition was part of those actions and offences arising from such possession are therefore also offences of a political character.

9.183   There is therefore, what appears to be a sharp distinction between those offences regarded as 'pure' political offences which automatically attract the exception and 'relative' offences, that is, criminal conduct that has a nexus to the political situation. It is in the instances where the latter category of offences is alleged that the difficulties arise. How is the court to determine whether or not the conduct falls within this exception? As stated above, this determination has been left to the national courts of the requested State. The first of such cases was determined by the Queen's Bench Division in *re Castioni* [1890] which expounded the 'incidence' test in respect of relative offences. This has been widely adopted and modified by various jurisdictions. The cases discussed below provide a distillation of that test.

In re Castioni, *Queen's Bench Division, November 1890*

9.184   On 11 September 1890 a number of citizens, one of whom was the applicant Castioni, seized the arsenal of the town, detained several people connected to the Government, and made them march to the municipal palace. The backdrop to this event was the general dissatisfaction in the town with the government administration. Upon arrival at the palace, the victim and another member of the

Government refused entry to the crowd. The applicant, who was armed, shot the victim. There was no evidence to suggest that the applicant knew the victim prior to the incident. The palace was occupied and several members of the Government were imprisoned.

The Swiss Government sought the extradition of Castioni in respect of the murder **9.185** and he contended that he should not be surrendered as the offence was 'one of a political character'. The magistrate rejected that argument and he was committed. Castioni lodged a petition for a writ of habeas corpus and the High Court in allowing the appeal considered the meaning of 'offence of a political nature':

> I think that in order to bring the case within the words of the Act and to exclude extradition for such an act as murder, which is one of the extradition offences, *it must at least be shewn that the act is done in furtherance of, done with intention of assistance, as a sort of overt act in the course of acting in a political matter, a political uprising, or a dispute between two parties in the State as to which is to have the government in its hands, before it can be brought within the meaning of the words used in the Act* ... I do not think it is intended that a scrap of a prima facie case on the one side should have the effect of throwing upon the other side the onus of proving or disproving his position ... there is nothing said as to upon whom is the onus probandi, or that it shall be made to appear by one side or the other in such a case. It is a restriction upon the surrender of a fugitive criminal ... wholly irrespective of any doctrine of onus on the one side or the other, that is within the restriction, and he cannot be surrendered ... I think it follows that this Court must have the power to go into the whole matter, and in some cases ... might take a different view of the matter from that taken by the magistrate. It seems to me that it is a question of mixed law and fact—mainly indeed fact—as to whether the facts are such as to bring the case within s. 3 and to shew that it was an offence of a political character[72] [emphasis added].

Hawkins J:

> It seems to me that the language of this part of the 9th section in itself shews that the onus is on the person who seeks to absolve himself or exonerate himself from the liability to be handed over. Now, I entirely dissent and I think all reasonable persons would dissent, from the proposition that any act done in the course of a political rising, or in the course o f any insurrection is necessarily of a political character. Everybody would agree, I think, with this—that it is not everything done during the period during which a political rising exists that could be said to be of a political character. A man might be joining in an insurrection ... if he were deliberately, for a matter of private revenge or for purposes of doing injury to another ... could not be said to have any relation at all to the political crime, namely, a crime which in law ought to be punished with the punishment awarded for such a crime ... Now what is the meaning of a crime of political character? I think therefore the expression in the Extradition Act ought to be interpreted to mean that fugitive criminals are not to be surrendered for extradition crimes, if those crimes were incidental to and formed a part of political disturbances.

---

[72] Per Denman J.

9.186 The Court therefore introduced the incidence test, which was followed in *Re Meunier*,[73] a request from France for an anarchist who had caused an explosion. In rejecting the applicant's argument that the conduct fell within the exception on the basis that the crime was committed towards private citizens, Cave J observed:

> It appears to me that, in order to constitute an offence of a political character, there must be two or more parties in the state, each seeking to impose the Government of their own choice on the other, and that if the offence is committed by one side or the other in the pursuance of that object, it is a political offence, otherwise not . . . their efforts are directed primarily against the general body of citizens.[74]

9.187 In *R v Governor of Brixton Prison ex p Schtraks*[75] [House of Lords], Israel sought the extradition of Schtraks to stand trial on charges of perjury and child stealing allegedly committed in Jerusalem. He was committed to await extradition to Israel.

9.188 Lord Reid introduced the subjective element in the determination of the exception, namely the 'motive and purpose of the accused in committing the offence must be relevant and may be decisive'[76] and cast some doubt on the hitherto requirement of a rigid incidence test—nexus to violent political uprising, insurrection etc. Lord Reid was of the view that:

> The use of force, or it may be other means, to compel a sovereign to change his advisers, or to compel a government to change its policy may be just as political in character as the use of force to achieve a revolution. And I do not see why it should be necessary that the refugee's party should have been trying to achieve power in the State. It would be enough if they were trying to make the government concede some measure of freedom . . .[77]

9.189 This approach was the subject of comment in the case of *Tzu-Tsai Cheng v Governor of Pentonville Prison, House of Lords*.[78] The cases so far had concerned conduct in the requesting State, however in *Cheng*, the Court considered the question of whether the political offence exception applied where the conduct alleged had no political nexus to the requesting State, in this case the US.

9.190 The applicant Cheng was convicted of murder in the US. The background to the offence is as follows—Cheng was the executive secretary of a political group (WUFI) which promoted as one its aims the exposure of the corruption and oppression of the Chiang Kai-shek regime in Taiwan to the public at large, but the US in particular. On 24 April 1970, Kai-shek's son visited New York and WUFI

---

[73] [1894] 2 QB 415.
[74] *Meunier* (n 73) 419.
[75] [1964] AC 556.
[76] *Schtraks* (n 75) 583–4.
[77] *Schtraks* (n 75) 583–4.
[78] [1973] AC 931.

planned a demonstration. During the course of the demonstration a shot was fired (not by the applicant) and he was arrested.

The applicant submitted that he had been convicted of an offence of a 'political character'. It was accepted that he was not engaged in any political activity against the US. The issue that arose was as follows: **9.191**

> Whether an offence committed within the jurisdiction of the state requesting extradition can amount to an offence of a political character where (a) the offence was committed in the course of a dispute between the governing party of another state, not the requesting state, on the one hand, and a movement dedicated to its overthrow; and (2) that the offence was committed directly to further the purpose of that movement and for no other purpose, or for any other motive.

The Divisional Court held that one looks to the requesting State in order to determine whether this is an offence of a political character or not, and it is not concerned with political character in relation to any other State than the requesting State. **9.192**

The question to be determined: Whether an offence committed within the jurisdiction of a State requesting the extradition of an offender is 'one of a political character' within the meaning of section 3(1) Extradition Act 1870 so as to stop the offender from being surrendered, his offence having been committed in the course of a dispute with the governing party of a State other than the requesting State. **9.193**

In dismissing the appeal, Their Lordships reiterated the incidence test and in their speeches made the following observations: **9.194**

Lord Hudson:

> Viscount Radcliffe In re Castioni stated: 'There is no authority which supports the argument of the applicant that his political activity vis-à-vis the Taiwan regime give the crime committed in the United States which is an offence against the State a political character so as to prevent an extradition order being made ... In my opinion the idea that lies behind the phrase 'offence of a political character' is that the fugitive is at odds with the State that applies for his extradition on some issue connected with the political control or government of the country. The analogy of 'political' in this context is with 'political' in such phrases as 'political refugee', 'political asylum' or 'political prisoner' To take the wide view contended for by the applicant, losing sight of the idea of political opposition as between fugitive and requesting state, would create an impossible situation ... Political character connotes the notion of opposition to the requesting state.

Lord Diplock:

> He is a fugitive criminal from the United States, not from Taiwan ... I would hold that prima facie an act committed in a foreign state was not an 'offence of a political character' unless the only purpose sought to be achieved by the offender in committing it were to change the government of the state in which it was committed, or to

induce it to change its policy, or to enable him to escape from the jurisdiction of the Government of whose political policies the offender disapproved but despaired of altering so long as he was there. I would not hold that an act constituted an 'offence of a political character' in the ordinary meaning of that phrase appearing in a Statute dealing with the trial and punishment of crimes committed in a foreign state if the only 'political purpose' which the offender sought to achieve by it was not directed against the government or governmental policies of that State within whose territory the offence is committed and which is the only other party to the trial and punishment of the offence.

Lord Salmon:

No exhaustive definition of an offence of a political character is possible and none has been attempted. I do not believe that in 1870 or before or afterwards this country or indeed any other country contemplated that a fugitive criminal should be immune from extradition unless his crime was a political offence directed against the requesting State . . . It seems to me that the benevolence with which it is said that the Act of 1870 should be construed in favour of a fugitive offender must surely have some rational limits. Otherwise, persons could, eg, bomb buildings . . . in, say the USA or any other country with which we have no extradition treaty, with the motive of obtaining some political end in a far off land, knowing that they could escape trial and punishment by escaping to England. This would act as an encouragement for the commission of crimes . . . Accordingly, if such crimes were committed here and criminals escaped abroad, there is no chance of them being surrendered if the Act of 1870 really bears the construction for which the Appellant contends . . . To hold otherwise would be to introduce a new and dangerous principle which the Act does not warrant.

The dissenting opinions were delivered by Lord Wilberforce and Lord Simon of Glaisdale, who observed that:

The difficulty of providing a definition of crimes which were to be non-extraditable because they were of a political character was already notorious. By 1870 France had entered into fifty-three extradition treaties, as compared with this country's three. All the French treaties . . . contained an exception for political offences and in none was the concept defined, France leaving it entirely to the State to whom the extradition request was made to decide whether the offence was of a political character . . . By reason of this primary and golden rule, therefore, the words 'offence of a political character' must be read in their natural ordinary and literal sense, without the addition of the words 'against (or, in respect of) the foreign State demanding such surrender' which are not in the Act . . . Indeed I cannot conceive that it would occur to anyone except a lawyer that the appellant's offence could possibly be described as other than of a political character . . . no jurist stipulates that the political character of the crime must be judged vis-à-vis the State seeking extradition. The appellant satisfies the most exacting relevant offence, namely [iii]—his crime was committed both from a political motive and for a political purpose. Against such an historical background it is impossible to suppose that Parliament intended section 3(1) to be construed other than benevolently in favour of the fugitive offender: certainly an artificially narrow construction is quite inadmissible.—Lord Simon of Glaisdale

In the US the political offence exception has been raised in both deportation and extradition matters and the courts have adopted a similar approach to the UK. The US Court of Appeals for the Fourth Circuit in the recent case of *Wilmer Yarleque Ordinola v John Hackman*[79] very helpfully sets out the position and historical development of the exception by the US courts[80] and is worthy of a detailed examination, particularly as the exception was raised by a former Government official. It will be recalled that hitherto the exception has been raised by those in some sort of opposition to the government of the day. It is somewhat regrettable that the Court did not seize the opportunity to examine this issue. Williams, Circuit Judge gave the leading opinion and concluded: **9.195**

> Unfortunately, the issue of whether the political offense exception should ever be applied to a former government actor is not technically before this court, the government having elected not to pursue the argument before the extradition court and on habeas review. Accordingly, we have no occasion to address this difficult problem directly and must assume the exception is theoretically available to an extraditee such as Ordinola. As a practical matter, however, the difficulty of assessing a former government agent's claim to the political offense exception persists in Ordinola's argument, which is essentially no different than the claim that any acts he committed under the auspices of the Colina Group were political. Indeed, the sole purpose for the existence of the Colina Group was political: to preserve the government from the revolutionary group that sought to overthrow it. Specifically, Ordinola takes the position that he is charged with political offenses because the underlying acts were politically motivated he was acting pursuant to directives from his superior officers. Thus, in Ordinola's mind, he was fighting an insurgency.[81]

The case concerns an extradition request from Peru to US for Ordinola, a former government official of Peru. He is sought for the crimes of aggravated homicide, aggravated kidnapping, forced disappearance of persons, inflicting major intentional injuries, and delinquent association. **9.196**

In 1991 the former President of Peru, Alberto Fujimori created a special operations paramilitary squad, Grupo Colina which was commissioned to combat the **9.197**

---

[79] US Court of Appeals for the Fourth Circuit No 06-6126 [22 December 2007].

[80] The Court examined the decisions in *Eain* 641 F 2d 504, 521(7th Cir 1981) and *Quinn* 783 F 2d 776, 54 USLW 2449, two earlier leading decisions. The approach in Eain had been at some variance with *Quinn* with regard to the killing of civilians and was then resolved in favour of the *Eain* approach in a decision by US Court of Appeals (9th Circuit) in the case of *Barapind v Enomoto* 1069 (9th Cir) 2004 which arose in the wake of Sikh militancy in the Punjab region of India in the 1980s: 'On balance, we believe that the Seventh Circuit's approach in *Eain* has the wiser of the arguments. As recognized by Judge Duniway in *Quinn*, 783 F 2d 819: 'the indiscriminate killings of civilians and police officers cannot and must not qualify for the political offense exception to extradition, even if "politically motivated". To hold otherwise is to open the door for our country to turn into "a social jungle and an encouragement to terrorists everywhere". *Eain*, 641 F 2d 520. In international affairs and multi-lateral situations, one cannot ignore the principle of reciprocity: what goes around comes around.'

[81] See 9.70 ff.

Shining Path. Ordinola was assigned to this group and later headed it. It is alleged that whilst serving on this Group, Ordinola on four separate occasions kidnapped and murdered non-combatant civilians.

9.198 Ordinola entered the US on 20 February 2001 and applied for political asylum in June 2001. On 12 November 2003 Peru submitted a request for his extradition. Ordinola was arrested and was committed by the Magistrate judge. At the hearing before the Magistrate Ordinola claimed that he could not be extradited as the offences fell into the political offence exception. The Magistrate rejected this argument and ruled that 'although Ordinola's alleged crimes occurred during a severe political uprising, the crimes were not sufficiently incidental to the uprising and thus did not fall within the exception. He reasoned that any political intentions Ordinola had in committing the alleged crimes were not enough to render the acts political offenses in light of the fact that Ordinola committed the crimes against noncombatant civilians' and certified Ordinola's extradition to the Secretary of State.

9.199 Ordinola filed a petition for a writ of habeas corpus which was granted by the US District Court for the Eastern District of Virginia. The District Court concluded that the Magistrate had erred in his conclusions on the issue of political offences as he was led to believe that the victims were terrorists and therefore had not knowingly killed civilians.

9.200 The Government appealed against this decision.

9.201 Williams, Circuit Judge gave the opinion of the Court and provided a helpful analysis of the US position as follows:

> The political offense exception to extradition forbids countries from extraditing people who are accused of offenses that are 'political' in nature. Like the vast majority of modern-day extradition treaties, the extradition Treaty between the United States and Peru provides a political offense exception:
>
>> Extradition shall not be granted if the offense for which extradition is requested constitutes a political offense.—Extradition Treaty, Art IV, sec 2.
>
> Although the exception has been ingrained in our country's extradition treaties for well over a century, this Circuit has never expressly addressed the exception. We do so now, beginning with an explanation of the exception's history and purpose.
>
> Unfortunately, however, these treaties do not define 'political offense'. Accordingly, we are forced to rely on judicial constructions, history, purpose, and State Department interpretations to determine the phrase's meaning.
>
> Extradition requests are of ancient origin. Extradition was the process by which states requested the surrender of 'pure' political offenders, ie, those accused of treason and contemptuous behavior toward the monarch. The political offense exception to extradition, however, is a far more recent development, tracing its beginnings to the Enlightenment ideals encapsulated in the French and American revolutions. These ideals supported a belief that people possessed an inalienable right to resist and

abolish tyrannical governments. See eg, The Declaration of Independence para 1 (US 1776) ('We hold these truths to be self-evident . . . That whenever any Form of Government becomes destructive of these ends, it is the Right of the People to alter or to abolish it . . .').

The theory underpinning the political offense exception, then, is as old as our country. The exception was deemed necessary to protect those people who justly fought back against their government oppressors to secure political change. In 1843, a decade after nations such as Belgium, France, and Switzerland included the political offense exception in their extradition treaties, the United States followed suit.

Traditionally, there have been two categories of political offenses: 'pure' and 'relative'. The core 'pure' political offenses are treason, sedition, and espionage. *Vo v Benov*, 447 F 3d 1235, 1241 (9th Cir 2006). 'Pure' political offenses do not have any of the elements of a common crime because '[s]uch laws exist solely because the very political entity, the state, has criminalized such conduct for its self-preservation'. Such crimes are perpetrated directly against the state and do not intend to cause private injury. Most extradition treaties preclude extradition for 'pure' political offenses. 'Relative' political offenses, on the other hand, are common crimes that are so intertwined with a political act that the offense itself becomes a political one. [. . .] As evidenced by this discussion, while 'pure' political offenses are easy to identify, determining whether a common offense is 'relatively' political requires close attention to the specific facts at issue.

Most American courts addressing 'relative' political offenses have developed a two-prong test to determine whether an offense is sufficiently political to fall within the exception. Known as 'the incidence test', it asks whether (1) there was a violent political disturbance or uprising in the requesting country at the time of the alleged offense, and if so, (2) whether the alleged offense was incidental to or in the furtherance of the uprising. See, eg, *Vo*, 447 F 3d at 1241. We, too, adopt the incidence test as our lodestar.

To fall within the political offense exception, Ordinola's alleged actions must have been incidental to or in furtherance of a violent political uprising in Peru. Although Ordinola's actions occurred in the course of a violent political uprising, he cannot show that the magistrate judge erred in finding that those actions were not in furtherance of quelling the uprising.

As an initial matter, we—like the magistrate judge and district court—have little trouble in agreeing that the alleged actions here occurred during the course of a violent political uprising. The Peruvian government and the Shining Path were engaged in a violent struggle for control of the country.

The more difficult question is whether Ordinola's alleged offenses were incident to the political uprising. First, we recognize that it makes little sense to ask whether his actions were in furtherance of or 'in aid' of the uprising. [. . .]. Ordinola, acting on behalf of the Peruvian government, was attempting to defeat, not aid, the uprising. Accordingly, we must slightly alter the question and instead ask whether Ordinola's actions were incident to or in furtherance of quelling the violent uprising. The parties disagree over the extent to which this test is subjective or objective.

We conclude that courts must look at the question both subjectively and objectively, although the objective view must usually carry more weight. Courts have long recognized the relevancy of subjective motives in the political offense context. See, eg, *In re Castioni* [1891] 1 QB 149, 158 (1890) (Opinion of Denman, J) 'It must at least be shown that the act is done in furtherance of, done with the intention of assistance, as a sort of overt act in the course of acting in a political matter, a political uprising, or a dispute between two parties in the State as to which is to have the government in its hands.' (emphasis added); Ornelas, 161 US at 511 (inquiring whether the acts 'were perpetrated with bona fide political or revolutionary designs'). We read these cases to mean that for a claimant to come within the protections of the political offense exception, it is necessary, but not sufficient, for the claimant to show that he was politically motivated. In other words, a claimant whose common crime was not subjectively politically motivated cannot come within the exception regardless of whether the offense itself could be described as an objectively 'political' one.

Aside from the subjective component, a claimant must also show that the offense was objectively political. See, eg, Bassiouni, supra [. . .] (explaining that a test that focuses solely on motives 'fails to appreciate the distinction between the nature of the offense and the motives of the actor'). This is because the Treaty itself exempts political offenses, and a political motivation does not turn every illegal action into a political offense. The Treaty, then, cannot be read to protect every act—no matter how unjustifiable and no matter the victim—simply because the suspect can proffer a political rationale for the action. See, eg, *Ahmad v Wigen*, 910 F 2d 1063, 1066 (2d Cir 1990) ('Political motivation does not convert every crime into a political offense.'); *Escobedo v United States*, 623 F 2d 1098, 1104 (5th Cir 1980) ('An offense is not of a political character simply because it was politically motivated.').

To determine whether a particular offense is political under the Treaty, we must look to the totality of the circumstances, focusing on such particulars as the mode of the attack and the identity of the victims . . .

The district court further suggested that the exception must apply to government actors seeking to protect their legal order as opposed to protecting a terrorist organization's violent attempts to overthrow the government. (JA at 522.) This distinction is nonsensical. There is no reason to assume that the two are mutually exclusive. First, one could decide that the political offense exception does not apply to 'terrorists' while at the same time deciding that it does not apply to government actors seeking to protect the legal order, or vice versa. Second, when government actors 'protect their legal order' through legal means, there can be no extradition. Extradition is only proper for acts that are criminalized in both nations. Regardless, to assuage the district court's fears of protecting terrorists, we note that the Treaty itself provides that 'offenses related to terrorism, as set forth in multilateral international agreements to which both Contracting States are parties' shall not be considered to be political offenses. Extradition Treaty, Art IV, sec 2.

We respectfully disagree with this conclusion and hold that there are in fact sound justifications for distinguishing between civilian and governmental—or in this case, revolutionary—targets. The first justification, of course, is that the Supreme Court has held that the civilian status of the 'persons killed' is relevant. Ornelas, 161 US at 511. Moreover, both the Second and Seventh Circuits have addressed the question and have concluded, like we do, that the status of the victims is relevant.

Second, it must be remembered that we are interpreting the Treaty to define the term 'political offense'. In doing so, we must afford 'great weight' to the meaning attributed to the provision by the State Department, as it is charged with enforcing the Treaty. *Sumitomo Shoji Am, Inc v Avagliano*, 457 US 176, 184–85 (1982); see also *Al-Hamdi*, 356 F 3d at 570 (granting 'substantial deference' to the State Department's interpretation of provisions of the Vienna Convention). The State Department has previously expressed the view that 'the political offense exception is not applicable to violent attacks on civilians', *Ahmad v Wigen*, 726 F Supp 389, 402 (EDNY 1989), aff'd, 910 F 2d 1063 (2d Cir 1990), and at oral argument, Government counsel informed us that the department continues to generally adhere to that view.

Third, the status of the victims has been an important factor since the inception of the political offense exception. See, eg, *Ahmad*, 726 F Supp at 404 ('In finding no distinction between targets, the Ninth Circuit ignored the fact that the civilian status of victims has been a significant factor in the political offense calculus since the nineteenth century.') In fact, aside from Ninth Circuit case law, we can find no other American authority stating that the civilian status of victims is irrelevant. Rather, the precedents and authorities stand firmly on the opposite front.

Fourth, by refusing to examine the scope of the attack, the mode of the attack, and the victims of the attack, the Ninth Circuit's approach results in defining a political offense as any common crime that occurs during a political uprising so long as the accused claims a political motive connected to the uprising. As explained above, we must reject such a subjective test.

Finally, both parties suggest that we make inferences based on the motives of the requesting government. For example, *Ordinola* contends that 'a new government seeks to punish [him as a] member[] of a former government for [his] conduct in suppressing a violent uprising' (Appellant's Br at 29.) The Government, for its part, points out that this is not a 'new government' comprised of the revolutionaries Ordinola once fought; rather, it is the same democratically elected government—albeit a different administration—that requests Ordinola's extradition. Although the Government's interpretation is correct on the facts, the motives of the requesting government are irrelevant to our decision. The Treaty states that extradition will be denied 'if the executive authority of the Requested State determines that the request was politically motivated'. Extradition Treaty, Art IV, sec 3. Any question into the Peruvian government's motivations is therefore well beyond this Court's legitimate realm of authority under the Treaty and must be addressed solely to the Secretary of State. [emphasis added]

'Pure' political offences such as espionage or treason are rarely, if ever, at issue in extradition litigation; it is the 'relative' category involving otherwise extraditable common crimes that produce significant 'definitional problems'.

The primary test for determining whether a crime is a relative political offence, as noted by the majority, involves two questions: '(1) whether, at the time of the alleged offense, there was a "violent political disturbance, such as war, revolution and rebellion"; and (2) whether the alleged offense was "committed in the course of and incidental to" the violent political disturbance. *Escobedo v United States*.[82] Virtually every court to encounter the question of whether the alleged crime is a relative political offense has applied this two-pronged test . . .'.

---

[82] 623 F 2d 1098, 1104 (5th Cir 1980).

9.202 In respect of the challenge raised by Ordinola regarding his position as a government official who was doing no more than was asked of him by his political masters in carrying out his duty, the Court concluded:

> Ordinola's defense to extradition raises an interesting theoretical issue about the application of the political offense exception to former government agents charged with crimes committed while there is an ongoing political uprising against the government.
>
> Rather, the heart of the inquiry when it comes to determining whether the charged offense falls within the political offense exception must be objective. See *Ornelas*, 161 US at 509–12. Factors such as 'the character of the foray, the mode of attack, [and] the persons killed or captured' are appropriate for courts to consider in determining whether, as an objective matter, the common crime at issue was 'incidental' to a major political disturbance or uprising. Id. at 511–12.
>
> I would agree that Ordinola failed to demonstrate that these actions were 'incidental' to a political disturbance. His argument is essentially that his conduct with respect to the Barrios Altos slayings was incidental to Peru's political upheaval because his actions were intended to further the Colinas' overarching objective of destroying the Shining Path. As suggested by the magistrate judge and explained in the majority opinion, Ordinola's subjective motivation, political though it may have been, does not alone convert his common crimes into political offenses. See *Ahmad*, 910 F 2d at 1066. Ordinola must show that his crimes were incidental to the political uprising from an objective vantage point, as well. He fails to do so.
>
> Instead, that evidence goes to what Ordinola subjectively believed and may be of relevance by way of defense to the charges if he is ultimately returned to Peru for trial. Here, however, it cannot avail him . . . [83]

9.203 It is however worth noting that in 1991 Germany[84] refused to extradite Reiner Jacobi on the grounds that the request disclosed offences of a 'political character'. The request related to the Marcos corruption investigation.

9.204 In Canada, the exception was examined in *Gil v Canada (Minister of Employment and Immigration)* (CA) in the context of refugee law, in particular the application and interpretation of Article 1F(b)[85] of the *United Nations Convention Relating to the Status of Refugees*,[86] the first such case to come before the Canadian courts.

9.205 During the time of the Khomeini regime in Iran in 1979, Gil, an Iranian citizen and supporter of the Shah was engaged in incidents of bombing and arson against

---

[83] At p 42.

[84] 17 July 1991, the 1st Criminal Panel of the Higher Regional Court of Munich.

[85] 'The provisions of this Convention shall not apply to any person with respect to whom there are serious reasons for considering that: (a) he has committed a crime against peace, a war crime, or a crime against humanity, as defined in the international instruments drawn up to make provision in respect of such crimes; (b) he has committed a serious non-political crime outside the country of refuge prior to his admission to that country as a refugee; (c) he has been guilty of acts contrary to the purposes and principles of the United Nations.'

[86] Adopted on 28 July 1951.

supporters of the regime. The incidents occurred in crowded bazaars consequently leading to the death and injury of innocent people. Gil subsequently left for Canada in 1986 and his refugee status was determined in 1991. The Immigration Board found that Gil had a well-founded fear of persecution if he were to be returned to Iran, however given the nature of the allegations against him he could not avail himself of the protection under the Convention under Article 1F(b).

The Court of Appeal in dismissing the application examined the nature of **9.206** 'political offence' and whether the meaning as understood under extradition law was *mutatis mutandis* applicable under refugee law. The Court held:

> Although the concept of 'political crime' is not normally thought of as known to Canadian criminal law, in two respects at least the laws of Canada recognize that the consequences of an otherwise criminal act may vary if that act can be characterized as political. In both instances the reference is to actions committed outside Canada but the standard to be applied is one which is mandated by Canadian law and administered by Canadian courts. The two exceptions are found in the law of refugee status and in extradition law. *Although they are said to be but two sides of the same coin and serve to complement one another, there are important differences between the two. These differences would seem to point to a need for even greater caution in characterizing a crime as political for the purposes of applying Article 1F(b) than for the purpose of denying extradition.* Case law on extradition, rather than refugee claims, in the United Kingdom, the United States and elsewhere has developed the so-called 'incidence' test for determining whether or not an offence was of political character. The first requirement of the test is that the alleged crimes must be committed in the course of and incidental to a violent political disturbance such as a war, revolution or rebellion. The 'political offense' exception is thus applicable only when a certain level of violence exists and when those resorting to violence are seeking to accomplish a particular objective such as to bring about political change or to combat violent political opposition. The second branch of the test is focused on the need for a nexus between the crime and the alleged political objective. The nature and purpose of the offense require examination, including whether it was committed out of genuine political motives or merely for personal reasons or gain, whether it was directed towards a modification of the political organization or the very structure of the state, and whether there is a close and direct causal link between the crime committed and its alleged political purpose and object. The political element should in principle outweigh the common law character of the offence, which may not be the case if the acts committed are grossly disproportionate to the objective, or are of an atrocious or barbarous nature . . . [emphasis added].

The breadth of the exception therefore, as it appears in the UN CT Conventions **9.207** reflects what has long been recognized as the position since the eighteenth century and seek only to address the 'relative' rather than the 'pure' offences. The latter being understood to attract an absolute prohibition for the purposes of extradition.

The UN CT instruments do, however, lay down a general prohibition to return/ **9.208** extradite 'if there are substantial grounds to believe that the request has been made for the purpose of prosecuting a person on ac of race religion, nationality, ethnic origin, or political opinion'.[87] This prohibition is also to be found in the various international[88] and regional[89] human rights instruments.

Other protections

Nothing in this Convention shall be interpreted as imposing an obligation to extradite or to afford mutual legal assistance if the requested State Party has substantial grounds for believing that the request for extradition for offences set forth in article 2 or for mutual legal assistance with respect to such offences has been made for the purpose of prosecuting or punishing a person on account of that person's race, religion, nationality, ethnic origin or political opinion or that compliance with the request would cause prejudice to that person's position for any of these reasons.[90]

9.209 Essentially these provisions seek to provide added safeguards in the extradition process and have come to be increasingly relied upon rather than the 'political offence exception'. The application of refugee law, in particular the principle of *non-refoulement*[91] is not unknown in the context of extradition and has come to be relied more often in extradition cases (discussed below). This rule imposes a mandatory prohibition on the return of an individual through any mechanism particularly save for the circumstances set out in Article 33(2) of the 1951 Convention.[92] No return/surrender is permitted if there is any danger of the person being subjected to torture, cruel, inhuman, or degrading treatment or punishment. If extradition is sought by a State other than the State from which

---

[87] Article 9 of the International Convention against the Taking of Hostages (1979); Article 12 of the International Convention for the Suppression of Terrorist Bombings (1997); Article 15 of the International Convention for the Suppression of the Financing of Terrorism (1999); Article 16 of the International Convention for the Suppression of Acts of Nuclear Terrorism (2005); Article 11B of the Amendment to the Convention on the Physical Protection of Nuclear Material (2005).

[88] For example: Convention against Torture and Other Cruel, Inhuman or Degrading Treatment or Punishment [1984]; Refugee Convention [1951].

[89] European Convention for the Protection of Human Rights and Fundamental Freedoms [1951]; Inter-American Convention on Extradition [1981]; London Scheme for Extradition within the Commonwealth [1966 as amended in 2002].

[90] Article 12 of the International Convention for the Suppression of Terrorist Bombings (1997). This principle is often referred to as the non-discrimination principle.

[91] Article 33(1) of the 1951 Convention which provides as follows: 'No Contracting State shall expel or return ("refouler") a refugee in any manner whatsoever to the frontiers of territories where his life or freedom would be threatened on account of his race, religion, nationality, membership of a particular social group or political opinion.'

[92] Article 33(2) provides as follows: 'the benefit of the present provision may not, however, be claimed by a refugee whom there are reasonable grounds for regarding as a danger to the security of the country in which he is, or who, having been convicted by a final judgment of a particularly serious crime, constitutes a danger to the community of that country'.

the person has fled, whilst there is no bar to extradition in those circumstances, an assurance must be sought fro m the requesting State that it will not re-extradite to the refugee/asylum-seeker's country of origin or indeed to any other country. Most States will consider extradition requests alongside any application for asylum.

A divergence of opinion is to be found in the approach of national courts. **9.210**

In, Mironescu v Costner (4th Circuit 2007), a US extradition case, the applicant **9.211** claimed that if he were returned to Romania he was in danger of being subjected to physical abuse.

Mironescu, a Roman national, was prosecuted in Romania. It was alleged he was **9.212** the head of a criminal gang responsible for theft of cars which were then resold in Moldova. During the course of proceedings M left Romania and came to the US. He was subsequently convicted in absence and sentenced to four years imprisonment.

Romania sought his extradition from US. In Dec 2003, the courts in the US **9.213** found him extraditable. Mironescu then asked the Secretary of State to consider the extradition request and not surrender him because he had been a local leader in Romania and both he and his family had been physically abused by Romanian authorities. He submitted that the charges were a sham and if returned he was in danger of being physically abused amounting to torture. He relied on Convention Against Torture (CAT).

The Department of Justice considered and rejected his submission. Mironescu **9.214** brought an application for habeas corpus before the District Court. The District Court ordered the Government to produce the information upon which they had placed reliance in order to determine if the Department of Justice/Secretary's decision on the torture aspect was not 'arbitrary, capricious, an abuse of discretion or otherwise not in accordance with law'.

On appeal the Department of Justice argued 'rule of non-inquiry' prevents the **9.215** District Court from hearing about the torture claims under CAT in a habeas application and such an inquiry falls foul of FARR Act (Foreign Affairs Reform & Restructuring Act) which only permits such a claim to be considered under immigration. As Mironescu was to be extradited and not deported, the court therefore had no jurisdiction.

The Court of Appeal (4th Circuit) ruled that they were indeed precluded from **9.216** reviewing a decision by Secretary of State to extradite, even where there were claims of torture in the requesting State but that the 'rule of non-inquiry' which shields the executive should be revisited or removed.

Mironescu has applied for certiorari and a decision is awaited from the US **9.217** Supreme Court.

9.218 By contrast, countries such as UK, Canada, and most common law countries whilst recognizing the principle of 'non-inquiry' still retain judicial oversight to ministerial decisions through the judicial review process. The European Court on Human Rights take a contrary view and have determined that where a request for the purpose of 'prosecuting or punishing a person on account of that person's race, religion, nationality, ethnic origin or political opinion', no return can lie whether through extradition or deportation.

Human rights considerations

Death penalty

9.219 Human rights considerations have always had an important role to perform in determining whether a request for extradition should be granted. In the UK, the Extradition Act 2003 specifically provides for human rights to be considered.[93] One of the main considerations that fall under this provision is the likelihood of the imposition of the death penalty for the offence for which extradition is sought.

9.220 As most European[94] and Commonwealth countries have abolished the death penalty, it is incumbent upon them not to surrender a person if he is likely to face the death penalty (see the South African case of *Khalfan Mohammed* discussed above). It is now agreed State practice that in such instances an assurance is to be sought from the requesting State that the death penalty will not be imposed, but in the event it is imposed, it will not be carried out.

9.221 In *Christopher St John v The United States of America and the Governor of HMP Brixton*,[95] the USA sought the extradition of St John (S) for offences of murder, manslaughter, grievous bodily harm, and actual bodily harm committed in Pennsylvania resulting from a course of violence by S against his wife's uncle. The violence was witnessed by S's wife and three of their children, as well as two other witnesses, all of whom swore affidavits. S was committed at Bow Street Magistrates' Court on 26 January 2001. He applied for habeas corpus.

9.222 He submitted that the potential death penalty meant that the crimes were not extradition crimes. This was the first occasion on which the court had considered a case involving the possibility of the death sentence since the Human Rights Act (HRA)

---

[93] Section 87 Human Rights:

    (i) If the judge is required to proceed under this section (by virtue of section 84, 85 or 86) he must decide whether the person's extradition would be compatible with the Convention rights within the meaning of the Human Rights Act 1988 (c. 42)

[94] The Sixth Protocol to the ECHR.

[95] [2001] EWHC Admin 543.

1998 came into force. Pennsylvania had the death penalty for murder and it was up to the jury to decide whether or not to impose it. S argued that this meant that murder was not an extradition crime when interpreted in the light of his ECHR rights because, in the absence of any assurances to the contrary, extradition would expose him to the risk of the death penalty in contravention of those rights.

In dismissing the appeal, the Court that the death penalty did not mean that the crimes were not extradition crimes. Harrison J said: **9.223**

> . . . the potential issue of violation of the applicant's Convention rights arises at the time when the Secretary of State decides whether to extradite the applicant. He may decide not to extradite, or he may obtain satisfactory assurances that the death penalty will not be carried out. In either of those situations, the issue of the violation of the applicant's Convention rights would not arise. In my judgment, it would be premature and wrong to reach conclusions now about potential violations of the applicant's Convention rights when they may never occur. If the Secretary of State were to decide to order the applicant's return without obtaining satisfactory assurances from the second respondent that the death penalty will not be carried out, it would be open to the applicant to seek permission to apply for judicial review of that decision. The availability of such a remedy, in my view, is sufficient to safeguard the applicant's position.

More recently the assurances received from the US were the subject of challenge in the UK in *Ahmad and Another v Government of the United States of America*.[96]   **9.224**

The United States of America sought the extradition of the appellants on charges relating to terrorism. The US provided diplomatic notes giving assurances that the appellants would be prosecuted before a federal court and granted full rights and protections. The note further confirmed that they would not be prosecuted before a military commission as specified in the President's Military Order of 13 November 2001, which permits trials of suspected international terrorists before a military tribunal.   **9.225**

At the extradition hearing the defence argued that if they were to be extradited there was a real prospect that they would be made subject to the military commission which could lead to violations of their human rights. The district judge relied on the assurances provided by the US and found that their rights under the European Convention on Human Rights would not be breached. He was equally assured that the death penalty would not be imposed and ruled them extraditable. The appellants appealed.   **9.226**

The appeals were dismissed and the Court held: **9.227**

> (1) Diplomatic notes should be treated as being effective to refute, for the purposes of the 2003 Act, the claims of potential violation of Convention rights and associated

---

[96] [2006] All ER (D) 418 (Nov).

bars to extradition. In the eye of international law such a note was regarded as binding on the State that issued it. There was also a fundamental assumption that the requesting State was acting in good faith unless displaced by evidence.

In the instant case, the assurances in the notes were given by a mature democracy and over a period of over 150 years there had been no instance of any assurance given by the USA in extradition proceedings having been dishonoured. Moreover, the USA would appreciate that their requests for the appellants' extradition had been acceded to expressly on the faith of the notes. It followed that the court should not conclude that the notes would not be fully honoured and the district judge had been correct to place confidence on them.

9.228 Similarly, in Canada, the extradition of a suspect in the absence of assurances of no death penalty were considered in two notable cases before the Supreme Court namely *Kindler v Canada (Minister of Justice)*[97] and *Re Ng Extradition (Can)*.[98]

9.229 *In Re Ng* an extradition request was submitted by the US for a number of offences, including twelve counts of murder. The offences attracted the death penalty. Before his trial, Ng escaped from prison and fled to Canada where he was arrested. The extradition judge found him extraditable and The Minister of Justice of Canada then ordered his extradition without seeking assurances from the US, under Article 6 of the Extradition Treaty between the two countries, that the death penalty would not be imposed, or if imposed, not carried out.

9.230 In dealing with both cases, as they raised the same issue, namely whether surrender in the absence of an assurance is in contravention of the Charter, the Court concluded:

> Both the reference questions and the constitutional questions raise the same issues considered in Kindler v Canada (Minister of Justice), [1991] 2 SCR 000. I would, therefore, answer these questions in accordance with my reasons in Kindler. It may be helpful to set out the summary given toward the end of those reasons. It reads (at p 000):
>
>> Capital punishment for murder is prohibited in Canada. Section 12 of the Charter provides that no one is to be subjected to cruel and unusual punishment. The death penalty is per se a cruel and unusual punishment. It is the ultimate denial of human dignity. No individual can be subjected to it in Canada. The decision of the Minister to surrender a fugitive who may be subject to execution without obtaining an assurance pursuant to Article 6 is one which can be reviewed under s. 12 of the Charter. It follows that the Minister must not surrender Kindler without obtaining the undertaking described in Article 6 of the Treaty. To do so would render s. 25 of the Extradition Act inconsistent with the Charter in its application to fugitives who would be subject to the death penalty.
>
> This conclusion is based upon the historical reluctance displayed by jurors over the centuries to impose the death penalty; the provisions of s. 12 of the Charter; the

---

[97] [1991] 2 SCR 779.
[98] [1991] 2 SCR 858.

decisions of this Court pertaining to that section; the pronouncements of this Court emphasizing the fundamental importance of human dignity; and the international statements and commitments made by Canada stressing the importance of the dignity of the individual and urging the abolition of the death penalty.

The Charter, the judicial pronouncements upon it and the international statements and commitments made by Canada reflect Canadian principles. The preservation of Canada's integrity and reputation in the international community require that extradition be refused unless an undertaking is obtained pursuant to Article 6. To take this position does not constitute an absolute refusal to extradite. It simply requires the requesting State to undertake that it will substitute a penalty of life imprisonment for the execution of the prisoner if that prisoner is found to be guilty of the crime . . . .

In the absence of obtaining an Article 6 assurance, the surrender order would contravene s. 12 of the Charter and could not be justified under s. 1 . . .

Torture, cruel, inhuman, and degrading treatment or punishment

An extradition[99] request must be refused if there is any danger that the person sought would be subject to torture, cruel, inhuman, or degrading treatment or punishment. The prohibition against torture is invariably contained in all human rights instruments—UN Convention against Torture [1984]; the Refugee Convention [1951]; Article 7 of the International Covenant on Civil and Political Rights; Article 3 of the European Convention for the Protection of Human Rights and Fundamental Freedoms [1950]; Article 5 of the American Convention on Human Rights [1969]; Article 5 of the African Charter on Human and Peoples' Rights [1981]; and customary international law. It is therefore an absolute bar to extradition. It is not proposed to analyse the well-known case law on this aspect as other writers have carried out detailed work save to remind the reader that when dealing with such a challenge, it is worth referring to the jurisprudence of all the regional human rights courts as well as the Human Rights Committee.[100] The recent Security Council Resolutions dealing with terrorism place a heavy emphasis on adherence to international human rights law, international humanitarian law, and refugee law.   **9.231**

Handing over of suspects

The possibility of handing over of suspects following an extradition request to the US Military Commissions has been the subject of some concern since their creation. Shortly after the US Embassy bombings in Kenya and Tanzania, an extradition request for three of the suspects (Khaled Al-Fawwaz, Abdel Bary, and Eidarous) was before the UK Courts. By the time the matter came before the   **9.232**

---

[99] The same principle applies in respect of deportation or any form of return/explusion.
[100] The Human Rights Committee also publishes General Comments on various topics and these must be considered as well.

House of Lords, the events of 11 September 2001 had occurred and the military commissions had been set up. At the hearing before their Lordships, the defence did not raise any concern of the possibility of a handover to these Commissions. However, despite that Lord Scott raised his concern at paragraph 121 of his speech as follows:

> Paragraph 8 of the first Schedule contains the final safeguard for the fugitive criminal whose extradition is sought. He will not be extradited unless the Secretary of State decides, as a matter of discretion, to order that the extradition may proceed. It has become the settled practice, as I understand it, for the Secretary of State, in a case where the law of the extraditing State might subject the extradited prisoner on conviction to the death penalty, to require a guarantee that a death sentence will not be imposed (see *Soering v United Kingdom* (1989) 11 EHRR 439). But there is, in the circumstances of the present cases a further matter of concern. The media have, over the past few weeks, carried reports of the intention of the President of the United States, acting under emergency executive powers, to establish military tribunals to try non-United States citizens who are accused of terrorist offences. The offences with which these appellants are charged might well fall within the category of offences proposed to be dealt with by military tribunals. It is reported that the proposed military tribunal will be presided over by military personnel, not judges, will be able to admit evidence that would not ordinarily be admissible before a criminal court of law and will be able to conduct the trial behind closed doors. The charges against the appellants that have led to the extradition requests were laid before the United States District Court for the Southern District of New York. If the appellants were to be extradited I imagine they will be tried before that court or some other Federal court and not before a military tribunal that will not sit in public and that need not observe the rules of evidence.

9.233 A similar concern of being handed to the military tribunals is the handing over of suspects to third States, unconnected to the extradition request which was raised in *Faraj Hassan Faraj v Government of Italy*.[101]

9.234 Faraj, a national of Libya was arrested and detained under the UK Prevention of Terrorism Act on his arrival in the United Kingdom in 2002. The following year Italy submitted a request for his extradition alleging that he conspired to commit terrorist offences in Italy between 1 December 2001 and September 2002 as part of an international terrorist gang engaged in the planning and preparation of terrorist attacks and the recruitment and training of those who would carry out such attacks both in and outside Italy. The gang was said to have the ability to procure false documents and raise funds for terrorists' use. It was also alleged that they carried out the necessary brainwashing of those who were to carry out atrocities.

9.235 They had come to the notice of the Italian authorities through intercept evidence and there was intelligence to suggest that the gang intended to carry out a terrorist atrocity, in an unidentified European country.

---

[101] [2004] EWHC 2950 (Admin).

Faraj claimed that if he were extradited to Italy, there was every possibility that he **9.236** would be expelled from Italy to Libya where he would be in grave personal danger. The Court considered two reports submitted by Faraj's legal representatives and concluded that on the face of those reports and the submissions made on his behalf, there was little evidence to support his claim and neither could it be shown that Italy had acted in bad faith:

> The reference to Treaty obligations reminds one, lest it should be lost sight of in the welter of other information contained in the papers, that Italy is a member of the European Union and the Council of Europe. The Union is founded on the principles of liberty, democracy, respect for human rights and fundamental freedoms, and the rule of law. Italy is a signatory of the 1951 Refugee Convention and its Protocol and the Human Rights Convention. Asylum is guaranteed under Article 10 of the Italian constitution. Italian law establishes procedures for applying for asylum with rights of appeal to the courts, although Miss Pargeter points to practical problems with the way in which the system operates, including difficulty in obtaining legal representation. Articles 2 and 3 of the Human Rights Convention should prevent any signatory to the Convention returning someone to a country where there was a real risk to his life or that he could be subjected to torture or inhuman or degrading treatment.—LJ Tuckey, para 19.

Similarly, in the recent request for surrender of *Mohamed Salah Ben Hamadi* **9.237** *Khemiri, Habib Ignaoua, Ali Ben Zidane Chehidi v The Court of Milan Italy,*[102] three appellants, all Tunisian nationals, were sought by Italy for under a EAW for offences of terrorism. Following the extradition order by the District Judge, the appellants appealed to the Administrative Court on the grounds that if they were surrendered to the Italy there was a real risk that they would be handed to the Tunisian authorities in breach of Article 3 of ECHR. The appellants relied on earlier deportations by Italy to Tunisia said to have occurred after the decision of the European Court (ECtHR) in *Saadi v Italy*.

At the hearing before the District Judge, the Prosecutor to the Republic provided **9.238** an assurance that the EAW had been issued for the purposes of prosecuting in Italy and not for the purpose of deporting to Tunisia. However, no assurance was provided by the Italian authorities on the possibility, or otherwise of onward deportation.

On the issue of lack of assurances, the Court was of the view that such assurances **9.239** are not necessary and Pill LJ in delivering the judgment observed:

> I do not and could not find that it would be possible for the Italian Government to give an assurance never to deport the appellants but, as did the District Judge, I acknowledge the difficulty in a Government binding itself to a course of conduct, even executive conduct, the implications of which could be broad and

---

[102] [2008] EWHC 1988 (Admin).

unpredictable . . . I do not regard the absence of a Governmental assurance in this case as an indication that the Italian Government does not intend to fulfil its legal obligations . . . [103]

9.240 The appellants had to satisfy the Court that there was a 'real risk' that they would be deported; there had been no instance of deportation from Italy to Tunisia where a person had been surrendered to Italy pursuant to the execution of the EAW. The appellants had failed to establish that there was a 'real risk' of deportation given the remoteness of such an event as criminal proceedings were still extant in Italy.

9.241 It is interesting to note that the submissions on behalf of the Milan Court rested on the importance of mutual recognition of judicial decisions amongst Member States and this meant the actions of the executive (as they would be for any deportation) fell outside the scope of consideration by the Court, thereby drawing a sharp line between the action of the two organs. The Administrative Court acknowledged the force of the argument but observed that the executive arm of a government was equally bound by the terms of the Framework Decision and should be seen to act consistently with it. Pill LJ [para 51 of the judgment] remarked:

> The submission that because the Framework Decision and the 2003 Act inaugurates a procedure between judicial authorities, and executive conduct is outside it, is not without force. However, courts must act on the basis that the confidence required extends to the conduct of the executive arm of the Government which is party to the Framework Decision. The separation and independence of the judiciary from the executive arm of the Government is fundamental to the rule of law, but the Framework Directive entitles an assumption that the conduct of the Italian judiciary and its role in protecting rights under the Convention is not to be nullified by parallel or subsequent action by the executive arm of Government.

9.242 Therefore in dealing with extradition requests in the context of terrorism, a number of challenges can arise, however, this does not mean that it militates against the extradition of suspects. On the contrary, it provides the safeguards necessary in such cases. As a concluding comment, practitioners must bear in mind that challenges in extradition cases, whether terrorist-related requests or otherwise, are being raised in most jurisdictions and that whilst case authorities or precedents from other jurisdictions, human rights courts, and committees may not be binding on their courts, they certainly are persuasive.

---

[103] Paras 44 and 45 of the judgment.

APPENDICES

1. UNSCR 1267, 1456, 1540, 1566, 1617, 1624, 1735   449

2. UNSCR 1373   479

3. Tokyo Convention   483

4. Hague Convention   491

5. Montreal Convention and Protocol   497

6. Diplomats Convention   509

7. Hostages Convention   515

8. Nuclear Materials Convention   521

9. Rome Convention and Protocols   531

10. Plastic Explosives Convention   561

11. Bombings Convention   567

12. International Convention for the Suppression of the Financing of Terrorism   575

13. International Convention for the Suppression of Acts of Nuclear Terrorism   587

14. The United Nations Global Counter-Terrorism Strategy   597

15. European Convention on the Suppression of Terrorism   605

16. American States Convention No. 24381   617

17. OAU Convention on the Prevention and Combating of Terrorism, 1999   621

18. The Arab Convention for the Suppression of Terrorism   631

19. Financial Action Task Force on Money Laundering Special Recommendations on Terrorist Financing   643

20. Commonwealth Secretariat Model Legislative Provisions on Measures to Combat Terrorism   645

21. Criminal Evidence (Witness Anonymity) Act 2008   689

22. Police & Criminal Evidence Act 1984 (PACE), Code H   697

23. Ratification Status and Depository Information on the UN Counter-Terrorism Legal Instruments   739

24. UNSC Resolution 1822   743

25. The USA PATRIOT Act   751

APPENDIX 1

UNSCR 1267, 1456, 1540, 1566, 1617, 1624, 1735
United Nations Security Council

S/RES/1267 (1999)
15 OCTOBER 1999

RESOLUTION 1267 (1999)

Adopted by
the Security Council at its 4051st meeting on 15 October 1999

The Security Council,

Reaffirming its previous resolutions, in particular resolutions 1189 (1998) of 13 August 1998, 1193 (1998) of 28 August 1998 and 1214 (1998) of 8 December 1998, and the statements of its President on the situation in Afghanistan,

Reaffirming its strong commitment to the sovereignty, independence, territorial integrity and national unity of Afghanistan, and its respect for Afghanistan's cultural and historical heritage,

Reiterating its deep concern over the continuing violations of international humanitarian law and of human rights, particularly discrimination against women and girls, and over the significant rise in the illicit production of opium, and stressing that the capture by the Taliban of the Consulate-General of the Islamic Republic of Iran and the murder of Iranian diplomats and a journalist in Mazar-e-Sharif constituted flagrant violations of established international law,

Recalling the relevant international counter-terrorism conventions and in particular the obligations of parties to those conventions to extradite or prosecute terrorists,

Strongly condemning the continuing use of Afghan territory, especially areas controlled by the Taliban, for the sheltering and training of terrorists and planning of terrorist acts, and reaffirming its conviction that the suppression of international terrorism is essential for the maintenance of international peace and security,

Deploring the fact that the Taliban continues to provide safe haven to Usama bin Laden and to allow him and others associated with him to operate a network of terrorist training camps from Taliban-controlled territory and to use Afghanistan as a base from which to sponsor international terrorist operations,

Noting the indictment of Usama bin Laden and his associates by the United States of America for, inter alia, the 7 August 1998 bombings of the United States embassies in Nairobi, Kenya, and Dar es Salaam, Tanzania and for conspiring to kill American nationals outside the United States, and noting also the request of the United States of America to the Taliban to surrender them for trial (S/1999/1021),

Determining that the failure of the Taliban authorities to respond to the demands in paragraph 13 of resolution 1214 (1998) constitutes a threat to international peace and security,

Stressing its determination to ensure respect for its resolutions,

Acting under Chapter VII of the Charter of the United Nations,

1. *Insists* that the Afghan faction known as the Taliban, which also calls itself the Islamic Emirate of Afghanistan, comply promptly with its previous resolutions and in particular cease the provision of sanctuary and training for international terrorists and their organizations, take appropriate effective measures to ensure that the territory under its control is not used for terrorist installations and camps, or for the preparation or organization of terrorist acts against other States or their citizens, and cooperate with efforts to bring indicted terrorists to justice;

2. *Demands* that the Taliban turn over Usama bin Laden without further delay to appropriate authorities in a country where he has been indicted, or to appropriate authorities in a country where he will be returned to such a country, or to appropriate authorities in a country where he will be arrested and effectively brought to justice;

3. *Decides* that on 14 November 1999 all States shall impose the measures set out in paragraph 4 below, unless the Council has previously decided, on the basis of a report of the Secretary-General, that the Taliban has fully complied with the obligation set out in paragraph 2 above;

4. *Decides further* that, in order to enforce paragraph 2 above, all States shall:

   (a) Deny permission for any aircraft to take off from or land in their territory if it is owned, leased or operated by or on behalf of the Taliban as designated by the Committee established by paragraph 6 below, unless the particular flight has been approved in advance by the Committee on the grounds of humanitarian need, including religious obligation such as the performance of the Hajj;

   (b) Freeze funds and other financial resources, including funds derived or generated from property owned or controlled directly or indirectly by the Taliban, or by any undertaking owned or controlled by the Taliban, as designated by the Committee established by paragraph 6 below, and ensure that neither they nor any other funds or financial resources so designated are made available, by their nationals or by any persons within their territory, to or for the benefit of the Taliban or any undertaking owned or controlled, directly or indirectly, by the Taliban, except as may be authorized by the Committee on a case-by-case basis on the grounds of humanitarian need;

5. *Urges* all States to cooperate with efforts to fulfil the demand in paragraph 2 above, and to consider further measures against Usama bin Laden and his associates;

6. *Decides* to establish, in accordance with rule 28 of its provisional rules of procedure, a Committee of the Security Council consisting of all the members of the Council to undertake the following tasks and to report on its work to the Council with its observations and recommendations:

   (a) To seek from all States further information regarding the action taken by them with a view to effectively implementing the measures imposed by paragraph 4 above;

   (b) To consider information brought to its attention by States concerning violations of the measures imposed by paragraph 4 above and to recommend appropriate measures in response thereto;

   (c) To make periodic reports to the Council on the impact, including the humanitarian implications, of the measures imposed by paragraph 4 above;

   (d) To make periodic reports to the Council on information submitted to it regarding alleged violations of the measures imposed by paragraph 4 above, identifying where possible persons or entities reported to be engaged in such violations;

   (e) To designate the aircraft and funds or other financial resources referred to in paragraph 4 above in order to facilitate the implementation of the measures imposed by that paragraph;

   (f) To consider requests for exemptions from the measures imposed by paragraph 4 above as provided in that paragraph, and to decide on the granting of an exemption to these measures in respect of the payment by the International Air Transport Association (IATA) to the aeronautical authority of Afghanistan on behalf of international airlines for air traffic control services;

(g) To examine the reports submitted pursuant to paragraph 9 below;

7. *Calls upon* all States to act strictly in accordance with the provisions of this resolution, notwithstanding the existence of any rights or obligations conferred or imposed by any international agreement or any contract entered into or any licence or permit granted prior to the date of coming into force of the measures imposed by paragraph 4 above;

8. *Calls upon* States to bring proceedings against persons and entities within their jurisdiction that violate the measures imposed by paragraph 4 above and to impose appropriate penalties;

9. *Calls upon* all States to cooperate fully with the Committee established by paragraph 6 above in the fulfilment of its tasks, including supplying such information as may be required by the Committee in pursuance of this resolution;

10. *Requests* all States to report to the Committee established by paragraph 6 above within 30 days of the coming into force of the measures imposed by paragraph 4 above on the steps they have taken with a view to effectively implementing paragraph 4 above;

11. *Requests* the Secretary-General to provide all necessary assistance to the Committee established by paragraph 6 above and to make the necessary arrangements in the Secretariat for this purpose;

12. *Requests* the Committee established by paragraph 6 above to determine appropriate arrangements, on the basis of recommendations of the Secretariat, with competent international organizations, neighbouring and other States, and parties concerned with a view to improving the monitoring of the implementation of the measures imposed by paragraph 4 above;

13. *Requests* the Secretariat to submit for consideration by the Committee established by paragraph 6 above information received from Governments and public sources on possible violations of the measures imposed by paragraph 4 above;

14. *Decides* to terminate the measures imposed by paragraph 4 above once the Secretary-General reports to the Security Council that the Taliban has fulfilled the obligation set out in paragraph 2 above;

15. *Expresses* its readiness to consider the imposition of further measures, in accordance with its responsibility under the Charter of the United Nations, with the aim of achieving the full implementation of this resolution;

16. *Decides* to remain actively seized of the matter.

United Nations Security Council

S/RES/1456 (2003)
20 JANUARY 2003

RESOLUTION 1456 (2003)

Adopted by
the Security Council at its 4688th meeting, on 20 January 2003

The Security Council,
Decides to adopt the attached declaration on the issue of combating terrorism.

ANNEX

The Security Council,

Meeting at the level of Ministers for Foreign Affairs on 20 January 2003 reaffirms that:

— terrorism in all its forms and manifestations constitutes one of the most serious threats to peace and security;

— any acts of terrorism are criminal and unjustifiable, regardless of their motivation, whenever and by whomsoever committed and are to be unequivocally condemned, especially when they indiscriminately target or injure civilians;

— there is a serious and growing danger of terrorist access to and use of nuclear, chemical, biological and other potentially deadly materials, and therefore a need to strengthen controls on these materials;

— it has become easier, in an increasingly globalized world, for terrorists to exploit sophisticated technology, communications and resources for their criminal objectives;

— measures to detect and stem the flow of finance and funds for terrorist purposes must be urgently strengthened;

— terrorists must also be prevented from making use of other criminal activities such as transnational organized crime, illicit drugs and drug trafficking, money-laundering and illicit arms trafficking;

— since terrorists and their supporters exploit instability and intolerance to justify their criminal acts the Security Council is determined to counter this by contributing to peaceful resolution of disputes and by working to create a climate of mutual tolerance and respect;

— terrorism can only be defeated, in accordance with the Charter of the United Nations and international law, by a sustained comprehensive approach involving the active participation and collaboration of all States, international and regional organizations, and by redoubled efforts at the national level.

* * *

The Security Council therefore calls for the following steps to be taken:

1. All States must take urgent action to prevent and suppress all active and passive support to terrorism, and in particular comply fully with all relevant resolutions of the Security Council, in particular resolutions 1373 (2001), 1390 (2002) and 1455 (2003);

2. The Security Council calls upon States to:

    (a) become a party, as a matter of urgency, to all relevant international conventions and protocols relating to terrorism, in particular the 1999 International Convention for the Suppression of the Financing of Terrorism and to support all international initiatives taken to that aim, and to make full use of the sources of assistance and guidance which are now becoming available;

(b) assist each other, to the maximum extent possible, in the prevention, investigation, prosecution and punishment of acts of terrorism, wherever they occur;

(c) cooperate closely to implement fully the sanctions against terrorists and their associates, in particular Al-Qaeda and the Taliban and their associates, as reflected in resolutions 1267 (1999), 1390 (2002) and 1455 (2003), to take urgent actions to deny them access to the financial resources they need to carry out their actions, and to cooperate fully with the Monitoring Group established pursuant to resolution 1363 (2001);

3. States must bring to justice those who finance, plan, support or commit terrorist acts or provide safe havens, in accordance with international law, in particular on the basis of the principle to extradite or prosecute;

4. The Counter-Terrorism Committee must intensify its efforts to promote the implementation by Member States of all aspects of resolution 1373 (2001), in particular through reviewing States' reports and facilitating international assistance and cooperation, and through continuing to operate in a transparent and effective manner, and in that regard the Council;

(i) stresses the obligation on States to report to the CTC, according to the timetable set by the CTC, calls on the 13 States who have not yet submitted a first report and on the 56 States who are late in submitting further reports to do so by 31 March, and requests the CTC to report regularly on progress;

(ii) calls on States to respond promptly and fully to the CTC's requests for information, comments and questions in full and on time, and instructs the CTC to inform the Council of progress, including any difficulties it encounters;

(iii) requests the CTC in monitoring the implementation of resolution 1373 (2001) to bear in mind all international best practices, codes and standards which are relevant to the implementation of resolution 1373 (2001), and underlines its support for the CTC's approach in constructing a dialogue with each State on further action required to fully implement resolution 1373 (2001);

5. States should assist each other to improve their capacity to prevent and fight terrorism, and notes that such cooperation will help facilitate the full and timely implementation of resolution 1373 (2001), and invites the CTC to step up its efforts to facilitate the provision of technical and other assistance by developing targets and priorities for global action;

6. States must ensure that any measure taken to combat terrorism comply with all their obligations under international law, and should adopt such measures in accordance with international law, in particular international human rights, refugee, and humanitarian law;

7. International organizations should evaluate ways in which they can enhance the effectiveness of their action against terrorism, including by establishing dialogue and exchanges of information with each other and with other relevant international actors, and directs this appeal in particular to those technical agencies and organizations whose activities relate to the control of the use of or access to nuclear, chemical, biological and other deadly materials; in this context the importance of fully complying with existing legal obligations in the field of disarmament, arms limitation and non-proliferation and, where necessary, strengthening international instruments in this field should be underlined;

8. Regional and subregional organizations should work with the CTC and other international organizations to facilitate sharing of best practice in the fight against terrorism, and to assist their members in fulfilling their obligation to combat terrorism;

9. Those participating in the Special Meeting of the Counter-Terrorism Committee with international regional and subregional organizations on 7 March 2003 should use that opportunity to make urgent progress on the matters referred to in this declaration which involve the work of such organizations;

* * *

The Security Council also:

10. *Emphasizes* that continuing international efforts to enhance dialogue and broaden the understanding among civilizations, in an effort to prevent the indiscriminate targeting of different religions and cultures, to further strengthen the campaign against terrorism, and to address unresolved regional conflicts and the full range of global issues, including development issues, will contribute to international cooperation and collaboration, which by themselves are necessary to sustain the broadest possible fight against terrorism;

11. Reaffirms its strong determination to intensify its fight against terrorism in accordance with its responsibilities under the Charter of the United Nations, and takes note of the contributions made during its meeting on 20 January 2003 with a view to enhancing the role of the United Nations in this regard, and invites Member States to make further contributions to this end;

12. Invites the Secretary General to present a report within 28 days summarizing any proposals made during its ministerial meeting and any commentary or response to these proposals by any Security Council member;

13. Encourages Member States of the United Nations to cooperate in resolving all outstanding issues with a view to the adoption, by consensus, of the draft comprehensive convention on international terrorism and the draft international convention for the suppression of acts of nuclear terrorism;

14. Decides to review actions taken towards the realization of this declaration at further meetings of the Security Council.

United Nations Security Council

S/RES/1540 (2004)
28 April 2004

RESOLUTION 1540 (2004)

Adopted by
the Security Council at its 4956th meeting, on 28 April 2004

The Security Council,

Affirming that proliferation of nuclear, chemical and biological weapons, as well as their means of delivery,* constitutes a threat to international peace and security,

Reaffirming, in this context, the Statement of its President adopted at the Council's meeting at the level of Heads of State and Government on 31 January 1992 (S/23500), including the need for all Member States to fulfil their obligations in relation to arms control and disarmament and to prevent proliferation in all its aspects of all weapons of mass destruction,

Recalling also that the Statement underlined the need for all Member States to resolve peacefully in accordance with the Charter any problems in that context threatening or disrupting the maintenance of regional and global stability,

Affirming its resolve to take appropriate and effective actions against any threat to international peace and security caused by the proliferation of nuclear, chemical and biological weapons and their means of delivery, in conformity with its primary responsibilities, as provided for in the United Nations Charter,

Affirming its support for the multilateral treaties whose aim is to eliminate or prevent the proliferation of nuclear, chemical or biological weapons and the importance for all States parties to these treaties to implement them fully in order to promote international stability,

Welcoming efforts in this context by multilateral arrangements which contribute to non-proliferation,

Affirming that prevention of proliferation of nuclear, chemical and biological weapons should not hamper international cooperation in materials, equipment and technology for peaceful purposes while goals of peaceful utilization should not be used as a cover for proliferation,

Gravely concerned by the threat of terrorism and the risk that non-State actors* such as those identified in the United Nations list established and maintained by the Committee established under Security Council Resolution 1267 and those to whom resolution 1373 applies, may acquire, develop, traffic in or use nuclear, chemical and biological weapons and their means of delivery,

Gravely concerned by the threat of illicit trafficking in nuclear, chemical, or biological weapons and their means of delivery, and related materials,* which adds a new dimension to the issue of proliferation of such weapons and also poses a threat to international peace and security,

---

* Definitions for the purpose of this resolution only:
    'Means of delivery': missiles, rockets and other unmanned systems capable of delivering nuclear, chemical, or biological weapons, that are specially designed for such use.
    'Non-State actor': individual or entity, not acting under the lawful authority of any State in conducting activities which come within the scope of this resolution.
    'Related materials': materials, equipment and technology covered by relevant multilateral treaties and arrangements, or included on national control lists, which could be used for the design, development, production or use of nuclear, chemical and biological weapons and their means of delivery.

Recognizing the need to enhance coordination of efforts on national, subregional, regional and international levels in order to strengthen a global response to this serious challenge and threat to international security,

Recognizing that most States have undertaken binding legal obligations under treaties to which they are parties, or have made other commitments aimed at preventing the proliferation of nuclear, chemical or biological weapons, and have taken effective measures to account for, secure and physically protect sensitive materials, such as those required by the Convention on the Physical Protection of Nuclear Materials and those recommended by the IAEA Code of Conduct on the Safety and Security of Radioactive Sources,

Recognizing further the urgent need for all States to take additional effective measures to prevent the proliferation of nuclear, chemical or biological weapons and their means of delivery,

Encouraging all Member States to implement fully the disarmament treaties and agreements to which they are party,

Reaffirming the need to combat by all means, in accordance with the Charter of the United Nations, threats to international peace and security caused by terrorist acts,

Determined to facilitate henceforth an effective response to global threats in the area of non-proliferation,

Acting under Chapter VII of the Charter of the United Nations,

1. *Decides that* all States shall refrain from providing any form of support to non-State actors that attempt to develop, acquire, manufacture, possess, transport, transfer or use nuclear, chemical or biological weapons and their means of delivery;

2. *Decides also* that all States, in accordance with their national procedures, shall adopt and enforce appropriate effective laws which prohibit any non-State actor to manufacture, acquire, possess, develop, transport, transfer or use nuclear, chemical or biological weapons and their means of delivery, in particular for terrorist purposes, as well as attempts to engage in any of the foregoing activities, participate in them as an accomplice, assist or finance them;

3. *Decides also* that all States shall take and enforce effective measures to establish domestic controls to prevent the proliferation of nuclear, chemical, or biological weapons and their means of delivery, including by establishing appropriate controls over related materials and to this end shall:

   (a) Develop and maintain appropriate effective measures to account for and secure such items in production, use, storage or transport;
   (b) Develop and maintain appropriate effective physical protection measures;
   (c) Develop and maintain appropriate effective border controls and law enforcement efforts to detect, deter, prevent and combat, including through international cooperation when necessary, the illicit trafficking and brokering in such items in accordance with their national legal authorities and legislation and consistent with international law;
   (d) Establish, develop, review and maintain appropriate effective national export and trans-shipment controls over such items, including appropriate laws and regulations to control export, transit, trans-shipment and re-export and controls on providing funds and services related to such export and trans-shipment such as financing, and transporting that would contribute to proliferation, as well as establishing end-user controls; and establishing and enforcing appropriate criminal or civil penalties for violations of such export control laws and regulations;

4. *Decides* to establish, in accordance with rule 28 of its provisional rules of procedure, for a period of no longer than two years, a Committee of the Security Council, consisting of all members of the Council, which will, calling as appropriate on other expertise, report to the Security Council for its examination, on the implementation of this resolution, and to this end calls upon States to present

a first report no later than six months from the adoption of this resolution to the Committee on steps they have taken or intend to take to implement this resolution;

5. *Decides* that none of the obligations set forth in this resolution shall be interpreted so as to conflict with or alter the rights and obligations of State Parties to the Nuclear Non-Proliferation Treaty, the Chemical Weapons Convention and the Biological and Toxin Weapons Convention or alter the responsibilities of the International Atomic Energy Agency or the Organization for the Prohibition of Chemical Weapons;

6. Recognizes the utility in implementing this resolution of effective national control lists and calls upon all Member States, when necessary, to pursue at the earliest opportunity the development of such lists;

7. *Recognizes* that some States may require assistance in implementing the provisions of this resolution within their territories and invites States in a position to do so to offer assistance as appropriate in response to specific requests to the States lacking the legal and regulatory infrastructure, implementation experience and/or resources for fulfilling the above provisions;

8. *Calls upon* all States:

   (a) To promote the universal adoption and full implementation, and, where necessary, strengthening of multilateral treaties to which they are parties, whose aim is to prevent the proliferation of nuclear, biological or chemical weapons;

   (b) To adopt national rules and regulations, where it has not yet been done, to ensure compliance with their commitments under the key multilateral non-proliferation treaties;

   (c) To renew and fulfil their commitment to multilateral cooperation, in particular within the framework of the International Atomic Energy Agency, the Organization for the Prohibition of Chemical Weapons and the Biological and Toxin Weapons Convention, as important means of pursuing and achieving their common objectives in the area of non-proliferation and of promoting international cooperation for peaceful purposes;

   (d) To develop appropriate ways to work with and inform industry and the public regarding their obligations under such laws;

9. *Calls upon* all States to promote dialogue and cooperation on non-proliferation so as to address the threat posed by proliferation of nuclear, chemical, or biological weapons, and their means of delivery;

10. Further to counter that threat, *calls upon* all States, in accordance with their national legal authorities and legislation and consistent with international law, to take cooperative action to prevent illicit trafficking in nuclear, chemical or biological weapons, their means of delivery, and related materials;

11. *Expresses* its intention to monitor closely the implementation of this resolution and, at the appropriate level, to take further decisions which may be required to this end;

12. *Decides* to remain seized of the matter.

United Nations Security Council

S/RES/1566 (2004)
8 OCTOBER 2004

RESOLUTION 1566 (2004)

Adopted by
the Security Council at its 5053rd meeting, on 8 October 2004

The Security Council,

Reaffirming its resolutions 1267 (1999) of 15 October 1999 and 1373 (2001) of 28 September 2001 as well as its other resolutions concerning threats to international peace and security caused by terrorism,

Recalling in this regard its resolution 1540 (2004) of 28 April 2004,

Reaffirming also the imperative to combat terrorism in all its forms and manifestations by all means, in accordance with the Charter of the United Nations and international law,

Deeply concerned by the increasing number of victims, including children, caused by acts of terrorism motivated by intolerance or extremism in various regions of the world,

Calling upon States to cooperate fully with the Counter-Terrorism Committee (CTC) established pursuant to resolution 1373 (2001), including the recently established Counter-Terrorism Committee Executive Directorate (CTED), the 'Al-Qaida/Taliban Sanctions Committee' established pursuant to resolution 1267 (1999) and its Analytical Support and Sanctions Monitoring Team, and the Committee established pursuant to resolution 1540 (2004), and *further calling* upon such bodies to enhance cooperation with each other,

Reminding States that they must ensure that any measures taken to combat terrorism comply with all their obligations under international law, and should adopt such measures in accordance with international law, in particular international human rights, refugee, and humanitarian law,

Reaffirming that terrorism in all its forms and manifestations constitutes one of the most serious threats to peace and security,

Considering that acts of terrorism seriously impair the enjoyment of human rights and threaten the social and economic development of all States and undermine global stability and prosperity,

Emphasizing that enhancing dialogue and broadening the understanding among civilizations, in an effort to prevent the indiscriminate targeting of different religions and cultures, and addressing unresolved regional conflicts and the full range of global issues, including development issues, will contribute to international cooperation, which by itself is necessary to sustain the broadest possible fight against terrorism,

Reaffirming its profound solidarity with victims of terrorism and their families,

Acting under Chapter VII of the Charter of the United Nations,

1. *Condemns* in the strongest terms all acts of terrorism irrespective of their motivation, whenever and by whomsoever committed, as one of the most serious threats to peace and security;

2. *Calls upon* States to cooperate fully in the fight against terrorism, especially with those States where or against whose citizens terrorist acts are committed, in accordance with their obligations under international law, in order to find, deny safe haven and bring to justice, on the basis of the principle to extradite or prosecute, any person who supports, facilitates, participates or attempts

to participate in the financing, planning, preparation or commission of terrorist acts or provides safe havens;

3. *Recalls* that criminal acts, including against civilians, committed with the intent to cause death or serious bodily injury, or taking of hostages, with the purpose to provoke a state of terror in the general public or in a group of persons or particular persons, intimidate a population or compel a government or an international organization to do or to abstain from doing any act, which constitute offences within the scope of and as defined in the international conventions and protocols relating to terrorism, are under no circumstances justifiable by considerations of a political, philosophical, ideological, racial, ethnic, religious or other similar nature, and *calls upon* all States to prevent such acts and, if not prevented, to ensure that such acts are punished by penalties consistent with their grave nature;

4. *Calls upon* all States to become party, as a matter of urgency, to the relevant international conventions and protocols whether or not they are a party to regional conventions on the matter;

5. *Calls upon* Member States to cooperate fully on an expedited basis in resolving all outstanding issues with a view to adopting by consensus the draft comprehensive convention on international terrorism and the draft international convention for the suppression of acts of nuclear terrorism;

6. *Calls upon* relevant international, regional and subregional organizations to strengthen international cooperation in the fight against terrorism and to intensify their interaction with the United Nations and, in particular, the CTC with a view to facilitating full and timely implementation of resolution 1373 (2001);

7. *Requests* the CTC in consultation with relevant international, regional and subregional organizations and the United Nations bodies to develop a set of best practices to assist States in implementing the provisions of resolution 1373 (2001) related to the financing of terrorism;

8. *Directs* the CTC, as a matter of priority and, when appropriate, in close cooperation with relevant international, regional and subregional organizations to start visits to States, with the consent of the States concerned, in order to enhance the monitoring of the implementation of resolution 1373 (2001) and facilitate the provision of technical and other assistance for such implementation;

9. *Decides* to establish a working group consisting of all members of the Security Council to consider and submit recommendations to the Council on practical measures to be imposed upon individuals, groups or entities involved in or associated with terrorist activities, other than those designated by the Al-Qaida/Taliban Sanctions Committee, including more effective procedures considered to be appropriate for bringing them to justice through prosecution or extradition, freezing of their financial assets, preventing their movement through the territories of Member States, preventing supply to them of all types of arms and related material, and on the procedures for implementing these measures;

10. *Requests* further the working group, established under paragraph 9 to consider the possibility of establishing an international fund to compensate victims of terrorist acts and their families, which might be financed through voluntary contributions, which could consist in part of assets seized from terrorist organizations, their members and sponsors, and submit its recommendations to the Council;

11. *Requests* the Secretary-General to take, as a matter of urgency, appropriate steps to make the CTED fully operational and to inform the Council by 15 November 2004;

12. *Decides* to remain actively seized of the matter.

United Nations Security Council

S/RES/1617 (2005)
29 JULY 2005

RESOLUTION 1617 (2005)

Adopted by
the Security Council at its 5244th meeting, on 29 July 2005

The Security Council,

Recalling its resolutions 1267 (1999) of 15 October 1999, 1333 (2000) of 19 December 2000, 1363 (2001) of 30 July 2001, 1373 (2001) of 28 September 2001, 1390 (2002) of 16 January 2002, 1452 (2002) of 20 December 2002, 1455 (2003) of 17 January 2003, 1526 (2004) of 30 January 2004 and 1566 (2004) of 8 October 2004, and the relevant statements of its President,

Reaffirming that terrorism in all its forms and manifestations constitutes one of the most serious threats to peace and security and that any acts of terrorism are criminal and unjustifiable regardless of their motivations, whenever and by whomsoever committed; and reiterating its unequivocal condemnation of Al-Qaida, Usama bin Laden, the Taliban—and associated individuals, groups, undertakings and entities—for ongoing and multiple criminal terrorist acts aimed at causing the death of innocent civilians and other victims, destruction of property and greatly undermining stability,

Expressing its concern over the use of various media, including the Internet, by Al-Qaida, Usama bin Laden, and the Taliban, and their associates, including for terrorist propaganda and inciting terrorist violence, and urging the working group established pursuant to resolution 1566 (2004) to consider these issues,

Reaffirming the need to combat by all means, in accordance with the Charter of the United Nations and international law, threats to international peace and security caused by terrorist acts, stressing in this regard the important role the United Nations plays in leading and coordinating this effort,

Emphasizing the obligation placed upon all Member States to implement, in full, resolution 1373 (2001), including with regard to the Taliban or Al-Qaida, and any individuals, groups, undertakings or entities associated with Al-Qaida, Usama bin Laden or the Taliban, who have participated in financing, planning, facilitating, recruiting for, preparing, perpetrating, or otherwise supporting terrorist activities or acts, as well as to facilitate the implementation of counter-terrorism obligations in accordance with relevant Security Council resolutions,

Stressing the importance of clarifying which individuals, groups, undertakings and entities are subject to listing in light of information regarding the changing nature of, and threat from, Al-Qaida, particularly as reported by the Analytical Support and Sanctions Monitoring Team ('Monitoring Team'),

Underscoring the importance of Member State designations pursuant to relevant resolutions and robust implementation of existing measures as a significant preventive measure in combating terrorist activity,

Noting that, in giving effect to the measures in paragraph 4 (b) of resolution 1267 (1999), paragraph 8 (c) of resolution 1333 (2000) and paragraphs 1 and 2 of resolution 1390 (2002), full account is to be taken of the provisions of paragraphs 1 and 2 of resolution 1452 (2002),

Welcoming the efforts of the International Civil Aviation Organization to prevent travel documents from being made available to terrorists and their associates,

Encouraging Member States to work in the framework of Interpol, in particular through the use of the Interpol database of stolen and lost travel documents, to reinforce the implementation of the measures against Al-Qaida, Usama bin Laden, and the Taliban, and their associates,

Expressing its concern over the possible use by Al-Qaida, Usama bin Laden, or the Taliban, and their associates of Man-Portable Air Defence Systems (MANPADS), commercially available explosives and chemical, biological, radiation or nuclear weapons and material, and encouraging Member States to consider possible action to reduce these threats,

Urging all States, international bodies, and regional organizations to allocate sufficient resources, including through international partnership, to meet the ongoing and direct threat posed by Al-Qaida, Usama bin Laden and the Taliban, and individuals, groups, undertakings and entities associated with them,

Stressing the importance of meeting the ongoing threat that Al-Qaida, Usama bin Laden and the Taliban, and individuals, groups, undertakings and entities associated with them represent to international peace and security,

Acting under Chapter VII of the Charter of the United Nations,

1. *Decides* that all States shall take the measures as previously imposed by paragraph 4 (b) of resolution 1267 (1999), paragraph 8 (c) of resolution 1333 (2000), and paragraphs 1 and 2 of resolution 1390 (2002) with respect to Al-Qaida, Usama bin Laden, and the Taliban and other individuals, groups, undertakings and entities associated with them, as referred to in the list created pursuant to resolutions 1267 (1999) and 1333 (2000) (the 'Consolidated List'):

   (a) Freeze without delay the funds and other financial assets or economic resources of these individuals, groups, undertakings and entities, including funds derived from property owned or controlled, directly or indirectly, by them or by persons acting on their behalf or at their direction, and ensure that neither these nor any other funds, financial assets or economic resources are made available, directly or indirectly, for such persons' benefit, by their nationals or by any persons within their territory;

   (b) Prevent the entry into or the transit through their territories of these individuals, provided that nothing in this paragraph shall oblige any State to deny entry or require the departure from its territories of its own nationals and this paragraph shall not apply where entry or transit is necessary for the fulfilment of a judicial process or the Committee established pursuant to resolution 1267 (1999) ('the Committee') determines on a case-by-case basis only that entry or transit is justified;

   (c) Prevent the direct or indirect supply, sale or transfer, to these individuals, groups, undertakings and entities from their territories or by their nationals outside their territories, or using their flag vessels or aircraft, of arms and related materiel of all types including weapons and ammunition, military vehicles and equipment, paramilitary equipment, and spare parts for the aforementioned and technical advice, assistance, or training related to military activities;

2. *Further decides* that acts or activities indicating that an individual, group, undertaking, or entity is 'associated with' Al-Qaida, Usama bin Laden or the Taliban include:

— participating in the financing, planning, facilitating, preparing, or perpetrating of acts or activities by, in conjunction with, under the name of, on behalf of, or in support of;

— supplying, selling or transferring arms and related materiel to;

— recruiting for; or

— otherwise supporting acts or activities of;

Al-Qaida, Usama bin Laden or the Taliban, or any cell, affiliate, splinter group or derivative thereof;

3. *Further decides* that any undertaking or entity owned or controlled, directly or indirectly, by, or otherwise supporting, such an individual, group, undertaking or entity associated with Al-Qaida, Usama bin Laden or the Taliban shall be eligible for designation;

4. *Decides* that, when proposing names for the Consolidated List, States shall act in accordance with paragraph 17 of resolution 1526 (2004) and henceforth also shall provide to the Committee a statement of case describing the basis of the proposal; and further encourages States to identify any undertakings and entities owned or controlled, directly or indirectly, by the proposed subject;

5. *Requests* relevant States to inform, to the extent possible, and in writing where possible, individuals and entities included in the Consolidated List of the measures imposed on them, the Committee's guidelines, and, in particular, the listing and delisting procedures and the provisions of resolution 1452 (2002);

6. *Decides* that the statement of case submitted by the designating State referred to in paragraph 4 above may be used by the Committee in responding to queries from Member States whose nationals, residents or entities have been included on the Consolidated List; decides also that the Committee may decide on a case-by-case basis to release the information to other parties, with the prior consent of the designating State, for example, for operational reasons or to aid the implementation of the measures; decides also that States may continue to provide additional information which shall be kept on a confidential basis within the Committee unless the submitting State agrees to the dissemination of such information;

7. *Strongly urges* all Member States to implement the comprehensive, international standards embodied in the Financial Action Task Force's (FATF) Forty Recommendations on Money Laundering and the FATF Nine Special Recommendations on Terrorist Financing;

8. *Requests* the Secretary-General to take the necessary steps to increase cooperation between the United Nations and Interpol in order to provide the Committee with better tools to fulfil its mandate more effectively and to give Member States better tools to implement the measures referred to in paragraph 1 above;

9. *Urges* all Member States, in their implementation of the measures called for in paragraph 1 above, to ensure that stolen and lost passports and other travel documents are invalidated as soon as possible and share information on those documents with other Member States through the Interpol database;

10. *Calls* on all Member States to use the checklist contained in annex II of this resolution to report by 1 March 2006 to the Committee on specific actions that they have taken to implement the measures outlined in paragraph 1 above with regard to individuals and entities henceforth added to the Consolidated List, and thereafter at intervals to be determined by the Committee;

11. *Directs* the Committee to encourage the submission of names and additional identifying information from Member States for inclusion on the Consolidated List;

12. *Calls upon* the Committee, working in cooperation with the Committee established pursuant to resolution 1373 (the 'Counter-Terrorism Committee' or 'CTC') to inform the Council of specific additional steps that States could take to implement the measures outlined in paragraph 1 above;

13. *Reiterates* the need for ongoing close cooperation and exchange of information among the Committee, the CTC, and the Committee established pursuant to resolution 1540 (2004), as well as their respective groups of experts, including enhanced information sharing, coordinated visits to countries, technical assistance, and other issues of relevance to all three committees;

14. *Further reiterates* the importance of having the Committee follow up via oral and/or written communications with Member States regarding effective implementation of the sanctions measures and provide Member States with an opportunity, at the Committee's request, to send representatives to meet the Committee for more in-depth discussion of relevant issues;

15. *Requests* the Committee to consider, where and when appropriate, visits to selected countries by the Chairman and/or Committee members to enhance the full and effective implementation of the measures referred to in paragraph 1 above, with a view to encouraging States to comply fully with this resolution and resolutions 1267 (1999), 1333 (2000), 1390 (2002), 1455 (2003) and 1526 (2004);

16. *Requests* the Committee to report orally, through its Chairman, at least every 120 days to the Council on the overall work of the Committee and the Monitoring Team, and, as appropriate, in conjunction with the reports by the Chairmen of the CTC and the Committee established pursuant to resolution 1540 (2004), including briefings for all interested Member States;

17. *Reminds* the Committee of its responsibilities as outlined in paragraph 14 of resolution 1455 (2003) and paragraph 13 of resolution 1526 (2004), and calls upon the Committee to provide the Council no later than 31 July 2006 with an update of the written assessment referred to in paragraph 13 of resolution 1526 (2004) of actions taken by Member States to implement the measures described in paragraph 1 above;

18. *Requests* that the Committee continue its work on the Committee's guidelines, including on listing and delisting procedures, and implementation of resolution 1452 (2002) and requests the Chairman, in his periodic reports to the Council pursuant to paragraph 16 above, to provide progress reports on the Committee's work on these issues;

19. *Decides*, in order to assist the Committee in the fulfilment of its mandate, to extend the mandate of the New York-based Monitoring Team for a period of 17 months, under the direction of the Committee with the responsibilities outlined in annex I;

20. *Requests* the Secretary-General, upon adoption of this resolution and acting in close consultation with the Committee, to appoint, consistent with United Nations rules and procedures, no more than eight members, including a coordinator, to the Monitoring Team, taking into account the areas of expertise referred to in paragraph 7 of resolution 1526 (2004);

21. *Decides* to review the measures described in paragraph 1 above with a view to their possible further strengthening in 17 months, or sooner if necessary;

22. *Decides* to remain actively seized of the matter.

ANNEX I TO RESOLUTION 1617 (2005)

In accordance with paragraph 19 of this resolution, the Monitoring Team shall operate under the direction of the Committee established pursuant to resolution 1267 (1999) and shall have the following responsibilities:

(a) To collate, assess, monitor and report on and make recommendations regarding implementation of the measures, to pursue case studies, as appropriate; and to explore in depth any other relevant issues as directed by the Committee;

(b) To submit a comprehensive programme of work to the Committee for its approval and review, as necessary, in which the Monitoring Team should detail the activities envisaged in order to fulfil its responsibilities, including proposed travel, based on close coordination with the CTC's Counter-Terrorism Executive Directorate to avoid duplication and reinforce synergies;

(c) To submit, in writing, three comprehensive, independent reports to the Committee, the first by 31 January 2006, the second by 31 July 2006, and the third by 10 December 2006, on implementation by States of the measures referred to in paragraph 1 of this resolution, including specific recommendations for improved implementation of the measures and possible new measures, as well as reporting on listing, de-listing, and exemptions pursuant to resolution 1452 (2003);

(d) To analyse reports submitted pursuant to paragraph 6 of resolution 1455 (2003), the checklists submitted pursuant to paragraph 10 of this resolution, and other information submitted by Member States to the Committee as instructed by the Committee;

(e) To work closely and share information with the CTC's Counter-Terrorism Executive Directorate and the 1540 Committee's group of experts to identify areas of convergence and to help facilitate concrete coordination among the three Committees;

(f) To develop a plan to assist the Committee with addressing noncompliance with the measures referred to in paragraph 1 of this resolution;

(g) To present to the Committee recommendations, which could be used by Member States to assist them with the implementation of the measures referred to in paragraph 1 of this resolution and in preparing proposed additions to the Consolidated List;

(h) To consult with Member States in advance of travel to selected Member States, based on its programme of work as approved by the Committee;

(i) To encourage Member States to submit names and additional identifying information for inclusion on the Consolidated List, as instructed by the Committee;

(j) To study and report to the Committee on the changing nature of the threat of Al-Qaida and the Taliban and the best measures to confront it;

(k) To consult with Member States, including regular dialogue with representatives in New York and in capitals, taking into account comments from Member States, especially regarding any issues that might be contained in the Monitoring Team's reports referred to in paragraph (c) of this annex;

(l) To report to the Committee, on a regular basis or when the Committee so requests, through oral and/or written briefings on the work of the Monitoring Team, including its visits to Member States and its activities;

(m) To assist the Committee in preparing oral and written assessments to the Council, in particular the analytical summaries referred to in paragraphs 17 and 18 of this resolution;

(n) Any other responsibility identified by the Committee.

Annex II to Resolution 1617 (2005)

1267 Committee Checklist

Please provide to the United Nations 1267 (Al-Qaida/Taliban Sanctions) Committee by XXX date information on the following individuals, groups, undertakings, and entities added in the last six months to the Committee's Consolidated List of those subject to the sanctions described in Security Council Resolution 1267 (1999) and successor resolutions.

This information is provided by the Government of _____ on XXX date.

YES   NO

1. Mr. Doe (Number _____ on Consolidated List)

    A. Name added to visa lookout list?

    B. Any visas denied?

    C. Financial institutions notified?

    D. Any assets frozen?

    E. Arms embargo ban implemented?

    F. Any attempts to purchase arms?

    Additional information, if available:

YES NO

2. The Doe Corp. (Number _____ on Consolidated List)

   A. Financial institutions notified?
   B. Any assets frozen?
   C. Arms embargo ban implemented?
   D. Any attempts to purchase arms?

   Additional information, if available:

United Nations Security Council

S/RES/1624 (2005)

14 SEPTEMBER 2005

RESOLUTION 1624 (2005)

Adopted by
the Security Council at its 5261st meeting, on 14 September 2005

The Security Council,

Reaffirming its resolutions 1267 (1999) of 15 October 1999, 1373 (2001) of 28 September 2001, 1535 (2004) of 26 March 2004, 1540 (2004) of 28 April 2004, 1566 (2004) of 8 October 2004, and 1617 (2005) of 29 July 2005, the declaration annexed to its resolution 1456 (2003) of 20 January 2003, as well as its other resolutions concerning threats to international peace and security caused by acts of terrorism,

Reaffirming also the imperative to combat terrorism in all its forms and manifestations by all means, in accordance with the Charter of the United Nations, and also *stressing* that States must ensure that any measures taken to combat terrorism comply with all their obligations under international law, and should adopt such measures in accordance with international law, in particular international human rights law, refugee law, and humanitarian law,

Condemning in the strongest terms all acts of terrorism irrespective of their motivation, whenever and by whomsoever committed, as one of the most serious threats to peace and security, and *reaffirming* the primary responsibility of the Security Council for the maintenance of international peace and security under the Charter of the United Nations,

Condemning also in the strongest terms the incitement of terrorist acts and *repudiating* attempts at the justification or glorification (*apologie*) of terrorist acts that may incite further terrorist acts,

Deeply concerned that incitement of terrorist acts motivated by extremism and intolerance poses a serious and growing danger to the enjoyment of human rights, threatens the social and economic development of all States, undermines global stability and prosperity, and must be addressed urgently and proactively by the United Nations and all States, and *emphasizing* the need to take all necessary and appropriate measures in accordance with international law at the national and international level to protect the right to life,

Recalling the right to freedom of expression reflected in Article 19 of the Universal Declaration of Human Rights adopted by the General Assembly in 1948 ('the Universal Declaration'), and recalling also the right to freedom of expression in Article 19 of the International Covenant on Civil and Political Rights adopted by the General Assembly in 1966 ('ICCPR') and that any restrictions thereon shall only be such as are provided by law and are necessary on the grounds set out in paragraph 3 of Article 19 of the ICCPR,

Recalling in addition the right to seek and enjoy asylum reflected in Article 14 of the Universal Declaration and the non-refoulement obligation of States under the Convention relating to the Status of Refugees adopted on 28 July 1951, together with its Protocol adopted on 31 January 1967 ('the Refugees Convention and its Protocol'), and also *recalling* that the protections afforded by the Refugees Convention and its Protocol shall not extend to any person with respect to whom there are serious reasons for considering that he has been guilty of acts contrary to the purposes and principles of the United Nations,

Reaffirming that acts, methods, and practices of terrorism are contrary to the purposes and principles of the United Nations and that knowingly financing, planning and inciting terrorist acts are also contrary to the purposes and principles of the United Nations,

Deeply concerned by the increasing number of victims, especially among civilians of diverse nationalities and beliefs, caused by terrorism motivated by intolerance or extremism in various regions of the world, *reaffirming* its profound solidarity with the victims of terrorism and their families, and *stressing* the importance of assisting victims of terrorism and providing them and their families with support to cope with their loss and grief,

Recognizing the essential role of the United Nations in the global effort to combat terrorism and *welcoming* the Secretary-General's identification of elements of a counter-terrorism strategy to be considered and developed by the General Assembly without delay with a view to adopting and implementing a strategy to promote comprehensive, coordinated and consistent responses at the national, regional and international level to counter terrorism,

Stressing its call upon all States to become party, as a matter of urgency, to the international counter-terrorism Conventions and Protocols whether or not they are party to regional Conventions on the matter, and to give priority consideration to signing the International Convention for the Suppression of Nuclear Terrorism adopted by the General Assembly on 13 April 2005,

Re-emphasizing that continuing international efforts to enhance dialogue and broaden understanding among civilizations, in an effort to prevent the indiscriminate targeting of different religions and cultures, and addressing unresolved regional conflicts and the full range of global issues, including development issues, will contribute to strengthening the international fight against terrorism,

Stressing the importance of the role of the media, civil and religious society, the business community and educational institutions in those efforts to enhance dialogue and broaden understanding, and in promoting tolerance and coexistence, and in fostering an environment which is not conducive to incitement of terrorism,

Recognizing the importance that, in an increasingly globalized world, States act cooperatively to prevent terrorists from exploiting sophisticated technology, communications and resources to incite support for criminal acts,

Recalling that all States must cooperate fully in the fight against terrorism, in accordance with their obligations under international law, in order to find, deny safe haven and bring to justice, on the basis of the principle of extradite or prosecute, any person who supports, facilitates, participates or attempts to participate in the financing, planning, preparation or commission of terrorist acts or provides safe havens,

1. *Calls upon* all States to adopt such measures as may be necessary and appropriate and in accordance with their obligations under international law to:

    (a) Prohibit by law incitement to commit a terrorist act or acts;
    (b) Prevent such conduct;
    (c) Deny safe haven to any persons with respect to whom there is credible and relevant information giving serious reasons for considering that they have been guilty of such conduct;

2. *Calls upon* all States to cooperate, inter alia, to strengthen the security of their international borders, including by combating fraudulent travel documents and, to the extent attainable, by enhancing terrorist screening and passenger security procedures with a view to preventing those guilty of the conduct in paragraph 1 (a) from entering their territory;

3. *Calls upon* all States to continue international efforts to enhance dialogue and broaden understanding among civilizations, in an effort to prevent the indiscriminate targeting of different religions and cultures, and to take all measures as may be necessary and appropriate and in

accordance with their obligations under international law to counter incitement of terrorist acts motivated by extremism and intolerance and to prevent the subversion of educational, cultural, and religious institutions by terrorists and their supporters;

4. *Stresses* that States must ensure that any measures taken to implement paragraphs 1, 2 and 3 of this resolution comply with all of their obligations under international law, in particular international human rights law, refugee law, and humanitarian law;

5. *Calls upon* all States to report to the Counter-Terrorism Committee, as part of their ongoing dialogue, on the steps they have taken to implement this resolution;

6. *Directs* the Counter-Terrorism Committee to:

(a) Include in its dialogue with Member States their efforts to implement this resolution;

(b) Work with Member States to help build capacity, including through spreading best legal practice and promoting exchange of information in this regard;

(c) Report back to the Council in twelve months on the implementation of this resolution.

7. *Decides* to remain actively seized of the matter.

United Nations Security Council

S/RES/1735 (2006)

22 DECEMBER 2006

RESOLUTION 1735 (2006)

Adopted by
the Security Council at its 5609th meeting, on 22 December 2006

The Security Council,

Recalling its resolutions 1267 (1999) of 15 October 1999, 1333 (2000) of 19 December 2000, 1363 (2001) of 30 July 2001, 1373 (2001) of 28 September 2001, 1390 (2002) of 16 January 2002, 1452 (2002) of 20 December 2002, 1455 (2003) of 17 January 2003, 1526 (2004) of 30 January 2004, 1566 (2004) of 8 October 2004, 1617 (2005) of 29 July 2005, 1624 (2005) of 14 September 2005, and 1699 (2006) of 8 August 2006, and the relevant statements of its President,

Reaffirming that terrorism in all its forms and manifestations constitutes one of the most serious threats to peace and security and that any acts of terrorism are criminal and unjustifiable regardless of their motivations, whenever and by whomsoever committed; and reiterating its unequivocal condemnation of Al-Qaida, Usama bin Laden, the Taliban, and other individuals, groups, under-takings, and entities associated with them, for ongoing and multiple criminal terrorist acts aimed at causing the death of innocent civilians and other victims, destruction of property and greatly undermining stability,

Expressing its deep concern about the increased violent and terrorist activities in Afghanistan of the Taliban and Al-Qaida, and other individuals, groups, undertakings, and entities associated with them,

Reaffirming the need to combat by all means, in accordance with the Charter of the United Nations and international law, threats to international peace and security caused by terrorist acts, stressing in this regard the important role the United Nations plays in leading and coordinating this effort,

Stressing that terrorism can only be defeated by a sustained and comprehensive approach involving the active participation and collaboration of all States, and international and regional organizations to impede, impair, isolate, and incapacitate the terrorist threat,

Emphasizing that dialogue between the Committee established pursuant to resolution 1267 (1999) ('the Committee') and Member States is vital to the full implementation of the measures,

Recognizing that one of the most effective means of dialogue between the Committee and Member States is through direct contact, including country visits,

Welcoming the expanded cooperation with Interpol, including the establishment of 'Interpol—UN Security Council Special Notices' and the passage of resolution 1699 (2006), and encouraging Member States to work in the framework of Interpol and other international and regional organizations in order to reinforce the implementation of the measures against Al-Qaida, Usama bin Laden, and the Taliban, and other individuals, groups, undertakings and entities associated with them,

Noting the need for robust implementation of the measures in paragraph 1 of this resolution as a significant tool in combating terrorist activity,

Reiterating that the measures referred to in paragraph 1 below, are preventative in nature and are not reliant upon criminal standards set out under national law,

469

Underscoring that, in giving effect to the measures in paragraph 1 of resolution 1617 (2005) and other relevant resolutions, full account is to be taken of the provisions regarding exemptions in paragraphs 1 and 2 of resolution 1452 (2002),

Taking note of the Committee's document on the arms embargo (SCA/2/06(20)), which is intended to be a useful tool to assist States in the implementation of the measures in paragraph 1(c) of this resolution,

Expressing its deep concern about criminal misuse of the internet by Al-Qaida, Usama bin Laden, and the Taliban, and other individuals, groups, undertakings, and entities associated with them, in furtherance of terrorist acts,

Noting with concern the changing nature of the threat presented by Al-Qaida, Usama bin Laden and the Taliban, and other individuals, groups, undertakings and entities associated with them, in particular the ways in which terrorist ideologies are promoted,

Stressing the importance of meeting all aspects of the threat that Al-Qaida, Usama bin Laden and the Taliban, and other individuals, groups, undertakings and entities associated with them represent to international peace and security,

Acting under Chapter VII of the Charter of the United Nations,

Measures

1. *Decides* that all States shall take the measures as previously imposed by paragraph 4 (b) of resolution 1267 (1999), paragraph 8 (c) of resolution 1333 (2000), paragraphs 1 and 2 of resolution *1390* (2002), with respect to Al-Qaida, Usama bin Laden, and the Taliban and other individuals, groups, undertakings and entities associated with them, as referred to in the list created pursuant to resolutions 1267 (1999) and 1333 (2000) (the 'Consolidated List'):

   (a) Freeze without delay the funds and other financial assets or economic resources of these individuals, groups, undertakings and entities, including funds derived from property owned or controlled, directly or indirectly, by them or by persons acting on their behalf or at their direction, and ensure that neither these nor any other funds, financial assets or economic resources are made available, directly or indirectly, for such persons' benefit, or by their nationals or by persons within their territory;

   (b) Prevent the entry into or the transit through their territories of these individuals, provided that nothing in this paragraph shall oblige any State to deny entry or require the departure from its territories of its own nationals and this paragraph shall not apply where entry or transit is necessary for the fulfilment of a judicial process or the Committee established pursuant to resolution 1267 (1999) ('the Committee') determines on a case-by-case basis only that entry or transit is justified;

   (c) Prevent the direct or indirect supply, sale, or transfer, to these individuals, groups, undertakings and entities from their territories or by their nationals outside their territories, or using their flag vessels or aircraft, of arms and related material of all types including weapons and ammunition, military vehicles and equipment, paramilitary equipment, and spare parts for the aforementioned and technical advice, assistance, or training related to military activities;

2. *Reminds* States of their obligation to freeze without delay the funds and other financial assets or economic resources pursuant to paragraph 1 (a) of this resolution;

3. *Confirms* that the requirements in paragraph 1 (a) of this resolution apply to economic resources of every kind;

4. *Calls upon* States to redouble their efforts to implement the measure in paragraph 1 (b) and 1 (c) of this resolution;

Listing

5. *Decides* that, when proposing names to the Committee for inclusion on the Consolidated List, States shall act in accordance with paragraph 17 of resolution 1526 (2004) and paragraph 4 of resolution 1617 (2005) and provide a statement of case; the statement of case should provide as much detail as possible on the basis(es) for the listing, including: (i) specific information supporting a determination that the individual or entity meets the criteria above; (ii) the nature of the information and (iii) supporting information or documents that can be provided; States should include details of any connection between the proposed designee and any currently listed individual or entity;

6. *Requests* designating States, at the time of submission, to identify those parts of the statement of case which may be publicly released for the purposes of notifying the listed individual or entity, and those parts which may be released upon request to interested States;

7. *Calls upon* States to use the cover sheet attached in Annex I when proposing names for the Consolidated List, in order to ensure clarity and consistency in requests for listing;

8. *Directs* the Committee to encourage the submission of names from Member States for inclusion on the Consolidated List;

9. *Directs* the Committee to encourage States to submit additional identifying and other information on listed individuals and entities, including updates on assets frozen and the movement of listed individuals as such information becomes available;

10. *Decides* that the Secretariat shall, after publication but within two weeks after a name is added to the Consolidated List, notify the Permanent Mission of the country or countries where the individual or entity is believed to be located and, in the case of individuals, the country of which the person is a national (to the extent this information is known), and include with this notification a copy of the publicly releasable portion of the statement of case, a description of the effects of designation, as set forth in the relevant resolutions, the Committee's procedures for considering delisting requests, and the provisions of resolution 1452 (2002);

11. *Calls upon* States receiving notification as in paragraph 10 to take reasonable steps according to their domestic laws and practices to notify or inform the listed individual or entity of the designation and to include with this notification a copy of the publicly releasable portion of the statement of case, a description of the effects of designation, as provided in the relevant resolutions, the Committee's procedures for considering delisting requests, the provisions of resolution 1452 (2002);

12. *Encourages* States to submit to the Committee for inclusion on the Consolidated List names of individuals and entities participating in the financing or support of acts or activities of Al-Qaida, Usama bin Laden and the Taliban, and other individuals, groups, undertakings and entities associated with them, as described in paragraph 2 of resolution 1617 (2005), by any means, including but not limited to using proceeds derived from illicit cultivation, production, and trafficking of narcotic drugs originating in Afghanistan, and their precursors;

Delisting

13. *Decides* that the Committee shall continue to develop, adopt, and apply guidelines regarding the de-listing of individuals and entities on the Consolidated List;

14. *Decides* that the Committee, in determining whether to remove names from the Consolidated List, may consider, among other things, (i) whether the individual or entity was placed on the Consolidated List due to a mistake of identity, or (ii) whether the individual or entity no longer meets the criteria set out in relevant resolutions, in particular resolution 1617 (2005); in making the evaluation in (ii) above, the Committee may consider, among other things, whether the individual is deceased, or whether it has been affirmatively shown that the individual or entity has severed all association, as defined in resolution 1617 (2005), with Al-Qaida, Usama bin Laden, the Taliban, and their supporters, including all individuals and entities on the Consolidated List;

Exemptions

15. *Decides* to extend the period for consideration by the Committee of notifications submitted pursuant to paragraph 1 (a) of resolution 1452 (2002) from 48 hours to 3 working days;

16. *Reiterates* that the Committee must make a negative decision on notifications submitted pursuant to paragraph 1 (a) of resolution 1452 (2002), in order to prevent the release of funds and other financial assets or economic resources that have been determined by the notifying State(s) to be necessary for basic expenses;

17. *Directs* the Committee to review its guidelines with respect to the provisions of paragraph 1(a) of resolution 1452 (2002) as reiterated in paragraph 15 above;

18. *Encourages* States that submit requests to the Committee, pursuant to paragraph 1 (b) of resolution 1452 (2002), to report in a timely way on the use of such funds, with a view to preventing such funds from being used to finance terrorism;

Measures implementation

19. *Encourages* States to identify, and if necessary introduce, adequate procedures to fully implement all aspects of the measures described in paragraph 1 of this resolution;

20. *Stresses* that the measures imposed by paragraph 1(a) of this resolution apply to all forms of financial resources, including but not limited to those used for the provision of Internet hosting or related services, used for the support of Al-Qaida, Usama bin Laden, and the Taliban and other individuals, groups, undertakings and entities associated with them;

21. *Directs* the Committee to identify possible cases of non-compliance with the measures pursuant to paragraph 1 above, and requests the Chairman, in his periodic reports to the Council pursuant to paragraph 31 below, to provide progress reports on the Committee's work on this issue;

22. *Requests* States to ensure that the most up to date version of the Consolidated List is promptly made available to relevant Government offices and other relevant bodies, in particular, those offices responsible for the assets freeze and border control;

23. *Requests* the Secretary General to take the necessary steps to increase cooperation between the United Nations and relevant international and regional organisations, including Interpol, ICAO, IATA, and the WCO, in order to provide the Committee with better tools to fulfil its mandate more effectively and to give Member States better tools to implement the measures referred to in paragraph 1 of this resolution;

Taliban

24. *Encourages* States to submit names of individuals and entities currently associated with the Taliban to the Committee for inclusion on the Consolidated List;

25. *Directs* the Committee to encourage States to provide additional identifying and other information on listed Taliban individuals and entities;

26. *Directs* the Committee to work, in accordance with its guidelines, to consider requests for inclusion on the Consolidated List, names of individuals and entities associated with the Taliban, and to consider petitions for the removal of listed members and/or associates of the Taliban who are no longer associated with the Taliban;

Coordination

27. *Reiterates* the need for ongoing close cooperation and exchange of information among the Committee, the Counter Terrorism Committee ('CTC'), and the Committee established pursuant to resolution 1540 (2004), as well as their respective groups of experts, including enhanced information sharing, coordinated visits to countries, technical assistance, and other issues of relevance to all three committees;

Outreach

28. *Further reiterates* the importance of having the Committee follow up via oral and/or written communications with Member States regarding effective implementation of the sanctions measures;

29. *Strongly encourages* Member States to send representatives to meet the Committee for more in-depth discussion of relevant issues;

30. *Requests* the Committee to consider, where and when appropriate, visits to selected countries by the Chairman and/or Committee members to enhance the full and effective implementation of the measures referred to in paragraph 1 above, with a view to encouraging States to comply fully with this resolution and resolutions 1267 (1999), 1333 (2000), 1390 (2002), 1455 (2003), 1526 (2004) and 1617 (2005);

31. *Requests* the Committee to report orally, through its Chairman, at least every 180 days to the Council on the overall work of the Committee and the Analytical Support and Sanctions Monitoring Team ('Monitoring Team'), and, as appropriate, in conjunction with the reports by the Chairmen of the CTC and the Committee established pursuant to resolution 1540 (2004), including briefings for all interested Member States;

Monitoring team and reviews

32. *Decides*, in order to assist the Committee in the fulfilment of its mandate, to extend the mandate of the current New York-based Monitoring Team, appointed by the Secretary-General pursuant to paragraph 20 of resolution 1617 (2005), for a further period of 18 months, under the direction of the Committee with the responsibilities outlined in Annex II, and requests the Secretary-General to make the necessary arrangements to this effect;

33. *Decides* to review the measures described in paragraph 1 of this resolution with a view to their possible further strengthening in 18 months, or sooner if necessary;

34. *Decides* to remain actively seized of the matter.

Annex I—Coversheet

CONSOLIDATED LIST: COVER SHEET FOR MEMBER STATE SUBMISSIONS TO THE COMMITTEE

Please complete as many of the following fields as possible:

CONSOLIDATED LIST: COVER SHEET FOR MEMBER STATE SUBMISSIONS TO THE COMMITTEE
Please complete as many of the following fields as possible:

I. IDENTIFIER INFORMATION – for Individuals

Where possible, note the nationality or cultural or ethnic sources of names/aliases. Provide all available spellings.		Surname/ Family Name/ Last Name	First Name	Additional name (e.g. father's name or middle name), where applicable	Additional name (e.g. grandfather's name), where applicable	Additional name, where applicable	Additional name, where applicable
Full Name: (in original and Latin script)							
Aliases/"Also Known As" (A.K.A.s): Note whether it is a strong or weak alias.	Current						
	Former						
Other nom de guerre, pseudonym:				**Title:** Honorary, professional, or religious title			
Employment/Occupation: Official title/position				**Nationality/ Citizenship:**			
Date of Birth: (DD/MM/YYYY)				**Passport Details:** (Number, issuing date & country, expiry date)			
Alternative Dates of Birth (if any): (DD/MM/YYYY)				**National Identification Number(s), Type(s):** (e.g. Identity card, Social Security)			
Place of Birth: (provide all known details including city, region, province/state, country)				**Address(es):** (provide all known details, including street address, city, province/state, country)			
Alternative Place(s) of Birth (if any): (city, region, province/state, country)				**Previous Address(es):** (provide all known details, including street address, city, province/state, country)			
Gender:				**Languages spoken:**			
Father's full name:				**Mother's full name:**			
Current location:				**Previous location(s):**			
Undertakings and entities owned or controlled, directly or indirectly by the individual (see UNSCR 1617 (2005), para. 3):							
Website Addresses:							
Other relevant detail: (such as physical description, distinguishing marks and characteristics)							

IDENTIFIER INFORMATION -- For Groups, Undertakings, or Entities	
Name:	
Also Known As (A.K.As): Where possible, note whether it is a strong or weak A.K.A.	**Now Known As (N.K.A.s)**
	Formerly Known As (F.K.A.s)
Address(es): Headquarters and/or branches. Provide all known details, including street address, city, province/state, country	
Tax Identification Number: (or local equivalent, type)	
Other Identification Number and type:	
Website Addresses:	
Other Information:	

II. BASIS FOR LISTING

May the Committee publicly release the following information?   Yes ☐   No ☐

May the Committee release the following information to Member States upon request?   Yes ☐   No ☐

Complete one or more of the following:

(a) participating in the financing, planning, facilitating, preparing, or perpetrating of acts or activities by, in conjunction with, under the name of, on behalf of, or in support of Al-Qaida (AQ), Usama bin Laden (UBL), or the Taliban, or any cell, affiliate, splinter group or derivative thereof.[1]
- Name(s) of cell, affiliate, splinter group or derivate thereof:

(b) supplying, selling or transferring arms and related materiel to AQ, UBL or the Taliban, or any cell, affiliate, splinter group or derivative thereof.[1]
- Name(s) of cell, affiliate, splinter group or derivate thereof:

(c) recruiting for AQ, UBL or the Taliban, or any cell, affiliate, splinter group or derivative thereof.[1]
- Name(s) of cell, affiliate, splinter group or derivate thereof:

(d) otherwise supporting acts or activities of AQ, UBL or the Taliban, or any cell, affiliate, splinter group or derivative thereof.[2]
- Name(s) of cell, affiliate, splinter group or derivate thereof:

(e) Other association with AQ, UBL or the Taliban, or any cell, affiliate, splinter group or derivative thereof.
- Briefly explain nature of association and provide name of cell, affiliate, splinter group or derivate thereof:

(f) Entity owned or controlled, directly or indirectly, by, or otherwise supporting, an individual or entity on the Consolidated List.[3]
- Name(s) of individual or entity on the Consolidated List:

Please attach a Statement of Case which should provide as much detail as possible on the basis(es) for listing indicated above, including: (1) specific findings demonstrating the association or activities alleged; (2) the nature of the supporting evidence (e.g., intelligence, law enforcement, judicial, media, admissions by subject, etc.) and (3) supporting evidence or documents that can be supplied. Include details of any connection with a currently listed individual or entity. Indicate what portion(s) of the Statement of Case the Committee may publicly release or release to Member States upon request.

[1] S/RES/1617 (2005), para. 2
[2] S/RES/1617 (2005), para. 2
[3] S/RES/1617 (2005), para. 3

III. POINT OF CONTACT *The individual(s) below may serve as a point-of-contact for further questions on this case:*
(THIS INFORMATION SHALL REMAIN CONFIDENTIAL)

Name: *Position/Title:*

ANNEX II

In accordance with paragraph 32 of this resolution, the Monitoring Team shall operate under the direction of the Committee established pursuant to resolution 1267 (1999) and shall have the following responsibilities:

a. To collate, assess, monitor and report on and make recommendations regarding implementation of the measures, including implementation of the measures in paragraph 1(a) of this resolution as it pertains to preventing the criminal misuse of the internet by Al-Qaida, Usama bin Laden, the Taliban, and other individuals, groups, undertakings, and entities associated with them, to pursue case studies, as appropriate; and to explore in depth any other relevant issues as directed by the Committee;

b. To submit a comprehensive program of work to the Committee for its review and approval, as necessary, in which the Monitoring Team should detail the activities, envisaged in order to fulfil its responsibilities, including proposed travel, based on close coordination with the CTC's Executive Directorate ('CTED') and the 1540 Committee's group of experts to avoid duplication and reinforce synergies;

c. To submit, in writing, two comprehensive, independent reports to the Committee, one by 30 September 2007 and the other by 31 March 2008, on implementation by States of the measures referred to in paragraph 1 of this resolution, including specific recommendations for improved implementation of the measures and possible new measures;

d. To analyze reports submitted pursuant to paragraph 6 of resolution 1455 (2003), the checklists submitted pursuant to paragraph 10 of resolution 1617 (2005), and other information submitted by Member States to the Committee as instructed by the Committee;

e. To work closely and share information with CTED and the 1540 Committee's group of experts to identify areas of convergence and overlap and to help facilitate concrete coordination, including in the area of reporting, among the three Committees;

f. To assist the Committee with its analysis of non-compliance with the measures referred to in paragraph 1 of this resolution by collating information collected from Member States and submitting case studies, both on its own initiative and upon the Committee's request, to the Committee for its review;

g. To present to the Committee recommendations, which could be used by Member States to assist them with the implementation of the measures referred to in paragraph 1 of this resolution and in preparing proposed additions to the Consolidated List;

h. To consult with Member States in advance of travel to selected Member States, based on its program of work as approved by the Committee;

i. To encourage Member States to submit names and additional identifying information for inclusion on the Consolidated List, as instructed by the Committee;

j. To study and report to the Committee on the changing nature of the threat of Al-Qaida and the Taliban and the best measures to confront it, including by developing a dialogue with relevant scholars and academic bodies, in consultation with the Committee;

k. To consult with Member States and other relevant organizations, including regular dialogue with representatives in New York and in capitals, taking into account their comments, especially regarding any issues that might be contained in the Monitoring Team's reports referred to in paragraph c of this annex;

l. To consult with Member States' intelligence and security services, including through regional fora, in order to facilitate the sharing of information and to strengthen enforcement of the measures;

m. To consult with relevant representatives of the private sector, including financial institutions, to learn about the practical implementation of the assets freeze and to develop recommendations for the strengthening of that measure;

n. To work with relevant international and regional organizations in order to promote awareness of, and compliance with, the measures;
o. To assist other subsidiary bodies of the Security Council, and their expert panels, upon request with enhancing their cooperation with Interpol, referred to in resolution 1699 (2006);
p. To report to the Committee, on a regular basis or when the Committee so requests, through oral and/or written briefings on the work of the Monitoring Team, including its visits to Member States and its activities;
q. Any other responsibility identified by the Committee

UNSCR 1373

United Nations Security Council

S/RES/1373 (2001)
28 SEPTEMBER 2001

RESOLUTION 1373 (2001)

Adopted by
the Security Council at its 4385th meeting, on 28 September 2001

The Security Council,

Reaffirming its resolutions 1269 (1999) of 19 October 1999 and 1368 (2001) of 12 September 2001,

Reaffirming also its unequivocal condemnation of the terrorist attacks which took place in New York, Washington, D.C. and Pennsylvania on 11 September 2001, and expressing its determination to prevent all such acts,

Reaffirming further that such acts, like any act of international terrorism, constitute a threat to international peace and security,

Reaffirming the inherent right of individual or collective self-defence as recognized by the Charter of the United Nations as reiterated in resolution 1368 (2001),

Reaffirming the need to combat by all means, in accordance with the Charter of the United Nations, threats to international peace and security caused by terrorist acts,

Deeply concerned by the increase, in various regions of the world, of acts of terrorism motivated by intolerance or extremism,

Calling on States to work together urgently to prevent and suppress terrorist acts, including through increased cooperation and full implementation of the relevant international conventions relating to terrorism,

Recognizing the need for States to complement international cooperation by taking additional measures to prevent and suppress, in their territories through all lawful means, the financing and preparation of any acts of terrorism,

Reaffirming the principle established by the General Assembly in its declaration of October 1970 (resolution 2625 (XXV)) and reiterated by the Security Council in its resolution 1189 (1998) of 13 August 1998, namely that every State has the duty to refrain from organizing, instigating, assisting or participating in terrorist acts in another State or acquiescing in organized activities within its territory directed towards the commission of such acts,

Acting under Chapter VII of the Charter of the United Nations,

1. *Decides* that all States shall:

   (a) Prevent and suppress the financing of terrorist acts;
   (b) Criminalize the wilful provision or collection, by any means, directly or indirectly, of funds by their nationals or in their territories with the intention that the funds should be used, or in the knowledge that they are to be used, in order to carry out terrorist acts;

(c) Freeze without delay funds and other financial assets or economic resources of persons who commit, or attempt to commit, terrorist acts or participate in or facilitate the commission of terrorist acts; of entities owned or controlled directly or indirectly by such persons; and of persons and entities acting on behalf of, or at the direction of such persons and entities, including funds derived or generated from property owned or controlled directly or indirectly by such persons and associated persons and entities;

(d) Prohibit their nationals or any persons and entities within their territories from making any funds, financial assets or economic resources or financial or other related services available, directly or indirectly, for the benefit of persons who commit or attempt to commit or facilitate or participate in the commission of terrorist acts, of entities owned or controlled, directly or indirectly, by such persons and of persons and entities acting on behalf of or at the direction of such persons;

2. *Decides* also that all States shall:

(a) Refrain from providing any form of support, active or passive, to entities or persons involved in terrorist acts, including by suppressing recruitment of members of terrorist groups and eliminating the supply of weapons to terrorists;

(b) Take the necessary steps to prevent the commission of terrorist acts, including by provision of early warning to other States by exchange of information;

(c) Deny safe haven to those who finance, plan, support, or commit terrorist acts, or provide safe havens;

(d) Prevent those who finance, plan, facilitate or commit terrorist acts from using their respective territories for those purposes against other States or their citizens;

(e) Ensure that any person who participates in the financing, planning, preparation or perpetration of terrorist acts or in supporting terrorist acts is brought to justice and ensure that, in addition to any other measures against them, such terrorist acts are established as serious criminal offences in domestic laws and regulations and that the punishment duly reflects the seriousness of such terrorist acts;

(f) Afford one another the greatest measure of assistance in connection with criminal investigations or criminal proceedings relating to the financing or support of terrorist acts, including assistance in obtaining evidence in their possession necessary for the proceedings;

(g) Prevent the movement of terrorists or terrorist groups by effective border controls and controls on issuance of identity papers and travel documents, and through measures for preventing counterfeiting, forgery or fraudulent use of identity papers and travel documents;

3. *Calls* upon all States to:

(a) Find ways of intensifying and accelerating the exchange of operational information, especially regarding actions or movements of terrorist persons or networks; forged or falsified travel documents; traffic in arms, explosives or sensitive materials; use of communications technologies by terrorist groups; and the threat posed by the possession of weapons of mass destruction by terrorist groups;

(b) Exchange information in accordance with international and domestic law and cooperate on administrative and judicial matters to prevent the commission of terrorist acts;

(c) Cooperate, particularly through bilateral and multilateral arrangements and agreements, to prevent and suppress terrorist attacks and take action against perpetrators of such acts;

(d) Become parties as soon as possible to the relevant international conventions and protocols relating to terrorism, including the International Convention for the Suppression of the Financing of Terrorism of 9 December 1999;

(e) Increase cooperation and fully implement the relevant international conventions and protocols relating to terrorism and Security Council resolutions 1269 (1999) and 1368 (2001);

(f) Take appropriate measures in conformity with the relevant provisions of national and international law, including international standards of human rights, before granting refugee status, for the purpose of ensuring that the asylum-seeker has not planned, facilitated or participated in the commission of terrorist acts;

(g) Ensure, in conformity with international law, that refugee status is not abused by the perpetrators, organizers or facilitators of terrorist acts, and that claims of political motivation are not recognized as grounds for refusing requests for the extradition of alleged terrorists;

4. *Notes* with concern the close connection between international terrorism and transnational organized crime, illicit drugs, money-laundering, illegal arms trafficking, and illegal movement of nuclear, chemical, biological and other potentially deadly materials, and in this regard *emphasizes* the need to enhance coordination of efforts on national, subregional, regional and international levels in order to strengthen a global response to this serious challenge and threat to international security;

5. *Declares* that acts, methods, and practices of terrorism are contrary to the purposes and principles of the United Nations and that knowingly financing, planning and inciting terrorist acts are also contrary to the purposes and principles of the United Nations;

6. *Decides* to establish, in accordance with rule 28 of its provisional rules of procedure, a Committee of the Security Council, consisting of all the members of the Council, to monitor implementation of this resolution, with the assistance of appropriate expertise, and *calls upon* all States to report to the Committee, no later than 90 days from the date of adoption of this resolution and thereafter according to a timetable to be proposed by the Committee, on the steps they have taken to implement this resolution;

7. *Directs* the Committee to delineate its tasks, submit a work programme within 30 days of the adoption of this resolution, and to consider the support it requires, in consultation with the Secretary-General;

8. *Expresses* its determination to take all necessary steps in order to ensure the full implementation of this resolution, in accordance with its responsibilities under the Charter;

9. *Decides* to remain seized of this matter.

APPENDIX 3

Tokyo Convention

No 10106

MULTILATERAL

**Convention on offences and certain other acts committed on board aircraft.
Signed at Tokyo on 14 September 1963**

Authentic texts: English, French and Spanish.

Registered by the International Civil Aviation Organization on 22 December 1969.

MULTILATÉRAL

**Convention relative aux infractions et à certains autres actes survenant à bord
des aéronefs. Signée à Tokyo le 14 septembre 1963**

Textes authentiques: anglais, français et espagnol.

Enregistrée par l'Organisation de l'aviation civile internationale le 22 décembre 1969.

CONVENTION[1] ON OFFENCES AND CERTAIN OTHER ACTS COMMITTED ON BOARD AIRCRAFT

The States Parties to this Convention

Have agreed as follows:

---

[1] Came into force on 4 December 1969 between the following States, ie, on the ninetieth day after the date of deposit with the International Civil Aviation Organization of the twelfth instrument of ratification by the said States, in accordance with article 21:

State	Date of deposit of the instrument
Portugal	25 November 1964[a]
Philippines	26 November 1965
Republic of China	28 February 1966
Denmark	17 January 1967[b]
Norway	17 January 1967[c]
Sweden	17 January 1967
Italy	18 October 1968
United Kingdom of Great Britain and Northern Ireland (With a declaration.)[d]	29 November 1968
Mexico	18 March 1969[e]
Upper Volta	6 June 1969
Niger	27 June 1969[f]
United States of America	5 September 1969

483

CHAPTER I

SCOPE OF THE CONVENTION

Article 1

1. This Convention shall apply in respect of:

   (*a*) offences against penal law;
   (*b*) acts which, whether or not they are offences, may or do jeopardize the safety of the aircraft or of persons or property therein or which jeopardize good order and discipline on board.

2. Except as provided in Chapter III, this Convention shall apply in respect of offences committed or acts done by a person on board any aircraft registered in a Contracting State, while that aircraft is in flight or on the surface of the high seas or of any other area outside the territory of any State.

3. For the purposes of this Convention, an aircraft is considered to be in flight from the moment when power is applied for the purpose of take-off until the moment when the landing run ends.

4. This Convention shall not apply to aircraft used in military, customs or police services.

Article 2

Without prejudice to the provisions of Article 4 and except when the safety of the aircraft or of persons or property on board so requires, no provision of this Convention shall be interpreted as authorizing or requiring any action in respect of offences against penal laws of a political nature or those based on racial or religious discrimination.

CHAPTER II

JURISDICTION

Article 3

1. The State of registration of the aircraft is competent to exercise jurisdiction over offences and acts committed on board.

2. Each Contracting State shall take such measures as may be necessary to establish its jurisdiction as the State of registration over offences committed on board aircraft registered in such State.

3. This Convention does not exclude any criminal jurisdiction exercised in accordance with national law.

Article 4

A Contracting State which is not the State of registration may not interfere with an aircraft in flight in order to exercise its criminal jurisdiction over an offence committed on board except in the following cases:

   (*a*) the offence has effect on the territory of such State;
   (*b*) the offence has been committed by or against a national or permanent resident of such State;

Subsequently, in accordance with article 21, the Convention came into force for the following State on the ninetieth day after the deposit of its instrument of ratification:

State	Date of deposit of the instrument
Israel..	19 September 1969 (With effect from 18 December 1969).

[a] Signature affixed on 11 March 1964: Ed. Brazão.
[b] Signature affixed on 21 November 1966: Mogens Juhl.
[c] Signature affixed on 19 April 1966: Bredo Stabell.
[d] [...]
[e] Signature affixed on 24 December 1968: José Rodríguez Torres.
[f] Signature affixed on 14 April 1969: Adamou Mayaki.

(c) the offence is against the security of such State;

(d) the offence consists of a breach of any rules or regulations relating to the flight or manœ uvre of aircraft in force in such State;

(e) the exercise of jurisdiction is necessary to ensure the observance of any obligation of such State under a multilateral international agreement.

CHAPTER III

POWERS OF THE AIRCRAFT COMMANDER

Article 5

1. The provisions of this Chapter shall not apply to offences and acts committed or about to be committed by a person on board an aircraft in flight in the airspace of the State of registration or over the high seas or any other area outside the territory of any State unless the last point of take-off or the next point of intended landing is situated in a State other than that of registration, or the aircraft subsequently flies in the airspace of a State other than that of registration with such person still on board.

2. Notwithstanding the provisions of Article 1, paragraph 3, an aircraft shall for the purposes of this Chapter, be considered to be in flight at any time from the moment when all its external doors are closed following embarkation until the moment when any such door is opened for disembarkation. In the case of a forced landing, the provisions of this Chapter shall continue to apply with respect to offences and acts committed on board until competent authorities of a State take over the responsibility for the aircraft and for the persons and property on board.

Article 6

1. The aircraft commander may, when he has reasonable grounds to believe that a person has committed, or is about to commit, on board the aircraft, an offence or act contemplated in Article 1, paragraph 1, impose upon such person reasonable measures including restraint which are necessary:

(a) to protect the safety of the aircraft, or of persons or property therein; or

(b) to maintain good order and discipline on board; or

(c) to enable him to deliver such person to competent authorities or to disembark him in accordance with the provisions of this Chapter.

2. The aircraft commander may require or authorize the assistance of other crew members and may request or authorize, but not require, the assistance of passengers to restrain any person whom he is entitled to restrain. Any crew member or passenger may also take reasonable preventive measures without such authorization when he has reasonable grounds to believe that such action is immediately necessary to protect the safety of the aircraft, or of persons or property therein.

Article 7

1. Measures of restraint imposed upon a person in accordance with Article 6 shall not be continued beyond any point at which the aircraft lands unless:

(a) such point is in the territory of a non-Contracting State and its authorities refuse to permit disembarkation of that person or those measures have been imposed in accordance with Article 6, paragraph 1 *(c)* in order to enable his delivery to competent authorities;

(b) the aircraft makes a forced landing and the aircraft commander is unable to deliver that person to competent authorities; or

(c) that person agrees to onward carriage under restraint.

2. The aircraft commander shall as soon as practicable, and if possible before landing in the territory of a State with a person on board who has been placed under restraint in accordance with the provisions of Article 6, notify the authorities of such State of the fact that a person on board is under restraint and of the reasons for such restraint.

Article 8

1. The aircraft commander may, in so far as it is necessary for the purpose of subparagraph *(a)* or *(b)* of paragraph 1 of Article 6, disembark in the territory of any State in which the aircraft lands any person who he has reasonable grounds to believe has committed, or is about to commit, on board the aircraft an act contemplated in Article 1, paragraph 1 *(b)*.

2. The aircraft commander shall report to the authorities of the State in which he disembarks any person pursuant to this Article, the fact of, and the reasons for, such disembarkation.

Article 9

1. The aircraft commander may deliver to the competent authorities of any Contracting State in the territory of which the aircraft lands any person who he has reasonable grounds to believe has committed on board the aircraft an act which, in his opinion, is a serious offence according to the penal law of the State of registration of the aircraft.

2. The aircraft commander shall as soon as practicable and if possible before landing in the territory of a Contracting State with a person on board whom the aircraft commander intends to deliver in accordance with the preceding paragraph, notify the authorities of such State of his intention to deliver such person and the reasons therefor.

3. The aircraft commander shall furnish the authorities to whom any suspected offender is delivered in accordance with the provisions of this Article with evidence and information which, under the law of the State of registration of the aircraft, are lawfully in his possession.

Article 10

For actions taken in accordance with this Convention, neither the aircraft commander, any other member of the crew, any passenger, the owner or operator of the aircraft, nor the person on whose behalf the flight was performed shall be held responsible in any proceeding on account of the treatment undergone by the person against whom the actions were taken.

CHAPTER IV

UNLAWFUL SEIZURE OF AIRCRAFT

Article 11

1. When a person on board has unlawfully committed by force or threat thereof an act of interference, seizure, or other wrongful exercise of control of an aircraft in flight or when such an act is about to be committed, Contracting States shall take all appropriate measures to restore control of the aircraft to its lawful commander or to preserve his control of the aircraft.

2. In the cases contemplated in the preceding paragraph, the Contracting State in which the aircraft lands shall permit its passengers and crew to continue their journey as soon as practicable, and shall return the aircraft and its cargo to the persons lawfully entitled to possession.

CHAPTER V

POWERS AND DUTIES OF STATES

Article 12

Any Contracting State shall allow the commander of an aircraft registered in another Contracting State to disembark any person pursuant to Article 8, paragraph 1.

Article 13

1. Any Contracting State shall take delivery of any person whom the aircraft commander delivers pursuant to Article 9, paragraph 1.

2. Upon being satisfied that the circumstances so warrant, any Contracting State shall take custody or other measures to ensure the presence of any person suspected of an act contemplated in Article 11, paragraph 1 and of any person of whom it has taken delivery. The custody and other measures shall be as provided in the law of that State but may only be continued for such time as is reasonably necessary to enable any criminal or extradition proceedings to be instituted.

3. Any person in custody pursuant to the previous paragraph shall be assisted in communicating immediately with the nearest appropriate representative of the State of which he is a national.

4. Any Contracting State, to which a person is delivered pursuant to Article 9, paragraph 1, or in whose territory an aircraft lands following the commission of an act contemplated in Article 11, paragraph 1, shall immediately make a preliminary enquiry into the facts.

5. When a State, pursuant to this Article, has taken a person into custody, it shall immediately notify the State of registration of the aircraft and the State of nationality of the detained person and, if it considers it advisable, any other interested State of the fact that such person is in custody and of the circumstances which warrant his detention. The State which makes the preliminary enquiry contemplated in paragraph 4 of this Article shall promptly report its findings to the said States and shall indicate whether it intends to exercise jurisdiction.

Article 14

1. When any person has been disembarked in accordance with Article 8, paragraph 1, or delivered in accordance with Article 9, paragraph 1, or has disembarked after committing an act contemplated in Article 11, paragraph 1, and when such person cannot or does not desire to continue his journey and the State of landing refuses to admit him, that State may, if the person in question is not a national or permanent resident of that State, return him to the territory of the State of which he is a national or permanent resident or to the territory of the State in which he began his journey by air.

2. Neither disembarkation, nor delivery, nor the taking of custody or other measures contemplated in Article 13, paragraph 2, nor return of the person concerned, shall be considered as admission to the territory of the Contracting State concerned for the purpose of its law relating to entry or admission of persons and nothing in this Convention shall affect the law of a Contracting State relating to the expulsion of persons from its territory.

Article 15

1. Without prejudice to Article 14, any person who has been disembarked in accordance with Article 8, paragraph 1, or delivered in accordance with Article 9, paragraph 1, or has disembarked after committing an act contemplated in Article 11, paragraph 1, and who desires to continue his journey shall be at liberty as soon as practicable to proceed to any destination of his choice unless his presence is required by the law of the State of landing for the purpose of extradition or criminal proceedings.

2. Without prejudice to its law as to entry and admission to, and extradition and expulsion from its territory, a Contracting State in whose territory a person has been disembarked in accordance with Article 8, paragraph 1, or delivered in accordance with Article 9, paragraph 1 or has disembarked and is suspected of having committed an act contemplated in Article 11, paragraph 1, shall accord to such person treatment which is no less favourable for his protection and security than that accorded to nationals of such Contracting State in like circumstances.

CHAPTER VI

OTHER PROVISIONS

Article 16

1. Offences committed on aircraft registered in a Contracting State shall be treated, for the purpose of extradition, as if they had been committed not only in the place in which they have occurred but also in the territory of the State of registration of the aircraft.

2. Without prejudice to the provisions of the preceding paragraph, nothing in this Convention shall be deemed to create an obligation to grant extradition.

Article 17

In taking any measures for investigation or arrest or otherwise exercising jurisdiction in connection with any offence committed on board an aircraft the Contracting States shall pay due regard to the safety and other interests of air navigation and shall so act as to avoid unnecessary delay of the aircraft, passengers, crew or cargo.

Article 18

If Contracting States establish joint air transport operating organizations or international operating agencies, which operate aircraft not registered in any one State those States shall, according to the circumstances of the case, designate the State among them which, for the purposes of this Convention, shall be considered as the State of registration and shall give notice thereof to the International Civil Aviation Organization which shall communicate the notice to all States Parties to this Convention.

CHAPTER VII

FINAL CLAUSES

Article 19

Until the date on which this Convention comes into force in accordance with the provisions of Article 21, it shall remain open for signature on behalf of any State which at that date is a Member of the United Nations or of any of the Specialized Agencies.

Article 20

1. This Convention shall be subject to ratification by the signatory States in accordance with their constitutional procedures.

2. The instruments of ratification shall be deposited with the International Civil Aviation Organization.

Article 21

1. As soon as twelve of the signatory States have deposited their instruments of ratification of this Convention, it shall come into force between them on the ninetieth day after the date of the deposit of the twelfth instrument of ratification. It shall come into force for each State ratifying thereafter on the ninetieth day after the deposit of its instrument of ratification.

2. As soon as this Convention comes into force, it shall be registered with the Secretary-General of the United Nations by the International Civil Aviation Organization.

Article 22

1. This Convention shall, after it has come into force, be open for accession by any State Member of the United Nations or of any of the Specialized Agencies.

2. The accession of a State shall be effected by the deposit of an instrument of accession with the International Civil Aviation Organization and shall take effect on the ninetieth day after the date of such deposit.

Article 23

1. Any Contracting State may denounce this Convention by notification addressed to the International Civil Aviation Organization.

2. Denunciation shall take effect six months after the date of receipt by the International Civil Aviation Organization of the notification of denunciation.

Article 24

1. Any dispute between two or more Contracting States concerning the interpretation or application of this Convention which cannot be settled through negotiation, shall, at the request of one of them, be submitted to arbitration. If within six months from the date of the request for arbitration the Parties are unable to agree on the organization of the arbitration, any one of those Parties may refer the dispute to the International Court of Justice by request in conformity with the Statute of the Court.

2. Each State may at the time of signature or ratification of this Convention or accession thereto, declare that it does not consider itself bound by the preceding paragraph. The other Contracting States shall not be bound by the preceding paragraph with respect to any Contracting State having made such a reservation.

3. Any Contracting State having made a reservation in accordance with the preceding paragraph may at any time withdraw this reservation by notification to the International Civil Aviation Organization.

Article 25

Except as provided in Article 24 no reservation may be made to this Convention.

Article 26

The International Civil Aviation Organization shall give notice to all States Members of the United Nations or of any of the Specialized Agencies:

(a) of any signature of this Convention and the date thereof;
(b) of the deposit of any instrument of ratification or accession and the date thereof;
(c) of the date on which this Convention comes into force in accordance with Article 21, paragraph 1;
(d) of the receipt of any notification of denunciation and the date thereof; and
(e) of the receipt of any declaration or notification made under Article 24 and the date thereof.

IN WITNESS WHEREOF the undersigned Plenipotentiaries, having been duly authorized, have signed this Convention.

DONE at Tokyo on the fourteenth day of September One Thousand Nine Hundred and Sixty-three in three authentic texts drawn up in the English, French and Spanish languages.

This Convention shall be deposited with the International Civil Aviation Organization with which, in accordance with Article 19, it shall remain open for signature and the said Organization shall send certified copies thereof to all States Members of the United Nations or of any Specialized Agency.

APPENDIX 4

Hague Convention

No 12325

MULTILATERAL

Convention for the suppression of unlawful seizure of aircraft.
Signed at The Hague on 16 December 1970

Authentic texts: English, French, Russian and Spanish.

Registered by the Union of Soviet Socialist Republics, the United Kingdom of Great Britain and Northern Ireland and the United States of America on 8 March 1973.

MULTILATÉRAL

Convention pour la répression de la capture illicite d'aéronefs.
Signée à La Haye le 16 décembre 1970

Textes authentiques: anglais, français, russe et espagnol.

Enregistrée par l'Union des Républiques socialistes soviétiques, le Royaume-Uni de Grande-Bretagne et d'Irlande du Nord et les États-Unis d'Amérique le 8 mars 1973.

CONVENTION[1] FOR THE SUPPRESSION OF UNLAWFUL SEIZURE OF AIRCRAFT

PREAMBLE

The States Parties to this Convention

Considering that unlawful acts of seizure or exercise of control of aircraft in flight jeopardize the safety of persons and property, seriously affect the operation of air services, and undermine the confidence of the peoples of the world in the safety of civil aviation;

---

[1] Came into force on 14 October 1971 for the States indicated hereafter, ie 30 days following the date (14 September 1971) by which the instruments of ratification of ten signatory States having participated in The Hague Conference had been deposited with the Governments of the Union of Soviet Socialist Republics, the United Kingdom of Great Britain and Northern Ireland or the United States of America, designated as the depositary Governments, in accordance with article 13 (3):

State	*Date of deposit of the instrument of ratification at London (L), Moscow (M) or Washington (W)*
Japan	19April 1971 (L, M, W)
Bulgaria	19 May 1971 (W)
	26 May 1971 (L)
	23 February 1972 (M)
Ecuador	14 June 1971 (W)
Sweden	7 July 1971 (L, M, W)

Considering that the occurrence of such acts is a matter of grave concern;

Considering that, for the purpose of deterring such acts, there is an urgent need to provide appropriate measures for punishment of offenders;

Have agreed as follows:

Article 1

Any person who on board an aircraft in flight:

- (*a*) unlawfully, by force or threat thereof, or by any other form of intimidation, seizes, or exercises control of, that aircraft, or attempts to perform any such act, or
- (*b*) is an accomplice of a person who performs or attempts to perform any such act commits an offence (hereinafter referred to as 'the offence').

Article 2

Each Contracting State undertakes to make the offence punishable by severe penalties.

Costa Rica	9 July 1971 (W)
Gabon	14 July 1971 (L)
Hungary	13 August 1971 (L, M, W)
Israel	16 August 1971 (L, M, W)
Norway	23 August 1971 (L, M, W)
Switzerland	14 September 1971 (L, M, W)
United States of America	14 September 1971 (W)
	21 September 1971 (L)
	23 September 1971 M)

Subsequently, the Convention came into force for each of the following States 30 days following the date of deposit of their instrument of ratification or accession, in accordance with article 13 (4):

State	*Date of deposit of the instrument of ratification or accession (a) at London (L), Moscow (M) or Washington (W)*	*Date of entry into force*
Argentina	11 September 1972 (W)	11 October 1972
	20 September 1972 (M)	
	21 September 1972 (L)	
Australia	9 November 1972 (L, M, W)	9 December 1972
Brazil	14 January 1972 (L, M, W)	13 February 1972
Byelorussian Soviet Socialist Republic	30 December 1971 (M)	29 January 1972
Canada	19 June 1972 (L)	19 July 1972
	20 June 1972 (W)	
	23 June 1972 (M)	
Chad	12 July 1972 (W)	11 August 1972
	12 July 1972 a (L)	
	17 August 1972 a (M)	
Chile	2 February 1972 (L)	3 March 1972
Cyprus	6 June 1972 a (L)	6 July 1972
	8 June 1972 a (M)	
	5 July 1972 a (W)	
Czechoslovakia	6 April 1972 (L, M, W)	6 May 1972
Dahomey	13 March 1972 (W)	12 April 1972
Denmark	17 October 1972 (L, M, W)	16 November 1972

(Decision reserved as regards the application of the Convention to the Faeroe Islands and Greenland.)

Article 3

1. For the purposes of this Convention, an aircraft is considered to be in flight at any time from the moment when all its external doors are closed following embarkation until the moment when any such door is opened for disembarkation. In the case of a forced landing, the flight shall be deemed to continue until the competent authorities take over the responsibility for the aircraft and for persons and property on board.

2. This Convention shall not apply to aircraft used in military, customs or police services.

3. This Convention shall apply only if the place of take-off or the place of actual landing of the aircraft on board which the offence is committed is situated outside the territory of the State of registration of that aircraft; it shall be immaterial whether the aircraft is engaged in an international or domestic flight.

State	*Date of deposit of the instrument of ratification or accession (a) at London (L), Moscow (M) or Washington (W)*	*Date of entry into force*
Fiji..................................	27 July 1972 (W) 14 August 1972 (L) 29 August 1972 (M)	26 August 1972
Finland	15 December 1971 (L, M, W)	14 January 1972
France...............................	18 September 1972 (L, M, W)	18 October 1972
German Democratic Republic..........	3 June 1971 (M)	14 October 1971
Iran.................................	25 January 1972 (L, W) 2 February 1972 (M)	24 February 1972
Iraq..................................	3 December 1971 (M) 4 January 1972 (L)	2 January 1972
Jordan..............................	16 November 1971 (M) 18 November 1971 (W) 1 December 1971 (L)	16 December 1971
Mali.................................	17 August 1971 a (M) 29 September 1971 a (W)	14 October 1971
Mexico..............................	19 July 1972 (L, M, W)	18 August 1972
Mongolia	8 October 1971 (M)	7 November 1971
Niger................................	15 October 1971 (W)	14 November 1971
Panama..............................	10 March 1972 (W)	9 April 1972
Paraguay	4 February 1972 (W)	5 March 1972
Poland	21 March 1972 (L, M, W)	20 April 1972
Portugal............................	27 November,1972 IL)	27 December 1972
Republic of China............................	27 July 1972 (W)	26 August 1972
Romania	10 July 1972 (L, M, W)	9 August 1972
South Africa........................	30 May 1972 (W)	29 June 1972
Spain	30 October 1972 (W)	29 November 1972
Trinidad and Tobago	31 January 1972 (L)	1 March 1972
Uganda..............................	27 March 1972 a (L)	26 April 1972
Ukrainian Soviet Socialist Republic	21 February 1972 (M)	22 March 1972
Union of Soviet Socialist Republics................................	24 September 1971 (L, M, W)	24 October 1971
United Kingdom of Great Britain and Northern Ireland	22 December 1971 (L, M, W)	21 January 1972

(In respect of the United Kingdom of Great Britain and Northern Ireland and Territories under the territorial sovereignty of the United Kingdom, as well as the British Solomon Islands Protectorate.)

Yugoslavia	2 October 1972 (L, M, W)	1 November 1972

4. In the cases mentioned in article 5, this Convention shall not apply if the place of take-off and the place of actual landing of the aircraft on board which the offence is committed are situated within the territory of the same State where that State is one of those referred to in that Article.

5. Notwithstanding paragraphs 3 and 4 of this article, articles 6, 7, 8 and 10 shall apply whatever the place of take-off or the place of actual landing of the aircraft, if the offender or the alleged offender is found in the territory of a State other than the State of registration of that aircraft.

Article 4

1. Each Contracting State shall take such measures as may be necessary to establish its jurisdiction over the offence and any other act of violence against passengers or crew committed by the alleged offender in connection with the offence, in the following cases:

   (a) when the offence is committed on board an aircraft registered in that State;
   (b) when the aircraft on board which the offence is committed lands in its territory with the alleged offender still on board;
   (c) when the offence is committed on board an aircraft leased without crew to a lessee who has his principal place of business or, if the lessee has no such place of business, his permanent residence, in that State.

2. Each Contracting State shall likewise take such measures as may be necessary to establish its jurisdiction over the offence in the case where the alleged offender is present in its territory and it does not extradite him pursuant to article 8 to any of the States mentioned in paragraph 1 of this article.

3. This Convention does not exclude any criminal jurisdiction exercised in accordance with national law.

Article 5

The Contracting States which establish joint air transport operating organizations or international operating agencies, which operate aircraft which are subject to joint or international registration shall, by appropriate means, designate for each aircraft the State among them which shall exercise the jurisdiction and have the attributes of the State of registration for the purpose of this Convention and shall give notice thereof to the International Civil Aviation Organization which shall communicate the notice to all States Parties to this Convention.

Article 6

1. Upon being satisfied that the circumstances so warrant, any Contracting State in the territory of which the offender or the alleged offender is present, shall take him into custody or take other measures to ensure his presence. The custody and other measures shall be as provided in the law of that State but may only be continued for such time as is necessary to enable any criminal or extradition proceedings to be instituted.

2. Such State shall immediately make a preliminary enquiry into the facts.

3. Any person in custody pursuant to paragraph 1 of this article shall be assisted in communicating immediately with the nearest appropriate representative of the State of which he is a national.

4. When a State, pursuant to this article, has taken a person into custody, it shall immediately notify the State of registration of the aircraft, the State mentioned in article 4, paragraph 1 *(c)*, the State of nationality of the detained person and, if it considers it advisable, any other interested States of the fact that such person is in custody and of the circumstances which warrant his detention. The State which makes the preliminary enquiry contemplated in paragraph 2 of this Article shall promptly report its findings to the said States and shall indicate whether it intends to exercise jurisdiction.

Article 7

The Contracting State in the territory of which the alleged offender is found shall, if it does not extradite him, be obliged, without exception whatsoever and whether or not the offence was committed in its territory, to submit the case to its competent authorities for the purpose of prosecution. Those authorities shall take their decision in the same manner as in the case of any ordinary offence of a serious nature under the law of that State.

Article 8

1. The offence shall be deemed to be included as an extraditable offence in any extradition treaty existing between Contracting States. Contracting States undertake to include the offence as an extraditable offence in every extradition treaty to be concluded between them.

2. If a Contracting State which makes extradition conditional on the existence of a treaty receives a request for extradition from another Contracting State with which it has no extradition treaty, it may at its option consider this Convention as the legal basis for extradition in respect of the offence. Extradition shall be subject to the other conditions provided by the law of the requested State.

3. Contracting States which do not make extradition conditional on the existence of a treaty shall recognize the offence as an extraditable offence between themselves subject to the conditions provided by the law of the requested State.

4. The offence shall be treated, for the purpose of extradition between Contracting States, as if it had been committed not only in the place in which it occurred but also in the territories of the States required to establish their jurisdiction in accordance with article 4, paragraph 1.

Article 9

1. When any of the acts mentioned in article 1 *(a)* has occurred or is about to occur, Contracting States shall take all appropriate measures to restore control of the aircraft to its lawful commander or to preserve his control of the aircraft.

2. In the cases contemplated by the preceding paragraph, any Contracting State in which the aircraft or its passengers or crew are present shall facilitate the continuation of the journey of the passengers and crew as soon as practicable, and shall without delay return the aircraft and its cargo to the persons lawfully entitled to possession.

Article 10

1. Contracting States shall afford one another the greatest measure of assistance in connection with criminal proceedings brought in respect of the offence and other acts mentioned in article 4. The law of the State requested shall apply in all cases.

2. The provisions of paragraph 1 of this article shall not affect obligations under any other treaty, bilateral or multilateral, which governs or will govern, in whole or in part, mutual assistance in criminal matters.

Article 11

Each Contracting State shall in accordance with its national law report to the Council of the International Civil Aviation Organization as promptly as possible any relevant information in its possession concerning:

  (a) the circumstances of the offence;
  (b) the action taken pursuant to article 9;
  (c) the measures taken in relation to the offender or the alleged offender, and, in particular, the results of any extradition proceedings or other legal proceedings.

Article 12

1. Any dispute between two or more Contracting States concerning the interpretation or application of this Convention which cannot be settled through negotiation, shall, at the request of one of them, be submitted to arbitration. If within six months from the date of the request for arbitration the Parties are unable to agree on the organization of the arbitration, any one of those Parties may refer the dispute to the International Court of Justice by request in conformity with the Statute of the Court.

2. Each State may at the time of signature or ratification of this Convention or accession thereto, declare that it does not consider itself bound by the preceding paragraph. The other Contracting States shall not be bound by the preceding paragraph with respect to any Contracting State having made such a reservation.

3. Any Contracting State having made a reservation in accordance with the preceding paragraph may at any time withdraw this reservation by notification to the Depositary Governments.

Article 13

1. This Convention shall be open for signature at The Hague on 16 December 1970, by States participating in the International Conference on Air Law held at The Hague from 1 to 16 December 1970 (hereinafter referred to as The Hague Conference). After 31 December 1970, the Convention shall be open to all States for signature in Moscow, London and Washington. Any State which does not sign this Convention before its entry into force in accordance with paragraph 3 of this article may accede to it at any time.

2. This Convention shall be subject to ratification by the signatory States. Instruments of ratification and instruments of accession shall be deposited with the Governments of the Union of Soviet Socialist Republics, the United Kingdom of Great Britain and Northern Ireland, and the United States of America, which are hereby designated the Depositary Governments.

3. This Convention shall enter into force thirty days following the date of the deposit of instruments of ratification by ten States signatory to this Convention which participated in The Hague Conference.

4. For other States, this Convention shall enter into force on the date of entry into force of this Convention in accordance with paragraph 3 of this article, or thirty days following the date of deposit of their instruments of ratification or accession, whichever is later.

5. The Depositary Governments shall promptly inform all signatory and acceding States of the date of each signature, the date of deposit of each instrument of ratification or accession, the date of entry into force of this Convention, and other notices.

6. As soon as this Convention comes into force, it shall be registered by the Depositary Governments pursuant to Article 102 of the Charter of the United Nations and pursuant to Article 83 of the Convention on International Civil Aviation (Chicago, 1944).

Article 14

1. Any Contracting State may denounce this Convention by written notification to the Depositary Governments.

2. Denunciation shall take effect six months following the date on which notification is received by the Depositary Governments.

IN WITNESS WHEREOF the undersigned Plenipotentiaries, being duly authorised thereto by their Governments, have signed this Convention.

DONE at The Hague, this sixteenth day of December, one thousand nine hundred and seventy, in three originals, each being drawn up in four authentic texts in the English, French, Russian and Spanish languages.

APPENDIX 5

Montreal Convention and Protocol

No 14118

MULTILATERAL

Convention for the suppression of unlawful acts against the safety of civil aviation
(with Final Act of the International Conference on Air Law held under the auspices of the
International Civil Aviation Organization at Montreal in September 1971).
Concluded at Montreal on 23 September 1971

Authentic texts: English, French, Russian and Spanish.

*Registered by the United States of America, the United Kingdom of Great Britain and Northern Ireland
and the Union of Soviet Socialist Republics on 18 July 1975.*

MULTILATÉRAL

Convention pour la répression d'actes illicites dirigés contre la sécurité de l'aviation civile
(avec Acte final de la Conférence internationale de droit aérien tenue sous les
auspices de l'Organisation de l'aviation civile internationale à Montréal
en septembre 1971). Conclue à Montréal le 23 septembre 1971

Textes authentiques: anglais, français, russe et espagnol.

*Enregistrée par les États-Unis d'Amérique, le Royaume-Uni de Grande-Bretagne et d'Irlande du Nord et
l'Union des Républiques socialistes soviétiques le 18 juillet 1975.*

CONVENTION[1] FOR THE SUPPRESSION OF UNLAWFUL ACTS
AGAINST THE SAFETY OF CIVIL AVIATION

The States Parties to the Convention,

Considering that unlawful acts against the safety of civil aviation jeopardize the safety of persons and
property, seriously affect the operation of air services, and undermine the confidence of the peoples
of the world in the safety of civil aviation;

---

[1] Came into force on 26 January 1973 in respect of the following States, on behalf of which an instrument of
ratification or accession had been deposited with the Governments of the Union of Soviet Socialist Republics,
the United Kingdom of Great Britain and Northern Ireland or the United States of America, ie 30 days following the date (27 December 1972) of deposit of the instruments of ratification of ten signatory States having
participated in the Montreal Conference, in accordance with article 15 (3):

State	Date of deposit of instrument of ratification or accession (a) at London (L), Moscow (M) or Washington (W)
Brazil	24 July 1972 (L, M, W)
Canada	19 June 1972 (L)
	20 June 1972 (W)
	23 July 1972 (M)

497

Considering that the occurrence of such acts is a matter of grave concern;

Considering that, for the purpose of deterring such acts, there is an urgent need to provide appropriate measures for punishment of offenders;

Have agreed as follows:

Article 1

1. Any person commits an offence if he unlawfully and intentionally:

   (a) performs an act of violence against a person on board an aircraft in flight if that act is likely to endanger the safety of that aircraft; or

   (b) destroys an aircraft in service or causes damage to such an aircraft which renders it incapable of flight or which is likely to endanger its safety in flight; or

   (c) places or causes to be placed on an aircraft in service, by any means whatsoever, a device or substance which is likely to destroy that aircraft, or to cause damage to it which renders it incapable of flight, or to cause damage to it which is likely to endanger its safety in flight; or

   (d) destroys or damages air navigation facilities or interferes with their operation, if any such act is likely to endanger the safety of aircraft in flight; or

   (e) communicates information which he knows to be false, thereby endangering the safety of an aircraft in flight.

Chad	12 July 1972 (L, W)
	17 August 1972 (M)
German Democratic Republic	9 July 1972 (M)
Guyana	21 December 1972 *a* (W)
Hungary	27 December 1972 (L, M, W)
Israel	30 June 1972 (L)
	6 July 1972 (W)
	10 July 1972 (M)
Malawi	21 December 1972 *a* (W)
Mali	24 August 1972 *a* (W)
Mongolia	5 September 1972 (W)
	14 September 1972 (L)
	20 October 1972 (M)
Niger	1 September 1972 (W)
Panama	24 April 1972 (W)
Republic of China	27 December 1972 (W)
South Africa	30 May 1972 (W)
Spain	30 October 1972 (W)
Trinidad and Tobago	9 February 1972 (W)
United States of America	1 November 1972 (W)
	15 November 1972 (L)
	22 November 1972 (M)
Yugoslavia	2 October 1972 (L, M, W)

Subsequently, the Convention came into force for the States listed below 30 days after the date of deposit of their instrument of ratification or accession with the Governments of the Union of Soviet Socialist Republics, the United Kingdom of Great Britain and Northern Ireland or the United States of America, in accordance with article 15 (4):

State	*Date of deposit of instrument of ratification or accession (a) at London (L), Moscow (M) or Washington (W)*
Argentina	26 November 1973 (L, M, W)
(With effect from 25 December 1973)	
Australia	12 July 1973 (L, M, W)
(With effect from 11 August 1973)	
Austria	11 February 1973 (L, M, W)
(With effect from 13 March 1974)	

2. Any person also commits an offence if he:

  (a) attempts to commit any of the offences mentioned in paragraph 1 of this Article; or

  (b) is an accomplice of a person who commits or attempts to commit any such offence.

Article 2

For the purposes of this Convention:

  (a) an aircraft is considered to be in flight at any time from the moment when all its external doors are closed following embarkation until the moment when any such door is opened for disembarkation; in the case of a forced landing, the flight shall be deemed to continue until the competent authorities take over the responsibility for the aircraft and for persons and property on board;

Bulgaria..	22 February 1973 (L)
(With effect from 24 March 1973)	28 March 1973 (W)
	20 March 1974 (M)
Byelorussian Soviet Socialist Republic.....................................	31 January 1973 (M)
(With effect from 2 March 1973)	
Chile..	28 February 1974 *a* (W)
(With effect from 30 March 1974)	
Costa Rica...	21 September 1973 (W)
(With effect from 21 October 1973)	
Cyprus	27 July 1973 (L)
(With effect from 14 September 1973)	30 July 1973 (M)
	15 August 1973 (W)
Czechoslovakia	10 August 1973 (L, M, W)
(With effect from 9 September 1973)	
Denmark..	17 January 1973 (L, M, W)
(With effect from 16 February 1973. Decision	
reserved as regards the application of the	
Convention to the Faroe Islands and Greenland)	
Dominican Republic..	28 November 1973 (W)
(With effect from 28 December 1973)	
Fiji	5 March 1973 (W)
(With effect from 4 April 1973)	18 April 1973 (L)
	28 April 1973 (M)
Finland..	13 July 1973 *a* (L, M, W)
(With effect from 12 August 1973)	
Ghana	12 December 1973 *a* (W)
(With effect from 11 January 1974)	
Greece..	15 January 1974 (W)
(With effect from 14 February 1974)	
Iceland	29 June 1973 (M)
(With effect from 29 July 1973)...	29 June 1973 *a* (L, W)
Iran	10 July 1973 *a* (L, M, W)
(With effect from 9 August 1973)	
Iraq	10 September 1974 *a* (M)
(With effect from 10 October 1974)	
Italy...	19 February 1974 (L, M, W)
(With effect from 21 March 1974)	
Ivory Coast..	9 January 1973 *a* (W)
(With effect from 8 February 1973)	
Japan...	12 June 1974 *a* (L, W)
(With effect from 12 July 1974)	
Jordan	13 February 1973 (L)
(With effect from 15 March 1973)...	19 February 1973 (M)
	25 April 1973 (W)

499

(b) an aircraft is considered to be in service from the beginning of the preflight preparation of the aircraft by ground personnel or by the crew for a specific flight until twenty-four hours after any landing; the period of service shall, in any event, extend for the entire period during which the aircraft is in flight as defined in paragraph *(a)* of this Article.

Article 3

Each Contracting State undertakes to make the offences mentioned in Article 1 punishable by severe penalties.

Libyan Arab Republic .... (With effect from 21 March 1974)	19 February 1974 *a* (W)
Mexico .... (With effect from 12 October 1974)	12 September 1974 (L, M, W)
Netherlands.. (With effect from 26 September 1973 for the Kingdom in Europe and Surinam, and with a declaration to the effect that the Convention shall apply to the Netherlands Antilles from 11 June 1974)	27 August 1973 (L, M, W)
New Zealand... (With effect from 14 March 1974)	12 February 1974 (L, M, W)
Nicaragua... (With effect from 6 December 1973)	6 November 1973 (W)
Nigeria... (With effect from 2 August 1973)	3 July 1973 *a* (W) 9 July 1973 *a* (L) 20 July 1973 *a* (M)
Norway .... (With effect from 31 August 1973)	1 August 1973 *a* (L, M, W)
Pakistan.. (With effect from 15 February 1974)	16 January 1974 *a* (M) 24 January 1974 *a* (L, W)
Paraguay... (With effect from 4 April 1974)	5 March 1974 (W)
Philippines .... (With effect from 25 April 1973)	26 March 1973 (W)
Poland.. (With effect from 27 February 1975)	26 January 1975 (L, M)
Portugal.. (With effect from 14 February 1973)	15 January 1973 (L)
Republic of Korea .... (With effect from 1 September 1973)	2 August 1973 *a* (W)
Saudi Arabia... (With effect from 14 July 1974)	14 June 1974 *a* (W)
Sweden.. (With effect from 9 August 1973)	10 July 1973 *a* (L, M, W)
Ukrainian Soviet Socialist Republic .... (With effect from 28 March 1973)	26 February 1973 (M)
Union of Soviet Socialist Republics..................................... (With effect from 21 March 1973)	19 February 1973 (L, M, W)
United Kingdom of Great Britain and Northern Ireland .... (With effect from 24 November 1973. In respect of the United Kingdom of Great Britain and Northern Ireland and Territories under the territorial sovereignty of the United Kingdom as well as the British Solomon Islands Protectorate)	25 October 1973 (L, M, W)
United Republic of Cameroon... (With effect from 10 August 1973)	11 July 1973 *a* (W)

Article 4

1. This Convention shall not apply to aircraft used in military, customs or police services.

2. In the cases contemplated in subparagraphs *(a)*, *(b)*, *(c)* and *(e)* of paragraph 1 of Article 1, this Convention shall apply, irrespective of whether the aircraft is engaged in an international or domestic flight, only if:

    (a) the place of take-off or landing, actual or intended, of the aircraft is situated outside the territory of the State of registration of that aircraft; or

    (b) the offence is committed in the territory of a State other than the State of registration of the aircraft.

3. Notwithstanding paragraph 2 of this Article, in the cases contemplated in subparagraphs *(a)*, *(b)*, *(c)* and *(e)* of paragraph 1 of Article 1, this Convention shall also apply if the offender or the alleged offender is found in the territory of a State other than the State of registration of the aircraft.

4. With respect to the States mentioned in Article 9 and in the cases mentioned in subparagraphs *(a)*, *(b)*, *(c)* and *(e)* of paragraph 1 of Article 1, this Convention shall not apply if the places referred to in subparagraph *(a)* of paragraph 2 of this Article are situated within the territory of the same State where that State is one of those referred to in Article 9, unless the offence is committed or the offender or alleged offender is found in the territory of a State other than that State.

5. In the cases contemplated in subparagraph *(d)* of paragraph 1 of Article 1, this Convention shall apply only if the air navigation facilities are used in international air navigation.

6. The provisions of paragraphs 2, 3, 4 and 5 of this Article shall also apply in the cases contemplated in paragraph 2 of Article 1.

Article 5

1. Each Contracting State shall take such measures as may be necessary to establish its jurisdiction over the offences in the following cases:

    (a) when the offence is committed in the territory of that State;

    (b) when the offence is committed against or on board an aircraft registered in that State;

    (c) when the aircraft on board which the offence is committed lands in its territory with the alleged offender still on board;

    (d) when the offence is committed against or on board an aircraft leased without crew to a lessee who has his principal place of business or, if the lessee has no such place of business, his permanent residence, in that State.

2. Each Contracting State shall likewise take such measures as may be necessary to establish its jurisdiction over the offences mentioned in Article 1, paragraph 1 *(a)*, *(b)* and *(c)*, and in Article 1, paragraph 2, in so far as that paragraph relates to those offences, in the case where the alleged offender is present in its territory and it does not extradite him pursuant to Article 8 to any of the States mentioned in paragraph 1 of this Article.

3. This Convention does not exclude any criminal jurisdiction exercised in accordance with national law.

Article 6

1. Upon being satisfied that the circumstances so warrant, any Contracting State in the territory of which the offender or the alleged offender is present, shall take him into custody or take other measures to ensure his presence. The custody and other measures shall be as provided in the law of that State but may only be continued for such time as is necessary to enable any criminal or extradition proceedings to be instituted.

2. Such State shall immediately make a preliminary enquiry into the facts.

3. Any person in custody pursuant to paragraph 1 of this Article shall be assisted in communicating immediately with the nearest appropriate representative of the State of which he is a national.

4. When a State, pursuant to this Article, has taken a person into custody, it shall immediately notify the States mentioned in Article 5, paragraph 1, the State of nationality of the detained person and, if it considers it advisable, any other interested State of the fact that such person is in custody and of the circumstances which warrant his detention. The State which makes the preliminary enquiry contemplated in paragraph 2 of this Article shall promptly report its findings to the said States and shall indicate whether it intends to exercise jurisdiction.

Article 7

The Contracting State in the territory of which the alleged offender is found shall, if it does not extradite him, be obliged, without exception whatsoever and whether or not the offence was committed in its territory, to submit the case to its competent authorities for the purpose of prosecution. Those authorities shall take their decision in the same manner as in the case of any ordinary offence of a serious nature under the law of that State.

Article 8

1. The offences shall be deemed to be included as extraditable offences in any extradition treaty existing between Contracting States. Contracting States undertake to include the offences as extraditable offences in every extradition treaty to be concluded between them.

2. If a Contracting State which makes extradition conditional on the existence of a treaty receives a request for extradition from another Contracting State with which it has no extradition treaty, it may at its option consider this Convention as the legal basis for extradition in respect of the offences. Extradition shall be subject to the other conditions provided by the law of the requested State.

3. Contracting States which do not make extradition conditional on the existence of a treaty shall recognize the offences as extraditable offences between themselves subject to the conditions provided by the law of the requested State.

4. Each of the offences shall be treated, for the purpose of extradition between Contracting States, as if it had been committed not only in the place in which it occurred but also in the territories of the States required to establish their jurisdiction in accordance with Article 5, paragraph 1 *(b)*, *(c)* and *(d)*.

Article 9

The Contracting States which establish joint air transport operating organizations or international operating agencies, which operate aircraft which are subject to joint or international registration shall, by appropriate means, designate for each aircraft the State among them which shall exercise the jurisdiction and have the attributes of the State of registration for the purpose of this Convention and shall give notice thereof to the International Civil Aviation Organization which shall communicate the notice to all States Parties to this Convention.

Article 10

1. Contracting States shall, in accordance with international and national law, endeavour to take all practicable measures for the purpose of preventing the offences mentioned in Article 1.

2. When, due to the commission of one of the offences mentioned in Article 1, a flight has been delayed or interrupted, any Contracting State in whose territory the aircraft or passengers or crew are present shall facilitate the continuation of the journey of the passengers and crew as soon as practicable, and shall without delay return the aircraft and its cargo to the persons lawfully entitled to possession.

Article 11

1. Contracting States shall afford one another the greatest measure of assistance in connection with criminal proceedings brought in respect of the offences. The law of the State requested shall apply in all cases.

2. The provisions of paragraph 1 of this Article shall not affect obligations under any other treaty, bilateral or multilateral, which governs or will govern, in whole or in part, mutual assistance in criminal matters.

Article 12

Any Contracting State having reason to believe that one of the offences mentioned in Article 1 will be committed shall, in accordance with its national law, furnish any relevant information in its possession to those States which it believes would be the States mentioned in Article 5, paragraph 1.

Article 13

Each Contracting State shall in accordance with its national law report to the Council of the International Civil Aviation Organization as promptly as possible any relevant information in its possession concerning:

    (a) the circumstances of the offence;
    (b) the action taken pursuant to Article 10, paragraph 2;
    (c) the measures taken in relation to the offender or the alleged offender and, in particular, the results of any extradition proceedings or other legal proceedings.

Article 14

1. Any dispute between two or more Contracting States concerning the interpretation or application of this Convention which cannot be settled through negotiation, shall, at the request of one of them, be submitted to arbitration. If within six months from the date of the request for arbitration the Parties are unable to agree on the organization of the arbitration, any one of those Parties may refer the dispute to the International Court of Justice by request in conformity with the Statute of the Court.

2. Each State may at the time of signature or ratification of this Convention or accession thereto, declare that it does not consider itself bound by the preceding paragraph. The other Contracting States shall not be bound by the preceding paragraph with respect to any Contracting State having made such a reservation.

3. Any Contracting State having made a reservation in accordance with the preceding paragraph may at any time withdraw this reservation by notification to the Depositary Governments.

Article 15

1. This Convention shall be open for signature at Montreal on 23 September 1971, by States participating in the International Conference on Air Law held at Montreal from 8 to 23 September 1971 (hereinafter referred to as the Montreal Conference). After 10 October 1971, the Convention shall be open to all States for signature in Moscow, London and Washington. Any State which does not sign this Convention before its entry into force in accordance with paragraph 3 of this Article may accede to it at any time.

2. This Convention shall be subject to ratification by the signatory States. Instruments of ratification and instruments of accession shall be deposited with the Governments of the Union of Soviet Socialist Republics, the United Kingdom of Great Britain and Northern Ireland, and the United States of America, which are hereby designated the Depositary Governments.

3. This Convention shall enter into force thirty days following the date of the deposit of instruments of ratification by ten States signatory to this Convention which participated in the Montreal Conference.

4. For other States, this Convention shall enter into force on the date of entry into force of this Convention in accordance with paragraph 3 of this Article, or thirty days following the date of deposit of their instruments of ratification or accession, whichever is later.

5. The Depositary Governments shall promptly inform all signatory and acceding States of the date of each signature, the date of deposit of each instrument of ratification or accession, the date of entry into force of this Convention, and other notices.

6. As soon as this Convention comes into force, it shall be registered by the Depositary Governments pursuant to Article 102 of the Convention on International Civil Aviation (Chicago, 1944).[2]

Article 16

1. Any Contracting State may denounce this Convention by written notification to the Depositary Governments.

2. Denunciation shall take effect six months following the date on which notification is received by the Depositary Governments.

IN WITNESS WHEREOF the undersigned Plenipotentiaries, being duly authorized thereto by their Governments, have signed this Convention.

DONE at Montreal, this twenty-third day of September, one thousand nine hundred and seventy-one, in three originals, each being drawn up in four authentic texts in the English, French, Russian and Spanish languages.

Montreal Protocol

No 14118

Convention for the Suppression of Unlawful Acts against the Safety of Civil Aviation. Concluded at Montreal on 23 September 1971[3]

Protocol[4] for the Supression of Unlawful Acts of Violence at Airports Serving International Civil Aviation, Supplementary to the Above-Mentioned Convention (With Final Act). Concluded at Montreal on 24 February 1988.

Authentic texts: English, French, Russian and Spanish.

Registered by the International Civil Aviation Organization on 22 December 1990.

---

[2] United Nations, *Treaty Series,* vol 15, p 295. For the texts of the Protocols amending this Convention, see vol 320, pp 209 and 217; vol 418, p 161; vol 514, p 209; vol 740, p 21, and vol 893, p 117.

[3] United Nations, *Treaty Series,* vol 974, p 177; for subsequent actions, see references in Cumulative Index No 17, as well as annex A in volumes 1058, 1107, 1126, 1144, 1195, 1214, 1217 (corrigendum to volume 974), 1259, 1286, 1297, 1308, 1338, 1484, 1491, 1505, 1510, 1511, 1563 and 1579.

[4] Came into force on 6 August 1989 in respect of the following States, on behalf of which an instrument of ratification had been deposited with the Governments of the Union of Soviet Socialist Republics, the United Kingdom of Great Britain and Northern Ireland and the United States of America or with the International Civil Aviation Organization, ie, the thirtieth day after the date of the deposit of the tenth instrument of ratification (7 July 1989), in accordance with article VI (1), provided that the deposit with the International Civil Aviation Organization of the relevant instruments was the effective deposit for the purpose of article VI (1):

State	Date of deposit of the instrument of ratification
Byelorussian Soviet Socialist Republic	1 May 1989
German Democratic Republic	31 January 1989
Hungary	7 September 1988
Kuwait	8 March 1989
Marshall Islands	30 May 1989
Peru	7 June 1989
Saudi Arabia	21 February 1989
Turkey	7 July 1989
Union of Soviet Socialist Republics	31 March 1989
United Arab Emirates	9 March 1989

The States Parties to this Protocol

Considering that unlawful acts of violence which endanger or are likely to endanger the safety of persons at airports serving international civil aviation or which jeopardize the safe operation of such airports undermine the confidence of the peoples of the world in safety at such airports and disturb the safe and orderly conduct of civil aviation for all States;

Considering that the occurrence of such acts is a matter of grave concern to the international community and that, for the purpose of deterring such acts, there is an urgent need to provide appropriate measures for punishment of offenders;

Considering that it is necessary to adopt provisions supplementary to those of the Convention for the Suppression of Unlawful Acts against the Safety of Civil Aviation, done at Montreal on 23 September 1971;[5] to deal with such unlawful acts of violence at airports serving international civil aviation;

Have agreed as follows:

Article I

This Protocol supplements the Convention for the Suppression of Unlawful Acts against the Safety of Civil Aviation, done at Montreal on 23 September 1971 (hereinafter referred to as 'the Convention'), and, as between the Parties to this Protocol, the Convention and the Protocol shall be read and interpreted together as one single instrument.

Article II

1. In Article 1 of the Convention, the following shall be added as new paragraph 1 *bis:*

'1 *bis.* Any person commits an offence if he unlawfully and intentionally, using any device, substance or weapon:
   (a) performs an act of violence against a person at an airport serving international civil aviation which causes or is likely to cause serious injury or death; or
   (b) destroys or seriously damages the facilities of an airport serving international civil aviation or aircraft not in service located thereon or disrupts the services of the airport,
if such an act endangers or is likely to endanger safety at that airport.'

Subsequently, the Protocol came into force for the following States on the thirtieth day after the date of deposit with the International Civil Aviation Organization of their instruments of ratification in accordance with article VI (1):

State	Date of deposit of the instrument of ratification
Chile...	15 August 1989

(With effect from 14 September 1989, provided that the deposit with the International Civil Aviation Organization was the effective deposit for the purpose of article VI (1) of the Protocol.)

Mauritius..	17 August 1989

(With effect from 16 September 1989, provided that the deposit with the International Civil Aviation Organization was the effective deposit for the purpose of article VI (1) of the Protocol.)

France*...	6 September 1989

(With effect from 6 October 1989, provided that the deposit with the International Civil Aviation Organization was the effective deposit for the purpose of article VI (1) of the Protocol.)

Denmark..	23 November 1989

(With a declaration of non-application to the Faeroe Islands. With effect from 23 December 1989, provided that the deposit with the International Civil Aviation Organization was the effective deposit for the purpose of article VI (1) of the Protocol.)

Austria...	28 December 1989

(With effect from 27 January 1990, provided that the deposit with the International Civil Aviation Organization was the effective deposit for the purpose of article VI (1) of the Protocol.)

* [...]

[5] United Nations, *Treaty Series,* vol 974, p 177.

2. In paragraph 2 (a) of Article 1 of the Convention, the following words shall be inserted after the words 'paragraph 1':
'or paragraph 1 *bis*'.

Article III

In Article 5 of the Convention, the following shall be added as paragraph 2 *bis:*

'2 *bis*. Each Contracting State shall likewise take such measures as may be necessary to establish its jurisdiction over the offences mentioned in Article 1, paragraph 1 *bis,* and in Article 1, paragraph 2, in so far as that paragraph relates to those offences, in the case where the alleged offender is present in its territory and it does not extradite him pursuant to Article 8 to the State mentioned in paragraph 1 (a) of this Article.'

Article IV

This Protocol shall be open for signature at Montreal on 24 February 1988 by States participating in the International Conference on Air Law held at Montreal from 9 to 24 February 1988. After 1 March 1988, the Protocol shall be open for signature to all States in London, Moscow, Washington and Montreal, until it enters into force in accordance with Article VI.

Article V

1. This Protocol shall be subject to ratification by the signatory States.

2. Any State which is not a Contracting State to the Convention may ratify this Protocol if at the same time it ratifies or accedes to the Convention in accordance with Article 15 thereof.

3. Instruments of ratification shall be deposited with the Governments of the Union of Soviet Socialist Republics, the United Kingdom of Great Britain and Northern Ireland and the United States of America or with the International Civil Aviation Organization, which are hereby designated the Depositaries.

Article VI

1. As soon as ten of the signatory States have deposited their instruments of ratification of this Protocol, it shall enter into force between them on the thirtieth day after the date of the deposit of the tenth instrument of ratification. It shall enter into force for each State which deposits its instrument of ratification after that date on the thirtieth day after deposit of its instrument of ratification.

2. As soon as this Protocol enters into force, it shall be registered by the Depositaries pursuant to Article 102 of the Charter of the United Nations and pursuant to Article 83 of the Convention on International Civil Aviation (Chicago, 1944).[5]

Article VII

1. This Protocol shall, after it has entered into force, be open for accession by any nonsignatory State.

2. Any State which is not a Contracting State to the Convention may accede to this Protocol if at the same time it ratifies or accedes to the Convention in accordance with Article 15 thereof.

3. Instruments of accession shall be deposited with the Depositaries and accession shall take effect on the thirtieth day after the deposit.

---

[5]   United Nations, *Treaty Series*, vol 15, p 295. For the texts of the Protocols amending this Convention, see vol 320, pp 209 and 217; vol 418, p 161; vol 514, p 209; vol 740, p 21; vol 893, p 117; vol 958, p 217; vol 1008, p 213, and vol 1175, p 297.

Article VIII

1. Any Party to this Protocol may denounce it by written notification addressed to the Depositaries.

2. Denunciation shall take effect six months following the date on which notification is received by the Depositaries.

3. Denunciation of this Protocol shall not of itself have the effect of denunciation of the Convention.

4. Denunciation of the Convention by a Contracting State to the Convention as supplemented by this Protocol shall also have the effect of denunciation of this Protocol.

Article IX

1. The Depositaries shall promptly inform all signatory and acceding States to this Protocol and all signatory and acceding States to the Convention:

    (a) of the date of each signature and the date of deposit of each instrument of ratification of, or accession to, this Protocol, and

    (b) of the receipt of any notification of denunciation of this Protocol and the date thereof.

2. The Depositaries shall also notify the States referred to in paragraph 1 of the date on which this Protocol enters into force in accordance with Article VI.

IN WITNESS WHEREOF the undersigned Plenipotentiaries, being duly authorized thereto by their Governments, have signed this Protocol.

DONE at Montreal on the twenty-fourth day of February of the year One Thousand Nine

Hundred and Eighty-eight, in four originals, each being drawn up in four authentic texts in the English, French, Russian and Spanish languages.

[…]

APPENDIX 6

Diplomats Convention

No 15410

MULTILATERAL

Convention on the prevention and punishment of crimes against internationally protected persons, including diplomatic agents (with resolution 3166 (XXVIII) of the General Assembly of the United Nations). Adopted by the General Assembly of the United Nations, at New York, on 14 December 1973

Authentic texts: English, French, Chinese, Russian and Spanish.

Registered ex officio *on 20 February 1977.*

MULTILATÉRAL

Convention sur la prévention et la répression des infractions contre les personnes jouissant d'une protection internationale, y compris les agents diplomatiques [avec résolution 3166 (XXVIII) de l'Assemblée générale des Nations Unies]. Adoptée par l'Assemblée générale des Nations Unies, à New York, le 14 décembre 1973

Textes authentiques: anglais, français, chinois, russe et espagnol.

Enregistrée d'office le 20 février 1977.

CONVENTION[1] ON THE PREVENTION AND PUNISHMENT OF CRIMES AGAINST INTERNATIONALLY PROTECTED PERSONS, INCLUDING DIPLOMATIC AGENTS

The States Parties to this Convention,

Having in mind the purposes and principles of the Charter of the United Nations concerning the maintenance of international peace and the promotion of friendly relations and co-operation among States,

---

[1] Came into force on 20 February 1977 in respect of the States listed hereafter, ie, the thirtieth day following the date of deposit of the twenty-second instrument of ratification or accession with the Secretary-General of the United Nations, in accordance with article 17 (1):

State	Date of deposit of the instrument of ratification, or accession (a)
Bulgaria	18 July 1974
Byelorussian Soviet Socialist Republic	5 February 1976
Canada	4 August 1976
Chile	21 January 1977 *a*
Cyprus	24 December 1975 *a*
Czechoslovakia	30 June 1975

509

Considering that crimes against diplomatic agents and other internationally protected persons jeopardizing the safety of these persons create a serious threat to the maintenance of normal international relations which are necessary for co-operation among States,

Believing that the commission of such crimes is a matter of grave concern to the international community,

Convinced that there is an urgent need to adopt appropriate and effective measures for the prevention and punishment of such crimes,

Have agreed as follows:

Article 1

For the purposes of this Convention:

1. 'Internationally protected person' means:

    (a) a Head of State, including any member of a collegial body performing the functions of a Head of State under the constitution of the State concerned, a Head of Government or a Minister for Foreign Affairs, whenever any such person is in a foreign State, as well as members of his family who accompany him;

    (b) any representative or official of a State or any official or other agent of an international organization of an intergovernmental character who, at the time when and in the place where a crime against him, his official premises, his private accommodation or his means of transport is committed, is entitled pursuant to international law to special protection from any attack on his person, freedom or dignity, as well as members of his family forming part of his household.

Denmark	1 July 1975
(With a declaration to the effect that, until further decision, the Convention shall not apply to the Faroe Islands and Greenland.)	
Ecuador	12 March 1975
German Democratic Republic	30 November 1976
Ghana	25 April 1975 *a*
Hungary	26 March 1975
Liberia	30 September 1975 *a*
Mongolia	8 August 1975
Nicaragua	10 March 1975
Pakistan	29 March 1976 *a*
Paraguay	24 November 1975
Philippines	26 November 1976 *a*
Sweden	1 July 1975
Tunisia	21 January 1977
Ukrainian Soviet Socialist Republic	20 January 1976
Union of Soviet Socialist Republics	15 January 1976
United States of America	26 October 1976
Yugoslavia	29 December 1976

Subsequently, the Convention came into force in respect of the State listed hereafter on the thirtieth day following the date of deposit of its instrument of ratification with the Secretary-General of the United Nations, in accordance with article 17 (2):

State	*Date of deposit of the instrument of ratification*
Germany, Federal Republic of	25 January 1977
(With effect from 24 February 1977. With a declaration of application to Berlin (West).)	

2. 'Alleged offender' means a person as to whom there is sufficient evidence to determine prima facie that he has committed or participated in one or more of the crimes set forth in article 2.

Article 2

1. The intentional commission of:

 (a) a murder, kidnapping or other attack upon the person or liberty of an internationally protected person;

 (b) a violent attack upon the official premises, the private accommodation or the means of transport of an internationally protected person likely to endanger his person or liberty;

 (c) a threat to commit any such attack;

 (d) an attempt to commit any such attack; and

 (e) an act constituting participation as an accomplice in any such attack shall be made by each State Party a crime under its internal law.

2. Each State Party shall make these crimes punishable by appropriate penalties which take into account their grave nature.

3. Paragraphs 1 and 2 of this article in no way derogate from the obligations of States Parties under international law to take all appropriate measures to prevent other attacks on the person, freedom or dignity of an internationally protected person.

Article 3

1. Each State Party shall take such measures as may be necessary to establish its jurisdiction over the crimes set forth in article 2 in the following cases:

 (a) when the crime is committed in the territory of that State or on board a ship or aircraft registered in that State;

 (b) when the alleged offender is a national of that State;

 (c) when the crime is committed against an internationally protected person as defined in article 1 who enjoys his status as such by virtue of functions which he exercises on behalf of that State.

2. Each State Party shall likewise take such measures as may be necessary to establish its jurisdiction over these crimes in cases where the alleged offender is present in its territory and it does not extradite him pursuant to article 8 to any of the States mentioned in paragraph 1 of this article.

3. This Convention does not exclude any criminal jurisdiction exercised in accordance with internal law.

Article 4

States Parties shall co-operate in the prevention of the crimes set forth in article 2, particularly by:

 (a) taking all practicable measures to prevent preparations in their respective territories for the commission of those crimes within or outside their territories;

 (b) exchanging information and co-ordinating the taking of administrative and other measures as appropriate to prevent the commission of those crimes.

Article 5

1. The State Party in which any of the crimes set forth in article 2 has been committed shall, if it has reason to believe that an alleged offender has fled from its territory, communicate to all other States concerned, directly or through the Secretary-General of the United Nations, all the pertinent facts regarding the crime committed and all available information regarding the identity of the alleged offender.

2. Whenever any of the crimes set forth in article 2 has been committed against an internationally protected person, any State Party which has information concerning the victim and the circumstances of the crime shall endeavour to transmit it, under the conditions provided for in its internal law, fully and promptly to the State Party on whose behalf he was exercising his functions.

Article 6

1. Upon being satisfied that the circumstances so warrant, the State Party in whose territory the alleged offender is present shall take the appropriate measures under its internal law so as to ensure his presence for the purpose of prosecution or extradition. Such measures shall be notified without delay directly or through the Secretary-General of the United Nations to:

- *(a)* the State where the crime was committed;
- *(b)* the State or States of which the alleged offender is a national or, if he is a stateless person, in whose territory he permanently resides;
- *(c)* the State or States of which the internationally protected person concerned is a national or on whose behalf he was exercising his functions;
- *(d)* all other States concerned; and
- *(e)* the international organization of which the internationally protected person concerned is an official or an agent.

2. Any person regarding whom the measures referred to in paragraph 1 of this article are being taken shall be entitled:

- *(a)* to communicate without delay with the nearest appropriate representative of the State of which he is a national or which is otherwise entitled to protect his rights or, if he is a stateless person, which he requests and which is willing to protect his rights; and
- *(b)* to be visited by a representative of that State.

Article 7

The State Party in whose territory the alleged offender is present shall, if it does not extradite him, submit, without exception whatsoever and without undue delay, the case to its competent authorities for the purpose of prosecution, through proceedings in accordance with the laws of that State.

Article 8

1. To the extent that the crimes set forth in article 2 are not listed as extraditable offences in any extradition treaty existing between States Parties, they shall be deemed to be included as such therein. States Parties undertake to include those crimes as extraditable offences in every future extradition treaty to be concluded between them.

2. If a State Party which makes extradition conditional on the existence of a treaty receives a request for extradition from another State Party with which it has no extradition treaty, it may, if it decides to extradite, consider this Convention as the legal basis for extradition in respect of those crimes. Extradition shall be subject to the procedural provisions and the other conditions of the law of the requested State.

3. States Parties which do not make extradition conditional on the existence of a treaty shall recognize those crimes as extraditable offences between themselves subject to the procedural provisions and the other conditions of the law of the requested State.

4. Each of the crimes shall be treated, for the purpose of extradition between States Parties, as if it had been committed not only in the place in which it occurred but also in the territories of the States required to establish their jurisdiction in accordance with paragraph 1 of article 3.

Article 9

Any person regarding whom proceedings are being carried out in connexion with any of the crimes set forth in article 2 shall be guaranteed fair treatment at all stages of the proceedings.

Article 10

1. States Parties shall afford one another the greatest measure of assistance in connexion with criminal proceedings brought in respect of the crimes set forth in article 2, including the supply of all evidence at their disposal necessary for the proceedings.

2. The provisions of paragraph 1 of this article shall not affect obligations concerning mutual judicial assistance embodied in any other treaty.

Article 11

The State Party where an alleged offender is prosecuted shall communicate the final outcome of the proceedings to the Secretary-General of the United Nations, who shall transmit the information to the other States Parties.

Article 12

The provisions of this Convention shall not affect the application of the Treaties on Asylum, in force at the date of the adoption of this Convention, as between the States which are parties to those Treaties; but a State Party to this Convention may not invoke those Treaties with respect to another State Party to this Convention which is not a party to those Treaties.

Article 13

1. Any dispute between two or more States Parties concerning the interpretation or application of this Convention which is not settled by negotiation shall, at the request of one of them, be submitted to arbitration. If within six months from the date of the request for arbitration the Parties are unable to agree on the organization of the arbitration, any one of those Parties may refer the dispute to the International Court of Justice by request in conformity with the Statute of the Court.

2. Each State Party may at the time of signature or ratification of this Convention or accession thereto declare that it does not consider itself bound by paragraph 1 of this article. The other States Parties shall not be bound by paragraph 1 of this article with respect to any State Party which has made such a reservation.

3. Any State Party which has made a reservation in accordance with paragraph 2 of this article may at any time withdraw that reservation by notification to the Secretary-General of the United Nations.

Article 14

This Convention shall be opened for signature by all States, until 31 December 1974, at United Nations Headquarters in New York.

Article 15

This Convention is subject to ratification. The instruments of ratification shall be deposited with the Secretary-General of the United Nations.

Article 16

This Convention shall remain open for accession by any State. The instruments of accession shall be deposited with the Secretary-General of the United Nations.

Article 17

1. This Convention shall enter into force on the thirtieth day following the date of deposit of the twenty-second instrument of ratification or accession with the Secretary-General of the United Nations.

2. For each State ratifying or acceding to the Convention after the deposit of the twenty-second instrument of ratification or accession, the Convention shall enter into force on the thirtieth day after deposit by such State of its instrument of ratification or accession.

Article 18

1. Any State Party may denounce this Convention by written notification to the Secretary-General of the United Nations.

2. Denunciation shall take effect six months following the date on which notification is received by the Secretary-General of the United Nations.

Article 19

The Secretary-General of the United Nations shall inform all States, inter alia:

  (a) of signatures to this Convention, of the deposit of instruments of ratification or accession in accordance with articles 14, 15 and 16 and of notifications made under article 18;

  (b) of the date on which this Convention will enter into force in accordance with article 17.

Article 20

The original of this Convention, of which the Chinese, English, French, Russian and Spanish texts are equally authentic, shall be deposited with the Secretary-General of the United Nations, who shall send certified copies thereof to all States.

IN WITNESS WHEREOF the undersigned, being duly authorized thereto by their respective Governments, have signed this Convention, opened for signature at New York on 14 December 1973.

APPENDIX 7

Hostages Convention

No 21931

MULTILATERAL

International Convention against the taking of hostages. Adopted by the General Assembly of the United Nations on 17 December 1979

Authentic texts: English, French, Arabic, Chinese, Russian and Spanish.

Registered ex officio on 3 June 1983.

MULTILATÉRAL

Convention internationale contre la prise d'otages. Adoptée par l'Assemblée générale des Nations Unies le 17 décembre 1979

Textes authentiques: anglais, français, arabe, chinois, russe et espagnol.

Enregistrée d'office le 3 juin 1983.

INTERNATIONAL CONVENTION[1] AGAINST THE TAKING OF HOSTAGES

The States Parties to this Convention,

Having in mind the purposes and principles of the Charter of the United Nations concerning the maintenance of international peace and security and the promotion of friendly relations and co-operation among States,

---

[1] Came into force on 3 June 1983 in respect of the following States, ie, on the thirtieth day following the date of deposit of the twenty-second instrument of ratification or accession with the Secretary-General of the United Nations, in accordance with article 18 (1):

State	Date of deposit of the instrument of ratification or accession (a)
Bahamas	4 June 1981 *a*
Barbados	9 March 1981 *a*
Bhutan	31 August 1981 *a*
Chile	12 November 1981
Egypt	2 October 1981
El Salvador	12 February 1981
(Confirming the reservation in respect of article 16 (1) made upon signature.)	
Finland	14 April 1983
Germany, Federal Republic of	15 December 1980
(With a declaration of application to Berlin (West).)	

Recognizing in particular that everyone has the right to life, liberty and security of person, as set out in the Universal Declaration of Human Rights[2] and the International Covenant on Civil and Political Rights,[3]

Reaffirming the principle of equal rights and self-determination of peoples as enshrined in the Charter of the United Nations and the Declaration on Principles of International Law concerning Friendly Relations and Co-operation among States in accordance with the Charter of the United Nations,[4] as well as in other relevant resolutions of the General Assembly,

Considering that the taking of hostages is an offence of grave concern to the international community and that, in accordance with the provisions of this Convention, any person committing an act of hostage-taking shall either be prosecuted or extradited,

Being convinced that it is urgently necessary to develop international cooperation between States in devising and adopting effective measures for the prevention, prosecution and punishment of all acts of taking of hostages as manifestations of international terrorism,

Have agreed as follows:

Article 1

1. Any person who seizes or detains and threatens to kill, to injure or to continue to detain another person (hereinafter referred to as the 'hostage') in order to compel a third party, namely, a State, an international intergovernmental organization, a natural or juridical person, or a group of persons, to do or abstain from doing any act as an explicit or implicit condition for the release of the hostage commits the offence of taking of hostages ('hostage-taking') within the meaning of this Convention.

2. Any person who:

   (a) Attempts to commit an act of hostage-taking, or
   (b) Participates as an accomplice of anyone who commits or attempts to commit an act of hostage-taking

   likewise commits an offence for the purposes of this Convention.

Article 2

Each State Party shall make the offences set forth in article 1 punishable by appropriate penalties which take into account the grave nature of those offences.

Guatemala	11 March 1983
Honduras	1 June 1981
Iceland	6 July 1981 *a*
Kenya	8 December 1981 *a*
(With a reservation in respect of article 16 (1).)	
Lesotho	5 November 1980
Mauritius	17 October 1980
Norway	2 July 1981
Panama	19 August 1982
Philippines	14 October 1980
Republic of Korea	4 May 1983 *a*
Suriname	5 November 1981
Sweden	15 January 1981
Trinidad and Tobago	1 April 1981 *a*
United Kingdom of Great Britain and Northern Ireland	22 December 1982
(In respect of the United Kingdom of Great Britain and Northern Ireland and the Territories under the territorial sovereignty of the United Kingdom.)	

[2] United Nations, *Treaty Series,* vol 213, p 222.
[3] *Ibid,* vol 999, p 171.
[4] United Nations, *Official Records of the General Assembly, Twenty-fifth Session, Supplement No 28 (A/8028)* p121.

Article 3

1. The State Party in the territory of which the hostage is held by the offender shall take all measures it considers appropriate to ease the situation of the hostage, in particular, to secure his release and, after his release, to facilitate, when relevant, his departure.

2. If any object which the offender has obtained as a result of the taking of hostages comes into the custody of a State Party, that State Party shall return it as soon as possible to the hostage or the third party referred to in article 1, as the case may be, or to the appropriate authorities thereof.

Article 4

States Parties shall co-operate in the prevention of the offences set forth in article 1, particularly by:

(*a*) Taking all practicable measures to prevent preparations in their respective territories for the commission of those offences within or outside their territories, including measures to prohibit in their territories illegal activities of persons, groups and organizations that encourage, instigate, organize or engage in the perpetration of acts of taking of hostages;

(*b*) Exchanging information and co-ordinating the taking of administrative and other measures as appropriate to prevent the commission of those offences.

Article 5

1. Each State Party shall take such measures as may be necessary to establish its jurisdiction over any of the offences set forth in article 1 which are committed:

(*a*) In its territory or on board a ship or aircraft registered in that State;

(*b*) By any of its nationals or, if that State considers it appropriate, by those stateless persons who have their habitual residence in its territory;

(*c*) In order to compel that State to do or abstain from doing any act; or

(*d*) With respect to a hostage who is a national of that State, if that State considers it appropriate.

2. Each State Party shall likewise take such measures as may be necessary to establish its jurisdiction over the offences set forth in article 1 in cases where the alleged offender is present in its territory and it does not extradite him to any of the States mentioned in paragraph 1 of this article.

3. This Convention does not exclude any criminal jurisdiction exercised in accordance with internal law.

Article 6

1. Upon being satisfied that the circumstances so warrant, any State Party in the territory of which the alleged offender is present shall, in accordance with its laws, take him into custody or take other measures to ensure his presence for such time as is necessary to enable any criminal or extradition proceedings to be instituted. That State Party shall immediately make a preliminary inquiry into the facts.

2. The custody or other measures referred to in paragraph 1 of this article shall be notified without delay directly or through the Secretary-General of the United Nations to:

(*a*) The State where the offence was committed;

(*b*) The State against which compulsion has been directed or attempted;

(*c*) The State of which the natural or juridical person against whom compulsion has been directed or attempted is a national;

(*d*) The State of which the hostage is a national or in the territory of which he has his habitual residence;

(*e*) The State of which the alleged offender is a national or, if he is a stateless person, in the territory of which he has his habitual residence;

(*f*) The international intergovernmental organization against which compulsion has been directed or attempted;

(*g*) All other States concerned.

3. Any person regarding whom the measures referred to in paragraph 1 of this article are being taken shall be entitled:

   (*a*) To communicate without delay with the nearest appropriate representative of the State of which he is a national or which is otherwise entitled to establish such communication or, if he is a stateless person, the State in the territory of which he has his habitual residence;

   (*b*) To be visited by a representative of that State.

4. The rights referred to in paragraph 3 of this article shall be exercised in conformity with the laws and regulations of the State in the territory of which the alleged offender is present subject to the proviso, however, that the said laws and regulations must enable full effect to be given to the purposes for which the rights accorded under paragraph 3 of this article are intended.

5. The provisions of paragraphs 3 and 4 of this article shall be without prejudice to the right of any State Party having a claim to jurisdiction in accordance with paragraph 1 (*b*) of article 5 to invite the International Committee of the Red Cross to communicate with and visit the alleged offender.

6. The State which makes the preliminary inquiry contemplated in paragraph 1 of this article shall promptly report its findings to the States or organization referred to in paragraph 2 of this article and indicate whether it intends to exercise jurisdiction.

Article 7

The State Party where the alleged offender is prosecuted shall in accordance with its laws communicate the final outcome of the proceedings to the Secretary-General of the United Nations, who shall transmit the information to the other States concerned and the international intergovernmental organizations concerned.

Article 8

1. The State Party in the territory of which the alleged offender is found shall, if it does not extradite him, be obliged, without exception whatsoever and whether or not the offence was committed in its territory, to submit the case to its competent authorities for the purpose of prosecution, through proceedings in accordance with the laws of that State. Those authorities shall take their decision in the same manner as in the case of any ordinary offence of a grave nature under the law of that State.

2. Any person regarding whom proceedings are being carried out in connexion with any of the offences set forth in article 1 shall be guaranteed fair treatment at all stages of the proceedings, including enjoyment of all the rights and guarantees provided by the law of the State in the territory of which he is present.

Article 9

1. A request for the extradition of an alleged offender, pursuant to this Convention, shall not be granted if the requested State Party has substantial grounds for believing:

   (*a*) That the request for extradition for an offence set forth in article 1 has been made for the purpose of prosecuting or punishing a person on account of his race, religion, nationality, ethnic origin or political opinion; or

   (*b*) That the person's position may be prejudiced:

   (i) For any of the reasons mentioned in subparagraph (*a*) of this paragraph, or

   (ii) For the reason that communication with him by the appropriate authorities of the State entitled to exercise rights of protection cannot be effected.

2. With respect to the offences as defined in this Convention, the provisions of all extradition treaties and arrangements applicable between States Parties are modified as between States Parties to the extent that they are incompatible with this Convention.

Article 10

1. The offences set forth in article 1 shall be deemed to be included as extraditable offences in any extradition treaty existing between States Parties. States Parties undertake to include such offences as extraditable offences in every extradition treaty to be concluded between them.

2. If a State Party which makes extradition conditional on the existence of a treaty receives a request for extradition from another State Party with which it has no extradition treaty, the requested State may at its option consider this Convention as the legal basis for extradition in respect of the offences set forth in article 1. Extradition shall be subject to the other conditions provided by the law of the requested State.

3. States Parties which do not make extradition conditional on the existence of a treaty shall recognize the offences set forth in article 1 as extraditable offences between themselves subject to the conditions provided by the law of the requested State.

4. The offences set forth in article 1 shall be treated, for the purpose of extradition between States Parties, as if they had been committed not only in the place in which they occurred but also in the territories of the States required to establish their jurisdiction in accordance with paragraph 1 of article 5.

Article 11

1. States Parties shall afford one another the greatest measure of assistance in connexion with criminal proceedings brought in respect of the offences set forth in article 1, including the supply of all evidence at their disposal necessary for the proceedings.

2. The provisions of paragraph 1 of this article shall not affect obligations concerning mutual judicial assistance embodied in any other treaty.

Article 12

In so far as the Geneva Conventions of 1949 for the protection of war victims[5] or the Protocols Additional to those Conventions[6] are applicable to a particular act of hostage-taking, and in so far as States Parties to this Convention are bound under those conventions to prosecute or hand over the hostage-taker, the present Convention shall not apply to an act of hostage-taking committed in the course of armed conflicts as defined in the Geneva Conventions of 1949 and the Protocols thereto, including armed conflicts mentioned in article 1, paragraph 4, of Additional Protocol I of 1977, in which peoples are fighting against colonial domination and alien occupation and against racist régimes in the exercise of their right of self-determination, as enshrined in the Charter of the United Nations and the Declaration on Principles of International Law concerning Friendly Relations and Co-operation among States in accordance with the Charter of the United Nations.

Article 13

This Convention shall not apply where the offence is committed within a single State, the hostage and the alleged offender are nationals of that State and the alleged offender is found in the territory of that State.

Article 14

Nothing in this Convention shall be construed as justifying the violation of the territorial integrity or political independence of a State in contravention of the Charter of the United Nations.

---

[5] United Nations, *Treaty Series,* vol 75, p 31, 85, 135 and 287.
[6] *Ibid,* vol 1125, pp 3 and 609.

Article 15

The provisions of this Convention shall not affect the application of the Treaties on Asylum, in force at the date of the adoption of this Convention, as between the States which are parties to those Treaties; but a State Party to this Convention may not invoke those Treaties with respect to another State Party to this Convention which is not a party to those treaties.

Article 16

1. Any dispute between two or more States Parties concerning the interpretation or application of this Convention which is not settled by negotiation shall, at the request of one of them, be submitted to arbitration. If within six months from the date of the request for arbitration the parties are unable to agree on the organization of the arbitration, any one of those parties may refer the dispute to the International Court of Justice by request in conformity with the Statute of the Court.

2. Each State may at the time of signature or ratification of this Convention or accession thereto declare that it does not consider itself bound by paragraph 1 of this article. The other States Parties shall not be bound by paragraph 1 of this article with respect to any State Party which has made such a reservation.

3. Any State Party which has made a reservation in accordance with paragraph 2 of this article may at any time withdraw that reservation by notification to the Secretary-General of the United Nations.

Article 17

1. This Convention is open for signature by all States until 31 December 1980 at United Nations Headquarters in New York.

2. This Convention is subject to ratification. The instruments of ratification shall be deposited with the Secretary-General of the United Nations.

3. This Convention is open for accession by any State. The instruments of accession shall be deposited with the Secretary-General of the United Nations.

Article 18

1. This Convention shall enter into force on the thirtieth day following the date of deposit of the twenty-second instrument of ratification or accession with the Secretary-General of the United Nations.

2. For each State ratifying or acceding to the Convention after the deposit of the twenty-second instrument of ratification or accession, the Convention shall enter into force on the thirtieth day after deposit by such State of its instrument of ratification or accession.

Article 19

1. Any State Party may denounce this Convention by written notification to the Secretary-General of the United Nations.

2. Denunciation shall take effect one year following the date on which notification is received by the Secretary-General of the United Nations.

Article 20

The original of this Convention, of which the Arabic, Chinese, English, French, Russian and Spanish texts are equally authentic, shall be deposited with the Secretary-General of the United Nations, who shall send certified copies thereof to all States.

IN WITNESS WHEREOF, the undersigned, being duly authorized thereto by their respective Governments, have signed this Convention, opened for signature at New York on 18 December 1979.

APPENDIX 8

Nuclear Materials Convention

No 24631

MULTILATERAL

**Convention on the physical protection of nuclear material (with annexes).
Adopted at Vienna on 26 October 1979 and opened for signature at
Vienna and New York on 3 March 1980**

Authentic texts: Arabic, Chinese, English, French, Russian and Spanish.

Registered by the International Atomic Energy Agency on 23 February 1987.

MULTILATÉRAL

**Convention sur la protection physique des matiéres nucléaires (avec annexes).
Adoptée à Vienne le 26 octobre 1979 et ouverte à la signature à Vienne et à
New York le 3 mars 1980**

Textes authentiques: arabe, chinois, anglais, français, russe et espagnol.

Enregistrée par l'Agence internationale de l'énergie atomique le 23 février 1987.

CONVENTION[1] ON THE PHYSICAL PROTECTION OF
NUCLEAR MATERIAL

The States Parties to this Convention,

Recognizing the right of all States to develop and apply nuclear energy for peaceful purposes
and their legitimate interests in the potential benefits to be derived from the peaceful application
of nuclear energy,

---

[1] Came into force on 8 February 1987, ie, the thirtieth day following the date of deposit with the Director-
General of the International Atomic Energy Agency of the twenty-first instrument of ratification, acceptance
or approval, in accordance with article 19 (1):

State	Date of deposit of the instrument of ratification
Brazil	17 October 1985
Bulgaria	10 April 1984
Canada	21 March 1986
Czechoslovakia	23 April 1982
German Democratic Republic	5 February 1981
Guatemala	23 April 1985
Hungary	4 May 1984
Indonesia	5 November 1986
Liechtenstein	25 November 1986
Mongolia	28 May 1986
Norway	15 August 1985

Convinced of the need for facilitating international co-operation in the peaceful application of nuclear energy,

Desiring to avert the potential dangers posed by the unlawful taking and use of nuclear material,

Convinced that offences relating to nuclear material are a matter of grave concern and that there is an urgent need to adopt appropriate and effective measures to ensure the prevention, detection and punishment of such offences,

Aware of the need for international co-operation to establish, in conformity with the national law of each State Party and with this Convention, effective measures for the physical protection of nuclear material,

Convinced that this Convention should facilitate the safe transfer of nuclear material,

Stressing also the importance of the physical protection of nuclear material in domestic use, storage and transport,

Recognizing the importance of effective physical protection of nuclear material used for military purposes, and understanding that such material is and will continue to be accorded stringent physical protection,

Have agreed as follows:

Article 1

For the purposes of this Convention:

(a) 'Nuclear material' means plutonium except that with isotopic concentration exceeding 80% in plutonium-238; uranium-233; uranium enriched in the isotopes 235 or 233; uranium containing the mixture of isotopes as occurring in nature other than in the form of ore or ore-residue; any material containing one or more of the foregoing;

(b) 'Uranium enriched in the isotope 235 or 233' means uranium containing the isotopes 235 or 233 or both in an amount such that the abundance ratio of the sum of these isotopes to the isotope 238 is greater than the ratio of the isotope 235 to the isotope 238 occurring in nature;

(c) 'International nuclear transport' means the carriage of a consignment of nuclear material by any means of transportation intended to go beyond the territory of the State where the shipment originates beginning with the departure from a facility of the shipper in that State and ending with the arrival at a facility of the receiver within the State of ultimate destination.

Article 2

1. This Convention shall apply to nuclear material used for peaceful purposes while in international nuclear transport.

Paraguay	6 February 1985
Philippines	22 September 1981
Poland	5 October 1983
Republic of Korea	7 April 1982
Sweden	1 August 1980
Switzerland	9 January 1987
Turkey	27 February 1985
Union of Soviet Socialist Republics	25 May 1983
United States of America	13 December 1982
Yugoslavia	14 May 1986

2. With the exception of articles 3 and 4 and paragraph 3 of article 5, this Convention shall also apply to nuclear material used for peaceful purposes while in domestic use, storage and transport.

3. Apart from the commitments expressly undertaken by States Parties in the articles covered by paragraph 2 with respect to nuclear material used for peaceful purposes while in domestic use, storage and transport, nothing in this Convention shall be interpreted as affecting the sovereign rights of a State regarding the domestic use, storage and transport of such nuclear material.

Article 3

Each State Party shall take appropriate steps within the framework of its national law and consistent with international law to ensure as far as practicable that, during international nuclear transport, nuclear material within its territory, or on board a ship or aircraft under its jurisdiction insofar as such ship or aircraft is engaged in the transport to or from that State, is protected at the levels described in Annex I.

Article 4

1. Each State Party shall not export or authorize the export of nuclear material unless the State Party has received assurances that such material will be protected during the international nuclear transport at the levels described in Annex I.

2. Each State Party shall not import or authorize the import of nuclear material from a State not party to this Convention unless the State Party has received assurances that such material will during the international nuclear transport be protected at the levels described in Annex I.

3. A State Party shall not allow the transit of its territory by land or internal waterways or through its airports or seaports of nuclear material between States that are not parties to this Convention unless the State Party has received assurances as far as practicable that this nuclear material will be protected during international nuclear transport at the levels described in Annex I.

4. Each State Party shall apply within the framework of its national law the levels of physical protection described in Annex I to nuclear material being transported from a part of that State to another part of the same State through international waters or airspace.

5. The State Party responsible for receiving assurances that the nuclear material will be protected at the levels described in Annex I according to paragraphs 1 to 3 shall identify and inform in advance States which the nuclear material is expected to transit by land or internal waterways, or whose airports or seaports it is expected to enter.

6. The responsibility for obtaining assurances referred to in paragraph 1 may be transferred, by mutual agreement, to the State Party involved in the transport as the importing State.

7. Nothing in this article shall be interpreted as in any way affecting the territorial sovereignty and jurisdiction of a State, including that over its airspace and territorial sea.

Article 5

1. States Parties shall identify and make known to each other directly or through the International Atomic Energy Agency their central authority and point of contact having responsibility for physical protection of nuclear material and for coordinating recovery and response operations in the event of any unauthorized removal, use or alteration of nuclear material or in the event of credible threat thereof.

2. In the case of theft, robbery or any other unlawful taking of nuclear material or of credible threat thereof, States Parties shall, in accordance with their national law, provide co-operation and assistance to the maximum feasible extent in the recovery and protection of such material to any State that so requests. In particular:

    (a) A State Party shall take appropriate steps to inform as soon as possible other States, which appear to it to be concerned, of any theft, robbery or other unlawful taking of nuclear material or credible threat thereof and to inform, where appropriate, international organizations.

(b) As appropriate, the States Parties concerned shall exchange information with each other or international organizations with a view to protecting threatened nuclear material, verifying the integrity of the shipping container, or recovering unlawfully taken nuclear material and shall:

(i)   Co-ordinate their efforts through diplomatic and other agreed channels;

(ii) Render assistance, if requested;

(iii) Ensure the return of nuclear material stolen or missing as a consequence of the above-mentioned events.

The means of implementation of this co-operation shall be determined by the States Parties concerned.

3. States Parties shall co-operate and consult as appropriate, with each other directly or through international organizations, with a view to obtaining guidance on the design, maintenance and improvement of systems of physical protection of nuclear material in international transport.

Article 6

1. States Parties shall take appropriate measures consistent with their national law to protect the confidentiality of any information which they receive in confidence by virtue of the provisions of this Convention from another State Party or through participation in an activity carried out for the implementation of this Convention. If States Parties provide information to international organizations in confidence, steps shall be taken to ensure that the confidentiality of such information is protected.

2. States Parties shall not be required by this Convention to provide any information which they are not permitted to communicate pursuant to national law or which would jeopardize the security of the State concerned or the physical protection of nuclear material.

Article 7

1. The intentional commission of:

(a) An act without lawful authority which constitutes the receipt, possession, use, transfer, alteration, disposal or dispersal of nuclear material and which causes or is likely to cause death or serious injury to any person or substantial damage to property;

(b) A theft or robbery of nuclear material;

(c) An embezzlement or fraudulent obtaining of nuclear material;

(d) An act constituting a demand for nuclear material by threat or use of force or by any other form of intimidation;

(e) A threat:

(i)   To use nuclear material to cause death or serious injury to any person or substantial property damage, or

(ii) To commit an offence described in sub-paragraph (b) in order to compel a natural or legal person, international organization or State to do or to refrain from doing any act;

(f) An attempt to commit any offence described in paragraphs (a), (b) or (c); and

(g) An act which constitutes participation in any offence described in paragraphs *(a)* to *(f)*

shall be made a punishable offence by each State Party under its national law.

2. Each State Party shall make the offences described in this article punishable by appropriate penalties which take into account their grave nature.

Article 8

1. Each State Party shall take such measures as may be necessary to establish its jurisdiction over the offences set forth in article 7 in the following cases:

(a) When the offence is committed in the territory of that State or on board a ship or aircraft registered in that State;

(b) When the alleged offender is a national of that State.

2. Each State Party shall likewise take such measures as may be necessary to establish its jurisdiction over these offences in cases where the alleged offender is present in its territory and it does not extradite him pursuant to article 11 to any of the States mentioned in paragraph 1.

3. This Convention does not exclude any criminal jurisdiction exercised in accordance with national law.

4. In addition to the States Parties mentioned in paragraphs 1 and 2, each State Party may, consistent with international law, establish its jurisdiction over the offences set forth in article 7 when it is involved in international nuclear transport as the exporting or importing State.

Article 9

Upon being satisfied that the circumstances so warrant, the State Party in whose territory the alleged offender is present shall take appropriate measures, including detention, under its national law to ensure his presence for the purpose of prosecution or extradition. Measures taken according to this article shall be notified without delay to the States required to establish jurisdiction pursuant to article 8 and, where appropriate, all other States concerned.

Article 10

The State Party in whose territory the alleged offender is present shall, if it does not extradite him, submit, without exception whatsoever and without undue delay, the case to its competent authorities for the purpose of prosecution, through proceedings in accordance with the laws of that State.

Article 11

1. The offences in article 7 shall be deemed to be included as extraditable offences in any extradition treaty existing between States Parties. States Parties undertake to include those offences as extraditable offences in every future extradition treaty to be concluded between them.

2. If a State Party which makes extradition conditional on the existence of a treaty receives a request for extradition from another State Party with which it has no extradition treaty, it may at its option consider this Convention as the legal basis for extradition in respect of those offences. Extradition shall be subject to the other conditions provided by the law of the requested State.

3. States Parties which do not make extradition conditional on the existence of a treaty shall recognize those offences as extraditable offences between themselves subject to the conditions provided by the law of the requested State.

4. Each of the offences shall be treated, for the purpose of extradition between States Parties, as if it had been committed not only in the place in which it occurred but also in the territories of the States Parties required to establish their jurisdiction in accordance with paragraph 1 of article 8.

Article 12

Any person regarding whom proceedings are being carried out in connection with any of the offences set forth in article 7 shall be guaranteed fair treatment at all stages of the proceedings.

Article 13

1. States Parties shall afford one another the greatest measure of assistance in connection with criminal proceedings brought in respect of the offences set forth in article 7, including the supply of evidence at their disposal necessary for the proceedings. The law of the State requested shall apply in all cases.

2. The provisions of paragraph 1 shall not affect obligations under any other treaty, bilateral or multilateral, which governs or will govern, in whole or in part, mutual assistance in criminal matters.

Article 14

1. Each State Party shall inform the depositary of its laws and regulations which give effect to this Convention. The depositary shall communicate such information periodically to all States Parties.

2. The State Party where an alleged offender is prosecuted shall, wherever practicable, first communicate the final outcome of the proceedings to the States directly concerned. The State Party shall also communicate the final outcome to the depositary who shall inform all States.

3. Where an offence involves nuclear material used for peaceful purposes in domestic use, storage or transport, and both the alleged offender and the nuclear material remain in the territory of the State Party in which the offence was committed, nothing in this Convention shall be interpreted as requiring that State Party to provide information concerning criminal proceedings arising out of such an offence.

Article 15

The Annexes constitute an integral part of this Convention.

Article 16

1. A conference of States Parties shall be convened by the depositary five years after the entry into force of this Convention to review the implementation of the Convention and its adequacy as concerns the preamble, the whole of the operative part and the annexes in the light of the then prevailing situation.

2. At intervals of not less than five years thereafter, the majority of States Parties may obtain, by submitting a proposal to this effect to the depositary, the convening of further conferences with the same objective.

Article 17

1. In the event of a dispute between two or more States Parties concerning the interpretation or application of this Convention, such States Parties shall consult with a view to the settlement of the dispute by negotiation, or by any other peaceful means of settling disputes acceptable to all parties to the dispute.

2. Any dispute of this character which cannot be settled in the manner prescribed in paragraph 1 shall, at the request of any party to such dispute, be submitted to arbitration or referred to the International Court of Justice for decision. Where a dispute is submitted to arbitration, if, within six months from the date of the request, the parties to the dispute are unable to agree on the organization of the arbitration, a party may request the President of the International Court of Justice or the Secretary-General of the United Nations to appoint one or more arbitrators. In case of conflicting requests by the parties to the dispute, the request to the Secretary-General of the United Nations shall have priority.

3. Each State Party may at the time of signature, ratification, acceptance or approval of this Convention or accession thereto declare that it does not consider itself bound by either or both of the dispute settlement procedures provided for in paragraph 2. The other States Parties shall not be bound by a dispute settlement procedure provided for in paragraph 2, with respect to a State Party which has made a reservation to that procedure.

4. Any State Party which has made a reservation in accordance with paragraph 3 may at any time withdraw that reservation by notification to the depositary.

Article 18

1. This Convention shall be open for signature by all States at the Headquarters of the International Atomic Energy Agency in Vienna and at the Headquarters of the United Nations in New York from 3 March 1980 until its entry into force.

2. This Convention is subject to ratification, acceptance or approval by the signatory States.

3. After its entry into force, this Convention will be open for accession by all States.

4. (a) This Convention shall be open for signature or accession by international organizations and regional organizations of an integration or other nature, provided that any such

organization is constituted by sovereign States and has competence in respect of the negotiation, conclusion and application of international agreements in matters covered by this Convention.

(b) In matters within their competence, such organizations shall, on their own behalf, exercise the rights and fulfil the responsibilities which this Convention attributes to States Parties.

(c) When becoming party to this Convention such an organization shall communicate to the depositary a declaration indicating which States are members thereof and which articles of this Convention do not apply to it:

(d) Such an organization shall not hold any vote additional to those of its Member States.

5. Instruments of ratification, acceptance, approval or accession shall be deposited with the depositary.

Article 19

1. This Convention shall enter into force on the thirtieth day following the date of deposit of the twenty-first instrument of ratification, acceptance or approval with the depositary.

2. For each State ratifying, accepting, approving or acceding to the Convention after the date of deposit of the twenty-first instrument of ratification, acceptance or approval, the Convention shall enter into force on the thirtieth day after the deposit by such State of its instrument of ratification, acceptance, approval or accession.

Article 20

1. Without prejudice to article 16 a State Party may propose amendments to this Convention. The proposed amendment shall be submitted to the depositary who shall circulate it immediately to all States Parties. If a majority of States Parties request the depositary to convene a conference to consider the proposed amendments, the depositary shall invite all States Parties to attend such a conference to begin not sooner than thirty days after the invitations are issued. Any amendment adopted at the conference by a two-thirds majority of all States Parties shall be promptly circulated by the depositary to all States Parties.

2. The amendment shall enter into force for each State Party that deposits its instrument of ratification, acceptance or approval of the amendment on the thirtieth day after the date on which two thirds of the States Parties have deposited their instruments of ratification, acceptance or approval with the depositary. Thereafter, the amendment shall enter into force for any other State Party on the day on which that State Party deposits its instrument of ratification, acceptance or approval of the amendment.

Article 21

1. Any State Party may denounce this Convention by written notification to the depositary.

2. Denunciation shall take effect one hundred and eighty days following the date on which notification is received by the depositary.

Article 22

The depositary shall promptly notify all States of:

(a) Each signature of this Convention;

(b) Each deposit of an instrument of ratification, acceptance, approval or accession;

(c) Any reservation or withdrawal in accordance with article 17;

(d) Any communication made by an organization in accordance with paragraph 4*(c)* of article 18;

(e) The entry into force of this Convention;

(f) The entry into force of any amendment to this Convention; and

(g) Any denunciation made under article 21.

Article 23

The original of this Convention, of which the Arabic, Chinese, English, French, Russian and Spanish texts are equally authentic, shall be deposited with the Director General of the International Atomic Energy Agency who shall send certified copies thereof to all States.

IN WITNESS WHEREOF, the undersigned, being duly authorized, have signed this Convention, opened for signature at Vienna and at New York on 3 March 1980.

ANNEX I

LEVELS OF PHYSICAL PROTECTION TO BE APPLIED IN INTERNATIONAL TRANSPORT OF NUCLEAR MATERIAL AS CATEGORIZED IN ANNEX II

1. Levels of physical protection for nuclear material during storage incidental to international nuclear transport include:

   (a) For Category III materials, storage within an area to which access is controlled;
   (b) For Category II materials, storage within an area under constant surveillance by guards or electronic devices, surrounded by a physical barrier with a limited number of points of entry under appropriate control or any area with an equivalent level of physical protection;
   (c) For Category I material, storage within a protected area as defined for Category II above, to which, in addition, access is restricted to persons whose trustworthiness has been determined, and which is under surveillance by guards who are in close communication with appropriate response forces. Specific measures taken in this context should have as their object the detection and prevention of any assault, unauthorized access or unauthorized removal of material.

2. Levels of physical protection for nuclear material during international transport include:

   (a) For Category II and [Category] III materials, transportation shall take place under special precautions including prior arrangements among sender, receiver, and carrier, and prior agreement between natural or legal persons subject to the jurisdiction and regulation of exporting and importing States, specifying time, place and procedures for transferring transport responsibility;
   (b) For Category I materials, transportation shall take place under special precautions identified above for transportation of Category II and [Category] III materials, and in addition, under constant surveillance by escorts and under conditions which assure close communication with appropriate response forces;
   (c) For natural uranium other than in the form of ore or ore-residue, transportation protection for quantities exceeding 500 kilograms U shall include advance notification of shipment specifying mode of transport, expected time of arrival and confirmation of receipt of shipment.

ANNEX II

TABLE. CATEGORIZATION OF NUCLEAR MATERIAL

Material	Form	Category		
		I	*II*	*III*[c]
1. Plutonium[a]	Unirradiated[b]	2 kg or more	Less than 2 kg but more than 500 g	500 g or less but more than 15 g
2. Uranium-235	Unirradiated[b] —uranium enriched to 20% ^{235}U or more	5 kg or more	Less than 5 kg but more than 1 kg	1 kg or less but more than 15 g
	—uranium enriched to 10% ^{235}U but less than 20%		10 kg or more	Less than 10 kg but more than 1 kg
	—uranium enriched above natural, but less than 10% ^{235}U			10 kg or more
3. Uranium-233	Unirradiated[b]	2 kg or more	Less than 2 kg but more than 500 g	500 g or less but more than 15 g
4. Irradiated fuel			Depleted or natural uranium, thorium or low-enriched fuel (less than 10% fissile content)[d, e]	

[a] All plutonium except that with isotopic concentration exceeding 80% in plutonium-238.

[b] Material not irradiated in a reactor or material irradiated in a reactor but with a radiation level equal to or less than 100 rads/hour at one metre unshielded.

[c] Quantities not falling in Category III and natural uranium should be protected in accordance with prudent management practice.

[d] Although this level of protection is recommended, it would be open to States, upon evaluation of the specific circumstances, to assign a different category of physical protection.

[e] Other fuel which by virtue of its original fissile material content is classified as Category I and [Category]II before irradiation may be reduced one category level while the radiation level from the fuel exceeds 100 rads/hour at one metre unshielded.

APPENDIX 9

Rome Convention and Protocols

No 29004

Multilateral

Convention for the suppression of unlawful acts against the safety of maritime navigation.
Concluded at Rome on 10 March 1988

Protocol to the above-mentioned Convention for the suppression of unlawful
acts against the safety of fixed platforms located on the continental shelf.
Concluded at Rome on 10 March 1988

Authentic texts: Arabic, Chinese, English, French, Russian and Spanish.

Registered by the International Maritime Organization on 26 June 1992.

Multilatéral

Convention pour la répression d'actes illicites contre la sécurité de la navigation maritime.
Conclu à Rome le 10 mars 1988

Protocole à la Convention susmentionnée pour la repression d'actes illicites contre la sécurité
des plates-formes fixes situées sur le plateau continental.
Conclu à Rome le 10 mars 1988

Textes authentiques: arabe, chinois, anglais, français, russe et espagnol.

Enregistrés par l'Organisation maritime internationale le 26 juin 1992.

CONVENTION[1] FOR THE SUPPRESSION OF UNLAWFUL ACTS AGAINST THE SAFETY OF MARITIME NAVIGATION

The States Parties to this Convention,

Having in mind the purposes and principles of the Charter of the United Nations concerning the maintenance of international peace and security and the promotion of friendly relations and co-operation among States,

---

[1] Came into force on 1 March 1992 in respect of the following States, ie, 90 days after the date on which at least 15 States had signed it without reservation as to ratification, acceptance or approval, or deposited the requisite instruments of ratification, acceptance, approval or accession with the Secretary-General of the International Maritime Organization, in accordance with article 18 (1):

Participant	*Date of deposit of the instrument of ratification, approval (AA) or accession (a)*
Austria	28 December 1989
China	20 August 1991
France	2 December 1991 *AA*
Gambia	1 November 1991 *a*

Recognizing in particular that everyone has the right to life, liberty and security of person, as set out in the Universal Declaration of Human Rights[2] and the International Covenant on Civil and Political Rights,[3]

Deeply concerned about the world-wide escalation of acts of terrorism in all its forms, which endanger or take innocent human lives, jeopardize fundamental freedoms and seriously impair the dignity of human beings,

Considering that unlawful acts against the safety of maritime navigation jeopardize the safety of persons and property, seriously affect the operation of maritime services, and undermine the confidence of the peoples of the world in the safety of maritime navigation,

Considering that the occurrence of such acts is a matter of grave concern to the international community as a whole,

Being convinced of the urgent need to develop international co-operation between States in devising and adopting effective and practical measures for the prevention of all unlawful acts against the safety of maritime navigation and the prosecution and punishment of their perpetrators,

Recalling resolution 40/61[4] of the General Assembly of the United Nations of 9 December 1985 which, inter alia, 'urges all States unilaterally and in co-operation with other States, as well as relevant United Nations organs, to contribute to the progressive elimination of causes underlying international terrorism and to pay special attention to all situations, including colonialism, racism and situations involving mass and flagrant violations of human rights and fundamental freedoms and those involving alien occupation, that may give rise to international terrorism and may endanger international peace and security',

Recalling further that resolution 40/61 'unequivocally condemns, as criminal, all acts, methods and practices of terrorism wherever and by whomever committed, including those which jeopardize friendly relations among States and their security',

Recalling also that by resolution 40/61, the International Maritime Organization was invited to 'study the problem of terrorism aboard or against ships with a view to making recommendations on appropriate measures',

Having in mind resolution A.584(14)[5] of 20 November 1985, of the Assembly of the International Maritime Organization, which called for development of measures to prevent unlawful acts which threaten the safety of ships and the security of their passengers and crews,

German Democratic Republic[1]	14 April 1989 *a*
Germany	6 November 1990 *a*
Hungary	9 November 1989
Italy	26 January 1990
Norway	18 April 1991
Oman	24 September 1990 *a*
Poland	25 June 1991
Seychelles	24 January 1989
Spain	7 July 1989
Sweden	13 September 1990
Trinidad and Tobago	27 July 1989 *a*
United Kingdom of Great Britain and Northern Ireland	3 May 1991

[1] Prior to the coming into effect of the accession, the German Democratic Republic acceded to the Federal Republic of Germany with effect from 3 October 1990.

[2] United Nations, *Official Records of the General Assembly, Third Session*, Part I, p 71.
[3] United Nations, *Treaty Series*, vol 999, p 171; vol 1057, p 407 (rectification of authentic Spanish text); vol 1059, p 451 (corrigendum to vol 999).
[4] United Nations, *Official Records of the General Assembly, Fortieth Session*, Supplement 53 (A/40/53), p 301.
[5] International Maritime Organization, *Resolutions and Other Decisions, Assembly, Fourteenth Session*, 11–22 November 1985, p 152.

Noting that acts of the crew which are subject to normal shipboard discipline are outside the purview of this Convention,

Affirming the desirability of monitoring rules and standards relating to the prevention and control of unlawful acts against ships and persons on board ships, with a view to updating them as necessary, and, to this effect, taking note with satisfaction of the Measures to Prevent Unlawful Acts against Passengers and Crews on Board Ships, recommended by the Maritime Safety Committee of the International Maritime Organization,

Affirming further that matters not regulated by this Convention continue to be governed by the rules and principles of general international law,

Recognizing the need for all States, in combating unlawful acts against the safety of maritime navigation, strictly to comply with rules and principles of general international law,

Have agreed as follows:

Article 1

For the purposes of this Convention, 'ship' means a vessel of any type whatsoever not permanently attached to the sea-bed, including dynamically supported craft, submersibles, or any other floating craft.

Article 2

1. This Convention does not apply to:

    (a) a warship; or
    (b) a ship owned or operated by a State when being used as a naval auxiliary or for customs or police purposes; or
    (c) a ship which has been withdrawn from navigation or laid up.

2. Nothing in this Convention affects the immunities of warships and other government ships operated for non-commercial purposes.

Article 3

1. Any person commits an offence if that person unlawfully and intentionally:

    (a) seizes or exercises control over a ship by force or threat thereof or any other form of intimidation; or
    (b) performs an act of violence against a person on board a ship if that act is likely to endanger the safe navigation of that ship; or
    (c) destroys a ship or causes damage to a ship or to its cargo which is likely to endanger the safe navigation of that ship; or
    (d) places or causes to be placed on a ship, by any means whatsoever, a device or substance which is likely to destroy that ship, or cause damage to that ship or its cargo which endangers or is likely to endanger the safe navigation of that ship; or
    (e) destroys or seriously damages maritime navigational facilities or seriously interferes with their operation, if any such act is likely to endanger the safe navigation of a ship; or
    (f) communicates information which he knows to be false, thereby endangering the safe navigation of a ship; or
    (g) injures or kills any person, in connection with the commission or the attempted commission of any of the offences set forth in subparagraphs (a) to (f).

2. Any person also commits an offence if that person:

    (a) attempts to commit any of the offences set forth in paragraph 1; or
    (b) abets the commission of any of the offences set forth in paragraph 1 perpetrated by any person or is otherwise an accomplice of a person who commits such an offence; or
    (c) threatens, with or without a condition, as is provided for under national law, aimed at compelling a physical or juridical person to do or refrain from doing any act, to commit

any of the offences set forth in paragraph 1, subparagraphs (b), (c) and (e), if that threat is likely to endanger the safe navigation of the ship in question.

Article 4

1. This Convention applies if the ship is navigating or is scheduled to navigate into, through or from waters beyond the outer limit of the territorial sea of a single State, or the lateral limits of its territorial sea with adjacent States.

2. In cases where the Convention does not apply pursuant to paragraph 1, it nevertheless applies when the offender or the alleged offender is found in the territory of a State Party other than the State referred to in paragraph 1.

Article 5

Each State Party shall make the offences set forth in article 3 punishable by appropriate penalties which take into account the grave nature of those offences.

Article 6

1. Each State Party shall take such measures as may be necessary to establish its jurisdiction over the offences set forth in article 3 when the offence is committed:

   (a) against or on board a ship flying the flag of the State at the time the offence is committed; or
   (b) in the territory of that State, including its territorial sea; or
   (c) by a national of that State.

2. A State Party may also establish its jurisdiction over any such offence when:

   (a) it is committed by a stateless person whose habitual residence is in that State; or
   (b) during its commission a national of that State is seized, threatened, injured or killed; or
   (c) it is committed in an attempt to compel that State to do or abstain from doing any act.

3. Any State Party which has established jurisdiction mentioned in paragraph 2 shall notify the Secretary-General of the International Maritime Organization (hereinafter referred to as 'the Secretary-General'). If such State Party subsequently rescinds that jurisdiction, it shall notify the Secretary-General.

4. Each State Party shall take such measures as may be necessary to establish its jurisdiction over the offences set forth in article 3 in cases where the alleged offender is present in its territory and it does not extradite him to any of the States Parties which have established their jurisdiction in accordance with paragraphs 1 and 2 of this article.

5. This Convention does not exclude any criminal jurisdiction exercised in accordance with national law.

Article 7

1. Upon being satisfied that the circumstances so warrant, any State Party in the territory of which the offender or the alleged offender is present shall, in accordance with its law, take him into custody or take other measures to ensure his presence for such time as is necessary to enable any criminal or extradition proceedings to be instituted.

2. Such State shall immediately make a preliminary inquiry into the facts, in accordance with its own legislation.

3. Any person regarding whom the measures referred to in paragraph 1 are being taken shall be entitled to:

   (a) communicate without delay with the nearest appropriate representative of the State of which he is a national or which is otherwise entitled to establish such communication or, if he is a stateless person, the State in the territory of which he has his habitual residence;
   (b) be visited by a representative of that State.

4. The rights referred to in paragraph 3 shall be exercised in conformity with the laws and regulations of the State in the territory of which the offender or the alleged offender is present, subject to the proviso that the said laws and regulations must enable full effect to be given to the purposes for which the rights accorded under paragraph 3 are intended.

5. When a State Party, pursuant to this article, has taken a person into custody, it shall immediately notify the States which have established jurisdiction in accordance with article 6, paragraph 1 and, if it considers it advisable, any other interested States, of the fact that such person is in custody and of the circumstances which warrant his detention. The State which makes the preliminary inquiry contemplated in paragraph 2 of this article shall promptly report its findings to the said States and shall indicate whether it intends to exercise jurisdiction.

Article 8

1. The master of a ship of a State Party (the 'flag State') may deliver to the authorities of any other State Party (the 'receiving State') any person who he has reasonable grounds to believe has committed one of the offences set forth in article 3.

2. The flag State shall ensure that the master of its ship is obliged, whenever practicable, and if possible before entering the territorial sea of the receiving State carrying on board any person whom the master intends to deliver in accordance with paragraph 1, to give notification to the authorities of the receiving State of his intention to deliver such person and the reasons therefor.

3. The receiving State shall accept the delivery, except where it has grounds to consider that the Convention is not applicable to the acts giving rise to the delivery, and shall proceed in accordance with the provisions of article 7. Any refusal to accept a delivery shall be accompanied by a statement of the reasons for refusal.

4. The flag State shall ensure that the master of its ship is obliged to furnish the authorities of the receiving State with the evidence in the master's possession which pertains to the alleged offence.

5. A receiving State which has accepted the delivery of a person in accordance with paragraph 3 may, in turn, request the flag State to accept delivery of that person. The flag State shall consider any such request, and if it accedes to the request it shall proceed in accordance with article 7. If the flag State declines a request, it shall furnish the receiving State with a statement of the reasons therefor.

Article 9

Nothing in this Convention shall affect in any way the rules of international law pertaining to the competence of States to exercise investigative or enforcement jurisdiction on board ships not flying their flag.

Article 10

1. The State Party in the territory of which the offender or the alleged offender is found shall, in cases to which article 6 applies, if it does not extradite him, be obliged, without exception whatsoever and whether or not the offence was committed in its territory, to submit the case without delay to its competent authorities for the purpose of prosecution, through proceedings in accordance with the laws of that State. Those authorities shall take their decision in the same manner as in the case of any other offence of a grave nature under the law of that State.

2. Any person regarding whom proceedings are being carried out in connection with any of the offences set forth in article 3 shall be guaranteed fair treatment at all stages of the proceedings, including enjoyment of all the rights and guarantees provided for such proceedings by the law of the State in the territory of which he is present.

Article 11

1. The offences set forth in article 3 shall be deemed to be included as extraditable offences in any extradition treaty existing between any of the States Parties. States Parties undertake to include such offences as extraditable offences in every extradition treaty to be concluded between them.

2. If a State Party which makes extradition conditional on the existence of a treaty receives a request for extradition from another State Party with which it has no extradition treaty, the requested State Party may, at its option, consider this Convention as a legal basis for extradition in respect of the offences set forth in article 3. Extradition shall be subject to the other conditions provided by the law of the requested State Party.

3. States Parties which do not make extradition conditional on the existence of a treaty shall recognize the offences set forth in article 3 as extraditable offences between themselves, subject to the conditions provided by the law of the requested State.

4. If necessary, the offences set forth in article 3 shall be treated, for the purposes of extradition between States Parties, as if they had been committed not only in the place in which they occurred but also in a place within the jurisdiction of the State Party requesting extradition.

5. A State Party which receives more than one request for extradition from States which have established jurisdiction in accordance with article [6]⁶ and which decides not to prosecute shall, in selecting the State to which the offender or alleged offender is to be extradited, pay due regard to the interests and responsibilities of the State Party whose flag the ship was flying at the time of the commission of the offence.

6. In considering a request for the extradition of an alleged offender pursuant to this Convention, the requested State shall pay due regard to whether his rights as set forth in article 7, paragraph 3, can be effected in the requesting State.

7. With respect to the offences as defined in this Convention, the provisions of all extradition treaties and arrangement applicable between States Parties are modified as between States Parties to the extent that they are incompatible with this Convention.

Article 12

1. State Parties shall afford one another the greatest measure of assistance in connection with criminal proceedings brought in respect of the offences set forth in article 3, including assistance in obtaining evidence at their disposal necessary for the proceedings.

2. States Parties shall carry out their obligations under paragraph 1 in conformity with any treaties on mutual assistance that may exist between them. In the absence of such treaties, States Parties shall afford each other assistance in accordance with their national law.

Article 13

1. States Parties shall co-operate in the prevention of the offences set forth in article 3, particularly by:

 (a) taking all practicable measures to prevent preparations in their respective territories for the commission of those offences within or outside their territories;
 (b) exchanging information in accordance with their national law, and co-ordinating administrative and other measures taken as appropriate to prevent the commission of offences set forth in article 3.

2. When, due to the commission of an offence set forth in article 3, the passage of a ship has been delayed or interrupted, any State Party in whose territory the ship or passengers or crew are present shall be bound to exercise all possible efforts to avoid a ship, its passengers, crew or cargo being unduly detained or delayed.

Article 14

Any State Party having reason to believe that an offence set forth in article 3 will be committed shall, in accordance with its national law, furnish as promptly as possible any relevant information in its

---

⁶ Text between brackets reflects corrections effected by procès-verbal of 21 December 1989.

possession to those States which it believes would be the States having established jurisdiction in accordance with article 6.

Article 15

1. Each State Party shall, in accordance with its national law, provide to the Secretary-General, as promptly as possible, any relevant information in its possession concerning:

(a) the circumstances of the offence;

(b) the action taken pursuant to article 13, paragraph 2;

(c) the measures taken in relation to the offender or the alleged offender and, in particular, the results of any extradition proceedings or other legal proceedings.

2. The State Party where the alleged offender is prosecuted shall, in accordance with its national law, communicate the final outcome of the proceedings to the Secretary-General.

3. The information transmitted in accordance with paragraphs 1 and 2 shall be communicated by the Secretary-General to all States Parties, to Members of the International Maritime Organization (hereinafter referred to as 'the Organization'), to the other States concerned, and to the appropriate international intergovernmental organizations.

Article 16

1. Any dispute between two or more States Parties concerning the interpretation or application of this Convention which cannot be settled through negotiation within a reasonable time shall, at the request of one of them, be submitted to arbitration. If, within six months from the date of the request for arbitration, the parties are unable to agree on the organization of the arbitration any one of those parties may refer the dispute to the International Court of Justice by request in conformity with the Statute of the Court.

2. Each State may at the time of signature or ratification, acceptance or approval of this Convention or accession thereto, declare that it does not consider itself bound by any or all of the provisions of paragraph 1. The other States Parties shall not be bound by those provisions with respect to any State Party which has made such a reservation.

3. Any State which has made a reservation in accordance with paragraph 2 may, at any time, withdraw that reservation by notification to the Secretary-General.

Article 17

1. This Convention shall be open for signature at Rome on 10 March 1988 by States participating in the International Conference on the Suppression of Unlawful Acts against the Safety of Maritime Navigation and at the Headquarters of the Organization by all States from 14 March 1988 to 9 March 1989. It shall thereafter remain open for accession.

2. States may express their consent to be bound by this Convention by:

(a) signature without reservation as to ratification, acceptance or approval; or

(b) signature subject to ratification, acceptance or approval, followed by ratification, acceptance or approval; or

(c) accession.

3. Ratification, acceptance, approval or accession shall be effected by the deposit of an instrument to that effect with the Secretary-General.

Article 18

1. This Convention shall enter into force ninety days following the date on which fifteen States have either signed it without reservation as to ratification, acceptance or approval, or have deposited an instrument of ratification, acceptance, approval or accession in respect thereof.

2. For a State which deposits an instrument of ratification, acceptance, approval or accession in respect of this Convention after the conditions for entry into force thereof have been met, the

ratification, acceptance, approval or accession shall take effect ninety days after the date of such deposit.

Article 19

1. This Convention may be denounced by any State Party at any time after the expiry of one year from the date on which this Convention enters into force for that State.

2. Denunciation shall be effected by the deposit of an instrument of denunciation with the Secretary-General.

3. A denunciation shall take effect one year, or such longer period as may be specified in the instrument of denunciation, after the receipt of the instrument of denunciation by the Secretary-General.

Article 20

1. A conference for the purpose of revising or amending this Convention may be convened by the Organization.

2. The Secretary-General shall convene a conference of the States Parties to this Convention for revising or amending the Convention, at the request of one third of the States Parties, or ten States Parties, whichever is the higher figure.

3. Any instrument of ratification, acceptance, approval or accession deposited after the date of entry into force of an amendment to this Convention shall be deemed to apply to the Convention as amended.

Article 21

1. This Convention shall be deposited with the Secretary-General.

2. The Secretary-General shall:

  (a) inform all States which have signed this Convention or acceded thereto, and all Members of the Organization, of:
   (i)   each new signature or deposit of an instrument of ratification, acceptance, approval or accession together with the date thereof;
   (ii) the date of the entry into force of this Convention;
   (iii) the deposit of any instrument of denunciation of this Convention together with the date on which it is received and the date on which the denunciation takes effect;
   (iv) the receipt of any declaration or notification made under this Convention;
  (b) transmit certified true copies of this Convention to all States which have signed this Convention or acceded thereto.

3. As soon as this Convention enters into force, a certified true copy thereof shall be transmitted by the Depositary to the Secretary-General of the United Nations for registration and publication in accordance with Article 102 of the Charter of the United Nations.

Article 22

This Convention is established in a single original in the Arabic, Chinese, English, French, Russian and Spanish languages, each text being equally authentic.

IN WITNESS WHEREOF the undersigned being duly authorized by their respective Governments for that purpose have signed this Convention.

DONE AT ROME this tenth day of March one thousand nine hundred and eighty-eight.

Protocol[7] for the Suppression of Unlawful Acts Against the Safety of Fixed Platforms Located on the Continental Shelf

The States Parties to this Protocol,

Being parties to the Convention for the Suppression of Unlawful Acts against the Safety of Maritime Navigation,

Recognizing that the reasons for which the Convention was elaborated also apply to fixed platforms located on the continental shelf,

Taking account of the provisions of that Convention,

Affirming that matters not regulated by this Protocol continue to be governed by the rules and principles of general international law,

Have agreed as follows:

Article 1

1. The provisions of articles 5 and 7 and of articles 10 to 16 of the Convention for the Suppression of Unlawful Acts against the Safety of Maritime Navigation (hereinafter referred to as 'the Convention') shall also apply *mutatis mutandis* to the offences set forth in article 2 of this Protocol where such offences are committed on board or against fixed platforms located on the continental shelf.

2. In cases where this Protocol does not apply pursuant to paragraph 1, it nevertheless applies when the offender or the alleged offender is found in the territory of a State Party other than the State in whose internal waters or territorial sea the fixed platform is located.

3. For the purposes of this Protocol, 'fixed platform' means an artificial island, installation or structure permanently attached to the sea-bed for the purpose of exploration or exploitation of resources or for other economic purposes.

---

[7] Came into force on 1 March 1992, ie, the date on which the above-mentioned Convention entered into force, in accordance with article 6 (1):

Participant	*Date of deposit of the instrument of ratification, approval (AA) or accession (a)*
Austria	28 December 1989 *a*
China	20 August 1991
France	2 December 1991 *AA*
German Democratic Republic[1]	14 April 1989 *a*
Germany	6 November 1990 *a*
Hungary	9 November 1989
Italy	26 January 1990
Norway	18 April 1991
Oman	24 September 1990 *a*
Poland	25 June 1991
Seychelles	24 January 1989
Spain	7 July 1989
Sweden	13 September 1990
Trinidad and Tobago	27 July 1989 *a*
United Kingdom of Great Britain and Northern Ireland	3 May 1991

[1] Prior to the coming into effect of the accession, the German Democratic Republic acceded to the Federal Republic of Germany with effect from 3 October 1990.

Article 2

1. Any person commits an offence if that person unlawfully and intentionally:

   (a) seizes or exercises control over a fixed platform by force or threat thereof or any other form of intimidation; or

   (b) performs an act of violence against a person on board a fixed platform if that act is likely to endanger its safety; or

   (c) destroys a fixed platform or causes damage to it which is likely to endanger its safety; or

   (d) places or causes to be placed on a fixed platform, by any means whatsoever, a device or substance which is likely to destroy that fixed platform or likely to endanger its safety; or

   (e) injures or kills any person in connection with the commission or the attempted commission of any of the offences set forth in subparagraphs (a) to (d).

2. Any person also commits an offence if that person:

   (a) attempts to commit any of the offences set forth in paragraph 1; or

   (b) abets the commission of any such offences perpetrated by any person or is otherwise an accomplice of a person who commits such an offence; or

   (c) threatens, with or without a condition, as is provided for under national law, aimed at compelling a physical or juridical person to do or refrain from doing any act, to commit any of the offences set forth in paragraph 1, subparagraphs (b) and (c), if that threat is likely to endanger the safety of the fixed platform.

Article 3

1. Each State Party shall take such measures as may be necessary to establish its jurisdiction over the offences set forth in article 2 when the offence is committed:

   (a) against or on board a fixed platform while it is located on the continental shelf of that State; or

   (b) by a national of that State.

2. A State Party may also establish its jurisdiction over any such offence when:

   (a) it is committed by a stateless person whose habitual residence is in that State;

   (b) during its commission a national of that State is seized, threatened, injured or killed; or

   (c) it is committed in an attempt to compel that State to do or abstain from doing any act.

3. Any State Party which has established jurisdiction mentioned in paragraph 2 shall notify the Secretary-General of the International Maritime Organization (hereinafter referred to as 'the Secretary-General'). If such State Party subsequently rescinds that jurisdiction, it shall notify the Secretary-General.

4. Each State Party shall take such measures as may be necessary to establish its jurisdiction over the offences set forth in article 2 in cases where the alleged offender is present in its territory and it does not extradite him to any of the States Parties which have established their jurisdiction in accordance with paragraphs 1 and 2 of this article.

5. This Protocol does not exclude any criminal jurisdiction exercised in accordance with national law.

Article 4

Nothing in this Protocol shall affect in any way the rules of international law pertaining to fixed platforms located on the continental shelf.

Article 5

1. This Protocol shall be open for signature at Rome on 10 March 1988 and at the Headquarters of the International Maritime Organization (hereinafter referred to as 'the Organization') from 14 March 1988 to 9 March 1989 by any State which has signed the Convention. It shall thereafter remain open for accession.

2. States may express their consent to be bound by this Protocol by:

(a) signature without reservation as to ratification, acceptance or approval; or

(b) signature subject to ratification, acceptance or approval, followed by ratification, acceptance or approval; or

(c) accession.

3. Ratification, acceptance, approval or accession shall be effected by the deposit of an instrument to that effect with the Secretary-General.

4. Only a State which has signed the Convention without reservation as to ratification, acceptance or approval, or has ratified, accepted, approved or acceded to the Convention may become a Party to this Protocol.

Article 6

1. This Protocol shall enter into force ninety days following the date on which three States have either signed it without reservation as to ratification, acceptance or approval, or have deposited an instrument of ratification, acceptance, approval or accession in respect thereof. However, this Protocol shall not enter into force before the Convention has entered into force.

2. For a State which deposits an instrument of ratification, acceptance, approval or accession in respect of this Protocol after the conditions for entry into force thereof have been met, the ratification, acceptance, approval or accession shall take effect ninety days after the date of such deposit.

Article 7

1. This Protocol may be denounced by any State Party at any time after the expiry of one year from the date on which this Protocol enters into force for that State.

2. Denunciation shall be effected by the deposit of an instrument of denunciation with the Secretary-General.

3. A denunciation shall take effect one year, or such longer period as may be specified in the instrument of denunciation, after the receipt of the instrument of denunciation by the Secretary-General.

4. A denunciation of the Convention by a State Party shall be deemed to be a denunciation of this Protocol by that Party.

Article 8

1. A conference for the purpose of revising or amending this Protocol may be convened by the Organization.

2. The Secretary-General shall convene a conference of the States Parties to this Protocol for revising or amending the Protocol, at the request of one third of the States Parties, or five States Parties, whichever is the higher figure.

3. Any instrument of ratification, acceptance, approval or accession deposited after the date of entry into force of an amendment to this Protocol shall be deemed to apply to the Protocol as amended.

Article 9

1. This Protocol shall be deposited with the Secretary-General.

2. The Secretary-General shall:

(a) inform all States which have signed this Protocol or acceded thereto, and all Members of the Organization, of:

(i) each new signature or deposit of an instrument of ratification, acceptance, approval or accession, together with the date thereof;

(ii) the date of entry into force of this Protocol;

(iii) the deposit of any instrument of denunciation of this Protocol together with the date on which it is received and the date on which the denunciation takes effect;

(iv) the receipt of any declaration or notification made under this Protocol or under the Convention, concerning this Protocol;

(b) transmit certified true copies of this Protocol to all States which have signed this Protocol or acceded thereto.

3. As soon as this Protocol enters into force, a certified true copy thereof shall be transmitted by the Depositary to the Secretary-General of the United Nations for registration and publication in accordance with Article 102 of the Charter of the United Nations.

Article 10

This Protocol is established in a single original in the Arabic, Chinese, English, French, Russian and Spanish languages, each text being equally authentic.

IN WITNESS WHEREOF the undersigned, being duly authorized by their respective Governments for that purpose, have signed this Protocol.

DONE AT ROME this tenth day of March one thousand nine hundred and eighty-eight.

INTERNATIONAL MARITIME ORGANIZATION

INTERNATIONAL CONFERENCE ON THE	LEG/CONF.15/22
REVISION OF THE SUA TREATIES	1 November 2005
Agenda item 8	Original: ENGLISH

ADOPTION OF THE FINAL ACT AND ANY INSTRUMENTS,
RECOMMENDATIONS AND RESOLUTIONS RESULTING FROM
THE WORK OF THE CONFERENCE

PROTOCOL OF 2005 TO THE PROTOCOL FOR THE SUPPRESSION
OF UNLAWFUL ACTS AGAINST THE SAFETY OF FIXED PLATFORMS
LOCATED ON THE CONTINENTAL SHELF

Text adopted by the Conference

The States Parties to this Protocol,

Being Parties to the Protocol for the Suppression of Unlawful Acts against the Safety of Fixed Platforms Located on the Continental Shelf done at Rome on 10 March 1988,

Recognizing that the reasons for which the Protocol of 2005 to the Convention for the Suppression of Unlawful Acts against the Safety of Maritime Navigation was elaborated also apply to fixed platforms located on the continental shelf,

Taking account of the provisions of those Protocols,

Have agreed as follows:

Article 1

For the purposes of this Protocol:

1. '1988 Protocol' means the Protocol for the Suppression of Unlawful Acts against the Safety of Fixed Platforms Located on the Continental Shelf, done at Rome on 10 March 1988.

2. 'Organization' means the International Maritime Organization.

3. 'Secretary-General' means the Secretary-General of the Organization.

Article 2

Article 1, paragraph 1, of the 1988 Protocol is replaced by the following text:

1. The provisions of article 1, paragraphs 1(c), (d), (e), (f), (g), (h) and 2(a), of articles 2*bis*, 5, 5*bis* and 7, and of articles 10 to 16, including articles 11*bis*, 11*ter* and 12*bis*, of the Convention for the Suppression of Unlawful Acts against the Safety of Maritime Navigation, as amended by the Protocol of 2005 to the Convention for the Suppression of Unlawful Acts against the Safety of Maritime Navigation, shall also apply *mutatis mutandis* to the offences set forth in articles 2, 2*bis* and 2*ter* of this Protocol where such offences are committed on board or against fixed platforms located on the continental shelf.

Article 3

1. Article 2, paragraph 1(d) of the 1988 Protocol is replaced by the following text:

(d) places or causes to be placed on a fixed platform, by any means whatsoever, a device or substance which is likely to destroy that fixed platform or likely to endanger its safety.

2. Article 2, paragraph 1(e) of the 1988 Protocol is deleted.

3. Article 2, paragraph 2 of the 1988 Protocol is replaced by the following text:

2. Any person also commits an offence if that person threatens, with or without a condition, as is provided for under national law, aimed at compelling a physical or juridical person to do or refrain from doing any act, to commit any of the offences set forth in paragraphs 1(b) and (c), if that threat is likely to endanger the safety of the fixed platform.

Article 4

1. The following text is inserted as article 2bis:

Article 2*bis*

Any person commits an offence within the meaning of this Protocol if that person unlawfully and intentionally, when the purpose of the act, by its nature or context, is to intimidate a population, or to compel a government or an international organization to do or to abstain from doing any act:

(a) uses against or on a fixed platform or discharges from a fixed platform any explosive, radio-active material or BCN weapon in a manner that causes or is likely to cause death or serious injury or damage; or
(b) discharges, from a fixed platform, oil, liquefied natural gas, or other hazardous or noxious substance, which is not covered by subparagraph (a), in such quantity or concentration that causes or is likely to cause death or serious injury or damage; or
(c) threatens, with or without a condition, as is provided for under national law, to commit an offence set forth in subparagraph (a) or (b).

2. The following text is inserted as article 2ter:

Article 2*ter*

Any person also commits an offence within the meaning of this Protocol if that person:

(a) unlawfully and intentionally injures or kills any person in connection with the commission of any of the offences set forth in article 2, paragraph 1, or article 2*bis*; or
(b) attempts to commit an offence set forth in article 2, paragraph 1, article 2*bis*, subparagraph (a) or (b), or subparagraph (a) of this article; or
(c) participates as an accomplice in an offence set forth in article 2, article 2*bis* or subparagraph (a) or (b) of this article; or
(d) organizes or directs others to commit an offence set forth in article 2, article 2*bis* or subparagraph (a) or (b) of this article; or

(e) contributes to the commission of one or more offences set forth in article 2, article 2*bis* or subparagraph (a) or (b) of this article, by a group of persons acting with a common purpose, intentionally and either:

    (i) with the aim of furthering the criminal activity or criminal purpose of the group, where such activity or purpose involves the commission of an offence set forth in article 2 or 2*bis*; or

    (ii) in the knowledge of the intention of the group to commit an offence set forth in article 2 or 2*bis*.

Article 5

1. Article 3, paragraph 1 of the 1988 Protocol is replaced by the following text:

1. Each State Party shall take such measures as may be necessary to establish its jurisdiction over the offences set forth in articles 2, 2*bis* and 2*ter* when the offence is committed:

    (a) against or on board a fixed platform while it is located on the continental shelf of that State; or

    (b) by a national of that State.

2. Article 3, paragraph 3 of the 1988 Protocol is replaced by the following text:

3. Any State Party which has established jurisdiction mentioned in paragraph 2 shall notify the Secretary-General. If such State Party subsequently rescinds that jurisdiction, it shall notify the Secretary-General.

3. Article 3, paragraph 4 of the 1988 Protocol is replaced by the following text:

4. Each State Party shall take such measures as may be necessary to establish its jurisdiction over the offences set forth in articles 2, 2*bis* and 2*ter* in cases where the alleged offender is present in its territory and it does not extradite the alleged offender to any of the States Parties which have established their jurisdiction in accordance with paragraphs 1 and 2.

Article 6

Interpretation and application

1. The 1988 Protocol and this Protocol shall, as between the Parties to this Protocol, be read and interpreted together as one single instrument.

2. Articles 1 to 4 of the 1988 Protocol, as revised by this Protocol, together with articles 8 to 13 of this Protocol shall constitute and be called the Protocol for the Suppression of Unlawful Acts against the Safety of Fixed Platforms Located on the Continental Shelf, 2005 (2005 SUA Fixed Platforms Protocol).

Article 7

The following text is added as Article 4 bis of the Protocol:

Final clauses of the Protocol for the Suppression of Unlawful Acts against the Safety of Fixed Platforms Located on the Continental Shelf, 2005

The final clauses of the Protocol for the Suppression of Unlawful Acts against the Safety of Fixed Platforms Located on the Continental Shelf, 2005, shall be articles 8 to 13 of the Protocol of 2005 to the Protocol for the Suppression of Unlawful Acts against the Safety of Fixed Platforms Located on the Continental Shelf. References in this Protocol to States Parties shall be taken to mean references to States Parties to the 2005 Protocol.

Final Clauses

Article 8

Signature, ratification, acceptance, approval and accession

1. This Protocol shall be open for signature at the Headquarters of the Organization from 14 February 2006 to 13 February 2007 and shall thereafter remain open for accession.

2. States may express their consent to be bound by this Protocol by:

   (a) signature without reservation as to ratification, acceptance or approval; or

   (b) signature subject to ratification, acceptance or approval, followed by ratification, acceptance or approval; or

   (c) accession.

3. Ratification, acceptance, approval or accession shall be effected by the deposit of an instrument to that effect with the Secretary-General.

4. Only a State which has signed the 1988 Protocol without reservation as to ratification, acceptance or approval, or has ratified, accepted, approved or acceded to the 1988 Protocol may become a Party to this Protocol.

Article 9

Entry into force

1. This Protocol shall enter into force ninety days following the date on which three States have either signed it without reservation as to ratification, acceptance or approval, or have deposited an instrument of ratification, acceptance, approval or accession with the Secretary-General. However, this Protocol shall not enter into force before the Protocol of 2005 to the Convention for the Suppression of Unlawful Acts against the Safety of Maritime Navigation has entered into force.

2. For a State which deposits an instrument of ratification, acceptance, approval or accession in respect of this Protocol after the conditions in paragraph 1 for entry into force thereof have been met, the ratification, acceptance, approval or accession shall take effect ninety days after the date of such deposit.

Article 10

Denunciation

1. This Protocol may be denounced by any State Party at any time after the date on which this Protocol enters into force for that State.

2. Denunciation shall be effected by the deposit of an instrument of denunciation with the Secretary-General.

3. A denunciation shall take effect one year, or such longer period as may be specified in the instrument of denunciation, after the deposit of the instrument with the Secretary-General.

Article 11

Revision and amendment

1. A conference for the purpose of revising or amending this Protocol may be convened by the Organization.

2. The Secretary-General shall convene a conference of States Parties to this Protocol for revising or amending the Protocol, at the request of one third of the States Parties, or five States Parties, whichever is the higher figure.

3. Any instrument of ratification, acceptance, approval or accession deposited after the date of entry into force of an amendment to this Protocol shall be deemed to apply to the Protocol as amended.

Article 12

Depositary

1. This Protocol and any amendments adopted under article 11 shall be deposited with the Secretary-General.

2. The Secretary-General shall:

    (a) inform all States which have signed this Protocol or acceded to this Protocol of:
        (i) each new signature or deposit of an instrument of ratification, acceptance, approval or accession together with the date thereof;
        (ii) the date of the entry into force of this Protocol;
        (iii) the deposit of any instrument of denunciation of this Protocol together with the date on which it is received and the date on which the denunciation takes effect;
        (iv) any communication called for by any article of this Protocol; and

    (b) transmit certified true copies of this Protocol to all States which have signed or acceded to this Protocol.

3. As soon as this Protocol enters into force, a certified true copy of the text shall be transmitted by the Secretary-General to the Secretary-General of the United Nations for registration and publication in accordance with Article 102 of the Charter of the United Nations.

Article 13

Languages

This Protocol is established in a single original in the Arabic, Chinese, English, French, Russian and Spanish languages, each text being equally authentic.

DONE AT LONDON this fourteenth day of October two thousand and five.

IN WITNESS WHEREOF the undersigned, being duly authorized by their respective Governments for that purpose, have signed this Protocol.

INTERNATIONAL MARITIME ORGANIZATION

INTERNATIONAL CONFERENCE ON THE	LEG/CONF.15/21
REVISION OF THE SUA TREATIES	1 November 2005
Agenda item 8	Original: ENGLISH

ADOPTION OF THE FINAL ACT AND ANY INSTRUMENTS,
RECOMMENDATIONS AND RESOLUTIONS RESULTING FROM
THE WORK OF THE CONFERENCE

PROTOCOL OF 2005 TO THE CONVENTION FOR
THE SUPPRESSION OF UNLAWFUL ACTS AGAINST
THE SAFETY OF MARITIME NAVIGATION

Text adopted by the Conference

PREAMBLE

The States Parties to this Protocol,

Being parties to the Convention for the Suppression of Unlawful Acts against the Safety of Maritime Navigation done at Rome on 10 March 1988,

Acknowledging that terrorist acts threaten international peace and security,

Mindful of resolution A.924(22) of the Assembly of the International Maritime Organization requesting the revision of existing international legal and technical measures and the consideration of new measures in order to prevent and suppress terrorism against ships and to improve security aboard and ashore, and thereby to reduce the risk to passengers, crews and port personnel on board ships and in port areas and to vessels and their cargoes,

Conscious of the Declaration on Measures to Eliminate International Terrorism, annexed to United Nations General Assembly resolution 49/60 of 9 December 1994, in which, inter alia, the States Members of the United Nations solemnly reaffirm their unequivocal condemnation of all acts, methods and practices of terrorism as criminal and unjustifiable, wherever and by whomever committed, including those which jeopardize the friendly relations among States and peoples and threaten the territorial integrity and security of States,

Noting United Nations General Assembly resolution 51/210 of 17 December 1996 and the Declaration to Supplement the 1994 Declaration on Measures to Eliminate International Terrorism annexed thereto,

Recalling resolutions 1368 (2001) and 1373 (2001) of the United Nations Security Council, which reflect international will to combat terrorism in all its forms and manifestations, and which assigned tasks and responsibilities to States, and taking into account the continued threat from terrorist attacks,

Recalling also resolution 1540 (2004) of the United Nations Security Council, which recognizes the urgent need for all States to take additional effective measures to prevent the proliferation of nuclear, chemical or biological weapons and their means of delivery,

Recalling further the Convention on Offences and Certain Other Acts Committed on Board Aircraft, done at Tokyo on 14 September 1963; the Convention for the Suppression of Unlawful Seizure of Aircraft, done at The Hague on 16 December 1970; the Convention for the Suppression of Unlawful Acts against the Safety of Civil Aviation, done at Montreal on 23 September 1971; the Convention on the Prevention and Punishment of Crimes against Internationally Protected Persons, including Diplomatic Agents, adopted by the General Assembly of the United Nations on 14 December 1973; the International Convention against the Taking of Hostages, adopted by the General Assembly of the United Nations on 17 December 1979; the Convention on the Physical Protection of Nuclear Material, done at Vienna on 26 October 1979 and amendments thereto adopted on 8 July 2005; the Protocol for the Suppression of Unlawful Acts of Violence at Airports Serving International Civil Aviation, supplementary to the Convention for the Suppression of Unlawful Acts against the Safety of Civil Aviation, done at Montreal on 24 February 1988; the Protocol for the Suppression of Unlawful Acts against the Safety of Fixed Platforms Located on the Continental Shelf, done at Rome on 10 March 1988; the Convention on the Marking of Plastic Explosives for the Purpose of Detection, done at Montreal on 1 March 1991; the International Convention for the Suppression of Terrorist Bombings, adopted by the General Assembly of the United Nations on 15 December 1997; the International Convention for the Suppression of the Financing of Terrorism, adopted by the General Assembly of the United Nations on 9 December 1999, and the International Convention for the Suppression of Acts of Nuclear Terrorism adopted by the General Assembly of the United Nations on 13 April 2005,

Bearing in mind the importance of the United Nations Convention on the Law of the Sea done at Montego Bay, on 10 December 1982, and of the customary international law of the sea,

Considering resolution 59/46 of the United Nations General Assembly, which reaffirmed that international co-operation as well as actions by States to combat terrorism should be conducted in conformity with the principles of the Charter of the United Nations, international law and relevant international conventions, and resolution 59/24 of the United Nations General Assembly, which urged States to become parties to the Convention for the Suppression of Unlawful Acts against the Safety of Maritime Navigation and its Protocol, invited States to participate in the review of those instruments by the Legal Committee of the International Maritime Organization to strengthen the means of combating such unlawful acts, including terrorist acts, and also urged States to take appropriate measures to ensure the effective implementation of those instruments, in particular through the adoption of legislation, where appropriate, aimed at ensuring that there is a proper framework for responses to incidents of armed robbery and terrorist acts at sea,

Considering also the importance of the amendments to the International Convention for the Safety of Life at Sea, 1974, and of the International Ship and Port Facility Security (ISPS) Code, both adopted by the 2002 Conference of Contracting Governments to that Convention, in establishing an appropriate international technical framework involving co-operation between Governments, Government agencies, national and local administrations and the shipping and port industries to detect security threats and take preventative measures against security incidents affecting ships or port facilities used in international trade,

Considering further resolution 58/187 of the United Nations General Assembly, which reaffirmed that States must ensure that any measure taken to combat terrorism complies with their obligations under international law, in particular international human rights, refugee and humanitarian law,

Believing that it is necessary to adopt provisions supplementary to those of the Convention, to suppress additional terrorist acts of violence against the safety and security of international maritime navigation and to improve its effectiveness,

Have agreed as follows:

Article 1

For the purposes of this Protocol:

1. 'Convention' means the Convention for the Suppression of Unlawful Acts against the Safety of Maritime Navigation, done at Rome on 10 March 1988.

2 'Organization' means the International Maritime Organization (IMO).

3 'Secretary-General' means the Secretary-General of the Organization.

Article 2

Article 1 of the Convention is amended to read as follows:

Article 1

1. For the purposes of this Convention:

   (a) 'ship' means a vessel of any type whatsoever not permanently attached to the sea-bed, including dynamically supported craft, submersibles, or any other floating craft.
   (b) 'transport' means to initiate, arrange or exercise effective control, including decision-making authority, over the movement of a person or item.
   (c) 'serious injury or damage' means:
      (i) serious bodily injury; or
      (ii) extensive destruction of a place of public use, State or government facility, infrastructure facility, or public transportation system, resulting in major economic loss; or
      (iii) substantial damage to the environment, including air, soil, water, fauna, or flora.
   (d) 'BCN weapon' means:
      (i) 'biological weapons', which are:
         (1) microbial or other biological agents, or toxins whatever their origin or method of production, of types and in quantities that have no justification for prophylactic, protective or other peaceful purposes; or
         (2) weapons, equipment or means of delivery designed to use such agents or toxins for hostile purposes or in armed conflict.

    (ii) 'chemical weapons', which are, together or separately:

      (1) toxic chemicals and their precursors, except where intended for:

        (A) industrial, agricultural, research, medical, pharmaceutical or other peaceful purposes; or

        (B) protective purposes, namely those purposes directly related to protection against toxic chemicals and to protection against chemical weapons; or

        (C) military purposes not connected with the use of chemical weapons and not dependent on the use of the toxic properties of chemicals as a method of warfare; or

        (D) law enforcement including domestic riot control purposes,

      as long as the types and quantities are consistent with such purposes;

      (2) munitions and devices specifically designed to cause death or other harm through the toxic properties of those toxic chemicals specified in subparagraph (ii)(1), which would be released as a result of the employment of such munitions and devices;

      (3) any equipment specifically designed for use directly in connection with the employment of munitions and devices specified in subparagraph (ii)(2).

    (iii) nuclear weapons and other nuclear explosive devices.

(e) 'toxic chemical' means any chemical which through its chemical action on life processes can cause death, temporary incapacitation or permanent harm to humans or animals. This includes all such chemicals, regardless of their origin or of their method of production, and regardless of whether they are produced in facilities, in munitions or elsewhere.

(f) 'precursor' means any chemical reactant which takes part at any stage in the production by whatever method of a toxic chemical. This includes any key component of a binary or multicomponent chemical system.

(g) 'Organization' means the International Maritime Organization (IMO).

(h) 'Secretary-General' means the Secretary-General of the Organization.

2 For the purposes of this Convention:

(a) the terms 'place of public use', 'State or government facility', 'infrastructure facility', and 'public transportation system' have the same meaning as given to those terms in the International Convention for the Suppression of Terrorist Bombings, done at New York on 15 December 1997; and

(b) the terms 'source material' and 'special fissionable material' have the same meaning as given to those terms in the Statute of the International Atomic Energy Agency (IAEA), done at New York on 26 October 1956.

Article 3

The following text is added as article 2bis of the Convention:

Article 2*bis*

1. Nothing in this Convention shall affect other rights, obligations and responsibilities of States and individuals under international law, in particular the purposes and principles of the Charter of the United Nations and international human rights, refugee and humanitarian law.

2. This Convention does not apply to the activities of armed forces during an armed conflict, as those terms are understood under international humanitarian law, which are governed by that law, and the activities undertaken by military forces of a State in the exercise of their official duties, inasmuch as they are governed by other rules of international law.

3. Nothing in this Convention shall affect the rights, obligations and responsibilities under the Treaty on the Non-Proliferation of Nuclear Weapons, done at Washington, London and Moscow on 1 July 1968, the Convention on the Prohibition of the Development, Production and Stockpiling of Bacteriological (Biological) and Toxin Weapons and on their Destruction, done at Washington,

London and Moscow on 10 April 1972, or the Convention on the Prohibition of the Development, Production, Stockpiling and Use of Chemical Weapons and on their Destruction, done at Paris on 13 January 1993, of States Parties to such treaties.

Article 4

1. *The chapeau of article 3, paragraph 1 of the Convention is replaced by the following text:*

Any person commits an offence within the meaning of this Convention if that person unlawfully and intentionally:

2. *Article 3, paragraph 1(f) of the Convention is replaced by the following text:*

(f) communicates information which that person knows to be false, thereby endangering the safe navigation of a ship.

3. *Article 3, paragraph 1(g) of the Convention is deleted.*

4. *Article 3, paragraph 2 of the Convention is replaced by the following text:*

2. Any person also commits an offence if that person threatens, with or without a condition, as is provided for under national law, aimed at compelling a physical or juridical person to do or refrain from doing any act, to commit any of the offences set forth in paragraphs 1 (b), (c), and (e), if that threat is likely to endanger the safe navigation of the ship in question.

5. *The following text is added as article 3bis of the Convention:*

Article 3bis

1. Any person commits an offence within the meaning of this Convention if that person unlawfully and intentionally:

(a) when the purpose of the act, by its nature or context, is to intimidate a population, or to compel a government or an international organization to do or to abstain from doing any act:

(i) uses against or on a ship or discharges from a ship any explosive, radioactive material or BCN weapon in a manner that causes or is likely to cause death or serious injury or damage; or

(ii) discharges, from a ship, oil, liquefied natural gas, or other hazardous or noxious substance, which is not covered by subparagraph (a)(i), in such quantity or concentration that causes or is likely to cause death or serious injury or damage; or

(iii) uses a ship in a manner that causes death or serious injury or damage; or

(iv) threatens, with or without a condition, as is provided for under national law, to commit an offence set forth in subparagraph (a)(i), (ii) or (iii); or

(b) transports on board a ship:

(i) any explosive or radioactive material, knowing that it is intended to be used to cause, or in a threat to cause, with or without a condition, as is provided for under national law, death or serious injury or damage for the purpose of intimidating a population, or compelling a government or an international organization to do or to abstain from doing any act; or

(ii) any BCN weapon, knowing it to be a BCN weapon as defined in article 1; or

(iii) any source material, special fissionable material, or equipment or material especially designed or prepared for the processing, use or production of special fissionable material, knowing that it is intended to be used in a nuclear explosive activity or in any other nuclear activity not under safeguards pursuant to an IAEA comprehensive safeguards agreement; or

   (iv) any equipment, materials or software or related technology that significantly contributes to the design, manufacture or delivery of a BCN weapon, with the intention that it will be used for such purpose.

2. It shall not be an offence within the meaning of this Convention to transport an item or material covered by paragraph 1(b)(iii) or, insofar as it relates to a nuclear weapon or other nuclear explosive device, paragraph 1(b)(iv), if such item or material is transported to or from the territory of, or is otherwise transported under the control of, a State Party to the Treaty on the Non-Proliferation of Nuclear Weapons where:

   (a) the resulting transfer or receipt, including internal to a State, of the item or material is not contrary to such State Party's obligations under the Treaty on the Non-Proliferation of Nuclear Weapons and,

   (b) if the item or material is intended for the delivery system of a nuclear weapon or other nuclear explosive device of a State Party to the Treaty on the Non-Proliferation of Nuclear Weapons, the holding of such weapon or device is not contrary to that State Party's obligations under that Treaty.

*6. The following text is added as article 3*ter *of the Convention:*

Article 3*ter*

Any person commits an offence within the meaning of this Convention if that person unlawfully and intentionally transports another person on board a ship knowing that the person has committed an act that constitutes an offence set forth in article 3, 3*bis* or 3*quater* or an offence set forth in any treaty listed in the Annex, and intending to assist that person to evade criminal prosecution.

*7. The following text is added as article 3*quater *of the Convention:*

Article 3*quater*

Any person also commits an offence within the meaning of this Convention if that person:

   (a) unlawfully and intentionally injures or kills any person in connection with the commission of any of the offences set forth in article 3, paragraph 1, article 3*bis*, or article 3*ter*; or

   (b) attempts to commit an offence set forth in article 3, paragraph 1, article 3*bis*, paragraph 1(a)(i), (ii) or (iii), or subparagraph (a) of this article; or

   (c) participates as an accomplice in an offence set forth in article 3, article 3*bis*, article 3*ter*, or subparagraph (a) or (b) of this article; or

   (d) organizes or directs others to commit an offence set forth in article 3, article 3*bis*, article 3*ter*, or subparagraph (a) or (b) of this article; or

   (e) contributes to the commission of one or more offences set forth in article 3, article 3*bis*, article 3*ter* or subparagraph (a) or (b) of this article, by a group of persons acting with a common purpose, intentionally and either:

      (i) with the aim of furthering the criminal activity or criminal purpose of the group, where such activity or purpose involves the commission of an offence set forth in article 3, 3*bis* or 3*ter*; or

      (ii) in the knowledge of the intention of the group to commit an offence set forth in article 3, 3*bis* or 3*ter*.

Article 5

1. Article 5 of the Convention is replaced by the following text:

Each State Party shall make the offences set forth in articles 3, 3*bis*, 3*ter* and 3*quater* punishable by appropriate penalties which take into account the grave nature of those offences.

2. The following text is added as article 5bis of the Convention:

Article 5bis

1. Each State Party, in accordance with its domestic legal principles, shall take the necessary measures to enable a legal entity located in its territory or organized under its laws to be held liable when a person responsible for management or control of that legal entity has, in that capacity, committed an offence set forth in this Convention. Such liability may be criminal, civil or administrative.

2. Such liability is incurred without prejudice to the criminal liability of individuals having committed the offences.

3. Each State Party shall ensure, in particular, that legal entities liable in accordance with paragraph 1 are subject to effective, proportionate and dissuasive criminal, civil or administrative sanctions. Such sanctions may include monetary sanctions.

Article 6

1. The chapeau of Article 6, paragraph 1 of the Convention is replaced by the following text:

1. Each State Party shall take such measures as may be necessary to establish its jurisdiction over the offences set forth in articles 3, 3*bis*, 3*ter* and 3*quater* when the offence is committed:

2. Article 6, paragraph 3 of the Convention is replaced by the following text:

3. Any State Party which has established jurisdiction mentioned in paragraph 2 shall notify the Secretary-General. If such State Party subsequently rescinds that jurisdiction, it shall notify the Secretary-General.

3. Article 6, paragraph 4 of the Convention is replaced by the following text:

4. Each State Party shall take such measures as may be necessary to establish its jurisdiction over the offences set forth in articles 3, 3*bis*, 3*ter* and 3*quater* in cases where the alleged offender is present in its territory and it does not extradite the alleged offender to any of the States Parties which have established their jurisdiction in accordance with paragraphs 1 and 2 of this article.

Article 7

The following text is added as the Annex to the Convention:

Annex

1. Convention for the Suppression of Unlawful Seizure of Aircraft, done at The Hague on 16 December 1970.

2. Convention for the Suppression of Unlawful Acts against the Safety of Civil Aviation, done at Montreal on 23 September 1971.

3. Convention on the Prevention and Punishment of Crimes against Internationally Protected Persons, including Diplomatic Agents, adopted by the General Assembly of the United Nations on 14 December 1973.

4. International Convention against the Taking of Hostages, adopted by the General Assembly of the United Nations on 17 December 1979.

5. Convention on the Physical Protection of Nuclear Material, done at Vienna on 26 October 1979.

6. Protocol for the Suppression of Unlawful Acts of Violence at Airports Serving International Civil Aviation, supplementary to the Convention for the Suppression of Unlawful Acts against the Safety of Civil Aviation, done at Montreal on 24 February 1988.

7. Protocol for the Suppression of Unlawful Acts against the Safety of Fixed Platforms Located on the Continental Shelf, done at Rome on 10 March 1988.

8. International Convention for the Suppression of Terrorist Bombings, adopted by the General Assembly of the United Nations on 15 December 1997.

9. International Convention for the Suppression of the Financing of Terrorism, adopted by the General Assembly of the United Nations on 9 December 1999.

Article 8

1. Article 8, paragraph 1 of the Convention is replaced by the following text:

1. The master of a ship of a State Party (the 'flag State') may deliver to the authorities of any other State Party (the 'receiving State') any person who the master has reasonable grounds to believe has committed an offence set forth in article 3, 3*bis*, 3*ter*, or 3*quater*.

*2. The following text is added as article 8*bis *of the Convention:*

Article 8*bis*

1. States Parties shall co-operate to the fullest extent possible to prevent and suppress unlawful acts covered by this Convention, in conformity with international law, and shall respond to requests pursuant to this article as expeditiously as possible.

2. Each request pursuant to this article should, if possible, contain the name of the suspect ship, the IMO ship identification number, the port of registry, the ports of origin and destination, and any other relevant information. If a request is conveyed orally, the requesting Party shall confirm the request in writing as soon as possible. The requested Party shall acknowledge its receipt of any written or oral request immediately.

3. States Parties shall take into account the dangers and difficulties involved in boarding a ship at sea and searching its cargo, and give consideration to whether other appropriate measures agreed between the States concerned could be more safely taken in the next port of call or elsewhere.

4. A State Party that has reasonable grounds to suspect that an offence set forth in article 3, 3*bis*, 3*ter* or 3*quater* has been, is being or is about to be committed involving a ship flying its flag, may request the assistance of other States Parties in preventing or suppressing that offence. The States Parties so requested shall use their best endeavours to render such assistance within the means available to them.

5. Whenever law enforcement or other authorized officials of a State Party ('the requesting Party') encounter a ship flying the flag or displaying marks of registry of another State Party ('the first Party') located seaward of any State's territorial sea, and the requesting Party has reasonable grounds to suspect that the ship or a person on board the ship has been, is or is about to be involved in the commission of an offence set forth in article 3, 3*bis*, 3*ter* or 3*quater*, and the requesting Party desires to board,

    (a) it shall request, in accordance with paragraphs 1 and 2 that the first Party confirm the claim of nationality, and

    (b) if nationality is confirmed, the requesting Party shall ask the first Party (hereinafter referred to as 'the flag State') for authorization to board and to take appropriate measures with regard to that ship which may include stopping, boarding and searching the ship, its cargo and persons on board, and questioning the persons on board in order to determine if an offence set forth in article 3, 3*bis*, 3*ter* or 3*quater* has been, is being or is about to be committed, and

    (c) the flag State shall either:

        (i) authorize the requesting Party to board and to take appropriate measures set out in subparagraph (b), subject to any conditions it may impose in accordance with paragraph 7; or

        (ii) conduct the boarding and search with its own law enforcement or other officials; or

> (iii) conduct the boarding and search together with the requesting Party, subject to any conditions it may impose in accordance with paragraph 7; or
>
> (iv) decline to authorize a boarding and search.

The requesting Party shall not board the ship or take measures set out in subparagraph (b) without the express authorization of the flag State.

> (d) Upon or after depositing its instrument of ratification, acceptance, approval or accession, a State Party may notify the Secretary-General that, with respect to ships flying its flag or displaying its mark of registry, the requesting Party is granted authorization to board and search the ship, its cargo and persons on board, and to question the persons on board in order to locate and examine documentation of its nationality and determine if an offence set forth in article 3, 3*bis*, 3*ter* or 3*quater* has been, is being or is about to be committed, if there is no response from the first Party within four hours of acknowledgement of receipt of a request to confirm nationality.
>
> (e) Upon or after depositing its instrument of ratification, acceptance, approval or accession, a State Party may notify the Secretary-General that, with respect to ships flying its flag or displaying its mark of registry, the requesting Party is authorized to board and search a ship, its cargo and persons on board, and to question the persons on board in order to determine if an offence set forth in article 3, 3*bis*, 3*ter* or 3*quater* has been, is being or is about to be committed.

The notifications made pursuant to this paragraph can be withdrawn at any time.

6. When evidence of conduct described in article 3, 3*bis*, 3*ter* or 3*quater* is found as the result of any boarding conducted pursuant to this article, the flag State may authorize the requesting Party to detain the ship, cargo and persons on board pending receipt of disposition instructions from the flag State. The requesting Party shall promptly inform the flag State of the results of a boarding, search, and detention conducted pursuant to this article. The requesting Party shall also promptly inform the flag State of the discovery of evidence of illegal conduct that is not subject to this Convention.

7. The flag State, consistent with the other provisions of this Convention, may subject its authorization under paragraph 5 or 6 to conditions, including obtaining additional information from the requesting Party, and conditions relating to responsibility for and the extent of measures to be taken. No additional measures may be taken without the express authorization of the flag State, except when necessary to relieve imminent danger to the lives of persons or where those measures derive from relevant bilateral or multilateral agreements.

8. For all boardings pursuant to this article, the flag State has the right to exercise jurisdiction over a detained ship, cargo or other items and persons on board, including seizure, forfeiture, arrest and prosecution. However, the flag State may, subject to its constitution and laws, consent to the exercise of jurisdiction by another State having jurisdiction under article 6.

9. When carrying out the authorized actions under this article, the use of force shall be avoided except when necessary to ensure the safety of its officials and persons on board, or where the officials are obstructed in the execution of the authorized actions. Any use of force pursuant to this article shall not exceed the minimum degree of force which is necessary and reasonable in the circumstances.

10. Safeguards:

> (a) Where a State Party takes measures against a ship in accordance with this article, it shall:
>
> > (i) take due account of the need not to endanger the safety of life at sea;
> >
> > (ii) ensure that all persons on board are treated in a manner which preserves their basic human dignity, and in compliance with the applicable provisions of international law, including international human rights law;
> >
> > (iii) ensure that a boarding and search pursuant to this article shall be conducted in accordance with applicable international law;

    (iv) take due account of the safety and security of the ship and its cargo;

    (v) take due account of the need not to prejudice the commercial or legal interests of the flag State;

    (vi) ensure, within available means, that any measure taken with regard to the ship or its cargo is environmentally sound under the circumstances;

    (vii) ensure that persons on board against whom proceedings may be commenced in connection with any of the offences set forth in article 3, *3bis*, *3ter* or *3quater* are afforded the protections of paragraph 2 of article 10, regardless of location;

    (viii) ensure that the master of a ship is advised of its intention to board, and is, or has been, afforded the opportunity to contact the ship's owner and the flag State at the earliest opportunity; and

    (ix) take reasonable efforts to avoid a ship being unduly detained or delayed.

(b) Provided that authorization to board by a flag State shall not per se give rise to its liability, States Parties shall be liable for any damage, harm or loss attributable to them arising from measures taken pursuant to this article when:

    (i) the grounds for such measures prove to be unfounded, provided that the ship has not committed any act justifying the measures taken; or

    (ii) such measures are unlawful or exceed those reasonably required in light of available information to implement the provisions of this article.

States Parties shall provide effective recourse in respect of such damage, harm or loss.

(c) Where a State Party takes measures against a ship in accordance with this Convention, it shall take due account of the need not to interfere with or to affect:

    (i) the rights and obligations and the exercise of jurisdiction of coastal States in accordance with the international law of the sea; or

    (ii) the authority of the flag State to exercise jurisdiction and control in administrative, technical and social matters involving the ship.

(d) Any measure taken pursuant to this article shall be carried out by law enforcement or other authorized officials from warships or military aircraft, or from other ships or aircraft clearly marked and identifiable as being on government service and authorized to that effect and, notwithstanding articles 2 and *2bis*, the provisions of this article shall apply.

(e) For the purposes of this article 'law enforcement or other authorized officials' means uniformed or otherwise clearly identifiable members of law enforcement or other government authorities duly authorized by their government. For the specific purpose of law enforcement under this Convention, law enforcement or other authorized officials shall provide appropriate government-issued identification documents for examination by the master of the ship upon boarding.

11. This article does not apply to or limit boarding of ships conducted by any State Party in accordance with international law, seaward of any State's territorial sea, including boardings based upon the right of visit, the rendering of assistance to persons, ships and property in distress or peril, or an authorization from the flag State to take law enforcement or other action.

12. States Parties are encouraged to develop standard operating procedures for joint operations pursuant to this article and consult, as appropriate, with other States Parties with a view to harmonizing such standard operating procedures for the conduct of operations.

13. States Parties may conclude agreements or arrangements between them to facilitate law enforcement operations carried out in accordance with this article.

14. Each State Party shall take appropriate measures to ensure that its law enforcement or other authorized officials, and law enforcement or other authorized officials of other States Parties acting on its behalf, are empowered to act pursuant to this article.

15. Upon or after depositing its instrument of ratification, acceptance, approval or accession, each State Party shall designate the authority, or, where necessary, authorities to receive and respond to

requests for assistance, for confirmation of nationality, and for authorization to take appropriate measures. Such designation, including contact information, shall be notified to the Secretary-General within one month of becoming a Party, who shall inform all other States Parties within one month of the designation. Each State Party is responsible for providing prompt notice through the Secretary-General of any changes in the designation or contact information.

Article 9

Article 10, paragraph 2 is replaced by the following text:

2. Any person who is taken into custody, or regarding whom any other measures are taken or proceedings are being carried out pursuant to this Convention, shall be guaranteed fair treatment, including enjoyment of all rights and guarantees in conformity with the law of the State in the territory of which that person is present and applicable provisions of international law, including international human rights law.

Article 10

1. Article 11, paragraphs 1, 2, 3 and 4 are replaced by the following text:

1. The offences set forth in articles 3, 3*bis*, 3*ter* and 3*quater* shall be deemed to be included as extraditable offences in any extradition treaty existing between any of the States Parties. States Parties undertake to include such offences as extraditable offences in every extradition treaty to be concluded between them.

2. If a State Party which makes extradition conditional on the existence of a treaty receives a request for extradition from another State Party with which it has no extradition treaty, the requested State Party may, at its option, consider this Convention as a legal basis for extradition in respect of the offences set forth in articles 3, 3*bis*, 3*ter* and 3*quater*. Extradition shall be subject to the other conditions provided by the law of the requested State Party.

3. States Parties which do not make extradition conditional on the existence of a treaty shall recognize the offences set forth in articles 3, 3*bis*, 3*ter* and 3*quater* as extraditable offences between themselves, subject to the conditions provided by the law of the requested State Party.

4. If necessary, the offences set forth in articles 3, 3*bis*, 3*ter* and 3*quater* shall be treated, for the purposes of extradition between States Parties, as if they had been committed not only in the place in which they occurred but also in a place within the jurisdiction of the State Party requesting extradition.

2. The following text is added as article 11bis, of the Convention:

Article 11*bis*

None of the offences set forth in article 3, 3*bis*, 3*ter* or 3*quater* shall be regarded for the purposes of extradition or mutual legal assistance as a political offence or as an offence connected with a political offence or as an offence inspired by political motives. Accordingly, a request for extradition or for mutual legal assistance based on such an offence may not be refused on the sole ground that it concerns a political offence or an offence connected with a political offence or an offence inspired by political motives.

3. The following text is added as article 11ter of the Convention:

Article 11*ter*

Nothing in this Convention shall be interpreted as imposing an obligation to extradite or to afford mutual legal assistance, if the requested State Party has substantial grounds for believing that the request for extradition for offences set forth in article 3, 3*bis*, 3*ter* or 3*quater* or for mutual legal assistance with respect to such offences has been made for the purpose of prosecuting or punishing a person on account of that person's race, religion, nationality, ethnic origin, political opinion or gender, or that compliance with the request would cause prejudice to that person's position for any of these reasons.

Article 11

1. Article 12, paragraph 1 of the Convention is replaced by the following text:

1. States Parties shall afford one another the greatest measure of assistance in connection with criminal proceedings brought in respect of the offences set forth in articles 3, 3*bis*, 3*ter* and 3*quater*, including assistance in obtaining evidence at their disposal necessary for the proceedings.

2. The following text is added as article 12bis of the Convention:

Article 12*bis*

1. A person who is being detained or is serving a sentence in the territory of one State Party whose presence in another State Party is requested for purposes of identification, testimony or otherwise providing assistance in obtaining evidence for the investigation or prosecution of offences set forth in article 3, 3*bis*, 3*ter* or 3*quater* may be transferred if the following conditions are met:

(a) the person freely gives informed consent; and
(b) the competent authorities of both States agree, subject to such conditions as those States may deem appropriate.

2. For the purposes of this article:

(a) the State to which the person is transferred shall have the authority and obligation to keep the person transferred in custody, unless otherwise requested or authorized by the State from which the person was transferred;
(b) the State to which the person is transferred shall without delay implement its obligation to return the person to the custody of the State from which the person was transferred as agreed beforehand, or as otherwise agreed, by the competent authorities of both States;
(c) the State to which the person is transferred shall not require the State from which the person was transferred to initiate extradition proceedings for the return of the person;
(d) the person transferred shall receive credit for service of the sentence being served in the State from which the person was transferred for time spent in the custody of the State to which the person was transferred.

3. Unless the State Party from which a person is to be transferred in accordance with this article so agrees, that person, whatever that person's nationality, shall not be prosecuted or detained or subjected to any other restriction of personal liberty in the territory of the State to which that person is transferred in respect of acts or convictions anterior to that person's departure from the territory of the State from which such person was transferred.

Article 12

Article 13 of the Convention is replaced by the following text:

1. States Parties shall co-operate in the prevention of the offences set forth in articles 3, 3*bis*, 3*ter* and 3*quater*, particularly by:

(a) taking all practicable measures to prevent preparation in their respective territories for the commission of those offences within or outside their territories;
(b) exchanging information in accordance with their national law, and co-ordinating administrative and other measures taken as appropriate to prevent the commission of offences set forth in articles 3, 3*bis*, 3*ter* and 3*quater*.

2. When, due to the commission of an offence set forth in article 3, 3bis, 3*ter* or 3*quater*, the passage of a ship has been delayed or interrupted, any State Party in whose territory the ship or passengers or crew are present shall be bound to exercise all possible efforts to avoid a ship, its passengers, crew or cargo being unduly detained or delayed.

Article 13

Article 14 of the Convention is replaced by the following text:

Any State Party having reason to believe that an offence set forth in article 3, 3*bis*, 3*ter* or 3*quater* will be committed shall, in accordance with its national law, furnish as promptly as possible any relevant information in its possession to those States which it believes would be the States having established jurisdiction in accordance with article 6.

Article 14

Article 15, paragraph 3 of the Convention is replaced by the following text:

3. The information transmitted in accordance with paragraphs 1 and 2 shall be communicated by the Secretary-General to all States Parties, to Members of the Organization, to other States concerned, and to the appropriate international intergovernmental organizations.

Article 15

Interpretation and application

1. The Convention and this Protocol shall, as between the Parties to this Protocol, be read and interpreted together as one single instrument.

2. Articles 1 to 16 of the Convention, as revised by this Protocol, together with articles 17 to 24 of this Protocol and the Annex thereto, shall constitute and be called the Convention for the Suppression of Unlawful Acts against the Safety of Maritime Navigation, 2005 (2005 SUA Convention).

Article 16

The following text is added as article 16bis of the Convention:

Final clauses of the Convention for the Suppression of Unlawful Acts against the Safety of Maritime Navigation, 2005

The final clauses of the Convention for the Suppression of Unlawful Acts against the Safety of Maritime Navigation, 2005 shall be articles 17 to 24 of the Protocol of 2005 to the Convention for the Suppression of Unlawful Acts against the Safety of Maritime Navigation. References in this Convention to States Parties shall be taken to mean references to States Parties to that Protocol.

Final Clauses

Article 17

Signature, ratification, acceptance, approval and accession

1. This Protocol shall be open for signature at the Headquarters of the Organization from 14 February 2006 to 13 February 2007 and shall thereafter remain open for accession.

2. States may express their consent to be bound by this Protocol by:

   (a) signature without reservation as to ratification, acceptance or approval; or
   (b) signature subject to ratification, acceptance or approval, followed by ratification, acceptance or approval; or
   (c) accession.

3. Ratification, acceptance, approval or accession shall be effected by the deposit of an instrument to that effect with the Secretary-General.

4. Only a State which has signed the Convention without reservation as to ratification, acceptance or approval, or has ratified, accepted, approved or acceded to the Convention may become a Party to this Protocol.

Article 18

Entry into force

1. This Protocol shall enter into force ninety days following the date on which twelve States have either signed it without reservation as to ratification, acceptance or approval, or have deposited an instrument of ratification, acceptance, approval or accession with the Secretary-General.

2. For a State which deposits an instrument of ratification, acceptance, approval or accession in respect of this Protocol after the conditions in paragraph 1 for entry into force thereof have been met, the ratification, acceptance, approval or accession shall take effect ninety days after the date of such deposit.

Article 19

Denunciation

1. This Protocol may be denounced by any State Party at any time after the date on which this Protocol enters into force for that State.

2. Denunciation shall be effected by the deposit of an instrument of denunciation with the Secretary-General.

3. A denunciation shall take effect one year, or such longer period as may be specified in the instrument of denunciation, after the deposit of the instrument with the Secretary-General.

Article 20

Revision and amendment

1. A conference for the purpose of revising or amending this Protocol may be convened by the Organization.

2. The Secretary-General shall convene a conference of States Parties to this Protocol for revising or amending the Protocol, at the request of one third of the States Parties, or ten States Parties, whichever is the higher figure.

3. Any instrument of ratification, acceptance, approval or accession deposited after the date of entry into force of an amendment to this Protocol shall be deemed to apply to the Protocol as amended.

Article 21

Declarations

1. Upon depositing its instrument of ratification, acceptance, approval or accession, a State Party which is not a party to a treaty listed in the Annex may declare that, in the application of this Protocol to the State Party, the treaty shall be deemed not to be included in article 3*ter*. The declaration shall cease to have effect as soon as the treaty enters into force for the State Party, which shall notify the Secretary-General of this fact.

2. When a State Party ceases to be a party to a treaty listed in the Annex, it may make a declaration as provided for in this article, with respect to that treaty.

3. Upon depositing its instrument of ratification, acceptance, approval or accession, a State Party may declare that it will apply the provisions of article 3*ter* in accordance with the principles of its criminal law concerning family exemptions of liability.

Article 22

Amendments to the Annex

1. The Annex may be amended by the addition of relevant treaties that:

    (a) are open to the participation of all States;
    (b) have entered into force; and

(c) have been ratified, accepted, approved or acceded to by at least twelve States Parties to this Protocol.

2. After the entry into force of this Protocol, any State Party thereto may propose such an amendment to the Annex. Any proposal for an amendment shall be communicated to the Secretary-General in written form. The Secretary-General shall circulate any proposed amendment that meets the requirements of paragraph 1 to all members of the Organization and seek from States Parties to this Protocol their consent to the adoption of the proposed amendment.

3. The proposed amendment to the Annex shall be deemed adopted after more than twelve of the States Parties to this Protocol consent to it by written notification to the Secretary-General.

4. The adopted amendment to the Annex shall enter into force thirty days after the deposit with the Secretary-General of the twelfth instrument of ratification, acceptance or approval of such amendment for those States Parties to this Protocol that have deposited such an instrument. For each State Party to this Protocol ratifying, accepting or approving the amendment after the deposit of the twelfth instrument with the Secretary-General, the amendment shall enter into force on the thirtieth day after deposit by such State Party of its instrument of ratification, acceptance or approval.

Article 23

Depositary

1. This Protocol and any amendments adopted under articles 20 and 22 shall be deposited with the Secretary-General.

2. The Secretary-General shall:

(a) inform all States which have signed this Protocol or acceded to this Protocol of:
   (i) each new signature or deposit of an instrument of ratification, acceptance, approval or accession together with the date thereof;
   (ii) the date of the entry into force of this Protocol;
   (iii) the deposit of any instrument of denunciation of this Protocol together with the date on which it is received and the date on which the denunciation takes effect;
   (iv) any communication called for by any article of this Protocol;
   (v) any proposal to amend the Annex which has been made in accordance with article 22, paragraph 2;
   (vi) any amendment deemed to have been adopted in accordance with article 22, paragraph 3;
   (vii) any amendment ratified, accepted or approved in accordance with article 22, paragraph 4, together with the date on which that amendment shall enter into force; and
(b) transmit certified true copies of this Protocol to all States which have signed or acceded to this Protocol.

3. As soon as this Protocol enters into force, a certified true copy of the text shall be transmitted by the Secretary-General to the Secretary-General of the United Nations for registration and publication in accordance with Article 102 of the Charter of the United Nations.

Article 24

Languages

This Protocol is established in a single original in the Arabic, Chinese, English, French, Russian and Spanish languages, each text being equally authentic.

DONE AT LONDON this fourteenth day of October two thousand and five.

IN WITNESS WHEREOF the undersigned, being duly authorized by their respective Governments for that purpose, have signed this Protocol.

APPENDIX 10

Plastic Explosives Convention

Convention on the Marking of Plastic Explosives for the Purpose of Detection

The States Parties to this Convention,

Conscious of the implications of acts of terrorism for international security;

Expressing deep concern regarding terrorist acts aimed at destruction of aircraft, other means of transportation and other targets;

Concerned that plastic explosives have been used for such terrorist acts;

Considering that the marking of such explosives for the purpose of detection would contribute significantly to the prevention of such unlawful acts;

Recognizing that for the purpose of deterring such unlawful acts there is an urgent need for an international instrument obliging States to adopt appropriate measures to ensure that plastic explosives are duly marked;

Considering United Nations Security Council Resolution 635 of 14 June 1989, and United Nations General Assembly Resolution 44/29 of 4 December 1989 urging the International Civil Aviation Organization to intensify its work on devising an international regime for the marking of plastic or sheet explosives for the purpose of detection;

Bearing in mind Resolution A27-8 adopted unanimously by the 27th Session of the Assembly of the International Civil Aviation Organization which endorsed with the highest and overriding priority the preparation of a new international instrument regarding the marking of plastic or sheet explosives for detection;

Noting with satisfaction the role played by the Council of the International Civil Aviation Organization in the preparation of the Convention as well as its willingness to assume functions related to its implementation;

Have agreed as follows:

Article I

For the purposes of this Convention:

1. 'Explosives' mean explosive products, commonly known as 'plastic explosives', including explosives in flexible or elastic sheet form, as described in the Technical Annex to this Convention.

2. 'Detection agent' means a substance as described in the Technical Annex to this Convention which is introduced into an explosive to render it detectable.

3. 'Marking' means introducing into an explosive a detection agent in accordance with the Technical Annex to this Convention.

4. 'Manufacture' means any process, including reprocessing, that produces explosives.

5. 'Duly authorized military devices' include, but are not restricted to, shells, bombs, projectiles, mines, missiles, rockets, shaped charges, grenades and perforators manufactured exclusively for military or police purposes according to the laws and regulations of the State Party concerned.

6. 'Producer State' means any State in whose territory explosives are manufactured.

Article II

Each State Party shall take the necessary and effective measures to prohibit and prevent the manufacture in its territory of unmarked explosives.

Article III

1. Each State Party shall take the necessary and effective measures to prohibit and prevent the movement into or out of its territory of unmarked explosives.

2. The preceding paragraph shall not apply in respect of movements for purposes not inconsistent with the objectives of this Convention, by authorities of a State Party performing military or police functions, of unmarked explosives under the control of that State Party in accordance with paragraph 1 of Article IV.

Article IV

1. Each State Party shall take the necessary measures to exercise strict and effective control over the possession and transfer of possession of unmarked explosives which have been manufactured in or brought into its territory prior to the entry into force of this Convention in respect of that State, so as to prevent their diversion or use for purposes inconsistent with the objectives of this Convention.

2. Each State Party shall take the necessary measures to ensure that all stocks of those explosives referred to in paragraph 1 of this Article not held by its authorities performing military or police functions are destroyed or consumed for purposes not inconsistent with the objectives of this Convention, marked or rendered permanently ineffective, within a period of three years from the entry into force of this Convention in respect of that State.

3. Each State Party shall take the necessary measures to ensure that all stocks of those explosives referred to in paragraph 1 of this Article held by its authorities performing military or police functions and that are not incorporated as an integral part of duly authorized military devices are destroyed or consumed for purposes not inconsistent with the objectives of this Convention, marked or rendered permanently ineffective, within a period of fifteen years from the entry into force of this Convention in respect of that State.

4. Each State Party shall take the necessary measures to ensure the destruction, as soon as possible, in its territory of unmarked explosives which may be discovered therein and which are not referred to in the preceding paragraphs of this Article, other than stocks of unmarked explosives held by its authorities performing military or police functions and incorporated as an integral part of duly authorized military devices at the date of the entry into force of this Convention in respect of that State.

5. Each State Party shall take the necessary measures to exercise strict and effective control over the possession and transfer of possession of the explosives referred to in paragraph II of Part 1 of the Technical Annex to this Convention so as to prevent their diversion or use for purposes inconsistent with the objectives of this Convention.

6. Each State Party shall take the necessary measures to ensure the destruction, as soon as possible, in its territory of unmarked explosives manufactured since the coming into force of this Convention in respect of that State that are not incorporated as specified in paragraph II d) of Part 1 of the Technical Annex to this Convention and of unmarked explosives which no longer fall within the scope of any other sub-paragraphs of the said paragraph II.

Article V

1. There is established by this Convention an International Explosives Technical Commission (hereinafter referred to as 'the Commission') consisting of not less than fifteen nor more than nineteen members appointed by the Council of the International Civil Aviation Organization (hereinafter referred to as 'the Council') from among persons nominated by States Parties to this Convention.

2. The members of the Commission shall be experts having direct and substantial experience in matters relating to the manufacture or detection of, or research in, explosives.

3. Members of the Commission shall serve for a period of three years and shall be eligible for re-appointment.

4. Sessions of the Commission shall be convened, at least once a year at the Headquarters of the International Civil Aviation Organization, or at such places and times as may be directed or approved by the Council.

5. The Commission shall adopt its rules of procedure, subject to the approval of the Council.

Article VI

1. The Commission shall evaluate technical developments relating to the manufacture, marking and detection of explosives.

2. The Commission, through the Council, shall report its findings to the States Parties and international organizations concerned.

3. Whenever necessary, the Commission shall make recommendations to the Council for amendments to the Technical Annex to this Convention. The Commission shall endeavour to take its decisions on such recommendations by consensus. In the absence of consensus the Commission shall take such decisions by a two-thirds majority vote of its members.

4. The Council may, on the recommendation of the Commission, propose to States Parties amendments to the Technical Annex to this Convention.

Article VII

1. Any State Party may, within ninety days from the date of notification of a proposed amendment to the Technical Annex to this Convention, transmit to the Council its comments. The Council shall communicate these comments to the Commission as soon as possible for its consideration. The Council shall invite any State Party which comments on or objects to the proposed amendment to consult the Commission.

2. The Commission shall consider the views of States Parties made pursuant to the preceding paragraph and report to the Council. The Council, after consideration of the Commission's report, and taking into account the nature of the amendment and the comments of States Parties, including producer States, may propose the amendment to all States Parties for adoption.

3. If a proposed amendment has not been objected to by five or more States Parties by means of written notification to the Council within ninety days from the date of notification of the amendment by the Council, it shall be deemed to have been adopted, and shall enter into force one hundred and eighty days thereafter or after such other period as specified in the proposed amendment for States Parties not having expressly objected thereto.

4. States Parties having expressly objected to the proposed amendment may, subsequently, by means of the deposit of an instrument of acceptance or approval, express their consent to be bound by the provisions of the amendment.

5. If five or more States Parties have objected to the proposed amendment, the Council shall refer it to the Commission for further consideration.

6. If the proposed amendment has not been adopted in accordance with paragraph 3 of this Article, the Council may also convene a conference of all States Parties.

Article VIII

1. States Parties shall, if possible, transmit to the Council information that would assist the Commission in the discharge of its functions under paragraph 1 of Article VI.

2. States Parties shall keep the Council informed of measures they have taken to implement the provisions of this Convention. The Council shall communicate such information to all States Parties and international organizations concerned.

Article IX

The Council shall, in co-operation with States Parties and international organizations concerned, take appropriate measures to facilitate the implementation of this Convention, including the provision of technical assistance and measures for the exchange of information relating to technical developments in the marking and detection of explosives.

Article X

The Technical Annex to this Convention shall form an integral part of this Convention.

Article XI

1. Any dispute between two or more States Parties concerning the interpretation or application of this Convention which cannot be settled through negotiation shall, at the request of one of them, be submitted to arbitration. If within six months from the date of the request for arbitration the Parties are unable to agree on the organization of the arbitration, any one of those Parties may refer the dispute to the International Court of Justice by request in conformity with the Statute of the Court.

2. Each State Party may, at the time of signature, ratification, acceptance or approval of this Convention or accession thereto, declare that it does not consider itself bound by the preceding paragraph. The other States Parties shall not be bound by the preceding paragraph with respect to any State Party having made such a reservation.

3. Any State Party having made a reservation in accordance with the preceding paragraph may at any time withdraw this reservation by notification to the Depositary.

Article XII

Except as provided in Article XI no reservation may be made to this Convention.

Article XIII

1. This Convention shall be open for signature in Montreal on 1 March 1991 by States participating in the International Conference on Air Law held at Montreal from 12 February to 1 March 1991. After 1 March 1991 the Convention shall be open to all States for signature at the Headquarters of the International Civil Aviation Organization in Montreal until it enters into force in accordance with paragraph 3 of this Article. Any State which does not sign this Convention may accede to it at any time.

2. This Convention shall be subject to ratification, acceptance, approval or accession by States. Instruments of ratification, acceptance, approval or accession shall be deposited with the International Civil Aviation Organization, which is hereby designated the Depositary. When depositing its instrument of ratification, acceptance, approval or accession, each State shall declare whether or not it is a producer State.

3. This Convention shall enter into force on the sixtieth day following the date of deposit of the thirty-fifth instrument of ratification, acceptance, approval or accession with the Depositary, provided that no fewer than five such States have declared pursuant to paragraph 2 of this Article that they are producer States. Should thirty-five such instruments be deposited prior to the deposit of their instruments by five producer States, this Convention shall enter into force on the sixtieth

day following the date of deposit of the instrument of ratification, acceptance, approval or accession of the fifth producer State.

4. For other States, this Convention shall enter into force sixty days following the date of deposit of their instruments of ratification, acceptance, approval or accession.

5. As soon as this Convention comes into force, it shall be registered by the Depositary pursuant to Article 102 of the Charter of the United Nations and pursuant to Article 83 of the Convention on International Civil Aviation (Chicago, 1944).

Article XIV

The Depositary shall promptly notify all signatories and States Parties of:

1. each signature of this Convention and date thereof;
2. each deposit of an instrument of ratification, acceptance, approval or accession and date thereof, giving special reference to whether the State has identified itself as a producer State;
3. the date of entry into force of this Convention;
4. the date of entry into force of any amendment to this Convention or its Technical Annex;
5. any denunciation made under Article XV; and
6. any declaration made under paragraph 2 of Article XI.

Article XV

1. Any State Party may denounce this Convention by written notification to the Depositary.

2. Denunciation shall take effect one hundred and eighty days following the date on which notification is received by the Depositary.

IN WITNESS WHEREOF the undersigned Plenipotentiaries, being duly authorized thereto by their Governments, have signed this Convention.

DONE at Montreal, this first day of March, one thousand nine hundred and ninety-one, in one original, drawn up in five authentic texts in the English, French, Russian, Spanish and Arabic languages.

APPENDIX 11

Bombings Convention

International Convention for the Suppression of Terrorist Bombings

The States Parties to this Convention,

Having in mind the purposes and principles of the Charter of the United Nations concerning the maintenance of international peace and security and the promotion of good-neighbourliness and friendly relations and cooperation among States,

Deeply concerned about the worldwide escalation of acts of terrorism in all its forms and manifestations,

Recalling the Declaration on the Occasion of the Fiftieth Anniversary of the United Nations of 24 October 1995,

Recalling also the Declaration on Measures to Eliminate International Terrorism, annexed to General Assembly resolution 49/60 of 9 December 1994, in which, inter alia, 'the States Members of the United Nations solemnly reaffirm their unequivocal condemnation of all acts, methods and practices of terrorism as criminal and unjustifiable, wherever and by whomever committed, including those which jeopardize the friendly relations among States and peoples and threaten the territorial integrity and security of States',

Noting that the Declaration also encouraged States 'to review urgently the scope of the existing international legal provisions on the prevention, repression and elimination of terrorism in all its forms and manifestations, with the aim of ensuring that there is a comprehensive legal framework covering all aspects of the matter',

Recalling further General Assembly resolution 51/210 of 17 December 1996 and the Declaration to Supplement the 1994 Declaration on Measures to Eliminate International Terrorism, annexed thereto,

Nothing also that terrorist attacks by means of explosives or other lethal devices have become increasingly widespread,

Noting further that existing multilateral legal provisions do not adequately address these attacks,

Being convinced of the urgent need to enhance international cooperation between States in devising and adopting effective and practical measures for the prevention of such acts of terrorism, and for the prosecution and punishment of their perpetrators,

Considering that the occurrence of such acts is a matter of grave concern to the international community as a whole,

Noting that the activities of military forces of States are governed by rules of international law outside the framework of this Convention and that the exclusion of certain actions from the coverage of this Convention does not condone or make lawful otherwise unlawful acts, or preclude prosecution under other laws,

Have agreed as follows:

Article 1

For the purposes of this Convention:

1. 'State or government facility' includes any permanent or temporary facility or conveyance that is used or occupied by representatives of a State, members of Government, the legislature or the judiciary or by officials or employees of a State or any other public authority or entity or by employees or officials of an intergovernmental organization in connection with their official duties.

2. 'Infrastructure facility' means any publicly or privately owned facility providing or distributing services for the benefit of the public, such as water, sewage, energy, fuel or communications.

3. 'Explosive or other lethal device' means:

   (a) An explosive or incendiary weapon or device that is designed, or has the capability, to cause death, serious bodily injury or substantial material damage; or
   (b) A weapon or device that is designed, or has the capability, to cause death, serious bodily injury or substantial material damage through the release, dissemination or impact of toxic chemicals, biological agents or toxins or similar substances or radiation or radioactive material.

4. 'Military forces of a State' means the armed forces of a State which are organized, trained and equipped under its internal law for the primary purpose of national defence or security, and persons acting in support of those armed forces who are under their formal command, control and responsibility.

5. 'Place of public use' means those parts of any building, land, street, waterway or other location that are accessible or open to members of the public, whether continuously, periodically or occasionally, and encompasses any commercial, business, cultural, historical, educational, religious, governmental, entertainment, recreational or similar place that is so accessible or open to the public.

6. 'Public transportation system' means all facilities, conveyances and instrumentalities, whether publicly or privately owned, that are used in or for publicly available services for the transportation of persons or cargo.

Article 2

1. Any person commits an offence within the meaning of this Convention if that person unlawfully and intentionally delivers, places, discharges or detonates an explosive or other lethal device in, into or against a place of public use, a State or government facility, a public transportation system or an infrastructure facility:

   (a) With the intent to cause death or serious bodily injury; or
   (b) With the intent to cause extensive destruction of such a place, facility or system, where such destruction results in or is likely to result in major economic loss.

2. Any person also commits an offence if that person attempts to commit an offence as set forth in paragraph 1.

3. Any person also commits an offence if that person:

   (a) Participates as an accomplice in an offence as set forth in paragraph 1 or 2; or
   (b) Organizes or directs others to commit an offence as set forth in paragraph 1 or 2; or
   (c) In any other way contributes to the commission of one or more offences as set forth in paragraph 1 or 2 by a group of persons acting with a common purpose; such contribution shall be intentional and either be made with the aim of furthering the general criminal activity or purpose of the group or be made in the knowledge of the intention of the group to commit the offence or offences concerned.

Article 3

This Convention shall not apply where the offence is committed within a single State, the alleged offender and the victims are nationals of that State, the alleged offender is found in the territory of that State and no other State has a basis under article 6, paragraph 1, or article 6, paragraph 2, of this Convention to exercise jurisdiction, except that the provisions of articles 10 to 15 shall, as appropriate, apply in those cases.

Article 4

Each State Party shall adopt such measures as may be necessary:

(a) To establish as criminal offences under its domestic law the offences set forth in article 2 of this Convention;
(b) To make those offences punishable by appropriate penalties which take into account the grave nature of those offences.

Article 5

Each State Party shall adopt such measures as may be necessary, including, where appropriate, domestic legislation, to ensure that criminal acts within the scope of this Convention, in particular where they are intended or calculated to provoke a state of terror in the general public or in a group of persons or particular persons, are under no circumstances justifiable by considerations of a political, philosophical, ideological, racial, ethnic, religious or other similar nature and are punished by penalties consistent with their grave nature.

Article 6

1. Each State Party shall take such measures as may be necessary to establish its jurisdiction over the offences set forth in article 2 when:

(a) The offence is committed in the territory of that State; or
(b) The offence is committed on board a vessel flying the flag of that State or an aircraft which is registered under the laws of that State at the time the offence is committed; or
(c) The offence is committed by a national of that State.

2. A State Party may also establish its jurisdiction over any such offence when:

(a) The offence is committed against a national of that State; or
(b) The offence is committed against a State or government facility of that State abroad, including an embassy or other diplomatic or consular premises of that State; or
(c) The offence is committed by a stateless person who has his or her habitual residence in the territory of that State; or
(d) The offence is committed in an attempt to compel that State to do or abstain from doing any act; or
(e) The offence is committed on board an aircraft which is operated by the Government of that State.

3. Upon ratifying, accepting, approving or acceding to this Convention, each State Party shall notify the Secretary-General of the United Nations of the jurisdiction it has established in accordance with paragraph 2 under its domestic law. Should any change take place, the State Party concerned shall immediately notify the Secretary-General.

4. Each State Party shall likewise take such measures as may be necessary to establish its jurisdiction over the offences set forth in article 2 in cases where the alleged offender is present in its territory and it does not extradite that person to any of the States Parties which have established their jurisdiction in accordance with paragraph 1 or 2.

5. This Convention does not exclude the exercise of any criminal jurisdiction established by a State Party in accordance with its domestic law.

Article 7

1. Upon receiving information that a person who has committed or who is alleged to have committed an offence as set forth in article 2 may be present in its territory, the State Party concerned shall take such measures as may be necessary under its domestic law to investigate the facts contained in the information.

2. Upon being satisfied that the circumstances so warrant, the State Party in whose territory the offender or alleged offender is present shall take the appropriate measures under its domestic law so as to ensure that person's presence for the purpose of prosecution or extradition.

3. Any person regarding whom the measures referred to in paragraph 2 are being taken shall be entitled to:

   (a) Communicate without delay with the nearest appropriate representative of the State of which that person is a national or which is otherwise entitled to protect that person's rights or, if that person is a stateless person, the State in the territory of which that person habitually resides;

   (b) Be visited by a representative of that State;

   (c) Be informed of that person's rights under subparagraphs (a) and (b).

4. The rights referred to in paragraph 3 shall be exercised in conformity with the laws and regulations of the State in the territory of which the offender or alleged offender is present, subject to the provision that the said laws and regulations must enable full effect to be given to the purposes for which the rights accorded under paragraph 3 are intended.

5. The provisions of paragraphs 3 and 4 shall be without prejudice to the right of any State Party having a claim to jurisdiction in accordance with article 6, subparagraph 1 (c) or 2 (c), to invite the International Committee of the Red Cross to communicate with and visit the alleged offender.

6. When a State Party, pursuant to this article, has taken a person into custody, it shall immediately notify, directly or through the Secretary-General of the United Nations, the States Parties which have established jurisdiction in accordance with article 6, paragraphs 1 and 2, and, if it considers it advisable, any other interested States Parties, of the fact that such person is in custody and of the circumstances which warrant that person's detention. The State which makes the investigation contemplated in paragraph 1 shall promptly inform the said States Parties of its findings and shall indicate whether it intends to exercise jurisdiction.

Article 8

1. The State Party in the territory of which the alleged offender is present shall, in cases to which article 6 applies, if it does not extradite that person, be obliged, without exception whatsoever and whether or not the offence was committed in its territory, to submit the case without undue delay to its competent authorities for the purpose of prosecution, through proceedings in accordance with the laws of that State. Those authorities shall take their decision in the same manner as in the case of any other offence of a grave nature under the law of that State.

2. Whenever a State Party is permitted under its domestic law to extradite or otherwise surrender one of its nationals only upon the condition that the person will be returned to that State to serve the sentence imposed as a result of the trial or proceeding for which the extradition or surrender of the person was sought, and this State and the State seeking the extradition of the person agree with this option and other terms they may deem appropriate, such a conditional extradition or surrender shall be sufficient to discharge the obligation set forth in paragraph 1.

Article 9

1. The offences set forth in article 2 shall be deemed to be included as extraditable offences in any extradition treaty existing between any of the States Parties before the entry into force of this Convention. States Parties undertake to include such offences as extraditable offences in every extradition treaty to be subsequently concluded between them.

2. When a State Party which makes extradition conditional on the existence of a treaty receives a request for extradition from another State Party with which it has no extradition treaty, the requested State Party may, at its option, consider this Convention as a legal basis for extradition in respect of the offences set forth in article 2. Extradition shall be subject to the other conditions provided by the law of the requested State.

3. States Parties which do not make extradition conditional on the existence of a treaty shall recognize the offences set forth in article 2 as extraditable offences between themselves, subject to the conditions provided by the law of the requested State.

4. If necessary, the offences set forth in article 2 shall be treated, for the purposes of extradition between States Parties, as if they had been committed not only in the place in which they occurred but also in the territory of the States that have established jurisdiction in accordance with article 6, paragraphs 1 and 2.

5. The provisions of all extradition treaties and arrangements between States Parties with regard to offences set forth in article 2 shall be deemed to be modified as between State Parties to the extent that they are incompatible with this Convention.

Article 10

1. States Parties shall afford one another the greatest measure of assistance in connection with investigations or criminal or extradition proceedings brought in respect of the offences set forth in article 2, including assistance in obtaining evidence at their disposal necessary for the proceedings.

2. States Parties shall carry out their obligations under paragraph 1 in conformity with any treaties or other arrangements on mutual legal assistance that may exist between them. In the absence of such treaties or arrangements, States Parties shall afford one another assistance in accordance with their domestic law.

Article 11

None of the offences set forth in article 2 shall be regarded, for the purposes of extradition or mutual legal assistance, as a political offence or as an offence connected with a political offence or as an offence inspired by political motives. Accordingly, a request for extradition or for mutual legal assistance based on such an offence may not be refused on the sole ground that it concerns a political offence or an offence connected with a political offence or an offence inspired by political motives.

Article 12

Nothing in this Convention shall be interpreted as imposing an obligation to extradite or to afford mutual legal assistance, if the requested State Party has substantial grounds for believing that the request for extradition for offences set forth in article 2 or for mutual legal assistance with respect to such offences has been made for the purpose of prosecuting or punishing a person on account of that person's race, religion, nationality, ethnic origin or political opinion or that compliance with the request would cause prejudice to that person's position for any of these reasons.

Article 13

1. A person who is being detained or is serving a sentence in the territory of one State Party whose presence in another State Party is requested for purposes of testimony, identification or otherwise

providing assistance in obtaining evidence for the investigation or prosecution of offences under this Convention may be transferred if the following conditions are met:

    (a) The person freely gives his or her informed consent; and

    (b) The competent authorities of both States agree, subject to such conditions as those States may deem appropriate.

2. For the purposes of this article:

    (a) The State to which the person is transferred shall have the authority and obligation to keep the person transferred in custody, unless otherwise requested or authorized by the State from which the person was transferred;

    (b) The State to which the person is transferred shall without delay implement its obligation to return the person to the custody of the State from which the person was transferred as agreed beforehand, or as otherwise agreed, by the competent authorities of both States;

    (c) The State to which the person is transferred shall not require the State from which the person was transferred to initiate extradition proceedings for the return of the person;

    (d) The person transferred shall receive credit for service of the sentence being served in the State from which he was transferred for time spent in the custody of the State to which he was transferred.

3. Unless the State Party from which a person is to be transferred in accordance with this article so agrees, that person, whatever his or her nationality, shall not be prosecuted or detained or subjected to any other restriction of his or her personal liberty in the territory of the State to which that person is transferred in respect of acts or convictions anterior to his or her departure from the territory of the State from which such person was transferred.

Article 14

Any person who is taken into custody or regarding whom any other measures are taken or proceedings are carried out pursuant to this Convention shall be guaranteed fair treatment, including enjoyment of all rights and guarantees in conformity with the law of the State in the territory of which that person is present and applicable provisions of international law, including international law of human rights.

Article 15

States Parties shall cooperate in the prevention of the offences set forth in article 2, particularly:

    (a) By taking all practicable measures, including, if necessary, adapting their domestic legislation, to prevent and counter preparations in their respective territories for the commission of those offences within or outside their territories, including measures to prohibit in their territories illegal activities of persons, groups and organizations that encourage, instigate, organize, knowingly finance or engage in the perpetration of offences as set forth in article 2;

    (b) By exchanging accurate and verified information in accordance with their national law, and coordinating administrative and other measures taken as appropriate to prevent the commission of offences as set forth in article 2;

    (c) Where appropriate, through research and development regarding methods of detection of explosives and other harmful substances that can cause death or bodily injury, consultations on the development of standards for marking explosives in order to identify their origin in post-blast investigations, exchange of information on preventive measures, cooperation and transfer of technology, equipment and related materials.

Article 16

The State Party where the alleged offender is prosecuted shall, in accordance with its domestic law or applicable procedures, communicate the final outcome of the proceedings to the Secretary-General of the United Nations, who shall transmit the information to the other States Parties.

Article 17

The States Parties shall carry out their obligations under this Convention in a manner consistent with the principles of sovereign equality and territorial integrity of States and that of non-intervention in the domestic affairs of other States.

Article 18

Nothing in this Convention entitles a State Party to undertake in the territory of another State Party the exercise of jurisdiction and performance of functions which are exclusively reserved for the authorities of that other State Party by its domestic law.

Article 19

1. Nothing in this Convention shall affect other rights, obligations and responsibilities of States and individuals under international law, in particular the purposes and principles of the Charter of the United Nations and international humanitarian law.

2. The activities of armed forces during an armed conflict, as those terms are understood under international humanitarian law, which are governed by that law, are not governed by this Convention, and the activities undertaken by military forces of a State in the exercise of their official duties, inasmuch as they are governed by other rules of international law, are not governed by this Convention.

Article 20

1. Any dispute between two or more States Parties concerning the interpretation or application of this Convention which cannot be settled through negotiation within a reasonable time shall, at the request of one of them, be submitted to arbitration. If, within six months from the date of the request for arbitration, the parties are unable to agree on the organization of the arbitration, any one of those parties may refer the dispute to the International Court of Justice, by application, in conformity with the Statute of the Court.

2. Each State may at the time of signature, ratification, acceptance or approval of this Convention or accession thereto declare that it does not consider itself bound by paragraph 1. The other States Parties shall not be bound by paragraph 1 with respect to any State Party which has made such a reservation.

3. Any State which has made a reservation in accordance with paragraph 2 may at any time withdraw that reservation by notification to the Secretary-General of the United Nations.

Article 21

1. This Convention shall be open for signature by all States from 12 January 1998 until 31 December 1999 at United Nations Headquarters in New York.

2. This Convention is subject to ratification, acceptance or approval. The instruments of ratification, acceptance or approval shall be deposited with the Secretary-General of the United Nations.

3. This Convention shall be open to accession by any State. The instruments of accession shall be deposited with the Secretary-General of the United Nations.

Article 22

1. This Convention shall enter into force on the thirtieth day following the date of the deposit of the twenty-second instrument of ratification, acceptance, approval or accession with the Secretary-General of the United Nations.

2. For each State ratifying, accepting, approving or acceding to the Convention after the deposit of the twenty-second instrument of ratification, acceptance, approval or accession, the Convention shall enter into force on the thirtieth day after deposit by such State of its instrument of ratification, acceptance, approval or accession.

Article 23

1. Any State Party may denounce this Convention by written notification to the Secretary-General of the United Nations.

2. Denunciation shall take effect one year following the date on which notification is received by the Secretary-General of the United Nations.

Article 24

The original of this Convention, of which the Arabic, Chinese, English, French, Russian and Spanish texts are equally authentic, shall be deposited with the Secretary-General of the United Nations, who shall send certified copies thereof to all States.

IN WITNESS WHEREOF, the undersigned, being duly authorized thereto by their respective Governments, have signed this Convention, opened for signature at New York on 12 January 1998.

APPENDIX 12

International Convention for the Suppression of the Financing of Terrorism

PREAMBLE

The States Parties to this Convention,

Bearing in mind the purposes and principles of the Charter of the United Nations concerning the maintenance of international peace and security and the promotion of good-neighbourliness and friendly relations and cooperation among States,

Deeply concerned about the worldwide escalation of acts of terrorism in all its forms and manifestations,

Recalling the Declaration on the Occasion of the Fiftieth Anniversary of the United Nations, contained in General Assembly resolution 50/6 of 24 October 1995,

Recalling also all the relevant General Assembly resolutions on the matter, including resolution 49/60 of 9 December 1994 and its annex on the Declaration on Measures to Eliminate International Terrorism, in which the States Members of the United Nations solemnly reaffirmed their unequivocal condemnation of all acts, methods and practices of terrorism as criminal and unjustifiable, wherever and by whomever committed, including those which jeopardize the friendly relations among States and peoples and threaten the territorial integrity and security of States,

Noting that the Declaration on Measures to Eliminate International Terrorism also encouraged States to review urgently the scope of the existing international legal provisions on the prevention, repression and elimination of terrorism in all its forms and manifestations, with the aim of ensuring that there is a comprehensive legal framework covering all aspects of the matter,

Recalling General Assembly resolution 51/210 of 17 December 1996, paragraph 3, subparagraph (f), in which the Assembly called upon all States to take steps to prevent and counteract, through appropriate domestic measures, the financing of terrorists and terrorist organizations, whether such financing is direct or indirect through organizations which also have or claim to have charitable, social or cultural goals or which are also engaged in unlawful activities such as illicit arms trafficking, drug dealing and racketeering, including the exploitation of persons for purposes of funding terrorist activities, and in particular to consider, where appropriate, adopting regulatory measures to prevent and counteract movements of funds suspected to be intended for terrorist purposes without impeding in any way the freedom of legitimate capital movements and to intensify the exchange of information concerning international movements of such funds,

Recalling also General Assembly resolution 52/165 of 15 December 1997, in which the Assembly called upon States to consider, in particular, the implementation of the measures set out in paragraphs 3 (a) to (f) of its resolution 51/210 of 17 December 1996,

Recalling further General Assembly resolution 53/108 of 8 December 1998, in which the Assembly decided that the Ad Hoc Committee established by General Assembly resolution 51/210 of 17 December 1996 should elaborate a draft international convention for the suppression of terrorist financing to supplement related existing international instruments,

Considering that the financing of terrorism is a matter of grave concern to the international community as a whole,

Noting that the number and seriousness of acts of international terrorism depend on the financing that terrorists may obtain,

Noting also that existing multilateral legal instruments do not expressly address such financing,

Being convinced of the urgent need to enhance international cooperation among States in devising and adopting effective measures for the prevention of the financing of terrorism, as well as for its suppression through the prosecution and punishment of its perpetrators,

Have agreed as follows:

Article 1

For the purposes of this Convention:

1. 'Funds' means assets of every kind, whether tangible or intangible, movable or immovable, however acquired, and legal documents or instruments in any form, including electronic or digital, evidencing title to, or interest in, such assets, including, but not limited to, bank credits, travellers cheques, bank cheques, money orders, shares, securities, bonds, drafts, letters of credit.

2. 'A State or governmental facility' means any permanent or temporary facility or conveyance that is used or occupied by representatives of a State, members of Government, the legislature or the judiciary or by officials or employees of a State or any other public authority or entity or by employees or officials of an intergovernmental organization in connection with their official duties.

3. 'Proceeds' means any funds derived from or obtained, directly or indirectly, through the commission of an offence set forth in article 2.

Article 2

1. Any person commits an offence within the meaning of this Convention if that person by any means, directly or indirectly, unlawfully and wilfully, provides or collects funds with the intention that they should be used or in the knowledge that they are to be used, in full or in part, in order to carry out:

   (a) An act which constitutes an offence within the scope of and as defined in one of the treaties listed in the annex; or
   (b) Any other act intended to cause death or serious bodily injury to a civilian, or to any other person not taking an active part in the hostilities in a situation of armed conflict, when the purpose of such act, by its nature or context, is to intimidate a population, or to compel a government or an international organization to do or to abstain from doing any act.

2. (a) On depositing its instrument of ratification, acceptance, approval or accession, a State Party which is not a party to a treaty listed in the annex may declare that, in the application of this Convention to the State Party, the treaty shall be deemed not to be included in the annex referred to in paragraph 1, subparagraph (a). The declaration shall cease to have effect as soon as the treaty enters into force for the State Party, which shall notify the depositary of this fact;
   (b) When a State Party ceases to be a party to a treaty listed in the annex, it may make a declaration as provided for in this article, with respect to that treaty.

3. For an act to constitute an offence set forth in paragraph 1, it shall not be necessary that the funds were actually used to carry out an offence referred to in paragraph 1, subparagraphs (a) or (b).

4. Any person also commits an offence if that person attempts to commit an offence as set forth in paragraph 1 of this article.

5. Any person also commits an offence if that person:

    (a) Participates as an accomplice in an offence as set forth in paragraph 1 or 4 of this article;

    (b) Organizes or directs others to commit an offence as set forth in paragraph 1 or 4 of this article;

    (c) Contributes to the commission of one or more offences as set forth in paragraphs 1 or 4 of this article by a group of persons acting with a common purpose. Such contribution shall be intentional and shall either:

        (i) Be made with the aim of furthering the criminal activity or criminal purpose of the group, where such activity or purpose involves the commission of an offence as set forth in paragraph 1 of this article; or

        (ii) Be made in the knowledge of the intention of the group to commit an offence as set forth in paragraph 1 of this article.

Article 3

This Convention shall not apply where the offence is committed within a single State, the alleged offender is a national of that State and is present in the territory of that State and no other State has a basis under article 7, paragraph 1, or article 7, paragraph 2, to exercise jurisdiction, except that the provisions of articles 12 to 18 shall, as appropriate, apply in those cases.

Article 4

Each State Party shall adopt such measures as may be necessary:

    (a) To establish as criminal offences under its domestic law the offences set forth in article 2;

    (b) To make those offences punishable by appropriate penalties which take into account the grave nature of the offences.

Article 5

1. Each State Party, in accordance with its domestic legal principles, shall take the necessary measures to enable a legal entity located in its territory or organized under its laws to be held liable when a person responsible for the management or control of that legal entity has, in that capacity, committed an offence set forth in article 2. Such liability may be criminal, civil or administrative.

2. Such liability is incurred without prejudice to the criminal liability of individuals having committed the offences.

3. Each State Party shall ensure, in particular, that legal entities liable in accordance with paragraph 1 above are subject to effective, proportionate and dissuasive criminal, civil or administrative sanctions. Such sanctions may include monetary sanctions.

Article 6

Each State Party shall adopt such measures as may be necessary, including, where appropriate, domestic legislation, to ensure that criminal acts within the scope of this Convention are under no circumstances justifiable by considerations of a political, philosophical, ideological, racial, ethnic, religious or other similar nature.

Article 7

1. Each State Party shall take such measures as may be necessary to establish its jurisdiction over the offences set forth in article 2 when:

    (a) The offence is committed in the territory of that State;

    (b) The offence is committed on board a vessel flying the flag of that State or an aircraft registered under the laws of that State at the time the offence is committed;

    (c) The offence is committed by a national of that State.

2. A State Party may also establish its jurisdiction over any such offence when:

(a) The offence was directed towards or resulted in the carrying out of an offence referred to in article 2, paragraph 1, subparagraph (a) or (b), in the territory of or against a national of that State;

(b) The offence was directed towards or resulted in the carrying out of an offence referred to in article 2, paragraph 1, subparagraph (a) or (b), against a State or government facility of that State abroad, including diplomatic or consular premises of that State;

(c) The offence was directed towards or resulted in an offence referred to in article 2, paragraph 1, subparagraph (a) or (b), committed in an attempt to compel that State to do or abstain from doing any act;

(d) The offence is committed by a stateless person who has his or her habitual residence in the territory of that State;

(e) The offence is committed on board an aircraft which is operated by the Government of that State.

3. Upon ratifying, accepting, approving or acceding to this Convention, each State Party shall notify the Secretary-General of the United Nations of the jurisdiction it has established in accordance with paragraph 2. Should any change take place, the State Party concerned shall immediately notify the Secretary-General.

4. Each State Party shall likewise take such measures as may be necessary to establish its jurisdiction over the offences set forth in article 2 in cases where the alleged offender is present in its territory and it does not extradite that person to any of the States Parties that have established their jurisdiction in accordance with paragraphs 1 or 2.

5. When more than one State Party claims jurisdiction over the offences set forth in article 2, the relevant States Parties shall strive to coordinate their actions appropriately, in particular concerning the conditions for prosecution and the modalities for mutual legal assistance.

6. Without prejudice to the norms of general international law, this Convention does not exclude the exercise of any criminal jurisdiction established by a State Party in accordance with its domestic law.

Article 8

1. Each State Party shall take appropriate measures, in accordance with its domestic legal principles, for the identification, detection and freezing or seizure of any funds used or allocated for the purpose of committing the offences set forth in article 2 as well as the proceeds derived from such offences, for purposes of possible forfeiture.

2. Each State Party shall take appropriate measures, in accordance with its domestic legal principles, for the forfeiture of funds used or allocated for the purpose of committing the offences set forth in article 2 and the proceeds derived from such offences.

3. Each State Party concerned may give consideration to concluding agreements on the sharing with other States Parties, on a regular or case-by-case basis, of the funds derived from the forfeitures referred to in this article.

4. Each State Party shall consider establishing mechanisms whereby the funds derived from the forfeitures referred to in this article are utilized to compensate the victims of offences referred to in article 2, paragraph 1, subparagraph (a) or (b), or their families.

5. The provisions of this article shall be implemented without prejudice to the rights of third parties acting in good faith.

Article 9

1. Upon receiving information that a person who has committed or who is alleged to have committed an offence set forth in article 2 may be present in its territory, the State Party concerned shall take such measures as may be necessary under its domestic law to investigate the facts contained in the information.

2. Upon being satisfied that the circumstances so warrant, the State Party in whose territory the offender or alleged offender is present shall take the appropriate measures under its domestic law so as to ensure that person's presence for the purpose of prosecution or extradition.

3. Any person regarding whom the measures referred to in paragraph 2 are being taken shall be entitled to:

  (a) Communicate without delay with the nearest appropriate representative of the State of which that person is a national or which is otherwise entitled to protect that person's rights or, if that person is a stateless person, the State in the territory of which that person habitually resides;
  (b) Be visited by a representative of that State;
  (c) Be informed of that person's rights under subparagraphs (a) and (b).

4. The rights referred to in paragraph 3 shall be exercised in conformity with the laws and regulations of the State in the territory of which the offender or alleged offender is present, subject to the provision that the said laws and regulations must enable full effect to be given to the purposes for which the rights accorded under paragraph 3 are intended.

5. The provisions of paragraphs 3 and 4 shall be without prejudice to the right of any State Party having a claim to jurisdiction in accordance with article 7, paragraph 1, subparagraph (b), or paragraph 2, subparagraph (b), to invite the International Committee of the Red Cross to communicate with and visit the alleged offender.

6. When a State Party, pursuant to the present article, has taken a person into custody, it shall immediately notify, directly or through the Secretary-General of the United Nations, the States Parties which have established jurisdiction in accordance with article 7, paragraph 1 or 2, and, if it considers it advisable, any other interested States Parties, of the fact that such person is in custody and of the circumstances which warrant that person's detention. The State which makes the investigation contemplated in paragraph 1 shall promptly inform the said States Parties of its findings and shall indicate whether it intends to exercise jurisdiction.

Article 10

1. The State Party in the territory of which the alleged offender is present shall, in cases to which article 7 applies, if it does not extradite that person, be obliged, without exception whatsoever and whether or not the offence was committed in its territory, to submit the case without undue delay to its competent authorities for the purpose of prosecution, through proceedings in accordance with the laws of that State. Those authorities shall take their decision in the same manner as in the case of any other offence of a grave nature under the law of that State.

2. Whenever a State Party is permitted under its domestic law to extradite or otherwise surrender one of its nationals only upon the condition that the person will be returned to that State to serve the sentence imposed as a result of the trial or proceeding for which the extradition or surrender of the person was sought, and this State and the State seeking the extradition of the person agree with this option and other terms they may deem appropriate, such a conditional extradition or surrender shall be sufficient to discharge the obligation set forth in paragraph 1.

Article 11

1. The offences set forth in article 2 shall be deemed to be included as extraditable offences in any extradition treaty existing between any of the States Parties before the entry into force of this

Convention. States Parties undertake to include such offences as extraditable offences in every extradition treaty to be subsequently concluded between them.

2. When a State Party which makes extradition conditional on the existence of a treaty receives a request for extradition from another State Party with which it has no extradition treaty, the requested State Party may, at its option, consider this Convention as a legal basis for extradition in respect of the offences set forth in article 2. Extradition shall be subject to the other conditions provided by the law of the requested State.

3. States Parties which do not make extradition conditional on the existence of a treaty shall recognize the offences set forth in article 2 as extraditable offences between themselves, subject to the conditions provided by the law of the requested State.

4. If necessary, the offences set forth in article 2 shall be treated, for the purposes of extradition between States Parties, as if they had been committed not only in the place in which they occurred but also in the territory of the States that have established jurisdiction in accordance with article 7, paragraphs 1 and 2.

5. The provisions of all extradition treaties and arrangements between States Parties with regard to offences set forth in article 2 shall be deemed to be modified as between States Parties to the extent that they are incompatible with this Convention.

Article 12

1. States Parties shall afford one another the greatest measure of assistance in connection with criminal investigations or criminal or extradition proceedings in respect of the offences set forth in article 2, including assistance in obtaining evidence in their possession necessary for the proceedings.

2. States Parties may not refuse a request for mutual legal assistance on the ground of bank secrecy.

3. The requesting Party shall not transmit nor use information or evidence furnished by the requested Party for investigations, prosecutions or proceedings other than those stated in the request without the prior consent of the requested Party.

4. Each State Party may give consideration to establishing mechanisms to share with other States Parties information or evidence needed to establish criminal, civil or administrative liability pursuant to article 5.

5. States Parties shall carry out their obligations under paragraphs 1 and 2 in conformity with any treaties or other arrangements on mutual legal assistance or information exchange that may exist between them. In the absence of such treaties or arrangements, States Parties shall afford one another assistance in accordance with their domestic law.

Article 13

None of the offences set forth in article 2 shall be regarded, for the purposes of extradition or mutual legal assistance, as a fiscal offence. Accordingly, States Parties may not refuse a request for extradition or for mutual legal assistance on the sole ground that it concerns a fiscal offence.

Article 14

None of the offences set forth in article 2 shall be regarded for the purposes of extradition or mutual legal assistance as a political offence or as an offence connected with a political offence or as an offence inspired by political motives. Accordingly, a request for extradition or for mutual legal assistance based on such an offence may not be refused on the sole ground that it concerns a political offence or an offence connected with a political offence or an offence inspired by political motives.

Article 15

Nothing in this Convention shall be interpreted as imposing an obligation to extradite or to afford mutual legal assistance, if the requested State Party has substantial grounds for believing that the request for extradition for offences set forth in article 2 or for mutual legal assistance with respect to such offences has been made for the purpose of prosecuting or punishing a person on account of that person's race, religion, nationality, ethnic origin or political opinion or that compliance with the request would cause prejudice to that person's position for any of these reasons.

Article 16

1. A person who is being detained or is serving a sentence in the territory of one State Party whose presence in another State Party is requested for purposes of identification, testimony or otherwise providing assistance in obtaining evidence for the investigation or prosecution of offences set forth in article 2 may be transferred if the following conditions are met:

   (a) The person freely gives his or her informed consent;
   (b) The competent authorities of both States agree, subject to such conditions as those States may deem appropriate.

2. For the purposes of the present article:

   (a) The State to which the person is transferred shall have the authority and obligation to keep the person transferred in custody, unless otherwise requested or authorized by the State from which the person was transferred;
   (b) The State to which the person is transferred shall without delay implement its obligation to return the person to the custody of the State from which the person was transferred as agreed beforehand, or as otherwise agreed, by the competent authorities of both States;
   (c) The State to which the person is transferred shall not require the State from which the person was transferred to initiate extradition proceedings for the return of the person;
   (d) The person transferred shall receive credit for service of the sentence being served in the State from which he or she was transferred for time spent in the custody of the State to which he or she was transferred.

3. Unless the State Party from which a person is to be transferred in accordance with the present article so agrees, that person, whatever his or her nationality, shall not be prosecuted or detained or subjected to any other restriction of his or her personal liberty in the territory of the State to which that person is transferred in respect of acts or convictions anterior to his or her departure from the territory of the State from which such person was transferred.

Article 17

Any person who is taken into custody or regarding whom any other measures are taken or proceedings are carried out pursuant to this Convention shall be guaranteed fair treatment, including enjoyment of all rights and guarantees in conformity with the law of the State in the territory of which that person is present and applicable provisions of international law, including international human rights law.

Article 18

1. States Parties shall cooperate in the prevention of the offences set forth in article 2 by taking all practicable measures, inter alia, by adapting their domestic legislation, if necessary, to prevent and counter preparations in their respective territories for the commission of those offences within or outside their territories, including:

   (a) Measures to prohibit in their territories illegal activities of persons and organizations that knowingly encourage, instigate, organize or engage in the commission of offences set forth in article 2;

(b) Measures requiring financial institutions and other professions involved in financial transactions to utilize the most efficient measures available for the identification of their usual or occasional customers, as well as customers in whose interest accounts are opened, and to pay special attention to unusual or suspicious transactions and report transactions suspected of stemming from a criminal activity. For this purpose, States Parties shall consider:

   (i) Adopting regulations prohibiting the opening of accounts the holders or beneficiaries of which are unidentified or unidentifiable, and measures to ensure that such institutions verify the identity of the real owners of such transactions;

   (ii) With respect to the identification of legal entities, requiring financial institutions, when necessary, to take measures to verify the legal existence and the structure of the customer by obtaining, either from a public register or from the customer or both, proof of incorporation, including information concerning the customer's name, legal form, address, directors and provisions regulating the power to bind the entity;

   (iii) Adopting regulations imposing on financial institutions the obligation to report promptly to the competent authorities all complex, unusual large transactions and unusual patterns of transactions, which have no apparent economic or obviously lawful purpose, without fear of assuming criminal or civil liability for breach of any restriction on disclosure of information if they report their suspicions in good faith;

   (iv) Requiring financial institutions to maintain, for at least five years, all necessary records on transactions, both domestic or international.

2. States Parties shall further cooperate in the prevention of offences set forth in article 2 by considering:

   (a) Measures for the supervision, including, for example, the licensing, of all money transmission agencies;

   (b) Feasible measures to detect or monitor the physical cross-border transportation of cash and bearer negotiable instruments, subject to strict safeguards to ensure proper use of information and without impeding in any way the freedom of capital movements.

3. States Parties shall further cooperate in the prevention of the offences set forth in article 2 by exchanging accurate and verified information in accordance with their domestic law and coordinating administrative and other measures taken, as appropriate, to prevent the commission of offences set forth in article 2, in particular by:

   (a) Establishing and maintaining channels of communication between their competent agencies and services to facilitate the secure and rapid exchange of information concerning all aspects of offences set forth in article 2;

   (b) Cooperating with one another in conducting inquiries, with respect to the offences set forth in article 2, concerning:

      (i) The identity, whereabouts and activities of persons in respect of whom reasonable suspicion exists that they are involved in such offences;

      (ii) The movement of funds relating to the commission of such offences.

4. States Parties may exchange information through the International Criminal Police Organization (Interpol).

Article 19

The State Party where the alleged offender is prosecuted shall, in accordance with its domestic law or applicable procedures, communicate the final outcome of the proceedings to the Secretary-General of the United Nations, who shall transmit the information to the other States Parties.

Article 20

The States Parties shall carry out their obligations under this Convention in a manner consistent with the principles of sovereign equality and territorial integrity of States and that of non-intervention in the domestic affairs of other States.

Article 21

Nothing in this Convention shall affect other rights, obligations and responsibilities of States and individuals under international law, in particular the purposes of the Charter of the United Nations, international humanitarian law and other relevant conventions.

Article 22

Nothing in this Convention entitles a State Party to undertake in the territory of another State Party the exercise of jurisdiction or performance of functions which are exclusively reserved for the authorities of that other State Party by its domestic law.

Article 23

1. The annex may be amended by the addition of relevant treaties that:
    (a) Are open to the participation of all States;
    (b) Have entered into force;
    (c) Have been ratified, accepted, approved or acceded to by at least twenty-two States Parties to the present Convention.

2. After the entry into force of this Convention, any State Party may propose such an amendment. Any proposal for an amendment shall be communicated to the depositary in written form. The depositary shall notify proposals that meet the requirements of paragraph 1 to all States Parties and seek their views on whether the proposed amendment should be adopted.

3. The proposed amendment shall be deemed adopted unless one third of the States Parties object to it by a written notification not later than 180 days after its circulation.

4. The adopted amendment to the annex shall enter into force 30 days after the deposit of the twenty-second instrument of ratification, acceptance or approval of such amendment for all those States Parties having deposited such an instrument. For each State Party ratifying, accepting or approving the amendment after the deposit of the twenty-second instrument, the amendment shall enter into force on the thirtieth day after deposit by such State Party of its instrument of ratification, acceptance or approval.

Article 24

1. Any dispute between two or more States Parties concerning the interpretation or application of this Convention which cannot be settled through negotiation within a reasonable time shall, at the request of one of them, be submitted to arbitration. If, within six months from the date of the request for arbitration, the parties are unable to agree on the organization of the arbitration, any one of those parties may refer the dispute to the International Court of Justice, by application, in conformity with the Statute of the Court.

2. Each State may at the time of signature, ratification, acceptance or approval of this Convention or accession thereto declare that it does not consider itself bound by paragraph 1. The other States Parties shall not be bound by paragraph 1 with respect to any State Party which has made such a reservation.

3. Any State which has made a reservation in accordance with paragraph 2 may at any time withdraw that reservation by notification to the Secretary-General of the United Nations.

Article 25

1. This Convention shall be open for signature by all States from 10 January 2000 to 31 December 2001 at United Nations Headquarters in New York.

2. This Convention is subject to ratification, acceptance or approval. The instruments of ratification, acceptance or approval shall be deposited with the Secretary-General of the United Nations.

3. This Convention shall be open to accession by any State. The instruments of accession shall be deposited with the Secretary-General of the United Nations.

Article 26

1. This Convention shall enter into force on the thirtieth day following the date of the deposit of the twenty-second instrument of ratification, acceptance, approval or accession with the Secretary-General of the United Nations.

2. For each State ratifying, accepting, approving or acceding to the Convention after the deposit of the twenty-second instrument of ratification, acceptance, approval or accession, the Convention shall enter into force on the thirtieth day after deposit by such State of its instrument of ratification, acceptance, approval or accession.

Article 27

1. Any State Party may denounce this Convention by written notification to the Secretary- General of the United Nations.

2. Denunciation shall take effect one year following the date on which notification is received by the Secretary-General of the United Nations.

Article 28

The original of this Convention, of which the Arabic, Chinese, English, French, Russian and Spanish texts are equally authentic, shall be deposited with the Secretary-General of the United Nations who shall send certified copies thereof to all States.

IN WITNESS WHEREOF, the undersigned, being duly authorized thereto by their respective Governments, have signed this Convention, opened for signature at United Nations Headquarters in New York on 10 January 2000.

Annex

1. Convention for the Suppression of Unlawful Seizure of Aircraft, done at The Hague on 16 December 1970.

2. Convention for the Suppression of Unlawful Acts against the Safety of Civil Aviation, done at Montreal on 23 September 1971.

3. Convention on the Prevention and Punishment of Crimes against Internationally Protected Persons, including Diplomatic Agents, adopted by the General Assembly of the United Nations on 14 December 1973.

4. International Convention against the Taking of Hostages, adopted by the General Assembly of the United Nations on 17 December 1979.

5. Convention on the Physical Protection of Nuclear Material, adopted at Vienna on 3 March 1980.

6. Protocol for the Suppression of Unlawful Acts of Violence at Airports Serving International Civil Aviation, supplementary to the Convention for the Suppression of Unlawful Acts against the Safety of Civil Aviation, done at Montreal on 24 February 1988.

7. Convention for the Suppression of Unlawful Acts against the Safety of Maritime Navigation, done at Rome on 10 March 1988.

8. Protocol for the Suppression of Unlawful Acts against the Safety of Fixed Platforms located on the Continental Shelf, done at Rome on 10 March 1988.

9. International Convention for the Suppression of Terrorist Bombings, adopted by the General Assembly of the United Nations on 15 December 1997.

APPENDIX 13

International Convention for the Suppression of Acts of Nuclear Terrorism

The States Parties to this Convention,

Having in mind the purposes and principles of the Charter of the United Nations concerning the maintenance of international peace and security and the promotion of good-neighbourliness and friendly relations and cooperation among States,

Recalling the Declaration on the Occasion of the Fiftieth Anniversary of the United Nations of 24 October 1995,

Recognizing the right of all States to develop and apply nuclear energy for peaceful purposes and their legitimate interests in the potential benefits to be derived from the peaceful application of nuclear energy,

Bearing in mind the Convention on the Physical Protection of Nuclear Material of 1980,

Deeply concerned about the worldwide escalation of acts of terrorism in all its forms and manifestations,

Recalling the Declaration on Measures to Eliminate International Terrorism annexed to General Assembly resolution 49/60 of 9 December 1994, in which, inter alia, the States Members of the United Nations solemnly reaffirm their unequivocal condemnation of all acts, methods and practices of terrorism as criminal and unjustifiable, wherever and by whomever committed, including those which jeopardize the friendly relations among States and peoples and threaten the territorial integrity and security of States,

Noting that the Declaration also encouraged States to review urgently the scope of the existing international legal provisions on the prevention, repression and elimination of terrorism in all its forms and manifestations, with the aim of ensuring that there is a comprehensive legal framework covering all aspects of the matter,

Recalling General Assembly resolution 51/210 of 17 December 1996 and the Declaration to Supplement the 1994 Declaration on Measures to Eliminate International Terrorism annexed thereto,

Recalling also that, pursuant to General Assembly resolution 51/210, an ad hoc committee was established to elaborate, inter alia, an international convention for the suppression of acts of nuclear terrorism to supplement related existing international instruments,

Noting that acts of nuclear terrorism may result in the gravest consequences and may pose a threat to international peace and security,

Noting also that existing multilateral legal provisions do not adequately address those attacks,

Being convinced of the urgent need to enhance international cooperation between States in devising and adopting effective and practical measures for the prevention of such acts of terrorism and for the prosecution and punishment of their perpetrators,

Noting that the activities of military forces of States are governed by rules of international law outside of the framework of this Convention and that the exclusion of certain actions from the coverage of this Convention does not condone or make lawful otherwise unlawful acts, or preclude prosecution under other laws,

Have agreed as follows:

Article 1

For the purposes of this Convention:

1. 'Radioactive material' means nuclear material and other radioactive substances which contain nuclides which undergo spontaneous disintegration (a process accompanied by emission of one or more types of ionizing radiation, such as alpha-, beta-, neutron particles and gamma rays) and which may, owing to their radiological or fissile properties, cause death, serious bodily injury or substantial damage to property or to the environment.

2. 'Nuclear material' means plutonium, except that with isotopic concentration exceeding 80 per cent in plutonium-238; uranium-233; uranium enriched in the isotope 235 or 233; uranium containing the mixture of isotopes as occurring in nature other than in the form of ore or ore residue; or any material containing one or more of the foregoing; Whereby 'uranium enriched in the isotope 235 or 233' means uranium containing the isotope 235 or 233 or both in an amount such that the abundance ratio of the sum of these isotopes to the isotope 238 is greater than the ratio of the isotope 235 to the isotope 238 occurring in nature.

3. 'Nuclear facility' means:

  (a) Any nuclear reactor, including reactors installed on vessels, vehicles, aircraft or space objects for use as an energy source in order to propel such vessels, vehicles, aircraft or space objects or for any other purpose;
  (b) Any plant or conveyance being used for the production, storage, processing or transport of radioactive material.

4. 'Device' means:

  (a) Any nuclear explosive device; or
  (b) Any radioactive material dispersal or radiation-emitting device which may, owing to its radiological properties, cause death, serious bodily injury or substantial damage to property or to the environment.

5. 'State or government facility' includes any permanent or temporary facility or conveyance that is used or occupied by representatives of a State, members of a Government, the legislature or the judiciary or by officials or employees of a State or any other public authority or entity or by employees or officials of an intergovernmental organization in connection with their official duties.

6. 'Military forces of a State' means the armed forces of a State which are organized, trained and equipped under its internal law for the primary purpose of national defence or security and persons acting in support of those armed forces who are under their formal command, control and responsibility.

Article 2

1. Any person commits an offence within the meaning of this Convention if that person unlawfully and intentionally:

  (a) Possesses radioactive material or makes or possesses a device:
    (i) With the intent to cause death or serious bodily injury; or
    (ii) With the intent to cause substantial damage to property or to the environment;
  (b) Uses in any way radioactive material or a device, or uses or damages a nuclear facility in a manner which releases or risks the release of radioactive material:
    (i) With the intent to cause death or serious bodily injury; or
    (ii) With the intent to cause substantial damage to property or to the environment; or

    (iii) With the intent to compel a natural or legal person, an international organization or a State to do or refrain from doing an act.

2. Any person also commits an offence if that person:

    (*a*) Threatens, under circumstances which indicate the credibility of the threat, to commit an offence as set forth in paragraph 1 (*b*) of the present article; or

    (*b*) Demands unlawfully and intentionally radioactive material, a device or a nuclear facility by threat, under circumstances which indicate the credibility of the threat, or by use of force.

3. Any person also commits an offence if that person attempts to commit an offence as set forth in paragraph 1 of the present article.

4. Any person also commits an offence if that person:

    (*a*) Participates as an accomplice in an offence as set forth in paragraph 1, 2 or 3 of the present article; or

    (*b*) Organizes or directs others to commit an offence as set forth in paragraph 1, 2 or 3 of the present article; or

    (*c*) In any other way contributes to the commission of one or more offences as set forth in paragraph 1, 2 or 3 of the present article by a group of persons acting with a common purpose; such contribution shall be intentional and either be made with the aim of furthering the general criminal activity or purpose of the group or be made in the knowledge of the intention of the group to commit the offence or offences concerned.

Article 3

This Convention shall not apply where the offence is committed within a single State, the alleged offender and the victims are nationals of that State, the alleged offender is found in the territory of that State and no other State has a basis under article 9, paragraph 1 or 2, to exercise jurisdiction, except that the provisions of articles 7, 12, 14, 15, 16 and 17 shall, as appropriate, apply in those cases.

Article 4

1. Nothing in this Convention shall affect other rights, obligations and responsibilities of States and individuals under international law, in particular the purposes and principles of the Charter of the United Nations and international humanitarian law.

2. The activities of armed forces during an armed conflict, as those terms are understood under international humanitarian law, which are governed by that law are not governed by this Convention, and the activities undertaken by military forces of a State in the exercise of their official duties, inasmuch as they are governed by other rules of international law, are not governed by this Convention.

3. The provisions of paragraph 2 of the present article shall not be interpreted as condoning or making lawful otherwise unlawful acts, or precluding prosecution under other laws.

4. This Convention does not address, nor can it be interpreted as addressing, in any way, the issue of the legality of the use or threat of use of nuclear weapons by States.

Article 5

Each State Party shall adopt such measures as may be necessary:

    (*a*) To establish as criminal offences under its national law the offences set forth in article 2;

    (*b*) To make those offences punishable by appropriate penalties which take into account the grave nature of these offences.

Article 6

Each State Party shall adopt such measures as may be necessary, including, where appropriate, domestic legislation, to ensure that criminal acts within the scope of this Convention, in particular where they are intended or calculated to provoke a state of terror in the general public or in a group of persons or particular persons, are under no circumstances justifiable by considerations of a political, philosophical, ideological, racial, ethnic, religious or other similar nature and are punished by penalties consistent with their grave nature.

Article 7

1. States Parties shall cooperate by:

    (*a*) Taking all practicable measures, including, if necessary, adapting their national law, to prevent and counter preparations in their respective territories for the commission within or outside their territories of the offences set forth in article 2, including measures to prohibit in their territories illegal activities of persons, groups and organizations that encourage, instigate, organize, knowingly finance or knowingly provide technical assistance or information or engage in the perpetration of those offences;

    (*b*) Exchanging accurate and verified information in accordance with their national law and in the manner and subject to the conditions specified herein, and coordinating administrative and other measures taken as appropriate to detect, prevent, suppress and investigate the offences set forth in article 2 and also in order to institute criminal proceedings against persons alleged to have committed those crimes. In particular, a State Party shall take appropriate measures in order to inform without delay the other States referred to in article 9 in respect of the commission of the offences set forth in article 2 as well as preparations to commit such offences about which it has learned, and also to inform, where appropriate, international organizations.

2. States Parties shall take appropriate measures consistent with their national law to protect the confidentiality of any information which they receive in confidence by virtue of the provisions of this Convention from another State Party or through participation in an activity carried out for the implementation of this Convention. If States Parties provide information to international organizations in confidence, steps shall be taken to ensure that the confidentiality of such information is protected.

3. States Parties shall not be required by this Convention to provide any information which they are not permitted to communicate pursuant to national law or which would jeopardize the security of the State concerned or the physical protection of nuclear material.

4. States Parties shall inform the Secretary-General of the United Nations of their competent authorities and liaison points responsible for sending and receiving the information referred to in the present article. The Secretary-General of the United Nations shall communicate such information regarding competent authorities and liaison points to all States Parties and the International Atomic Energy Agency. Such authorities and liaison points must be accessible on a continuous basis.

Article 8

For purposes of preventing offences under this Convention, States Parties shall make every effort to adopt appropriate measures to ensure the protection of radioactive material, taking into account relevant recommendations and functions of the International Atomic Energy Agency.

Article 9

1. Each State Party shall take such measures as may be necessary to establish its jurisdiction over the offences set forth in article 2 when:

   (*a*) The offence is committed in the territory of that State; or

   (*b*) The offence is committed on board a vessel flying the flag of that State or an aircraft which is registered under the laws of that State at the time the offence is committed; or

   (*c*) The offence is committed by a national of that State.

2. A State Party may also establish its jurisdiction over any such offence when:

   (*a*) The offence is committed against a national of that State; or

   (*b*) The offence is committed against a State or government facility of that State abroad, including an embassy or other diplomatic or consular premises of that State; or

   (*c*) The offence is committed by a stateless person who has his or her habitual residence in the territory of that State; or

   (*d*) The offence is committed in an attempt to compel that State to do or abstain from doing any act; or

   (*e*) The offence is committed on board an aircraft which is operated by the Government of that State.

3. Upon ratifying, accepting, approving or acceding to this Convention, each State Party shall notify the Secretary-General of the United Nations of the jurisdiction it has established under its national law in accordance with paragraph 2 of the present article. Should any change take place, the State Party concerned shall immediately notify the Secretary-General.

4. Each State Party shall likewise take such measures as may be necessary to establish its jurisdiction over the offences set forth in article 2 in cases where the alleged offender is present in its territory and it does not extradite that person to any of the States Parties which have established their jurisdiction in accordance with paragraph 1 or 2 of the present article.

5. This Convention does not exclude the exercise of any criminal jurisdiction established by a State Party in accordance with its national law.

Article 10

1. Upon receiving information that an offence set forth in article 2 has been committed or is being committed in the territory of a State Party or that a person who has committed or who is alleged to have committed such an offence may be present in its territory, the State Party concerned shall take such measures as may be necessary under its national law to investigate the facts contained in the information.

2. Upon being satisfied that the circumstances so warrant, the State Party in whose territory the offender or alleged offender is present shall take the appropriate measures under its national law so as to ensure that person's presence for the purpose of prosecution or extradition.

3. Any person regarding whom the measures referred to in paragraph 2 of the present article are being taken shall be entitled:

   (*a*) To communicate without delay with the nearest appropriate representative of the State of which that person is a national or which is otherwise entitled to protect that person's rights or, if that person is a stateless person, the State in the territory of which that person habitually resides;

   (*b*) To be visited by a representative of that State;

   (*c*) To be informed of that person's rights under subparagraphs (*a*) and (*b*).

591

4. The rights referred to in paragraph 3 of the present article shall be exercised in conformity with the laws and regulations of the State in the territory of which the offender or alleged offender is present, subject to the provision that the said laws and regulations must enable full effect to be given to the purposes for which the rights accorded under paragraph 3 are intended.

5. The provisions of paragraphs 3 and 4 of the present article shall be without prejudice to the right of any State Party having a claim to jurisdiction in accordance with article 9, paragraph 1 (*c*) or 2 (*c*), to invite the International Committee of the Red Cross to communicate with and visit the alleged offender.

6. When a State Party, pursuant to the present article, has taken a person into custody, it shall immediately notify, directly or through the Secretary-General of the United Nations, the States Parties which have established jurisdiction in accordance with article 9, paragraphs 1 and 2, and, if it considers it advisable, any other interested States Parties, of the fact that that person is in custody and of the circumstances which warrant that person's detention. The State which makes the investigation contemplated in paragraph 1 of the present article shall promptly inform the said States Parties of its findings and shall indicate whether it intends to exercise jurisdiction.

Article 11

1. The State Party in the territory of which the alleged offender is present shall, in cases to which article 9 applies, if it does not extradite that person, be obliged, without exception whatsoever and whether or not the offence was committed in its territory, to submit the case without undue delay to its competent authorities for the purpose of prosecution, through proceedings in accordance with the laws of that State. Those authorities shall take their decision in the same manner as in the case of any other offence of a grave nature under the law of that State.

2. Whenever a State Party is permitted under its national law to extradite or otherwise surrender one of its nationals only upon the condition that the person will be returned to that State to serve the sentence imposed as a result of the trial or proceeding for which the extradition or surrender of the person was sought, and this State and the State seeking the extradition of the person agree with this option and other terms they may deem appropriate, such a conditional extradition or surrender shall be sufficient to discharge the obligation set forth in paragraph 1 of the present article.

Article 12

Any person who is taken into custody or regarding whom any other measures are taken or proceedings are carried out pursuant to this Convention shall be guaranteed fair treatment, including enjoyment of all rights and guarantees in conformity with the law of the State in the territory of which that person is present and applicable provisions of international law, including international law of human rights.

Article 13

1. The offences set forth in article 2 shall be deemed to be included as extraditable offences in any extradition treaty existing between any of the States Parties before the entry into force of this Convention. States Parties undertake to include such offences as extraditable offences in every extradition treaty to be subsequently concluded between them.

2. When a State Party which makes extradition conditional on the existence of a treaty receives a request for extradition from another State Party with which it has no extradition treaty, the requested State Party may, at its option, consider this Convention as a legal basis for extradition in respect of the offences set forth in article 2. Extradition shall be subject to the other conditions provided by the law of the requested State.

3. States Parties which do not make extradition conditional on the existence of a treaty shall recognize the offences set forth in article 2 as extraditable offences between themselves, subject to the conditions provided by the law of the requested State.

4. If necessary, the offences set forth in article 2 shall be treated, for the purposes of extradition between States Parties, as if they had been committed not only in the place in which they occurred but also in the territory of the States that have established jurisdiction in accordance with article 9, paragraphs 1 and 2.

5. The provisions of all extradition treaties and arrangements between States Parties with regard to offences set forth in article 2 shall be deemed to be modified as between States Parties to the extent that they are incompatible with this Convention.

Article 14

1. States Parties shall afford one another the greatest measure of assistance in connection with investigations or criminal or extradition proceedings brought in respect of the offences set forth in article 2, including assistance in obtaining evidence at their disposal necessary for the proceedings.

2. States Parties shall carry out their obligations under paragraph 1 of the present article in conformity with any treaties or other arrangements on mutual legal assistance that may exist between them. In the absence of such treaties or arrangements, States Parties shall afford one another assistance in accordance with their national law.

Article 15

None of the offences set forth in article 2 shall be regarded, for the purposes of extradition or mutual legal assistance, as a political offence or as an offence connected with a political offence or as an offence inspired by political motives. Accordingly, a request for extradition or for mutual legal assistance based on such an offence may not be refused on the sole ground that it concerns a political offence or an offence connected with a political offence or an offence inspired by political motives.

Article 16

Nothing in this Convention shall be interpreted as imposing an obligation to extradite or to afford mutual legal assistance if the requested State Party has substantial grounds for believing that the request for extradition for offences set forth in article 2 or for mutual legal assistance with respect to such offences has been made for the purpose of prosecuting or punishing a person on account of that person's race, religion, nationality, ethnic origin or political opinion or that compliance with the request would cause prejudice to that person's position for any of these reasons.

Article 17

1. A person who is being detained or is serving a sentence in the territory of one State Party whose presence in another State Party is requested for purposes of testimony, identification or otherwise providing assistance in obtaining evidence for the investigation or prosecution of offences under this Convention may be transferred if the following conditions are met:

    (*a*) The person freely gives his or her informed consent; and

    (*b*) The competent authorities of both States agree, subject to such conditions as those States may deem appropriate.

2. For the purposes of the present article:

    (*a*) The State to which the person is transferred shall have the authority and obligation to keep the person transferred in custody, unless otherwise requested or authorized by the State from which the person was transferred;

    (*b*) The State to which the person is transferred shall without delay implement its obligation to return the person to the custody of the State from which the person was transferred as agreed beforehand, or as otherwise agreed, by the competent authorities of both States;

(c) The State to which the person is transferred shall not require the State from which the person was transferred to initiate extradition proceedings for the return of the person;

(d) The person transferred shall receive credit for service of the sentence being served in the State from which he or she was transferred for time spent in the custody of the State to which he or she was transferred.

3. Unless the State Party from which a person is to be transferred in accordance with the present article so agrees, that person, whatever his or her nationality, shall not be prosecuted or detained or subjected to any other restriction of his or her personal liberty in the territory of the State to which that person is transferred in respect of acts or convictions anterior to his or her departure from the territory of the State from which such person was transferred.

Article 18

1. Upon seizing or otherwise taking control of radioactive material, devices or nuclear facilities, following the commission of an offence set forth in article 2, the State Party in possession of such items shall:

(a) Take steps to render harmless the radioactive material, device or nuclear facility;

(b) Ensure that any nuclear material is held in accordance with applicable International Atomic Energy Agency safeguards; and

(c) Have regard to physical protection recommendations and health and safety standards published by the International Atomic Energy Agency.

2. Upon the completion of any proceedings connected with an offence set forth in article 2, or sooner if required by international law, any radioactive material, device or nuclear facility shall be returned, after consultations (in particular, regarding modalities of return and storage) with the States Parties concerned to the State Party to which it belongs, to the State Party of which the natural or legal person owning such radioactive material, device or facility is a national or resident, or to the State Party from whose territory it was stolen or otherwise unlawfully obtained.

3. (a) Where a State Party is prohibited by national or international law from returning or accepting such radioactive material, device or nuclear facility or where the States Parties concerned so agree, subject to paragraph 3 (b) of the present article, the State Party in possession of the radioactive material, devices or nuclear facilities shall continue to take the steps described in paragraph 1 of the present article; such radioactive material, devices or nuclear facilities shall be used only for peaceful purposes;

(b) Where it is not lawful for the State Party in possession of the radioactive material, devices or nuclear facilities to possess them, that State shall ensure that they are placed as soon as possible in the possession of a State for which such possession is lawful and which, where appropriate, has provided assurances consistent with the requirements of paragraph 1 of the present article in consultation with that State, for the purpose of rendering it harmless; such radioactive material, devices or nuclear facilities shall be used only for peaceful purposes.

4. If the radioactive material, devices or nuclear facilities referred to in paragraphs 1 and 2 of the present article do not belong to any of the States Parties or to a national or resident of a State Party or was not stolen or otherwise unlawfully obtained from the territory of a State Party, or if no State is willing to receive such items pursuant to paragraph 3 of the present article, a separate decision concerning its disposition shall, subject to paragraph 3 (b) of the present article, be taken after consultations between the States concerned and any relevant international organizations.

5. For the purposes of paragraphs 1, 2, 3 and 4 of the present article, the State Party in possession of the radioactive material, device or nuclear facility may request the assistance and cooperation of other States Parties, in particular the States Parties concerned, and any relevant international organizations, in particular the International Atomic Energy Agency. States Parties and the relevant

international organizations are encouraged to provide assistance pursuant to this paragraph to the maximum extent possible.

6. The States Parties involved in the disposition or retention of the radioactive material, device or nuclear facility pursuant to the present article shall inform the Director General of the International Atomic Energy Agency of the manner in which such an item was disposed of or retained. The Director General of the International Atomic Energy Agency shall transmit the information to the other States Parties.

7. In the event of any dissemination in connection with an offence set forth in article 2, nothing in the present article shall affect in any way the rules of international law governing liability for nuclear damage, or other rules of international law.

Article 19

The State Party where the alleged offender is prosecuted shall, in accordance with its national law or applicable procedures, communicate the final outcome of the proceedings to the Secretary-General of the United Nations, who shall transmit the information to the other States Parties.

Article 20

States Parties shall conduct consultations with one another directly or through the Secretary-General of the United Nations, with the assistance of international organizations as necessary, to ensure effective implementation of this Convention.

Article 21

The States Parties shall carry out their obligations under this Convention in a manner consistent with the principles of sovereign equality and territorial integrity of States and that of non-intervention in the domestic affairs of other States.

Article 22

Nothing in this Convention entitles a State Party to undertake in the territory of another State Party the exercise of jurisdiction and performance of functions which are exclusively reserved for the authorities of that other State Party by its national law.

Article 23

1. Any dispute between two or more States Parties concerning the interpretation or application of this Convention which cannot be settled through negotiation within a reasonable time shall, at the request of one of them, be submitted to arbitration. If, within six months of the date of the request for arbitration, the parties are unable to agree on the organization of the arbitration, any one of those parties may refer the dispute to the International Court of Justice, by application, in conformity with the Statute of the Court.

2. Each State may, at the time of signature, ratification, acceptance or approval of this Convention or accession thereto, declare that it does not consider itself bound by paragraph 1 of the present article. The other States Parties shall not be bound by paragraph 1 with respect to any State Party which has made such a reservation.

3. Any State which has made a reservation in accordance with paragraph 2 of the present article may at any time withdraw that reservation by notification to the Secretary-General of the United Nations.

Article 24

1. This Convention shall be open for signature by all States from 14 September 2005 until 31 December 2006 at United Nations Headquarters in New York.

2. This Convention is subject to ratification, acceptance or approval. The instruments of ratification, acceptance or approval shall be deposited with the Secretary-General of the United Nations.

3. This Convention shall be open to accession by any State. The instruments of accession shall be deposited with the Secretary-General of the United Nations.

Article 25

1. This Convention shall enter into force on the thirtieth day following the date of the deposit of the twenty-second instrument of ratification, acceptance, approval or accession with the Secretary-General of the United Nations.

2. For each State ratifying, accepting, approving or acceding to the Convention after the deposit of the twenty-second instrument of ratification, acceptance, approval or accession, the Convention shall enter into force on the thirtieth day after deposit by such State of its instrument of ratification, acceptance, approval or accession.

Article 26

1. A State Party may propose an amendment to this Convention. The proposed amendment shall be submitted to the depositary, who circulates it immediately to all States Parties.

2. If the majority of the States Parties request the depositary to convene a conference to consider the proposed amendments, the depositary shall invite all States Parties to attend such a conference to begin no sooner than three months after the invitations are issued.

3. The conference shall make every effort to ensure amendments are adopted by consensus. Should this not be possible, amendments shall be adopted by a two-thirds majority of all States Parties. Any amendment adopted at the conference shall be promptly circulated by the depositary to all States Parties.

4. The amendment adopted pursuant to paragraph 3 of the present article shall enter into force for each State Party that deposits its instrument of ratification, acceptance, accession or approval of the amendment on the thirtieth day after the date on which two thirds of the States Parties have deposited their relevant instrument. Thereafter, the amendment shall enter into force for any State Party on the thirtieth day after the date on which that State deposits its relevant instrument.

Article 27

1. Any State Party may denounce this Convention by written notification to the Secretary-General of the United Nations.

2. Denunciation shall take effect one year following the date on which notification is received by the Secretary-General of the United Nations .

Article 28

The original of this Convention, of which the Arabic, Chinese, English, French, Russian and Spanish texts are equally authentic, shall be deposited with the Secretary-General of the United Nations, who shall send certified copies thereof to all States.

IN WITNESS WHEREOF, the undersigned, being duly authorized thereto by their respective Governments, have signed this Convention, opened for signature at United Nations Headquarters in New York on 14 September 2005.

APPENDIX 14

The United Nations Global Counter-Terrorism Strategy
United Nations General Assembly

DISTR: GENERAL
20 SEPTEMBER 2006

SIXTIETH SESSION
AGENDA ITEMS 46 AND 120

Resolution adopted by

the General Assembly

[*without reference to a Main Committee (A/60/L.62)*]

60/288. THE UNITED NATIONS GLOBAL COUNTER-TERRORISM STRATEGY

The General Assembly,

Guided by the purposes and principles of the Charter of the United Nations, and reaffirming its role under the Charter, including on questions related to international peace and security,

Reiterating its strong condemnation of terrorism in all its forms and manifestations, committed by whomever, wherever and for whatever purposes, as it constitutes one of the most serious threats to international peace and security,

Reaffirming the Declaration on Measures to Eliminate International Terrorism, contained in the annex to General Assembly resolution 49/60 of 9 December 1994, the Declaration to Supplement the 1994 Declaration on Measures to Eliminate International Terrorism, contained in the annex to General Assembly resolution 51/210 of 17 December 1996, and the 2005 World Summit Outcome,[1] in particular its section on terrorism,

Recalling all General Assembly resolutions on measures to eliminate international terrorism, including resolution 46/51 of 9 December 1991, and Security Council resolutions on threats to international peace and security caused by terrorist acts, as well as relevant resolutions of the General Assembly on the protection of human rights and fundamental freedoms while countering terrorism,

Recalling also that, in the 2005 World Summit Outcome, world leaders rededicated themselves to support all efforts to uphold the sovereign equality of all States, respect their territorial integrity and political independence, to refrain in their international relations from the threat or use of force in any manner inconsistent with the purposes and principles of the United Nations, to uphold the resolution of disputes by peaceful means and in conformity with the principles of justice

---

[1] See resolution 60/1.

and international law, the right to self-determination of peoples which remain under colonial domination or foreign occupation, non-interference in the internal affairs of States, respect for human rights and fundamental freedoms, respect for the equal rights of all without distinction as to race, sex, language or religion, international cooperation in solving international problems of an economic, social, cultural or humanitarian character, and the fulfilment in good faith of the obligations assumed in accordance with the Charter,

Recalling further the mandate contained in the 2005 World Summit Outcome that the General Assembly should develop without delay the elements identified by the Secretary-General for a counter-terrorism strategy, with a view to adopting and implementing a strategy to promote comprehensive, coordinated and consistent responses, at the national, regional and international levels, to counter terrorism, which also takes into account the conditions conducive to the spread of terrorism,

Reaffirming that acts, methods and practices of terrorism in all its forms and manifestations are activities aimed at the destruction of human rights, fundamental freedoms and democracy, threatening territorial integrity, security of States and destabilizing legitimately constituted Governments, and that the international community should take the necessary steps to enhance cooperation to prevent and combat terrorism,

Reaffirming also that terrorism cannot and should not be associated with any religion, nationality, civilization or ethnic group,

Reaffirming further Member States' determination to make every effort to reach an agreement on and conclude a comprehensive convention on international terrorism, including by resolving the outstanding issues related to the legal definition and scope of the acts covered by the convention, so that it can serve as an effective instrument to counter terrorism,

Continuing to acknowledge that the question of convening a high-level conference under the auspices of the United Nations to formulate an international response to terrorism in all its forms and manifestations could be considered,

Recognizing that development, peace and security, and human rights are interlinked and mutually reinforcing,

Bearing in mind the need to address the conditions conducive to the spread of terrorism,

Affirming Member States' determination to continue to do all they can to resolve conflict, end foreign occupation, confront oppression, eradicate poverty, promote sustained economic growth, sustainable development, global prosperity, good governance, human rights for all and rule of law, improve intercultural understanding and ensure respect for all religions, religious values, beliefs or cultures,

1. *Expresses its appreciation* for the report entitled 'Uniting against terrorism: recommendations for a global counter-terrorism strategy' submitted by the Secretary-General to the General Assembly;[2]

2. *Adopts* the present resolution and its annex as the United Nations Global Counter-Terrorism Strategy ('the Strategy');

3. *Decides*, without prejudice to the continuation of the discussion in its relevant committees of all their agenda items related to terrorism and counterterrorism, to undertake the following steps for the effective follow-up of the Strategy:

   (*a*) To launch the Strategy at a high-level segment of its sixty-first session;
   (*b*) To examine in two years progress made in the implementation of the Strategy, and to con-
         sider updating it to respond to changes, recognizing that many of the measures contained
         in the Strategy can be achieved immediately, some will require sustained work through the
         coming few years and some should be treated as long-term objectives;

---

[2] A/60/825.

(*c*) To invite the Secretary-General to contribute to the future deliberations of the General Assembly on the review of the implementation and updating of the Strategy;

(*d*) To encourage Member States, the United Nations and other appropriate international, regional and subregional organizations to support the implementation of the Strategy, including through mobilizing resources and expertise;

(*e*) To further encourage non-governmental organizations and civil society to engage, as appropriate, on how to enhance efforts to implement the Strategy;

4. *Decides* to include in the provisional agenda of its sixty-second session an item entitled 'The United Nations Global Counter-Terrorism Strategy'.

99th plenary meeting
8 September 2006

Annex

Plan of Action

We, the States Members of the United Nations, resolve:

1. To consistently, unequivocally and strongly condemn terrorism in all its forms and manifestations, committed by whomever, wherever and for whatever purposes, as it constitutes one of the most serious threats to international peace and security;

2. To take urgent action to prevent and combat terrorism in all its forms and manifestations and, in particular:

(*a*) To consider becoming parties without delay to the existing international conventions and protocols against terrorism, and implementing them, and to make every effort to reach an agreement on and conclude a comprehensive convention on international terrorism;

(*b*) To implement all General Assembly resolutions on measures to eliminate international terrorism and relevant General Assembly resolutions on the protection of human rights and fundamental freedoms while countering terrorism;

(*c*) To implement all Security Council resolutions related to international terrorism and to cooperate fully with the counter-terrorism subsidiary bodies of the Security Council in the fulfilment of their tasks, recognizing that many States continue to require assistance in implementing these resolutions;

3. To recognize that international cooperation and any measures that we undertake to prevent and combat terrorism must comply with our obligations under international law, including the Charter of the United Nations and relevant international conventions and protocols, in particular human rights law, refugee law and international humanitarian law.

I. Measures to Address the Conditions Conducive to the Spread of Terrorism

We resolve to undertake the following measures aimed at addressing the conditions conducive to the spread of terrorism, including but not limited to prolonged unresolved conflicts, dehumanization of victims of terrorism in all its forms and manifestations, lack of the rule of law and violations of human rights, ethnic, national and religious discrimination, political exclusion, socio-economic marginalization and lack of good governance, while recognizing that none of these conditions can excuse or justify acts of terrorism:

1. To continue to strengthen and make best possible use of the capacities of the United Nations in areas such as conflict prevention, negotiation, mediation, conciliation, judicial settlement, rule of law, peacekeeping and peacebuilding, in order to contribute to the successful prevention and

peaceful resolution of prolonged unresolved conflicts. We recognize that the peaceful resolution of such conflicts would contribute to strengthening the global fight against terrorism;

2. To continue to arrange under the auspices of the United Nations initiatives and programmes to promote dialogue, tolerance and understanding among civilizations, cultures, peoples and religions, and to promote mutual respect for and prevent the defamation of religions, religious values, beliefs and cultures. In this regard, we welcome the launching by the Secretary-General of the initiative on the Alliance of Civilizations. We also welcome similar initiatives that have been taken in other parts of the world;

3. To promote a culture of peace, justice and human development, ethnic, national and religious tolerance and respect for all religions, religious values, beliefs or cultures by establishing and encouraging, as appropriate, education and public awareness programmes involving all sectors of society. In this regard, we encourage the United Nations Educational, Scientific and Cultural Organization to play a key role, including through inter-faith and intra-faith dialogue and dialogue among civilizations;

4. To continue to work to adopt such measures as may be necessary and appropriate and in accordance with our respective obligations under international law to prohibit by law incitement to commit a terrorist act or acts and prevent such conduct;

5. To reiterate our determination to ensure the timely and full realization of the development goals and objectives agreed at the major United Nations conferences and summits, including the Millennium Development Goals. We reaffirm our commitment to eradicate poverty and promote sustained economic growth, sustainable development and global prosperity for all;

6. To pursue and reinforce development and social inclusion agendas at every level as goals in themselves, recognizing that success in this area, especially on youth unemployment, could reduce marginalization and the subsequent sense of victimization that propels extremism and the recruitment of terrorists;

7. To encourage the United Nations system as a whole to scale up the cooperation and assistance it is already conducting in the fields of rule of law, human rights and good governance to support sustained economic and social development;

8. To consider putting in place, on a voluntary basis, national systems of assistance that would promote the needs of victims of terrorism and their families and facilitate the normalization of their lives. In this regard, we encourage States to request the relevant United Nations entities to help them to develop such national systems. We will also strive to promote international solidarity in support of victims and foster the involvement of civil society in a global campaign against terrorism and for its condemnation. This could include exploring at the General Assembly the possibility of developing practical mechanisms to provide assistance to victims.

II. Measures to Prevent and Combat Terrorism

We resolve to undertake the following measures to prevent and combat terrorism, in particular by denying terrorists access to the means to carry out their attacks, to their targets and to the desired impact of their attacks:

1. To refrain from organizing, instigating, facilitating, participating in, financing, encouraging or tolerating terrorist activities and to take appropriate practical measures to ensure that our respective territories are not used for terrorist installations or training camps, or for the preparation ororganization of terrorist acts intended to be committed against other States or their citizens;

2. To cooperate fully in the fight against terrorism, in accordance with our obligations under international law, in order to find, deny safe haven and bring to justice, on the basis of the principle of extradite or prosecute, any person who supports, facilitates, participates or attempts to participate in the financing, planning, preparation or perpetration of terrorist acts or provides safe havens;

3. To ensure the apprehension and prosecution or extradition of perpetrators of terrorist acts, in accordance with the relevant provisions of national and international law, in particular human rights law, refugee law and international humanitarian law. We will endeavour to conclude and implement to that effect mutual judicial assistance and extradition agreements and to strengthen cooperation between law enforcement agencies;

4. To intensify cooperation, as appropriate, in exchanging timely and accurate information concerning the prevention and combating of terrorism;

5. To strengthen coordination and cooperation among States in combating crimes that might be connected with terrorism, including drug trafficking in all its aspects, illicit arms trade, in particular of small arms and light weapons, including man-portable air defence systems, money-laundering and smuggling of nuclear, chemical, biological, radiological and other potentially deadly materials;

6. To consider becoming parties without delay to the United Nations Convention against Transnational Organized Crime[3] and to the three protocols supplementing it,[4] and implementing them;

7. To take appropriate measures, before granting asylum, for the purpose of ensuring that the asylum-seeker has not engaged in terrorist activities and, after granting asylum, for the purpose of ensuring that the refugee status is not used in a manner contrary to the provisions set out in section II, paragraph 1, above;

8. To encourage relevant regional and subregional organizations to create or strengthen counter-terrorism mechanisms or centres. Should they require cooperation and assistance to this end, we encourage the Counter-Terrorism Committee and its Executive Directorate and, where consistent with their existing mandates, the United Nations Office on Drugs and Crime and the International Criminal Police Organization, to facilitate its provision;

9. To acknowledge that the question of creating an international centre to fight terrorism could be considered, as part of international efforts to enhance the fight against terrorism;

10. To encourage States to implement the comprehensive international standards embodied in the Forty Recommendations on Money-Laundering and Nine Special Recommendations on Terrorist Financing of the Financial Action Task Force, recognizing that States may require assistance in implementing them;

11. To invite the United Nations system to develop, together with Member States, a single comprehensive database on biological incidents, ensuring that it is complementary to the biocrimes database contemplated by the International Criminal Police Organization. We also encourage the Secretary-General to update the roster of experts and laboratories, as well as the technical guidelines and procedures, available to him for the timely and efficient investigation of alleged use. In addition, we note the importance of the proposal of the Secretary-General to bring together, within the framework of the United Nations, the major biotechnology stakeholders, including industry, the scientific community, civil society and Governments, into a common programme aimed at ensuring that biotechnology advances are not used for terrorist or other criminal purposes but for the public good, with due respect for the basic international norms on intellectual property rights;

12. To work with the United Nations with due regard to confidentiality, respecting human rights and in compliance with other obligations under international law, to explore ways and means to:

    (*a*) Coordinate efforts at the international and regional levels to counter terrorism in all its forms and manifestations on the Internet;

    (*b*) Use the Internet as a tool for countering the spread of terrorism, while recognizing that States may require assistance in this regard;

---

[3] Resolution 55/25, annex I.
[4] Resolution 55/25, annexes II and III; and resolution 55/255, annex.

13. To step up national efforts and bilateral, subregional, regional and international cooperation, as appropriate, to improve border and customs controls in order to prevent and detect the movement of terrorists and prevent and detect the illicit traffic in, inter alia, small arms and light weapons, conventional ammunition and explosives, and nuclear, chemical, biological or radiological weapons and materials, while recognizing that States may require assistance to that effect;

14. To encourage the Counter-Terrorism Committee and its Executive Directorate to continue to work with States, at their request, to facilitate the adoption of legislation and administrative measures to implement the terrorist travel-related obligations and to identify best practices in this area, drawing whenever possible on those developed by technical international organizations, such as the International Civil Aviation Organization, the World Customs Organization and the International Criminal Police Organization;

15. To encourage the Committee established pursuant to Security Council resolution 1267 (1999) to continue to work to strengthen the effectiveness of the travel ban under the United Nations sanctions regime against Al-Qaida and the Taliban and associated individuals and entities, as well as to ensure, as a matter of priority, that fair and transparent procedures exist for placing individuals and entities on its lists, for removing them and for granting humanitarian exceptions. In this regard, we encourage States to share information, including by widely distributing the International Criminal Police Organization/United Nations special notices concerning people subject to this sanctions regime;

16. To step up efforts and cooperation at every level, as appropriate, to improve the security of manufacturing and issuing identity and travel documents and to prevent and detect their alteration or fraudulent use, while recognizing that States may require assistance in doing so. In this regard, we invite the International Criminal Police Organization to enhance its database on stolen and lost travel documents, and we will endeavour to make full use of this tool, as appropriate, in particular by sharing relevant information;

17. To invite the United Nations to improve coordination in planning a response to a terrorist attack using nuclear, chemical, biological or radiological weapons or materials, in particular by reviewing and improving the effectiveness of the existing inter-agency coordination mechanisms for assistance delivery, relief operations and victim support, so that all States can receive adequate assistance. In this regard, we invite the General Assembly and the Security Council to develop guidelines for the necessary cooperation and assistance in the event of a terrorist attack using weapons of mass destruction;

18. To step up all efforts to improve the security and protection of particularly vulnerable targets, such as infrastructure and public places, as well as the response to terrorist attacks and other disasters, in particular in the area of civil protection, while recognizing that States may require assistance to this effect.

III. Measures to Build States' Capacity to Prevent and Combat Terrorism and to Strengthen the Role of the United Nations System in This Regard

We recognize that capacity-building in all States is a core element of the global counter-terrorism effort, and resolve to undertake the following measures to develop State capacity to prevent and combat terrorism and enhance coordination and coherence within the United Nations system in promoting international cooperation in countering terrorism:

1. To encourage Member States to consider making voluntary contributions to United Nations counter-terrorism cooperation and technical assistance projects, and to explore additional sources of funding in this regard. We also encourage the United Nations to consider reaching out to the private sector for contributions to capacity-building programmes, in particular in the areas of port, maritime and civil aviation security;

2. To take advantage of the framework provided by relevant international, regional and subregional organizations to share best practices in counter-terrorism capacity-building, and to facilitate their contributions to the international community's efforts in this area;

3. To consider establishing appropriate mechanisms to rationalize States' reporting requirements in the field of counter-terrorism and eliminate duplication of reporting requests, taking into account and respecting the different mandates of the General Assembly, the Security Council and its subsidiary bodies that deal with counter-terrorism;

4. To encourage measures, including regular informal meetings, to enhance, as appropriate, more frequent exchanges of information on cooperation and technical assistance among Member States, United Nations bodies dealing with counter-terrorism, relevant specialized agencies, relevant international, regional and subregional organizations and the donor community, to develop States' capacities to implement relevant United Nations resolutions;

5. To welcome the intention of the Secretary-General to institutionalize, within existing resources, the Counter-Terrorism Implementation Task Force within the Secretariat in order to ensure overall coordination and coherence in the counterterrorism efforts of the United Nations system;

6. To encourage the Counter-Terrorism Committee and its Executive Directorate to continue to improve the coherence and efficiency of technical assistance delivery in the field of counter-terrorism, in particular by strengthening its dialogue with States and relevant international, regional and subregional organizations and working closely, including by sharing information, with all bilateral and multilateral technical assistance providers;

7. To encourage the United Nations Office on Drugs and Crime, including its Terrorism Prevention Branch, to enhance, in close consultation with the Counter-Terrorism Committee and its Executive Directorate, its provision of technical assistance to States, upon request, to facilitate the implementation of the international conventions and protocols related to the prevention and suppression of terrorism and relevant United Nations resolutions;

8. To encourage the International Monetary Fund, the World Bank, the United Nations Office on Drugs and Crime and the International Criminal Police Organization to enhance cooperation with States to help them to comply fully with international norms and obligations to combat money-laundering and the financing of terrorism;

9. To encourage the International Atomic Energy Agency and the Organization for the Prohibition of Chemical Weapons to continue their efforts, within their respective mandates, in helping States to build capacity to prevent terrorists from accessing nuclear, chemical or radiological materials, to ensure security at related facilities and to respond effectively in the event of an attack using such materials;

10. To encourage the World Health Organization to step up its technical assistance to help States to improve their public health systems to prevent and prepare for biological attacks by terrorists;

11. To continue to work within the United Nations system to support the reform and modernization of border management systems, facilities and institutions at the national, regional and international levels;

12. To encourage the International Maritime Organization, the World Customs Organization and the International Civil Aviation Organization to strengthen their cooperation, work with States to identify any national shortfalls in areas of transport security and provide assistance, upon request, to address them;

13. To encourage the United Nations to work with Member States and relevant international, regional and subregional organizations to identify and share best practices to prevent terrorist attacks on particularly vulnerable targets. We invite the International Criminal Police Organization to work with the Secretary-General so that he can submit proposals to this effect. We also recognize the importance of developing public-private partnerships in this area.

IV. Measures to Ensure Respect for Human Rights for All and the Rule of Law as the Fundamental Basis of the Fight against Terrorism

We resolve to undertake the following measures, reaffirming that the promotion and protection of human rights for all and the rule of law is essential to all components of the Strategy, recognizing that effective counter-terrorism measures and the protection of human rights are not conflicting goals, but complementary and mutually reinforcing, and stressing the need to promote and protect the rights of victims of terrorism:

1. To reaffirm that General Assembly resolution 60/158 of 16 December 2005 provides the fundamental framework for the 'Protection of human rights and fundamental freedoms while countering terrorism';

2. To reaffirm that States must ensure that any measures taken to combat terrorism comply with their obligations under international law, in particular human rights law, refugee law and international humanitarian law;

3. To consider becoming parties without delay to the core international instruments on human rights law, refugee law and international humanitarian law, and implementing them, as well as to consider accepting the competence of international and relevant regional human rights monitoring bodies;

4. To make every effort to develop and maintain an effective and rule of law-based national criminal justice system that can ensure, in accordance with our obligations under international law, that any person who participates in the financing, planning, preparation or perpetration of terrorist acts or in support of terrorist acts is brought to justice, on the basis of the principle to extradite or prosecute, with due respect for human rights and fundamental freedoms, and that such terrorist acts are established as serious criminal offences in domestic laws and regulations. We recognize that States may require assistance in developing and maintaining such effective and rule of law-based criminal justice systems, and we encourage them to resort to the technical assistance delivered, inter alia, by the United Nations Office on Drugs and Crime;

5. To reaffirm the important role of the United Nations system in strengthening the international legal architecture by promoting the rule of law, respect for human rights and effective criminal justice systems, which constitute the fundamental basis of our common fight against terrorism;

6. To support the Human Rights Council and to contribute, as it takes shape, to its work on the question of the promotion and protection of human rights for all in the fight against terrorism;

7. To support the strengthening of the operational capacity of the Office of the United Nations High Commissioner for Human Rights, with a particular emphasis on increasing field operations and presences. The Office should continue to play a lead role in examining the question of protecting human rights while countering terrorism, by making general recommendations on the human rights obligations of States and providing them with assistance and advice, in particular in the area of raising awareness of international human rights law among national law enforcement agencies, at the request of States;

8. To support the role of the Special Rapporteur on the promotion and protection of human rights and fundamental freedoms while countering terrorism. The Special Rapporteur should continue to support the efforts of States and offer concrete advice by corresponding with Governments, making country visits, liaising with the United Nations and regional organizations and reporting on these issues.

APPENDIX 15

European Convention on the Suppression of Terrorism
No 17828

MULTILATERAL

European Convention on the suppression of terrorism.
Concluded at Strasbourg on 27 January 1977

Authentic texts: English and French.

Registered by the Secretary-General of the Council of Europe, acting on behalf of the Parties, on 30 May 1979.

MULTILATÉRAL

Convention européenne pour la répression du terrorisme.
Conclue à Strasbourg le 27 janvier 1977

Textes authentiques: anglais et français.

Enregistrée par le Secrétaire général du Conseil de l'Europe, agissant au nom

des Parties, le 30 mai 1979.

EUROPEAN CONVENTION[1] ON THE SUPPRESSION OF TERRORISM

The member States of the Council of Europe, signatory hereto,

---

[1] Came into force on 4 August 1978, ie, three months after the date of deposit with the Secretary-General of the Council of Europe of the third instrument of ratification, acceptance or approval, in accordance with article 11 (1) and (2). Instruments of ratification, acceptance or approval were deposited as follows:

State	Date of deposit of the instrument of ratification
Austria	11 August 1977
Sweden	15 September 1977
Germany, Federal Republic of	3 May 1978

(With a declaration of application to *Land Berlin*.)

Subsequently, the Convention came into force for the following States three months after the date of deposit of their instruments of ratification, acceptance or approval with the Secretary-General of the Council of Europe, in accordance with article 11 (1) and (3):

State	Date of deposit of the instrument of ratification
Denmark	27 June 1978

(With effect from 28 September 1978. With a declaration of non-application to the Faroe Islands and Greenland.)

United Kingdom of Great Britain and Northern Ireland	24 July 1978

(With effect from 25 October 1978. With a declaration of application to the bailiwick of Jersey, the bailiwick of Guernsey and the Isle of Man.)

Cyprus	26 February 1979

(With effect from 27 May 1979.)

Considering that the aim of the Council of Europe is to achieve a greater unity between its members,

Aware of the growing concern caused by the increase in acts of terrorism,

Wishing to take effective measures to ensure that the perpetrators of such acts do not escape prosecution and punishment,

Convinced that extradition is a particularly effective measure for achieving this result,

Have agreed as follows:

Article 1

For the purposes of extradition between Contracting States, none of the following offences shall be regarded as a political offence or as an offence connected with a political offence or as an offence inspired by political motives:

    (a) An offence within the scope of the Convention for the Suppression of Unlawful Seizure of Aircraft, signed at The Hague on 16 December 1970;[2]

    (b) An offence within the scope of the Convention for the Suppression of Unlawful Acts against the Safety of Civil Aviation, signed at Montreal on 23 September 1971;[3]

    (c) A serious offence involving an attack against the life, physical integrity or liberty of internationally protected persons, including diplomatic agents;

    (d) An offence involving kidnapping, the taking of a hostage or serious unlawful detention;

    (e) An offence involving the use of a bomb, grenade, rocket, automatic firearm or letter or parcel bomb if this use endangers persons;

    (f) An attempt to commit any of the foregoing offences or participation as an accomplice of a person who commits or attempts to commit such an offence.

Article 2

1. For the purposes of extradition between Contracting States, a Contracting State may decide not to regard as a political offence or as an offence connected with a political offence or as an offence inspired by political motives a serious offence involving an act of violence, other than one covered by article 1, against the life, physical integrity or liberty of a person.

2. The same shall apply to a serious offence involving an act against property, other than one covered by article 1, if the act created a collective danger for persons.

3. The same shall apply to an attempt to commit any of the foregoing offences or participation as an accomplice of a person who commits or attempts to commit such an offence.

Article 3

The provisions of all extradition treaties and arrangements applicable between Contracting States, including the European Convention on Extradition,[4] are modified as between Contracting States to the extent that they are incompatible with this Convention.

Article 4

For the purposes of this Convention and to the extent that any offence mentioned in article 1 or 2 is not listed as an extraditable offence in any extradition convention or treaty existing between Contracting States, it shall be deemed to be included as such therein.

---

[2] United Nations, *Treaty Series*, vol 860, p 105.

[3] *Ibid,* vol 974, p 177.

[4] United Nations, *Treaty Series*, vol 359, p 273; see also 'Additional Protocol to the European Convention on extradition, signed at Strasbourg on 15 October 1975', *Ibid,* vol 1161, No A-5146.

Article 5

Nothing in this Convention shall be interpreted as imposing an obligation to extradite if the requested State has substantial grounds for believing that the request for extradition for an offence mentioned in article 1 or 2 has been made for the purpose of prosecuting or punishing a person on account of his race, religion, nationality or political opinion, or that that person's position may be prejudiced for any of these reasons.

Article 6

1. Each Contracting State shall take such measures as may be necessary to establish its jurisdiction over an offence mentioned in article 1 in the case where the suspected offender is present in its territory and it does not extradite him after receiving a request for extradition from a Contracting State whose jurisdiction is based on a rule of jurisdiction existing equally in the law of the requested State.

2. This Convention does not exclude any criminal jurisdiction exercised in accordance with national law.

Article 7

A Contracting State in whose territory a person suspected to have committed an offence mentioned in article 1 is found and which has received a request for extradition under the conditions mentioned in article 6, paragraph 1, shall, if it does not extradite that person, submit the case, without exception whatsoever and without undue delay, to its competent authorities for the purpose of prosecution. Those authorities shall take their decision in the same manner as in the case of any offence of a serious nature under the law of that State.

Article 8

1. Contracting States shall afford one another the widest measure of mutual assistance in criminal matters in connection with proceedings brought in respect of the offences mentioned in article 1 or 2. The law of the requested State concerning mutual assistance in criminal matters shall apply in all cases. Nevertheless this assistance may not be refused on the sole ground that it concerns a political offence or an offence connected with a political offence or an offence inspired by political motives.

2. Nothing in this Convention shall be interpreted as imposing an obligation to afford mutual assistance if the requested State has substantial grounds for believing that the request for mutual assistance in respect of an offence mentioned in article 1 or 2 has been made for the purpose of prosecuting or punishing a person on account of his race, religion, nationality or political opinion or that that person's position may be prejudiced for any of these reasons.

3. The provisions of all treaties and arrangements concerning mutual assistance in criminal matters applicable between Contracting States, including the European Convention on Mutual Assistance in Criminal Matters, are modified as between Contracting States to the extent that they are incompatible with this Convention.

Article 9

1. The European Committee on Crime Problems of the Council of Europe shall be kept informed regarding the application of this Convention.

2. It shall do whatever is needful to facilitate a friendly settlement of any difficulty which may arise out of its execution.

Article 10

1. Any dispute between Contracting States concerning the interpretation or application of this Convention, which has not been settled in the framework of article 9, paragraph 2, shall, at the request of any Party to the dispute, be referred to arbitration. Each Party shall nominate an arbitrator and the two arbitrators shall nominate a referee. If any Party has not nominated its arbitrator within

the three months following the request for arbitration, he shall be nominated at the request of the other Party by the President of the European Court of Human Rights. If the latter should be a national of one of the Parties to the dispute, this duty shall be carried out by the Vice-President of the Court or, if the Vice-President is a national of one of the Parties to the dispute, by the most senior judge of the Court not being a national of one of the Parties to the dispute. The same procedure shall be observed if the arbitrators cannot agree on the choice of referee.

2. The arbitration tribunal shall lay down its own procedure. Its decisions shall be taken by majority vote. Its award shall be final.

Article 11

1. This Convention shall be open to signature by the member States of the Council of Europe. It shall be subject to ratification, acceptance or approval. Instruments of ratification, acceptance or approval shall be deposited with the Secretary General of the Council of Europe.

2. The Convention shall enter into force three months after the date of the deposit of the third instrument of ratification, acceptance or approval.

3. In respect of a signatory State ratifying, accepting or approving subsequently, the Convention shall come into force three months after the date of the deposit of its instrument of ratification, acceptance or approval.

Article 12

1. Any State may, at the time of signature or when depositing its instrument of ratification, acceptance or approval, specify the territory or territories to which this Convention shall apply.

2. Any State may, when depositing its instrument of ratification, acceptance or approval or at any later date, by declaration addressed to the Secretary General of the Council of Europe, extend this Convention to any other territory or territories specified in the declaration and for whose international relations it is responsible or on whose behalf it is authorized to give undertakings.

3. Any declaration made in pursuance of the preceding paragraph may, in respect of any territory mentioned in such declaration, be withdrawn by means of a notification addressed to the Secretary General of the Council of Europe. Such withdrawal shall take effect immediately or at such later date as may be specified in the notification.

Article 13

1. Any State may, at the time of signature or when depositing its instrument of ratification, acceptance or approval, declare that it reserves the right to refuse extradition in respect of any offence mentioned in article 1 which it considers to be a political offence, an offence connected with a political offence or an offence inspired by political motives, provided that it undertakes to take into due consideration, when evaluating the character of the offence, any particularly serious aspects of the offence, including:

    (a) That it created a collective danger to the life, physical integrity or liberty of persons; or
    (b) That it affected persons foreign to the motives behind it; or
    (c) That cruel or vicious means have been used in the commission of the offence.

2. Any State may wholly or partly withdraw a reservation it has made in accordance with the foregoing paragraph by means of a declaration addressed to the Secretary General of the Council of Europe which shall become effective as from the date of its receipt.

3. A State which has made a reservation in accordance with paragraph 1 of this article may not claim the application of article 1 by any other State; it may, however, if its reservation is partial or conditional, claim the application of that article in so far as it has itself accepted it.

Article 14

Any Contracting State may denounce this Convention by means of a written notification addressed to the Secretary General of the Council of Europe. Any such denunciation shall take effect immediately or at such later date as may be specified in the notification.

Article 15

This Convention ceases to have effect in respect of any Contracting State which withdraws from or ceases to be a Member of the Council of Europe.

Article 16

The Secretary General of the Council of Europe shall notify the member States of the Council of:

- *(a)* Any signature;
- *(b)* Any deposit of an instrument of ratification, acceptance or approval;
- *(c)* Any date of entry into force of this Convention in accordance with article 11 thereof;
- *(d)* Any declaration or notification received in pursuance of the provisions of article 12;
- *(e)* Any reservation made in pursuance of the provisions of article 13, paragraph 1;
- *(f)* The withdrawal of any reservation effected in pursuance of the provisions of article 13, paragraph 2;
- *(g)* Any notification received in pursuance of article 14 and the date on which denunciation takes effect;
- *(h)* Any cessation of the effects of the Convention pursuant to article 15.

IN WITNESS WHEREOF, the undersigned, being duly authorized thereto, have signed this Convention.

DONE at Strasbourg, this 27th day of January 1977, in English and in French, both texts being equally authoritative, in a single copy which shall remain deposited in the archives of the Council of Europe. The Secretary General of the Council of Europe shall transmit certified copies to each of the signatory States.

EN FOI DE QUOI, les soussignés, dûment autorisés à cet effet, ont signé la présente Convention.

FAIT à Strasbourg, le 27 janvier 1977, en français et en anglais, les deux textes faisant également foi, en un seul exemplaire qui sera déposé dans les archives du Conseil de l'Europe. Le Secrétaire général du Conseil de l'Europe en communiquera copie certifiée conforme à chacun des Etats signataires.

For the Government of the Republic of Austria:

Pour le Gouvernement de la République d'Autriche:

WILLIBALD PAHR

For the Government of the Kingdom of Belgium:

Pour le Gouvernement du Royaume de Belgique:

RENAAT VAN ELSLANDE

For the Government of the Republic of Cyprus:

Pour le Gouvernement de la République de Chypre:

IOANNIS CHRISTOPHIDES

For the Government of the Kingdom of Denmark:

Pour le Gouvernement du Royaume de Danemark:

K B ANDERSEN

For the Government of the French Republic:	Pour le Gouvernement de la République française:

P C TAITTINGER

For the Government of the Federal Republic of Germany:	Pour le Gouvernement de la République fédérale d'Allemagne:

HANS-DIETRICH GENSCHER

For the Government of the Hellenic Republic:	Pour le Gouvernement de la République hellénique:

DIMITRI S BITSIOS

For the Government of the Icelandic Republic:	Pour le Gouvernement de la République islandaise:

EINAR AGUSTSSON

For the Government of Ireland:	Pour le Gouvernement d'Irlande:
For the Government of the Italian Republic:	Pour le Gouvernement de la République italienne:

GHERARDO CORNAGGIA MEDICI CASTIGLIONI

For the Government of the Principality of Liechtenstein:	Pour le Gouvernement de la Principauté de Liechtenstein:

Strasbourg, le 22 janvier 1979

NIKOLAUS VON LIECHTENSTEIN

For the Government of the Grand Duchy of Luxembourg:	Pour le Gouvernement du Grand-Duché de Luxembourg:

GASTON THORN

For the Government of Malta:	Pour le Gouvernement de Malte:
For the Government of the Kingdom of the Netherlands:	Pour le Gouvernement du Royaume des Pays-Bas:

MAX VAN DER STOEL

For the Government of the Kingdom of Norway:	Pour le Gouvernement du Royaume de Norvège:

KNUT FRYDENLUND

For the Government of the Portuguese Republic:	Pour le Gouvernement de la République portugaise:

JOSÉ MEDEIROS FERREIRA

For the Government of the Kingdom
of Spain:

Pour le Gouvernement du Royaume de
l'Espagne:

Strasbourg, le 27 avril 1978

MARCELINO OREJA AGUIRRE

For the Government of the Kingdom of
Sweden:

Pour le Gouvernement du Royaume de Suède:

KARIN SÖDER

For the Government of the Swiss
Confederation:

Pour le Gouvernement de la Confédération
suisse:

PIERRE GRABER

For the Government of the Turkish
Republic:

Pour le Gouvernement de la République
turque:

I S ÇAGLAYANGIL

For the Government of the United Kingdom
of Great Britain and Northern Ireland:

Pour le Gouvernement du Royaume-Uni de
Grande-Bretagne et d'Irlande du Nord:

ANTHONY CROSLAND

RESERVATIONS AND DECLARATIONS
MADE UPON SIGNATURE

FRANCE

[Translation[1]—Traduction[2]]

In deciding to sign the European Convention
on the Suppression of Terrorism today, the
Government wished to demonstrate its
solidarity with the other European
countries in combating a danger which has
created—and continues to create—a number
of innocent victims and very properly
arouses public feeling.

This signature is the logical consequence of
the action we have been taking for several
years and which has caused us on several
occasions to strengthen our internal
legislation and to ratify The Hague[3] and
Montreal[4] Conventions on air terrorism.

RÉSERVES ET DÉCLARATIONS FAITES
LORS DE LA SIGNATURE

FRANCE

«En décidant de signer aujourd'hui la
Convention européenne sur la répression
du terrorisme, le gouvernement a entendu
marquer sa solidarité avec les autres pays
européens dans la lutte contre un fléau qui a
fait—et continue de faire—nombre de victimes
innocentes et soulève à juste titre l'émotion
de l'opinion publique.

«Cette signature est la suite logique d'une action
entreprise depuis plusieurs années
et qui nous a amenés à renforcer à différentes
reprises notre législation interne aussi bien qu'à
ratifier les conventions de La Haye[1] et de
Montréal,[2] dans le domaine du terrorisme aérien.

---

[1] Translation supplied by the Council of Europe.
[2] Traduction fournie par le Conseil de l'Europe.
[3] United Nations, *Treaty Series*, vol 860, p 105.
[4] *Ibid*, vol 974, p 177.

[1] Nations Unies, *Recueil des Traités*, vol 860, p 105.
[2] *Ibid*, vol 974, p 177.

It is self-evident that efficiency in this struggle must be reconciled with respect for the fundamental principles of our criminal law and of our Constitution, which states in its preamble that 'anyone persecuted on account of his action for the cause of liberty has the right to asylum on the territory of the Republic'.

It is also clear that such a high degree of solidarity as is provided for in the Council of Europe Convention[5] can only apply between States sharing the same ideals of freedom and democracy.

France will therefore subject the application of the Convention to certain conditions. On ratification it will make the reservations necessary to ensure that the considerations I have just mentioned will be taken into account and that human rights will at no time be endangered.

There is a further point of very special importance to the Government: this is the success of the work of the Nine in the same field following the decisions of the European Council on 13 July 1976. We wish to avoid risks of conflict between the two texts and the Government therefore does not intend to ratify the Strasbourg Convention before the instrument which will be prepared by the Nine.

Furthermore, taking action against terrorism does not absolve us from tackling the political problem of the causes of terrorism. For in many respects the real struggle against terrorism is a struggle for a just peace which guarantees everyone's legitimate rights.

«Il va de soi que l'efficacité de la lutte à mener doit se concilier avec le respect des principes fondamentaux de notre droit pénal et de notre Constitution, laquelle proclame dans son préambule que «tout homme persécuté en raison de son action en faveur de la liberté a droit d'asile sur les territoires de la République».

«Il est bien évident aussi qu'une solidarité aussi poussée que celle qui est prévue par la Convention du Conseil de l'Europe[3] ne peut s'exercer qu'entre Etats qui partagent les mêmes idéaux de liberté et de démocratic.

«La France mettra donc à l'application de la Convention certaines conditions. Elle formulera, lors de la ratification, les réserves voulues pour que soient prises en compte les préoccupations que je viens d'exprimer et qu'à aucun moment les Droits de l'Homme ne risquent d'être mis en danger.

«Il y a aussi un point qui revêt pour le gouvernement une importance toute particuliére: c'est le succès des travaux engages à Neuf dans le même domaine, à la suite des décisions du Conseil Européen du 13 juillet 1976. Nous voulons éviter les risques de conflit entre les deux textes; le gouvernement n'a donc pas l'intention de ratifier la Convention de Strasbourg avant l'instrument qui sera élaboré par les Neuf.

«Une action contre les manifestations du terrorisme ne nous dispensera d'ailleurs pas de nous attaquer au problème politique, qui est celui des causes du terrorisme. A bien des égards, en effet, le vrai combat contre ce dernier est avant tout le combat pour une paix juste, qui garantisse les droits légitimes de chacun.»

---

[5] *Ibid*, vol 87, p 103.

[3] *Ibid*, vol 87, p 103.

ITALY

[TRANSLATION[1]—TRADUCTION[2]]

Italy declares that it reserves the right to refuse extradition and mutual assistance in criminal matters in respect to any offence mentioned in article 1 which it considers to be a political offence, an offence connected with a political offence or an offence inspired by political motives: in this case Italy undertakes to take into due consideration, when evaluating the character of the offence, any particularly serious aspects of the offence, including:

- *(a)* That it created a collective danger to the life, physical integrity or liberty of persons; or
- *(b)* That it affected persons foreign to the motives behind it; or
- *(c)* That cruel or vicious means have been used in the commission of the offence.

---

[1] Translation supplied by the Council of Europe.
[2] Traduction fournie par le Conseil de l'Europe.

ITALIE

«L'Italie déclare qu'elle se réserve le droit de refuser l'extradition, ainsi que l'entraide judiciaire, en ce qui concerne toute infraction énumérée dans l'article 1er qu'elle considère comme une infraction politique, comme une infraction connexe à une infraction politique ou comme une infraction inspirée par des mobiles politiques; dans ces cas, l'Italie s'engage à prendre dûment en considération, lors de l'évaluation du caractère de l'infraction, son caractère de particulière gravité, y compris:

- «*a*) Qu'elle a créé un danger collectif pour la vie, l'intégrité corporelle ou la liberté des personnes; ou bien
- «*b*) Qu'elle a atteint des personnes étrangèes aux mobiles qui l'ont inspirée; ou bien
- «c) Que des moyens cruels ou perfides ont été utilisés pour sa réalisation.»

NORWAY

'The Kingdom of Norway declares that it reserves the right to refuse, in conformity with the provisions laid down in article 13, paragraph 1, of the Convention, extradition in respect of any offences mentioned in article 1 if it considers it to be a political offence or connected with a political offence or inspired by political motives.

'The Kingdom of Norway does not consider itself bound by the provisions of article 8 and reserves the right to refuse requests for assistance in criminal matters in which the offence is regarded by Norwegian authorities to be a political offence or connected with a political offence or inspired by political motives.'

NORVÈGE

[TRADUCTION[1]—TRANSLATION[2]]

Le Royaume de Norvège déclare qu'il se réserve le droit de refuser l'extradition, en conformité avec les dispositions de l'article 13, paragraphe 1, de la Convention, en ce qui concerne toute infraction énumérée dans l'article 1er qu'il considère comme une infraction politique ou comme une infraction connexe à une infraction politique ou comme une infraction inspirée par des mobiles politiques.

Le Royaume de Norvège ne se considère pas lié par les dispositions de l'article 8 et se réserve le droit de refuser des demandes d'entraide judiciaire en matière pénale lorsque le Gouvernement norvégien considère l'infraction comme une infraction politique ou comme une infraction inspirée par des mobiles politiques.

---

[1] Traduction fournie par le Conseil de l'Europe.
[2] Translation supplied by the Council of Europe.

PORTUGAL

[TRANSLATION[1]—TRADUCTION[2]]

As requested State, Portugal will not grant extradition for offences punishable by death in the requesting State, this is, in accordance with article 11 of the European Convention on Extradition to which Portugal is not a Contracting Party.

Portugal is signing the Convention subject to the safeguard of the provisions of its constitution relating to non-extradition on political grounds.

---

[1] Translation supplied by the Council of Europe.
[2] Traduction fournie par le Conseil de l'Europe.

PORTUGAL

«Le Portugal n'acceptera pas l'extradition comme Etat requis quand les infractions sont punies de la peine de mort dans l'Etat requérant, en conformité avec l'article 11 de la Convention européenne d'extradition à laquelle le Portugal n'est pas Partie Contractante.

«Le Portugal signe la Convention sous réserve que soient sauvegardées les dispositions constitutionnelles relatives à la non-extradition pour des motifs politiques.»

RESERVATIONS AND DECLARATIONS MADE UPON RATIFICATION

CYPRUS

'The Government of the Republic of Cyprus reserves the right to refuse extradition in respect of any offence mentioned in article 1 which it considers to be a political offence.

'*(a)* With respect to Article 7 of the Convention and pursuant to the Republic of Cyprus the Extension of Jurisdiction of National Courts with respect to certain Terrorist Offences Law of 1979 which has been enacted by the House of Representatives of the Republic of Cyprus on the 18th January 1979, the national courts of Cyprus can prosecute a person suspected to have committed an offence mentioned in article 1 of this Convention.
'*(b)* In this regard, the Government of the Republic of Cyprus wishes further to notify that its reservations and declarations made on 22nd January 1971[1] when depositing its instrument of ratification with regard to the European Convention on Extradition of 13th December 1957 are still valid.'

---

[1] United Nations, *Treaty Series*, vol 789, p 292.

RÉSERVES ET DÉCLARATIONS FAITES LORS DE LA RATIFICATION

CHYPRE

«Le Gouvernement de la République de Chypre se réserve le droit de refuser l'extradition en ce qui concerne toute infraction énumérée dans l'article 1 qu'il considère comme une infraction politique.

«*a)* En ce qui concerne l'article 7 de la Convention et conformément à *l'Extension of Jurisdiction of National Courts with respect to certain Terrorist Offences Law of 1979* qui à été adoptée par la Chambre des Représentants de la République de Chypre le 18 janvier 1979, les juridictions nationales de Chypre peuvent poursuivre une personne soupçonnée d'avoir commis l'une des infractions énumérées à l'article 1 de la Convention.
«*b)* A ce sujet, le Gouvernement de la République de Chypre désire également notifier que les réserves et déclarations qu'il a faites le 22 janvier 1971[1] lors du dépôt de l'instrument de ratification de la Convention européenne d'Extradition demeurent valables.»

---

[1] Nations Unies, *Recueil des Traités*, vol 789, p 293.

DENMARK

'The Danish Government, in accordance with the provisions of article 13 of this Convention and subject to the undertaking contained in that article, reserves the right to refuse extradition in respect of any offence mentioned in article 1 which it considers to be a political offence.'

FEDERAL REPUBLIC OF GERMANY

'With effect from the date on which the said Convention enters into force for the Federal Republic of Germany, it shall also apply to *Land Berlin,* subject to the rights, responsibilities and legislation of the French Republic, the United Kingdom of Great Britain and Northern Ireland and the United States of America.

'In particular, nationals of the French Republic, the United Kingdom of Great Britain and Northern Ireland or the United States of America shall not be extradited without the consent of the appropriate Sector Commander.'

SWEDEN

'The Swedish Government, in accordance with the provisions of article 13 of this Convention and subject to the undertaking contained in that article, reserves the right to refuse extradition in respect of any offence mentioned in article 1 which it considers to be a political offence.'

DANEMARK

«Le Gouvernement danois, en conformité avec les dispositions de l'article 13 de cette Convention et tenant compte de l'engagement contenu dans cet article, se réserve le droit de refuser l'extradition en ce qui concerne toute infraction énumérée dans l'article 1 qu'il considère comme une infraction politique.»

RÉPUBLIQUE FÉDÉRALE D'ALLEMAGNE

«Avec effet de la date à laquelle la Convention entrera en vigueur pour la République fédérale d'Allemagne, elle s'appliquera également au Land de Berlin, sous réserve des droits, responsabilités et législations de la République française, du Royaume-Uni de Grande-Bretagne et d'Irlande du Nord et des Etats-Unis d'Amérique.

«En particulier, des ressortissants de la République française, du Royaume-Uni de Grande-Bretagne et d'Irlande du Nord ou des Etats-Unis d'Amérique ne devront pas être extradés sans l'assentiment du Commandant de secteur compétent.

SUÈDE

[TRADUCTION—TRANSLATION]

Le Gouvernement suédois, en conformité avec les dispositions de l'article 13 de cette Convention, et tenant compte de l'engagement contenu dans cet article, se réserve le droit de refuser l'extradition en ce qui concerne toute infraction énumérée dans l'article 1 qu'il considère comme une infraction politique.

APPENDIX 16

American States Convention
No 24381

MULTILATERAL

Convention to prevent and punish the acts of terrorism taking the form of crimes
against persons and related extortion that are of international significance.
Concluded at Washington on 2 February 1971

Authentic texts: Spanish, English, French and Portuguese.

Registered by the Organization of American States on 23 October 1986.

MULTILATÉRAL

Convention pour la prévention ou la répression des actes de terrorisme qui prennent
la forme de délits contre les personnes ainsi que de l'extorsion connexe
a ces délits lorsque de tels actes ont des répercussions internationales.
Conclue à Washington le 2 février 1971

Textes authentiques: espagnol, anglais, français et portugais.

Enregistrée par l'Organisation des États américains le 23 octobre 1986.

CONVENTION[1] TO PREVENT AND PUNISH THE ACTS OF TERRORISM TAKING THE FORM OF CRIMES AGAINST PERSONS AND RELATED EXTORTION THAT ARE OF INTERNATIONAL SIGNIFICANCE

Whereas:

The defense of freedom and justice and respect for the fundamental rights of the individual that
are recognized by the American Declaration of the Rights and Duties of Man and the Universal
Declaration of Human Rights are primary duties of states;

---

[1] Came into force in respect of the following States on the date of deposit with the General Secretariat of the
Organization of American States of their respective instruments of ratification, in accordance with article 12:

State	*Date of deposit of the instrument of ratification*
Costa Rica	16 October 1973
Dominican Republic	25 May 1976
El Salvador	1 May 1980
Guatemala	19 February 1980
Mexico	17 March 1975
Nicaragua	8 March 1973
United States of America	20 October 1976
Uruguay	17 March 1978
Venezuela	7 November 1973

The General Assembly of the Organization, in Resolution 4, of June 30, 1970, strongly condemned acts of terrorism, especially the kidnapping of persons and extortion in connection with that crime, which it declared to be serious common crimes;

Criminal acts against persons entitled to special protection under international law are occurring frequently, and those acts are of international significance because of the consequences that may flow from them for relations among states;

It is advisable to adopt general standards that will progressively develop international law as regards cooperation in the prevention and punishment of such acts; and

In the application of those standards the institution of asylum should be maintained and, likewise the principle of nonintervention should not be impaired,

The Member States of the Organization of American States

Have agreed upon the following articles:

Article 1

The contracting states undertake to cooperate among themselves by taking all the measures that they may consider effective, under their own laws, and especially those established in this convention, to prevent and punish acts of terrorism, especially kidnapping, murder, and other assaults against the life or physical integrity of those persons to whom the state has the duty according to international law to give special protection, as well as extortion in connection with those crimes.

Article 2

For the purposes of this convention, kidnapping, murder, and other assaults against the life or personal integrity of those persons to whom the state has the duty to give special protection according to international law, as well as extortion in connection with those crimes, shall be considered common crimes of international significance, regardless of motive.

Article 3

Persons who have been charged or convicted for any of the crimes referred to in Article 2 of this convention shall be subject to extradition under the provisions of the extradition treaties in force between the parties or, in the case of states that do not make extradition dependent on the existence of a treaty, in accordance with their own laws.

In any case, it is the exclusive responsibility of the state under whose jurisdiction or protection such persons are located to determine the nature of the acts and decide whether the standards of this convention are applicable.

Article 4

Any person deprived of his freedom through the application of this convention shall enjoy the legal guarantees of due process.

Article 5

When extradition requested for one of the crimes specified in Article 2 is not in order because the person sought is a national of the requested state, or because of some other legal or constitutional impediment, that state is obliged to submit the case to its competent authorities for prosecution, as if the act had been committed in its territory. The decision of these authorities shall be communicated to the state that requested extradition. In such proceedings, the obligation established in Article 4 shall be respected.

Article 6

None of the provisions of this convention shall be interpreted so as to impair the right of asylum.

Article 7

The contracting states undertake to include the crimes referred to in Article 2 of this convention among the punishable acts giving rise to extradition in any treaty on the subject to which they agree among themselves in the future. The contracting states that do not subject extradition to the existence of a treaty with the requesting state shall consider the crimes referred to in Article 2 of this convention as crimes giving rise to extradition, according to the conditions established by the laws of the requested state.

Article 8

To cooperate in preventing and punishing the crimes contemplated in Article 2 of this convention, the contracting states accept the following obligations:

   a. To take all measures within their power, and in conformity with their own laws, to prevent and impede the preparation in their respective territories of the crimes mentioned in Article 2 that are to be carried out in the territory of another contracting state;

   b. To exchange information and consider effective administrative measures for the purpose of protecting the persons to whom Article 2 of this convention refers;

   c. To guarantee to every person deprived of his freedom through the application of this convention every right to defend himself;

   d. To endeavor to have the criminal acts contemplated in this convention included in their penal laws, if not already so included;

   e. To comply most expeditiously with the requests for extradition concerning the criminal acts contemplated in this convention.

Article 9

This convention shall remain open for signature by the Member States of the Organization of American States, as well as by any other state that is a member of the United Nations or any of its specialized agencies, or any state that is a party to the Statute of the International Court of Justice, or any other state that may be invited by the General Assembly of the Organization of American States to sign it.

Article 10

This convention shall be ratified by the signatory states in accordance with their respective constitutional procedures.

Article 11

The original instrument of this convention, the English, French, Portuguese, and Spanish texts of which are equally authentic, shall be deposited in the General Secretariat of the Organization of American States, which shall send certified copies to the signatory governments for purposes of ratification. The instruments of ratification shall be deposited in the General Secretariat of the Organization of American States, which shall notify the signatory governments of such deposit.

Article 12

This convention shall enter into force among the states that ratify it when they deposit their respective instruments of ratification.

Article 13

This convention shall remain in force indefinitely, but any of the contracting states may denounce it. The denunciation shall be transmitted to the General Secretariat of the Organization of American States, which shall notify the other contracting states thereof. One year following the denunciation, the convention shall cease to be in force for the denouncing state, but shall continue to be in force for the other contracting states.

IN WITNESS WHEREOF, the undersigned plenipotentiaries, having presented their full powers, which have been found to be in due and proper form, sign this convention on behalf of their respective governments, at the city of Washington this second day of February of the year one thousand nine hundred seventy-one.

OAU Convention on the Prevention and Combating of Terrorism, 1999

Adopted at

Algiers on 14 July 1999

Entry into force in accordance with Article 20

Depositary: Secretary-General of the Organization of African Unity

The Member States of the Organization of African Unity:

Considering the purposes and principles enshrined in the Charter of the Organization of African Unity, in particular its clauses relating to the security, stability, development of friendly relations and cooperation among its Member States;

Recalling the provisions of the Declaration on the Code of Conduct for Inter African Relations, adopted by the Thirtieth Ordinary Session of the Assembly of Heads of State and Government of the Organization of African Unity, held in Tunis, Tunisia, from 13 to 15 June 1994;

Aware of the need to promote human and moral values based on tolerance and rejection of all forms of terrorism irrespective of their motivations;

Believing in the principles of international law, the provisions of the Charters of the Organization of African Unity and of the United Nations and the latter's relevant resolutions on measures aimed at combating international terrorism and, in particular, resolution 49/60 of the General Assembly of 9 December 1994, together with the annexed Declaration on Measures to Eliminate International Terrorism as well as resolution 51/210 of the General Assembly of 17 December 1996 and the Declaration to Supplement the 1994 Declaration on Measures to Eliminate International Terrorism, annexed thereto;

Deeply concerned over the scope and seriousness of the phenomenon of terrorism and the dangers it poses to the stability and security of States;

Desirous of strengthening cooperation among Member States in order to forestall and combat terrorism;

Reaffirming the legitimate right of peoples for self-determination and independence pursuant to the principles of international law and the provisions of the Charters of the Organization of African Unity and the United Nations as well as the African Charter on Human and Peoples' Rights;

Concerned that the lives of innocent women and children are most adversely affected by terrorism;

Convinced that terrorism constitutes a serious violation of human rights and, in particular, the rights to physical integrity, life, freedom and security, and impedes socio-economic development through destabilization of States;

Convinced further that terrorism cannot be justified under any circumstances and, consequently, should be combated in all its forms and manifestations, including those in which States are involved directly or indirectly, without regard to its origin, causes and objectives;

Aware of the growing links between terrorism and organized crime, including the illicit traffic of arms, drugs and money laundering;

Determined to eliminate terrorism in all its forms and manifestations;

Have agreed as follows:

PART I
SCOPE OF APPLICATION
Article 1

For the purposes of this Convention:

1. 'Convention' means the OAU Convention on the Prevention and Combating of Terrorism.

2. 'State Party' means any Member State of the Organization of African Unity which has ratified or acceded to this Convention and has deposited its instrument of ratification or accession with the Secretary General of the Organization of African Unity.

3. 'Terrorist act' means:

    (a) any act which is a violation of the criminal laws of a State Party and which may endanger the life, physical integrity or freedom of, or cause serious injury or death to, any person, any number or group of persons or causes or may cause damage to public or private property, natural resources, environmental or cultural heritage and is calculated or intended to:

        (i) intimidate, put in fear, force, coerce or induce any government, body, institution, the general public or any segment thereof, to do or abstain from doing any act, or to adopt or abandon a particular standpoint, or to act according to certain principles; or

        (ii) disrupt any public service, the delivery of any essential service to the public or to create a public emergency; or

        (iii) create general insurrection in a State;

    (b) any promotion, sponsoring, contribution to, command, aid, incitement, encouragement, attempt, threat, conspiracy, organizing, or procurement of any person, with the intent to commit any act referred to in paragraph (a) (i) to (iii).

Article 2

States Parties undertake to:

    (a) review their national laws and establish criminal offences for terrorist acts as defined in this Convention and make such acts punishable by appropriate penalties that take into account the grave nature of such offences;

    (b) consider, as a matter of priority, the signing or ratification of, or accession to, the international instruments listed in the Annexure, which they have not yet signed, ratified or acceded to; and

    (c) implement the actions, including enactment of legislation and the establishment as criminal offences of certain acts as required in terms of the international instruments referred to in paragraph (b) and that States have ratified and acceded to and make such acts punishable by appropriate penalties which take into account the grave nature of those offences;

    (d) notify the Secretary General of the OAU of all the legislative measures it has taken and the penalties imposed on terrorist acts within one year of its ratification of, or accession to, the Convention.

Article 3

1. Notwithstanding the provisions of Article 1, the struggle waged by peoples in accordance with the principles of international law for their liberation or self-determination, including armed struggle against colonialism, occupation, aggression and domination by foreign forces shall not be considered as terrorist acts.

2. Political, philosophical, ideological, racial, ethnic, religious or other motives shall not be a justifiable defence against a terrorist act.

PART II
AREAS OF COOPERATION
Article 4

1. States Parties undertake to refrain from any acts aimed at organizing, supporting, financing, committing or inciting to commit terrorist acts, or providing havens for terrorists, directly or indirectly, including the provision of weapons and their stockpiling in their countries and the issuing of visas and travel documents.

2. States Parties shall adopt any legitimate measures aimed at preventing and combating terrorist acts in accordance with the provisions of this Convention and their respective national legislation, in particular, they shall do the following:

   (a) prevent their territories from being used as a base for the planning, organization or execution of terrorist acts or for the participation or collaboration in these acts in any form whatsoever;

   (b) develop and strengthen methods of monitoring and detecting plans or activities aimed at the illegal cross-border transportation, importation, export, stockpiling and use of arms, ammunition and explosives and other materials and means of committing terrorist acts;

   (c) develop and strengthen methods of controlling and monitoring land, sea and air borders and customs and immigration check-points in order to pre-empt any infiltration by individuals or groups involved in the planning, organization and execution of terrorist acts;

   (d) strengthen the protection and security of persons, diplomatic and consular missions, premises of regional and international organizations accredited to a State Party, in accordance with the relevant conventions and rules of international law;

   (e) promote the exchange of information and expertise on terrorist acts and establish data bases for the collection and analysis of information and data on terrorist elements, groups, movements and organizations;

   (f) take all necessary measures to prevent the establishment of terrorist support networks in any form whatsoever;

   (g) ascertain, when granting asylum, that the asylum seeker is not involved in any terrorist act;

   (h) arrest the perpetrators of terrorist acts and try them in accordance with national legislation, or extradite them in accordance with the provisions of this Convention or extradition treaties concluded between the requesting State and the requested State and, in the absence of a treaty, consider facilitating the extradition of persons suspected of having committed terrorist acts; and

   (i) establish effective cooperation between relevant domestic security officials and services and the citizens of the States Parties in a bid to enhance public awareness of the scourge of terrorist acts and the need to combat such acts, by providing guarantees and incentives that will encourage the population to give information on terrorist acts or other acts which may help to uncover such acts and arrest their perpetrators.

Article 5

States Parties shall cooperate among themselves in preventing and combating terrorist acts in conformity with national legislation and procedures of each State in the following areas:

1. States Parties undertake to strengthen the exchange of information among them regarding:

    (a) acts and crimes committed by terrorist groups, their leaders and elements, their headquarters and training camps, their means and sources of funding and acquisition of arms, the types of arms, ammunition and explosives used, and other means in their possession;

    (b) the communication and propaganda methods and techniques used by the terrorists groups, the behaviour of these groups, the movement of their leaders and elements, as well as their travel documents.

2. States Parties undertake to exchange any information that leads to:

    (a) the arrest of any person charged with a terrorist act against the interests of a State Party or against its nationals, or attempted to commit such an act or participated in it as an accomplice or an instigator;

    (b) the seizure and confiscation of any type of arms, ammunition, explosives, devices or funds or other instrumentalities of crime used to commit a terrorist act or intended for that purpose.

3. States Parties undertake to respect the confidentiality of the information exchanged among them and not to provide such information to another State that is not party to this Convention, or to a third State Party, without the prior consent of the State from where such information originated.

4. States Parties undertake to promote cooperation among themselves and to help each other with regard to procedures relating to the investigation and arrest of persons suspected of, charged with or convicted of terrorist acts, in conformity with the national law of each State.

5. States Parties shall cooperate among themselves in conducting and exchanging studies and researches on how to combat terrorist acts and to exchange expertise relating to control of terrorist acts.

6. States Parties shall cooperate among themselves, where possible, in providing any available technical assistance in drawing up programmes or organizing, where necessary and for the benefit of their personnel, joint training courses involving one or several States Parties in the area of control of terrorist acts, in order to improve their scientific, technical and operational capacities to prevent and combat such acts.

PART III
STATE JURISDICTION
Article 6

1. Each State Party has jurisdiction over terrorist acts as defined in Article 1 when:

    (a) the act is committed in the territory of that State and the perpetrator of the act is arrested in its territory or outside it if this is punishable by its national law;

    (b) the act is committed on board a vessel or a ship flying the flag of that State or an aircraft which is registered under the laws of that State at the time the offence is committed; or

    (c) the act is committed by a national or a group of nationals of that State.

2. A State Party may also establish its jurisdiction over any such offence when:

    (a) the act is committed against a national of that State; or

    (b) the act is committed against a State or government facility of that State abroad, including an embassy or other diplomatic or consular premises, and any other property, of that State; or

624

(c) the act is committed by a stateless person who has his or her habitual residence in the territory of that State; or

(d) the act is committed on board an aircraft which is operated by any carrier of that State; and

(e) the act is committed against the security of the State Party.

3. Upon ratifying or acceding to this Convention, each State Party shall notify the Secretary General of the Organization of African Unity of the jurisdiction it has established in accordance with paragraph 2 under its national law. Should any change take place, the State Party concerned shall immediately notify the Secretary General.

4. Each State Party shall likewise take such measures as may be necessary to establish its jurisdiction over the acts set forth in Article 1 in cases where the alleged offender is present in its territory and it does not extradite that person to any of the States Parties which have established their jurisdiction in accordance with paragraphs 1 or 2.

Article 7

1. Upon receiving information that a person who has committed or who is alleged to have committed any terrorist act as defined in Article 1 may be present in its territory, the State Party concerned shall take such measures as may be necessary under its national law to investigate the facts contained in the information.

2. Upon being satisfied that the circumstances so warrant, the State Party in whose territory the offender or alleged offender is present shall take the appropriate measures under its national law so as to ensure that person's presence for the purpose of prosecution.

3. Any person against whom the measures referred to in paragraph 2 are being taken shall be entitled to:

(a) communicate without delay with the nearest appropriate representative of the State of which that person is a national or which is otherwise entitled to protect that person's rights or, if that person is a stateless person, the State in whose territory that person habitually resides;

(b) be visited by a representative of that State;

(c) be assisted by a lawyer of his or her choice;

(d) be informed of his or her rights under sub-paragraphs (a), (b) and (c).

4. The rights referred to in paragraph 3 shall be exercised in conformity with the national law of the State in whose territory the offender or alleged offender is present, subject to the provision that the said laws must enable full effect to be given to the purposes for which the rights accorded under paragraph 3 are intended.

PART IV
EXTRADITION
Article 8

1. Subject to the provisions of paragraphs 2 and 3 of this Article, the States Parties shall undertake to extradite any person charged with or convicted of any terrorist act carried out on the territory of another State Party and whose extradition is requested by one of the States Parties in conformity with the rules and conditions provided for in this Convention or under extradition agreements between the States Parties and within the limits of their national laws.

2. Any State Party may, at the time of the deposit of its instrument of ratification or accession, transmit to the Secretary General of the OAU the grounds on which extradition may not be granted and shall at the same time indicate the legal basis in its national legislation or international

conventions to which it is a party which excludes such extradition. The Secretary General shall forward these grounds to the States Parties.

3. Extradition shall not be granted if final judgement has been passed by a competent authority of the requested State upon the person in respect of the terrorist act or acts for which extradition is requested. Extradition may also be refused if the competent authority of the requested State has decided either not to institute or terminate proceedings in respect of the same act or acts.

4. A State Party in whose territory an alleged offender is present shall be obliged, whether or not the offence was committed in its territory, to submit the case without undue delay to its competent authorities for the purpose of prosecution if it does not extradite that person.

Article 9

Each State Party undertakes to include as an extraditable offence any terrorist act as defined in Article 1, in any extradition treaty existing between any of the States Parties before or after the entry into force of this Convention.

Article 10

Exchange of extradition requests between the States Parties to this Convention shall be effected directly either through diplomatic channels or other appropriate organs in the concerned States.

Article 11

Extradition requests shall be in writing, and shall be accompanied in particular by the following:

(a) an original or authenticated copy of the sentence, warrant of arrest or any order or other judicial decision made, in accordance with the procedures laid down in the laws of the requesting State;

(b) a statement describing the offences for which extradition is being requested, indicating the date and place of its commission, the offence committed, any convictions made and a copy of the provisions of the applicable law; and

(c) as comprehensive a description as possible of the wanted person together with any other information which may assist in establishing the person's identity and nationality.

Article 12

In urgent cases, the competent authority of the State making the extradition may, in writing, request that the State seized of the extradition request arrest the person in question provisionally. Such provisional arrest shall be for a reasonable period in accordance with the national law of the requested State.

Article 13

1. Where a State Party receives several extradition requests from different States Parties in respect of the same suspect and for the same or different terrorist acts, it shall decide on these requests having regard to all the prevailing circumstances, particularly the possibility of subsequent extradition, the respective dates of receipt of the requests, and the degree of seriousness of the crime.

2. Upon agreeing to extradite, States Parties shall seize and transmit all funds and related materials purportedly used in the commission of the terrorist act to the requesting State as well as relevant incriminating evidence.

3. Such funds, incriminating evidence and related materials, upon confirmation of their use in the terrorist act by the requested State, shall be transmitted to the requesting State even if, for reasons of death or escape of the accused, the extradition in question cannot take place.

4. The provisions in paragraphs 1, 2 and 3 of this Article shall not affect the rights of any of the States Parties or bona fide third parties regarding the materials or revenues mentioned above.

Part V
Extra-Territorial Investigations (Commission Rogatoire) and Mutual Legal Assistance
Article 14

1. Any State Party may, while recognizing the sovereign rights of States Parties in matters of criminal investigation, request any other State Party to carry out, with its assistance and cooperation, on the latter's territory, criminal investigations related to any judicial proceedings concerning alleged terrorist acts and, in particular:

   (a) the examination of witnesses and transcripts of statements made as evidence;
   (b) the opening of judicial information;
   (c) the initiation of investigation processes;
   (d) the collection of documents and recordings or, in their absence, authenticated copies thereof;
   (e) conducting inspections and tracing of assets for evidentiary purposes;
   (f) executing searches and seizures; and
   (g) service of judicial documents.

Article 15

A commission rogatoire may be refused:

   (a) where each of the States Parties has to execute a commission rogatoire relating to the same terrorist acts;
   (b) if that request may affect efforts to expose crimes, impede investigations or the indictment of the accused in the country requesting the commission rogatoire; or
   (c) if the execution of the request would affect the sovereignty of the requested State, its security or public order.

Article 16

The extra-territorial investigation (commission rogatoire) shall be executed in compliance with the provisions of national laws of the requested State. The request for an extra-territorial investigation (commission rogatoire) relating to a terrorist act shall not be rejected on the grounds of the principle of confidentiality of bank operations or financial institutions, where applicable.

Article 17

The States Parties shall extend to each other the best possible mutual police and judicial assistance for any investigation, criminal prosecution or extradition proceedings relating to the terrorist acts as set forth in this Convention.

Article 18

The States Parties undertake to develop, if necessary, especially by concluding bilateral and multilateral agreements and arrangements, mutual legal assistance procedures aimed at facilitating and speeding up investigations and collecting evidence, as well as cooperation between law enforcement agencies in order to detect and prevent terrorist acts.

Part VI
Final Provisions
Article 19

1. This Convention shall be open to signature, ratification or accession by the Member States of the Organization of African Unity.

2. The instruments of ratification or accession to the present Convention shall be deposited with the Secretary General of the Organization of African Unity.

3. The Secretary General of the Organization of African Unity shall inform Member States of the Organization of the deposit of each instrument of ratification or accession.

4. No State Party may enter a reservation which is incompatible with the object and purposes of this Convention.

5. No State Party may withdraw from this Convention except on the basis of a written request addressed to the Secretary General of the Organization of African Unity. The withdrawal shall take effect six months after the date of receipt of the written request by the Secretary General of the Organization of African Unity.

Article 20

1. This Convention shall enter into force thirty days after the deposit of the fifteenth instrument of ratification with the Secretary General of the Organization of African Unity.

2. For each of the States that shall ratify or accede to this Convention shall enter into force thirty days after the date of the deposit by that State Party of its instrument of ratification or accession.

Article 21

1. Special protocols or agreements may, if necessary, supplement the provisions of this Convention.

2. This Convention may be amended if a State Party makes a written request to that effect to the Secretary General of the Organization of African Unity. The Assembly of Heads of State and Government may only consider the proposed amendment after all the States Parties have been duly informed of it at least three months in advance.

3. The amendment shall be approved by a simple majority of the States Parties. It shall come into force for each State which has accepted it in accordance with its constitutional procedures three months after the Secretary General has received notice of the acceptance.

Article 22

1. Nothing in this Convention shall be interpreted as derogating from the general principles of international law, in particular the principles of international humanitarian law, as well as the African Charter on Human and Peoples' Rights.

2. Any dispute that may arise between the States Parties regarding the interpretation or application of this Convention shall be amicably settled by direct agreement between them. Failing such settlement, any one of the States Parties may refer the dispute to the International Court of Justice in conformity with the Statute of the Court or by arbitration by other States Parties to this Convention.

Article 23

The original of this Convention, of which the Arabic, English, French and Portuguese texts are equally authentic, shall be deposited with the Secretary General of the Organization of African Unity.

ANNEX
LIST OF INTERNATIONAL INSTRUMENTS

(a) Tokyo Convention on Offences and Certain Other Acts Committed on Board Aircraft of 1963;

(b) Montreal Convention for the Suppression of Unlawful Acts against the Safety of Civil Aviation of 1971 and the Protocol thereto of 1984;

(c) New York Convention on the Prevention and Punishment of Crimes against Internationally Protected Persons, including Diplomatic Agents of 1973;

(d) International Convention against the Taking of Hostages of 1979;

(e) Convention on the Physical Protection of Nuclear Material of 1979;

(f) United Nations Convention on the Law of the Sea 1982;

(g) Protocol for the Suppression of Unlawful Acts of Violence at Airports Serving International Civil Aviation, supplementary to the Convention for the Suppression of Unlawful Acts against the Safety of Civil Aviation of 1988;

(h) Protocol for the Suppression of Unlawful Acts against the Safety of Fixed Platforms located on the Continental Shelf of 1988;

(i) Convention for the Suppression of Unlawful Acts against Maritime Navigation of 1988;

(j) Convention on the Marking of Plastic Explosives of 1991;

(k) International Convention for the Suppression of Terrorist Explosive Bombs of 1997;

(l) Convention on the Prohibition of the Use, Stockpiling, Production and Transfer of Anti-Personnel Mines and on their Destruction of 1997.

APPENDIX 18

The Arab Convention for the Suppression of Terrorism

League of Arab States
April 1998

*Translated from
Arabic by the United Nations English translation service
(Unofficial translation) 29 May 2000*

League of Arab States
The Arab Convention for the Suppression of Terrorism

Adopted by
the Council of Arab Ministers of the Interior
and the Council of Arab Ministers of Justice Cairo, April 1998

PREAMBLE

The Arab states signatory hereto,

Desiring to promote mutual cooperation in the suppression of terrorist offences, which pose a threat to the security and stability of the Arab Nation and endanger its vital interests,

Being committed to the highest moral and religious principles and, in particular, to the tenets of the Islamic Sharia, as well as to the humanitarian heritage of an Arab Nation that rejects all forms of violence and terrorism and advocates the protection of human rights, with which precepts the principles of international law conform, based as they are on cooperation among peoples in the promotion of peace,

Being further committed to the Pact of the League of Arab States, the Charter of the United Nations and all the other international convents and instruments to which the Contracting States to this Convention are parties,

Affirming the right of peoples to combat foreign occupation and aggression by whatever means, including armed struggle, in order to liberate their territories and secure their right to self-determination, and independence and to do so in such a manner as to preserve the territorial integrity of each Arab country, of the foregoing being in accordance with the purposes and principles of the Charter of the United Nations and with the Organization's resolutions.

Have agreed to conclude this convention and to invite any Arab State that did not participate in its conclusion to accede hereto.

PART ONE

DEFINITIONS AND GENERAL PROVISIONS

Article 1

Each of the following terms shall be understood in the light of the definition give;

1. Contracting State

   Any member State of the League of Arab States that has ratified this Convention and that has deposited its instruments of ratification with the General Secretariat of the League.

2. Terrorism

   Any act or threat of violence, whatever its motives or purposes, that occurs in the advancement of an individual or collective criminal agenda and seeking to sow panic among people, causing fear by harming them, or placing their lives, liberty or security in danger, or seeking to cause damage to the environment or to public or private installations or property or to occupying or seizing them, or seeking to jeopardize a national resources.

3. Terrorist offence

   Any offence or attempted offence committed in furtherance of a terrorist objective in any of the Contracting States, or against their nationals, property or interests, that is punishable by their domestic law. The offences stipulated in the following conventions, except where conventions have not been ratified by Contracting States or where offences have been excluded by their legislation, shall also be regarded as terrorist offences:

   a. The Tokyo Convention on offences and Certain Other Acts Committed on Board Aircraft, of 14 September 1963;

   b. The Hague Convention for the Suppression of Unlawful Seizure of Aircraft, of 16 December 1970;

   c. The Montreal Convention for the Suppression of Unlawful Acts against the Safety of Civil Aviation, of 23 September 1971, and the Protocol thereto of 10 May 1984;

   d. The Convention on the Prevention and Punishment of Crimes against Internationally Protected Persons, including Diplomatic Agents, of 14 December 1973;

   e. The International Convention against the Taking of Hostages, of 17 December 1979;

   f. The provisions of the United Nations Convention on the Law of the Sea, of 1982, relating to piracy on the high seas.

Article 2

a. All cases of struggle by whatever means, including armed struggle, against foreign occupation and aggression for liberation and self-determination, in accordance with the principles of international law, shall not be regarded as an offence. This provision shall not apply to any act prejudicing the territorial integrity of any Arab State.

b. None of the terrorist offences indicated in the preceding article shall be regarded as a political offence. In the application of this Convention, none of the following offences shall be regarded as a political offence, even if committed for political motives:

c. Attacks on the kings, Heads of State or rulers of the Contracting States or on their spouses and families;

d. Attacks on crown princes, vice-presidents, prime ministers or ministers in any of the Contracting States;

e. Attacks on persons enjoying diplomatic immunity, including ambassadors and diplomats serving in or accredited to the Contracting States;

f. Premeditated murder or theft accompanied by the use of force directed against individuals, the authorities or means of transport and communications;

g.   Acts of sabotage and destruction of public property and property assigned to a public service, even if owned by another Contracting State;

h.   The manufacture, illicit trade in or possession of weapons, munitions or explosives, or other items that may be used to commit terrorist offences.

PART TWO

PRINCIPLES OF ARAB COOPERATION FOR THE
SUPPRESSION OF TERRORISM

CHAPTER I: THE SECURITY FIELD

Section I: Measures for the prevention and suppression of terrorist offences

Article 3

Contracting States undertake not to organize, finance or commit terrorist acts or to be accessories thereto in any manner whatsoever. In their commitment to the prevention and suppression of terrorist offence in accordance with their domestic laws and procedures, they shall endeavour:

I.   Preventive Measure:

1.   To prevent the use of their territories as a base for planning, organizing, executing, attempting or taking part in terrorist crime in any manner whatsoever. This includes the prevention of terrorists; infiltration into, or residence in their territories either as individuals or groups, receiving or giving refuge to them, training, arming, financing, or providing any facilitation to them;

2.   To cooperate and coordinate action among Contracting States, particularly neighbouring countries suffering from similar or common terrorist offences;

3.   To develop and strengthen systems for the detection of the movement, importation, exportation, stockpiling and use of weapons, munitions and explosives and of other means of aggression, murder and destruction as well as procedures for monitoring their passage through customs and across borders in order to prevent their transfer from one Contracting State to another or to third-party States other than for lawful purposes;

4.   To develop and strengthen systems concerned with surveillance procedures and the securing of borders and points of entry overland and by air in order to prevent illicit entry thereby;

5.   To strengthen mechanisms for the security and protection of eminent persons, vital installations and means of public transportation,

6.   To enhance the protection, security and safety of diplomatic and consular persons and missions and international and regional organizations accredited to Contracting Stages, in accordance with the relevant international agreements, which govern this subject;

7.   To reinforce security-related information activities and to coordinate them with those of each State in accordance with its information policy, with a view to exposing the objectives of terrorist groups and organizations, thwarting their schemes and demonstrating the danger they pose to security and stability;

8.   To establish, in each Contracting State, a database for the accumulation and analysis of information relating to terrorist elements, groups, movements and organizations and for the monitoring of developments with respect to the terrorist phenomenon and of successful experiences in counterterrorism, and to keep such information up to date and make it available to the competent authorities of Contracting States, within the limits established by the domestic laws and procedures of each State;

II. Measures of Suppression

1.   To arrest the perpetrators of terrorist offences and to prosecute them in accordance with national law or extradite them in accordance with the provision's of this Convention or of any bilateral treaty between the requesting State and the requested State;

633

2. To provide effective protection for those working in the criminal justice field;
3. To provide effective protection for sources of information concerning terrorist offences and for witnesses thereof;
4. To extend necessary assistance to victims of terrorism;
5. To establish effective cooperation between the relevant agencies and the public in countering terrorism by, inter alia, establishing appropriate guarantees and incentives to encourage the reporting of terrorist acts, the provision of information to assist in their investigation, and cooperation in the arrest of perpetrators.

Section II: Arab cooperation for the prevention and suppression of terrorist offences
Article 4

Contracting States shall cooperate for the prevention and suppression of terrorist offences, in accordance with the domestic laws and regulations of each State, as set forth hereunder:

I. Exchanging of Information
    1. Contracting States shall undertake to promote the exchange of information between and among them concerning:

        a. The activities and crimes of terrorist groups and of their leaders and members; their headquarters and training; the means and sources by which they are funded and armed; the types of weapons, munitions and explosives used by them; and other means of aggression, murder and destruction;
        b. The means of communication and propaganda used by terrorist groups, their modus operandi; the movements of their leaders and members; and the travel documents that they use.

    2. Each contracting State shall undertake to notify any other Contracting State in an expeditious manner of the information it has concerning any terrorist offence that takes place in its territory and is intended to harm the interests of that State or of its nationals and to include in such notification statements concerning the circumstances surrounding the offence, those who committed it, its victims, the losses occasioned by it and the devices and methods used in its perpetration, to the extent compatible with the requirements of the investigation and inquiry.
    3. Contracting States shall undertake to cooperate with each other in the exchange of information for the suppression of terrorist offences and promptly to notify other Contracting States of all the information or data in their possession that may prevent the occurrence of terrorist offences in their territory, against their nationals or residents or against their interests.
    4. Each Contracting State shall undertake to furnish any other Contracting State with any information or data in its possession that may:

        a. Assist in the arrest of a person or persons accused of committing a terrorist offence against the interests of that State or of being implicated in such an offence whether by aiding and abetting, collusion or incitement;
        b. Lead to the seizure of any weapons, munitions or explosives or any devices or funds used or intended for use to commit a terrorist offence.

    5. Contracting States shall undertake to maintain the confidentiality of the information that they exchange among themselves and not to furnish it to any State that is not a Contracting State or any other party without the prior consent of the State that was the source of the information.

II. Investigations:
    Contracting States shall undertake to promote cooperation among themselves and to provide assistance with respect to measures for the investigation and arrest of fugitives suspected or convicted of terrorist offences in accordance with the laws and regulations of each state.

III. Exchange of expertise:

    1. Contracting States shall cooperate in the conduct and exchange of research studies for the suppression of terrorist offences and shall exchange expertise in the counterterrorism field.

    2. Contracting States shall cooperate, within the limits of their resources, in providing all possible technical assistance for the formulation of programmes or the holding of joint training courses or training courses intended for one state or for a group of Contracting States, as required for the benefit of those working in counterterrorism with the aim of developing their scientific and practical abilities and enhancing their performance.

CHAPTER II: THE JUDICIAL FIELD

Section I: Extradition of Offenders

Article 5

Contracting States shall undertake to extradite those indicated for or convicted of terrorist offences whose extradition is requested by any of these states in accordance with the rules and conditions stipulated in this convention.

Article 6

Extradition shall not be permissible in any of the following circumstances:

    a. If the offence for which extradition is requested is regarded under the laws in force in the requested State as an offence of a political nature;

    b. If the offence for which extradition is requested relates solely to a dereliction of military duties;

    c. If the offence for which extradition is requested was committed in the territory of the requested contracting State, except where the offence has harmed the interests of the requesting State and its laws provide for the prosecution and punishment for such offences and where the requested State has not initiated any investigation or prosecution;

    d. If a final judgement having the force of *res judicata* has been rendered in respect of the offence in the requested Contracting State or in a third Contracting State;

    e. If, on delivery of the request for extradition, proceedings have been terminated or punishment has, under the law of the requesting State, lapsed because of the passage of time;

    f. If the offence was committed outside the territory of the requesting State by a person who is not a national of that State and the law of the requested State does not allow prosecution for the same category of offence when committed outside its territory by such a person;

    g. If the requesting State has granted amnesty to perpetrators of offences that include the offence in question;

    h. If the legal system of the requested State does not allow it to extradite its nationals. In this case, the requested State shall prosecute any such persons who commit in any of the other Contracting States a terrorist offence that is punishable in both States by deprivation of liberty for a period of at least one year or more. The nationality of the person whose extradition is sought shall be determined as at the date on which the offence in question was committed, and use shall be made in this regard of the investigation conducted by the requesting state.

Article 7

Should the person whose extradition is sought be under investigation, on trial or already convicted for another offence in the requested State, his concluded, the trial is completed or the sentence is imposed. The requested State may nevertheless extradite him on an interim basis for questioning or trial provided that he is returned to that State before serving the sentence imposed on him in the requesting State.

Article 8

For purposes of the extradition of offenders under this Convention, no account shall be taken of any difference there may be in the domestic legislation of Contracting States in the legal designation of the offence as a felony or a misdemeanour or in the penalty assigned to it, provided that it is punishable under the laws of both States by deprivation of liberty for a period of at least one year or more.

Section II: Judicial Delegation

Article 9

Each Contracting State may request any other Contracting State to undertake in its territory and on its behalf any judicial procedure relating to an action arising out of a terrorist offence and, in particular:

a. To hear the testimony of witnesses and take depositions as evidence;
b. To effect service of judicial documents;
c. To execute searches and seizures;
d. To examine and inspect evidence;
e. To obtain relevant documents and records or certified copies thereof.

Article 10

Each of the Contracting States shall undertake to implement judicial delegations relating to terrorist offences, but such assistance may be refused in either of the two following cases:

a. Where the request relates to an offence that is subject to investigation or prosecution in the requested State;
b. Where granting the request might be prejudicial to the sovereignty, security or public order of the requested State.

Article 11

The request for judicial delegation shall be granted promptly in accordance with the provisions of the domestic law of the requested State. The latter may postpone the execution of the request until such time as any ongoing investigation or prosecution involving the same matter are completed or any compelling reasons for postponement cease to exist, provided that the requesting State is notified of such postponement.

Article 12

a. A measure that is undertaken by means of a judicial delegation, in accordance with the provisions of this Conventions, shall have the same legal effect as if it had been taken by the competent authority of the requesting State
b. The result of implementing the judicial delegation may be used only for the purpose for which the delegation is issued.

Section III: Judicial cooperation

Article 13

Each contracting State shall provide the other States with all possible and necessary assistance for investigations or prosecutions relating to terrorist offences.

Article 14

a. Where one of the Contracting States has jurisdiction to prosecute a person suspected of a terrorist offence, it may request the State in which the suspect is present to take proceedings against him for that offence, subject to the agreement of that State and provided that the offence is punishable in the prosecuting State by deprivation of liberty for a period of at least one your or more. The requesting state shall, in this event, provide the requested state with all the investigation documents and evidence relating to the offence.

b.   The investigation or prosecution shall be conducted on the basis of the charge or charges made by the requesting state against the suspect, in accordance with the provisions and procedures of the law of the prosecuting state.

Article 15

The submission by the requesting state of a request for prosecution in accordance with paragraph (a) of the preceding article shall entail the suspension of the measures taken by it to pursue, investigate and prosecute the suspect whose prosecution is being requested, with the exception of those required for the purposes of the judicial cooperation and assistance, or the judicial delegation, sought by the State requested to conduct the prosecution.

Article 16

a.   The measures taken in either the requesting State or that in which the prosecution takes place shall be subject to the law of the State in which they are taken and they shall have the force accorded to them by that law.

b.   The requesting State may try or retry a person whose prosecution it has requested only if the requested State declines to prosecute him.

c.   The State requested to take proceedings shall in all cases undertake to notify the requesting State of what action it has taken with regard to the request and of the outcome of the investigation or prosecution.

Article 17

The State requested to take proceedings may take all the measures and steps established by its law with respect to the accused both before the request to take proceedings reaches it and subsequently.

Article 18

The transfer of competence for prosecution shall not prejudice the rights of the victim of the offence, who reserves the right to approach the courts of the requesting State or the prosecuting State with a view to claiming his civil-law rights as a result of the offence.

Section IV: Seizure of assets and proceeds derived from the offence

Article 19

a.   If it is decided to extradite the requested person, any Contracting State shall undertake to seize and hand over to the requesting State the property used and proceeds derived from or relating to the terrorist offence, whether in the possession of the person whose extradition is sought or that of a third party.

b.   Once it has been established that they relate to the terrorist offence, the items indicated in the preceding paragraph shall be surrendered even if the person to be extradited is not handed over because he has absconded or died or for any other reason.

c.   The provisions of the two preceding paragraphs shall be without prejudice to the rights of any Contracting State or of bona fide third parties in the property or proceeds in question.

Article 20

The State requested to hand over property and proceeds may take all the precautionary measures necessary to discharge its obligation to hand them over. It may also retain such property or proceeds on a temporary basis if they are required for pending criminal proceedings or may, for the same reason, hand them over to the requesting State on condition that they are returned.

Section V: Exchange of evidence
Article 21

Contracting States shall undertake to have the evidence of any terrorist offence committed in their territory against another Contracting State examined by their competent agencies, and they may seek the assistance of any other Contracting State in doing so. They shall take the necessary measures to preserve such evidence and ensure its legal validity. They alone shall examination to the State against whose interests the offence was committed, and the Contracting State or States whose assistance is sought shall not pass this information to any third party.

PART THREE
MECHANISMS FOR IMPLEMENTING COOPERATION
CHAPTER I: EXTRADITION PROCEDURES

Article 22

Requests for extradition shall be made between the competent authorities in the Contracting States directly, through their ministries of justice or the equivalent or through the diplomatic channel.

Article 23

The request for extradition shall be made in writing and shall be accompanied by the following:

a. The original or an authenticated copy of the indictment or detention order or any other documents having the same effect and issued in accordance with the procedure laid down in the law of the requesting State;

b. A statement of the offences for which extradition is requested, showing the time and place of their commission, their legal designation and a reference to the legal provisions applicable thereto, together with a copy of the relevant provisions;

c. As accurate a description as possible of the person whose extradition is sought, together with any other information that may serve to establish his identity and nationality.

Article 24

1. The judicial authorities in the requesting State may apply to the requested State by any of the means of written communication for the provisional detention of the person being sought pending the presentation of the request for extradition.

2. In this case, the State from which extradition is requested may detain the person being sought on a provisional basis. If the request for extraction is not presented together with the necessary documents specified in the preceding article, the person whose extradition is being sought may not be detained for more than 30 days from the date of his arrest.

Article 25

The requesting State shall submit a request accompanied by the documents specified in article 23 of this Convention. If the requested State determines that the request is in order, its competent authorities shall grant the request in accordance with its own law and its decision shall be promptly communicated to the requesting State.

Article 26

1. In all of the cases stipulated in the two preceding articles, the period of provisional detention shall not exceed 60 days from the date of arrest.

2. During the period specified in the preceding paragraph, the possibility of provisional release is not excluded provided that the State from which extradition is requested takes any measures it considers necessary to prevent the escape of the person sought.

3. Such release shall not prevent the rearrest of the person concerned or his extradition if a request for extradition is received subsequently.

Article 27

Should the requested State consider that it requires supplementary information in order to ascertain whether the conditions stipulated in this Chapter has been met, it shall notify the requesting State accordingly and a date for the provision of such information shall be established.

Article 28

Should the requested State receive several requests for extradition from different States, either for the same offence or for different offences, it shall make its decision having regard to all the circumstances and, in particular, the possibility of subsequent extradition, the respective dates o when the requests were received, the relative seriousness of the offences and the place where the offences were committed.

CHAPTER II: PROCEDURES FOR JUDICIAL DELEGATION

Article 29

Request relating to judicial delegations shall contain the following information:

a. The authority presenting the request;
b. The subject of and reason for the request;
c. An exact statement, to the extent possible, of the identity and nationality of the person concerned;
d. A description of the offence in connection with which the request for a judicial delegation is being made, its legal designation, the penalty established for its commission, and as much information as possible on the circumstances so as to facilitate the proper functioning of the judicial delegation.

Article 30

1. The request for a judicial delegation shall be addressed by the Ministry of Justice of the requesting State to the Ministry of Justice of the requested State and shall be returned through the same channel.
2. In case of urgency, the request for a judicial delegation shall be addressed by the judicial authorities of the requesting State directly to the judicial authorities of the requested State, and a copy of the request shall be sent at the same time to the Ministry of Justice of the requested State. The request, accompanied by the documents relating to its implementation, shall be returned through the channel stipulated in the preceding paragraph.
3. The request for a judicial delegation may be sent by the judicial authorities directly to the competent authority in the requested State, and replies may be forwarded directly through this authority.

Article 31

Requests for judicial delegation and their accompanying documents must be signed and must bear the seal of the competent authority or be authenticated by it. Such documents shall be exempt from all formalities that may be required by the legislation of the requested State.

Article 32

Should an authority that receives a request for a judicial delegation not have the competence to deal with it, it shall automatically refer it to the competent authority in its State. In the event the request has been sent directly, it shall notify the requesting State in the same manner.

Article 33

Every refusal of a request for a judicial delegation must be accompanied by a statement of the grounds for such refusal.

CHAPTER III: MEASURES FOR THE PROTECTION OF WITNESSES AND EXPERTS

Article 34

If, in the estimation of a requesting State, the appearance of a witness or expert before its judicial authority is of particular importance, it shall indicate this fact in its request. The request or summons to appear shall indicate the approximate amount of the allowances and the travel and subsistence expenses and shall include an undertaking to pay them. The requested State shall invite the witness or expert to appear and shall inform the requesting State of the response.

Article 35

1. A witness or an expert who does not comply with a summons to appear shall not be subject to any penalty or coercive measure, not withstanding any contrary statement in the summons.
2. Where a witness or an expert travels to the territory of the requesting State of his own accord, he should be summoned to appear in accordance with the provisions of the domestic legislation of that State.

Article 36

1. A witness or an expert shall not be prosecuted, detained or subjected to any restrictions on his personal liberty in the territory of the requesting State in respect of any acts or convictions that preceded the person's departure from the requested State, regardless of his nationality, as long as his appearance before the judicial authorities of that State is in response to a summons.
2. No witness or expert, regardless of his nationality, who appears before the judicial authorities of a requesting State in response to a summons may be prosecuted, detained or subjected to any restriction on his personal liberty in the territory of that State in respect of any acts or convictions not specified in the summons and that preceded the person's departure from the territory of the requested State.
3. The immunity stipulated in this article shall lapse if the witness or expert sought, being free to leave, remains in the territory of the requesting State for a period of 30 consecutive days after his presence is not longer required by the judicial authorities or, having left the territory of the requesting State, has voluntarily returned.

Article 37

1. The requesting State shall take all necessary measures to protect witnesses and experts from any publicity that might endanger them, their families or their property as a result of their provision of testimony or expertise and shall, in particular, guarantee confidentiality with respect to:
   a. The date, place and means of their arrival in the requesting state;
   b. Their place of residence, their movements and the places they frequent;
   c. Their testimony and the information they provide before the competent judicial authorities.
2. The requesting State shall undertake to provide the necessary protection for the security of witnesses and experts and of members of their families that is required by their situation, the circumstances of the case in connection with which they are sought and the types of risks that can be anticipated.

Article 38

1. Where a witness or expert whose appearance, is sought by a requesting State is in custody in the requested State, he may be temporarily transferred to the location of the hearing where he is requested to provide his testimony under conditions and at times to be determined by the requested State. Such transfer may be refused if:
   a. The witness or expert in custody objects;
   b. His presence is required for criminal proceedings in the territory of the requested State;

    c.   His transfer would prolong the term of his detention;

    d.   There are considerations militating against his transfer.

2. The witness or expert thus transferred shall continue to be held in custody in the territory of the requesting State until such time as he is returned to the requested State unless the latter State requests that he be released.

PART FOUR

FINAL PROVISIONS

Article 39

This Convention is subject to ratification, acceptance or approval by the signatory States, and instruments of ratification, acceptance or approval shall be deposited with the General Secretariat of the League of Arab States within 30 days of the date of such ratification, acceptance or approval. The General Secretariat shall notify member States of the deposit of each such instrument and of its date.

Article 40

1. This convention shall enter into force on the thirtieth day after the date as of which instruments of ratification, acceptance or approval have been deposited by seven Arab States.

2. This Convention shall enter into force for any other Arab State only after the instrument of ratification, acceptance or approval has been deposited and 30 days have elapsed from the date of that deposit.

Article 41

No Contracting State may make any reservation that explicitly or implicitly violates the provisions of this Convention or is incompatible with its objectives.

Article 42

A Contracting State may denounce this Convention only by written request addressed to the Secretary-General of the League of Arab States.

Denunciation shall take effect six months from the date the request is addressed to the Secretary-General of the League of Arab States.

The provisions of this Convention shall remain in force in respect of requests submitted before this period expires.

DONE AT Cairo, this twenty-second day of April 1998, in a single copy, which shall be deposited with the General Secretariat of the League of Arab States. A certified copy shall be kept at the General Secretariat of the Council of Arab Ministers of the Interior, and certified copies shall be transmitted to each of the parties that are signatories to this Convention or that accede hereto.

IN WITNESS WHEREOF, the Arab Ministers of the Interior and Ministers of Justice have signed this Convention on behalf of their respective states.

APPENDIX 19

Financial Action Task Force on Money Laundering Special Recommendations on Terrorist Financing

Recognising the vital importance of taking action to combat the financing of terrorism, the FATF has agreed these Recommendations, which, when combined with the FATF Forty Recommendations on money laundering, set out the basic framework to detect, prevent and suppress the financing of terrorism and terrorist acts.

I. RATIFICATION AND IMPLEMENTATION OF UN INSTRUMENTS

Each country should take immediate steps to ratify and to implement fully the 1999 United Nations International Convention for the Suppression of the Financing of Terrorism.

Countries should also immediately implement the United Nations resolutions relating to the prevention and suppression of the financing of terrorist acts, particularly United Nations Security Council Resolution 1373.

II. CRIMINALISING THE FINANCING OF TERRORISM AND ASSOCIATED MONEY LAUNDERING

Each country should criminalise the financing of terrorism, terrorist acts and terrorist organisations. Countries should ensure that such offences are designated as money laundering predicate offences.

III. FREEZING AND CONFISCATING TERRORIST ASSETS

Each country should implement measures to freeze without delay funds or other assets of terrorists, those who finance terrorism and terrorist organisations in accordance with the United Nations resolutions relating to the prevention and suppression of the financing of terrorist acts.

Each country should also adopt and implement measures, including legislative ones, which would enable the competent authorities to seize and confiscate property that is the proceeds of, or used in, or intended or allocated for use in, the financing of terrorism, terrorist acts or terrorist organisations.

IV. REPORTING SUSPICIOUS TRANSACTIONS RELATED TO TERRORISM

If financial institutions, or other businesses or entities subject to anti-money laundering obligations, suspect or have reasonable grounds to suspect that funds are linked or related to, or are to be used for terrorism, terrorist acts or by terrorist organisations, they should be required to report promptly their suspicions to the competent authorities.

V. INTERNATIONAL CO-OPERATION

Each country should afford another country, on the basis of a treaty, arrangement or other mechanism for mutual legal assistance or information exchange, the greatest possible measure of assistance in connection with criminal, civil enforcement, and administrative investigations, inquiries and proceedings relating to the financing of terrorism, terrorist acts and terrorist organisations.

Countries should also take all possible measures to ensure that they do not provide safe havens for individuals charged with the financing of terrorism, terrorist acts or terrorist organisations, and should have procedures in place to extradite, where possible, such individuals.

VI. Alternative Remittance

Each country should take measures to ensure that persons or legal entities, including agents, that provide a service for the transmission of money or value, including transmission through an informal money or value transfer system or network, should be licensed or registered and subject to all the FATF Recommendations that apply to banks and non-bank financial institutions. Each country should ensure that persons or legal entities that carry out this service illegally are subject to administrative, civil or criminal sanctions.

VII. Wire Transfers

Countries should take measures to require financial institutions, including money remitters, to include accurate and meaningful originator information (name, address and account number) on funds transfers and related messages that are sent, and the information should remain with the transfer or related message through the payment chain.

Countries should take measures to ensure that financial institutions, including money remitters, conduct enhanced scrutiny of and monitor for suspicious activity funds transfers which do not contain complete originator information (name, address and account number).

VIII. Non-profit Organisations

Countries should review the adequacy of laws and regulations that relate to entities that can be abused for the financing of terrorism. Non-profit organisations are particularly vulnerable, and countries should ensure that they cannot be misused:

(i)   by terrorist organisations posing as legitimate entities;
(ii) to exploit legitimate entities as conduits for terrorist financing, including for the purpose of escaping asset freezing measures; and
(iii) to conceal or obscure the clandestine diversion of funds intended for legitimate purposes to terrorist organisations.

IX. Cash Couriers

Countries should have measures in place to detect the physical cross-border transportation of currency and bearer negotiable instruments, including a declaration system or other disclosure obligation.

Countries should ensure that their competent authorities have the legal authority to stop or restrain currency or bearer negotiable instruments that are suspected to be related to terrorist financing or money laundering, or that are falsely declared or disclosed.

Countries should ensure that effective, proportionate and dissuasive sanctions are available to deal with persons who make false declaration(s) or disclosure(s). In cases where the currency or bearer negotiable instruments are related to terrorist financing or money laundering, countries should also adopt measures, including legislative ones consistent with Recommendation 3 and Special Recommendation III, which would enable the confiscation of such currency or instruments.

APPENDIX 20

Commonwealth Secretariat Model Legislative Provisions on Measures to Combat Terrorism

INTRODUCTION

The following Model Legislative Provisions on Measures to Combat Terrorism were prepared on the basis of the Commonwealth Secretariat document: *Report of the Expert Working Group on Legislative and Administrative Measures to Combat Terrorism.* Excerpts from that report are included in the Explanatory Guide, which is at the end of this document and the full report is available from the Secretariat. As the model provisions were prepared on the basis of the expert group analysis of the Security Council resolution, they reflect that group's interpretation of the obligations as explained in their report.

These model legislative provisions do not represent a single approach to counter-terrorism legislation that is to be adopted within the Commonwealth. In accordance with the Heads of Government Statement on Terrorism and the Plan of Action developed by the Commonwealth Committee on Terrorism, the provisions were developed to assist countries with implementation of United Nations Security Council Resolution 1373. They illustrate the legislative measures that are required under the resolution and also include measures that are not mandatory but are very useful in combating terrorism.

As any legislative measures adopted by countries would need to be considered and adapted to existing laws and structures, there are notes throughout the model provisions highlighting considerations in that regard. The Explanatory Guide at the end of the model provisions also sets outs excerpts from the Expert Group Report to explain the background and intent of the clauses and provide additional notes of explanation.

As indicated, the model legislative provisions need to be assessed with regard to existing law and the requirements of the Security Council resolution. Some countries already may have enacted legislation in response to the resolution, such that existing law will be sufficient to meet the relevant obligations. Other countries may need only to add to or amend existing legislation and could use portions of the model for that purpose. Still others may require extensive legislative action, in which case the model provisions, in whole or in part, could be adopted to implement Security Council Resolution 1373. Finally, there may be some countries that wish simply to draw from the ideas in the model legislative provisions, the explanatory guide and Expert Group Report to develop domestic policy and legislation. The intention is to provide a flexible tool that countries can use in preparing and enacting domestic law to meet their obligations under the Security Council resolution.

The Criminal Law Section of the Legal and Constitutional Affairs Division of the Secretariat would be pleased to provide additional assistance to member countries with the use of the model legislative provisions for the development of domestic law in this area.

The model legislative provisions were prepared on the basis of funding provided by the Government of Canada.

Criminal Law Section

Legal and Constitutional Affairs Division

Commonwealth Secretariat   September 2002

Draft Model Legislation on Measures to Combat Terrorism

PREAMBLE

WHEREAS terrorist acts in all their forms threaten the stability of the institutions and economy of . . . . (name of country), its development, the rule of law, pluralism and the right of its citizens to live in peace, freedom and security;

AND WHEREAS it is necessary to strengthen . . . . 's (name of country) capacity to suppress and detect terrorist acts, and to bring to trial or extradite, persons committing those acts;

AND WHEREAS it is necessary to take comprehensive measures to prevent the territory, resources and financial services of . . . . (name of country) from being used to commit terrorist acts;

AND WHEREAS it is necessary to cooperate with other states in suppressing terrorism by implementing the United Nations and other international instruments relating to the combating of terrorism;

Now be it enacted by the Parliament of . . . . (name of country).

NOTE
Name of country in which the legislation is enacted to be inserted in the blank spaces.

PART I
INTERPRETATION

1. In this Act, unless the context otherwise requires—

'communication' means a communication received or transmitted by post or a telegraphic, telephonic or other communication received or transmitted by electricity, magnetism, or other means;

'communications service provider' means a person who provides services for the transmission or reception of communications;

'counter-terrorism convention' means any of the following Conventions:

(a) Convention on Offences and Certain Other Acts Committed on Board Aircraft signed at Tokyo on 14 September 1963;

(b) Convention for the Suppression of Unlawful Seizure of Aircraft done at The Hague on 16 December 1970;

(c) Convention for the Suppression of Unlawful Acts Against the Safety of Civil Aviation, done at Montreal on 23 September 1971;

(d) Convention on the Prevention and Punishment of Crimes Against Internationally Protected Persons, including Diplomatic Agents, adopted by the General Assembly of the United Nations on 14 December 1973;

(e) International Convention against the taking of Hostages, adopted by the General Assembly of the United Nations on 17 December 1979;

(f) Convention on the Physical Protection of Nuclear Material, adopted at Vienna on 3 March 1980;

(g) Protocol for the Suppression of Unlawful Acts of Violence at Airports Serving International Civil Aviation, supplementary to the Convention for the Suppression of Unlawful Acts against the Safety of Civil Aviation, done at Montreal on 24 February 1988;

(h) Convention for the Suppression of Unlawful Acts against the Safety of Maritime Navigation, done at the Rome on 10 March 1988;

(i) Protocol for the Suppression of Unlawful Acts against the Safety of Fixed Platforms located on the Continental Shelf, done at Rome on 10 March 1988;

(j) Convention on the Marking of Plastic Explosives for the Purposes of Detection, signed at Montreal, on 1 March 1991;

(k) International Convention for the Suppression of Terrorist Bombings, adopted by the General Assembly of the United Nations on 15 December 1997;

(l) International Convention for the Suppression of the Financing of Terrorism, adopted by the General Assembly of the United Nations on 9 December 1999. (Not yet in force);

'entity' means a person, group, trust, partnership, fund or an unincorporated association or organisation;

'explosive or other lethal device' means:

(a) an explosive or incendiary weapon or device that is designed or has the capability to cause death, serious bodily injury or substantial material damage;

(b) a weapon or device that is designed or has the capability to cause death, serious bodily injury or substantial material damage.

'financial institution' means a commercial bank, or any other institution which makes loans, advances or investments or accepts deposits of money from the public;

647

'Master' in relation to a vessel, means the owner or person (except a harbour master or pilot) having for the time being command or charge of the vessel;

'operator' in relation to an aircraft, means the owner or person for the time being in charge or command or control of the aircraft

---

NOTE

The Convention for the Suppression of the Financing of Terrorism defines the term 'funds' as opposed to 'property'. Other conventions such as the United Nations Convention against Transnational Organized Crime use the term 'property'. Countries should use the term most consistent with domestic legislation but in either event the actual definition is the same.

'property' means any asset of every kind, whether corporeal or incorporeal, moveable or immovable, tangible or intangible, and legal documents or instruments in any form including electronic or digital, evidencing title to, or interest in, such assets, including but not limited to bank credits, travellers cheques, bank cheques, money orders, shares, securities, bonds, drafts, letters of credit;

'specified entity' means an entity in respect of which an Order under section 2 has been made, or is deemed by reason of the operation of section 3(2) to have been made, and is for the time being in force;

NOTE

The legislative scheme to implement UN SCR requires some definition of terrorist act or activities. The content of that definition needs to be decided within each country, as there is no international agreement on a specific definition. The following options for the definition of terrorist act have been included as illustrations of possible definitions. The difference between options 1 and 2 is that option 2 has an additional element of purpose of the act, captured in subsection 2(iii). Countries may choose to adopt a much narrower definition, for example, confined only to subsections 2(a) and (b) or to expand on the listed conduct. Countries may also wish to include specific exclusion clauses such as those relating to self-determination or national liberation movements.

'terrorist act' means—;

Option 1

(1) an act or omission in or outside . . . . (name of country) which constitutes an offence within the scope of a counter-terrorism convention; or

(2) an act or threat of action in or outside . . . . (name of country) which—

    (a) involves serious bodily harm to a person;

    (b) involves serious damage to property;

    (c) endangers a person's life;

    (d) creates a serious risk to the health or safety of the public or a section of the public;

    (e) involves the use of firearms or explosives;

    (f) involves releasing into the environment or any part thereof or distributing or exposing the public or any part thereof to—

        (i) any dangerous, hazardous, radioactive or harmful substance;

        (ii) any toxic chemical;

        (iii) any microbial or other biological agent or toxin;

(g) is designed or intended to disrupt any computer system or the provision of services directly related to communications infrastructure, banking or financial services, utilities, transportation or other essential infrastructure;

(h) is designed or intended to disrupt the provision of essential emergency services such as police, civil defence or medical services;

(i) involves prejudice to national security or public safety;

and is intended, or by its nature and context, may reasonably be regarded as being intended to:

    (i) intimidate the public or a section of the public; or

    (ii) compel a government or an international organization to do, or refrain from doing, any act.

(3) an act which—

(a) disrupts any services; and

(b) is committed in pursuance of a protest, demonstration or stoppage of work, shall be deemed not to be a terrorist act within the meaning of this definition, so long and so long only as the act is not intended to result in any harm referred to in paragraphs, (a), (b), (c) or (d) of subsection (2).

Option 2

'terrorist act' means—

(1) an act or omission in or outside . . . . (name of country) which constitutes an offence within the scope of a counter-terrorism convention;

(2) an act or threat of action in or outside . . . . (name of country) which—

(a) involves serious bodily harm to a person;

(b) involves serious damage to property;

(c) endangers a person's life;

(d) creates a serious risk to the health or safety of the public or a section of the public;

(e) involves the use of firearms or explosives;

(f) involves releasing into the environment or any part thereof or distributing or exposing the public or any part thereof to—

    (i) any dangerous, hazardous, radioactive or harmful substance;

    (ii) any toxic chemical;

    (iii) any microbial or other biological agent or toxin;

(g) is designed or intended to disrupt any computer system or the provision of services directly related to communications infrastructure, banking or financial services, utilities, transportation or other essential infrastructure;

(h) is designed or intended to disrupt the provision of essential emergency services such as police, civil defence or medical services;

(j) involves prejudice to national security or public safety;

and is intended, or by its nature and context, may reasonably be regarded as being intended to—

    (i) intimidate the public or a section of the public; or

    (ii) compel a government or an international organization to do, or refrain from doing, any act, and

    (iii) is made for the purpose of advancing a political, ideological, or religious cause.

(3) An act which—

(a) disrupts any services; and

(b) is committed in pursuance of a protest, demonstration or stoppage of work, shall be deemed not to be a terrorist act within the meaning of this definition, so long and so long only as the act is not intended to result in any harm referred to in paragraphs, (a), (b), (c) or (d) of subsection (2).

NOTE

While jurisdiction over the individual offences is dealt with later in clause 24, the definition of 'terrorist act' includes acts and omissions wherever committed (within or outside named country) as the Security Council obligations in respect of financing, support etc are not limited to terrorist acts committed within the territory of the state and in fact under 2(d) are specifically aimed at the financing and support of terrorism in another state. As indicated, this is distinct from the question of jurisdiction over the individual offences created under the Act, which is addressed later.

NOTE

Countries concerned about the use of incorporation by reference of the counter-terrorism conventions in subsection (1) above may wish to specifically list the convention offences in the body of the text or in a schedule.

'terrorist group' means—
  (a) an entity that has as one of it's activities and purposes, the committing of, or the facilitation of the commission of, a terrorist act; or
  (b) a specified entity;
'terrorist property' means—
  (a) proceeds from the commission of a terrorist act;
  (b) property which has been, is being, or is likely to be used to commit a terrorist act;
  (c) property which has been, is being, or is likely to be used by a terrorist group;
  (d) property owned or controlled by or on behalf of a terrorist group; or
  (e) property which has been collected for the purpose of providing support to a terrorist group or funding a terrorist act.
  'vessel' means any thing made or adapted for the conveyance by water, of people or property;
  'weapon' includes a firearm, explosive, chemical, biological or nuclear weapon.

PART II

SPECIFIED ENTITIES

NOTE

The 'Attorney General' and 'Minister' have been selected as illustrative of the types of authorities that should be accorded the legislative powers under this section. Countries may wish to use other competent authorities more appropriate to the legal structure within a particular jurisdiction. The Supreme Court represents the High Court or a Superior Court within the jurisdiction.

The choice as between grounds to believe or suspect is dependent on the standard normally employed for search warrants and other similar orders under domestic law.

Orders Declaring Certain Entities to be Specified Entities

2. (1) Where the Attorney General has reasonable grounds to [believe] [suspect] that—
    (a) an entity has knowingly—
        (i) committed;
        (ii) attempted to commit;
        (iii) participated in committing; or
        (iv) facilitated the commission of a terrorist act, or
    (b) an entity is knowingly acting—
        (i) on behalf of;
        (ii) at the direction of;
        (iii) in association with;
    an entity referred to in paragraph (a), he or she may recommend to the Minister that an Order be made under subsection (2) in respect of that entity.
    (2) If the Minister is satisfied that there is evidence to support a recommendation made under the subsection (1), he or she may, by Order published in the *Gazette*, declare the entity in respect of which the recommendation has been made, to be a specified entity.
    (3) Within [60] days of publication in the *Gazette*, a specified entity may make an application in writing to the Minister for the revocation of an Order made under subsection (2), or deemed under section 3 to have been made, in respect of that entity.
    (4) Prior to deciding on an application made under subsection (3) the Minister shall consult with the Attorney General.
    (5) If, on an application made under subsection (3), the Minister—
        (a) decides that there are reasonable grounds for revocation he or she shall revoke the Order, and publish a notice of revocation in the *Gazette*,
        (b) decides that there are no reasonable grounds for revocation, he or she shall refuse the application and shall, within 60 days of receiving the application, inform the applicant of his or her decision.
    (6) Within 60 days of receiving information of the decision referred to in subsection (5) the applicant may apply, on notice to the Attorney General, to a Judge of the Supreme Court for a review of that decision.
    (7) Upon an application being made under subsection (6), the judge shall—
        (a) examine in chambers, any security or intelligence reports considered in recommending or making an Order under subsection (2) in respect of the applicant and hear any other evidence or information that may be presented by or on behalf of the Attorney General and may, at the request of the Attorney General, hear all or part of that evidence or information in the absence of the applicant or any counsel representing the applicant, if the judge is of the opinion that the disclosure of the information would be prejudicial to national security or endanger the safety of any person;

     (b) provide the applicant with a statement summarizing the information available to the judge, so as to enable the applicant to be reasonably informed of the reasons for the decision, without disclosing any information the disclosure of which would, in the judge's opinion, be prejudicial to national security or endanger the safety of any person;

     (c) provide the applicant with a reasonable opportunity to be heard; and

     (d) determine whether the decision is reasonable on the basis of the information available to the judge and, if found not to be reasonable, make an order compelling the Minister to revoke the Order made, or deemed to have been made, under subsection (2) in respect of the applicant.

(8) The judge may receive in evidence, anything (including information obtained from the government or institution or agency of a foreign state or an international organisation), that, in the opinion of the judge, is reliable and relevant, even if the thing would not otherwise be admissible in law, and may base his or her decision on that evidence.

(9) The Attorney General shall review all the Orders made under subsection (2) every six months to determine whether there are still reasonable grounds, as set out in subsection (1), for any such Order to continue to apply to a specified entity, and if he or she determines that there are no such reasonable grounds, shall recommend to the Minister, the revocation of the Order made under subsection (2) in respect of that specified entity.

NOTE

The publication of the list of specified entities in the *Gazette* is intended to constitute sufficient notice such that persons and in particular financial and related institutions would have knowledge that any property held by or on behalf of the specified entities would fall within the prohibitions set out in sections 4,5,7 and 8 below. If there is any doubt as to effectiveness of this 'constructive notice' a country may wish to provide that the Financial Intelligence Unit or other similar authority shall transmit a copy of the list to specified financial and related institutions to ensure that the funds will be effectively frozen by the institutions in accordance with the requirements of the resolution.

Similarly a country may wish to include a provision requiring notice to the specified entity, upon their being listed.

Orders for the Implementation of Measures to Give Effect to
Resolutions of the Security Council

3. (1) Where the Security Council of the United Nations decides, in pursuance of Article 41 of the Charter of the United Nations, on the measures to be employed to give effect to any of it's decisions and calls upon the Government of . . . . (name of country) to apply those measures, the Minister responsible for Foreign Affairs may, by Order published in the *Gazette*, make such provision as may appear to him or her to be necessary or expedient to enable those measures to be effectively applied.

(2) Where an Order under subsection (1), makes provision to the effect that there are reasonable grounds to believe that an entity specified in the Order is engaged in terrorist activity, that entity shall be deemed, with effect from the date of the Order, to have been declared a specified entity under section 2.

PART III

OFFENCES

NOTE

The applicable penalty for the offences is to be determined by each country, given the variation in approaches between various jurisdictions. However, while no terms have been included in the model, it is strongly recommended that specific maximum penalties be included for each offence and that those penalties, consistent with the resolution, reflect the grave nature of the offences.

NOTE

Under the model legislative scheme outlined below, no offence is created for the commission of a 'terrorist act' per se on the basis of the assumption that such acts will in and of themselves constitute a criminal offence. A country could choose however to create an offence of 'terrorist act' or alternatively provide for an enhanced penalty (life imprisonment for example) where a person commits an offence that also constitutes a 'terrorist act'. If a country chooses to create an offence of 'terrorist act' consideration should be given to whether the offence provision will also apply to acts or omissions wherever committed.

NOTE

The offences set out in sections 4–19 are illustrative of the types of 'support' conduct that needs to be prohibited. Countries may choose, however, to combine some of the provisions into more general offences.

Provision or Collection of Property to Commit Terrorist Acts

4. Every person who—

   (a) provides,
   (b) collects; or
   (c) makes available

by any means, directly or indirectly, any property, intending, knowing or having reasonable grounds to believe that the property will be used in full or in part to carry out a terrorist act commits an offence and shall on conviction be liable to imprisonment for a term not exceeding ( ) years.

Provision of Services for Commission of Terrorist Acts

5. (1) Every person who, directly or indirectly, provides or makes available, financial or other related services—

   (a) intending that they be used, in whole or in part, for the purpose of committing or facilitating the commission of, a terrorist act or for the purpose of benefiting any person who is committing or facilitating the commission of, a terrorist act; or
   (b) knowing that in whole or part, they will be used by, or will benefit, a terrorist group,

commits an offence and shall on conviction, be liable to imprisonment for a term not exceeding ( ) years.

653

Use of Property for Commission of Terrorist Acts

6. Every person who—

   (a) uses property, directly or indirectly, in whole or in part, for the purpose of committing or facilitating the commission of a terrorist act; or

   (b) possesses property intending that it be used or knowing that it will be used, directly or indirectly, in whole or in part, for the purpose of committing or facilitating the commission of a terrorist act,

commits an offence and shall on conviction, be liable to imprisonment for a term not exceeding ( ) years.

Arrangements for Retention or Control of Terrorist Property

7. Every person who knowingly enters into, or becomes concerned in, an arrangement which facilitates the acquisition, retention or control by or on behalf of another person of terrorist property—

   (a) by concealment,

   (b) by a removal out of jurisdiction,

   (c) by transfer to a nominee, or

   (d) in any other way,

commits an offence and shall on conviction, be liable to imprisonment for a term not exceeding ( ) years.

Dealing with Terrorist Property

8. (1) Every person who knowingly—

   (a) deals, directly or indirectly, in any terrorist property;

   (b) acquires or possesses terrorist property;

   (c) enters into, or facilitates, directly or indirectly, any transaction in respect of terrorist property;

   (d) converts, conceals or disguises terrorist property; or

   (e) provides financial or other services in respect of terrorist property at the direction of a terrorist group,

commits an offence and shall on conviction, be liable to imprisonment for a term not exceeding ( ) years.

Soliciting and Giving of Support to Terrorist Groups or for the Commission of Terrorist Acts

9. (1) Every person who knowingly, and in any manner—

   (a) solicits support for, or gives support to, any terrorist group, or

   (b) solicits support for, or gives support to, the commission of a terrorist act,

commits an offence and shall on conviction, be liable to imprisonment for a term not exceeding ( ) years.

(2) Support under subsection (1) includes but is not limited to:

   (a) an offer to provide, or the provision of, forged or falsified travel documents to a member of a terrorist group;

   (b) an offer to provide, or the provision of a skill or an expertise for the benefit of, at the direction of or in association with a terrorist group; or

   (c) entering or remaining in any country for the benefit of, or at the direction of or in association with a terrorist group.

Harbouring of Persons Committing Terrorist Acts

10. Every person who harbours or conceals, or prevents, hinders or interferes with the apprehension of, any other person knowing, or having reason to believe that such other person—

    (a)   has committed or is planning or likely to commit a terrorist act; or

    (b)   is a member of a terrorist group;

commits an offence and shall on conviction, be liable to imprisonment for a term not exceeding ( ) years.

Provision of Devices to Terrorist Groups

11. Every person who knowingly offers to provide, or provides any explosive or other lethal device to—

    (a)   a terrorist group;

    (b)   a member of a terrorist group;

    (c)   any other person for use by, or for the benefit of, a terrorist group or a member of a terrorist group,

commits an offence and shall on conviction, be liable to imprisonment for ( ) years.

Recruitment of Persons to be Members of Terrorist Groups or to Participate in Terrorist Acts

12. Every person who knowingly agrees to recruit, or recruits, another person—

    (a)   to be a member of a terrorist group; or

    (b)   to participate in the commission of a terrorist act,

commits an offence and shall on conviction be liable to imprisonment for a term not exceeding ( ) years.

Provision of Training and Instruction to Terrorist Groups and Persons Committing Terrorist Acts

13. Every person who, knowingly agrees to provide training or instruction, or provides training or instruction—

    (a)   in the making or use of any explosive or other lethal device,

    (b)   in carrying out a terrorist act,

    (c)   in the practice of military exercises or movements,

to a member of a terrorist group or a person engaging in, or preparing to engage in, the commission of a terrorist act commits an offence and shall on conviction, be liable to imprisonment for ( ) years.

Incitement, Promotion or Solicitation of Property for the Commission of Terrorist Acts

14. Every person who, knowingly—

    (a)   incites or promotes the commission of a terrorist act;

    (b)   incites or promotes membership in a terrorist group; or

    (c)   solicits property for the benefit of a terrorist group or for the commission of a terrorist act

commits an offence and shall on conviction, be liable to imprisonment for a period of term not exceeding ( ) years.

Providing Facilities in Support of Terrorist Acts

15. Every person who being—

   (a) the owner, occupier, lessee or person in charge of any building, premises, room, or place knowingly permits a meeting of persons to be held in that building, premises, room or place;

   (b) the owner, charterer, lessee, operator, agent, or master of a vessel or the owner, charterer, lessee, operator, agent or pilot in charge of an air craft knowingly permits that vessel or aircraft to be used;

   (c) the owner, lessee or person in charge of any equipment or facility that allows for recording or conferencing or meetings via technology knowingly permits that equipment or facility to be used;

for the purposes of committing an offence under section 14, or planning, promoting or supporting the commission of a terrorist act, commits an offence and shall on conviction, be liable to imprisonment for a term not exceeding ( ) years.

Conspiracy to Commit Offences under this Act

16. (1) Every person who conspires with another person in . . . . (name of country) to do any act in any place outside . . . . (name of country), being an act, which if done in . . . . (name of country) would have constituted an offence under this Act shall be deemed to have conspired to do that act in . . . . (name of country).

(2) Every person who conspires with another person in a place outside (name of country) to do any act in . . . . (name of country) which constitutes an offence under this Act shall be deemed to have conspired in . . . . (name of country) to do that act.

NOTE
Name of the country in which the legislation is enacted to be inserted in the blank space.

NOTE
Countries will need to consider if prohibition of membership in and of itself is possible within constitutional constraints.

Membership of Terrorist Groups

17. (1) Every person who—

   (a) is a member of,

   (b) professes to be a member of,

a terrorist group commits an offence and shall, on conviction, be liable to imprisonment for term not exceeding ( ) years.

(2) It shall be a defence for a person charged with an offence under this section to prove that the entity in respect of which the charge is brought was not a terrorist group at or on the date that he or she—

   (a) became a member of, or

   (b) professed to be a member of,

that entity, or that he or she has not taken part in the activities of that entity, after it became a terrorist group.

Arrangements of Meetings in Support of Terrorist Groups

18. (1) Every person who arranges, manages or assists in arranging or managing a meeting which he or she knows is—

    (a) to support a terrorist group,

    (b) to further the activities of a terrorist group,

    (c) to be addressed by a person who belongs or professes to belong to a terrorist group,

commits an offence and shall on conviction be liable to imprisonment for a term not exceeding ( ) years.

(2) In this section 'meeting' means a meeting of 2 or more persons, whether or not the public are admitted.

Participation in the Commission of Offences under this Act

19. Every person who—

    (a) aids and abets the commission;

    (b) attempts to commit;

    (c) conspires to commit;

    (d) counsels or procures the commission of;

an offence under this Act commits an offence and shall on conviction, be liable to the same punishment as is prescribed for the first mentioned offence.

PART IV

INVESTIGATION OF OFFENCES

> NOTE
>
> The provisions in sections 20–23 are not mandated by SCR 1373 and are provided solely to illustrate the types of investigative tools that have been adopted in other jurisdictions for use in terrorism investigations. Countries may wish to consider these for inclusion in counter-terrorism legislation.

Powers of Arrest

20. *Any police officer may arrest without warrant any person who has committed or is committing or whom he or she has reasonable grounds for suspecting to have committed or to be committing an offence under this Act.*

Detention Orders

21. (1) *Subject to subsection (2), a police officer may, for the purpose of preventing the commission of an offence under this Act or preventing interference in the investigation of an offence under this Act, apply ex parte, to a Judge of the High Court for a detention order.*

(2) *A police officer may make an application under subsection (1) only with the prior written consent of the Attorney General.*

(3) *A judge to whom an application is made under subsection (1) may make an order for the detention of the person named in the application if the judge is satisfied that the written consent of the Attorney General has been obtained as required by subsection (2) and that there are reasonable grounds to[believe] [suspect] that—*

    (a) *the person is preparing to commit an offence under this Act, or*

    (b) *is interfering, or is likely to interfere with, an investigation into an offence under this Act.*

(4) *An order under subsection (3) shall be for a period not exceeding 48 hours in the first instance and may, on application made by a police officer, be extended for a further period, provided that maximum period of detention under the order does not exceed 5 days.*

(5) *An order under subsection (3) shall specify the place at which the person named in the order is to be detained and the conditions subject to which he or she is to be detained (including conditions relating to access to a government medical officer and the video recording of the person in detention so as to constitute an accurate, continuous and uninterrupted record of his or her detention for the whole period of his or her detention).*

> NOTE
>
> The references in this section and in subsequent sections to High Court, is a reference to the highest court exercising original criminal jurisdiction.

Power to gather information

22. (1) *Subject to subsection (2), a police officer may, for the purpose of an investigation of an offence under this Act, apply ex parte to a Judge of the High Court for an order for the gathering of information.*

(2) *A police officer may make an application under subsection (1) only with the prior written consent of the Attorney General.*

(3) *A judge to whom an application is made under subsection (1) may make an order for the gathering of information if the judge is satisfied that the written consent of the Attorney General has been obtained as required by subsection (2) and—*

   (a) *that there are reasonable grounds to[believe] [suspect] that*

      (i) *an offence under this Act has been committed, and*

      (ii) *information concerning the offence, or information that may reveal the whereabouts of a person suspected by the police officer of having committed the offence, is likely to be obtained as a result of the order; or*

   (b) *that—*

      (i) *there are reasonable grounds to[believe] [suspect] that an offence under this Act will be committed,*

      (ii) *there are reasonable grounds to [believe] [suspect] that a person has direct and material information that relates to an offence referred to in subparagraph (i), or that may reveal the whereabouts of a person who the police officer suspects may commit the offence referred to in this paragraph, and*

      (iii) *reasonable attempts have been made to obtain the information referred to in subparagraph (ii) from the person referred to in that subparagraph.*

(4) *An order made under subsection (3) may—*

   (a) *order the examination, on oath or not, of a person named in the order;*

   (b) *order the person to attend at the place fixed by the judge, or by the judge designated under paragraph (d), as the case may be, for the examination and to remain in attendance until excused by the presiding judge;*

   (c) *order the person to bring to the examination any document or thing in his or her possession or control, and produce it to the presiding judge;*

   (d) *designate another judge as the judge before whom the examination is to take place; and*

   (e) *include any other terms or conditions that the judge considers desirable, including terms or conditions for the protection of the interests of the person named in the order and of third parties or for the protection of any on going investigation.*

(5) *An order made under subsection (3) may be executed anywhere in . . . . (name of country).*

(6) *The judge who made the order under subsection (3), or another judge of the same court, may vary its terms and conditions.*

(7) *A person named in an order made under subsection (3) shall answer questions put to the person by the Attorney General or the Attorney General's representative, and shall produce to the presiding judge documents or things that the person was ordered to bring, but may refuse to do so if answering a question or producing a document or thing would disclose information that is protected by the law relating to non disclosure of information or privilege.*

(8) *The presiding judge shall rule on an objection or other issue relating to a refusal to answer a question or to produce a document or thing.*

(9) *No person shall be excused from answering a question or producing a document or thing under subsection (7) on the ground that the answer or document or thing may tend to incriminate the person or subject the person to any proceedings or penalty, but*

   (a) *no answer given or document or thing produced under subsection (7) shall be used or received against the person in any criminal proceedings against that person, other than in a prosecution for perjury or giving false evidence; and*

   (b) *no evidence derived from the evidence obtained from the person shall be used or received against the person in any criminal proceedings against that person, other than in a prosecution for perjury or giving false evidence.*

(10) *A person has the right to retain and instruct counsel at any stage of the proceedings under this section.*

(11) *The presiding judge, if satisfied that any document or thing produced during the course of the examination is likely to be relevant to the investigation of any offence under this Act, shall order that the document or thing be given into the custody of the police officer or someone acting in the police officer's behalf.*

Power to intercept communications and the admissibility of intercepted communications

23. (1) *Subject to subsection (2), a police officer may, for the purpose of obtaining evidence of the commission of an offence under this Act, apply, ex parte, to a Judge of the High Court, for an interception of communications order.*

(2) *A police officer may make an application under subsection (1) only with the prior written consent of the Attorney General.*

(3) *A judge to whom an application is made under subsection (1) may make an order-*

   (a) *requiring a communications service provider to intercept and retain a specified communication or communications of a specified description received or transmitted, or about to be received or transmitted by that communications service provider,*

   (b) *authorizing the police officer to enter any premises and to install on such premises, any device for the interception and retention of a specified communication or communications of a specified description and to remove and retain such device,*

if the judge is satisfied that the written consent of the Attorney General has been obtained as required by subsection (2) and that there are reasonable grounds to believe that material information relating to—

   (i) *the commission of an offence under this Act, or*

   (ii) *the whereabouts of the person suspected by the police officer to have committed the offence,*

is contained in that communication or communications of that description.

(4) *Any information contained in a communication—*

   (a) *intercepted and retained pursuant to an order under subsection (3);*

   (b) *intercepted and retained in a foreign state in accordance with the law of that foreign state and certified by a Judge of that foreign state to have been so intercepted and retained,*

shall be admissible in proceedings for an offence under this Act, as evidence of the truth of its contents notwithstanding the fact that it contains hearsay.

PART V

TRIAL OF OFFENCES

> **NOTE**
>
> The High Court is used to illustrate that the offences would most appropriately be tried before a superior court within the relevant jurisdiction. The designation of such a court should be made in accordance with the practice within each country with respect to serious offences.

Jurisdiction to Try Offences under this Act

24. (1) The High Court shall have jurisdiction to try offences under this Act.

(2) The High Court shall have jurisdiction to try an offence under this Act if the act or omission constituting the offence is committed in. . . . . (name of country)

> **NOTE**
>
> The Security Council resolution does not mandate the extension of jurisdiction beyond clause 24(1) territorial jurisdiction and clause 24(3)a(i) on nationals for some of the support offences. However, there is under subparagraphs 2(c) and (e) of the resolution, obligations to deny safe haven and to ensure that those who commit the offences are brought to justice. In the absence of extended jurisdiction beyond territory and nationals there is a danger that countries will be unable to meet these obligations if extradition of an alleged offender is not possible. Further, several of the counter-terrorism conventions include a prosecute or extradite obligation which cannot be met in the absence of such extended jurisdiction. For that reason subparagraph 3—two optional approaches—has been included, albeit parts of it are denoted by italics as not strictly mandated by SCR 1373.

(3) For the purposes of subsection (2) an act or omission committed outside . . . . (name of country) and which would if committed in . . . . (name of country) constitute an offence under this Act shall be deemed to have been committed in . . . . (name of country) if—

    (a) the person committing the act or omission is—

Option 1

        (i) a citizen of . . . . (name of country);
        (ii) *not a citizen of any country but is ordinarily resident in* . . . . *(name of country);*
    (b) *the act or omission is committed to compel the government of* . . . . *(name of country) to do or refrain from doing any act;*
    (c) *the act or omission is committed against a citizen of* . . . . *(name of country);*
    (d) *the act or omission is committed against property belonging to the Government of* . . . . *(name of country) outside* . . . . *(name of country); or*
    (e) *the person who commits the act or omission is after its commission, present in* . . . . *(name of country).*

OR

Option 2

(3) (b) *if the person committing the act or omission is present in* . . . . *(name of country) and cannot be extradited to a foreign state having jurisdiction over the offence constituted by such act or omission.*

661

NOTE

Name of the country in which the legislation is enacted to be inserted in the blank space.

Evidence by Certificate

25. Where in any proceedings for an offence under this Act, a question arises as to whether any thing or substance is a weapon, a hazardous, radioactive or a harmful substance, a toxic chemical or microbial or other biological agent or toxin, a certificate purporting to be signed by an appropriate authority to the effect that the thing or substance described in the certificate is a weapon, hazardous, radioactive or harmful substance, a toxic chemical or microbial or other biological agent or toxin, shall be admissible in evidence without proof of the signature or authority of the person appearing to have signed it and shall, in the absence of evidence to the contrary, be proof of the facts stated therein.

PART VI

INFORMATION SHARING, EXTRADITION AND MUTUAL
ASSISTANCE IN CRIMINAL MATTERS

NOTE

The Commissioner of Police is used below to illustrate that this power should be accorded to a senior law enforcement authority. The designation of that authority within a particular jurisdiction will depend on the applicable legal structure. This power can also be assigned to a relevant Minister responsible for policing if appropriate within the domestic context. This exchange of information provision is separate and apart from formal mutual legal assistance powers which are also mandated under SCR 1373 and should be incorporated by way of separate general mutual legal assistance legislation.

Exchange of Information Relating to Terrorist
Groups and Terrorist Acts

26. The Commissioner of Police may, on a request made by the appropriate authority of a foreign state, disclose to that authority, any information in his or her possession or in the possession of any other government department or agency, relating to any of the following—

   (a) the actions or movements of terrorist groups or persons suspected of involvement in the commission of terrorist acts;
   (b) the use of forged or falsified travel papers by persons suspected of involvement in the commission of terrorist acts;
   (c) traffic in explosives or other lethal devices or sensitive materials by terrorist groups or persons suspected of involvement in the commission of terrorist acts;
   (d) the use of communication technologies by terrorist groups;

if the disclosure is not prohibited by any provision of law and will not, in the Commissioner's view be prejudicial to national security or public safety.

NOTE

The references to 'Extradition Act' and 'Mutual Assistance in Criminal Matters Act' below are reference to applicable legislation governing extradition and mutual assistance within the Commonwealth, though the name of the applicable legislation will vary as between jurisdictions.

Counter-terrorism Conventions to be used
as Basis for Extradition

27. (1) Where . . . . (name of country) becomes a party to a counter-terrorism convention and there is in force, an extradition arrangement between the Government of . . . . (name of country) and another state which is a party to that counter-terrorism Convention, the extradition arrangement shall be deemed, for the purposes of the Extradition Act, to include provision for extradition in respect of offences falling within the scope of that counter-terrorism convention.

(2) Where . . . . (name of country) becomes a party to a counter-terrorism convention and there is no extradition arrangement between the government of . . . . (name of country) and another state which is a party to that counter-terrorism convention, the Minister may, by Order published in the *Gazette*, treat the counter-terrorism convention, for the purposes of the Extradition Act, as an extradition arrangement between the Government of . . . . (name of

country) and that state, providing for extradition in respect of offences falling within the scope of that counter-terrorism convention.

NOTE

Name of the country in which the legislation is enacted to be inserted in the blank space.

Counter-terrorism Convention to be used as Basis for
Mutual Assistance in Criminal Matters

28. (1) Where . . . . (name of country) becomes a party to a counter-terrorism convention and there is in force, an arrangement between the government of . . . . (name of country) and another state which is a party to that counter-terrorism convention, for mutual assistance in criminal matters, the arrangement shall be deemed, for the purposes of the Mutual Assistance in Criminal Matters Act, to include provision for mutual assistance in criminal matters in respect of offences falling within the scope of that counter-terrorism convention.

(2) Where . . . . (name of country) becomes a party to a counter-terrorism convention and there is no arrangement between the government of . . . . (name of country) and another state which is a party to that counter-terrorism convention for mutual assistance in criminal matters, the Minister may, by Order published in the *Gazette*, treat the counter-terrorism convention as an arrangement between the Government of . . . . (name of country) and that state providing for mutual assistance in criminal matters in respect of offences falling within the scope of that counter-terrorism convention.

NOTE

Name of the country in which the legislation is enacted to be inserted in the blank space.

Offences under this Act Deemed not to be Offences of a
Political Character for the Purposes of Extradition

29. (1) Notwithstanding anything in the Extradition Act or Mutual Assistance Act, an offence under this Act or an offence under any other Act where the act or omission constituting the offence also constitutes a terrorist act, shall, for the purposes of extradition or mutual assistance, be deemed not to be:

  (a) an offence of a political character or an offence connected with a political offence or an offence inspired by political motives; or
  (b) *a fiscal offence.*

(2) *Notwithstanding anything in the Mutual Assistance Act, no request for mutual assistance in relation to an offence under this Act or an offence under any other act where the act or omission also constitutes a terrorist act may be declined solely on the basis of bank secrecy.*

NOTE

While SCR 1373 does not strictly mandate the exclusion of the fiscal offence ground of refusal and the overriding of bank secrecy, these are obligations arising under the Convention for the Suppression of the Financing of Terrorism and are directly related to some of the obligations in SCR 1373. For that reason subparagraph 29(1) b and paragraph 29(2) have been included though they are denoted by italics as not specifically mandated under SCR 1373.

In addition, the necessity of sections 27–29 would depend on the content and application of existing mutual assistance and extradition legislation.

PART VII
DISCLOSURE AND SHARING OF INFORMATION

> **NOTE**
>
> Each country will need to determine the appropriate authority for receipt of the disclosures, depending on domestic structures and context.

Duty to Disclose Information Relating to Offences and Terrorist Acts

30. (1) Every person who has any information which will be of assistance in—

   (a) preventing the commission by another person, of a terrorist act,
   (b) securing the arrest or prosecution of another person for an offence under this Act, or an offence under any other act where the act or omission also constitutes a terrorist act,

shall forthwith disclose the information to an officer not below the rank of ... (insert appropriate rank or level of police officer)

(2) Nothing in subsection (1) requires the disclosure of any information which is protected by privilege.

(3) No civil or criminal proceedings shall lie against any person for disclosing any information, in good faith, under subsection (1).

(4) Any person who fails to comply with subsection (1) commits an offence and shall on conviction, be liable to imprisonment for a term not exceeding ( ) years.

> **NOTE**
>
> The obligation below requires disclosure of information to a Financial Intelligence Unit given that most countries have or are in the process of establishing such a unit. In the absence of a FIU an alternative authority should be named.
>
> Paragraphs (3) and (4) have been included as an additional obligation that some countries have imposed with respect to financial institutions and other related persons or entities dealing in financial matters. Its appropriateness and usefulness would be dependent on the local financial structure and thus it is designated by italics as an optional approach.
>
> The term 'financial institution' is used below to illustrate the obligation that can be imposed. However the scope of its application can and should be extended beyond financial institutions to other businesses or entities dealing in financial matters.

Duty to Disclose Information Relating to Property of Terrorist
Groups or Property Used for Commission of Offences under this Act

31. (1) Every person shall forthwith disclose to the Financial Intelligence Unit—

   (a) the existence of any property in his or her possession or control, which to his or her knowledge, is terrorist property, or for which there are reasonable grounds to [believe] [suspect] is terrorist property;
   (b) the existence of any property in his or her possession or control, owned or controlled by or on behalf of a specified entity or for which there are reasonable grounds to [believe] [suspect] is owned or controlled by or on behalf of a specified entity;
   (c) any information regarding a transaction or proposed transaction in respect of terrorist property; or

(d) any information regarding a transaction or proposed transaction for which there are reasonable grounds to [believe] [suspect] may involve terrorist property.

(2) The Financial Intelligence Unit shall disclose to the Financial Intelligence Unit of a foreign state or the appropriate authority of a foreign state, as the case may be, any information in its possession relating to any property owned or controlled by or on behalf of a terrorist group, if such information is requested or if the Financial Intelligence Unit in . . . . (name of country) is of the view that the information would be relevant to a foreign state.

(3) *Every financial institution shall report, every three months, to the Financial Intelligence Unit and any body authorized by law to supervise and regulate its activities—*

  (a) *that it is not in possession or control of any property owned or controlled by or on behalf of a terrorist group;*
  (b) *that it is in possession or control of such property, and the particulars relating to the persons, accounts, and transactions involved and the total value of the property.*

(4) *In addition to the requirements of subsection (3), every financial Institution shall report, to the Financial Intelligence Unit, every transaction which occurs within the course of its activities, and in respect of which there are reasonable grounds to suspect that the transaction is related to the commission of a terrorist act.*

(5) No civil or criminal proceedings shall lie against any person for making a disclosure or report, in good faith, under subsection (1) or (2), or (3) or (4).

(6) Every person who fails to comply with subsection (1) or (3) or (4) commits an offence and shall on conviction, be liable to imprisonment for a term not exceeding ( ) years.

PART VIII
SEIZURE AND FORFEITURE OF TERRORIST PROPERTY

> NOTE
> The reference to Commissioner of Police is illustrative of a senior police official. The selection of an appropriate authority within each country will depend on local context and circumstances.

> NOTE
> There is an obligation under SCR 1373 to freeze assets. There is as well under the Convention for the Suppression of the Financing of Terrorism an obligation to forfeit or confiscate. Sections 32–35 are examples of provisions that can be used separately or in combination to meet the relevant obligations. This is in addition to the 'freezing' of assets that will result from the combined effect of the listing process under Clauses 2 and 3 and the prohibitions in Clauses 4, 5, 7 and 8.

Power to Seize Property Used in Commission of Terrorist Acts

32. (1) Where the Commissioner of Police has reasonable grounds to [believe] [suspect] that any property has been, is being, or may be used to commit an offence under this Act, he or she may seize the property.

(2) The Commissioner of Police may exercise his or her powers under subsection (1) whether or not any proceedings have been instituted for an offence under this Act in respect of that property.

(3) The Commissioner of Police, shall as soon as practicable after seizing any property under subsection (1), and in any event within 10 days, make an application, ex parte, to a Judge of the High Court for a detention order in respect of that property.

(4) A judge to whom an application is made under subsection (3), shall not make a detention order in respect of the property referred to in the application unless he or she—

  (a) has given every person appearing to have an interest in the property, a reasonable opportunity of being heard;
  (b) has reasonable grounds to believe that the property has been, is being, or may be used to commit an offence under this Act.

(5) Subject to subsection (6), every detention order made under subsection (4), shall be valid for a period of 60 days, and may, on application, be renewed by a Judge of the High Court, for a further period of 60 days until such time as the property referred to in the order is produced in court in proceedings for an offence under this Act in respect of that property.

(6) A Judge of the High Court may release any property referred to in a detention order made under subsection (4) if—

  (a) he or she no longer has reasonable grounds to suspect that the property has been, is being or will be used to commit an offence under this Act; or
  (b) no proceedings are instituted in the High Court for an offence under this Act in respect of that property within 6 months of the date of the detention order.

(7) No civil or criminal proceedings shall lie against the Commissioner of Police for a seizure of property, made in good faith, under subsection (1).

Orders for Forfeiture of Property on Conviction
for Offences under this Act

33. (1) Where any person is convicted of an offence under this Act, or an offence under any other Act where the act or omission also constitutes a terrorist act, the court may order that any property—

(a) used for, or in connection with; or

(b) obtained as proceeds from,

the commission of that offence, be forfeited to the State.

(2) Before making an order under subsection (1), the court shall give every person appearing to have an interest in the property in respect of which the order is proposed to be made, an opportunity of being heard.

(3) Property forfeited to the State under subsection (1) shall vest in the State—

(a) if no appeal has been made against the order, at the end of the period within which an appeal may be made against the order; and

(b) if an appeal has been made against the order, on the final determination of the appeal.

Orders for Seizure and Restraint of Property

34. (1) Where a judge of the High Court is satisfied, on an ex parte application made to the judge in chambers, that there are reasonable grounds to [believe] [suspect] that there is in any building, place or vessel, any property in respect of which an order of forfeiture may be made under section 35, the judge may issue—

(a) a warrant authorising a police officer to search the building, place or vessel for that property and to seize that property if found, and any other property in respect of which that police officer believes, on reasonable grounds, that an order of forfeiture may be made under section 35;

(b) a restraint order prohibiting any person from disposing of, or otherwise dealing with any interest in, that property, other than as may be specified in the order.

(2) On an application made under subsection (1), the judge may, at the request of the Attorney General and if the judge is of the opinion that the circumstances so require—

(a) appoint a person to take control of, and manage or otherwise deal with, the whole or a part of the property, in accordance with the directions of the judge;

(b) require any person having possession of the property to give possession thereof to the person appointed under paragraph (a)

(3) The power to manage or otherwise deal with property under subsection (2) includes—

(a) in the case of perishable or rapidly depreciating property, the power to sell that property; and

(b) in the case of property that has little or no value, the power to destroy that property.

(4) Before a person appointed under subsection (2) destroys any property referred to subsection 3 (b), he or she shall apply to a Judge of the High Court for a destruction order.

(5) Before making a destruction order in relation to any property, the judge shall require notice to be given, in such manner as the judge may direct, to any person who, in the opinion of the judge, appears to have an interest in the property and may provide that person with a reasonable opportunity to be heard.

(6) A judge may order that any property in respect of which an application is made under subsection (4), be destroyed if he or she is satisfied that the property has little or no financial or other value.

(7) A management order under subsection (2) shall cease to have effect when the property which is the subject of the management order is returned to an applicant in accordance with the law or forfeited to the State.

(8) The Attorney General may at any time apply to a Judge of the High Court to cancel or vary a warrant or order issued under this section.

Orders for Forfeiture of Property

35. (1) The Attorney General may make an application to a Judge of the High Court for an order of forfeiture in respect of terrorist property.

(2) The Attorney General shall be required to name as respondents to an application under subsection (1) only those persons who are known to own or control the property that is the subject of the application.

(3) The Attorney General shall give notice of an application under subsection (1) to the respondents named in the application in such manner as the judge may direct.

(4) If a judge is satisfied, on a balance of probabilities, that the property which is the subject of the application is terrorist property, the judge shall order that the property be forfeited to the State to be disposed of as directed by the judge.

(5) Where a judge refuses an application under subsection (1), the judge shall make an order that describes the property and declare that it is not property referred to in that subsection.

(6) On an application under subsection (1), a judge may require notice to be given to any person, who in the opinion of the judge, appears to have an interest in the property, and any such person shall be entitled to be added as a respondent to the application.

(7) If a judge is satisfied that a person referred to in subsection (6)—

    (a) has an interest in the property which is the subject of the application,

    (b) has exercised reasonable care to ensure that the property is not the proceeds of a terrorist act, would not be used to commit or facilitate the commission of a terrorist act and would not be used by a terrorist group; and

    (c) is not a member of a terrorist group,

the judge shall order that the interest shall not be affected by the order. The order shall also declare the nature and extent of the interest in question.

(8) A person who claims an interest in property that has been forfeited and who has not been given notice under subsection (6) may make an application to the Supreme Court to vary or set aside an order made under subsection (4) not later than 60 days after the day on which the forfeiture order was made.

(9) Pending the determination of an appeal against an order of forfeiture made under this section, property restrained under section 34 shall continue to be restrained, property seized under a warrant issued under that section shall continue to be detained, and any person appointed to manage, control or otherwise deal with the property under that section shall continue in that capacity.

(10) The provisions of this section shall not affect the operation of any other provision of this Act respecting forfeiture.

PART IX

CHARITIES

NOTE

Though not strictly required under the resolution, as the abuse of charities for financing of terrorism has been identified as a concern these provisions are included as one of the possible measures that can be adopted. However, the need for and nature of legislation relating to charities will depend on domestic structures and laws governing such entities.

Refusal of Applications for Registration, and the Revocation of the Registration, of Charities Linked to Terrorist Groups

36. (1) *The Minister and the Minister of Finance may sign a certificate refusing or revoking registration of a charity, based on information received including any security or criminal intelligence reports, where there are reasonable grounds to [believe] [suspect] that an applicant for registration as a registered charity (in this section referred to as 'the applicant') or a registered charity has made, is making, or is likely to make available, any resources, directly or indirectly, to a terrorist group.*

(2) *A copy of the signed certificate shall be served on the applicant or the registered charity, personally or by registered letter sent to its last known address, with a copy of the certificate.*

(3) *The certificate or any matter arising out of it shall not be subject to review or be restrained, prohibited, removed, set aside or otherwise dealt with, except in accordance with this section.*

(4) *Within (30) thirty days of receipt of the copy of the notice under subsection (2), the applicant or the registered charity may make an application to the High Court to review the decision of the Minister.*

(5) *Upon the filing of an application under sub section (4), a judge of that court shall—*

    (a) *examine in chambers, the information, including any security or criminal or intelligence reports, considered by the Minister and the Minister of Finance before signing the certificate and hear any evidence or information that may be presented by or on behalf of those Ministers (whether or not such information is admissible in a court of law), and may, on the request of the Minister, hear all or part of that evidence or information in the absence of the applicant or registered charity, or any counsel representing the applicant or the registered charity, if the judge is of the opinion that the disclosure of the information would be prejudicial to national security or endanger the safety of any person.*

    (b) *provide the applicant or the registered charity with a statement summarising the information available to the judge so as to enable the applicant or the registered charity to be reasonably informed of the circumstances giving rise to the certificate, without disclosing any information the disclosure of which would, in the judges opinion, be prejudicial to national security or endanger the safety of any person,*

    (c) *provide the applicant or registered charity with a reasonable opportunity to be heard, and*

    (d) *determine whether the certificate is reasonable on the basis of all the information available to the judge or if found not reasonable, quash it.*

(6) *A determination under subsection (5) shall not be subject to appeal or review by any court.*

(7) *Where the judge determines, under subsection (5), that a certificate is reasonable, or if no application is brought upon the expiry of (30) thirty days from the date of service of the notice, the Minister shall cause the certificate to be published in the Gazette.*

(8) *A certificate determined to be reasonable under subsection (5), shall be deemed for all purposes to be sufficient grounds for the refusal of the application for registration of the charity referred to in the certificate or the revocation of the registration of the charity referred to in the certificate.*

(9) *Where the judge determines that the certificate is not reasonable, he or she shall order the registration or continued registration of the charity.*

PART X
MISCELLANEOUS POWERS

Provision of Information Relating to Passengers of Vessels and Aircraft and Persons Entering and Leaving the Country

37. (1) The—

(a) operator of an aircraft or master of a vessel, departing from . . . . (name of country); or

(b) operator of an aircraft registered in . . . . (name of country) or master of a vessel registered in . . . . (name of country), departing from any place outside . . . . (name of country),

may subject to regulations made under subsection (5), provide—

(i) to the Commissioner of Police any information in his or her possession, relating to persons on board, or expected to be on board, the aircraft or vessel, as the case may be;

(ii) to the competent authority in a foreign state, any information in his or her possession, relating to persons on board, or expected to be on board, the aircraft or vessel, as the case may be, and required by the laws of that foreign state.

(2) The Commissioner of Immigration may, subject to regulations made under subsection (5), provide to the competent authority in a foreign state any information in his or her possession relating to persons entering or leaving . . . . (name of country), by land, and that is required by the laws of that foreign state.

(3) The provision of any information under subsection (1) or (2), subject to regulations made under subsection (5), shall be deemed not to be a contravention of any provision of law prohibiting the disclosure of the information.

(4) No information provided to the Commissioner of Police under subsection (1) shall be used or disclosed by the Commissioner of Police except for the purpose of protecting national security or public safety.

(5) The Minister may make regulations generally to give effect to the purposes of this section, including regulations—

(a) respecting the types or classes of information that may be provided under this section,

(b) specifying the foreign states to which the information may be provided.

NOTE
The name of the country in which the legislation is enacted to be inserted in blank space.

Power to Prevent Entry and Order the Removal of Persons

38. (1) The Commissioner of Immigration or other authorized officer under the laws relating to immigration shall not grant an endorsement or other authority permitting a person to enter . . . . . . (name of country) if he or she has reasonable grounds to [suspect] [believe] that that person has been, is, or will be, involved in the commission of a terrorist act.

(2) Where the Minister in charge of Immigration has reasonable grounds to believe that a person in . . . . (name of country) has been, is or will be, involved in the commission of a terrorist act, he or she may make an order requiring that person to leave . . . . (name of country) and remain thereafter out of . . . . (name of country).

(3) A person with respect to whom an order under subsection (2) is made shall leave . . . . (name of country) and shall, so long as the order is in force, remain out of . . . . (name of country).

(4) A person with respect to whom an order under subsection (2) is made may be detained in such manner as may be directed by the Minister in charge of Immigration and may be placed on a vessel or aircraft leaving . . . . (name of country).

NOTE

The name of the country in which the legislation is enacted to be inserted in blank space.

The reference to the Minister in charge of Immigration is in case that Minister is not the same as the Minister charged with the enforcement of this Act.

Power to Refuse Refugee Application

39. The Minster in charge of Immigration may, having regard to the interests of national security and public safety, refuse the application of any person applying for status as a refugee, if he or she has reasonable grounds to believe that the applicant has committed a terrorist act or is or is likely to be, involved in the commission of a terrorist act.

NOTE

The name of the country in which the legislation is enacted to be inserted in blank space.

Power to Make Regulations

40. (1) The Minister may make regulations in respect of all matters for which regulations are required or authorized to be made by this Act.

(2) Every regulation made under subsection (1) shall be published in the *Gazette* and shall come into operation on the date of such publication or on such later date as may be specified in the regulation.

(3) Every regulation made under subsection (1), shall, as soon as convenient after its publication in the *Gazette,* be brought before Parliament for approval. Any regulation which is not so approved shall be deemed to be rescinded as from the date of disapproval, but without prejudice to anything previously done thereunder.

(4) Where an Order is deemed to be rescinded by reason of the operation of subsection (3), the Minister shall cause notice of such rescission to be published in the *Gazette.*

NOTE

In the absence of implementing legislation, some countries have chosen to respond to UNSCR 1373 by issuing detailed regulations under a provision equivalent to Clause 3 of the model legislation above or pursuant to separate legislation relating to resolutions of the UN Security Council. The following sample regulation is provided solely to illustrate an alternate approach that may be adopted either in the short term or as general implementing legislation. Some countries may have difficulty with this approach because of restrictions on the use of the regulation power.

SAMPLE REGULATION UNDER CLAUSE 3

Whereas the Security Council of the United Nations, acting under section 41 of the Charter of the United Nations, adopted Security Council Resolution 1373(2001) on September 28, 2001;

And Whereas it appears to me to be necessary to make provision for enabling the measures set out in that resolution to be effectively applied in . . . . (name of country);

Now therefore I . . . ., Minister responsible for Foreign Affairs, in the exercise of the powers conferred on me by section 3 (1) of the Measures to Combat Terrorism Act, make the Order set out hereunder.

Minister responsible for Foreign Affairs

UNITED NATIONS SUPPRESSION OF TERRORISM ORDER

Interpretation

1. This Order may be cited as the United Nations Suppression of Terrorism Order.

2. In this Order—

   'entity' means a body corporate, trust, partnership of fund or an unincorporated association or organization;

   'listed person' means—

   (a) a person whose name is listed in the Schedule to this Order in accordance with section 3;

   'Minister' means the Minister responsible for Foreign Affairs;

   'person' means an individual or an entity;

   'property' means any asset of every kind, whether corporeal or incorporeal, movable or immovable, tangible or intangible, and legal documents or instruments in any form including electronic or digital, evidencing title to or interest in, such assets, including but not limited to bank credits, travellers cheques, bank cheques, money orders, shares, securities, bonds, drafts, letters of credit;

List

3. (1) A person whose name is listed in the Schedule to this Order is a person who there are reasonable grounds to believe—

   (a) has carried out, attempted to carry out, participated in or facilitated the carrying out of, a terrorist activity;

   (b) is controlled directly or indirectly by any person conducting any of the activities set out in paragraph (a); or

   (c) is acting on behalf of, or at the direction of, or in association with any person conducting any of the activities set out in paragraph (a).

(2) Any listed person may apply in writing to the Minister to be removed from the list.

(3) The Minister shall consider and decide on any application made under subsection (2) and advise the applicant in writing of his or her decision. If the Minister decides to remove the person from the list, the schedule shall be amended accordingly.

Providing or Collecting Funds

4. No citizen of . . . . (name of country) and no body corporate incorporated in . . . . (name of country) shall outside . . . . (name of country) knowingly provide or collect by any means, directly or indirectly, funds with the intention that the funds be used, or in the knowledge that the funds are to be used, by a listed person.

Freezing Property

5. No citizen of . . . . (name of country) and no body corporate incorporated in . . . . (name of country) shall outside . . . . (name of country) knowingly—

  (a) deal directly or indirectly in any property of a listed person, including funds derived or generated from property owned or controlled directly or indirectly by that person;
  (b) enter into or facilitate, directly or indirectly, any transaction related to a dealing referred to in paragraph (a);
  (c) provide any financial or other related service in respect of the property referred to in paragraph (a); or
  (d) make any property or any financial or other related service available, directly or indirectly, for the benefit of a listed person.

6. All secured and unsecured rights and interests held by a person, other than a listed person or their agent, in the frozen property are entitled to the same ranking as they would have been entitled to had the property not been frozen.

Causing, Assisting or Promoting

7. No citizen of . . . . (name of country) and no body corporate incorporated in . . . . (name of country) shall outside . . . . (name of country) knowingly do anything that causes, assists or promotes, or is intended to cause, assist or promote, any activity prohibited by section 4 or 5, unless the person has a certificate issued by the Minister under section 12.

Disclosure

8. Every citizen of . . . . (name of country) and every body corporate incorporated in . . . . (name of country), outside . . . . (name of country) shall disclose forthwith to the Commissioner of Police—

  (a) the existence of property in their possession or control that they have reason to believe is owned or controlled by or on behalf of a listed person; and
  (b) information about a transaction or proposed transaction in respect of property referred to in paragraph (a).

Offences and Punishment

9. Any person who contravenes sections 4, 5, 7, or 8 is guilty of an offence and liable, on conviction after trial to a fine not exceeding . . . . or to imprisonment, for a term not exceeding . . . . years.

Certificate

10. No offence is committed under Section 9 by doing any act or thing that may be prohibited by this Order or omitting to do any act or thing that may be required by this Order if, before that person

does or omits to do that act or thing, the Minister issues a certificate to the person stating that Minister has reasonable grounds to believe that—

(a) the Security Council of the United Nations Resolution 1373 adopted September 28, 2001, does not intend that that act or thing be prohibited,

(b) the act or thing has been approved by the Security Council of the United Nations or by the Committee of the Security Council; or

(c) the person named in the certificate is not a listed person.

Coming into Force

10. This order shall come into force on the day on which it is published in the *Gazette*.

SCHEDULE
(SECTIONS 2 AND 3)

List persons and entities as identified in the relevant resolution

EXPLANATORY GUIDE TO MODEL LEGISLATIVE PROVISIONS
PREAMBLE

Expert Group Report

Each country will need to decide whether to include a preamble or use other explanatory tools in the legislation that is adopted. A decision on this issue will depend on policy towards legislative drafting and the Group noted that there were differing views as to the usefulness and value of such provisions.

Note

The Preamble should reflect the fundamental issues to be addressed by the legislation from the perspective of the enacting country.

CLAUSE I

Expert Group Report

At law, it is not possible to make the provision and collection of funds for terrorism a criminal offence without defining the underlying concept, with enough certainty to allow for prosecution of the offence. Thus, before considering the content of the specific offence, the Group deliberated on legislative approaches to a definition of 'terrorism' or 'terrorist acts' to which the specific offences will apply.

The members of the Expert Group emphasized that in this exercise, they were not in any way attempting to arrive at an acceptable international definition of terrorism, recognizing that this was a serious and complex question, which was still under consideration by the United Nations. Further in the domestic context, it is for each country to decide upon the sensitive and complex policy considerations relating to a definition and to adopt a legislative provision appropriate for that country.

At the same time, the Group was of the view that it was important to provide countries with some guidance and information as to the general structure of and existing legislative approaches to such a definition. It was noted that this would hopefully be of some assistance to those countries with no previous legislation of this nature and may also allow for some uniformity of approach that will enhance international cooperation to combat terrorism.

Much guidance was drawn from the various Security Council and General Assembly resolutions on terrorism, existing UN counter-terrorism conventions, and the legislation of Singapore, Canada, the United Kingdom and the Mauritius Bill.

An analysis of this documentation revealed that the legislative approaches were quite consistent. Generally, the definitions were comprised of a list of underlying acts and a requirement that the act was threatened or committed to intimidate or threaten the population or to compel a government or international organization to do or refrain from doing an act. A third element, found in some of the legislative provisions, was an additional requirement that the act is motivated by a political, religious or ideological cause.

The Group considered each component of the definition. It was agreed that the list of underlying acts should include, as a minimum, conduct that constitutes an offence as described in the existing UN counter-terrorism conventions. However, consistent with the Convention for the Suppression of the Financing of Terrorism, all of the definition provisions examined also covered other acts not addressed specifically in the counter-terrorism conventions. As to the scope of the acts to be covered, it was accepted that this would need to be determined based on domestic policy. The list could range from acts which are intended to cause death or serious bodily harm, as in Article 2 of the Convention for the Suppression of the Financing of Terrorism, to a broader range of acts covering matters such as serious property damage or attacks on essential services.

The fundamental problem, which was discussed at length, was how to craft a provision that was sufficiently comprehensive and flexible to capture the various activities of terrorists and yet avoid an overly broad definition that would extend well beyond real terrorist acts and have the potential for abuse.

The Group noted particular concerns about the relationship of the definition to matters such as lawful protest or strike action.

After discussion, the Group concluded that in order to provide countries with a comprehensive view of the issue, it would be best to incorporate an extensive, rather than limited, list of underlying acts, drawn from all of the legislative provisions examined. This would be accompanied by an explanatory note, which would outline that this was an illustrative list and countries would need to decide what acts to cover in domestic law. Because of particular concerns regarding lawful protests and strikes, a provision drawn from the Canadian legislation has also been included as paragraph 3 for consideration.

As to the purpose of the act, there was consensus that it should generally follow Article 2 of the Convention on the Suppression of the Financing of Terrorism, which was the approach adopted in most of the existing and proposed legislation.

The Group went on to consider the additional element of 'for political, ideological or religious motivation', focusing on the reasoning behind the absence or inclusion of this as a further component of the definition. The inclusion of a 'motivation' element provides the special characterization to the offence that separates terrorist acts and activity from other criminal acts, such as those related to organized crime groups. It also provides parameters that will narrow the application of the offence to some extent, such that it is less likely that it can be subject to abuse in its application.

Alternatively, there were reasons supporting a definition without this additional requirement. In particular, it reflects a policy approach where the act and purpose alone constitute 'terrorism' and the motivation is of no relevance. This approach is also easier to apply in practice, as there is no requirement to prove motivation as an element of the offence. As well, such an approach is consistent with the definition in the Convention on the Suppression of the Financing of Terrorism as noted above.

The Group considered that ultimately this was a fundamental policy decision that each country would need to make when developing implementing legislation and therefore, two optional approaches have been included.

Note

Clause 1 sets out the definitions that apply in the Act.

The definition of 'Explosive or other lethal devices' is taken from the International Convention on the Suppression of Terrorist Financing and includes weapons and other devices.

The term 'property' is defined using the definition for 'funds' found in the Convention on the Suppression of Terrorist Financing. As indicated in the model, countries may choose to use either term depending on consistency with other domestic legislation. Countries that have implemented the United Nations Convention against Illicit Traffic in Narcotic Drugs and Psychotropic Substances or the United Nations Convention against Transnational Organized Crime may wish to use the term 'property' that is used in those conventions but which carries the same definition, with some detail added, as the term 'funds' in the Financing Convention.

The background to the definition of 'terrorist act' is outlined above by the expert group report. It is important to emphasize that while 'terrorist act' is included in the definitions because of the link to the financing and support offences, it is not made a criminal offence itself under the Act. The assumption is made that countries will already have in place offences to governing the underlying 'terrorist act'. Instead, it is defined in order that the relevant supporting conduct can be criminalized. Nothing however precludes a country from creating, in addition, a separate offence of 'terrorist act'.

As noted in the model, terrorist act includes extraterritorial acts because the intent and scope of UN SCR is such that the support offences were clearly intended to cover support to both domestic and foreign terrorist acts. This is a distinct concept from the jurisdictional provisions relating to the offences created under the act.

CLAUSE 2

Expert Group Report

For the prohibition on making funds available and the general support offences under para 1(d) of the Security Council resolution, it is also useful to adopt a domestic process by which persons and entities can be proscribed as terrorists or terrorist groups by executive action. This will avoid the requirement to establish a link to terrorist acts in each individual case. The requirements for and process adopted for the 'listing' of individuals and groups will be dependent upon the requirements of domestic law in this regard.

Note

As indicated the design of the 'listing process' will be dependent on domestic law. Clause 2 provides an example of a procedure that can be employed to designate specified or prohibited entities. It is important that the process adopted strikes an appropriate balance between effective law enforcement, including according protections to national security and other secure information and the rights of the individual. Clause 2 is designed to balance those competing interests.

Under the legislative scheme of the model provisions Clause 2 is integral to implementation of the obligation to 'freeze assets' that is discussed below under Clauses 32–36 and the Sample Regulation. Once an entity is listed the various prohibitions in the offence section with respect to dealing in any manner with property or providing financial or other services will become operative. If a country chooses not to adopt a 'listing' process then another mechanism such as regulations under Security Council legislation will have to be employed to meet the critical obligation of freezing the assets of those entities listed by the Security Council.

CLAUSE 3

Expert Group Report

SCR 1(c)—Freezing of Assets

Subparagraph 1(c) of the resolution requires countries to have mechanisms under domestic law that will allow for the freezing of funds and assets related to terrorists and terrorist activities. It was noted that the most critical and challenging aspect of this obligation is the requirement to act expeditiously to freeze assets and funds of persons or entities named by the Security Council. The Group discussed the legal issues surrounding this obligation at some length.

One approach, adopted by several countries to deal with freezing, particularly on the basis of lists, is to pass regulations under legislation that allows for implementation of Security Council resolutions. These regulations provide for the freezing of assets of named individuals and entities and thus freezing action would be available in relation to the lists provided by the Security Council, which can be annexed to or form part of the regulation.

One approach that may facilitate the use of the lists is to provide that where a person or entity is included in the list they are deemed to have been involved in terrorist activity or there is deemed to be reasonable grounds to believe or a prima facie case against them. The freezing action is then based on that deeming provision. Canada used this technique in adopting implementing regulations by providing in section 2 that the persons in the list are persons for whom there are reasonable grounds to believe are involved in terrorist activity.

The Group concluded that in terms of implementing the obligations with respect to 'listed' persons or entities, each country would have to determine how best to do so, given the constraints and limitations that exist under their domestic laws. However, it was emphasized that whatever path is chosen, countries must have in place a scheme to allow for quick and effective action to be taken with reference to any lists issued by the Security Council. On this point, the Group recommended that countries adopt a regime of regulations under general United Nations Security Council legislation for that purpose.

Note

Clause 3 is tied to the requirement under the Security Council resolution to freeze the assets of persons named by the Security Council. In accordance with the expert group recommendation, a general power for regulations to implement Security Council resolutions has been incorporated. In addition, paragraph 2 allows for entities named by the Security Council to be included in the prohibited list by a deeming process. As noted, each country will need to consider if this approach is feasible under domestic law and constitutional restrictions.

CLAUSE 4

Expert Group Report

In this subparagraph of the resolution, States are obligated to ensure that the conduct of wilfully providing or collecting funds for terrorist activity is made criminal, on a broad basis. The Group looked at some of the existing or proposed legislation, noting the different approaches that can be used to meet the obligation. In particular, a country may choose to enact one general offence or a series of separate offences.

The Group chose to recommend a simple but effective option of basing the offence on Article 2 of the Convention for the Suppression of the Financing of Terrorism, which parallels the language used in this subparagraph of the resolution, but including a mental element of intent, knowledge or objective basis to believe.

Note

Subparagraph 1(b) of the resolution requires the criminalization of the provision and collection of funds for terrorism. As noted above, the term used in the legislation is property, consistent with other international instruments, but the definition accords with that of 'funds' in the Financing Convention. The term property as defined is also sufficiently broad so as to cover the terms used in the resolution which include 'financial assets' and 'economic resources'.

CLAUSES 5–8

Expert Group Report

Under SCR (1) d, countries are required to prohibit making funds, financial assets, or economic resources or financial or other related services available for the benefit of persons who commit or attempt to commit or facilitate or participate in the commission of terrorist acts.

The Group noted that in enacting legislation to implement this aspect of the resolution countries should give careful consideration to the interpretation given to the words 'for the benefit of persons' and in particular what the concept of 'benefit' will cover. There are also questions as to the applicable intent or level of knowledge required in relation to the offence.

The Group noted that to meet this obligation a country may wish to establish one general offence or several separate offences or both, to capture all of the elements contained in the resolution.

Note

As indicated, there are alternate approaches that can be taken to implement this aspect of the resolution. Clauses 5–8 of the model legislative provisions, combined with clause 4 (making property available) illustrate the use of several specific offences to cover the obligation comprehensively. As an alternative a country could employ one general offence covering these various elements of 'making available'.

CLAUSES 9–13 AND 18

Expert Group Report

The Group noted that paragraph 2 of the resolution is broadly framed placing obligations on states to undertake or refrain from the action specified in each subparagraph. In so far as the obligations are

680

directed to State activity, the Group considered that this would need to be addressed at the executive level of each state.

However, by placing obligations on States, for example, to refrain from providing support or to deny safe haven, there are legislative provisions that can be adopted to prevent individuals of that State from providing such assistance or to ensure that individuals will not find safe haven there. The legislative recommendations on paragraph 2 relate to this second application of the obligations.

There are several types of offences that can be created in response to the obligation under subparagraph 2(a) to refrain from providing support to terrorist groups. As the subparagraph highlights assistance by way of recruitment and the supply of weapons, the Group recommended that countries consider a combination of specific recruitment, training and weapons offences, along with a general 'support' offence or offences. This combination should ensure that the obligations under sub paragraph 2(a) can be met in that all 'support' activities will be criminalized.

The Group noted that a country could choose to adopt several specific support offences or a few that could be used in combination with existing conspiracy, and aiding and abetting provisions. If the latter approach is adopted, a country should ensure that the combination of provisions provides a sufficiently broad basis for prosecution of terrorist support activity.

Note

In these clauses, the model provides examples of the types of conduct that should be criminalized to fully implement this obligation under the resolution. Again, countries might wish to combine some of these into more general offences.

CLAUSES 14, 15 AND 16

Expert Group Report

Subparagraph 2(d) places an obligation on states to prevent acts against other states and the citizens of those states. The Group was of the opinion that implementation of this obligation clearly requires improvements to investigation and intelligence gathering capacity (addressed in a separate part of the Expert Group Report). In addition, some countries have in place laws that specifically criminalize planning and preparation activity aimed at the commission of offences against another country or its citizens.

Note

Clauses 14 and 15 implement both subparagraph 2(a) on support and subparagraph 2(d) on preventing acts against other states by criminalizing various acts such as incitement and promotion of terrorist acts and provision of property or services for the commission of the offences or meetings at the planning stage. As the definition of 'terrorist act' is not territorially limited, these offences can be used to implement this obligation with respect to the protection of other states.

Clause 16 widens the scope of the conspiracy provisions to create offences for both conspiring in one country to do something in another and vice versa. This clearly extends countries' powers in respect of this obligation of the resolution.

CLAUSE 17

Expert Group Report

A central issue that must be considered in implementing the obligation to prohibit the provision of support to terrorist groups is whether or not to create an offence of 'membership' in a terrorist group. It was noted that this approach has been adopted in several jurisdictions and does provide an effective means to prevent terrorists from receiving training, obtaining weapons or recruiting members, as any involvement in the prohibited group is criminal in and of itself. However, some countries might face constitutional problems with the creation of a membership offence. Countries facing possible challenges of this nature may wish to consider the approach adopted by Canada, which combines the listing of persons and groups with a broad range of 'support' offences but does not make membership, per se, an offence.

Note

As indicated it is for each country to determine if membership alone in an organization can be made the subject of a criminal offence.

Clause 19

Expert Group Report

The Group recommended that all of the offences adopted should cover those who participate in the act. As the actual content of such a 'participation' clause may vary from country to country, a comprehensive list has been included from which a country may make specific selections if it considers the content to be duplicative.

Clauses 20 and 21

Expert Group Report

One of the obligations in subparagraph 2(e) is to ensure that those who engage in terrorist activity face trial. In that regard, the Group examined the question of investigative detention provisions, which have been adopted or are under consideration by some countries. Clearly in the context of terrorism investigations, there may be circumstances where concerns for public safety or the need to prevent interference with an investigation require swift action by authorities, including the immediate detention of individuals prior to the institution of charges.

At the same time, there are justifiable concerns about the rights of the individual and the need to guard against arbitrary arrest and detention. After lengthy discussion, the Group concluded that, depending on the particular circumstances in the country, it may be important to have such a power in order to react effectively in some situations. However, any such power would need to be limited in scope and application and restricted to detention periods of short duration. Therefore, the Group recommended the inclusion of an optional investigative detention power for a short period (36–48 hours), with a possible extension by court order for up to 5 days. To reduce the possibility of abuse of such a power the Group further recommended that the power be restricted in application to where there are reasonable grounds to belief that detention is necessary to prevent an act of terrorism or interference with an investigation relating to terrorism. The Group also noted the added protections of the Mauritius draft bill of ensuring access by a government medical officer and the use of video taping.

Clauses 22 and 23

Expert Group Report

With regard to the obligation under subparagraph 2(e) to bring terrorists to justice, consideration should be given not only to the offence provisions but also the powers available to law enforcement authorities to investigate terrorist activities. While SCR 1373 does not require the adoption of any specific forms of investigative measures, the Group recommended consideration, on a purely optional basis, of powers to take investigative statements from witnesses under court order and the interception of communications under court authorization.

In the realm of communication interception, problems can arise where the interception evidence is lawfully gathered in one country and a second country seeks to rely on that evidence in its prosecution. This issue can be of particular concern in the context of investigations relating to terrorism. To avoid arguments as to the admissibility of the evidence in these circumstances, the Group recommended consideration, again on an optional basis, of providing by legislation for the admission of evidence in those circumstances.

The model law includes optional provisions for these investigative powers, and an evidentiary clause for the admission of intercept evidence lawfully gathered in a foreign country.

CLAUSE 24

Expert Group Report

The Group discussed the approach on jurisdiction in relation to the offences in the model legislative provisions.

The Group noted that the Security Council resolution requires, in relation to some obligations, that jurisdiction be extended to nationals.[1] Thus, for those offences, countries need to adopt legislation that allows for prosecution of nationals for those offences, wherever they may have occurred. The Group recognized that the resolution itself does not require specifically that states provide for universal jurisdiction[2] over the relevant offences. However, the Group considered that because of the international nature of terrorism, in particular the global reach of terrorist financing, consideration should be given to establishing universal jurisdiction over the relevant offences. The Group highlighted that this approach was consistent with resolutions 1373 and 1269, both of which require states to deny safe haven to those who carry out terrorist acts.

The Group further highlighted that some of the offences required by SCR 1373 are also contained in the UN counter-terrorism conventions. Most of those conventions obligate countries to either prosecute or extradite persons alleged to have committed the convention offences and mandate countries to provide for jurisdiction over the offences, where extradition is refused. One way to ensure that these obligations can be met is to have universal jurisdiction over the relevant offences such that if the situation requires it, the State will be able to prosecute an offender who cannot be extradited, regardless of the fact that there is no direct connection between the offence or offender and the country in question, aside from his or her presence there. An alternative approach would be to provide for jurisdiction over the offence in instances where extradition is refused. Therefore, while not a strict requirement, the Group recommended that implementing legislation should provide for extraterritorial jurisdiction over the relevant offences on the basis of the universality principle or alternatively allow for jurisdiction in circumstances where the person is not extradited.

Note

As indicated while the extended jurisdiction in the model is not mandated by SCR 1373, countries may wish to consider taking such jurisdiction, particularly in relation to offences also governed by the counter-terrorism conventions which contain a prosecute or extradite obligation.

CLAUSE 26

Expert Group Report

The Group reiterated the need for countries to review and enhance existing mechanisms for the gathering and sharing of information, both domestically and internationally, regarding not only terrorist activities but also related criminal activity, such as that outlined in subparagraph 3(a) of the resolution. Countries need to ensure that, if required, a proper legislative framework is in place to allow for such information exchange.

---

[1] See SCR paragraphs 1(b), and 1(d).

[2] The term 'universal jurisdiction' is used here to denote that a country may assert jurisdiction over an offence on the basis that the person is found in that country, without the requirement for any other nexus between the country and the offence.

Note

Clause 26 in the model is illustrative of the types of provisions that can be made in domestic law to allow for the sharing of information. Countries may wish to substitute other authorities depending on domestic laws and structures. Further, the information sharing provisions will need to be consistent with any applicable privacy and data protection laws.

CLAUSES 27 AND 28

Expert Group Report

Paragraph 3(c) of the resolution relates to the use of bilateral and multilateral instruments for cooperation. The expert group stressed that countries need to ensure that existing laws will permit full implementation of the mutual legal assistance and extradition obligations under the UN counter-terrorism conventions. One way to achieve this objective is through general provisions in extradition and mutual legal assistance laws that defines treaty to include a multilateral treaty, to which that country is party and which contains a provision on mutual assistance or extradition.

CLAUSE 29

Expert Group Report

Under subparagraph 3(g) countries must ensure that claims of political motivation are not recognized as grounds for refusing requests for the extradition of alleged terrorists. Consideration was also given to the obligation to ensure that alleged terrorists cannot rely on the political offence exception as a basis for the refusal of extradition. In so far as this exception is recognized under existing extradition laws, countries need to amend the legislation to ensure that it does not apply to any person accused or convicted of a terrorist offence.

CLAUSES 30 AND 31

Expert Group Report

Various provisions of the resolution require enhanced information gathering and sharing, both domestically and internationally. The obligation under this subparagraph to share information and cooperate in administrative and judicial matters requires powers both to obtain the relevant information and to share it. In establishing such powers, countries need to ensure that a proper balance is struck between the need for information gathering and dissemination and appropriate safeguards for privacy and data protection. Each country will have to consider how best to achieve this balance within the context of its legal system.

The important role that a Financial Intelligence Unit (FIU) can play in gathering information was emphasized. While such units have a general mandate respecting all money laundering matters, they can be particularly useful for the gathering of information relating to the financing of terrorism. The Group recommended that those countries that have yet to establish such a unit take steps to do so and those with existing units ensure that their powers and mandate are sufficient to be effective with respect to the terrorist financing. As well, in terms of distributing information, if the FIU does not have a specific power to share information internationally with other similar bodies, that power should be created.

In addition to information sharing by FIU's, all relevant regulatory agencies should have a similar power to exchange information that may be relevant to combating terrorist financing.

The Group also noted that because of the special nature and concerns surrounding terrorist activities, some countries have chosen to require the disclosure of information regarding terrorist activities or at least with respect to terrorist property and assets. While such an obligation is contrary to the position at common law that generally no individual is required to report an offence that he or she may have witnessed or be aware of, it can be of critical importance in combating the activities of terrorists. For this reason, such a provision is included in the model law, albeit some countries may face legal challenges to it.

684

In summary, the Group was of the view that countries should adopt a series of measures related to information sharing, including effective mutual legal assistance legislation, specific powers that provide for the sharing of information between police, regulatory and other relevant agencies and powers to compel disclosure of information.

CLAUSES 32–35 AND SAMPLE REGULATION UNDER CLAUSE 3

Expert Group Report

Subparagraph 1(c) requires countries to have mechanisms under domestic law that will allow for the freezing of funds and assets related to terrorists and terrorist activities. It was noted that the most critical and challenging aspect of this obligation is the requirement to act expeditiously to freeze assets and funds of persons or entities named by the Security Council. The Group discussed the legal issues surrounding this obligation at some length.

One approach, adopted by several countries to deal with freezing, particularly on the basis of lists, is to pass regulations under legislation that allows for implementation of Security Council resolutions. These regulations provide for the freezing of assets of named individuals and entities and thus freezing action would be available in relation to the lists provided by the Security Council, which can be annexed to or form part of the regulation.

While several countries have used this regulatory approach, there are variations as to the extent and scope of the regulations and whether the regulations are used in addition to a separate legislative scheme. For example, Singapore has adopted extensive regulations to implement the obligations regarding the freezing of assets and other requirements of the resolution. Other countries have passed regulations solely for the freezing of assets and some have adopted the regulations only as an interim measure, pending introduction of legislation allowing for the freezing and confiscation of such assets. Each country will need to decide which approach will be best, given the applicable laws and the legal system context.

Additional approaches to freezing action were identified. Some countries, like Australia, have used the existing powers of their Financial Intelligence Units (FIU) to issue directives to financial institutions, calling for the tracing and freezing of funds of listed persons or entities and prohibiting any dealing with such funds. In other countries, where the existing FIU had no such power, that power has been created through legislation. Canada has amended its laws to place a positive obligation on listed financial and related institutions to determine if they are in possession of any assets or funds of identified persons or entities and report accordingly. This is coupled with an offence for dealing in any manner with such assets or funds. Mauritius proposes under its Bill to extend the existing powers for temporary freezing (90 days), vested in the Commissioner of Police for general proceeds of crime, to terrorist financing. Any subsequent extension of the freezing takes place through court proceedings.

In the case of both Canada and Mauritius a power has been created under domestic law to proscribe or list persons or entities. The effect of this domestic power is that the lists relied upon are adopted on the basis of a decision taken by domestic authorities.

The Group highlighted and discussed the serious problems, constitutional and otherwise, that many Commonwealth countries may face with freezing action that is based solely on a list. It was noted that in the event of a court challenge, while judges may be prepared to give considerable weight to a list provided by the Security Council, ultimately that may not be sufficient, without the production of underlying evidence. Examples were cited of challenges that have already been brought in some jurisdictions. One approach that may facilitate the use of the lists is to provide that where a person or entity is included in the list they are deemed to have been involved in terrorist activity or there is deemed to be reasonable grounds to believe or a prima facie case against them. The freezing action is then based on that deeming provision. Canada used this technique in adopting implementing regulations by providing in section 2 that the persons in the list are persons for whom there are reasonable grounds to believe are involved in terrorist activity.

The problem is even more significant where the list emanates from another country, as the court is even less likely to accept that as a basis for proceeding without underlying evidence to support the suspicion or believe that the person or entity is involved in terrorist activity. Many countries may be unable to obtain the relevant supporting evidence from the country that has submitted the list or the evidence may be protected by national security requirements.

It was also noted that countries which elect to issue directives on the basis of the existing powers of the FIU may face problems if that power is not clearly established by legislation, as happened in one jurisdiction where such action has been successfully challenged.[3] While the decision is currently under appeal, countries need to carefully consider whether such an administrative power will withstand challenge in their jurisdictions and if so, whether a more clear and detailed legislative scheme should be created for this purpose.

The Group concluded that in terms of implementing the obligations with respect to 'listed' persons or entities, each country would have to determine how best to do so, given the constraints and limitations that exist under their domestic laws. However, it was emphasized that whatever path is chosen, countries must have in place a scheme to allow for quick and effective action to be taken with reference to any lists issued by the Security Council. On this point, the Group recommended that countries adopt a regime of regulations under general United Nations Security Council legislation for that purpose. In addition, if possible under domestic law, countries should use existing powers or adopt new legislative powers to allow for the issuance of directives by the FIU's or other similar authorities. If the domestic law will not allow for the use of administrative powers without court approval for the freezing of assets, a country would need to extend existing powers for freezing proceeds of crime or create a new regime to allow for the freezing of funds and assets related to terrorism, as required by the resolution. Provisions for all of these approaches have been included in the model law.

Strictly, SCR 1373 does not require countries to adopt measures for the confiscation of assets or funds that have been frozen. However, the Group recommended that, in addition to any administrative freezing powers adopted, particularly to deal with lists, countries should put in place a full scheme for the freezing and confiscation of assets related to terrorist activities and to persons involved in such activities. It was noted that this was an obligation of the International Convention for the Suppression of the Financing of Terrorism and thus countries would be required to implement those obligations in domestic law in any event. The Group also considered that the freezing of assets indefinitely, without a capacity for confiscation, could result in legal challenges and present significant legal problems.

A sample scheme has been included in the model. However, countries need to consider their existing laws and approaches to restraint and confiscation of proceeds of crime. There are a variety of systems currently employed to freeze and ultimately confiscate proceeds of crime. It is important to ensure that there is some consistency under domestic law as to the process used in relation to proceeds of crime and procedures adopted to freeze and confiscate assets and funds related to the financing of terrorism. At the same time, countries will want to ensure that the procedures adopted in relation to terrorist financing provide for a comprehensive, speedy and effective scheme.

Note

As indicated under Clause 2 above, in addition to the specific provisions on seizing and forfeiting terrorist property, the combination of the listing process in Clause 2 and the offences relating to dealing in property or providing financial services will also operate to allow the effective 'freezing' of terrorist property of those entities identified by the UN Security Council.

---

[3] See *Financial Clearing Corporation v Attorney General* 27, November 2001, Supreme Court of the Bahamas.

CLAUSE 36

Expert Group Report

In respect of the prohibition on making property available, if applicable, countries should consider possible amendments to laws relating to charities or non-profit organizations to ensure that these cannot be abused for terrorist financing.

Note

Clause 36 is illustrative of a scheme that can be employed in the regulation of charities and non-profit organizations to prevent abuse of such entities for the financing of terrorism. The type of scheme implemented would vary considerably depending on the domestic legal structure relating to charities.

CLAUSE 37

Expert Group Report

Subparagraph 2(g) requires that steps be taken to prevent the movement of terrorists

The Group recommended various legislative measures that could be adopted to implement this obligation. These would include providing for the transmission of passenger information from private industry, in particular airline companies, to relevant government authorities and ensuring adequate powers for sharing of information by border control officers. They were of the view that each country would have to adopt an approach that was most appropriate, within the particular context of the country and region and taking into account resource and capacity restrictions. The Group also noted that careful consideration would have to be given to the relationship between these provisions and any applicable privacy/data protection laws and an appropriate balance struck in that regard.

With respect to any legislation allowing for the dissemination of information, particularly information held by private industry, the Group highlighted the need for legislative protections in terms of use limitations, confidentiality and the scope of information available.

Note

Clause 37 again utilizes authorities such as the Commissioner of Immigration and Commissioner of Police to illustrate the appropriate type of authorities for these powers. Each country would need to select the domestic authority most suitable within the legal context and structure.

CLAUSE 38

Expert Group Report

Subparagraph 2(a) requires the denial of safe haven to terrorists. In order to effectively implement this obligation, countries need to carefully review and consider the application and operation of existing laws relating to immigration and extradition, to determine their efficacy in application to those involved in terrorist activity. With respect to immigration, the Group noted that many existing laws provide for the exclusion and removal of persons on the basis of reasonable grounds to believe that they have, are or will be involved in criminal activity. The Group recommended that if existing laws do not allow for exclusion and removal on this basis, amendments should be made to introduce such a provision either limited to terrorist activity or extended to criminal activity generally.

CLAUSE 39

Expert Group Report

SCR 3(f) and (g) require that in conformity with international law and standards countries take steps to prevent the granting of refugee status or abuse of refugee statues by those committing or facilitating the commission of terrorist acts.

There are a number of sensitive and difficult issues in this area, which the Group discussed at some length. As parties to international conventions, many countries have existing obligations with respect refugee claimants. At the same time, countries need to ensure that the refugee process established to implement those obligations is not misused by individuals involved in terrorist activities to obtain safe haven. In both legislative and administrative action in this area it is necessary that countries find an approach that strikes an appropriate balance between the various important interests and obligations involved.

The Group recognized that in some instances, the existing legislative schemes may be sufficient and the main emphasis will be on the administration and implementation of the laws. However, other countries may need to enhance their legislative structure to deal more effectively with individuals involved in terrorist activity, who seek refugee status. The Group considered the approaches adopted in existing and proposed legislation. Of particular note in some legislation was the executive power to preclude consideration of a refugee claim where the authority was of the view that the individual had, is or would be involved in terrorist activity. The Group was of the view that such provisions were necessary because of legitimate concerns for national security and public safety and the need to prevent safe havens. At the same time, the existing powers of judicial review would serve to protect the rights of the individual in such cases.

Note

The provision extends the power of refusal beyond those who have committed or facilitated commission to those who are or may be involved at a future time. It is consistent with the intent of the resolution. It also provides a broader protection for countries. At the same time, the rights of the individual are protected in that there must be reasonable grounds to believe and there will be a right of judicial review flowing from the decision under the general application of law.

APPENDIX 21

Criminal Evidence (Witness Anonymity) Act 2008

CHAPTER 15

CONTENTS

Introduction

1 New rules relating to anonymity of witnesses

Witness anonymity orders

2 Witness anonymity orders
3 Applications
4 Conditions for making order
5 Relevant considerations
6 Discharge or variation of order
7 Warning to jury
8 Special provisions for service courts

Application of provisions etc

9 Proceedings to which new rules apply
10 Pre-commencement anonymity orders: existing proceedings
11 Pre-commencement anonymity orders: appeals

Supplementary

12 Interpretation
13 Commencement
14 Expiry of power to make witness anonymity orders
15 Short title and extent

Criminal Evidence (Witness Anonymity) Act 2008

2008 CHAPTER 15

An Act to make provision for the making of orders for securing the anonymity of witnesses in criminal proceedings. [21st July 2008]

BE IT ENACTED by the Queen's most Excellent Majesty, by and with the advice and consent of the Lords Spiritual and Temporal, and Commons, in this present Parliament assembled, and by the authority of the same, as follows:—

Introduction

1 New rules relating to anonymity of witnesses

(1) This Act provides for the making of witness anonymity orders in relation to witnesses in criminal proceedings.

(2) The common law rules relating to the power of a court to make an order for securing that the identity of a witness in criminal proceedings is withheld from the defendant (or, on a defence application, from other defendants) are abolished.

(3) Nothing in this Act affects the common law rules as to the withholding of information on the grounds of public interest immunity.

Witness anonymity orders

2 Witness anonymity orders

(1) In this Act a 'witness anonymity order' is an order made by a court that requires such specified measures to be taken in relation to a witness in criminal proceedings as the court considers appropriate to ensure that the identity of the witness is not disclosed in or in connection with the proceedings.

(2) The kinds of measures that may be required to be taken in relation to a witness include measures for securing one or more of the following—

    (a) that the witness's name and other identifying details may be—
        (i) withheld;
        (ii) removed from materials disclosed to any party to the proceedings;
    (b) that the witness may use a pseudonym;
    (c) that the witness is not asked questions of any specified description that might lead to the identification of the witness;
    (d) that the witness is screened to any specified extent;
    (e) that the witness's voice is subjected to modulation to any specified extent.

(3) Subsection (2) does not affect the generality of subsection (1).

(4) Nothing in this section authorises the court to require—

    (a) the witness to be screened to such an extent that the witness cannot be seen by—
        (i) the judge or other members of the court (if any);
        (ii) the jury (if there is one); or
        (iii) any interpreter or other person appointed by the court to assist the witness;
    (b) the witness's voice to be modulated to such an extent that the witness's natural voice cannot be heard by any persons within paragraph (a)(i) to (iii).

(5) In this section 'specified' means specified in the witness anonymity order concerned.

3 Applications

(1) An application for a witness anonymity order to be made in relation to a witness in criminal proceedings may be made to the court by the prosecutor or the defendant.

(2) Where an application is made by the prosecutor, the prosecutor—

    (a) must (unless the court directs otherwise) inform the court of the identity of the witness, but

    (b) is not required to disclose in connection with the application—

        (i) the identity of the witness, or

        (ii) any information that might enable the witness to be identified,

    to any other party to the proceedings or his or her legal representatives.

(3) Where an application is made by the defendant, the defendant—

    (a) must inform the court and the prosecutor of the identity of the witness, but

    (b) (if there is more than one defendant) is not required to disclose in connection with the application—

        (i) the identity of the witness, or

        (ii) any information that might enable the witness to be identified,

    to any other defendant or his or her legal representatives.

(4) Accordingly, where the prosecutor or the defendant proposes to make an application under this section in respect of a witness, any relevant material which is disclosed by or on behalf of that party before the determination of the application may be disclosed in such a way as to prevent—

    (a) the identity of the witness, or

    (b) any information that might enable the witness to be identified,

    from being disclosed except as required by subsection (2)(a) or (3)(a).

(5) 'Relevant material' means any document or other material which falls to be disclosed, or is sought to be relied on, by or on behalf of the party concerned in connection with the proceedings or proceedings preliminary to them.

(6) The court must give every party to the proceedings the opportunity to be heard on an application under this section.

(7) But subsection (6) does not prevent the court from hearing one or more parties in the absence of a defendant and his or her legal representatives, if it appears to the court to be appropriate to do so in the circumstances of the case.

(8) Nothing in this section is to be taken as restricting any power to make rules of court.

4 Conditions for making order

(1) This section applies where an application is made for a witness anonymity order to be made in relation to a witness in criminal proceedings.

(2) The court may make such an order only if it is satisfied that Conditions A to C below are met.

(3) Condition A is that the measures to be specified in the order are necessary—

    (a) in order to protect the safety of the witness or another person or to prevent any serious damage to property, or

    (b) in order to prevent real harm to the public interest (whether affecting the carrying on of any activities in the public interest or the safety of a person involved in carrying on such activities, or otherwise).

(4) Condition B is that, having regard to all the circumstances, the taking of those measures would be consistent with the defendant receiving a fair trial.

(5) Condition C is that it is necessary to make the order in the interests of justice by reason of the fact that it appears to the court that—

  (a) it is important that the witness should testify, and

  (b) the witness would not testify if the order were not made.

(6) In determining whether the measures to be specified in the order are necessary for the purpose mentioned in subsection (3)(a), the court must have regard (in particular) to any reasonable fear on the part of the witness—

  (a) that the witness or another person would suffer death or injury, or

  (b) that there would be serious damage to property,

  if the witness were to be identified.

5 Relevant considerations

(1) When deciding whether Conditions A to C in section 4 are met in the case of an application for a witness anonymity order, the court must have regard to—

  (a) the considerations mentioned in subsection (2) below, and

  (b) such other matters as the court considers relevant.

(2) The considerations are—

  (a) the general right of a defendant in criminal proceedings to know the identity of a witness in the proceedings;

  (b) the extent to which the credibility of the witness concerned would be a relevant factor when the weight of his or her evidence comes to be assessed;

  (c) whether evidence given by the witness might be the sole or decisive evidence implicating the defendant;

  (d) whether the witness's evidence could be properly tested (whether on grounds of credibility or otherwise) without his or her identity being disclosed;

  (e) whether there is any reason to believe that the witness—

    (i) has a tendency to be dishonest, or

    (ii) has any motive to be dishonest in the circumstances of the case,

    having regard (in particular) to any previous convictions of the witness and to any relationship between the witness and the defendant or any associates of the defendant;

  (f) whether it would be reasonably practicable to protect the witness's identity by any means other than by making a witness anonymity order specifying the measures that are under consideration by the court.

6 Discharge or variation of order

(1) A court that has made a witness anonymity order in relation to any criminal proceedings may subsequently discharge or vary (or further vary) the order if it appears to the court to be appropriate to do so in view of the provisions of sections 4 and 5 that applied to the making of the order.

(2) The court may do so—

  (a) on an application made by a party to the proceedings if there has been a material change of circumstances since the relevant time, or

  (b) on its own initiative.

(3) 'The relevant time' means—

    (a) the time when the order was made, or

    (b) if a previous application has been made under subsection (2), the time when the application (or the last application) was made.

7 Warning to jury

(1) Subsection (2) applies where, on a trial on indictment with a jury, any evidence has been given by a witness at a time when a witness anonymity order applied to the witness.

(2) The judge must give the jury such warning as the judge considers appropriate to ensure that the fact that the order was made in relation to the witness does not prejudice the defendant.

8 Special provisions for service courts

(1) Subsections (2) and (3) apply in relation to criminal proceedings before a service court consisting of a judge advocate and other members.

(2) Any decision falling to be made by the court in such proceedings under sections 2 to 6 is to be made by the judge advocate alone.

(3) If any evidence is given by a witness in such proceedings at a time when a witness anonymity order applies to the witness, the judge advocate must give the other members such warning as the judge advocate considers appropriate to ensure that the fact that the order was made in relation to the witness does not prejudice the defendant.

(4) Each of the provisions mentioned in subsection (5) has effect with the modification set out in that subsection in a case where—

   (a) a witness anonymity order is made by a service court to which that provision applies, and
   (b) a person does anything in relation to the order which would, if the court had been a court of law having power to commit for contempt, have been contempt of that court.

(5) In such a case—

   (a) section 101(1) of the Army Act 1955 (3 & 4 Eliz 2 c 18) has effect with the omission of the words 'not subject to military law';
   (b) section 101(1) of the Air Force Act 1955 (3 & 4 Eliz 2 c 19) has effect with the omission of the words 'not subject to air-force law'; and
   (c) section 65(1) of the Naval Discipline Act 1957 (c 53) has effect with the omission of the words 'not subject to this Act'.

Application of provisions etc.

9 Proceedings to which new rules apply

(1) Sections 2 to 8 apply to criminal proceedings in cases where—

   (a) the trial or hearing begins on or after the day on which this Act is passed, or
   (b) the trial or hearing has begun, but has not ended, before that day.

(2) Section 10 applies to certain proceedings falling within subsection (1)(b).

10 Pre-commencement anonymity orders: existing proceedings

(1) This section has effect in relation to criminal proceedings in cases where—

   (a) the trial or hearing has begun, but has not ended, before commencement, and
   (b) the court has made a pre-commencement anonymity order in relation to a witness at the trial or hearing.

(2) Subsection (3) applies if the witness has not begun to give evidence under the terms of that order before commencement.

(3) In such a case the court—

   (a) must consider whether that order was one that the court could have made if this Act had been in force at the material time,
   (b) if it considers that that order was one that it could have made in those circumstances, may direct that the order is to remain in place, and
   (c) otherwise, must discharge the order and consider whether instead it should make a witness anonymity order in relation to the witness in accordance with sections 2 to 5.

(4) Any witness anonymity order made by virtue of subsection (3)(c) must be made so as to come into effect immediately on the discharge of the precommencement anonymity order.

(5) Subsections (6) and (7) apply if the witness began before commencement to give evidence under the terms of the order mentioned in subsection (1)(b) (whether or not he or she has finished doing so).

(6) In such a case the court must consider whether the effect of that order is that the defendant has been prevented from receiving a fair trial, having regard (in particular) to—

(a) whether the order was one that the court could have made if this Act had been in force at the material time, and

(b) whether the court should exercise any power to give a direction to the jury (if there is one) regarding the evidence given under the terms of the order.

(7) If the court determines that the defendant has been prevented from receiving a fair trial, it must give such directions as it considers appropriate for and in connection with bringing the trial or hearing to a conclusion.

(8) In this section—

'commencement' means the day on which this Act is passed;
'pre-commencement anonymity order' means an order made before commencement that falls within section 1(2).

11 Pre-commencement anonymity orders: appeals

(1) This section applies where—

(a) an appeal court is considering an appeal against a conviction in criminal proceedings in a case where the trial ended before commencement, and

(b) the court from which the appeal lies ('the trial court') made a pre-commencement anonymity order in relation to a witness at the trial.

(2) The appeal court—

(a) may not treat the conviction as unsafe solely on the ground that the trial court had no power at common law to make the order mentioned in subsection (1)(b), but

(b) must treat the conviction as unsafe if it considers—

(i) that the order was not one that the trial court could have made if this Act had been in force at the material time, and

(ii) that, as a result of the order, the defendant did not receive a fair trial.

(3) In this section—

'appeal court' means—
(a) the Court of Appeal;
(b) the Court of Appeal in Northern Ireland; or
(c) the Courts-Martial Appeal Court or the Court Martial Appeal Court;
'commencement' and 'pre-commencement anonymity order' have the meanings given by section 10(8).

Supplementary

12 Interpretation

(1) In this Act—

'court' means—
(a) in relation to England and Wales, a magistrates' court, the Crown Court or the criminal division of the Court of Appeal;
(b) in relation to Northern Ireland, a magistrates' court, the Crown Court, a county court exercising its criminal jurisdiction or the Court of Appeal in Northern Ireland; or
(c) a service court;

'criminal proceedings' means—

    (a) in relation to a court within paragraph (a) or (b) above, criminal proceedings consisting of a trial or other hearing at which evidence falls to be given;

    (b) in relation to a service court, proceedings in respect of a service offence consisting of a trial or other hearing at which evidence falls to be given;

'the defendant', in relation to any criminal proceedings, means any person charged with an offence to which the proceedings relate (whether or not convicted);

'prosecutor' means an individual or body charged with duties to conduct criminal prosecutions;

'service court' has the meaning given by subsection (2);

'service offence' has the meaning given by subsection (3);

'witness', in relation to any criminal proceedings, means any person called, or proposed to be called, to give evidence at the trial or hearing in question;

'witness anonymity order' has the meaning given by section 2.

(2) In this Act 'service court' means—

    (a) a court-martial constituted under the Army Act 1955 (3 & 4 Eliz 2 c 18), the Air Force Act 1955 (3 & 4 Eliz 2 c 19) or the Naval Discipline Act 1957 (c 53) or the Court Martial established by the Armed Forces Act 2006 (c 52);

    (b) the Summary Appeal Court established by any of those Acts;

    (c) a Standing Civilian Court established under the Armed Forces Act 1976 (c 52) or the Service Civilian Court established by the Armed Forces Act 2006; or

    (d) the Courts-Martial Appeal Court or the Court Martial Appeal Court.

(3) In this Act 'service offence' means—

    (a) any offence against any provision of Part 2 of the Army Act 1955, Part 2 of the Air Force Act 1955 or Part 1 of the Naval Discipline Act 1957; or

    (b) any offence under Part 1 of the Armed Forces Act 2006.

13 Commencement

This Act comes into force on the day on which it is passed.

14 Expiry of power to make witness anonymity orders

(1) No witness anonymity order may be made under this Act after the relevant date.

(2) Subject to subsection (3), the relevant date is 31 December 2009.

(3) The Secretary of State may by order provide for the relevant date to be a date specified in the order that falls not more than 12 months after—

    (a) 31 December 2009, or

    (b) (if an order has already been made under this subsection) the date specified in the last order.

(4) Nothing in this section affects—

    (a) the continuation in effect of a witness anonymity order made before the relevant date, or

    (b) the power to discharge or vary such an order under section 6.

(5) An order under subsection (3)—

    (a) is to be made by statutory instrument; and

    (b) may not be made unless a draft of the instrument containing the order has been laid before and approved by a resolution of each House of Parliament.

15 Short title and extent

(1) This Act may be cited as the Criminal Evidence (Witness Anonymity) Act 2008.

(2) Subject to subsection (3), this Act extends to England and Wales and Northern Ireland.

(3) The service courts provisions of this Act extend to England and Wales, Scotland and Northern Ireland; and in section 384 of the Armed Forces Act 2006 (c 52) (extent to Channel Islands etc) any reference to that Act includes a reference to the service courts provisions of this Act.

(4) In subsection (3) 'the service courts provisions of this Act' means the provisions of this Act so far as having effect in relation to service courts.

Police & Criminal Evidence Act 1984 (PACE)

CODE H

Code of practice in connection with the detention, treatment and questioning by police officers of persons under section 41 of, and Schedule 8 to, the Terrorism Act 2000

COMMENCEMENT—TRANSITIONAL ARRANGEMENTS

This Code applies to people in police detention following their arrest under section 41 of the Terrorism Act 2000, after midnight (on 24 July 2006), notwithstanding that they may have been arrested before that time.

1. General

1.1 Terrorism Act 2000 (TACT) and detained in police custody under those provisions and Schedule 8 of the Act. References to detention under this provision that were previously included in PACE Code C—Code for the Detention, Treatment, and Questioning of Persons by Police Officers, no longer apply.

1.2 The Code ceases to apply at any point that a detainee is:

    (a) charged with an offence
    (b) released without charge, or
    (c) transferred to a prison see *section 14.5.*

1.3 References to an offence in this Code include being concerned in the commission, preparation or instigation of acts of terrorism.

1.4 This Code's provisions do not apply to detention of individuals under any other terrorism legislation. This Code does not apply to people:

    (i) detained under section 5(1) of the Prevention of Terrorism Act 2005.
    (ii) detained for examination under TACT Schedule 7 and to whom the Code of Practice issued under that Act, Schedule 14, paragraph 6 applies;
    (iii) detained for searches under stop and search powers.

The provisions for the detention, treatment and questioning by police officers of persons other than those in police detention following arrest under section 41 of TACT, are set out in Code C issued under section 66(1) of the Police & Criminal Evidence Act (PACE)1984 (PACE Code C).

1.5 All persons in custody must be dealt with expeditiously, and released as soon as the need for detention no longer applies.

1.6 There is no provision for bail under TACT prior to charge.

1.7 An officer must perform the assigned duties in this Code as soon as practicable. An officer will not be in breach of this Code if delay is justifiable and reasonable steps are taken to prevent unnecessary delay. The custody record shall show when a delay has occurred and the reason. See *Note 1H*.

1.8 This Code of Practice must be readily available at all police stations for consultation by:

- police officers
- police staff
- detained persons
- members of the public.

1.9 The provisions of this Code:

- include the *Annexes*
- do not include the *Notes for Guidance*.

1.10 If an officer has any suspicion, or is told in good faith, that a person of any age may be mentally disordered or otherwise mentally vulnerable, in the absence of clear evidence to dispel that suspicion, the person shall be treated as such for the purposes of this Code. See *Note 1G*.

1.11 For the purposes of this Code, a juvenile is any person under the age of 17. If anyone appears to be under 17, and there is no clear evidence that they are 17 or over, they shall be treated as a juvenile for the purposes of this Code.

1.12 If a person appears to be blind, seriously visually impaired, deaf, unable to read or speak or has difficulty orally because of a speech impediment, they shall be treated as such for the purposes of this Code in the absence of clear evidence to the contrary.

1.13 'The appropriate adult' means, in the case of a:

    (a) juvenile:
        (i) the parent, guardian or, if the juvenile is in local authority or voluntary organisation care, or is otherwise being looked after under the Children Act 1989, a person representing that authority or organisation;
        (ii) a social worker of a local authority social services department;
        (iii) failing these, some other responsible adult aged 18 or over who is not a police officer or employed by the police.
    (b) person who is mentally disordered or mentally vulnerable: See *Note 1D*.
        (i) a relative, guardian or other person responsible for their care or custody;
        (ii) someone experienced in dealing with mentally disordered or mentally vulnerable people but who is not a police officer or employed by the police;
        (iii) failing these, some other responsible adult aged 18 or over who is not a police officer or employed by the police.

1.14 If this Code requires a person be given certain information, they do not have to be given it if at the time they are incapable of understanding what is said, are violent or may become violent or in urgent need of medical attention, but they must be given it as soon as practicable.

1.15 References to a custody officer include any:

- police officer; or
- designated staff custody officer acting in the exercise or performance of the powers and duties conferred or imposed on them by their designation, performing the functions of a custody officer. See *Note 1J*.

1.16 When this Code requires the prior authority or agreement of an officer of at least inspector or superintendent rank, that authority may be given by a sergeant or chief inspector authorised by section 107 of PACE to perform the functions of the higher rank under TACT.

1.17 In this Code:

(a) 'designated person' means a person other than a police officer, designated under the Police Reform Act 2002, Part 4 who has specified powers and duties of police officers conferred or imposed on them;

(b) reference to a police officer includes a designated person acting in the exercise or performance of the powers and duties conferred or imposed on them by their designation.

1.18 Designated persons are entitled to use reasonable force as follows:

(a) when exercising a power conferred on them which allows a police officer exercising that power to use reasonable force, a designated person has the same entitlement to use force; and

(b) at other times when carrying out duties conferred or imposed on them that also entitle them to use reasonable force, for example:

- when at a police station carrying out the duty to keep detainees for whom they are responsible under control and to assist any other police officer or designated person to keep any detainee under control and to prevent their escape.
- when securing, or assisting any other police officer or designated person in securing, the detention of a person at a police station.
- when escorting, or assisting any other police officer or designated person in escorting, a detainee within a police station.
- for the purpose of saving life or limb; or
- preventing serious damage to property.

1.19 Nothing in this Code prevents the custody officer, or other officer given custody of the detainee, from allowing police staff who are not designated persons to carry out individual procedures or tasks at the police station if the law allows. However, the officer remains responsible for making sure the procedures and tasks are carried out correctly in accordance with the Codes of Practice. Any such person must be:

(a) a person employed by a police authority maintaining a police force and under the control and direction of the Chief Officer of that force;

(b) employed by a person with whom a police authority has a contract for the provision of services relating to persons arrested or otherwise in custody.

1.20 Designated persons and other police staff must have regard to any relevant provisions of this Code.

1.21 References to pocket books include any official report book issued to police officers or other police staff.

Notes for guidance

1A Although certain sections of this Code apply specifically to people in custody at police stations, those there voluntarily to assist with an investigation should be treated with no less consideration, eg offered refreshments at appropriate times, and enjoy an absolute right to obtain legal advice or communicate with anyone outside the police station.

1B A person, including a parent or guardian, should not be an appropriate adult if they:

- *are*
  - *suspected of involvement in the offence or involvement in the commission, preparation or instigation of acts of terrorism*
  - *the victim*
  - *a witness*
  - *involved in the investigation*
- *received admissions prior to attending to act as the appropriate adult.*

Note: If a juvenile's parent is estranged from the juvenile, they should not be asked to act as the appropriate adult if the juvenile expressly and specifically objects to their presence.

1C If a juvenile admits an offence to, or in the presence of, a social worker or member of a youth offending team other than during the time that person is acting as the juvenile's appropriate adult, another appropriate adult should be appointed in the interest of fairness.

1D In the case of people who are mentally disordered or otherwise mentally vulnerable, it may be more satisfactory if the appropriate adult is someone experienced or trained in their care rather than a relative lacking such qualifications. But if the detainee prefers a relative to a better qualified stranger or objects to a particular person their wishes should, if practicable, be respected.

1E A detainee should always be given an opportunity, when an appropriate adult is called to the police station, to consult privately with a solicitor in the appropriate adult's absence if they want. An appropriate adult is not subject to legal privilege.

1F A solicitor or independent custody visitor (formerly a lay visitor) present at the police station in that capacity may not be the appropriate adult.

1G 'Mentally vulnerable' applies to any detainee who, because of their mental state or capacity, may not understand the significance of what is said, of questions or of their replies. 'Mental disorder' is defined in the Mental Health Act 1983, section 1(2) as 'mental illness, arrested or incomplete development of mind, psychopathic disorder and any other disorder or disability of mind'. When the custody officer has any doubt about the mental state or capacity of a detainee, that detainee should be treated as mentally vulnerable and an appropriate adult called.

1H Paragraph 1.7 is intended to cover delays which may occur in processing detainees eg if:

- *a large number of suspects are brought into the station simultaneously to be placed in custody;*
- *interview rooms are all being used;*
- *there are difficulties contacting an appropriate adult, solicitor or interpreter.*

1I The custody officer must remind the appropriate adult and detainee about the right to legal advice and record any reasons for waiving it in accordance with section 6.

1J The designation of police staff custody officers applies only in police areas where an order commencing the provisions of the Police Reform Act 2002, section 38 and Schedule 4A, for designating police staff custody officers is in effect.

1K This Code does not affect the principle that all citizens have a duty to help police officers to prevent crime and discover offenders. This is a civic rather than a legal duty; but when a police officer is trying to discover whether, or by whom, an offence has been committed he is entitled to question any person from whom he thinks useful information can be obtained, subject to the restrictions imposed by this Code. A person's declaration that he is unwilling to reply does not alter this entitlement.

1L If a person is moved from a police station to receive medical treatment, or for any other reason, the period of detention is still calculated from the time of arrest under section 41 of TACT (or, if a person was being detained under TACT Schedule 7 when arrested, from the time at which the examination under Schedule 7 began).

1M Under Paragraph 1 of Schedule 8 to TACT, all police stations are designated for detention of persons arrested under section 41 of TACT. Paragraph 4 of Schedule 8 requires that the constable who arrests a person under section 41 takes him as soon as practicable to the police station which he considers is 'most appropriate'.

2. Custody records

2.1 When a person is brought to a police station:

- under TACT section 41 arrest, or
- is arrested under TACT section 41 at the police station having attended there voluntarily,

they should be brought before the custody officer as soon as practicable after their arrival at the station or, if appropriate, following arrest after attending the police station voluntarily *see Note 3H*. A person is deemed to be 'at a police station' for these purposes if they are within the boundary of any building or enclosed yard which forms part of that police station.

2.2 A separate custody record must be opened as soon as practicable for each person brought to a police station under arrest or arrested at the station having gone there voluntarily. All information recorded under this Code must be recorded as soon as practicable in the custody record unless otherwise specified. Any audio or video recording made in the custody area is not part of the custody record.

2.3 If any action requires the authority of an officer of a specified rank, this must be noted in the custody record, subject to paragraph 2.8.

2.4 The custody officer is responsible for the custody record's accuracy and completeness and for making sure the record or copy of the record accompanies a detainee if they are transferred to another police station. The record shall show the:

- time and reason for transfer;
- time a person is released from detention.

2.5 A solicitor or appropriate adult must be permitted to consult a detainee's custody record as soon as practicable after their arrival at the station and at any other time whilst the person is detained. Arrangements for this access must be agreed with the custody officer and may not unreasonably interfere with the custody officer's duties or the justifiable needs of the investigation.

2.6 When a detainee leaves police detention or is taken before a court they, their legal representative or appropriate adult shall be given, on request, a copy of the custody record as soon as practicable. This entitlement lasts for 12 months after release.

2.7 The detainee, appropriate adult or legal representative shall be permitted to inspect the original custody record once the detained person is no longer held under the provisions of TACT section 41 and Schedule 8, provided they give reasonable notice of their request. Any such inspection shall be noted in the custody record.

2.8 All entries in custody records must be timed and identified by the maker. Nothing in this Code requires the identity of officers or other police staff to be recorded or disclosed in the case of enquiries linked to the investigation of terrorism. In these cases, they shall use their warrant or other identification numbers and the name of their police station *see Note 2A*. If records are entered on computer these shall also be timed and contain the operator's identification.

2.9 The fact and time of any detainee's refusal to sign a custody record, when asked in accordance with this Code, must be recorded.

Note for guidance

2A The purpose of paragraph 2.8 is to protect those involved in terrorist investigations or arrests of terrorist suspects from the possibility that those arrested, their associates or other individuals or groups may threaten or cause harm to those involved.

3. Initial action

(a) Detained persons—normal procedure

3.1 When a person is brought to a police station under arrest or arrested at the station having gone there voluntarily, the custody officer must make sure the person is told clearly about the following continuing rights which may be exercised at any stage during the period in custody:

(i) the right to have someone informed of their arrest as in *section 5*;
(ii) the right to consult privately with a solicitor and that free independent legal advice is available;
(iii) the right to consult this Code of Practice. See *Note 3D*

3.2 The detainee must also be given:

- a written notice setting out:
  — the above three rights;
  — the arrangements for obtaining legal advice;
  — the right to a copy of the custody record as in *paragraph 2.6;*
  — the caution in the terms prescribed in *section 10.*
- an additional written notice briefly setting out their entitlements while in custody, see *Notes 3A* and *3B.*

Note: The detainee shall be asked to sign the custody record to acknowledge receipt of these notices. Any refusal must be recorded on the custody record.

3.3 A citizen of an independent Commonwealth country or a national of a foreign country, including the Republic of Ireland, must be informed as soon as practicable about their rights of communication with their High Commission, Embassy or Consulate. See *section 7.*

3.4 The custody officer shall:

- record that the person was arrested under section 41 of TACT and the reason(s) for the arrest on the custody record. See *paragraph 10.2 and Note for Guidance 3G.*
- note on the custody record any comment the detainee makes in relation to the arresting officer's account but shall not invite comment. If the arresting officer is not physically present when the detainee is brought to a police station, the arresting officer's account must be made available to the custody officer remotely or by a third party on the arresting officer's behalf;
- note any comment the detainee makes in respect of the decision to detain them but shall not invite comment;
- not put specific questions to the detainee regarding their involvement in any offence, nor in respect of any comments they may make in response to the arresting officer's account or the decision to place them in detention *See paragraphs 14.1* and *14.2* and *Notes for Guidance 3H, 14A* and *14B.* Such an exchange is likely to constitute an interview as in *paragraph 11.1* and require the associated safeguards in *section 11.*

See *paragraph 5.9 of the Code of Practice issued under TACT Schedule 8 Paragraph 3* in respect of unsolicited comments.

If the first review of detention is carried out at this time, see paragraphs 14.1 and 14.2, and Part II of Schedule 8 to the Terrorism Act 2000 in respect of action by the review officer.

3.5 The custody officer shall:

- (a) ask the detainee, whether at this time, they:
  - (vii) would like legal advice, see *section 6;*
  - (viii) want someone informed of their detention, see *section 5*
- (b) ask the detainee to sign the custody record to confirm their decisions in respect of (*a*);
- (c) determine whether the detainee:
  - (i)   is, or might be, in need of medical treatment or attention, see *section 9;*
  - (ii) requires:
    - an appropriate adult;
    - help to check documentation;
    - an interpreter;
- (d) record the decision in respect of (*c*).

3.6 When determining these needs the custody officer is responsible for initiating an assessment to consider whether the detainee is likely to present specific risks to custody staff, any individual who may have contact with detainee (eg, legal advisers, medical staff), or themselves. Such assessments should always include a check on the Police National Computer, to be carried out as soon as practicable, to identify any risks highlighted in relation to the detainee. Although such assessments are primarily the custody officer's responsibility, it will be necessary to obtain information from other sources, especially the investigation team *See Note 3E*, the arresting officer or an appropriate health care professional, see *paragraph 9.15*. Reasons for delaying the initiation or completion of the assessment must be recorded.

3.7 Chief Officers should ensure that arrangements for proper and effective risk assessments required by *paragraph 3.6* are implemented in respect of all detainees at police stations in their area.

3.8 Risk assessments must follow a structured process which clearly defines the categories of risk to be considered and the results must be incorporated in the detainee's custody record. The custody officer is responsible for making sure those responsible for the detainee's custody are appropriately briefed about the risks. The content of any risk assessment and any analysis of the level of risk relating to the person's detention is not required to be shown or provided to the detainee or any person acting on behalf of the detainee. If no specific risks are identified by the assessment, that should be noted in the custody record. See *Note 3F* and *paragraph 9.15*.

3.9 Custody officers are responsible for implementing the response to any specific risk assessment, which should include for example:

- reducing opportunities for self harm;
- calling a health care professional;
- increasing levels of monitoring or observation;
- reducing the risk to those who come into contact with the detainee. *See Note for Guidance 3F*.

3.10 Risk assessment is an ongoing process and assessments must always be subject to review if circumstances change.

3.11 If video cameras are installed in the custody area, notices shall be prominently displayed showing cameras are in use. Any request to have video cameras switched off shall be refused.

3.12 A constable, prison officer or other person authorised by the Secretary of State may take any steps which are reasonably necessary for:

(a) photographing the detained person
(b) measuring him, or
(c) identifying him.

3.13 Paragraph 3.12 concerns the power in TACT Schedule 8 Paragraph 2. The power in TACT Schedule 8 Paragraph 2 does not cover the taking of fingerprints, intimate samples or non-intimate samples, which is covered in TACT Schedule 8 paragraphs 10–15.

(b) Detained persons—special groups

3.14 If the detainee appears deaf or there is doubt about their hearing or speaking ability or ability to understand English, and the custody officer cannot establish effective communication, the custody officer must, as soon as practicable, call an interpreter for assistance in the action under *paragraphs 3.1–3.5*. See *section 13*.

3.15 If the detainee is a juvenile, the custody officer must, if it is practicable, ascertain the identity of a person responsible for their welfare. That person:

- may be:
  — the parent or guardian;
  — if the juvenile is in local authority or voluntary organisation care, or is otherwise being looked after under the Children Act 1989, a person appointed by that authority or organisation to have responsibility for the juvenile's welfare;
  — any other person who has, for the time being, assumed responsibility for the juvenile's welfare.

- must be informed as soon as practicable that the juvenile has been arrested, why they have been arrested and where they are detained. This right is in addition to the juvenile's right in *section 5* not to be held incommunicado. See *Note 3C*.

3.16 If a juvenile is known to be subject to a court order under which a person or organisation is given any degree of statutory responsibility to supervise or otherwise monitor them, reasonable steps must also be taken to notify that person or organisation (the 'responsible officer'). The responsible officer will normally be a member of a Youth Offending Team, except for a curfew order which involves electronic monitoring when the contractor providing the monitoring will normally be the responsible officer.

3.17 If the detainee is a juvenile, mentally disordered or otherwise mentally vulnerable, the custody officer must, as soon as practicable:

- inform the appropriate adult, who in the case of a juvenile may or may not be a person responsible for their welfare, as in *paragraph 3.15,* of:
  — the grounds for their detention;
  — their whereabouts.
- ask the adult to come to the police station to see the detainee.

3.18 If the appropriate adult is:

- already at the police station, the provisions of *paragraphs 3.1* to *3.5* must be complied with in the appropriate adult's presence;
- not at the station when these provisions are complied with, they must be complied with again in the presence of the appropriate adult when they arrive.

3.19 The detainee shall be advised that:

- the duties of the appropriate adult include giving advice and assistance;
- they can consult privately with the appropriate adult at any time.

3.20 If the detainee, or appropriate adult on the detainee's behalf, asks for a solicitor to be called to give legal advice, the provisions of *section 6* apply.

3.21 If the detainee is blind, seriously visually impaired or unable to read, the custody officer shall make sure their solicitor, relative, appropriate adult or some other person likely to take an interest in them and not involved in the investigation is available to help check any documentation. When this Code requires written consent or signing the person assisting may be asked to sign instead, if the detainee prefers. This paragraph does not require an appropriate adult to be called solely to assist in checking and signing documentation for a person who is not a juvenile, or mentally disordered or otherwise mentally vulnerable (see *paragraph 3.17*).

(c) **Documentation**

3.22 The grounds for a person's detention shall be recorded, in the person's presence if practicable.

3.23 Action taken under *paragraphs 3.14* to *3.22* shall be recorded.

Notes for guidance

3A The notice of entitlements should:

- *list the entitlements in this Code, including:*
  — *visits and contact with outside parties where practicable, including special provisions for Commonwealth citizens and foreign nationals;*
  — *reasonable standards of physical comfort;*
  — *adequate food and drink;*
  — *access to toilets and washing facilities, clothing, medical attention, and exercise when practicable.*

- *mention the:*
    - *— provisions relating to the conduct of interviews;*
    - *— circumstances in which an appropriate adult should be available to assist the detainee and their statutory rights to make representation whenever the period of their detention is reviewed.*

3B In addition to notices in English, translations should be available in Welsh, the main minority ethnic languages and the principal European languages whenever they are likely to be helpful. Audio versions of the notice should also be made available.

3C If the juvenile is in local authority or voluntary organisation care but living with their parents or other adults responsible for their welfare, although there is no legal obligation to inform them, they should normally be contacted, as well as the authority or organisation unless suspected of involvement in the offence concerned. Even if the juvenile is not living with their parents, consideration should be given to informing them.

3D The right to consult this or other relevant Codes of Practice does not entitle the person concerned to delay unreasonably any necessary investigative or administrative action whilst they do so. Examples of action which need not be delayed unreasonably include:

- *searching detainees at the police station;*
- *taking fingerprints or non-intimate samples without consent for evidential purposes.*

3E The investigation team will include any officer involved in questioning a suspect, gathering or analysing evidence in relation to the offences of which the detainee is suspected of having committed. Should a custody officer require information from the investigation team, the first point of contact should be the officer in charge of the investigation.

3F Home Office Circular 32/2000 provides more detailed guidance on risk assessments and identifies key risk areas which should always be considered. This should be read with the Guidance on Safer Detention & Handling of Persons in Police Custody issued by the National Centre for Policing Excellence in conjunction with the Home Office and Association of Chief Police Officers.

3G Arrests under TACT section 41 can only be made where an officer has reasonable grounds to suspect that the individual concerned is a 'terrorist'. This differs from the PACE power of arrest in that it need not be linked to a specific offence. There may also be circumstances where an arrest under TACT is made on the grounds of sensitive information which can not be disclosed. In such circumstances, the grounds for arrest may be given in terms of the interpretation of a 'terrorist' set out in TACT sections 40(1)(a) or 40(1)(b).

3H For the purpose of arrests under TACT section 41, the review officer is responsible for authorising detention (see Paragraphs 14.1 and 14.2, and Notes for Guidance 14A and 14B). The review officer's role is explained in TACT Schedule 8 Part II. A person may be detained after arrest pending the first review, which must take place as soon as practicable after the person's arrest.

4 Detainee's property

(a) Action

4.1 The custody officer is responsible for:

- (a) ascertaining what property a detainee:
    - (i) has with them when they come to the police station, either on first arrival at the police station or any subsequent arrivals at a police station in connection with that detention.
    - (ii) might have acquired for an unlawful or harmful purpose while in custody;
- (b) the safekeeping of any property taken from a detainee which remains at the police station.

The custody officer may search the detainee or authorise their being searched to the extent they consider necessary, provided a search of intimate parts of the body or involving the removal of more than outer clothing is only made as in *Annex A*. A search may only be carried out by an officer of the same sex as the detainee. See *Note 4A*.

4.2 Detainees may retain clothing and personal effects at their own risk unless the custody officer considers they may use them to cause harm to themselves or others, interfere with evidence, damage property, effect an escape or they are needed as evidence. In this event the custody officer may withhold such articles as they consider necessary and must tell the detainee why.

4.3 Personal effects are those items a detainee may lawfully need, use or refer to while in detention but do not include cash and other items of value.

(b) Documentation

4.4 It is a matter for the custody officer to determine whether a record should be made of the property a detained person has with him or had taken from him on arrest (see *Note for Guidance 4D*). Any record made is not required to be kept as part of the custody record but the custody record should be noted as to where such a record exists. Whenever a record is made the detainee shall be allowed to check and sign the record of property as correct. Any refusal to sign shall be recorded.

4.5 If a detainee is not allowed to keep any article of clothing or personal effects, the reason must be recorded.

Notes for guidance

4A PACE, Section 54(1) and paragraph 4.1 require a detainee to be searched when it is clear the custody officer will have continuing duties in relation to that detainee or when that detainee's behaviour or offence makes an inventory appropriate. They do not require every detainee to be searched, eg if it is clear a person will only be detained for a short period and is not to be placed in a cell, the custody officer may decide not to search them. In such a case the custody record will be endorsed 'not searched', paragraph 4.4 will not apply, and the detainee will be invited to sign the entry. If the detainee refuses, the custody officer will be obliged to ascertain what property they have in accordance with paragraph 4.1.

4B Paragraph 4.4 does not require the custody officer to record on the custody record property in the detainee's possession on arrest if, by virtue of its nature, quantity or size, it is not practicable to remove it to the police station.

4C Paragraph 4.4 does not require items of clothing worn by the person be recorded unless withheld by the custody officer as in paragraph 4.2.

4D Section 43(2) of TACT allows a constable to search a person who has been arrested under section 41 to discover whether he has anything in his possession that may constitute evidence that he is a terrorist.

5 Right not to be held incommunicado

(a) Action

5.1 Any person arrested and held in custody at a police station or other premises may, on request, have one named person who is a friend, relative or a person known to them who is likely to take an interest in their welfare informed at public expense of their whereabouts as soon as practicable. If the person cannot be contacted the detainee may choose up to two alternatives. If they cannot be contacted, the person in charge of detention or the investigation has discretion to allow further attempts until the information has been conveyed. See *Notes 5D* and *5E*.

5.2 The exercise of the above right in respect of each person nominated may be delayed only in accordance with *Annex B*.

5.3 The above right may be exercised each time a detainee is taken to another police station or returned to a police station having been previously transferred to prison. This Code does not afford such a right to a person on transfer to a prison, where a detainee's rights will be governed by Prison Rules *see paragraph 14.8*.

5.4 If the detainee agrees, they may receive visits from friends, family or others likely to take an interest in their welfare, at the custody officer's discretion. Custody Officers should liaise closely with the investigation team (see *Note 3E*) to allow risk assessments to be made where particular visitors have been requested by the detainee or identified themselves to police. In circumstances where the nature of the investigation means that such requests can not be met, consideration should be given, in conjunction with a representative of the relevant scheme, to increasing the frequency of visits from independent visitor schemes. See *Notes 5B* and *5C*.

5.5 If a friend, relative or person with an interest in the detainee's welfare enquires about their whereabouts, this information shall be given if the suspect agrees and *Annex B* does not apply. See *Note 5E*.

5.6 The detainee shall be given writing materials, on request, and allowed to telephone one person for a reasonable time, see *Notes 5A* and *5F.* Either or both these privileges may be denied or delayed if an officer of inspector rank or above considers sending a letter or making a telephone call may result in any of the consequences in *Annex B paragraphs 1* and *2*, particularly in relation to the making of a telephone call in a language which an officer listening to the call (see paragraph 5.7) does not understand. See *Note 5G*.

Nothing in this paragraph permits the restriction or denial of the rights in *paragraphs 5.1* and *6.1*.

5.7 Before any letter or message is sent, or telephone call made, the detainee shall be informed that what they say in any letter, call or message (other than in a communication to a solicitor) may be read or listened to and may be given in evidence. A telephone call may be terminated if it is being abused *see Note 5G*. The costs can be at public expense at the custody officer's discretion.

5.8 Any delay or denial of the rights in this section should be proportionate and should last no longer than necessary.

(b) Documentation

5.9 A record must be kept of any:

(a) request made under this section and the action taken;

(b) letters, messages or telephone calls made or received or visit received;

(c) refusal by the detainee to have information about them given to an outside enquirer, or any refusal to see a visitor. The detainee must be asked to countersign the record accordingly and any refusal recorded.

Notes for guidance

5A A person may request an interpreter to interpret a telephone call or translate a letter.

5B At the custody officer's discretion (and subject to the detainee's consent), visits from friends, family or others likely to take an interest in the detainee's welfare, should be allowed when possible, subject to sufficient personnel being available to supervise a visit and any possible hindrance to the investigation. Custody Officers should bear in mind the exceptional nature of prolonged TACT detention and consider the potential benefits that visits may bring to the health and welfare of detainees who are held for extended periods.

5C Official visitors should be given access following consultation with the officer who has overall responsibility for the investigation provided the detainee consents, and they do not compromise safety or security or unduly delay or interfere with the progress of an investigation. Official visitors should still be required to provide appropriate identification and subject to any screening process in place at the place of detention. Official visitors may include:

- *An accredited faith representative*
- *Members of either House of Parliament*
- *Public officials needing to interview the prisoner in the course of their duties*

- *Other persons visiting with the approval of the officer who has overall responsibility for the investigation*
- *Consular officials visiting a detainee who is a national of the country they represent subject to Annex F.*

Visits from appropriate members of the Independent Custody Visitors Scheme should be dealt with in accordance with the separate Code of Practice on Independent Custody Visiting.

5D If the detainee does not know anyone to contact for advice or support or cannot contact a friend or relative, the custody officer should bear in mind any local voluntary bodies or other organisations that might be able to help. Paragraph 6.1 applies if legal advice is required.

5E In some circumstances it may not be appropriate to use the telephone to disclose information under paragraphs 5.1 and 5.5.

5F The telephone call at paragraph 5.6 is in addition to any communication under paragraphs 5.1 and 6.1. Further calls may be made at the custody officer's discretion.

5G The nature of terrorism investigations means that officers should have particular regard to the possibility of suspects attempting to pass information which may be detrimental to public safety, or to an investigation.

6 Right to legal advice

(a) Action

6.1 Unless *Annex B* applies, all detainees must be informed that they may at any time consult and communicate privately with a solicitor, whether in person, in writing or by telephone, and that free independent legal advice is available from the duty solicitor.

Where an appropriate adult is in attendance, they must also be informed of this right. See *paragraph 3.1, Note 1I, Note 6B* and *Note 6I.*

6.2 A poster advertising the right to legal advice must be prominently displayed in the charging area of every police station. See *Note 6G.*

6.3 No police officer should, at any time, do or say anything with the intention of dissuading a detainee from obtaining legal advice.

6.4 The exercise of the right of access to legal advice may be delayed exceptionally only as in *Annex B*. Whenever legal advice is requested, and unless *Annex B* applies, the custody officer must act without delay to secure the provision of such advice. If, on being informed or reminded of this right, the detainee declines to speak to a solicitor in person, the officer should point out that the right includes the right to speak with a solicitor on the telephone (see *paragraph 5.6*). If the detainee continues to waive this right the officer should ask them why and any reasons should be recorded on the custody record or the interview record as appropriate. Reminders of the right to legal advice must be given as in *paragraphs 3.5, 11.3,* and the PACE Code D on the Identification of Persons by Police Officers (PACE Code D), *paragraphs 3.19(ii)* and *6.2*. Once it is clear a detainee does not want to speak to a solicitor in person or by telephone they should cease to be asked their reasons. See *Note 6J*.

6.5 An officer of the rank of Commander or Assistant Chief Constable may give a direction under TACT Schedule 8 paragraph 9 that a detainee may only consult a solicitor within the sight and hearing of a qualified officer. Such a direction may only be given if the officer has reasonable grounds to believe that if it were not, it may result in one of the consequences set out in TACT Schedule 8 paragraphs 8(4) or 8(5)(c). See *Annex B paragraph 3* and *Note 6I*. A 'qualified officer' means a police officer who:

    (a) is at least the rank of inspector;
    (b) is of the uniformed branch of the force of which the officer giving the direction is a member, and

(c) in the opinion of the officer giving the direction, has no connection with the detained person's case.

Officers considering the use of this power should first refer to Home Office Circular 40/2003.

6.6 In the case of a juvenile, an appropriate adult should consider whether legal advice from a solicitor is required. If the juvenile indicates that they do not want legal advice, the appropriate adult has the right to ask for a solicitor to attend if this would be in the best interests of the person. However, the detained person cannot be forced to see the solicitor if he is adamant that he does not wish to do so.

6.7 A detainee who wants legal advice may not be interviewed or continue to be interviewed until they have received such advice unless:

(a) *Annex B* applies, when the restriction on drawing adverse inferences from silence in *Annex C* will apply because the detainee is not allowed an opportunity to consult a solicitor; or

(b) an officer of superintendent rank or above has reasonable grounds for believing that:

  (i) the consequent delay might:
   • lead to interference with, or harm to, evidence connected with an offence;
   • lead to interference with, or physical harm to, other people;
   • lead to serious loss of, or damage to, property;
   • lead to alerting other people suspected of having committed an offence but not yet arrested for it;
   • hinder the recovery of property obtained in consequence of the commission of an offence.

  (ii) when a solicitor, including a duty solicitor, has been contacted and has agreed to attend, awaiting their arrival would cause unreasonable delay to the process of investigation.

Note: In these cases the restriction on drawing adverse inferences from silence in *Annex C* will apply because the detainee is not allowed an opportunity to consult a solicitor.

(c) the solicitor the detainee has nominated or selected from a list:

  (i) cannot be contacted;
  (ii) has previously indicated they do not wish to be contacted; or
  (iii) having been contacted, has declined to attend; and the detainee has been advised of the Duty Solicitor Scheme but has declined to ask for the duty solicitor.

In these circumstances the interview may be started or continued without further delay provided an officer of inspector rank or above has agreed to the interview proceeding.

Note: The restriction on drawing adverse inferences from silence in *Annex C* will not apply because the detainee is allowed an opportunity to consult the duty solicitor;

(d) the detainee changes their mind, about wanting legal advice.

In these circumstances the interview may be started or continued without delay provided that:

  (i) the detainee agrees to do so, in writing or on the interview record made in accordance with the Code of Practice issued under TACT Schedule 8 Paragraph 3; and
  (ii) an officer of inspector rank or above has inquired about the detainee's reasons for their change of mind and gives authority for the interview to proceed.

Confirmation of the detainee's agreement, their change of mind, the reasons for it if given and, subject to *paragraph 2.8*, the name of the authorising officer shall be recorded in the written interview record or the interview record made in accordance with the Code of Practice issued under Paragraph 3 of Schedule 8 to the Terrorism Act. See *Note 6H*.

Note: In these circumstances the restriction on drawing adverse inferences from silence in *Annex C* will not apply because the detainee is allowed an opportunity to consult a solicitor if they wish.

6.8 If *paragraph 6.7(a)* applies, where the reason for authorising the delay ceases to apply, there may be no further delay in permitting the exercise of the right in the absence of a further authorisation unless *paragraph 6.7 (b), (c)* or *(d)* applies.

6.9 A detainee who has been permitted to consult a solicitor shall be entitled on request to have the solicitor present when they are interviewed unless one of the exceptions in *paragraph 6.7* applies.

6.10 The solicitor may only be required to leave the interview if their conduct is such that the interviewer is unable properly to put questions to the suspect. See *Notes 6C* and *6D*.

6.11 If the interviewer considers a solicitor is acting in such a way, they will stop the interview and consult an officer not below superintendent rank, if one is readily available, and otherwise an officer not below inspector rank not connected with the investigation. After speaking to the solicitor, the officer consulted will decide if the interview should continue in the presence of that solicitor. If they decide it should not, the suspect will be given the opportunity to consult another solicitor before the interview continues and that solicitor given an opportunity to be present at the interview. See *Note 6D*.

6.12 The removal of a solicitor from an interview is a serious step and, if it occurs, the officer of superintendent rank or above who took the decision will consider if the incident should be reported to the Law Society. If the decision to remove the solicitor has been taken by an officer below superintendent rank, the facts must be reported to an officer of superintendent rank or above who will similarly consider whether a report to the Law Society would be appropriate. When the solicitor concerned is a duty solicitor, the report should be both to the Law Society and to the Legal Services Commission.

6.13 'Solicitor' in this Code means:

- a solicitor who holds a current practising certificate
- an accredited or probationary representative included on the register of representatives maintained by the Legal Services Commission.

6.14 An accredited or probationary representative sent to provide advice by, and on behalf of, a solicitor shall be admitted to the police station for this purpose unless an officer of inspector rank or above considers such a visit will hinder the investigation and directs otherwise. Hindering the investigation does not include giving proper legal advice to a detainee as in *Note 6C*. Once admitted to the police station, *paragraphs 6.7* to *6.11* apply.

6.15 In exercising their discretion under *paragraph 6.14*, the officer should take into account in particular:

- whether:
  — the identity and status of an accredited or probationary representative have been satisfactorily established;
  — they are of suitable character to provide legal advice,
  — any other matters in any written letter of authorisation provided by the solicitor on whose behalf the person is attending the police station. See *Note 6E*.

6.16 If the inspector refuses access to an accredited or probationary representative or a decision is taken that such a person should not be permitted to remain at an interview, the inspector must notify the solicitor on whose behalf the representative was acting and give them an opportunity to make alternative arrangements. The detainee must be informed and the custody record noted.

6.17 If a solicitor arrives at the station to see a particular person, that person must, unless *Annex B* applies, be so informed whether or not they are being interviewed and asked if they would like to see the solicitor. This applies even if the detainee has declined legal advice or, having requested it, subsequently agreed to be interviewed without receiving advice. The solicitor's attendance and the detainee's decision must be noted in the custody record.

(b) Documentation

6.18 Any request for legal advice and the action taken shall be recorded.

6.19 A record shall be made in the interview record if a detainee asks for legal advice and an interview is begun either in the absence of a solicitor or their representative, or they have been required to leave an interview.

Notes for guidance

6A If paragraph 6.7(b) applies, the officer should, if practicable, ask the solicitor for an estimate of how long it will take to come to the station and relate this to the time detention is permitted, the time of day (ie, whether the rest period under paragraph 12.2 is imminent) and the requirements of other investigations. If the solicitor is on their way or is to set off immediately, it will not normally be appropriate to begin an interview before they arrive. If it appears necessary to begin an interview before the solicitor's arrival, they should be given an indication of how long the police would be able to wait so there is an opportunity to make arrangements for someone else to provide legal advice. Nothing within this section is intended to prevent police from ascertaining immediately after the arrest of an individual whether a threat to public safety exists (see paragraph 11.2).

6B A detainee who asks for legal advice should be given an opportunity to consult a specific solicitor or another solicitor from that solicitor's firm or the duty solicitor. If advice is not available by these means, or they do not want to consult the duty solicitor, the detainee should be given an opportunity to choose a solicitor from a list of those willing to provide legal advice. If this solicitor is unavailable, they may choose up to two alternatives.

If these attempts are unsuccessful, the custody officer has discretion to allow further attempts until a solicitor has been contacted and agrees to provide legal advice. Apart from carrying out these duties, an officer must not advise the suspect about any particular firm of solicitors.

6C A detainee has a right to free legal advice and to be represented by a solicitor. The solicitor's only role in the police station is to protect and advance the legal rights of their client. On occasions this may require the solicitor to give advice which has the effect of the client avoiding giving evidence which strengthens a prosecution case. The solicitor may intervene in order to seek clarification, challenge an improper question to their client or the manner in which it is put, advise their client not to reply to particular questions, or if they wish to give their client further legal advice. Paragraph 6.9 only applies if the solicitor's approach or conduct prevents or unreasonably obstructs proper questions being put to the suspect or the suspect's response being recorded. Examples of unacceptable conduct include answering questions on a suspect's behalf or providing written replies for the suspect to quote.

6D An officer who takes the decision to exclude a solicitor must be in a position to satisfy the court the decision was properly made. In order to do this they may need to witness what is happening.

6E If an officer of at least inspector rank considers a particular solicitor or firm of solicitors is persistently sending probationary representatives who are unsuited to provide legal advice, they should inform an officer of at least superintendent rank, who may wish to take the matter up with the Law Society.

6F Subject to the constraints of Annex B, a solicitor may advise more than one client in an investigation if they wish. Any question of a conflict of interest is for the solicitor under their professional code of conduct. If, however, waiting for a solicitor to give advice to one client may lead to unreasonable delay to the interview with another, the provisions of paragraph 6.7(b) may apply.

6G In addition to a poster in English, a poster or posters containing translations into Welsh, the main minority ethnic languages and the principal European languages should be displayed wherever they are likely to be helpful and it is practicable to do so.

6H Paragraph 6.7(d) requires the authorisation of an officer of inspector rank or above to the continuation of an interview when a detainee who wanted legal advice changes their mind. It is permissible for such authorisation to be given over the telephone, if the authorising officer is able to satisfy themselves about the reason for the detainee's change of mind and is satisfied it is proper to continue the interview in those circumstances.

6I Whenever a detainee exercises their right to legal advice by consulting or communicating with a solicitor, they must be allowed to do so in private. This right to consult or communicate in private is fundamental. Except as allowed by the Terrorism Act 2000, Schedule 8, paragraph 9, if the requirement for privacy is compromised because what is said or written by the detainee or solicitor for the purpose of giving and receiving legal advice is overheard, listened to, or read by others without the informed consent of the detainee, the right will effectively have been denied. When a detainee chooses to speak to a solicitor on the telephone, they should be allowed to do so in private unless a direction under Schedule 8, paragraph 9 of the Terrorism Act 2000 has been given or this is impractical because of the design and layout of the custody area, or the location of telephones. However, the normal expectation should be that facilities will be available, unless they are being used, at all police stations to enable detainees to speak in private to a solicitor either face to face or over the telephone.

6J A detainee is not obliged to give reasons for declining legal advice and should not be pressed to do so.

7 Citizens of independent Commonwealth countries or foreign nationals

(a) Action

7.1 Any citizen of an independent Commonwealth country or a national of a foreign country, including the Republic of Ireland, may communicate at any time with the appropriate High Commission, Embassy or Consulate. The detainee must be informed as soon as practicable of:

- this right;
- their right, upon request, to have their High Commission, Embassy or Consulate told of their whereabouts and the grounds for their detention. Such a request should be acted upon as soon as practicable.

7.2 If a detainee is a citizen of a country with which a bilateral consular convention or agreement is in force requiring notification of arrest, the appropriate High Commission, Embassy or Consulate shall be informed as soon as practicable, subject to *paragraph 7.4*. The countries to which this applies as at 1 April 2003 are listed in *Annex F*.

7.3 Consular officers may visit one of their nationals in police detention to talk to them and, if required, to arrange for legal advice. Such visits shall take place out of the hearing of a police officer.

7.4 Notwithstanding the provisions of consular conventions, if the detainee is a political refugee whether for reasons of race, nationality, political opinion or religion, or is seeking political asylum, consular officers shall not be informed of the arrest of one of their nationals or given access or information about them except at the detainee's express request.

(b) Documentation

7.5 A record shall be made when a detainee is informed of their rights under this section and of any communications with a High Commission, Embassy or Consulate.

Note for guidance

7A The exercise of the rights in this section may not be interfered with even though Annex B applies.

8 Conditions of detention

(a) Action

8.1 So far as it is practicable, not more than one detainee should be detained in each cell.

8.2 Cells in use must be adequately heated, cleaned and ventilated. They must be adequately lit, subject to such dimming as is compatible with safety and security to allow people detained overnight to sleep. No additional restraints shall be used within a locked cell unless absolutely necessary and then only restraint equipment, approved for use in that force by the Chief Officer, which is reasonable and necessary in the circumstances having regard to the detainee's demeanour and with a view to ensuring their safety and the safety of others. If a detainee is deaf, mentally disordered or otherwise mentally vulnerable, particular care must be taken when deciding whether to use any form of approved restraints.

8.3 Blankets, mattresses, pillows and other bedding supplied shall be of a reasonable standard and in a clean and sanitary condition.

8.4 Access to toilet and washing facilities must be provided.

8.5 If it is necessary to remove a detainee's clothes for the purposes of investigation, for hygiene, health reasons or cleaning, replacement clothing of a reasonable standard of comfort and cleanliness shall be provided. A detainee may not be interviewed unless adequate clothing has been offered.

8.6 At least two light meals and one main meal should be offered in any 24 hour period. See *Note 8B*. Drinks should be provided at meal times and upon reasonable request between meals. Whenever necessary, advice shall be sought from the appropriate health care professional, see *Note 9A*, on medical and dietary matters. As far as practicable, meals provided shall offer a varied diet and meet any specific dietary needs or religious beliefs the detainee may have. Detainees should also be made aware that the meals offered meet such needs. The detainee may, at the custody officer's discretion, have meals supplied by their family or friends at their expense. See *Note 8A*.

8.7 Brief outdoor exercise shall be offered daily if practicable. Where facilities exist, indoor exercise shall be offered as an alternative if outside conditions are such that a detainee can not be reasonably expected to take outdoor exercise (eg, in cold or wet weather) or if requested by the detainee or for reasons of security, *see Note 8C*.

8.8 Where practicable, provision should be made for detainees to practice religious observance. Consideration should be given to providing a separate room which can be used as a prayer room. The supply of appropriate food and clothing, and suitable provision for prayer facilities, such as uncontaminated copies of religious books, should also be considered. *See Note 8D*.

8.9 A juvenile shall not be placed in a cell unless no other secure accommodation is available and the custody officer considers it is not practicable to supervise them if they are not placed in a cell or that cell provides more comfortable accommodation than other secure accommodation in the station. A juvenile may not be placed in a cell with a detained adult.

8.10 Police stations should keep a reasonable supply of reading material available for detainees, including but not limited to, the main religious texts. *See Note 8D*. Detainees should be made aware that such material is available and reasonable requests for such material should be met as soon as practicable unless to do so would:

   (i)   interfere with the investigation; or
   (ii)   prevent or delay an officer from discharging his statutory duties, or those in this Code.

If such a request is refused on the grounds of (i) or (ii) above, this should be noted in the custody record and met as soon as possible after those grounds cease to apply.

(b) Documentation

8.11 A record must be kept of replacement clothing and meals offered.

8.12 The use of any restraints on a detainee whilst in a cell, the reasons for it and, if appropriate, the arrangements for enhanced supervision of the detainee whilst so restrained, shall be recorded. See *paragraph 3.9*.

Notes for guidance

8A In deciding whether to allow meals to be supplied by family or friends, the custody officer is entitled to take account of the risk of items being concealed in any food or package and the officer's duties and responsibilities under food handling legislation. If an officer needs to examine food or other items supplied by family and friends before deciding whether they can be given to the detainee, he should inform the person who has brought the item to the police station of this and the reasons for doing so.

8B Meals should, so far as practicable, be offered at recognised meal times, or at other times that take account of when the detainee last had a meal.

8C In light of the potential for detaining individuals for extended periods of time, the overriding principle should be to accommodate a period of exercise, except where to do so would hinder the investigation, delay the detainee's release or charge, or it is declined by the detainee.

8D Police forces should consult with representatives of the main religious communities to ensure the provision for religious observance is adequate, and to seek advice on the appropriate storage and handling of religious texts or other religious items.

9 Care and treatment of detained persons

(a) General

9.1 Notwithstanding other requirements for medical attention as set out in this section, detainees who are held for more than 96 hours must be visited by a healthcare professional at least once every 24 hours.

9.2 Nothing in this section prevents the police from calling the police surgeon or, if appropriate, some other health care professional, to examine a detainee for the purposes of obtaining evidence relating to any offence in which the detainee is suspected of being involved. See *Note 9A.*

9.3 If a complaint is made by, or on behalf of, a detainee about their treatment since their arrest, or it comes to notice that a detainee may have been treated improperly, a report must be made as soon as practicable to an officer of inspector rank or above not connected with the investigation. If the matter concerns a possible assault or the possibility of the unnecessary or unreasonable use of force, an appropriate health care professional must also be called as soon as practicable.

9.4 Detainees should be visited at least every hour. If no reasonably foreseeable risk was identified in a risk assessment, see *paragraphs 3.6—3.10*, there is no need to wake a sleeping detainee. Those suspected of being intoxicated through drink or drugs or having swallowed drugs, see *Note 9C*, or whose level of consciousness causes concern must, subject to any clinical directions given by the appropriate health care professional, see *paragraph 9.15*:

- be visited and roused at least every half hour
- have their condition assessed as in *Annex H*
- and clinical treatment arranged if appropriate.

See *Notes 9B, 9C* and *9G.*

9.5 When arrangements are made to secure clinical attention for a detainee, the custody officer must make sure all relevant information which might assist in the treatment of the detainee's condition is made available to the responsible health care professional. This applies whether or not the health care professional asks for such information. Any officer or police staff with relevant information must inform the custody officer as soon as practicable.

(b) Clinical treatment and attention

9.6 The custody officer must make sure a detainee receives appropriate clinical attention as soon as reasonably practicable if the person:

(a) appears to be suffering from physical illness; or
(b) is injured; or
(c) appears to be suffering from a mental disorder; or
(d) appears to need clinical attention.

9.7 This applies even if the detainee makes no request for clinical attention and whether or not they have already received clinical attention elsewhere. If the need for attention appears urgent, eg, when indicated as in *Annex H*, the nearest available health care professional or an ambulance must be called immediately.

9.8 The custody officer must also consider the need for clinical attention as set out in *Note 9C* in relation to those suffering the effects of alcohol or drugs.

9.9 If it appears to the custody officer, or they are told, that a person brought to a station under arrest may be suffering from an infectious disease or condition, the custody officer must take reasonable steps to safeguard the health of the detainee and others at the station. In deciding what action to take, advice must be sought from an appropriate health care professional. See *Note 9D*. The custody officer has discretion to isolate the person and their property until clinical directions have been obtained.

9.10 If a detainee requests a clinical examination, an appropriate health care professional must be called as soon as practicable to assess the detainee's clinical needs. If a safe and appropriate care plan cannot be provided, the police surgeon's advice must be sought. The detainee may also be examined by a medical practitioner of their choice at their expense.

9.11 If a detainee is required to take or apply any medication in compliance with clinical directions prescribed before their detention, the custody officer must consult the appropriate health care professional before the use of the medication. Subject to the restrictions in *paragraph 9.12*, the custody officer is responsible for the safekeeping of any medication and for making sure the detainee is given the opportunity to take or apply prescribed or approved medication. Any such consultation and its outcome shall be noted in the custody record.

9.12 No police officer may administer or supervise the self-administration of medically prescribed controlled drugs of the types and forms listed in the Misuse of Drugs Regulations 2001, Schedule 2 or 3. A detainee may only self-administer such drugs under the personal supervision of the registered medical practitioner authorising their use. Drugs listed in Schedule 4 or 5 may be distributed by the custody officer for self-administration if they have consulted the registered medical practitioner authorising their use, this may be done by telephone, and both parties are satisfied self-administration will not expose the detainee, police officers or anyone else to the risk of harm or injury.

9.13 When appropriate health care professionals administer drugs or other medications, or supervise their self-administration, it must be within current medicines legislation and the scope of practice as determined by their relevant professional body.

9.14 If a detainee has in their possession, or claims to need, medication relating to a heart condition, diabetes, epilepsy or a condition of comparable potential seriousness then, even though *paragraph 9.6* may not apply, the advice of the appropriate health care professional must be obtained.

9.15 Whenever the appropriate health care professional is called in accordance with this section to examine or treat a detainee, the custody officer shall ask for their opinion about:

- any risks or problems which police need to take into account when making decisions about the detainee's continued detention;
- when to carry out an interview if applicable; and
- the need for safeguards.

9.16 When clinical directions are given by the appropriate health care professional, whether orally or in writing, and the custody officer has any doubts or is in any way uncertain about any aspect of the directions, the custody officer shall ask for clarification. It is particularly important that directions concerning the frequency of visits are clear, precise and capable of being implemented. See *Note 9E*.

(c) Documentation

9.17 A record must be made in the custody record of:

(a) the arrangements made for an examination by an appropriate health care professional under *paragraph 9.3* and of any complaint reported under that paragraph together with any relevant remarks by the custody officer;

(b) any arrangements made in accordance with *paragraph 9.6*;

(c) any request for a clinical examination under *paragraph 9.10* and any arrangements made in response;

(d) the injury, ailment, condition or other reason which made it necessary to make the arrangements in (*a*) to (*c*), see *Note 9F*;

(e) any clinical directions and advice, including any further clarifications, given to police by a health care professional concerning the care and treatment of the detainee in connection with any of the arrangements made in (*a*) to (*c*), see *Note 9E*;

(f) if applicable, the responses received when attempting to rouse a person using the procedure in *Annex H*, see *Note 9G*.

9.18 If a health care professional does not record their clinical findings in the custody record, the record must show where they are recorded. See *Note 9F*. However, information which is necessary to custody staff to ensure the effective ongoing care and well being of the detainee must be recorded openly in the custody record, see *paragraph 3.8* and *Annex G, paragraph 7*.

9.19 Subject to the requirements of *Section 4*, the custody record shall include:

- a record of all medication a detainee has in their possession on arrival at the police station;
- a note of any such medication they claim to need but do not have with them.

Notes for guidance

9A A 'health care professional' means a clinically qualified person working within the scope of practice as determined by their relevant professional body. Whether a health care professional is 'appropriate' depends on the circumstances of the duties they carry out at the time.

9B Whenever possible juveniles and mentally vulnerable detainees should be visited more frequently.

9C A detainee who appears drunk or behaves abnormally may be suffering from illness, the effects of drugs or may have sustained injury, particularly a head injury which is not apparent. A detainee needing or dependent on certain drugs, including alcohol, may experience harmful effects within a short time of being deprived of their supply. In these circumstances, when there is any doubt, police should always act urgently to call an appropriate health care professional or an ambulance. Paragraph 9.6 does not apply to minor ailments or injuries which do not need attention. However, all such ailments or injuries must be recorded in the custody record and any doubt must be resolved in favour of calling the appropriate health care professional.

9D It is important to respect a person's right to privacy and information about their health must be kept confidential and only disclosed with their consent or in accordance with clinical advice when it is necessary to protect the detainee's health or that of others who come into contact with them.

9E The custody officer should always seek to clarify directions that the detainee requires constant observation or supervision and should ask the appropriate health care professional to explain precisely what action needs to be taken to implement such directions.

9F Paragraphs 9.17 and 9.18 do not require any information about the cause of any injury, ailment or condition to be recorded on the custody record if it appears capable of providing evidence of an offence.

9G The purpose of recording a person's responses when attempting to rouse them using the procedure in Annex H is to enable any change in the individual's consciousness level to be noted and clinical treatment arranged if appropriate.

10 Cautions

(a) When a caution must be given

10.1 A person whom there are grounds to suspect of an offence, see *Note 10A,* must be cautioned before any questions about an offence, or further questions if the answers provide the grounds for suspicion, are put to them if either the suspect's answers or silence, (ie, failure or refusal to answer or answer satisfactorily) may be given in evidence to a court in a prosecution.

10.2 A person who is arrested, or further arrested, must be informed at the time, or as soon as practicable thereafter, that they are under arrest and the grounds for their arrest, see paragraph 3.4, *Note 3G* and *Note 10B.*

10.3 As per *section 3* of PACE Code G, a person who is arrested, or further arrested, must also be cautioned unless:

(a) it is impracticable to do so by reason of their condition or behaviour at the time;
(b) they have already been cautioned immediately prior to arrest as in *paragraph 10.1.*

(b) Terms of the cautions

10.4 The caution which must be given on:

(a) arrest;
(b) all other occasions before a person is charged or informed they may be prosecuted, see *PACE Code C*, section 16.

should, unless the restriction on drawing adverse inferences from silence applies, see *Annex C*, be in the following terms:

'You do not have to say anything. But it may harm your defence if you do not mention when questioned something which you later rely on in Court. Anything you do say may be given in evidence.'

See *Note 10F.*

10.5 *Annex C, paragraph 2* sets out the alternative terms of the caution to be used when the restriction on drawing adverse inferences from silence applies.

10.6 Minor deviations from the words of any caution given in accordance with this Code do not constitute a breach of this Code, provided the sense of the relevant caution is preserved. See *Note 10C.*

10.7 After any break in questioning under caution, the person being questioned must be made aware they remain under caution. If there is any doubt the relevant caution should be given again in full when the interview resumes. See *Note 10D.*

10.8 When, despite being cautioned, a person fails to cooperate or to answer particular questions which may affect their immediate treatment, the person should be informed of any relevant consequences and that those consequences are not affected by the caution. Examples are when a person's refusal to provide:

• their name and address when charged may make them liable to detention;
• particulars and information in accordance with a statutory requirement.

(c) Special warnings under the Criminal Justice and Public Order Act 1994, sections 36 and 37

10.9 When a suspect interviewed at a police station or authorised place of detention after arrest fails or refuses to answer certain questions, or to answer satisfactorily, after due warning, see *Note 10E*, a court or jury may draw such inferences as appear proper under the Criminal Justice and Public Order Act 1994, sections 36 and 37. Such inferences may only be drawn when:

(a) the restriction on drawing adverse inferences from silence, see Annex C, does not apply; and

(b) the suspect is arrested by a constable and fails or refuses to account for any objects, marks or substances, or marks on such objects found:
  • on their person;
  • in or on their clothing or footwear;
  • otherwise in their possession; or
  • in the place they were arrested;

(c) the arrested suspect was found by a constable at a place at or about the time the offence for which that officer has arrested them is alleged to have been committed, and the suspect fails or refuses to account for their presence there.

When the restriction on drawing adverse inferences from silence applies, the suspect may still be asked to account for any of the matters in (*b*) or (*c*) but the special warning described in *paragraph 10.10* will not apply and must not be given.

10.10 For an inference to be drawn when a suspect fails or refuses to answer a question about one of these matters or to answer it satisfactorily, the suspect must first be told in ordinary language:

(a) what offence is being investigated;
(b) what fact they are being asked to account for;
(c) this fact may be due to them taking part in the commission of the offence;
(d) a court may draw a proper inference if they fail or refuse to account for this fact;
(e) a record is being made of the interview and it may be given in evidence if they are brought to trial.

(d) Juveniles and persons who are mentally disordered or otherwise mentally vulnerable

10.11 If a juvenile or a person who is mentally disordered or otherwise mentally vulnerable is cautioned in the absence of the appropriate adult, the caution must be repeated in the adult's presence.

(e) Documentation

10.12 A record shall be made when a caution is given under this section, either in the interviewer's pocket book or in the interview record.

Notes for guidance

10A There must be some reasonable, objective grounds for the suspicion, based on known facts or information which are relevant to the likelihood the offence has been committed and the person to be questioned committed it.

10B An arrested person must be given sufficient information to enable them to understand that they have been deprived of their liberty and the reason they have been arrested, eg when a person is arrested on suspicion of committing an offence they must be informed of the suspected offence's nature, when and where it was committed see Note 3G. The suspect must also be informed of the reason or reasons why the arrest is considered necessary. Vague or technical language should be avoided.

10C If it appears a person does not understand the caution, the person giving it should explain it in their own words.

10D It may be necessary to show to the court that nothing occurred during an interview break or between interviews which influenced the suspect's recorded evidence. After a break in an interview or at the beginning of a subsequent interview, the interviewing officer should summarise the reason for the break and confirm this with the suspect.

10E The Criminal Justice and Public Order Act 1994, sections 36 and 37 apply only to suspects who have been arrested by a constable or Customs and Excise officer and are given the relevant warning by the police or customs officer who made the arrest or who is investigating the offence. They do not apply to any interviews with suspects who have not been arrested.

10F Nothing in this Code requires a caution to be given or repeated when informing a person not under arrest they may be prosecuted for an offence. However, a court will not be able to draw any inferences under the Criminal Justice and Public Order Act 1994, section 34, if the person was not cautioned.

11 Interviews—general

(a) Action

11.1 An interview in this Code is the questioning of a person arrested on suspicion of being a terrorist which, under *paragraph 10.1*, must be carried out under caution. Whenever a person is interviewed they must be informed of the grounds for arrest *see Note 3G*.

11.2 Following a decision to arrest a suspect, they must not be interviewed about the relevant offence except at a place designated for detention under Schedule 8 paragraph 1 of the Terrorism Act 2000, unless the consequent delay would be likely to:

(a) lead to:
- interference with, or harm to, evidence connected with an offence;
- interference with, or physical harm to, other people; or
- serious loss of, or damage to, property;

(b) lead to alerting other people suspected of committing an offence but not yet arrested for it; or

(c) hinder the recovery of property obtained in consequence of the commission of an offence.

Interviewing in any of these circumstances shall cease once the relevant risk has been averted or the necessary questions have been put in order to attempt to avert that risk.

11.3 Immediately prior to the commencement or re-commencement of any interview at a designated place of detention, the interviewer should remind the suspect of their entitlement to free legal advice and that the interview can be delayed for legal advice to be obtained, unless one of the exceptions in *paragraph 6.7* applies. It is the interviewer's responsibility to make sure all reminders are recorded in the interview record.

11.4 At the beginning of an interview the interviewer, after cautioning the suspect, see *section 10*, shall put to them any significant statement or silence which occurred in the presence and hearing of a police officer or other police staff before the start of the interview and which have not been put to the suspect in the course of a previous interview. See *Note 11A*. The interviewer shall ask the suspect whether they confirm or deny that earlier statement or silence and if they want to add anything.

11.5 A significant statement is one which appears capable of being used in evidence against the suspect, in particular a direct admission of guilt. A significant silence is a failure or refusal to answer a question or answer satisfactorily when under caution, which might, allowing for the restriction on drawing adverse inferences from silence, see *Annex C*, give rise to an inference under the Criminal Justice and Public Order Act 1994, Part III.

11.6 No interviewer may try to obtain answers or elicit a statement by the use of oppression. Except as in *paragraph 10.8*, no interviewer shall indicate, except to answer a direct question, what action will be taken by the police if the person being questioned answers questions, makes a statement or refuses to do either. If the person asks directly what action will be taken if they answer questions, make a statement or refuse to do either, the interviewer may inform them what action the police propose to take provided that action is itself proper and warranted.

11.7 The interview or further interview of a person about an offence with which that person has not been charged or for which they have not been informed they may be prosecuted, must cease when:

(a) the officer in charge of the investigation is satisfied all the questions they consider relevant to obtaining accurate and reliable information about the offence have been put to the suspect, this includes allowing the suspect an opportunity to give an innocent explanation and asking questions to test if the explanation is accurate and reliable, eg to clear up ambiguities or clarify what the suspect said;

(b) the officer in charge of the investigation has taken account of any other available evidence; and

(c) the officer in charge of the investigation, or in the case of a detained suspect, the custody officer, see *PACE Code C paragraph 16.1*, reasonably believes there is sufficient evidence to provide a realistic prospect of conviction for that offence. See *Note 11B*.

(b) Interview records

11.8 Interview records should be made in accordance with the Code of Practice issued under Schedule 8 Paragraph 3 to the Terrorism Act where the interview takes place at a designated place of detention.

(c) Juveniles and mentally disordered or otherwise mentally vulnerable people

11.9 A juvenile or person who is mentally disordered or otherwise mentally vulnerable must not be interviewed regarding their involvement or suspected involvement in a criminal offence or offences, or asked to provide or sign a written statement under caution or record of interview, in the absence of the appropriate adult unless *paragraphs 11.2, 11.11 to 11.13* apply. See *Note 11C*.

11.10 If an appropriate adult is present at an interview, they shall be informed:

- they are not expected to act simply as an observer; and
- the purpose of their presence is to:
  — advise the person being interviewed;
  — observe whether the interview is being conducted properly and fairly;
  — facilitate communication with the person being interviewed.

The appropriate adult may be required to leave the interview if their conduct is such that the interviewer is unable properly to put questions to the suspect. This will include situations where the appropriate adult's approach or conduct prevents or unreasonably obstructs proper questions being put to the suspect or the suspect's responses being recorded. If the interviewer considers an appropriate adult is acting in such a way, they will stop the interview and consult an officer not below superintendent rank, if one is readily available, and otherwise an officer not below inspector rank not connected with the investigation. After speaking to the appropriate adult, the officer consulted will decide if the interview should continue without the attendance of that appropriate adult. If they decide it should not, another appropriate adult should be obtained before the interview continues, unless the provisions of paragraph 11.11 below apply.

(d) Vulnerable suspects—urgent interviews at police stations

11.11 The following persons may not be interviewed unless an officer of superintendent rank or above considers delay will lead to the consequences in *paragraph 11.2(a)* to *(c)*, and is satisfied the interview would not significantly harm the person's physical or mental state (see Annex G):

(a) a juvenile or person who is mentally disordered or otherwise mentally vulnerable if at the time of the interview the appropriate adult is not present;

(b) anyone other than in *(a)* who at the time of the interview appears unable to:
  - appreciate the significance of questions and their answers; or
  - understand what is happening because of the effects of drink, drugs or any illness, ailment or condition;

(c) a person who has difficulty understanding English or has a hearing disability, if at the time of the interview an interpreter is not present.

11.12 These interviews may not continue once sufficient information has been obtained to avert the consequences in *paragraph 11.2(a)* to *(c)*.

11.13 A record shall be made of the grounds for any decision to interview a person under *paragraph 11.11*.

Notes for guidance

11A Paragraph 11.4 does not prevent the interviewer from putting significant statements and silences to a suspect again at a later stage or a further interview.

11B The Criminal Procedure and Investigations Act 1996 Code of Practice, paragraph 3.4 states 'In conducting an investigation, the investigator should pursue all reasonable lines of enquiry, whether these point towards or away from the suspect. What is reasonable will depend on the particular circumstances'. Interviewers should keep this in mind when deciding what questions to ask in an interview.

11C Although juveniles or people who are mentally disordered or otherwise mentally vulnerable are often capable of providing reliable evidence, they may, without knowing or wishing to do so, be particularly prone in certain circumstances to provide information that may be unreliable, misleading or self-incriminating. Special care should always be taken when questioning such a person, and the appropriate adult should be involved if there is any doubt about a person's age, mental state or capacity. Because of the risk of unreliable evidence it is also important to obtain corroboration of any facts admitted whenever possible.

11D Consideration should be given to the effect of extended detention on a detainee and any subsequent information they provide, especially if it relates to information on matters that they have failed to provide previously in response to similar questioning see Annex G.

11E Significant statements described in paragraph 11.4 will always be relevant to the offence and must be recorded. When a suspect agrees to read records of interviews and other comments and sign them as correct, they should be asked to endorse the record with, eg 'I agree that this is a correct record of what was said' and add their signature. If the suspect does not agree with the record, the interviewer should record the details of any disagreement and ask the suspect to read these details and sign them to the effect that they accurately reflect their disagreement. Any refusal to sign should be recorded.

12 Interviews in police stations

(a) Action

12.1 If a police officer wants to interview or conduct enquiries which require the presence of a detainee, the custody officer is responsible for deciding whether to deliver the detainee into the officer's custody.

12.2 Except as below, in any period of 24 hours a detainee must be allowed a continuous period of at least 8 hours for rest, free from questioning, travel or any interruption in connection with the investigation concerned. This period should normally be at night or other appropriate time which takes account of when the detainee last slept or rested. If a detainee is arrested at a police station after going there voluntarily, the period of 24 hours runs from the time of their arrest (or, if a person was being detained under TACT Schedule 7 when arrested, from the time at which the examination under Schedule 7 began) and not the time of arrival at the police station. The period may not be interrupted or delayed, except:

   (a) when there are reasonable grounds for believing not delaying or interrupting the period would:

   (i)   involve a risk of harm to people or serious loss of, or damage to, property;
   (ii) delay unnecessarily the person's release from custody;
   (iii) otherwise prejudice the outcome of the investigation;

   (b) at the request of the detainee, their appropriate adult or legal representative;
   (c) when a delay or interruption is necessary in order to:

   (i)   comply with the legal obligations and duties arising under *section 14*;
   (ii) to take action required under *section 9* or in accordance with medical advice.

If the period is interrupted in accordance with *(a)*, a fresh period must be allowed. Interruptions under *(b)* and *(c)*, do not require a fresh period to be allowed.

12.3 Before a detainee is interviewed the custody officer, in consultation with the officer in charge of the investigation and appropriate health care professionals as necessary, shall assess whether the detainee is fit enough to be interviewed. This means determining and considering the risks to the detainee's physical and mental state if the interview took place and determining what safeguards are needed to allow the interview to take place. The custody officer shall not allow a detainee to be interviewed if the custody officer considers it would cause significant harm to the detainee's physical or mental state. Vulnerable suspects listed at *paragraph 11.11* shall be treated as always being at some risk during an interview and these persons may not be interviewed except in accordance with *paragraphs 11.11* to *11.13*.

12.4 As far as practicable interviews shall take place in interview rooms which are adequately heated, lit and ventilated.

12.5 A suspect whose detention without charge has been authorised under TACT Schedule 8, because the detention is necessary for an interview to obtain evidence of the offence for which they have been arrested, may choose not to answer questions but police do not require the suspect's consent or agreement to interview them for this purpose. If a suspect takes steps to prevent themselves being questioned or further questioned, eg by refusing to leave their cell to go to a suitable interview room or by trying to leave the interview room, they shall be advised their consent or agreement to interview is not required. The suspect shall be cautioned as in *section 10*, and informed if they fail or refuse to cooperate, the interview may take place in the cell and that their failure or refusal to cooperate may be given in evidence. The suspect shall then be invited to cooperate and go into the interview room.

12.6 People being questioned or making statements shall not be required to stand.

12.7 Before the interview commences each interviewer shall, subject to the qualification at *paragraph 2.8,* identify themselves and any other persons present to the interviewee.

12.8 Breaks from interviewing should be made at recognised meal times or at other times that take account of when an interviewee last had a meal. Short refreshment breaks shall be provided at approximately two hour intervals, subject to the interviewer's discretion to delay a break if there are reasonable grounds for believing it would:

   (i) involve a:
- risk of harm to people;
- serious loss of, or damage to, property;

   (ii) unnecessarily delay the detainee's release;

   (iii) otherwise prejudice the outcome of the investigation.

See *Note 12B.*

12.9 During extended periods where no interviews take place, because of the need to gather further evidence or analyse existing evidence, detainees and their legal representative shall be informed that the investigation into the relevant offence remains ongoing. If practicable, the detainee and legal representative should also be made aware in general terms of any reasons for long gaps between interviews. Consideration should be given to allowing visits, more frequent exercise, or for reading or writing materials to be offered *see paragraph 5.4, section 8* and *Note 12C.*

12.10 If during the interview a complaint is made by or on behalf of the interviewee concerning the provisions of this Code, the interviewer should:

   (i) record it in the interview record;

   (ii) inform the custody officer, who is then responsible for dealing with it as in *section 9.*

(b) Documentation

12.11 A record must be made of the:

- time a detainee is not in the custody of the custody officer, and why
- reason for any refusal to deliver the detainee out of that custody

12.12 A record shall be made of:

(a) the reasons it was not practicable to use an interview room; and

(b) any action taken as in *paragraph 12.5*.

The record shall be made on the custody record or in the interview record for action taken whilst an interview record is being kept, with a brief reference to this effect in the custody record.

12.13 Any decision to delay a break in an interview must be recorded, with reasons, in the interview record.

12.14 All written statements made at police stations under caution shall be written on forms provided for the purpose.

12.15 All written statements made under caution shall be taken in accordance with *Annex D*. Before a person makes a written statement under caution at a police station they shall be reminded about the right to legal advice. See *Note 12A*.

Notes for guidance

12A It is not normally necessary to ask for a written statement if the interview was recorded in writing and the record signed in accordance with the Code of Practice issued under TACT Schedule 8 Paragraph 3. Statements under caution should normally be taken in these circumstances only at the person's express wish. A person may however be asked if they want to make such a statement.

12B Meal breaks should normally last at least 45 minutes and shorter breaks after two hours should last at least 15 minutes. If the interviewer delays a break in accordance with paragraph 12.8 and prolongs the interview, a longer break should be provided. If there is a short interview, and another short interview is contemplated, the length of the break may be reduced if there are reasonable grounds to believe this is necessary to avoid any of the consequences in paragraph 12.8(i) to (iii).

12C Consideration should be given to the matters referred to in paragraph 12.9 after a period of over 24 hours without questioning. This is to ensure that extended periods of detention without an indication that the investigation remains ongoing do not contribute to a deterioration of the detainee's well-being.

13 Interpreters

(a) General

13.1 Chief officers are responsible for making sure appropriate arrangements are in place for provision of suitably qualified interpreters for people who:

- are deaf;
- do not understand English.

Whenever possible, interpreters should be drawn from the National Register of Public Service Interpreters (NRPSI) or the Council for the Advancement of Communication with Deaf People (CACDP) Directory of British Sign Language/English Interpreters.

(b) Foreign languages

13.2 Unless *paragraphs 11.2, 11.11* to *11.13* apply, a person must not be interviewed in the absence of a person capable of interpreting if:

(a) they have difficulty understanding English;

(b) the interviewer cannot speak the person's own language;

(c) the person wants an interpreter present.

13.3 The interviewer shall make sure the interpreter makes a note of the interview at the time in the person's language for use in the event of the interpreter being called to give evidence, and certifies its accuracy. The interviewer should allow sufficient time for the interpreter to note each question and answer after each is put, given and interpreted. The person should be allowed to read the record or have it read to them and sign it as correct or indicate the respects in which they consider it inaccurate. If the interview is audibly recorded or visually recorded with sound, the Code of Practice issued under paragraph 3 of Schedule 8 to the Terrorism Act 2000 will apply.

13.4 In the case of a person making a statement to a police officer or other police staff other than in English:

    (a) the interpreter shall record the statement in the language it is made;

    (b) the person shall be invited to sign it;

    (c) an official English translation shall be made in due course.

(c) Deaf people and people with speech difficulties

13.5 If a person appears to be deaf or there is doubt about their hearing or speaking ability, they must not be interviewed in the absence of an interpreter unless they agree in writing to being interviewed without one or *paragraphs 11.2, 11.11 to 11.13* apply.

13.6 An interpreter should also be called if a juvenile is interviewed and the parent or guardian present as the appropriate adult appears to be deaf or there is doubt about their hearing or speaking ability, unless they agree in writing to the interview proceeding without one or *paragraphs 11.2, 11.11 to 11.13* apply.

13.7 The interviewer shall make sure the interpreter is allowed to read the interview record and certify its accuracy in the event of the interpreter being called to give evidence. If the interview is audibly recorded or visually recorded, the Code of Practice issued under TACT Schedule 8 Paragraph 3 will apply.

(d) Additional rules for detained persons

13.8 All reasonable attempts should be made to make the detainee understand that interpreters will be provided at public expense.

13.9 If *paragraph 6.1* applies and the detainee cannot communicate with the solicitor because of language, hearing or speech difficulties, an interpreter must be called. The interpreter may not be a police officer or any other police staff when interpretation is needed for the purposes of obtaining legal advice. In all other cases a police officer or other police staff may only interpret if the detainee and the appropriate adult, if applicable, give their agreement in writing or if the interview is audibly recorded or visually recorded as in the Code of Practice issued under TACT Schedule 8 Paragraph 3.

13.10 When the custody officer cannot establish effective communication with a person charged with an offence who appears deaf or there is doubt about their ability to hear, speak or to understand English, arrangements must be made as soon as practicable for an interpreter to explain the offence and any other information given by the custody officer.

(e) Documentation

13.11 Action taken to call an interpreter under this section and any agreement to be interviewed in the absence of an interpreter must be recorded.

14 Reviews and extensions of detention

(a) Reviews and extensions of detention

14.1 The powers and duties of the review officer are in the Terrorism Act 2000, Schedule 8, Part II. See *Notes 14A* and *14B*. A review officer should carry out his duties at the police station where the detainee is held, and be allowed such access to the detainee as is necessary for him to exercise those duties.

14.2 For the purposes of reviewing a person's detention, no officer shall put specific questions to the detainee:

- regarding their involvement in any offence; or
- in respect of any comments they may make:
  — when given the opportunity to make representations; or
  — in response to a decision to keep them in detention or extend the maximum period of detention.

Such an exchange could constitute an interview as in *paragraph 11.1* and would be subject to the associated safeguards in *section 11* and, in respect of a person who has been charged see *PACE Code C Section 16.8.*

14.3 If detention is necessary for longer than 48 hours, a police officer of at least superintendent rank, or a Crown Prosecutor may apply for warrants of further detention under the Terrorism Act 2000, Schedule 8, Part III.

14.4 When an application for a warrant of further or extended detention is sought under Paragraph 29 or 36 of Schedule 8, the detained person and their representative must be informed of their rights in respect of the application. These include:

a) the right to a written or oral notice of the warrant See *Note 14G.*
b) the right to make oral or written representations to the judicial authority about the application.
c) the right to be present and legally represented at the hearing of the application, unless specifically excluded by the judicial authority.
d) their right to free legal advice (see section 6 of this Code).

(b) Transfer of detained persons to prison

14.5 Where a warrant is issued which authorises detention beyond a period of 14 days from the time of arrest (or if a person was being detained under TACT Schedule 7, from the time at which the examination under Schedule 7 began), the detainee must be transferred from detention in a police station to detention in a designated prison as soon as is practicable, unless:

a) the detainee specifically requests to remain in detention at a police station and that request can be accommodated, or
b) there are reasonable grounds to believe that transferring a person to a prison would:
   i) significantly hinder a terrorism investigation;
   ii) delay charging of the detainee or his release from custody, or
   iii) otherwise prevent the investigation from being conducted diligently and expeditiously.

If any of the grounds in (b)(i) to (iii) above are relied upon, these must be presented to the judicial authority as part of the application for the warrant that would extend detention beyond a period of 14 days from the time of arrest (or if a person was being detained under TACT Schedule 7, from the time at which the examination under Schedule 7 began) *See Note 14J.*

14.6 If a person remains in detention at a police station under a warrant of further detention as described at section 14.5, they must be transferred to a prison as soon as practicable after the grounds at (b)(i) to (iii) of that section cease to apply.

14.7 Police should maintain an agreement with the National Offender Management Service (NOMS) that stipulates named prisons to which individuals may be transferred under this section. This should be made with regard to ensuring detainees are moved to the most suitable prison for the purposes of the investigation and their welfare, and should include provision for the transfer of male, female and juvenile detainees. Police should ensure that the Governor of a prison to which they intend to transfer a detainee is given reasonable notice of this. Where practicable, this should be no later than the point at which a warrant is applied for that would take the period of detention beyond 14 days.

14.8 Following a detained person's transfer to a designated prison, their detention will be governed by the terms of Schedule 8 and Prison Rules, and this Code of Practice will not apply during any period that the person remains in prison detention. The Code will once more apply if a detained person is transferred back from prison detention to police detention. In order to enable the Governor to arrange for the production of the detainee back into police custody, police should give notice to the Governor of the relevant prison as soon as possible of any decision to transfer a detainee from prison back to a police station. Any transfer between a prison and a police station should be conducted by police, and this Code will be applicable during the period of transit See *Note 14K*. A detainee should only remain in police custody having been transferred back from a prison, for as long as is necessary for the purpose of the investigation.

14.9 The investigating team and custody officer should provide as much information as necessary to enable the relevant prison authorities to provide appropriate facilities to detain an individual. This should include, but not be limited to:

    i)   medical assessments
    ii) security and risk assessments
    iii) details of the detained person's legal representatives
    iv) details of any individuals from whom the detained person has requested visits, or who have requested to visit the detained person.

14.10 Where a detainee is to be transferred to prison, the custody officer should inform the detainee's legal adviser beforehand that the transfer is to take place (including the name of the prison). The custody officer should also make all reasonable attempts to inform:

    • family or friends who have been informed previously of the detainee's detention;
    • the person who was initially informed of the detainee's detention as at *paragraph 5.1.*

(c) **Documentation**

14.11 It is the responsibility of the officer who gives any reminders as at *paragraph 14.4*, to ensure that these are noted in the custody record, as well any comments made by the detained person upon being told of those rights.

14.12 The grounds for, and extent of, any delay in conducting a review shall be recorded.

14.13 Any written representations shall be retained.

14.14 A record shall be made as soon as practicable about the outcome of each review or determination whether to extend the maximum detention period without charge or an application for a warrant of further detention or its extension.

14.15 Any decision not to transfer a detained person to a designated prison under paragraph *14.5*, must be recorded, along with the reasons for this decision. If a request under paragraph *14.5(a)* is not accommodated, the reasons for this should also be recorded.

Notes for guidance

14A TACT Schedule 8 Part II sets out the procedures for review of detention up to 48 hours from the time of arrest under TACT section 41 (or if a person was being detained under TACT Schedule 7, from the time at which the examination under Schedule 7 began). These include provisions for the requirement to review detention, postponing a review, grounds for continued detention, designating a review officer, representations, rights of the detained person and keeping a record. The review officer's role ends after a warrant has been issued for extension of detention under Part III of Schedule 8.

14B Section 24(1) of the Terrorism Act 2006, amended the grounds contained within the 2000 Act on which a review officer may authorise continued detention. Continued detention may be authorised if it is necessary—

   a) *to obtain relevant evidence whether by questioning him or otherwise*
   b) *to preserve relevant evidence*
   c) *while awaiting the result of an examination or analysis of relevant evidence*
   d) *for the examination or analysis of anything with a view to obtaining relevant evidence*
   e) *pending a decision to apply to the Secretary of State for a deportation notice to be served on the detainee, the making of any such application, or the consideration of any such application by the Secretary of State*
   f) *pending a decision to charge the detainee with an offence.*

14C Applications for warrants to extend detention beyond 48 hours, may be made for periods of 7 days at a time (initially under TACT Schedule 8 paragraph 29, and extensions thereafter under TACT Schedule 8, Paragraph 36), up to a maximum period of 28 days from the time of arrest (or if a person was being detained under TACT Schedule 7, from the time at which the examination under Schedule 7 began). Applications may be made for shorter periods than 7 days, which must be specified. The judicial authority may also substitute a shorter period if he feels a period of 7 days is inappropriate.

14D Unless Note 14F applies, applications for warrants that would take the total period of detention up to 14 days or less should be made to a judicial authority, meaning a District Judge (Magistrates' Court) designated by the Lord Chancellor to hear such applications.

14E Any application for a warrant which would take the period of detention beyond 14 days from the time of arrest (or if a person was being detained under TACT Schedule 7, from the time at which the examination under Schedule 7 began), must be made to a High Court Judge.

14F If an application has been made to a High Court judge for a warrant which would take detention beyond 14 days, and the High Court judge instead issues a warrant for a period of time which would not take detention beyond 14 days, further applications for extension of detention must also be made to a High Court judge, regardless of the period of time to which they refer.

14G TACT Schedule 8 Paragraph 31 requires a notice to be given to the detained person if a warrant is sought for further detention. This must be provided before the judicial hearing of the application for that warrant and must include:

   a) *notification that the application for a warrant has been made*
   b) *the time at which the application was made*
   c) *the time at which the application is to be heard*
   d) *the grounds on which further detention is sought.*

A notice must also be provided each time an application is made to extend an existing warrant.

14H An officer applying for an order under TACT Schedule 8 Paragraph 34 to withhold specified information on which he intends to rely when applying for a warrant of further detention, may make the application for the order orally or in writing. The most appropriate method of application will depend on the circumstances of the case and the need to ensure fairness to the detainee.

14I Where facilities exist, hearings relating to extension of detention under Part III of Schedule 8 may take place using video conferencing facilities provided that the requirements set out in Schedule 8 are still met. However, if the judicial authority requires the detained person to be physically present at any hearing, this should be complied with as soon as practicable. Paragraphs 33(4) to 33(9) of TACT Schedule 8 govern the relevant conduct of hearings.

14J Transfer to prison is intended to ensure that individuals who are detained for extended periods of time are held in a place designed for longer periods of detention than police stations. Prison will provide detainees with a greater range of facilities more appropriate to longer detention periods.

14K The Code will only apply as is appropriate to the conditions of detention during the period of transit. There is obviously no requirement to provide such things as bed linen or reading materials for the journey between prison and police station.

15 Charging

15.1 Charging of detained persons is covered by PACE and guidance issued under PACE by the Director of Public Prosecutions. General guidance on charging can be found in section 16 of PACE Code C.

16 Testing persons for the presence of specified Class A drugs

16.1 The provisions for drug testing under section 63B of PACE (as amended by section 5 of the Criminal Justice Act 2003 and section 7 of the Drugs Act 2005), do not apply to detention under TACT section 41 and Schedule 8. Guidance on these provisions can be found in section 17 of PACE Code C.

ANNEX A—INTIMATE AND STRIP SEARCHES

A Intimate search

1. An intimate search consists of the physical examination of a person's body orifices other than the mouth. The intrusive nature of such searches means the actual and potential risks associated with intimate searches must never be underestimated.

(a) Action

2. Body orifices other than the mouth may be searched only if authorised by an officer of inspector rank or above who has reasonable grounds for believing that the person may have concealed on themselves anything which they could and might use to cause physical injury to themselves or others at the station and the officer has reasonable grounds for believing that an intimate search is the only means of removing those items.

3. Before the search begins, a police officer, designated detention officer or staff custody officer, must tell the detainee:

   (a) that the authority to carry out the search has been given;
   (b) the grounds for giving the authorisation and for believing that the article cannot be removed without an intimate search.

4. An intimate search may only be carried out by a registered medical practitioner or registered nurse, unless an officer of at least inspector rank considers this is not practicable, in which case a police officer may carry out the search. See *Notes A1 to A5*.

5. Any proposal for a search under *paragraph 2* to be carried out by someone other than a registered medical practitioner or registered nurse must only be considered as a last resort and when the authorising officer is satisfied the risks associated with allowing the item to remain with the detainee outweigh the risks associated with removing it. See *Notes A1 to A5*.

6. An intimate search at a police station of a juvenile or mentally disordered or otherwise mentally vulnerable person may take place only in the presence of an appropriate adult of the same sex, unless the detainee specifically requests a particular adult of the opposite sex who is readily available. In the case of a juvenile the search may take place in the absence of the appropriate adult only if the juvenile signifies in the presence of the appropriate adult they do not want the adult present during the search and the adult agrees. A record shall be made of the juvenile's decision and signed by the appropriate adult.

7. When an intimate search under *paragraph 2* is carried out by a police officer, the officer must be of the same sex as the detainee. A minimum of two people, other than the detainee, must be present during the search. Subject to *paragraph 6*, no person of the opposite sex who is not a medical

practitioner or nurse shall be present, nor shall anyone whose presence is unnecessary. The search shall be conducted with proper regard to the sensitivity and vulnerability of the detainee.

(b) Documentation

8. In the case of an intimate search under paragraph 2, the following shall be recorded as soon as practicable, in the detainee's custody record:

- the authorisation to carry out the search;
- the grounds for giving the authorisation;
- the grounds for believing the article could not be removed without an intimate search
- which parts of the detainee's body were searched
- who carried out the search
- who was present
- the result.

9. If an intimate search is carried out by a police officer, the reason why it was impracticable for a registered medical practitioner or registered nurse to conduct it must be recorded.

B Strip search

10. A strip search is a search involving the removal of more than outer clothing. In this Code, outer clothing includes shoes and socks.

(a) Action

11. A strip search may take place only if it is considered necessary to remove an article which a detainee would not be allowed to keep, and the officer reasonably considers the detainee might have concealed such an article. Strip searches shall not be routinely carried out if there is no reason to consider that articles are concealed.

The conduct of strip searches

12. When strip searches are conducted:

(a) a police officer carrying out a strip search must be the same sex as the detainee;

(b) the search shall take place in an area where the detainee cannot be seen by anyone who does not need to be present, nor by a member of the opposite sex except an appropriate adult who has been specifically requested by the detainee;

(c) except in cases of urgency, where there is risk of serious harm to the detainee or to others, whenever a strip search involves exposure of intimate body parts, there must be at least two people present other than the detainee, and if the search is of a juvenile or mentally disordered or otherwise mentally vulnerable person, one of the people must be the appropriate adult. Except in urgent cases as above, a search of a juvenile may take place in the absence of the appropriate adult only if the juvenile signifies in the presence of the appropriate adult that they do not want the adult to be present during the search and the adult agrees. A record shall be made of the juvenile's decision and signed by the appropriate adult. The presence of more than two people, other than an appropriate adult, shall be permitted only in the most exceptional circumstances;

(d) the search shall be conducted with proper regard to the sensitivity and vulnerability of the detainee in these circumstances and every reasonable effort shall be made to secure the detainee's cooperation and minimise embarrassment. Detainees who are searched shall not normally be required to remove all their clothes at the same time, eg a person should be allowed to remove clothing above the waist and redress before removing further clothing;

(e) if necessary to assist the search, the detainee may be required to hold their arms in the air or to stand with their legs apart and bend forward so a visual examination may be made of the genital and anal areas provided no physical contact is made with any body orifice;

    (f) if articles are found, the detainee shall be asked to hand them over. If articles are found within any body orifice other than the mouth, and the detainee refuses to hand them over, their removal would constitute an intimate search, which must be carried out as in *Part A*;

    (g) a strip search shall be conducted as quickly as possible, and the detainee allowed to dress as soon as the procedure is complete.

(b) Documentation

13. A record shall be made on the custody record of a strip search including the reason it was considered necessary, those present and any result.

Notes for guidance

A1 Before authorising any intimate search, the authorising officer must make every reasonable effort to persuade the detainee to hand the article over without a search. If the detainee agrees, a registered medical practitioner or registered nurse should whenever possible be asked to assess the risks involved and, if necessary, attend to assist the detainee.

A2 If the detainee does not agree to hand the article over without a search, the authorising officer must carefully review all the relevant factors before authorising an intimate search. In particular, the officer must consider whether the grounds for believing an article may be concealed are reasonable.

A3 If authority is given for a search under paragraph 2, a registered medical practitioner or registered nurse shall be consulted whenever possible. The presumption should be that the search will be conducted by the registered medical practitioner or registered nurse and the authorising officer must make every reasonable effort to persuade the detainee to allow the medical practitioner or nurse to conduct the search.

A4 A constable should only be authorised to carry out a search as a last resort and when all other approaches have failed. In these circumstances, the authorising officer must be satisfied the detainee might use the article for one or more of the purposes in paragraph 2 and the physical injury likely to be caused is sufficiently severe to justify authorising a constable to carry out the search.

A5 If an officer has any doubts whether to authorise an intimate search by a constable, the officer should seek advice from an officer of superintendent rank or above.

Annex B—Delay in Notifying Arrest or Allowing Acces to Legal Advice for Persons Detained Under the Terrorism Act 2000

A Delays under TACT Schedule 8

1. The rights as in *sections 5* or *6,* may be delayed if the person is detained under the Terrorism Act 2000, section 41, has not yet been charged with an offence and an officer of superintendent rank or above has reasonable grounds for believing the exercise of either right will have one of the following consequences:

    (a) interference with or harm to evidence of a serious offence,

    (b) interference with or physical injury to any person,

    (c) the alerting of persons who are suspected of having committed a serious offence but who have not been arrested for it,

    (d) the hindering of the recovery of property obtained as a result of a serious offence or in respect of which a forfeiture order could be made under section 23,

    (e) interference with the gathering of information about the commission, preparation or instigation of acts of terrorism,

    (f) the alerting of a person and thereby making it more difficult to prevent an act of terrorism, or

    (g) the alerting of a person and thereby making it more difficult to secure a person's apprehension, prosecution or conviction in connection with the commission, preparation or instigation of an act of terrorism.

2. These rights may also be delayed if the officer has reasonable grounds for believing that:

(a) the detained person has benefited from his criminal conduct (to be decided in accordance with Part 2 of the Proceeds of Crime Act 2002), and

(b) the recovery of the value of the property constituting the benefit will be hindered by—

(i) informing the named person of the detained person's detention (in the case of an authorisation under Paragraph 8(1)(a) of Schedule 8 to TACT, or

(ii) the exercise of the right under paragraph 7 (in the case of an authorisation under Paragraph 8(1)(b) of Schedule 8 to TACT.

3. Authority to delay a detainee's right to consult privately with a solicitor may be given only if the authorising officer has reasonable grounds to believe the solicitor the detainee wants to consult will, inadvertently or otherwise, pass on a message from the detainee or act in some other way which will have any of the consequences specified under *paragraph 8 of Schedule 8 to the Terrorism Act 2000.* In these circumstances the detainee must be allowed to choose another solicitor. See *Note B3.*

4. If the detainee wishes to see a solicitor, access to that solicitor may not be delayed on the grounds they might advise the detainee not to answer questions or the solicitor was initially asked to attend the police station by someone else. In the latter case the detainee must be told the solicitor has come to the police station at another person's request, and must be asked to sign the custody record to signify whether they want to see the solicitor.

5. The fact the grounds for delaying notification of arrest may be satisfied does not automatically mean the grounds for delaying access to legal advice will also be satisfied.

6. These rights may be delayed only for as long as is necessary but not beyond 48 hours from the time of arrest (or if a person was being detained under TACT Schedule 7, from the time at which the examination under Schedule 7 began). If the above grounds cease to apply within this time the detainee must as soon as practicable be asked if they wish to exercise either right, the custody record noted accordingly, and action taken in accordance with the relevant section of this Code.

7. A person must be allowed to consult a solicitor for a reasonable time before any court hearing.

B Documentation

8. The grounds for action under this Annex shall be recorded and the detainee informed of them as soon as practicable.

9. Any reply given by a detainee under *paragraph 6* must be recorded and the detainee asked to endorse the record in relation to whether they want to receive legal advice at this point.

C Cautions and special warnings

10. When a suspect detained at a police station is interviewed during any period for which access to legal advice has been delayed under this Annex, the court or jury may not draw adverse inferences from their silence.

Notes for guidance

B1 Even if Annex B applies in the case of a juvenile, or a person who is mentally disordered or otherwise mentally vulnerable, action to inform the appropriate adult and the person responsible for a juvenile's welfare if that is a different person, must nevertheless be taken as in paragraph 3.15 and 3.17.

B2 In the case of Commonwealth citizens and foreign nationals, see Note 7A.

B3 A decision to delay access to a specific solicitor is likely to be a rare occurrence and only when it can be shown the suspect is capable of misleading that particular solicitor and there is more than a substantial risk that the suspect will succeed in causing information to be conveyed which will lead to one or more of the specified consequences.

Annex C—Restriction on Drawing Adverse Inferences From Silence and Terms of the Caution When the Restriction Applies

(a) The restriction on drawing adverse inferences from silence

1. The Criminal Justice and Public Order Act 1994, sections 34, 36 and 37 as amended by the Youth Justice and Criminal Evidence Act 1999, section 58 describe the conditions under which adverse inferences may be drawn from a person's failure or refusal to say anything about their involvement in the offence when interviewed, after being charged or informed they may be prosecuted. These provisions are subject to an overriding restriction on the ability of a court or jury to draw adverse inferences from a person's silence. This restriction applies:

(a) to any detainee at a police station who, before being interviewed, see section 11 or being charged or informed they may be prosecuted, see section 15, has:
(i) asked for legal advice, see *section 6, paragraph 6.1*;
(ii) not been allowed an opportunity to consult a solicitor, including the duty solicitor, as in this Code; and
(iii) not changed their mind about wanting legal advice, see *section 6, paragraph 6.7(c)*
Note the condition in (ii) will
— apply when a detainee who has asked for legal advice is interviewed before speaking to a solicitor as in *section 6, paragraph 6.6(a)* or *(b)*.
— not apply if the detained person declines to ask for the duty solicitor, see *section 6, paragraphs 6.7(b)* and *(c)*;

(b) to any person charged with, or informed they may be prosecuted for, an offence who:
(i) has had brought to their notice a written statement made by another person or the content of an interview with another person which relates to that offence, see PACE Code C *section 16, paragraph 16.6*;
(ii) is interviewed about that offence, see PACE Code C *section 16, paragraph 16.8*; or
(iii) makes a written statement about that offence, see *Annex D paragraphs 4* and *9*.

(b) Terms of the caution when the restriction applies

2. When a requirement to caution arises at a time when the restriction on drawing adverse inferences from silence applies, the caution shall be:

'You do not have to say anything, but anything you do say may be given in evidence.'

3. Whenever the restriction either begins to apply or ceases to apply after a caution has already been given, the person shall be re-cautioned in the appropriate terms. The changed position on drawing inferences and that the previous caution no longer applies shall also be explained to the detainee in ordinary language. See *Note C1*.

Notes for guidance

C1 The following is suggested as a framework to help explain changes in the position on drawing adverse inferences if the restriction on drawing adverse inferences from silence:

(a) begins to apply:
'The caution you were previously given no longer applies. This is because after that caution:
(i) you asked to speak to a solicitor but have not yet been allowed an opportunity to speak to a solicitor. See paragraph 1(a); or
(ii) you have been charged with/informed you may be prosecuted. See paragraph 1(b).
'This means that from now on, adverse inferences cannot be drawn at court and your defence will not be harmed just because you choose to say nothing. Please listen carefully to the caution I am about to give you because it will apply from now on. You will see that it does not say anything about your defence being harmed.'

(b) ceases to apply before or at the time the person is charged or informed they may be prosecuted, see paragraph 1(a);

'The caution you were previously given no longer applies. This is because after that caution you have been allowed an opportunity to speak to a solicitor. Please listen carefully to the caution I am about to give you because it will apply from now on. It explains how your defence at court may be affected if you choose to say nothing.'

ANNEX D—WRITTEN STATEMENTS UNDER CAUTION

(a) Written by a person under caution

1. A person shall always be invited to write down what they want to say.

2. A person who has not been charged with, or informed they may be prosecuted for, any offence to which the statement they want to write relates, shall:

 (a) unless the statement is made at a time when the restriction on drawing adverse inferences from silence applies, see Annex C, be asked to write out and sign the following before writing what they want to say:

 'I make this statement of my own free will. I understand that I do not have to say anything but that it may harm my defence if I do not mention when questioned something which I later rely on in court. This statement may be given in evidence.';

 (b) if the statement is made at a time when the restriction on drawing adverse inferences from silence applies, be asked to write out and sign the following before writing what they want to say;

 'I make this statement of my own free will. I understand that I do not have to say anything. This statement may be given in evidence.'

3. When a person, on the occasion of being charged with or informed they may be prosecuted for any offence, asks to make a statement which relates to any such offence and wants to write it they shall:

 (a) unless the restriction on drawing adverse inferences from silence, see Annex C, applied when they were so charged or informed they may be prosecuted, be asked to write out and sign the following before writing what they want to say:

 'I make this statement of my own free will. I understand that I do not have to say anything but that it may harm my defence if I do not mention when questioned something which I later rely on in court. This statement may be given in evidence.';

 (b) if the restriction on drawing adverse inferences from silence applied when they were so charged or informed they may be prosecuted, be asked to write out and sign the following before writing what they want to say:

 'I make this statement of my own free will. I understand that I do not have to say anything. This statement may be given in evidence.'

4. When a person, who has already been charged with or informed they may be prosecuted for any offence, asks to make a statement which relates to any such offence and wants to write it they shall be asked to write out and sign the following before writing what they want to say:

 'I make this statement of my own free will. I understand that I do not have to say anything. This statement may be given in evidence.';

5. Any person writing their own statement shall be allowed to do so without any prompting except a police officer or other police staff may indicate to them which matters are material or question any ambiguity in the statement.

(b) Written by a police officer or other police staff

6. If a person says they would like someone to write the statement for them, a police officer, or other police staff shall write the statement.

7. If the person has not been charged with, or informed they may be prosecuted for, any offence to which the statement they want to make relates they shall, before starting, be asked to sign, or make their mark, to the following:

(a) unless the statement is made at a time when the restriction on drawing adverse inferences from silence applies, see *Annex C*:

'*I,............................, wish to make a statement. I want someone to write down what I say. I understand that I do not have to say anything but that it may harm my defence if I do not mention when questioned something which I later rely on in court. This statement may be given in evidence.*';

(b) if the statement is made at a time when the restriction on drawing adverse inferences from silence applies:

'*I,............................, wish to make a statement. I want someone to write down what I say. I understand that I do not have to say anything. This statement may be given in evidence.*'

8. If, on the occasion of being charged with or informed they may be prosecuted for any offence, the person asks to make a statement which relates to any such offence they shall before starting be asked to sign, or make their mark to, the following:

(a) unless the restriction on drawing adverse inferences from silence applied, see *Annex C,* when they were so charged or informed they may be prosecuted:

'*I,............................, wish to make a statement. I want someone to write down what I say. I understand that I do not have to say anything but that it may harm my defence if I do not mention when questioned something which I later rely on in court. This statement may be given in evidence.*';

(b) if the restriction on drawing adverse inferences from silence applied when they were so charged or informed they may be prosecuted:

'*I,............................, wish to make a statement. I want someone to write down what I say. I understand that I do not have to say anything. This statement may be given in evidence.*'

9. If, having already been charged with or informed they may be prosecuted for any offence, a person asks to make a statement which relates to any such offence they shall before starting, be asked to sign, or make their mark to:

'*I,............................, wish to make a statement. I want someone to write down what I say. I understand that I do not have to say anything. This statement may be given in evidence.*'

10. The person writing the statement must take down the exact words spoken by the person making it and must not edit or paraphrase it. Any questions that are necessary, eg to make it more intelligible, and the answers given must be recorded at the same time on the statement form.

11. When the writing of a statement is finished the person making it shall be asked to read it and to make any corrections, alterations or additions they want. When they have finished reading they shall be asked to write and sign or make their mark on the following certificate at the end of the statement:

'*I have read the above statement, and I have been able to correct, alter or add anything I wish. This statement is true. I have made it of my own free will.*'

12. If the person making the statement cannot read, or refuses to read it, or to write the above mentioned certificate at the end of it or to sign it, the person taking the statement shall read it to them and ask them if they would like to correct, alter or add anything and to put their signature or make their mark at the end. The person taking the statement shall certify on the statement itself what has occurred.

ANNEX E—SUMMARY OF PROVISIONS RELATING TO MENTALLY DISORDERED AND OTHERWISE MENTALLY VULNERABLE PEOPLE

1. If an officer has any suspicion, or is told in good faith, that a person of any age may be mentally disordered or otherwise mentally vulnerable, or mentally incapable of understanding the significance of questions or their replies that person shall be treated as mentally disordered or otherwise mentally vulnerable for the purposes of this Code. See *paragraph 1.10*.

2. In the case of a person who is mentally disordered or otherwise mentally vulnerable, 'the appropriate adult' means:

    (a) a relative, guardian or other person responsible for their care or custody;
    (b) someone experienced in dealing with mentally disordered or mentally vulnerable people but who is not a police officer or employed by the police;
    (c) failing these, some other responsible adult aged 18 or over who is not a police officer or employed by the police.

See *paragraph 1.13(b) and Note 1D*.

3. If the detention of a person who is mentally vulnerable or appears to be suffering from a mental disorder is authorised by the review officer (see *paragraphs 14.1* and *14.2* and *Notes for Guidance 14A* and *14B)*, the custody officer must as soon as practicable inform the appropriate adult of the grounds for detention and the person's whereabouts, and ask the adult to come to the police station to see them. If the appropriate adult:

    • is already at the station when information is given as in *paragraphs 3.1* to *3.5* the information must be given in their presence
    • is not at the station when the provisions of *paragraph 3.1* to *3.5* are complied with

these provisions must be complied with again in their presence once they arrive.

See *paragraphs 3.15* to *3.16*.

4. If the appropriate adult, having been informed of the right to legal advice, considers legal advice should be taken, the provisions of *section 6* apply as if the mentally disordered or otherwise mentally vulnerable person had requested access to legal advice. See *paragraph 3.20* and *Note E1*.

5. The custody officer must make sure a person receives appropriate clinical attention as soon as reasonably practicable if the person appears to be suffering from a mental disorder or in urgent cases immediately call the nearest health care professional or an ambulance. It is not intended these provisions delay the transfer of a detainee to a place of safety under the Mental Health Act 1983, section 136 if that is applicable. If an assessment under that Act is to take place at a police station, the custody officer must consider whether an appropriate health care professional should be called to conduct an initial clinical check on the detainee. See *paragraph 9.6* and *9.8*.

6. If a mentally disordered or otherwise mentally vulnerable person is cautioned in the absence of the appropriate adult, the caution must be repeated in the appropriate adult's presence. See *paragraph 10.11*.

7. A mentally disordered or otherwise mentally vulnerable person must not be interviewed or asked to provide or sign a written statement in the absence of the appropriate adult unless the provisions of *paragraphs 11.2* or *11.11* to *11.13* apply. Questioning in these circumstances may not continue in the absence of the appropriate adult once sufficient information to avert the risk has been obtained. A record shall be made of the grounds for any decision to begin an interview in these circumstances. See *paragraphs 11.2, 11.9* and *11.11* to *11.13*.

8. If the appropriate adult is present at an interview, they shall be informed they are not expected to act simply as an observer and the purposes of their presence are to:

    • advise the interviewee
    • observe whether or not the interview is being conducted properly and fairly
    • facilitate communication with the interviewee.

See *paragraph 11.10*.

9. If the custody officer charges a mentally disordered or otherwise mentally vulnerable person with an offence or takes such other action as is appropriate when there is sufficient evidence for a prosecution this must be done in the presence of the appropriate adult. The written notice embodying any charge must be given to the appropriate adult. See *paragraphs PACE Code C Section 16*.

10. An intimate or strip search of a mentally disordered or otherwise mentally vulnerable person may take place only in the presence of the appropriate adult of the same sex, unless the detainee specifically requests the presence of a particular adult of the opposite sex. A strip search may take place in the absence of an appropriate adult only in cases of urgency when there is a risk of serious harm to the detainee or others. See *Annex A, paragraphs 6* and *12(c)*.

11. Particular care must be taken when deciding whether to use any form of approved restraints on a mentally disordered or otherwise mentally vulnerable person in a locked cell. See *paragraph 8.2*.

Notes for guidance

E1 The purpose of the provision at paragraph 3.20 is to protect the rights of a mentally disordered or otherwise mentally vulnerable detained person who does not understand the significance of what is said to them. If the detained person wants to exercise the right to legal advice, the appropriate action should be taken and not delayed until the appropriate adult arrives. A mentally disordered or otherwise mentally vulnerable detained person should always be given an opportunity, when an appropriate adult is called to the police station, to consult privately with a solicitor in the absence of the appropriate adult if they want.

E2 Although people who are mentally disordered or otherwise mentally vulnerable are often capable of providing reliable evidence, they may, without knowing or wanting to do so, be particularly prone in certain circumstances to provide information that may be unreliable, misleading or self-incriminating. Special care should always be taken when questioning such a person, and the appropriate adult should be involved if there is any doubt about a person's mental state or capacity. Because of the risk of unreliable evidence, it is important to obtain corroboration of any facts admitted whenever possible.

E3 Because of the risks referred to in Note E2, which the presence of the appropriate adult is intended to minimise, officers of superintendent rank or above should exercise their discretion to authorise the commencement of an interview in the appropriate adult's absence only in exceptional cases, if it is necessary to avert an immediate risk of serious harm. See paragraphs 11.2, 11.11 to 11.13.

ANNEX F—COUNTRIES WITH WHICH BILATERAL CONSULAR CONVENTIONS OR AGREEMENTS REQUIRING NOTIFICATION OF THE ARREST AND DETENTION OF THEIR NATIONALS ARE IN FORCE

Armenia	German Federal Republic
Austria	Greece
Azerbaijan	Hungary
Belarus	Italy
Belgium	Japan
Bosnia-Herzegovina	Kazakhstan
Bulgaria	Macedonia
China*	Mexico
Croatia	Moldova
Cuba	Mongolia
Czech Republic	Norway
Denmark	Poland
Egypt	Romania
France	Russia
Georgia	Slovak Republic

Slovenia	Ukraine
Spain	USA
Sweden	Uzbekistan
Tajikistan	Yugoslavia
Turkmenistan	

* Police are required to inform Chinese officials of arrest/detention in the Manchester consular district only. This comprises Derbyshire, Durham, Greater Manchester, Lancashire, Merseyside, North South and West Yorkshire, and Tyne and Wear.

ANNEX G—FITNESS TO BE INTERVIEWED

1. This Annex contains general guidance to help police officers and health care professionals assess whether a detainee might be at risk in an interview.

2. A detainee may be at risk in a interview if it is considered that:

   (a) conducting the interview could significantly harm the detainee's physical or mental state;

   (b) anything the detainee says in the interview about their involvement or suspected involvement in the offence about which they are being interviewed **might** be considered unreliable in subsequent court proceedings because of their physical or mental state.

3. In assessing whether the detainee should be interviewed, the following must be considered:

   (a) how the detainee's physical or mental state might affect their ability to understand the nature and purpose of the interview, to comprehend what is being asked and to appreciate the significance of any answers given and make rational decisions about whether they want to say anything;

   (b) the extent to which the detainee's replies may be affected by their physical or mental condition rather than representing a rational and accurate explanation of their involvement in the offence;

   (c) how the nature of the interview, which could include particularly probing questions, might affect the detainee.

4. It is essential health care professionals who are consulted consider the functional ability of the detainee rather than simply relying on a medical diagnosis, eg it is possible for a person with severe mental illness to be fit for interview.

5. Health care professionals should advise on the need for an appropriate adult to be present, whether reassessment of the person's fitness for interview may be necessary if the interview lasts beyond a specified time, and whether a further specialist opinion may be required.

6. When health care professionals identify risks they should be asked to quantify the risks.

They should inform the custody officer:

   • whether the person's condition:
     — is likely to improve
     — will require or be amenable to treatment; and
   • indicate how long it may take for such improvement to take effect.

7. The role of the health care professional is to consider the risks and advise the custody officer of the outcome of that consideration. The health care professional's determination and any advice or recommendations should be made in writing and form part of the custody record.

8. Once the health care professional has provided that information, it is a matter for the custody officer to decide whether or not to allow the interview to go ahead and if the interview is to proceed,

to determine what safeguards are needed. Nothing prevents safeguards being provided in addition to those required under the Code. An example might be to have an appropriate health care professional present during the interview, in addition to an appropriate adult, in order constantly to monitor the person's condition and how it is being affected by the interview.

ANNEX H—DETAINED PERSON: OBSERVATION LIST

1. If any detainee fails to meet any of the following criteria, an appropriate health care professional or an ambulance must be called.

2. When assessing the level of rousability, consider:

Rousability—can they be woken?

- go into the cell
- call their name
- shake gently

Response to questions—can they give appropriate answers to questions such as:

- What's your name?
- Where do you live?
- Where do you think you are?

Response to commands—can they respond appropriately to commands such as:

- Open your eyes!
- Lift one arm, now the other arm!

3. Remember to take into account the possibility or presence of other illnesses, injury, or mental condition, a person who is drowsy and smells of alcohol may also have the following:

- Diabetes
- Epilepsy
- Head injury
- Drug intoxication or overdose
- Stroke

Ratification Status and Depository Information on the UN Counter-Terrorism Legal Instruments

Instrument	Date of entry into force	No of ratifications (as of 31 December 2007)	Depository information
Convention on Offences and Certain Other Acts Committed on Board Aircraft (1963)	4 December 1969	182	Secretary-General of the International Civil Aviation Organization (ICAO) 999 University Street, Montreal, Quebec H3C 5H7, Canada
Convention for the Suppression of Unlawful Seizure of Aircraft (1970)	14 October 1971	182	Russian Federation, United Kingdom of Great Britain and Northern Ireland, United States of America
Convention for the Suppression of Unlawful Acts against the Safety of Civil Aviation (1971)	26 January 1973	185	Russian Federation, United Kingdom of Great Britain and Northern Ireland, United States of America
Convention on the Prevention and Punishment of Crimes against Internationally Protected Persons, including Diplomatic Agents (1973)	20 February 1977	166	Secretary-General of the United Nations CONTACT: Treaty Section Office of Legal Affairs United Nations New York, NY 10017 United States
International Convention against the Taking of Hostages (1979)	3 June 1983	164	Secretary-General of the United Nations CONTACT: Treaty Section Office of Legal Affairs United Nations New York, NY 10017 United States

Instrument	Date of entry into force	No of ratifications (as of 31 December 2007)	Depository information
Convention on the Physical Protection of Nuclear Material (1979)	8 February 1987	129	Director-General of the International Atomic Energy Agency (IAEA) PO Box 100, Wagramer Strasse 5 A-1400 Vienna, Austria
Protocol for the Suppression of Unlawful Acts of Violence at Airports Serving International Civil Aviation (1988)	6 August 1989	161	Russian Federation, United Kingdom of Great Britain and Northern Ireland, United States of America OR Secretary-General of the International Civil Aviation Organization (ICAO) 999 University Street, Montreal, Quebec H3C 5H7, Canada
Convention for the Suppression of Unlawful Acts against the Safety of Maritime Navigation (1988)	1 March 1992	146	Secretary-General of the International Maritime Organization (IMO) 4 Albert Embankment London SE1 7SR United Kingdom
Protocol for the Suppression of Unlawful Acts against the Safety of Fixed Platforms Located on the Continental Shelf (1988)	1 March 1992	134	Secretary-General of the International Maritime Organization (IMO) 4 Albert Embankment London SE1 7SR United Kingdom
Convention on the Marking of Plastic Explosives for the Purpose of Detection (1991)	21 June 1998	137	Secretary-General of the International Civil Aviation Organization (ICAO) 999 University Street, Montreal, Quebec H3C 5H7, Canada
International Convention for the Suppression of Terrorist Bombings (1997)	23 May 2001	153	Secretary-General of the United Nations CONTACT: Treaty Section Office of Legal Affairs United Nations New York, NY 10017 United States

Instrument	Date of entry into force	No of ratifications (as of 31 December 2007)	Depository information
International Convention for the Suppression of the Financing of Terrorism (1999)	10 April 2002	160	Secretary-General of the United Nations CONTACT: Treaty Section Office of Legal Affairs United Nations New York, NY 10017 United States
International Convention for the Suppression of Acts of Nuclear Terrorism (2005)	7 July 2007	29	Secretary-General of the United Nations CONTACT: Treaty Section Office of Legal Affairs United Nations New York, NY 10017 United States
Amendment to the Convention on the Physical Protection of Nuclear Material (2005)	Not yet in force (will enter force thirteen days after the deposit of ratification by two thirds of State Parties)	13	Director-General of the International Atomic Energy Agency (IAEA) PO Box 100, Wagramer Strasse 5 A-1400 Vienna, Austria
Protocol of 2005 to the Convention for the Suppression of Unlawful Acts against the Safety of Maritime Navigation (2005)	Not yet in force (will enter force 90 days after the twelfth deposit of ratification)	3	Secretary-General of the International Maritime Organization (IMO) 4 Albert Embankment London SE1 7SR United Kingdom
Protocol for the Suppression of Unlawful Acts against the Safety of Fixed Platforms Located on the Continental Shelf (2005)	Not yet in force (will enter force 90 days after the twelfth deposit of ratification)	0	Secretary-General of the International Maritime Organization (IMO) 4 Albert Embankment London SE1 7SR United Kingdom

UNSC Resolution 1822

United Nations Security Council

Distr:
General
S/RES/1822 (2008)
30 June 2008

Resolution 1822 (2008)

Adopted by
the Security Council at its 5928th meeting, on 30 June 2008

The Security Council,

Recalling its resolutions 1267 (1999), 1333 (2000), 1363 (2001), 1373 (2001), 1390 (2002), 1452 (2002), 1455 (2003), 1526 (2004), 1566 (2004), 1617 (2005), 1624 (2005), 1699 (2006), 1730 (2006), and 1735 (2006), and the relevant statements of its President,

Reaffirming that terrorism in all its forms and manifestations constitutes one of the most serious threats to peace and security and that any acts of terrorism are criminal and unjustifiable regardless of their motivations, whenever and by whomsoever committed, and *reiterating* its unequivocal condemnation of Al-Qaida, Usama bin Laden, the Taliban, and other individuals, groups, undertakings, and entities associated with them, for ongoing and multiple criminal terrorist acts aimed at causing the death of innocent civilians and other victims, destruction of property and greatly undermining stability,

Reaffirming the need to combat by all means, in accordance with the Charter of the United Nations and international law, including applicable international human rights, refugee, and humanitarian law, threats to international peace and security caused by terrorist acts, stressing in this regard the important role the United Nations plays in leading and coordinating this effort,

Welcoming the adoption by the General Assembly of the United Nations Global Counter-Terrorism Strategy (A/60/288) of 8 September 2006 and the creation of the Counter-Terrorism Implementation Task Force (CTITF) to ensure overall coordination and coherence in the counter-terrorism efforts of the United Nations system,

Reiterating its deep concern about the increased violent and terrorist activities in Afghanistan of the Taliban and Al-Qaida and other individuals, groups, undertakings and entities associated with them,

Recalling its resolution 1817 (2008) and *reiterating* its support for the fight against illicit production and trafficking of drugs from and chemical precursors to Afghanistan, in neighbouring countries, countries on trafficking routes, drug destination countries and precursors producing countries,

Expressing its deep concern about criminal misuse of the Internet by Al-Qaida, Usama bin Laden and the Taliban, and other individuals, groups, undertakings, and entities associated with them, in furtherance of terrorist acts,

Stressing that terrorism can only be defeated by a sustained and comprehensive approach involving the active participation and collaboration of all States, and international and regional organizations to impede, impair, isolate, and incapacitate the terrorist threat,

Emphasizing that sanctions are an important tool under the Charter of the United Nations in the maintenance and restoration of international peace and security, and stressing in this regard the need for robust implementation of the measures in paragraph 1 of this resolution as a significant tool in combating terrorist activity,

Urging all Member States, international bodies, and regional organizations to allocate sufficient resources to meet the ongoing and direct threat posed by Al-Qaida, Usama bin Laden and the Taliban, and other individuals, groups, undertakings, and entities associated with them, including by participating actively in identifying which individuals, groups, undertakings and entities should be subject to the measures referred to in paragraph 1 of this resolution,

Reiterating that dialogue between the Committee established pursuant to resolution 1267 (1999) ('the Committee') and Member States is vital to the full implementation of the measures,

Taking note of challenges to measures implemented by Member States in accordance with the measures referred to in paragraph 1 of this resolution and *recognizing* continuing efforts of Member States and the Committee to ensure that fair and clear procedures exist for placing individuals, groups, undertakings, and entities on the list created pursuant to resolutions 1267 (1999) and 1333 (2000) (the 'Consolidated List') and for removing them, as well as for granting humanitarian exemptions,

Reiterating that the measures referred to in paragraph 1 of this resolution, are preventative in nature and are not reliant upon criminal standards set out under national law,

Emphasizing the obligation placed upon all Member States to implement, in full, resolution 1373 (2001), including with regard to the Taliban or Al-Qaida, and any individuals, groups, undertakings or entities associated with Al-Qaida, Usama bin Laden or the Taliban, who have participated in financing, planning, facilitating, recruiting for, preparing, perpetrating, or otherwise supporting terrorist activities or acts, as well as to facilitate the implementation of counter-terrorism obligations in accordance with relevant Security Council resolutions,

Welcoming the establishment by the Secretary-General pursuant to resolution 1730 (2006) of the Focal Point within the Secretariat to receive delisting requests, and *taking note* with appreciation of the ongoing cooperation between the Focal Point and the Committee,

Welcoming the continuing cooperation of the Committee and INTERPOL, in particular on the development of Special Notices, which assists Member States in their implementation of the measures, and recognizing the role of the Analytical Support and Sanctions Implementation Monitoring Team ('the Monitoring Team') in this regard,

Welcoming the continuing cooperation of the Committee with the United Nations Office on Drugs and Crime, in particular on technical assistance and capacity-building, to assist Member States in implementing their obligations under this and other relevant resolutions and international instruments,

Noting with concern the continued threat posed to international peace and security by Al-Qaida, Usama bin Laden and the Taliban, and other individuals, groups, undertakings and entities associated with them, and *reaffirming* its resolve to address all aspects of that threat,

Acting under Chapter VII of the Charter of the United Nations,

Measures

1. *Decides* that all States shall take the measures as previously imposed by paragraph 4(b) of resolution 1267 (1999), paragraph 8(c) of resolution 1333 (2000), and paragraphs 1 and 2 of resolution 1390 (2002), with respect to Al-Qaida, Usama bin Laden and the Taliban, and other individuals,

groups, undertakings, and entities associated with them, as referred to in the list created pursuant to resolutions 1267 (1999) and 1333 (2000) (the 'Consolidated List'):

(a) Freeze without delay the funds and other financial assets or economic resources of these individuals, groups, undertakings and entities, including funds derived from property owned or controlled directly or indirectly, by them or by persons acting on their behalf or at their direction, and ensure that neither these nor any other funds, financial assets or economic resources are made available, directly or indirectly for such persons' benefit, or by their nationals or by persons within their territory;

(b) Prevent the entry into or transit through their territories of these individuals, provided that nothing in this paragraph shall oblige any State to deny entry or require the departure from its territories of its own nationals and this paragraph shall not apply where entry or transit is necessary for the fulfilment of a judicial process or the Committee determines on a case-by-case basis only that entry or transit is justified;

(c) Prevent the direct or indirect supply, sale, or transfer, to these individuals, groups, under- takings and entities from their territories or by their nationals outside their territories, or using their flag vessels or aircraft, of arms and related materiel of all types including weapons and ammunition, military vehicles and equipment paramilitary equipment, and spare parts for the aforementioned and technical advice, assistance, or training related to military activities;

2. *Reaffirms* that acts or activities indicating that an individual, group, undertaking, or entity is 'associated with' Al-Qaida, Usama bin Laden or the Taliban include:

(a) participating in the financing, planning, facilitating, preparing, or perpetrating of acts or activities by, in conjunction with, under the name of, on behalf of, or in support of;

(b) supplying, selling or transferring arms and related materiel to;

(c) recruiting for; or

(d) otherwise supporting acts or activities of;

Al-Qaida, Usama bin Laden or the Taliban, or any cell, affiliate, splinter group or derivative thereof;

3. *Further reaffirms* that any undertaking or entity owned or controlled, directly or indirectly, by, or otherwise supporting, such an individual, group, undertaking or entity associated with Al-Qaida, Usama bin Laden or the Taliban shall be eligible for designation;

4. *Confirms* that the requirements in paragraph 1(a) above apply to financial and economic resources of every kind, including but not limited to those used for the provision of Internet hosting or related services, used for the support of Al-Qaida, Usama bin Laden, and the Taliban and other individuals, groups, undertakings, or entities associated with them;

5. *Encourages* Member States to continue their efforts to act vigorously and decisively to cut the flow of funds and other financial assets and economic resources to Al-Qaida, Usama bin Laden and the Taliban and other individuals, group, undertakings and entities associated with them;

6. *Decides* that Member States may permit the addition to accounts frozen pursuant to the provi- sions of paragraph 1 above of any payment in favour of listed individuals, groups, undertakings or entities, provided that any such payments continue to be subject to the provisions in paragraph 1 above and are frozen;

7. *Reaffirms* the provisions regarding available exemptions to the measures in paragraph 1(a) above, set out in paragraphs 1 and 2 of resolution 1452 (2002), as amended by resolution 1735 (2006), and *reminds* Member States to use the procedures for exemptions as set out in the Committee's guidelines;

8. *Reiterates* the obligation of all Member States to implement and enforce the measures set out in paragraph 1 above, and *urges* all States to redouble their efforts in this regard;

Listing

9. *Encourages* all Member States to submit to the Committee for inclusion on the Consolidated List names of individuals, groups, undertakings, and entities participating, by any means, in the financing or support of acts or activities of Al-Qaida, Usama bin Laden and the Taliban, and other individuals, groups, undertakings, and entities associated with them, as described in paragraph 2 of resolution 1617 (2005) and reaffirmed in paragraph 2 above;

10. *Notes* that such means of financing or support include but are not limited to the use of proceeds derived from illicit cultivation, production, and trafficking of narcotic drugs originating in Afghanistan, and their precursors;

11. *Reiterates* its call for continued cooperation between the Committee and the Government of Afghanistan and the United Nations Assistance Mission in Afghanistan (UNAMA), including by identifying individuals and entities participating in the financing or support of acts or activities of Al-Qaida and the Taliban as described in paragraph 30 of resolution 1806 (2008);

12. *Reaffirms* that, when proposing names to the Committee for inclusion on the Consolidated List, Member States shall act in accordance with paragraph 5 of resolution 1735 (2006) and provide a detailed statement of case, and *decides further* that for each such proposal Member States shall identify those parts of the statement of case that may be publicly released, including for use by the Committee for development of the summary described in paragraph 13 below or for the purpose of notifying or informing the listed individual or entity, and those parts which may be released upon request to interested States;

13. *Directs* the Committee, with the assistance of the Monitoring Team and in coordination with the relevant designating States, after a name is added to the Consolidated List, to make accessible on the Committee's website a narrative summary of reasons for listing for the corresponding entry or entries on the Consolidated List, and *further directs* the Committee, with the assistance of the Monitoring Team and in coordination with the relevant designating States, to make accessible on the Committee's website narrative summaries of reasons for listing for entries that were added to the Consolidated List before the date of adoption of this resolution;

14. *Calls upon* Member States, when proposing names to the Committee for inclusion on the Consolidated List to use the cover sheet in annex I of resolution 1735 (2006) and requests that they provide the Committee with as much relevant information as possible on the proposed name, in particular sufficient identifying information to allow for the positive identification of individuals, groups, undertakings, and entities by Member States, and directs the Committee to update the cover sheet in line with the provisions outlined in paragraphs 12 and 13 above;

15. *Decides* that the Secretariat shall, after publication but within one week after a name is added to the Consolidated List, notify the Permanent Mission of the country or countries where the individual or entity is believed to be located and, in the case of individuals; the country of which the person is a national (to the extent this information is known) in accordance with paragraph 10 of resolution 1735 (2006);

16. *Underlines* the need for the prompt update of the Consolidated List on the Committee's website;

17. *Demands* that Member States receiving notification as in paragraph 15 above take, in accordance with their domestic laws and practices, all possible measures to notify or inform in a timely manner the listed individual or entity of the designation and to include with this notification a copy of the publicly releasable portion of the statement of case, any information on reasons for listing available on the Committee's website, a description of the effects of designation, as provided in the relevant resolutions, the Committee's procedures for considering delisting requests, and the provisions of resolution 1452 (2002) regarding available exemptions;

18. *Encourages* Member States receiving notification as in paragraph 15 above to inform the Committee on steps they have taken to implement the measures set out in paragraph 1 above, and

on the measures taken in accordance with paragraph 17 above, and further encourages Member States to use the tools provided on the Committee's website to provide this information;

Delisting

19. *Welcomes* the establishment within the Secretariat of the Focal Point, pursuant to resolution 1730 (2006), that provides listed individuals, groups, undertakings or entities with the option to submit a petition for de-listing directly to the Focal Point;

20. *Urges* designating States and States of citizenship and residence to review de-listing petitions received through the Focal Point, in accordance with the procedures outlined in the annex to resolution 1730 (2006), in a timely manner and to indicate whether they support or oppose the request in order to facilitate the Committee's review;

21. *Directs* the Committee to continue to work, in accordance with its guidelines, to consider petitions for the removal from the Consolidated List of members and/or associates of Al-Qaida, Usama bin Laden, the Taliban who no longer meet the criteria established in the relevant resolutions;

22. *Directs* the Committee to consider an annual review of the names on the Consolidated List of individuals reported to be deceased, in which the names are circulated to the relevant states pursuant to the procedures set forth in the Committee guidelines, in order to ensure the Consolidated List is as updated and accurate as possible and to confirm that listing remains appropriate;

23. *Decides* that the Secretariat shall, within one week after a name is removed from the Consolidated List, notify the Permanent Mission of the country or countries where the individual or entity is believed to be located and, in the case of individuals, the country of which the person is a national (to the extent this information is known), and *demands* that States receiving such notification take measures, in accordance with their domestic laws and practices, to notify or inform the concerned individual or entity of the delisting in a timely manner;

Review and maintenance of the Consolidated List

24. *Encourages* all Member States, in particular designating states and states of residence or nationality, to submit to the Committee additional identifying and other information, along with supporting documentation, on listed individuals, groups, undertakings, and entities, including updates on the operating status of listed entities, groups and undertakings, the movement, incarceration or death of listed individuals and other significant events, as such information becomes available;

25. *Directs* the Committee to conduct a review of all names on the Consolidated List at the date of adoption of this resolution by 30 June 2010 in which the relevant names are circulated to the designating states and states of residence and/or citizenship, where known, pursuant to the procedures set forth in the Committee guidelines, in order to ensure the Consolidated List is as updated and accurate as possible and to confirm that listing remains appropriate;

26. *Further directs* the Committee, upon completion of the review described in paragraph 25 above, to conduct an annual review of all names on the Consolidated List that have not been reviewed in three or more years, in which the relevant names are circulated to the designating states and states of residence and/or citizenship, where known, pursuant to the procedures set forth in the Committee guidelines, in order to ensure the Consolidated List is as updated and accurate as possible and to confirm that listing remains appropriate;

Measures implementation

27. *Reiterates* the importance of all States identifying, and if necessary introducing, adequate procedures to implement fully all aspects of the measures described in paragraph 1 above;

28. *Encourages* the Committee to continue to ensure that fair and clear procedures exist for placing individuals and entities on the Consolidated List and for removing them as well as for granting

humanitarian exemptions, and directs the Committee to keep its guidelines under active review in support of these objectives;

29. *Directs* the Committee, as a matter of priority, to review its guidelines with respect to the provisions of this resolution, in particular paragraphs 6, 12, 13, 17, 22, and 26 above;

30. *Encourages* Member States to send representatives to meet the Committee for more in-depth discussion of relevant issues and welcomes voluntary briefings from interested Member States on their efforts to implement the measures referred to in paragraph 1 above, including particular challenges that hinder full implementation of the measures;

31. *Requests* the Committee to report to the Council on its findings regarding Member States' implementation efforts, and identify and recommend steps necessary to improve implementation;

32. *Directs* the Committee to identify possible cases of non-compliance with the measures pursuant to paragraph 1 above and to determine the appropriate course of action on each case, and *requests* the Chairman, in periodic reports to the Council pursuant to paragraph 38 below, to provide progress reports on the Committee's work on this issue;

33. *Urges* all Member States, in their implementation of the measures set out in paragraph 1 above, to ensure that fraudulent, counterfeit, stolen, and lost passports and other travel documents are invalidated and removed from circulation, in accordance with domestic laws and practices, as soon as possible, and to share information on those documents with other Member States through the INTERPOL database;

34. *Encourages* Member States to share, in accordance with their domestic laws and practices, with the private sector information in their national databases related to fraudulent, counterfeit, stolen, and lost identity or travel documents pertaining to their own jurisdictions, and, if a listed party is found to be using a false identity including to secure credit or fraudulent travel documents, to provide the Committee with information in this regard;

Coordination and outreach

35. *Reiterates* the need to enhance ongoing cooperation among the Committee, the Counter Terrorism Committee (CTC), and the Committee established pursuant to resolution 1540 (2004), as well as their respective groups of experts, including through, as appropriate, enhanced information-sharing, coordination on visits to countries within their respective mandates, on technical assistance, on relations with international and regional organizations and agencies and on other issues of relevance to all three committees, and *expresses its intention* to provide guidance to the committees on areas of common interest in order better to coordinate their efforts;

36. *Encourages* the Monitoring Team, and the United Nations Office on Drugs and Crime, to continue their joint activities, in cooperation with CTED and 1540 Committee experts to assist Member States in their efforts to comply with their obligations under the relevant resolutions, including through organizing subregional workshops;

37. *Requests* the Committee to consider, where and when appropriate, visits to selected countries by the Chairman and/or Committee members to enhance the full and effective implementation of the measures referred to in paragraph 1 above, with a view to encouraging States to comply fully with this resolution and resolutions 1267 (1999), 1333 (2000), 1390 (2002), 1455 (2003), 1526 (2004), 1617 (2005), and 1735 (2006);

38. *Requests* the Committee to report orally, through its Chairman, at least every 180 days to the Council on the overall work of the Committee and the Monitoring Team, and, as appropriate, in conjunction with the reports by the Chairmen of the CTC and the Committee established pursuant to resolution 1540 (2004), including briefings for all interested Member States;

Monitoring Team

39. *Decides*, in order to assist the Committee in the fulfilment of its mandate, to extend the mandate of the current New York-based Monitoring Team, appointed by the Secretary-General pursuant to paragraph 20 of resolution 1617 (2005), for a further period of 18 months, under the direction of the Committee with the responsibilities outlined in Annex 1, and requests the Secretary-General to make the necessary arrangements to this effect;

Reviews

40. *Decides* to review the measures described in paragraph 1 above with a view to their possible further strengthening in 18 months, or sooner if necessary;

41. *Decides* to remain actively seized of the matter.

ANNEX I

In accordance with paragraph 39 of this resolution, the Monitoring Team shall operate under the direction of the Committee established pursuant to resolution 1267 (1999) and shall have the following responsibilities:

(a) To submit, in writing, two comprehensive, independent reports to the Committee, one by 28 February 2009 and the second by 31 July 2009, on implementation by States of the measures referred to in paragraph 1 of this resolution, including specific recommendations for improved implementation of the measures and possible new measures;

(b) To analyse reports submitted pursuant to paragraph 6 of resolution 1455 (2003), the checklists submitted pursuant to paragraph 10 of resolution 1617 (2005), and other information submitted by Member States to the Committee as instructed by the Committee;

(c) To assist the Committee in following-up on requests to Member States for information, including with respect to implementation of the measures referred to in paragraph 1 of this resolution;

(d) To submit a comprehensive program of work to the Committee for its review and approval, as necessary, in which the Monitoring Team should detail the activities, envisaged in order to fulfil its responsibilities, including proposed travel, based on close coordination with the CTC's Executive Directorate ('CTED') and the 1540 Committee's group of experts to avoid duplication and reinforce synergies;

(e) To work closely and share information with CTED and the 1540 Committee's group of experts to identify areas of convergence and overlap and to help facilitate concrete coordination, including in the area of reporting, among the three Committees;

(f) To participate actively in and support all relevant activities under the United Nations Global Counter-Terrorism Strategy including within the Counter-Terrorism Implementation Task Force established to ensure overall coordination and coherence in the counter-terrorism efforts of the United Nations system;

(g) To assist the Committee with its analysis of non-compliance with the measures referred to in paragraph 1 of this resolution by collating information collected from Member States and submitting case studies, both on its own initiative and upon the Committee's request, to the Committee for its review;

(h) To present to the Committee recommendations, which could be used by member States to assist them with the implementation of the measures referred to in paragraph 1 of this resolution and in preparing proposed additions to the Consolidated List;

(i) To assist the Committee in compiling publicly releasable information referred to in paragraph 13;

(j) To consult with Member States in advance of travel to selected Member States, based on its program of work as approved by the Committee;

(k) To encourage Member States to submit names and additional identifying information for inclusion on the Consolidated List, as instructed by the Committee;

(l) To present to the Committee additional identifying and other information to assist the Committee in its efforts to keep the Consolidated List as updated and accurate as possible;

(m) To study and report to the Committee on the changing nature of the threat of Al-Qaida and the Taliban and the best measures to confront it, including by developing a dialogue with relevant scholars and academic bodies, in consultation with the Committee;

(n) To collate, assess, monitor and report on and make recommendations regarding implementation of the measures, including implementation of the measure in paragraph 1(a) of this resolution as it pertains to preventing the criminal misuse of the Internet by Al-Qaida, Usama bin Laden, and the Taliban and other individuals, groups, undertakings and entities associated with them; to pursue case studies, as appropriate; and to explore in depth any other relevant issues as directed by the Committee;

(o) To consult with Member States and other relevant organizations, including regular dialogue with representatives in New York and in capitals, taking into account their comments, especially regarding any issues that might be contained in the Monitoring Team's reports referred to in paragraph (a) of this Annex;

(p) To consult with Member States' intelligence and security services, including through regional forums, in order to facilitate the sharing of information and to strengthen enforcement of the measures;

(q) To consult with relevant representatives of the private sector, including financial institutions, to learn about the practical implementation of the assets freeze and to develop recommendations for the strengthening of that measure;

(r) To work with relevant international and regional organizations in order to promote awareness of, and compliance with, the measures;

(s) To work with INTERPOL and Member States to obtain photographs of listed individuals for possible inclusion in INTERPOL Special Notices;

(t) To assist other subsidiary bodies of the Security Council, and their expert panels, upon request with enhancing their cooperation with INTERPOL, referred to in resolution 1699 (2006);

(u) To report to the Committee, on a regular basis or when the Committee so requests, through oral and/or written briefings on the work of the Monitoring Team, including its visits to Member States and its activities;

(v) Any other responsibility identified by the Committee.

The USA PATRIOT Act ('Uniting and Strengthening America by Providing Appropriate Tools Required to Intercept and Obstruct Terrorism')

The USA PATRIOT Act entered into law on 26 October 2001. The Act contained certain provisions with 'sunset clauses'; consequently, following a review of the working of the Act, Congress passed the USA PATRIOT Improvement and Re-authorization Act of 2005 on 2 March 2006, the main provisions of the USA PATRIOT Act are as follows:

1. Certain investigative tools previously available in the investigation of organized crime and drug trafficking have been extended to allow use in counter-terrorism investigations. The tools thus extended include:

   i. The deployment of roving wiretap authorized by a federal judge for deployment against a particular suspect rather than in respect of a particular phone line or communications device, along with the extension of wiretap deployment to the full range of terrorism-related offences.

   ii. The delayed notification to a subject that a judicially-approved search warrant has been executed. Such delay previously being available in drug and organized crime cases.

   iii. Allowing a federal agent to ask a federal court (the Foreign Intelligence Surveillance Court, FISA) to order the production of business records in order to assist a national security terrorism investigation. Previously such records could be obtained in terrorism cases only through grand jury subpoena. In order for such an order to be made, it must be demonstrated that the records concerned are sought for an organized investigation to obtain foreign intelligence information not concerning a US person, or to protect against international terrorism or clandestine intelligence activities. (Provided, in each case, that such investigation of a US person is not conducted solely on the basis of activities protected by the First Amendment).

2. The Act facilitates information-sharing and coordination between US government agencies. In particular, it seems to break down the organizational barriers that may exist between police officers, federal agents, federal prosecutors, and the intelligence service.

3. The USA PATRIOT Act amends existing law to reflect the increasingly trans-jurisdictional nature of terrorism investigations. In particular, the Act allows for a search warrant to be obtained in any district in which terrorism-related activities have occurred, irrespective of where the warrant will actually be executed. It also seeks to make the law 'technology-neutral' by placing hackers or 'electronic trespassers' on the same footing as a person who commits a physical trespass.

4. The Act has created new offences and has increased penalties for some existing offences where a terrorist crime is committed. A new offence of knowingly harbouring a person who has committed or is about to commit a terrorist offence has been introduced, along with specific provisions addressing terrorist attacks on mass transit systems and bio-terrorism. As to the introduction of increased penalties, these have been increased for a variety of crimes which could be committed as part of terrorist activity, including arson, destruction of energy facilities, and the destruction of national defence materials. In addition to addressing substantive offences, the Act has also made changes to the

offence of conspiracy: Under existing law much terrorism legislation did not specifically criminalize conspiracies, leaving the prosecution with only the option of indicting under the general federal provisions which carry a maximum sentence of 5 years' imprisonment.

THE PROVISIONS OF THE USA PATRIOT ACT

TABLE OF CONTENTS

The table of contents for this Act is as follows:

Sec. 1. Short title and table of contents.
Sec. 2. Construction; severability.

TITLE I—ENHANCING DOMESTIC SECURITY AGAINST TERRORISM

Sec. 101. Counterterrorism fund.
Sec. 102. Sense of Congress condemning discrimination against Arab and Muslim Americans.
Sec. 103. Increased funding for the technical support center at the Federal Bureau of Investigation.
Sec. 104. Requests for military assistance to enforce prohibition in certain emergencies.
Sec. 105. Expansion of National Electronic Crime Task Force Initiative.
Sec. 106. Presidential authority.

TITLE II—ENHANCED SURVEILLANCE PROCEDURES

Sec. 201. Authority to intercept wire, oral, and electronic communications relating to terrorism.
Sec. 202. Authority to intercept wire, oral, and electronic communications relating to computer fraud and abuse offenses.
Sec. 203. Authority to share criminal investigative information.
Sec. 204. Clarification of intelligence exceptions from limitations on interception and disclosure of wire, oral, and electronic communications.
Sec. 205. Employment of translators by the Federal Bureau of Investigation.
Sec. 206. Roving surveillance authority under the Foreign Intelligence Surveillance Act of 1978.
Sec. 207. Duration of FISA surveillance of non-United States persons who are agents of a foreign power.
Sec. 208. Designation of judges.
Sec. 209. Seizure of voice-mail messages pursuant to warrants.
Sec. 210. Scope of subpoenas for records of electronic communications.
Sec. 211. Clarification of scope.
Sec. 212. Emergency disclosure of electronic communications to protect life and limb.
Sec. 213. Authority for delaying notice of the execution of a warrant.
Sec. 214. Pen register and trap and trace authority under FISA.
Sec. 215. Access to records and other items under the Foreign Intelligence Surveillance Act.
Sec. 216. Modification of authorities relating to use of pen registers and trap and trace devices.
Sec. 217. Interception of computer trespasser communications.
Sec. 218. Foreign intelligence information.
Sec. 219. Single-jurisdiction search warrants for terrorism.
Sec. 220. Nationwide service of search warrants for electronic evidence.
Sec. 221. Trade sanctions.
Sec. 222. Assistance to law enforcement agencies.
Sec. 223. Civil liability for certain unauthorized disclosures.
Sec. 224. Sunset.
Sec. 225. Immunity for compliance with FISA wiretap.

Title III—International Money Laundering Abatement and
Anti-Terrorist Financing Act of 2001

Sec. 301. Short title.
Sec. 302. Findings and purposes.
Sec. 303. 4–year congressional review; expedited consideration.

Subtitle A—International Counter Money Laundering and Related Measures

Sec. 311. Special measures for jurisdictions, financial institutions, or international transactions of primary money laundering concern.
Sec. 312. Special due diligence for correspondent accounts and private banking accounts.
Sec. 313. Prohibition on United States correspondent accounts with foreign shell banks.
Sec. 314. Cooperative efforts to deter money laundering.
Sec. 315. Inclusion of foreign corruption offenses as money laundering crimes.
Sec. 316. Anti-terrorist forfeiture protection.
Sec. 317. Long-arm jurisdiction over foreign money launderers.
Sec. 318. Laundering money through a foreign bank.
Sec. 319. Forfeiture of funds in United States interbank accounts.
Sec. 320. Proceeds of foreign crimes.
Sec. 321. Financial institutions specified in subchapter II of chapter 53 of title 31, United States code.
Sec. 322. Corporation represented by a fugitive.
Sec. 323. Enforcement of foreign judgments.
Sec. 324. Report and recommendation.
Sec. 325. Concentration accounts at financial institutions.
Sec. 326. Verification of identification.
Sec. 327. Consideration of anti-money laundering record.
Sec. 328. International cooperation on identification of originators of wire transfers.
Sec. 329. Criminal penalties.
Sec. 330. International cooperation in investigations of money laundering, financial crimes, and the finances of terrorist groups.

Subtitle B—Bank Secrecy Act Amendments and Related Improvements

Sec. 351. Amendments relating to reporting of suspicious activities.
Sec. 352. Anti-money laundering programs.
Sec. 353. Penalties for violations of geographic targeting orders and certain recordkeeping requirements, and lengthening effective period of geographic targeting orders.
Sec. 354. Anti-money laundering strategy.
Sec. 355. Authorization to include suspicions of illegal activity in written employment references.
Sec. 356. Reporting of suspicious activities by securities brokers and dealers; investment company study.
Sec. 357. Special report on administration of bank secrecy provisions.
Sec. 358. Bank secrecy provisions and activities of United States intelligence agencies to fight international terrorism.
Sec. 359. Reporting of suspicious activities by underground banking systems.
Sec. 360. Use of authority of United States Executive Directors.
Sec. 361. Financial crimes enforcement network.
Sec. 362. Establishment of highly secure network.
Sec. 363. Increase in civil and criminal penalties for money laundering.
Sec. 364. Uniform protection authority for Federal Reserve facilities.
Sec. 365. Reports relating to coins and currency received in non-financial trade or business.
Sec. 366. Efficient use of currency transaction report system.

Subtitle C—Currency Crimes and Protection

Sec. 371. Bulk cash smuggling into or out of the United States.

Sec. 372. Forfeiture in currency reporting cases.

Sec. 373. Illegal money transmitting businesses.

Sec. 374. Counterfeiting domestic currency and obligations.

Sec. 375. Counterfeiting foreign currency and obligations.

Sec. 376. Laundering the proceeds of terrorism.

Sec. 377. Extraterritorial jurisdiction.

TITLE IV—PROTECTING THE BORDER

Subtitle A—Protecting the Northern Border

Sec. 401. Ensuring adequate personnel on the northern border.

Sec. 402. Northern border personnel.

Sec. 403. Access by the Department of State and the INS to certain identifying information in the criminal history records of visa applicants and applicants for admission to the United States.

Sec. 404. Limited authority to pay overtime.

Sec. 405. Report on the integrated automated fingerprint identification system for ports of entry and overseas consular posts.

Subtitle B—Enhanced Immigration Provisions

Sec. 411. Definitions relating to terrorism.

Sec. 412. Mandatory detention of suspected terrorists; habeas corpus; judicial review.

Sec. 413. Multilateral cooperation against terrorists.

Sec. 414. Visa integrity and security.

Sec. 415. Participation of Office of Homeland Security on Entry-Exit Task Force.

Sec. 416. Foreign student monitoring program.

Sec. 417. Machine readable passports.

Sec. 418. Prevention of consulate shopping.

Subtitle C—Preservation of Immigration Benefits for Victims of Terrorism

Sec. 421. Special immigrant status.

Sec. 422. Extension of filing or reentry deadlines.

Sec. 423. Humanitarian relief for certain surviving spouses and children.

Sec. 424. 'Age-out' protection for children.

Sec. 425. Temporary administrative relief.

Sec. 426. Evidence of death, disability, or loss of employment.

Sec. 427. No benefits to terrorists or family members of terrorists.

Sec. 428. Definitions.

TITLE V—REMOVING OBSTACLES TO INVESTIGATING TERRORISM

Sec. 501. Attorney General's authority to pay rewards to combat terrorism.

Sec. 502. Secretary of State's authority to pay rewards.

Sec. 503. DNA identification of terrorists and other violent offenders.

Sec. 504. Coordination with law enforcement.

Sec. 505. Miscellaneous national security authorities.

Sec. 506. Extension of Secret Service jurisdiction.

Sec. 507. Disclosure of educational records.

Sec. 508. Disclosure of information from NCES surveys.

Title VI—Providing for Victims of Terrorism, Public Safety Officers, and Their Families

Subtitle A—Aid to Families of Public Safety Officers

Sec. 611. Expedited payment for public safety officers involved in the prevention, investigation, rescue, or recovery efforts related to a terrorist attack.

Sec. 612. Technical correction with respect to expedited payments for heroic public safety officers.

Sec. 613. Public safety officers benefit program payment increase.

Sec. 614. Office of Justice programs.

Subtitle B—Amendments to the Victims of Crime Act of 1984

Sec. 621. Crime victims fund.

Sec. 622. Crime victim compensation.

Sec. 623. Crime victim assistance.

Sec. 624. Victims of terrorism.

Title VII—Increased Information Sharing for Critical Infrastructure Protection

Sec. 711. Expansion of regional information sharing system to facilitate federal–State–local law enforcement response related to terrorist attacks.

Title VIII—Strengthening the Criminal Laws Against Terrorism

Sec. 801. Terrorist attacks and other acts of violence against mass transportation systems.

Sec. 802. Definition of domestic terrorism.

Sec. 803. Prohibition against harboring terrorists.

Sec. 804. Jurisdiction over crimes committed at U.S. facilities abroad.

Sec. 805. Material support for terrorism.

Sec. 806. Assets of terrorist organizations.

Sec. 807. Technical clarification relating to provision of material support to terrorism.

Sec. 808. Definition of federal crime of terrorism.

Sec. 809. No statute of limitation for certain terrorism offenses.

Sec. 810. Alternate maximum penalties for terrorism offenses.

Sec. 811. Penalties for terrorist conspiracies.

Sec. 812. Post-release supervision of terrorists.

Sec. 813. Inclusion of acts of terrorism as racketeering activity.

Sec. 814. Deterrence and prevention of cyberterrorism.

Sec. 815. Additional defense to civil actions relating to preserving records in response to Government requests.

Sec. 816. Development and support of cybersecurity forensic capabilities.

Sec. 817. Expansion of the biological weapons statute.

Title IX—Improved Intelligence

Sec. 901. Responsibilities of Director of Central Intelligence regarding foreign intelligence collected under Foreign Intelligence Surveillance Act of 1978.

Sec. 902. Inclusion of international terrorist activities within scope of foreign intelligence under National Security Act of 1947.

Sec. 903. Sense of Congress on the establishment and maintenance of intelligence relationships to acquire information on terrorists and terrorist organizations.

Sec. 904. Temporary authority to defer submittal to Congress of reports on intelligence and intelligence-related matters.

Sec. 905. Disclosure to Director of Central Intelligence of foreign intelligence-related information with respect to criminal investigations.

Sec. 906. Foreign terrorist asset tracking center.

Sec. 907. National Virtual Translation Center.

Sec. 908. Training of government officials regarding identification and use of foreign intelligence.

Title X—Miscellaneous

Sec. 1001. Review of the Department of Justice.

Sec. 1002. Sense of congress.

Sec. 1003. Definition of 'electronic surveillance'.

Sec. 1004. Venue in money laundering cases.

Sec. 1005. First responders assistance act.

Sec. 1006. Inadmissibility of aliens engaged in money laundering.

Sec. 1007. Authorization of funds for DEA police training in South and Central Asia.

Sec. 1008. Feasibility study on use of biometric identifier scanning system with access to the FBI integrated automated fingerprint identification system at overseas consular posts and points of entry to the United States.

Sec. 1009. Study of access.

Sec. 1010. Temporary authority to contract with local and State governments for performance of security functions at United States military installations.

Sec. 1011. Crimes against charitable Americans.

Sec. 1012. Limitation on issuance of hazmat licenses.

Sec. 1013. Expressing the sense of the senate concerning the provision of funding for bioterrorism preparedness and response.

Sec. 1014. Grant program for State and local domestic preparedness support.

Sec. 1015. Expansion and reauthorization of the crime identification technology act for antiterrorism grants to States and localities.

Sec. 1016. Critical infrastructures protection.

Focusing on just some of the key provisions of the Act, particularly in respect of investigations and terrorism financing:

Title I contains provisions to enhance domestic security against terrorism. It includes (at section 105) the expansion of the National Electronic Crime Taskforce Initiative.

Title II addressed enhanced surveillance procedures. The effect of the Act at Title II is, inter alia:

i   Permit pen register, and trap and trace order for electronic communications (including email);

ii Authorize nationwide execution of court orders for pen registers etc, and also for access to stored communications data (including email records);

iii To put stored voicemail on the same footing as stored email (in other words, to take stored voice communication outside or wiretap);

iv Permit the investigative authorities to intercept telecommunications to and from a trespasser within a computer system where permission of the system's owner has been obtained;

In respect of the above powers, section 216, addressing pen registers and trap and trace devices, should in particular be noted. It provides for court orders authorizing trap and pen registers and trace devices to be used to capture source and addressee information for email contact as well as telephone conversations. Under this provision a court with a jurisdiction over the crime under investigation may issue an order to be executed anywhere in the US.

Other provisions to be noted in relation to the provisions above, section 210 adds credit card and bank account numbers to the type of information that law enforcement officials may subpoena from a communications service provider's customer records. Section 220 widens the jurisdiction as to access to the content of stored email material under a court order. Under section 220, federal courts in the district where an offence under investigation occurred may issue an order which is applicable without any geographical limitation.

Title II also amends the Foreign Intelligence Surveillance Act (FISA) in relation to the access by criminal investigators to foreign intelligence information. Section 218 provides that a foreign intelligence gathering be a 'significant purpose' for the request for surveillance or physical search orders under the FISA.

Title III addresses the financing of terrorism.

Title III enlarges the role of the Secretary of the Treasury over reporting requirements. In accordance with sections 321 and 356, the Secretary is to promulgate regulations under which securities brokers and dealers, as well as commodity merchants, advisors, and pool operators, must file suspicious activity reports (SARs). Businesses which previously were required to report transactions only if more than $10,000 was involved (reporting to the IRS) are now required by the Act to complete a SAR as well. Sections 351 and 355 address liability for disclosure of SARs. Before the Act, there was a prohibition under federal law for financial institutions and their officers and employees from tipping off any of those involved in a suspicious transaction. However, federal law also provided immunity to institutions and their officers and employees from liability from filing a SAR and for failing to disclose that they had done so. Section 351 makes changes to the prohibition and the immunity. Government officials who have access to the SAR are added to those prohibited to from tipping off, and institutions are allowed, but not required, to reveal SAR information in the context of employment references provided to other financial institutions. In addition, it is made plain that the immunity does not extend to immunity from governmental action. Section 355, meanwhile, expands the immunity to cover disclosure in employment references to other insured depository financial institutions, provided disclosure is done in good faith.

The body responsible for money laundering reporting and for record keeping requirements is the Financial Crimes Enforcement Network (FinCEN). The effect of section 361 is to make FinCEN a bureau within the Treasury Department. Section 362 also charges it with the responsibility for establishing a secure network allowing financial institutions to file the required reports electronically and to permit FinCEN to provide those financial institutions with alerts and other information concerning money laundering measures.

Section 311 provides for 'special measures' in which the Secretary of the Treasury is given the power to issue regulations and orders that involve additional measures and due diligence requirements to combat money laundering and terrorist financing. In addition section 312 requires that all US financial institutions have policies, procedures, and controls in place to identify instances where their correspondent and private banking accounts with foreign individuals and entities might be used for money laundering purposes. The effect is enhance due diligence requirements for correspondent accounts held for offshore banking institutions or institutions located in money laundering jurisdictions as designated by the Secretary of the Treasury or by international watchdogs such as FATF. The enhanced standard of due diligence expected is that there must be at least reasonable effects to identify the ownership of foreign institutions which are not publicly held, to closely monitor the accounts for money laundering activity and hold any foreign bank, for whom the US institutions has a correspondent account, to the same standards in relation to other correspondent accounts maintained by the foreign bank. Meanwhile, in the case of private banking accounts of $1,000,000 or more, US financial institutions must keep records of the owners of the accounts and the sources of funds deposited in those accounts. They must, in particular, report suspicious transactions and, when an account is held for a foreign official of PEP, guard against transactions involving foreign bribery.

Title III reflects, in its content, concern as to the capability of law enforcement in the US to trace money transfers to the US from foreign jurisdictions. Accordingly, section 328 instructs the Secretary of the Treasury, the Secretary of State, and the Attorney General to make every effort to encourage other governments to require identification of the originator of international wire transfers. Section 330, meanwhile, encourages the Administration to seek to negotiate international agreements to enable US law enforcement officials to track and trace the financials activities of foreign terrorist organizations, money launderers, and others involved in criminal activity.

Prior to the Act, there was a full framework of federal money laundering criminalization, addressing both concealing the proceeds of past offending and financing new offences. The Act creates new offences, however, and also increases penalties for some existing crimes. Section 315 adds further offences to the federal money laundering predicate offence list. The additional offences include crimes in violation of the laws of other States in circumstances where the proceeds are involved in financial transactions in the US and the unlawful importation of firearms, firearms trafficking, computer fraud, and abuse and felony violations of the Foreign Agents Registration Act.

Section 376 also adds to the list predicate offences, with the addition of the offence of providing material support to a terrorist organization.

INDEX

9/11
  financial issues arising, 6.02–6.03
  increased prioritization of terrorism
    afterwards, 1.03
  not the origins of terrorism, 1.06–1.08
  proliferation of national responses, 1.43
  Security Council Resolution 1373, 6.35
  Security Council response, 2.11–2.14
  US response, 1.14
  use of torture to obtain evidence, 4.87

Abu Dhabi Conferences, 7.22–7.27
Accomplices
  aircraft hijacking, 3.11, 3.37
  evidence form, 4.03–4.7
  nuclear terrorism, 3.103
Active personality principle, 3.141–3.145
Actus reus
  forms of participation evolved by UN, 2.38–2.41
  identification by UNSCR, 1.45
Admissions and confessions
  illegal detention, 4.74–4.84
  obtained by trickery, 4.103–4.106
  oppression
    Sri Lanka, 4.96–4.100
    United Kingdom, 4.93–4.95
  procedure for challenge, 4.107–4.111
  silence as acknowledgment of truth, 4.101–4.102
  use of torture, 4.85–4.92
Aiding and abetting terrorism
  maritime safety, 3.79
  need for appropriate response, 1.17
  UK jurisdictional approach, 3.192
Aircraft safety
  Airports Protocol, 2.73–2.74
  criminalization
    Hague Convention, 3.2–3.11
    Montreal Convention, 3.28–3.37
    Montreal Protocol, 3.40–3.44
    UK incorporation of Hague
      Convention, 3.12–3.27
    UK incorporation of Montreal
      Convention, 3.38–3.39
  Hague Convention
    aut dedere aut judicare, 2.58–2.61
    cooperation, 2.58–2.61
    criminalization, 2.53–2.55

  due process, 2.57
  full text, App 4
  jurisdiction, 2.56
  jurisdictional approach
    active personality principle, 3.144
    based on registration, 3.134, 3.136
    extra-territorial jurisdiction, 3.133
    Hague Convention, 3.161–3.163
    Montreal Convention, 3.164–3.165
    persons present in territory, 3.189
    Tokyo Convention, 3.158–3.160
    United Kingdom, 3.192
  Montreal Convention
    cooperation, 2.69–2.72
    criminalization, 2.63–2.66
    due process, 2.68
    jurisdiction, 2.67
  Montreal Protocol
    full text, App 5
    political offences, 9.170
    Security Council response to Pan Am and UTA
      flights, 2.10
  Tokyo Convention
    applicability, 2.48
    exclusions, 2.49
    full text, App 3
    jurisdiction, 2.50–2.51
    UN requirement for cooperation, 2.46
Al-Qaida
  challenges to financing provisions, 6.44–6.48
  communications interception, 4.139–4.145
  jurisdictional approach, 3.148
  most well-known terrorist group, 1.13
  Security Council Resolution 1267, 6.24–6.28
  Security Council Resolution 1373, 6.35
  Security Council Resolution 1390, 6.29
  Security Council Resolution 1617, App 1
  Security Council Resolution 1735, App 1, 6.32
  Security Council response to Taliban's extradition
    refusals, 2.10
  US response to 9/11, 1.14–1.15
Alternative remittance systems
  Abu Dhabi Conferences, 7.22–7.27
  advantages, 7.12–7.14
  conclusions, 7.33
  FATF Special Recommendations, 6.55, 7.15–7.20
  hawala system, 7.08–7.11

759

Alternative remittance systems (*cont.*)
meaning, 7.07
other payment methods
New Payment Methods, 7.31–7.32
wire transfers, 7.29–7.30
relationship with funding, 7.01–7.06
Anonymous witnesses
Criminal Evidence (Witness Anonymity)
Act 2008, App 21
general approach, 4.30–4.35
recent developments, 4.36–4.56
Arab League Convention, App 18
Armed conflicts
Bombings Convention, 3.84–3.86
criminalization by UK law, 3.110
immunity for warships, 3.66–3.67
meaning and scope of terrorism, 1.39
Arrest powers
broad UK approach to criminalization, 3.115
European Arrest Warrants, 9.138–9.147
UK provisions, 4.65–4.66
universal jurisdiction, 3.175–3.185
Asset freezing and forfeiture
FATF Special Recommendations, 6.55
Financing Convention, 6.20–6.22
human rights challenges, 6.43–6.50
key extracts from Security Council Resolutions
1267 (1999), 6.27
1373 (2001), 6.36–6.39
1390 (2002), 6.29
1735 (2006), 6.32
summary table, 6.42
Security Council Resolutions, App 1
Atomic energy. *see* **Nuclear materials**
Attempts
aircraft hijacking, 3.07
financing, 3.92
forms of participation evolved by UN, 2.38–2.41
international treaty crimes, 1.31
nuclear terrorism, 3.103, 3.107
Aut dedere aut judicare
aircraft hijacking
Hague Convention, 2.58–2.61
Montreal Convention, 2.69–2.72
Bombings Convention, 2.134–2.140
civilian protection
Diplomats Convention, 2.108–2.113
Hostages Convention, 2.121–2.125
Financing Convention, 2.151–2.158
jurisdiction over persons present in
territory, 3.188–3.191
maritime safety, 2.83–2.87
nuclear materials
Nuclear Material Convention, 2.97–2.102

Nuclear Terrorism Convention, 2.168–2.174
objectives, 9.162–9.167
UN instruments generally
basis of UN approach, 2.26
common element, 2.31
development of UN provisions, 2.44–2.46
Aviation. *see* **aircraft hijacking**

Banking. *see also* **Alternative remittance systems**
Egmont Group, 6.58–6.61
International Monetary Fund, 6.56
problems with mutual legal assistance, 9.99
Wolfsberg Group, 6.62–6.63
Biological weapons
growing challenge of terrorism, 1.02
Security Council resolution, 2.18
UK jurisdictional approach, 3.192
Bombings
aut dedere aut judicare, 9.165
Bombings Convention
aut dedere aut judicare, 2.134–2.140
cooperation, 2.134–2.140
criminalization, 2.127–2.130, 3.83–3.91
due process, 2.132–2.133
full text, App 11
jurisdiction, 2.131
extra-territoriality reach of human rights, 8.16
forms of participation evolved by UN, 2.40–2.41
intent to cause injury, 2.33
jurisdictional approach
Bombings Convention, 3.171
extra-territorial approach, 3.136
passive personality principle, 3.149
persons present in territory, 3.190
protective personality principle, 3.149
Plastic Explosives Convention, App 10
political offences, 9.172
scene management
CCTV, 4.121–4.122
cordons, 4.116
interviewing witnesses, 4.120
media strategies, 4.123
post-incident investigations, 4.113
scene examiners, 4.117
Senior Investigating Officers, 4.114–4.115
zoning, 4.118–4.119
Security Council response to US embassy
bombings, 2.10
UK burden of proof, 5.49
UK jurisdictional approach, 3.192
Burden of proof
legal or evidential burden of proof, 5.19–5.41
reverse burden of proof
cause for concern, 5.03

human rights, 5.01–5.02
UK approach, 5.04–5.18
UK counter-terrorism legislation, 5.42–5.49

Case management
adverse comment from media, 5.86–5.107
disclosure of evidence
consequences of non-disclosure, 5.71
importance to fair trial, 5.52–5.54
material forming part of prosecution
case, 5.55–5.57
material held by foreign authorities, 5.84
ongoing duty, 5.85
relevant information, 5.74–5.77
revelation by investigators, 5.72–5.73
sensitive material, 5.82–5.83
third party material, 5.79–5.81
unrepresented accused, 5.78
unused prosecution material, 5.58–5.70
hearings in camera, 5.108–5.109
overview, 5.50
*Protocol on the Management of Terrorism
Cases*, 5.51

Chemical weapons
growing challenge of terrorism, 1.02
Security Council resolution, 2.18
UK jurisdictional approach, 3.192

Civilian protection
basis of terrorism, 1.06
criminalization
Diplomats Convention, 3.46–3.50
Diplomats Convention
applicability, 2.103
aut dedere aut judicare, 2.108–2.113
cooperation, 2.108–2.113
criminalization, 2.104–2.105
due process, 2.107
full text, App 6
jurisdiction, 2.106
jurisdictional approach, 2.106, 3.166
extra-territoriality reach of human
rights, 8.17–8.21
Financing Convention, 6.12
Hostages Convention
active personality principle, 3.145
applicability, 2.114
aut dedere aut judicare, 2.121–2.125
cooperation, 2.121–2.125
due process, 2.120
full text, App 7
jurisdictional approach, 2.119, 3.167
present-day acts of terrorism, 1.13
terrorism by States, 1.26

Commonwealth

Expert Group, 3.118, 3.121–3.122
Model Legislative Provisions, App 20
Communications interception
general reliance, 4.130–4.138
UK approach, 4.151–4.160
US approach, 4.139–4.150
Confessions. *see* **Admissions and confessions**
Confidentiality, 8.113–8.124
Conspiracy
international treaty crimes, 1.31
UK jurisdictional approach, 3.192
Conventions. *see* **Treaties and conventions**
Cooperation, *see* **International cooperation**
Counter-Terrorism Committee (CTC), 2.13
Covert investigations
broad UK approach to criminalization, 3.115
communications interception
general reliance, 4.130–4.138
UK approach, 4.151–4.160
US approach, 4.139–4.150
entrapment
importance, 4.248–4.249
UK approach, 4.250–4.265
human rights
fair trial, 4.174–4.176
legality principle, 4.169–4.170
necessity, 4.171
overview, 4.161–4.164
permissive regime, 4.167
privacy, 4.165–4.166, 8.113–8.124
proportionality, 4.172–4.173
surveillance
directed surveillance, 4.218–4.224
general reliance, 4.213
interference with property, 4.240–4.247
intrusive surveillance, 4.225–4.239
statutory provisions, 4.213–4.217
undercover agents
best practice handling model, 4.199–4.212
overview, 4.177–4.182
UK approach, 4.183–4.198
Criminalization
aircraft hijacking, 2.74
Hague Convention, 2.53–2.55
Montreal Convention, 2.63–2.66
Bombings Convention, 2.127–2.130
civilian protection
Diplomats Convention, 2.104–2.105
Hostages Convention, 2.115–2.118
elements common to UN instruments
definitions and terminology, 2.32
intent, 2.33
motive, 2.33–2.34
overview, 2.31

Criminalization (*cont.*)
  financing
    FATF Special Recommendations, 6.55
    Financing Convention, 2.142–2.146,
      6.11–6.16
    summary table, 6.42
  maritime safety
    1988 Safety Convention, 2.76–2.78
    2005 Protocols, 2.90–2.92
  national law
    Barbados, 3.113
    Commonwealth Expert Group, 3.118,
      3.121–3.122
    inclusion of motive, 3.120
    need for definition, 3.117
    reliance on treaty formulation, 3.119
    United Kingdom, 3.108–3.112, 3.114–3.6,
      3.125
  need for appropriate response to terrorism, 1.16
  nuclear materials
    Nuclear Material Convention, 2.94
    Nuclear Terrorism Convention, 2.159–2.164
  Security Council Resolution, 3.123–3.124
  treaties and conventions
    2005 Protocols, 3.76–3.82
    Bombings Convention, 3.83–3.91
    Diplomats Convention, 3.46–3.50
    Financing Convention, 3.92–3.102
    Hague Convention, 3.02–3.11
    Hostages Convention, 3.51–3.57
    Montreal Convention, 3.28–3.39
    Montreal Protocol, 3.40–3.44
    Nuclear Material Convention, 3.58–3.60
    Nuclear Terrorism Convention, 3.103–3.107
    Rome Convention, 3.61–3.71
    Rome Protocol, 3.72–3.75
Customary international law
  meaning and scope of terrorism, 1.38
  universal jurisdiction, 3.181–3.185

Death penalty
  bar to extradition, 9.232–9.242
  refusal of mutual legal assistance, 9.26
Detention
  evidence for further detention, 4.72–4.73
  extra-territoriality reach of human
    rights, 8.22–8.28
  failure to identify detainee, 4.67–4.71
  illegal detention amounting to
    torture, 8.94–8.106
  international responses to Guantanamo Bay, 1.15
  PACE Code of Practice, App 22
  torture and forced confessions, 4.74–4.84
Diplomats

Diplomats Convention
  applicability, 2.103
  aut dedere aut judicare, 2.108–2.113
  cooperation, 2.108–2.113
  criminalization, 2.104–2.105, 3.46–3.50
  due process, 2.107
  full text, App 6
  jurisdictional approach, 2.106, 3.166
  UK jurisdictional approach, 3.192
Directed surveillance, 4.218–4.224
Disclosure of evidence
  consequences of non-disclosure, 5.71
  importance to fair trial, 5.52–5.54
  material forming part of prosecution
    case, 5.55–5.57
  material held by foreign authorities, 5.84
  ongoing duty, 5.85
  relevant information, 5.74–5.77
  revelation by investigators, 5.72–5.73
  sensitive material, 5.82–5.83
  third party material, 5.79–5.81
  UK burden of proof, 5.49
  unrepresented accused, 5.78
  unused prosecution material
    civil law approach, 5.70
    common law approach, 5.60–5.69
    divergence of treatment, 5.58–5.-59
Dual criminality
  European Arrest Warrants, 9.143–9.144
  extradition
    conduct test, 9.154–9.155
    essential safeguard, 9.152–9.153
    list test, 9.156–9.161
  mutual legal assistance, 9.21–9.22
Dual jeopardy, 9.27
Due process. *see* **Fair trial**

Egmont Group, 6.58–6.61
Entrapment
  admissions and confessions obtained by
    trickery, 4.103–4.106
  illegal extradition, 9.137
  importance, 4.248–4.249
  UK approach, 4.250–4.265
European Union. *see also* **Human rights**
  Convention on the Suppression of
    Terrorism, App 15
  European Arrest Warrants, 9.138–9.147
Evidence. *see also* **Mutual legal assistance**
  from accomplices, 4.03–4.7
  Criminal Evidence (Witness Anonymity) Act
    2008, App 21
  disclosure
    consequences of non-disclosure, 5.71

importance to fair trial, 5.52–5.54
material forming part of prosecution
    case, 5.55–5.57
material held by foreign authorities, 5.84
ongoing duty, 5.85
relevant information, 5.74–5.77
revelation by investigators, 5.72–5.73
sensitive material, 5.82–5.83
third party material, 5.79–5.81
UK burden of proof, 5.49
unrepresented accused, 5.78
unused prosecution material, 5.58–5.70
further detention of suspects, 4.72–4.73
interrogation techniques amounting to
    torture, 8.53–8.93
legal or evidential burden of proof, 5.19–5.41
reverse burden of proof
    cause for concern, 5.03
    human rights, 5.01–5.02
    UK approach, 5.04–5.18
scene management
    CCTV, 4.121–4.122
    cordons, 4.116
    interviewing witnesses, 4.120
    post-incident investigations, 4.113
    scene examiners, 4.117
    Senior Investigating Officers, 4.114–4.115
    zoning, 4.118–4.119
witness protection
    anonymity, 4.30–4.56
    general principles, 4.21–4.22
    resident informants, 4.08–4.20
    special measures, 4.23–4.29
Explosives. *see* **Bombings**
Extra-territoriality
human rights, 8.15–8.29
jurisdictional approach, 3.137–3.140
Extradition. *see also* **Aut dedere aut judicare**
comity, 9.113–9.118
common element of UN instruments, 2.31
dual criminality
    conduct test, 9.154–9.155
    essential safeguard, 9.152–9.153
    list test, 9.156–9.161
European Arrest Warrants, 9.138–9.147
human rights considerations
    death penalty, 9.219–9.230
    handing over suspects, 9.232–9.242
    torture, 9.231
meaning and background, 9.113–9.118
need for appropriate response to terrorism, 1.16
objectives, 9.162–9.167
other protections, 9.209–9.218
political offence exception

absence of express references, 9.171
aircraft hijacking, 9.170
bombings, 9.172
financing, 9.173
meaning and scope, 9.174–9.208
protective personality principle, 3.147–3.148
Security Council response to Taliban's extradition
    refusals, 2.10
UN instruments
    framework Conventions, 9.148–9.149
    legal basis, 9.150–9.151

Fair trial
admissions and confessions by oppression
    Sri Lanka, 4.96–4.100
    United Kingdom, 4.93–4.95
aircraft hijacking
    Hague Convention, 2.57
    Montreal Convention, 2.68
Bombings Convention, 2.132–2.133
civilian protection
    Diplomats Convention, 2.107
    Hostages Convention, 2.120
covert investigations, 4.165–4.166
extra-territoriality reach of human rights, 8.22–8.25
Financing Convention, 2.148–2.150
maritime safety, 2.80–2.82
meaning and scope, 8.107–8.112
need for appropriate response to terrorism, 1.16
nuclear materials
    Nuclear Material Convention, 2.96
    Nuclear Terrorism Convention, 2.166–2.167
presumption of innocence, 5.19–5.41
reverse burden of proof, 5.15
Financial Action Task Force
alternative remittance systems, 7.15–7.20
establishment, 6.51
international efforts to combat terrorism, 6.07
leading role, 6.53
Money Laundering Recommendations, App 19
procedures, 6.54
scope includes financing, 6.52
Special Recommendations, 6.55
Financing
Egmont Group, 6.58–6.61
Financial Action Task Force, 6.52
Financing Convention
    applicability, 2.141
    asset freezing and forfeiture, 6.20–6.22
    aut dedere aut judicare, 2.151–2.158
    cooperation, 2.151–2.158, 6.19
    criminalization, 2.142–2.146, 3.92–3.107,
        6.11–6.16
    due process, 2.148–2.150

Financing (*cont.*)
  Financing Convention (*cont.*)
    full text, App 12
    international legal regime, 6.09
    jurisdictional approach, 2.147, 3.172, 6.18
    key provisions, 6.22
    legal liability, 6.17
  human rights challenges, 6.43–6.50
  international efforts to combat, 6.07–6.8
  International Monetary Fund, 6.56
  jurisdictional approach
    Financing Convention, 3.147, 3.172
    United States, 3.148
  key extracts from Security Council Resolutions
    1267 (1999), 6.24–6.28
    1373 (2001), 6.33–6.41
    1390 (2002), 6.29
    1452 (2002), 6.30
    1730 (2006), 6.31
    1735 (2006), 6.32
    summary table, 6.42
  money laundering distinguished, 6.04–6.06
  need for appropriate response to terrorism, 1.17
  overview, 6.01–6.06
  Palermo Convention, 6.23
  political offences, 9.173
  problems with mutual legal assistance, 9.99
  relationship with movement
    of funds, 7.01–7.06
  Security Council Resolution 1373, App 1
  Security Council Resolution 1566, App 1
  Security Council response to 9/11, 2.13
  specific intent, 2.33
  Task Force Money Laundering
    Recommendations, App 19
  UK burden of proof, 5.43
  Wolfsberg Group, 6.62–6.63
Fiscal offences, 9.24–9.25
Freedom fighters, 1.20, 1.25
Freedom of expression, 8.121–8.122

General Assembly
  Counter-Terrorism Strategy, App 14
  development of global legal regime, 2.02–2.08

Hawala **remittance system**
  Abu Dhabi Conferences, 7.22–7.27
  advantages, 7.12–7.14
  meaning and use, 7.08–7.11
Hearings in camera, 5.108–5.109
Hijacking. *see* **Aircraft hijacking**
Hostage taking
  active personality principle, 3.145
  aut dedere aut judicare, 9.164–9.165

  cooperation, 2.121–2.125
  criminalization, 2.115–2.118
  full text of Hostages Convention, App 7
  intent, 2.33
  jurisdictional approach, 2.119, 3.167
Human intelligence sources
  best practice handling model, 4.199–4.212
  overview, 4.177–4.182
  UK approach, 4.183–4.198
Human rights
  available mechanisms, 1.04
  bars to extradition
    death penalty, 9.219–9.230
    handing over suspects, 9.232–9.242
    torture, 9.231
  challenges to financing provisions, 6.43–6.50
  covert investigations
    fair trial, 4.174–4.176
    legality principle, 4.169–4.170
    necessity, 4.171
    overview, 4.161–4.164
    permissive regime, 4.167
    privacy, 4.165–4.166
    proportionality, 4.172–4.173
  extra-territoriality, 8.15–8.29
  failure of UN to define terrorism, 1.44–1.45
  freedom of expression, 8.121–8.122
  international humanitarian law
    compared, 8.02–8.06
  need for appropriate response to
    terrorism, 1.16–1.17
  particular rights engaged
    fair trial, 8.107–8.112
    life, right to, 8.46–8.51
    prohibition against torture, 8.52–8.106
  permitted derogations, 8.31–8.41
  presumption of innocence, 5.19–5.41
  privacy
    meaning and scope of protection, 8.113–8.124
  problems with mutual legal assistance, 9.99
  removal, 9.128
  reverse burden of proof, 5.01–5.02, 5.14–5.15
  right to silence, 5.115, 5.116–5.141,
    5.135–5.141
  Security Council 'flagship' resolution, 2.17
  State obligations, 8.42–8.45
  stop and search powers, 4.57–4.59
  witness protection, 4.24–4.27
Humanitarian law. *see* **International**
  humanitarian law

Inchoate crimes
  aircraft hijacking, 3.37
  attempts

aircraft hijacking, 3.07
financing, 3.92
forms of participation evolved by
    UN, 2.38–2.41
nuclear terrorism, 3.103
conspiracy
    international treaty crimes, 1.31
    UK jurisdictional approach, 3.192
forms of participation evolved by UN, 2.38–2.41
incitement
    international treaty crimes, 1.31
    Security Council Resolution 1624, App 1
international treaty crimes, 1.31
nuclear terrorism, 3.103, 3.107
Incitement
international treaty crimes, 1.31
Security Council Resolution 1624, App 1
Informants
best practice handling model, 4.199–4.212
overview, 4.177–4.182
UK approach, 4.183–4.198
Intent
Bombings Convention, 3.84
common element of UN instruments, 2.33
nuclear terrorism, 3.104–3.105
International cooperation
aircraft hijacking
    Hague Convention, 2.58–2.61
    Montreal Convention, 2.69–2.72
Bombings Convention, 2.134–2.140
civilian protection
    Diplomats Convention, 2.108–2.113
    Hostages Convention, 2.121–2.125
common element of UN instruments, 2.31
extradition
    aut dedere aut judicare, 9.162–9.167
    comity, 9.119–9.137
    dual criminality, 9.152–9.161
    European Arrest Warrants, 9.138–9.147
    human rights considerations, 9.219–9.242
    meaning and background, 9.113–9.118
    other protections, 9.209–9.218
    political offences, 9.168–9.208
    UN instruments, 9.148–9.151
financing
    FATF Special Recommendations, 6.55
    Financing Convention, 2.151–2.158, 6.19
informal mutual assistance, 9.60–9.69
maritime safety, 2.83–2.87
mutual legal assistance
    adducing evidence from abroad, 9.101
    execution of requests, 9.28–9.59
    formal requests, 9.70–9.98
    foundation of global strategy, 9.04

grounds for refusal, 9.20–9.27
importance, 9.03
legal basis, 9.17–9.19
problems experienced, 9.99
refusals to execute letter of
    request, 9.102–9.112
sensitive material, 9.100
UN instruments, 9.05–9.16
need for appropriate response to terrorism, 1.16
nuclear materials
    Nuclear Material Convention, 2.97–2.102
    Nuclear Terrorism Convention, 2.168–2.174
proactive approach to investigations
    strategic coordination, 4.126–4.127
    tactical coordination, 4.128–4.129
scope, 9.02
Security Council resolution, 2.19
Security Council Resolution 1456, App 1
UN impetus, 9.01
UN instruments generally
    common element, 2.29
    development of UN provisions, 2.44–2.46
International humanitarian law
armed conflicts, 1.39
available mechanisms, 1.04
human rights compared, 8.02–8.06
Security Council 'flagship' resolution, 2.17
sources, 8.07–8.14
International law. *see also* **national law**
available mechanisms, 1.04
development of global regime by UN
    General Assembly, 2.01–2.08
    Global Counter-Terrorism Strategy, 2.21–2.22
    Security Council, 2.09–2.20
legal effect of Security Council resolutions, 2.20
meaning and scope of terrorism
    customary international law, 1.38
    international humanitarian law, 1.39
    international treaty crime, 1.28–1.37
International Monetary Fund, 6.56–6.57
International responses
Intrusive surveillance, 4.225–4.239
Investigations
arrest powers, 4.65–4.66
covert methodologies
    communications interception, 4.130–4.160
    entrapment, 4.248–4.265
    human rights, 4.161–4.176
    surveillance, 4.213–4.247
    undercover agents, 4.177–4.212
detention of suspects
    evidence for further detention, 4.72–4.73
    failure to identify detainee, 4.67–4.71
    torture and confessions, 4.74–4.84

Investigations (*cont.*)
  growing challenge of terrorism, 1.02
  obtaining evidence
    from accomplices, 4.03–4.7
    from resident sources, 4.08–4.20
  proactive approach
    importance, 4.124–4.125
    strategic coordination, 4.126–4.127
    tactical coordination, 4.128–4.129
  scene management for bombings and explosions
    CCTV, 4.121–4.122
    cordons, 4.116
    interviewing witnesses, 4.120
    media strategies, 4.123
    post-incident investigations, 4.113
    scene examiners, 4.117
    Senior Investigating Officers, 4.114–4.115
    zoning, 4.118–4.119
  stop and search powers, 4.57–4.64
  witness protection
    anonymity, 4.30–4.56
    general principles, 4.21–4.22
    resident informants, 4.08–4.20
    special measures, 4.23–4.29

Jurisdiction
  active personality, 3.141–3.145
  aircraft hijacking
    Hague Convention, 2.56
    Montreal Convention, 2.67
    Tokyo Convention, 2.50–2.51
  based on registration
    aircraft, 3.134, 3.136
    ships, 3.135
  Bombings Convention, 2.131
  civilian protection
    Diplomats Convention, 2.106
    Hostages Convention, 2.119
  extra-territoriality, 3.137–3.140
  Financing Convention, 2.147, 6.18
  general principles, 3.127
  growing challenge of terrorism, 1.02
  importance, 3.126
  maritime safety, 2.79
  nuclear materials
    Nuclear Material Convention, 2.95
    Nuclear Terrorism Convention, 2.165
  persons present in territory, 3.188–3.191
  territoriality, 3.128–3.133
  UK approach, 3.192
  UN approach
    Bombings Convention, 3.171
    Diplomats Convention, 3.166
    Financing Convention, 3.172

    Hague Convention, 3.161–3.163
    Hostages Convention, 3.167
    Montreal Convention, 3.164–3.165
    Nuclear Material Convention, 3.168
    overview, 3.155–3.157
    Rome Convention, 3.169
    Tokyo Convention, 3.158–3.160
  UN instruments generally
    common elements, 2.31
    development of UN provisions,
      2.42–2.43
  universal jurisdiction
    arrest powers, 3.175–3.185
    maritime safety, 3.186
    meaning, 3.174
    recognition, 3.173

Law. *see* **International law; national law**
Legal advice
  disclosure of evidence, 5.78
  right to silence, 5.116–5.141
Liberty, right to
  stop and search powers, 4.57–4.59
Life, right to
  death penalty
    bar to extradition, 9.232–9.242
    refusal of mutual legal assistance, 9.26
  meaning and scope, 8.46–8.51
  non-derogable right, 8.33

Maritime safety
  1988 Safety Convention
    applicability, 2.75
    cooperation, 2.83–2.87
    criminalization, 2.76–2.78
    due process, 2.80–2.82
    jurisdiction, 2.79
  criminalization
    2005 Protocols, 3.76–3.91
    Rome Convention, 3.61–3.71
    Rome Protocol, 3.72–3.75
  jurisdictional approach
    based on registration, 3.135
    extra-territorial jurisdiction, 3.128–3.130
    Rome Convention, 3.169
    United Kingdom, 3.192
    universal jurisdiction, 3.175–3.185
  Rome Convention
    2005 Protocols, 2.90–2.92
    full text, App 9
Media
  management and effect of adverse
    comment, 5.86–5.107
  scene management, 4.123

Mens rea
Bombings Convention, 3.84
common element of UN instruments, 2.33
identification by UNSCR, 1.45
Money laundering
Financial Action Task Force
establishment, 6.51
leading role, 6.53
procedures, 6.54
scope includes financing, 6.52
Special Recommendations, App 19, 6.55
financing distinguished, 6.04–6.06
Motive
defining terrorism, 1.25
elements common to UN
instruments, 2.33–2.34
Mutual legal assistance
adducing evidence from abroad, 9.101
common element of UN instruments, 2.31
execution of requests, 9.28–9.59
absence of express treaty provisions, 9.53–9.59
in accordance with laws of requested
State, 9.28–9.44
limitations and delay, 9.47–9.48
pronouncement of indictments, 9.52
silence, right of, 9.49–9.51
trials in absence, 9.45–9.46
formal requests
form of letter, 9.77–9.98
key principle, 9.70–9.74
foundation of global strategy, 9.04
grounds for refusal
death penalty, 9.26
dual criminality, 9.21–9.-22
dual jeopardy, 9.27
fiscal offences, 9.24–9.25
permissive approach, 9.20
political offences, 9.23
importance, 9.03
informal assistance, 9.60–9.69
legal basis, 9.17–9.19
need for appropriate response to terrorism, 1.16
problems experienced, 9.99
sensitive material, 9.100
UN instruments, 9.05–9.16

National law. *see also* **International law; United**
Kingdom; United States
aircraft hijacking
UK incorporation of Hague
Convention, 3.12–3.27
UK incorporation of Montreal
Convention, 3.38–3.39
UK incorporation of Montreal Protocol, 3.45

available mechanisms, 1.04
criminalization
Barbados, 3.113
Commonwealth Expert Group, 3.118,
3.121–3.122
inclusion of motive, 3.120
need for definition, 3.117
reliance on treaty formulation, 3.119
United Kingdom, 3.108–3.112, 3.114–3.6,
3.125
incorporation of international treaty crimes, 1.31,
1.33–1.37
meaning and scope of terrorism, 1.40–1.47
UK jurisdictional approach, 3.192
National liberation movements, 1.20, 1.25
Nationality
basis of jurisdiction
offender, 3.141–3.145
victim, 3.146–3.154
UK jurisdictional approach, 3.192
Non bis in idem, 9.27
Nuclear materials. *see also* **Atomic energy**
increasing threat from terrorism, 1.02
maritime safety, 3.78
Nuclear Material Convention
applicability, 2.93
cooperation, 2.97–2.102
criminalization, 2.94, 3.58–3.60
due process, 2.96
full text, App 8
jurisdictional approach, 2.95, 3.168
Nuclear Terrorism Convention
aut dedere aut judicare, 2.168–2.174
cooperation, 2.168–2.174
criminalization, 2.159–2.164, 3.103–3.107
due process, 2.166–2.167
full text, App 13
jurisdiction, 2.165
overview, 2.158
Security Council resolution, 2.18
UK jurisdictional approach, 3.192

Oppression
Sri Lanka, 4.96–4.100
United Kingdom, 4.93–4.95
Organisation of African Unity Convention, App 17
Organizing or directing others
forms of participation evolved by UN, 2.40–2.41
maritime safety, 3.80
nuclear terrorism, 3.103
Osama Bin Laden. *see* **Usama Bin Laden**

Passive personality principle, 3.146–3.154
Payment systems. *see* **Alternative remittance systems**

Piracy. *see* Maritime safety
Political offences
  bar to extradition
    absence of express references, 9.171
    aircraft hijacking, 9.170
    bombings, 9.172
    financing, 9.173
    historical exception, 9.168–9.169
    meaning and scope, 9.174–9.208
  refusal of mutual legal assistance, 9.23
Presumption of innocence
  human rights, 5.04
  interference justified and proportionate, 5.19
  minimum standard of justice, 8.108
Privacy
  covert investigations, 4.165–4.166
  meaning and scope of protection, 8.113–8.124
  stop and search powers, 4.57–4.59
Prohibition against torture
  bar to extradition, 9.231
  meaning and scope
    illegal detention, 8.94–8.106
    interrogation techniques, 8.53–8.93
Proof
  legal or evidential burden of proof, 5.19–5.41
  reverse burden of proof
    cause for concern, 5.03
    human rights, 5.01–5.02
    UK approach, 5.04–5.18
    UK counter-terrorism legislation, 5.42–5.49
Proscribed organizations
  identification, 4.268–4.270
  importance, 4.266–4.267
  UK burden of proof, 5.43, 5.49
  UK jurisdictional approach, 3.192
Protective personality principle, 3.146–3.154
Protocol on the Management of Terrorism Cases, 5.51
Protocols. *see* Treaties and conventions

Remittance systems. *see* Alternative remittance systems
Resident informants, 4.08–4.20

Scene management
  CCTV, 4.121–4.122
  cordons, 4.116
  interviewing witnesses, 4.120
  media strategies, 4.123
  post-incident investigations, 4.113
  scene examiners, 4.117
  Senior Investigating Officers, 4.114–4.115
  zoning, 4.118–4.119
Search powers
  general principles, 4.57–4.64
  problems with mutual legal assistance, 9.99

Security Council
  definition of terrorism, 1.44–1.45
  developments after Cold War, 2.09–2.10
  key extracts on financing from various resolutions
    1267 (1999), 6.24–6.28
    1390 (2002), 6.29
    1452 (2002), 6.30
    1730 (2006), 6.31
    1735 (2006), 6.32
  relevant resolutions
    criminalization, 3.123–3.124
    full texts, App 1
    human and humanitarian rights, 2.17
    legal effect, 2.20
    Taliban sanctions, 2.16
    weapons of mass destruction, 2.18
  response to 9/11, 2.11–2.14
Sensitive material
  disclosure of evidence, 5.82–5.83
  hearings in camera, 5.108–5.109
  mutual legal assistance, 9.100
Ships. *see* Maritime safety
Silence, right of
  human rights obligations, 5.115
  mutual legal assistance, 9.49–9.51
  right to silence
    access to legal advice, 5.116–5.141
    silence as acknowledgment of truth, 4.101–4.102
  UK approach
    common law position, 5.111
    special provisions for terrorist
      suspects, 5.116–5.117
    statutory provisions, 5.112–5.113
State terrorism
  reluctance to define as terrorists, 1.26
  State support distinguished, 1.27
Stop and search powers, 4.57–4.64
Strategies
  media strategies, 4.123
  mutual legal assistance, 9.04
  need for legal development, 1.05
  proactive approach to investigations, 4.126–4.127
  UN Global Counter-Terrorism
    Strategy, 2.21–2.22
Support for terrorism. *see also* Financing
  Security Council Resolution 1540, App 1
  Security Council response to 9/11, 2.13
  State support distinguished from State
    terrorism, 1.27
  UK burden of proof, 5.43, 5.49
  UK jurisdictional approach, 3.192
Surveillance
  directed surveillance, 4.218–4.224
  general reliance, 4.213

intrusive surveillance, 4.225–4.239
statutory provisions, 4.213–4.217

Taliban
challenges to financing provisions, 6.44–6.48
Security Council Resolution 1267, App 1,
  6.24–6.28
Security Council Resolution 1390, 6.29
Security Council Resolution 1735, App 1, 6.32
Security Council sanctions, 2.16
US response to 9/11, 1.14
Territoriality, 3.128–3.133
Terrorism
increased prioritization after 9/11, 1.03
increasing threat, 1.01
meaning and scope
  armed conflicts, 1.39
  customary international law, 1.38
  general points, 1.06–1.08
  international law definition, 1.18–1.27
  international treaty crime, 1.28–1.37
  national law, 1.40–1.47
origins and development, 1.10–1.13
responses to 9/11, 1.14–1.16
Torture, prohibition against
illegal detention, 4.74–4.84
non-derogable human right, 8.33
whether legal to obtain evidence, 4.85–4.92
Transport. *see* **Aircraft safety; Marine safety**
Treaties and conventions
aircraft hijacking
  Airports Protocol, 2.73–2.74
  Montreal Convention, 2.62–2.72
  Tokyo Convention, 2.47–2.61
criminalization
  2005 Protocols, 3.76–3.82
  Bombings Convention, 3.83–3.91
  Diplomats Convention, 3.46–3.50
  Financing Convention, 3.92–3.102
  Hague Convention, 3.02–3.11
  Hostages Convention, 3.51–3.57
  Montreal Convention, 3.28–3.39
  Montreal Protocol, 3.40–3.44
  Nuclear Material Convention, 3.58–3.60
  Nuclear Terrorism Convention, 3.103–3.107
  Rome Protocol, 3.72–3.75
establishment of terrorism as international
  crime, 1.28–1.37
Financing Convention
  asset freezing and forfeiture, 6.20–6.22
  cooperation, 6.19
  criminalization, 6.11–6.16
  international legal regime, 6.09
  jurisdictional approach, 6.18

key provisions, 6.22
legal liability, 6.17
uniqueness, 6.10
Hostages Convention
  applicability, 2.114
  aut dedere aut judicare, 2.121–2.125
  cooperation, 2.121–2.125
  due process, 2.120
  jurisdiction, 2.119
incorporation into national law, 1.31, 1.33–1.37
jurisdictional approach
  Bombings Convention, 3.171
  Diplomats Convention, 3.166
  Financing Convention, 3.172
  Hague Convention, 3.161–3.163
  Hostages Convention, 3.167
  Montreal Convention, 3.164–3.165
  Nuclear Material Convention, 3.168
  overview, 3.155–3.157
  Rome Convention, 3.169
  Tokyo Convention, 3.158–3.160
maritime safety
  2005 Protocols, 2.88–2.92
  Maritime Safety Convention, 2.75–2.87
nuclear materials
  Nuclear Material Convention, 2.94–2.102
  Nuclear Terrorism Convention, 2.158–2.174
overview of UN instruments
  based on *aut dedere aut judicare*, 2.26
  common elements, 2.29–2.31
  cooperation, 2.44–2.46
  criminalization, 2.32–2.37
  elaboration by relevant organizations, 2.24
  forms of participation, 2.38–2.41
  jurisdiction provisions, 2.42–2.43
  legal effect, 2.28
  part of broader response, 2.27
  role of Ad Hoc Committee, 2.25
  summary table, 2.23
Palermo Convention, 6.23
Rome Convention, 3.61–3.71

Undercover agents
best practice handling model, 4.199–4.212
overview, 4.177–4.182
UK approach, 4.183–4.198
United Kingdom
admissions and confessions
  obtained by trickery, 4.103–4.106
  oppression, 4.93–4.95
  procedure for challenge, 4.107
  silence as acknowledgment of
    truth, 4.101–4.102
  use of torture to obtain evidence, 4.87

769

United Kingdom (*cont.*)
aircraft hijacking
  incorporation of Hague
    Convention, 3.12–3.27
  incorporation of Montreal
    Convention, 3.38–3.39
  incorporation of Montreal Protocol, 3.37, 3.45
arrest powers, 4.65–4.66
burden of proof imposed by counter-terrorism
    legislation, 5.42–5.49
covert investigations
  communications interception, 4.151–4.160
  entrapment, 4.250–4.265
  human intelligence sources, 4.183–4.198
  surveillance, 4.213–4.247
criminalization
  acts of war, 3.110
  attempts at definition, 3.109
  foreign terrorism, 3.116
  meaning and scope, 3.108
  narrow approach, 3.115
  table of instruments, 3.125
  threats designed to influence
    government, 3.111–3.112
detention of suspects
  evidence for further detention, 4.72–4.73
  failure to identify detainee, 4.67–4.71
  PACE Code of Practice, App 22
jurisdictional approach
  active personality principle, 3.141–3.142
  extension for terrorist offences, 3.192
  usually local in effect, 3.139
political offences, 9.187–9.195
right to silence
  access to legal advice, 5.116–5.141
  common law position, 5.111
  special provisions for terrorist
    suspects, 5.116–5.117
  statutory provisions, 5.112–5.113
scene management for bombings and explosions
  CCTV, 4.121–4.122
  cordons, 4.116
  interviewing witnesses, 4.120
  media strategies, 4.123
  post-incident investigations, 4.113
  scene examiners, 4.117
  Senior Investigating Officers, 4.114–4.115
  zoning, 4.118–4.119
sentencing of accomplices who give
    evidence, 4.06–4.7
stop and search powers, 4.57–4.64
witnesses
  anonymity, 4.30–4.35
  protective measures, 4.24–4.27

recent developments, 4.36–4.56
resident informants, 4.08–4.20
United Nations
aircraft hijacking
  Airports Protocol, 2.73–2.74
  Hague Convention, 2.52–2.61
  Montreal Convention, 2.62–2.72
  Tokyo Convention, 2.47–2.51
Bombings Convention
  aut dedere aut judicare, 2.134–2.140
  cooperation, 2.134–2.140
  criminalization, 2.127–2.130
  due process, 2.132–2.133
  jurisdiction, 2.131
Counter-Terrorism Strategy
  General Assembly, App 14
development of global legal regime
  General Assembly, 2.01–2.08
  Global Counter-Terrorism Strategy, App 14,
    2.21–2.22
  Security Council, 2.09–2.20
Diplomats Convention
  applicability, 2.103
  aut dedere aut judicare, 2.108–2.113
  cooperation, 2.108–2.113
  criminalization, 2.104–2.105
  due process, 2.107
  jurisdiction, 2.106
extradition
  framework Conventions, 9.148–9.149
  legal basis, 9.150–9.151
Financing Convention
  applicability, 2.141
  aut dedere aut judicare, 2.151–2.158
  cooperation, 2.151–2.158
  criminalization, 2.142–2.146
  due process, 2.148–2.150
  jurisdiction, 2.147
Hostages Convention
  applicability, 2.114
  aut dedere aut judicare, 2.121–2.125
  cooperation, 2.121–2.125
  due process, 2.120
  jurisdiction, 2.119
maritime safety
  1988 Safety Convention, 2.75–2.87
  2005 Protocols, 2.88–2.92
mutual legal assistance
  foundation of global strategy, 9.04
  importance, 9.03
  particular instruments, 9.05–9.16
Nuclear Material Convention
  applicability, 2.93
  cooperation, 2.97–2.102

criminalization, 2.94
due process, 2.96
jurisdiction, 2.95
Nuclear Terrorism Convention
  aut dedere aut judicare, 2.168–2.174
  cooperation, 2.168–2.174
  criminalization, 2.159–2.164
  due process, 2.166–2.167
  jurisdiction, 2.165
  overview, 2.158
overview of treaties conventions and protocols
  based on *aut dedere aut judicare*, 2.26
  elaboration by relevant organizations, 2.24
  legal effect, 2.28
  part of broader response, 2.27
  role of Ad Hoc Committee, 2.25
  summary table, 2.23
overview of UN instruments
  common elements, 2.29–2.31
  criminalization, 2.32–2.37
  forms of participation, 2.38–2.41
  jurisdiction provisions, 2.42–2.43
  ratification status and depository
    information, App 23
Security Council Resolutions, App 1
  Al-Qaida, App 1
  cooperation, App 1
  criminalization, 3.123–3.124
  financing, App 1
  'flagship' resolution on human and
    humanitarian rights, 2.17
  incitement, App 1
  legal effect, 2.20
  support for terrorism, App 1
  Taliban, App 1
  Taliban sanctions, 2.16
  weapons of mass destruction, 2.18
source of IHRL, 8.07–8.14
United States
9/11
  financial issues arising, 6.02–6.03
  increased prioritization of terrorism
    afterwards, 1.03
  not the origins of terrorism, 1.06–1.08
  proliferation of national responses, 1.43
  Security Council Resolution 1373, 6.35

Security Council response, 2.11–2.14
US response, 1.14
use of torture to obtain evidence, 4.87
American States Convention, App 16
bars to extradition
  handing over suspects, 9.232–9.233
  political offences, 9.196–9.202
communications interception, 4.139–4.150
Guantanamo Bay, 1.15
jurisdictional approach, 3.147–3.149
response to 9/11, 1.14
Universal jurisdiction
arrest powers, 3.175–3.185
maritime safety, 3.186
meaning, 3.174
recognition, 3.173
Usama Bin Laden
jurisdictional approach, 3.148
Security Council Resolution 1390, 6.29
Security Council Resolution 1617, App 1
Security Council Resolution 1735, App 1, 6.32
Security Council response to Taliban's extradition
  refusals, 2.10

War. *see* **Armed conflicts**
Weapons of mass destruction
growing challenge of terrorism, 1.02
Security Council resolution, 2.18
Wire transfers
alternative remittance system, 7.29–7.30
FATF Special Recommendations, 6.55
Witnesses
accomplices, 4.03–4.7
anonymity
  general approach, 4.30–4.35
  recent developments, 4.36–4.56
  Criminal Evidence (Witness Anonymity) Act
    2008, App 21
protection
  resident informants, 4.20
  special measures, 4.23–4.29
  vulnerable witnesses, 4.21–4.22
resident informants, 4.08–4.20
scene management, 4.120
Wolfsberg Group, 6.62–6.63